Lecture Notes in Computer Science 11442

Commenced Publication in 1973
Founding and Former Series Editors:
Gerhard Goos, Juris Hartmanis, and Jan van Leeuwen

More information about this series at http://www.springer.com/series/7410

Dongdai Lin · Kazue Sako (Eds.)

Public-Key Cryptography – PKC 2019

22nd IACR International Conference
on Practice and Theory of Public-Key Cryptography
Beijing, China, April 14–17, 2019
Proceedings, Part I

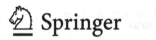 Springer

Editors
Dongdai Lin
SKLOIS, Institute of Information
Engineering
Chinese Academy of Sciences
Beijing, China

Kazue Sako
Security Research Laboratories
NEC Corporation
Kawasaki, Japan

ISSN 0302-9743   ISSN 1611-3349   (electronic)
Lecture Notes in Computer Science
ISBN 978-3-030-17252-7   ISBN 978-3-030-17253-4   (eBook)
https://doi.org/10.1007/978-3-030-17253-4

Library of Congress Control Number: 2019936577

LNCS Sublibrary: SL4 – Security and Cryptology

This Springer imprint is published by the registered company Springer Nature Switzerland AG
The registered company address is: Gewerbestrasse 11, 6330 Cham, Switzerland

Preface

The 22nd IACR International Conference on Practice and Theory of Public-Key Cryptography (PKC 2019) was held April 14–17, 2019, in Beijing, China. The conference is sponsored by the International Association for Cryptologic Research (IACR) and focuses on all technical aspects of public-key cryptography. These proceedings consist of two volumes including 42 papers that were selected by the Program Committee from 173 submissions. Each submission was assigned to at least three reviewers while submissions co-authored by Program Committee members received at least five reviews. During the discussion phase, the Program Committee used quite intensively a recent feature of the review system, which allows Program Committee members to anonymously ask questions to the authors. The reviewing and selection process was a challenging task and we are deeply grateful to the Program Committee members and external reviewers for their hard and thorough work. Many thanks also to Shai Halevi for his assistance with the Web submission and review software. We thank the authors for promptly responding to the questions raised by the committee, which helped us understand the content of their submissions.

The conference program also included an invited talk by Tatsuaki Okamoto (NTT). We would like to thank the invited speaker as well as all the other speakers and the authors of all submissions for their contributions to the program and conference. Finally, we would like to thank Xiaoyun Wang, the general chair, and all the members of local Organizing Committee for organizing a great conference and all the conference attendees for making this conference a truly intellectually stimulating event through their active participation.

April 2019

Dongdai Lin
Kazue Sako

PKC 2019

22nd IACR International Conference on Practice and Theory of Public-Key Cryptography

Beijing, China
April 14–17, 2019

Sponsored and Organized by

International Association for Cryptologic Research
State Key Laboratory of Information Security
State Key Laboratory of Cryptology
TopSec Technologies Inc.
Institute of Information Engineering, Chinese Academy of Sciences
Chinese Association for Cryptologic Research

General Chair

Xiaoyun Wang   Tsinghua University, China

Program Co-chairs

Dongdai Lin	SKLOIS, Institute of Information Engineering, Chinese Academy of Sciences, China
Kazue Sako	Security Research Laboratories, NEC Corporation, Japan

Steering Committee

Michel Abdalla	Ecole Normale Supérieure, France
Yvo Desmedt	University of Texas at Dallas, USA
Goichiro Hanaoka	National Institute of Advanced Industrial Science and Technology, Japan
Aggelos Kiayias	University of Edinburgh, UK
Dongdai Lin	Chinese Academy of Sciences, China
David Naccache	Ecole Normale Supérieure, France
Tatsuaki Okamoto	NTT Labs, Japan
David Pointcheval	Ecole Normale Supérieure, France
Kazue Sako	NEC Security Research Laboratories, Japan
Moti Yung	Google and Columbia University, USA
Yuliang Zheng	University of Alabama at Birmingham, USA

Program Committee

Erdem Alkim	Ondokuz Mayis University, Turkey
Diego F. Aranha	Aarhus University, Denmark and University of Campinas, Brazil
Chris Brzuska	Alto University, Finland
Dario Catalano	University of Catania, Italy
Nishanth Chandran	Microsoft, India
Sanjit Chatterjee	Indian Institute of Sciences, India
Jie Chen	East China Normal University, China
Jung Hee Cheon	Seoul National University, Korea
Craig Costello	Microsoft Research, USA
Yi Deng	Chinese Academy of Sciences, China
Leo Ducas	CWI Amsterdam, The Netherlands
Nico Döttling	Cispa Helmholtz Center (i.G.), Germany
Dario Fiore	IMDEA Software Institute, Spain
Pierre-Alain Fouque	Rennes University, France
Feng Hao	University of Warwick, UK
Tibor Jager	Paderborn University, Germany
Marc Joye	OneSpan, Belgium
Tancrède Lepoint	SRI International, USA
Benoît Libert	CNRS and ENS de Lyon, France
Helger Lipmaa	University of Tartu, Estonia
Feng-Hao Liu	Florida Atlantic University, USA
Takahiro Matsuda	AIST, Japan
Pratyay Mukherjee	Visa Research, USA
Satoshi Obana	Hosei University, Japan
Miyako Okubo	NICT, Japan
Arpita Patra	Indian Institute of Science, India
Ludovic Perret	Sorbonne University, France
Thomas Peters	UC Louvain, Belgium
Benny Pinkas	Bar-Ilan University, Israel
Bertram Poettering	Royal Holloway, University of London, UK
Antigoni Polychroniadou	Cornell Tech, USA
Alessandra Scafuro	NC State University, USA
Jae Hong Seo	Hanyang University, South Korea
Qiang Tang	New Jersey Institute of Technology, USA
Huaxiong Wang	Nanyang Technological University, Singapore
Yu Yu	Shanghai Jiaotong University, China

Organizing Committee

Xiaofeng Chen	Xidian University, China
Yu Chen	SKLOIS, Institute of Information Engineering, CAS, China
Shuqin Fan	State Key Laboratory of Cryptology, China

Xinyi Huang	Fujian Normal University, China
Ming Li	SKLOIS, Institute of Information Engineering, CAS, China
Zhe Liu	Nanjing University of Aeronautics and Astronautics, China
Chunming Tang	Guangzhou University, China
Anyu Wang	SKLOIS, Institute of Information Engineering, CAS, China
Jian Weng	Jinan University, China
Baofeng Wu	SKLOIS, Institute of Information Engineering, CAS, China
Fangguo Zhang	Sun Yat-sen University, China
Yunlei Zhao	Fudan University, China

Additional Reviewers

Benjamin Dowling
Behzad Abdolmaleki
Masayuki Abe
Martin R. Albrecht
Pedro G. M. R. Alves
Gilad Asharov
Nuttapong Attrapadung
Karim Baghery
Shi Bai
Marshall Ball
Manuel Barbosa
Hridam Basu
Carsten Baum
Pascal Bemmann
Fabrice Benhamouda
Pauline Bert
Francesco Berti
Ward Beullens
Sauvik Bhattacharya
Olivier Blazy
Katharina Boudgoust
Florian Bourse
Xavier Bultel
Olive Chakraborty
Biniy Chen
Long Chen
Rongmao Chen
Yu Chen
Wonhee Cho

Ashish Choudhury
Peter Chvojka
Sadro Coretti
Geoffroy Couteau
Edouard Cuvelier
Prem Laxman Das
Bernardo David
Amit Deo
Apoorvaa Deshpande
Julien Devigne
Ning Ding
Lucas Enloe
Jieun Eom
Naomi Ephraim
Xiong Fan
Antonio Faonio
Luca De Feo
Daniele Friolo
Georg Fuchsbauer
Ben Fuller
Tommaso Gagliardoni
Steven Galbraith
Tatiana Galibus
Chaya Ganesh
Romain Gay
Peter Gazi
Kai Gellert
Nicholas Genise
Satrajit Ghosh

Irene Giacomelli
Junqing Gong
Alonso Gonzalez
Jens Groth
Fabrice Ben Hammouda
Kyoohyung Han
Abida Haque
Javier Herranz
Clemens Heuberger
Minki Hhan
Hyunsook Hong
Seungwan Hong
Jingwei Hu
Qiong Huang
Xinyi Huang
Huisu Jang
Christian Janson
Jinhyuck Jeong
Yun-Seong Ji
Shaoquan Jiang
Zhang Jiang
Charanjit Jutla
R. Kabaleeshwaran
Saqib A. Kakvi
Koray Karabina
Shuichi Katsumata
Yutaka Kawai
Hamidreza Khoshakhlagh
Dongwoo Kim
Duhyeong Kim
Jaeyun Kim
Jiseung Kim
Minkyu Kim
Fuyuki Kitagawa
Susumu Kiyoshima
Kamil Kluczniak
François Koeune
Yashvanth Kondi
Toomas Krips
Shravan Kumar
Rafael Kurek
Fabien Laguillaumie
Junzuo Lai
Qiqi Lai
Hyung Tae Lee
Joohee Lee

Kiwoo Lee
Jiangtao Li
Jie Li
Changlu Lin
Fuchun Lin
Qipeng Liu
Shengli Liu
Zhe Liu
Zhen Liu
Patrick Longa
Steve Lu
Yuan Lu
Lin Lyu
Shunli Ma
Varun Madathil
Monosij Maitra
Giulio Malavolta
Mark Manulis
Chloe Martindale
Daniel Masny
Peihan Miao
Rafael Misoczki
Payman Mohassel
Fabrice Mouhartem
Yi Mu
Sayantan Mukherjee
Pierrick Méaux
Michael Naehrig
Kartik Nayak
Khoa Nguyen
David Niehues
Ryo Nishimaki
Luca Nizzardo
Ariel Nof
Koji Nuida
Sai Lakshmi Bhavana Obbattu
Cristina Onete
Emmanuella Orsini
Jiaxin Pan
Tapas Pandit
Lorenz Panny
Jong Hwan Park
Alain Passelègue
Sikhar Patranabis
Alice Pellet–Mary
Geovandro Pereira

Olivier Pereira
Rachel Player
S. Puria
Erick Purwanto
Baodong Qin
Chen Qian
Mario Di Raimondo
Somindu C. Ramanna
Divya Ravi
Joost Renes
Amanda Cristina Davi Resende
Melissa Rossi
Arnab Roy
Paul Rösler
Mohamed Sabt
Yusuke Sakai
Jonas Schneider
Peter Scholl
Jacob Schuldt
Sven Schäge
Adam Sealfon
Sruthi Sekar
Minhye Seo
Akash Shah
Kazumasa Shinagawa
Adam Shull
Janno Siim
Luisa Siniscalchi
Benjamin Smith
Azam Soleimanian
Yongha Son
Katerina Sotiraki
Shifeng Sun
Willy Susilo
Koutarou Suzuki
Benjamin Hong Meng Tan
Radu Titiu
Junichi Tomida
Rotem Tsabary
Daniel Tschudi

Anselme Tueno
Dominque Unruh
Muthuramakrishnan Venkitasubramaniam
Daniele Venturi
Sameer Wagh
Michael Walter
Hailong Wang
Liping Wang
Luping Wang
Yu-chen Wang
Yuyu Wang
Zhedong Wang
Weiqiang Wen
Joanne Woodage
Shota Yamada
Takashi Yamakawa
Avishay Yanay
Guomin Yang
Kang Yang
Rupeng Yang
Xu Yanhong
Donggeon Yhee
Jingyue Yu
Yang Yu
Zuoxia Yu
Aaram Yun
Michal Zajac
Ming Zeng
Cong Zhang
Jiang Zhang
Juanyang Zhang
Kai Zhang
Liang Feng Zhang
Mingwu Zhang
Rui Zhang
Xiaojun Zhang
Qian Zhao
Yunlei Zhao
Linfeng Zhou
Giorgos Zirdelis

Contents – Part I

Identity-Based Encryption

Fundamental Primitives (I)

Contents – Part II

Re-encryption Schemes

Fundamental Primitives (II)

Post Quantum Cryptography

Cryptographic Protocols

Sub-logarithmic Distributed Oblivious RAM with Small Block Size

Eyal Kushilevitz and Tamer Mour$^{(\boxtimes)}$

Computer Science Department, Technion, 32000 Haifa, Israel
eyalk@cs.technion.ac.il, tamer.mour@technion.ac.il

Abstract. *Oblivious RAM* (ORAM) is a cryptographic primitive that allows a client to securely execute RAM programs over data that is stored in an untrusted server. *Distributed Oblivious RAM* is a variant of ORAM, where the data is stored in $m > 1$ servers. Extensive research over the last few decades have succeeded to reduce the bandwidth overhead of ORAM schemes, both in the single-server and the multi-server setting, from $O(\sqrt{N})$ to $O(1)$. However, all known protocols that achieve a sub-logarithmic overhead either require heavy server-side computation (e.g. homomorphic encryption), or a large block size of at least $\Omega(\log^3 N)$.

In this paper, we present a family of distributed ORAM constructions that follow the hierarchical approach of Goldreich and Ostrovsky [17]. We enhance known techniques, and develop new ones, to take better advantage of the existence of multiple servers. By plugging efficient known hashing schemes in our constructions, we get the following results:

1. For any number $m \geq 2$ of servers, we show an m-server ORAM scheme with $O(\log N/\log\log N)$ overhead, and block size $\Omega(\log^2 N)$. This scheme is private even against an $(m-1)$-server collusion.
2. A three-server ORAM construction with $O(\omega(1) \cdot \log N/\log\log N)$ overhead and a block size almost logarithmic, i.e. $\Omega(\log^{1+\epsilon} N)$.

We also investigate a model where the servers are allowed to perform a linear amount of light local computations, and show that constant overhead is achievable in this model, through a simple four-server ORAM protocol. From theoretical viewpoint, this is the first ORAM scheme with asymptotic constant overhead, and polylogarithmic block size, that does not use homomorphic encryption. Practically speaking, although we do not provide an implementation of the suggested construction, evidence from related work (e.g. [12]) confirms that despite the linear computational overhead, our construction is practical, in particular when applied to secure computation.

Keywords: Oblivious RAM · Multi-server setting ·
Secure computation · Private storage

A full version is available on arXiv.org e-Print archive as arXiv:1802.05145 [cs.CR]. Research supported by ISF grant 1709/14, BSF grant 2012378, NSF-BSF grant 2015782, and a grant from the Ministry of Science and Technology, Israel, and the Department of Science and Technology, Government of India.

© International Association for Cryptologic Research 2019
D. Lin and K. Sako (Eds.): PKC 2019, LNCS 11442, pp. 3–33, 2019.
https://doi.org/10.1007/978-3-030-17253-4_1

1   Introduction

Since it was first introduced by Goldreich and Ostrovsky [17], the *Oblivious RAM* problem has attracted a lot of attention (see, e.g. [22,33,35]). Throughout the past three decades, efficient ORAM protocols were constructed (e.g. [18,34]), their various applications, such as secure storage [4,28], secure processors [32], and secure multi-party computation [20,25], were studied, and their limits were considered [1,17,24].

Standard Model. The standard ORAM model considers a setting where a client outsources his data to an untrusted server that supports read and write operations only. The goal of an *ORAM simulation* is to simulate any RAM program that the client executes over the remote data, so that the same computation is performed, but the view of the server during the interaction would provide no information about the client's private input and the program executed, except their length. Clearly, encryption can be employed to hide the *content* of the data, but the sequence of reads and write locations itself might leak information as well. Thus, the focus of ORAM protocols is to hide the *access pattern* made to the server. The main metric considered in ORAM research is the *bandwidth overhead* of an ORAM scheme (shortly referred to as "overhead"), which is the multiplicative increase in the amount of communication incurred by an oblivious simulation relative to a regular run of the simulated program. In this standard model, researchers have been able to improve the overhead from $O(\log^3 N)$ [17] to $O(\log N)$ [5,34,35], where N is the number of data blocks in storage, and thus reaching the optimal overhead in that model due to the matching impossibility results of Goldreich and Ostrovsky [17] and Larsen and Nielsen [24].

In an attempt to achieve sub-logarithmic overhead, research has deviated from the standard model (e.g. [4,19,25]). For instance, by allowing the server to perform some local computation, multiple works [4,11,14] could achieve a constant overhead. However, this improvement comes at a cost: the server performs heavy homomorphic encryption computation which practically becomes the actual bottleneck of such schemes.

Distributed Oblivious RAM. Another interesting line of work, often referred to as *Distributed Oblivious RAM* [1,19,38, etc.], was initiated by Ostrovsky and Shoup [28] and later refined by Lu and Ostrovsky [25], and considers the multi-server setting. We denote by (m,t)-*ORAM* an ORAM scheme that involves $m > 1$ servers, out of which $t < m$ servers might collude. In the two-server setting, Zhang et al. [38] and Abraham et al. [1] construct $(2,1)$-ORAMs with sub-logarithmic overhead. In order to achieve $O(\log_d N)$ overhead (for any $d \in \mathbb{N}$) using their construction, Abraham et al. require that the size of a memory block, i.e. the data unit retrieved in a single query to the RAM, is $\Omega(d\log^2 N)$ (with larger blocks the asymptotic overhead increases). For example, for an overhead of $O(\log N/\log\log N)$, one has to work with blocks of relatively large size of $\Omega(\log^3 N)$, which may be undesired in many applications. Zhang et al. require a polynomial block size of $\Omega(N^\epsilon)$ for a constant bandwidth blowup.

Other attempts to achieve low overhead in the multi-server setting [26] were shown to be vulnerable to concrete attacks [1]. These recent developments in distributed ORAM raise the following question, which we address in this paper:

Can we construct a sub-logarithmic distributed ORAM with a small block size?

Known sub-logarithmic ORAMs [1,38] belong to the family of *tree-based ORAMs* [33]. One of the key components in tree-based ORAMs is a *position map* that is maintained through a recursive ORAM. Such a recursion imposes the requirement for a large polylogarithmic block size[1]. Thus, it seems that a positive answer to the question above will come, if at all, from constructions of the other well-studied type of ORAMs, those based on the hierarchical solution of [17]. By applying the hierarchical approach to the distributed setting, Lu and Ostrovsky [25] obtained the first logarithmic *hierarchical* ORAM scheme. In this paper, we show how to take a further advantage of the multiple servers in order to beat the logarithmic barrier, and still use a relatively small block size, with constructions in both the two-server and three-server settings. In addition, we consider the case where $t > 1$, and show how to generalize our two-server solution to an $(m, m-1)$-ORAM, with the same asymptotic complexity, for any $m > 2$.

ORAM for Secure Computation. An interesting application of ORAM is its integration in multi-party computation (MPC) protocols for RAM programs on large data. The possibility of using ORAM for MPC was first pointed out by Ostrovsky and Shoup [28], and was revisited by more recent works [20,25] due to the increasing interest in applied secure computation. Despite the extensive improvements in the practicality of secure circuit evaluation protocols, the theoretical framework for MPC protocols for RAM evaluation, given in [20,25,28] and other works, encountered major obstacles toward achieving practical efficiency.

A new line of work [12,19,36,37] studies the practicality of (distributed) ORAM in MPC, and observes that the traditional ORAM approaches were designed for the client-server model, and that in the MPC context, a focus on a different set of efficiency measures and optimizations is required in order to achieve better performance. For instance, constructions where the client complexity is optimized, even in exchange for server-side work that is linear in N per read/write, perform better than classic schemes, where server work is usually limited. In this context, the new cryptographic primitive of *function secret sharing* (FSS), introduced by Boyle et al. [7], was shown to be useful for constructing schemes that are practically efficient [12], or that have low interaction [19]. However, despite their practical efficiency, none of the mentioned schemes achieve sub-logarithmic overhead, thus leaving us with the following question:

Can we achieve sub-logarithmic ORAM that is "optimized for MPC"?

---

[1] To the best of our knowledge, the only tree-based ORAM that bypasses recursion, due to Wang et al. [19], works in a different model where linear server work is allowed (see preceding discussion).

Table 1. Comparison of ORAM schemes.

Scheme	m	t	Overhead	Block size	Server work
Goldreich-Ostrovsky [17]	1	-	$O(\log^3 N)$	$\Omega(\log N)$	-
Kushilevitz et al. [22]	1	-	$O(\frac{\log^2 N}{\log\log N})$	$\Omega(\log N)$	-
Wang et al. [35]	1	-	$O(\log N \cdot \omega(1))$	$\Omega(\log^2 N)$	-
Asharov et al. [5]	1	-	$O(\log N)$	$\Omega(\log N)$	-
Lu-Ostrovsky [25]	2	1	$O(\log N)$	$\Omega(\log N)$	polylog
Chan et al. [9]	3	1	$O(\log^2 N)$	$\Omega(\log N)$	-
Zhang et al. [38]	2	1	$O(1)$	$\Omega(N^\epsilon)$	polylog
Abraham et al. [1]	2	1	$O(\log_d N)$	$\omega(d\log^2 N)$	polylog
Doerner-Shelat [12]	2	1	$O(\sqrt{N})$	$\Omega(\log N)$	linear
Gordon et al. [19]	2	1	$O(\log N)$	$\Omega(\log N)$	linear
Our 4-server construction					
Instantiation 1	4	1	$O(1)$	$\Omega(\lambda \log N)$	linear
Our 3-server construction					
Instantiation 2 $d = \log^\epsilon N$	3	1	$O(\log_d N \cdot \omega(1))$ $O(\frac{\log N}{\log\log N} \cdot \omega(1))$	$\Omega(d\log N)$ $\Omega(\log^{1+\epsilon} N)$	polylog
Instantiation 3 $d = \log^\epsilon N$	3	1	$O(\log_d N)$ $O(\frac{\log N}{\log\log N})$	$\Omega(d\log^{1.5} N)$ $\Omega(\log^{1.5+\epsilon} N)$	polylog
Our m-server construction					
Instantiation 4	$m \geq 2$	$m-1$	$O(\frac{\log N}{\log\log N})$	$\Omega(\log^2 N)$	polylog

We show that by allowing the servers to perform linear computations per RAM step, we can achieve a four-server ORAM scheme with a small *constant* overhead. Our constructions strictly improve over the two-server ORAM schemes from [12,19], which were shown to perform well in practical implementations, in terms of overhead and computation, both asymptotically and concretely.

1.1 Our Contribution and Technical Overview

Sub-logarithmic Distributed ORAM Constructions. Our main contribution is a family of distributed hierarchical ORAM constructions with any number of servers. Our constructions make a black-box use of hashing schemes. Instantiating our constructions with hashing schemes that were previously used in ORAM [8,18,25], yields state-of-the-art results (see Table 1). We elaborate.

A Three-Server ORAM Protocol. By using techniques from [25] over the balanced hierarchy from [22], and using two-server PIR [10] as a black box, we are able to construct an efficient $(3,1)$-ORAM scheme. Instantiating the scheme with cuckoo hash tables (similarly to [18,22,25]) achieves an overhead of $O(\omega(1) \cdot \log_d N)$ with a block size of $B = \Omega(d\log N)$. Thus, for any $\epsilon > 0$, we achieve $O(\omega(1) \cdot \log N / \log\log N)$ overhead with $B = \Omega(\log^{1+\epsilon} N)$.

In the classic hierarchical solution from [17], the data is stored in $\log N$ levels, and the protocol consists of two components: *queries*, in which target virtual blocks are retrieved, and *reshuffles*, which are performed to properly maintain the data structure. Roughly speaking, in a query, a single block is downloaded from every level, resulting in $\log N$ overhead per query. The reshuffles cost $\log N$ overhead per level, and $\log^2 N$ overall. Kushilevitz et al. [22] suggest to balance the hierarchy by reducing the number of levels to $\log N / \log \log N$. In the balanced hierarchy, however, one has to download $\log N$ blocks from a level in every query. Thus, balancing the hierarchy "balances", in some sense, the asymptotic costs of the queries and reshuffles, as they both become $\log^2 N / \log \log N$.

At a high level, we carefully apply two-server techniques to reduce the overhead, both of the queries and the reshuffles, from the single-server ORAM of [22]. More specifically, to reduce the queries cost, we use two-server PIR to allow the client to efficiently read the target block from the $\log N$ positions, it had otherwise have to download, from every level. By requiring the right (relatively small) block size, the cost of PIRs can be made constant per level and, therefore, $\log N / \log \log N$ in total. To reduce the reshuffles cost, we replace the single-server reshuffles with cheaper two-server reshuffles, that were first used by Lu and Ostrovsky [25], and that incur only a constant overhead per level.

So far, it sounds like we are already able to achieve $\log N / \log \log N$ overhead using two servers only. However, combining two-server PIR and two-server reshuffles is tricky: each assumes a different distribution of the data. In standard two-server PIR, the data is assumed to be identically replicated among the two servers. On the other hand, it is essential for the security of the two-server reshuffles from [25] that every level in the hierarchy is held only by one of the two servers, so that the other server, which is used to reshuffle the data, does not see the access pattern to the level. We solve this problem by combining the two settings using three servers: every level is held only by two of the three servers in a way that preserves the security of the two-server reshuffles and, at the same time, provides the required setting for two-server PIR.

An $(m, m - 1)$-ORAM Protocol. We take further advantage of the existence of multiple servers and construct, for any integer $m \geq 2$, an m-server ORAM scheme that is private against a collusion of up to $m - 1$ servers. Using oblivious two-tier hashing [8], our scheme achieves an overhead of $O(\log N / \log \log N)$, for which it requires $B = \Omega(\log^2 N)$ (see Theorem 4 and Instantiation 4).

We begin by describing a $(2, 1)$-ORAM scheme, then briefly explain how to extend it to any number of servers $m > 2$. Let us take a look back at our three-server construction. We were able to use both two-server PIR and two-server reshuffles using only a three-server setting. Now that we restrict ourselves to using two servers, we opt for the setting where the two servers store identical replicates of the entire data structure. Performing PIR is clearly still possible, but now that the queries in all levels are made to the same two servers, we cannot perform Lu and Ostrovsky's [25] two-server reshuffles securely. Instead, we use *oblivious sort* (or, more generally, oblivious hashing) to reshuffle the levels. Oblivious sort is a sorting protocol in the client-server setting, where the server involved learns nothing about the obtained order of blocks. Oblivious sort is used in many single-server hierarchical ORAMs (e.g. [17, 22]), where it incurs $\log N$ overhead per level. Since we aim for a sub-logarithmic overhead, we avoid this undesired blowup by performing oblivious sort over the tags of the blocks only (i.e. their identities) which are much shorter, rather than over the blocks themselves. We require a block size large enough such that the gap between the size of the tags and the size of the blocks cancels out the multiplicative overhead of performing oblivious sort. Once the tags are shuffled into a level, it remains to match them with the blocks with the data. That is where the second server is used. We apply a secure two-server "matching procedure" which, at a high level, lets the second server to randomly permute the data blocks and send them to the server holding the shuffled tags. The latter can then match the data to the tags in an oblivious manner. Of course, the data exchange during the matching has to involve a subtle cryptographic treatment to preserve security.

The above scheme can be generalized to an $(m, m-1)$-ORAM, for any $m > 2$. The data is replicated in all servers involved, and m-server PIR is used. The matching procedure is extended to an m-server procedure, where all the servers participate in randomly permuting the data.

ORAM with Constant Overhead for Secure Computation. We also investigate "ORAM for practical MPC", where we allow linear server-side work and focus on client efficiency, and show that constant overhead is achievable in this model (see Table 1). The proposed scheme, described below, applies function secret sharing over secret-shared data, thus avoiding the need for encrypting the data using symmetric encryption (unlike existing schemes, e.g. [12, 19]).

A Simple Four-Server ORAM Protocol. Inspired by an idea first suggested in [28], we combine private information retrieval (PIR) [10], and PIR-write [28], to obtain a four-server ORAM. To implement the PIR and PIR-write protocols efficiently, we make a black-box use of *distributed point functions* (DPFs) [7, 16], i.e. function secret sharing schemes for the class of point functions. Efficient DPFs can be used to construct (i) a (computational) two-server PIR protocol if the data is replicated among the two servers, or (ii) a two-server PIR-write protocol for when the data is additively secret-shared among the two servers. These two applications of DPFs are combined as follows: we create two additive shares of the data, and replicate each share twice. We send each of the four shares (two pairs of identical shares) to one of the four servers. A read is simulated with two instances of PIR, each invoked with a different pair of servers holding the same share. A write is simulated with two instance of PIR-write, each invoked with a different pair of servers holding different shares.

We stress that the client in all of our constructions can be described using a simple small circuit, and therefore, our schemes can be used to obtain efficient secure multi-party protocols, following [25].

1.2   Related Work

Classic Hierarchical Solution. The first hierarchical ORAM scheme appeared in the work of Ostrovsky [27] and later in [17]. In this solution, the server holds the data in a hierarchy of levels, growing geometrically in size, where the ith level is a standard hash table with 2^i buckets of logarithmic size, and a hash function $h_i(\cdot)$, which is used to determine the location of blocks in the hash table: block of address v may be found in level i (if at all) in bucket $h_i(v)$. The scheme is initiated when all blocks are in the lowest level. An access to a block with a virtual address v is simulated by downloading bucket $h_i(v)$ from every level i. Once the block is found, it is written back to the appropriate bucket in the smallest level ($i = 0$). As a level fills up, it is merged down with the subsequent (larger) level $i + 1$, which is reshuffled with a new hash function h_{i+1} using oblivious sorting. Thus, a block is never accessed twice in the same level with the same hash function, hence the obliviousness of the scheme. Using AKS sorting network [3] for the oblivious sort achieves an $O(\log^3 N)$ overhead.

Balanced Hierarchy. Up until recently, the best known single-server ORAM scheme for general block size, with constant client memory, was obtained by Kushilevitz et al. [22], using an elegant "balancing technique", that reduces the number of levels in the hierarchy of [17], in exchange for larger levels. Their scheme achieves an overhead of $O(\log^2 / \log \log N)$, using *oblivious cuckoo hashing* (first applied to ORAM in [18,31]). An alternative construction, recently proposed by Chan et al. [8], follows the same idea, but replaces the relatively complex cuckoo hashing with a simpler oblivious hashing that is based on a variant of the two-tier hashing scheme from [2].

Tree-Based ORAM. Another well-studied family of ORAM schemes is tree-based ORAMs (e.g. [33,35]), where, as the name suggests, the data is stored in a tree structure. The first ORAMs with a logarithmic overhead, in the single-server model, were tree-based [34,35]. However, tree-based ORAMs usually require a large block size of at least $B = \Omega(\log^2 N)$.

Optimal ORAM with General Block Size. The recent work of Asharov et al. [5], which improves upon the work of Patel et al. [30], succeeds to achieve optimal logarithmic overhead with general block size (due to known lower bounds [17,24]). Both results are based on the solution from [17] and use non-trivial properties of the data in the hierarchy to optimize the overhead.

Distributed ORAM Constructions. Ostrovsky and Shoup [28] were the first to construct a distributed private-access storage scheme (that is not read-only). Their solution is based on the hierarchical ORAM from [17]. However, their model is a bit different than ours: they were interested in the amount of communication required for a single query (rather than a sequence of queries), and they did not limit the work done by the servers. Lu and Ostrovsky [25] considered the more general ORAM model, defined in Sect. 2.1. They presented the first two-server oblivious RAM scheme, and achieved a logarithmic overhead with a logarithmic block size by bypassing oblivious sort, and replacing it with an efficient reshuffling procedure that uses the two servers.

The tree approach was also studied in the multi-server model. Contrary to the hierarchical schemes, known distributed tree-based ORAMs [1,38] beat the logarithmic barrier. The improvement in overhead could be achieved by using k-ary tree data structures, for some parameter $k = \omega(1)$. However, these constructions suffer from a few drawbacks, most importantly, they require a large polylogarithmic (sometimes polynomial) block size.

ORAM Constructions for MPC with Linear Computational Overhead. The work of Ostrovsky and Shoup [28], as well as some recent works [12,19] have considered the model where the servers are allowed to perform a linear amount of light computations. Both the works of Doerner and Shelat [12] and Wang et al. [19] elegantly implement techniques from the standard model (square-root construction, and tree structure, respectively), and use the efficient PIR protocol from [7], to construct practically efficient two-server ORAM schemes with linear server-side computation per access and bandwidth overhead matching their analogues in the single-server setting (see Table 1).

1.3   Paper Organization

Section 2 contains formal definitions and introduces cryptographic tools that we use. In Sect. 3, we present our four-server ORAM. In Sect. 4, we provide an overview of the hierarchical ORAM framework, on which our main distributed ORAM constructions are based. In Sects. 5 and 6, we present these constructions. Due to space limit, de-amortization of our constructions, and a discussion of their application to secure computation, are left to the full version.

2   Preliminaries

2.1   Model and Problem Definition

The RAM Model. We work in the RAM model, where a RAM machine consists of a CPU that interacts with a (supposedly remote) RAM storage. The CPU has a small number of registers, therefore it uses the RAM storage for computations over large data, by performing reads and writes to memory locations in the RAM. A sequence of ℓ queries is a list of ℓ tuples $(op_1, v_1, x_1), \ldots, (op_\ell, v_\ell, x_\ell)$, where op_i is either Read or Write, v_i is the location of the memory cell to be read or written to, and x_i is the data to be written to v_i in case of a Write. For simplicity of notation, we unify both types of operations into an operation known as an *access*, namely "Read then Write". Hence, the *access pattern* of the RAM machine is the sequence of the memory locations and the data $(v_1, x_1), \ldots, (v_\ell, x_\ell)$.

Oblivious RAM Simulation. A *(single-server) oblivious RAM simulation*, shortly *ORAM simulation*, is a simulation of a RAM machine, held by a client as a CPU, and a server as RAM storage. The client communicates with the server, and thus can query its memory. The server is untrusted but is assumed to be *semi-honest*, i.e. it follows the protocol but attempts to learn as much information as possible from its view about the client's input and program. We also assume that the server is not just a memory machine with I/O functionality, but that it can perform basic local computations over its storage (e.g. shuffle arrays, compute simple hash functions, etc.). We refer to the access pattern of the RAM machine that is simulated as the *virtual* access pattern. The access pattern that is produced by the oblivious simulation is called the *actual* access pattern. The goal of ORAM is to simulate the RAM machine correctly, in a way that the distribution of the view of the server, i.e. the actual access pattern, would look independent of the virtual access pattern.

Definition 1 (ORAM, informal). *Let RAM be a RAM machine. We say that a (probabilistic) RAM machine ORAM is an oblivious RAM simulation of RAM, if (i) (correctness) for any virtual access pattern $y := ((v_1, x_1), \ldots, (v_\ell, x_\ell))$, the output of RAM and ORAM at the end of the client-server interaction is equal with probability $\geq 1 - negl(\ell)$, and (ii) (security) for any two virtual access patterns, y, z, of length ℓ, the corresponding distribution of the actual access patterns produced by ORAM, denoted $\tilde{y}$ and $\tilde{z}$, are computationally indistinguishable.*

An alternative interpretation of the security requirement is as follows: the view of the server, during an ORAM simulation, can be simulated in a way that is indistinguishable from the actual view of the server, given only ℓ.

Distributed Oblivious RAM. A *distributed oblivious RAM simulation* is the analogue of ORAM simulation in the multi-server setting. To simulate a RAM machine, the client now communicates with m semi-honest servers. With the involvement of more servers, we can hope to achieve schemes that are more efficient as well as schemes that protect against collusions of t servers.

Definition 2 (Distributed ORAM, informal). *An (m, t)-ORAM simulation $(0 < t < m)$ is an oblivious RAM simulation of a RAM machine, that is invoked by a CPU client and m remote storage servers, and that is private against a collusion of t corrupt servers. Namely, for any two actual access patterns y, z of length ℓ, the corresponding combined view of any t servers during the ORAM simulation (that consists of the actual access queries made to the t servers) are computationally indistinguishable.*

Parameters and Complexity Measures. The main complexity measure in which ORAM schemes compete is the *bandwidth overhead* (or, shortly, *overhead*). When the ORAM protocol operates in the "balls and bins" manner [17], where the only type of data exchanged between the client and servers is actual memory blocks, it is convenient to define the overhead as the amount of actual memory blocks that are queried in the ORAM simulation to simulate a virtual query to a single block. However, in general, overhead is defined as the blowup in the number of information bits exchanged between the parties, relative to a non-oblivious execution of the program. Following the more general definition, the overhead is sometimes a function of the block size B. Clearly, we aim to achieve a small asymptotic overhead with block size as small as possible.

Other metrics include the size of the server storage and the client's local memory (in blocks), and the amount and type of the computations performed by the servers (e.g. simple arithmetics vs. heavy cryptography). We note that all of these notions are best defined in terms of overhead, compared to a non-oblivious execution of the program, e.g. storage overhead, computational overhead, etc.

2.2 Private Information Retrieval

Private information retrieval (PIR) [10] is a cryptographic primitive that allows a client to query a database stored in a remote server, without revealing the identity of the queried data block. Specifically, an array of n blocks $X = (x_1, \ldots, x_n)$ is stored in a server. The client, with input $i \in [n]$, wishes to retrieve x_i, while keeping i private. PIR protocols allow the client to do that while minimizing the number of bits exchanged between the client and server. PIR is studied in two main settings: single-server PIR, where the database is stored in a single server, and the multi-server setting, where the database is replicated and stored in all servers, with which the client communicates simultaneously. More specifically, an (m, t)-PIR is a PIR protocol that involves $m > 1$ servers and that is secure against any collusion of $t < m$ servers. It was shown in [10] that non-trivial single-server PIRs cannot achieve information-theoretic security. Such schemes are possible with two servers (or more). Moreover, many known two-server PIRs (both information theoretic and computational, e.g. [6,7,10,13]) do not involve heavy server-side computation, like homomorphic encryption or number theoretic computations, as opposed to known single-server protocols (e.g. [15,23]).

3   A Simple Four-Server ORAM with Constant Overhead

We present our four-server ORAM protocol with constant bandwidth overhead and linear server-side computation per access. The protocol bypasses the need for symmetric encryption as it secret-shares the data among the servers. We use distributed point functions [16] (see Sect. 3.1 below) as a building block.

Theorem 1 (Four-server ORAM). *Assume the existence of a two-party DPF scheme for point functions $\{0,1\}^n \to \{0,1\}^m$ with share length $\Lambda(n, m)$ bits. Then, there exists a $(4, 1)$-ORAM scheme with linear² server-side computation per access and bandwidth overhead of $O(\Lambda(\log N, B)/B)$ for a block size of $B = \Omega(\Lambda(\log N, 1))$.*

---

² Up to polylogarithmic factors.

Instantiating our scheme with the DPF from [7] obtains the following.

Instantiation 1. *Assume the existence of one-way functions. Then, there exists a $(4,1)$-ORAM scheme with linear server-side computation per access and constant bandwidth overhead for a block size of $B = \Omega(\lambda \log N)$, where λ is a security parameter.*

3.1 Building Block: Distributed Point Functions

Distributed Point Functions (DPF), introduced by Gilboa and Ishai [16], are a special case of the broader cryptographic primitive called *Function Secret Sharing* (FSS) [7]. Analogous to standard secret sharing, an FSS allows a dealer to secret-share a function f among two (or more) participants. Each participant is given a share that does not reveal any information about f. Using his share, each participant p_i, for $i \in \{0,1\}$, can compute a value $f_i(x)$ on any input x in f's domain. The value $f(x)$ can be computed by combining $f_0(x)$ and $f_1(x)$. In fact, $f(x) = f_0(x) + f_1(x)$. Distributed point function is an FSS for the class of point functions, i.e., all functions $P_{a,b} : \{0,1\}^n \rightarrow \{0,1\}^m$ that are defined by $P_{a,b}(a) = b$ and $P_{a,b}(a') = 0^m$ for all $a' \neq a$. Boyle et al. [7] construct a DPF scheme where the shares given to the parties are of size $O(\lambda n + m)$, where λ is a security parameter, that is the length of a PRG seed. We are mainly interested in the application of DPFs to PIR and PIR-write [7,16].

3.2 Overview

Similarly to the schemes of [12,19], we apply DPF-based PIR [7] to allow the client to efficiently read records from a replicated data. If we allow linear server-side computation per access, the task of oblivious reads becomes trivial by using DPFs. The remaining challenge is how to efficiently perform oblivious writes to the data.

The core idea behind the scheme is to apply DPFs not only for PIR, but also for a variant of *PIR-write*. PIR-write (a variant of which was first investigated in [28]) is the write-only analog of PIR. We use DPFs to construct a simple two-server PIR-write where every server holds an additive share of the data. Our PIR-write protocol is limited in the sense that the client can only modify an existing record by some difference of his specification (rather than specifying the new value to be written). If the client has the ability to read the record in a private manner, then this limitation becomes irrelevant.

We combine the read-only PIR and the write-only PIR-write primitives to obtain a four-server ORAM scheme that enables both private reads and writes. In the setup, the client generates two additive shares of the initial data, X^0, X^1 s.t. $X = X^0 \oplus X^1$, and replicates each of the shares. Each of the four shares obtained is given to one of the servers. For a private read, the client retrieves each of the shares X^0, X^1, using the DPF-based PIR protocol, with the two servers that hold the share. For a private write, the proposed PIR-write protocol is invoked with pairs of servers holding different shares of the data.

We remark that our method to combine PIR and PIR-write for ORAM is inspired by the 8-server ORAM scheme presented in [28], in which an elementary 4-server PIR-write protocol was integrated with the PIR from [10].

3.3 Oblivious Read-Only and Write-Only Schemes

Basic PIR and PIR-Write. Recall the classic two-server PIR protocol, proposed in [10]. To securely retrieve a data block x_i from an array $X = (x_1, \ldots, x_N)$ that is stored in two non-colluding servers $\mathcal{S}_0$ and $\mathcal{S}_1$, the client generates two random N-bit vectors, e_i^0 and e_i^1 such that $e_i^0 \oplus e_i^1 = e_i$, where e_i is the ith unit vector, and sends e_i^b to $\mathcal{S}_b$. In other words, the client secret-shares the vector e_i among the two servers. Then, each server, computes the inner product $x_i^b := X \cdot e_i^b$ and sends it to the client. It is easy to see that $x_i = x_i^0 \oplus x_i^1$.

The same approach can be used for two-server PIR-write. However, now we require that the data is shared, rather than replicated, among the two servers. Namely, server $\mathcal{S}_b$ holds a share of the data X^b, such that $X^0 \oplus X^1 = X$. In order to write a new value $\hat{x}_i$ to the ith block in the array, the client secret-shares the vector $(\hat{x}_i \oplus x_i)e_i$ to the two servers. Each of the servers adds his share to X^b, and obtains a new array $\hat{X}^b$. After this update, the servers have additive shares of X with the updated value of x_i. Notice that we assume that the client already read and knows x_i; this is not standard in the PIR-write model.

Efficient PIR and PIR-Write via DPFs. In the heart of the PIR and PIR-write protocols described above is the secret sharing of vectors of size N. Applying standard additive secret sharing yields protocols with linear communication cost. Since we share a very specific type of vectors, specifically, unit vectors and their multiples, standard secret sharing is an overkill. Instead, we use DPFs. The values of a point function $P_{i,x} : [N] \rightarrow \{0,1\}^m$ (that evaluates x at i, and zero elsewhere) can be represented by a multiple of a unit vector $v_{i,x} := xe_i$. Hence, one can view distributed point functions as a means to "compress" shares of unit vectors and their multiples. We can use DPFs to share such a vector among two participants p_0 and p_1, as follows. We secret-share the function $P_{i,x}$ using a DPF scheme, and generate two shares $P_{i,x}^0$ and $P_{i,x}^1$. For $b \in \{0,1\}$, share $P_{i,x}^b$ is sent to participant p_b. The participants can compute their shares of the vector $v_{i,x}$ by evaluating their DPF share on every input in $[N]$. Namely, p_b computes his share $v_{i,x}^b := (P_{i,x}^b(1), \ldots, P_{i,x}^b(n))$. From the correctness of the underlying DPF scheme, it holds that $v_{i,x}^0 \oplus v_{i,x}^1 = v_{i,x}$. Further, from the security of the DPF, the participants do not learn anything about the vector $v_{i,x}$ except the fact that it is a multiple of a unit vector. Using the DPF construction from [7], we have a secret sharing scheme for unit vectors and their multiples, with communication complexity $O(\lambda \log N + m)$, assuming the existence of a PRG $G : \{0,1\}^\lambda \rightarrow \{0,1\}^m$.

3.4 Construction of Four-Server ORAM

Initial Server Storage. Let $\mathcal{S}_0^0, \mathcal{S}_1^0, \mathcal{S}_0^1$ and $\mathcal{S}_1^1$ be the four servers involved in the protocol. Let $X = (x_1, \ldots, x_N)$ be the data consisting of N blocks, each of size $B = \Omega(\Lambda(\log N, 1))$ bits. In initialization, the client generates two additive shares of the data, $X^0 = (x_1^0, \ldots, x_N^0)$ and $X^1 = (x_1^1, \ldots, x_N^1)$. That is, X^0 and X^1 are two random vectors of N blocks, satisfying $X^0 \oplus X^1 = X$. For $b \in \{0, 1\}$, the client sends X^b to both $\mathcal{S}_0^b$ and $\mathcal{S}_1^b$. Throughout the ORAM simulation, we maintain the following invariant: for $b \in \{0, 1\}$, $\mathcal{S}_0^b$ and $\mathcal{S}_1^b$ have an identical array X^b, such that X^0 and X^1 are random additive shares of X.

Query Protocol. To obliviously simulate a read/write query to the ith block in the data, the client first reads the value x_i via two PIR queries: a two-server PIR with $\mathcal{S}_0^0$ and $\mathcal{S}_1^0$ to retrieve x_i^0, and a two-server PIR with $\mathcal{S}_0^1$ and $\mathcal{S}_1^1$ to retrieve x_i^1. The client then computes x_i using the two shares. Second, to write a new value $\hat{x}_i$ to the data (which can possibly be equal to x_i), the client performs two *identical* invocations of two-server PIR-write, each with servers $\mathcal{S}_b^0$ and $\mathcal{S}_b^1$ for $b \in \{0, 1\}$. It is important that $\mathcal{S}_0^b, \mathcal{S}_1^b$ (for $b \in \{0, 1\}$) receive an identical PIR-write query, since otherwise, they will no longer have two identical replicates.

3.5 Analysis

The security of the scheme follows directly from the security of the underlying DPF protocol from [7]. It remains to analyze the bandwidth cost. To simulate a query, the client sends each of the servers two DPF shares: one for reading of length $\Lambda(\log N, 1)$ bits, and another for writing of length $\Lambda(\log N, B)$. With a block size of $B = \Omega(\Lambda(\log N, 1))$ this translates to $O(\Lambda(\log N, B)/B)$ bandwidth overhead. Each of the servers, in return, answers by sending two blocks.

4 The Balanced Hierarchical ORAM Framework

In this section, we lay the groundwork for our constructions in the standard distributed ORAM model, that are presented later in Sects. 5 and 6.

4.1 Main Building Block: Hashing

Hashing, or more accurately, oblivious hashing, has been a main building block of hierarchical ORAM schemes since their first appearance in [27]. Various types of hashing schemes, each with different parameters and properties, were plugged in ORAM constructions in an attempt to achieve efficient protocols (e.g. [8,17,18]). Hashing stands at the heart of our constructions as well. However, since we make a generic black-box use of hashing, we do not limit ourselves to a specific scheme, but rather take a modular approach.

We consider an (n, m, s)-*hashing scheme*[3], H, to be defined by three procedures: Gen for key generation, Build for constructing a hash table T of size m that contains n given data elements, using the generated key, and Lookup for querying T for a target value. The scheme may also use a stash to store at most

---

[3] Implicitly stated parameters may be omitted for brevity.

s elements that could not be inserted into T. In a context where a collection of hashing schemes operate simultaneously (e.g. ORAMs), a *shared stash* may be used by all hash tables. We denote by $C_{\mathsf{Build}}(H)$ and $C_{\mathsf{Lookup}}(H)$, the build-up complexity and the query complexity of H (resp.) in terms of communication (in the client-server setting).

An *oblivious* hashing scheme is a scheme whose Build and Lookup procedures are oblivious of the stored data and the queried elements (respectively). In the full version, we provide formal definitions and notation for the above, and survey a few of the schemes that were used in prior ORAM works.

4.2   Starting Point: Single-Server ORAM of Kushilevitz et al. [22]

Overview. The starting point of our distributed ORAM constructions in Sects. 5 and 6 is the single-server scheme from [22]. In standard hierarchical ORAMs, the server stores the data in $\log N$ levels, where every level is a hash table, larger by a factor of 2 than the preceding level. Kushilevitz et al. changed this by having $L = \log_d N$ levels, where the size of the ith level is proportional to $(d-1) \cdot d^{i-1}$. Having less levels eventually leads to the efficiency in overhead, however, since level $i+1$ is larger by a factor of d (no longer constant) than level i, merging level i with level $i+1$ becomes costly (shuffling an array of size $(d-1) \cdot d^i$ every $(d-1) \cdot d^{i-1}$ queries). To solve this problem, every level is stored in $d-1$ separate hash tables of equal size in a way that allows us to reshuffle every level into a single hash table in the subsequent level.

Theorem 2 ([8,22]). *Let d be a parameter, and define $L = \log_d N$. Assume the existence of one-way functions, and a collection $\{H_i\}_{i=1}^{L}$, where H_i is an oblivious $(d^{i-1}k, \cdot, \cdot)$-hashing scheme, with a shared stash of size s. Then there exists a single-server ORAM scheme that achieves the following overhead for block size $B = \Omega(\log N)$.*

$$O\left(k + s + \sum_{i=1}^{L} d \cdot C_{\mathsf{Lookup}}(H_i) + \sum_{i=1}^{L} \frac{C_{\mathsf{Build}}(H_i)}{d^{i-1}k} \right)$$

A special variant of the theorem was proven by Kushilevitz et al. [22]. In their work, they use a well-specified collection of hashing schemes (consisting of both standard and cuckoo hashing [29]), and obtain an overhead of $O(\log^2 N / \log \log N)$. The modular approach to hierarchical ORAM was taken by Chan et al. [8], in light of their observations regarding the conceptual complexity of cuckoo hashing, and their construction of a simpler oblivious hashing scheme that achieves a similar result. Our results in the distributed setting fit perfectly in this generic framework, as they are independent of the underlying hashing schemes. Below, we elaborate the details of the construction from [22], as a preparation towards the following sections.

Data Structure. The top level, indexed $i = 0$, is stored as a plain array of size k. As for the rest of the hierarchy, the ith level ($i = 1 \dots L$) is stored in $d-1$

hash tables, generated by an oblivious $(d^{i-1}k, \cdot, \cdot)$-hashing scheme H_i. For every $i = 1, \ldots, L$ and $j = 1, \ldots, d - 1$, let T_i^j be the jth table in the ith level, and let κ_i^j be its corresponding key. All hashing schemes in the hierarchy share a stash S^4. The keys κ_i^j can be encrypted and stored remotely in the server. Also, the client stores and maintains a counter t that starts at zero, and increments by one after every virtual access is simulated. The ORAM simulation starts with the initial data stored entirely in the lowest level.

Blocks Positioning Invariant. Throughout the ORAM simulation, every data block in the virtual memory resides either in the top level, or in one of the hash tables in the hierarchy, or in the shared stash. The blocks are hashed according to their virtual addresses. The data structure does not contain duplicated records.

Blocks Flow and Reshuffles. Once a block is queried, it is inserted into the top level, therefore the level fills up after k queries. Reshuffles are used to push blocks down the hierarchy and prevent overflows in the data structure. Basically, every time we try to insert blocks to a full level, we clear the level by reshuffling its blocks to a lower level. For instance, the top level is reshuffled every k queries.

In every reshuffle, blocks are inserted into the first empty hash table in the highest level possible, using the corresponding Build procedure, with a freshly generated key. Thus, the first time the top level is reshuffled (after round k), its blocks are inserted to the first table in the next level, i.e. T_1^1, which becomes full. The top level fills up again after k queries. This time, the reshuffle is made to T_1^2, as T_1^1 is not empty anymore. After $d - 1$ such reshuffles, the entire first level becomes full, therefore, after $d \cdot k$ queries, we need to reshuffle both the top level and the first level. This time, we insert all blocks in these levels into T_2^1.

Observe that this mechanism is analogous to counting in base d: every level represents a digit, whose value is the number of full hash tables in the level. An increment of a digit with value $d - 1$, equivalently - insertion to a full level, is done by resetting the digit to zero, and incrementing the next digit by 1, that is, reshuffling the level to a hash table in the next level (see Fig. 1). We formalize the process as follows: in every round $t = t' \cdot k$, levels $0, \ldots, i$ are reshuffled down to hash table T_{i+1}^j, where i is the maximal integer for which $d^i \mid t'$, and $j = (t' \bmod d^{i+1})/d^i$. Notice that level i is reshuffled every $k \cdot d^i$ queries.

$d = 6$
$t = 360 \cdot k = 1400_6 \cdot k$

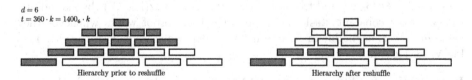

Hierarchy prior to reshuffle   Hierarchy after reshuffle

Fig. 1. A demonstration of the flow of blocks during an ORAM simulation with $d = 6$. A gray cell indicates a full hash table, a white one is an empty table.

---

[4] In the scheme of [22], the shared stash is 'virtualized', and is re-inserted into the hierarchy. We roll-back this optimization in preparation to our constructions.

Query. In order to retrieve a data block with virtual address v, the client searches for the block in the top level and the stash first. Then, for every level i, the client scans hash tables T_i^j using H_i.Lookup procedure, *in reverse order*, starting with the table that was last reshuffled into. Once the target block was found, the scan continues with dummy queries. This is important for security (see Claim 4).

5   A Three-Server ORAM Scheme

Below, we formally state our first result in the standard distributed ORAM model: an efficient three-server ORAM scheme.

Theorem 3 (Three-server ORAM using regular hashing). *Let d be a parameter, and define $L = \log_d N$. Assume the existence of one-way functions, and a collection $\{H_i\}_{i=1}^{L}$, where H_i is a $(d^{i-1}(k + s), m_i, s)$-hashing scheme. Then, there exists a $(3,1)$-ORAM scheme that achieves an overhead of*

$$O\left(k + L + \sum_{i=1}^{L} \frac{m_i}{d^{i-1}k}\right)$$

for block size $B = \Omega(\alpha d \log N + s \log d)$, where $\alpha := \max_i C_{\mathsf{Lookup}}(H_i)$.

We propose two different instantiations of our construction, each with a different collection of hashing schemes that was used in prior ORAM works [8,18,22]. Both instantiations yield sub-logarithmic overhead, and their parameters are very close. However, Instantiation 3 may be conceptually simpler (due to [8]). More details about the used hashing schemes can be found in the full version.

First, we plug in the collection of hashing schemes used by Goodrich and Mitzenmacher [18], and later by Kushilevitz et al. [22]. The collection mainly consists of cuckoo hashing schemes, however, since stashed cuckoo hashing was shown to have a negligible failure probability only when the size of the hash table is polylogarithmic in N (specifically, $\Omega(\log^7 N)$) [18], standard hashing with bucket size $\log N / \log \log N$ is used in the first $\Theta(\log_d \log N)$ levels. We point out that in both mentioned works [18,22], the stash size for cuckoo hashing is logarithmic. In our instantiation, we use a stash of size $\Theta(\omega(1) \cdot \log N / \log \log N)$. Although [18] proved that failure probability is negligible in N when the stash is of size $s = \Theta(\log N)$ and the size of the table is $m = \Omega(\log^7 N)$ (by extending the proof for constant stash size from [21]), their proof works whenever the value $m^{-\Theta(s)}$ is negligible in N, and in particular, when we choose $s = \Theta(\omega(1) \cdot \log N / \log \log N)$.

Instantiation 2 (Three-server ORAM using cuckoo hashing). *Assume the existence of one-way functions. Let d be a parameter at most polylogarithmic in N. Then, there exists a three-server ORAM scheme that achieves overhead of $O(\log_d N \cdot \omega(1))$ for $B = \Omega(d \log N)$.*

When $d = \log^\epsilon N$ for a constant $\epsilon \in (0, 1)$, we achieve an overhead of $O(\omega(1) \cdot \log N / \log \log N)$ with $B = O(\log^{1+\epsilon} N)$.

Alternatively, we can use the simple two-tier hashing scheme from [2], with buckets of size $\log^{0.5+\epsilon} N$, to achieve the following parameters.

Instantiation 3 (Three-server ORAM using two-tier hashing). *Assume the existence of one-way functions. Let d be a parameter at most polylogarithmic in N. Then, there exists a three-server ORAM scheme that achieves overhead of $O(\log_d N)$ for block size $B = \Omega(d \log^{1.5+\epsilon} N)$.*

For $d = \log^\epsilon N$, we obtain an overhead of $O(\log N / \log \log N)$ with $B = O(\log^{1.5+2\epsilon} N)$.

5.1 Overview

Our three-server scheme is based on the single-server balanced hierarchical structure of Kushilevitz et al. [22] (described in Sect. 4). We take advantage of the existence of multiple servers and reduce the overhead as follows.

Reduce Query Cost Using PIR. One of the consequences of balancing the hierarchy is having multiple hash tables in a level, in any of which a target block can reside. More specifically, if $T_i^1, \ldots, T_i^{d-1}$ are the hash tables at level i, then a block with address v can possibly reside in any of the positions in $T_i^j[H_i.\text{Lookup}(v, \kappa_i^j)]$ for $j = 1, \cdots, d-1$. To retrieve such a block, we could basically download all blocks in these positions, i.e. $\sum_{i=1}^{L}(d-1)C_{\text{Lookup}}(H_i)$ blocks in total. This already exceeds the promised overhead. Instead, we use PIR to extract the block efficiently without compromising the security of the scheme. For every level i, starting from the top, we invoke a PIR protocol over the array that consists of the $(d-1)C_{\text{Lookup}}(H_i)$ possible positions for v in the level.

Performing PIR queries requires that the client knows the exact position of the target block in the queried array, namely, in which bucket, out of the $d-1$ possibilities, block v resides, if at all. Therefore, the client first downloads the addresses of all blocks in the array, and only then performs the PIR query. Although some PIR protocols in the literature (e.g. [7]) do not impose this requirement, we still need to download the addresses since it is essential for the security of the protocol that the client re-writes the address of the queried block.

An address of a block can be represented using $\log N$ bits. Thus, downloading the addresses of all possible positions in all levels costs us $\sum_{i=1}^{L}(d-1)C_{\text{Lookup}}(H_i) \log N$ bits of communication. If we choose $B = \Omega(\alpha d \log N)$ for $\alpha = \max_i C_{\text{Lookup}}(H_i)$, this cost translates to the desirable $O(L)$ overhead. Two-server PIRs work in the model where the data is replicated and stored in two non-colluding servers. Thus, every level in the hierarchy, except the top level, will be stored, accessed, and modified simultaneously in two of the three servers.

Reduce Reshuffles Cost by Bypassing Oblivious Hashing. We use a variant of the reshuffle procedure suggested by Lu and Ostrovsky [25]. Their protocol works in a model with two non-colluding servers, where one server stores the odd levels, and the other stores the even levels. Before reshuffling a level, the servers gather all blocks to be reshuffled, permute them randomly, and exchange them through the client, who re-encrypts them and tags them with pseudorandom tags. The level is then reshuffled by one server using some *regular* hashing scheme (not necessarily oblivious), and is sent to the other server, record by record, through the client. The security of their scheme follows from the following observations:

(i) the blocks are re-encrypted and permuted randomly before the reshuffle, eliminating any dependency on prior events,

(ii) the blocks are hashed according to pseudorandom tags, hence their order is (computationally) independent of their identities,

(iii) the server that holds a level cannot distinguish between dummy queries and real ones since he was not involved in the reshuffle, and

(iv) the server that reshuffles the level (and can tell a dummy query) does not see the accesses to the level at all.

Applying this method naively when each of the servers holds the entire hierarchy might reveal information about the access pattern since (iii) and (iv) no longer hold. Therefore, we should adapt their method wisely, while having two replicates of every level, to allow performing PIR queries. A straight forward implementation would require four servers: two holding replicates of the odd levels, and two holding replicates of the even levels. However, this can be done using three servers only by having every pair of servers (out of the three possible pairs) hold every third level.

5.2   Full Construction

Data Structure. The data is virtually viewed as an array of N blocks, each of size $\Omega(\alpha d \log N)$ bits. Every block therefore has a virtual address in $[N]$.

Distributed Server Storage. The data structure is identical to that from [22], however, our scheme uses three servers, S_0, S_1, and S_2, to store the data. The top level is stored in all servers. Every other level is held by two servers only: for $j = 0, \ldots, \lfloor \frac{L}{3} \rfloor$, S_0 and S_1 share replicates of levels $i = 3j$, S_1 and S_2 share replicates of levels $3j + 1$, and S_2 and S_0 both hold all levels $i = 3j + 2$.

Dummy Blocks. Dummy blocks are blocks that are not "real" (not part of the virtual memory), but are treated as such, and assigned dummy virtual addresses. From the point of view of the 'reshuffler' server, a dummy block, unlike an empty block, cannot be distinguished from a real block. We use two types of dummy blocks, both essential for the security of the scheme.

(i) *Dummy Hash Blocks.* Dummy hash blocks replace real blocks once they are read and written to the top level. The security of our scheme relies on the fact that all blocks in the hierarchy are of distinct addresses, hence the importance of this replacement.

(ii) *Dummy Stash Blocks.* Dummy stash blocks are created by the client to fill in empty entries in the hierarchy. Since our scheme uses a stash to handle overflows, the number of blocks in the stash and in each of the hash tables is not deterministic and is dependent on the access pattern. To hide this information from the server that performs the reshuffling of a level, we fill all empty entries in the stash, and some of the empty entries in the hash tables, with dummy stash blocks.

Block Headers. To properly manage the data, the client needs to know the identity of every block it downloads (i.e. its virtual address). Therefore, every entry in the server storage contains, besides the data of the block, a header that consists of the virtual address of the block, which can be either an address in $[N]$, a numbered dummy address, such as '$dummyHash \circ t$' or '$dummyStash \circ r$', or just '$empty$'. The length of the header is $O(\log N)$ bits, thus does not affect the asymptotic block size. Unless explicitly stated otherwise, the headers are downloaded, uploaded and re-encrypted together with the data. An entry with a block of virtual address v and data x is denoted by the tuple (v, x).

Tags. Since we use the servers for reshuffling the levels, we wish to hide the virtual addresses of the blocks to be reshuffled. We use pseudorandom tags to replace these addresses, as first suggested in [25]. The tags are computed using a keyed PRF, F_s, that is known to the client only. When generating a new hash table, the server hashes the blocks according to their tags (rather than their virtual addresses). Furthermore, to eliminate any dependency between tags that are seen in different reshuffles, the client keeps an *epoch* e_i^j for every hash table T_i^j in the hierarchy. The epoch of a table is updated prior to every reshuffle, and is used, together with i and j, to compute fresh tags for blocks in the table. The epochs can be stored remotely in the servers to avoid large client storage.

Protocol. We refer to the balanced hierarchy of [22] as our starting point.

Query. We replace the reads performed by the client with PIR protocols that are executed over arrays in the data. Specifically, the first PIR is performed over the stash to retrieve the target block if it is found there. The top level can be downloaded entirely since it has to be re-written anyway. The search continues to the other levels in the hierarchy in the order specified in Sect. 4. The target block can possibly reside in any of the $d - 1$ hash tables in a level, therefore, the client invokes a PIR protocol to extract the target block out of the many possible positions. Every PIR in the procedure is preceded by downloading the headers in the queried array, using which the client knows the position of the target block. A technical detailed description is provided in Algorithm 1.

Algorithm 1. Three-Server Construction: Query
***
1: Allocate a local register of the size of a single record.

2: Initialize a flag found $\leftarrow 0$.

3: Download the top level, one record at a time. If v is found at some entry (v, x) then store x in the local register, and mark $found \leftarrow 1$.

4: Download all headers from S. If v was found among these headers, let p be its position, and mark found $\leftarrow 1$. Otherwise, let p be a position of a random entry in the stash. Invoke $\text{PIR}(S, p)$ to fetch (v, x) with any two of the three servers, and store x in the register.

5: **for** every level $i = 1 \ldots L$ **do**

6:     $t' \leftarrow \lfloor t/k \rfloor$

7:     $r \leftarrow \lfloor (t' \bmod d^i)/d^{i-1} \rfloor$

8:     $headers \leftarrow \emptyset$

9:     **for** every hash table $j = r \ldots 1$ **do**

10:         If found $= false$, compute the corresponding tag of v, $\tau \leftarrow F_s(i, j, e_i^j, v)$. Otherwise, assign $\tau \leftarrow F_s(i, j, e_i^j, dummy \circ t)$.

11:         $Q_i^j \leftarrow H_i.\text{Lookup}(\tau, \kappa_i^j)$

12:         Download all headers of entries in $T_i^j[Q_i^j]$, and append them to $headers$. If one of the headers says v, mark found $\leftarrow true$.

13:     **end for**

14:     Let p be the position of v in $headers$ if it was found there, or a random value in $\{1, \ldots, |headers|\}$ otherwise.

15:     Let A be the array of entries corresponding to headers in $headers$.

16:     Invoke $\text{PIR}(A, p)$ to fetch (v, x) with the two servers holding level i, and store x in the register (if v was not found in $headers$ this would be a dummy PIR).

17:     Re-encrypt $headers$, and upload it back to the two servers, while changing v to $dummyHash \circ t$.

18: **end for**

19: If the query is a write query, overwrite x in the register.

20: Read each entry of the entire top level from both servers one at a time, re-encrypt it, then write it back, with the following exception: if the entry (v, x) was first found at the top level, then overwrite x with the (possibly) new value from the register, otherwise, write (v, x) in the first empty spot of the form $(empty, \cdot)$.

21: Increment the counter t, and reshuffle the appropriate levels.
***

Reshuffles. Let $\mathcal{S}_a$ and $\mathcal{S}_b$ be the two servers holding level $i + 1$, and let $\mathcal{S}_c$ be the other server. Reshuffling levels $0, \ldots, i$ into hash table T_{i+1}^j is performed as follows. As a first step, we send all non-empty blocks that should be reshuffled (including stash) to $\mathcal{S}_c$, by having the servers exchange the blocks they hold in levels $0, \ldots, i$ and the stash, through the client, one block at a time, in a random order. Besides forwarding the blocks to $\mathcal{S}_c$, the client also re-encrypts every block and re-tags it with a fresh tag (using epochs, as already mentioned). Once $\mathcal{S}_c$ has all tagged blocks, he can create a new hash table and stash using the appropriate Build procedure. He then sends the hash table and stash, one record at a time, to the client. The client re-encrypts all records, and forwards them to the other two servers, who store the hash table in T_{i+1}^j, and the stash to its place.

Algorithm 2. Three-Server Construction: Reshuffle

Reshuffling into table T_{i+1}^j

Let $\mathcal{S}_a$ and $\mathcal{S}_b$ be the servers holding level $i+1$, and let $\mathcal{S}_c$ be the other server.

1: Every server of the three allocates a temporary array. For every level ℓ between levels 1 and i, let $\mathcal{S}^\ell$ be the server with the smallest id that holds level ℓ. For every such ℓ, $\mathcal{S}^\ell$ inserts all records in level ℓ to its temporary array. In addition, one of the servers, say $\mathcal{S}_0$, inserts all stash records into its temporary array.

2: $\mathcal{S}_c$ applies a random permutation on its temporary array, and sends the records one by one to the client. The client re-encrypts each record and sends it to $\mathcal{S}_b$. $\mathcal{S}_b$ inserts all records it receives to its array. $\mathcal{S}_b$ permutes its array randomly, and forwards it to $\mathcal{S}_a$ through the client (who re-encrypts them). $\mathcal{S}_a$, in his turn, also inserts all received records, applies a random permutation, and sends them one by one to the client.

3: The client re-encrypts every non-empty record (v,x) and sends it to $\mathcal{S}_c$, together with a tag, which is the output of the PRF $F_s(i+1, j, e_{i+1}^j, v)$, where e_{i+1} is the new epoch of T_{i+1}^j. Note that v may be a virtual memory address, or a dummy value. In this step, dummy records are treated as real records and only empty records are discarded.

4: $\mathcal{S}_c$ receives $d^i(k+s)$ tagged records, which are all records that should be reshuffled into T_{i+1}^j. It generates a new key $\kappa_i^j \leftarrow H_i.\mathsf{Gen}(N)$, and constructs a hash table and a stash $(T_i^j, S) \leftarrow H_i.\mathsf{Build}(\kappa_i^j, Y)$, where Y is the set of tagged records received from the client. If the insertion fails, a new key is generated (this happens with a negligible probability). $\mathcal{S}_c$ then informs the client about the number of elements inside the stash, σ, and the key κ_i^j, then sends both the hash table T_i^j and the stash one record at a time to the client.

5: As the client receives entries from $\mathcal{S}_c$ one at a time, it re-encrypts each record and sends it to both $\mathcal{S}_a$ and $\mathcal{S}_b$ without modifying the contents except:
   (a) The first σ empty records in the table the client receives from $\mathcal{S}_c$ are encrypted as $(dummyStash \circ r, \cdot)$, incrementing r each time.
   (b) Subsequent empty records from the table are encrypted as $(empty, \cdot)$.
   (c) Every empty record in the stash is re-encrypted as $(dummyStash \circ r, \cdot)$, incrementing r each time.

6: $\mathcal{S}_a$ and $\mathcal{S}_b$ store the table records in level $i+1$ in the order in which they were received, and store the stash records at the top level.

The client uses dummy stash blocks to replace as many empty blocks as needed to get a full hash table, and a full stash. This is important since we do not want to reveal the load of the stash to the server that does the next reshuffle. The reshuffle procedure is described in full details in Algorithm 2.

5.3 Analysis

Complexity. We begin with analyzing the complexity of the described scheme.

Storage Complexity. The combined server storage contains a stash of size s, a top level of size k, and two duplicates of every other level i, consisting of $d-1$ hash tables of size m_i each. In total, we have $O\left(s + k + \sum_{i=1}^{L} dm_i\right)$.

The client uses constant working memory as he only receives and forwards records, one at a time. The client does not need to keep the headers he downloads prior to PIR queries, as it is sufficient to keep the position of the target block.

Overhead. We now analyze the cost of performing a single query. First, consider the communication cost of downloading the headers for the PIRs. The PIRs are performed over the stash and each of the levels $i = 1, \ldots, L$. The number of headers downloaded amounts to $s + \sum_{i=1}^{L}(d-1)C_{\text{Lookup}}(H_i) \leq s + \alpha L(d-1)$, which is equivalent to $O(L)$ blocks of the required minimum size. Overall, $L+1$ PIR queries are invoked. For levels $i = 1, \ldots, L$, the PIR queries are performed over arrays of size at most $(d-1)C_{\text{Lookup}}(H_i)$. By using the classic two-server PIR from [10], this costs $(d-1)C_{\text{Lookup}}(H_i) < \alpha d$ bits and a single block per level. The stash adds s bits and a block. All of this sums up to no more than $O(L)$ data blocks. The client also downloads $O(k)$ blocks from the top level.

Next, consider the reshuffles. Blocks are reshuffled down to some hash table in the ith level if i is the smallest integer for which $(t/k) \bmod d^i \neq 0$. This occurs whenever t/k is a multiple of d^{i-1}, but not of d^i, i.e., at most once every $k \cdot d^{i-1}$ queries. During the reshuffle of a hash table T_i^j, the number of blocks transmitted is asymptotically bounded by the size of T_i^j and the size of the stash, which is $O(m_i)$. Hence, the amortized overhead of the reshuffles is $O(\sum_{i=1}^{L} \frac{m_i}{d^{i-1}k})$.

Security. Next, we present the security proof for our construction. We prove that the access pattern to any of the servers is oblivious and independent on the input. We describe a simulator Sim_a (for $a \in \{0,1,2\}$), that produces an output that is indistinguishable from the view of server $\mathcal{S}_a$ during the execution of the protocol, upon any sequence of virtual queries, given only its length.

Lemma 1 (Security of the three-server ORAM). *Let* $\text{View}_a(\boldsymbol{y})$ *be the view of server* $\mathcal{S}_a$ *during the execution of the three-server ORAM protocol, described in Algorithms 1 and 2, over a virtual access pattern* $\boldsymbol{y} = ((v_1, x_1), \ldots, (v_\ell, x_\ell))$. *For* $a \in \{0,1,2\}$, *there exists a simulator* Sim_a, *such that for every* $\boldsymbol{y}$ *of length* ℓ, *the distributions* $\text{Sim}_a(\ell)$ *and* $\text{View}_a(\boldsymbol{y})$ *are computationally indistinguishable.*

Proof Sketch. As in all previous works, we assume that the client uses one-way functions to encrypt and authenticate the data held in the servers, and therefore, encrypted data is indistinguishable by content (notice that the client re-encrypts every piece of data before sending it). We replace the keyed tagging functions, that are modeled as PRFs, with random functions. These steps can be formalized using proper standard hybrid arguments, which we avoid for brevity.

We begin by inspecting the view of the servers during the reshuffles. The procedure starts with the servers exchanging all blocks stored in levels $1, \ldots, i$

and in the stash, and sending them to $\mathcal{S}_c$. It is essential for security that the number of these blocks is independent of the input, as argued in Claims 1 and 2. We refer the reader to the full version for full proofs for these two claims, and all claims to follow.

Claim 1. *Throughout the ORAM simulation, the stash is always full.*

Claim 2. *Let t be a multiple of k, and denote $t' = t/k$. For every $1 \leq i \leq L$, define $r_i^t := \lfloor (t' \bmod d^i)/d^{i-1} \rfloor$. Then,*

(i) the top level is full prior to the reshuffle at round t, and is empty afterwards.
(ii) for every other level $1 \leq i \leq L$, once the reshuffle is completed, the first r_i^t tables in level i (i.e., $T_i^1, \ldots, T_i^{r_i^t}$) are full (contain $d^i(k+s)$ records each), and all other tables in level i are empty.

Claim 1 follows immediately from Step 5 of Algorithm 2. For Claim 2 follows from the analogy of the reshuffles to counting in base d (see Sect. 4) (notice that r_i^t can be also defined as the ith digit in the base d representation of t').

Having shown that the amount of data exchanged during the first steps of the reshuffling procedure depends only on t, we can simulate the view of any of the servers by a sequence of arbitrary encrypted data of the appropriate length. Next, $\mathcal{S}_c$ receives $(k+s) \cdot d^i$ tagged encrypted records (Claim 2). Since dummy records are numbered uniquely, and virtual records are never duplicated, these records always have unique addresses. We formalize this in Claim 3 below.

Claim 3. *At all times during the execution, any non-empty record of the form $(v, \cdot)$ will appear at most once in all hash tables in the hierarchy.*

Since the addresses of the records are unique, their tags will be unique as well (with overwhelming probability). This implies the following.

Corollary 1. *The tagging function $F_s(\cdot)$ will not be computed twice on the same input throughout the executions of Algorithm 2 during the ORAM simulation.*

Hence, by assuming F_s is a random function, the view of $\mathcal{S}_c$ can be simulated as a sequence of $(k+s) \cdot d^i$ arbitrary encrypted records with random distinct tags. Once $\mathcal{S}_c$ successfully creates the hash table, it sends it to $\mathcal{S}_a$ and $\mathcal{S}_b$ via the client. The size of the hash table is fixed. The entries of the hash tables are encrypted, and can be simulated as an arbitrary sequence of encrypted records.

To summarize, to simulate the view of the servers during the reshuffling phase, $\mathsf{Sim}_a(\ell)$ and $\mathsf{Sim}_b(\ell)$ output a sequence of encrypted arbitrary records of the appropriate length (which is fixed due to Claims 1 and 2), whereas $\mathsf{Sim}_c(\ell)$ outputs a sequence of encrypted arbitrary records that are tagged using distinct uniform values (a, b, c alternate between $0, 1, 2$ throughout the phases). From Corollary 1 and the security of the underlying symmetric encryption and PRFs, these outputs are indistinguishable from the views of the servers at the reshuffles.

We proceed to simulating the access pattern during queries. A query for a block v begins, independently of v, with downloading all blocks in the top level, and all headers in the stash. Next, a PIR is invoked over the stash. From the security of the underlying PIR, there exist two simulators $\mathsf{Sim}_0^{\mathrm{PIR}}(m), \mathsf{Sim}_1^{\mathrm{PIR}}(m)$, that simulate the individual views of the two servers (resp.) involved in the protocol, given only the size of the queried array, m. We use these simulators to simulate the view of the servers involved in the this and all following PIRs.

It remains to show that the identity of the blocks over which the PIRs are called, i.e. the values Q_i^j that a server $\mathcal{S}_a$ sees during the execution of Algorithm 1, can be simulated as well. Recall that, at every execution of the algorithm, Q_i^j is computed, for every i, j, as $H_i.\mathsf{Lookup}(\tau, \kappa_i^j)$, where τ is a tag computed using F_s, and κ_i^j is the used hash key. We denote by $\langle Q_i^j \rangle_a$ the sequence of Q_i^j values seen by $\mathcal{S}_a$ at *all* executions of Algorithm 1 during the ORAM simulation (these values correspond to levels i that are stored in $\mathcal{S}_a$). We also denote by $\langle \tau \rangle_a$ and $\langle \kappa_i^j \rangle_a$ the values used to compute $\langle Q_i^j \rangle_a$.

Claim 4. *The same v will not be queried upon twice at the same hash table (in Algorithm 1) between two reshuffles of the table during the ORAM execution.*

Dummy queries are numbered uniquely. The order in which we traverse the hierarchy, and the fact that no real queries are made after the block is found, ensure that Claim 4 is true for real queries as well. Hence, the following holds.

Corollary 2. *The tagging function F_s will not be computed twice on the same input throughout the executions of Algorithm 1 during the ORAM simulation.*

From Corollary 2, and since $\mathcal{S}_a$ is not involved in the hashing of $\langle \tau \rangle_a$, we get:

Claim 5. *The sequence $\langle \tau \rangle_a$, defined above, is comp. indistinguishable from a uniform sequence of unique tags, given the view of $\mathcal{S}_a$ during the reshuffles.*

Claim 6. *The sequence $\langle \kappa_i^j \rangle_a$, defined above, is comp. indistinguishable from a uniform sequence of hash keys, given the view of $\mathcal{S}_a$ during the reshuffles.*

In Claims 5 and 6, we show that $\langle \tau \rangle_a$ and $\langle \kappa_i^j \rangle_a$ are indistinguishable from sequences of uniformly chosen values, given the view of $\mathcal{S}_a$. Therefore, to simulate the values $\langle Q_i^j \rangle_a$, the simulator $\mathsf{Sim}_a(\ell)$ computes the output of $H_i.\mathsf{Lookup}$ for uniformly random tags and hash keys. This completes the proof of Lemma 1.

6   A Family of Multi-server ORAM Schemes

We present our following last result.

Theorem 4 ($(m, m-1)$-*ORAM* using oblivious hashing). *Let d be a parameter, and define $L = \log_d N$. Assume the existence of one-way functions, and a collection $\{H_i\}_{i=1}^L$, where H_i is an oblivious $(d^{i-1}(k+s), m_i, s)$-hashing scheme. Then, for any $m \geq 2$, there exists an $(m, m-1)$-ORAM scheme that achieves the following overhead for block size $B = \Omega(\beta \log N + \alpha d \log N)$*

$$O\left(k + L + \sum_{i=1}^{L} \frac{m_i}{d^{i-1}k} \right)$$

where $\alpha := \max_i C_{\mathsf{Lookup}}(H_i)$ and $\beta := \max_i \frac{C_{\mathsf{Build}}(H_i)}{d^{i-1}k}$.

Here, oblivious two-tier hashing [8] performs slightly better than other candidates (e.g. oblivious cuckoo hashing [18]).

Instantiation 4 $((m, m-1)$**-ORAM using two-tier hashing).** *Assuming the existence of one-way functions, there exists, for any* $m \geq 2$, *a* $(m,m-1)$-*ORAM scheme with overhead of* $O(\log N / \log \log N)$ *for block size of* $B = \Omega(\log^2 N)$.

We first present the special case of our construction in the two-server setting, and then generalize it the case where $m > 2$.

6.1   Two-Server ORAM: Overview

We base our two-server construction on the the $(3, 1)$-ORAM from Sect. 5.

Back to Oblivious Hashing. Now that we limit ourselves to using two servers only, each of which has to hold a replicate of the data for the PIR queries, we lose the ability to perform the reshuffles through a "third-party". Hence, we require now that the underlying hashing schemes are oblivious, and the build-up of the hash table is done using the oblivious Build procedures, where the client is the CPU, and one of the servers takes the role of the RAM.

Recall that the tags were essential for the security of the three-server scheme since the reshuffles were made by one of the servers, to which we did not want to reveal the identity of the blocks being reshuffled. Now that the reshuffling is done using oblivious hashing that hides any information about the records that are being hashed, or the hash keys used to hash them, using tags is not necessary anymore. Instead, the blocks are hashed, and accessed, by their headers.

Optimizing the Reshuffles. Naively creating a hash table at level i using H_i.Build, incurs an overhead of $C_{\mathsf{Build}}(H_i)$. We observe that in any hashing scheme, the only input relevant for the build-up of a hash table is the tags or, in our case, the headers of the blocks being reshuffled. Thus, we suggest the following solution. The reshuffles are modified so that the build-up of the hash tables is given, as input, the set of headers, rather than the blocks themselves. Since the headers are smaller than the blocks by a factor of at least $\beta := \max_i \frac{C_{\mathsf{Build}}(H_i)}{d^{i-1}k}$, the overhead incurred by the build-ups is cut by β, making it linear in $d^{i-1}k$.

Matching Data to Headers. As the headers are hashed, we still have to move the data to the new hash table. We securely match the data elements to the headers, by tagging them, and letting the servers to permute them randomly.

6.2   Two-Server ORAM: Full Construction

Data Structure. We start with the scheme from Sect. 5. The server storage remains as is, except the entire data structure is now replicated in the two servers. This is guaranteed to be the case at the end of every round in the protocol.

Query. Every virtual access is simulated as described in Algorithm 1, with the exception that the target block is queried upon in the hash tables by its virtual address, rather than its tag: $H_i.\mathsf{Lookup}(v, \kappa_i^j)$ rather than $H_i.\mathsf{Lookup}(\tau, \kappa_i^j)$. Also, all reads and writes, as well as the PIR queries, are made now to $\mathcal{S}_0$ and $\mathcal{S}_1$.

Reshuffles. The reshuffles are still performed in the same frequency. However, the roles of the servers change, as only two servers participate in the protocol. First, $\mathcal{S}_0$ prepares all headers of blocks that have to be reshuffled into the destination hash table, and, together with the client, invokes the appropriate oblivious Build procedure to hash the blocks into a new hash table.

We now match the data to the headers using our matching procedure. We begin by tagging the headers. $\mathcal{S}_0$ sends the shuffled headers, one by one to the client, who decrypts every header and tags it using a new epoch, then sends it back to $\mathcal{S}_0$. The headers corresponding to empty slots are tagged using numbered values, e.g. '*empty* ∘ 1'. Notice that the number of empty slots in the hash table and stash, combined, is fixed and independent of the input. Next, $\mathcal{S}_1$ sends the records (headers and data) that correspond to the shuffled headers, one by one, in a random order. Among the actual records, $\mathcal{S}_1$ also sends as many (numbered) empty records as required to match the number of empty slots in the hash table. The client tags every record he receives from $\mathcal{S}_1$, and forwards it $\mathcal{S}_0$ together with its tag. $\mathcal{S}_0$ now matches every record he receives to a header in the hash table or stash, according to the tags. He then sends the new hash table and stash to $\mathcal{S}_1$, through the client. See Algorithm 3 for full details.

6.3   Two-Server ORAM: Analysis

Complexity. The query complexity is identical to that of the three-server construction, and is equal to $O(k + L)$. To obliviously construct a hash table and a stash for a level i, the client and the servers exchange $C_{\mathsf{Build}}(H_i) = O(\beta d^{i-1}k)$ records (recall $\beta := \max_i \frac{C_{\mathsf{Build}}(H_i)}{d^{i-1}k}$). However, since the build-up is done over tags of size $\log N$ bits, rather than whole blocks of size $\Omega(\beta \log N)$, this translates to $O(d^{i-1}k)$ overhead in blocks. The matching procedure has a linear cost in the size of the level, that is $O(m_i)$. This amortizes to $O(1 + m_i/d^{i-1}k)$ overhead per level, and $O(L + \sum_{i=1}^{L} \frac{m_i}{d^{i-1}k})$ overall.

Security. Following Definition 2, it suffices to prove the following Lemma.

Lemma 2 (Security of the two-server ORAM). *Let* $\mathsf{View}_a(\boldsymbol{y})$ *be the view of server* $\mathcal{S}_a$ *during the execution of the two-server ORAM protocol, described in Sect. 6, over a virtual access pattern* $\boldsymbol{y} = ((v_1, x_1), \ldots, (v_\ell, x_\ell))$. *There exist simulators* $\mathsf{Sim}_0, \mathsf{Sim}_1$, *such that for every* $\boldsymbol{y}$ *of length* ℓ, *and every* $a \in \{0, 1\}$ *the distributions* $\mathsf{Sim}_a(\ell)$ *and* $\mathsf{View}_a(\boldsymbol{y})$ *are computationally indistinguishable.*

Algorithm 3. Two-Server Construction: Reshuffle

Reshuffling headers into table T_{i+1}^j

1: S_0 sends all records in levels $1, \ldots, i$ and the stash, one by one, to the client. The client re-encrypts every record he receives and forwards it to S_1, while eliminating all empty records. S_1 inserts every record he receives to a temporary array Y. Server S_1 now sends every header in Y back to S_0, through the client.

2: Let $\hat{Y}$ be the array of encrypted headers received by S_0. The client generates a fresh hashing key $\kappa_i^j \leftarrow H_i.\mathsf{Gen}(N)$, and, together with S_0, invokes $(\hat{T}, \hat{S}) \leftarrow H_i.\mathsf{Build}(\kappa_i^j, \hat{Y})$ to obliviously hash the headers into a hash table and stash.

Matching data to headers.

3: S_0 sends $(\hat{T}, \hat{S})$, record by record, to the client. The client decrypts every header v he receives, and computes a tag $\tau \leftarrow F_s(i+1, j, e_{i+1}^j, v)$. If the header is empty, then $\tau \leftarrow F_s(i+1, j, e_{i+1}^j, empty \circ z)$, where z is a counter that starts at 1 and and increments after every empty header. Notice that the number of empty headers, denoted by Z, depends only on i. The client sends the tag back to S_0.

4: S_1 inserts Z empty records $(empty \circ 1, \cdot), \ldots, (empty \circ Z, \cdot)$ to Y. Server S_1 permutes Y randomly, and sends it, one record at a time, to the client.

5: The client re-encrypts every record (v, x) it receives, and sends it to S_0 with a tag τ, that is the output of F_s on v with the appropriate epoch.

6: S_0 matches every tagged record it receives to one of the tags it received in Step 3, and inserts the corresponding record to its appropriate slot (either in $\hat{T}$ or $\hat{S}$).

7: At this point, S_0 holds the newly reshuffled hash table and stash, headers and data. The tags are discarded. S_0 sends both the table and the stash to S_1, via the client. Both servers replace the old stash and T_{i+1}^j with the new data.

Proof Sketch. Again, we assume that encryption is secure and tagging functions are random. Consider the view of the servers at the reshuffles. Claims 1 and 2 hold true here as well, therefore, the amount of encrypted data exchanged in Step 1 of Algorithm 3 is oblivious. From the obliviousness of the hashing scheme, the view seen in Step 2 can be simulated with an access pattern for an arbitrary execution of the oblivious $H_i.\mathsf{Build}$ procedure. As for the matching procedure, the view of S_1 consists of the new hash table and stash, both encrypted and of fixed size. S_0 receives a sequence of tags computed using F_s for a sequence of headers. We claim that these headers are unique. A proof of the claim is also provided in the full version.

Claim 7. *The tagging function $F_s(\cdot)$ will not be computed twice on the same input in Step 3 of Algorithm 3 throughout the executions of the algorithms during the ORAM simulation.*

Hence, the tags seen by S_0 are indistinguishable from uniform distinct values, and Sim_0 simulates them as such. Lastly, S_0 receives a sequence of tagged records. The records are encrypted and can be simulated. The tags were obtained by tagging the same set of unique headers, however, in an order that is uniformly and independently chosen by S_1 and that is not known to S_0. Therefore, we let Sim_0 to output the tags he has previously generated, permuted randomly.

To simulate the access pattern for the queries we rely on the obliviousness of the Lookup procedure: the sequence of $H_i.\mathsf{Lookup}(v, \kappa_i^j)$ values is indistinguishable from a sequence generated for an arbitrary sequence of addresses v using random hash keys. Thus, Sim_A just generates random keys using Gen, and computes Lookup for arbitrary inputs. The transcripts of the PIRs can be simulated from the definition of two-server PIR.

6.4   From Two Servers to m Servers

Lastly, we briefly show how to transform our two-server ORAM to an $(m, m-1)$-ORAM for $m > 2$. Please refer to the full version for a detailed analysis.

Query Using Multi-server PIR. To obliviously simulate a query to a block, the client follows the protocol used in the two-server construction (Algorithm 1). However, now that we want to achieve privacy against any colluding subset of corrupt servers, we use an m-server PIR protocol which guarantees such a privacy. That is, instead of invoking two-server PIRs to query blocks from the stash and hierarchy levels, the client now uses an $(m, m-1)$-PIR protocol involving all m servers, where the joint view of any $m-1$ servers is (computationally) independent of the target index. In particular, we can use the straight-forward m-server generalization of the basic PIR protocol from [10]. Since this protocol, as well as many known m-server PIRs, follow the standard PIR setting where the data is assumed to be replicated in all of the servers, the servers during the ORAM execution will hold identical replicates of the same data structure.

Extending the Matching Procedure. Reshuffles of levels are done in the same frequency, and in a very similar manner as in the two-server protocol. We only change the matching procedure. To match the content to the tags, we cannot rely only on two servers, since they might be both corrupt. Instead, all servers participate. The reshuffling procedure from Algorithm 3 is followed up to Step 5. After the client receives the permuted records from $\mathcal{S}_1$, he re-encrypts them and forwards them to $\mathcal{S}_2$. $\mathcal{S}_2$, in its turn, randomly permutes the records it receives, and forwards them to $\mathcal{S}_3$ (if it exists), through the client. This continues until all servers, except $\mathcal{S}_0$, have received the records and permuted them. Once they all had, the client tags the records and sends them to $\mathcal{S}_0$, who matches them to the shuffled headers. Lastly, the final hash table and stash are sent to all servers.

Acknowledgments. We thank Yuval Ishai, Rafail Ostrovsky and Benny Pinkas for useful comments.

References

1. Abraham, I., Fletcher, C.W., Nayak, K., Pinkas, B., Ren, L.: Asymptotically tight bounds for composing ORAM with PIR. In: Fehr, S. (ed.) PKC 2017. LNCS, vol. 10174, pp. 91–120. Springer, Heidelberg (2017). https://doi.org/10.1007/978-3-662-54365-8_5
2. Adler, M., Chakrabarti, S., Mitzenmacher, M., Rasmussen, L.: Parallel randomized load balancing. In: Proceedings of the Twenty-Seventh Annual ACM Symposium on Theory of Computing, STOC 1995, pp. 238–247. ACM, New York (1995)
3. Ajtai, M., Komlós, J., Szemerédi, E.: An O(n log n) sorting network. In: Proceedings of the Fifteenth Annual ACM Symposium on Theory of Computing, STOC 1983, pp. 1–9. ACM, New York (1983)
4. Apon, D., Katz, J., Shi, E., Thiruvengadam, A.: Verifiable oblivious storage. In: Krawczyk, H. (ed.) PKC 2014. LNCS, vol. 8383, pp. 131–148. Springer, Heidelberg (2014). https://doi.org/10.1007/978-3-642-54631-0_8
5. Asharov, G., Komargodski, I., Lin, W.-K., Nayak, K., Shi, E.: OptORAMa: optimal oblivious RAM. Cryptology ePrint Archive, Report 2018/892 (2018)
6. Barkol, O., Ishai, Y., Weinreb, E.: On locally decodable codes, self-correctable codes, and t-private PIR. In: Charikar, M., Jansen, K., Reingold, O., Rolim, J.D.P. (eds.) APPROX/RANDOM -2007. LNCS, vol. 4627, pp. 311–325. Springer, Heidelberg (2007). https://doi.org/10.1007/978-3-540-74208-1_23
7. Boyle, E., Gilboa, N., Ishai, Y.: Function secret sharing. In: Oswald, E., Fischlin, M. (eds.) EUROCRYPT 2015. LNCS, vol. 9057, pp. 337–367. Springer, Heidelberg (2015). https://doi.org/10.1007/978-3-662-46803-6_12
8. Chan, T.-H.H., Guo, Y., Lin, W.-K., Shi, E.: Oblivious hashing revisited, and applications to asymptotically efficient ORAM and OPRAM. Cryptology ePrint Archive, Report 2017/924 (2017)
9. Chan, T.-H.H, Katz, J., Nayak, K., Polychroniadou, A., Shi, E.: More is less: perfectly secure oblivious algorithms in the multi-server setting. Cryptology ePrint Archive, Report 2018/851 (2018)
10. Chor, B., Goldreich, O., Kushilevitz, E., Sudan, M.: Private information retrieval. J. ACM 45(6), 965–981 (1998)
11. Devadas, S., van Dijk, M., Fletcher, C.W., Ren, L., Shi, E., Wichs, D.: Onion ORAM: a constant bandwidth blowup oblivious RAM. In: Kushilevitz, E., Malkin, T. (eds.) TCC 2016. LNCS, vol. 9563, pp. 145–174. Springer, Heidelberg (2016). https://doi.org/10.1007/978-3-662-49099-0_6
12. Doerner, J., Shelat, A.: Scaling ORAM for secure computation. In: Proceedings of the 2017 ACM SIGSAC Conference on Computer and Communications Security, CCS 2017, pp. 523–535. ACM, New York (2017)
13. Dvir, Z., Gopi, S.: 2-Server PIR with subpolynomial communication. J. ACM 63(4), 39:1–39:15 (2016)
14. Fletcher, C.W., Naveed, M., Ren, L., Shi, E., Stefanov, E.: Bucket ORAM: single online roundtrip, constant bandwidth oblivious RAM. IACR Cryptology ePrint Archive, 2015:1065 (2015)
15. Gentry, C., Ramzan, Z.: Single-database private information retrieval with constant communication rate. In: Caires, L., Italiano, G.F., Monteiro, L., Palamidessi, C., Yung, M. (eds.) ICALP 2005. LNCS, vol. 3580, pp. 803–815. Springer, Heidelberg (2005). https://doi.org/10.1007/11523468_65
16. Gilboa, N., Ishai, Y.: Distributed point functions and their applications. In: Nguyen, P.Q., Oswald, E. (eds.) EUROCRYPT 2014. LNCS, vol. 8441, pp. 640–658. Springer, Heidelberg (2014). https://doi.org/10.1007/978-3-642-55220-5_35

17. Goldreich, O., Ostrovsky, R.: Software protection and simulation on oblivious RAMs. J. ACM **43**(3), 431–473 (1996)
18. Goodrich, M.T., Mitzenmacher, M.: Privacy-preserving access of outsourced data via oblivious RAM simulation. In: Aceto, L., Henzinger, M., Sgall, J. (eds.) ICALP 2011. LNCS, vol. 6756, pp. 576–587. Springer, Heidelberg (2011). https://doi.org/10.1007/978-3-642-22012-8_46
19. Gordon, D., Katz, J., Wang, X.: Simple and efficient two-server ORAM. Cryptology ePrint Archive, Report 2018/005 (2018)
20. Gordon, S.D., et al.: Secure two-party computation in sublinear (amortized) time. In: Proceedings of the 2012 ACM Conference on Computer and Communications Security, CCS 2012, pp. 513–524. ACM, New York (2012)
21. Kirsch, A., Mitzenmacher, M., Wieder, U.: More robust hashing: cuckoo hashing with a stash. SIAM J. Comput. **39**(4), 1543–1561 (2009)
22. Kushilevitz, E., Lu, S., Ostrovsky, R.: On the (in)security of hash-based oblivious RAM and a new balancing scheme. In: Proceedings of the Twenty-Third Annual ACM-SIAM Symposium on Discrete Algorithms, SODA 2012, pp. 143–156. Society for Industrial and Applied Mathematics, Philadelphia (2012)
23. Kushilevitz, E., Ostrovsky, R.: Replication is not needed: single database, computationally-private information retrieval. In: Proceedings of the 38th Annual Symposium on Foundations of Computer Science, FOCS 1997, p. 364. IEEE Computer Society, Washington, DC (1997)
24. Larsen, K.G., Nielsen, J.B.: Yes, there is an oblivious RAM lower bound!. In: Shacham, H., Boldyreva, A. (eds.) CRYPTO 2018. LNCS, vol. 10992, pp. 523–542. Springer, Cham (2018). https://doi.org/10.1007/978-3-319-96881-0_18
25. Lu, S., Ostrovsky, R.: Distributed oblivious RAM for secure two-party computation. In: Sahai, A. (ed.) TCC 2013. LNCS, vol. 7785, pp. 377–396. Springer, Heidelberg (2013). https://doi.org/10.1007/978-3-642-36594-2_22
26. Moataz, T., Blass, E., Mayberry, T.: CHf-ORAM: a constant communication ORAM without homomorphic encryption. Cryptology ePrint Archive, Report 2015/1116 (2015)
27. Ostrovsky, R.: Efficient computation on oblivious RAMs. In: Proceedings of the Twenty-Second Annual ACM Symposium on Theory of Computing, STOC 1990, pp. 514–523. ACM, New York (1990)
28. Ostrovsky, R., Shoup, V.: Private information storage (extended abstract). In: Proceedings of the Twenty-Ninth Annual ACM Symposium on Theory of Computing, STOC 1997, pp. 294–303. ACM, New York (1997)
29. Pagh, R., Rodler, F.F.: Cuckoo hashing. J. Algorithms **51**(2), 122–144 (2004)
30. Patel, S., Persiano, G., Raykova, M., Yeo, K.: PanORAMa: oblivious RAM with logarithmic overhead. Cryptology ePrint Archive, Report 2018/373 (2018)
31. Pinkas, B., Reinman, T.: Oblivious RAM revisited. In: Rabin, T. (ed.) CRYPTO 2010. LNCS, vol. 6223, pp. 502–519. Springer, Heidelberg (2010). https://doi.org/10.1007/978-3-642-14623-7_27
32. Ren, L., Yu, X., Fletcher, C.W., van Dijk, M., Devadas, S.: Design space exploration and optimization of path oblivious RAM in secure processors. SIGARCH Comput. Archit. News **41**(3), 571–582 (2013)
33. Shi, E., Chan, T.-H.H., Stefanov, E., Li, M.: Oblivious RAM with $O((\log N)^3)$ worst-case cost. In: Lee, D.H., Wang, X. (eds.) ASIACRYPT 2011. LNCS, vol. 7073, pp. 197–214. Springer, Heidelberg (2011). https://doi.org/10.1007/978-3-642-25385-0_11

34. Stefanov, E., et al.: Path ORAM: an extremely simple oblivious RAM protocol. In: Proceedings of the 2013 ACM SIGSAC Conference on Computer Communications Security, CCS 2013, pp. 299–310. ACM, New York (2013)

35. Wang, X., Chan, H., Shi, E.: Circuit ORAM: on tightness of the Goldreich-Ostrovsky lower bound. In: Proceedings of the 22nd ACM SIGSAC Conference on Computer and Communications Security, CCS 2015, pp. 850–861. ACM, New York (2015)

36. Wang, X., Huang, Y., Chan, T.-H., Shelat, A., Shi, E.: SCORAM: oblivious RAM for secure computation. In: Proceedings of the 2014 ACM SIGSAC Conference on Computer and Communications Security, CCS 2014, pp. 191–202. ACM, New York (2014)

37. Zahur, S., et al.: Revisiting square-root ORAM: efficient random access in multi-party computation. In: 2016 IEEE Symposium on Security and Privacy (SP), pp. 218–234, May 2016

38. Zhang, J., Ma, Q., Zhang, W., Qiao, D.: MSKT-ORAM: a constant bandwidth ORAM without homomorphic encryption. Cryptology ePrint Archive, Report 2016/882 (2016)

Lossy Algebraic Filters with Short Tags

Benoît Libert[1,2(✉)] and Chen Qian[3]

[1] CNRS, Laboratoire LIP, Lyon, France
[2] ENS de Lyon, Laboratoire LIP (U. Lyon, CNRS, ENSL, Inria, UCBL),
Lyon, France
benoit.libert@ens-lyon.fr
[3] Univ Rennes, CNRS, IRISA, Rennes, France

Abstract. Lossy algebraic filters (LAFs) are function families where each function is parametrized by a tag, which determines if the function is injective or lossy. While initially introduced by Hofheinz (Eurocrypt 2013) as a technical tool to build encryption schemes with key-dependent message chosen-ciphertext (KDM-CCA) security, they also find applications in the design of robustly reusable fuzzy extractors. So far, the only known LAF family requires tags comprised of $\Theta(n^2)$ group elements for functions with input space $\mathbb{Z}_p^n$, where p is the group order. In this paper, we describe a new LAF family where the tag size is only linear in n and prove it secure under simple assumptions in asymmetric bilinear groups. Our construction can be used as a drop-in replacement in all applications of the initial LAF system. In particular, it can shorten the ciphertexts of Hofheinz's KDM-CCA-secure public-key encryption scheme by 19 group elements. It also allows substantial space improvements in a recent fuzzy extractor proposed by Wen and Liu (Asiacrypt 2018). As a second contribution, we show how to modify our scheme so as to prove it (almost) tightly secure, meaning that security reductions are not affected by a concrete security loss proportional to the number of adversarial queries.

Keywords: Lossy algebraic filters · Efficiency · Tight security · Standard assumptions

1 Introduction

As introduced by Peikert and Waters a decade ago [39], lossy trapdoor functions (LTFs) are function families where injective functions – which are efficiently invertible using a trapdoor - are computationally indistinguishable from many-to-one functions, wherein the image is drastically smaller than the domain. Since their introduction, they drew a lot of attention [19,23,24,43,45] and revealed powerful enough to imply chosen-ciphertext (IND-CCA2) security [39], deterministic public-key encryption in the standard model [9,15,41], as well as encryption schemes achieving the best possible security against selective-opening (SO) adversaries [2,5] or using imperfect randomness [1].

D. Lin and K. Sako (Eds.): PKC 2019, LNCS 11442, pp. 34–65, 2019.
https://doi.org/10.1007/978-3-030-17253-4_2

LOSSY ALGEBRAIC FILTERS. Lossy algebraic filters (LAFs) are a variant LTFs introduced by Hofheinz [25] as a tool enabling the design of chosen-ciphertext-secure encryption schemes with key-dependent message (KDM-CCA) security [6]. Recently, they were also used by Wen and Liu [44] in the construction of robustly reusable fuzzy extractors. In LAF families, each function takes as arguments an input x and a tag t, which determines if the function behaves as a lossy or an injective function. More specifically, each tag $t = (t_c, t_a)$ is comprised of an auxiliary component t_a, which may consist of any public data, and a core component t_c. For any auxiliary component t_a, there should exist at least one t_c such that $t = (t_c, t_a)$ induces a lossy function $f_{\mathsf{LAF}}(t, \cdot)$. LAFs strengthen the requirements of lossy trapdoor functions in that, for any lossy tag t, the function $f_{\mathsf{LAF}}(t, x)$ always reveals the same information about the input x, regardless of which tag is used. In particular, for a given evaluation key ek, multiple evaluations $f_{\mathsf{LAF}}(t_1, x), \ldots, f_{\mathsf{LAF}}(t_n, x)$ for distinct lossy tags do not reveal any more information about x than a single evaluation. On the other hand, LAFs depart from lossy trapdoor functions in that they need not be efficiently invertible using a trapdoor. For their applications to KDM-CCA security [25] and fuzzy extractors [44], lossy algebraic filters are expected to satisfy two security properties. The first one, called *indistinguishability*, requires that lossy tags be indistinguishable from random tags. The second one, named *evasiveness*, captures that lossy tags should be hard to come by without a trapdoor.

So far, the only known LAF realization is a candidate, suggested by Hofheinz [25], which relies on the Decision Linear assumption (DLIN) [12] in groups with a bilinear map. While efficient and based on a standard assumption, it incurs relatively large tags comprised of a quadratic number of group elements in the number of input symbols. More precisely, for functions admitting inputs $\mathbf{x} = (x_1, \ldots, x_n)^\top \in \mathbb{Z}_p^n$, where p is the order of a pairing-friendly $\mathbb{G}$, the core components t_c contain $\Theta(n^2)$ elements of $\mathbb{G}$. For the application to KDM-CCA security [25] (where t_c should be part of ciphertexts), quadratic-size tags are not prohibitively expensive as the encryption scheme of [25, Section 4] can make do with a constant n (typically, $n = 6$). In the application to fuzzy extractors [44], however, it is desirable to reduce the tag length. In the robustly reusable fuzzy extractor of [44], the core tag component t_c is included in the public helper string P that allows reconstructing a secret key from a noisy biometric reading w. The latter lives in a metric space that should be small enough to fit in the input space $\mathbb{Z}_p^n$ of the underlying LAF family. Even if p is exponentially large in the security parameter λ, a constant n would restrict biometric readings to have linear length in λ. Handling biometric readings of polynomial length thus incurs $n = \omega(1)$, which results in large tags and longer public helper strings. This motivates the design of new LAF candidates with smaller tags.

OUR RESULTS. The contribution of this paper is two-fold. We first construct a new LAF with linear-size tags and prove it secure under simple, constant-size assumptions (as opposed to q-type assumptions, which are described using a linear number of elements in the number of adversarial queries) in bilinear groups. The indistinguishability and evasiveness properties of our scheme are implied by the Decision 3-party Diffie-Hellman assumption (more precisely, its natural analogue in asymmetric bilinear maps), which posits the pseudorandomness of tuples $(g, g^a, g^b, g^c, g^{abc})$, for random $a, b, c \in_R \mathbb{Z}_p$. For inputs in $\mathbb{Z}_p^n$, where p is the group order, our core tag components only consist of $O(n)$ group elements. These shorter tags are obtained without inflating evaluation keys, which remain of length $O(n)$ (as in [25]).

As a second contribution, we provide a second LAF realization with $O(n)$-size tags where the indistinguishability and evasiveness properties are both *almost tightly* related to the underlying hardness assumption. Namely, our security proofs are tight – or almost tight in the terminology of Chen and Wee [16] – in that the gap between the advantages of the adversary and the reduction only depends on the security parameter, and not on the number of adversarial queries. In the LAF suggested by Hofheinz [25], the proof of evasiveness relies on the unforgeability of Waters signatures [42]. As a result, the reduction loses a linear factor in the number of lossy tags obtained by the adversary. In our second construction, we obtain tight reductions by replacing Waters signatures with (a variant of) a message authentication code (MAC) due to Blazy, Kiltz and Pan [7]. As a result, our proof of evasiveness only loses a factor $O(\lambda)$ with respect to the Symmetric eXternal Diffie-Hellman assumption (SXDH). If our scheme is plugged into the robustly reusable fuzzy extractor of Wen and Liu [44], it immediately translates into a tight proof of robustness in the sense of the definition of [44]. While directly using our second LAF in the KDM-CCA-secure scheme of [25] does not seem sufficient to achieve tight key-dependent message security, it may still provide a building block for future constructions of tightly KDM-CCA-secure encryption schemes with short ciphertexts.

TECHNIQUES. Like the DLIN-based solution given by Hofheinz [25], our evaluation algorithms proceed by computing a matrix-vector product in the exponent, where the matrix is obtained by pairing group elements taken from the core tag t_c with elements of the evaluation key. Here, we reduce the size of t_c from $O(n^2)$ to $O(n)$ group elements using a technique suggested by Boyen and Waters [14] in order to compress the evaluation keys of DDH-based lossy trapdoor functions.

In the pairing-based LTF of [14], the evaluation key contains group elements $\{(R_i, S_i) = (g^{r_i}, (h^i \cdot u)^{r_i})\}_{i=1}^n$, $\{(V_j = g^{v_j}, H_j = (h^j \cdot u)^{v_j})\}_{j=1}^n$. Using a symmetric bilinear maps $e : \mathbb{G} \times \mathbb{G} \to \mathbb{G}_T$, these make it possible to compute the off-diagonal elements of a matrix

$$M_{i,j} = e(g, h)^{r_i \cdot v_j} = \left(\frac{e(R_i, H_j)}{e(S_i, V_j)}\right)^{1/(j-i)} \qquad \forall (i,j) \in [n] \times [n] \setminus \{(i,i)\}_{i=1}^n \qquad (1)$$

via a "two equation" technique borrowed from the revocation system of Lewko, Sahai and Waters [33]. By including $\{D_i = e(g, g)^{r_i \cdot v_i} \cdot e(g, g)\}_{i=1}^n$ in the evaluation key, the LTF of [14] allows the evaluator to compute a matrix $(M_{i,j})_{i,j \in [n]}$ such that $M_{i,j} = e(g, g)^{r_i \cdot v_j}$ if $i \neq j$ and $M_{i,i} = e(g, g)^{r_i \cdot v_i} \cdot e(g, g)^{m_i}$ and for which $m_i = 1$ (resp. $m_i = 0$), for all $i \in [n]$, in injective (resp. lossy) functions. The indistinguishability of lossy and injective evaluation keys relies on the fact that (1) is only computable when $i \neq j$, making it infeasible to distinguish $\{D_i = e(g, h)^{r_i \cdot v_i} \cdot e(g, g)\}_{i=1}^n$ from $\{D_i = e(g, h)^{r_i \cdot v_i}\}_{i=1}^n$.

Our first LAF construction relies on the "two equation" technique of [33] in a similar way with the difference that we include $\{(V_j = g^{v_j}, H_j = (h^j \cdot u)^{v_j}\}_{j=1}^n$ in the evaluation key ek, but $\{(R_i, S_i) = (g^{r_i}, (h^i \cdot u)^{r_i})\}_{i=1}^n$ is now part of the core tag components t_c. This makes it possible to compute off-diagonal elements of $(M_{i,j})_{i,j\in[n]}$ by pairing elements of ek with those of t_c. To enable the computation of diagonal elements $\{M_{i,i}\}_{i=1}^n$, we augment core tag components by introducing pairs $(D_i, E_i) \in \mathbb{G}^2$, which play the same role as $\{D_i = e(g, g)^{r_i \cdot v_i} \cdot e(g, g)\}_{i=1}^n$ in the LTF of [14]. In lossy tags, $\{(D_i, E_i)\}_{i=1}^n$ are of the form

$$(D_i, E_i) = (h^{r_i \cdot v_i} \cdot H_{\mathbb{G}}(\tau)^{\rho_i}, g^{\rho_i}), \tag{2}$$

for a random $\rho_i \in_R \mathbb{Z}_p$, where τ is a chameleon hashing of all tag components. Such pairs $\{(D_i, E_i)\}_{i=1}^n$ allow the evaluator to compute

$$M_{i,i} = \frac{e(D_i, g)}{e(H_{\mathbb{G}}(\tau), E_i)} = e(g, h)^{r_i \cdot v_i} \qquad \forall i \in [n],$$

which results in a rank-one matrix $(M_{i,j})_{i,j\in[n]}$, where $M_{i,j} = e(g, h)^{r_i \cdot v_j}$. When computed as per (2), $\{(D_i, E_i)\}_{i=1}^n$ can be seen as "blinded" Waters signatures [42]. Namely, $(g, h, V_i = g^{v_i})$ can be seen as a verification key; h^{v_i} is the corresponding secret key; and $r_i \in \mathbb{Z}_p$ serves as a blinding factor that ensures the indistinguishability of (D_i, E_i) from random pairs. Indeed, the Decision 3-party Diffie-Hellman (D3DH) assumption allows proving that $h^{r_i \cdot v_i}$ is computationally indistinguishable from random given (g, h, g^{v_i}, g^{r_i}). In our proof of indistinguishability, however, we need to rely on the proof technique of the Boneh-Boyen IBE [11] in order to apply a hybrid argument that allows gradually replacing pairs $\{(D_i, E_i)\}_{i=1}^n$ by random group elements.

In our proof of evasiveness, we rely on the fact that forging a pair of the form $(D_i, E_i) = (h^{r_i \cdot v_i} \cdot H_{\mathbb{G}}(\tau)^{\rho_i}, g^{\rho_i})$ on input of (g, h, g^{v_i}) is as hard as solving the 2-3-Diffie-Hellman problem [32], which consist in finding a non-trivial pair $(g^r, g^{r \cdot ab}) \in \mathbb{G}^* \times \mathbb{G}^*$ on input of (g, g^a, g^b). In turn, this problem is known to be at least as hard as breaking the Decision 3-party Diffie-Hellman assumption.

The above techniques allow us to construct a LAF with $O(n)$-size tags and evaluation keys made of $O(n + \lambda)$ group elements under a standard assumption. Our first LAF is actually described in terms of asymmetric pairings, but it can be instantiated in all types (i.e., symmetric or asymmetric) of bilinear groups. Our second LAF construction requires asymmetric pairing configurations and the Symmetric eXternal Diffie-Hellman (SXDH) assumption. It is very similar to our first construction with the difference that we obtain a tight proof of evasiveness by replacing Waters signatures with a variant of a MAC proposed by Blazy, Kiltz and Pan [7]. In order for the proofs to go through, we need to include n MAC instances (each with its own keys) in lossy tags, which incurs evaluation keys made of $O(n \cdot \lambda)$ group elements. We leave it is an interesting open problem to achieve tight security using shorter evaluation keys.

RELATED WORK. All-but-one lossy trapdoor functions (ABO-LTFs) [39] are similar to LAFs in that they are lossy function families where each function is parametrized by a tag that determines if the function is injective or lossy. They differ from LAFs in two aspects: (i) They should be efficiently invertible using a trapdoor; (ii) For a given evaluation key ek, there exists only one tag for which the function is lossy. The main motivation of ABO-LTFs is the construction of chosen-ciphertext [40] encryption schemes. *All-but-many* lossy trapdoor functions (ABM-LTFs) are an extension of ABO-LTFs introduced by Hofheinz [24]. They are very similar to LAFs in that a trapdoor makes it possible to dynamically create arbitrarily many lossy tags using. In particular, each tag $t = (t_c, t_a)$ consists of an auxiliary component t_a and a core component t_c so that, by computing t_c as a suitable function of t_a, the pair $t = (t_c, t_a)$ can be made lossy, but still random-looking. The motivation of ABM-LTFs is the construction chosen-ciphertext-secure public-key encryption schemes in scenarios, such as the selective-opening setting [2,18], which involve multiple challenge ciphertexts [24]. They also found applications in the design of universally composable commitments [20]. Lossy algebraic filters differ from ABM-LTFs in that they may not have a trapdoor enabling efficient inversion but, for any lossy tag $t = (t_c, t_a)$, the information revealed by $f_{\mathsf{LAF}}(t, x)$ is always the same (i.e., it is completely determined by x and the evaluation key ek).

LAFs were first introduced by Hofheinz [25] as a building block for KDM-CCA-secure encryption schemes, where they enable some form of "plaintext awareness". In the security proofs of KDM-secure encryption schemes (e.g., [10]), the reduction must be able to simulate encryptions of (functions of) the secret key. When the adversary is equipped with a decryption oracle, the ability to publicly compute encryptions of the decryption key may be a problem as decryption queries could end up revealing that key. LAFs provide a way reconcile the conflicting requirements of KDM and CCA2-security by introducing in each ciphertext a LAF-evaluation of the secret key. By having the simulator encrypt a lossy function of the secret key, one can keep encryption queries from leaking too much secret information. At the same time, adversarially-generated ciphertexts always contain an injective function of the key, which prevents the adversary from learning the secret key by publicly generating encryptions of that key.

Recently, Wen and Liu [44] appealed to LAFs in the design of robustly reusable fuzzy extractors. As defined by Dodis *et al.* [17], fuzzy extractors allow one to generate a random cryptographic key R – together with some public helper string P – out of a noisy biometric reading w. The key R need not be stored as it can be reproduced from the public helper string P and a biometric reading w' which is sufficiently close to w. Reusable fuzzy extractors [13] make it possible to safely generate multiple keys $R_1, \ldots, R_t$ (each with its own public helper string P_i) from correlated readings $w_1, \ldots, w_t$ of the same biometric source. Wen and Liu [44] considered the problem of achieving robustness in reusable fuzzy extractors. In short, robustness prevents adversaries from covertly tampering with the public helper string P_i in order to affect the reproducibility of R_i. The Wen-Liu [44] fuzzy extractor relies on LAFs to simultaneously achieve reusability and robustness assuming a common reference string. Their solution requires the LAF to be homomorphic, meaning that function outputs should live in a group and, for any tag t and inputs x_1, x_2, we have $f_{\mathsf{LAF}}(t, x_1 + x_2) = f_{\mathsf{LAF}}(t, x_1) \cdot f_{\mathsf{LAF}}(t, x_2)$. The candidate proposed by Hofheinz [25] and ours are both usable in robustly reusable fuzzy extractors as they both satisfy this homomorphic property. Our scheme offers the benefit of shorter public helper strings P since these have to contain a LAF tag in the fuzzy extractor of [44].

The tightness of cryptographic security proofs was first considered by Bellare and Rogaway [4] in the random oracle model [3]. In the standard model, it drew a lot of attention in digital signatures and public-key encryption the recent years (see, e.g., [7,16,21,22,26–28,34,35]). In the context of all-but-many lossy trapdoor functions, a construction with tight evasiveness was put forth by Hofheinz [24]. A tightly secure lattice-based ABM-LTF was described by Libert et al. [36] as a tool enabling tight chosen-ciphertext security from lattice assumptions. To our knowledge, the only other prior work considering tight reductions for lossy trapdoor functions is a recent result of Hofheinz and Nguyen [29]. In particular, tight security has never been obtained in the context of LAFs, nor in fuzzy extractors based on public-key techniques.

2   Background

2.1   Lossy Algebraic Filters

We recall the definition of Lossy Algebraic Filter (LAF) from [25], in which the distribution over the function domain may not be the uniform one.

Definition 1. *For integers* $\ell_{\mathsf{LAF}}(\lambda), n(\lambda) > 0$, *an* (ℓ_{LAF}, n)-*lossy algebraic filter (LAF) with security parameter* λ *consists of the following PPT algorithms:*

Key Generation. $\mathsf{LAF.Gen}(1^\lambda)$ *outputs an evaluation key* ek *and a trapdoor key* tk. *The evaluation key* ek *specifies an* ℓ_{LAF}-*bit prime* p *as well as the description of a tag space* $\mathcal{T} = \mathcal{T}_c \times \mathcal{T}_a$, *where* $\mathcal{T}_c$ *is efficiently samplable. The disjoint sets of injective and non-injective tags are called* $\mathcal{T}_{\mathsf{inj}}$ *and* $\mathcal{T}_{\mathsf{non\text{-}inj}} = \mathcal{T} \setminus \mathcal{T}_{\mathsf{inj}}$, *respectively. We also define the subset of lossy tags* $\mathcal{T}_{\mathsf{loss}}$ *to be a subset of* $\mathcal{T}_{\mathsf{non\text{-}inj}}$, *which induce very lossy functions. A tag* $t = (t_c, t_a)$ *is described by a core part* $t_c \in \mathcal{T}_c$ *and an auxiliary part* $t_a \in \mathcal{T}_a$. *A tag may be injective, or lossy, or neither. The trapdoor* tk *allows sampling lossy tags.*
Evaluation. $\mathsf{LAF.Eval}(ek, t, X)$ *takes as inputs an evaluation key* ek, *a tag* $t \in \mathcal{T}$ *and a function input* $X \in \mathbb{Z}_p^n$. *It outputs an image* $Y = f_{ek,t}(X)$.
Lossy Tag Generation. $\mathsf{LAF.LTag}(tk, t_a)$ *takes as input the trapdoor key* tk, *an auxiliary part* $t_a \in \mathcal{T}_a$ *and outputs a core part* t_c *such that* $t = (t_c, t_a) \in \mathcal{T}_{\mathsf{loss}}$ *forms a lossy tag.*

In addition, LAF *has to meet the following requirements:*

Lossiness. *For any* $(ek, tk) \xleftarrow{R} \mathsf{LAF.Gen}(1^\lambda)$, *the following conditions should be satisfied.*

a. *For any* $t \in \mathcal{T}_{\mathsf{inj}}$, $f_{ek,t}(.)$ *should behave as an injective function (note that* $f_{ek,t}^{-1}(.)$ *is not required to be efficiently computable given tk).*
b. *For any auxiliary tag* $t_{\mathsf{a}} \in \mathcal{T}_{\mathsf{a}}$ *and any* $t_{\mathsf{c}} \overset{R}{\leftarrow} \mathsf{LAF.LTag}(tk, t_{\mathsf{a}})$, *we have* $t = (t_{\mathsf{c}}, t_{\mathsf{a}}) \in \mathcal{T}_{\mathsf{loss}}$, *meaning that* $f_{ek,t}(.)$ *is a lossy function. Moreover, for any input* $X = (x_1, \ldots, x_n) \in \mathbb{Z}_p^n$ *and any* $t = (t_{\mathsf{c}}, t_{\mathsf{a}}) \in \mathcal{T}_{\mathsf{loss}}$, $f_{ek,t}(X)$ *is completely determined by* $\sum_{i=1}^n v_i \cdot x_i \bmod p$ *for coefficients* $\{v_i\}_{i=1}^n$ *that only depend on* ek.

Indistinguishability. *Multiple lossy tags are computationally indistinguishable from random tags, namely:*

$$\mathbf{Adv}_Q^{\mathcal{A},\mathsf{ind}}(\lambda) := \big| \Pr[\mathcal{A}(1^\lambda, ek)^{\mathsf{LAF.LTag}(tk,\cdot)} = 1] - \Pr[\mathcal{A}(1^\lambda, ek)^{\mathcal{O}_{\mathcal{T}_{\mathsf{c}}}(\cdot)} = 1] \big|$$

is negligible for any PPT algorithm $\mathcal{A}$, *where* $(ek, tk) \overset{R}{\leftarrow} \mathsf{LAF.Gen}(1^\lambda)$ *and* $\mathcal{O}_{\mathcal{T}_{\mathsf{c}}}(\cdot)$ *is an oracle that assigns a random core tag* $t_{\mathsf{c}} \overset{R}{\leftarrow} \mathcal{T}_{\mathsf{c}}$ *to each auxiliary tag* $t_{\mathsf{a}} \in \mathcal{T}_{\mathsf{a}}$ *(rather than a core tag that makes* $t = (t_{\mathsf{c}}, t_{\mathsf{a}})$ *lossy). Here* Q *denotes the number of oracle queries made by* $\mathcal{A}$.

Evasiveness. *Non-injective tags are computationally hard to find, even with access to an oracle outputting multiple lossy tags, namely:*

$$\mathbf{Adv}_{Q_1,Q_2}^{\mathcal{A},\mathsf{eva}}(\lambda) := \Pr[\mathcal{A}(1^\lambda, ek)^{\mathsf{LAF.LTag}(tk,\cdot),\ \mathsf{LAF.IsInjective}(tk,\cdot)} \in \mathcal{T}_{\mathsf{non\text{-}inj}}]$$

is negligible for legitimate adversary $\mathcal{A}$, *where* $(ek, ik, tk) \overset{R}{\leftarrow} \mathsf{LAF.Gen}(1^\lambda)$ *and* $\mathcal{A}$ *is given access to the following oracle:*

- $\mathsf{LAF.LTag}(tk, \cdot)$ *which acts exactly as the lossy tag generation algorithm.*
- $\mathsf{LAF.IsInjective}(tk, \cdot)$ *that takes as input a tag* $t = (t_{\mathsf{c}}, t_{\mathsf{a}})$. *It outputs* 0 *if* $t \in \mathcal{T}_{\mathsf{non\text{-}inj}} = \mathcal{T} \backslash \mathcal{T}_{\mathsf{inj}}$ *and* 1 *if* $t \in \mathcal{T}_{\mathsf{inj}}$. *If* $t \notin \mathcal{T}$, *the oracle outputs* $\perp$.

We denote by Q_1 *and* Q_2 *the number of queries to* $\mathsf{LAF.LTag}(tk, \cdot)$ *and* $\mathsf{LAF.IsInjective}(tk, \cdot)$, *respectively. By "legitimate adversary", we mean that* $\mathcal{A}$ *is PPT and never outputs a tag* $t = (t_{\mathsf{c}}, t_{\mathsf{a}})$ *such that* t_{c} *was obtained by invoking the* $\mathsf{LAF.LTag}$ *oracle on* t_{a}.

In our construction, the tag space $\mathcal{T}$ will not be dense (i.e., not all elements of the ambient algebraic structure are potential tags). However, elements of the tag space $\mathcal{T}$ will be efficiently recognizable given ek.

We note that the above definition of evasiveness departs from the one used by Hofheinz [25] in that it uses an additional $\mathsf{LAF.IsInjective}(tk, \cdot)$ oracle that uses the trapdoor tk to decide whether a given tag is injective or not. However, this oracle will only be used in our tightly secure LAF (and not in our first construction). Its only purpose is to enable a modular use of our tightly evasive LAF in applications to KDM security [25] or robustly reusable fuzzy extractors [44]. Specifically, by invoking the $\mathsf{LAF.IsInjective}(tk, \cdot)$ oracle, the reduction from the security of a primitive to the underlying LAF's evasiveness does not have to guess which adversarial query involves a non-lossy tag.

2.2   Chameleon Hash Functions

A chameleon hash function [31] is a tuple of algorithms $\mathsf{CMH} = (\mathsf{CMKg}, \mathsf{CMhash},$ $\mathsf{CMswitch})$ which contains an algorithm CMKg that, given a security parameter 1^λ, outputs a key pair $(hk, td) \leftarrow \mathcal{G}(1^\lambda)$. The randomized hashing algorithm outputs $y = \mathsf{CMhash}(hk, m, r)$ given the public key hk, a message m and random coins $r \in \mathcal{R}_{hash}$. On input of messages m, m', random coins $r \in \mathcal{R}_{hash}$ and the trapdoor key td, the switching algorithm $r' \leftarrow \mathsf{CMswitch}(td, m, r, m')$ computes $r' \in \mathcal{R}_{hash}$ such that $\mathsf{CMhash}(hk, m, r) = \mathsf{CMhash}(hk, m', r')$. The collision-resistance property mandates that it be infeasible to come up with pairs $(m', r') \neq (m, r)$ such that $\mathsf{CMhash}(hk, m, r) = \mathsf{CMhash}(hk, m', r')$ without knowing the trapdoor key tk. Uniformity guarantees that the distribution of hash values is independent of the message m: in particular, for all hk, and all messages m, m', the distributions $\{r \leftarrow \mathcal{R}_{hash} : \mathsf{CMHash}(hk, m, r)\}$ and $\{r \leftarrow \mathcal{R}_{hash} : \mathsf{CMHash}(hk, m', r)\}$ are identical.

2.3   Hardness Assumptions

Definition 2. *Let* $(\mathbb{G}, \hat{\mathbb{G}}, \mathbb{G}_T)$ *be bilinear groups of order* p. *The* **First Decision 3-Party Diffie-Hellman** *(D3DH1) assumption holds in* $(\mathbb{G}, \hat{\mathbb{G}}, \mathbb{G}_T)$ *if no PPT distinguisher can distinguish the distribution*

$$D_1 := \{(g, \hat{g}, g^a, g^b, g^c, \hat{g}^a, \hat{g}^b, \hat{g}^c, g^{abc}) \mid g \xleftarrow{R} \mathbb{G}, \hat{g} \xleftarrow{R} \hat{\mathbb{G}}, \ a, b, c \xleftarrow{R} \mathbb{Z}_p\}$$
$$D_0 := \{(g, \hat{g}, g^a, g^b, g^c, \hat{g}^a, \hat{g}^b, \hat{g}^c, g^z) \mid g \xleftarrow{R} \mathbb{G}, \hat{g} \xleftarrow{R} \hat{\mathbb{G}}, \ a, b, c, z \xleftarrow{R} \mathbb{Z}_p\}.$$

The D3DH1 assumption has a natural analogue where the pseudorandom value lives in $\hat{\mathbb{G}}$ instead of $\mathbb{G}$.

Definition 3. *The* **Second Decision 3-Party Diffie-Hellman** *(D3DH2) assumption holds in* $(\mathbb{G}, \hat{\mathbb{G}}, \mathbb{G}_T)$ *if no PPT algorithm can distinguish between the distribution*

$$D_1 := \{(g, \hat{g}, g^a, g^b, g^c, \hat{g}^a, \hat{g}^b, \hat{g}^c, \hat{g}^{abc}) \mid g \xleftarrow{R} \mathbb{G}, \hat{g} \xleftarrow{R} \hat{\mathbb{G}}, \ a, b, c \xleftarrow{R} \mathbb{Z}_p\}$$
$$D_0 := \{(g, \hat{g}, g^a, g^b, g^c, \hat{g}^a, \hat{g}^b, \hat{g}^c, \hat{g}^z) \mid g \xleftarrow{R} \mathbb{G}, \hat{g} \xleftarrow{R} \hat{\mathbb{G}}, \ a, b, c, z \xleftarrow{R} \mathbb{Z}_p\}.$$

We also need a computational assumption which is implied by D3DH2. The 2-3-CDH was initially introduced [32] in ordinary (i.e., non-pairing-friendly) discrete-logarithm hard groups. Here, we extend it to asymmetric bilinear groups.

Definition 4 ([32]). *Let* $(\mathbb{G}, \hat{\mathbb{G}})$ *be a bilinear groups of order* p *with generators* $g \in \mathbb{G}$ *and* $\hat{g} \in \hat{\mathbb{G}}$. *The* **2-out-of-3 Computational Diffie-Hellman** *(2-3-CDH) assumption says that, given* $(g, g^a, \hat{g}^a, g^b, \hat{g}^b)$ *for randomly chosen* $a, b \xleftarrow{R} \mathbb{Z}_p$, *no PPT algorithm can find a pair* $(g^r, g^{r \cdot ab})$ *such that* $r \neq 0$.

It is known (see, e.g., [37]) that any algorithm solving the 2-3-CDH problem can be used to break the D3DH2 assumption. On input of $(g, \hat{g}, g^a,$ $g^b, g^c, \hat{g}^a, \hat{g}^b, \hat{g}^c, \hat{g}^z)$, where $z = abc$ or $z \in_R \mathbb{Z}_p$, the reduction can simply run a 2-3-CDH solver on input of $(g, g^a, g^b, \hat{g}^a, \hat{g}^b)$. If the solver outputs a non-trivial pair of the form $(R_1, R_2) = (g^r, g^{r \cdot ab})$, the D3DH2 distinguisher decides that $z = abc$ if and only if $e(R_1, \hat{g}^z) = e(R_2, \hat{g}^c)$.

In our constructions, we actually rely on a weaker variant of D3HD1, called wD3HD1, where $\hat{g}^a$ is not given. In our tightly secure construction (which requires asymmetric pairings), we need to rely on the following variant of wD3HD1.

Definition 5. *Let $(\mathbb{G}, \hat{\mathbb{G}}, \mathbb{G}_T)$ be bilinear groups of order p. The **Randomized weak Decision 3-Party Diffie-Hellman** (R-wD3DH1) assumption holds in $(\mathbb{G}, \hat{\mathbb{G}}, \mathbb{G}_T)$ if no PPT distinguisher can distinguish the distribution*

$$D_1 := \left\{ \{(g, \hat{g}, g^{a_i}, g^b, g^c, \hat{g}^b, \hat{g}^c, g^{a_i bc})\}_{i=1}^Q \mid g \xleftarrow{R} \mathbb{G}, \hat{g} \xleftarrow{R} \hat{\mathbb{G}}, \right.$$
$$\left. a_1, \ldots, a_Q, b, c \xleftarrow{R} \mathbb{Z}_p \} \right\}$$

$$D_0 := \left\{ \{(g, \hat{g}, g^{a_i}, g^b, g^c, \hat{g}^b, \hat{g}^c, g^{z_i})\}_{i=1}^Q \mid g \xleftarrow{R} \mathbb{G}, \hat{g} \xleftarrow{R} \hat{\mathbb{G}}, \right.$$
$$\left. a_1, \ldots, a_Q, z_1, \ldots, z_Q, b, c \xleftarrow{R} \mathbb{Z}_p \} \right\}.$$

We do not know if D3DH1 or wD3DH1 can be tightly reduced to R-wD3DH1 (the only reduction we are aware of proceeds via a hybrid argument). In asymmetric pairings, however, we can give a tight reduction between R-wD3DH1 and a combination of wD3DH1 and SXDH.

Lemma 1. *There is a tight reduction from the wD3DH1 assumption and the DDH assumption in $\mathbb{G}$ to the R-wD3DH1 assumption. More precisely, for any R-wD3DH1 adversary $\mathcal{B}$, there exist distinguishers $\mathcal{B}_1$ and $\mathcal{B}_2$ which run in about the same time as $\mathcal{B}$ and such that*

$$\mathbf{Adv}_{\mathcal{B}}^{\text{R-wD3DH1}}(\lambda) \leq \mathbf{Adv}_{\mathcal{B}_1}^{\text{wD3DH1}}(\lambda) + \mathbf{Adv}_{\mathcal{B}_2}^{\text{DDH}_1}(\lambda),$$

where the second term denotes $\mathcal{B}_2$'s advantage as a DDH distinguisher in $\mathbb{G}$.

Proof. To prove the result, we consider the following distribution:

$$D_{int} := \left\{ \{(g, \hat{g}, g^{a \cdot \alpha_i}, g^b, g^c, \hat{g}^b, \hat{g}^c, g^{z \cdot \alpha_i})\}_{i=1}^Q \mid g \xleftarrow{R} \mathbb{G}, \hat{g} \xleftarrow{R} \hat{\mathbb{G}}, \right.$$
$$\left. \alpha_1, \ldots, \alpha_Q, b, c, z \xleftarrow{R} \mathbb{Z}_p, a \xleftarrow{R} \mathbb{Z}_p^\star \} \right\}$$

A straightforward reduction shows that, under the wD3DH1 assumption, D_1 is computationally indistinguishable from D_{int}. We show that, under the DDH assumption in $\mathbb{G}$, D_{int} is computationally indistinguishable from D_0. Moreover, the reduction is tight in that the two distinguishers have the same advantage.

First, we show that, under the wD3DH1 assumption, D_{int} is computationally indistinguishable from D_1.

We can build a wD3DH1 distinguisher $\mathcal{B}_1$ from any distinguisher for D_1 and D_{int}. With $(g, \hat{g}, g^a, g^b, g^c, \hat{g}^b, \hat{g}^c, T)$ as input where $g \xleftarrow{R} \mathbb{G}$, $\hat{g} \xleftarrow{R} \hat{\mathbb{G}}$ and $a, b, c \xleftarrow{R} \mathbb{Z}_p$, $\mathcal{B}_1$ uniformly draws $\alpha_i, \ldots, \alpha_Q \xleftarrow{R} \mathbb{Z}_p$ and computes

$$D_{\mathcal{B}_1} := \left\{ \{(g, \hat{g}, g^{a \cdot \alpha_i}, g^b, g^c, \hat{g}^b, \hat{g}^c, T^{\alpha_i})\}_{i=1}^Q \mid \alpha_1, \ldots, \alpha_Q \xleftarrow{R} \mathbb{Z}_p \right\}.$$

It is easy to see that if $T = g^{abc}$, then $D_{\mathcal{B}_1}$ is identical to D_1. If $T \in_R \mathbb{G}$, then $D_{\mathcal{B}_1}$ is distributed as D_{int}. Hence, any distinguisher between D_1 and D_{int} with $D_{\mathcal{B}_1}$ implies a distinguisher $\mathcal{B}_1$ for the wD3DH1 problem.

Next, we show that, under the DDH assumption in $\mathbb{G}$, D_{int} is computationally indistinguishable from D_0. In order to build a DDH distinguisher $\mathcal{B}_2$ out of a distinguisher between D_{int} and D_0, we use the random self-reducibility of the DDH assumption.

Lemma 2 (Random Self-Reducibility [38]**).** *Letting $\mathbb{G}$ be a group of prime order p, there exists a PPT algorithm R that takes as input $(g, g^a, g^b, g^c) \in \mathbb{G}^4$, for any $a, b, c \in \mathbb{Z}_p$, and returns a triple $(g^a, g^{b'}, g^{c'}) \in \mathbb{G}^3$ such that:*

- *If $c = ab \mod q$, then b' is uniformly random in $\mathbb{Z}_p$ and $c' = ab'$.*
- *If $c \neq ab \mod q$, then $b', c' \in_R \mathbb{Z}_p$ are independent and uniformly random.*

On input of $(g, g^z, g^\alpha, T) \in \mathbb{G}^4$, where $g \xleftarrow{R} \mathbb{G}$ and $z, \alpha \xleftarrow{R} \mathbb{Z}_p$, $\mathcal{B}_2$ uses algorithm R to generate Q instances $\{(g^z, g^{\alpha_i}, T_i)\}_{i=1}^Q$. Next, $\mathcal{B}_2$ draws $\hat{g} \xleftarrow{R} \hat{\mathbb{G}}$, $a, b, c \xleftarrow{R} \mathbb{Z}_p$ and defines the following distribution:

$$D_{\mathcal{B}_2} := \left\{ \{(g, \hat{g}, (g^{\alpha_i})^a, g^b, g^c, \hat{g}^b, \hat{g}^c, T_i)\}_{i=1}^Q \mid \hat{g} \xleftarrow{R} \hat{\mathbb{G}}, a, b, c \xleftarrow{R} \mathbb{Z}_p \right\}.$$

We observe that, if $T = g^{z \cdot \alpha}$, we have $T_i = g^{z \cdot \alpha_i}$ for all $i \in [Q]$. In this case, $D_{\mathcal{B}_2}$ is identical to D_{int}. In contrast, if $T \in_R \mathbb{G}$, the random self-reducibility ensures that $T_1, \ldots, T_Q \in_R \mathbb{G}$ are i.i.d, meaning that $D_{\mathcal{B}_2}$ is identical to D_0. Using a distinguisher between D_{int} and D_0 and feeding it with $D_{\mathcal{B}_2}$, we obtain a distinguisher $\mathcal{B}_2$ for the DDH problem in $\mathbb{G}$. $\square$

3   A Lossy Algebraic Filter with Linear-Size Tags

We present a LAF based on DDH-like assumptions with tags of size $O(n)$, where n is the number of input symbols when the input is viewed as a vector over $\mathbb{Z}_p$. Our tags are comprised of $4n$ elements of $\mathbb{G}$, which outperforms the construction of [25] for $n > 4$. In his application to KDM-CCA security [25], Hofheinz uses a LAF scheme with $n = 6$, in which case we decrease the tag size from 43 to 24 group elements[1] and thus shorten ciphertexts by 19 group elements.

---

[1] The LAF of [25] was described in terms of symmetric pairings but it extends to asymmetric pairings $e : \mathbb{G} \times \hat{\mathbb{G}} \to \mathbb{G}_T$ where tags are comprised of elements in $\mathbb{G}$.

The construction is inspired by the lossy TDF of [14] and relies on the revocation technique of Lewko, Sahai and Waters [33] (LSW) in the same way. In asymmetric pairings $e : \mathbb{G} \times \hat{\mathbb{G}} \to \mathbb{G}_T$, the evaluation key contains a set of LSW ciphertexts $\{(\hat{V}_j = \hat{g}^{v_j}, \hat{H}_j = (\hat{h}^j \cdot \hat{u})^{v_j})\}_{j=1}^n$, while each core tag component t_c can be seen as containing a set of LSW secret keys $\{(R_i, S_i) = (g^{r_i}, (h^i \cdot u)^{r_i})\}_{i=1}^n$, allowing the evaluator compute $M_{i,j} = e(g, \hat{h})^{r_i \cdot v_j}$ for any pairwise distinct indices $i \neq j$. In lossy tags (t_c, t_a), diagonal elements $\{M_{i,i}\}_{i=1}^n$ are handled by having t_c contain Waters signatures $(D_i, E_i) = (h^{r_i \cdot v_i} \cdot H_{\mathbb{G}}(\tau)^{\rho_i}, g^{\rho_i})$, where $\rho_i \in_R \mathbb{Z}_p$ and $H_{\mathbb{G}} : \{0,1\}^L \to \mathbb{G}$ is an algebraic hash function mapping the output τ of a chameleon hash function to the group $\mathbb{G}$. For indistinguishability purposes, pairs $\{(D_i, E_i)\}_{i=1}^n$ are not immediately recognizable as Waters signatures because the underlying secret key h^{v_i} is blinded by a random exponent $r_i = \log_g(R_i)$. Still, running the verification algorithm of Waters signatures on (D_i, E_i) allows the evaluation algorithm to derive $M_{i,i} = e(g, \hat{h})^{r_i \cdot v_i}$, so that $(M_{i,j})_{i,j \in [n]}$ forms a rank-1 matrix. In injective tags, $\{(D_i, E_i)\}_{i=1}^n$ are uniformly distributed in $\mathbb{G}$, so that $(M_{i,j})_{i,j \in [n]}$ is the sum of a rank-1 matrix and a diagonal matrix.

3.1   Description

Key Generation. LAF.Gen(1^λ) conducts the following steps.

1. Choose bilinear groups $(\mathbb{G}, \hat{\mathbb{G}}, \mathbb{G}_T)$ of prime order $p > 2^\lambda$ with random generators $g, h, u \xleftarrow{R} \mathbb{G}$ and $\hat{g}, \hat{h}, \hat{u} \xleftarrow{R} \hat{\mathbb{G}}$ subject to the constraints $\log_g(h) = \log_{\hat{g}}(\hat{h})$ and $\log_g(u) = \log_{\hat{g}}(\hat{u})$.
2. Choose a chameleon hash function $\mathsf{CMH} = (\mathsf{CMKg}, \mathsf{CMhash}, \mathsf{CMswitch})$, where the hashing algorithm $\mathsf{CMhash} : \{0,1\}^* \times \mathcal{R}_{hash} \to \{0,1\}^L$ has output length $L \in \mathsf{poly}(\lambda)$. Generate a pair $(hk_{\mathsf{CMH}}, td_{\mathsf{CMH}}) \leftarrow \mathsf{CMKg}(1^\lambda)$ made of a hashing key hk_{CMH} and a trapdoor td_{CMH}.
3. Choose random exponents $w_0, \ldots, w_L \xleftarrow{R} \mathbb{Z}_p$ and define

$$W_k = g^{w_k}, \qquad \hat{W}_k = \hat{g}^{w_k} \qquad \forall k \in [0, L]$$

that will be used to instantiate two hash functions $H_{\mathbb{G}} : \{0,1\}^L \to \mathbb{G}$, $H_{\hat{\mathbb{G}}} : \{0,1\}^L \to \hat{\mathbb{G}}$ which map any string $\mathsf{m} \in \{0,1\}^L$ to

$$H_{\mathbb{G}}(\mathsf{m}) = W_0 \cdot \prod_{k=1}^L W_k^{\mathsf{m}[k]}, \qquad H_{\hat{\mathbb{G}}}(\mathsf{m}) = \hat{W}_0 \cdot \prod_{k=1}^L \hat{W}_k^{\mathsf{m}[k]},$$

respectively. Note that $e(g, H_{\hat{\mathbb{G}}}(\mathsf{m})) = e(H_{\mathbb{G}}(\mathsf{m}), \hat{g})$ for any $\mathsf{m} \in \{0,1\}^L$.
4. Let $n \in \mathsf{poly}(n)$ be the desired input length. For each $j \in [n]$, choose $v_j \xleftarrow{R} \mathbb{Z}_p$ and define

$$\hat{V}_j = \hat{g}^{v_j}, \qquad \hat{H}_j = (\hat{h}^j \cdot \hat{u})^{v_j} \qquad \forall j \in [n].$$

5. Output the evaluation key ek and the lossy tag generation key tk, which consist of

$$ek := \left(hk_{\mathsf{CMH}}, \ g, \ h, \ u, \ \hat{g}, \ \hat{h}, \ \hat{u}, \ \{W_k, \hat{W}_k\}_{k=0}^L, \ \{\hat{V}_j, \hat{H}_j\}_{j=1}^n \right),$$

$$tk := \left(td_{\mathsf{CMH}}, \ \{v_j\}_{j=1}^n \right).$$

The tag space $\mathcal{T} = \mathcal{T}_c \times \mathcal{T}_{aux}$ is defined as a product of $\mathcal{T}_a = \{0,1\}^*$ and

$$\mathcal{T}_c := \{(\{R_i, S_i, D_i, E_i\}_{i=1}^n, r_{hash}) \mid r_{hash} \in \mathcal{R}_{\mathsf{CMH}} \wedge$$
$$\forall i \in [n] : (R_i, S_i, D_i, E_i) \in \mathbb{G}^{*4} \wedge e(R_i, \hat{h}^i \cdot \hat{u}) = e(S_i, \hat{g})\},$$

where $\mathbb{G}^* := \mathbb{G} \setminus \{1_{\mathbb{G}}\}$. The range of the function family is $\mathsf{Rng}_\lambda = \mathbb{G}_T^{n+1}$ and its domain is $\mathbb{Z}_p^n$.

Lossy Tag Generation. $\mathsf{LAF.LTag}(tk, t_a)$ takes in an auxiliary tag component $t_a \in \{0,1\}^*$ and uses $tk = (td_{\mathsf{CMH}}, \{v_j\}_{j=1}^n, \{w_k\}_{k=0}^L)$ to generate a lossy tag as follows.

1. For each $i \in [n]$, choose $r_i \xleftarrow{R} \mathbb{Z}_p^*$ and compute

$$R_i = g^{r_i}, \qquad S_i = (h^i \cdot u)^{r_i} \qquad \forall i \in [n]. \qquad (3)$$

2. For each $i \in [n]$, choose $\rho_i \xleftarrow{R} \mathbb{Z}_p$ and compute

$$D_i = h^{r_i \cdot v_i} \cdot H_{\mathbb{G}}(\tau)^{\rho_i}, \qquad E_i = g^{\rho_i} \qquad \forall i \in [n],$$

where $\tau \in \{0,1\}^L$ is chosen uniformly in the range of CMhash.
3. Use the trapdoor td_{CMH} to find $r_{hash} \in \mathcal{R}_{hash}$ such that

$$\tau = \mathsf{CMhash}(hk_{hash}, (t_a, \{R_i, S_i, D_i, E_i\}_{i=1}^n), r_{hash}) \in \{0,1\}^L$$

and output the tag $t = (t_c, t_a)$, where $t_c = (\{R_i, S_i, D_i, E_i\}_{i=1}^n, r_{hash})$.

Each lossy tag is associated with a matrix $(M_{i,j})_{i,j \in [n]} = (e(g, \hat{h})^{r_i \cdot v_j})_{i,j}$, which is a rank-1 matrix in the exponent. Its diagonal entries consist of

$$M_{i,i} = \frac{e(D_i, \hat{g})}{e(E_i, H_{\hat{\mathbb{G}}}(\tau))} = e(g, \hat{h})^{r_i \cdot v_i} \qquad \forall i \in [n], \qquad (4)$$

while its non-diagonal entries

$$M_{i,j} = \left(\frac{e(R_i, \hat{H}_j)}{e(S_i, \hat{V}_j)}\right)^{1/(j-i)} = e(g, \hat{h})^{r_i \cdot v_j} \qquad \forall (i,j) \in [n] \times [n] \setminus \{(i,i)\}_{i=1}^n, \qquad (5)$$

are obtained by pairing tag component (R_i, S_i) with evaluation key components $(\hat{V}_j, \hat{H}_j)$.

Random Tags. A random tag can be publicly sampled as follows.

1. For each $i \in [n]$, choose $r_i \xleftarrow{R} \mathbb{Z}_p^*$ and compute $\{R_i, S_i\}_{i=1}^n$ as in (3).
2. For each $i \in [n]$, choose $(D_i, E_i) \xleftarrow{R} \mathbb{G}^* \times \mathbb{G}^*$ uniformly at random.
3. Choose $r_{hash} \xleftarrow{R} \mathcal{R}_{hash}$.

Finally, output the tag $t = (t_c, t_a)$, where $t_c = (\{R_i, S_i, D_i, E_i\}_{i=1}^n, r_{hash})$.

We note that, in both random and lossy tags, we have $e(R_i, \hat{u}^i \cdot \hat{h}) = e(S_i, \hat{g})$ for all $i \in [n]$, so that elements of $\mathcal{T}$ are publicly recognizable.

Evaluation. LAF.Eval$(ek, t, \mathbf{x})$ takes in the function input $\mathbf{x} \in \mathbb{Z}_p^n$ as well as the tag $t = (t_c, t_a)$. It parses t_c as $(\{R_i, S_i, D_i, E_i\}_{i=1}^n, r_{hash})$ and proceeds as follows.

1. Return $\bot$ if there exists $i \in [n]$ such that $e(R_i, \hat{h}^i \cdot \hat{u}) \neq e(S_i, \hat{g})$.
2. Compute the matrix $(M_{i,j})_{i,j\in[n]} \in \mathbb{G}_T^{n\times n}$ as

$$M_{i,i} = \frac{e(D_i, \hat{g})}{e(E_i, H_{\hat{G}}(\tau))} \qquad \forall i \in [n] \quad , \tag{6}$$

where $\tau = \mathsf{CMhash}\big(hk_{hash}, (t_a, \{R_i, S_i, D_i, E_i\}_{i=1}^n), r_{hash}\big)$, and

$$M_{i,j} = \Big(\frac{e(R_i, \hat{H}_j)}{e(S_i, \hat{V}_j)}\Big)^{1/(j-i)} \qquad \forall (i,j) \in [n] \times [n] \setminus \{(i,i)\}_{i=1}^n, \tag{7}$$

Note that, since $R_i = g^{r_i}$ and $S_i = (h^i \cdot u)^{r_i}$ for some $r_i \in \mathbb{Z}_q$, we have

$$M_{i,i} = e(g, \hat{h})^{r_i \cdot v_i + \omega_i}, \qquad \forall i \in [n] \tag{8}$$
$$M_{i,j} = e(g, \hat{h})^{r_i \cdot v_j}, \qquad \forall i \neq j,$$

for some vector $(\omega_1, \ldots, \omega_n)^\top \in \mathbb{Z}_p^n$ that only contains non-zero entries if $t = (t_c, t_a)$ is injective.
3. Compute the vector $(V_{T,j})_{j\in[n]}$ as $V_{T,j} = e(h, \hat{V}_j) = e(g, \hat{h})^{v_j}$ for each $j \in [n]$.
4. Use the input $\mathbf{x} = (x_1, \ldots, x_n)^\top \in \mathbb{Z}_p^n$ to compute

$$Y_0 = \prod_{j=1}^n V_{T,j}^{x_j} \tag{9}$$

$$Y_i = \prod_{j=1}^n M_{i,j}^{x_j} \qquad \forall i \in [n]$$

and output $\mathbf{Y} = (Y_0, Y_1, \ldots, Y_n)^\top \in \mathbb{G}_T^{n+1}$.

While the above construction inherits the $\Theta(\lambda)$-size public keys of Waters signatures [42], we believe that it can be adapted to other signature schemes in the standard model (e.g., [8,30]) so as to obtain shorter evaluation keys.

INJECTIVITY AND LOSSINESS. For any injective tag, all entries of the vector $(\omega_1, \ldots, \omega_n)^\top$ are non-zero in (8). We can use Y_0 to ensure that the function is injective. As long as $\omega_i \neq 0$ for all $i \in [n]$, the evaluation algorithm (9) yields a vector $\mathbf{Y} = (Y_0, Y_1, \ldots, Y_n) \in \mathbb{G}_T^{n+1}$ of the form

$$Y_0 = e(g, \hat{h})^{\sum_{j=1}^n v_j \cdot x_j}$$
$$Y_i = e(g, \hat{h})^{\omega_i \cdot x_i + r_i \cdot \sum_{j=1}^n v_j \cdot x_j} \qquad \forall i \in [n],$$

meaning that $x_i \in \mathbb{Z}_p$ is uniquely determined by (Y_0, Y_i) and (R_i, D_i, E_i) (note that the triple (R_i, D_i, E_i) uniquely defines ω_i).

For any lossy tag, the evaluation outputs $\mathbf{Y} = (Y_0, Y_1, \ldots, Y_n) \in \mathbb{G}_T^{n+1}$ such that

$$Y_0 = e(g, \hat{h})^{\sum_{j=1}^n v_j \cdot x_j}$$
$$Y_i = e(g, \hat{h})^{r_i \cdot \sum_{j=1}^n v_j \cdot x_j} \qquad \forall i \in [n],$$

which always reveals the same information $\sum_{j=1}^n v_j \cdot x_j \bmod p$ about the input vector $\mathbf{x} = (x_1, \ldots, x_n)^\top$, no matter which tag is used.

3.2 Security

The proof of indistinguishability relies on the wD3DH1 assumption via a hybrid argument over the queries to the LAF.LTag$(tk, \cdot)$ oracle and over the pairs $\{(D_i, E_i)\}_{i=1}^n$ produced by LAF.LTag$(tk, \cdot)$ at each query. Using the R-wD3DH1 assumption, it is possible to modify the proof so as to use a hybrid argument over the pairs $\{(D_i, E_i)\}_{i=1}^n$ only (meaning that all queries to LAF.LTag$(tk, \cdot)$ are processed in parallel at each game transition). However, this proof would require the SXDH assumption – which only holds in asymmetric pairings – to apply the result of Lemma 1. In contrast, the proof of Theorem 1 allows instantiations in all bilinear group configurations, even in symmetric pairings.

The proof of Theorem 1 uses a hybrid argument to gradually replace pairs $\{(D_i, E_i)\}_{i=1}^n$ by truly random group elements in outputs of the lossy tag generation oracle. To this end, it relies on the proof technique of the Boneh-Boyen IBE [11] in the proof of Lemma 3. Namely, in order to embed a D3DH1 instance $(g, h, g^{v_k}, g^{r_k}, T \overset{?}{=} h^{r_k \cdot v_k})$ in the k-th pair (D_k, E_k), for indexes $i > k$, the reduction has to simulate $h^{r_i \cdot v_k}$ for a known $r_i \in \mathbb{Z}_p$ and an unknown h^{v_k}.

Theorem 1. *The above LAF provides indistinguishability under the wD3DH1 assumption in $(\mathbb{G}, \hat{\mathbb{G}}, \mathbb{G}_T)$.*

Proof. We first recall that, for any injective or non-injective tag $t = (t_c, t_a)$, the core component $t_c = (\{R_i, S_i, D_i, E_i\}_{i=1}^n, r_{hash})$ imply a matrix $(M_{i,j})_{i,j \in [n]}$ where the off-diagonal entries are $M_{i,j} = e(g, \hat{h})^{r_i \cdot v_j}$ and the diagonal entries are of the form (8). In injective tags, the vector $(\omega_1, \ldots, \omega_n)^\top \in \mathbb{Z}_p^n$ only contains non-zero entries. In lossy tags, we have $(\omega_1, \ldots, \omega_n)^\top = \mathbf{0}^n$. We define a sequence of hybrid games. In Game$_{(0,0)}$, the adversary has access to the real oracle LAF.LTag$(tk, .)$ that always outputs lossy tags. In Game$_{(Q,n)}$, the adversary is given access to an oracle $\mathcal{O}_{T_c}(.)$ that always outputs random tags.

Game$_{(\ell,k)}$ $(1 \le \ell \le Q, 1 \le k \le n)$: In this game, the adversary interacts with a hybrid oracle LAF.LTag$^{(\ell,k)}(tk, .)$. At the μ-th query, this oracle outputs tags $t^{(\mu)} = (t_c^{(\mu)}, t_a^{(\mu)})$ such that
- If $\mu < \ell$, the tag $t_c^{(\mu)} = (\{R_i, S_i, D_i, E_i\}_{i=1}^n, r_{hash})$ implies a matrix $(M_{i,j}^{(\mu)})_{i,j \in [n]}$ of the form (8) where $(\omega_1^{(\mu)}, \ldots, \omega_n^{(\mu)})^\top$ is uniform over $\mathbb{Z}_p^n$.

- If $\mu = \ell$, $t_c^{(\mu)} = (\{R_i, S_i, D_i, E_i\}_{i=1}^n, r_{hash})$ implies a matrix $\left(M_{i,j}^{(\mu)}\right)_{i,j \in [n]}$ of the form (8) where the first k entries of $(\omega_1^{(\mu)}, \ldots, \omega_n^{(\mu)})^\top$ are uniform over $\mathbb{Z}_p$ and its last $n - k$ entries are zeroes.
- If $\mu > \ell$, the matrix $\left(M_{i,j}^{(\mu)}\right)_{i,j \in [n]}$ implied by the core tag component $t_c^{(\mu)} = (\{R_i, S_i, D_i, E_i\}_{i=1}^n, r_{hash})$ is a rank-1 matrix in the exponent since $(\omega_1^{(\mu)}, \ldots, \omega_n^{(\mu)})^\top = \mathbf{0}^n$.

Lemma 3 shows that, for all pairs $(\ell, k) \in [Q] \times [n]$, these games are computationally indistinguishable from one another, which yields the stated result. $\square$

Lemma 3. *For each $k \in [n]$ and $\ell \in [Q]$, $\mathsf{Game}_{(\ell,k)}$ is computationally indistinguishable from $\mathsf{Game}_{(\ell,k-1)}$ if the wD3DH1 assumption holds. Under the same assumption, $\mathsf{Game}_{(\ell,1)}$ is computationally indistinguishable from $\mathsf{Game}_{(\ell-1,n)}$.*

Proof. For the sake of contradiction, assume that there exists $\ell \in [Q]$, $k \in [n]$ such that the adversary $\mathcal{A}$ can distinguish $\mathsf{Game}_{(\ell,k)}$ from $\mathsf{Game}_{(\ell,k-1)}$ with noticeable advantage (the indistinguishability of $\mathsf{Game}_{(\ell-1,n)}$ and $\mathsf{Game}_{(\ell,1)}$ can be proved in a completely similar way). We build a wD3DH1 distinguisher $\mathcal{B}$ that inputs $(g, \hat{g}, g^a, g^b, g^c, \hat{g}^b, \hat{g}^c, T)$ with the goal of deciding if $T = g^{abc}$ or $T \in_R \mathbb{G}$.

To this end, $\mathcal{B}$ defines $h = g^b$, $\hat{h} = \hat{g}^b$ and $\hat{V}_k = \hat{g}^c$. It picks $\alpha \xleftarrow{R} \mathbb{Z}_p$ and defines $\hat{u} = \hat{h}^{-k} \cdot \hat{g}^\alpha$ as well as $u = h^{-k} \cdot g^\alpha$, which implicitly sets $v_k = c$. This allows defining

$$\hat{H}_k = (\hat{h}^k \cdot \hat{u})^c = (\hat{g}^c)^\alpha,$$

In addition, $\mathcal{B}$ defines $(W_0, W_1, \ldots, W_L) \in \mathbb{G}^{L+1}$ and $(\hat{W}_0, \hat{W}_1, \ldots, \hat{W}_L) \in \hat{\mathbb{G}}^{L+1}$ by setting

$$W_i = (g^b)^{\alpha_i} \cdot g^{\beta_i}, \qquad\qquad \hat{W}_i = (\hat{g}^b)^{\alpha_i} \cdot \hat{g}^{\beta_i} \quad \forall i \in \{0, \ldots, L\}$$

for randomly chosen $\alpha_0, \ldots, \alpha_L \xleftarrow{R} \mathbb{Z}_p$, $\beta_0, \ldots, \beta_L \xleftarrow{R} \mathbb{Z}_p$. Then, $\mathcal{B}$ chooses $v_i \xleftarrow{R} \mathbb{Z}_p$ for each $i \in [n] \setminus \{k\}$ and defines the rest of the evaluation key ek by setting

$$\hat{V}_i = \hat{g}^{v_i}, \qquad\qquad \hat{H}_i = (\hat{h}^i \cdot \hat{u})^{v_i}, \qquad\qquad \forall i \in [n] \setminus \{k\}$$

Then, at each invocation of the $\mathsf{LAF.LTag}(tk, .)$ oracle, $\mathcal{B}$ responds as follows. At the μ-th query $t_a^{(\mu)}$, it generates a core tag $t_c^{(\mu)}$ such that

- If $\mu < \ell$, $t_c^{(\mu)} = (\{R_i, S_i, D_i, E_i\}_{i=1}^n, r_{hash})$ contains $\{\hat{D}_i, \hat{E}_i\}_{i=1}^n$ uniformly random pairs whereas $\{R_i, \hat{S}_i\}_{i=1}^n$ are chosen as in the real algorithm sampling random tags.
- If $\mu = \ell$, $t_c^{(\mu)} = (\{R_i, S_i, D_i, E_i\}_{i=1}^n, r_{hash})$ is generated as follows. It sets

$$R_k = g^a, \qquad\qquad S_k = (g^a)^\alpha.$$

As for indexes $i \neq k$, it chooses $r_1, \ldots, r_{k-1}, r_{k+1}, \ldots, r_n \xleftarrow{R} \mathbb{Z}_p$ and sets

$$R_i = g^{r_i}, \qquad S_i = (h^i \cdot u)^{r_i} \qquad \forall i \in [n] \setminus \{k\}.$$

It generates the pairs $\{D_i, E_i\}_{i=1}^n$ by choosing $(D_i, E_i) \xleftarrow{R} \mathbb{G}^2$ at random for each $i \in [k-1]$. The k-th pair (D_k, E_k) is defined as

$$D_k = T \cdot H_{\mathbb{G}}(\tau)^{\rho_k}, \qquad E_k = g^{\rho_k}. \qquad (10)$$

for a randomly chosen $\rho_k \xleftarrow{R} \mathbb{Z}_p$. As for $\{D_i, E_i\}_{i=k+1}^n$, they are obtained by choosing a random $\tau = \tau[1] \ldots \tau[L] \in \{0,1\}^L$ in the range of CMhash and choosing $\rho_i \xleftarrow{R} \mathbb{Z}_p$ before setting

$$D_i = H_{\mathbb{G}}(\tau)^{\rho_i} \cdot (g^c)^{-r_i \cdot \frac{\beta_0 + \sum_{i=1}^L \beta_i \cdot \tau[i]}{\alpha_0 + \sum_{i=1}^L \alpha_i \cdot \tau[i]}} \qquad (11)$$

$$E_i = g^{\rho_i} \cdot (g^c)^{-\frac{r_i}{\alpha_0 + \sum_{i=1}^L \alpha_i \cdot \tau[i]}}$$

which can be written

$$D_i = g^{bc \cdot r_i} \cdot H_{\mathbb{G}}(\tau)^{\tilde{\rho}_i} = h^{v_k \cdot r_i} \cdot H_{\mathbb{G}}(\tau)^{\tilde{\rho}_i}$$
$$E_i = g^{\tilde{\rho}_i}$$

if we define $\tilde{\rho}_i = \rho_i - \frac{c \cdot r_i}{\alpha_0 + \sum_{i=1}^L \alpha_i \cdot \tau[i]}$. Note that the reduction $\mathcal{B}$ fails if $\alpha_0 + \sum_{i=1}^L \alpha_i \cdot \tau[i] = 0$ but this only occurs with negligible chance since the coordinates $(\alpha_0, \ldots, \alpha_L) \in \mathbb{Z}_p^L$ are independent of $\mathcal{A}$'s view. Finally, $\mathcal{B}$ uses the trapdoor td_{CMH} of the chameleon hash function to find coins $r_{hash} \in \mathcal{R}_{\mathsf{CMH}}$ such that $\tau = \mathsf{CMhash}(hk_{hash}, (t_a, \{R_i, S_i, D_i, E_i\}_{i=1}^n), r_{hash})$.
- If $\mu > \ell$, the tags are generated as lossy tags. To this end, $\mathcal{B}$ proceeds as in the previous case, except that all elements $\{D_i, E_i\}_{i=1}^n$ (and not only the last $n - k$ ones) are generated as per (11).

It is easy to see that, if $T = g^{abc}$, the pair (D_k, E_k) of (10) can be written

$$D_k = h^{v_k \cdot r_k} \cdot H_{\mathbb{G}}(\tau)^{\rho_k}, \qquad E_k = g^{\rho_k},$$

meaning that $\mathcal{A}$'s view is the same as in $\mathsf{Game}_{(\ell, k-1)}$. In contrast, if $T \in_R \mathbb{G}$, then (D_k, E_k) can be written

$$D_k = h^{\omega_k + v_k \cdot r_k} \cdot H_{\mathbb{G}}(\tau)^{\rho_k}, \qquad E_k = g^{\rho_k},$$

for some uniformly random $\omega_k \in_R \mathbb{Z}_p$. In this case, $\mathcal{A}$'s view corresponds to $\mathsf{Game}_{(\ell, k)}$. □

The evasiveness property is established by Theorem 2 for which a proof is given in the full version of the paper.

Theorem 2. *The above LAF provides evasiveness assuming that: (i)* CMH *is a collision-resistant chameleon hash function; (ii) The wD3DH1 and 2-3-CDH assumptions both hold in* $(\mathbb{G}, \hat{\mathbb{G}}, \mathbb{G}_T)$.

Recall that the wD3DH1 and 2-3-CDH assumptions are implied by the D3DH1 and D3DH2 assumptions, respectively. Theorems 1 and 2 thus guarantee the D3DH1 and D3DH2 assumptions suffice to ensure the indistinguishability and evasiveness properties of our LAF construction (indeed, chameleon hash functions also exist under these assumptions).

3.3   Towards All-But-Many Lossy Trapdoor Functions

Our LAF construction can be modified to construct an all-but-many lossy trapdoor function [24]. Recall that ABM-LTFs do not require evaluations on lossy tags to always output the same information about the input: on any lossy tag, the image size is only required to be much smaller. On the other hand, ABM-LTFs require that, for any injective tag, the function be efficiently invertible using a trapdoor.

Our construction can be turned into an ABM-LTF in the following way. In the evaluation algorithm, a binary input vector $\mathbf{x} = (x_1, \ldots, x_n)^\top \in \{0,1\}^n$ is mapped to the output $(Y_0, \ldots, Y_n) \in \mathbb{G}_T^{n+1}$, where $Y_0 = \prod_{i=1}^n e(R_i, \hat{h})^{x_i}$ and

$$Y_j = \prod_{i=1}^n M_{i,j}^{x_i} \qquad \forall j \in [n],$$

which can be written

$$Y_0 = e(g, \hat{h})^{\sum_{i=1}^n r_i \cdot x_i}$$
$$Y_j = e(g, \hat{h})^{\omega_j \cdot x_j + v_j \cdot \sum_{i=1}^n r_i \cdot x_i} \qquad \forall j \in [n].$$

Using $ik = (v_1, \ldots, v_n) \in \mathbb{Z}_p^n$ as an inversion key, one can decode the j-th input bit as $x_j = 0$ (resp. $x_j = 1$) if $Y_j/Y_0^{v_j} = 1_{\mathbb{G}_T}$ (resp. $Y_j/Y_0^{v_j} \neq 1_{\mathbb{G}_T}$).

Unfortunately, the above ABM-LTF does not seem immediately usable in the application to selective-opening chosen-ciphertext security, which was suggested in [24]. The reason is that our tags have a special and publicly recognizable structure, where (R_i, S_i) both depend on the same exponent $r_i \in \mathbb{Z}_p$. In the selective-opening setting, the problem arises when the adversary chooses to corrupt some senders, at which point the reduction should reveal the random coins used to create lossy/injective tags. In our construction, this would entail to reveal $r_i \in \mathbb{Z}_p$, which is incompatible with our proofs of indistinguishability and evasiveness. In the ABM-LTF constructions of [24,36], lossy tags are explainable because they are pseudorandom, which allows the reduction to pretend that they have been randomly sampled in their ambient space. Here, the special structure of lossy/injective tags prevents us from explaining the generation of lossy tags in the same way for corrupted senders. The only apparent way to sample a pair (R_i, S_i) satisfying $e(R_i, \hat{h}^i \cdot \hat{u}) = e(S_i, \hat{g})$ is to choose $r_i \in \mathbb{Z}_p$ and compute $(R_i, S_i) = (g^{r_i}, (h^i \cdot u)^{r_i})$.

We thus leave it as an open problem to build an ABM-LTF with explainable linear-size tags under DDH-like assumptions.

4   A Lossy Algebraic Filter With Tight Security

In this section, we modify our first LAF construction in such a way that we can prove it tightly secure under constant-size assumptions.[2] To this end, we replace Waters signatures by a variant of the MAC described by Blazy, Kiltz and Pan [7], which is itself inspired by the Naor-Reingold PRF [38].

4.1   A Variant of the BKP MAC

The MAC construction below is identical to the signature scheme implied by the IBE scheme of [7, Appendix D] with two differences which prevent public verification in order to obtain a pseudo-random MAC instead of a digital signature. The signature scheme of [7] was actually designed by transposing a pseudo-random MAC from standard DDH-hard groups to bilinear groups in order to enable public verification. Here, we cannot immediately use the MAC of [7] because we need bilinear maps in the evaluation algorithm of our LAF.

In order to obtain a pseudo-random MAC, we thus modify the signature scheme of [7] by introducing an additional randomizer $r \in \mathbb{Z}_p$ and an extra group element h, of which the discrete logarithm $\log_g(h)$ serves as a private verification key.

Keygen$(1^\lambda, 1^L)$: Given a security parameter λ and a message length $L \in \mathsf{poly}(\lambda)$, choose asymmetric bilinear groups $(\mathbb{G}, \hat{\mathbb{G}}, \mathbb{G}_T)$ of prime order $p > 2^\lambda$ with generators $g, h \xleftarrow{R} \mathbb{G}$, $\hat{g} \xleftarrow{R} \hat{\mathbb{G}}$.

1. Choose $\theta, \alpha, \beta \xleftarrow{R} \mathbb{Z}_p$ and compute $\hat{g}^\theta \in \hat{\mathbb{G}}$. For each $\mu \in \{0,1\}$, choose vectors $\boldsymbol{x}_\mu = (x_{1,\mu}, \ldots, x_{L,\mu}) \xleftarrow{R} \mathbb{Z}_p^L$, $\boldsymbol{y}_\mu = (y_{1,\mu}, \ldots, y_{L,\mu}) \xleftarrow{R} \mathbb{Z}_p^L$.
2. Set $v = \alpha + \theta \cdot \beta$ and $\boldsymbol{z}_\mu = \boldsymbol{x}_\mu + \theta \cdot \boldsymbol{y}_\mu \in \mathbb{Z}_p^L$. Compute $\hat{V} = \hat{g}^v$ and, for each $\mu \in \{0,1\}$, define $\hat{\boldsymbol{Z}}_\mu = (\hat{Z}_{1,\mu}, \ldots, \hat{Z}_{L,\mu}) = \hat{g}^{\boldsymbol{z}_\mu}$.

Output a secret key $\mathsf{sk}_{mac} = (\alpha, \beta, \boldsymbol{x}_0, \boldsymbol{x}_1, \boldsymbol{y}_0, \boldsymbol{y}_1, \eta)$, where $\eta = \log_g(h)$, and public parameters consisting of $\mathsf{pp} = ((\mathbb{G}, \hat{\mathbb{G}}, \mathbb{G}_T), g, \hat{g}, h, \hat{g}^\theta, (\hat{V}, \hat{\boldsymbol{Z}}_0, \hat{\boldsymbol{Z}}_1))$.

Mac.Sig$(\mathsf{pp}, \mathsf{sk}_{mac}, M)$: To generate a MAC for $M = m[1] \ldots m[L] \in \{0,1\}^L$ using $\mathsf{sk}_{mac} = (x, y, \boldsymbol{x}_0, \boldsymbol{x}_1, \boldsymbol{y}_0, \boldsymbol{y}_1, \eta)$, choose $r, \rho \xleftarrow{R} \mathbb{Z}_p$ and compute

$$\sigma_1 = h^{\alpha \cdot r} \cdot g^{\rho \cdot (\sum_{k=1}^L x_{k,m[k]})}$$
$$\sigma_2 = h^{\beta \cdot r} \cdot g^{\rho \cdot (\sum_{k=1}^L y_{k,m[k]})}$$
$$\sigma_3 = g^\rho$$
$$\sigma_4 = g^r$$

---

[2] While the assumption of Definition 5 is described using $O(Q)$ group elements, it tightly reduces to wD3DH1 and DDH which both take a constant number of group elements to describe.

Mac.Ver(pp, sk$_{mac}$, M, σ): Given sk$_{mac}$ = $(\alpha, \beta, \boldsymbol{x}_0, \boldsymbol{x}_1, \boldsymbol{y}_0, \boldsymbol{y}_1, \eta)$ and an L-bit message $M = m[1] \ldots m[L]$, a purported MAC $\sigma = (\sigma_1, \sigma_2, \sigma_3, \sigma_4)$ is accepted if and only if

$$e(\sigma_1, \hat{g}) \cdot e(\sigma_2, \hat{g}^\theta) = e(\sigma_4, \hat{V})^\eta \cdot e(\sigma_3, \prod_{k=1}^{L} \hat{Z}_{k,m[k]}). \tag{12}$$

We note that the verification algorithm can be modified in such a way that it does not require any pairing evaluation. The above description is just meant to simplify the presentation of the security proof of our LAF construction.

The proof is essentially identical to that of [7] but we give it for completeness. We note that, in the security definitions of MACs, the adversary is generally allowed to make verification queries. Here, for simplicity, we prove unforgeability in a game where the adversary knows $\eta = \log_g(h)$, which allows it to run the verification oracle itself. This dispenses us with the need for a verification oracle.

Lemma 4. *The above construction is an unforgeable MAC assuming that the SXDH assumption holds in $(\mathbb{G}, \hat{\mathbb{G}})$. Namely, any forger $\mathcal{A}$ making Q MAC queries and Q_V verification queries within running time $t_\mathcal{A}$ has advantage at most*

$$\mathbf{Adv}_\mathcal{A}^{\text{uf-mac}}(\lambda) \leq \mathbf{Adv}_{\mathcal{B}_1}^{\text{DDH}_2}(\lambda) + 2L \cdot \mathbf{Adv}_{\mathcal{B}_2}^{\text{DDH}_1}(\lambda),$$

where $\mathcal{B}_1$ and $\mathcal{B}_2$ are PPT distinguishers against the DDH assumption in $\mathbb{G}_1$ and $\mathbb{G}_2$, respectively, which run in time $t_\mathcal{A} + (Q + Q_V) \cdot \text{poly}(\lambda)$.

Proof. To prove the result, we consider a sequence of games. For each index i, we call W_i the event that the challenger outputs 1 in Game$_i$.

Game$_0$: This is the real game MAC security game, where the adversary $\mathcal{A}$ is additionally given $\eta = \log_g(h)$ in such a way that it can run the verification algorithm (and test whether Eq. (12) holds) by itself. The challenger outputs 1 if and only if $\mathcal{A}$ eventually outputs a pair $(M^\star, \sigma^\star = (\sigma_1^\star, \sigma_2^\star, \sigma_3^\star, \sigma_4^\star))$ satisfying

$$e(\sigma_1^\star, \hat{g}) \cdot e(\sigma_2^\star, \hat{g}^\theta) = e(\sigma_4^\star, \hat{V})^\eta \cdot e(\sigma_3^\star, \prod_{k=1}^{L} \hat{Z}_{k,m^\star[k]}), \tag{13}$$

where $M^\star = m^\star[1] \ldots m^\star[L] \in \{0,1\}^L$, although $M^\star$ was not previously queried to the MAC oracle. By definition, $\Pr[W_0] = \mathbf{Adv}_\mathcal{A}^{\text{uf-mac}}(\lambda)$.

Game$_1$: In this game, we modify again the verification oracle as follows. When $\mathcal{A}$ outputs a pair $(M^\star, \sigma^\star = (\sigma_1^\star, \sigma_2^\star, \sigma_3^\star, \sigma_4^\star))$ such that $M^\star$ was not queried to the MAC oracle but $(M^\star, \sigma^\star)$ still satisfies (13), the challenger checks if

$$\sigma_1^\star = \sigma_4^{\star\eta\cdot\alpha} \cdot \sigma_3^{\star\sum_{k=1}^{L} x_{k,m^\star[k]}} \tag{14}$$
$$\sigma_2^\star = \sigma_4^{\star\eta\cdot\beta} \cdot \sigma_3^{\star\sum_{k=1}^{L} y_{k,m^\star[k]}}.$$

We call E_1 the event that equalities (14) are satisfied. If they are not satisfied, the challenger outputs 0. Otherwise, it outputs 1 as it did in Game_0. If we denote by E_0 the analogue of event E_1 in Game_0, we have

$$\Pr[W_0] = \Pr[W_0 \wedge E_0] + \Pr[W_0 \wedge \neg E_0]$$
$$= \Pr[W_1 \wedge E_1] + \Pr[W_0 \wedge \neg E_0] = \Pr[W_1] + \Pr[W_0 \wedge \neg E_0]$$

since $\Pr[W_1 \wedge \neg E_1] = 0$. Lemma 5 shows that event $W_0 \wedge \neg E_0$ would contradict the DDH assumption in $\hat{\mathbb{G}}$: namely, we have $\Pr[W_0 \wedge \neg E_0] \leq \mathbf{Adv}^{\mathrm{DDH}_2}(\lambda)$, which implies $|\Pr[W_1] - \Pr[W_0]| \leq \mathbf{Adv}^{\mathrm{DDH}_2}(\lambda)$.

We now use a sub-sequence of L hybrid games over the input bits of queried messages. For convenience, we define $\mathsf{Game}_{2.0}$ to be identical to Game_1.

$\mathsf{Game}_{2.i}$ ($1 \leq i \leq L$): In this sub-sequence of games, we modify the key generation phase and the MAC oracle in the following way.
- At the beginning of the game, the challenge defines $\hat{V} = \hat{g}^v$ for a random $v \xleftarrow{R} \mathbb{Z}_p$.
- MAC queries are handled as follows. Let $R : \{0,1\}^i \to \mathbb{Z}_p$ be a truly random function mapping i-bit input to $\mathbb{Z}_p$. At each message M queried by $\mathcal{A}$, the challenger computes $(\sigma_3, \sigma_4) = (g^\rho, g^r)$ for random $\rho, r \xleftarrow{R} \mathbb{Z}_p$. Then, it outputs $(\sigma_1, \sigma_2, \sigma_3, \sigma_4)$, where

$$\sigma_1 = h^{(v - \theta \cdot R(m[1]\dots m[i])) \cdot r} \cdot g^{\rho \cdot (\sum_{k=1}^{L} x_{k, m[k]})}$$
$$\sigma_2 = h^{R(m[1]\dots m[i]) \cdot r} \cdot g^{\rho \cdot (\sum_{k=1}^{L} y_{k, m[k]})}$$

When the adversary outputs $(M^\star, \sigma^\star = (\sigma_1^\star, \sigma_2^\star, \sigma_3^\star, \sigma_4^\star))$ satisfying (13) for a new message $M^\star$, the challenger checks if the following equalities are satisfied:

$$\sigma_1^\star = \sigma_4^{\star \eta \cdot (v - \theta \cdot R(m^\star[1]\dots m^\star[i]))} \cdot \sigma_3^{\star \sum_{k=1}^{L} x_{k, m^\star[k]}} \tag{15}$$
$$\sigma_2^\star = \sigma_4^{\star \eta \cdot R(m^\star[1]\dots m^\star[i])} \cdot \sigma_3^{\star \sum_{k=1}^{L} y_{k, m^\star[k]}}.$$

If so, the challenger outputs 1. Otherwise, it outputs 0. Lemma 6 shows that $\mathsf{Game}_{2.i}$ is indistinguishable from $\mathsf{Game}_{2.(i-1)}$ under the DDH assumption in $\mathbb{G}$. Namely, $|\Pr[W_{2.i}] - \Pr[W_{2.(i-1)}]| \leq \mathbf{Adv}^{\mathrm{DDH}_1}(\lambda)$.

In $\mathsf{Game}_{2.L}$, we claim that $\Pr[W_{2.L}] = 1/p$. Indeed, the equalities (15) can only hold by pure chance when $i = L$ because $m^\star[1]\dots m^\star[L]$ was never involved in an output of the MAC oracle. Hence, the random function output $R(m^\star[1]\dots m^\star[L])$ is perfectly independent of $\mathcal{A}$'s view. Since $\Pr[W_{2.0}] = \Pr[W_1]$, we obtain the claimed upper bound for $\Pr[W_0]$. $\square$

Lemma 5. *In Game_0, we have $\Pr[W_0 \wedge \neg E_0] \leq \mathbf{Adv}^{\mathrm{DDH}_2}(\lambda)$.*

Proof. Towards a contradiction, let us assume that, in Game_1, the adversary $\mathcal{A}$ can output a pair $(M^\star, \sigma^\star = (\sigma_1^\star, \sigma_2^\star, \sigma_3^\star, \sigma_4^\star))$ satisfying (13) but not (14). We construct a distinguisher $\mathcal{B}$ for the DDH assumption in $\hat{\mathbb{G}}$. Our distinguisher $\mathcal{B}$ takes as input $(\hat{g}, \hat{g}^\theta, \hat{g}^\omega, \hat{T}) \in \hat{\mathbb{G}}^4$ and decides if $\hat{T} = \hat{g}^{\alpha \cdot \omega}$ or $\hat{T} \in_R \hat{\mathbb{G}}$. To this end, $\mathcal{B}$ will compute a pair of the form $(w, w^\theta) \in \mathbb{G}^2$ with $w \neq 1_{\mathbb{G}}$, which allows solving the given DDH instance in $\hat{\mathbb{G}}$ by testing if $e(w, \hat{T}) = e(w^\theta, \hat{g}^\omega)$. Indeed, the latter equality holds if and only if $\hat{T} = \hat{g}^{\alpha \cdot \omega}$.

The reduction $\mathcal{B}$ runs the real key generation algorithm and answers all MAC and verification queries exactly as in Game_1. By hypothesis, $\mathcal{B}$ has non-negligible probability of outputting a pair $(M^\star, \sigma^\star = (\sigma_1^\star, \sigma_2^\star, \sigma_3^\star, \sigma_4^\star))$ satisfying (13) although

$$\sigma_1^\star \neq \sigma_4^{\star \eta \cdot \alpha} \cdot \sigma_3^{\star \sum_{k=1}^L x_{k,m^\star[k]}}, \qquad \sigma_2^\star \neq \sigma_4^{\star \eta \cdot \beta} \cdot \sigma_3^{\star \sum_{k=1}^L y_{k,m^\star[k]}}.$$

At this point, $\mathcal{B}$ uses sk_{mac} to construct a different valid MAC $(\sigma_1', \sigma_2', \sigma_3^\star, \sigma_4^\star)$ satisfying (13) and such that $(\sigma_1', \sigma_2') \neq (\sigma_1^\star, \sigma_2^\star)$. Namely, $\mathcal{B}$ computes

$$\sigma_1' = \sigma_4^{\star \eta \cdot \alpha} \cdot \sigma_3^{\star \sum_{k=1}^L x_{k,m^\star[k]}}, \qquad \sigma_2' = \sigma_4^{\star \eta \cdot \beta} \cdot \sigma_3^{\star \sum_{k=1}^L y_{k,m^\star[k]}}.$$

By dividing the two verification equations for $(\sigma_1', \sigma_2', \sigma_3^\star, \sigma_4^\star)$ and $(\sigma_1^\star, \sigma_2^\star, \sigma_3^\star, \sigma_4^\star)$, we get

$$e(\sigma_1^\star/\sigma_1', \hat{g}) \cdot e(\sigma_2^\star/\sigma_2', \hat{g}^\theta) = 1_{\mathbb{G}_T}$$

meaning that $\sigma_1^\star/\sigma_1' = (\sigma_2'/\sigma_2^\star)^\theta$. Since $\sigma_1^\star \neq \sigma_1'$, this provides $\mathcal{B}$ with a non-trivial pair $(w, w^\theta) = (\sigma_2'/\sigma_2^\star, \sigma_1^\star/\sigma_1')$, which is sufficient to solve DDH in $\hat{\mathbb{G}}$. □

Lemma 6. *Under the DDH assumption in $\mathbb{G}$, the challenger outputs 1 with about the same probabilities in $\mathsf{Game}_{3.(i-1)}$ and $\mathsf{Game}_{3.i}$. We have*

$$|\Pr[W_{2.i}] - \Pr[W_{2.(i-1)}]| \leq 2 \cdot \mathbf{Adv}^{\mathrm{DDH}_1}(\lambda).$$

(The proof is given in the full version of the paper.)

4.2   The LAF Construction

In order to apply a hybrid argument in our proof of indistinguishability, we need to use n instances of the MAC of Sect. 4.1, each of which has its own secret key $\mathsf{sk}_{mac,j}$ and its own set of public parameters $\mathsf{pp}_j = (g, \hat{g}, h, \hat{g}^{\theta_j}, (\hat{V}_j, \hat{Z}_{j,0}, \hat{Z}_{j,1}))$. As a result, we need an evaluation key containing $\Theta(n \cdot L)$ group elements. We leave it as an open problem to shorter the evaluation while retaining tight security and short tags.

Key Generation. LAF.Gen(1^λ) conducts the following steps.

1. Choose asymmetric bilinear groups $(\mathbb{G}, \hat{\mathbb{G}}, \mathbb{G}_T)$ of prime order $p > 2^\lambda$ with generators $g, h \xleftarrow{R} \mathbb{G}$, $\hat{g} \xleftarrow{R} \hat{\mathbb{G}}$ and let $\eta = \log_g(h)$.

2. Choose a chameleon hash function CMH $=$ (CMKg, CMhash, CMswitch), where the hashing algorithm CMhash $: \{0,1\}^* \times \mathcal{R}_{hash} \rightarrow \{0,1\}^L$ has output length $L \in \mathsf{poly}(\lambda)$. Generate a pair $(hk_{\mathsf{CMH}}, td_{\mathsf{CMH}}) \leftarrow \mathsf{CMKg}(1^\lambda)$ made of a hashing key hk_{CMH} and a trapdoor td_{CMH}.

3. Generate n keys for the MAC of Sect. 4.1 which all share the same parameters $g, h \in \mathbb{G}$, $\hat{g} \in \hat{\mathbb{G}}$. Namely, for each $j \in [n]$, conduct the following steps.

   a. Choose $\theta_j \xleftarrow{R} \mathbb{Z}_p$ and compute $\hat{g}^{\theta_j} \in \hat{\mathbb{G}}$.
   b. For each $\mu \in \{0,1\}$, choose vectors $\boldsymbol{x}_{j,\mu} = (x_{j,1,\mu}, \ldots, x_{j,L,\mu}) \xleftarrow{R} \mathbb{Z}_p^L$ and $\boldsymbol{y}_{j,\mu} = (y_{j,1,\mu}, \ldots, y_{j,L,\mu}) \xleftarrow{R} \mathbb{Z}_p^L$.
   c. Compute $\boldsymbol{z}_{j,\mu} = \boldsymbol{x}_{j,\mu} + \theta_j \cdot \boldsymbol{y}_{j,\mu}$ and $\hat{\boldsymbol{Z}}_{j,\mu} = \hat{g}^{\boldsymbol{z}_{j,\mu}} = (\hat{g}^{z_{j,1,\mu}}, \ldots, g^{z_{j,L,\mu}})$ for each $\mu \in \{0,1\}$.
   d. Choose $\alpha_j, \beta_j \xleftarrow{R} \mathbb{Z}_p$ and compute $\hat{V}_j = \hat{g}^{\alpha_j + \theta_j \cdot \beta_j}$.
   e. Define $\mathsf{sk}_{mac,j} = (\alpha_j, \beta_j, \boldsymbol{x}_{j,0}, \boldsymbol{x}_{j,1}, \boldsymbol{y}_{j,0}, \boldsymbol{y}_{j,1})$.

4. Choose $u \xleftarrow{R} \mathbb{G}$ and $\hat{h}, \hat{u} \xleftarrow{R} \hat{\mathbb{G}}$ subject to the constraints $\log_g(h) = \log_{\hat{g}}(\hat{h})$ and $\log_g(u) = \log_{\hat{g}}(\hat{u})$.

5. Define

$$\hat{H}_j = (\hat{h}^j \cdot \hat{u})^{\alpha_j + \theta_j \cdot \beta_j} \qquad \forall j \in [n].$$

6. Output the evaluation key ek and the lossy tag generation key tk, which consist of

$$ek := \Big(g, h, u, \hat{g}, \hat{h}, \hat{u}, \{\hat{g}^{\theta_j}\}_{j=1}^n, \{\hat{\boldsymbol{Z}}_{j,\mu}\}_{j\in[n],\mu\in\{0,1\}}, \{\hat{V}_j, \hat{H}_j\}_{j=1}^n, hk_{\mathsf{CMH}} \Big),$$
$$tk := (\{\mathsf{sk}_{mac,j}\}_{j=1}^n, \eta, td_{\mathsf{CMH}}).$$

The tag space $\mathcal{T} = \mathcal{T}_c \times \mathcal{T}_{aux}$ is defined as a product of $\mathcal{T}_a = \{0,1\}^*$ and

$$\mathcal{T}_c := \{(\{R_i, S_i, D_i, E_i, F_i\}_{i=1}^n, r_{hash}) \mid r_{hash} \in \mathcal{R}_{hash} \wedge$$
$$\forall i \in [n] : (R_i, S_i, D_i, E_i, F_i) \in \mathbb{G}^5 \wedge e(R_i, \hat{h}^i \cdot \hat{u}) = e(S_i, \hat{g})\}.$$

The range of the function family is $\mathsf{Rng}_\lambda = \mathbb{G}_T^{n+1}$ and its domain is $\mathbb{Z}_p^n$.

Lossy Tag Generation. LAF.LTag(tk, t_a) takes in an auxiliary tag component $t_a \in \{0,1\}^*$ and uses $tk = (\{\mathsf{sk}_{mac,j}\}_{j=1}^n, \eta)$ to generate a lossy tag as follows.

1. For each $i \in [n]$, choose $r_i \xleftarrow{R} \mathbb{Z}_p$ and compute

$$R_i = g^{r_i}, \qquad\qquad S_i = (h^i \cdot u)^{r_i} \qquad\qquad \forall i \in [n]. \qquad (16)$$

2. Choose a random string $\tau \in \{0,1\}^L$ in the range of CMhash. Then, for each $i \in [n]$, choose $\rho_i \xleftarrow{R} \mathbb{Z}_p$ and compute

$$
\begin{aligned}
D_i &= h^{\alpha_i \cdot r_i} \cdot g^{\rho_i \cdot (\sum_{k=1}^{L} x_{i,k,\tau[k]})}, \\
E_i &= h^{\beta_i \cdot r_i} \cdot g^{\rho_i \cdot (\sum_{k=1}^{L} y_{i,k,\tau[k]})}, \qquad \forall i \in [n] \qquad (17) \\
F_i &= g^{\rho_i}.
\end{aligned}
$$

3. Use the trapdoor td_{CMH} of the chameleon hash function to find random coins $r_{hash} \in \mathcal{R}_{hash}$ such that

$$\tau = \mathsf{CMhash}(hk_{\mathsf{CMH}}, (t_{\mathsf{a}}, \{R_i, S_i, D_i, E_i, F_i\}_{i=1}^n), r_{hash}) \in \{0,1\}^L.$$

4. Output the tag $t = (t_{\mathsf{c}}, t_{\mathsf{a}})$, where $t_{\mathsf{c}} = (\{R_i, S_i, D_i, E_i, F_i\}_{i=1}^n, r_{hash})$.

Each lossy tag corresponds to a matrix $\left(M_{i,j}\right)_{i,j\in[n]} = \left(e(g, \hat{h})^{r_i \cdot (\alpha_j + \theta_j \cdot \beta_j)}\right)_{i,j}$, which forms a rank-1 matrix in the exponent. Its diagonal entries consist of

$$M_{i,i} = \frac{e(D_i, \hat{g}) \cdot e(E_i, \hat{g}^{\theta_i})}{e(F_i, \prod_{k=1}^{L} \hat{Z}_{i,k,\tau[k]})} = e(g, \hat{h})^{r_i \cdot (\alpha_i + \theta_i \cdot \beta_i)} \qquad \forall i \in [n], \qquad (18)$$

while its non-diagonal entries

$$
\begin{aligned}
M_{i,j} &= \left(\frac{e(R_i, \hat{H}_j)}{e(S_i, \hat{V}_j)}\right)^{1/(j-i)} \qquad\qquad\qquad (19) \\
&= e(g, \hat{h})^{r_i \cdot (\alpha_j + \theta_j \cdot \beta_j)} \qquad \forall (i,j) \in [n] \times [n] \setminus \{(i,i)\}_{i=1}^n,
\end{aligned}
$$

are obtained by pairing tag component (R_i, S_i) with evaluation key components $(\hat{V}_j, \hat{H}_j)$.

Random Tags. A random tag can be publicly sampled as follows.

1. For each $i \in [n]$, choose $r_i \xleftarrow{R} \mathbb{Z}_p$ and compute $\{R_i, S_i\}_{i=1}^n$ as in (16).
2. For each $i \in [n]$, choose $(D_i, E_i, F_i) \xleftarrow{R} \mathbb{G}^3$ uniformly at random.
3. Choose $r_{hash} \xleftarrow{R} \mathcal{R}_{hash}$.

Output the tag $t = (t_{\mathsf{c}}, t_{\mathsf{a}})$, where $t_{\mathsf{c}} = (\{R_i, S_i, D_i, E_i, F_i\}_{i=1}^n, r_{hash})$.

We note that, in both random and lossy tags, we have $e(R_i, \hat{u}^i \cdot \hat{h}) = e(S_i, \hat{g})$ for all $i \in [n]$, so that elements of $\mathcal{T}$ are publicly recognizable.

Evaluation. $\mathsf{LAF.Eval}(ek, t, \mathbf{x})$ takes in the input $\mathbf{x} \in \mathbb{Z}_p^n$ and the tag $t = (t_{\mathsf{c}}, t_{\mathsf{a}})$. It parses t_{c} as $(\{R_i, S_i, D_i, E_i, F_i\}_{i=1}^n, r_{hash})$ and does the following.

1. Return $\perp$ if there exists $i \in [n]$ such that $e(R_i, \hat{h}^i \cdot \hat{u}) \neq e(S_i, \hat{g})$.
2. Compute the matrix $\left(M_{i,j}\right)_{i,j\in[n]} \in \mathbb{G}_T^{n\times n}$ as

$$M_{i,i} = \frac{e(D_i, \hat{g}) \cdot e(E_i, \hat{g}^{\theta_i})}{e(F_i, \prod_{k=1}^{L} \hat{Z}_{i,k,\tau[k]})} \qquad \forall i \in [n] \qquad , \qquad (20)$$

where $\tau = \mathsf{CMhash}(hk_{\mathsf{CMH}}, (t_{\mathsf{a}}, \{R_i, S_i, D_i, E_i, F_i\}_{i=1}^n), r_{hash}) \in \{0,1\}^L$, and

$$M_{i,j} = \left(\frac{e(R_i, \hat{H}_j)}{e(S_i, \hat{V}_j)}\right)^{1/(j-i)} \qquad \forall (i,j) \in [n] \times [n] \setminus \{(i,i)\}_{i=1}^n, \qquad (21)$$

Since $R_i = g^{r_i}$ and $S_i = (h^i \cdot u)^{r_i}$ for some $r_i \in \mathbb{Z}_q$, we have

$$M_{i,i} = e(g, \hat{h})^{r_i \cdot (\alpha_i + \theta_i \cdot \beta_i) + \omega_i}, \qquad \forall i \in [n] \qquad (22)$$
$$M_{i,j} = e(g, \hat{h})^{r_i \cdot (\alpha_j + \theta_j \cdot \beta_j)}, \qquad \forall i \neq j,$$

for some vector $(\omega_1, \ldots, \omega_n)^\top \in \mathbb{Z}_p^n$ that only contains non-zero entries if $t = (t_{\mathsf{c}}, t_{\mathsf{a}})$ is injective.

3. Compute the vector $(V_{T,j})_{j \in [n]}$ as $V_{T,j} = e(h, \hat{V}_j) = e(g, \hat{h})^{\alpha_j + \theta_j \cdot \beta_j}$ for each $j \in [n]$.

4. Use the input $\mathbf{x} = (x_1, \ldots, x_n)^\top \in \mathbb{Z}_p^n$ to compute

$$Y_0 = \prod_{j=1}^n V_{T,j}^{x_j} \qquad (23)$$

$$Y_i = \prod_{j=1}^n M_{i,j}^{x_j} \qquad \forall i \in [n]$$

and output $\mathbf{Y} = (Y_0, Y_1, \ldots, Y_n)^\top \in \mathbb{G}_T^{n+1}$.

The lossiness/injectivity properties can be analyzed exactly in the same way as in the construction of Sect. 3. Indeed, by defining $v_j = \alpha_j + \theta_j \cdot \beta_j$ for each $j \in [n]$, we find that $\{\hat{V}\}_{j=1}^n$ and $(M_{ij})_{i,j \in [n]}$ are distributed as in Sect. 3.

4.3   Security

Theorem 3. *The above LAF provides indistinguishability assuming that the wD3DH1 assumption holds in $(\mathbb{G}, \hat{\mathbb{G}}, \mathbb{G}_T)$ and that the DDH assumptions holds in $\mathbb{G}$. The advantage of any PPT distinguisher $\mathcal{A}$ making Q queries within time $t_\mathcal{A}$ is bounded by*

$$\mathbf{Adv}^{indist}(\lambda) \le n \cdot (\mathbf{Adv}_{\mathcal{B}_1}^{\mathrm{wD3DH1}}(\lambda) + \mathbf{Adv}_{\mathcal{B}_2}^{\mathrm{DDH1}}(\lambda))$$

for PPT algorithm $\mathcal{B}_1$, $\mathcal{B}_2$ running in time $t_\mathcal{A} + Q \cdot \mathsf{poly}(\lambda)$.

Proof. We define a sequence of hybrid games. In Game_0, the adversary has access to the real oracle $\mathsf{LAF.LTag}(tk, .)$ oracle that always outputs lossy tags. In Game_n, the adversary is given access to an oracle $\mathcal{O}_{\mathcal{T}_c}(.)$ that always outputs random tags in the tag space $\mathcal{T}$.

Game$'_\xi$ $(1 \le \xi \le n)$**:** The adversary interacts with an oracle LAF.LTag$^{(\ell,k)}(tk,.)$ that outputs tags $t = (t_c, t_a)$ with the following hybrid distribution. In the core component $t_c = (\{R_i, S_i, D_i, E_i, F_i\}_{i=1}^n, r_{hash})$, the first $\xi - 1$ tuples $\{(R_i, S_i, D_i, E_i, F_i)\}_{i=1}^\xi$ of t_c are random group elements satisfying the equality $e(R_i, \hat{h}^i \cdot \hat{u}) = e(S_i, \hat{g})$. The last $n - \xi$ tuples $\{(R_i, S_i, D_i, E_i, F_i)\}_{i=\xi+1}^n$ are generated exactly as in lossy tags. The ξ-th tuple $(R_\xi, S_\xi, D_\xi, E_\xi, F_\xi)$ has a special distribution where $e(R_\xi, \hat{h}^\xi \cdot \hat{u}) = e(S_\xi, \hat{g})$, D_ξ is completely random in $\mathbb{G}$ and

$$E_\xi = h^{\beta_\xi \cdot \log_g(R_\xi)} \cdot g^{\rho_\xi \cdot \sum_{k=1}^L y_{\xi,k,\tau[k]}},$$
$$F_\xi = g^{\rho_\xi}$$

Game$_\xi$ $(1 \le \xi \le n)$**:** The adversary interacts with an oracle LAF.LTag$^{(\ell,k)}(tk,.)$ that outputs $t = (t_c, t_a)$ such that the first ξ tuples $\{(R_i, S_i, D_i, E_i, F_i)\}_{i=1}^\xi$ of t_c are random subject to the constraint $e(R_i, \hat{h}^i \cdot \hat{u}) = e(S_i, \hat{g})$ while $\{(R_i, S_i, D_i, E_i, F_i)\}_{i=\xi+1}^n$ are generated as in lossy tags.

For each index $\xi \in [n]$, Lemma 7 shows that Game$'_\xi$ is computationally indistinguishable from Game$_{\xi-1}$ if the R-wD3DH1 assumption holds. In a second step, Lemma 8 shows that Game$'_\xi$ is indistinguishable from Game$_\xi$ under the DDH assumption in $\mathbb{G}$. By applying Lemma 1, we obtain that the scheme provides indistinguishability under tight reductions from the hardness of wD3DH1 and that of the DDH problem in $\mathbb{G}$.   □

Lemma 7. *Game$'_\xi$ is computationally indistinguishable from Game$_{\xi-1}$ under the R-wD3DH1 assumption. The advantage of any PPT distinguisher between the two games can be bounded by* $\mathbf{Adv}^{\xi' - (\xi-1)}(\lambda) \le \mathbf{Adv}^{\text{R-wD3DH1}}(\lambda)$.

Proof. Let us assume that there exists $\xi \in [n]$ such that the adversary $\mathcal{A}$ can distinguish Game$'_\xi$ from Game$_{\xi-1}$ with non-negligible advantage. We build a R-wD3DH1 distinguisher $\mathcal{B}$ that takes as input $\{(g, \hat{g}, g^{a_i}, g^b, g^c, \hat{g}^b, \hat{g}^c, T_i)\}_{i=1}^Q$ with the goal of deciding if $T_i = g^{a_i bc}$ for each $i \in [Q]$ or if $\{T_i\}_{i=1}^Q$ are all independent and uniformly distributed over $\mathbb{G}$.

To this end, $\mathcal{B}$ defines $h = g^b$, $\hat{h} = \hat{g}^b$. It also picks $\theta'_\xi, \beta'_\xi \xleftarrow{R} \mathbb{Z}_p$ uniformly and sets

$$\hat{g}^{\theta_\xi} = (\hat{g}^b)^{\theta'_\xi}, \qquad \hat{V}_\xi = (\hat{g})^c \cdot \hat{g}^{\theta'_\xi \cdot \beta'_\xi},$$

which implicitly defines

$$\alpha_\xi = c, \qquad \beta_\xi = \beta'_\xi / b, \qquad \theta_\xi = b \cdot \theta'_\xi.$$

It chooses $\nu \xleftarrow{R} \mathbb{Z}_p$ and defines $\hat{u} = \hat{h}^{-\xi} \cdot \hat{g}^\nu$ as well as $u = h^{-\xi} \cdot g^\nu$. This allows defining

$$\hat{H}_\xi = (\hat{h}^\xi \cdot \hat{u})^{c + \theta'_\xi \cdot \beta'_\xi} = (\hat{V}_\xi)^\nu,$$

For all indexes $j \in [n] \setminus \{\xi\}$, it chooses $\alpha_j, \beta_j, \theta_j \overset{R}{\leftarrow} \mathbb{Z}_p$ and faithfully computes $\hat{V}_j = \hat{g}^{\alpha_j + \theta_j \cdot \beta_j}$ and

$$\hat{H}_j = (\hat{h}^j \cdot \hat{u})^{\alpha_j + \theta_j \cdot \beta_j}.$$

Then, it constructs the MAC secret keys $\{\boldsymbol{x}_{j,\mu}, \boldsymbol{y}_{j,\mu}\}_{j=1}^n$ for randomly chosen vectors $\boldsymbol{x}_{j,\mu} = (x_{j,1,\mu}, \ldots, x_{j,L,\mu}) \overset{R}{\leftarrow} \mathbb{Z}_p^L$, $\boldsymbol{y}_{j,\mu} = (y_{j,1,\mu}, \ldots, y_{j,L,\mu}) \overset{R}{\leftarrow} \mathbb{Z}_p^L$. For each $j \in [n]$, it defines

$$\hat{\boldsymbol{Y}}_{j,\mu} = (\hat{Y}_{j,1,\mu}, \ldots, \hat{Y}_{j,L,\mu}) = \hat{g}^{\boldsymbol{y}_{j,\mu}}, \qquad \boldsymbol{Y}_{j,\mu} = (Y_{j,1,\mu}, \ldots, Y_{j,L,\mu}) = g^{\boldsymbol{y}_{j,\mu}}$$
$$\hat{\boldsymbol{X}}_{j,\mu} = (\hat{X}_{j,1,\mu}, \ldots, \hat{X}_{j,L,\mu}) = \hat{g}^{\boldsymbol{x}_{j,\mu}}, \qquad \boldsymbol{X}_{j,\mu} = (X_{j,1,\mu}, \ldots, X_{j,L,\mu}) = g^{\boldsymbol{x}_{j,\mu}}.$$

Then, it computes

$$\hat{\boldsymbol{Z}}_{j,\mu} = \hat{\boldsymbol{X}}_{j,\mu} \cdot \hat{\boldsymbol{Y}}_{j,\mu}^{\theta_j} \qquad \forall j \in [n] \setminus \{\xi\}$$
$$\hat{\boldsymbol{Z}}_{\xi,\mu} = \hat{\boldsymbol{X}}_{\xi,\mu} \cdot (\hat{g}^b)^{\boldsymbol{y}_{\xi,\mu} \cdot \theta_\xi'}$$

At the t-th invocation of the LAF.LTag$(tk,.)$ oracle, $\mathcal{B}$ sets

$$R_\xi = g^{a_t}, \qquad S_\xi = (g^{a_t})^\nu = (h^\xi \cdot u)^{a_t},$$

where g^{a_t} is fetched from the t-th input tuple $(g, \hat{g}, g^{a_t}, g^b, g^c, \hat{g}^b, \hat{g}^c, T_t)$. For all indexes $i \neq \xi$, it chooses $r_1, \ldots, r_{\xi-1}, r_{\xi+1}, \ldots, r_n \overset{R}{\leftarrow} \mathbb{Z}_p$ and sets

$$R_i = g^{r_i}, \qquad S_i = (h^i \cdot u)^{r_i} \qquad \forall i \in [n] \setminus \{\xi\}.$$

It generates the triples $\{D_i, E_i, F_i\}_{i=1}^n$ by choosing $(D_i, E_i, F_i) \overset{R}{\leftarrow} \mathbb{G}^3$ at random for each $i \in [\xi - 1]$. The ξ-th triple (D_k, E_k, F_k) is defined as

$$D_\xi = T_t \cdot \left(\prod_{k=1}^L \hat{Y}_{\xi,k,\tau[k]} \right)^{\rho_\xi},$$

$$E_\xi = (g^{a_t})^{\beta_\xi'} \cdot \left(\prod_{k=1}^L \hat{Y}_{\xi,k,\tau[k]} \right)^{\rho_\xi},$$

$$F_\xi = g^{\rho_\xi}.$$

for a randomly chosen $\rho_\xi \overset{R}{\leftarrow} \mathbb{Z}_p$ and $\tau \overset{R}{\leftarrow} \{0,1\}^L$. As for $\{D_i, E_i, F_i\}_{i=\xi+1}^n$, they are obtained by choosing choosing $\rho_i, r_i \overset{R}{\leftarrow} \mathbb{Z}_p$ before setting

$$D_i = (g^b)^{\alpha_i \cdot r_i} \left(\prod_{k=1}^L X_{\xi,k,\tau[k]} \right)^{\rho_i}, \qquad E_i = (g^b)^{\beta_i \cdot r_i} \left(\prod_{k=1}^L Y_{\xi,k,\tau[k]} \right)^{\rho_i}, \qquad F_i = g^{\rho_i}.$$

Then, it uses the trapdoor td_{CMH} of the chameleon hash function to find coins $r_{hash} \in \mathcal{R}_{hash}$ such that $\tau = \mathsf{CMhash}(hk_{\mathsf{CMH}}, (t_{\mathsf{a}}, \{R_i, S_i, D_i, E_i, F_i\}_{i=1}^n), r_{hash})$.

It is easy to see that, if $T_t = g^{a_t bc}$, the triple (D_ξ, E_ξ, F_ξ) can be written

$$D_\xi = h^{\alpha_\xi \cdot r_\xi} \cdot \Big(\prod_{k=1}^L \hat{X}_{\xi,k,\tau[k]} \Big)^{\rho_\xi},$$

$$E_\xi = h^{\beta_\xi \cdot r_\xi} \cdot \Big(\prod_{k=1}^L \hat{Y}_{\xi,k,\tau[k]} \Big)^{\rho_\xi}$$

$$F_\xi = g^{\rho_\xi},$$

meaning that $\mathcal{A}$'s view is the same as in $\mathsf{Game}_{\xi-1}$. In contrast, if $T_t \in_R \mathbb{G}$, it can be written $T_t = g^{a_t bc + z_t}$ for some uniformly random $z_t \in_R \mathbb{Z}_p$. In this case, (D_ξ, E_ξ, F_ξ) can be written

$$D_\xi = h^{z_t + \alpha_\xi \cdot r_\xi} \cdot \Big(\prod_{k=1}^L \hat{X}_{\xi,k,\tau[k]} \Big)^{\rho_\xi},$$

$$E_\xi = h^{\beta_\xi \cdot r_\xi} \cdot \Big(\prod_{k=1}^L \hat{Y}_{\xi,k,\tau[k]} \Big)^{\rho_\xi},$$

$$F_\xi = g^{\rho_\xi},$$

for some random $z_t \in_R \mathbb{Z}_p$ that does not appear anywhere else. In this case, $\mathcal{A}$'s view corresponds to Game'_ξ. $\qquad\square$

Lemma 8. Game_ξ *is computationally indistinguishable from* Game'_ξ *under the DDH assumption in* $\mathbb{G}$. *The advantage of any PPT distinguisher between the two games can be bounded by* $\mathbf{Adv}^{\xi\text{-}\xi'}(\lambda) \leq \mathbf{Adv}^{\mathrm{DDH_1}}(\lambda)$.

Proof. We assume that there exists $\xi \in [n]$ such that $\mathcal{A}$ can tell apart Game'_ξ from Game_ξ with noticeable advantage. We build a distinguisher $\mathcal{B}$ that takes as input Q tuples $\{(g, g^{a_i}, g^{a_i \cdot b}, g^b, T_i)\}_{i=1}^Q$ in $\mathbb{G}^5$ with the goal of deciding if $T_i = g^{a_i b}$ for each $i \in [Q]$ or if $\{T_i\}_{i=1}^Q$ are independent and uniformly distributed over $\mathbb{G}$. This assumption is known (see, e.g., [38, Lemma 4.4]) to have a tight reduction from the DDH assumption.

To this end, $\mathcal{B}$ defines $h = g^\eta$, $\hat{h} = \hat{g}^\eta$ for a random $\eta \xleftarrow{R} \mathbb{Z}_p$. It also computes $\hat{g}^{\theta_\xi}$ for a randomly chosen $\theta_\xi \xleftarrow{R} \mathbb{Z}_p$. Then, it picks $v_\xi \xleftarrow{R} \mathbb{Z}_p$ uniformly and sets

$$\hat{V}_\xi = \hat{g}^{v_\xi}.$$

Implicitly, $\mathcal{B}$ will define

$$\beta_\xi = b, \qquad \alpha_\xi = v_\xi - b \cdot \theta_\xi$$

although it does not know (α_ξ, β_ξ). It chooses $\hat{u} \in \hat{\mathbb{G}}$ and $u \in \mathbb{G}$ by setting $u = g^\nu$ and $\hat{u} = \hat{g}^\nu$ for a random $\nu \xleftarrow{R} \mathbb{Z}_p$. Then, $\mathcal{B}$ defines

$$\hat{H}_\xi = (\hat{h}^\xi \cdot \hat{u})^{v_\xi}.$$

For all indexes $j \in [n] \setminus \{\xi\}$, it chooses $\alpha_j, \beta_j, \theta_j \xleftarrow{R} \mathbb{Z}_p$ and faithfully computes $\hat{V}_j = \hat{g}^{\alpha_j + \theta_j \cdot \beta_j}$ and

$$\hat{H}_j = (\hat{h}^j \cdot \hat{u})^{\alpha_j + \theta_j \cdot \beta_j}.$$

Then, it constructs the MAC secret keys $\{x_{j,\mu}, y_{j,\mu}\}_{j=1}^n$ by for randomly chosen vectors $x_{j,\mu} = (x_{j,1,\mu}, \ldots, x_{j,L,\mu}) \xleftarrow{R} \mathbb{Z}_p^L$, $y_{j,\mu} = (y_{j,1,\mu}, \ldots, y_{j,L,\mu}) \xleftarrow{R} \mathbb{Z}_p^L$. For each $j \in [n]$, it defines

$$\hat{Y}_{j,\mu} = (\hat{Y}_{j,1,\mu}, \ldots, \hat{Y}_{j,L,\mu}) = \hat{g}^{y_{j,\mu}}, \qquad Y_{j,\mu} = (Y_{j,1,\mu}, \ldots, Y_{j,L,\mu}) = g^{y_{j,\mu}}$$
$$\hat{X}_{j,\mu} = (\hat{X}_{j,1,\mu}, \ldots, \hat{X}_{j,L,\mu}) = \hat{g}^{x_{j,\mu}}, \qquad X_{j,\mu} = (X_{j,1,\mu}, \ldots, X_{j,L,\mu}) = g^{x_{j,\mu}}.$$

Then, it computes

$$\hat{Z}_{j,\mu} = \hat{X}_{j,\mu} \cdot \hat{Y}_{j,\mu}^{\theta_j} \qquad \forall j \in [n].$$

For each $t \in [Q]$, the t-th invocation of the LAF.LTag$(tk,.)$ oracle is handled by setting

$$R_\xi = g^{a_t}, \qquad S_\xi = (g^{a_t})^{\eta \cdot \xi + \nu} = (h^\xi \cdot u)^{a_t},$$

where g^{a_t} is fetched from the t-th input tuple $(g, g^{a_t}, g^{a_t \cdot b}, g^b, T_t)$. For all indexes $i \neq \xi$, it chooses $r_1, \ldots, r_{\xi-1}, r_{\xi+1}, \ldots, r_n \xleftarrow{R} \mathbb{Z}_p$ and sets

$$R_i = g^{r_i}, \qquad S_i = (h^i \cdot u)^{r_i} \qquad \forall i \in [n] \setminus \{\xi\}.$$

It generates the triples $\{D_i, E_i, F_i\}_{i=1}^n$ by choosing $(D_i, E_i, F_i) \xleftarrow{R} \mathbb{G}^3$ at random for each $i \in [\xi - 1]$. The ξ-th triple (D_k, E_k, F_k) is defined by sampling $D_\xi \xleftarrow{R} \mathbb{G}$ uniformly and setting

$$E_\xi = T_t^\eta \cdot \Big(\prod_{k=1}^L \hat{Y}_{\xi,k,\tau[k]} \Big)^{\rho_\xi},$$
$$F_\xi = g^{\rho_\xi}.$$

for randomly chosen $\rho_\xi \xleftarrow{R} \mathbb{Z}_p$ and $\tau \xleftarrow{R} \{0,1\}^L$. As for $\{D_i, E_i, F_i\}_{i=\xi+1}^n$, they are obtained by choosing choosing $\rho_i, r_i \xleftarrow{R} \mathbb{Z}_p$ before setting

$$D_i = h^{\alpha_i \cdot r_i} \Big(\prod_{k=1}^L X_{\xi,k,\tau[k]} \Big)^{\rho_i}, \qquad E_i = h^{\beta_i \cdot r_i} \Big(\prod_{k=1}^L Y_{\xi,k,\tau[k]} \Big)^{\rho_i}, \qquad F_i = g^{\rho_i}.$$

Then, it uses the trapdoor td_{CMH} of the chameleon hash function to obtain coins $r_{hash} \in \mathcal{R}_{hash}$ such that $\tau = \text{CMhash}(hk_{\text{CMH}}, (t_a, \{R_i, S_i, D_i, E_i, F_i\}_{i=1}^n), r_{hash})$.

We observe that, if $T_t = g^{a_t \cdot b}$ for each $t \in [Q]$, the triples (D_ξ, E_ξ, F_ξ) are distributed as $D_\xi \in_R \mathbb{G}$ and

$$E_\xi = h^{\beta_\xi \cdot \log_g(R_\xi)} \cdot \Big(\prod_{k=1}^L \hat{Y}_{\xi,k,\tau[k]} \Big)^{\rho_\xi}$$
$$F_\xi = g^{\rho_\xi},$$

so that $\mathcal{A}$'s view is the same as in Game'_ξ. In contrast, if $T_t \in_R \mathbb{G}$, it can be written $T_t = g^{a_t b + z_t}$ for some uniformly random $z_t \in_R \mathbb{Z}_p$ that does not appear anywhere else. In this case, (D_ξ, E_ξ, F_ξ) is just a triple of uniformly random group elements, meaning that $\mathcal{A}$'s view is the same as in Game_ξ. $\qquad\square$

Theorem 4. *The above LAF provides evasiveness under the SXDH and wD3DH1 assumptions, assuming that* CMH *is a collision-resistant chameleon hash function. Namely, for any PPT evasiveness adversary, there exist efficient algorithms* $\mathcal{B}_0$, $\mathcal{B}_1$, $\mathcal{B}_2$, $\mathcal{B}_3$ *with comparable running time and such that*

$$\mathbf{Adv}_Q^{\mathcal{A},\mathsf{eva}} \leq \mathbf{Adv}_{\mathcal{B}_0}^{\mathsf{CMH\text{-}CR}}(\lambda) + n \cdot \mathbf{Adv}_{\mathcal{B}_1}^{\mathsf{wD3DH1}}(\lambda)$$
$$+ n \cdot \mathbf{Adv}_{\mathcal{B}_2}^{\mathsf{DDH}_2}(\lambda) + 2n \cdot (1+L) \cdot \mathbf{Adv}_{\mathcal{B}_3}^{\mathsf{DDH}_1}(\lambda),$$

(The proof is given in the full version of the paper.)

Acknowledgements. We thank the reviewers for their careful reading. This work was funded in part by the French ANR ALAMBIC project (ANR-16-CE39-0006).

References

1. Bellare, M., et al.: Hedged public-key encryption: how to protect against bad randomness. In: Matsui, M. (ed.) ASIACRYPT 2009. LNCS, vol. 5912, pp. 232–249. Springer, Heidelberg (2009). https://doi.org/10.1007/978-3-642-10366-7_14
2. Bellare, M., Hofheinz, D., Yilek, S.: Possibility and impossibility results for encryption and commitment secure under selective opening. In: Joux, A. (ed.) EUROCRYPT 2009. LNCS, vol. 5479, pp. 1–35. Springer, Heidelberg (2009). https://doi.org/10.1007/978-3-642-01001-9_1
3. Bellare, M., Rogaway, P.: Random oracles are practical: a paradigm for designing efficient protocols. In: ACM-CCS (1993)
4. Bellare, M., Rogaway, P.: The exact security of digital signatures-how to sign with RSA and Rabin. In: Maurer, U. (ed.) EUROCRYPT 1996. LNCS, vol. 1070, pp. 399–416. Springer, Heidelberg (1996). https://doi.org/10.1007/3-540-68339-9_34
5. Bellare, M., Yilek, S.: Encryption schemes secure under selective opening attack. Cryptology ePrint Archive: Report 2009/101 (2009)
6. Black, J., Rogaway, P., Shrimpton, T.: Encryption-scheme security in the presence of key-dependent messages. In: Nyberg, K., Heys, H. (eds.) SAC 2002. LNCS, vol. 2595, pp. 62–75. Springer, Heidelberg (2003). https://doi.org/10.1007/3-540-36492-7_6
7. Blazy, O., Kiltz, E., Pan, J.: (Hierarchical) identity-based encryption from affine message authentication. In: Garay, J.A., Gennaro, R. (eds.) CRYPTO 2014. LNCS, vol. 8616, pp. 408–425. Springer, Heidelberg (2014). https://doi.org/10.1007/978-3-662-44371-2_23
8. Böhl, F., Hofheinz, D., Jager, T., Koch, J., Seo, J.H., Striecks, C.: Practical signatures from standard assumptions. In: Johansson, T., Nguyen, P.Q. (eds.) EUROCRYPT 2013. LNCS, vol. 7881, pp. 461–485. Springer, Heidelberg (2013). https://doi.org/10.1007/978-3-642-38348-9_28

9. Boldyreva, A., Fehr, S., O'Neill, A.: On notions of security for deterministic encryption, and efficient constructions without random oracles. In: Wagner, D. (ed.) CRYPTO 2008. LNCS, vol. 5157, pp. 335–359. Springer, Heidelberg (2008). https://doi.org/10.1007/978-3-540-85174-5_19

10. Boneh, D., Halevi, S., Hamburg, M., Ostrovsky, R.: Circular-secure encryption from decision Diffie-Hellman. In: Wagner, D. (ed.) CRYPTO 2008. LNCS, vol. 5157, pp. 108–125. Springer, Heidelberg (2008). https://doi.org/10.1007/978-3-540-85174-5_7

11. Boneh, D., Boyen, X.: Efficient selective-ID secure identity-based encryption without random oracles. In: Cachin, C., Camenisch, J.L. (eds.) EUROCRYPT 2004. LNCS, vol. 3027, pp. 223–238. Springer, Heidelberg (2004). https://doi.org/10.1007/978-3-540-24676-3_14

12. Boneh, D., Boyen, X., Shacham, H.: Short group signatures. In: Franklin, M. (ed.) CRYPTO 2004. LNCS, vol. 3152, pp. 41–55. Springer, Heidelberg (2004). https://doi.org/10.1007/978-3-540-28628-8_3

13. Boyen, X.: Reusable cryptographic fuzzy extractors. In ACM-CCS (2004)

14. Boyen, X., Waters, B.: Shrinking the keys of discrete-log-type lossy trapdoor functions. In: Zhou, J., Yung, M. (eds.) ACNS 2010. LNCS, vol. 6123, pp. 35–52. Springer, Heidelberg (2010). https://doi.org/10.1007/978-3-642-13708-2_3

15. Brakerski, Z., Segev, G.: Better security for deterministic public-key encryption: the auxiliary-input setting. In: Rogaway, P. (ed.) CRYPTO 2011. LNCS, vol. 6841, pp. 543–560. Springer, Heidelberg (2011). https://doi.org/10.1007/978-3-642-22792-9_31

16. Chen, J., Wee, H.: Fully, (almost) tightly secure IBE and dual system groups. In: Canetti, R., Garay, J.A. (eds.) CRYPTO 2013. LNCS, vol. 8043, pp. 435–460. Springer, Heidelberg (2013). https://doi.org/10.1007/978-3-642-40084-1_25

17. Dodis, Y., Reyzin, L., Smith, A.: Fuzzy extractors: how to generate strong keys from biometrics and other noisy data. In: Cachin, C., Camenisch, J.L. (eds.) EUROCRYPT 2004. LNCS, vol. 3027, pp. 523–540. Springer, Heidelberg (2004). https://doi.org/10.1007/978-3-540-24676-3_31

18. Dwork, C., Naor, M., Reingold, O., Stockmeyer, L.: Magic functions. J. ACM 50(6), 852–921 (2003)

19. Freeman, D., Goldreich, O., Kiltz, E., Rosen, A., Segev, G.: More constructions of lossy and correlation-secure trapdoor functions. J. Cryptol. 26(1), 39–74 (2013)

20. Fujisaki, E.: All-but-many encryption. In: Sarkar, P., Iwata, T. (eds.) ASIACRYPT 2014. LNCS, vol. 8874, pp. 426–447. Springer, Heidelberg (2014). https://doi.org/10.1007/978-3-662-45608-8_23

21. Gay, R., Hofheinz, D., Kiltz, E., Wee, H.: Tightly CCA-secure encryption without pairings. In: Fischlin, M., Coron, J.-S. (eds.) EUROCRYPT 2016. LNCS, vol. 9665, pp. 1–27. Springer, Heidelberg (2016). https://doi.org/10.1007/978-3-662-49890-3_1

22. Gay, R., Hofheinz, D., Kohl, L.: Kurosawa-Desmedt meets tight security. In: Katz, J., Shacham, H. (eds.) CRYPTO 2017. LNCS, vol. 10403, pp. 133–160. Springer, Cham (2017). https://doi.org/10.1007/978-3-319-63697-9_5

23. Hemenway, B., Ostrovsky, R.: Extended-DDH and lossy trapdoor functions. In: Fischlin, M., Buchmann, J., Manulis, M. (eds.) PKC 2012. LNCS, vol. 7293, pp. 627–643. Springer, Heidelberg (2012). https://doi.org/10.1007/978-3-642-30057-8_37

24. Hofheinz, D.: All-but-many lossy trapdoor functions. In: Pointcheval, D., Johansson, T. (eds.) EUROCRYPT 2012. LNCS, vol. 7237, pp. 209–227. Springer, Heidelberg (2012). https://doi.org/10.1007/978-3-642-29011-4_14

25. Hofheinz, D.: Circular chosen-ciphertext security with compact ciphertexts. In: Johansson, T., Nguyen, P.Q. (eds.) EUROCRYPT 2013. LNCS, vol. 7881, pp. 520–536. Springer, Heidelberg (2013). https://doi.org/10.1007/978-3-642-38348-9_31. Cryptology ePrint Archive: Report 2012/150

26. Hofheinz, D.: Algebraic partitioning: fully compact and (almost) tightly secure cryptography. In: Kushilevitz, E., Malkin, T. (eds.) TCC 2016. LNCS, vol. 9562, pp. 251–281. Springer, Heidelberg (2016). https://doi.org/10.1007/978-3-662-49096-9_11

27. Hofheinz, D.: Adaptive partitioning. In: Coron, J.-S., Nielsen, J.B. (eds.) EUROCRYPT 2017. LNCS, vol. 10212, pp. 489–518. Springer, Cham (2017). https://doi.org/10.1007/978-3-319-56617-7_17

28. Hofheinz, D., Jager, T.: Tightly secure signatures and public-key encryption. In: Safavi-Naini, R., Canetti, R. (eds.) CRYPTO 2012. LNCS, vol. 7417, pp. 590–607. Springer, Heidelberg (2012). https://doi.org/10.1007/978-3-642-32009-5_35

29. Hofheinz, D., Nguyen, N.-K.: On tightly secure primitives in the multi-instance setting. Cryptology ePrint Archive: Report 2018/958 (2018)

30. Jutla, C.S., Roy, A.: Shorter quasi-adaptive NIZK proofs for linear subspaces. In: Sako, K., Sarkar, P. (eds.) ASIACRYPT 2013. LNCS, vol. 8269, pp. 1–20. Springer, Heidelberg (2013). https://doi.org/10.1007/978-3-642-42033-7_1

31. Krawczyk, H., Rabin, T.: Chameleon signatures. In: NDSS (2000)

32. Kunz-Jacques, S., Pointcheval, D.: About the security of MTI/C0 and MQV. In: De Prisco, R., Yung, M. (eds.) SCN 2006. LNCS, vol. 4116, pp. 156–172. Springer, Heidelberg (2006). https://doi.org/10.1007/11832072_11

33. Lewko, A., Sahai, A., Waters, B.: Revocation systems with very small private keys. In: IEEE Symposium on Security and Privacy (2010)

34. Libert, B., Joye, M., Yung, M., Peters, T.: Concise multi-challenge CCA-secure encryption and signatures with almost tight security. In: Sarkar, P., Iwata, T. (eds.) ASIACRYPT 2014. LNCS, vol. 8874, pp. 1–21. Springer, Heidelberg (2014). https://doi.org/10.1007/978-3-662-45608-8_1

35. Libert, B., Peters, T., Joye, M., Yung, M.: Compactly hiding linear spans. In: Iwata, T., Cheon, J.H. (eds.) ASIACRYPT 2015. LNCS, vol. 9452, pp. 681–707. Springer, Heidelberg (2015). https://doi.org/10.1007/978-3-662-48797-6_28

36. Libert, B., Sakzad, A., Stehlé, D., Steinfeld, R.: All-but-many lossy trapdoor functions and selective opening chosen-ciphertext security from LWE. In: Katz, J., Shacham, H. (eds.) CRYPTO 2017. LNCS, vol. 10403, pp. 332–364. Springer, Cham (2017). https://doi.org/10.1007/978-3-319-63697-9_12

37. Libert, B., Vergnaud, D.: Multi-use unidirectional proxy re-signatures. In: ACM-CCS (2008)

38. Naor, M., Reingold, O.: Number-theoretic constructions of efficient pseudo-random functions. In: FOCS (1997)

39. Peikert, C., Waters, B.: Lossy trapdoor functions and their applications. In: STOC (2008)

40. Rackoff, C., Simon, D.R.: Non-interactive zero-knowledge proof of knowledge and chosen ciphertext attack. In: Feigenbaum, J. (ed.) CRYPTO 1991. LNCS, vol. 576, pp. 433–444. Springer, Heidelberg (1992). https://doi.org/10.1007/3-540-46766-1_35

41. Raghunathan, A., Segev, G., Vadhan, S.: Deterministic public-key encryption for adaptively chosen plaintext distributions. In: Johansson, T., Nguyen, P.Q. (eds.) EUROCRYPT 2013. LNCS, vol. 7881, pp. 93–110. Springer, Heidelberg (2013). https://doi.org/10.1007/978-3-642-38348-9_6

42. Waters, B.: Efficient identity-based encryption without random oracles. In: Cramer, R. (ed.) EUROCRYPT 2005. LNCS, vol. 3494, pp. 114–127. Springer, Heidelberg (2005). https://doi.org/10.1007/11426639_7

43. Wee, H.: Dual projective hashing and its applications—lossy trapdoor functions and more. In: Pointcheval, D., Johansson, T. (eds.) EUROCRYPT 2012. LNCS, vol. 7237, pp. 246–262. Springer, Heidelberg (2012). https://doi.org/10.1007/978-3-642-29011-4_16

44. Wen, Y., Liu, S.: Robustly reusable fuzzy extractor from standard assumptions. In: Peyrin, T., Galbraith, S. (eds.) ASIACRYPT 2018. LNCS, vol. 11274, pp. 459–489. Springer, Cham (2018). https://doi.org/10.1007/978-3-030-03332-3_17

45. Zhandry, M.: The magic of ELFs. In: Robshaw, M., Katz, J. (eds.) CRYPTO 2016. LNCS, vol. 9814, pp. 479–508. Springer, Heidelberg (2016). https://doi.org/10.1007/978-3-662-53018-4_18

Non-interactive Keyed-Verification Anonymous Credentials

Geoffroy Couteau$^{(\boxtimes)}$ and Michael Reichle

Karlsruhe Institute of Technology, Karlsruhe, Germany
geoffroy.couteau@kit.edu, m.reichle95@outlook.com

Abstract. Anonymous credential (AC) schemes are protocols which allow for authentication of authorized users without compromising their privacy. Of particular interest are non-interactive anonymous credential (NIAC) schemes, where the authentication process only requires the user to send a single message that still conceals its identity. Unfortunately, all known NIAC schemes in the standard model require pairing based cryptography, which limits them to a restricted set of specific assumptions and requires expensive pairing computations. The notion of keyed-verification anonymous credential (KVAC) was introduced in (Chase et al., CCS'14) as an alternative to standard anonymous credential schemes allowing for more efficient instantiations; yet, making existing KVAC non-interactive either requires pairing-based cryptography, or the Fiat-Shamir heuristic.

In this work, we construct the first non-interactive keyed-verification anonymous credential (NIKVAC) system in the standard model, without pairings. Our scheme is efficient, attribute-based, supports multi-show unlinkability, and anonymity revocation. We achieve this by building upon a combination of algebraic MAC with the recent designated-verifier non-interactive zero-knowledge (DVNIZK) proof of knowledge of (Couteau and Chaidos, Eurocrypt'18). Toward our goal of building NIKVAC, we revisit the security analysis of a MAC scheme introduced in (Chase et al., CCS'14), strengthening its guarantees, and we introduce the notion of *oblivious* non-interactive zero-knowledge proof system, where the prover can generate non-interactive proofs for statements that he *cannot check by himself*, having only a part of the corresponding witness, and where the proof can be checked efficiently given the missing part of the witness. We provide an efficient construction of an oblivious DVNIZK, building upon the specific properties of the DVNIZK proof system of (Couteau and Chaidos, Eurocrypt'18).

Keywords: Anonymous credentials ·
Keyed-verification anonymous credentials ·
Non-interactive anonymous credentials ·
Designated-verifier non-interactive zero-knowledge proofs

© International Association for Cryptologic Research 2019
D. Lin and K. Sako (Eds.): PKC 2019, LNCS 11442, pp. 66–96, 2019.
https://doi.org/10.1007/978-3-030-17253-4_3

1   Introduction

1.1   Anonymous Credentials

Anonymous credentials, introduced in the seminal work of Chaum [14], allow users to authenticate in an anonymous way to a variety of services. Each user can receive credentials from authorities, and register pseudonyms with authorities and verifiers. These pseudonyms are associated to the identity of the user, but should be *unlinkable* to its exact identity. That is, another entity should not be able to check whether two pseudonyms are associated with the same identity. Authorities can issue credentials to users which can be shown to verifiers, and the presentation of a credential should only leak the information that the user knows the identity associated to the pseudonym, and owns a credential from the authority for this identity. This guarantees the *anonymity* of users. In order for credentials to make sense, they must be *unforgeable*: a user should not be able to present a credential without having received one from the authority first. Due to their wide range of real-world applications, anonymous credentials have received a constant attention from the cryptographic community [1,2,4,6–9,13,17,21,23,24,26,29].

Non-interactive Anonymous Credentials. Non-interactive anonymous credentials (NIAC) are anonymous credentials where the process of showing possession of a valid credential to a verifier requires sending a single message from the user to the verifier. Non-interactivity in anonymous credentials is considered to be a highly desirable security property, and was the focus on an important research effort [3,4,24]. However, a downside of existing NIAC scheme is that all known constructions in the standard model require the use of pairing based cryptography, which limits their efficiency (since pairing are a relatively expensive cryptographic operation) and restricts the set of assumptions their security can be based on. While some interactive anonymous credential schemes can be made non-interactive in the random oracle model under the Fiat-Shamir transform, this is known to provide only heuristic security arguments in the standard model [10,20,22].

Keyed-Verification Anonymous Credential. Most commonly, anonymous credential schemes allow for a single credential to be shown more than once to multiple verifiers. The notion of *keyed-verification anonymous credentials* (KVAC) was introduced in [13]; it restricts credential to only be valid with respect to one verifier and requires the authority and verifier to share a secret key. The key observation of [13] is that such restricted anonymous credentials can be instantiated very efficiently, using algebraic message authentication codes. Therefore, in numerous applications where the restriction to keyed-verification is not an issue, they can be used to allow for more efficient instantiations. Think for example of a bus company issuing monthly pass, where the pass must be shown each time a user boards a bus; here, it is reasonable to assume that the bus device can share a secret-key with the bus company (since both belong to the same organisation).

A downside of the KVAC scheme of [13], however, is that the process of showing possession of a credential requires an interactive protocol between the user and the verifier. This protocol can be made non-interactive, but this either requires the Fiat-Shamir transform (leading to a protocol secure in the random oracle model only), or the use of pairing-based cryptography, nullifying the efficiency advantages of KVAC with respect to their publicly verifiable counterpart.

1.2 Our Contribution

In this work, we construct the first non-interactive keyed-verification anonymous credential scheme (NIKVAC) in the standard model, without relying on pairing-based cryptography. Our NIKVAC is very expressive: it natively supports multi-show unlinkability (*i.e.*, when showing possession of a credential multiple time to a verifier, the latter cannot tell whether these correspond to the same user) or pseudonyms (the verifier knows a pseudonym that he can link a credential to, but that he cannot link to the actual identity of the user), without any additional cost (*i.e.*, we do not require to generate an additional commitment to the identity and prove knowledge of its content to obtain pseudonyms, as in most alternative approaches; rather, such commitments are natively and implicitly defined by our scheme). Our NIKVAC is also attribute-based (it supports vectors of attributes as opposed to identities, and can handle a variety of relations on the attributes), and supports anonymity revocation (there exists a global trapdoor which a trusted authority can use to revoke the anonymity of a misbehaving user, efficiently extracting his identity from any accepting credential).

While our scheme is the first NIKVAC in the standard model without pairings, we observe (this is in fact the starting point of our work) that there is a relatively natural construction of a NIKVAC which is obtained by starting with the (interactive) scheme of [13], and replacing the underlying zero-knowledge proof system by the designated-verifier non-interactive zero-knowledge proof system of [11]. While this observation is interesting in itself, the security analysis of the resulting construction does not present major technical difficulties (although it is not entirely straightforward). In this work, we refine this approach, adopting a different strategy to better exploit the structural properties of the proof system of [11]. Our optimized approach provides strong efficiency improvements (which we detail in Sect. 1.6) over the previous alternative.

1.3 Our Approach

Our starting point is the interactive KVAC scheme of [13]. In this scheme, a credential is an algebraic MAC signature on the identity of the user. Anonymous presentation of a credential is done (informally) by masking the credential, and providing some zero-knowledge proofs of knowledge of the identity together with the masking informations satisfying the appropriate relation, which allows the verifier (who knows the secret MAC key) to check that the masked credential does indeed verify correctly with respect to the (hidden) identity of the user.

To make this scheme non-interactive, the basic observation is that it suffices to rely on a *designated-verifier* non-interactive zero-knowledge (DVNIZK) proof of knowledge of the appropriate values. Unlike their publicly-verifiable counterpart, there exists efficient constructions of DVNIZK proof systems which does not rely on pairings. However, until recently, all known constructions of DVNIZK proof systems [12,16,18] suffered from two important downside, each of them preventing their use in a NIKVAC scheme:

- they can only deal with *existential* statements, while anonymous credentials crucially rely on proving *knowledge* of the signed identity, and
- they only satisfy a *bounded* notion of security, where the soundness of the proof is only guaranteed to hold if the prover is restricted to query a verification oracle an a priori bounded number of times. In an anonymous credential system, however, the users can interact freely with a verifier and receive feedback on whether proofs of credential possession was accepted or not; hence, for all of these scheme, a malicious user could forge a credential which is accepted by the verifier even though it was not issued by the authority, by interacting a sufficient (polynomial) number of times with the verifier.

This situation recently changed with the introduction in [11] of the first DVNIZK proof system which allows to provide proofs of *knowledge* of a witness, for a wide variety of algebraic statements, where soundness is *unbounded* (it holds even if the prover is given arbitrary access to a verification oracle). Furthermore, the framework of [11] allows for efficient DVNIZK proofs, directly proportional to the size of the algebraic statement to be proven.

A natural approach toward building a NIKVAC scheme is therefore to rely on the KVAC scheme of [13], and to replace the underlying zero-knowledge proofs by appropriate DVNIZK, using the framework of [11]. However, while this approach should lead to a secure NIKVAC, it misses the opportunity to exploit the specific structure of the scheme of [11] to get improved efficiency guarantees. Therefore, we choose instead to tackle the problem directly and construct an optimized NIKVAC system, heavily building upon the specific structure of the DVNIZK of [11].

1.4 Our Techniques

To describe our strategy, it is helpful to start from a natural but insecure approach. As in [13], a credential will simply be a signature on the identity of the user using an algebraic MAC. To show possession of a credential, the user can simply send this credential (but not his identity) and prove with a DVNIZK that he knows an identity such that the MAC verification algorithm returns 1 when given as input this identity and the credential. A first observation is that this approach allows for a straightforward optimization: in the most common setting, the verifier must know a pseudonym associated to the user (which cannot be linked to his identity), which will usually take the form of a commitment to the identity of the user. We observe, however, that a DVNIZK proof of knowledge within the framework of [11] does already include an encryption of the witness, and the proof of knowledge property does in particular guarantee that the witness whose knowledge is proven is indeed the one encrypted in the proof. Therefore, it is not necessary to add a commitment to the identity and prove that the committed value is the one for which the user knows a credential; rather, the user can simply compute this encryption ahead of time (this does not require knowing the credential) and send it to the verifier, which will store it as being the user pseudonym. Then, each time the user wants to authenticate, he only have to generate the "missing part" of the proof with respect to this encryption. This strongly reduces the size of the proof (since the proof does not need to include an explicit proof regarding a commitment anymore), and allows to reuse a significant portion of the proof across many authentications.

However, the natural approach of disclosing a credential σ and proving knowledge of an identity that verifies correctly with respect to σ fails, for two reasons:

– First, the above approach does not guarantee anonymity, because the verifier (who knows the secret MAC key) could find out the identity of the user simply by colluding with the authority, and evaluating the MAC verification algorithms on all identities previously submitted to the authority, to find out which one verifies correctly with respect to this credential.
– Second, and more importantly, the MAC verification requires knowledge of the secret MAC key, which the user does not know; hence, he cannot possibly issue a proof that his credential verifies correctly, since checking this statement does already require knowing the secret MAC key.

We first explain how we address the second concern. Our idea is to build upon the specific malleability property of the DVNIZK proof system of [11] to build an *oblivious* DVNIZK proof system, which allows the prover to issue a proof for a statement *even if he does not know himself whether the statement does hold*. This does not contradict the security of the MAC scheme, since the proof system is not publicly verifiable: hence, even after he builds the proof, the prover cannot check by himself whether this proof verifies correctly. Intuitively, the prover will construct a "partial non-interactive proof" which is malleable in the following sense: given this proof and the secret MAC key, the verifier can reconstruct himself the complete proof that the credential verifies correctly. If the prover does not know the appropriate witness, the reconstructed proof will not verify correctly. The partial proof should not leak any more information about the witness held by the prover than what is leaked by the reconstructed proof; hence, by the zero-knowledge property of the DVNIZK proof system, this proof will only reveal whether the statement (which depends on both the prover witness and the secret key known to the verifier) is true. We believe that the concept of non-interactive oblivious proofs, which allows to prove that a statement is true while knowing only a part of the witness to a verifier knowing the "missing part" of the witness, might be of independent interest (we briefly elaborate on this in Sect. 1.5); in particular, it formalizes the approach taken (in the interactive setting) in previous works on keyed-verification anonymous credentials [13].

To tackle the first concern, the prover will randomize his credential and mask it with appropriate random values, and issue a partial proof that the *unmasked* credential does verify with respect to the secret key. We formalize both properties at once by introducing a new primitive, oblivious designated-verifier non-interactive zero-knowledge proofs of knowledge, which can be used to prove statements non-interactively even when the prover only knows a part of the witness, and can be simulated by a simulator that does not know neither the witness nor the word for which the proof is constructed, guaranteeing that the verifier will not only be unable to recover the witness, but also that he cannot possibly recover the credential, which would allow him to break anonymity by colluding with the authority.

Next, we provide an optimized construction of an oblivious DVNIZK proof system for the language of valid credentials, building upon the DVNIZK proof system of [11]. Proving security of the resulting proof system, however, runs into a subtle issue: when considering the more general setting of *attribute-based* anonymous credentials, where the user will have a secret *vector of attributes* instead of a secret identity, the unforgeability property of the underlying MAC scheme does not suffice to prove the soundness of the oblivious proof system. We provide two alternatives to overcome this issue:

- When the vector of attributes is of length one (*i.e.*, when we restrict our attention to non-attribute-based anonymous credentials, where the secret of the user is only his identity), we show that the public parameters of the MAC scheme suffice to reduce the security directly to the unforgeability of the MAC scheme. This setting already captures many possible applications.
- In the general setting, where the vector of attributes can be longer than 1, we show that the security can be proven if the MAC scheme satisfies a stronger notion of unforgeability, which we call *extended unforgeability*. Then, we revisit the security analysis of one of the two MAC schemes constructed in [13], which is secure in the generic group model, and prove that this scheme does in fact already satisfy extended unforgeability. While the second MAC scheme constructed in [13] (which is based on the decisional Diffie-Hellman assumption) does plausibly satisfy extended unforgeability, we leave it as an interesting open problem to prove it under a standard assumption, or to construct a MAC scheme with extended unforgeability under the DDH assumption. We note that considering algebraic MACs with stronger unforgeability guarantees is a relatively natural approach in the setting of anonymous credentials (see e.g. [3,4]), but the specific strengthening we require in our construction was not, to our knowledge, considered in previous works.

There is an additional requirement which we must take care of: the MAC schemes of [13] are only proven secure in groups of prime order, while the most natural instantiation of the DVNIZK proof system of [11] typically requires composite-order groups. While the security of their DDH-based MAC easily extends to the composite order setting by assuming in addition that it is infeasible for any polytime adversary to find a generator of a strict subgroup (which is a standard and well-studied assumption), the proof of their generic-group-model-based (GGM-based) MAC is unconditional, hence it assumes that the adversary is unbounded, in which case there is an explicit attack on the composite-order variant of the scheme where the unbounded adversary constructs an invalid MAC signature in a strict subgroup of the group. We therefore revisit the security proof of the GGM-based MAC, and show that it holds in the generic group model assuming in addition that the adversary is polynomially bounded, and that the computational subgroup assumption holds. Altogether, we show that this gives rise to a highly optimized NIKVAC. In the next section, we discuss in more details the efficiency of our scheme.

1.5   Applications of Oblivious DVNIZK

Given the intermediate abstraction of oblivious designated non-interactive zero-knowledge proofs, the construction of NIKVAC follows very naturally. In fact, we could have provided a direct construction of NIKVAC from this approach, without formalizing the intermediate primitive. However, we believe that oblivious DVNIZKs can be interesting in their own right. We elaborate below.

Secure computation protocols allow a group of parties to securely evaluate a public function on their joint private input. We focus in this discussion on the case of two parties for simplicity. A common approach to secure two-party computation is to first design a scheme secure against passive adversaries, which do not deviate from the specifications of the protocol, and then to use zero-knowledge proofs to let all adversaries prove their honest behavior throughout the protocol. This transformation makes the protocol secure against malicious adversaries, which can deviate arbitrarily from the specifications of the protocol. To obtain round-efficient compilation of passively secure computation protocols into maliciously secure protocols, the most natural strategy is to rely on (designated-verifier) non-interactive zero-knowledge proofs (an alternative is to use implicit zero-knowledge proofs [5], but this adds two more rounds to the protocol) to prove honest behavior of each user after each round.

Oblivious DVNIZK allow for an alternative compilation strategy, which starts from a protocol with stronger security guarantees, but is in general more efficient. Let us call (informally) *half-maliciously secure* a secure computation protocol which is passively secure, and such that no malicious adversary can compromise the *privacy* of the inputs (but can possibly compromise the *correctness* of the computation). Let Π be a half-maliciously secure protocol, securely computing a function f. Let (x_1, x_2) denote the inputs of the parties. To convert Π into a fully secure protocol, we first modify Π to include commitments (c_1, c_2) to the inputs (if Π does not already include them). Then, to guarantee full security, one of the parties, which we call the prover, must send a single oblivious DVNIZK to the other party (the receiver) at the very end of the protocol, which is a proof that $y = f(x_1, x_2)$, where y is the output of the protocol, and (x_1, x_2) is committed in (c_1, c_2). Note that the prover does not have the full witness for this statement (since it depends, in particular, on the private input of the verifier), but the prover and the verifier jointly have the full witness, allowing the verifier to check the proof without further interaction. This is in contrast with DVNIZK-based compilation, which requires proving honest behavior of all users at each round (here, we only prove *correctness* of the computation in the last round). We leave the formal proof of this observation to future work.

1.6 Efficiency

There is, to our knowledge, no existing previous construction of NIKVAC in the standard model. However, as we pointed out previously, there is a relatively natural construction which is obtained by starting from the scheme of [13], and replacing the underlying zero-knowledge proofs by DVNIZKs instantiated with [11]. Let us call this construction the CMZ + CC construction. We use CMZ + CC as a basis for comparison with our improved construction. We focus on the communication cost of showing possession of a credential, since the computation is directly proportional to the communication (hence, an improvement factor with respect to communication translates to a comparable improvement factor with respect to computation), and since the cost of issuing a credential depends on the specific secure computation scheme used to implement it, which is not the focus of our work (we require the same blind issuance of an algebraic MAC as in previous works on KVAC).

For simplicity, we focus on the cost obtained when implementing the MAC with the more efficient GGM-based MAC scheme of [13]; when using the other, DDH-based MAC scheme, all costs must be roughly scaled up by 50% (up to constants), and the improvement factor of our method compared to the naive approach will be essentially identical. Let β denote the length of the vector of attributes. In the minimal setting where the verifier knows a pseudonym, implemented as a commitment to the user's vector of attributes, instantiating the zero-knowledge proofs in [13] using the DVNIZK proof system of [11] leads to a proof size of $3\beta + 3$ group elements, and $6\beta + 2$ ciphertexts (in a typical instantiation of the DVNIZK of [11], the group will be a composite order abelian group, and the encryption scheme will be the Paillier encryption scheme).

In comparison, our proof of credential possession requires sending $\beta + 2$ group elements, and $2\beta + 2$ ciphertexts. Furthermore, all the ciphertexts can be sent once for all to the verifier (they form the pseudonym of the prover); each new credential presentation then requires only generating and sending $\beta + 2$ group elements (in comparison, the pseudonym in [13] is a tuple of β commitments, hence sending the pseudonym ahead of time saves only β group elements). For the important case of $\beta = 1$ attribute, and instantiating the DVNIZK with Paillier and a 2048-bit modulus, this corresponds to a factor of improvement of more than 7 in the proof size compared to [13]. In addition, using an optimization which we describe in the full version [15], the number of ciphertexts can be further reduced, from $2\beta + 2$ to 2β. We summarize the comparison between our scheme and CMZ+CC in the Table 1.

Table 1. Comparison of our optimized NIKVAC to a direct construction from [13] with the DVNIZK of [11].

NIKVAC[a]	CMZ+CC	This work	This work (full version [15])
β attributes, group element length n, ciphertext size m			
Pseudonym size	βn	$(2\beta + 2)m$	$2\beta m$
Proof size	$(2\beta + 3)n + (6\beta + 2)m$	$(\beta + 2)n$	$(\beta + 2)n$
Prover computation[b]	$(5\beta + 2)A + (3\beta + 1)(B + C)$	$(2\beta + 3)A$	$(2\beta + 3)A$
Assumption	GGM+IND-CPA	GGM+IND-CPA	GGM+IND-CPA + short-exp dlog
(with Paillier) 1 attribute, group element length 2048, ciphertext size 4096			
Pseudonym size	256 Byte	2048 Byte	1024 Byte
Proof size	5,38 kB	756 Byte	756 Byte
Prover computation	$7A + 4(B + C)$	$5A$	$5A$
Assumption	GGM+Paillier	GGM+Paillier	GGM+Paillier + short-exp dlog

[a] We consider a minimal setting where the prover shows possession of a valid credential with respect to an identity committed in a *pseudonym* known to the verifier. We use the GGM-based scheme of [13] as the underlying algebraic MAC (the efficiency gain of our approach is essentially the same if one uses the DDH-based MAC of [13]).

[b] A denotes the cost of an exponentiation in the group $\mathbb{G}$, B denotes the cost of an encryption, C denotes the cost of an homomorphic scalar multiplication. We note that, under the short-exponent discrete logarithm assumptions, all exponentiations in $\mathbb{G}$ (resp. all homomorphic scalar multiplications) can be performed with exponents (resp. scalars) of length at most 256 bits.

Eventually, we sketch a straightforward computational optimization (assuming an instantiation with the Paillier scheme and a 2048-bit modulus for concreteness): the exponents manipulated when constructing and verifying the proof are either attributes, random coins, or masks. If attributes are, say, up to 128-bit long, then under the short-exponent discrete logarithm assumption (which states that it is hard to find x from g^x even if x is random but *short*, e.g. 128-bit long), all exponents can be taken either 128-bit long (for the attributes and the random coins) or 256-bit long (for the masks, since they must statistically mask the attributes over the integers). This makes computing exponentiations and scalar multiplications considerably more efficient than with full-size (i.e., 2048-bit) values.

Comparison with Plain [13]. We briefly comment on the comparison with the plain scheme of [13] (which is either interactive, or non-interactive in the random oracle model). Our main efficiency bottleneck is the fact that we use the DVNIZK of [11], which requires to use a large order group.[1] Therefore, using natural parameters, we manipulate group elements of size 2048 bits, and ciphertexts of size 4096 bits. In constrast, [13] can work exclusively with group elements and exponents over any DDH-hard group, e.g. of size 256 bits. However, the proof size of [13] (not counting the size of the pseudonym) is $\beta + 2$ group elements and $3\beta + 2$ 256-bit exponents, for a total of 256 Byte. Our proof system achieves a proof size 756 Byte, less than three times larger in spite of our use of an 8-time larger group - and unlike [13], it is secure in the standard model

---

[1] In [11], the size of the group must be equal to the size of the plaintext space of a DVNIZK-friendly encryption scheme, such as Paillier.

(the ratio remains essentially the same if we instantiate instead the underlying MAC scheme with the DDH-based scheme of [13]).

1.7 Organization

In Sect. 2, we recall necessary preliminaries (further preliminaries are given in the full version [15]). In Sect. 3, we recall the definition of MAC schemes, introduce a general algebraic MAC scheme, and define the stronger notion of extended unforgeability. In Sect. 4, we formally define non-interactive keyed-verification anonymous credentials and their security properties. In Sect. 5, we introduce the concept of oblivious DVNIZK and their security properties, provide an explicit instantiation tailored to our application, and formally prove its security. In Sect. 6, we show how to construct a non-interactive keyed-verification anonymous credential from a MAC scheme and an oblivious DVNIZK proof system. Eventually, in the full version [15], we prove that the first MAC scheme of [13] satisfies extended unforgeability in the generic group model (with composite order groups), and we describe further improvements to our NIKVAC construction relying on the short-exponent discrete logarithm assumption.

2 Preliminaries

Throughout this paper, λ denotes the security parameter. A probabilistic polynomial time algorithm (PPT, also denoted *efficient* algorithm) runs in time polynomial in the (implicit) security parameter λ. A positive function f is *negligible* if for any polynomial p there exists a bound $B > 0$ such that, for any integer $k \geq B$, $f(k) \leq 1/|p(k)|$. An event depending on λ occurs with *overwhelming probability* when its probability is at least $1 - \mathrm{negl}(\lambda)$ for a negligible function negl. Given a finite set S, the notation $x \xleftarrow{\$} S$ means a uniformly random assignment of an element of S to the variable x. We represent adversaries as interactive probabilistic Turing machines; the notation $\mathscr{A}^{\mathcal{O}}$ indicates that the machine $\mathscr{A}$ is given oracle access to $\mathcal{O}$. Adversaries will sometime output an arbitrary state st to capture stateful interactions.

Abelian Groups and Modules. We use additive notation for groups for convenience, and write $(\mathbb{G}, +)$ for an abelian group of order k. When it is clear from the context, we denote 0 its neutral element (otherwise, we denote it $0_\mathbb{G}$). We denote by $ord(\mathbb{G})$ the order of $\mathbb{G}$. We denote by $\bullet$ the scalar-multiplication algorithm (*i.e.* for any $(x, G) \in \mathbb{Z}_k \times \mathbb{G}$, $x \bullet G = G + G + \ldots + G$, where the sum contains x terms). Observe that we can naturally view $\mathbb{G}$ as a $\mathbb{Z}_k$-module $(\mathbb{G}, +, \bullet)$, for the ring $(\mathbb{Z}_k, +, \cdot)$. For simplicity, we write $-G$ for $(-1) \bullet G$. We use lower case to denote elements of $\mathbb{Z}_k$, upper case to denote elements of $\mathbb{G}$, and bold notations to denote vectors. We extend the notations $(+, -)$ to vectors and matrices in the natural way, and write $\boldsymbol{x} \bullet \boldsymbol{G}$ to denote the scalar product $x_1 \bullet G_1 + \ldots + x_t \bullet G_t$ (where $\boldsymbol{x}, \boldsymbol{G}$ are vectors of the same length t). For a vector

v, we denote by v^{T} its transpose. By $\mathsf{GGen}(1^\lambda)$, we denote a probabilistic efficient algorithm that, given the security parameter λ, generates an abelian group $\mathbb{G}$ in which the CSG and DLSE assumption defined below holds in respect to λ. Note that this implies that the normal discrete log problem is hard in this group, as well. In the following, we write $(\mathbb{G}, k) \xleftarrow{\$} \mathsf{GGen}(1^\lambda)$. Additionally, we denote by $\mathsf{GGen}(1^\lambda, k)$ a group generation algorithm that allows us to select the order k beforehand.

RSA Groups. A *strong prime* is a prime $p = 2p' + 1$ such that p' is also a prime. We call *RSA modulus* a product $n = pq$ of two strong primes. We denote by φ Euler's totient function; it holds that $\varphi(n) = (p-1)(q-1)$. We denote by $\mathbb{J}_n$ the cyclic subgroup of $\mathbb{Z}_n^*$ of elements with Jacobi symbol 1 (the order of this group is $\varphi(n)/2$), and by QR_n the cyclic subroup of squares of $\mathbb{Z}_n^*$ (which is also a subgroup of $\mathbb{J}_n$ and has order $\varphi(n)/4$). By $\mathsf{Gen}(1^\lambda)$, we denote a probabilistic efficient algorithm that, given the security parameter λ, generates a strong RSA modulus n and secret parameters (p, q) where $n = pq$, such that the best known algorithm for factoring n takes time 2^λ. In the following, we write $(n, (p, q)) \xleftarrow{\$} \mathsf{Gen}(1^\lambda)$ and call abelian groups with order n composite order groups, if n is a RSA modulus.

Generic Group Model. The generic group model (GGM) was introduced in [31] and is an idealized model of groups. It captures groups with no additional structure apart from being a group. In such generic groups, the only possibility of attacking a cryptographic primitive is utilizing generic algorithms which only make use of group operations.

In proofs, the generic group model is captured by giving an adversary access to the group through random encodings of the group elements as bitstrings and a group operation oracle. Note that if a cryptographic primitive is proven secure in the GGM, it only ensures that it can not be broken with generic algorithms. In order to simulate the oracle in this work, we will require the following lemma, based on [30].

Lemma 1 (Generalised Schwartz-Zippel). *Let* $(\mathsf{n}, (p, q)) \xleftarrow{\$} \mathsf{Gen}(1^\lambda), \mathbb{G} \xleftarrow{\$} \mathsf{GGen}(1^\lambda, \mathsf{n})$ *and* $F \in \mathbb{Z}_\mathsf{n}[\overline{x_1}, \overline{x_2}, .., \overline{x_l}]$ *with* $F \neq 0 \wedge deg(F) = d \geq 0$. *Let* $p' \in \{p, q\}$ *and* $\mathbb{P}$ *a subgroup of* $\mathbb{G}$ *of order* p'. *It holds that*

$$\Pr\left[x = (x_1, x_2, .., x_l) \xleftarrow{\$} \mathbb{P}^l : F(x) = 0\right] \leq \frac{d}{p'}$$

2.1 Assumptions

Computational Subgroup Assumption (CSG). The computational subgroup assumption states that no bounded adversary can output a generator for a non-trivial subgroup. Or more formally, for all PPT adversaries $\mathscr{A}$, it holds that

$$\Pr \begin{bmatrix} (n, (p,q)) \xleftarrow{\$} \mathsf{Gen}(1^\lambda), \\ \mathbb{G} \xleftarrow{\$} \mathsf{GGen}(1^\lambda, n), \\ G \leftarrow \mathscr{A}(\mathbb{G}, n), \end{bmatrix} : G \neq 0_\mathbb{G} \wedge (p \bullet G = 0_\mathbb{G} \vee q \bullet G = 0_\mathbb{G}) \end{bmatrix} \leq \mu(\lambda)$$

where $\mu(\lambda) = \mathrm{negl}(\lambda)$.

Decisional-Diffie-Hellman (DDH) **Assumption.** Let $\mathbb{G}$ be a group with order n. For all PPT adversaries $\mathscr{A}$ it holds that

$$\left| \Pr \begin{bmatrix} a, b, c \xleftarrow{\$} \mathbb{Z}_n & : \mathscr{A}(G, A, B, C) = 1 \\ A \leftarrow a \bullet G, B \leftarrow b \bullet G, C \leftarrow ab \bullet G \end{bmatrix} - \Pr \begin{bmatrix} a, b, c \xleftarrow{\$} \mathbb{Z}_n & : \mathscr{A}(G, A, B, C) = 1 \\ A \leftarrow a \bullet G, B \leftarrow b \bullet G, C \leftarrow c \bullet G \end{bmatrix} \right| \leq \mu(\lambda)$$

2.2   Encryption Schemes

A public-key encryption scheme S is a triple of PPT algorithms ($S.\mathsf{KeyGen}$, $S.\mathsf{Enc}, S.\mathsf{Dec}$), such that $S.\mathsf{KeyGen}$ generates encryption and decryption keys $(\mathsf{ek}, \mathsf{dk})$, $S.\mathsf{Enc}_\mathsf{ek}$, given a plaintext, outputs a (randomized) ciphertext, and $S.\mathsf{Dec}_\mathsf{dk}$, given a ciphertext, outputs a plaintext. An encryption scheme must be correct ($S.\mathsf{Enc}_\mathsf{dk}(S.\mathsf{Enc}_\mathsf{ek}(m)) = m$ for every message m) and IND-CPA secure (no adversary can distinguish between the encryptions of two messages of its choice). Because of space constraints, we defer to the full version [15] the formal definition of encryption schemes and their security properties.

In this work, we will focus on additively homomorphic encryption schemes, which are homomorphic for both the message and the random coin. More formally, we require that the message space $\mathcal{M}$ and the random source $\mathcal{R}$ are integer sets ($\mathbb{Z}_M, \mathbb{Z}_R$) for some integers (M, R), and that there exists an efficient operation $\oplus$ such that for any $(\mathsf{ek}, \mathsf{sk}) \xleftarrow{\$} \mathsf{KeyGen}(1^\lambda)$, any $(m_1, m_2) \in \mathbb{Z}_M^2$ and $(r_1, r_2) \in \mathbb{Z}_R^2$, denoting $(C_i)_{i \leq 2} \leftarrow (S.\mathsf{Enc}_\mathsf{ek}(m_i; r_i))_{i \leq 2}$, it holds that $C_1 \oplus C_2 = S.\mathsf{Enc}_\mathsf{ek}(m_1 + m_2 \bmod M; r_1 + r_2 \bmod R)$. We say an encryption scheme is *strongly additive* if it satisfies these requirements. Note that the existence of $\oplus$ implies (via a standard square-and-multiply method) the existence of an algorithm that, on input a ciphertext $C = S.\mathsf{Enc}_\mathsf{ek}(m; r)$ and an integer $\rho \in \mathbb{Z}$, outputs a ciphertext $C' = S.\mathsf{Enc}_\mathsf{ek}(\rho m \bmod M; \rho r \bmod R)$. We denote by $\rho \odot C$ the external multiplication of a ciphertext C by an integer ρ, and by $\ominus$ the operation $C \oplus (-1) \odot C'$ for two ciphertexts (C, C'). We will sometimes slightly abuse these notations, and write $C \oplus m$ (resp. $C \ominus m$) for a plaintext m to denote $C \oplus S.\mathsf{Enc}_\mathsf{ek}(m; 0)$ (resp. $C \ominus S.\mathsf{Enc}_\mathsf{ek}(m; 0)$). We extend in a natural way the algorithm Enc over vectors: for vectors $\boldsymbol{m} = (m_i)_i \in \mathbb{Z}_M^*$ and $\boldsymbol{r} = (r_i)_i \in \mathbb{Z}_R^*$ of the same size, $S.\mathsf{Enc}_\mathsf{ek}(\boldsymbol{m}; \boldsymbol{r})$ denotes the vector $(S.\mathsf{Enc}_\mathsf{ek}(m_i, r_i))_i$. We extend the algorithm Dec to vectors of ciphertexts in a similar way.

The Paillier Encryption Scheme. The Paillier encryption scheme [27] is a well-known additively homomorphic encryption scheme over $\mathbb{Z}_n$ for an RSA modulus n. We describe here a standard variant [19,25], where the random coin is an exponent over $\mathbb{J}_n$ rather than a group element. Note that the exponent space of $\mathbb{J}_n$ is $\mathbb{Z}_{\varphi(n)/2}$, which is a group of unknown order; however, it suffices to draw exponents at random from $\mathbb{Z}_{n/2}$ to get a distribution statistically close from uniform over $\mathbb{Z}_{\varphi(n)/2}$. The IND-CPA security of the Paillier encryption scheme reduces to the DCR assumption, which states that it is computationally infeasible to distinguish random n'th powers over $\mathbb{Z}_{n^2}^*$ from random elements of $\mathbb{Z}_{n^2}^*$.

- KeyGen(1^λ): run $(n, (p,q)) \xleftarrow{\$} \mathsf{Gen}(1^\lambda)$, pick $g \xleftarrow{\$} \mathbb{J}_n$, set $h \leftarrow g^n \bmod n^2$, and compute $\delta \leftarrow n^{-1} \bmod \varphi(n)$ (n and $\varphi(n)$ are relatively prime). Return $\mathsf{ek} = (n, h)$ and $\mathsf{dk} = \delta$;
- Enc($\mathsf{ek}, m; r$): given $m \in \mathbb{Z}_n$, for a random $r \xleftarrow{\$} \mathbb{Z}_{n/2}$, compute and output $c \leftarrow (1+n)^m \cdot h^r \bmod n^2$;
- Dec(dk, c): compute $x \leftarrow c^{\mathsf{dk}} \bmod n$ and $c_0 \leftarrow [c \cdot x^{-n} \bmod n^2]$. Return $m \leftarrow (c_0 - 1)/n$.

DVNIZK-Friendly Encryption Scheme. We say that a strongly additive encryption scheme is DVNIZK *-friendly*, when it satisfies the following additional properties:

- Coprimality Property: we require that the size M of the plaintext space and the size R of the random source are coprime, *i.e.*, $\gcd(M, R) = 1$;
- Decodable: for any $(\mathsf{ek}, \mathsf{sk}) \xleftarrow{\$} \mathsf{KeyGen}(1^\lambda)$, the function $f_{\mathsf{ek}} : m \mapsto \mathsf{Enc}_{\mathsf{ek}}(m; 0)$ must be efficiently invertible (*i.e.*, there is a PPT algorithm, which is given ek, computing f_{ek}^{-1} on any value from the image of f_{ek}).

Note that the Paillier cryptosystem is DVNIZK-friendly: $(\gcd(n, \varphi(n)) = 1$, and any message m can be efficiently recovered from $\mathsf{Enc}_{\mathsf{ek}}(m; 0) = (1+n)^m \bmod n^2)$.

2.3 Non-interactive Zero-Knowledge Proof of Knowledge Systems

A (designated-verifier) non-interactive zero-knowledge (DVNIZK) proof system for a language $\mathscr{L}$ is a quadruple $(\Pi.\mathsf{Setup}, \Pi.\mathsf{KeyGen}, \Pi.\mathsf{Prove}, \Pi.\mathsf{Verify})$, as follows: $\Pi.\mathsf{Setup}$ generates the setup parameters; $\Pi.\mathsf{KeyGen}$ generate the (public) proving key and the verification key (which is private in a designated-verifier scheme, and public in a publicly-verifiable one); $\Pi.\mathsf{Prove}$, given the proving key, a word x an a witness w for $x \in \mathscr{L}$, outputs a proof π; and $\Pi.\mathsf{Verify}$, given the verification key, x, and π, outputs either accept or reject.

A DVNIZK proof system must be complete (if $x \in \mathscr{L}$, the verifier accept), sound (if $x \notin \mathscr{L}$, no malicious prover can cause the verifier to accept; we usually want a stronger security notion, *unbounded extractability*, which states that a polytime extractor can extract a valid witness from any accepting proof, even if the proof was adversarially generated with arbitrary access to a verification oracle), and *zero-knowledge* (the proof can be simulated without knowledge of the witness). Because of space constraints, we defer to the full version [15] the formal definition of DVNIZKs and their security properties.

The DVNIZK of Chaidos and Couteau. This DVNIZK proof of knowledge system was introduced in [11] and satisfies composable zero-knowledge, and statistical adaptive unbounded knowledge-extractability. The proofs are generated for statements defined by a linear map over $\mathbb{G}$:

Let k be an integer, $(\mathbb{G}, +)$ be an abelian group of order k, and (α, β, γ) be three integers. Let $\boldsymbol{G} \in \mathbb{G}^{\alpha}$ denote a vector of *public parameters*, and let $\boldsymbol{C} \in \mathbb{G}^{\beta}$ denote a public *word*. This system considers statements $\mathsf{St}_{\Gamma}(\boldsymbol{G}, \boldsymbol{C})$ defined by a linear map $\Gamma : (\mathbb{G}^{\alpha}, \mathbb{G}^{\beta}) \mapsto \mathbb{G}^{\gamma \times \beta}$ such that $\mathsf{St}_{\Gamma}(\boldsymbol{G}, \boldsymbol{C}$ corresponds to the statement "I know $\boldsymbol{x} \in \mathbb{Z}_k^{\gamma}$ such that $\boldsymbol{x} \bullet \Gamma(\boldsymbol{G}, \boldsymbol{C}) = \boldsymbol{C}$". Let $S = (S.\mathsf{KeyGen}, S.\mathsf{Enc}, S.\mathsf{Dec})$ denote a DVNIZK-friendly encryption scheme with plaintext space $\mathbb{Z}_k$. The algorithms $(\Pi_{\mathsf{K}}.\mathsf{Setup}, \Pi_{\mathsf{K}}.\mathsf{KeyGen}, \Pi_{\mathsf{K}}.\mathsf{Prove}, \Pi_{\mathsf{K}}.\mathsf{Verify})$ form a DVNIZK of knowledge Π_{K} for a statement $\mathsf{St}_{\Gamma}(\boldsymbol{G}, \boldsymbol{C})$ over a word $\boldsymbol{C} \in \mathbb{G}^{\beta}$, with public parameters $\boldsymbol{G} \in \mathbb{G}^{\alpha}$, defined by a linear map $\Gamma : (\mathbb{G}^{\alpha}, \mathbb{G}^{\beta}) \mapsto \mathbb{G}^{\gamma \times \beta}$:

- $\Pi_{\mathsf{K}}.\mathsf{Setup}(1^{\lambda})$: compute $(\mathsf{ek}, \mathsf{dk}) \xleftarrow{\$} S.\mathsf{KeyGen}(1^{\lambda})$. Output $\mathsf{crs} \leftarrow \mathsf{ek}$. Note that ek defines a plaintext space $\mathbb{Z}_k$ and a random source $\mathbb{Z}_R$. As the IND-CPA and strong additive properties of S require R to be unknown, we assume that a bound B on R is publicly available. We denote $\ell \leftarrow 2^{\lambda} k B$.
- $\Pi_{\mathsf{K}}.\mathsf{KeyGen}(1^{\lambda})$: pick $e \leftarrow \mathbb{Z}_{\ell}$, set $\mathsf{pk} \leftarrow S.\mathsf{Enc}_{\mathsf{ek}}(0; e)$ and $\mathsf{vk} \leftarrow e$.
- $\Pi_{\mathsf{K}}.\mathsf{Prove}(\mathsf{pk}, \boldsymbol{C}, \boldsymbol{x})$: on a word $\boldsymbol{C} \in \mathbb{Z}_k^{\beta}$, with witness $\boldsymbol{x}$ for the statement $\mathsf{St}_{\Gamma}(\boldsymbol{G}, \boldsymbol{C})$, pick $\boldsymbol{x'} \xleftarrow{\$} \mathbb{Z}_k^{\gamma}$, $\boldsymbol{r} \xleftarrow{\$} \mathbb{Z}_{2^{\lambda}B}^{\gamma}$, compute

$$\boldsymbol{X} \leftarrow S.\mathsf{Enc}_{\mathsf{ek}}(\boldsymbol{x}; \boldsymbol{r}),$$
$$\boldsymbol{X'} \leftarrow S.\mathsf{Enc}_{\mathsf{ek}}(\boldsymbol{x'}; 0) \ominus (\boldsymbol{r} \odot \mathsf{pk}) = S.\mathsf{Enc}_{\mathsf{ek}}(\boldsymbol{x'}; -e \cdot \boldsymbol{r}),$$
$$\boldsymbol{C'} \leftarrow \boldsymbol{x'} \bullet \Gamma(\boldsymbol{G}, \boldsymbol{C}),$$

and output $\boldsymbol{\pi} \leftarrow (\boldsymbol{X}, \boldsymbol{X'}, \boldsymbol{C'})$.
- $\Pi_{\mathsf{K}}.\mathsf{Verify}(\mathsf{pk}, \mathsf{vk}, \boldsymbol{C}, \boldsymbol{\pi})$: parse $\boldsymbol{\pi}$ as $(\boldsymbol{X}, \boldsymbol{X'}, \boldsymbol{C'})$. Check that $e \odot \boldsymbol{X} \oplus \boldsymbol{X'}$ is decodable, and decode it to a vector $\boldsymbol{d} \in \mathbb{Z}_k^{\gamma}$. Check that

$$\boldsymbol{d} \bullet \Gamma(\boldsymbol{G}, \boldsymbol{C}) = e \bullet \boldsymbol{C} + \boldsymbol{C'}.$$

If all checks succeeded, accept. Otherwise, reject.

3   Message Authentication Codes

In this section, we recall the definition of message authentication codes (MAC), and outline a general MAC scheme (which we call "abstract MAC"), which unifies several existing MAC scheme with a natural algebraic structure. Then, we introduce a stronger unforgeability notion for this abstract MAC scheme. In the full version [15], we prove that one of the MAC schemes of [13] does satisfy this security notion in the generic group model.

3.1 Definition

Definition 1 (Message Authentication Code). We recall the definition of
a message authentication code. A message authentication code (MAC) M is a
quadruple of PPT algorithms $(M.\mathsf{Setup}, M.\mathsf{KeyGen}, M.\mathsf{Sign}, M.\mathsf{Verify})$, such that

- $M.\mathsf{Setup}(1^\lambda)$ generates the public parameters pp of the MAC. We assume that
  pp specifies the tag space $\mathcal{S}$ and the message space $\mathcal{M}$;
- $M.\mathsf{KeyGen}(\mathsf{pp})$ generates and outputs a key sk and optionally public issuer
  parameters ipp.
- $M.\mathsf{Sign}_{\mathsf{sk}}(m)$ given the message $m \in \mathcal{M}$, outputs a tag σ;
- $M.\mathsf{Verify}_{\mathsf{sk}}(m, \sigma)$ given the message $m \in \mathcal{M}$ and a tag $\sigma \in \mathcal{S}$, outputs a bit b
  whose value depends on the validity of the tag σ with respect to m.

We assume for simplicity that once generated, the public parameters pp are
implicitly passed as an argument to the algorithms $(M.\mathsf{KeyGen}, M.\mathsf{Sign},$
$M.\mathsf{Verify})$.

Definition 2 (Correctness of a MAC). A Message Authentication Code M
is *correct* if for any $\mathsf{pp} \xleftarrow{\$} M.\mathsf{Setup}(1^\lambda)$, any $\mathsf{sk} \xleftarrow{\$} M.\mathsf{KeyGen}(\mathsf{pp})$, any message
$m \in \mathcal{M}$ and for $\sigma \xleftarrow{\$} M.\mathsf{Sign}_{\mathsf{sk}}(m)$, it holds that $M.\mathsf{Verify}_{\mathsf{sk}}(m, \sigma) = 1$.

Definition 3 (UF-CMVA Security of a MAC). A MAC M is UF-CMVA *secure*
if for any PPT adversary $\mathscr{A}$, it holds that

$$\Pr \begin{bmatrix} Q \leftarrow \emptyset, \mathsf{pp} \xleftarrow{\$} M.\mathsf{Setup}(1^\lambda), \\ \mathsf{sk} \xleftarrow{\$} M.\mathsf{KeyGen}(\mathsf{pp}), \\ (m, \sigma) \xleftarrow{\$} \mathscr{A}^{\mathcal{O}_{\mathsf{sk}}[Q]}(\mathsf{pp}) \end{bmatrix} : M.\mathsf{Verify}_k(m, \sigma) = 1 \wedge m \notin Q \end{bmatrix} \leq \frac{1}{2} + \mu(\lambda)$$

for some function $\mu(\lambda) = \mathsf{negl}(\lambda)$. $\mathscr{A}$ has access to an oracle $\mathcal{O}_{\mathsf{sk}}[Q]$ which answers
to verification and signing queries:

- $\mathcal{O}.\mathsf{Sign}(m)$ sets $Q \leftarrow Q \cup \{m\}$ and outputs $M.\mathsf{Sign}_{\mathsf{sk}}(m)$;
- $\mathcal{O}.\mathsf{Verify}(m, \sigma)$ outputs $M.\mathsf{Verify}_{\mathsf{sk}}(m, \sigma)$.

In this paper we will need algebraic MACs which means that the signing and
verification algorithms require only group operations to be performed.

3.2 An Abstract MAC Scheme

Let $\mathbb{G}$ be an abelian group of order n. Given a vector $\boldsymbol{x} = (x_0, \cdots, x_\beta)$ for some
integer β, we denote by $H_{\boldsymbol{x}} : \mathbb{Z}_n^\beta \mapsto \mathbb{Z}_n$ the affine function which, on input
$(m_1, \cdots, m_\beta)$, outputs $x_0 + \sum_{i=1}^\beta x_i \cdot m_i$. Consider now the following generic
MAC scheme, parametrized with integers (α, β):

- $M.\mathsf{Setup}(1^\lambda)$: pick a generator G of $\mathbb{G}$ and output $\mathsf{pp} \leftarrow (\mathbb{G}, \mathsf{n}, G, \alpha, \beta)$;

- $M.\mathsf{KeyGen}(\mathsf{pp})$: pick α vectors $(\mathbf{k}_i)_{i \leq \alpha} \in (\mathbb{Z}_n^{\beta+1})^\alpha$ (which can be either random or fixed) of length $\beta + 1$, and α random group elements $(G_i)_{i \leq \alpha} \xleftarrow{\$} \mathbb{G}^\alpha$. Set $H_{i,j} \leftarrow \mathsf{k}_{i,j}^{-1} \bullet G$ for $i \in [1..\alpha], j \in [1..\beta]$, $G_i' \leftarrow \mathsf{k}_{i,0} \bullet G_i$ for $i \in [1..\alpha]$, and $\mathsf{ipp} \leftarrow ((H_{i,j})_{1 \leq j \leq \beta})_{i \leq \alpha}, (G_i, G_i')_{i \leq \alpha})$. Output $\mathsf{sk} = (\mathbf{k}_i)_{i \leq \alpha}$ and ipp.
- $M.\mathsf{Sign}_{\mathsf{sk}}(\boldsymbol{m})$: given a message $\boldsymbol{m} = (m_1, .., m_\beta) \in \mathbb{Z}_n^\beta$, pick a random group element $U \xleftarrow{\$} \mathbb{G}$ and output

$$\sigma \leftarrow (U, (H_{\mathbf{k}_i}(\boldsymbol{m}) \bullet U)_{i \leq \alpha}).$$

- $M.\mathsf{Verify}_{\mathsf{sk}}(\boldsymbol{m}, \sigma)$: parse σ as $(U, (V_i)_{i \leq \alpha})$ and check that for $i = 1$ to α, $V_i = H_{\mathbf{k}_i}(\boldsymbol{m}) \bullet U$.

Example 1. The scheme $\mathsf{MAC_{GGM}}$ from [13] is obtained by setting $\alpha = 1$, and sampling the key $\mathbf{k}$ uniformly at random. This scheme is $\mathsf{UF\text{-}CMVA}$-secure in the generic group model. Similarly, we recover the scheme $\mathsf{MAC_{DDH}}$ from [13] by setting $\alpha = 3$, sampling $\mathbf{k}_1, \mathbf{k}_2$ at random, and setting $\mathbf{k}_3 \leftarrow (\mathsf{k}_{3,0}, 0, \cdots, 0)$ for a uniformly random $\mathsf{k}_{3,0}$. This scheme is $\mathsf{UF\text{-}CMVA}$-secure under the decisional Diffie-Hellman assumption.

Note that for our construction of an anonymous credential scheme, we will require the security of the underlying MAC scheme to hold in a group of composite order. In the full version [15], we slightly modify $\mathsf{MAC_{GGM}}$ and prove that the modified version is secure in non-prime order groups in the generic group model.

3.3   Extended Unforgeability

The $\mathsf{UF\text{-}CMVA}$ security property states that no PPT adversary should be able to forge a MAC on a message, even given access to signing and verification oracles, as long as this message was never queried to the signing oracle. One can consider stronger notions of unforgeability, where the adversary is given access to an additional oracle. In particular, it will be useful in our setting to consider the following *extended unforgeability* property for the abstract MAC scheme defined above:

Definition 4 (Extended   Unforgeability). An   abstract   MAC M is $\mathsf{XUF\text{-}CMVA}$ *secure* if for any PPT adversary $\mathscr{A}$, it holds that

$$\Pr \left[\begin{array}{l} Q \leftarrow \emptyset, \mathsf{pp} \xleftarrow{\$} M.\mathsf{Setup}(1^\lambda), \\ \mathsf{sk} \xleftarrow{\$} M.\mathsf{KeyGen}(\mathsf{pp}), \\ (m, \sigma) \xleftarrow{\$} \mathscr{A}^{\mathcal{O}_{\mathsf{sk}}[Q]}(\mathsf{pp}) \end{array} : M.\mathsf{Verify}_{\mathsf{sk}}(m, \sigma) = 1 \wedge m \notin Q \right] \leq \frac{1}{2} + \mu(\lambda)$$

for some function $\mu(\lambda) = \mathsf{negl}(\lambda)$. $\mathscr{A}$ has access to an oracle $\mathcal{O}_{\mathsf{sk}}[Q]$ which answers to verification and signing queries, as well as another specific type of query:

- $\mathcal{O}.\mathsf{Sign}(m)$ sets $Q \leftarrow Q \cup \{m\}$ and outputs $M.\mathsf{Sign}_{\mathsf{sk}}(m)$;
- $\mathcal{O}.\mathsf{Verify}(m, \sigma)$ outputs $M.\mathsf{Verify}_{\mathsf{sk}}(m, \sigma)$;

– $\mathcal{O}.\mathsf{Check}((A_{i,j})_{i\leq\alpha,j\leq\beta},(B_{i,j})_{i\leq\alpha,j\leq\beta})$ checks $\sum_{j=1}^{\beta}\mathsf{k}_{i,j}\bullet A_{i,j} = \sum_{j=1}^{\beta}\mathsf{k}_{i,j}\bullet B_{i,j}$ for all $i \leq \alpha$, and outputs 1 iff all checks succeed (note: the $\mathcal{O}.\mathsf{Check}$ oracle could equivalently check whether $\sum_{j=1}^{\beta}\mathsf{k}_{i,j}\bullet A_{i,j} = 0$).

In the full version [15], we will prove that the scheme $\mathsf{MAC_{GGM}}$ from [13], which was proven UF-CMVA-secure over prime order groups in the generic group model in [13], is in fact XUF-CMVA -*secure* in the generic group model over *composite order groups* (the use of groups of composite order is required for compatibility of the MAC scheme with the DVNIZK scheme of [11]), under the computational subgroup assumption. Note that, while it is uncommon to prove security in the GGM under an additional assumption, it is necessary here: there exists an explicit attack against the security of the MAC if the adversary is able to compute a generator of a strict subgroup of $\mathbb{G}$. However, in the usual formulation of the GGM, the adversary is unbounded and receives as input the order of the group, hence he can trivially factor this order and efficiently compute generators of strict subgroups of $\mathbb{G}$, showing that $\mathsf{MAC_{GGM}}$ is in fact *not* unconditionally secure in the GGM over composite order groups.

4 Non-interactive Keyed-Verification Anonymous Credentials

In this section, we formally introduce non-interactive keyed-verification anonymous credentials and their security properties. Our definition mostly follows the blueprint of [13].

Definition 5 (Non-interactive Keyed-Verification Anonymous Credentials). An non-interactive keyed-verification anonymous credentials (NIKVAC) scheme Θ is a set of algorithms ($\Theta.\mathsf{Setup}, \Theta.\mathsf{CredKeyGen}, \Theta.\mathsf{BlindIssue}, \Theta.\mathsf{BlindObtain}, \Theta.\mathsf{Show}, \Theta.\mathsf{ShowVerify}$) such that

– $\Theta.\mathsf{Setup}(1^\lambda)$, outputs the public parameters pp of the AC and a trapdoor td, the public parameters fix the set of supported statements $\mathbf{\Phi}$, the universe of attributes $\mathcal{U}$ and are passed to the following algorithms implicitly, the trapdoor can be used to revoke anonymity;
– $\Theta.\mathsf{CredKeyGen}(\mathsf{pp})$, generates a secret key sk and public issuer parameters ipp for an issuing organization;
– $\Theta.\mathsf{BlindIssue}(\mathsf{sk}, S) \leftrightarrow \Theta.\mathsf{BlindObtain}(\mathsf{ipp}, (m_1, ..., m_l))$, interactively generates a credential cred for the attributes $(m_1, .., m_l) \in \mathcal{U}$, where $S \subset \{m_1, .., m_l\}$ (here, S refers to the subset of attributes that the user wants to keep private; it allows to flexibly choose which attributes should be revealed, and which should not);
– $\Theta.\mathsf{Show}(\mathsf{ipp}, \mathsf{cred}, (m_1, ..., m_l), \Phi)$, outputs a proof of possession π of a credential cred for organization with issuer parameters ipp in respect to the attributes $(m_1, .., m_l) \in \mathcal{U}$ with associated statements $\Phi \in \mathbf{\Phi}$;
– $\Theta.\mathsf{ShowVerify}(\mathsf{sk}, \pi, \Phi)$, checks the proof π with sk with respect to the statements $\Phi \in \mathbf{\Phi}$;

which satisfies the *correctness, anonymity, unforgeability, blind issuance* and *key-parameter consistency* properties defined below.

We define two extra algorithms to simplify the security definitions:

- Issue(sk, $(m_1, .., m_l)$): generates a credential for the attributes $(m_1, .., m_l)$ using sk;
- CredVerify(sk, $(m_1, .., m_l)$, cred): verifies the credential cred using sk.

Here we define correctness, which guarantees that Issue always outputs proper credentials and that a proof of possession for a valid credential verifies correctly.

Definition 6 (Correctness). A NIKVAC scheme Θ is *correct* if it holds that

$$\Pr\left[\begin{array}{l}(\text{pp}, \text{td}) \xleftarrow{\$} \Theta.\text{Setup}(1^\lambda), (m_1, .., m_l) \xleftarrow{\$} \mathcal{U}, \\ (\text{sk}, \text{ipp}) \xleftarrow{\$} \Theta.\text{CredKeyGen}(1^\lambda), \\ \text{cred} \xleftarrow{\$} \text{Issue}(\text{sk}, (m_1, .., m_l)), \\ b \xleftarrow{\$} \text{CredVerify}(\text{sk}, (m_1, .., m_l), \text{cred})\end{array} : b = 1\right] = 1$$

and

$$\Pr\left[\begin{array}{l}(\text{pp}, \text{td}) \xleftarrow{\$} \Theta.\text{Setup}(1^\lambda), \\ \Phi \in \mathbf{\Phi}, (m_1, .., m_l) \xleftarrow{\$} \mathcal{U} \text{ with } \Phi(m_1, .., m_l) = 1, \\ (\text{sk}, \text{ipp}) \xleftarrow{\$} \Theta.\text{CredKeyGen}(1^\lambda), \\ \text{cred} \xleftarrow{\$} \text{Issue}(\text{sk}, (m_1, .., m_l)), \\ \pi \xleftarrow{\$} \Theta.\text{Show}(\text{ipp}, \text{cred}, (m_1, ..., m_l), \Phi) \\ b \xleftarrow{\$} \Theta.\text{ShowVerify}(\text{sk}, \pi, \Phi),\end{array} : b = 1\right] = 1$$

Unforgeability ensures that users cannot successfully show credentials without having received one from the authority.

Definition 7 (Unforgeability). A NIKVAC scheme Θ is *unforgeable* if for any PPT adversary $\mathscr{A}$ it holds that

$$\Pr\left[\begin{array}{l}\text{pp} \xleftarrow{\$} \text{Setup}(1^\lambda), Q \leftarrow \emptyset, \\ (\text{sk}, \text{ipp}) \xleftarrow{\$} \Theta.\text{CredKeyGen}(1^\lambda), \\ (\Phi, \pi) \xleftarrow{\$} \mathscr{A}^{\mathcal{O}_{\text{sk}}[Q]}(\text{pp}, \text{ipp}), \\ b \xleftarrow{\$} \Theta.\text{ShowVerify}(\text{sk}, \pi, \Phi),\end{array} : \begin{array}{l} b = 1 \wedge \forall (m_1, .., m_l) \in Q : \\ \Phi(m_1, .., m_l) = 0 \end{array}\right] \leq \mu(\lambda)$$

for some function $\mu(\lambda) = \text{negl}(\lambda)$. $\mathscr{A}$ has access to an oracle $\mathcal{O}_{\text{sk}}[Q]$ which answers to issuing and verification queries:

- $\mathcal{O}.\text{Issue}(m_1, .., m_l)$ sets $Q \leftarrow Q \cup \{m_1, .., m_l\}$ and outputs Issue(sk, ipp, $(m_1, .., m_l)$);
- $\mathcal{O}.\text{Verify}(\Phi, \pi)$ outputs $\Theta.\text{ShowVerify}(\text{sk}, \pi, \Phi)$.

Anonymity ensures that a user that shows a credential stays anonymous. Note that, as observed in [13], this simulation-style notion of anonymity implies in particular the standard notion of multi-show unlinkability, which states that anonymity is preserved throughout multiple presentations of the credential (a property which is not satisfied by e.g. U-Prove [28]).

Definition 8 (Anonymity). A NIKVAC scheme Θ is *anonymous* if for any PPT adversary $\mathcal{A}$, there exists a PPT simulator Sim such that it holds that

$$\left| \Pr \left[\begin{array}{l} (\mathsf{pp}, \mathsf{td}) \xleftarrow{\$} \Theta.\mathsf{Setup}(1^\lambda), \\ (\mathsf{sk}, \mathsf{ipp}) \xleftarrow{\$} \Theta.\mathsf{CredKeyGen}(1^\lambda), \\ (\Phi, \mathsf{cred}, (m_1, .., m_l), \mathsf{st}) \xleftarrow{\$} \mathcal{A}(\mathsf{pp}, \mathsf{ipp}, \mathsf{sk}), \\ \pi \xleftarrow{\$} \Theta.\mathsf{Show}(\mathsf{ipp}, \mathsf{cred}, (m_1, ..., m_l), \Phi) \end{array} \right. \left| \begin{array}{l} \mathsf{CredVerify}(\mathsf{sk}, (m_1, .., m_l), \mathsf{cred}) \\ := \quad 1 \ \wedge \ \Phi(m_1, .., m_l) \quad = \quad 1 \ \wedge \\ \mathcal{A}(\mathsf{st}, \pi) = 1 \end{array} \right] - \right.$$
$$\left. \Pr \left[\begin{array}{l} (\mathsf{pp}, \mathsf{td}) \xleftarrow{\$} \Theta.\mathsf{Setup}(1^\lambda), \\ (\mathsf{sk}, \mathsf{ipp}) \xleftarrow{\$} \Theta.\mathsf{CredKeyGen}(1^\lambda), \\ (\Phi, \mathsf{cred}, (m_1, .., m_l), \mathsf{st}) \xleftarrow{\$} \mathcal{A}(\mathsf{pp}, \mathsf{ipp}, \mathsf{sk}), \\ \pi \xleftarrow{\$} \mathsf{Sim}(\mathsf{ipp}, \mathsf{sk}, \Phi) \end{array} \right. \left| \begin{array}{l} \mathsf{CredVerify}(\mathsf{sk}, (m_1, .., m_l), \mathsf{cred}) \\ := \quad 1 \ \wedge \ \Phi(m_1, .., m_l) \quad = \quad 1 \ \wedge \\ \mathcal{A}(\mathsf{st}, \pi) = 1 \end{array} \right] \right| \le \mu(\lambda)$$

for some function $\mu(\lambda) = \mathrm{negl}(\lambda)$.

Blind Issuance. The protocol BlindIssue $\leftrightarrow$ BlindObtain defines a secure two-party protocol for the function $f((S, \mathsf{pp}, \mathsf{ipp}), (\mathsf{sk}, r), (m_1, .., m_l))$ for shared input $(S, \mathsf{pp}, \mathsf{ipp})$, issuer input (sk, r) and user input $(m_1, .., m_l)$ which returns $\mathsf{cred} \leftarrow \mathsf{Issue}(\mathsf{sk}, (m_1, .., m_l); r)$ to the user, if the input is correct. Since we will not cover this property explicitly in this paper, refer to [13] for more details.

Definition 9 (Key-Parameter Consistency). A NIKVAC scheme Θ fulfills the *key-parameter consistency* property if for any PPT adversary $\mathcal{A}$, it holds that

$$\Pr \left[\begin{array}{ll} (\mathsf{pp}, \mathsf{td}) \xleftarrow{\$} \Theta.\mathsf{Setup}(1^\lambda), & \text{for } i \in \{0, 1\}, \\ (\mathsf{ipp}, \mathsf{sk}_0, \mathsf{sk}_1) \xleftarrow{\$} \mathcal{A}(\mathsf{pp}) \ : \ (\mathsf{ipp}, \mathsf{sk}_i) \in \{x \mid x \xleftarrow{\$} \Theta.\mathsf{CredKeyGen}(1^\lambda)\} \end{array} \right] \le \mu(\lambda)$$

for some function $\mu(\lambda) = \mathrm{negl}(\lambda)$.

4.1 Additional Properties

Anonymity Revocation. The following property would allow a trusted third party to revoke anonymity if desired.

Definition 10 (Extractability). A NIKVAC scheme Θ is *extractable* if there exists an efficient extractor Ext such that

$$\Pr \left[\begin{array}{l} (\mathsf{pp}, \mathsf{td}) \xleftarrow{\$} \Theta.\mathsf{Setup}(1^\lambda), \\ \Phi \in \mathbf{\Phi}, (m_1, .., m_l) \xleftarrow{\$} \mathcal{U}, \\ (\mathsf{sk}, \mathsf{ipp}) \xleftarrow{\$} \Theta.\mathsf{CredKeyGen}(1^\lambda), \\ \mathsf{cred} \xleftarrow{\$} \mathsf{Issue}(\mathsf{sk}, (m_1, .., m_l)), \\ \pi \xleftarrow{\$} \Theta.\mathsf{Show}(\mathsf{ipp}, \mathsf{cred}, (m_1, ..., m_l), \Phi) \end{array} \ : \ (m_1, .., m_l) \leftarrow \mathsf{Ext}(\mathsf{td}, \pi) \right] = 1$$

5   Oblivious Designated-Verifier Non-interactive Zero-Knowledge

In this section, we introduce oblivious (designated-verifier, non-interactive) zero-knowledge proof system. Intuitively, an oblivious DVNIZK enhances the security and the functionality of a DVNIZK with two properties:

- First, the oblivious DVNIZK on a word x can be used to show knowledge of a witness w such that $R_{sk}(x, w) = 1$, where R_{sk} is a *secret* witness relation, which depends on a secret information which is not known to the prover. The knowledge of sk is not required to generate a proof – but it is, obviously, necessary to verify the proof.
- Second, we consider words x which can be divided in subwords (x_0, x_1), such that x_0 is a *public subword*, while x_1 is a *private subword*. The privacy of x_1 is ensured by requiring, for the zero-knowledge property, the existence of a simulator which can simulate a proof without knowing the witness w and/or x_1. Note that this formalism is mainly chosen for notational convenience: the word x_1 could always be thought of as being part of the witness. However, defining it as a part of the word allows us to set the secret relation R_{sk} to be exactly the MAC verification, where the word is the signature and the witness is the message, in our concrete instantiation.

5.1   Definition

Definition 11 (Oblivious DVNIZK). An oblivious designated-verifier non-interactive zero-knowledge proof of knowledge Π for a family of *secret* witness relations $\{R_{crs}(\cdot, \cdot, \cdot)\}_{crs}$ (which take as input triples (sk, x, w) where sk is a *secret relation key*, x is a word, and w is a witness for the relation $R_{crs}(sk, \cdot, \cdot)$) is a five-tuple $(\Pi.\text{Setup}, \Pi.\text{RelSetup}, \Pi.\text{KeyGen}, \Pi.\text{Prove}, \Pi.\text{Verify})$ of efficient algorithms such that

- $\Pi.\text{Setup}(1^\lambda)$, on input the security parameter in unary, outputs a pair (crs, td) where crs is a *common reference string* and td is a *trapdoor*;
- $\Pi.\text{RelSetup}(crs)$, on input crs, outputs a pair (sk, ipp), where sk is a secret *relation key*, and ipp are public issuer parameters;
- $\Pi.\text{KeyGen}(crs)$, on input crs, outputs a pair (pk, vk) where pk is a public *proving key*, and vk is a secret *verification key*;
- $\Pi.\text{Prove}(crs, pk, ipp, (x_0, x_1), w)$, on input crs, the public key pk, the issuer parameters ipp, a word (x_0, x_1), where x_0 is a public subword and x_1 is a secret subword, and a witness w such that $R_{crs}(sk, (x_0, x_1), w) = 1$, outputs a proof π;
- $\Pi.\text{Verify}(crs, pk, ipp, x_0, vk, sk, \pi)$, on input crs, the public key pk, the issuer parameters ipp, the public subword x_0, the verification key vk, the secret relation key sk, and a proof π, outputs a bit $b \in \{0, 1\}$;

which satisfies the completeness, oblivious zero-knowledge, and oblivious knowledge-extractability properties defined below.

Definition 12 (Completeness). An oblivious DVNIZK proof system $\Pi = (\Pi.\mathsf{Setup}, \Pi.\mathsf{RelSetup}, \Pi.\mathsf{KeyGen}, \Pi.\mathsf{Prove}, \Pi.\mathsf{Verify})$ for a family of secret witness relations $\{R_{\mathsf{crs}}\}_{\mathsf{crs}}$ satisfies *completeness* if for every $(\mathsf{crs}, \mathsf{td})$ in the image of $\Pi.\mathsf{Setup}(1^\lambda)$, every $(\mathsf{sk}, \mathsf{ipp})$ in the image of $\Pi.\mathsf{RelSetup}(\mathsf{crs})$, every $(\mathsf{pk}, \mathsf{vk}, \mathsf{sk})$ in the image of $\Pi.\mathsf{KeyGen}(\mathsf{crs})$, every $((x_0, x_1), w)$ such that $R_{\mathsf{crs}}(\mathsf{sk}, (x_0, x_1), w) = 1$, and every π in the image of $\Pi.\mathsf{Prove}(\mathsf{pk}, \mathsf{ipp}, (x_0, x_1), w)$, it holds that $\Pi.\mathsf{Verify}(\mathsf{pk}, \mathsf{ipp}, x_0, \mathsf{vk}, \mathsf{sk}, \pi) = 1$.

Definition 13 (Oblivious Zero-Knowledge). An oblivious DVNIZK proof system $\Pi = (\Pi.\mathsf{Setup}, \Pi.\mathsf{RelSetup}, \Pi.\mathsf{KeyGen}, \Pi.\mathsf{Prove}, \Pi.\mathsf{Verify})$ for a family of witness relations $\{R_{\mathsf{crs}}\}_{\mathsf{crs}}$ satisfies *oblivious zero-knowledge* if for any stateful PPT Adv, there exists a probabilistic polynomial-time simulator Sim such that

$$\left| \Pr \left[\begin{array}{l} (\mathsf{crs}, \mathsf{td}) \xleftarrow{\$} \Pi.\mathsf{Setup}(1^\lambda), \\ (\mathsf{pk}, \mathsf{vk}) \xleftarrow{\$} \Pi.\mathsf{KeyGen}(\mathsf{crs}), \\ ((x_0, x_1), w, \mathsf{ipp}, \mathsf{sk}) \leftarrow \mathscr{A}(\mathsf{crs}, \mathsf{pk}, \mathsf{vk}), \\ \pi \leftarrow \Pi.\mathsf{Prove}(\mathsf{crs}, \mathsf{pk}, \mathsf{ipp}, (x_0, x_1), w), \end{array} \!\!: \begin{array}{l} (R_{\mathsf{crs}}(\mathsf{sk}, (x_0, x_1), w) = 1) \\ \wedge (\mathscr{A}(\pi) = 1) \end{array} \right] - \right.$$

$$\left. \Pr \left[\begin{array}{l} (\mathsf{crs}, \mathsf{td}) \xleftarrow{\$} \Pi.\mathsf{Setup}(1^\lambda), \\ (\mathsf{pk}, \mathsf{vk}, \mathsf{sk}) \xleftarrow{\$} \Pi.\mathsf{KeyGen}(\mathsf{crs}), \\ ((x_0, x_1), w, \mathsf{sk}, \mathsf{ipp}) \leftarrow \mathscr{A}(\mathsf{crs}, \mathsf{pk}, \mathsf{vk}), \\ \pi \leftarrow \mathsf{Sim}(\mathsf{crs}, \mathsf{pk}, \mathsf{ipp}, x_0, \mathsf{vk}, \mathsf{sk}), \end{array} \!\!: \begin{array}{l} (R_{\mathsf{crs}}(\mathsf{sk}, (x_0, x_1), w) = 1) \\ \wedge (\mathscr{A}(\pi) = 1) \end{array} \right] \right| \le \mu(\lambda)$$

where $\mu(\lambda) = \mathsf{negl}(\lambda)$.

Definition 14 $((\mathcal{O}_0, \mathcal{O}_1)$-Knowledge-Extractability). An oblivious DVNIZK proof system $\Pi = (\Pi.\mathsf{Setup}, \Pi.\mathsf{RelSetup}, \Pi.\mathsf{KeyGen}, \Pi.\mathsf{Prove}, \Pi.\mathsf{Verify})$ for a family of secret witness relations $\{R_{\mathsf{crs}}\}_{\mathsf{crs}}$ satisfies $(\mathcal{O}_0, \mathcal{O}_1)$-*knowledge-extractability* if the following two conditions hold:

- for every PPT adversary $\mathscr{A}$, there is an efficient extractor Ext such that

$$\Pr \left[\begin{array}{l} (\mathsf{crs}, \mathsf{td}) \xleftarrow{\$} \mathsf{Setup}(1^\lambda), \\ (\mathsf{sk}, \mathsf{ipp}) \xleftarrow{\$} \mathsf{RelSetup}(\mathsf{crs}), \\ (\mathsf{pk}, \mathsf{vk}) \xleftarrow{\$} \Pi.\mathsf{KeyGen}(\mathsf{crs}), \\ (\pi, x_0) \leftarrow \mathscr{A}^{\mathcal{V}, \mathcal{O}_0[\mathsf{sk}]}(\mathsf{crs}, \mathsf{pk}, \mathsf{ipp}), \\ (x_1, w) \leftarrow \mathsf{Ext}(\mathsf{crs}, \mathsf{pk}, \mathsf{ipp}, x_0, \mathsf{td}, \pi), \end{array} \!\!: \begin{array}{l} R_{\mathsf{crs}}(\mathsf{sk}, (x_0, x_1), w) = 0 \wedge \\ \Pi.\mathsf{Verify}(\mathsf{crs}, \mathsf{pk}, \mathsf{ipp}, x_0, \mathsf{vk}, \\ \mathsf{sk}, \pi) = 1 \end{array} \right] \approx 0,$$

where $\mathcal{V}$ denotes $\Pi.\mathsf{Verify}(\mathsf{crs}, \mathsf{pk}, \mathsf{ipp}, \cdot, \mathsf{vk}, \mathsf{sk}, \cdot)$;
- there exists an efficient simulator that simulates the answers of $\Pi.\mathsf{Verify}(\mathsf{crs}, \mathsf{pk}, \mathsf{ipp}, \cdot, \mathsf{vk}, \mathsf{sk}, \cdot)$, which is not given sk but is instead given oracle access to $\mathcal{O}_1[\mathsf{sk}]$.

5.2   Instantiation

We now provide an instantiation of an oblivious DVNIZK suitable for our construction. At a high level, the secret witness relation we consider will be the one that checks, for triples (sk, x, w), that the message w is the one signed in the credential x (with respect to the secret key sk of the abstract MAC scheme defined in Sect. 3.1). Our construction heavily builds upon the DVNIZK proof system of [11]. Let $S = (S.\mathsf{KeyGen}, S.\mathsf{Enc}, S.\mathsf{Dec})$ denote a DVNIZK-friendly encryption scheme with plaintext space $\mathbb{Z}_n$ and $M = (M.\mathsf{Setup}, M.\mathsf{KeyGen}, M.\mathsf{Sign}, M.\mathsf{Verify})$ be a MAC scheme, which we assume to have the abstract structure given in Sect. 3.1, over a group $\mathbb{G}$ of order n with generator G. We will consider the following witness relation: $R_{\mathsf{crs}}(\mathsf{sk}, x, w)$, given as input a vector $x = (U, (V_i)_{i \leq \alpha}) \in \mathbb{G}^{\alpha+1}$ of group elements, a witness $w = (m_1, \cdots, m_\beta)$, and given sk, checks that $M.\mathsf{Ver}_{\mathsf{sk}}(m_1, \cdots, m_\beta, x) = 1$, where $\mathsf{sk} = (\mathbf{k}_i)_{i \leq \alpha}$ is the MAC key. Since the purpose of the public word x_0 is mainly to allow more expressivity when considering a more complex relation, and we focus here on the most basic relation (the scheme can be enhanced to work with more complex relations), we simply consider that $x = x_1$ is entirely a secret word. The scheme works as follows:

- $\Pi.\mathsf{Setup}(1^\lambda)$: compute $(\mathsf{ek}, \mathsf{dk}) \xleftarrow{\$} S.\mathsf{KeyGen}(1^\lambda)$ and $\mathsf{pp} \xleftarrow{\$} M.\mathsf{Setup}(1^\lambda)$. Output $\mathsf{crs} \leftarrow (\mathsf{ek}, \mathsf{pp})$. Note that ek defines a plaintext space $\mathbb{Z}_n$ and a random source $\mathbb{Z}_R$. As the IND-CPA and strong additive properties of S require R to be unknown, we assume that a bound B on R is publicly available. We denote $\ell \leftarrow 2^\lambda n B$.
- $\Pi.\mathsf{RelSetup}(\mathsf{crs})$: same as $M.\mathsf{KeyGen}$, namely: pick α vectors $(\mathbf{k}_i)_{i \leq \alpha} \in (\mathbb{Z}_n^\beta)^\alpha$ (which can be either random or fixed) of length β, and α random group elements $(G_i)_{i \leq \alpha} \xleftarrow{\$} \mathbb{G}^\alpha$. Set $H_{i,j} \leftarrow \mathbf{k}_{i,j}^{-1} \bullet G$ for $i \in [1..\alpha], j \in [1..\beta]$, $G_i' \leftarrow \mathbf{k}_{i,0} \bullet G_i$ for $i \in [1..\alpha]$, and $\mathsf{ipp} \leftarrow ((H_{i,j})_{1 \leq j \leq \beta})_{i \leq \alpha}, (G_i, G_i')_{i \leq \alpha})$. Output $\mathsf{sk} = (\mathbf{k}_i)_{i \leq \alpha}$ and ipp.
- $\Pi.\mathsf{KeyGen}(\mathsf{crs})$: pick $e \leftarrow \mathbb{Z}_\ell$, set $\mathsf{pk} \leftarrow S.\mathsf{Enc}_{\mathsf{ek}}(0; e)$ and $\mathsf{vk} \leftarrow e$. Output $(\mathsf{pk}, \mathsf{vk})$.
- $\Pi.\mathsf{Prove}(\mathsf{crs}, \mathsf{pk}, \mathsf{ipp}, x, w)$: given $x = (U, (V_i)_{i \leq \alpha})$ and a witness $w = \mathbf{m}$, pick $(\mathbf{m}', \mathbf{t}, \mathbf{t}') \xleftarrow{\$} \mathbb{Z}_n^\beta \times (\mathbb{Z}_n^\alpha)^2$, $(\mathbf{r}_m, \mathbf{r}_t) \xleftarrow{\$} \mathbb{Z}_{2^\lambda B}^\beta \times \mathbb{Z}_{2^\lambda B}^\alpha$, $z \xleftarrow{\$} \mathbb{Z}_n$. Let $(\mathbf{t}_j')_{j \leq \beta} = (t_{1,j}', \cdots, t_{\alpha,j}')_{j \leq \beta}$ denote uniformly random additive shares of $\mathbf{t}'$ over $\mathbb{Z}_n^\alpha$. Compute

$$(U', (V_i')_{i \leq \alpha}) \leftarrow (z \bullet U, ((z \bullet V_i) + (t_i \bullet G))_{i \leq \alpha})$$
$$W_{i,j} \leftarrow m_j' \bullet U' + (t_{i,j}' \bullet H_{i,j}) \text{ for } i \in [1..\alpha], j \in [1..\beta]$$
$$(\mathbf{X}_m, \mathbf{X}_t) \leftarrow (S.\mathsf{Enc}_{\mathsf{ek}}(\mathbf{m}; \mathbf{r}_m), S.\mathsf{Enc}_{\mathsf{ek}}(\mathbf{t}; \mathbf{r}_t)),$$
$$\mathbf{X}_m' \leftarrow S.\mathsf{Enc}_{\mathsf{ek}}(\mathbf{m}'; 0) \ominus (\mathbf{r}_m \odot \mathsf{pk}) = S.\mathsf{Enc}_{\mathsf{ek}}(\mathbf{m}'; -e \cdot \mathbf{r}_m),$$
$$\mathbf{X}_t' \leftarrow S.\mathsf{Enc}_{\mathsf{ek}}(\mathbf{t}'; 0) \ominus (\mathbf{r}_t \odot \mathsf{pk}) = S.\mathsf{Enc}_{\mathsf{ek}}(\mathbf{t}'; -e \cdot \mathbf{r}_t),$$

and output $\pi \leftarrow (U', (V_i')_{i \leq \alpha}, (W_{i,j})_{i \leq \alpha, j \leq \beta}, \mathbf{X}_m, \mathbf{X}_t, \mathbf{X}_m', \mathbf{X}_t')$.
- $\Pi.\mathsf{Verify}(\mathsf{crs}, \mathsf{pk}, \mathsf{ipp}, \mathsf{vk}, \mathsf{sk}, \pi)$: parse π as

$$(U', (V_i')_{i \leq \alpha}, (W_{i,j})_{i \leq \alpha, j \leq \beta}, \mathbf{X}_m, \mathbf{X}_t, \mathbf{X}_m', \mathbf{X}_t').$$

Check that $e \odot \boldsymbol{X}_m \oplus \boldsymbol{X}'_m$ and $e \odot \boldsymbol{X}_t \oplus \boldsymbol{X}'_t$ are decodable, and decode them to vectors $\boldsymbol{d}_m, \boldsymbol{d}_t$. Reconstruct

$$(W'_i)_{i \leq \alpha} \leftarrow \left(\sum_{j=1}^{\beta} \mathsf{k}_{i,j} \bullet W_{i,j} \right)_{i \leq \alpha}$$

and check that

$$(e \bullet (V'_i - (\mathsf{k}_{i,0} \bullet U')) + W'_i)_{i \leq \alpha} = (\boldsymbol{d}_m \bullet (\mathsf{k}_{i,j} \bullet U')_{1 \leq j \leq \beta})_{i \leq \alpha} + \boldsymbol{d}_t \bullet G.$$

Output 1 if and only if all checks succeeded.

Theorem 2. *The scheme Π is an oblivious designated-verifier zero-knowledge proof of knowledge for the family of secret witness relations $\{R_{\mathsf{crs}}\}_{\mathsf{crs}}$, whose oblivious zero-knowledge property reduces to the semantic security of the DVNIZK-friendly encryption scheme S, and which satisfies statistical $(\mathcal{O}_0, \mathcal{O}_1)$-knowledge extractability for the oracle $\mathcal{O}_0[\mathsf{sk}] \equiv M.\mathsf{Sign}_{\mathsf{sk}}$, and an oracle $\mathcal{O}_1[\mathsf{sk}]$ which is either*

- $M.\mathsf{Verify}_{\mathsf{sk}}(\cdot, \cdot)$ *if $\beta = 1$, or*
- $M.\mathsf{Verify}_{\mathsf{sk}}(\cdot, \cdot)$ *together with* $M.\mathsf{Check}_{\mathsf{sk}}(\cdot, \cdot)$ *otherwise.*

5.3 Extensions and Optimizations

In itself, the above oblivious DVNIZK does not seem to provide a strong unforgeability guarantee. Indeed, recall that the unforgeability of keyed-verification anonymous credential states (informally) that it should be infeasible to come up with a pair $(\boldsymbol{m}, \sigma)$ such that $M.\mathsf{Ver}_{\mathsf{sk}}(\boldsymbol{m}, \sigma) = 1$ and $\Phi(\boldsymbol{m}) = 1$, if all previous queries to the signing authority where on vectors $\boldsymbol{m}'$ such that $\Phi(\boldsymbol{m}') = 0$. The exact choice of Φ depends on the particular application; typically, $\Phi(\boldsymbol{m})$ could correspond to the statement that $\boldsymbol{m}$ is the value committed in some *pseudonym* known to the verifier; that way, the condition "all previous queries to the signing authority where on vectors $\boldsymbol{m}'$ such that $\Phi(\boldsymbol{m}') = 0$" boils down to the standard guarantee of anonymous credentials: it should be infeasible to come up with an accepting credential on a vector that was never signed before by the authority. But Φ can also check a more complex statement on the vector of attributes (e.g. it could check that the attribute "age" is above 18).

In the construction given above, we directly focus on enforcing $M.\mathsf{Ver}_{\mathsf{sk}}(\boldsymbol{m}, \sigma) = 1$; there is no additional Φ to, for example, bind $\boldsymbol{m}$ to a commitment. However, we observe that this typical choice of Φ is *for free* in our construction above. Indeed, a proof π does contain, by construction, a perfectly binding commitment (in fact, an encryption with S) of the vector $\boldsymbol{m}$, which is $\boldsymbol{X}_m$. Furthermore, it will immediately follow from the security analysis that the proof does not only guarantee the knowledge of a witness $w = \boldsymbol{m}$ (recovered by the extractor): it further guarantees that this witness is exactly the one encrypted in $\boldsymbol{X}_m$. Therefore, to bind the user to a pseudonym known to the verifier, it is unnecessary to add a commitment to $\boldsymbol{m}$. Instead, the user can simply compute $(\boldsymbol{X}_m, \boldsymbol{X}_t, \boldsymbol{X}'_m, \boldsymbol{X}'_t)$ in advance (observe that this does not require the knowledge of a credential) and send it to the verifier, who will simply define it to be the pseudonym of the user. Then, each time he wants to show possession of a credential $(U, (V_i)_{i \leq \alpha})$, the user only needs to compute the *missing part* of the proof, $(U', (V'_i)_{i \leq \alpha}, (W_{i,j})_{i \leq \alpha, j \leq \beta})$. This significantly reduces the size of a proof of possession, and in scenario where Φ is only intended to check that the vector matches with a pseudonym, the basic construction suffices as is. Of course, it can be extended to more complex statements Φ, as long as they fit in the framework of statements handled by [11].

5.4   Security Analysis

Completeness follows from a straightforward (although tedious) inspection. We now establish oblivious zero-knowledge and $(\mathcal{O}_0, \mathcal{O}_1)$-knowledge extractability.

Oblivious Zero-Knowledge. We exhibit a simulator Sim which simulates a proof π given $(\mathsf{crs}, \mathsf{pk}, \mathsf{ipp}, x_0, \mathsf{vk} = e, \mathsf{sk} = (\mathsf{k}_i)_{i \leq \alpha})$. Note that Sim is not given the witness w nor x_1. The simulator Sim proceeds as follows:

Pick $(\tilde{m}, m', d_m, t, t', d_t) \xleftarrow{\$} (\mathbb{Z}_n^\beta)^3 \times (\mathbb{Z}_n^\beta)^3$, $(r_m, r_t) \xleftarrow{\$} \mathbb{Z}_{2^\lambda B}^\beta \times \mathbb{Z}_{2^\lambda B}^\alpha$. Let $(t'_j)_{j \leq \beta} = (t'_{1,j}, \cdots, t'_{\alpha,j})_{j \leq \beta}$ denote uniformly random additive shares of t' over $\mathbb{Z}_n^\alpha$. Compute

$(U', (V'_i)_{i \leq \alpha}) \xleftarrow{\$} \mathbb{G}^{\alpha+1}$

$(W'_i)_{i \leq \alpha} \leftarrow (d_m \bullet (\mathsf{k}_{i,j} \bullet U')_{1 \leq j \leq \beta})_{i \leq \alpha} + d_t \bullet G - e \bullet (V'_i - (\mathsf{k}_{i,0} \bullet U'))_{i \leq \alpha}$

$(\boldsymbol{X}_m, \boldsymbol{X}_t) \leftarrow (S.\mathsf{Enc}_{\mathsf{ek}}(\tilde{m}; r_m), S.\mathsf{Enc}_{\mathsf{ek}}(t; r_t))$,

$(\boldsymbol{X}'_m, \boldsymbol{X}'_t) \leftarrow (S.\mathsf{Enc}_{\mathsf{ek}}(d_m - e \cdot \tilde{m}; -e \cdot r_m), S.\mathsf{Enc}_{\mathsf{ek}}(d_t - e \cdot t; -e \cdot r_t))$.

Then, for $i \in [1..\alpha], j \in [1..\beta]$, pick random $W_{i,j}$ conditioned on

$$W'_i = \sum_{j=1}^{\beta} \mathsf{k}_{i,j} \bullet W_{i,j},$$

and output $\pi \leftarrow (U', (V'_i)_{i \leq \alpha}, (W_{i,j})_{i \leq \alpha, j \leq \beta}, \boldsymbol{X}_m, \boldsymbol{X}_t, \boldsymbol{X}'_m, \boldsymbol{X}'_t)$.

We now show how to use an adversary Adv which outputs $((x_0, x_1), w, \mathsf{ipp}, \mathsf{sk})$ and distinguishes $\pi \leftarrow \Pi.\mathsf{Prove}(\mathsf{crs}, \mathsf{pk}, \mathsf{ipp}, (x_0, x_1), w)$ from $\pi \leftarrow \mathsf{Sim}(\mathsf{crs}, \mathsf{pk}, \mathsf{ipp}, , x_0, \mathsf{vk}, \mathsf{sk})$ conditioned on $R_{\mathsf{crs}}(\mathsf{sk}, (x_0, x_1), w) = 1$ to break the semantic security of S. The reduction obtains m from Adv, samples a random $\tilde{m}$, and sends $(m, \tilde{m})$ to a challenger for the IND-CPA game of S. It receives a ciphertext $\boldsymbol{X}_m$. It samples $(m', d_m, t, t', d_t) \xleftarrow{\$} (\mathbb{Z}_n^\beta)^2 \times (\mathbb{Z}_n^\alpha)^3$, $r_t \xleftarrow{\$} \mathbb{Z}_{2^\lambda B}^\alpha$ as before, and sets $\boldsymbol{X}'_m \leftarrow S.\mathsf{Enc}_{\mathsf{ek}}(d_m; 0) \ominus \boldsymbol{X}_m \odot e$. Finally, it computes $(U', (V'_i)_{i \leq \alpha})$, $(W_{i,j})_{i \leq \alpha, j \leq \beta}$, and $(\boldsymbol{X}_t, \boldsymbol{X}'_t)$ as before. Observe that $(U', (V'_i)_{i \leq \alpha})$ are distributed identically in the real game and the simulated game; direct calculations show that when $\boldsymbol{X}_m$ encrypts m, the proof π is distributed exactly as in the real game, while when $\boldsymbol{X}_m$ encrypts $\tilde{m}$, the proof π is distributed exactly as in the simulated game.

$((\mathcal{O}_0, \mathcal{O}_1)$-**Knowledge-Extractability).** We now turn our attention to the $(\mathcal{O}_0, \mathcal{O}_1)$-knowledge extractability property. The extractor Ext proceeds as follows: given a proof $\pi = (U', (V_i')_{i \leq \alpha}, (W_{i,j})_{i \leq \alpha, j \leq \beta}, \boldsymbol{X}_m, \boldsymbol{X}_t, \boldsymbol{X}_m', \boldsymbol{X}_t')$, it computes $\boldsymbol{m} \leftarrow S.\mathsf{Dec}_{\mathsf{td}}(\boldsymbol{X}_m)$, $\boldsymbol{t} \leftarrow S.\mathsf{Dec}_{\mathsf{td}}(\boldsymbol{X}_t)$, and outputs $x \leftarrow (U', (V_i' - t_i \bullet G)_{i \leq \alpha})$, and $w \leftarrow \boldsymbol{m}$. We now analyze the probability that $R_{\mathsf{crs}}(\mathsf{sk}, (x_0, x_1), w) = 0 \wedge \Pi.\mathsf{Verify}(\mathsf{crs}, \mathsf{pk}, \mathsf{ipp}, x_0, \mathsf{vk}, \mathsf{sk}, \pi) = 1$. To do so, we proceed in two steps:

Game 1. In this game, we modify the behavior of the oracle $\Pi.\mathsf{Verify}(\mathsf{crs}, \mathsf{pk}, \mathsf{ipp}, \mathsf{vk}, \cdot, \mathsf{sk}, \cdot)$ that Adv is given access to. Namely, the oracle is not given vk anymore. Rather, we generate vk as before, and set $e_R \leftarrow \mathsf{vk} \bmod R$. Each time Adv sends a query π to the oracle, we proceed as follows: we parse π as

$$\pi = (U', (V_i')_{i \leq \alpha}, (W_{i,j})_{i \leq \alpha, j \leq \beta}, \boldsymbol{X}_m, \boldsymbol{X}_t, \boldsymbol{X}_m', \boldsymbol{X}_t'),$$

and use td to decrypt $(\boldsymbol{X}_m, \boldsymbol{X}_t, \boldsymbol{X}_m', \boldsymbol{X}_t')$, obtaining vectors $(\boldsymbol{m}, \boldsymbol{t}, \boldsymbol{m}', \boldsymbol{t}')$. Then, we perform the following checks:

1. we check that $-e_R \odot (\boldsymbol{X}_m \ominus \boldsymbol{m}) = \boldsymbol{X}_m' \ominus \boldsymbol{m}'$;
2. we check that $-e_R \odot (\boldsymbol{X}_t \ominus \boldsymbol{t}) = \boldsymbol{X}_t' \ominus \boldsymbol{t}'$;
3. we check $V_i' - t_i \bullet G = H_{\mathsf{k}_i}(\boldsymbol{m}) \bullet U'$ for every $i \leq \alpha$ (that is, we run $M.\mathsf{Ver}_{\mathsf{sk}}(\boldsymbol{m}, \sigma)$ on the MAC $\sigma = (U'(V_i' - t_i \bullet G)_{i \leq \alpha}))$;
4. we reconstruct $(W_i')_{i \leq \alpha} \leftarrow \left(\sum_{j=1}^{\beta} \mathsf{k}_{i,j} \bullet W_{i,j} \right)_{i \leq \alpha}$ and check $W_i' - t_i' \bullet G = \sum_{j=1}^{\beta} (\mathsf{k}_{i,j} \cdot m_j') \bullet U'$ for every $i \leq \alpha$.

Note that this follows exactly the proof strategy of [11, Section 3.3]. It follows by the exact same argument that it is statistically infeasible to distinguish the simulated oracle in Game 1 from the real oracle, and the distinguishing advantage is at most $Q(\alpha+1)p$, where p is the smallest prime factor of n and Q is the number of queries of Adv to the oracle. Intuitively, the argument stems from the fact that if Adv ever submits a proof that would be accepted by the oracle, but not by the simulated oracle (or the converse), then this proof information-theoretically determines vk. However, even given $e_R = \mathsf{vk} \bmod R$, it follows from the chinese remainder theorem that the value $\mathsf{vk} \bmod \mathsf{n}$ remains *statistically hidden*, since vk was initially picked at random in $\mathbb{Z}_\ell$ and ℓ satisfies $\ell > 2^\lambda \mathsf{n} R$. Observe that game already suffices to establish that the probability of $R_{\mathsf{crs}}(\mathsf{sk}, (x_0, x_1), w) = 0 \wedge \Pi.\mathsf{Verify}(\mathsf{pk}, \mathsf{vk}, \mathsf{sk}, \pi) = 1$ must be negligible, since in this game the simulation of $\Pi.\mathsf{Verify}$ does in particular check that $R_{\mathsf{crs}}(\mathsf{sk}, (x_0, x_1), w) = 1$. However, the simulation of $\Pi.\mathsf{Verify}$ still uses sk; to establish the second property of the $(\mathcal{O}_0, \mathcal{O}_1)$-knowledge-extractability, we proceed with a second game.

Game 2. In this game, we further modify the simulated oracle, so that it does not use sk anymore. Instead, the simulation will itself rely on the MAC verification oracle. More precisely, the key sk is only used in the checks 3 and 4 of Game 1. The third check is straightforward given oracle access to $M.\mathsf{Verify}_{\mathsf{sk}}(\cdot, \cdot)$: just call $M.\mathsf{Verify}_{\mathsf{sk}}(\boldsymbol{m}, \sigma)$ with $\sigma = (U', (V_i' - t_i \bullet G)_{i \leq \alpha})$ (this is perfectly identical to the third check in the previous game).

The fourth check, however, is more problematic, since it's not clear how to reconstruct the $(W_i')_{i \leq \alpha}$ without knowing sk. Rewriting a bit the fourth check, we need to check is

$$\sum_{j=1}^{\beta} k_{i,j} \bullet W_{i,j} - t_i' \bullet G = \sum_{j=1}^{\beta} k_{i,j} \bullet (m_j' \bullet U')$$

for every $i \leq \alpha$. Letting $(t_{i,1}', \cdots, t_{i,\beta}')$ denote an arbitrary additive sharing of t_i' for every $i \leq \alpha$, this equation can be rewritten as

$$\sum_{j=1}^{\beta} k_{i,j} \bullet (W_{i,j} - t_{i,j}' \bullet H_{i,j}) = \sum_{j=1}^{\beta} k_{i,j} \bullet (m_j' \bullet U')$$

Now, we distinguish two cases:

- **Case 1.** If it holds that $\beta = 1$, corresponding to the case where the vector of attributes has length 1 (or, equivalently, we consider a simplified scenario without attributes, and credentials computed directly on the identity of the user), then the equation becomes

$$k_{i,1} \bullet (m_1' \bullet U' - W_{i,1}) = t_i' \bullet G.$$

  Observe that this check can be performed efficiently: since we are given $H_{i,1} = k_{i,1}^{-1} \bullet G$, this is perfectly equivalent to checking

$$m_1' \bullet U' - W_{i,1} = t_i' \bullet H_{i,1}$$

  for every $i \leq \alpha$, which does not require the knowledge of sk.
- **Case 2.** In the general case, where β can be larger than 1, there is no immediate shortcut. In this case, we have to rely on a MAC with a stronger unforgeability property, the XUF-CMVA security property defined in Sect. 3, and we simulate the verification using the following two oracles:
  - $M.\mathsf{Verify}(m, \sigma)$ outputs $M.\mathsf{Verify}_{\mathsf{sk}}(m, \sigma)$;
  - $M.\mathsf{Check}((A_{i,j})_{i \leq \alpha, j \leq \beta} (B_{i,j})_{i \leq \alpha, j \leq \beta})$ checks $\sum_{j=1}^{\beta} k_{i,j} \bullet A_{i,j} = \sum_{j=1}^{\beta} k_{i,j} \bullet B_{i,j}$ for all $i \leq \alpha$, and outputs 1 iff all checks succeed,

  where the first oracle allows to check the third equation, and the second oracle allows to check the last equation.

In both cases, it is immediate to see that the answers of the simulated oracle are distributed exactly as in Game 1. Furthermore, the simulation only requires access to an oracle $\mathcal{O}_1[\mathsf{sk}]$, which is $M.\mathsf{Verify}$ in case 1, and the pair of oracles $M.\mathsf{Verify}, M.\mathsf{Check}$ in case 2.

6   A Construction of **NIKVAC** from Algebraic **MAC** and Oblivious **DVNIZK**

In this section, we will use the system introduced in Sect. 5 to construct a NIKVAC scheme Θ.

6.1   Construction

Let M be a MAC and Φ a set of statements for attributes $m_1, .., m_l$. Let Π_Φ be an oblivious DVNIZK system which runs on a common Setup algorithm with M for the relation R_{crs}, for crs $\xleftarrow{\$} M.\mathsf{Setup}(1^\lambda)$, defined as

$$R_{crs}((x_0, x_1), (m_1, .., m_l), \mathsf{k}) = 1 \text{ iff } M.\mathsf{Verify}_\mathsf{k}((m_1, .., m_l), x_1) = 1 \wedge \Phi(m_1, .., m_l),$$

where x_0 is a public word needed to prove the statements Φ and $\Pi_\Phi.\mathsf{RelSetup} = M.\mathsf{KeyGen}$. We assume Π_Φ satisfies $(\mathcal{O}_0, \mathcal{O}_1)$-knowledge-extractability, where $\mathcal{O}_0[\mathsf{k}](\cdot) = M.\mathsf{Sign}_\mathsf{k}(\cdot)$ and $\mathcal{O}_1[\mathsf{k}]$ is either the MAC verification oracle, if M is UF-CMVA secure (and the attribute vectors are of length 1), or the MAC verification and additional check oracle, if M is XUF-CMVA secure. Since x_0 depends on the choice of Φ, we omit it entirely in the following and simply set $x = x_1$. Note that $\Pi_\Phi.\mathsf{Setup}, \Pi_\Phi.\mathsf{CredKeyGen}$ do not rely on the choice of Φ, so we simply write $\Pi.\mathsf{Setup}, \Pi.\mathsf{CredKeyGen}$. We now construct a NIKVAC scheme using $\{\Pi_\Phi\}_\Phi$.

- $\Theta.\mathsf{Setup}(1^\lambda)$, outputs $(\mathsf{pp}, \mathsf{td}) \xleftarrow{\$} \Pi.\mathsf{Setup}(1^\lambda)$, we assume that pp fixes the supported statements Φ, the universe of attributes $\mathcal{U}$ is the message space of M;
- $\Theta.\mathsf{CredKeyGen}(\mathsf{pp})$, runs $(\mathsf{pk}, \mathsf{vk}) \xleftarrow{\$} \Pi.\mathsf{KeyGen}(\mathsf{pp})$, $(\mathsf{k}, \mathsf{ipp}_M) \xleftarrow{\$} \Pi.\mathsf{RelSetup}(\mathsf{pp})$, outputs secret key $\mathsf{sk} \leftarrow (\mathsf{vk}, \mathsf{k})$ and issuer parameters $\mathsf{ipp} \leftarrow (\mathsf{pk}, \mathsf{ipp}_M)$, we assume that $\mathsf{CredKeyGen}$ satisfies key-parameter consistency;
- $\Theta.\mathsf{BlindIssue}(\mathsf{sk}, S) \leftrightarrow \Theta.\mathsf{BlindObtain}(\mathsf{ipp}, (m_1, ..., m_l))$, performs a secure two-party computation that issues a tag of M to the user on valid input, we assume that this protocol satisfies *blind issuance* property[2];
- $\Theta.\mathsf{Show}(\mathsf{ipp}, \mathsf{cred}, (m_1, ..., m_l), \Phi)$, parses ipp as $(\mathsf{pk}, \mathsf{ipp}_M)$ outputs $\pi \xleftarrow{\$} \Pi_\Phi.\mathsf{Prove}(\mathsf{pk}, \mathsf{ipp}_M, \mathsf{cred}, (m_1, ..., m_l))$;
- $\Theta.\mathsf{ShowVerify}(\mathsf{sk}, \pi, \Phi)$, parses sk as $(\mathsf{vk}, \mathsf{k})$ and ipp as $(\mathsf{pk}, \mathsf{ipp}_M)$, checks $\Pi_\Phi.\mathsf{Verify}(\mathsf{pk}, \mathsf{ipp}_M, \mathsf{vk}, \mathsf{k}, \pi)$.

6.2   Security Analysis

For Θ, the functions Issue and CredVerify are defined as follows:

- $\mathsf{Issue}(\mathsf{sk}, (m_1, .., m_l))$: for $\mathsf{sk} = (\mathsf{vk}, \mathsf{k})$ outputs $M.\mathsf{Sign}_\mathsf{k}(m_1, .., m_l)$;
- $\mathsf{CredVerify}(\mathsf{sk}, (m_1, .., m_l), \mathsf{cred})$: for $\mathsf{sk} = (\mathsf{vk}, \mathsf{k})$ outputs $M.\mathsf{Verify}_\mathsf{k}((m_1, .., m_l), \mathsf{cred})$.

Theorem 3 (Correctness). *The NIKVAC scheme Θ satisfies correctness if M is correct and Π_Φ is complete.*

---

[2] The protocol depends highly on the chosen MAC scheme. Thus, we omit details in abstract instantiation.

Proof. Let $(\mathsf{pp}, \mathsf{td}) \leftarrow \Theta.\mathsf{Setup}(1^\lambda)$, $(m_1, .., m_l) \xleftarrow{\$} \mathcal{U}$, $(\mathsf{sk}, \mathsf{ipp}) \xleftarrow{\$} \Theta.\mathsf{CredKeyGen}$ (pp) and $\mathsf{credIssue}(\mathsf{sk}, (m_1, .., m_l))$. It follows that $\mathsf{CredVerify}(\mathsf{sk}, (m_1, .., m_l),$ $\mathsf{cred}) = 1$ from the correctness of the MAC scheme M.

Now, let $(\mathsf{pp}, \mathsf{td}) \leftarrow \Theta.\mathsf{Setup}(1^\lambda)$, $\Phi \xleftarrow{\$} \mathbf{\Phi}, (m_1, .., m_l) \xleftarrow{\$} \mathcal{U}$ with $\Phi(m_1, ..,$ $m_l) = 1$, $(\mathsf{sk} = (\mathsf{vk}, \mathsf{k}), \mathsf{ipp}) \xleftarrow{\$} \Theta.\mathsf{CredKeyGen}(\mathsf{pp})$ and $\mathsf{cred} \xleftarrow{\$} \mathsf{Issue}(\mathsf{sk},$ $(m_1, .., m_l))$. Let $\pi \xleftarrow{\$} \Theta.\mathsf{Show}(\mathsf{ipp}, \mathsf{cred}, (m_1, .., m_l), \Phi)$. Note that $R_\mathsf{k}(\mathsf{cred},$ $(m_1, .., m_l)) = 1$ and thus $\Theta.\mathsf{ShowVerify}(\mathsf{sk}, \pi, \Phi) = 1$ by the completeness of Π_Φ.

Theorem 4 (Unforgeability). *The* NIKVAC *scheme Θ is unforgeable if M is unforgeable and Π_Φ is $(\mathcal{O}_0, \mathcal{O}_1)$-knowledge-extractable for all $\Phi \in \mathbf{\Phi}$.*

Proof. Let $\mathscr{A}$ be a PPT adversary on the unforgeability of Θ. We build an adversary $\mathscr{B}$ which either breaks the unforgeability of M (so either the UF-CMVA or XUF-CMVA security) or the $(\mathcal{O}_0, \mathcal{O}_1)$-knowledge-extractability of Π_Φ for some $\Phi \in \mathbf{\Phi}$.

$\mathscr{B}$ receives $(\mathsf{crs}, \mathsf{pk}, \mathsf{ipp}_M)^3$ and access to a proof verification oracle $\mathcal{V}_\Phi$ and an MAC issuing oracle $\mathcal{O}_0$ (defined in Sect. 6.1) from the $(\mathcal{O}_0, \mathcal{O}_1)$-knowledge-extractability[4] game with Π_Φ for $\Phi \in \mathbf{\Phi}$. $\mathscr{B}$ sends $\mathsf{pp} \leftarrow \mathsf{crs}, \mathsf{ipp} \leftarrow (\mathsf{pk}, \mathsf{ipp}_M)$ to $\mathscr{A}$ and gives access to the following issuing and verification oracle $\mathcal{O}$:

- $\mathcal{O}.\mathsf{Issue}(m_1, .., m_l)$ sets $Q \leftarrow Q \cup \{m_1, .., m_l\}$ and outputs $\mathcal{O}_0(m_1, .., m_l)$;
- $\mathcal{O}.\mathsf{Verify}(\Phi, \pi)$ outputs $\mathcal{V}_\Phi(\pi)$.

By the second property of definition 14, $\mathcal{V}_\Phi(\cdot)$ can be simulated only using $\mathcal{O}_1$ without access to the secret key. Now, all answers to queries which require the secret MAC key can be computed using solely access to the MAC oracles. Note that $\mathscr{B}$ simulates the unforgeability game of Θ with overwhelming probability. At some point, if $\mathscr{A}$ is successful, he will output π, Φ such that the pair (π, Φ) verifies correctly and for all queried $(m_1, .., m_l) \in Q : \Phi(m_1, .., m_l) = 0$. Subsequently, $\mathscr{B}$ forwards π to the $(\mathcal{O}_0, \mathcal{O}_1)$-knowledge-extractability game for Π_Φ, which in turn forwards the extracted values (x_1, w) to the MAC unforgeability game.

We now analyze the success probability of $\mathscr{B}$ assuming $\mathscr{A}$ is successful. If $\mathscr{B}$ won the $(\mathcal{O}_0, \mathcal{O}_1)$-knowledge-extractability game, we are finished. In the other case, the MAC unforgeability game receives $(x_1 = \sigma, w = (m_1, .., m_l))$. Because $\mathscr{A}$ is successful, π verifies correctly with regards to Θ and thus also verifies correctly with regards to Π_Φ. Because $\mathscr{B}$ failed the first game, it necessarily holds that $R(\sigma, (m_1, .., m_l)) = 1$. Since $\forall (m'_1, .., m'_l) \in Q : \Phi(m'_1, .., m'_l) = 0$ and $\Phi(m_1, .., m_l) = 1$, it holds that $(m_1, .., m_l) \notin Q$ and σ verifies correctly. Thus, $\mathscr{B}$ breaks the unforgeability of M. $\qquad\square$

Theorem 5 (Anonymity). *The* NIKVAC *scheme Θ is anonymous if Π_Φ satisfies oblivious zero-knowledge.*

---

[3] The parameters $(\mathsf{crs}, \mathsf{pk}, \mathsf{ipp}_M)$ are fixed for all $\Phi \in \mathbf{\Phi}$, since they do not depend on the particular choice of Φ.

[4] In this proof, this refers to the first property of definition 14.

G. Couteau and M. Reichle

Proof. Let $\mathscr{A}$ be an adversary on the anonymity of Θ. We construct an adversary $\mathscr{B}$ that breaks the oblivious zero-knowledge property of Π_Φ for some $\Phi \in \mathbf{\Phi}$ with overwhelming probability if $\mathscr{A}$ is successful.

$\mathscr{B}$ receives $\mathsf{crs}, \mathsf{pk}, \mathsf{vk}$ from the zero-knowledge game with Π_Φ for some arbitrary $\Phi \in \mathbf{\Phi}$. Note that these values are independent of the particular choice of Φ. $\mathscr{B}$ then runs $(\mathsf{k}, \mathsf{ipp}_M) \xleftarrow{\$} M.\mathsf{KeyGen}(\mathsf{crs})$ and sends $\mathsf{pp} \leftarrow \mathsf{crs}, \mathsf{ipp} \leftarrow (\mathsf{pk}, \mathsf{ipp}_M), \mathsf{sk} \leftarrow (\mathsf{vk}, \mathsf{k})$ to $\mathscr{A}$. In turn, $\mathscr{B}$ receives $(\Phi, \mathsf{cred}, (m_1, .., m_l))$ from $\mathscr{A}$. Next, $\mathscr{B}$ outputs $(\mathsf{cred}, (m_1, .., m_l), \mathsf{k}, \mathsf{ipp}_M)$ to the oblivious zero-knowledge game for the now fixed Φ and receives π in return which he forwards to $\mathscr{A}$. Note that $\mathscr{B}$ simulates the anonymity game with overwhelming probability. Also, $R_{\mathsf{crs}}(\mathsf{sk}, \mathsf{cred}, (m_1, .., m_l)) = 1 \iff \mathsf{CredVerify}(\mathsf{sk}, (m_1, .., m_l), \mathsf{cred}) = 1 \wedge \Phi(m_1, .., m_l)$. The simulation of π in the zero-knowledge game only uses $\mathsf{ipp}, \mathsf{sk}, \Phi$ and will thus be a simulation for the anonymity game. Otherwise, π is built honestly in both games and thus, if $\mathscr{A}$ is successful, $\mathscr{B}$ is successful with overwhelming probability. $\qquad\square$

Missing Properties. The missing properties are *blind issuance* and *key-parameter consistency*. In practice, *key-parameter consistency* can easily be fulfilled by adding additional commitments to the components of the secret key and the two-party computation for *blind issuance* depends highly on the structure of the MAC scheme and can be implemented with any standard two party computation protocol; we briefly outline a possible candidate for an optimized version of our scheme in the full version [15].

References

1. Acar, T., Nguyen, L.: Revocation for delegatable anonymous credentials. In: Catalano, D., Fazio, N., Gennaro, R., Nicolosi, A. (eds.) PKC 2011. LNCS, vol. 6571, pp. 423–440. Springer, Heidelberg (2011). https://doi.org/10.1007/978-3-642-19379-8_26

2. Barki, A., Brunet, S., Desmoulins, N., Traoré, J.: Improved algebraic MACs and practical keyed-verification anonymous credentials. In: Avanzi, R., Heys, H. (eds.) SAC 2016. LNCS, vol. 10532, pp. 360–380. Springer, Cham (2017). https://doi.org/10.1007/978-3-319-69453-5_20

3. Belenkiy, M., Camenisch, J., Chase, M., Kohlweiss, M., Lysyanskaya, A., Shacham, H.: Randomizable proofs and delegatable anonymous credentials. In: Halevi, S. (ed.) CRYPTO 2009. LNCS, vol. 5677, pp. 108–125. Springer, Heidelberg (2009). https://doi.org/10.1007/978-3-642-03356-8_7

4. Belenkiy, M., Chase, M., Kohlweiss, M., Lysyanskaya, A.: P-signatures and non-interactive anonymous credentials. In: Canetti, R. (ed.) TCC 2008. LNCS, vol. 4948, pp. 356–374. Springer, Heidelberg (2008). https://doi.org/10.1007/978-3-540-78524-8_20

5. Benhamouda, F., Couteau, G., Pointcheval, D., Wee, H.: Implicit zero-knowledge arguments and applications to the malicious setting. In: Gennaro, R., Robshaw, M. (eds.) CRYPTO 2015, Part II. LNCS, vol. 9216, pp. 107–129. Springer, Heidelberg (2015). https://doi.org/10.1007/978-3-662-48000-7_6

6. Camenisch, J., Kohlweiss, M., Soriente, C.: An accumulator based on bilinear maps and efficient revocation for anonymous credentials. In: Jarecki, S., Tsudik, G. (eds.) PKC 2009. LNCS, vol. 5443, pp. 481–500. Springer, Heidelberg (2009). https://doi.org/10.1007/978-3-642-00468-1_27
7. Camenisch, J., Lysyanskaya, A.: An efficient system for non-transferable anonymous credentials with optional anonymity revocation. Cryptology ePrint Archive, Report 2001/019 (2001). http://eprint.iacr.org/2001/019
8. Camenisch, J., Lysyanskaya, A.: Dynamic accumulators and application to efficient revocation of anonymous credentials. In: Yung, M. (ed.) CRYPTO 2002. LNCS, vol. 2442, pp. 61–76. Springer, Heidelberg (2002). https://doi.org/10.1007/3-540-45708-9_5
9. Camenisch, J., Lysyanskaya, A.: Signature schemes and anonymous credentials from bilinear maps. In: Franklin, M. (ed.) CRYPTO 2004. LNCS, vol. 3152, pp. 56–72. Springer, Heidelberg (2004). https://doi.org/10.1007/978-3-540-28628-8_4
10. Canetti, R., Goldreich, O., Halevi, S.: The random oracle methodology, revisited (preliminary version). In: 30th ACM STOC, pp. 209–218. ACM Press, May 1998
11. Chaidos, P., Couteau, G.: Efficient designated-verifier non-interactive zero-knowledge proofs of knowledge. In: Nielsen, J.B., Rijmen, V. (eds.) EUROCRYPT 2018, Part III. LNCS, vol. 10822, pp. 193–221. Springer, Cham (2018). https://doi.org/10.1007/978-3-319-78372-7_7
12. Chaidos, P., Groth, J.: Making Sigma-protocols non-interactive without random oracles. In: Katz, J. (ed.) PKC 2015. LNCS, vol. 9020, pp. 650–670. Springer, Heidelberg (2015). https://doi.org/10.1007/978-3-662-46447-2_29
13. Chase, M., Meiklejohn, S., Zaverucha, G.: Algebraic MACs and keyed-verification anonymous credentials. In: Ahn, G.J., Yung, M., Li, N. (eds.) ACM CCS 2014, pp. 1205–1216. ACM Press, November 2014
14. Chaum, D.: Showing credentials without identification. In: Pichler, F. (ed.) EUROCRYPT 1985. LNCS, vol. 219, pp. 241–244. Springer, Heidelberg (1986). https://doi.org/10.1007/3-540-39805-8_28
15. Couteau, G., Reichle, M.: Non-interactive keyed-verification anonymous credentials (2018, to appear)
16. Cramer, R., et al.: Bounded CCA2-secure encryption. In: Kurosawa, K. (ed.) ASIACRYPT 2007. LNCS, vol. 4833, pp. 502–518. Springer, Heidelberg (2007). https://doi.org/10.1007/978-3-540-76900-2_31
17. Damgård, I.B.: Payment systems and credential mechanisms with provable security against abuse by individuals. In: Goldwasser, S. (ed.) CRYPTO 1988. LNCS, vol. 403, pp. 328–335. Springer, New York (1990). https://doi.org/10.1007/0-387-34799-2_26
18. Damgård, I., Fazio, N., Nicolosi, A.: Non-interactive zero-knowledge from homomorphic encryption. In: Halevi, S., Rabin, T. (eds.) TCC 2006. LNCS, vol. 3876, pp. 41–59. Springer, Heidelberg (2006). https://doi.org/10.1007/11681878_3
19. Damgård, I., Jurik, M., Nielsen, J.B.: A generalization of paillier's public-key system with applications to electronic voting. Int. J. Inf. Secur. 9(6), 371–385 (2010)
20. Dwork, C., Naor, M., Reingold, O., Stockmeyer, L.J.: Magic functions. In: 40th FOCS, pp. 523–534. IEEE Computer Society Press, October 1999
21. Garman, C., Green, M., Miers, I.: Decentralized anonymous credentials. In: NDSS 2014. The Internet Society, February 2014
22. Goldwasser, S., Kalai, Y.T.: On the (in)security of the Fiat-Shamir paradigm. In: 44th FOCS, pp. 102–115. IEEE Computer Society Press, October 2003

23. Hanser, C., Slamanig, D.: Structure-preserving signatures on equivalence classes and their application to anonymous credentials. In: Sarkar, P., Iwata, T. (eds.) ASIACRYPT 2014, Part I. LNCS, vol. 8873, pp. 491–511. Springer, Heidelberg (2014). https://doi.org/10.1007/978-3-662-45611-8_26

24. Izabachène, M., Libert, B., Vergnaud, D.: Block-wise P-signatures and non-interactive anonymous credentials with efficient attributes. In: Chen, L. (ed.) IMACC 2011. LNCS, vol. 7089, pp. 431–450. Springer, Heidelberg (2011). https://doi.org/10.1007/978-3-642-25516-8_26

25. Lipmaa, H.: Optimally sound sigma protocols under DCRA. Cryptology ePrint Archive, Report 2017/703 (2017). http://eprint.iacr.org/2017/703

26. Lysyanskaya, A., Rivest, R.L., Sahai, A., Wolf, S.: Pseudonym systems. In: Heys, H., Adams, C. (eds.) SAC 1999. LNCS, vol. 1758, pp. 184–199. Springer, Heidelberg (2000). https://doi.org/10.1007/3-540-46513-8_14

27. Paillier, P.: Public-key cryptosystems based on composite degree residuosity classes. In: Stern, J. (ed.) EUROCRYPT 1999. LNCS, vol. 1592, pp. 223–238. Springer, Heidelberg (1999). https://doi.org/10.1007/3-540-48910-X_16

28. Paquin, C., Zaverucha, G.: U-prove cryptographic specification V1.1 (revision 2) (2013). www.microsoft.com/uprove

29. Sadiah, S., Nakanishi, T., Funabiki, N.: Anonymous credential system with efficient proofs for monotone formulas on attributes. In: Tanaka, K., Suga, Y. (eds.) IWSEC 2015. LNCS, vol. 9241, pp. 262–278. Springer, Cham (2015). https://doi.org/10.1007/978-3-319-22425-1_16

30. Schwartz, J.T.: Fast probabilistic algorithms for verification of polynomial identities. J. ACM (JACM) **27**(4), 701–717 (1980)

31. Shoup, V.: Lower bounds for discrete logarithms and related problems. In: Fumy, W. (ed.) EUROCRYPT 1997. LNCS, vol. 1233, pp. 256–266. Springer, Heidelberg (1997). https://doi.org/10.1007/3-540-69053-0_18

Digital Signatures

Shorter Ring Signatures from Standard Assumptions

Alonso González[(✉)]

ENS de Lyon, Laboratoire LIP (U. Lyon, CNRS,
ENSL, Inria, UCBL), Lyon, France
alonso.gonzalez@ens-lyon.fr

Abstract. Ring signatures, introduced by Rivest, Shamir and Tauman (ASIACRYPT 2001), allow to sign a message on behalf of a set of users while guaranteeing authenticity and anonymity. Groth and Kohlweiss (EUROCRYPT 2015) and Libert et al. (EUROCRYPT 2016) constructed schemes with signatures of size logarithmic in the number of users. An even shorter ring signature, of size independent from the number of users, was recently proposed by Malavolta and Schröder (ASIACRYPT 2017). However, all these short signatures are obtained relying on strong and controversial assumptions. Namely, the former schemes are both proven secure in the random oracle model while the later requires non-falsifiable assumptions.

The most efficient construction under mild assumptions remains the construction of Chandran et al. (ICALP 2007) with a signature of size $\Theta(\sqrt{n})$, where n is the number of users, and security is based on the Diffie-Hellman assumption in bilinear groups (the SXDH assumption in asymmetric bilinear groups).

In this work we construct an asymptotically shorter ring signature from the hardness of the Diffie-Hellman assumption in bilinear groups. Each signature comprises $\Theta(\sqrt[3]{n})$ group elements, signing a message requires computing $\Theta(\sqrt[3]{n})$ exponentiations, and verifying a signature requires $\Theta(n^{2/3})$ pairing operations. To the best of our knowledge, this is the first ring signature based on bilinear groups with $o(\sqrt{n})$ signatures and sublinear verification complexity.

1 Introduction

Ring signatures, introduced by Rivest, Shamir and Tauman [28], allow to anonymously sign a message on behalf of a ring of users $R = \{P_1, \ldots, P_n\}$, only if the signer belongs to that ring. That is, no one outside R can forge a valid signature and an honestly computed signature reveals no information about the actual signer. Unlike other similar primitives such as group signatures [7], ring signatures are not coordinated: each user generates secret/public keys on his

This work was funded in part by the French ANR ALAMBIC project (ANR-16-CE39-0006).

D. Lin and K. Sako (Eds.): PKC 2019, LNCS 11442, pp. 99–126, 2019.
https://doi.org/10.1007/978-3-030-17253-4_4

own—i.e. no central authorities—and might sign on behalf of a ring without the approval or assistance of the other members.

The original motivation for ring signatures was anonymous leakage of secrets. Suppose a high rank officer wants to leak some sensitive document to a journalist without revealing its identity. To do so, it signs this document using a ring signature where the ring contains all other high rank officers. The journalist is convinced that some high rank officer signed the document, but it has no clue who, while this leakage might go unnoticed for the rest of officers.

More recently, ring signatures have also found applications in the construction of confidential transactions for cryptocurrencies. In a usual (non-anonymous) transaction the user computes a signature that assesses if is allowed to spend coins. In cryptocurrencies like Monero, a user form a ring from public keys in the blockchain to issue a ring signature on the transaction. Thereby, the anonymity properties of the ring signature guarantee untraceability of the transaction and fungibility, i.e. two coins can be mutually substituted. Given the practical usefulness of ring signatures, it becomes crucial to study and improve its efficiency and security.

1.1 Related Work

The efficiency of a ring signature might be splitted into three parameters: the signature size, the time required for computing a signature, and the time required for verifying a signature. Among these metrics, the signature size has received the most attention and improvements in the size usually imply improvement in the other metrics. In terms of signature size, two of the most efficient constructions have signature size logarithmic in the size of the ring [18,23]. Both constructions rely on the random oracle model, which is an idealization of hash functions with known theoretical inconsistencies [13]. Malavolta et al. constructed a constant size ring signature without random oracles [24] using SNARKS [8,11,17] as a subroutine, which are known to require controversial non-falsifiable assumptions such as the knowledge of exponent assumption [12,26]. Unlike traditional falsifiable assumptions (e.g. DDH), is not possible to efficiently check whether the adversary effectively breaks the assumption yielding non-explicit security reductions [26]. In practice, random oracles and non-falsifiable assumptions offer great efficiency at the price of less understood security guarantees. Therefore, we believe that it is important and challenging to explore practical constructions from milder assumptions.

Using only standard assumptions like RSA, Chase and Lysyanskaya proposed a ring signature scheme whose size is independent from the number of users [6]. Their ring signature is built on top of signatures of knowledge and accumulators, following Dodis et al. [9]. The scheme description is only sketched and no proof of security is given but, for fairness (as also noted in [24]), their work is previous to the (now standard) formal definition of ring signatures of Bender et al. [2]. Anyway, signatures of knowledge are built on top of simulation sound NIZK which in turn is built from standard NIZK. The underlying statements involve multiplications modulo $\phi(N)$ and exponentiations modulo N, where N

an RSA modulus. To the best of our knowledge, no efficient NIZK schemes under standard assumptions are known for statements of this kind. Thus, the only alternative under standard assumptions seems the NIZK for circuit satisfiability of Groth, Ostrovsky and Sahai [20]. A naive implementation of this protocol would require, at least, perfectly binding bit-by-bit commitments of integers in $\mathbb{Z}_N$. Typically, N requires 1024 bits so this solution requires at least 1024 elements of a bilinear group. On contrast, our construction is far more efficient than that for any $n < 10^4$. Although it might be possible to avoid committing bit-by-bit, there would be still many challenges. For example, it would require a NIZK proof that $a = b^y \mod N$, for $a, b \in \mathbb{Z}_N, y \in \mathbb{Z}_{\phi(N)}$, for which the only solution seems to be committing to y bit-by-bit (in order to use binary exponentiation) leading again to proofs of ~ 1024 group elements. Our conclusion is that is not clear how to implement Chase and Lysyanskaya's ring signature in a practical way.

Despite Chase and Lysyanskaya's construction, without random oracles or non-falsifiable assumptions all constructions have signatures of size linear in the size of the ring, being the sole exception the $\Theta(\sqrt{n})$ ring signature of Chandran et al. [5]. They construct a simple and elegant ring signature which at its core implements a *set-membership proof*, i.e. a proof that some committed public key belongs to the set of public keys of the ring users. Their set-membership proof is quite strong, in the sense that the verification keys may be even chosen by the adversary. Going a step forward, we will build a more efficient but weaker set-membership proof which is still useful for building ring signatures.

We note that no improvements in the signature size have been made within a decade. In fact, although two previous works claim to construct signatures of constant [4] or logarithmic [16] size, in the full version (see [15]) of this work we show that one construction fails to give a correct proof of security and the other is in fact of size $\Theta(n)$. The only (non-asymptotic) improvements we are aware of are [14,27].

1.2 Our Contribution

In this work we present the first ring signature based on bilinear groups whose signature size is asymptotically smaller than Chandran et al.'s, and whose security is proven under falsifiable assumptions and without random oracles. The signature consists of $\Theta(\sqrt[3]{n})$ group elements, computing a signature requires $\Theta(\sqrt[3]{n})$ exponentiations, and verifying a signature requires $\Theta(n^{2/3})$ pairings. Our ring signature is perfectly anonymous, i.e. it completely hides the identity of the actual signer, and is computationally infeasible to forge signatures for non-members of the ring.

As a first step, we construct a $\Theta(\sqrt[3]{n})$ ring signature whose security relies on a security assumption—the permutation pairing assumption—introduced by Groth and Lu [19] in an unrelated setting: proofs of correctness of a shuffle. While the assumption is "non-standard", in the sense that is not a "DDH like" assumption, it is a falsifiable assumption and it was proven hard in generic symmetric bilinear groups by Groth and Lu. We work on asymmetric groups (Type III groups

[10]) and thus we give a natural translation of the permutation pairing assumption which we also prove secure in generic asymmetric bilinear groups.

We give a second construction which is solely based on the security of the DDH assumption in both base groups (the so called SXDH assumption). The construction is highly inspired in the first construction, but we manage to get rid of the permutation pairing assumption and further shorten the size of the signature. A comparison of our ring signatures and Chandran et al.'s is given in Table 1.

Table 1. Comparison of Chandran et al.'s ring signature and ours for a ring of size n. 'Signature generation' is given in number of exponentiations, 'Verification' is given in number of pairings, and all other rows are given in number of group elements. The security of the three schemes is proved under the unforgeability of the Boneh-Boyen signature scheme plus the corresponding assumption indicated in the row 'Assumption'. The last row states if the key generation algorithm erases its random coins after generating the verification and secret keys.

	Chandran et al. [5]	Section 3.2	Section 4.2
CRS size $\mathbb{G}_1/\mathbb{G}_2$	4/4	4/4	4/8
Verification key size $\mathbb{G}_1/\mathbb{G}_2$	1/0	2/5	10/9
Signature size $\mathbb{G}_1/\mathbb{G}_2$	$12\sqrt{n}+10/15\sqrt{n}+8$	$24\sqrt[3]{n}+36/34\sqrt[3]{n}+24$	$18\sqrt[3]{n}+30/34\sqrt[3]{n}+18$
Signature generation #exps.	$37\sqrt{n}+23$	$80\sqrt[3]{n}+71$	$72\sqrt[3]{n}+61$
Verification #pairings	$2n+60\sqrt{n}+38$	$8n^{2/3}+162\sqrt[3]{n}+118$	$8n^{2/3}+122\sqrt[3]{n}+94$
Assumption	SXDH	PPA	SXDH
Erasures	No	Yes	No

1.3 Technical Overview

Most ring signature constructions have followed the next approach. Given a ring of users, defined by the set of their verification keys, and a message: (a) sign the message, (b) prove in zero-knowledge knowledge of a signature which can be verified using some committed/randomized verification key, and then (c) prove in zero-knowledge that this verification key belongs to the set of public keys in the ring. The most expensive part is (c) and is sometimes called a *set-membership proof*.

We observe that, when proving unforgeability, *all the verification keys forming the ring are honestly generated*. Indeed, it only makes sense to guarantee unforgeability when all the members of the ring are honest (otherwise the adversary knows at least one secret key) and thus the set-membership proof might assume that all verification keys were honestly generated. It turns out that all the schemes we are aware of, in particular Chandran et al.'s, obviate this property, meaning that their set-membership proofs work even for adversarially chosen verification keys. We ask the following natural question.

Can we construct more efficient set membership proofs (without random oracles or non-falsifiable assumptions) when verification keys are sampled from a known distribution?

We answer this question in the affirmative constructing a $\Theta(\sqrt[3]{n})$ set membership proof specially tailored to the case when the verification keys are honestly sampled. In contrast, Chandran et al.'s proof is of size $\Theta(\sqrt{n})$ but it makes no assumption on the verification keys distribution.

Our Construction from the Permutation Pairing Assumption. Our main technical tools are two hash functions compatible with Groth-Sahai proofs.

The first function, h, is *second-preimage resistant* under a slightly different notion of collision. Given $\mathbf{A} = (\boldsymbol{a}_1, \ldots, \boldsymbol{a}_m)$ randomly sampled from the domain of h, it is hard to find $\mathbf{A}'$ such that $h(\mathbf{A}') = h(\mathbf{A})$ whenever $\mathbf{A}'$ is not a permutation of $\mathbf{A}$. We give a simple instantiation of h based on the permutation pairing assumption (PPA). For simplicity, consider a symmetric bilinear group $\mathbb{G}$ of order q and generated by $\mathcal{P}$ (it can be extended to asymmetric bilinear groups as we show in Sect. 2.1). This assumption states that, given $\boldsymbol{a}_1 = (x_1\mathcal{P}, x_1^2\mathcal{P}), \ldots, \boldsymbol{a}_m = (x_m\mathcal{P}, x_m^2\mathcal{P})$, for $x_1, \ldots, x_m \leftarrow \mathbb{Z}_q$, the only way to compute $\boldsymbol{a}_1' = (y_1\mathcal{P}, y_1^2\mathcal{P}), \ldots, \boldsymbol{a}_m' = (y_m\mathcal{P}, y_m^2\mathcal{P})$ such that $\sum_{i=1}^m \boldsymbol{a}_i' = \sum_{i=1}^m \boldsymbol{a}_i$ is to take $\mathbf{A}'$ as a permutation of the columns of $\mathbf{A}$. It is straightforward to note that $h(\mathbf{A}) := \sum_{i=1}^m \boldsymbol{a}_i$ is second-preimage resistant "modulo permutations", given the hardness of PPA.

Our second function, g, is collision-resistant in the traditional sense. It uses $\mathbf{A}$ as key and returns $g_{\mathbf{A}}(vk_1, \ldots, vk_m) = \sum_{i=1}^m e(\boldsymbol{a}_i, vk_i)$ for $vk_1, \ldots, vk_m \in \mathbb{G}$. Groth and Lu conjectured that it is hard to find non-trivial $vk_1, \ldots, vk_m \in \mathbb{G}$ such that $\sum_{i=1}^m e(\boldsymbol{a}_i, vk_i) = 0$ when each $\boldsymbol{a}_i$ is of the form $(x_i\mathcal{P}, x_i^2\mathcal{P})$ and $x_i \leftarrow \mathbb{Z}_q$ [19]. They give some evidence that this assumption might be true proving its hardness in the generic bilinear group model. It follows that g is collision resistant given the hardness of the aforementioned assumption. In order to be more compatible with Groth-Sahai proofs (say, structure-preserving) we compute g's outputs in the base group, instead of the target group $\mathbb{G}_T$. To render $g_{\mathbf{A}}(\boldsymbol{vk}) \in \mathbb{G}$ efficiently computable we make $sk_i\boldsymbol{a}_i$ publicly available, where $vk_i = sk_i\mathcal{P}$, and redefine g as $g_{\mathbf{A}}(\boldsymbol{vk}) = \sum_i sk_i\boldsymbol{a}_i$. Note that the discrete logarithm in base $\mathcal{P}_T = e(\mathcal{P}, \mathcal{P})$ of g defined over $\mathbb{G}_T$ and the discrete logarithm in base $\mathcal{P}$ of g defined over $\mathbb{G}$ remain the same.

Each $\boldsymbol{a}_i$ will be taken from the ring member's verification key and hence, since all these verification keys are honestly sampled, when proving unforgeability we may assume that $\mathbf{A}$ is honestly sampled from the PPA distribution.

The Basic Construction. In our ring signature, each user possesses an "extended verification key" which contains the verification key of a Boneh-Boyen signature scheme $vk = sk\mathcal{P}$ plus $\boldsymbol{a}$ and $sk\boldsymbol{a}$, where sk is the corresponding secret key.[1] We want to show that some commitment c opens to vk and

---

[1] Although any signature scheme compatible with Groth-Sahai proofs suffices (e.g. structure preserving signatures), we would rather keep it simple and stick to Boneh-Boyen signature which, since the verification key is just one group element, simplifies the notation and reduces the size of the final signature.

$vk \in \{vk_1, \ldots, vk_n\}$. To do so, we arrange the n elements of the ring into $n^{2/3}$ blocks of size $m = \sqrt[3]{n}$. We use the following notation: for $\{s_1, \ldots, s_n\}$ define $s_{i,j} := s_{(i-1)m+j}$, where $1 \le i \le n^{2/3}, 1 \le j \le m$. Assume that $vk = vk_{\mu,\nu}$.

Split $(a_1, \ldots, a_n)$ into $\mathbf{A}_i := (a_{i,1}, \ldots, a_{i,m})$ and $(vk_1, \ldots, vk_n)$ into $\boldsymbol{vk}_i = (vk_{i,1}, \ldots, vk_{i,m})$, for $1 \le i \le n^{2/3}$, and define $H := \{h(\mathbf{A}_1), \ldots, h(\mathbf{A}_{n^{2/3}})\}$ and $G := \{g_{\mathbf{A}_1}(\boldsymbol{vk}_1), \ldots, g_{\mathbf{A}_{n^{2/3}}}(\boldsymbol{vk}_{n^{2/3}})\}$. We use Chandran et al.'s set-membership proof of size $\Theta(\sqrt{n})$ to prove knowledge of some $h(\mathbf{A}_\mu) \in H$. Since $|H| = n^{2/3}$, this proof is of size $\Theta(\sqrt[3]{n})$. Then we prove knowledge of $\mathbf{A}'$, a preimage of $h(\mathbf{A}_\mu)$ such that $a_1' = a_{\mu,\nu}$. Using Groth-Sahai proofs it requires commitments to the $\sqrt[3]{n}$ columns of $\mathbf{A}'$ plus a $\Theta(1)$ proof that $h(\mathbf{A}') = h(\mathbf{A}_\mu)$. Hence, this part of the proof adds up to $\Theta(\sqrt[3]{n})$ group elements.

We give a second set-membership proof of knowledge of some $g_{\mathbf{A}_{\mu'}}(\boldsymbol{vk}_{\mu'}) \in G$ such that $\mu' = \mu$ (this is straightforward to do with Chandran et al.'s set-membership proof). We commit to $\boldsymbol{vk}'$, a permutation of $\boldsymbol{vk}_\mu$ such that $vk_1' = vk_{\mu,\nu}$ (and consistent with $\mathbf{A}'$), and we prove using Groth-Sahai proofs that $g_{\mathbf{A}_{\mu'}}(\boldsymbol{vk}_{\mu'}) = g_{\mathbf{A}'}(\boldsymbol{vk}')$. Again, this part of the proof adds $\Theta(\sqrt[3]{n})$ group elements.

The proof that $h(\mathbf{A}') = h(\mathbf{A}_\mu)$ implies that $\mathbf{A}'$ is a permutation of $\mathbf{A}_\mu$, which can be equivalently written as $\mathbf{A}' = \mathbf{A}_\mu \mathbf{P}$, where $\mathbf{P}$ is some permutation matrix. Given that $e(g_{\mathbf{A}'}(\boldsymbol{vk}'), \mathcal{P}) = e(\mathbf{A}_\mu \mathbf{P}, \boldsymbol{vk}') = e(g_{\mathbf{A}_\mu}(\mathbf{P}\boldsymbol{vk}'), \mathcal{P}) = e(g_{\mathbf{A}_\mu}(\boldsymbol{vk}_\mu), \mathcal{P})$, the collision resistance of g implies that $vk_1', \ldots, vk_m'$ is a permutation of $vk_{\mu,1}, \ldots, vk_{\mu,m}$. We conclude that $vk_{\mu,\nu} = vk_1'$ is in the ring.

Getting Rid of the Permutation Pairing Assumption. The PPA-based ring signature has the disadvantage that the PPA is not a constant-size assumption and belongs to the class of the so called q-assumptions (such as the Strong Diffie-Hellman assumption among others). It is then desirable to have a similar construction under more standard constant-size assumptions such as the SXDH assumption.

Consider the set of binary vectors of size m and the function h defined as the hamming weight of a binary vector $h(\boldsymbol{\beta}) = \sum_{i=1}^m \beta_i$. Analogously as with the PPA, $h(\boldsymbol{\beta}) = h(\boldsymbol{\beta}')$ and $\boldsymbol{\beta}, \boldsymbol{\beta}' \in \{0,1\}^m$ implies that $\boldsymbol{\beta}'$ is a permutation of $\boldsymbol{\beta}$. (Note that in this case $\boldsymbol{\beta}'$ is a permutation of $\boldsymbol{\beta}$ unconditionally.) We use this property of binary vectors as a replacement of the PPA. Define also $g_{\boldsymbol{\beta}}(\boldsymbol{vk}) := \sum_i \beta_i vk_i$. Although g is longer collision resistant, it turns out that proofs that $h(\boldsymbol{\beta}') = h(\boldsymbol{\beta})$ and $g_{\boldsymbol{\beta}'}(\boldsymbol{vk}') = g_{\boldsymbol{\beta}}(\boldsymbol{vk})$ will still allow us to prove unforgeability.[2]

Each possible ring member generates a single $\beta \in \{0,1\}$ and her extended verification key contains commitments $\boldsymbol{a} = \mathsf{Com}(\beta)$, $\boldsymbol{d} = \mathsf{Com}(\beta vk)$, and vk. Additionally it contains π, a Groth-Sahai proof that $\beta \in \{0,1\}$, and θ, a

---

[2] Even when the adversary only knows a commitment to β, as it will be in our case, g is not collision resistant. For small rings, the adversary may guess β with non-negligible probability and solve $\sum_i \beta_i(vk_i - vk_i') = 0$ for some non trivial $\boldsymbol{vk}'$. However, this adversary is not even not aware that it has found a collision.

Groth-Sahai proof that $y = \beta vk$ where y is $\boldsymbol{d}$'s opening. Although g and h are not efficiently computable from the extended verification keys, it is possible to compute commitments to $h(\boldsymbol{\beta})$ and $g_{\beta}(\boldsymbol{vk})$ using the homomorphic properties of Groth-Sahai commitments. Indeed $\mathsf{Com}(h(\boldsymbol{\beta})) = \sum_i \boldsymbol{a}_i$ and $\mathsf{Com}(g_{\beta}(\boldsymbol{vk})) = \sum_i \boldsymbol{d}_i$. Using this fact together with the re-randomizability of Groth-Sahai proofs (see [1]) we will emulate the ring signature in the PPA setting.

Assume the signer wish to sign on behalf of the ring $R = \{vk_{1,1}, \ldots, vk_{n^{2/3},m}\}$ knowing the secret key corresponding to $vk_{\mu,\nu}$. Define $\mathbf{A}_1, \ldots, \mathbf{A}_{n^{2/3}}$ as in the PPA construction and let $\beta_1, \ldots, \beta_{n^{2/3}}$ the respective openings. In the first part of the signature, the signer proves knowledge of some $\mathsf{Com}(h(\boldsymbol{\beta}_{\mu}))$ from $H = \{\mathsf{Com}(h(\boldsymbol{\beta}_1)), \ldots, \mathsf{Com}(h(\boldsymbol{\beta}_{n^{2/3}}))\}$ and then commits to $\mathbf{A}'$, a permutation of a re-randomization of $\mathbf{A}_{\mu}$ such that $\boldsymbol{a}'_1$ is a re-randomization of $\boldsymbol{a}_{\mu,\nu}$. Then it shows with a Groth-Sahai proof that (a) $\sum_i \boldsymbol{a}'_i - \mathsf{Com}(h(\boldsymbol{\beta}_{\mu})) = \mathsf{Com}(0)$, and (b) $\beta'_1 \ldots, \beta'_m \in \{0,1\}$ re-randomizing proofs $\pi_{\mu,1}, \ldots, \pi_{\mu,m}$. It follows that $\boldsymbol{\beta}'$, the vector of openings of $\mathbf{A}'$, is a permutation of $\boldsymbol{\beta}_{\mu}$, the vector of openings of $\mathbf{A}_{\mu}$.

In the second part the signer proves knowledge of some $\mathsf{Com}(g_{\beta_{\mu}}(\boldsymbol{vk}_{\mu}))$ from $G = \{\mathsf{Com}(g_{\beta_1}(\boldsymbol{vk}_1)), \ldots, \mathsf{Com}(g_{\beta_{n^{2/3}}}(\boldsymbol{vk}_{n^{2/3}}))\}$ and computes commitments $\boldsymbol{c}'_1, \ldots, \boldsymbol{c}'_m$ to $vk'_1 = vk_{\mu,1}, \ldots, vk'_m = vk_{\mu,m}$, respectively. In Sect. 4.1 we show that, from $\boldsymbol{d}_{\mu,1}, \ldots, \boldsymbol{d}_{\mu,m}$ and $\theta_{\mu,1}, \ldots, \theta_{\mu,m}$ one can derive a proof that $\sum_i \beta'_i vk'_i = \sum_i \beta_{\mu,i} vk_{\mu,i}$, or equivalently a proof that $g_{\beta'}(\boldsymbol{vk}') = g_{\beta_{\mu}}(\boldsymbol{vk}_{\mu})$.

Zero-knowledge of the set-membership proof implies perfect anonymity of the ring signature, and follows from the fact that all proofs are statistically independent of vk when the Groth-Sahai CRS is perfectly hiding. Soundness implies unforgeability, and follows from the following argument.

Without loss of generality, we may assume that $\boldsymbol{vk}_{\mu}$ has not repeated entries since the verifier might drop all repeated entries in R without changing the statement. Suppose an adversary wish to convince the verifier that $vk = vk'_1$ is in R while in fact $vk \notin R$. In particular, this implies that vk'_1 is different from each of $vk_{\mu,1}, \ldots, vk_{\mu,m}$. By the pigeonhole principle, there must be also some $vk_{\mu,i}$ that is different from each of $vk'_1, \ldots, vk'_m$.

Since we can guess such μ, i pair beforehand with non negligible probability $1/Q$, where Q is the maximum number of verification keys. We can jump to a game where we program $\mathbf{A} = (\boldsymbol{a}_1, \ldots, \boldsymbol{a}_Q)$ such that its opening $\beta \in \{0,1\}^Q$ is of hamming weight 1 and $\beta_{\mu,i} = 1$. By the hiding property of the commitment scheme, which is based on the SXDH assumption, the adversary notices such change in $\mathbf{A}$ only with negligible probability. Given that β' is a permutation of β, in this game the equation $\sum_i \beta'_i vk'_i = \sum_i \beta_{\mu,i} vk_{\mu,i}$ is in fact $vk'_j = vk_{\mu,i}$, for some $1 \leq j \leq m$, and hence the adversary has 0 probability of winning.

The Erasures Assumption. A ring signature must tolerate the adaptive corruption of the verification keys. That is, an adversary may adaptively ask for the random coins used for generating the verification keys. In the PPA-based ring signature, this amounts to reveal x_i and x_i^2 which is incompatible with the

PPA (unless one considers a much stronger interactive assumption). The only alternative seems to be assume that the key generation algorithm can erase its random coins.[3]

But this is not the case for the SXDH-based construction. To avoid erasures, each possible ring member samples the extended verification key with $\beta = 0$. Thereby, Every answer to a corruption query is of the form $0, sk$ plus all the random coins used to generate the extended verification key.

We can argue as before that an adversary may produce some $vk \notin R$ with roughly the same probability even if $\mathbf{A}$ is computed from a random binary vector $\boldsymbol{\beta}$ of hamming weight 1 with the unique 1 in the right place. In this case we can answer all corruption queries with the exception of the unique verification key for which $\beta = 1$. But anyway, the probability that the adversary corrupts this verification key is no greater than $1/Q$ so we can safely abort if this is the case. The rest of the argument is exactly as before.

Relation to [14]. Our construction is similar to the set membership proof of González et al. [14, Appendix D.2] also of size $\Theta(\sqrt[3]{n})$. There, the CRS contains a matrix $\mathbf{A}$ of size $2 \times m$ that is used to compute $\sqrt[3]{n}$ hashes of $n^{2/3}$ of subsets of verification keys of size $\sqrt[3]{n}$. Then some hidden hash is shown to belong to the set for $n^{2/3}$ hashes. These hashes are computed as a linear combination of the columns of $\mathbf{A}$ with the verification keys.

One could turn this construction into a ring signature including $vk\mathbf{A}$ in each verification key. However, the fact that $\mathbf{A}$ is fixed implies that signatures of size $\Theta(\sqrt[3]{n})$ can be obtained only when $n \le m^3$. So, asymptotically, this is not a $\Theta(\sqrt[3]{n})$ signature. Furthermore, the verification key will be of size $\Theta(m)$. In contrast, our ring signature verification keys are of size $\Theta(1)$ and the size of the ring is unbounded.

2   Preliminaries

We write PPT as a shortcut for probabilistic polynomial time Turing machine.

Let Gen_a be some PPT which on input 1^λ, where λ is the security parameter, returns the *group key* which is the description of an asymmetric bilinear group $gk := (q, \mathbb{G}_1, \mathbb{G}_2, \mathbb{G}_T, e, \mathcal{P}_1, \mathcal{P}_2, \mathcal{P}_T = e(\mathcal{P}_1, \mathcal{P}_2), q)$, where $\mathbb{G}_1$, $\mathbb{G}_2$, and $\mathbb{G}_T$ are groups of prime order q, the element $\mathcal{P}_s$ is a generator of $\mathbb{G}_s$, and $e : \mathbb{G}_1 \times \mathbb{G}_2 \to \mathbb{G}_T$ is an efficiently computable and non-degenerated bilinear map. We will use additive notation for the group operation of all groups.

Elements in $\mathbb{G}_s$ are denoted implicitly as $[a]_s := a\mathcal{P}_s$, where $a \in \mathbb{Z}_q$, $s \in \{1, 2, T\}$. The pairing operation is written as a product $\cdot$, that is $[a]_1 \cdot [b]_2 = [a]_1[b]_2 = [b]_2[a]_1 = e([a]_1, [b]_2) = [ab]_T$. Vectors and matrices are denoted in boldface. Given a matrix $\mathbf{T} = (t_{i,j})$, $[\mathbf{T}]_s$ is the natural embedding of $\mathbf{T}$ in $\mathbb{G}_s$, that is, the matrix whose (i, j)th entry is $t_{i,j}\mathcal{P}_s$. Given a matrix $\mathbf{S}$ with the same number of rows as $\mathbf{T}$, we define $\mathbf{S}|\mathbf{T}$ as the concatenation of $\mathbf{S}$ and $\mathbf{T}$.

---

[3] We elaborate more on the erasures assumption for ring signatures in the full version of this work [15].

2.1 Hardness Assumptions

We use a natural translation to asymmetric groups of the permutation pairing assumption introduced by Groth and Lu.

Definition 1 (Permutation Pairing Assumption [19]). *Let* $\mathcal{Q}_m = \overbrace{\mathcal{Q}|\dots|\mathcal{Q}}^{m\ times}$, *where concatenation of distributions is defined in the natural way and* $\mathcal{Q} : \boldsymbol{a} = \left(\begin{smallmatrix} x \\ x^2 \end{smallmatrix}\right)$, $x \leftarrow \mathbb{Z}_q$. *We say that the m-permutation pairing assumption holds relative to* Gen_a *if for any adversary* A

$$\Pr\left[\begin{array}{l} gk \leftarrow \mathsf{Gen}_a(1^\lambda); \mathbf{A} \leftarrow \mathcal{Q}_m; \\ ([\mathbf{Z}]_1, [\underline{z}]_2) \leftarrow \mathsf{A}(gk, [\mathbf{A}]_1, [\mathbf{A}]_2): \\ \text{(i) } \sum_{i=1}^m [z_i]_1 = \sum_{i=1}^m [a_i]_1, \\ \text{(ii) } \forall i \in [m]\ [z_{1,i}]_1[1]_2 = [1]_1[\underline{z}_i]_2 \ and\ [z_{2,i}]_1[1]_2 = [z_{1,i}]_1[\underline{z}_i]_2, \\ and\ \mathbf{Z}\ is\ not\ a\ permutation\ of\ the\ columns\ of\ \mathbf{A} \end{array}\right],$$

where $[\mathbf{Z}] = [z_1|\cdots|z_m]_1 \in \mathbb{G}_1^{2\times m}$, $[\mathbf{A}]_1 = [a_1|\cdots|a_m]_1 \in \mathbb{G}_1^{2\times m}$, $[\underline{z}]_2 = [(\underline{z}_1,\dots, \underline{z}_m)]_2 \in \mathbb{G}_2^{1\times m}$, *is negligible in* λ.

Groth and Lu proved the hardness of the PPA in generic symmetric bilinear groups [19]. In the full version of this work we show that the m-PPA in generic asymmetric groups is as hard as the PPA in generic symmetric groups [15].

For constructing the function g in the PPA instantiation we require the assumption that is hard to find $[\boldsymbol{x}]_2 \in \mathbb{G}_2^m \setminus \{0\}$ such that $[\boldsymbol{x}^\top]_2[\mathbf{A}^\top]_1 = 0$, where $\mathbf{A} \leftarrow \mathcal{Q}_m$. Groth and Lu proved the generic hardness of the natural translation of this assumption to symmetric groups [19]. We observe that this assumption corresponds to a kernel assumption [25], the $\mathcal{Q}_m^\top$-KerMDH assumption in symmetric groups.

Definition 2 (Kernel Diffie-Hellman Assumption in $\mathbb{G}$ [25]). *Let* $gk \leftarrow \mathsf{Gen}_a(1^\lambda)$ *and* $\mathcal{D}_{\ell,k}$ *a distribution over* $\mathbb{Z}_q^{\ell\times k}$. *The Kernel Diffie-Hellman assumption in* $\mathbb{G}$ *(*$\mathcal{D}_{\ell,k}$-$\mathsf{KerMDH}_{\mathbb{G}_s}$*) says that every PPT Algorithm has negligible advantage in the following game: given* $[\mathbf{A}]$, *where* $\mathbf{A} \leftarrow \mathcal{D}_{\ell,k}$, *find* $[\boldsymbol{x}] \in \mathbb{G}^\ell$, $\boldsymbol{x} \neq \mathbf{0}$, *such that* $[\boldsymbol{x}]^\top[\mathbf{A}] = [\mathbf{0}]_T$.

Our assumption is the natural translation of the $Q_m^\top$-KerMDH assumption to asymmetric groups, where $[\mathbf{A}]_s$ is also given in $\mathbb{G}_{3-s}$. Such assumption is a weaker variant of a *split* KerMDH assumption, introduced in [14], where the adversary might find an element in $\mathrm{Ker}(\mathbf{A})$ which is splitted between $\mathbb{G}_1$ and $\mathbb{G}_2$.

Definition 3 (Split Kernel Diffie-Hellman Assumption [14]). *Let* $gk \leftarrow \mathsf{Gen}_a(1^\lambda)$ *and* $\mathcal{D}_{\ell,k}$ *a distribution over* $\mathbb{Z}_q^{\ell\times k}$. *The Split Kernel Diffie-Hellman assumption (*$\mathcal{D}_{\ell,k}$-$\mathsf{SKerMDH}$*) says that every PPT Algorithm has negligible advantage in the following game: given* $[\mathbf{A}]_1, [\mathbf{A}]_2$, *where* $\mathbf{A} \leftarrow \mathcal{D}_{\ell,k}$, *find* $[\boldsymbol{x}]_1 \in \mathbb{G}_1^\ell, [\boldsymbol{y}]_2 \in \mathbb{G}_2^\ell$, $\boldsymbol{x} \neq \boldsymbol{y}$, *such that* $[\boldsymbol{x}]_1^\top[\mathbf{A}]_1 = [\boldsymbol{y}]_2^\top[\mathbf{A}]_2$.

Our weaker variant restricts the adversary to give solutions only in $\mathbb{G}_1$ (i.e. $[\boldsymbol{y}]_2 = 0$), while we simply refer to it as the $Q_m^\top$-SKerMDH. González et al. proved that, in generic asymmetric groups, the $\mathcal{D}_{\ell,k}$-SKerMDH is as hard as the $\mathcal{D}_{\ell,k}$-KerMDH assumption in symmetric groups, for any distribution $\mathcal{D}_{\ell,k}$ [14]. We conclude that the $Q_m^\top$-SKerMDH is hard in generic asymmetric groups (and of course, the weaker variant that we will be using).

Finally, we recall also the definition of the Decisional Diffie-Hellman assumption (in matrix notation).

Definition 4 (Decisional Diffie-Hellman (DDH) in $\mathbb{G}_s$). *Let $gk \leftarrow$* *$\mathsf{Gen}_a(1^\lambda)$ and let $\mathbf{A} := (a,1)^\top$, $a \leftarrow \mathbb{Z}_q$. We say that the DDH assumption holds relative to Gen_a if for all PPT adversaries D*

$$\mathbf{Adv}_{\mathrm{DDH},\mathsf{Gen}_s}(\mathsf{D}) := |\Pr[\mathsf{D}(gk,[\mathbf{A}]_s,[\mathbf{A}w]_s) = 1] - \Pr[\mathsf{D}(gk,[\mathbf{A}]_s,[\mathbf{z}]_s) = 1]|$$

is negligible in λ, where the probability is taken over $gk \leftarrow \mathsf{Gen}_a(1^\lambda)$, $a \leftarrow \mathbb{Z}_q$, $w \leftarrow \mathbb{Z}_q$, $[\mathbf{z}]_2 \leftarrow \mathbb{G}_s^2$, and the coin tosses of the adversary. We say that the Symmetric eXternal Diffie-Hellman (SXDH) assumption holds if the DDH assumption holds in both $\mathbb{G}_1$ and $\mathbb{G}_2$.

2.2 Ring Signature Definition

We follow Chandran et al.'s definitions [5], which extends the original definition of Bender et al. [2] by including a CRS and perfect anonymity. We allow erasures in the key generation algorithm.

Definition 5 (Ring Signature). *A ring signature scheme consists of a quadruple of PPT algorithms (CRSGen, KeyGen, Sign, Verify) that respectively, generate the common reference string, generate keys for a user, sign a message, and verify the signature of a message. More formally:*

- *CRSGen(gk), where gk is the group key, outputs the common reference string ρ.*
- *KeyGen(ρ) is run by the user. It outputs a public verification key vk and a private signing key sk.*
- *Sign$_{\rho,sk}(m, R)$ outputs a signature σ on the message m with respect to the ring $R = \{vk_1, \ldots, vk_n\}$. We require that (vk, sk) is a valid key-pair output by KeyGen and that $vk \in R$.*
- *Verify$_{\rho,R}(m, \sigma)$ verifies a purported signature σ on a message m with respect to the ring of public keys R and reference string ρ. It outputs 1 if σ is a valid signature for m with respect to R and ρ, and 0 otherwise.*

The quadruple (CRSGen, KeyGen, Sign, Verify) is a ring signature with perfect anonymity if it has perfect correctness, computational unforgeability and perfect anonymity as defined below.

Definition 6 (Perfect Correctness). *We require that a user can sign any message on behalf of a ring where she is a member. A ring signature (CRSGen, KeyGen, Sign, Verify) has perfect correctness if for any unbounded adversary A we have:*

$$\Pr\left[\begin{array}{l} gk \leftarrow \mathsf{Gen}(1^\lambda); \rho \leftarrow \mathsf{CRSGen}(gk); (vk, sk) \leftarrow \mathsf{KeyGen}(\rho); \\ (m, R) \leftarrow \mathsf{A}(\rho, vk, sk); \sigma \leftarrow \mathsf{Sign}_{\rho, sk}(m; R): \\ \mathsf{Verify}_{\rho, R}(m, \sigma) = 1 \ or \ vk \notin R \end{array}\right] = 1$$

Definition 7 (Computational Unforgeability). *A ring signature scheme* (CRSGen, KeyGen, Sign, Verify) *is unforgeable if it is infeasible to forge a ring signature on a message without controlling one of the members in the ring. Formally, it is unforgeable when for all PPT adversaries* A *we have that*

$$\Pr\left[\begin{array}{l} gk \leftarrow \mathsf{Gen}(1^\lambda); \rho \leftarrow \mathsf{CRSGen}(gk); (m, R, \sigma) \leftarrow \mathsf{A}^{\mathsf{VKGen},\mathsf{Sign},\mathsf{Corrupt}}(\rho): \\ \mathsf{Verify}_{\rho, R}(m, \sigma) = 1 \end{array}\right]$$

is negligible in λ, *where*

- VKGen *on query number* i *selects randomness* w_i, *computes* $(vk_i, sk_i) :=$ KeyGen$(\rho; w_i)$ *and returns* vk_i.
- Sign(i, m, R) *returns* $\sigma \leftarrow \mathsf{Sign}_{\rho, sk_i}(m, R)$, *provided* (vk_i, sk_i) *has been generated by* VKGen *and* $vk_i \in R$.
- Corrupt(i) *returns* sk_i *provided* (vk_i, sk_i) *has been generated by* VKGen. *(The fact that* w_i *is not revealed allows the erasure of the random coins used in the generation of* (vk_i, sk_i).)
- A *outputs* (m, R, σ) *such that* Sign *has not been queried with* $(*, m, R)$ *and* R *only contains keys* vk_i *generated by* VKGen *where* i *has not been corrupted.*

Definition 8 (Perfect Anonymity). *A ring signature scheme* (CRSGen, KeyGen, Sign, Verify) *has perfect anonymity, if a signature on a message* m *under a ring* R *and key* vk_{i_0} *looks exactly the same as a signature on the message* m *under the ring* R *and key* vk_{i_1}, *where* $vk_{i_0}, vk_{i_1} \in R$. *This means that the signer's key is hidden among all the honestly generated keys in the ring. Formally, we require that for any unbounded adversary* A:

$$\Pr\left[\begin{array}{l} gk \leftarrow \mathsf{Gen}(1^\lambda); \rho \leftarrow \mathsf{CRSGen}(gk); \\ (m, i_0, i_1, R) \leftarrow \mathsf{A}^{\mathsf{KeyGen}(\rho)}(\rho); \sigma \leftarrow \mathsf{Sign}_{\rho, sk_{i_0}}(m, R): \\ \mathsf{A}(\sigma) = 1 \end{array}\right] =$$

$$\Pr\left[\begin{array}{l} gk \leftarrow \mathsf{Gen}(1^\lambda); \rho \leftarrow \mathsf{CRSGen}(gk); \\ (m, i_0, i_1, R) \leftarrow \mathsf{A}^{\mathsf{KeyGen}(\rho)}(\rho); \sigma \leftarrow \mathsf{Sign}_{\rho, sk_{i_1}}(m, R): \\ \mathsf{A}(\sigma) = 1 \end{array}\right]$$

where A *chooses* i_0, i_1 *such that* $(vk_{i_0}, sk_{i_0}), (vk_{i_1}, sk_{i_1})$ *have been generated by the oracle* KeyGen(ρ).

2.3 Groth-Sahai Proofs in the SXDH Instantiation

The Groth Sahai (GS) proof system is a non-interactive witness indistinguishable proof system (and in some cases also zero-knowledge) for the language of quadratic equations over a bilinear group. The admissible equation types must be in the following form:

$$\sum_{j=1}^{m_y} f(\alpha_j, \mathsf{y}_j) + \sum_{i=1}^{m_x} f(\mathsf{x}_i, \beta_i) + \sum_{i=1}^{m_x} \sum_{j=1}^{m_y} f(\mathsf{x}_i, \gamma_{i,j} \mathsf{y}_j) = t, \tag{1}$$

where $\boldsymbol{\alpha} \in A_1^{m_y}$, $\boldsymbol{\beta} \in A_2^{m_x}$, $\boldsymbol{\Gamma} = (\gamma_{i,j}) \in \mathbb{Z}_q^{m_x \times m_y}$, $t \in A_T$, and $A_1, A_2, A_T \in \{\mathbb{Z}_q, \mathbb{G}_1, \mathbb{G}_2, \mathbb{G}_T\}$ are equipped with some bilinear map $f : A_1 \times A_2 \to A_T$.

The GS proof system is a *commit-and-prove* proof system, that is, the prover first commits to solutions of Eq. (1) using the GS commitments, and then computes a proof that the committed values satisfies Eq. (1).

GS proofs are perfectly sound when the CRS is sampled from the perfectly binding distribution, and perfectly witness-indistinguishable when sampled from the perfectly hiding distribution. Computational indistinguishability of both distributions implies either perfect soundness and computational witness indistinguishability or computational soundness and perfect witness-indistinguishability.

Further, Belenky et al. noted that Groth-Sahai proofs can be *re-randomized* [1]. This means that, given commitments and proofs showing the satisfiability of some equation, on can compute new proofs which looks exactly as fresh proofs (i.e. computed with fresh randomness) for the same equation, even without knowing the commitment openings nor the randomness. In this work compute such proofs for integer equations $\beta(\beta - 1) = 0$ and $\beta x = y$.

2.4   Groth-Sahai Commitments

Following Groth and Sahai's work [21], in asymmetric groups and using the SXDH assumption, GS commitments are vectors in $\mathbb{G}_\gamma^2$, $\gamma \in \{1, 2\}$, the form

$$\mathsf{GS.Com}_{ck_\gamma}([x]_\gamma; \boldsymbol{r}) := \begin{pmatrix} [0]_\gamma \\ [x]_\gamma \end{pmatrix} + r_1 \left[\boldsymbol{u}_1 - \begin{pmatrix} 0 \\ 1 \end{pmatrix} \right]_\gamma + r_2 [\boldsymbol{u}_2]_\gamma$$

$$\mathsf{GS.Com}_{ck_\gamma}(x; \boldsymbol{r}) := x[\boldsymbol{u}_1]_\gamma + r[\boldsymbol{u}_2]_\gamma$$

where $ck_\gamma := [\boldsymbol{u}_1 | \boldsymbol{u}_2]_\gamma$, and $\boldsymbol{u}_2$ are sampled from the same distribution as $\mathbf{A}$, the matrix from Definition 4. The GS reference string is formed by the commitment keys ck_1, ck_2 and $\boldsymbol{u}_1 := w\boldsymbol{u}_2 + \boldsymbol{e}_2$ in the perfectly binding setting, and $\boldsymbol{u}_1 := w\boldsymbol{u}_2$ in the perfectly hiding setting, for $w \leftarrow \mathbb{Z}_q$.

We define commitments to row vectors as the horizontal concatenation of commitments to each of the coordinates. That is, for $\boldsymbol{x} \in \mathbb{Z}_q^m$ and $\boldsymbol{r} \in \mathbb{Z}_q^m$

$$\mathsf{GS.Com}_{ck_\gamma}(\boldsymbol{x}^\top; \boldsymbol{r}^\top) := [\boldsymbol{u}_1]_\gamma \boldsymbol{x}^\top + [\boldsymbol{u}_2]_\gamma \boldsymbol{r}^\top \in \mathbb{G}_\gamma^{2 \times m}.$$

Given a Groth-Sahai commitment $[\boldsymbol{c}]_\gamma$, we will say that $[\boldsymbol{c}']_\gamma$ is a re-randomization of $[\boldsymbol{c}]_\gamma$ if $[\boldsymbol{c}']_\gamma = [\boldsymbol{c}]_\gamma + \mathsf{GS.Com}_{ck_s}(0; \delta)$, for $\delta \leftarrow \mathbb{Z}_q$.

2.5   Boneh-Boyen Signatures

Boneh and Boyen introduced a short signature—each signature consists of only one group element—which is secure against existential forgery under weak chosen message attacks without random oracles [3]. The verification of the validity of any signature-message pair can be written as a set of pairing product equations. Thereby, using Groth-Sahai proofs one can show the possession of a valid signature without revealing the actual signature.

We construct our ring signature using Boneh-Boyen signatures, but we could replace the Boneh-Boyen signature scheme with any structure preserving signature scheme secure under milder assumptions (e.g. [22]). We rather keep it simple and stick to Boneh-Boyen signature which, since the verification key is just one group element, simplifies the notation and reduces the size of the final signature.

Definition 9 (weak Existential Unforgeability (wUF-CMA)). *We say that a signature scheme* $\Sigma = (\mathsf{KGen}, \mathsf{Sign}, \mathsf{Ver})$ *is wUF-CMA if for any PPT adversary* A

$$\Pr \left[\begin{array}{l} gk \leftarrow \mathsf{Gen}_a(1^\lambda), (m_1, \ldots, m_{q_{\mathsf{sig}}}) \leftarrow \mathsf{A}(gk), (sk, vk) \leftarrow \mathsf{KGen}(1^\lambda), \\ (m, \sigma) \leftarrow \mathsf{A}(\mathsf{Sign}_{sk}(m_1), \ldots, \mathsf{Sign}_{sk}(m_{q_{\mathsf{sig}}})) : \\ \mathsf{Ver}_{vk}(m, \sigma) = 1 \ and \ m \notin \{m_1, \ldots, m_{q_{\mathsf{sig}}}\} \end{array} \right]$$

is negligible in λ.

The Boneh-Boyen signature described bellow is wUF-CMA under the m-*strong Diffie-Hellman* assumption.

BB.KeyGen: Given a group key gk, pick $x \leftarrow \mathbb{Z}_q$. The secret/public key pair is defined as $(sk, vk) := (x, [x]_{3-s})$.

BB.Sign: Given a secret key $sk \in \mathbb{Z}_q$ and a message $m \in \mathbb{Z}_q$, output the signature $[\sigma]_s := \left[\frac{1}{x+m} \right]_s$. In the unlikely case that $x + m = 0$ we let $[\sigma]_s := [0]_s$.

BB.Ver: On input the verification key $[vk]_{3-s}$, a message $m \in \mathbb{Z}_q$, and a signature $[\sigma]_s$, verify that $[m + x]_{3-s}[\sigma]_s = [1]_T$.

It is direct to prove knowledge of a Boneh-Boyen signature for some message m under some committed verification key with a Groth-Sahai proof for the verification equation. In our SXDH based ring signature we need to prove a slightly different statement. Since we have a commitment to the secret key $[c]_2 = \mathsf{Com}_{ck_2}(x; s) = x[w_1]_2 + s[w_2]_2$ we need to show that

$$e([\sigma]_1, m[w_1]_2 + [c]_2) - [w_1]_T = e([\tilde{s}]_1, [w_2]_2), \tag{2}$$

for some $[\tilde{s}]_1 \in \mathbb{G}_1$.

2.6 Chandran et al.'s Set-Membership Proof

The core of Chandran et al.'s ring signature is a set-membership proof of size $\Theta(\sqrt{n})$ for a set $S \subset \mathbb{G}_\gamma, \gamma \in \{1, 2\}$, of size n. Assume that $S = \{[s_1]_\gamma, \ldots, [s_n]_\gamma\}$. The proof arranges elements of the set in a matrix of size $m \times m$, where $m := \sqrt{n}$,

$$[\mathbf{S}]_\gamma := \begin{pmatrix} [s_{1,1}]_\gamma & \cdots & [s_{1,m}]_\gamma \\ \vdots & \ddots & \vdots \\ [s_{m,1}]_\gamma & \cdots & [s_{m,m}]_\gamma \end{pmatrix} \text{ where } s_{i,j} := s_{(i-1)m+j} \text{ for } 1 \le i, j \le m.$$

Let $[s_\alpha]_\gamma$ the element for which the prover wants to show that $[s_\alpha]_\gamma \in S$ and let i_α, j_α such that $s_\alpha = s_{i_\alpha, j_\alpha}$. The prover selects the j_α th column of $[\mathbf{S}]_\gamma$ and then the i_α th element of that column. To do so, the prover commits to

1. $b_1, \ldots, b_m \in \{0, 1\}$ such that $b_j = 1$ iff $j = j_\alpha$,
2. $b'_1, \ldots, b'_m \in \{0, 1\}$ such that $b'_i = 1$ iff $i = i_\alpha$,
3. $[\kappa_1]_\gamma := [s_{1,j_\alpha}]_\gamma, \ldots, [\kappa_m]_\gamma := [s_{m,j_\alpha}]_\gamma$.

Using Groth-Sahai proofs, the prover proves that

  i. $b_1(b_1 - 1) = 0, \ldots, b_m(b_m - 1) = 0, b'_1(b'_m - 1) = 0, \ldots, b'_m(b'_m - 1) = 0$,
 ii. $\sum_{i=1}^{m} b_i = 1$ and $\sum_{i=1}^{m} b'_i = 1$,
iii. $[\kappa_1]_\gamma = \sum_{j=1}^{m} b_j[s_{1,j}]_\gamma, \ldots, [\kappa_m]_\gamma = \sum_{j=1}^{m} b_j[s_{m,j}]_\gamma$,
 iv. $[s_\alpha]_\gamma = \sum_{i=1}^{m} b'_i[\kappa_i]_\gamma$.

Equations i and ii prove that $(b_1, \ldots, b_m)$ and $(b'_1, \ldots, b'_m)$ are unitary vectors, equation iii proves that $([\kappa_1]_\gamma, \ldots, [\kappa_m]_\gamma)^\top$ is a column of $[\mathbf{S}]_\gamma$, and equation iv proves that $[s_\alpha]_\gamma$ is an element of $([\kappa_1]_\gamma, \ldots, [\kappa_m]_\gamma)$.

In our SXDH based ring signature we need this set-membership to show that some vector $[s]_\gamma$ is the re-randomization of one of the elements of the set of commitments $S = \{[s]_\gamma, \ldots, [s_n]_\gamma\} \subseteq \mathbb{G}_\gamma^2$. That is, there exists some $\delta \in \mathbb{Z}_q$ such that $[s]_\gamma - \mathsf{GS.Com}_{ck_\gamma}(0; \delta) \in S$. The proof remains the same but now the prover computes re-randomizations

3'. $[\kappa_1]_\gamma := [s_{1,j_\alpha}]_\gamma + \mathsf{GS.Com}_{ck_\gamma}(0; \delta_1), \ldots, [\kappa_m]_\gamma := [s_{m,j_\alpha}]_\gamma + \mathsf{GS.Com}_{ck_\gamma}(0; \delta_m)$,

and Groth-Sahai proofs that

iii'. $[\kappa_1]_\gamma - \sum_{j=1}^{m} b_j[s_{1,j}]_\gamma = \mathsf{GS.Com}_{ck_\gamma}(0; \delta_1), \ldots, [\kappa_m]_\gamma - \sum_{j=1}^{m} b_j[s_{m,j}]_\gamma = \mathsf{GS.Com}_{ck_\gamma}(0; \delta_m)$,
 iv'. $[s]_\gamma - \sum_{i=1}^{m} b'_i[\kappa_i]_\gamma = \mathsf{GS.Com}_{ck_\gamma}(0; \delta - \delta_{i_\alpha})$.

2.7 Hash Functions

We recall the definition of a hash function plus a weaker notion where the adversary needs to find a second preimage (see [29]). We consider a function $h : \mathcal{K} \times \mathcal{M} \to \mathcal{Y}$ and an algorithm KGen which on input a group key randomly samples an element from $\mathcal{K}$.

Definition 10 (Collision Resistance). *We say that h is a hash-function family with collision resistance if for all PPT adversary* A

$$\mathbf{Adv}_h^{\mathsf{Col}}(\mathsf{A}) := \Pr[k \leftarrow \mathsf{KGen}(1^\lambda), (x, x') \leftarrow \mathsf{A}(k) : x \neq x' \text{ and } h_k(x) = h_k(x')]$$

is negligible in λ.

We use a weaker variant of collision resistance for our hash function based on the PPA assumption.

Definition 11 (Second-Preimage Resistance). *We say that h is a hash-function family with always second-preimage resistance if for all PPT adversary* A

$$\mathbf{Adv}_h^{\mathsf{Sec}}(\mathsf{A}) := \Pr\left[\begin{array}{c} k \leftarrow \mathsf{KGen}(gk), x \leftarrow \mathcal{M}, x' \leftarrow \mathsf{A}(k, x) : \\ x \neq x' \text{ and } h_k(x) = h_k(x') \end{array} \right]$$

is negligible in λ.

3 Our Construction in the PPA Setting

The high level description of our PPA based ring signature was already given in Sect. 1.3. Next we proceed to formally define the hash functions h and g a then we give the formal description and security proof of the protocol.

3.1 The Hash Functions h and g

We instantiate Definition 10 with the function g and 11 with h defined as follows. For h, $\mathcal{M} = Q_m$, $\mathcal{Y} = \mathbb{G}_1^2$, $\mathsf{KGen} = \mathsf{Gen}_a$, and

$$h(A) := \sum_{([\boldsymbol{a}]_1, [\boldsymbol{a}]_2) \in A} [\boldsymbol{a}]_1, \text{ where}$$

$\mathcal{Q}_m := \{\mathbf{A} \in \mathbb{Z}_q^{2 \times m} : A = (\boldsymbol{a}_1 | \cdots | \boldsymbol{a}_m) \text{ and } \boldsymbol{a}_i = (a_{i,1}, a_{i,2})^\top \text{ s.t. } a_{i,2} = a_{i,1}^2\}$ and $Q_m = \{A : \exists \mathbf{A} \in \mathcal{Q}_m \text{ s.t. } A' = \cup_{i=1}^m ([\boldsymbol{a}_i]_1, [\boldsymbol{a}_i]_2)\}$.

It might seem odd to define Q_m as sets of vectors in both groups while h only require elements in one group. However, this will be crucial in the security proof of our ring signature, where we need to compute $[vk\boldsymbol{a}]_2$, for some $vk \in \mathbb{Z}_q$, without knowledge of $\boldsymbol{a}$. For simplicity, we may just write $h(A)$ for $A \subseteq \mathbb{G}_1^2$ (which is still well defined).

   Given a second preimage h, it is trivial to construct an adversary breaking the m-PPA assumption. Indeed, Let $[\mathbf{A}]_1, [\mathbf{A}]_2$ the challenge of the m-PPA assumption and let A the set of columns of $[\mathbf{A}]_1$ and $[\mathbf{A}]_2$, which is clearly uniformly distributed in Q_m. Then given any $A' \in Q_m$ such that $A' \neq A$ and $h(A) = h(A')$, it holds that $[\mathbf{A}']_1$, the matrix whose columns are the first components of the elements of A', is not a permutation of $[\mathbf{A}]_1$ and hence breaks m-PPA assumption. Then for any adversary A there is an adversary B such that $\mathbf{Adv}^{\mathsf{aPre}_g}(\mathsf{A}) = \mathbf{Adv}_{m\text{-PPA}}(\mathsf{B})$.

   In the case of g, $\mathcal{M} = \mathbb{G}_2^m$, $\mathcal{Y} = \mathbb{G}_2^2$, and $\mathsf{KGen}_{\mathsf{global}}$ picks a group description $gk \leftarrow \mathsf{Gen}_a(1^\lambda)$, while $\mathsf{KGen}_{\mathsf{local}}$ picks $[\boldsymbol{a}]_1 \in \mathbb{G}_1^{2 \times m}$, where $\boldsymbol{a} \leftarrow \mathcal{Q}_1$, and the function is defined as

$$g_{[\mathbf{A}]_1}([\boldsymbol{x}]_2) := [\mathbf{A}\boldsymbol{x}]_2.$$

Although not efficiently computable, one can efficiently check if $g_{[\mathbf{A}]_1}([\boldsymbol{x}]_2) = g_{[\mathbf{A}]_1}([\boldsymbol{x}']_2)$ using the pairing operation. Further, in our scheme we will publish values of the form $[a_i x_i]_2$ which will render g efficiently computable.

   Given a collision $[\boldsymbol{x}]_2, [\boldsymbol{x}']_2$ for g, then $([\boldsymbol{x}]_2 - [\boldsymbol{x}']_2) \neq [\mathbf{0}]$ is in the kernel of $[\mathbf{A}]_1$. Therefore, is trivial to prove that for any adversary A against static collision resistance there is an adversary B such that $\mathbf{Adv}^{\mathsf{Col}_g}(\mathsf{A}) = \mathbf{Adv}_{\mathcal{Q}_m^\top\text{-SKerMDH}}(\mathsf{B})$, whenever $\mathbf{A} \leftarrow \mathcal{Q}_m$.

   We note that given $A \in Q_m, [\mathbf{A}]_1 \in \mathbb{G}_1^{2 \times m}, [\boldsymbol{x}]_2 \in \mathbb{G}_2^m, [\boldsymbol{y}]_1 \in \mathbb{G}_1^2$ and $[\boldsymbol{y}']_1 \in \mathbb{G}_2^1$ one can express the statements $A \in Q_m, g_{[\mathbf{A}]_1}([\boldsymbol{x}]_2) = [\boldsymbol{y}]_2$, and $h(A) = [\boldsymbol{y}']_1$ as (3), (4), and (5), respectively.

$$e([a_1]_1, [1]_2) = e([1]_1, [b_1]_2) \text{ and}$$

$$e([a_2]_1, [1]_2) = e([a_1]_1, [b_1]_2) \text{ for each } ([\boldsymbol{a}]_1, [\boldsymbol{b}]_2) \in A \tag{3}$$

$$\sum_{j=1}^{m} e([a_{i,j}]_1, [x_i]_1) = e([1]_1, [y_i]_2) \text{ for each } i \in \{1,2\} \tag{4}$$

$$\sum_{([\boldsymbol{a}]_1, [\boldsymbol{a}]_2) \in A} [a_i]_1 = [y_i']_1 \text{ for each } i \in \{1,2\}. \tag{5}$$

Hence, one can compute Groth-Sahai proofs of size $\Theta(m), \Theta(1)$, and $\Theta(1)$, respectively, for the satisfiability of each statement.

Finally, we prove a simple lemma that relates both functions.

Lemma 1. *Let* $A \leftarrow Q_m, A' \in Q_m, [\boldsymbol{x}]_2, [\boldsymbol{x}']_2 \in \mathbb{G}_2^m$, *and* $[\mathbf{A}]_1, [\mathbf{A}']_1$ *the matrices whose columns are the first component of the elements of* A *and* A', *respectively. Then* $h(A) = h(A')$ *and* $g_{[\mathbf{A}]_1}([\boldsymbol{x}]_2) = g_{[\mathbf{A}']_1}([\boldsymbol{x}']_2)$ *implies that* A' *is a second preimage of* $h(A)$ *or there exists a permutation matrix* $\mathbf{P}$ *such that* $g_{[\mathbf{A}]_1}([\boldsymbol{x}]_2) = g_{[\mathbf{A}]_1}([\mathbf{P}\boldsymbol{x}']_2)$.

Proof. If $A \neq A'$, then A' is a second preimage of $h(A)$. Else, there is a permutation matrix $\mathbf{P}$ such that $[\mathbf{A}']_1 = [\mathbf{AP}]_1$. Then

$$g_{[\mathbf{A}]_1}([\boldsymbol{x}]_2) = g_{[\mathbf{A}']_1}([\boldsymbol{x}']_2) \iff g_{[\mathbf{A}]_1}([\boldsymbol{x}]_2) = g_{[\mathbf{AP}]_1}([\boldsymbol{x}']_2) = g_{[\mathbf{A}]_1}([\mathbf{P}\boldsymbol{x}']_2).$$

3.2 Our Ring Signature

In the following let $n := |R|, m := \sqrt[3]{n}$, and for $1 \leq \alpha \leq n$ define $1 \leq \mu \leq n^{2/3}$ and $1 \leq \nu \leq m$ such that $\alpha = (\mu-1)m + \nu$. For a sequence $\{s\}_{1 \leq i \leq n}$ we define $s_{\mu,\nu} := s_{(\mu-1)m+\nu}$. Consider $\mathsf{OT} = (\mathsf{OT.KeyGen}, \mathsf{OT.Sign}, \mathsf{OT.Ver})$ a one-time signature scheme.

$\mathsf{CRSGen}(gk)$: Pick a perfectly hiding CRS for the Groth-Sahai proof system $\mathsf{crs}_{\mathsf{GS}}$ and define $(ck_1, ck_2) := \mathsf{crs}_{\mathsf{GS}}$. Note that $\mathsf{crs}_{\mathsf{GS}}$ can be also used for the $\Theta(\sqrt{n})$ set-membership of Chandran et al. The CRS is $\rho := (gk, \mathsf{crs}_{\mathsf{GS}})$.

$\mathsf{KeyGen}(\rho)$: Pick $\boldsymbol{a} \leftarrow Q$ and $(sk, [vk]_2) \leftarrow \mathsf{BB.KeyGen}(gk)$, compute $[\boldsymbol{a}]_1, [\boldsymbol{a}]_2$ and then erase $\boldsymbol{a}$ (but if not erased we prove security under the (ℓ, m)-PPA). The secret key is sk and the extended verification key is $\tilde{vk} := ([vk]_2, [\boldsymbol{a}]_1, [\boldsymbol{a}]_2, \boldsymbol{a}[vk]_2)$.

$\mathsf{Sign}_{\rho, sk}(m, R)$: Let α the index of the signer with respect to R.
1. Compute $(sk_{\mathsf{ot}}, vk_{\mathsf{ot}}) \leftarrow \mathsf{OT.KeyGen}(gk)$ and $\sigma_{\mathsf{ot}} \leftarrow \mathsf{OT.Sign}_{sk_{\mathsf{ot}}}(m, R)$.
2. Compute $[\boldsymbol{c}]_2 := \mathsf{GS.Com}_{ck_2}([vk_\alpha]_2; \boldsymbol{r})$, $\boldsymbol{r} \leftarrow \mathbb{Z}_q^2$, $[\sigma]_1 \leftarrow \mathsf{BB.Sign}_{sk_\alpha}(vk_{\mathsf{ot}})$, $[\boldsymbol{d}]_1 := \mathsf{GS.Com}_{ck_1}([\sigma]_1; \boldsymbol{s})$, $\boldsymbol{s} \leftarrow \mathbb{Z}_q^2$, and a GS proof π_{BB} that $\mathsf{BB.Ver}_{[vk]_2}([\sigma]_1, vk_{\mathsf{ot}}) = 1$.
3. For $1 \leq i \leq n^{2/3}$, let $[\boldsymbol{\kappa}_i]_2 = ([vk_{i,1}]_2, \ldots, [vk_{i,m}]_2)^\top$, $A_i = \{([\boldsymbol{a}_{i,1}]_1, [\boldsymbol{a}_{i,1}]_2), \ldots, ([\boldsymbol{a}_{i,m}]_1, [\boldsymbol{a}_{i,m}]_2)\}$, and $[\mathbf{A}_i]_1 := [\boldsymbol{a}_{i,1}|\cdots|\boldsymbol{a}_{i,m}]_1$. Define the sets $H = \{h(A_1), \ldots, h(A_{n^{2/3}})\}$ and $G = \{g_{[\mathbf{A}_1]_1}([\boldsymbol{\kappa}_1]_2) \ldots, g_{[\mathbf{A}_{n^{2/3}}]_1}([\boldsymbol{\kappa}_{n^{2/3}}]_2)\}$.

4. Let $[\boldsymbol{x}]_1 := h(A_\mu)$ and $[\boldsymbol{y}]_2 = g_{[\mathbf{A}_\mu]_1}([\boldsymbol{\kappa}_\mu]_2)$. Compute GS commitments to $[\boldsymbol{x}]_1$ and $[\boldsymbol{y}]_2$ and compute proofs π_G and π_H that they belong to G and H, respectively. It is also proven that they appear in the same positions reusing the commitments to $b_1, \dots, b_m$ and $b'_1, \dots, b'_m$, used in the set-membership proof of Chandran et al., which define $[\boldsymbol{x}]_1$'s and $[\boldsymbol{y}]_2$'s position in H and G respectively.

5. Let $[\boldsymbol{\kappa}']_2 := ([vk_\alpha]_2, [vk_{\mu,1}]_2, \dots, [vk_{\alpha-1}]_2, [vk_{\alpha+1}]_2, \dots, [vk_{\mu,m}]_2)^\top \in \mathbb{G}_2^m$, $[\mathbf{A}']_1 := [\boldsymbol{a}_\alpha | \boldsymbol{a}_{\mu,1} | \cdots | \boldsymbol{a}_{\alpha-1} | \boldsymbol{a}_{\alpha+1} | \cdots | \boldsymbol{a}_{\mu,m}]_1 \in \mathbb{G}_1^{2\times m}$ and $A' = \{([\boldsymbol{a}_{\mu,1}]_1, [\boldsymbol{a}_{\mu,1}]_2), \dots, ([\boldsymbol{a}_{\mu,1}]_1, [\boldsymbol{a}_{\mu,1}]_2)\}$. Compute GS commitments to all but the first element of $[\boldsymbol{\kappa}']_2$ (note that $[\boldsymbol{c}]_2$ is a commitment to the first element of $[\boldsymbol{\kappa}']_2$). Compute also a GS proof π_g that $g_{[\mathbf{A}']_1}([\boldsymbol{\kappa}']_2) = [\boldsymbol{y}]_2$, a GS proof π_h that $h(A') = [\boldsymbol{x}]_1$, and a GS proof π_{Q_m} that $A' \in Q_m$.

6. Return the signature $\boldsymbol{\sigma} := (vk_{\mathsf{ot}}, \sigma_{\mathsf{ot}}, [\boldsymbol{c}]_2, [\boldsymbol{d}]_1, \pi_{\mathsf{BB}}, \pi_G, \pi_H, \pi_g, \pi_h, \pi_{Q_m})$. (GS proofs include commitments to variables).

Verify$_{\rho, R}(m, \boldsymbol{\sigma})$: Verify the validity of the one-time signature and of all the proofs. Return 0 if any of these checks fails and 1 otherwise.

We prove the following theorem which states the security of our construction.

Theorem 1. *The scheme presented in this section is a ring signature scheme with perfect correctness, perfect anonymity and computational unforgeability under the Q_{gen}-permutation pairing assumption, the $Q_{Q_{\mathsf{gen}}}^\top$-SKerMDH assumption, the SXDH assumption, and the assumption that the one-time signature and the Boneh-Boyen signature are unforgeable. Concretely, for any PPT adversary A against the unforgeability of the scheme, there exist adversaries $\mathsf{B}_1, \mathsf{B}_2, \mathsf{B}_3, \mathsf{B}_4, \mathsf{B}_5$ such that*

$$\mathbf{Adv}(\mathsf{A}) \le \mathbf{Adv}_{\mathrm{SXDH}}(\mathsf{B}_1) + \mathbf{Adv}_{Q_{\mathsf{gen}}\text{-PPA}}(\mathsf{B}_2) + \mathbf{Adv}_{Q_{Q_{\mathsf{gen}}}^\top\text{-SKerMDH}}(\mathsf{B}_3)$$
$$+ Q_{\mathsf{gen}}(Q_{\mathsf{sign}}\mathbf{Adv}_{\mathrm{OT}}(\mathsf{B}_4) + \mathbf{Adv}_{\mathrm{BB}}(\mathsf{B}_5)),$$

where Q_{gen} and Q_{sign} are, respectively, upper bounds for the number of queries that A makes to its VKGen and Sign oracles.

Proof. Perfect correctness follows directly from the definitions. Perfect anonymity follows from the fact that the perfectly hiding Groth-Sahai CRS defines perfectly hiding commitments and perfect witness-indistinguishable proofs, information theoretically hiding any information about $\tilde{vk}$.

We say that an unforgeability adversary is "eager" if makes all its queries to the VKGen oracle at the beginning. Note that any non-eager adversary A' can be perfectly simulated by an eager adversary that makes Q_{gen} queries to VKGen and answers A' queries to VKGen "on demand". This is justified by the fact that the output of VKGen is independent of all previous outputs.

W.l.o.g. we assume that A is an eager adversary. Computational unforgeability follows from the indistinguishability of the following games

Game$_0$: This is the real unforgeability experiment. Game$_0$ returns 1 if the adversary A produces a valid forgery and 0 if not.

Game$_1$: This is game exactly as Game$_0$ with the following differences:
  - The Groth-Sahai CRS is sampled together with its discrete logarithms from the perfectly binding distribution. Note that the discrete logarithms of the CRS allow to open the Groth-Sahai commitments.
  - At the beginning, variables err$_2$ and err$_3$ are initialized to 0 and a random index i^* is chosen from $\{1, \ldots, Q_{\mathsf{gen}}\}$.
  - On a query to Corrupt with argument i, if $i = i^*$ set err$_3 \leftarrow 1$ and proceed as in Game$_0$.
  - Let (m, R, σ) the purported forgery output by A. If $[vk]_2$, the opening of commitment $[c_{\mu,\nu}]_2$ from σ, is not equal to $[vk_{i^*}]_2$, set err$_3 \leftarrow 1$. If $[vk]_2 \notin R$, then set err$_2 = 1$.

Game$_2$: This is game exactly as Game$_1$ except that, if err$_2$ is set to 1, Game$_2$ aborts.

Game$_3$: This is game exactly as Game$_2$ except that, if err$_3$ is set to 1, Game$_3$ aborts.

Since in Game$_1$ variables err$_2$ and err$_3$ are just dummy variables, the only difference with Game$_0$ comes from the Groth-Sahai CRS distribution. It follows that there is an adversary B$_1$ against SXDH such that $|\Pr[\mathsf{Game}_0 = 1] - \Pr[\mathsf{Game}_1 = 1]| \leq \mathbf{Adv}_{\mathrm{SXDH}}(\mathsf{B}_1)$.

Lemma 2. *There exist adversaries* B$_2$ *and* B$_3$ *against the* Q_{gen}-*permutation pairing assumption and against the* $\mathcal{Q}_{Q_{\mathsf{gen}}}^\top$-*KerMDH assumption, respectively, such that*

$$|\Pr[\mathsf{Game}_2 = 1] - \Pr[\mathsf{Game}_1 = 1]| \leq \mathbf{Adv}_{Q_{\mathsf{gen}}\text{-PPA}}(\mathsf{B}_2) + \mathbf{Adv}_{\mathcal{Q}_{Q_{\mathsf{gen}}}^\top\text{-SKerMDH}}(\mathsf{B}_3).$$

Proof. Note that

$$
\begin{aligned}
\Pr[\mathsf{Game}_1 = 1] &= \Pr[\mathsf{Game}_1 = 1|\mathsf{err}_2 = 0]\Pr[\mathsf{err}_2 = 0] \\
&\quad + \Pr[\mathsf{Game}_1 = 1|\mathsf{err}_2 = 1]\Pr[\mathsf{err}_2 = 1] \\
&\leq \Pr[\mathsf{Game}_2 = 1] + \Pr[\mathsf{Game}_1 = 1|\mathsf{err}_2 = 0] \\
&\Longrightarrow |\Pr[\mathsf{Game}_2 = 1] - \Pr[\mathsf{Game}_1 = 1]| \leq \Pr[\mathsf{Game}_1 = 1|\mathsf{err}_2 = 1].
\end{aligned}
$$

We proceed to bound this last probability constructing two adversaries against collision resistance of g and preimage resistance of h. Let $1 \leq \mu \leq n^{2/3}$ the index defined in π_G and π_S.

Consider an adversary A$_h$ that finds a second preimage of h when $\mathcal{M} = Q_{Q_{\mathsf{gen}}}$. A$_h$ receives as challenge $B \in Q_{Q_{\mathsf{gen}}}$ and honestly simulates Game$_1$ with the following exception. On the i th query of A to VKGen picks $(sk, [vk]) \leftarrow$ BB.KeyGen(1^λ) and sets $(sk_i, \tilde{vk}_i) := (sk, ([vk]_2, [b_i]_1, [b_i]_2, sk[b_i]_2))$, where $([b_i]_1, [b_i]_2)$ is the i th element of B. When A corrupts the i th party, it returns sk_i but it might also request a_i to its oracle if we are proving security under the (ℓ, m)-PPA assumption. When A outputs and π_{Q_m}, A$_h$ extracts $A' = \{([a'_1]_1, [a'_1]_2), \ldots, ([a'_m]_1, [a'_m]_2)\}$ and returns $A' \cup \bar{A}_\mu$, where $\bar{A}_\mu := B \setminus A_\mu$.

Consider another adversary A_g against the collision resistance of g when $\mathcal{M} = \mathbb{G}^{Q_{\mathrm{gen}}}$. B receives as challenge $[\mathbf{B}]_1 \in \mathbb{G}_1^{2 \times Q_{\mathrm{gen}}}$ and $[\mathbf{B}]_2 \in \mathbb{G}_2^{2 \times Q_{\mathrm{gen}}}$ and honestly simulates Game_1 embedding $[\mathbf{B}]_1, [\mathbf{B}]_2$ in the user keys in the same way as A_h. When A outputs $[c]_2, \mathsf{GS.Com}_{ck_2}([\kappa_2']_2), \ldots, \mathsf{GS.Com}_{ck_2}([\kappa_m']_2)$, A_g extracts $[vk], [\kappa_2'], \ldots, [\kappa_m']$. W.l.o.g. assume that $\mathbf{B} = \mathbf{A}_\mu | \bar{\mathbf{A}}_\mu$, where $\bar{\mathbf{A}}_\mu$ is some matrix whose rows are the discrete logs of the elements of $\bar{A}_\mu$. A_g attempts to extract a permutation matrix $\mathbf{P}$ such that $[\mathbf{A}']_1 = [\mathbf{A}_\mu]_1 \mathbf{P}$. If there is no such permutation matrix, then A_g aborts. Else, A_g returns $\begin{pmatrix} [\kappa_\mu]_2 \\ [\mathbf{0}]_2 \end{pmatrix}$, $\begin{pmatrix} \mathbf{P}[\kappa']_2 \\ [\mathbf{0}]_2 \end{pmatrix} \in \mathbb{G}_2^{Q_{\mathrm{gen}}}$, where $[\kappa_1']$ is the opening of $[c]$.

Perfect soundness of proof π_g (recall that the Groth-Sahai CRS is perfectly binding) implies that

$$g_{[\mathbf{A}']_1}([\kappa']_2) = [\boldsymbol{y}]_2.$$

Perfect soundness of proof π_g and π_{Q_m} implies that

$$h(A') = [\boldsymbol{x}]_1 \text{ and } A' \in Q_m.$$

Given perfect soundness of proofs π_G, π_H, it holds that

$$g_{[\mathbf{A}']_1}([\kappa']_2) = g_{[\mathbf{A}_\mu]_1}([\kappa_\mu]_2)$$
$$h(A') = h(A_\mu).$$

By Lemma 1 we get that either $A' \neq A_\mu$ is a second preimage for $h(A_\mu)$, thus $A' \cup \bar{A}_\mu \neq B$ and A_h is successful, or there exists a permutation matrix $\mathbf{P}$, which is the one that A_g searches, such that $g_{[\mathbf{A}_\mu]_1}(\mathbf{P}[\kappa']_2) = g_{[\mathbf{A}_\mu]_1}([\kappa_\mu]_2)$. $\mathrm{err}_2 = 1$ implies that $[vk]_2 = [\kappa_1']_2 \neq [\kappa_{\mu,i}]_2$, for all $1 \leq i \leq m$, and thus $\mathbf{P}[\kappa']_2 \neq [\kappa_\mu]_2$ and, since $[\mathbf{B}]_1 = [\mathbf{A}_\mu | \bar{\mathbf{A}}_\mu]_1$,

$$g_{[\mathbf{A}_\mu]_1}(\mathbf{P}[\kappa']_2) = g_{[\mathbf{B}]_1}\begin{pmatrix} \mathbf{P}[\kappa']_2 \\ [\mathbf{0}]_2 \end{pmatrix} = g_{[\mathbf{A}_\mu]_1}([\kappa_\mu]_2) = g_{[\mathbf{B}]_1}\begin{pmatrix} [\kappa_\mu]_2 \\ [\mathbf{0}]_2 \end{pmatrix}$$

and A_g is successful.

As stated in Sect. 2.7, from A_h we can construct an adversary B_2 that breaks the Q_{gen}-PPA assumption and from A_g we can construct an adversary B_3 that breaks the $\mathcal{Q}_m^\top$-SKerMDH assumption, with the same advantages. We conclude that

$$\Pr[\mathsf{Game}_1 = 1 | \mathrm{err}_2 = 1] \leq \mathbf{Adv}_{Q_{\mathrm{gen}}\text{-PPA}}(B_2) + \mathbf{Adv}_{\mathcal{Q}_{Q_{\mathrm{gen}}}^\top\text{-SKerMDH}}(B_3)$$

Lemma 3.
$$\Pr[\mathsf{Game}_3 = 1] \geq \frac{1}{Q_{\mathrm{gen}}} \Pr[\mathsf{Game}_2 = 1].$$

Proof. It holds that

$$\Pr[\mathsf{Game}_3 = 1] = \Pr[\mathsf{Game}_3 = 1 | \mathrm{err}_3 = 0] \Pr[\mathrm{err}_3 = 0]$$
$$= \Pr[\mathsf{Game}_2 = 1 | \mathrm{err}_3 = 0] \Pr[\mathrm{err}_3 = 0]$$
$$= \Pr[\mathrm{err}_3 = 0 | \mathsf{Game}_2 = 1] \Pr[\mathsf{Game}_2 = 1].$$

The probability that $\mathsf{err}_3 = 0$ given $\mathsf{Game}_2 = 1$ is the probability that the Q_{cor} calls to Corrupt do not abort and that $[vk]_2 = [vk_{i^*}]_2$. Since A is an eager adversary, at the i th call to Corrupt the index i^* is uniformly distributed over the $Q_{\mathsf{gen}} - i + 1$ indices of uncorrupted users. Similarly, when A outputs its purported forgery, the probability that $[vk]_2 = [vk_{i^*}]_2$ is $1/(Q_{\mathsf{gen}} - Q_{\mathsf{cor}})$, since $[vk]_2 \in R$ (or otherwise Game_2 would have aborted). Therefore

$$\Pr[\mathsf{err}_2 = 1|\mathsf{Game}_2 = 1] = \frac{Q_{\mathsf{gen}} - 1}{Q_{\mathsf{gen}}} \frac{Q_{\mathsf{gen}} - 2}{Q_{\mathsf{gen}} - 1} \cdots \frac{Q_{\mathsf{gen}} - Q_{\mathsf{cor}}}{Q_{\mathsf{gen}} - Q_{\mathsf{cor}} + 1} \frac{1}{Q_{\mathsf{gen}} - Q_{\mathsf{cor}}} = \frac{1}{Q_{\mathsf{gen}}}.$$

Lemma 4. *There exist adversaries B_4 and B_5 against the unforgeability of the one-time signature scheme and the weak unforgeability of the Boneh-Boyen signature scheme such that*

$$\Pr[\mathsf{Game}_3 = 1] \leq Q_{\mathsf{sig}}\mathbf{Adv}_{\mathsf{OT}}(\mathsf{B}_4) + \mathbf{Adv}_{\mathsf{BB}}(\mathsf{B}_5)$$

Proof. We construct adversaries B_4 and B_5 as follows.

B_4 receives $vk_{\mathsf{ot}}^\dagger$ and simulates Game_3 honestly but with the following differences. It chooses a random $j^* \in \{1, \ldots, Q_{\mathsf{sig}}\}$ and answer the j^* th query to $\mathsf{Sign}(i, m^\dagger, R^\dagger)$ honestly but computing $\sigma_{\mathsf{ot}}^\dagger$ querying on $(m^\dagger, R^\dagger)$ its oracle and setting $vk_{\mathsf{ot}}^\dagger$ as the corresponding one-time verification key. Finally, when A outputs its purported forgery $(m, R, (\sigma_{\mathsf{ot}}, vk_{\mathsf{ot}}, \ldots))$, B_4 outputs the corresponding one-time signature.

B_5 receives $[vk]_2$ and simulates Game_3 honestly but with the following differences. Let $i := 0$. B_5 computes $(sk_{\mathsf{ot}}^i, vk_{\mathsf{ot}}^i) \leftarrow \mathsf{OT.KeyGen}(gk)$, for each $1 \leq i \leq Q_{\mathsf{sig}}$ and queries its signing oracle on $(vk_{\mathsf{ot}}^1, \ldots, vk_{\mathsf{ot}}^{Q_{\mathsf{sig}}})$ obtaining $[\sigma_1]_1, \ldots, [\sigma_{Q_{\mathsf{sig}}}]_1$. On the i^* th query of A to the key generation algorithm, B_5 picks $\boldsymbol{a} \leftarrow \mathcal{Q}$ and outputs $\tilde{vk} := ([vk]_2, [\boldsymbol{a}]_1, [\boldsymbol{a}]_2, \boldsymbol{a}[vk]_2)$. When A queries the signing oracle on input (i^*, m, R), B_5 computes an honest signature but replaces vk_{ot} with vk_{ot}^i and $[\sigma]_1$ with $[\sigma_i]_2$, and then adds 1 to i. Finally, when A outputs its purported forgery $(m, R, (\sigma_{\mathsf{ot}}, vk_{\mathsf{ot}}, [\boldsymbol{c}]_2, [\boldsymbol{d}]_1, \ldots))$, it extracts $[\sigma]_1$ from $[\boldsymbol{d}]_1$ as its forgery for vk_{ot}.

Let E be the event where vk_{ot}, from the purported forgery of A, has been previously output by Sign. We have that

$$\Pr[\mathsf{Game}_3 = 1] \leq \Pr[\mathsf{Game}_3 = 1|E] + \Pr[\mathsf{Game}_3 = 1|\neg E].$$

Since (m, R) has never been signed by a one-time signature and that, conditioned on E, the probability of $vk_{\mathsf{ot}} = vk_{\mathsf{ot}}^\dagger$ is $1/Q_{\mathsf{sig}}$, then

$$Q_{\mathsf{sig}}\mathbf{Adv}_{\mathsf{OT}}(\mathsf{B}_4) \geq \Pr[\mathsf{Game}_3 = 1|E]$$

Finally, if $\neg E$ holds, then $[\sigma]$ is a forgery for vk_{ot} and thus

$$\mathbf{Adv}_{\mathsf{BB}}(\mathsf{B}_5) \geq \Pr[\mathsf{Game}_3 = 1|\neg E]$$

4   Our Construction in the SXDH Setting

Our construction follow the high-level description depicted in Sect. 1.3 with the only difference that we do not use the verification key of the Boneh-Boyen signature vk, but a commitment to the secret key x. The only reason is efficiency since in this way we use Groth-Sahai proofs for integer equations instead of equations involving group elements.

For $\beta \in \{0,1\}^m$ we define $h(\beta) := \sum_{i=1}^m \beta_i$ and $g_\beta(x) := \sum_{i=1}^m \beta_i x_i$. Unlike the PPA-based construction, we do not prove collision resistance of h or g (g is not collision resistant). Instead, these functions are only used as shorthand and to keep an intuitive link with the PPA-based construction.

In the high level description of our ring signature in the SXDH setting from Sect. 1.3 it was left to show how to derive a proof that $g_{\beta'}(x') = g_{\beta_\mu}(x_\mu)$, which is described in following section.

4.1   NIZK Proof that $g_{\beta'}(x') = g_\beta(x)$

Let $[\mathbf{U}]_1$ and $[\mathbf{W}]_2$ Groth-Sahai commitment keys. Consider $[a_i]_1 = \mathsf{Com}(\beta_i; r_i)$, $[c_i]_2 = \mathsf{Com}_{[\mathbf{W}]_2}(x_i; s)$, and $[d_i] = \mathsf{Com}_{[\mathbf{U}]_1}(y_i; t)$, where $y_i = \beta_i x_i$, $\beta \in \{0,1\}$, $r, s, t \in \mathbb{Z}_q$, and $1 \leq i \leq m$. Consider also $[g]_1$, a re-randomization of $\sum_{i=1}^m [d_i]_1 = \mathsf{Com}(g_\beta(x))$, and $[\mathbf{A}']_1$ and $[\mathbf{C}']_2$ permutations of re-randomizations of $[\mathbf{A}]_1 := ([a_1]|\cdots|[a_m])$ and $[\mathbf{C}]_2 := ([c_1]_2|\cdots|[c_m]_2)$, respectively. We want to construct a proof that $g_{\beta'}(x') = g_\beta(x)$, or equivalently $\sum_{i=1}^m \beta_i' x_i' = \sum_{i=1}^m \beta_i x_i$, only from the extended verification keys and the random coins used in the re-randomizations.

Apart from $[a_i]_1, [c_i]_2, [d_i]_1$, the extended verification key contains Groth-Sahai proofs $[\psi_i]_2, [\omega_i]_1$ for the equation $\beta_i x_i = y_i$. Each of these proofs satisfy the verification equation

$$[a_i]_1[c_i^\top]_2 - [d_i]_1[w_1^\top]_2 = [u_2]_1[\psi_i^\top]_2 + [\omega_i]_1[w_2^\top]_2.$$

$[\mathbf{A}']_1$, $[\mathbf{C}']_2$ and $[g]_1$ are computed as $[\mathbf{A}']_1 = [\mathbf{A}]_1\mathbf{P} + [u_2]_1\delta_a^\top$, $[\mathbf{C}']_2 = [\mathbf{C}]_2\mathbf{P} + [w_2]_2\delta_c^\top$, and $[g]_1 = \sum_{i=1}^m [d_i]_1 + [u_2]_1\delta_g$, where $\mathbf{P}$ is a permutation matrix and $\delta_a, \delta_c \in \mathbb{Z}_q^m$ and $\delta_g \in \mathbb{Z}_q$. The right side of the verification equation for equation $\sum_{i=1}^m \beta_i' x_i' - y = 0$, where $y = \sum_{i=1}^n \beta_i x_i$ is the opening of $[d']_1$ and β', x' are the openings of $[\mathbf{A}']_1$ and $[\mathbf{C}']_2$ respectively, is equal to

$$[\mathbf{A}']_1[\mathbf{C}'^\top]_2 - [d']_1[w_1^\top]_2$$

$$= [\mathbf{A}]_1\mathbf{PP}^\top[\mathbf{C}^\top]_2 + [\mathbf{A}]_1\mathbf{P}\delta_c[w_2^\top]_2 + [u_2]_1\delta_a^\top[\mathbf{C}'^\top]_2 - [d']_1[w_2^\top]_2$$

$$= \sum_{i=1}^m ([a_i]_1[c_i^\top]_2 - [d_i]_1[w_1^\top]) + [\mathbf{A}]_1\mathbf{P}\delta_c[w_2^\top]_2 + [u_2]_1(\delta_a^\top[\mathbf{C}'^\top]_2 - \delta_g[w_1^\top]_2)$$

$$= [u_2]_1\left(\sum_{i=1}^m [\psi_i]_1 + [\mathbf{C}']_2\delta_a - \delta_g[w_1]_2\right)^\top + \left(\sum_{i=1}^m [\omega_i]_1 + [\mathbf{A}]_1\mathbf{P}\delta_c\right)[w_2^\top]_2.$$

The last equation indicates that the proof must be the terms multiplying $[\boldsymbol{u}_2]_1$ and $[\boldsymbol{w}_2^{\top}]_2$ plus randomization terms. That is, for $\xi \leftarrow \mathbb{Z}_q$

$$[\boldsymbol{\psi}']_2 = \sum_{i=1}^{m}[\boldsymbol{\psi}_i]_1 + [\mathbf{C}']_2\boldsymbol{\delta}_a - \delta_g[\boldsymbol{w}_1]_2 + \xi[\boldsymbol{w}_2]_2$$

$$[\boldsymbol{\omega}']_1 = \sum_{i=1}^{m}[\boldsymbol{\omega}_i]_1 + [\mathbf{A}]_1\mathbf{P}\boldsymbol{\delta}_c - \xi[\boldsymbol{u}_2]_1. \tag{6}$$

Assuming $[\boldsymbol{d}']_1$ is correctly computed, the proof is sound because it satisfy the Groth-Sahai verification equation for $\sum_{i=1}^{m}\beta'_i x'_i - \sum_{i=1}^{m}\beta_i x_i = 0$. Furthermore, the proof is uniformly distributed conditioned on satisfying the verification equation and thus follows exactly the same distribution as a fresh Groth-Sahai proof.

4.2 Our Ring Signature

In the following let $n := |R|$, $m := \sqrt[3]{n}$, and for $1 \leq \alpha \leq n$ define $1 \leq \mu \leq n^{2/3}$ and $1 \leq \nu \leq m$ such that $\alpha = (\mu-1)m + \nu$. For a sequence $\{s\}_{1 \leq i \leq n}$ we define $s_{\mu,\nu} := s_{(\mu-1)m+\nu}$. Consider $\mathsf{OT} = (\mathsf{OT.KeyGen}, \mathsf{OT.Sign}, \mathsf{OT.Ver})$ a one-time signature scheme. We assume that ring descriptions don't contain repeated elements.

$\mathsf{CRSGen}(gk)$: Pick three perfectly hiding CRS for the Groth-Sahai proof system ck_1, ck_2, ck'_2, where $ck_1 := [\mathbf{U}]_1, ck_2 := [\mathbf{V}]_2, ck'_2 := [\mathbf{W}]_2$. We use ck_1, ck_2 for the $\Theta(\sqrt{n})$ set-membership of Chandran et al. The CRS is $\rho := (gk, ck_1, ck_2, ck'_2)$.

$\mathsf{KeyGen}(\rho)$: Pick $(x, [x]_2) \leftarrow \mathsf{BB.KeyGen}(gk)$, compute $[\boldsymbol{a}]_1 := \mathsf{Com}_{[\mathbf{U}]_1}(\beta = 0; r)$, where $r \leftarrow \mathbb{Z}_q$, plus a Groth-Sahai proof π that $\beta(\beta - 1) = 0$. Compute also $[\boldsymbol{c}]_2 = \mathsf{GS.Com}_{ck'_2}(x; s), [\boldsymbol{d}]_1 := \mathsf{GS.Com}_{ck_1}(y; t)$, where $s, t \leftarrow \mathbb{Z}_q$, and a proof $[\boldsymbol{\psi}]_2, [\boldsymbol{\omega}]_1$ that $\beta x = y$. The secret key is x and the extended verification key is $\widetilde{vk} := ([x]_2, [\boldsymbol{a}]_1, [\boldsymbol{c}]_2, [\boldsymbol{d}]_1, \pi, [\boldsymbol{\psi}]_2, [\boldsymbol{\omega}]_1)$.

$\mathsf{Sign}_{\rho,x}(m, R)$: Let $\alpha = (\mu - 1)m + \nu$ the index of the signer with respect to R.
  1. Compute $(sk_{\mathsf{ot}}, vk_{\mathsf{ot}}) \leftarrow \mathsf{OT.KeyGen}(gk)$ and $\sigma_{\mathsf{ot}} \leftarrow \mathsf{OT.Sign}_{sk_{\mathsf{ot}}}(m, R)$.
  2. For $1 \leq i \leq n^{2/3}$, let $[\mathbf{A}_i]_1 := [\boldsymbol{a}_{i,1}|\dots|\boldsymbol{a}_{i,m}]_1$, $[\boldsymbol{h}_i]_1 := \sum_{j=1}^{m}[\boldsymbol{a}_{i,j}]_1$ and $[\boldsymbol{g}_i]_1 := \sum_{j=1}^{m}[\boldsymbol{d}_{i,j}]_1$. Define the sets $H = \{[\boldsymbol{h}_1]_2, \dots, [\boldsymbol{h}_{n^{2/3}}]_2\}$ and $G = \{[\boldsymbol{g}_1]_2 \dots, [\boldsymbol{g}_{n^{2/3}}]_2\}$.
  3. Let $[\boldsymbol{h}]_1 := [\boldsymbol{h}_\mu] + \delta_h[\boldsymbol{u}_1]_1$ and $[\boldsymbol{g}]_1 = [\boldsymbol{g}_\mu]_1 + \delta_g[\boldsymbol{u}_2]_1$, $\delta_g, \delta_h \leftarrow \mathbb{Z}_q$. Compute proofs π_G and π_H that they belong to G and H, respectively. It is also proven that they appear in the same positions reusing the commitments to $b_1, \dots, b_m$ and $b'_1, \dots, b'_m$, used in the set-membership proof of Chandran et al., which define $[\boldsymbol{h}]_1$'s and $[\boldsymbol{g}]_2$'s positions in H and G respectively.
  4. Let $[\mathbf{C}']_2 := [\boldsymbol{c}_{\mu,\nu}|\boldsymbol{c}_{\mu,1}|\cdots|\boldsymbol{c}_{\mu,m}]_2 + [\boldsymbol{w}_2]_2\boldsymbol{\delta}_c^{\top}$ and $[\mathbf{A}']_1 := [\boldsymbol{a}_{\mu,\nu}|\boldsymbol{a}_{\mu,1}|\cdots|\boldsymbol{a}_{\mu,m}]_1 + [\boldsymbol{u}_2]_1\boldsymbol{\delta}_a^{\top} \in \mathbb{G}_1^{2\times m}$, where $\boldsymbol{\delta}_a, \boldsymbol{\delta}_c \leftarrow \mathbb{Z}_q^m$ (the ν-th row is moved to the front of each matrix). Use $[\mathbf{A}_\mu]_1, [\mathbf{C}']_2, \mathbf{P}$ the permutation matrix that swaps the first element with the ν-th element, and $[\boldsymbol{\psi}_{\mu,i}]_2, [\boldsymbol{\omega}_{\mu,i}]_1$ plus $\boldsymbol{\delta}_a, \boldsymbol{\delta}_c, \delta_g$ to derive $\pi_g = ([\boldsymbol{\psi}']_2, [\boldsymbol{\omega}']_1)$, a proof that $g_{\beta'}(\boldsymbol{x}') = g_\beta(\boldsymbol{x})$, as in Eq. (6).

5. Compute a proof π_h that $h(\beta') = h(\beta_\mu)$ as the GS proof that $\sum_{i=1}^{m} [a'_i]_1 - [h]_1 = \tilde{\delta}_h [u_2]$, where $\tilde{\delta}_h = \sum_{i=1}^{m} \delta_{a,i} - \delta_h$.

6. Compute a GS proof π_{bits} that β', the vector of openings of $\mathbf{A}'$, belongs to $\{0,1\}^m$ re-randomizing proofs $\pi_{\mu,\nu}, \pi_{\mu,1}, \ldots, \pi_{\mu,m}$.

7. Compute $[\sigma]_1 \leftarrow \text{BB.Sign}_{x_{\mu,\nu}}(vk_{\text{ot}})$, $[f]_1 \leftarrow \text{GS.Com}_{ck_1}([\sigma]_1)$, and a GS proof π_{BB} of satisfiability of Eq. (2) with $[c_{\mu,\nu}]_2$ the commitment to the secret key.

8. Return the signature $\boldsymbol{\sigma} := (vk_{\text{ot}}, \sigma_{\text{ot}}, [f]_1, [\mathbf{A}']_2, [\mathbf{C}']_2, [g]_1, [h]_1, \pi_G, \pi_H, \pi_g, \pi_h, \pi_{\text{bits}}, \pi_{\text{BB}})$. (GS proofs include commitments to variables).

Verify$_{\rho,R}(m, \boldsymbol{\sigma})$: Verify the validity of the one-time signature and of all the proofs. Return 0 if any of these checks fails and 1 otherwise.

We prove the following theorem which states the security of our construction.

Theorem 2. *The scheme presented in this section is a ring signature scheme with perfect correctness, perfect anonymity and computational unforgeability under the* SXDH *assumption, and the assumption that the one-time signature and the Boneh-Boyen signature are unforgeable. Concretely, for any PPT adversary* A *against the unforgeability of the scheme, there exist adversaries* B_1, B_2, B_3 *such that*

$$\mathbf{Adv}(\mathsf{A}) \le (Q_{\text{gen}}^2 + 1)\mathbf{Adv}_{\text{SXDH}}(\mathsf{B}_1) + Q_{\text{gen}}Q_{\text{sig}}\mathbf{Adv}_{\text{OT}}(\mathsf{B}_2) + Q_{\text{gen}}\mathbf{Adv}_{\text{BB}}(\mathsf{B}_3),$$

where Q_{gen} *and* Q_{sign} *are, respectively, upper bounds for the number of queries that* A *makes to its* VKGen *and* Sign *oracles.*

Proof. Perfect correctness follows directly from the definitions. Perfect anonymity follows from the fact that the perfectly hiding Groth-Sahai commitment keys defines perfectly hiding commitments and perfect witness-indistinguishable proofs, information theoretically hiding any information about $\widetilde{vk}$ and x. Further, the re-randomized commitments are random elements $\mathbb{G}_2^1$ or $\mathbb{G}_2^2$, and hence independent of the original commitments, and the re-randomized proofs follows the same distribution of the honest proofs and hence, they don't reveal any information about $\widetilde{vk}$ and x.

We say that an unforgeability adversary is "eager" if makes all its queries to the VKGen oracle at the beginning. Note that any non-eager adversary A′ can be perfectly simulated by an eager adversary that makes Q_{gen} queries to VKGen and answers A′ queries to VKGen "on demand". This is justified by the fact that the output of VKGen is independent of all previous outputs.

W.l.o.g. we assume that A is an eager adversary. Computational unforgeability follows from the indistinguishability of the following games

Game$_0$: This is the real unforgeability experiment. Game$_0$ returns 1 if the adversary A produces a valid forgery and 0 if not.

Game$_1$: This is game exactly as Game$_0$ with the following differences:
  - The commitment key ck'_2 is sampled together with its discrete logarithms from the perfectly binding distribution. Note that the discrete logarithms of ck'_2 allow to open commitments $[c_i]_2$ and $[c_j]_2$ for $i \in [Q_{\text{gen}}]$ and $j \in [m]$.

- At the beginning, variables $\mathsf{err}_1, \mathsf{err}_2$, err_3 and err_4 are initialized to 0 and random index i^* from $\{1, \ldots, Q_{\mathsf{gen}}\}$ is chosen.
- On a query to Corrupt with argument i, if $i = i^*$ set $\mathsf{err}_3 \leftarrow 1$.
- Let (m, R, σ) the purported forgery output by A.
  * If $[x]_2 \notin R$, then set $\mathsf{err}_1 = 1$.
  * If $i^* \neq (m-1)\mu + i$ for all $i \in [m]$, where μ is the index defined in π_G and π_H, or there is some $j \in [m]$ such that $[x_{i^*}]_2 = [x'_j]_2$, then set $\mathsf{err}_2 \leftarrow 1$.
  * If $[x'_1]_2$, the opening of commitment $[c'_1]_2$ from σ, is not equal to $[x_{i^*}]_2$, set $\mathsf{err}_4 \leftarrow 1$.

Game$_2$: This is game exactly as Game$_1$ except that, if err_1 is set to 1, Game$_2$ aborts.

Game$_{2,1}$: This game is exactly as Game$_1$ except that, if at the onset $\mathsf{err}_1 = 0$ or $\mathsf{err}_2 = 1$, Game$_{2,1}$ aborts.

Game$_{2,2}$: This game is exactly as Game$_{2,1}$ except that in the i^*th query to VKGen commitment $[a_{i^*}]_1$ is set to $\mathsf{Com}_{[\mathbf{U}]_1}(\beta_{i^*} = 1; r_{i^*})$, $r_{i^*} \leftarrow \mathbb{Z}_q$. Additionally, if err_3 is set to 1 abort.

Game$_{2,3}$: This game is exactly as Game$_{2,2}$ except that ck_1 and ck_2 are sampled from the perfectly binding distribution.

Game$_3$: This is game exactly as Game$_2$ except that, if err_3 or err_4 are set to 1, Game$_3$ aborts.

Game$_4$: This is game exactly as Game$_3$ except that, if err_3 is set to 1, Game$_4$ aborts.

Since in Game$_1$ variables $\mathsf{err}_1, \mathsf{err}_2$ and err_3 are just dummy variables, the only difference with Game$_0$ comes from ck'_2 distribution. Similarly, the only difference between Game$_{2,2}$ and Game$_{2,3}$ comes from ck_1 and ck_2 distribution. It follows that there an adversaries $\mathsf{B}_1, \mathsf{B}_2$ against SXDH such that $|\Pr[\mathsf{Game}_0 = 1] - \Pr[\mathsf{Game}_1 = 1]| \leq \mathbf{Adv}_{\mathrm{SXDH}}(\mathsf{B}_1)$ and $|\Pr[\mathsf{Game}_{2,2} = 1] - \Pr[\mathsf{Game}_{2,3} = 1]| \leq \mathbf{Adv}_{\mathrm{SXDH}}(\mathsf{B}_2)$.

Lemma 5.

$$\Pr[\mathsf{Game}_1 = 1] \leq \Pr[\mathsf{Game}_2 = 1] + Q_{\mathsf{gen}} \Pr[\mathsf{Game}_{2,1} = 1]$$

Proof.

$$\begin{aligned}
\Pr[\mathsf{Game}_1 = 1] &= \Pr[\mathsf{Game}_1 = 1 | \mathsf{err}_1 = 0] \Pr[\mathsf{err}_1 = 0] \\
&\quad + \Pr[\mathsf{Game}_1 = 1 | \mathsf{err}_1 = 1] \Pr[\mathsf{err}_1 = 1] \\
&\leq \Pr[\mathsf{Game}_2 = 1] + \Pr[\mathsf{Game}_1 = 1 | \mathsf{err}_1 = 1] \Pr[\mathsf{err}_1 = 1]
\end{aligned}$$

Now we proceed to bound $\Pr[\mathsf{Game}_1 = 1 | \mathsf{err}_1 = 1] \Pr[\mathsf{err}_1 = 1]$. It holds that

$$\begin{aligned}
\Pr[\mathsf{Game}_{2,1} = 1] &= \Pr[\mathsf{Game}_1 = 1, \mathsf{err}_1 = 1, \mathsf{err}_2 = 0] \\
&= \Pr[\mathsf{err}_2 = 0 | \mathsf{Game}_1 = 1, \mathsf{err}_1 = 1] \Pr[\mathsf{Game}_1 = 1, \mathsf{err}_1 = 1] \\
&\geq \frac{1}{Q_{\mathsf{gen}}} \Pr[\mathsf{Game}_1 = 1 | \mathsf{err}_1 = 1] \Pr[\mathsf{err}_1 = 1].
\end{aligned}$$

where the last inequality follows from the fact that $\mathrm{err}_1 = 1$ implies that $[x'_1]_2 \notin R$ and then $x'_i \neq x_{\mu,k}$ for all $k \in [m]$. Given that all entries of $\boldsymbol{x}_\mu$ must be different, there is least one $j \in [m]$ such that $x_{\mu,j} \neq x'_k$ for all $k \in [m]$. Since j^* is completely hidden to the adversary, it follows that $\Pr[\mathrm{err}_2 = 0 | \mathsf{Game}_1 = 1, \mathrm{err}_1 = 1] \geq \Pr[j^* = (m-1)\mu + j] = 1/Q_{\mathsf{gen}}$.

Lemma 6. $\Pr[\mathsf{Game}_{2,1} = 1] \leq Q_{\mathsf{gen}} \Pr[\mathsf{Game}_{2,2} = 1]$

Proof. Since ck_1 and ck_2 are perfectly hiding there is no information revealed about β through the extended verification keys or the signatures. Then, it holds that $\Pr[\mathsf{Game}_{2,2} = 1] = \Pr[\mathrm{err}_3 = 0 | \mathsf{Game}_{2,1} = 1] \Pr[\mathsf{Game}_{2,1} = 1]$ and $\Pr[\mathrm{err}_3 = 0 | \mathsf{Game}_{2,1} = 1]$ is the probability that the Q_{corr} calls to Corrupt do not abort. Since A is an eager adversary, the probability that i^* doesn't hit any of the Q_{corr} corrupted users is $(Q_{\mathsf{gen}} - Q_{\mathsf{corr}})/Q_{\mathsf{gen}} \geq 1/Q_{\mathsf{gen}}$ and then $\Pr[\mathsf{Game}_{2,2} = 1] \geq 1/Q_{\mathsf{gen}} \Pr[\mathsf{Game}_{2,1} = 1]$.

Lemma 7. $\Pr[\mathsf{Game}_{2,3} = 1] = 0$

Proof. Since ck_1, ck_2 and ck'_2 are perfectly binding, all Groth-Sahai proofs are perfectly sound. If π_{bits} and π_h are valid proofs, then $\boldsymbol{\beta}'$, the opening of $[\mathbf{A}']$, is a permutation of $\boldsymbol{\beta}_\mu$. Since $\mathrm{err}_1 = 1$ and $\mathrm{err}_2 = 0$, it holds that $x_{i^*} = x_{\mu,i^*_\mu}$, for some $i^*_\mu \in [m]$, and $x_{\mu,i^*} \neq x'_j$ for all j. Furthermore, since $\beta_{i^*} = \beta_{\mu,i^*_\mu} = 1$, then $\beta_{j^*} = 1$ for some unique $j^* \in [m]$.

Finally, equation $\sum_{i=1}^m \beta'_i x'_i = \sum_{i=1}^m \beta_{\mu,i} x_{\mu,i}$ becomes $x'_{j^*} = x_{\mu,i^*_\mu}$, and therefore can't be satisfied. We conclude that $\pi_{\mathsf{bits}}, \pi_h$, and π_g can't be valid proofs simultaneously and thus $\Pr[\mathsf{Game}_{2,3} = 1] = 0$.

Lemma 8.
$$\Pr[\mathsf{Game}_2 = 1] \leq Q_{\mathsf{gen}} \Pr[\mathsf{Game}_3 = 1].$$

Proof. It holds that

$$\Pr[\mathsf{Game}_3 = 1] = \Pr[\mathsf{Game}_3 = 1 | \mathrm{err}_3 = 0, \mathrm{err}_4 = 0] \Pr[\mathrm{err}_3 = 0, \mathrm{err}_4 = 0]$$
$$= \Pr[\mathsf{Game}_2 = 1 | \mathrm{err}_3 = 0, \mathrm{err}_4 = 0] \Pr[\mathrm{err}_3 = 0, \mathrm{err}_4 = 1]$$
$$= \Pr[\mathrm{err}_3 = 0, \mathrm{err}_4 = 0 | \mathsf{Game}_2 = 1] \Pr[\mathsf{Game}_2 = 1].$$

The probability that $\mathrm{err}_3 = 0$ and $\mathrm{err}_4 = 0$ given $\mathsf{Game}_3 = 1$ is the probability that the Q_{corr} calls to Corrupt do not abort and that $[x'_1]_2 = [x_{i^*}]_2$. Since A is an eager adversary, the probability that i^* doesn't hit any of the Q_{corr} corrupted users is $Q_{\mathsf{gen}} - Q_{\mathsf{corr}}/Q_{\mathsf{gen}}$. Similarly, when A outputs its purported forgery, the probability that $[x'_1]_2 = [x_{i^*}]_2$ is $1/(Q_{\mathsf{gen}} - Q_{\mathsf{corr}})$, since $[x'_1]_2 \in R$ (or otherwise Game_3 would have aborted). Therefore

$$\Pr[\mathrm{err}_3 = 0, \mathrm{err}_4 = 0 | \mathsf{Game}_2 = 1] = \frac{Q_{\mathsf{gen}} - Q_{\mathsf{corr}}}{Q_{\mathsf{gen}}} \frac{1}{Q_{\mathsf{gen}} - Q_{\mathsf{corr}}} = \frac{1}{Q_{\mathsf{gen}}}.$$

Lemma 9. *There exist adversaries* B_3 *and* B_4 *against the unforgeability of the one-time signature scheme and the weak unforgeability of the Boneh-Boyen signature scheme such that*

$$\Pr[\mathsf{Game}_3 = 1] \leq Q_{\mathsf{sig}} \mathbf{Adv}_{\mathsf{OT}}(\mathsf{B}_3) + \mathbf{Adv}_{\mathsf{BB}}(\mathsf{B}_4)$$

124   A. González

Proof. We construct adversaries B_3 and B_4 as follows.

B_3 receives $vk_{\mathsf{ot}}^\dagger$ and simulates Game_3 honestly but with the following differences. It chooses a random $j^* \in \{1, \ldots, Q_{\mathsf{sig}}\}$ and answer the j^* th query to $\mathsf{Sign}(i, m^\dagger, R^\dagger)$ honestly but computing $\sigma_{\mathsf{ot}}^\dagger$ querying on $(m^\dagger, R^\dagger)$ its oracle and setting $vk_{\mathsf{ot}}^\dagger$ as the corresponding one-time verification key. Finally, when A outputs its purported forgery $(m, R, (\sigma_{\mathsf{ot}}, vk_{\mathsf{ot}}, \ldots))$, B_3 outputs the corresponding one-time signature.

B_4 receives $[x]_2$ and simulates Game_3 honestly but with the following differences. Let $i := 0$. B_4 computes $(sk_{\mathsf{ot}}^i, vk_{\mathsf{ot}}^i) \leftarrow \mathsf{OT.KeyGen}(gk)$, for each $1 \le i \le Q_{\mathsf{sig}}$ and queries its signing oracle on $(vk_{\mathsf{ot}}^1, \ldots, vk_{\mathsf{ot}}^{Q_{\mathsf{sig}}})$ obtaining $[\sigma_1]_1, \ldots, [\sigma_{Q_{\mathsf{sig}}}]_1$. On the i^* th query of A to the key generation algorithm, B_4 it computes $[\boldsymbol{a}]_1 := \beta[\boldsymbol{u}_1]_1 + r[\boldsymbol{u}_2]$, for $\beta = 0$, $[\boldsymbol{c}]_2 = [x]_2\boldsymbol{w}_1 + s[\boldsymbol{w}_2]_2$ and $[\boldsymbol{d}]_1 = y[\boldsymbol{u}_1]_1 + t[\boldsymbol{u}_2]_1$ and $[\boldsymbol{\psi}]_2, [\boldsymbol{\omega}]_1$ as a Groth-Sahai proof for equation $\beta x = y$, for $\beta = y = 0$. The proof π_{bits} that $\boldsymbol{\beta} \in \{0,1\}$ is honestly computed and A outputs $\boldsymbol{vk} := ([x]_2, [\boldsymbol{a}]_1, [\boldsymbol{c}]_2, [\boldsymbol{d}]_1, [\boldsymbol{\psi}]_2, [\boldsymbol{\omega}]_1, \pi)$. When A queries the signing oracle on input (i^*, m, R), B_4 computes an honest signature but replaces vk_{ot} with vk_{ot}^i and $[\sigma]_1$ with $[\sigma_i]_2$, and then adds 1 to i. Finally, when A outputs its purported forgery $(m, R, (\sigma_{\mathsf{ot}}, vk_{\mathsf{ot}}, [\boldsymbol{f}]_2, [\mathbf{A}']_1, \ldots))$, it extracts $[\sigma]_1$ from $[\boldsymbol{f}]_1$ as its forgery for vk_{ot}.

Let E be the event where vk_{ot}, from the purported forgery of A, has been previously output by Sign. We have that

$$\Pr[\mathsf{Game}_4 = 1] \le \Pr[\mathsf{Game}_4 = 1|E] + \Pr[\mathsf{Game}_4 = 1|\neg E].$$

Since (m, R) has never been signed by a one-time signature and that, conditioned on E, the probability of $vk_{\mathsf{ot}} = vk_{\mathsf{ot}}^\dagger$ is $1/Q_{\mathsf{sig}}$, then

$$Q_{\mathsf{sig}}\mathbf{Adv}_{\mathsf{OT}}(B_4) \ge \Pr[\mathsf{Game}_4 = 1|E]$$

Finally, if $\neg E$ holds, then $[\sigma]_1$ is a forgery for vk_{ot} and thus

$$\mathbf{Adv}_{\mathsf{BB}}(B_4) \ge \Pr[\mathsf{Game}_4 = 1|\neg E].$$

Acknowledgments. We thank to the anonymous reviewers for the constructive feedback. It was very useful for simplifying the SXDH-based construction. We also thanks Carla Ràfols and Mojtaba Khalili for their comments on earlier versions of this work. This work was funded in part by the French ANR ALAMBIC project (ANR-16-CE39-0006).

References

1. Belenkiy, M., Camenisch, J., Chase, M., Kohlweiss, M., Lysyanskaya, A., Shacham, H.: Randomizable proofs and delegatable anonymous credentials. In: Halevi, S. (ed.) CRYPTO 2009. LNCS, vol. 5677, pp. 108–125. Springer, Heidelberg (2009). https://doi.org/10.1007/978-3-642-03356-8_7
2. Bender, A., Katz, J., Morselli, R.: Ring signatures: stronger definitions, and constructions without random oracles. In: Halevi, S., Rabin, T. (eds.) TCC 2006. LNCS, vol. 3876, pp. 60–79. Springer, Heidelberg (2006). https://doi.org/10.1007/11681878_4

3. Boneh, D., Boyen, X.: Short signatures without random oracles. In: Cachin, C., Camenisch, J.L. (eds.) EUROCRYPT 2004. LNCS, vol. 3027, pp. 56–73. Springer, Heidelberg (2004). https://doi.org/10.1007/978-3-540-24676-3_4
4. Bose, P., Das, D., Rangan, C.P.: Constant size ring signature without random oracle. In: Foo, E., Stebila, D. (eds.) ACISP 2015. LNCS, vol. 9144, pp. 230–247. Springer, Cham (2015). https://doi.org/10.1007/978-3-319-19962-7_14
5. Chandran, N., Groth, J., Sahai, A.: Ring signatures of sub-linear size without random oracles. In: Arge, L., Cachin, C., Jurdziński, T., Tarlecki, A. (eds.) ICALP 2007. LNCS, vol. 4596, pp. 423–434. Springer, Heidelberg (2007). https://doi.org/10.1007/978-3-540-73420-8_38
6. Chase, M., Lysyanskaya, A.: On signatures of knowledge. In: Dwork, C. (ed.) CRYPTO 2006. LNCS, vol. 4117, pp. 78–96. Springer, Heidelberg (2006). https://doi.org/10.1007/11818175_5
7. Chaum, D., van Heyst, E.: Group signatures. In: Davies, D.W. (ed.) EUROCRYPT 1991. LNCS, vol. 547, pp. 257–265. Springer, Heidelberg (1991). https://doi.org/10.1007/3-540-46416-6_22
8. Danezis, G., Fournet, C., Groth, J., Kohlweiss, M.: Square span programs with applications to succinct NIZK arguments. In: Sarkar, P., Iwata, T. (eds.) ASIACRYPT 2014, Part I. LNCS, vol. 8873, pp. 532–550. Springer, Heidelberg (2014). https://doi.org/10.1007/978-3-662-45611-8_28
9. Dodis, Y., Kiayias, A., Nicolosi, A., Shoup, V.: Anonymous identification in *Ad hoc* groups. In: Cachin, C., Camenisch, J.L. (eds.) EUROCRYPT 2004. LNCS, vol. 3027, pp. 609–626. Springer, Heidelberg (2004). https://doi.org/10.1007/978-3-540-24676-3_36
10. Galbraith, S., Paterson, K., Smart, N.: Pairings for cryptographers. Cryptology ePrint Archive, Report 2006/165 (2006). http://eprint.iacr.org/2006/165
11. Gennaro, R., Gentry, C., Parno, B., Raykova, M.: Quadratic span programs and succinct NIZKs without PCPs. In: Johansson, T., Nguyen, P.Q. (eds.) EUROCRYPT 2013. LNCS, vol. 7881, pp. 626–645. Springer, Heidelberg (2013). https://doi.org/10.1007/978-3-642-38348-9_37
12. Gentry, C., Wichs, D.: Separating succinct non-interactive arguments from all falsifiable assumptions. In: Fortnow, L., Vadhan, S.P. (eds.) 43rd ACM STOC, San Jose, CA, USA, 6–8 June 2011, pp. 99–108. ACM Press (2011)
13. Goldwasser, S., Kalai, Y.T.: On the (in)security of the Fiat-Shamir paradigm. In: 44th FOCS, Cambridge, MA, USA, 11–14 October 2003, pp. 102–115. IEEE Computer Society Press (2003)
14. González, A., Hevia, A., Ràfols, C.: QA-NIZK arguments in asymmetric groups: new tools and new constructions. In: Iwata, T., Cheon, J.H. (eds.) ASIACRYPT 2015, Part I. LNCS, vol. 9452, pp. 605–629. Springer, Heidelberg (2015). https://doi.org/10.1007/978-3-662-48797-6_25
15. González, A.: Shorter ring signatures from standard assumptions. Cryptology ePrint Archive, Report 2017/905 (2017). https://eprint.iacr.org/2017/905
16. Gritti, C., Susilo, W., Plantard, T.: Logarithmic size ring signatures without random oracles. IET Inf. Secur. **10**(1), 1–7 (2016)
17. Groth, J.: On the size of pairing-based non-interactive arguments. In: Fischlin, M., Coron, J.-S. (eds.) EUROCRYPT 2016, Part II. LNCS, vol. 9666, pp. 305–326. Springer, Heidelberg (2016). https://doi.org/10.1007/978-3-662-49896-5_11
18. Groth, J., Kohlweiss, M.: One-out-of-many proofs: or how to leak a secret and spend a coin. In: Oswald, E., Fischlin, M. (eds.) EUROCRYPT 2015, Part II. LNCS, vol. 9057, pp. 253–280. Springer, Heidelberg (2015). https://doi.org/10.1007/978-3-662-46803-6_9

126   A. González

19. Groth, J., Lu, S.: A non-interactive shuffle with pairing based verifiability. In: Kurosawa, K. (ed.) ASIACRYPT 2007. LNCS, vol. 4833, pp. 51–67. Springer, Heidelberg (2007). https://doi.org/10.1007/978-3-540-76900-2_4
20. Groth, J., Ostrovsky, R., Sahai, A.: Perfect non-interactive zero knowledge for NP. In: Vaudenay, S. (ed.) EUROCRYPT 2006. LNCS, vol. 4004, pp. 339–358. Springer, Heidelberg (2006). https://doi.org/10.1007/11761679_21
21. Groth, J., Sahai, A.: Efficient non-interactive proof systems for bilinear groups. In: Smart, N. (ed.) EUROCRYPT 2008. LNCS, vol. 4965, pp. 415–432. Springer, Heidelberg (2008). https://doi.org/10.1007/978-3-540-78967-3_24
22. Jutla, C.S., Roy, A.: Improved structure preserving signatures under standard bilinear assumptions. Cryptology ePrint Archive, Report 2017/025 (2017). http://eprint.iacr.org/2017/025
23. Libert, B., Ling, S., Nguyen, K., Wang, H.: Zero-knowledge arguments for lattice-based accumulators: logarithmic-size ring signatures and group signatures without trapdoors. In: Fischlin, M., Coron, J.-S. (eds.) EUROCRYPT 2016, Part II. LNCS, vol. 9666, pp. 1–31. Springer, Heidelberg (2016). https://doi.org/10.1007/978-3-662-49896-5_1
24. Malavolta, G., Schröder, D.: Efficient ring signatures in the standard model. In: Takagi, T., Peyrin, T. (eds.) ASIACRYPT 2017, Part II. LNCS, vol. 10625, pp. 128–157. Springer, Cham (2017). https://doi.org/10.1007/978-3-319-70697-9_5
25. Morillo, P., Ràfols, C., Villar, J.L.: The kernel matrix Diffie-Hellman assumption. In: Cheon, J.H., Takagi, T. (eds.) ASIACRYPT 2016, Part I. LNCS, vol. 10031, pp. 729–758. Springer, Heidelberg (2016). https://doi.org/10.1007/978-3-662-53887-6_27
26. Naor, M.: On cryptographic assumptions and challenges. In: Boneh, D. (ed.) CRYPTO 2003. LNCS, vol. 2729, pp. 96–109. Springer, Heidelberg (2003). https://doi.org/10.1007/978-3-540-45146-4_6
27. Ràfols, C.: Stretching Groth-Sahai: NIZK proofs of partial satisfiability. In: Dodis, Y., Nielsen, J.B. (eds.) TCC 2015, Part II. LNCS, vol. 9015, pp. 247–276. Springer, Heidelberg (2015). https://doi.org/10.1007/978-3-662-46497-7_10
28. Rivest, R.L., Shamir, A., Tauman, Y.: How to leak a secret. In: Boyd, C. (ed.) ASIACRYPT 2001. LNCS, vol. 2248, pp. 552–565. Springer, Heidelberg (2001). https://doi.org/10.1007/3-540-45682-1_32
29. Rogaway, P., Shrimpton, T.: Cryptographic hash-function basics: definitions, implications, and separations for preimage resistance, second-preimage resistance, and collision resistance. In: Roy, B.K., Meier, W. (eds.) FSE 2004. LNCS, vol. 3017, pp. 371–388. Springer, Heidelberg (2004). https://doi.org/10.1007/978-3-540-25937-4_24

Efficient Attribute-Based Signatures for Unbounded Arithmetic Branching Programs

Pratish Datta[1(✉)], Tatsuaki Okamoto[1], and Katsuyuki Takashima[2]

[1] NTT Secure Platform Laboratories, 3-9-11 Midori-cho,
Musashino-shi, Tokyo 180-8585, Japan
pratish.datta.yg@hco.ntt.co.jp, tatsuaki.okamoto@gmail.com
[2] Mitsubishi Electric, 5-1-1 Ofuna, Kamakura, Kanagawa 247-8501, Japan
Takashima.Katsuyuki@aj.MitsubishiElectric.co.jp

Abstract. This paper presents the *first attribute-based signature* (ABS) scheme in which the correspondence between signers and signatures is captured in an *arithmetic* model of computation. Specifically, we design a *fully* secure, i.e., *adaptively* unforgeable and *perfectly* signer-private ABS scheme for signing policies realizable by *arithmetic branching programs* (ABP), which are a *quite expressive* model of arithmetic computations. On a more positive note, the proposed scheme places *no bound* on the *size* and *input length* of the supported signing policy ABP's, and at the same time, supports the use of an input attribute for an *arbitrary* number of times inside a signing policy ABP, i.e., the so called *unbounded multi-use* of attributes. The size of our public parameters is *constant* with respect to the sizes of the signing attribute vectors and signing policies available in the system. The construction is built in (asymmetric) bilinear groups of prime order, and its unforgeability is derived in the standard model under (asymmetric version of) the *well-studied decisional linear* (DLIN) assumption coupled with the existence of standard *collision resistant hash functions*. Due to the use of the arithmetic model as opposed to the boolean one, our ABS scheme not only *excels significantly* over the existing state-of-the-art constructions in terms of *concrete efficiency*, but also achieves *improved applicability* in various practical scenarios. Our principal technical contributions are (a) extending and refining the techniques of Okamoto and Takashima [PKC 2011, PKC 2013], which were originally developed in the context of boolean span programs, to the arithmetic setting; and (b) innovating new ideas to allow unbounded multi-use of attributes inside ABP's, which themselves are of unbounded size and input length.

Keywords: Attribute-based signatures ·
Arithmetic branching programs · Arithmetic span programs ·
Concrete efficiency · Unbounded multi-use of attributes ·
Bilinear groups

© International Association for Cryptologic Research 2019
D. Lin and K. Sako (Eds.): PKC 2019, LNCS 11442, pp. 127–158, 2019.
https://doi.org/10.1007/978-3-030-17253-4_5

1   Introduction

Attribute-based signatures (ABS), introduced in the seminal work of Maji et al. [19], is an ambitious variant of digital signatures that simultaneously enforce fine-grained control over authentication rights and conceal the identity of signers. An ABS scheme is associated with a predicate family $\mathcal{R} = \{R(Y, \cdot) : \mathcal{X} \to \{0, 1\} \mid Y \in \mathcal{Y}\}$, where $\mathcal{X}$ is a universe of possible signing attributes and $\mathcal{Y}$ is a collection of admissible signing policies over the attributes of $\mathcal{X}$. A central authority holds a master signing key and publishes system public parameters. Using its master signing key, the authority can issue restricted signing keys to individual signers corresponding to the attributes $X \in \mathcal{X}$ possessed by them. Such a constrained signing key associated with some attribute $X \in \mathcal{X}$ allows a signer to sign messages under only those signing policies $Y \in \mathcal{Y}$ which are satisfied by X, i.e., for which $R(Y, X) = 1$. The signatures can be verified by any one using solely the public parameters.

In an ABS scheme, by verifying a signature on some message with respect to some claimed signing policy, a verifier gets convinced that the signature is indeed generated by someone holding some attributes satisfying the policy. In particular, generating a valid signature on any message under any signing policy is (computationally) infeasible for any group of colluding signers, none of whom individually possesses a signing attribute that satisfies the signing policy, by pooling their attributes together. This is the so called *unforgeability* property of an ABS scheme. The second property of an ABS scheme, which ensures that given a signature, it is impossible to trace the exact signer or signing attributes used to create it, is known as *signer privacy*. This notion of ABS is sometimes referred to as a *message-policy* ABS. Another flavor of this notion that interchanges the roles of signing attributes and signing policies is called a *key-policy* ABS. In addition to being an exciting cryptographic primitive in its own right, ABS has found countless important practical applications ranging from attribute-based messaging and attribute-based authentication to anonymous credential systems, trust negotiations, and leaking secrets (see [19–21,31] for more details). In this paper, we will deal with the message-policy variant since this variant is more natural and better suited in most of the aforementioned real-life applications of ABS.

Since their inception, ABS have been intensively studied in a long sequence of interesting works, and just like any other access-control primitive, a central theme of research in those works has been to expand the expressiveness of the allowable class of signing policies in view of implementing this delicate signature paradigm in scenarios where the relationship between the signing attributes and policies is more and more sophisticated. Starting with the early works [10,17–19,31], which can handle threshold signing policies, the class of admissible signing policies has been progressively enlarged to boolean formulas or span programs by Maji et al. [20], Okamoto and Takashima [22,23] as well as El Kaafarani et al. [5,6], and further to general circuits by Tang et al. [33], Sakai et al. [29], Tsabary [34], as well as El Kaafarani and Katsumata [7], based on various computational assumptions on bilinear groups and lattices, as well as in different security models such as random oracle model, generic group model, and standard model. Very recently, Datta et al. [4] and Sakai et al. [30] have constructed ABS schemes which can even realize Turing machines as signing policies. On the other hand, Bellare and Fuchsbauer [3] have put forward a versatile signature primitive termed as *policy-based signatures* (PBS) and have presented a generic construction of an ABS scheme from a PBS scheme. This generic construction, when instantiated with their proposed PBS scheme for general NP languages, results in an ABS scheme which can realize any NP relation as signing policy.

Two other important parameters determining the quality and applicability of ABS schemes are (a) supporting signing policies of unbounded polynomial size and input length, and (b) allowing the use of a signing attribute for a unbounded polynomial number of times inside a signing policy, i.e., the so called unbounded multi-use of attributes. Here, the term "unbounded" means not fixed by the public parameters. Out of the existing ABS schemes mentioned above, the only schemes which achieves both these parameters simultaneously and are somewhat practicable are the constructions due to Sakai et al. [29,30]. While Okamoto and Takashima were able to realize unbounded multi-use of attributes in an updated version of their ABS scheme [23], namely, [24], their scheme cannot handle signing policies of unbounded size and input length. On the other hand, the ABS scheme of Datta et al. [4] features both the above properties, but are based on heavy-duty cryptographic tools such as indistinguishability obfuscation.

From the above review of the available ABS schemes, it is evident that research in the field of ABS has already reached the pinnacle in terms of expressiveness and unboundedness of the supported signing policies, as well as in terms of accommodating unbounded multi-use of attributes. Despite of this massive progress, one significant limitation that still persists in the current state of the art in this area is that all the existing ABS constructions consider the relationship between the signing attributes and policies only in some *boolean* model of computation, i.e., in those schemes the signing attributes are treated as bit strings and the policies are defined by sets of boolean operations. This raises the following natural question:

Can we construct an ABS scheme which captures the relationship between the signing attributes and policies in some arithmetic model of computation, while at the same time, supports signing policies having unbounded size and input length, as well as unbounded multi-use of attributes?

In an arithmetic-model-based ABS scheme, signing attributes are considered to be elements of some finite field $\mathbb{F}_q$, and signing policies are represented by collections of field operations, i.e., additions and multiplications over the field $\mathbb{F}_q$. The above question is not only intriguing from a theoretical perspective as the arithmetic model is a more structured one compared to its boolean counterpart, it is also of a high significance from several practical view points. Most importantly, since arithmetic computations arise in many real-life scenarios, this question has a natural motivation when the concrete efficiency of most of the applications of ABS discussed above is considered. For instance, note that it is possible to capture any arithmetic relationships between the signing attributes and policies by employing the state-of-the-art ABS schemes of Sakai et al. for general circuits and Turing machines [29,30] by representing an arithmetic computation by an equivalent boolean computation that replaces each field operation by a corresponding boolean sub-computation. Given the bit representation of the signing attributes, this approach can be used to simulate any arithmetic relation with an overhead which depends on the boolean complexity of the field operations. While providing reasonable asymptotic efficiency in theory (e.g., via fast integer multiplication techniques [8]), the concrete overhead of this approach is enormous. Moreover, scenarios may arise where one does not have access to the bits of the signing attributes and must treat them as atomic field elements. Note that in view of similar efficiency and applicability issues with boolean computations, arithmetic variants of various important cryptographic primitives have already been considered in the last few years. Examples include arithmetic garbled circuits [2], arithmetic multi-party computations [15], verifiable arithmetic computations [28], and so on. An even more fascinating aspect of the above question is to simultaneously support unbounded signing policies and unbounded multi-use of attributes in the arithmetic setting. These properties are especially significant for making the scheme resilient to potential usage situations which may arise after the scheme is setup. It can be readily inferred from the scarcity of existing ABS schemes supporting unbounded signing policies and unbounded multi-use of attributes simultaneously, even in the boolean setting, that achieving both these properties at the same time is a rather challenging task in any computational model.

Our Contribution

In this paper, we provide an *affirmative* answer to the above important question. For the *first* time in the literature, we design an ABS scheme where the relationship between the signing attributes and policies are considered in an *arithmetic* model of computation. More specifically, we construct an ABS scheme in which signing attributes are represented as elements of a finite field $\mathbb{F}_q$ and the signing policies are expressed as *arithmetic branching programs* (ABP) [11,12] of *unbounded* polynomial *size* and *input length* over $\mathbb{F}_q$. While not capable of capturing most general relations like arbitrary circuits or Turing machines, ABP's are a *quite powerful* model for realizing a wide range of relations that arise in practice, namely, the relations which can be expressed as polynomials over some finite field. In particular, note that there is a linear-time algorithm that can convert any Boolean formula, Boolean branching program, or arithmetic formula to an ABP only with a constant blow-up in the representation size. Thus, in terms of expressiveness of supported signing policies, our ABS scheme subsumes all the existing ABS schemes except those for general circuits or Turing machines. On a more positive note, we place *no restriction* on the *number of times* an attribute can be used inside the description of a signing policy ABP.

The proposed scheme enjoys *perfect* signer privacy and unforgeability against adversaries which are allowed to make an *arbitrary* polynomial number of signing key and signature queries *adaptively*. Our scheme is built in asymmetric bilinear groups of prime order, and its unforgeability is derived under the *simultaneous external decisional linear* (SXDLIN) assumption [1], which is the asymmetric version of and in fact equivalent to the *well-studied decisional linear* (DLIN) assumption, coupled with the existence of standard *collision resistant hash functions*. Observe that asymmetric bilinear groups of prime order are now considered to be both faster and more secure in the cryptographic community following the recent progress of analysing bilinear groups of composite order and symmetric bilinear groups instantiated with elliptic curves of small characteristics.

While our ABS construction is less expressive compared to the state-of-the-art schemes of Sakai et al. [29,30], due to the use of the arithmetic model as opposed to the boolean one, our scheme *outperforms* those constructions by a *large margin* in terms of *concrete efficiency*. In fact, as we demonstrate in Table 1 and explain in Remark 3.1, even for a very simple signing policy such as an equality test over some finite field $\mathbb{F}_q$, where q is a 128-bit prime integer, our scheme can give more than 136 times better results compared to the one of [29], which is also built in asymmetric prime-order bilinear group setting under the symmetric external Diffie-Hellman (SXDH) assumption. Hence, it is evident that our scheme is a far more advantageous choice in most real-life applications of ABS, which often do not require the most general forms of signing policies but do require high performance.

Our ABS construction is developed *directly* from the scratch. On the technical side, our contribution is two fold: Firstly, we extend and refine the ABS construction techniques devised by Okamoto and Takashima [22,23] in the context of boolean formulas to the arithmetic setting. Secondly and more interestingly, we develop new ideas to support unbounded multi-use of attributes inside arithmetic signing policies, which themselves can be of an arbitrary size and input length.

Table 1. Comparison of concrete efficiency for 128-bit prime q

Schemes	Computational assumptions	Signature size	Pairings needed in verification
[29]	SXDH	At least $4102\,|g|$	At least 4102
Ours	SXDLIN	$26\,|g|$	30

The values presented in this table is for the signing policy ABP $f : \mathbb{F}_q \rightarrow \mathbb{F}_q$ defined by $f(x_1) = x_1 - a_1$, where a_1 is a constant belonging to $\mathbb{F}_q$.

In this table, $|g|$ represents the size of a group element.

Overview of Our Techniques

In order to design our ABS scheme for ABP's, we start with the high level approach adopted by Okamoto and Takashima [22,23]. At the top level of strategy, this approach considers an extension of the Naor's paradigm, which was originally proposed for converting an identity-based encryption (IBE) scheme to a digital signature scheme. The idea is to build a message-policy ABS scheme by augmenting a ciphertext-policy attribute-based encryption (ABE) scheme [25,35].

Just like a message-policy ABS scheme, a ciphertext-policy ABE scheme has an associated predicate family $\mathcal{R} = \{R(Y, \cdot) : \mathcal{X} \to \{0, 1\} \mid Y \in \mathcal{Y}\}$, where $\mathcal{X}$ and $\mathcal{Y}$ comprise respectively of the admissible decryption attributes and policies. A central authority holds a master secret key and publishes public system parameters. Anyone can encrypt a message, which is also referred to as a payload, with respect to any decryption policy $Y \in \mathcal{Y}$ using solely the public parameters. A decrypter may obtain a restricted decryption key from the authority corresponding to the attributes $X \in \mathcal{X}$ it possesses. Using such a restricted decryption key for $X \in \mathcal{X}$ the decrypter can recover the payload from only those ciphertexts which are generated with respect to a policy $Y \in \mathcal{Y}$ such that $R(Y, X) = 1$. In particular, it is (computationally) infeasible to decrypt a ciphertext generated with respect to some decryption policy $Y \in \mathcal{Y}$ for any collection of colluding decrypters, none of whom individually possesses an attribute that satisfies Y, by pooling their attributes together. An ABE ciphertext contains the associated decryption policy in the clear, and hence this security property of an ABE scheme is referred to as *payload hiding*.

Roughly speaking, in the approach of Okamoto and Takashima [22,23], a signing key for some signing attribute $X \in \mathcal{X}$ in the ABS scheme corresponds to a decryption key for X in the underlying ABE scheme. On the other hand, a signature on some message MSG under some claimed signing policy $Y \in \mathcal{Y}$ is verified by generating a verification-text that corresponds to a ciphertext of MSG under Y in the underlying ABE scheme. The most challenging part of this approach is that no straightforward counterpart of a signature in ABS exists in ABE, and moreover, the privacy property of signatures, which is a vital requirement of an ABS scheme has no corresponding notion in ABE. In order to tackle these issues, Okamoto and Takashima [22,23] devised a novel technique, which they termed as "rerandomization with specialized delegation", where a signature in the ABS scheme generated with respect to some signing policy Y using a signing key for some attribute X can be interpreted to be a random ABE decryption key specialized to decrypt only those ABE ciphertexts which have Y as the associated decryption policy. As for the security of the resulting ABS scheme, the idea is to reduce the unforgeability of the ABS scheme to the payload-hiding security of the underlying ABE scheme. On the other hand, the signer privacy is ensured by the careful rerandomized delegation procedure employed in the generation of signatures. While this high level description of the approach may sound quite simple, the actual realization, however, is quite delicate and involves many subtle aspects. Okamoto and Takashima [22,23] addressed those technical huddles in the context of boolean span programs by using various additional ideas.

We first explain how we adopt the above high level construction methodology to the context of ABP's, which is a rather non-trivial task. In order to design our scheme, we utilize the machineries of the *dual pairing vector spaces* (DPVS) [25,27]. A highly powerful feature of DPVS is that one can completely or partially hide a linear subspace of the whole vector space by concealing the basis of that subspace or the basis of its dual subspace respectively from the public parameters. In DPVS-based constructions, a collection of pairs of mutually dual vector spaces $\{\mathbb{V}_\imath, \mathbb{V}_\imath^*\}_{\imath \in [N]}$ along with a bilinear pairing $e : \mathbb{V}_\imath \times \mathbb{V}_\imath^* \to \mathbb{G}_T$ for all $\imath \in [N]$, constructed from a standard bilinear group $\mathsf{params}_{\mathbb{G}} = (q, \mathbb{G}_1, \mathbb{G}_2, \mathbb{G}_T, g_1, g_2, e)$ of prime order q is used. Typically, for all $\imath \in [N]$, a pair of dual orthonormal bases $(\mathbb{B}_\imath, \mathbb{B}_\imath^*)$ of $(\mathbb{V}_\imath, \mathbb{V}_\imath^*)$ is generated using a secret random invertible linear transformation $\boldsymbol{B}^{(\imath)}$ over $\mathbb{F}_q$ during setup, and portions of $(\mathbb{B}_\imath, \mathbb{B}_\imath^*)$, say $(\widehat{\mathbb{B}}_\imath, \widehat{\mathbb{B}}_\imath^*)$ for $\imath \in [N]$ is used as the public parameters. Thus, the remaining portions of the bases $(\mathbb{B}_\imath \backslash \widehat{\mathbb{B}}_\imath, \mathbb{B}_\imath^* \backslash \widehat{\mathbb{B}}_\imath^*)$ for $\imath \in [N]$ remain hidden from the outside world. This provides a strong framework for various kinds of information-theoretic tricks in the public-key setting by exploiting various nice properties of linear transformations.

In order to extend the techniques of Okamoto and Takashima [22,23] to the setting of ABP's, we first look for a representation of ABP's using some span program like structure, which supports "linear reconstruction". The linear reconstruction property is important for our scheme since we need to reconstruct some secrets in the exponents of group elements. We observe that Ishai and Wee [13] have devised a polynomial-time algorithm that given an ABP f, outputs an *arithmetic span program* (ASP) $\mathbb{S} = (\mathbb{U}, \rho)$ such that for any $\vec{x} \in \mathbb{F}_q^n$, $f(\vec{x}) = 0 \iff \mathbb{S}$ accepts $\vec{x}$. ASP's are the arithmetic counterpart of boolean span programs. An ASP $\mathbb{S}$ is described as a pair $\mathbb{S} = (\mathbb{U}, \rho)$, where $\mathbb{U}$ is a set of pairs of vectors $\mathbb{U} = \{(\vec{y}^{(j)}, \vec{z}^{(j)})\}_{j \in [m]} \subset (\mathbb{F}_q^\ell)^2$ for some $\ell, m \in \mathbb{N}$ and ρ is a mapping $\rho : [m] \to [n]$. $\mathbb{S}$ accepts $\vec{x} \in \mathbb{F}_q^n \iff \vec{e}^{(\ell, \ell)} \in \mathrm{SPAN}\langle x_{\rho(j)} \vec{y}^{(j)} + \vec{z}^{(j)} \mid j \in [m]\rangle$,

where $\vec{e}^{(\ell, \ell)} = (\overbrace{0, \ldots, 0}^{\ell-1}, 1)$ and SPAN refers to the standard linear span of vectors. With this representation at hand, we proceed to extending the ABS scheme of Okamoto and Takashima [22,23] to the ABP setting.

The most important difficulty we face here is with the application of the rerandomization with special delegation technique to generate the signatures due to a fundamental difference in the structures of the boolean and arithmetic span programs. Recall that a boolean span program over n boolean variables is represented as $\mathbb{P} = (\boldsymbol{P} \in \mathbb{F}_q^{m \times \ell}, \rho : [m] \to [n])$, and $\mathbb{P}$ accepts a boolean string $\vec{x} \in \mathbb{F}_2^n \iff \vec{e}^{(\ell, \ell)} \in \mathrm{SPAN}\langle \vec{p}^{(j)} \mid j \in [m] \wedge x_{\rho(j)} = 1\rangle$, where $\vec{p}^{(j)} \in \mathbb{F}_q^\ell$ is the jth row vector of $\boldsymbol{P}$. This means while evaluating a boolean span program on some input, the input only determines which vectors are to be included in the linear span and does not affect the description of the included vectors as such. Roughly speaking, in the ABS construction of [22,23], the randomized special delegation is applied by masking the actual coefficients $(\Omega_j)_{j \in [m]} \in \mathbb{F}_q^m$ of the linear span of the vectors $\{\vec{p}^{(j)}\}_{j \in [m]}$ of a signing policy $\mathbb{P} = (\boldsymbol{P} \in \mathbb{F}_q^{m \times \ell}, \rho)$ resulting in the vector $\vec{e}^{(\ell, \ell)}$ when $\mathbb{P}$ accepts some boolean signing attribute string $\vec{x} \in \mathbb{F}_2^n$, with the coefficients $(\Omega_j')_{j \in [m]} \in \mathbb{F}_q^m$ of some random linear combination of the vectors $\{\vec{p}^{(j)}\}_{j \in [m]}$ that results in the zero vector $\vec{0}^\ell$. More precisely, while generating a signature under $\mathbb{P} = (\boldsymbol{P}, \rho)$ using a secret key for $\vec{x} \in \mathbb{F}_2^n$, one computes $\Omega_j + \Omega_j'$ for all $j \in [m]$. This rerandomization works for ensuring signer privacy, i.e., for erasing the information of the specific signing attribute string $\vec{x} \in \mathbb{F}_2^n$ from the signature for boolean span programs because seeing the rerandomized coefficients $(\Omega_j + \Omega_j')_{j \in [m]}$, one cannot decide which Ω_j's were 0 in the real linear span, and hence the information of the actual boolean attribute string $\vec{x} \in \mathbb{F}_2^n$ is completely erased via this rerandomization.

This rerandomization technique is, however, no longer sufficient in case of ASP's. This is because, while evaluating an ASP $\mathbb{S} = (\mathbb{U} = \{(\vec{y}^{(j)}, \vec{z}^{(j)})\}_{j \in [m]} \subset (\mathbb{F}_q^\ell)^2, \rho : [m] \rightarrow [n])$ on some input vector $\vec{x} \in \mathbb{F}_q^n$, the description of the vectors, whose linear span needs to be considered, namely, the vectors $\{x_{\rho(j)} \vec{y}^{(j)} + \vec{z}^{(j)}\}_{j \in [m]}$ itself depends on the specific input vector $\vec{x} \in \mathbb{F}_q^n$ used. Therefore, even if the above randomized masking is applied, the result would still leak information of the specific vector $\vec{x}$ used.

In order to overcome this issue, we apply a more clever rerandomization. Roughly speaking, we randomize not only the linear-combination-coefficients, but also the input values $\{x_{\rho(j)}\}_{j \in [m]}$. We consider a random linear combination of the vectors $\{\vec{y}^{(j)}, \vec{z}^{(j)}\}_{j \in [m]}$ that leads to the zero vector $\vec{0}^\ell$, i.e., we compute random $((\Omega_j')_{j \in [m]}, (\Omega_j'')_{j \in [m]})$ such that $\sum_{j \in [m]} (\Omega_j' \vec{y}^{(j)} + \Omega_j'' \vec{z}^{(j)}) = \vec{0}^\ell$. Then, we use the scalars $(\Omega_j')_{j \in [m]}$ to mask $(\Omega_j x_{\rho(j)})_{j \in [m]}$ and $(\Omega_j'')_{j \in [m]}$ to mask $(\Omega_j)_{j \in [m]}$, where $(\Omega_j)_{j \in [m]}$ are the coefficients of the vectors $\{x_{\rho(j)} \vec{y}^{(j)} + \vec{z}^{(j)}\}_{j \in [m]}$ in the linear combination resulting in $\vec{e}^{(\ell, \ell)}$. More precisely, while generating a signature under some ASP $\mathbb{S}$ using a signing key for $\vec{x} \in \mathbb{F}_q^n$, we compute $\Omega_j x_{\rho(j)} + \Omega_j'$ and $\Omega_j + \Omega_j''$ for all $j \in [m]$. Observe that this rerandomization not only erases the actual values of the linear combination coefficients $(\Omega_j)_{j \in [m]}$ but also the information of the actual input $\vec{x}$ for which the linear combination is evaluated.

Now, note that unlike the schemes of [22,23], in which the size and input length of the supported span programs are bounded by the public parameters, our goal is to support ABP's, and hence ASP's by the above discussion, of unbounded size and input length. For this, we start by extending the techniques called "indexing" and "consistent randomness amplification", developed by Okamoto and Takashima in [26] in the context of ABE for boolean span programs, to our setting of ASP's. Roughly speaking, in the ABS constructions of [22,23], once parts of a set of pairs of dual orthonormal bases $\{\widehat{\mathbb{B}}_\iota, \widehat{\mathbb{B}}_\iota^*\}_{\iota \in [n]}$ are published as the public parameters, the input length of the signing policy span programs becomes fixed to n. The proof of adaptive unforgeability of the scheme follows the so called "dual system encryption" methodology [36], and crucially makes use of certain information-theoretic arguments. The randomness of the secret linear transformations $\{\boldsymbol{B}^{(\iota)}\}_{\iota \in [n]}$ used to generate the bases $\{\mathbb{B}_\iota, \mathbb{B}_\iota^*\}_{\iota \in [n]}$, whose parts are included in the public parameters, acts as the source of entropy for those information-theoretic arguments.

In contrast, in the unbounded setting, the input length of the signing policy span programs are not fixed by the public parameters. In particular, in our unbounded ABS scheme, the public parameters would only consist of a constant number of pairs of dual orthonormal bases. Thus, the randomness contained in the public parameters (which is just a constant amount with respect to the length of the input attribute vectors n) is clearly insufficient for the dual system encryption arguments on adaptive security. To supply the additional randomness required for the security reduction, we adopt the indexing technique of [26], and for all $\iota \in [n]$, embed two dimensional prefix vectors $\sigma_\iota(1, \iota)$ and $\mu_j(\iota, -1)$ within the components corresponding to the ιth attribute in signing keys and verification-texts respectively, where σ_ι and μ_j are freshly sampled random elements of $\mathbb{F}_q$. However, this method of supplying linear-in-n amount of additional randomness is still not sufficient. This is because, for the application of the dual system encryption methodology, such randomness introduced by the indexing technique needs to be expanded to the hidden subspaces of signing keys and verification-texts, and the distribution of the expanded randomness should also be adjusted to the conditions imposed on the queries of the adversary in the unforgeability experiment. To resolve the problem, we attempt to employ the consistent randomness amplification technique similar to [26].

However, recall that our objective is not limited to only supporting signing policies of unbounded size and input length. We additionally want to allow unbounded multi-use of attributes inside the signing policies. As we explain below, the consistent randomness amplification technique of Okamoto and Takashima [26] does not suffice for achieving both these goals simultaneously. Therefore, we need to innovate new technical ideas to accomplish our target. In terms of technicality, this is the most sophisticated part of this paper. In fact, the techniques we devise in this segment are pretty much general, and we strongly believe they will find more applications in various other DPVS-based construction in the future.

Roughly speaking, the single use restriction in DPVS-based adaptively secure constructions of attribute-based primitives arise from the use of a crucial information-theoretic lemma, the so called "pairwise independence lemma" (Lemma 3 in [25]), while employing the dual system encryption paradigm in the security proofs. This technique requires a one-to-one correspondence between a pair of a key part and a verification-text or ciphertext part through the map ρ of the policy span program considered. However, in the multi-use scenario, one key part corresponds to multiple verification-text or ciphertext parts. Even when a generalized version of the pairwise independence lemma [25] is used, the maximum number of times an attribute can be used inside a policy span program remains bounded by the public parameters. While some attempts were made to mitigate the issue in the context of ABE [16,32], those were only partially successful.

On the other hand, Okamoto and Takashima successfully resolved the multi-use issue in the context of ABS in an updated version of [23], namely, [24] by introducing a new technique, which they termed as "one-dimensional localization of inner product values". The main idea of this technique is to embed a specific inner product value for an unbounded (with respect to the public parameters) number of times in a certain one-dimension of the hidden subspace of a signing key or verification-text, while erasing all informations of the inner product value from all the remaining dimensions of the hidden subspace. This technique is applied in two steps. First a "special linear transformation" step is applied over the hidden segments of a signing key and a verification-text. This step localizes the inner product values in certain one-dimension of the hidden subspace. But, some informations of the inner product values still remain in the other dimensions of the hidden subspace. To completely remove those informations, random values are "injected" into those dimensions of the hidden subspace. This second step is executed via a computational transition based on the underlying computational assumption, and thus is not problematic to directly extend to the unbounded setting. However, the first step, i.e., the special linear transformation step is information theoretic, and crucially relies on the secret randomness used to generate the public parameters. Since the public parameters only uses a constant amount of secret randomness in the unbounded setting, such an information-theoretic transition cannot be applied.

The most intuitive way-out to the above issue is to use the indexing and consistent randomness amplification techniques of [26] to supply the additional randomness required for the transition just as it is used to resolve similar issues in extending the dual system encryption proof technique to the unbounded setting. Unfortunately, the consistent randomness amplification technique of [26] is only capable of computationally simulating the application of a *random* linear transformation to the hidden segment of a key component and the corresponding segment of a verification-text component. Such a random linear transformation suffices for the application of the pairwise independence lemma to complete a security proof based on the dual system encryption paradigm. However, the one-dimensional localization technique requires the application of certain *specific* linear transformations over the hidden segments of a signing key and a verification-text that crucially depend on the associated signing attribute vector of the signing key being considered.

To resolve this issue, we devise a more sophisticated technique. Very roughly, we first computationally simulate the effect of random linear transformations over the hidden subspaces on the verification-text side. This step corresponds to the transition between the hybrid experiments $\mathsf{Hyb}_{0'}$ and Hyb_1 in the proof of unforgeability of our ABS construction (proof of Theorem 4.2). Next, we computationally amplify the randomness provided by the two-dimensional prefix vectors to the hidden subspaces on the signing key side. This is the transition from $\mathsf{Hyb}_{2\text{-}(\chi-1)\text{-}9}$ to $\mathsf{Hyb}_{2\text{-}\chi\text{-}1}$ in the unforgeability proof. After this step, we computationally alter the random linear transformations to specific ones on the verification-text side. This step is executed while moving from $\mathsf{Hyb}_{2\text{-}\chi\text{-}1}$ to $\mathsf{Hyb}_{2\text{-}\chi\text{-}2}$ in the proof of unforgeability. Finally, we computationally adjust the randomness expanded to the hidden segments on the signing key side to match the specific linear transformations to be applied on that side. This transformation is achieved via the transition between $\mathsf{Hyb}_{2\text{-}\chi\text{-}2}$ and $\mathsf{Hyb}_{2\text{-}\chi\text{-}3}$ in our unforgeability proof. We stress that the above explanation of our highly involved techniques is merely a bird's eye-view. For a comprehensive understanding of our techniques please refer to our detail security proof presented in Sect. 4.

2 Preliminaries

In this section we present the backgrounds required for the rest of this paper.

2.1 Notations

Let $\lambda \in \mathbb{N}$ denotes the security parameter and 1^λ be its unary encoding. Let $\mathbb{F}_q$ for any prime $q \in \mathbb{N}$ denotes the finite field of integers modulo q. For $d \in \mathbb{N}$ and $c \in \mathbb{N} \cup \{0\}$ (with $c < d$), we let $[d] = \{1, \ldots, d\}$ and $[c, d] = \{c, \ldots, d\}$. For any set Z, $z \xleftarrow{\mathsf{U}} Z$ represents the process of uniformly sampling an element z from the set Z, and $\sharp Z$ signifies the size or cardinality of the set Z. For a probabilistic algorithm $\mathcal{P}$, we denote by $\Pi \xleftarrow{\mathsf{R}} \mathcal{P}(\Theta)$ the process of sampling Π from the output distribution of $\mathcal{P}$ with a uniform random tape on input Θ. Similarly, for any deterministic algorithm $\mathcal{D}$, we write $\Pi = \mathcal{D}(\Theta)$ to denote the output of $\mathcal{D}$ on input Θ. We use the abbreviation PPT to mean probabilistic polynomial-time. We assume that all the algorithms are given the unary representation 1^λ of the security parameter λ as input, and will not write 1^λ explicitly as input of the algorithms when it is clear from the context. For any finite field $\mathbb{F}_q$ and $d \in \mathbb{N}$, let $\vec{v}$ denote the (row) vector $(v_1, \ldots, v_d) \in \mathbb{F}_q^d$, where $v_i \in \mathbb{F}_q$ for all $i \in [d]$. The all zero vector in $\mathbb{F}_q^d$ will be denoted by $\vec{0}^d$, while the canonical basis vectors in $\mathbb{F}_q^d$ will be represented by $\vec{e}^{(d,i)} = (\overbrace{0, \ldots, 0}^{i-1}, 1, \overbrace{0, \ldots, 0}^{d-i})$ for $i \in [d]$. For any two vectors $\vec{v}, \vec{w} \in \mathbb{F}_q^d$, $\vec{v} \cdot \vec{w}$ stands for the inner product of the vectors $\vec{v}$ and $\vec{w}$, i.e., $\vec{v} \cdot \vec{w} = \sum_{i \in [d]} v_i w_i \in \mathbb{F}_q$. For any $s \in \mathbb{N}$ and any collection of s vectors $\{\vec{v}^{(i)}\}_{i \in [s]} \subset \mathbb{F}_q^d$, we denote by $\mathrm{SPAN}\langle \vec{v}^{(i)} \mid i \in [s] \rangle$ the subspace of $\mathbb{F}_q^d$ spanned by $\{\vec{v}^{(i)}\}_{i \in [s]}$. For any multiplicative group $\mathbb{G}$, let $\boldsymbol{v}$ represents a d-dimensional (row) vector of group elements, i.e., $\boldsymbol{v} = (g^{v_1}, \ldots, g^{v_d}) \in \mathbb{G}^d$ for some $d \in \mathbb{N}$, where $\vec{v} = (v_1, \ldots, v_d) \in \mathbb{F}_q^d$. We use $\boldsymbol{M} = (m_{k,i})$ to represent a $d \times r$ matrix for some $d, r \in \mathbb{N}$ with entries $m_{k,i} \in \mathbb{F}_q$. By $\boldsymbol{M}^\top$ we will signify the transpose of the matrix $\boldsymbol{M}$ and by $\det(\boldsymbol{M})$ the determinant of the matrix $\boldsymbol{M}$. Let $\mathsf{GL}(d, \mathbb{F}_q)$ denote the set of all $d \times d$ invertible matrices over $\mathbb{F}_q$. A function $\mathsf{negl} : \mathbb{N} \to \mathbb{R}^+$ is said to be *negligible* if for every $c \in \mathbb{N}$, there exists $T \in \mathbb{N}$ such that for all $\lambda \in \mathbb{N}$ with $\lambda > T$, $|\mathsf{negl}(\lambda)| < 1/\lambda^c$.

2.2 Arithmetic Branching Programs and Arithmetic Span Programs

Here we formally define the notions of arithmetic branching programs (ABP) and arithmetic span programs (ASP), and explain the connection between them. These computational models will be used to represent the signing policies in our ABS construction.

Definition 2.1 (Arithmetic Branching Programs: ABP [11,12]**):** A *branching program* (BP) Γ is defined by a 5-tuple $\Gamma = (V, E, \text{V}_0, \text{V}_1, \phi)$, where (V, E) is a directed acyclic graph, $\text{V}_0, \text{V}_1 \in V$ are two special vertices called the source and the sink respectively, and ϕ is a labeling function for the edges in E. An *arithmetic branching program* (ABP) Γ over a finite field $\mathbb{F}_q$ computes a function $f : \mathbb{F}_q^n \to \mathbb{F}_q$ for some $n \in \mathbb{N}$. In this case, the labeling function ϕ assigns to each edge in E either a degree one polynomial function in one of the input variables with coefficients in $\mathbb{F}_q$ or a constant in $\mathbb{F}_q$. Let $\wp$ be the set of all V_0-V_1 paths in Γ. The output of the function f computed by the ABP Γ on some input $\vec{x} = (x_1, \ldots, x_n) \in \mathbb{F}_q^n$ is defined as $f(\vec{x}) = \sum\limits_{P \in \wp} \left[\prod\limits_{\text{E} \in P} \phi(\text{E})|_{\vec{x}} \right]$, where for any $\text{E} \in E$, $\phi(\text{E})|_{\vec{x}}$ represents the evaluation of the function $\phi(\text{E})$ at $\vec{x}$. We refer to $\sharp V + \sharp E$ as the size of the ABP Γ.

Ishai and Kushilevitz [11,12] showed how to relate the computation performed by an ABP to the computation of the determinant of a matrix.

Lemma 2.1 ([11]): *Given an ABP $\Gamma = (V, E, \text{V}_0, \text{V}_1, \phi)$ computing a function $f : \mathbb{F}_q^n \to \mathbb{F}_q$, we can efficiently and deterministically compute a function $\boldsymbol{L}$ mapping an input $\vec{x} \in \mathbb{F}_q^n$ to a $(\sharp V - 1) \times (\sharp V - 1)$ matrix $\boldsymbol{L}(\vec{x})$ over $\mathbb{F}_q$ such that the following holds:*

- $\det(\boldsymbol{L}(\vec{x})) = f(\vec{x})$.
- *Each entry of $\boldsymbol{L}(\vec{x})$ is either a degree one polynomial in a single input variable x_i $(i \in [n])$ with coefficients in $\mathbb{F}_q$ or a constant in $\mathbb{F}_q$.*
- *$\boldsymbol{L}(\vec{x})$ contains only -1's in the subdiagonal, i.e., the diagonal just below the main diagonal, and 0's below the subdiagonal.*

Specifically, $\boldsymbol{L}$ is obtained by removing the column corresponding to V_0 and the row corresponding to V_1 in the matrix $\boldsymbol{A}_\Gamma - \boldsymbol{I}$, where $\boldsymbol{A}_\Gamma$ is the adjacency matrix for Γ and $\boldsymbol{I}$ is the identity matrix of the same size as $\boldsymbol{A}_\Gamma$.

Note that there is a linear-time algorithm that converts any Boolean formula, Boolean branching program, or arithmetic formula to an ABP with a constant blow-up in the representation size. Thus, ABP's can be viewed as a stronger computational model than all the others mentioned above.

Definition 2.2 (Arithmetic Span Programs: ASP [13,14]**):** An *arithmetic span program* (ASP) $\mathbb{S} = (\mathbb{U}, \rho)$ over n variables is a collection of pairs of vectors $\mathbb{U} = \{(\vec{y}^{(j)}, \vec{z}^{(j)})\}_{j \in [m]}$ for some $m \in \mathbb{N}$, where for all $j \in [m]$, $(\vec{y}^{(j)}, \vec{z}^{(j)}) \in (\mathbb{F}_q^\ell)^2$ for some $\ell \in \mathbb{N}$, and a function $\rho : [m] \to [n]$. We say that $\vec{x} \in \mathbb{F}_q^n$ satisfies $\mathbb{S}$ if and only if $\vec{e}^{(\ell, \ell)} \in \text{SPAN}\langle x_{\rho(j)}\vec{y}^{(j)} + \vec{z}^{(j)} \mid j \in [m]\rangle$.

The following lemma shows a connection between the two arithmetic computational models defined above.

Lemma 2.2 ([13]): *There exists an efficient algorithm that given an ABP $\Gamma = (V, E, \text{V}_0, \text{V}_1, \phi)$ of size $m + 1$ computing some function $f : \mathbb{F}_q^n \to \mathbb{F}_q$ for some $n, m \in \mathbb{N}$, constructs an ASP $\mathbb{S} = (\mathbb{U} = \{(\vec{y}^{(j)}, \vec{z}^{(j)})\}_{j \in [m]} \subset (\mathbb{F}_q^{(m+1)})^2, \rho : [m] \to [n])$ such that for all $\vec{x} \in \mathbb{F}_q^n$, $f(\vec{x}) = 0 \iff \mathbb{S}$ accepts $\vec{x}$.*

Proof: The algorithm starts with constructing a modified ABP Γ' for f from the input ABP Γ, by first replacing each edge $\text{E} \in E$ with a pair of edges labeled $\phi(\text{E})$ and 1, and then adding an edge labeled 1 connecting the sink in Γ to a newly created sink node. Clearly, the modified ABP Γ' has $m+2$ vertices, where every vertex has at most one incoming edge having a label of degree 1. Next, it applies the transformation of Lemma 2.1 to Γ' to obtain the $(m+1) \times (m+1)$ matrix representation $\boldsymbol{L}$ of Γ'. By Lemma 2.1, we clearly have $\det(\boldsymbol{L}(\vec{x})) = f(\vec{x})$ for all $\vec{x} \in \mathbb{F}_q^n$, and $\boldsymbol{L}$ is of the following form:

$$\boldsymbol{L} = \begin{pmatrix} \bigstar & \bigstar & \bigstar & \cdots & \bigstar & \bigstar & 0 \\ -1 & \bigstar & \bigstar & \cdots & \bigstar & \bigstar & 0 \\ 0 & -1 & \bigstar & \cdots & \bigstar & \bigstar & 0 \\ \vdots & \vdots & \vdots & \ddots & \vdots & \vdots & \vdots \\ 0 & 0 & 0 & \cdots & -1 & \bigstar & 0 \\ 0 & 0 & 0 & \cdots & 0 & -1 & 1 \end{pmatrix},$$

where the $\bigstar$'s indicates polynomial functions of degree at most 1 in some input variable x_i ($i \in [n]$). Also, observe that since each vertex in Γ' has at most one incoming edge having a label of degree one, for all $j \in [m]$, each entry of the jth column of the matrix $\boldsymbol{L}$ depends on one and the same input variable x_i ($i \in [n]$) and hence can be expressed as $x_i \vec{y}^{(j)} + \vec{z}^{(j)}$ for some pair of vectors $(\vec{y}^{(j)}, \vec{z}^{(j)}) \in (\mathbb{F}_q^{(m+1)})^2$. Further, it is immediate from the structure of $\boldsymbol{L}$ that the first m columns of $\boldsymbol{L}$ are linearly independent. Now, observe that $f(\vec{x}) = 0 \iff \det(\boldsymbol{L}(\vec{x})) = 0 \iff \vec{e}^{(m+1,m+1)}$, which is the $(m+1)^{\text{th}}$ column of $\boldsymbol{L}$, lies in the linear span of the first m columns of $\boldsymbol{L}$, i.e., $\vec{e}^{(m+1,m+1)} \in \text{SPAN}\langle x_i \vec{y}^{(j)} + \vec{z}^{(j)} \mid j \in [m] \wedge \text{the } j^{\text{th}} \text{ column of } \boldsymbol{L} \text{ depends on } x_i \ (i \in [n])\rangle$. The algorithm outputs the ASP $\mathbb{S} = (\mathbb{U} = \{(\vec{y}^{(j)}, \vec{z}^{(j)})\}_{j \in [m]} \subset (\mathbb{F}_q^{(m+1)})^2, \rho : [m] \to [n])$, where $\rho : [m] \to [n]$ is defined by $\rho(j) = i$ if the jth column of $\boldsymbol{L}$ depends on x_i. This ASP $\mathbb{S}$ is clearly the desired one by the above explanation. Hence Lemma 2.2 follows. □

2.3   Bilinear Groups and Dual Pairing Vector Spaces

In this section, we will provide the necessary backgrounds on bilinear groups and dual pairing vector spaces, which are the primary building blocks of our ABS construction.

Definition 2.3 (Bilinear Group): A bilinear group $\mathsf{params}_\mathbb{G} = (q, \mathbb{G}_1, \mathbb{G}_2, \mathbb{G}_T, g_1, g_2, e)$ is a tuple of a prime $q \in \mathbb{N}$; cyclic multiplicative groups $\mathbb{G}_1, \mathbb{G}_2, \mathbb{G}_T$ of order q each with polynomial-time computable group operations; generators $g_1 \in \mathbb{G}_1$, $g_2 \in \mathbb{G}_2$; and a polynomial-time computable non-degenerate bilinear map $e : \mathbb{G}_1 \times \mathbb{G}_2 \to \mathbb{G}_T$, i.e., e satisfies the following two properties:

- *Bilinearity:* $e(g_1^\Upsilon, g_2^{\hat{\Upsilon}}) = e(g_1, g_2)^{\Upsilon \hat{\Upsilon}}$ for all $\Upsilon, \hat{\Upsilon} \in \mathbb{F}_q$.
- *Non-degeneracy:* $e(g_1, g_2) \neq 1_{\mathbb{G}_T}$, where $1_{\mathbb{G}_T}$ denotes the identity element of the group $\mathbb{G}_T$.

A *bilinear group* is said to be asymmetric if no efficiently computable isomorphism exists between $\mathbb{G}_1$ and $\mathbb{G}_2$. Let $\mathcal{G}_{\text{BPG}}$ be an algorithm that on input the unary encoded security parameter 1^λ, outputs a description $\text{params}_{\mathbb{G}} = (q, \mathbb{G}_1, \mathbb{G}_2, \mathbb{G}_T, g_1, g_2, e)$ of a bilinear group.

Definition 2.4 (Dual Pairing Vector Spaces: DPVS [25,27]): A *dual pairing vector space* (DPVS) $\text{params}_{\mathbb{V}} = (q, \mathbb{V}, \mathbb{V}^*, \mathbb{G}_T, \mathbb{A}, \mathbb{A}^*, e)$ formed by the direct product of a bilinear group $\text{params}_{\mathbb{G}} = (q, \mathbb{G}_1, \mathbb{G}_2, \mathbb{G}_T, g_1, g_2, e)$ is a tuple of a prime $q \in \mathbb{N}$; d-dimensional vector spaces $\mathbb{V} = \mathbb{G}_1^d$, $\mathbb{V}^* = \mathbb{G}_2^d$ over $\mathbb{F}_q$ for some $d \in \mathbb{N}$, under vector addition and scalar multiplication defined componentwise in the usual manner; canonical bases $\mathbb{A} = \{a^{(i)} = (\overbrace{1_{\mathbb{G}_1}, \ldots, 1_{\mathbb{G}_1}}^{i-1}, g_1, \overbrace{1_{\mathbb{G}_1}, \ldots, 1_{\mathbb{G}_1}}^{d-i})\}_{i\in[d]}$

and $\mathbb{A}^* = \{a^{*(i)} = (\overbrace{1_{\mathbb{G}_2}, \ldots, 1_{\mathbb{G}_2}}^{i-1}, g_2, \overbrace{1_{\mathbb{G}_2}, \ldots, 1_{\mathbb{G}_2}}^{d-i})\}_{i\in[d]}$ of $\mathbb{V}$ and $\mathbb{V}^*$ respectively, where $1_{\mathbb{G}_1}$ and $1_{\mathbb{G}_2}$ are the identity elements of the groups $\mathbb{G}_1$ and $\mathbb{G}_2$ respectively; and a pairing $e : \mathbb{V} \times \mathbb{V}^* \to \mathbb{G}_T$ defined by $e(v, w) = \prod_{i\in[d]} e(g_1^{v_i}, g_2^{w_i}) \in \mathbb{G}_T$

for all $v = (g_1^{v_1}, \ldots, g_1^{v_d}) \in \mathbb{V}$, $w = (g_2^{w_1}, \ldots, g_2^{w_d}) \in \mathbb{V}^*$. Observe that the newly defined map e is also non-degenerate bilinear, i.e., e also satisfies the following two properties:

- *Bilinearity*: $e(\Upsilon v, \widehat{\Upsilon} w) = e(v, w)^{\Upsilon\widehat{\Upsilon}}$ for all $\Upsilon, \widehat{\Upsilon} \in \mathbb{F}_q$, $v \in \mathbb{V}$, and $w \in \mathbb{V}^*$.

- *Non-degeneracy*: If $e(v, w) = 1_{\mathbb{G}_T}$ for all $w \in \mathbb{V}^*$, then $v = (\overbrace{1_{\mathbb{G}_1}, \ldots, 1_{\mathbb{G}_1}}^{d})$. Similar statement also holds with the vectors v and w interchanged.

For any ordered basis $\mathbb{W} = \{w^{(1)}, \ldots, w^{(d)}\}$ of $\mathbb{V}$ (or $\mathbb{V}^*$), and any vector $\vec{v} \in \mathbb{F}_q^d$, let $(\vec{v})_{\mathbb{W}}$ represent the vector in $\mathbb{V}$ (or $\mathbb{V}^*$ accordingly) formed by the linear combination of the members of $\mathbb{W}$ with the components of $\vec{v}$ as the coefficients, i.e., $(\vec{v})_{\mathbb{W}} = \sum_{i\in[d]} v_i w^{(i)} \in \mathbb{V}$ (or $\mathbb{V}^*$ accordingly). Also, for any $s \in \mathbb{N}$ and any collection of s vectors $\{v^{(i)}\}_{i\in[s]}$ of $\mathbb{V}$ (or $\mathbb{V}^*$), we will denote by $\text{SPAN}\langle v^{(i)} \mid i \in [s]\rangle$ the subspace of $\mathbb{V}$ (or $\mathbb{V}^*$ accordingly) spanned by the set of vectors $\{v^{(i)}\}_{i\in[s]}$. The DPVS generation algorithm $\mathcal{G}_{\text{DPVS}}$ takes in the unary encoded security parameter 1^λ, a dimension value $d \in \mathbb{N}$, along with a bilinear group $\text{params}_{\mathbb{G}} = (q, \mathbb{G}_1, \mathbb{G}_2, \mathbb{G}_T, g_1, g_2, e) \xleftarrow{\text{R}} \mathcal{G}_{\text{BPG}}()$, and outputs a description $\text{params}_{\mathbb{V}} = (q, \mathbb{V}, \mathbb{V}^*, \mathbb{G}_T, \mathbb{A}, \mathbb{A}^*, e)$ of DPVS with d-dimensional $\mathbb{V}$ and $\mathbb{V}^*$.

We now describe random *dual orthonormal basis* generator $\mathcal{G}_{\text{OB}}$ [25,27] in Fig. 1. This algorithm will be utilized as a sub-routine in our ABS construction.

2.4 Collision-Resistant Hash Functions

Here we will formally describe the notion of collision-resistant hash functions which will be used as an ingredient of our ABS construction.

$\mathcal{G}_{\mathsf{OB}}(N, (d_0, \ldots, d_N))$: This algorithm takes as input the unary encoded security parameter 1^λ, a number $N \in \mathbb{N}$, and the respective dimensions $d_0, \ldots, d_N \in \mathbb{N}$ of the $N+1$ pairs of bases to be generated. It executes the following operations:

1. It first generates $\mathsf{params}_{\mathbb{G}} = (q, \mathbb{G}_1, \mathbb{G}_2, \mathbb{G}_T, g_1, g_2, e) \xleftarrow{\mathsf{R}} \mathcal{G}_{\mathsf{BPG}}()$.
2. Next, it samples $\psi \xleftarrow{\mathsf{U}} \mathbb{F}_q \backslash \{0\}$ and computes $g_T = e(g_1, g_2)^\psi$.
3. Then, for $\imath \in [0, N]$, it performs the following:
   (a) It constructs $\mathsf{params}_{\mathbb{V}_\imath} = (q, \mathbb{V}_\imath, \mathbb{V}_\imath^*, \mathbb{G}_T, \mathbb{A}_\imath, \mathbb{A}_\imath^*, e) \xleftarrow{\mathsf{R}} \mathcal{G}_{\mathsf{DPVS}}(d_\imath, \mathsf{params}_{\mathbb{G}})$.
   (b) It samples $\boldsymbol{B}^{(\imath)} = \left(b_{k,\imath}^{(\imath)} \right) \xleftarrow{\mathsf{U}} \mathsf{GL}(d_\imath, \mathbb{F}_q)$.
   (c) It computes $\boldsymbol{B}^{*(\imath)} = \left(b_{k,\imath}^{*(\imath)} \right) = \psi((\boldsymbol{B}^{(\imath)})^{-1})^\top$.
   (d) For all $k \in [d_\imath]$, let $\vec{b}^{(\imath,k)}$ and $\vec{b}^{*(\imath,k)}$ represent the kth rows of $\boldsymbol{B}^{(\imath)}$ and $\boldsymbol{B}^{*(\imath)}$ respectively. It computes $\boldsymbol{b}^{(\imath,k)} = (\vec{b}^{(\imath,k)})_{\mathbb{A}_\imath}, \boldsymbol{b}^{*(\imath,k)} = (\vec{b}^{*(\imath,k)})_{\mathbb{A}_\imath^*}$ for $k \in [d_\imath]$, and sets
   $$\mathbb{B}_\imath = \{\boldsymbol{b}^{(\imath,1)}, \ldots, \boldsymbol{b}^{(\imath,d_\imath)}\}, \mathbb{B}_\imath^* = \{\boldsymbol{b}^{*(\imath,1)}, \ldots, \boldsymbol{b}^{*(\imath,d_\imath)}\}.$$

   Clearly $\mathbb{B}_\imath$ and $\mathbb{B}_\imath^*$ form bases of the vector spaces $\mathbb{V}_\imath$ and $\mathbb{V}_\imath^*$ respectively. Also, note that $\mathbb{B}_\imath$ and $\mathbb{B}_\imath^*$ are dual orthonormal in the sense that for all $k, k' \in [d_\imath]$,

   $$e(\boldsymbol{b}^{(\imath,k)}, \boldsymbol{b}^{*(\imath,k')}) = \begin{cases} g_T & \text{if } k = k', \\ 1_{\mathbb{G}_T} & \text{otherwise.} \end{cases}$$

4. Next, it sets $\mathsf{params} = (\{\mathsf{params}_{\mathbb{V}_\imath}\}_{\imath \in [0,N]}, g_T)$.
5. It returns $(\mathsf{params}, \{\mathbb{B}_\imath, \mathbb{B}_\imath^*\}_{\imath \in [0,N]})$.

Fig. 1. Dual orthonormal basis generator $\mathcal{G}_{\mathsf{OB}}$

▶ **Syntax:** A hash function family $\mathbb{H}$ associated with a bilinear group generator $\mathcal{G}_{\mathsf{BPG}}$ and a polynomial $\mathsf{poly}(\cdot)$ consists of the following two polynomial-time algorithms:

KGen(): The hashing key generation algorithm is a probabilistic algorithm that takes as input the unary encoded security parameter 1^λ, and samples a hashing key hk from the key space $\mathbb{HK}_\lambda$, which is a probability space over bit strings parameterized by λ.

$\mathsf{H}_{\mathsf{hk}}^{(\lambda, \mathsf{poly})} : \mathbb{D} = \{0, 1\}^{\mathsf{poly}(\lambda)} \to \mathbb{F}_q \backslash \{0\}$: A deterministic function that maps an element of $\mathbb{D} = \{0, 1\}^{\mathsf{poly}}$ to an element of $\mathbb{F}_q \backslash \{0\}$ with q being the first element of the output $\mathsf{params}_{\mathbb{G}} = (q, \mathbb{G}_1, \mathbb{G}_2, \mathbb{G}_T, g_1, g_2, e)$ of $\mathcal{G}_{\mathsf{BPG}}$ on input 1^λ.

▶ **Collision Resistance:** A hash function family $\mathbb{H}$ associated with $\mathcal{G}_{\mathsf{BPG}}$ and $\mathsf{poly}(\cdot)$ is said to be collision resistant if for any PPT adversary $\mathcal{M}$, for any security parameter λ and any $\mathsf{hk} \xleftarrow{\mathsf{R}} \mathsf{KGen}()$, the advantage of $\mathcal{M}$ in finding a collision, defined as

$$\mathsf{Adv}_{\mathcal{M}}^{\mathsf{H,CR}}(\lambda) = \Pr[\varUpsilon_1, \varUpsilon_2 \in \mathbb{D} = \{0, 1\}^{\mathsf{poly}(\lambda)} \wedge \varUpsilon_1 \neq \varUpsilon_2 \wedge$$

$$\mathsf{H}_{\mathsf{hk}}^{(\lambda, \mathsf{poly})}(\varUpsilon_1) = \mathsf{H}_{\mathsf{hk}}^{(\lambda, \mathsf{poly})}(\varUpsilon_2) \mid (\varUpsilon_1, \varUpsilon_2) \xleftarrow{\mathsf{R}} \mathcal{M}(\mathsf{hk}, \mathbb{D})]$$

is negligible, i.e., $\mathsf{Adv}_{\mathcal{M}}^{\mathsf{H,CR}}(\lambda) \leq \mathsf{negl}(\lambda)$, where negl is some negligible function.

2.5 The Notion of Attribute-Based Signatures for Arithmetic Branching Programs

Let for some prime $q \in \mathbb{N}$, $\mathcal{F}_{\text{ABP}}^{(q)}$ denote the class of all functions $f : \mathbb{F}_q^n \to \mathbb{F}_q$ for any $n = \mathsf{p}(\lambda) \in \mathbb{N}$, where p is an arbitrary polynomial, realizable by some ABP of polynomial size over $\mathbb{F}_q$. In this section, we will formally define the notion of an attribute-based signature (ABS) scheme for the predicate family $\mathcal{R}_{\text{Z-ABP}}^{(q)}$ defined as $\mathcal{R}_{\text{Z-ABP}}^{(q)} = \{R_{\text{Z-ABP}}^{(q)}(f, \cdot) : \mathbb{F}_q^n \to \{0, 1\} \mid f : \mathbb{F}_q^n \to \mathbb{F}_q \in \mathcal{F}_{\text{ABP}}^{(q)}\}$, where $R_{\text{Z-ABP}}^{(q)}(f, \vec{x}) = 1$ if $f(\vec{x}) = 0$, and $R_{\text{Z-ABP}}^{(q)}(f, \vec{x}) = 0$ otherwise for all $f : \mathbb{F}_q^n \to \mathbb{F}_q \in \mathcal{F}_{\text{ABP}}^{(q)}$ and $\vec{x} \in \mathbb{F}_q^n$. As stated in Lemma 2.2, there exists a polynomial-time algorithm that on input any $f : \mathbb{F}_q^n \to \mathbb{F}_q \in \mathcal{F}_{\text{ABP}}^{(q)}$, constructs an ASP $\mathbb{S} = (\mathbb{U}, \rho)$ such that for any $\vec{x} \in \mathbb{F}_q^n$, it holds that $R_{\text{Z-ABP}}^{(q)}(f, \vec{x}) = 1 \iff f(\vec{x}) = 0 \iff \mathbb{S}$ accepts $\vec{x}$. Therefore, for the rest of this paper, we will identify predicates $R_{\text{Z-ABP}}^{(q)}(f, \cdot) \in \mathcal{R}_{\text{Z-ABP}}^{(q)}$ by their corresponding ASP-representations $\mathbb{S} = (\mathbb{U}, \rho)$ computed using the algorithm of Lemma 2.2.

▶ **Syntax:** An *attribute-based signature* (ABS) scheme for some predicate family $\mathcal{R}_{\text{Z-ABP}}^{(q)}$ consists of an associated message space $\mathbb{M} \subseteq \{0, 1\}^*$, a signature space Σ, along with the following PPT algorithms:

ABS.Setup(): The setup algorithm takes as input the unary encoded security parameter 1^λ. It outputs the public parameters MPK and the master signing key MSK.

ABS.KeyGen(MPK, MSK, $\vec{x}$): The signing key generation algorithm takes as input the public parameters MPK, the master signing key MSK, along with a signing attribute vector $\vec{x} \in \mathbb{F}_q^n$ for some $n = \mathsf{p}(\lambda) \in \mathbb{N}$. It outputs a signing key SK($\vec{x}$).

ABS.Sign(MPK, $\vec{x}$, SK($\vec{x}$), $\mathbb{S}$, MSG): The signing algorithm takes as input the public parameters MPK, a signing attribute string $\vec{x} \in \mathbb{F}_q^n$ for some $n = \mathsf{p}(\lambda) \in \mathbb{N}$, a signing key SK($\vec{x}$) for $\vec{x}$, a signing policy $R_{\text{Z-ABP}}^{(q)}(f, \cdot) : \mathbb{F}_q^n \to \{0, 1\} \in \mathcal{R}_{\text{Z-ABP}}^{(q)}$ represented as an ASP $\mathbb{S} = (\mathbb{U}, \rho)$, and a message MSG $\in \mathbb{M}$. It outputs either a signature sig $\in \Sigma$ or the distinguished symbol $\perp$ indicating failure.

ABS.Verify(MPK, $\mathbb{S}$, (MSG, sig)): The verification algorithm takes as input the public parameters MPK, a signing policy $R_{\text{Z-ABP}}^{(q)}(f, \cdot) \in \mathcal{R}_{\text{Z-ABP}}^{(q)}$ represented as an ASP $\mathbb{S} = (\mathbb{U}, \rho)$, and a message-signature pair (MSG, sig) $\in \mathbb{M} \times \Sigma$. It outputs either 1 or 0.

▶ **Correctness:** An ABS scheme for some predicate family $\mathcal{R}_{\text{Z-ABP}}^{(q)}$ is said to be correct if for any security parameter λ, any $n = \mathsf{p}(\lambda) \in \mathbb{N}$, any signing policy predicate $R_{\text{Z-ABP}}^{(q)}(f, \cdot) : \mathbb{F}_q^n \to \{0, 1\} \in \mathcal{R}_{\text{Z-ABP}}^{(q)}$ represented as an ASP $\mathbb{S} = (\mathbb{U}, \rho)$, any signing attribute vector $\vec{x} \in \mathbb{F}_q^n$, any (MPK, MSK) $\xleftarrow{\text{R}}$ ABS.Setup(), and any SK($\vec{x}$) $\xleftarrow{\text{R}}$ ABS.KeyGen(MPK, MSK, $\vec{x}$), if $\mathbb{S}$ accepts $\vec{x}$, then

$$\Pr[1 \xleftarrow{\text{R}} \text{ABS.Verify(MPK, } \mathbb{S}, (\text{MSG, sig})) \mid \text{sig} \xleftarrow{\text{R}} \text{ABS.Sign(MPK, } \vec{x}, \text{SK}(\vec{x}), \mathbb{S}, \text{MSG})]$$
$$\geq 1 - \mathsf{negl}(\lambda),$$

where negl is some negligible function, and the probability is taken over the random coins of ABS.Sign and ABS.Verify.

▶ **Signer Privacy:** An ABS scheme for some predicate family $\mathcal{R}_{\text{Z-ABP}}^{(q)}$ is said to achieve *perfect* signer privacy if for any security parameter λ, any $n = \mathsf{p}(\lambda) \in \mathbb{N}$, any message MSG $\in \mathbb{M}$, any (MPK, MSK) $\xleftarrow{\text{R}}$ ABS.Setup(), any signing policy $R_{\text{Z-ABP}}^{(q)}(f, \cdot) : \mathbb{F}_q^n \to \{0, 1\} \in \mathcal{R}_{\text{Z-ABP}}^{(q)}$ having ASP representation $\mathbb{S} = (\mathbb{U}, \rho)$, any two signing attribute vectors $\vec{x}, \vec{x}' \in \mathbb{F}_q^n$ such that $\mathbb{S}$ accepts both $\vec{x}$ and $\vec{x}'$, any signing keys SK$(\vec{x}) \xleftarrow{\text{R}}$ ABS.KeyGen(MPK, MSK, $\vec{x}$), SK$(\vec{x}') \xleftarrow{\text{R}}$ ABS.KeyGen(MPK, MSK, $\vec{x}'$), the distributions of the signatures outputted by ABS.Sign(MPK, $\vec{x}$, SK$(\vec{x})$, $\mathbb{S}$, MSG) and ABS.Sign(MPK, $\vec{x}'$, SK$(\vec{x}')$, $\mathbb{S}$, MSG) are equivalent.

▶ **Existential unforgeability:** Existential unforgeability of an ABS scheme for some predicate class $\mathcal{R}_{\text{Z-ABP}}^{(q)}$ against adaptive-predicate-adaptive-message attack is defined through the following experiment between a stateful probabilistic adversary $\mathcal{A}$ and a stateful probabilistic challenger $\mathcal{B}$:

- $\mathcal{B}$ generates (MPK, MSK) $\xleftarrow{\text{R}}$ ABS.Setup() and sends MPK to $\mathcal{A}$.
- $\mathcal{A}$ may adaptively make any polynomial number of queries of the following types to $\mathcal{B}$:
  - *Signing Key Generation Query*: When $\mathcal{A}$ requests the generation of a signing key for some signing attribute vector $\vec{x} \in \mathbb{F}_q^n$ for some $n = \mathsf{p}(\lambda) \in \mathbb{N}$, $\mathcal{B}$ generates a signing key SK$(\vec{x}) \xleftarrow{\text{R}}$ ABS.KeyGen(MPK, MSK, $\vec{x}$) and stores the signing key SK$(\vec{x})$.
  - *Signature Generation Query*: When $\mathcal{A}$ specifies a signing key for some signing attribute vector $\vec{x} \in \mathbb{F}_q^n$ for some $n = \mathsf{p}(\lambda) \in \mathbb{N}$ that it has already requested $\mathcal{B}$ to generate, and requests the generation of a signature using that signing key on some message MSG $\in \mathbb{M}$ under some signing policy $R_{\text{Z-ABP}}^{(q)}(f, \cdot) : \mathbb{F}_q^n \to \{0, 1\} \in \mathcal{R}_{\text{Z-ABP}}^{(q)}$ represented as an ASP $\mathbb{S} = (\mathbb{U}, \rho)$ such that $\mathbb{S}$ accepts $\vec{x}$, $\mathcal{B}$ creates a signature sig $\xleftarrow{\text{R}}$ ABS.Sign(MPK, $\vec{x}$, SK$(\vec{x})$, $\mathbb{S}$, MSG) and stores it.
  - *Signing key/Signature Reveal Query*: When $\mathcal{A}$ requests $\mathcal{B}$ to reveal an already created signing key corresponding to some signing attribute vector $\vec{x} \in \mathbb{F}_q^n$ for some $n = \mathsf{p}(\lambda) \in \mathbb{N}$ or an already created signature on some message MSG $\in \mathbb{M}$ under some signing policy $R_{\text{Z-ABP}}^{(q)}(f, \cdot) : \mathbb{F}_q^n \to \{0, 1\} \in \mathcal{R}_{\text{Z-ABP}}^{(q)}$ for some $n = \mathsf{p}(\lambda) \in \mathbb{N}$ represented by an ASP $\mathbb{S} = (\mathbb{U}, \rho)$, $\mathcal{B}$ provides $\mathcal{A}$ with the respective queried item.

  We would like to emphasize that when a signing key or signature generation query is made, $\mathcal{A}$ does not receives the signing key or signature that $\mathcal{B}$ creates. $\mathcal{A}$ receives it only when it makes a reveal query for that signing key or signature.
- At the end of interaction $\mathcal{A}$ outputs a triplet ($\mathbb{S}$, MSG, sig), where $\mathbb{S}$ is the ASP-representation of a signing policy $R_{\text{Z-ABP}}^{(q)}(f, \cdot) : \mathbb{F}_q^n \to \{0, 1\} \in \mathcal{R}_{\text{Z-ABP}}^{(q)}$ for

some $n = \mathsf{p}(\lambda) \in \mathbb{N}$, MSG $\in \mathbb{M}$, and sig $\in \Sigma$. $\mathcal{A}$ wins if the following conditions hold simultaneously:

(a) $1 = \mathsf{ABS.Verify}(\text{MPK}, \mathbb{S}, (\text{MSG}, \text{sig}))$.

(b) $\mathcal{A}$ has not made a signature reveal query on MSG under $\mathbb{S}$.

(c) $\mathbb{S}$ does not accept any signing attribute string $\vec{x} \in \mathbb{F}_q^n$ for which $\mathcal{A}$ has requested to reveal a signing key.

An ABS scheme for some predicate family $\mathcal{R}_{\text{Z-ABP}}^{(q)}$ is said to be existentially unforgeable against adaptive-predicate-adaptive-message attack if for any PPT adversary $\mathcal{A}$, for any security parameter λ, the advantage of $\mathcal{A}$ in the above experiment, defined as

$$\mathsf{Adv}_{\mathcal{A}}^{\mathsf{ABS,UF}}(\lambda) = \Pr[\mathcal{A} \text{ wins in the unforgeability experiment}]$$

is negligible in λ, i.e., $\mathsf{Adv}_{\mathcal{A}}^{\mathsf{ABS,UF}}(\lambda) \leq \mathsf{negl}(\lambda)$, where negl is some negligible function.

3   The Proposed **ABS** Scheme

In this section, we will present our ABS scheme for a predicate family $\mathcal{R}_{\text{Z-ABP}}^{(q)}$ parameterized by some prime $q \in \mathbb{N}$ as defined in Sect. 2.5. Let $\mathbb{M} \subset \{0,1\}^*$ be the message space associated with our ABS scheme. We emphasize that in our construction the functions ρ included within the description of ASP's are not necessarily injective, and thus our ABS scheme supports *unbounded* multi-use of attributes within the signing policies. In our scheme description and in the proof of security $n = \mathsf{p}(\lambda) \in \mathbb{N}$ for an arbitrary polynomial p.

$\mathsf{ABS.Setup}()$: The setup algorithm takes as input the unary encoded security parameter 1^λ. It proceeds as follows:

1. It first generates $(\mathsf{params}, \{\mathbb{B}_\imath, \mathbb{B}_\imath^*\}_{\imath \in [0,2]}) \xleftarrow{\mathsf{R}} \mathcal{G}_{\mathrm{OB}}(2, (4, 14, 8))$.

2. Then, it sets the following:

$$\widehat{\mathbb{B}}_0 = \{b^{(0,1)}, b^{(0,4)}\},$$

$$\widehat{\mathbb{B}}_0^* = \{b^{*(0,3)}\},$$

$$\widehat{\mathbb{B}}_1 = \{b^{(1,1)}, \ldots, b^{(1,4)}, b^{(1,13)}, b^{(1,14)}\},$$

$$\widehat{\mathbb{B}}_1^* = \{b^{*(1,1)}, \ldots, b^{*(1,4)}, b^{*(1,11)}, b^{*(1,12)}\},$$

$$\widehat{\mathbb{B}}_2 = \{b^{(2,1)}, b^{(2,2)}, b^{(2,7)}, b^{(2,8)}\},$$

$$\widehat{\mathbb{B}}_2^* = \{b^{*(2,1)}, b^{*(2,2)}, b^{*(2,5)}, b^{*(2,6)}\}.$$

3. Next, it samples a hashing key $\mathsf{hk} \xleftarrow{\mathsf{R}} \mathsf{KGen}()$ for a hash function family $\mathbb{H}$ associated with the bilinear group generator $\mathcal{G}_{\mathrm{BPG}}$ used as a subroutine of $\mathcal{G}_{\mathrm{OB}}$ and a polynomial $\mathsf{poly}(\cdot)$, where poly represents the length of the bit string formed by concatenating a message belonging to $\mathbb{M}$ and the binary representation of an ASP representing a signing policy predicate in $\mathcal{R}_{\text{Z-ABP}}^{(q)}$.

4. It outputs the public parameters $\text{MPK} = (\text{hk}, \text{params}, \{\widehat{\mathbb{B}}_\iota, \widehat{\mathbb{B}}_\iota^*\}_{\iota \in [0,2]})$ and the master signing key $\text{MSK} = \boldsymbol{b}^{*(0,1)}$.

$\text{ABS.KeyGen}(\text{MPK}, \text{MSK}, \vec{x})$: The signing key generation algorithm takes as input the public parameters MPK, the master signing key MSK, and a signing attribute vector $\vec{x} \in \mathbb{F}_q^n$. It executes the following steps:

1. First, it samples $\omega \xleftarrow{\mathsf{U}} \mathbb{F}_q \backslash \{0\}$, $\varphi_0 \xleftarrow{\mathsf{U}} \mathbb{F}_q$, and computes

$$\boldsymbol{k}^{*(0)} = (\omega, 0, \varphi_0, 0)_{\mathbb{B}_0^*}.$$

2. Next, for $\iota \in [n]$, it samples $\sigma_\iota \xleftarrow{\mathsf{U}} \mathbb{F}_q$, $\vec{\varphi}^{(\iota)} \xleftarrow{\mathsf{U}} \mathbb{F}_q^2$, and computes

$$\boldsymbol{k}^{*(\iota)} = (\sigma_\iota(1, \iota), \omega(1, x_\iota), \vec{0}^6, \vec{\varphi}^{(\iota)}, \vec{0}^2)_{\mathbb{B}_1^*}.$$

3. Then, it samples $\vec{\varphi}^{(n+1,1)}, \vec{\varphi}^{(n+1,2)} \xleftarrow{\mathsf{U}} \mathbb{F}_q^2$, and computes

$$\boldsymbol{k}^{*(n+1,1)} = (\omega(1,0), \vec{0}^2, \vec{\varphi}^{(n+1,1)}, \vec{0}^2)_{\mathbb{B}_2^*},$$
$$\boldsymbol{k}^{*(n+1,2)} = (\omega(0,1), \vec{0}^2, \vec{\varphi}^{(n+1,2)}, \vec{0}^2)_{\mathbb{B}_2^*}.$$

4. It outputs the signing key $\text{SK}(\vec{x}) = (\boldsymbol{k}^{*(0)}, \ldots, \boldsymbol{k}^{*(n)}, \boldsymbol{k}^{*(n+1,1)}, \boldsymbol{k}^{*(n+1,2)})$.

$\text{ABS.Sign}(\text{MPK}, \vec{x}, \text{SK}(\vec{x}), \mathbb{S}, \text{MSG})$: The signing algorithm takes in the public parameters MPK, a signing attribute string $\vec{x} \in \mathbb{F}_q^n$, a signing key $\text{SK}(\vec{x}) = (\boldsymbol{k}^{*(0)}, \ldots, \boldsymbol{k}^{*(n)}, \boldsymbol{k}^{*(n+1,1)}, \boldsymbol{k}^{*(n+1,2)})$ for $\vec{x}$, a signing policy predicate $R_{\text{Z-ABP}}^{(q)}(f, \cdot) : \mathbb{F}_q^n \rightarrow \{0, 1\} \in \mathcal{R}_{\text{Z-ABP}}^{(q)}$ with ASP representation $\mathbb{S} = (\mathbb{U} = \{(\vec{y}^{(j)}, \vec{z}^{(j)})\}_{j \in [m]} \subset (\mathbb{F}_q^\ell)^2, \rho : [m] \rightarrow [n])$, along with a message $\text{MSG} \in \mathbb{M}$. If $\mathbb{S}$ does not accept $\vec{x}$, it outputs $\perp$. Otherwise, i.e., if $\mathbb{S}$ accepts $\vec{x}$, it operates as follows:

1. It first computes $(\Omega_j)_{j \in [m]} \in \mathbb{F}_q^m$ such that $\vec{e}^{(\ell, \ell)} = \sum_{j \in [m]} \Omega_j (x_{\rho(j)} \vec{y}^{(j)} + \vec{z}^{(j)})$.

2. Next, it samples $\xi \xleftarrow{\mathsf{U}} \mathbb{F}_q \backslash \{0\}$, and $((\Omega_j')_{j \in [m]}, (\Omega_j'')_{j \in [m]}) \xleftarrow{\mathsf{U}} (\mathbb{F}_q^m)^2$ such that $\sum_{j \in [m]} (\Omega_j' \vec{y}^{(j)} + \Omega_j'' \vec{z}^{(j)}) = \vec{0}^\ell$.

3. After that, it samples $\boldsymbol{r}^{*(0)} \xleftarrow{\mathsf{U}} \text{SPAN}\langle \boldsymbol{b}^{*(0,3)} \rangle$ and computes

$$\boldsymbol{s}^{*(0)} = \xi \boldsymbol{k}^{*(0)} + \boldsymbol{r}^{*(0)}.$$

4. Then, for $j \in [m]$, it samples $\sigma_j' \xleftarrow{\mathsf{U}} \mathbb{F}_q$, $\boldsymbol{r}^{*(j)} \xleftarrow{\mathsf{U}} \text{SPAN}\langle \boldsymbol{b}^{*(1,11)}, \boldsymbol{b}^{*(1,12)} \rangle$, and computes

$$\boldsymbol{s}^{*(j)} = \xi \Omega_j \boldsymbol{k}^{*(\rho(j))} + \sigma_j'(\boldsymbol{b}^{*(1,1)} + \rho(j) \boldsymbol{b}^{*(1,2)}) + \Omega_j'' \boldsymbol{b}^{*(1,3)} + \Omega_j' \boldsymbol{b}^{*(1,4)} + \boldsymbol{r}^{*(j)}.$$

5. Next, it samples $\boldsymbol{r}^{*(m+1)} \xleftarrow{\mathsf{U}} \text{SPAN}\langle \boldsymbol{b}^{*(2,5)}, \boldsymbol{b}^{*(2,6)} \rangle$ and computes

$$\boldsymbol{s}^{*(m+1)} = \xi(\boldsymbol{k}^{*(n+1,1)} + \mathsf{H}_{\text{hk}}^{(\lambda, \text{poly})}(\text{MSG} \| \mathbb{S}) \boldsymbol{k}^{*(n+1,2)}) + \boldsymbol{r}^{*(m+1)}.$$

6. It outputs the signature sig $= (\boldsymbol{s}^{*(0)}, \ldots, \boldsymbol{s}^{*(m+1)})$.

ABS.Verify(MPK, $\mathbb{S}$, (MSG, sig)): The verification algorithm takes as input the public parameters MPK, a signing policy predicate $R_{\text{Z-ABP}}^{(q)}(f, \cdot) : \mathbb{F}_q^n \to \{0,1\} \in \mathcal{R}_{\text{Z-ABP}}^{(q)}$ having ASP-representation $\mathbb{S} = (\mathbb{U} = \{(\vec{y}^{(j)}, \vec{z}^{(j)})\}_{j \in [m]} \subset (\mathbb{F}_q^\ell)^2, \rho : [m] \to [n])$, a message-signature pair (MSG $\in \mathbb{M}$, sig $= (\boldsymbol{s}^{*(0)}, \ldots, \boldsymbol{s}^{*(m+1)}))$. It proceeds as follows:

1. It generates a verification-text $(\boldsymbol{c}^{(0)}, \ldots, \boldsymbol{c}^{(m+1)})$ as follows:

   (a) It first samples $\vec{u} = (u_1, \ldots, u_\ell) \xleftarrow{\mathsf{U}} \mathbb{F}_q^\ell$, and computes $s_j = \vec{u} \cdot \vec{y}^{(j)}$, $s_j' = \vec{u} \cdot \vec{z}^{(j)}$ for $j \in [m]$.

   (b) Next, it samples $u, \eta_0 \xleftarrow{\mathsf{U}} \mathbb{F}_q$, and computes
   $$\boldsymbol{c}^{(0)} = (-u - u_\ell, 0, 0, \eta_0)_{\mathbb{B}_0}.$$

   (c) Then, for $j \in [m]$, if $\boldsymbol{s}^{*(j)} \notin \mathbb{V}_1^*$, then it outputs 0. Otherwise, it samples $\mu_j \xleftarrow{\mathsf{U}} \mathbb{F}_q$, $\vec{\eta}^{(j)} \xleftarrow{\mathsf{U}} \mathbb{F}_q^2$, and computes
   $$\boldsymbol{c}^{(j)} = (\mu_j(\rho(j), -1), (s_j', s_j), \vec{0}^6, \vec{0}^2, \vec{\eta}^{(j)})_{\mathbb{B}_1}.$$

   (d) Then, it samples $\kappa \xleftarrow{\mathsf{U}} \mathbb{F}_q$, $\vec{\eta}^{(m+1)} \xleftarrow{\mathsf{U}} \mathbb{F}_q^2$, and computes
   $$\boldsymbol{c}^{(m+1)} = ((u - \kappa \mathsf{H}_{\mathsf{hk}}^{(\lambda, \mathsf{poly})}(\text{MSG} \| \mathbb{S}), \kappa), \vec{0}^2, \vec{0}^2, \vec{\eta}^{(m+1)})_{\mathbb{B}_2}.$$

2. It outputs 0 if $e(\boldsymbol{b}^{(0,1)}, \boldsymbol{s}^{*(0)}) = 1_{\mathbb{G}_T}$.
3. It outputs 1 if $\prod_{j \in [0,m+1]} e(\boldsymbol{c}^{(j)}, \boldsymbol{s}^{*(j)}) = 1_{\mathbb{G}_T}$. It outputs 0 otherwise. Here, $1_{\mathbb{G}_T}$ is the identity element of the group $\mathbb{G}_T$.

▶ **Correctness:** The correctness of the proposed ABS construction can be verified as follows: For any signature sig $= (\boldsymbol{s}^{*(0)}, \ldots, \boldsymbol{s}^{*(m+1)})$ on a message MSG $\in \mathbb{M}$ under a signing policy predicate $R_{\text{Z-ABP}}^{(q)}(f, \cdot) : \mathbb{F}_q^n \to \{0,1\} \in \mathcal{R}_{\text{Z-ABP}}^{(q)}$ having ASP representation $\mathbb{S} = (\mathbb{U} = \{(\vec{y}^{(j)}, \vec{z}^{(j)})\}_{j \in [m]} \subset (\mathbb{F}_q^\ell)^2, \rho : [m] \to [n])$ generated using a signing key SK$(\vec{x}) = (\boldsymbol{k}^{*(0)}, \ldots, \boldsymbol{k}^{*(n)}, \boldsymbol{k}^{*(n+1,1)}, \boldsymbol{k}^{*(n+1,2)})$ for a signing attribute vector $\vec{x} \in \mathbb{F}_q^n$ such that $\mathbb{S}$ accepts $\vec{x}$, and any verification-text $(\boldsymbol{c}^{(0)}, \ldots, \boldsymbol{c}^{(m+1)})$ generated while executing ABS.Verify, we have

$$\prod_{j \in [0,m+1]} e(\boldsymbol{c}^{(j)}, \boldsymbol{s}^{*(j)})$$

$$= e(\boldsymbol{c}^{(0)}, \boldsymbol{k}^{*(0)})^\xi \prod_{j \in [m]} e(\boldsymbol{c}^{(j)}, \boldsymbol{k}^{*(\rho(j))})^{\xi \Omega_j} \prod_{j \in [m]} [e(\boldsymbol{c}^{(j)}, \boldsymbol{b}^{*(1,3)})^{\Omega_j''} e(\boldsymbol{c}^{(j)}, \boldsymbol{b}^{*(1,4)})^{\Omega_j'}].$$

$$[e(\boldsymbol{c}^{(m+1)}, \boldsymbol{k}^{*(n+1,1)}) e(\boldsymbol{c}^{(m+1)}, \boldsymbol{k}^{*(n+1,2)})^{\mathsf{H}_{\mathsf{hk}}^{(\lambda,\mathsf{poly})}(\text{MSG} \| \mathbb{S})}]^\xi$$

$$= g_T^{\xi \omega(-u-u_\ell)} \prod_{j \in [m]} g_T^{\xi \omega \Omega_j (x_{\rho(j)} s_j + s_j')} \prod_{j \in [m]} g_T^{(\Omega_j' s_j + \Omega_j'' s_j')} g_T^{\xi \omega u}$$

$$= g_T^{\xi \omega(-u-u_\ell)} g_T^{\xi \omega (\vec{u} \cdot \sum_{j \in [m]} \Omega_j(x_{\rho(j)} \vec{y}^{(j)} + \vec{z}^{(j)}))} g_T^{\vec{u} \cdot \sum_{j \in [m]} (\Omega_j' \vec{y}^{(j)} + \Omega_j'' \vec{z}^{(j)})} g_T^{\xi \omega u}$$

$$= g_T^{\xi \omega(-u-u_\ell)} g_T^{\xi \omega(\vec{u} \cdot \vec{e}^{(\ell,\ell)})} g_T^{\vec{u} \cdot \vec{0}^\ell} g_T^{\xi \omega u} = g_T^{\xi \omega(-u-u_\ell)} g_T^{\xi \omega u_\ell} 1_{\mathbb{G}_T} g_T^{\xi \omega u} = 1_{\mathbb{G}_T}.$$

The above follows from the expressions of $(\boldsymbol{c}^{(0)}, \ldots, \boldsymbol{c}^{(m+1)})$, $(\boldsymbol{s}^{*(0)}, \ldots, \boldsymbol{s}^{*(m+1)})$, $(\boldsymbol{k}^{*(0)}, \ldots, \boldsymbol{k}^{*(n)}, \boldsymbol{k}^{*(n+1,1)}, \boldsymbol{k}^{*(n+1,2)})$, and the dual orthonormality property of $\{\mathbb{B}_\imath, \mathbb{B}_\imath^*\}_{\imath \in [0,2]}$; in conjunction with the facts that $\sum\limits_{j \in [m]} \Omega_j (x_{\rho(j)} \vec{y}^{(j)} + \vec{z}^{(j)}) = \vec{e}^{(\ell,\ell)}$ (since $\mathbb{S}$ accepts $\vec{x}$), and $\sum\limits_{j \in [m]} (\Omega_j' \vec{y}^{(j)} + \Omega_j'' \vec{z}^{(j)}) = \vec{0}^\ell$ (by selection).

Remark 3.1 (Discussion on the Concrete Efficiency of the Proposed ABS Scheme): In order to understand the concrete efficiency gains of our ABS scheme over the state-of-the-art scheme of [29], let us consider the performance of both the schemes for a simple signing policy ABP $f : \mathbb{F}_q \to \mathbb{F}_q$ defined by $f(x_1) = x_1 - a_1$ for all $x_1 \in \mathbb{F}_q$, where q is a 128-bit prime integer and a_1 is a constant belonging to $\mathbb{F}_q$. We have already presented the summary of this efficiency analysis in Table 1 in the Introduction section. For the considered ABP, we have $R_{\text{Z-ABP}}^{(q)}(f, x_1) = 1 \iff f(x_1) = 0 \iff x_1 = a_1$. By applying the algorithm of [13], we can represent the ABP f by the ASP $\mathbb{S} = (\mathbb{U} = \{(\vec{y}^{(1)} = (1,0), \vec{z}^{(1)} = (-a, -1))\}, \rho \mid 1 \mapsto 1)$. Hence, it can be readily verified from the description of the proposed ABS scheme above that in this scheme, a signature $\text{SIG} = (\boldsymbol{s}^{*(0)}, \boldsymbol{s}^{*(1)}, \boldsymbol{s}^{*(2)})$ on some message $\text{MSG} \in \mathbb{M}$ under $R_{\text{Z-ABP}}^{(q)}(f, \cdot)$ would consist of only 26 group elements, namely, 4 group elements for $\boldsymbol{s}^{*(0)}$, 14 group elements for $\boldsymbol{s}^{*(1)}$, while 8 group elements for $\boldsymbol{s}^{*(2)}$. On the other hand, to verify the signature, a verifier would have to compute 30 pairing operations, namely, 4 pairing operations to verify whether $e(\boldsymbol{b}^{(0,1)}, \boldsymbol{s}^{*(0)}) = 1_{\mathbb{G}_T}$ and 26 pairing operations to verify whether $\prod\limits_{j \in [0,2]} e(\boldsymbol{c}^{(j)}, \boldsymbol{s}^{*(j)}) = 1_{\mathbb{G}_T}$, where $(\boldsymbol{c}^{(0)}, \boldsymbol{c}^{(1)}, \boldsymbol{c}^{(2)})$ is the verification-text computed during the verification procedure.

Now, let us look into the size of a signature computed for the same signing policy using the ABS scheme of Sakai et al. [29]. Observe that in this scheme, signing policies are considered as boolean circuits. So, we must express $R_{\text{Z-ABP}}^{(q)}(f, \cdot)$ as a boolean circuit. Clearly, the boolean circuit that simulates $R_{\text{Z-ABP}}^{(q)}(f, \cdot)$ would have 128 input gates to take as input the bit representation of x_1. Moreover, in order to simulate the equality test $x_1 = a_1$ over $\mathbb{F}_q$ using boolean operations, the circuit would need to implement 127 boolean AND gates, where the first boolean AND gate would connect the first and second bits of x_1, the second one would connect the earlier AND gate with the third bit of x_1, and so on. Also, for all $i \in [128]$, the wire connecting the ith bit of x_1 to an AND gate must pass through a NOT gate if the ith bit of a_1 is 0. For instance, if we represent the ith bit of an element $b \in \mathbb{F}_q$ by $b[i]$ for all $i \in [128]$, and some $a_1 \in \mathbb{F}_q$ has binary representation $110 \ldots 01$, then the boolean circuit simulating $R_{\text{Z-ABP}}^{(q)}(f, \cdot)$ with this a_1 would be

$$(((\ldots((x_1[1] \text{ AND } x_1[2]) \text{ AND } (\text{NOT } x_1[3])) \ldots)$$
$$\text{AND } (\text{NOT } x_1[127])) \text{ AND } x_1[128]).$$

Hence, it follows that the boolean circuit that realizes $R_{\text{Z-ABP}}^{(q)}(f, \cdot)$ would have 128 input gates, 127 AND gates along with some additional NOT gates. Further, note that the ABS scheme of [29] considers representing signing policies using boolean circuits consisting of NAND gates only. Since 3 NAND gates are required to simulate each AND gate, and 1 NAND gate is needed to simulate each NOT gate, it follows that the boolean circuit simulating $R_{\text{Z-ABP}}^{(q)}(f, \cdot)$ using only NAND gates would consist of at least 128 input gates and at least 127 NAND gates. Now, notice that a signature in the scheme of [29] consists of Groth-Sahai commitments and proofs [9] for each wire of the signing policy circuit for which it is being generated, and verification requires checking all those proofs. Therefore, it is immediate from the performance figures presented in Tables 1 and 2 of [29] that a signature on some message with respect to the boolean circuit simulating $R_{\text{Z-ABP}}^{(q)}(f, \cdot)$ in this scheme would include at least 4102 group elements, and verification of the signature would require at least 4102 pairing operations.

Thus, it is clear that in terms of concrete efficiency, even for a very simple signing policy such as an equality test over $\mathbb{F}_q$, our ABS scheme gives more than 136 times better results compared to the one of [29].

4   Security

Theorem 4.1 (Signer Privacy): *The proposed* ABS *scheme achieves perfect signer privacy (as per the security model described in Sect. 2.5).*

Proof: In order to prove Theorem 4.1, we introduce the following signing algorithm, we call ABS.AltSign, that generates signatures on messages using the master signing key MSK and do not use any attribute-specific signing key SK($\vec{x}$).

ABS.AltSign(MPK, MSK, $\mathbb{S}$, MSG): This algorithm takes in the public parameters MPK, the master signing key MSK, a signing policy predicate $R_{\text{Z-ABP}}^{(q)}(f, \cdot)$: $\mathbb{F}_q^n \to \{0,1\} \in \mathcal{R}_{\text{Z-ABP}}^{(q)}$ having ASP-representation $\mathbb{S} = (\mathbb{U} = \{(\vec{y}^{(j)}, \vec{z}^{(j)})\}_{j \in [m]} \subset (\mathbb{F}_q^\ell)^2, \rho : [m] \to [n])$, and a message MSG $\in \mathbb{M}$. It proceeds as follows:

1. If $S = \{((\widehat{\Omega}_j)_{j \in [m]}, (\widehat{\Omega}'_j)_{j \in [m]}) \in (\mathbb{F}_q^m)^2 \mid \sum_{j \in [m]} (\widehat{\Omega}_j \vec{y}^{(j)} + \widehat{\Omega}'_j \vec{z}^{(j)}) = \vec{e}^{(\ell, \ell)}\} = \varnothing$, then it outputs $\perp$ indicating failure. Otherwise, it samples $((\widehat{\Omega}_j)_{j \in [m]}, (\widehat{\Omega}'_j)_{j \in [m]}) \xleftarrow{\mathsf{U}} S$.

2. Next, it samples $\widehat{\omega} \xleftarrow{\mathsf{U}} \mathbb{F}_q \backslash \{0\}$, $\widehat{v}_0 \xleftarrow{\mathsf{U}} \mathbb{F}_q$, and computes

$$\boldsymbol{s}^{*(0)} = (\widehat{\omega}, 0, \widehat{v}_0, 0)_{\mathbb{B}_0^*}.$$

3. For $j \in [m]$, it samples $\widehat{\sigma}_j \xleftarrow{\mathsf{U}} \mathbb{F}_q$, $\vec{\widehat{v}}_j \xleftarrow{\mathsf{U}} \mathbb{F}_q^2$, and computes

$$\boldsymbol{s}^{*(j)} = (\widehat{\sigma}_j (1, \rho(j)), (\widehat{\Omega}'_j, \widehat{\Omega}_j), \vec{0}^6, \vec{\widehat{v}}^{(j)}, \vec{0}^2)_{\mathbb{B}_1^*}.$$

4. Then, it samples $\vec{v}^{(m+1)} \xleftarrow{\mathsf{U}} \mathbb{F}_q^2$ and computes

$$\boldsymbol{s}^{*(m+1)} = (\widehat{\omega}(1, \mathsf{H}_{\mathsf{hk}}^{(\lambda,\mathrm{poly})}(\mathrm{MSG}\|\mathbb{S})), \vec{0}^2, \vec{v}^{(m+1)}, \vec{0}^2)_{\mathbb{B}_2^*}.$$

5. It outputs the signature sig $= (\boldsymbol{s}^{*(0)}, \ldots, \boldsymbol{s}^{*(m+1)})$.

Remark 4.1: Note that using the ABS.AltSign algorithm, one can generate a correctly verifiable signature on any message MSG $\in$ M under any signing policy predicate $R_{\mathrm{Z\text{-}ABP}}^{(q)}(f, \cdot) : \mathbb{F}_q^n \to \{0,1\} \in \mathcal{R}_{\mathrm{Z\text{-}ABP}}^{(q)}$ having ASP-representation $\mathbb{S} = (\mathbb{U} = \{(\vec{y}^{(j)}, \vec{z}^{(j)})\}_{j \in [m]} \subset (\mathbb{F}_q^\ell)^2, \rho : [m] \to [n])$ even without knowing any signing attribute string $\vec{x} \in \mathbb{F}_q^n$ accepted by $\mathbb{S}$. However, in order to execute this algorithm, one should have access to the master signing key MSK – something which a signer does not have access to in the real world (and an adversary in the unforgeability experiment). Hence, the above algorithm should only be viewed as a virtual one used in the security proof. Also, note that if the set S defined in the ABS.AltSign algorithm above is empty, then it is impossible that there exists some signing attribute string $\vec{x} \in \mathbb{F}_q^n$ accepted by $\mathbb{S}$, and hence no signature can ever be generated under $\mathbb{S}$, even in the real world.

Clearly, in order to prove Theorem 4.1 it is enough to show that the following statement is true:
For any security parameter $\lambda \in \mathbb{N}$, any message MSG $\in$ M, *any signing attribute string* $\vec{x} \in \mathbb{F}_q^n$, *any signing policy predicate* $R_{\mathrm{Z\text{-}ABP}}^{(q)}(f, \cdot) : \mathbb{F}_q^n \to \{0,1\} \in \mathcal{R}_{\mathrm{Z\text{-}ABP}}^{(q)}$ *having* ASP-*representation* $\mathbb{S} = (\mathbb{U} = \{(\vec{y}^{(j)}, \vec{z}^{(j)})\}_{j \in [m]} \subset (\mathbb{F}_q^\ell)^2, \rho : [m] \to [n])$ *such that* $\mathbb{S}$ *accepts* $\vec{x}$, *any* (MPK, MSK) $\xleftarrow{\mathsf{R}}$ ABS.Setup(1^n), *and any* SK$(\vec{x}) \xleftarrow{\mathsf{R}}$ ABS.KeyGen(MPK, MSK, $\vec{x}$), *the distributions of the signatures outputted by* ABS.Sign(MPK, $\vec{x}$, SK$(\vec{x})$, $\mathbb{S}$, MSG) *and those outputted by* ABS.AltSign(MPK, MSK, $\mathbb{S}$, MSG) *are equivalent.*
In the proposed ABS scheme, sig $= (\boldsymbol{s}^{*(0)}, \ldots, \boldsymbol{s}^{*(m+1)}) \xleftarrow{\mathsf{R}}$ ABS.Sig(MPK, $\vec{x}$, SK$(\vec{x})$, $\mathbb{S}$, MSG) is computed as

$$\boldsymbol{s}^{*(0)} = (p_0, 0, 0, v_0)_{\mathbb{B}_0^*},$$
$$\boldsymbol{s}^{*(j)} = (\bar{\sigma}_j(1, \rho(j)), \vec{p}^{(j)}, \vec{0}^6, \vec{v}^{(j)}, \vec{0}^2)_{\mathbb{B}_1^*} \text{ for } j \in [m],$$
$$\boldsymbol{s}^{*(m+1)} = (\vec{p}^{(m+1)}, \vec{0}^2, \vec{v}^{(m+1)}, \vec{0}^2)_{\mathbb{B}_2^*},$$

such that $p_0 = \xi\omega$, $\bar{\sigma}_j = \xi\sigma_{\rho(j)}\Omega_j + \sigma_j'$, $\vec{p}^{(j)} = (\xi\omega\Omega_j + \Omega_j'', \xi\omega x_{\rho(j)}\Omega_j + \Omega_j')$ for $j \in [m]$, and $\vec{p}^{(m+1)} = \xi\omega(1, \mathsf{H}_{\mathsf{hk}}^{(\lambda,\mathrm{poly})}(\mathrm{MSG}\|\mathbb{S}))$, where $\omega, \xi \xleftarrow{\mathsf{U}} \mathbb{F}_q \backslash \{0\}$, $\{\sigma_\iota\}_{\iota \in [n]}, \{\sigma_j'\}_{j \in [m]}, v_0 \xleftarrow{\mathsf{U}} \mathbb{F}_q$, $\{\vec{v}^{(j)}\}_{j \in [m+1]} \xleftarrow{\mathsf{U}} \mathbb{F}_q^2$, $(\Omega_j)_{j \in [m]} \in \mathbb{F}_q^\ell$ with $\sum_{j \in [m]} \Omega_j(x_{\rho(j)}\vec{y}^{(j)} + \vec{z}^{(j)}) = \vec{e}^{(\ell,\ell)}$, and $((\Omega_j')_{j \in [m]}, (\Omega_j'')_{j \in [m]}) \xleftarrow{\mathsf{U}} (\mathbb{F}_q^m)^2$ with $\sum_{j \in [m]} (\Omega_j'\vec{y}^{(j)} + \Omega_j''\vec{z}^{(j)}) = \vec{0}^\ell$.

On the other hand sig $= (s^{*(0)}, \ldots, s^{*(m+1)}) \xleftarrow{\text{R}} \text{ABS.AltSign}(\text{MPK}, \text{MSK}, \mathbb{S},$ $\text{MSG})$ is computed as

$$s^{*(0)} = (\widehat{p}_0, 0, \widehat{v}_0, 0)_{\mathbb{B}_0^*},$$

$$s^{*(j)} = (\widehat{\sigma}_j(1, \rho(j)), \vec{\widehat{p}}^{(j)}, \vec{0}^6, \vec{\widehat{v}}^{(j)}, \vec{0}^2)_{\mathbb{B}_1^*} \text{ for } j \in [m],$$

$$s^{*(m+1)} = (\vec{\widehat{p}}^{(m+1)}, \vec{0}^2, \vec{\widehat{v}}^{(m+1)}, \vec{0}^2)_{\mathbb{B}_2^*},$$

such that $\widehat{p}_0 = \widehat{\omega}, \vec{\widehat{p}}^{(j)} = (\widehat{\Omega}'_j, \widehat{\Omega}_j)$ for $j \in [m]$, and $\vec{\widehat{p}}^{(m+1)} = \widehat{\omega}(1, \text{H}_{\text{hk}}^{(\lambda, \text{poly})}$ $(\text{MSG}\|\mathbb{S}))$, where $\widehat{\omega} \xleftarrow{\text{U}} \mathbb{F}_q \backslash \{0\}, \{\widehat{\sigma}_j\}_{j \in [m]}, \widehat{v}_0 \xleftarrow{\text{U}} \mathbb{F}_q, \{\vec{\widehat{v}}^{(j)}\}_{j \in [m+1]} \xleftarrow{\text{U}} \mathbb{F}_q^2$, and $((\widehat{\Omega}_j)_{j \in [m]}, (\widehat{\Omega}'_j)_{j \in [m]}) \xleftarrow{\text{U}} S = \{((\widehat{\Omega}_j)_{j \in [m]}, (\widehat{\Omega}'_j)_{j \in [m]}) \in (\mathbb{F}_q^m)^2 \mid \sum_{j \in [m]} (\widehat{\Omega}_j \vec{y}^{(j)} + \widehat{\Omega}'_j \vec{z}^{(j)}) = \vec{e}^{(\ell, \ell)}\}$.

Observe that the distributions $\{(\xi\omega, (\xi\omega x_{\rho(j)} \Omega_j + \Omega'_j)_{j \in [m]}, (\xi\omega\Omega_j + \Omega''_j)_{j \in [m]}) \mid \omega, \xi \xleftarrow{\text{U}} \mathbb{F}_q \backslash \{0\}, ((\Omega'_j)_{j \in [m]}, (\Omega''_j)_{j \in [m]}) \xleftarrow{\text{U}} (\mathbb{F}_q^m)^2 \text{ with } \sum_{j \in [m]} (\Omega'_j \vec{y}^{(j)} + \Omega''_j \vec{z}^{(j)}) = \vec{0}^\ell, (\Omega_j)_{j \in [m]} \in \mathbb{F}_q^m \text{ with } \sum_{j \in [m]} \Omega_j(x_{\rho(j)} \vec{y}^{(j)} + \vec{z}^{(j)}) = \vec{e}^{(\ell, \ell)}\}$ and $\{(\widehat{\omega}, (\widehat{\Omega}_j)_{j \in [m]}, (\widehat{\Omega}'_j)_{j \in [m]}) \mid \widehat{\omega} \xleftarrow{\text{U}} \mathbb{F}_q \backslash \{0\}, ((\widehat{\Omega}_j)_{j \in [m]}, (\widehat{\Omega}'_j)_{j \in [m]}) \xleftarrow{\text{U}} S\}$ are equivalent. Also, the distributions $\{(\bar{\sigma}_j = \xi\Omega_j \sigma_{\rho(j)} + \sigma'_j)_{j \in [m]} \mid \xi \xleftarrow{\text{U}} \mathbb{F}_q \backslash \{0\}, \{\sigma_\iota\}_{\iota \in [n]}, \{\sigma'_j\}_{j \in [m]} \xleftarrow{\text{U}} \mathbb{F}_q, (\Omega_j)_{j \in [m]} \in \mathbb{F}_q^m \text{ with } \sum_{j \in [m]} \Omega_j(x_{\rho(j)} \vec{y}^{(j)} + \vec{z}^{(j)}) = \vec{e}^{(\ell, \ell)}\}$ and $\{(\widehat{\sigma}_j)_{j \in [m]} \mid \{\widehat{\sigma}_j\}_{j \in [m]} \xleftarrow{\text{U}} \mathbb{F}_q\}$ are equivalent. Thus, the distributions of sig $\xleftarrow{\text{R}} \text{ABS.Sign}(\text{MPK}, \vec{x}, \text{SK}(\vec{x}), \mathbb{S}, \text{MSG})$ and that of sig $\xleftarrow{\text{R}} \text{ABS.AltSign}(\text{MPK}, \text{MSK}, \mathbb{S}, \text{MSG})$ are equivalent. This completes the proof of Theorem 4.1. ☐

Theorem 4.2 (Existential Unforgeability): *The proposed* ABS *scheme is existentially unforgeable against adaptive-predicate-adaptive-message attack (as per the security model described in Sect. 2.5) under the* SXDLIN *assumption* [1].

Proof: In order to prove Theorem 4.2, we consider a sequence of hybrid experiments which differ from one another in the construction of the signing keys/signatures queried by the adversary $\mathcal{A}$ and/or the verification-text used by the challenger $\mathcal{B}$ to verify the validity of the forged signature outputted by $\mathcal{A}$ at the end of the experiment. The first hybrid corresponds to the real unforge-ability experiment described in Sect. 2.5, while the last hybrid corresponds to one in which the probability that a forged signature outputted by $\mathcal{A}$ passes the verification is negligible. We argue that $\mathcal{A}$'s winning probability changes only by a negligible amount in each successive hybrid experiment, thereby establishing Theorem 4.2. The overall structure of our reduction is demonstrated in Fig. 2. The intermediate computational problems, e.g., Problem 1, Problem 2 etc. used in the reduction (as can be seen in Fig. 2) are presented in the full version of the paper. Let q_{key} and q_{sig} be the total number of signing keys and signatures $\mathcal{A}$ requests $\mathcal{B}$ to reveal during the experiment. The sequence of hybrid experiments are described below. In the description of the hybrids a part framed by a box indicates coefficients which are altered in a transition from its previous hybrid.

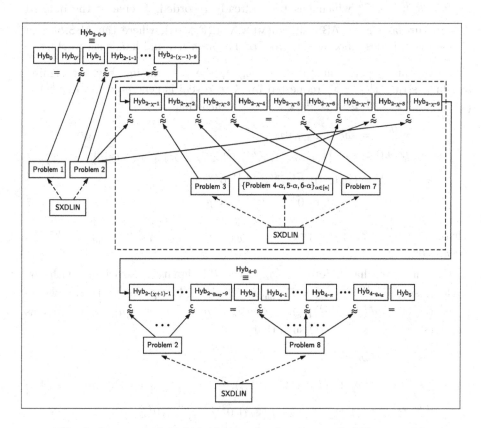

Fig. 2. Structure of the hybrid reduction for the proof of Theorem 4.2

■ Sequence of Hybrid Experiments

Hyb$_0$: This is the real unforgeability experiment described in Sect. 2.5.

Hyb$_{0'}$: This experiment is the same as Hyb$_0$ except the following:

1. When $\mathcal{A}$ makes a signing key generation query for some signing attribute string $\vec{x} \in \mathbb{F}_q^n$, $\mathcal{B}$ only records $\vec{x}$, but creates no actual signing key.
2. When a signature query is made by $\mathcal{A}$ on some message MSG $\in \mathbb{M}$ under some signing policy predicate $R_{\text{Z-ABP}}^{(q)}(f, \cdot) : \mathbb{F}_q^n \to \{0, 1\} \in \mathcal{R}_{\text{Z-ABP}}^{(q)}$ having ASP-representation $\mathbb{S} = (\mathbb{U}, \rho)$ to be created using a signing key for some signing attribute string $\vec{x} \in \mathbb{F}_q^n$ for which it has already made a signing key generation query, $\mathcal{B}$ simply records the triple (MSG, $\mathbb{S}, \vec{x}$), but creates no actual signature.

3. When $\mathcal{A}$ issues a signing key reveal query for some signing attribute string $\vec{x} \in \mathbb{F}_q^n$ which has been already recorded, $\mathcal{B}$ creates the queried signing key as $\mathrm{SK}(\vec{x}) \xleftarrow{\mathrm{R}} \mathsf{ABS.KeyGen}(\mathrm{MPK}, \mathrm{MSK}, \vec{x})$, and returns it to $\mathcal{A}$. On the other hand, when $\mathcal{A}$ issues a signature reveal query for some triple $(\mathrm{MSG}, \mathbb{S}, \vec{x}) \in \mathbb{M} \times \mathcal{R}_{\mathrm{Z\text{-}ABP}}^{(q)} \times \mathbb{F}_q^n$ which has been already recorded, $\mathcal{B}$ creates the queried signature as $\mathrm{sig} \xleftarrow{\mathrm{R}} \mathsf{ABS.AltSign}(\mathrm{MPK}, \mathrm{MSK}, \mathbb{S}, \mathrm{MSG})$, where the $\mathsf{ABS.AltSign}$ algorithm is described in the proof of Theorem 4.1, and hands sig to $\mathcal{A}$.

Thus, in this experiment for $h \in [q_{\mathrm{key}}]$, the hth signing key for signing attribute string $\vec{x}^{(h)} \in \mathbb{F}_q^n$ requested by $\mathcal{A}$ to reveal is generated as $\mathrm{SK}(\vec{x}^{(h)}) = (\boldsymbol{k}^{*(h,0)}, \ldots, \boldsymbol{k}^{*(h,n)}, \boldsymbol{k}^{*(h,n+1,1)}, \boldsymbol{k}^{*(h,n+1,2)})$ such that

$$
\begin{aligned}
\boldsymbol{k}^{*(h,0)} &= (\omega_h, 0, \varphi_{h,0}, 0)_{\mathbb{B}_0^*}, \\
\boldsymbol{k}^{*(h,\iota)} &= (\sigma_{h,\iota}(1,\iota), \omega_h(1, x_\iota^{(h)}), \vec{0}^6, \vec{\varphi}^{(h,\iota)}, \vec{0}^2)_{\mathbb{B}_1^*} \text{ for } \iota \in [n], \\
\boldsymbol{k}^{*(h,n+1,1)} &= (\omega_h(1,0), \vec{0}^2, \vec{\varphi}^{(h,n+1,1)}, \vec{0}^2)_{\mathbb{B}_2^*}, \\
\boldsymbol{k}^{*(h,n+1,2)} &= (\omega_h(0,1), \vec{0}^2, \vec{\varphi}^{(h,n+1,2)}, \vec{0}^2)_{\mathbb{B}_2^*},
\end{aligned}
\tag{4.1}
$$

where $\omega_h \xleftarrow{\mathrm{U}} \mathbb{F}_q \backslash \{0\}$, $\{\sigma_{h,\iota}\}_{\iota \in [n]}, \varphi_{h,0} \xleftarrow{\mathrm{U}} \mathbb{F}_q$, $\{\vec{\varphi}^{(h,\iota)}\}_{\iota \in [n]}, \vec{\varphi}^{(h,n+1,1)}, \vec{\varphi}^{(h,n+1,2)} \xleftarrow{\mathrm{U}} \mathbb{F}_q^2$.

On the other hand, for $t \in [q_{\mathrm{sig}}]$, the tth signature associated with the triple $(\mathrm{MSG}_t, \mathbb{S}_t, \vec{x}^{(t)}) \in \mathbb{M} \times \mathcal{R}_{\mathrm{Z\text{-}ABP}}^{(q)} \times \mathbb{F}_q^n$ that $\mathcal{A}$ requests to reveal, where $\mathbb{S}_t = (\mathbb{U}_t = \{(\vec{y}^{(t,j)}, \vec{z}^{(t,j)})\}_{j \in [m_t]} \subset (\mathbb{F}_q^{\ell_t})^2, \rho_t : [m_t] \rightarrow [n])$, is created as $\mathrm{sig}_t = (\boldsymbol{s}^{*(t,0)}, \ldots, \boldsymbol{s}^{*(t,m_t+1)})$ such that

$$
\begin{aligned}
\boldsymbol{s}^{*(t,0)} &= (\widehat{\omega}_t, 0, \widehat{v}_{t,0}, 0)_{\mathbb{B}_0^*}, \\
\boldsymbol{s}^{*(t,j)} &= (\widehat{\sigma}_{t,j}(1, \rho_t(j)), (\widehat{\Omega}_{t,j}', \widehat{\Omega}_{t,j}), \vec{0}^6, \vec{v}^{(t,j)}, \vec{0}^2)_{\mathbb{B}_1^*} \text{ for } j \in [m_t], \\
\boldsymbol{s}^{*(t,m_t+1)} &= (\widehat{\omega}(1, \mathsf{H}_{\mathrm{hk}}^{(\lambda,\mathrm{poly})}(\mathrm{MSG}_t \| \mathbb{S}_t)), \vec{0}^2, \vec{v}^{(t,m_t+1)}, \vec{0}^2)_{\mathbb{B}_2^*},
\end{aligned}
\tag{4.2}
$$

where $\widehat{\omega}_t \xleftarrow{\mathrm{U}} \mathbb{F}_q \backslash \{0\}$, $\{\widehat{\sigma}_{t,j}\}_{j \in [m_t]}, \widehat{v}_{t,0} \xleftarrow{\mathrm{U}} \mathbb{F}_q$, $\{\vec{v}^{(t,j)}\}_{j \in [m_t+1]} \xleftarrow{\mathrm{U}} \mathbb{F}_q^2$, and $((\widehat{\Omega}_{t,j})_{j \in [m_t]}, (\widehat{\Omega}_{t,j}')_{j \in [m_t]}) \xleftarrow{\mathrm{U}} S_t = \{((\widehat{\Omega}_{t,j})_{j \in [m_t]}, (\widehat{\Omega}_{t,j}')_{j \in [m_t]}) \in (\mathbb{F}_q^{m_t})^2 \mid \sum_{j \in [m_t]} (\widehat{\Omega}_{t,j} \vec{y}^{(t,j)} + \widehat{\Omega}_{t,j}' \vec{z}^{(t,j)}) = \vec{e}^{(\ell_t, \ell_t)}\}$.

Finally, in this experiment, the verification-text used to verify the forged signature outputted by $\mathcal{A}$ on some message $\mathrm{MSG} \in \mathbb{M}$ under some signing policy predicate $R_{\mathrm{Z\text{-}ABP}}^{(q)}(f, \cdot) : \mathbb{F}_q^n \rightarrow \{0,1\} \in \mathcal{R}_{\mathrm{Z\text{-}ABP}}^{(q)}$ having ASP-representation $\mathbb{S} = (\mathbb{U} = \{(\vec{y}^{(j)}, \vec{z}^{(j)})\}_{j \in [m]} \subset (\mathbb{F}_q^\ell)^2, \rho : [m] \rightarrow [n])$ is generated as $(\boldsymbol{c}^{(0)}, \ldots, \boldsymbol{c}^{(m+1)})$ such that

$$
\begin{aligned}
\boldsymbol{c}^{(0)} &= (-u - u_\ell, 0, 0, \eta_0)_{\mathbb{B}_0}, \\
\boldsymbol{c}^{(j)} &= (\mu_j(\rho(j), -1), (s_j', s_j), \vec{0}^6, \vec{0}^2, \vec{\eta}^{(j)})_{\mathbb{B}_1} \text{ for } j \in [m], \\
\boldsymbol{c}^{(m+1)} &= ((u - \kappa \mathsf{H}_{\mathrm{hk}}^{(\lambda,\mathrm{poly})}(\mathrm{MSG} \| \mathbb{S}), \kappa), \vec{0}^2, \vec{0}^2, \vec{\eta}^{(m+1)})_{\mathbb{B}_2},
\end{aligned}
\tag{4.3}
$$

where $\vec{u} = (u_1, \ldots, u_\ell) \xleftarrow{\mathsf{U}} \mathbb{F}_q^\ell$, $s_j = \vec{u} \cdot \vec{y}^{(j)}$, $s_j' = \vec{u} \cdot \vec{z}^{(j)}$ for $j \in [m]$, $u, \{\mu_j\}_{j \in [m]}$, $\kappa, \eta_0 \xleftarrow{\mathsf{U}} \mathbb{F}_q$, and $\{\vec{\eta}^{(j)}\}_{j \in [m+1]} \xleftarrow{\mathsf{U}} \mathbb{F}_q^2$.

Here $\{\mathbb{B}_\iota, \mathbb{B}_\iota^*\}_{\iota \in [0,2]}$ is the collection of dual orthonormal bases generated by $\mathcal{B}$ during the setup phase of the experiment.

Hyb$_1$: This experiment is analogous to Hyb$_{0'}$ except that in this experiment, the verification-text used to verify the forged signature outputted by $\mathcal{A}$ on some message MSG $\in \mathbb{M}$ under some signing policy predicate $R_{\text{Z-ABP}}^{(q)}(f, \cdot) : \mathbb{F}_q^n \to \{0, 1\} \in \mathcal{R}_{\text{Z-ABP}}^{(q)}$ having ASP-representation $\mathbb{S} = (\mathbb{U} = \{(\vec{y}^{(j)}, \vec{z}^{(j)})\}_{j \in [m]} \subset (\mathbb{F}_q^\ell)^2, \rho : [m] \to [n])$ is generated as $(\boldsymbol{c}^{(0)}, \ldots, \boldsymbol{c}^{(m+1)})$ such that

$$\boldsymbol{c}^{(0)} = (-u - u_\ell, \boxed{-\widetilde{u}_\ell}, 0, \eta_0)_{\mathbb{B}_0},$$

$$\boldsymbol{c}^{(j)} = (\mu_j(\rho(j), -1), (s_j', s_j), \boxed{(\widetilde{s}_j', \widetilde{s}_j)}, \vec{0}^2, \boxed{\vec{r}^{(j)}}, \vec{0}^2, \vec{\eta}^{(j)})_{\mathbb{B}_1} \text{ for } j \in [m], \quad (4.4)$$

$$\boldsymbol{c}^{(m+1)} = ((u - \kappa \mathsf{H}_{\mathsf{hk}}^{(\lambda, \mathsf{poly})}(\text{MSG}\|\mathbb{S}), \kappa), \boxed{\vec{r}^{(m+1)}}, \vec{0}^2, \vec{\eta}^{(m+1)})_{\mathbb{B}_2},$$

where $\widetilde{\vec{u}} = (\widetilde{u}_1, \ldots, \widetilde{u}_\ell) \xleftarrow{\mathsf{U}} \mathbb{F}_q^\ell$, $\widetilde{s}_j = \widetilde{\vec{u}} \cdot \vec{y}^{(j)}$, $\widetilde{s}_j' = \widetilde{\vec{u}} \cdot \vec{z}^{(j)}$ for $j \in [m]$, $\{\vec{r}^{(j)}\}_{j \in [m+1]} \xleftarrow{\mathsf{U}} \mathbb{F}_q^2$, and all the other variables are generated as in Hyb$_{0'}$.

Hyb$_{2\text{-}\chi\text{-}1}$ $(\chi \in [q_{\mathbf{key}}])$: Hyb$_{2\text{-}0\text{-}9}$ coincides with Hyb$_1$. This experiment is the same as Hyb$_{2\text{-}(\chi-1)\text{-}9}$ with the only exception that in this experiment, the χth signing key for signing attribute string $\vec{x}^{(\chi)} \in \mathbb{F}_q^n$ requested by $\mathcal{A}$ to reveal is generated as $\text{SK}(\vec{x}^{(\chi)}) = (\boldsymbol{k}^{*(\chi,0)}, \ldots, \boldsymbol{k}^{*(\chi,n)}, \boldsymbol{k}^{*(\chi,n+1,1)}, \boldsymbol{k}^{*(\chi,n+1,2)})$ such that $\boldsymbol{k}^{*(\chi,n+1,1)}, \boldsymbol{k}^{*(\chi,n+1,2)}$ are given by Eq. (4.1), and

$$\boldsymbol{k}^{*(\chi,0)} = (\omega_\chi, \boxed{\widetilde{\omega}_\chi}, \varphi_{\chi,0}, 0)_{\mathbb{B}_0^*},$$

$$\boldsymbol{k}^{*(\chi,\iota)} = (\sigma_{\chi,\iota}(1, \iota), \omega_\chi(1, x_\iota^{(\chi)}), \boxed{\widetilde{\omega}_\chi(1, x_\iota^{(\chi)})}, \vec{0}^4, \vec{\varphi}^{(\chi,\iota)}, \vec{0}^2)_{\mathbb{B}_1^*} \text{ for } \iota \in [n], \quad (4.5)$$

where $\widetilde{\omega}_\chi \xleftarrow{\mathsf{U}} \mathbb{F}_q \backslash \{0\}$ and all the other variables are generated as in Hyb$_{2\text{-}(\chi-1)\text{-}9}$.

Hyb$_{2\text{-}\chi\text{-}2}$ $(\chi \in [q_{\mathbf{key}}])$: This experiment is analogous to Hyb$_{2\text{-}\chi\text{-}1}$ except that in this experiment, the verification-text used to verify the forged signature outputted by $\mathcal{A}$ on some message MSG $\in \mathbb{M}$ under some signing policy predicate $R_{\text{Z-ABP}}^{(q)}(f, \cdot) : \mathbb{F}_q^n \to \{0, 1\} \in \mathcal{R}_{\text{Z-ABP}}^{(q)}$ having ASP-representation $\mathbb{S} = (\mathbb{U} = \{(\vec{y}^{(j)}, \vec{z}^{(j)})\}_{j \in [m]} \subset (\mathbb{F}_q^\ell)^2, \rho : [m] \to [n])$ is generated as $(\boldsymbol{c}^{(0)}, \ldots, \boldsymbol{c}^{(m+1)})$ such that $\boldsymbol{c}^{(0)}, \boldsymbol{c}^{(m+1)}$ have the same form as in Eq. (4.4) and

$$\boldsymbol{c}^{(j)} = (\mu_j(\rho(j), -1), (s_j', s_j), (\widetilde{s}_j', \widetilde{s}_j), \vec{0}^2, \boxed{(\widetilde{s}_j', \widetilde{s}_j) \boldsymbol{Z}^{(\rho(j))}}, \vec{0}^2, \vec{\eta}^{(j)})_{\mathbb{B}_1} \text{ for } j \in [m], \quad (4.6)$$

where $\boldsymbol{Z}^{(\iota)} \in \{\boldsymbol{Z} \in \mathsf{GL}(2, \mathbb{F}_q) \mid \vec{e}^{(2,2)} = (1, x_\iota^{(\chi)})(\boldsymbol{Z}^{-1})^\top\}$ for $\iota \in [n]$, and all the other variables are generated as in Hyb$_{2\text{-}\chi\text{-}1}$.

Hyb$_{2\text{-}\chi\text{-}3}$ $(\chi \in [q_{\mathbf{key}}])$: This experiment is the same as Hyb$_{2\text{-}\chi\text{-}2}$ with the only exception that in this experiment, the χth signing key for signing attribute string $\vec{x}^{(\chi)} \in \mathbb{F}_q^n$ requested by $\mathcal{A}$ to reveal is generated as $\mathrm{SK}(\vec{x}^{(\chi)}) = (\boldsymbol{k}^{*(\chi,0)}, \ldots, \boldsymbol{k}^{*(\chi,n)}, \boldsymbol{k}^{*(\chi,n+1,1)}, \boldsymbol{k}^{*(\chi,n+1,2)})$ such that $\boldsymbol{k}^{*(\chi,0)}$ is given by Eq. (4.5), $\boldsymbol{k}^{*(\chi,n+1,1)}, \boldsymbol{k}^{*(\chi,n+1,2)}$ are given by Eq. (4.1), and

$$\boldsymbol{k}^{*(\chi,\iota)} = (\sigma_{\chi,\iota}(1,\iota), \omega_\chi(1, x_\iota^{(\chi)}), \boxed{\vec{0}^2}, \vec{0}^2, \boxed{(0, \widetilde{\omega}_\chi)}, \varphi^{(\chi,\iota)}, \vec{0}^2)_{\mathbb{B}_1^*} \text{ for } \iota \in [n], \quad (4.7)$$

where all the variables are generated as in $\mathsf{Hyb}_{2\text{-}\chi\text{-}2}$.

$\mathsf{Hyb}_{2\text{-}\chi\text{-}4}$ ($\chi \in [q_{\mathbf{key}}]$): This experiment is identical to $\mathsf{Hyb}_{2\text{-}\chi\text{-}3}$ except that in this experiment, the verification-text used to verify the forged signature outputted by $\mathcal{A}$ on some message $\mathrm{MSG} \in \mathbb{M}$ under some signing policy predicate $R_{\mathrm{Z\text{-}ABP}}^{(q)}(f, \cdot)$: $\mathbb{F}_q^n \to \{0,1\} \in \mathcal{R}_{\mathrm{Z\text{-}ABP}}^{(q)}$ having ASP-representation $\mathbb{S} = (\mathbb{U} = \{(\vec{y}^{(j)}, \vec{z}^{(j)})\}_{j \in [m]} \subset (\mathbb{F}_q^\ell)^2, \rho : [m] \to [n])$ is generated as $(\boldsymbol{c}^{(0)}, \ldots, \boldsymbol{c}^{(m+1)})$ such that $\boldsymbol{c}^{(0)}, \boldsymbol{c}^{(m+1)}$ have the same form as in Eq. (4.4) and

$$\begin{aligned} \boldsymbol{c}^{(j)} = (\mu_j(\rho(j), -1), (s_j', s_j), \boxed{\vec{a}^{(j)}}, \vec{0}^2, (\boxed{\widetilde{a}_j}, \vec{\widetilde{u}} \cdot (x_{\rho(j)}^{(\chi)} \vec{y}^{(j)} + \vec{z}^{(j)})), \\ \vec{0}^2, \vec{\eta}^{(j)})_{\mathbb{B}_1} \text{ for } j \in [m], \end{aligned} \quad (4.8)$$

where $\{\widetilde{a}_j\}_{j \in [m]} \xleftarrow{\mathsf{U}} \mathbb{F}_q$, $\{\vec{a}^{(j)}\}_{j \in [m]} \xleftarrow{\mathsf{U}} \mathbb{F}_q^2$, and all the other variables are generated as in $\mathsf{Hyb}_{2\text{-}\chi\text{-}3}$.

$\mathsf{Hyb}_{2\text{-}\chi\text{-}5}$ ($\chi \in [q_{\mathbf{key}}]$): This experiment is the same as $\mathsf{Hyb}_{2\text{-}\chi\text{-}4}$ with the only exception that in this experiment, the χth signing key for signing attribute string $\vec{x}^{(\chi)} \in \mathbb{F}_q^n$ requested by $\mathcal{A}$ to reveal is generated as $\mathrm{SK}(\vec{x}^{(\chi)}) = (\boldsymbol{k}^{*(\chi,0)}, \ldots, \boldsymbol{k}^{*(\chi,n)}, \boldsymbol{k}^{*(\chi,n+1,1)}, \boldsymbol{k}^{*(\chi,n+1,2)})$ such that $\{\boldsymbol{k}^{*(\chi,\iota)}\}_{\iota \in [n]}$ are given by Eq. (4.7), $\boldsymbol{k}^{*(\chi,n+1,1)}, \boldsymbol{k}^{*(\chi,n+1,2)}$ are given by Eq. (4.1), and

$$\boldsymbol{k}^{*(\chi,0)} = (\omega_\chi, \boxed{\Im_\chi}, \varphi_{\chi,0}, 0)_{\mathbb{B}_0^*}, \quad (4.9)$$

where $\Im_\chi \xleftarrow{\mathsf{U}} \mathbb{F}_q$, and all the other variables are generated as in $\mathsf{Hyb}_{2\text{-}\chi\text{-}4}$.

$\mathsf{Hyb}_{2\text{-}\chi\text{-}6}$ ($\chi \in [q_{\mathbf{key}}]$): This experiment is analogous to $\mathsf{Hyb}_{2\text{-}\chi\text{-}5}$ except that in this experiment, the verification-text used to verify the forged signature outputted by $\mathcal{A}$ on some message $\mathrm{MSG} \in \mathbb{M}$ under some signing policy predicate $R_{\mathrm{Z\text{-}ABP}}^{(q)}(f, \cdot) : \mathbb{F}_q^n \to \{0,1\} \in \mathcal{R}_{\mathrm{Z\text{-}ABP}}^{(q)}$ having ASP-representation $\mathbb{S} = (\mathbb{U} = \{(\vec{y}^{(j)}, \vec{z}^{(j)})\}_{j \in [m]} \subset (\mathbb{F}_q^\ell)^2, \rho : [m] \to [n])$ is generated as $(\boldsymbol{c}^{(0)}, \ldots, \boldsymbol{c}^{(m+1)})$ such that $\boldsymbol{c}^{(0)}, \boldsymbol{c}^{(m+1)}$ have the same form as in Eq. (4.4) and $\{\boldsymbol{c}^{(j)}\}_{j \in [m]}$ are given by Eq. (4.6) where $\widetilde{s}_j = \vec{\widetilde{u}} \cdot \vec{y}^{(j)}$, $\widetilde{s}_j' = \vec{\widetilde{u}} \cdot \vec{z}^{(j)}$ for $j \in [m]$, $\boldsymbol{Z}^{(\iota)} \in \{\boldsymbol{Z} \in \mathsf{GL}(2, \mathbb{F}_q) \mid \vec{e}^{(2,2)} = (1, x_\iota^{(\chi)})(\boldsymbol{Z}^{-1})^\top\}$ for $\iota \in [n]$, and all the other variables are generated as in $\mathsf{Hyb}_{2\text{-}\chi\text{-}5}$.

$\mathsf{Hyb}_{2\text{-}\chi\text{-}7}$ ($\chi \in [q_{\mathbf{key}}]$): This experiment is analogous to $\mathsf{Hyb}_{2\text{-}\chi\text{-}6}$ with the only exception that in this experiment, the χth signing key for signing attribute string $\vec{x}^{(\chi)} \in \mathbb{F}_q^n$ requested by $\mathcal{A}$ to reveal is generated as $\mathrm{SK}(\vec{x}^{(\chi)}) = (\boldsymbol{k}^{*(\chi,0)}, \ldots, \boldsymbol{k}^{*(\chi,n)}, \boldsymbol{k}^{*(\chi,n+1,1)}, \boldsymbol{k}^{*(\chi,n+1,2)})$ such that $\boldsymbol{k}^{*(0)}$ is given by Eq. (4.9), $\{k^{*(\chi,\iota)}\}_{\iota\in[n]}$ are given by Eq. (4.5), and $k^{*(\chi,n+1,1)}, k^{*(\chi,n+1,2)}$ are given by Eq. (4.1), where all the variables are generated as in $\mathsf{Hyb}_{2\text{-}\chi\text{-}6}$.

$\mathsf{Hyb}_{2\text{-}\chi\text{-}8}$ ($\chi \in [q_{\mathsf{key}}]$): This experiment is analogous to $\mathsf{Hyb}_{2\text{-}\chi\text{-}7}$ except that in this experiment, the verification-text used to verify the forged signature outputted by $\mathcal{A}$ on some message $\mathrm{MSG} \in \mathbb{M}$ under some signing policy predicate $R_{\text{Z-ABP}}^{(q)}(f,\cdot) : \mathbb{F}_q^n \to \{0,1\} \in \mathcal{R}_{\text{Z-ABP}}^{(q)}$ having ASP-representation $\mathbb{S} = (\mathbb{U} = \{(\vec{y}^{(j)}, \vec{z}^{(j)})\}_{j\in[m]} \subset (\mathbb{F}_q^\ell)^2, \rho : [m] \to [n])$ is generated as $(c^{(0)}, \ldots, c^{(m+1)})$ such that $\{c^{(j)}\}_{j\in[0,m+1]}$ have the same form as in Eq. (4.4), where $\{\vec{r}^{(j)}\}_{j\in[m]} \xleftarrow{\mathsf{U}} \mathbb{F}_q^2$, and all the other variables are generated as in $\mathsf{Hyb}_{2\text{-}\chi\text{-}7}$.

$\mathsf{Hyb}_{2\text{-}\chi\text{-}9}$ ($\chi \in [q_{\mathsf{key}}]$): This experiment is analogous to $\mathsf{Hyb}_{2\text{-}\chi\text{-}8}$ with the only exception that in this experiment, the χth signing key for signing attribute string $\vec{x}^{(\chi)} \in \mathbb{F}_q^n$ requested by $\mathcal{A}$ to reveal is generated as $\mathrm{SK}(\vec{x}^{(\chi)}) = (k^{*(\chi,0)}, \ldots, k^{*(\chi,n)}, k^{*(\chi,n+1,1)}, k^{*(\chi,n+1,2)})$ such that $k^{*(0)}$ is given by Eq. (4.9), and $\{k^{*(\chi,\iota)}\}_{\iota\in[n]}, k^{*(\chi,n+1,1)}, k^{*(\chi,n+1,2)}$ are given by Eq. (4.1), where all the variables are generated as in $\mathsf{Hyb}_{2\text{-}\chi\text{-}8}$.

Hyb_3: This experiment is identical to $\mathsf{Hyb}_{2\text{-}q_{\mathsf{key}}\text{-}9}$ except that in this experiment, the verification-text used to verify the forged signature outputted by $\mathcal{A}$ on some message $\mathrm{MSG} \in \mathbb{M}$ under some signing policy predicate $R_{\text{Z-ABP}}^{(q)}(f,\cdot) : \mathbb{F}_q^n \to \{0,1\} \in \mathcal{R}_{\text{Z-ABP}}^{(q)}$ having ASP-representation $\mathbb{S} = (\mathbb{U} = \{(\vec{y}^{(j)}, \vec{z}^{(j)})\}_{j\in[m]} \subset (\mathbb{F}_q^\ell)^2, \rho : [m] \to [n])$ is generated as $(c^{(0)}, \ldots, c^{(m+1)})$ such that $\{c^{(j)}\}_{j\in[m+1]}$ have the same form as in Eq. (4.4), and

$$c^{(0)} = (-u - u_\ell, \boxed{v}, 0, \eta_0)_{\mathbb{B}_0}, \tag{4.10}$$

where $v \xleftarrow{\mathsf{U}} \mathbb{F}_q$, and all the other variables are generated as in $\mathsf{Hyb}_{2\text{-}q_{\mathsf{key}}\text{-}9}$.

$\mathsf{Hyb}_{4\text{-}\pi}$ ($\pi \in [q_{\mathsf{sig}}]$): $\mathsf{Hyb}_{4\text{-}0}$ coincides with Hyb_3. This experiment is the same as $\mathsf{Hyb}_{4\text{-}(\pi-1)}$ except that in this experiment, the πth signature associated with the triple $(\mathrm{MSG}_\pi, \mathbb{S}_\pi, \vec{x}^{(\pi)}) \in \mathbb{M} \times \mathcal{R}_{\text{Z-ABP}}^{(q,n)} \times \mathbb{F}_q^n$ that $\mathcal{A}$ requests to reveal, where $\mathbb{S}_\pi = (\mathbb{U}_\pi = \{(\vec{y}^{(\pi,j)}, \vec{z}^{(\pi,j)})\}_{j\in[m_\pi]} \subset (\mathbb{F}_q^{\ell_\pi})^2, \rho_\pi : [m_\pi] \to [n])$, is created as $\mathrm{sig}_\pi = (s^{*(\pi,0)}, \ldots, s^{*(\pi,m_\pi+1)})$ such that $\{s^{*(\pi,j)}\}_{j\in[m_\pi]}$ have the same form as in Eq. (4.2), and

$$s^{*(\pi,0)} = (\widehat{\omega}_\pi, \boxed{\zeta_{\pi,0}}, \widehat{v}_{\pi,0}, 0)_{\mathbb{B}_0^*},$$

$$s^{*(\pi,m_\pi+1)} = (\widehat{\omega}_\pi(1, \mathsf{H}_{\mathsf{hk}}^{(\lambda,\mathsf{poly})}(\mathrm{MSG}_\pi\|\mathbb{S}_\pi)), \boxed{\vec{\zeta}^{(\pi,m_\pi+1)}}, \vec{v}^{(\pi,m_\pi+1)}, \vec{0}^2)_{\mathbb{B}_2^*}, \tag{4.11}$$

where $\zeta_{\pi,0} \xleftarrow{\mathsf{U}} \mathbb{F}_q$, $\vec{\zeta}^{(\pi,m_\pi+1)} \xleftarrow{\mathsf{U}} \mathbb{F}_q^2$, and all the other variables are generated as in $\mathsf{Hyb}_{4\text{-}(\pi-1)}$.

Hyb_5: This experiment is identical to $\mathsf{Hyb}_{4\text{-}q_{\mathsf{sig}}}$ except that in this experiment, the verification-text used to verify the forged signature outputted by $\mathcal{A}$ on some message $\mathrm{MSG} \in \mathbb{M}$ under some signing policy predicate

$R_{\text{Z-ABP}}^{(q)}(f, \cdot) : \mathbb{F}_q^n \to \{0, 1\} \in \mathcal{R}_{\text{Z-ABP}}^{(q)}$ having ASP-representation $\mathbb{S} = (\mathbb{U} = \{(\vec{y}^{(j)}, \vec{z}^{(j)})\}_{j \in [m]} \subset (\mathbb{F}_q^\ell)^2, \rho : [m] \to [n])$ is generated as $(\boldsymbol{c}^{(0)}, \ldots, \boldsymbol{c}^{(m+1)})$ such that $\{\boldsymbol{c}^{(j)}\}_{j \in [m+1]}$ have the same form as in Eq. (4.4), and

$$\boldsymbol{c}^{(0)} = (\boxed{w}, v, 0, \eta_0)_{\mathbb{B}_0}, \tag{4.12}$$

where $w \xleftarrow{\mathsf{U}} \mathbb{F}_q$, and all the other variables are generated as in $\mathsf{Hyb}_{5\text{-}q_{\text{sig}}}$.

■ **Analysis**

Let us now denote by $\mathsf{Adv}_{\mathcal{A}}^{(i)}(\lambda)$ the probability that $\mathcal{A}$ wins in Hyb_i for $i \in \{0, 0', 1, \{2\text{-}\chi\text{-}k\}_{\chi \in [q_{\text{key}}], k \in [9]}, 3, \{4\text{-}\pi\}_{\pi \in [q_{\text{sig}}]}, 5\}$. By definition, we clearly have $\mathsf{Adv}_{\mathcal{A}}^{\text{ABS,UF}}(\lambda) \equiv \mathsf{Adv}_{\mathcal{A}}^{(0)}(\lambda)$, $\mathsf{Adv}_{\mathcal{A}}^{(1)}(\lambda) \equiv \mathsf{Adv}_{\mathcal{A}}^{(2\text{-}0\text{-}9)}(\lambda)$, and $\mathsf{Adv}_{\mathcal{A}}^{(3)}(\lambda) \equiv \mathsf{Adv}_{\mathcal{A}}^{(4\text{-}0)}(\lambda)$. Hence, we have

$$
\begin{aligned}
\mathsf{Adv}_{\mathcal{A}}^{\text{ABS,UF}}(\lambda) \leq{} & \left| \mathsf{Adv}_{\mathcal{A}}^{(0)}(\lambda) - \mathsf{Adv}_{\mathcal{A}}^{(0')}(\lambda) \right| + \left| \mathsf{Adv}_{\mathcal{A}}^{(0')}(\lambda) - \mathsf{Adv}_{\mathcal{A}}^{(1)}(\lambda) \right| + \\
& \sum_{\chi \in [q_{\text{key}}]} \left[\left| \mathsf{Adv}_{\mathcal{A}}^{(2\text{-}(\chi-1)\text{-}9)}(\lambda) - \mathsf{Adv}_{\mathcal{A}}^{(2\text{-}\chi\text{-}1)}(\lambda) \right| + \right. \\
& \left. \sum_{k \in [8]} \left| \mathsf{Adv}_{\mathcal{A}}^{(2\text{-}\chi\text{-}K)}(\lambda) - \mathsf{Adv}_{\mathcal{A}}^{(2\text{-}\chi\text{-}(K+1))}(\lambda) \right| \right] + \\
& \left| \mathsf{Adv}_{\mathcal{A}}^{(2\text{-}q_{\text{key}}\text{-}9)}(\lambda) - \mathsf{Adv}_{\mathcal{A}}^{(3)}(\lambda) \right| + \\
& \sum_{\pi \in [q_{\text{sig}}]} \left| \mathsf{Adv}_{\mathcal{A}}^{(4\text{-}(\pi-1))}(\lambda) - \mathsf{Adv}_{\mathcal{A}}^{(4\text{-}\pi)}(\lambda) \right| + \\
& \left| \mathsf{Adv}_{\mathcal{A}}^{(4\text{-}q_{\text{sig}})}(\lambda) - \mathsf{Adv}_{\mathcal{A}}^{(5)}(\lambda) \right| + \mathsf{Adv}_{\mathcal{A}}^{(5)}(\lambda).
\end{aligned}
\tag{4.13}
$$

We prove that each term on the RHS of Eq. (4.13) is negligible under the SXDLIN assumption. See the full version for details. Hence Theorem 4.2 follows.   □

References

1. Abe, M., Chase, M., David, B., Kohlweiss, M., Nishimaki, R., Ohkubo, M.: Constant-size structure-preserving signatures: generic constructions and simple assumptions. In: Wang, X., Sako, K. (eds.) ASIACRYPT 2012. LNCS, vol. 7658, pp. 4–24. Springer, Heidelberg (2012). https://doi.org/10.1007/978-3-642-34961-4_3
2. Applebaum, B., Ishai, Y., Kushilevitz, E.: How to garble arithmetic circuits. SIAM J. Comput. **43**(2), 905–929 (2014)
3. Bellare, M., Fuchsbauer, G.: Policy-based signatures. In: Krawczyk, H. (ed.) PKC 2014. LNCS, vol. 8383, pp. 520–537. Springer, Heidelberg (2014). https://doi.org/10.1007/978-3-642-54631-0_30
4. Datta, P., Dutta, R., Mukhopadhyay, S.: Attribute-based signatures for turing machines. Cryptology ePrint Archive, Report 2017/801

5. El Kaafarani, A., El Bansarkhani, R.: Post-quantum attribute-based signatures from lattice assumptions. Cryptology ePrint Archive, Report 2016/823
6. El Kaafarani, A., Ghadafi, E., Khader, D.: Decentralized traceable attribute-based signatures. In: Benaloh, J. (ed.) CT-RSA 2014. LNCS, vol. 8366, pp. 327–348. Springer, Cham (2014). https://doi.org/10.1007/978-3-319-04852-9_17
7. El Kaafarani, A., Katsumata, S.: Attribute-based signatures for unbounded circuits in the ROM and efficient instantiations from lattices. In: Abdalla, M., Dahab, R. (eds.) PKC 2018. LNCS, vol. 10770, pp. 89–119. Springer, Cham (2018). https://doi.org/10.1007/978-3-319-76581-5_4
8. Fürer, M.: Faster integer multiplication. SIAM J. Comput. **39**(3), 979–1005 (2009)
9. Groth, J., Sahai, A.: Efficient non-interactive proof systems for bilinear groups. In: Smart, N. (ed.) EUROCRYPT 2008. LNCS, vol. 4965, pp. 415–432. Springer, Heidelberg (2008). https://doi.org/10.1007/978-3-540-78967-3_24
10. Herranz, J., Laguillaumie, F., Libert, B., Ràfols, C.: Short attribute-based signatures for threshold predicates. In: Dunkelman, O. (ed.) CT-RSA 2012. LNCS, vol. 7178, pp. 51–67. Springer, Heidelberg (2012). https://doi.org/10.1007/978-3-642-27954-6_4
11. Ishai, Y., Kushilevitz, E.: Perfect constant-round secure computation via perfect randomizing polynomials. In: Widmayer, P., Eidenbenz, S., Triguero, F., Morales, R., Conejo, R., Hennessy, M. (eds.) ICALP 2002. LNCS, vol. 2380, pp. 244–256. Springer, Heidelberg (2002). https://doi.org/10.1007/3-540-45465-9_22
12. Ishai, Y., Kushilevitz, E.: Private simultaneous messages protocols with applications. In: ITCS 1997, pp. 174–183. IEEE (1997)
13. Ishai, Y., Wee, H.: Partial garbling schemes and their applications. In: Esparza, J., Fraigniaud, P., Husfeldt, T., Koutsoupias, E. (eds.) ICALP 2014. LNCS, vol. 8572, pp. 650–662. Springer, Heidelberg (2014). https://doi.org/10.1007/978-3-662-43948-7_54
14. Karchmer, M., Wigderson, A.: On span programs. In: Structure in Complexity Theory Conference 1993, pp. 102–111. IEEE (1993)
15. Keller, M., Orsini, E., Scholl, P.: Mascot: faster malicious arithmetic secure computation with oblivious transfer. In: ACM-CCS 2016, pp. 830–842. ACM (2016)
16. Kowalczyk, L., Liu, J., Malkin, T., Meiyappan, K.: Mitigating the one-use restriction in attribute-based encryption. Cryptology ePrint Archive, Report 2018/645
17. Li, J., Au, M.H., Susilo, W., Xie, D., Ren, K.: Attribute-based signature and its applications. In: ASIACCS 2010, pp. 60–69. ACM (2010)
18. Li, J., Kim, K.: Attribute-based ring signatures. Cryptology ePrint Archive, Report 2008/394
19. Maji, H., Prabhakaran, M., Rosulek, M.: Attribute-based signatures: achieving attribute-privacy and collusion-resistance. Cryptology ePrint Archive, Report 2008/328
20. Maji, H.K., Prabhakaran, M., Rosulek, M.: Attribute-based signatures. In: Kiayias, A. (ed.) CT-RSA 2011. LNCS, vol. 6558, pp. 376–392. Springer, Heidelberg (2011). https://doi.org/10.1007/978-3-642-19074-2_24
21. Maji, H.K., Prabhakaran, M., Rosulek, M.: Attribute-based signatures. Cryptology ePrint Archive, Report 2010/595
22. Okamoto, T., Takashima, K.: Decentralized attribute-based signatures. In: Kurosawa, K., Hanaoka, G. (eds.) PKC 2013. LNCS, vol. 7778, pp. 125–142. Springer, Heidelberg (2013). https://doi.org/10.1007/978-3-642-36362-7_9

23. Okamoto, T., Takashima, K.: Efficient attribute-based signatures for non-monotone predicates in the standard model. In: Catalano, D., Fazio, N., Gennaro, R., Nicolosi, A. (eds.) PKC 2011. LNCS, vol. 6571, pp. 35–52. Springer, Heidelberg (2011). https://doi.org/10.1007/978-3-642-19379-8_3

24. Okamoto, T., Takashima, K.: Efficient attribute-based signatures for non-monotone predicates in the standard model. Cryptology ePrint Archive, Report 2011/700

25. Okamoto, T., Takashima, K.: Fully secure functional encryption with general relations from the decisional linear assumption. In: Rabin, T. (ed.) CRYPTO 2010. LNCS, vol. 6223, pp. 191–208. Springer, Heidelberg (2010). https://doi.org/10.1007/978-3-642-14623-7_11

26. Okamoto, T., Takashima, K.: Fully secure unbounded inner-product and attribute-based encryption. In: Wang, X., Sako, K. (eds.) ASIACRYPT 2012. LNCS, vol. 7658, pp. 349–366. Springer, Heidelberg (2012). https://doi.org/10.1007/978-3-642-34961-4_22

27. Okamoto, T., Takashima, K.: Hierarchical predicate encryption for inner-products. In: Matsui, M. (ed.) ASIACRYPT 2009. LNCS, vol. 5912, pp. 214–231. Springer, Heidelberg (2009). https://doi.org/10.1007/978-3-642-10366-7_13

28. Parno, B., Howell, J., Gentry, C., Raykova, M.: Pinocchio: nearly practical verifiable computation. Commun. ACM **59**(2), 103–112 (2016)

29. Sakai, Y., Attrapadung, N., Hanaoka, G.: Attribute-based signatures for circuits from bilinear map. In: Cheng, C.-M., Chung, K.-M., Persiano, G., Yang, B.-Y. (eds.) PKC 2016. LNCS, vol. 9614, pp. 283–300. Springer, Heidelberg (2016). https://doi.org/10.1007/978-3-662-49384-7_11

30. Sakai, Y., Katsumata, S., Attrapadung, N., Hanaoka, G.: Attribute-based signatures for unbounded languages from standard assumptions. Cryptology ePrint Archive, Report 2018/842

31. Shahandashti, S.F., Safavi-Naini, R.: Threshold attribute-based signatures and their application to anonymous credential systems. In: Preneel, B. (ed.) AFRICACRYPT 2009. LNCS, vol. 5580, pp. 198–216. Springer, Heidelberg (2009). https://doi.org/10.1007/978-3-642-02384-2_13

32. Takashima, K.: New proof techniques for DLIN-based adaptively secure attribute-based encryption. In: Pieprzyk, J., Suriadi, S. (eds.) ACISP 2017. LNCS, vol. 10342, pp. 85–105. Springer, Cham (2017). https://doi.org/10.1007/978-3-319-60055-0_5

33. Tang, F., Li, H., Liang, B.: Attribute-based signatures for circuits from multilinear maps. In: Chow, S.S.M., Camenisch, J., Hui, L.C.K., Yiu, S.M. (eds.) ISC 2014. LNCS, vol. 8783, pp. 54–71. Springer, Cham (2014). https://doi.org/10.1007/978-3-319-13257-0_4

34. Tsabary, R.: An equivalence between attribute-based signatures and homomorphic signatures, and new constructions for both. In: Kalai, Y., Reyzin, L. (eds.) TCC 2017. LNCS, vol. 10678, pp. 489–518. Springer, Cham (2017). https://doi.org/10.1007/978-3-319-70503-3_16

35. Waters, B.: Ciphertext-policy attribute-based encryption: an expressive, efficient, and provably secure realization. In: Catalano, D., Fazio, N., Gennaro, R., Nicolosi, A. (eds.) PKC 2011. LNCS, vol. 6571, pp. 53–70. Springer, Heidelberg (2011). https://doi.org/10.1007/978-3-642-19379-8_4

36. Waters, B.: Dual system encryption: realizing fully secure IBE and HIBE under simple assumptions. In: Halevi, S. (ed.) CRYPTO 2009. LNCS, vol. 5677, pp. 619–636. Springer, Heidelberg (2009). https://doi.org/10.1007/978-3-642-03356-8_36

Efficient Invisible and Unlinkable Sanitizable Signatures

Xavier Bultel[1]([✉]), Pascal Lafourcade[2], Russell W. F. Lai[3], Giulio Malavolta[3], Dominique Schröder[3], and Sri Aravinda Krishnan Thyagarajan[3]

[1] Univ Rennes, CNRS, IRISA, Rennes, France
xavier.bultel@uca.fr
[2] University Clermont Auvergne, LIMOS, Clermont-Ferrand, France
[3] Friedrich-Alexander University Erlangen-Nürnberg, Erlangen, Germany

Abstract. Sanitizable signatures allow designated parties (the sanitizers) to apply arbitrary modifications to some restricted parts of signed messages. A secure scheme should not only be unforgeable, but also protect privacy and hold both the signer and the sanitizer accountable. Two important security properties that are seemingly difficult to achieve simultaneously and efficiently are invisibility and unlinkability. While invisibility ensures that the admissible modifications are hidden from external parties, unlinkability says that sanitized signatures cannot be linked to their sources. Achieving both properties simultaneously is crucial for applications where sensitive personal data is signed with respect to data-dependent admissible modifications. The existence of an efficient construction achieving both properties was recently posed as an open question by Camenisch et al. (PKC'17). In this work, we propose a solution to this problem with a two-step construction. First, we construct (non-accountable) invisible and unlinkable sanitizable signatures from signatures on equivalence classes and other basic primitives. Second, we put forth a generic transformation using verifiable ring signatures to turn any non-accountable sanitizable signature into an accountable one while preserving all other properties. When instantiating in the generic group and random oracle model, the efficiency of our construction is comparable to that of prior constructions, while providing stronger security guarantees.

1 Introduction

Sanitizable signature schemes introduced by Ateniese *et al.* [1] are signature schemes that allow a certain degree of controlled malleability: The signer signs messages along with some "admissible modifications" with respect to another party called the sanitizer. The sanitizer can (only) convert a given message-signature pair into one that is admissible. When necessary, the signer can (dis)prove the authorship of a given signature to the public which is modelled by a party called the judge. Over the years, the originally informal security properties [1] were formalized [6,7] and strengthened [25]. Beyond unforgeability,

© International Association for Cryptologic Research 2019
D. Lin and K. Sako (Eds.): PKC 2019, LNCS 11442, pp. 159–189, 2019.
https://doi.org/10.1007/978-3-030-17253-4_6

sanitizable signatures provide one with meaningful privacy guarantees, which are important when signing and sanitizing sensitive data. Furthermore, accountability of the signatures prevents the parties from misbehaving as they may eventually get caught. New properties, such as invisibility, were recently proposed [2,10]. To summarize, we recall the security properties which we consider in this work:

Immutability: The sanitizer cannot modify non-admissible messages.
Accountability: The signer cannot accuse the sanitizer (vice versa) of signing.
Transparency: Non-sanitized and sanitized signatures are indistinguishable.
Invisibility: The class of admissible modifications are hidden from external parties.
Unlinkability: Sanitized signatures cannot be linked to their sources.

Applications. Ateniese *et al.* [1] suggested a wide range of applications of sanitizable signatures, including multicast transmission, database outsourcing, protecting health information, and secure routing. As an example, we highlight the importance of invisibility and unlinkability of sanitizable signatures for signing medical records. Suppose that a physician signs medical records of patients using a sanitizable signature scheme. The patients can then sanitize the medical record for different purposes. For example, they may (1) remove the personal information and delegate the anonymized record for analysis; (2) remove everything except for the personal information for financing purposes, in such a way that the receivers are convinced of the authenticity of the record. As discussed in [7], *unlinkability* ensures that colluding receivers cannot reconstruct the full medical records since they cannot link records sanitized from the same source.

However, suppose that the admissible modifications chosen by the physician, are data-dependent. For instance, patients suffering from certain sensitive medical condition that might possibly lead them to be discriminated against, may be allowed to change the fields corresponding to these conditions to NO, while other patients not suffering from any of these conditions are not allowed to change any of the fields to YES. Such a policy of assigning admissible modifications prevents the former patients from facing discrimination when revealing such conditions is not necessary, while preventing the latter patients from getting hold of drugs which are otherwise only issued to patients suffering from those conditions. The security property *invisibility* is crucial for such a scenario, since the receiver of a sanitized medical record can otherwise easily tell whether the corresponding patient suffers from a sensitive condition by just checking whether changing the corresponding field in the record is modifiable or not.

1.1 Open Problem

As discussed above, achieving both unlinkability and invisibility is desirable for certain applications. Obviously, realizing both notions simultaneously is rather easy from a theoretical point of view using common "encrypt and prove" techniques. Although the feasibility is clear, doing so efficiently turns out to be challenging.

One obvious starting point to answer this question is the idea to lift an existing invisible sanitizable signature scheme to an unlinkable one. Following this path does not seem to be fruitful, because existing invisible constructions adopt the "chameleon-hash-then-sign" paradigm: The main ingredients in this approach are a signature scheme for which the signer has the secret key, and a chameleon hashing scheme[1] for which the sanitizer has the trapdoor. To sign a message, the signer first splits the message into ℓ message blocks, some of which are "admissible", meaning that they are allowed to be changed by the sanitizer, while some are not. The signer then computes the chameleon hashes of the individual message blocks, in such a way that the sanitizer can recover the trapdoors corresponding to the admissible blocks, and sign the hash values. Later, the sanitizer can change the admissible blocks by using the trapdoors to "explain" the hash values with new messages.

Under the "chameleon-hash-then-sign" paradigm, we can see that signatures are inherently linkable. This is because all signatures which are sanitized from a fresh signature contain the same set of hash values. One can of course hide the hash values by using generic non-interactive zero-knowledge arguments, but that would not yield a practical scheme. Therefore, [10] and [2] posed the following open problem:

"How to construct (efficient) sanitizable signature schemes which are simultaneously unlinkable and invisible?"

In this work, we answer this question by constructing the first efficient invisible and unlinkable sanitizable signature scheme.

1.2 Our Techniques

To solve the problem of constructing an efficient unlinkable and invisible sanitizable signature scheme, we suggest a modular approach visualized with the help of Fig. 1.

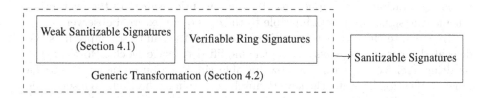

Fig. 1. Outline of our approach.

First, we decouple the problem by presenting a generic transformation that turns any "weak" sanitizable signature scheme, which is not accountable, into an

---

[1] A chameleon hashing scheme allows to generate a probabilistic hash function H together with a trapdoor. With the latter, one can efficiently compute a randomness r when given any message m and hash value h such that $h = H(m, r)$.

accountable one while preserving or upgrading all other properties. Our transformation is very efficient as it only requires a verifiable [28] ring signature[2]. Recall that a ring signature scheme allows a signer to sign messages on behalf of an ad-hoc group picked during signature generation. Verifiability in this context means that a signer can (dis)prove the authorship of a given signature a posteriori. The basic idea of our transformation is as follows.

To sign (resp. sanitize), the signer (resp. the sanitizer) runs the sign (resp. sanitize) algorithm of the weak sanitizable signature scheme, and signs the whole output (ignoring the underlying structure) with a verifiable ring signature scheme, where the ring is composed by the verification keys of the signer and the sanitizer. The resulting scheme is accountable because the signer can (dis)prove the authorship of a certain signature using the accountability property of the ring signature itself. Our transformation does not only preserve the underlying properties of the (non-accountable) sanitizable signature scheme, but it also strengthens some of them: If the underling scheme is weakly immutable (resp. weakly unlinkable), then the resulting scheme is immutable (resp. unlinkable). Loosely speaking, weak immutability considers a forgery as legitimate if it corresponds to a pre-determined sanitizer, as opposed to *any* sanitizer. On the other hand, weak unlinkability restricts the queries of the adversary to the sanitization oracle to consist exclusively of honestly generated signatures.

Next, we tackle the main problem of constructing an invisible and unlinkable (non-accountable) sanitizable signature scheme. The (long-term) public and secret keys of the signer are the verification and signing keys of a certain signature scheme, which we refer to as the outer-layer scheme. To sign a message, the signer splits the message into ℓ message blocks, and generates ℓ pairs of signing and verification keys of an inner-layer signature scheme. Naturally, the signer signs each message block with the corresponding inner signing key, and signs the verification keys with its (long-term) outer secret key. To allow sanitization, the signer additionally delegates the inner signing keys corresponding to the admissible blocks by encrypting them under the sanitizer public key. Note that all message blocks are treated equally, which is critical for invisibility, except for the generation of the ciphertext. By the semantic security of the encryption scheme, the signature is still invisible to the eyes of an external observer.

To generate signatures for sanitized messages, the sanitizer simply uses the delegated inner signing keys to sign the modified message blocks. However, the resulting sanitized signature is now linkable since the outer signature on the inner verification keys and the keys themselves remain unchanged. To resolve this issue, we need to craft an inner signature scheme with some special properties. Our inner signatures scheme is very similar to the Boneh–Lynn–Shacham (BLS) signature scheme [4] and works as follows: The public key consists of two group

---

[2] We remark that verifiable ring signatures can be implemented from unique [18], linkable [27], accountable [35], or traceable [21] ring signatures, so the transformation also works with these kinds of signature.

elements (G_1^x, G_1^{xy}) and the secret key $y \in \mathbb{Z}_q$ can be used to sign a message m by computing $\sigma := \mathsf{H}(m)^y \in G_2$. The verification is done using the pairing

$$e\left(G_1^x, \sigma\right) = e\left(G_1^{xy}, \mathsf{H}(m)\right).$$

The difference with respect to BLS lies in the extra term of the public key whose role will appear clear in a moment. The property that we need is that the keys and the signatures are publicly re-randomizable, i.e., one can compute consistent scalings of both the signature and the public key

$$\left(\sigma, \left(G_1^x, G_1^{xy}\right)\right) \mapsto \left(\sigma, \left(G_1^x, G_1^{xy}\right)\right)^r := \left(\sigma^r, \left(G_1^{rx}, G_1^{rx \cdot y}\right)\right).$$

It is easy to see that the resulting key-signature pair is still consistent, i.e., the verification checks out. Unfortunately, it turns out that the re-randomization strategy of above is too simplistic and it is prone to mix-and-match attacks. We therefore devise a slightly more sophisticated re-randomization procedure

$$\left(\sigma, \left(G_1^x, G_1^{xy}\right)\right) \mapsto \left(\sigma^s, \left(G_1^{rx}, G_1^{rx \cdot sy}\right)\right).$$

which scales the two elements of the public keys by two different scalars r and rs respectively. Fortunately, this does not affect the correctness of the scheme.

Table 1. Size of the parameters.

Sig. SK	San. SK	Sig. PK	San. PK	Signature	Proof
$(\ell + 1)\, \mathbb{Z}_q^*$	$2\, \mathbb{Z}_q^*$	$1\, G_1 +$ $\ell\, G_2$	$2\, G_1$	$(\ell + 5)\, \mathbb{Z}_q^* +$ $(2\ell + 11)\, G_1 +$ $(\ell + 2)\, G_2$	$2\, \mathbb{Z}_q^* +$ $3\, G_1$

The last obstacle towards decorrelating signed and sanitized signatures is a mechanism to publicly rerandomize the outer signature so that it is consistent with the rerandomized inner verification keys. More concretely, the problem is to rerandomize signatures of $(G_1^{x_1}, \ldots, G_1^{x_\ell})$ and $(G_1^{x_1 y_1}, \ldots, G_1^{x_\ell y_\ell})$ to signatures of $(G_1^{rx_1}, \ldots, G_1^{rx_\ell})$ and $(G_1^{rsx_1 y_1}, \ldots, G_1^{rsx_\ell y_\ell})$ respectively. It turns out that equivalence class signatures (EQS) [22] provide exactly such functionality.

1.3 Our Results

To summarize, in this paper we present the following results:

- We present the first *efficient* sanitizable signature scheme which simultaneously achieves unlinkability and invisibility. This resolves an open problem posed by Camenisch et al. [10]. Our construction is over type-III pairing groups. It uses an equivalence class signature (EQS) scheme, a public-key encryption (PKE) scheme, a hash function (modeled as a random oracle) with images living in G_2, and a verifiable ring signature (VRS) scheme.

We suggest to instantiate our construction with the EQS scheme of Fuchs-bauer, Hanser, and Slamanig [19], the PKE scheme obtained by applying the Fujisaki-Okamoto transformation [20] to the ElGamal encryption scheme [15], and the VRS scheme of Bultel and Lafourcade [9]. The efficiency of such an instantiation is summarized in Tables 1 and 2.

- We construct weak sanitizable signatures from equivalence class signatures and other basic primitives. The scheme is weak in the sense that it satisfies weak immutability, weak unlinkability, strong proof-restricted transparency[3], and strong invisibility, but not accountability.
- We present a generic transformation from weak sanitizable signatures to fully-fledged sanitizable signatures, using VRS. Fully-fledged sanitizable signatures satisfy immutability, unlinkability, strong proof-restricted transparency, strong invisibility, and strong accountability. The transformation is very efficient as it ignores the structure of the underlying weak sanitizable signature scheme. This allows the future design of sanitizable signatures to focus on achieving other properties while not worrying about accountability.

Table 2. Dominating operations in algorithms.

Op.	Signing	Sanitizing	Verifying	Proving	Judging
Exp.	$(4\ell + 11)\ \mathbb{G}_1 +$ $(\ell + 2)\ \mathbb{G}_2$	$(2\ell + 14)\ \mathbb{G}_1 +$ $(\ell + 2)\ \mathbb{G}_2$	$8\ \mathbb{G}_1$	$3\ \mathbb{G}_1$	$4\ \mathbb{G}_1$
Pairings	-	-	$4\ell + 6$	-	-

1.4 Related Work

An alternative definition of accountability called *non-interactive public account-ability* was given by Brzuska *et al.* [8]. This variant of accountability is mutually exclusive with transparency. Several existing works [7,9,17,26] proposed schemes that are both transparent and unlinkable. Recently, Krenn *et al.* [25] propose the "strong" versions of unforgeability, (non-interactive public) accountability, and transparency.

The above works do not consider the notion of invisibility which dates back to the original work by Ateniese *et al.* [1], and was formalized by Camenisch *et al.* [10]. Beck *et al.* [2] refined the notion to strong invisibility and proposed a scheme that is both strongly invisible and strongly account-able. Recently Fischlin *et al.* [16] show that an invisible (but not unlinkable nor transparent) sanitizable signature scheme can be obtained from any public key encryption scheme.

Miyazaki *et al.* [29] also considered "invisible sanitizable signatures" which is actually a different primitive known as *redactable signatures* [13] as discussed in [10]. Extensions of sanitizable signatures such as the multi-sanitizer setting [12]

---

[3] Our construction actually achieves perfect strong (non-proof-restricted) transparency.

and a setting where the modification capabilities of the sanitizer are limited [11] were also considered. Other primitives related to sanitizable signatures include homomorphic signatures [23,24], redactable signatures [5,13,31], and proxy signatures [30,32,34]. To the best of our knowledge, none of the existing works present an efficient sanitizable signature scheme that simultaneously achieves all of the five security properties, and in particular unlinkability and invisibility together.

2   Preliminaries

Throughout this work we denote by $\lambda \in \mathbb{N}$ the security parameter and by $\mathsf{poly}(\lambda)$ any function that is bounded by a polynomial in λ. We denote any function that is negligible in the security parameter by $\mathsf{negl}(\lambda)$. We say that an algorithm is PPT if it is modelled as a probabilistic Turing machine whose running time is bounded by some function $\mathsf{poly}(\lambda)$. Given a set S, we denote by $x \leftarrow S$ the sampling of and element uniformly at random from S, and we denote by $x \leftarrow \mathcal{A}(\text{in})$ the output of the algorithm $\mathcal{A}$ on input in. The elements of the set $\{1, \ldots, n\}$ are succinctly represented as $[n]$. Next we define the necessary notions for understanding our constructions.

2.1   Class-Hiding Groups

Let $\mathcal{BG} := (\mathbb{G}_1, \mathbb{G}_2, \mathbb{G}_T, g_1, g_2, g_T, e, q) \leftarrow \mathsf{BGGen}(1^\lambda)$ be the description of a multiplicative bilinear group of prime order q generated by some efficient PPT algorithm $\mathsf{BGGen}(1^\lambda)$. Let $\bar{X} = (X_1, \ldots, X_\ell) \in \mathbb{G}_1^\ell$ and $\rho \in \mathbb{Z}_q$. We write $\bar{X} := (X_1, \ldots, X_\ell)^\rho := (X_1^\rho, \ldots, X_\ell^\rho)$. We then define the equivalence relation

$$\mathcal{R} := \{(\bar{M}, \bar{N}) : \exists \ell > 1, \ \rho \in \mathbb{Z}_q^* \ s.t. \ (\bar{M}, \bar{N}) \in \mathbb{G}_1^\ell \times \mathbb{G}_1^\ell \wedge \bar{N} = \bar{M}^\rho\}.$$

For a vector $\bar{M} \in \mathbb{G}_1^\ell$ for some $\ell > 1$, its equivalence class is defined by

$$[\bar{M}]_\mathcal{R} := \{\bar{N} \in \mathbb{G}_1^\ell : (\bar{M}, \bar{N}) \in \mathcal{R}\}.$$

Next we define the notion of class hiding for a relation $\mathcal{R}$, which intuitively says that it should be hard to distinguish elements from the same equivalence class from randomly sampled group elements[4].

Definition 1 (Class-Hiding). *A relation $\mathcal{R}$ is said to be class-hiding if for all $\ell > 1$ and for all PPT adversaries $\mathcal{A}$ there exists a negligible function $\mathsf{negl}(\lambda)$ such that*

$$\left| \Pr\left[b' = b : \begin{array}{l} b \leftarrow \{0,1\}; \mathcal{BG} \leftarrow \mathsf{BGGen}(1^\lambda); (M, M_0) \leftarrow (\mathbb{G}_1^\ell)^2; \\ M_1 \leftarrow [M]_\mathcal{R}; b' \leftarrow \mathcal{A}(\mathcal{BG}, M, M_b) \end{array} \right] - \frac{1}{2} \right| \leq \mathsf{negl}(\lambda).$$

The following lemma was proven (in different wordings) by Hanser and Slamanig [22]:

Lemma 1 ([22]). *$\mathcal{R}$ is class-hiding if and only if the DDH assumption holds in $\mathbb{G}_1$.*

---

[4] Class-hiding was originally introduced [22] as a property of equivalence class signatures.

2.2   Equivalence Class Signatures

Equivalence class signatures allow users to sign representatives of the equivalence classes defined above, such that a representative and its corresponding signature can be adapted to give a fresh signature of a random representative in the same class. Below, we recall the formal definition of equivalence class signatures [22].

Definition 2 (EQS). *An equivalence class signature (EQS) scheme is defined with respect to a bilinear group description $\mathcal{BG}$ and a message length $\ell > 1$. An EQS scheme is a tuple of* PPT *algorithms* (KGen, Sign, ChgRep, Vf, VfKey) *defined as follows:*

$(\mathsf{pk}, \mathsf{sk}) \leftarrow \mathsf{KGen}(\mathcal{BG}, 1^\ell)$: *The key generation algorithm inputs a group $\mathcal{BG}$ and the message length 1^ℓ. It outputs a key pair* $(\mathsf{pk}, \mathsf{sk})$.

$\sigma \leftarrow \mathsf{Sign}(\mathsf{sk}, \bar{M})$: *The signing algorithm inputs the secret key* sk *and a message* $\bar{M} \in \mathbb{G}_1^\ell$. *It outputs a signature σ on the equivalence class* $[\bar{M}]_\mathcal{R}$.

$\sigma' \leftarrow \mathsf{ChgRep}(\mathsf{pk}, \bar{M}, \sigma, \rho)$: *The change representation algorithm inputs the public key* pk, *a message* $\bar{M} \in \mathbb{G}_1^\ell$, *a signature σ on the equivalence class* $[\bar{M}]_\mathcal{R}$, *and a scalar ρ. It outputs a new signature σ' on the (same) equivalence class* $[\bar{M}^\rho]_\mathcal{R} = [\bar{M}]_\mathcal{R}$.

$b \leftarrow \mathsf{Vf}(\mathsf{pk}, \bar{M}, \sigma)$: *The signature verification algorithm inputs the public key* pk, *a message* $\bar{M} \in \mathbb{G}_1^\ell$, *and a signature σ. It returns $b = 1$ if σ is a valid signature under* pk *on the equivalence class* $[\bar{M}]_\mathcal{R}$, *and $b = 0$ otherwise.*

$b \leftarrow \mathsf{VfKey}(\mathsf{pk}, \mathsf{sk})$: *The key verification algorithm inputs a public key* pk *and a secret key* sk. *It returns $b = 1$ if the keys are consistent and $b = 0$ otherwise.*

We refer the reader to [22] for a formal treatment of correctness. We define existential unforgeability under random message attacks (EUF-CMA) in the following.

Definition 3 (EUF-CMA). *An EQS scheme is said to be existentially unforgeable under chosen message attacks (EUF-CMA) if for all $\ell > 1$, for all $n \in \mathsf{poly}(\lambda)$, and for all PPT adversaries $\mathcal{A}$,*

$$\Pr\left[\begin{array}{l} 1 = \mathsf{Vf}(\mathsf{pk}, M^*, \sigma^*) \wedge \\ \forall M \in Q : [M]_\mathcal{R} \neq [M^*]_\mathcal{R} \end{array} : \begin{array}{l} \mathcal{BG} \leftarrow \mathsf{BGGen}(1^\lambda); \\ (\mathsf{pk}, \mathsf{sk}) \leftarrow \mathsf{KGen}(\mathcal{BG}, 1^\ell); \\ (M^*, \sigma^*) \leftarrow \mathcal{A}^{\mathsf{Sign}(\mathsf{sk}, \cdot)}(\mathsf{pk}) \end{array} \right] \leq \mathsf{negl}(\lambda).$$

Next we recall the notion of signature adaptation which captures the fact that signatures output by ChgRep are distributed like fresh signatures on the new representative.

Definition 4 (Perfect Signature Adaptation). *An EQS scheme is said to perfectly adapt signatures if for all tuples* $(\mathsf{sk}, \mathsf{pk}, \bar{M}, \sigma, \rho)$ *such that* $\mathsf{VfKey}(\mathsf{pk}, \mathsf{sk}) = 1$, $\mathsf{Vf}(\mathsf{pk}, \bar{M}, \sigma) = 1$, $\bar{M} \in \mathbb{G}_1^\ell$ *for some $\ell > 1$, and $\rho \leftarrow \mathbb{Z}_q^*$ it holds that*

$$\mathsf{ChgRep}(\mathsf{pk}, \bar{M}, \sigma, \rho) \text{ and } \mathsf{Sign}(\mathsf{sk}, \bar{M}^\rho)$$

are identically distributed.

2.3 Verifiable Ring Signatures

Ring Signatures allow users to sign a message anonymously within a group of users, where the group is chosen upon signature creation in an ad-hoc way. *Verifiable Ring Signatures* (VRS) allow each user of the group to prove *a posteriori* whether he is the signer of a given message or not. VRS was formally defined and constructed in [28]. Below, we recall the syntax of VRS.

Definition 5 (Verifiable Ring Signature (VRS)). *A* Verifiable Ring Signature *(VRS) scheme is a tuple of six algorithms* VRS = (Setup, KGen, Sign, Verify, Prove, Judge) *defined as follows:*

pp ← Setup(1^λ): *On input the security parameter* 1^λ, *return the public parameters* pp.

(pk, sk) ← KGen(pp): *On input the public parameters* pp, *return a pair of signer public/private keys* (pk, sk).

σ ← Sign(sk, L, m): *On input the secret key* sk, *a ring* L, *and a message* m, *return a signature* σ *on the message* m *under the set of public keys* L.

b ← Verify(L, m, σ): *On input a ring* L, *a message* m, *and a signature* σ, *return a bit* b *or the distinguished symbol* ⊥.

π ← Prove(L, m, σ, pk, sk): *On input a ring* L, *a message* m, *a signature* σ, *a public key* pk, *and a secret key* sk, *return a proof* π.

b ← Judge(L, m, σ, pk, π): *On input a ring* L, *a message* m, *a signature* σ, *a public key* pk, *and a proof* π, *return a bit* b *or the distinguished symbol* ⊥. *By convention, if* $b = 1$ *(resp. 0) then* π *proves that* σ *was (resp. was not) generated by the signer corresponding to the public key* pk.

A VRS is required to be (strongly) unforgeable, (strongly) accountable, anonymous, and (strongly) non-seizable. For their formal definitions we refer to the full version.

3 Definition of Sanitizable Signatures

In the following we recall the syntax of sanitizable signatures. Let the signer and the sanitizer be denoted by S and Z respectively. Throughout this work we consider messages $m = (m_1, \ldots, m_\ell)$ to be tuples of ℓ parts for some $\ell > 1$, where $m_k \in \{0,1\}^*$ for all $k \in \ell$, and represent the admissible modification as a bit string $\alpha = \alpha_1 \| \ldots \| \alpha_\ell \in \{0,1\}^\ell$. We write $\alpha_k = 1$ if and only if the k-th block is admissible. For ease of exposition, we sometimes write $k \in \alpha$ instead of $\alpha_k = 1$.

Let δ be a function which maps a message m to another message $m' = \delta(m)$. Also, we say that δ is an admissible modification, denoted by $\alpha(\delta) = 1$, if and only if for all messages m and $m' = \delta(m)$, it holds that $m'_k = m_k$ for all $k \in \alpha$.

Definition 6 (Sanitizable Signature Scheme). *A sanitizable signature scheme consists of the* PPT *algorithms* (Setup, KGen$_S$, KGen$_Z$, Sign, San, Verify, Prove, Judge).

pp ← Setup($1^\lambda, 1^\ell$): *The setup algorithm inputs the security parameter 1^λ and the (maximum) length 1^ℓ of the messages and creates a public parameter* pp.

($\mathsf{pk_S}, \mathsf{sk_S}$) ← KGen$_\mathsf{S}$(pp): *The signer key generation algorithm inputs the public parameter* pp *and outputs* ($\mathsf{pk_S}, \mathsf{sk_S}$), *the public and secret key of the signer respectively.*

($\mathsf{pk_Z}, \mathsf{sk_Z}$) ← KGen$_\mathsf{Z}$(pp): *The sanitizer key generation algorithm inputs the public parameter* pp *and outputs* ($\mathsf{pk_Z}, \mathsf{sk_Z}$), *the public and secret key of the sanitizer respectively.*

σ ← Sign($\mathsf{sk_S}, \mathsf{pk_Z}, m, \alpha$): *The signing algorithm inputs a message $m \in (\{0,1\}^*)^\ell$, a signer private key $\mathsf{sk_S}$, a sanitizer public key $\mathsf{pk_Z}$, as well as a description α of the admissible modifications to m by the sanitizer and outputs a signature σ.*

σ' ← San($\mathsf{pk_S}, \mathsf{sk_Z}, m, \delta, \sigma$): *The sanitizing algorithm takes as input a message $m \in (\{0,1\}^*)^\ell$, a description δ of the desired modifications to m, a signature σ, the signer public key $\mathsf{pk_S}$, and a sanitizer private key $\mathsf{sk_Z}$. It outputs a new signature σ'.*

b ← Verify($\mathsf{pk_S}, \mathsf{pk_Z}, m, \sigma$): *The verification algorithm inputs a message m, a signature σ, a signer public key $\mathsf{pk_S}$, as well as a sanitizer public key $\mathsf{pk_Z}$ and outputs a bit b.*

π ← Prove($\mathsf{sk_S}, \mathsf{pk_Z}, m, \sigma$): *The proof algorithm takes as input a signer private key $\mathsf{sk_S}$, a message m, a signature σ, and a sanitizer public key $\mathsf{pk_Z}$ and outputs a proof π.*

d ← Judge($\mathsf{pk_S}, \mathsf{pk_Z}, m, \sigma, \pi$): *The judge algorithm inputs a message m, a signature σ, signer and sanitizer public keys $\mathsf{pk_S}, \mathsf{pk_Z}$, and proof π. It outputs a decision $d \in \{\mathsf{S}, \mathsf{Z}\}$ indicating whether the message-signature pair was created by the signer or the sanitizer.*

For a sanitizable signature scheme the usual correctness properties should hold, saying that genuinely signed or sanitized messages are accepted and that a genuinely created proof by the signer leads the judge to decide in favor of the signer. For a formal approach to correctness see [6].

3.1   Unlinkability and Invisibility

In the original definition of unlinkability by Brzuska *et al.* [7], the property was modeled using an experiment where the adversary gets access to, among other oracles, a "left-or-right sanitize" oracle LoRSanit$\mathcal{O}$, which inputs two message-modification-signature tuples and outputs a sanitized signature produced from one of the tuples. The adversary's task is to decide which tuple is used for the sanitization.

To define LoRSanit$\mathcal{O}$, Brzuska *et al.* assumed that the description of admissible modifications α can be recovered from a valid signature, so that LoRSanit$\mathcal{O}$ can recover the admissible modifications from both input signatures and check whether they are equal. Note that if this check is omitted, then the adversary can trivially decide which signature is used by querying the sanitize oracle San$\mathcal{O}$ on the output of LoRSanit$\mathcal{O}$.

$\mathsf{Sign}\mathcal{O}(\mathsf{pk}_Z, m, \alpha)$
___
$\sigma \leftarrow \mathsf{Sign}(\mathsf{sk}_S^\dagger, \mathsf{pk}_Z, m, \alpha)$
$L := L \| \{(\mathsf{pk}_S^\dagger, \mathsf{pk}_Z, m, \alpha, \sigma)\}$
return σ

$\mathsf{Prove}\mathcal{O}(\mathsf{pk}_Z, m, \sigma)$
___
if $\begin{cases} \mathsf{pk}_Z = \mathsf{pk}_Z^\dagger \\ (m, \sigma) \in \mathcal{Q} \end{cases}$ **then return** $\bot$

/ Only triggered in transparency experiment.
$\beta := \mathsf{Vf}(\mathsf{pk}_S^\dagger, \mathsf{pk}_Z, m, \sigma)$
if $\beta = 0$ **then return** $\bot$
$\pi \leftarrow \mathsf{Prove}(\mathsf{sk}_S^\dagger, \mathsf{pk}_Z, m, \sigma)$
return π

$\mathsf{San}\mathcal{O}'(\mathsf{pk}_S, m, \delta, \sigma)$
___
if $\mathsf{pk}_S \neq \mathsf{pk}_S^\dagger$ **then**
  $(m', \sigma') \leftarrow \mathsf{San}(\mathsf{pk}_S, \mathsf{sk}_Z^\dagger, m, \delta, \sigma)$
  return (m', σ')
elseif $\exists \alpha \ s.t.\ (m, \sigma, \alpha) \in \mathcal{R} \wedge \delta \in \alpha$ **then**
  $(m', \sigma') \leftarrow \mathsf{San}(\mathsf{pk}_S, \mathsf{sk}_Z^\dagger, m, \delta, \sigma)$
  $\mathcal{R} \leftarrow \mathcal{R} \| \{(m', \sigma', \alpha)\}$
  return (m', σ')
endif
return $\bot$

$\mathsf{wLoRSanit}\mathcal{O}_b(i_0, \delta_0, i_1, \delta_1)$
___
if $L[i_0] = \epsilon \vee L[i_1] = \epsilon$ **then**
  return $\bot$
endif
$(\mathsf{pk}_{S,0}, \mathsf{pk}_{Z,0}, m_0, \alpha_0, \sigma_0) := L[i_0]$
$(\mathsf{pk}_{S,1}, \mathsf{pk}_{Z,1}, m_1, \alpha_1, \sigma_1) := L[i_1]$
foreach $\beta \in \{0, 1\}$ **do**
  $\sigma'_\beta \leftarrow \mathsf{San}(\mathsf{pk}_S^\dagger, \mathsf{sk}_Z^\dagger, m_\beta, \delta_\beta, \sigma_\beta)$
endfor
if $\begin{cases} \alpha_0 = \alpha_1 \\ \delta_0 \in \alpha_0 \wedge \delta_1 \in \alpha_1 \\ \delta_0(m_0) = \delta_1(m_1) \end{cases}$ **then**
  $L := L \| \{(\mathsf{pk}_S^\dagger, \mathsf{pk}_Z^\dagger, m_b, \alpha_b, \sigma_b)\}$
  return σ_b
endif
return $\bot$

$\mathsf{San}\mathcal{O}(\mathsf{pk}_S, m, \delta, \sigma)$
___
$\alpha \leftarrow \mathsf{ExtAdm}(\mathsf{pk}_S, \mathsf{sk}_Z^\dagger, \sigma)$
if $\begin{cases} \mathsf{Verify}(\mathsf{pk}_S, \mathsf{pk}_Z^\dagger, m, \sigma) = 1 \\ \delta \in \alpha \end{cases}$ **then**
  $\sigma' \leftarrow \mathsf{San}(\mathsf{pk}_S, \mathsf{sk}_Z^\dagger, m, \delta, \sigma)$
  $L := L \| \{(\mathsf{pk}_S, \mathsf{pk}_Z^\dagger, \delta(m), \alpha, \sigma')\}$
  return σ'
endif
return $\bot$

$\mathsf{LoRAdm}\mathcal{O}_b(\mathsf{pk}_Z, m, \alpha_0, \alpha_1)$
___
if $\begin{cases} |\alpha_0| = |\alpha_1| = |m| \\ \mathsf{pk}_Z = \mathsf{pk}_Z^\dagger \vee \alpha_0 = \alpha_1 \end{cases}$ **then**
  $\sigma \leftarrow \mathsf{Sign}(\mathsf{sk}_S^\dagger, \mathsf{pk}_Z, m, \alpha_b)$
  if $\mathsf{pk}_Z = \mathsf{pk}_Z^\dagger$ **then**
    $\mathcal{R} := \mathcal{R} \| \{(m, \sigma, \alpha_0 \circ \alpha_1)\}$
  endif
  return σ
endif
return $\bot$

$\mathsf{Sign/San}\mathcal{O}_b(m, \delta, \alpha)$
___
if $\delta \notin \alpha$ **then return** $\bot$
$\sigma \leftarrow \mathsf{Sign}(\mathsf{sk}_S^\dagger, \mathsf{pk}_S^\dagger, m, \alpha)$
$\sigma'_\beta \leftarrow \begin{cases} \mathsf{Sign}(\mathsf{sk}_S^\dagger, \mathsf{pk}_S^\dagger, \delta(m), \alpha) & b = 0 \\ \mathsf{San}(\mathsf{pk}_S^\dagger, \mathsf{sk}_Z^\dagger, m, \delta, \alpha) & b = 1 \end{cases}$
$\boxed{\mathcal{Q} = \mathcal{Q} \| (\delta(m), \sigma')}$
return σ'

$\mathsf{LoRSanit}\mathcal{O}_b(m_0, \delta_0, \sigma_0, m_1, \delta_1, \sigma_1)$
___
$b_\beta \leftarrow \mathsf{Verify}(\mathsf{pk}_S^\dagger, \mathsf{pk}_Z^\dagger, m_\beta, \sigma_\beta), \ \forall \beta \in \{0, 1\}$
if $b_0 = 0 \vee b_1 = 0$ **then return** $\bot$
foreach $\beta \in \{0, 1\}$ **do**
  $\alpha_\beta \leftarrow \mathsf{ExtAdm}(\mathsf{pk}_S^\dagger, \mathsf{sk}_Z^\dagger, \sigma_\beta)$
  $\sigma'_\beta \leftarrow \mathsf{San}(\mathsf{pk}_S^\dagger, \mathsf{sk}_Z^\dagger, m_\beta, \delta_\beta, \sigma_\beta)$
endfor
if $\begin{cases} \alpha_0 = \alpha_1 \\ \delta_0 \in \alpha_0 \wedge \delta_1 \in \alpha_1 \\ \delta_0(m_0) = \delta_1(m_1) \end{cases}$ **then**
  $L := L \| \{(\mathsf{pk}_S^\dagger, \mathsf{pk}_Z^\dagger, m_b, \alpha_b, \sigma_b)\}$
  return σ_b
endif
return $\bot$

Fig. 2. Oracles for sanitizable signatures

$\overline{\mathsf{wExpImmutability}}_{\mathcal{A},\Pi}(1^\lambda)$

$L := \epsilon,\ \mathcal{Q} := \epsilon,\ \mathsf{pp} \leftarrow \mathsf{Setup}(1^\lambda)$

$(\mathsf{pk}_\mathsf{S}^\dagger, \mathsf{sk}_\mathsf{S}^\dagger) \leftarrow \mathsf{KGen}_\mathsf{S}(\mathsf{pp})$

$(\mathsf{pk}_\mathsf{Z}^*, m^*, \sigma^*) \leftarrow \mathcal{A}^{\mathsf{Sign}\mathcal{O},\mathsf{Prove}\mathcal{O}}(\mathsf{pp}, \mathsf{pk}_\mathsf{S}^\dagger)$

parse L **as** $\{(\mathsf{pk}_{\mathsf{S},i}, \mathsf{pk}_{\mathsf{Z},i}, m_i, \alpha_i, \sigma_i)\}_{i=1}^{|L|}$

$b_0 := \mathsf{Verify}(\mathsf{pk}_\mathsf{S}^\dagger, \mathsf{pk}_\mathsf{Z}^*, m^*, \sigma^*)$

$b_1 := \left(\begin{array}{l} \exists i \in [|L|],\ \delta \in \alpha_i\ s.t. \\ \left\{ \begin{array}{l} \overline{\mathsf{pk}_\mathsf{Z}^* = \mathsf{pk}_{\mathsf{Z},i}} \\ m^* = \delta(m_i) \end{array} \right. \end{array} \right)$

return $b_0 \wedge \neg b_1$

$\mathsf{ExpSanAcc}_{\mathcal{A},\Pi}(1^\lambda)$

$L := \epsilon,\ \mathcal{Q} := \epsilon,\ \mathsf{pp} \leftarrow \mathsf{Setup}(1^\lambda)$

$(\mathsf{pk}_\mathsf{S}^\dagger, \mathsf{sk}_\mathsf{S}^\dagger) \leftarrow \mathsf{KGen}_\mathsf{S}(\mathsf{pp})$

$(\mathsf{pk}_\mathsf{Z}^*, m^*, \sigma^*) \leftarrow \mathcal{A}^{\mathsf{Sign}\mathcal{O},\mathsf{Prove}\mathcal{O}}(\mathsf{pp}, \mathsf{pk}_\mathsf{S}^\dagger)$

$\pi^* \leftarrow \mathsf{Prove}(\mathsf{sk}_\mathsf{S}^\dagger, \mathsf{pk}_\mathsf{Z}^*, m^*, \sigma^*)$

parse L **as** $\{(\mathsf{pk}_{\mathsf{S},i}, \mathsf{pk}_{\mathsf{Z},i}, m_i, \alpha_i, \sigma_i)\}_{i=1}^{|L|}$

$b_0 := \mathsf{Verify}(\mathsf{pk}_\mathsf{S}^\dagger, \mathsf{pk}_\mathsf{Z}^*, m^*, \sigma^*)$

$b_1 := \left((\mathsf{pk}_\mathsf{Z}^*, m^*, \sigma^*) \notin \{(\mathsf{pk}_{\mathsf{Z},i}, m_i, \sigma_i)\}_{i=1}^{|L|} \right)$

$b_2 := (\mathsf{Judge}(\mathsf{pk}_\mathsf{S}^\dagger, \mathsf{pk}_\mathsf{Z}^*, m^*, \sigma^*, \pi^*) \neq Z)$

return $b_0 \wedge b_1 \wedge b_2$

$\mathsf{ExpSigAcc}_{\mathcal{A},\Pi}(1^\lambda)$

$L := \epsilon,\ \mathcal{Q} := \epsilon,\ \mathcal{R} := \epsilon,\ \mathsf{pp} \leftarrow \mathsf{Setup}(1^\lambda)$

$(\mathsf{pk}_\mathsf{Z}^\dagger, \mathsf{sk}_\mathsf{Z}^\dagger) \leftarrow \mathsf{KGen}_\mathsf{Z}(\mathsf{pp})$

$(\mathsf{pk}_\mathsf{S}^*, m^*, \sigma^*, \pi^*) \leftarrow \mathcal{A}^{\mathsf{San}\mathcal{O}}(\mathsf{pp}, \mathsf{pk}_\mathsf{Z}^\dagger)$

parse L **as** $\{(\mathsf{pk}_{\mathsf{S},i}, \mathsf{pk}_{\mathsf{Z},i}, m_i, \alpha_i, \sigma_i)\}_{i=1}^{|L|}$

$b_0 := \mathsf{Verify}(\mathsf{pk}_\mathsf{S}^*, \mathsf{pk}_\mathsf{Z}^\dagger, m^*, \sigma^*)$

$b_1 := \left((\mathsf{pk}_\mathsf{S}^*, m^*, \sigma^*) \notin \{(\mathsf{pk}_{\mathsf{S},i}, m_i, \sigma_i)\}_{i=1}^{|L|} \right)$

$b_2 := (\mathsf{Judge}(\mathsf{pk}_\mathsf{S}^*, \mathsf{pk}_\mathsf{Z}^\dagger, m^*, \sigma^*, \pi^*) \neq S)$

return $b_0 \wedge b_1 \wedge b_2$

$\mathsf{ExpTransparency}_{\mathcal{A},\Pi}^b(1^\lambda)$

$L := \epsilon,\ \mathcal{Q} := \epsilon,\ \mathsf{pp} \leftarrow \mathsf{Setup}(1^\lambda)$

$(\mathsf{pk}_\mathsf{S}^\dagger, \mathsf{sk}_\mathsf{S}^\dagger) \leftarrow \mathsf{KGen}_\mathsf{S}(\mathsf{pp}),\ (\mathsf{pk}_\mathsf{Z}^\dagger, \mathsf{sk}_\mathsf{Z}^\dagger) \leftarrow \mathsf{KGen}_\mathsf{Z}(\mathsf{pp})$

$\mathbb{O} := \left\{ \begin{array}{l} \mathsf{Sign}\mathcal{O},\ \mathsf{San}\mathcal{O}, \\ \mathsf{Prove}\mathcal{O},\ \mathsf{Sign/San}\mathcal{O}_b \end{array} \right\}$

$b' \leftarrow \mathcal{A}^\mathbb{O}(\mathsf{pp}, \mathsf{pk}_\mathsf{S}^\dagger, \mathsf{pk}_\mathsf{Z}^\dagger)$

return b'

$\mathsf{wExpUnlink}_{\mathcal{A},\Pi}^b(1^\lambda)$

$L := \epsilon,\ \mathsf{pp} \leftarrow \mathsf{Setup}(1^\lambda)$

$(\mathsf{pk}_\mathsf{S}^\dagger, \mathsf{sk}_\mathsf{S}^\dagger) \leftarrow \mathsf{KGen}_\mathsf{S}(\mathsf{pp}),\ (\mathsf{pk}_\mathsf{Z}^\dagger, \mathsf{sk}_\mathsf{Z}^\dagger) \leftarrow \mathsf{KGen}_\mathsf{Z}(\mathsf{pp})$

$\mathbb{O} := \left\{ \begin{array}{l} \mathsf{Sign}\mathcal{O},\ \mathsf{San}\mathcal{O}, \\ \mathsf{Prove}\mathcal{O},\ \mathsf{wLoRSanit}\mathcal{O}_b \end{array} \right\}$

$b' \leftarrow \mathcal{A}^\mathbb{O}(\mathsf{pp}, \mathsf{pk}_\mathsf{S}^\dagger, \mathsf{pk}_\mathsf{Z}^\dagger)$

return b'

$\mathsf{ExpUnlink}_{\mathcal{A},\Pi}^b(1^\lambda)$

$L := \epsilon,\ \mathsf{pp} \leftarrow \mathsf{Setup}(1^\lambda)$

$(\mathsf{pk}_\mathsf{S}^\dagger, \mathsf{sk}_\mathsf{S}^\dagger) \leftarrow \mathsf{KGen}_\mathsf{S}(\mathsf{pp}),\ (\mathsf{pk}_\mathsf{Z}^\dagger, \mathsf{sk}_\mathsf{Z}^\dagger) \leftarrow \mathsf{KGen}_\mathsf{Z}(\mathsf{pp})$

$\mathbb{O} := \left\{ \begin{array}{l} \mathsf{Sign}\mathcal{O},\ \mathsf{San}\mathcal{O}, \\ \mathsf{Prove}\mathcal{O},\ \mathsf{LoRSanit}\mathcal{O}_b \end{array} \right\}$

$b' \leftarrow \mathcal{A}^\mathbb{O}(\mathsf{pp}, \mathsf{pk}_\mathsf{S}^\dagger, \mathsf{pk}_\mathsf{Z}^\dagger)$

return b'

$\mathsf{ExpInvisibility}_{\mathcal{A},\Pi}^b(1^\lambda)$

$L := \epsilon,\ \mathcal{Q} := \epsilon,\ \mathcal{R} := \epsilon,\ \mathsf{pp} \leftarrow \mathsf{Setup}(1^\lambda)$

$(\mathsf{pk}_\mathsf{S}^\dagger, \mathsf{sk}_\mathsf{S}^\dagger) \leftarrow \mathsf{KGen}_\mathsf{S}(\mathsf{pp}),\ (\mathsf{pk}_\mathsf{Z}^\dagger, \mathsf{sk}_\mathsf{Z}^\dagger) \leftarrow \mathsf{KGen}_\mathsf{Z}(\mathsf{pp})$

$\mathbb{O} := \{ \mathsf{San}\mathcal{O}',\ \mathsf{Prove}\mathcal{O},\ \mathsf{LoRAdm}\mathcal{O}_b \}$

$b' \leftarrow \mathcal{A}^\mathbb{O}(\mathsf{pp}, \mathsf{pk}_\mathsf{S}^\dagger, \mathsf{pk}_\mathsf{Z}^\dagger)$

return b'

Fig. 3. Security experiments for sanitizable signatures. Oracles are defined in Fig. 2.

Brzuska *et al.* did not explicitly state if such recovery can be done publicly or requires a secret key. Indeed, in all existing constructions of unlinkable sanitizable signatures [7], the recovery mechanism is public, which violates invisibility. Therefore, to achieve unlinkability and invisibility simultaneously, we must explicitly state that the admissible modifications can be recovered from a valid signature (hopefully only) with the corresponding sanitizer secret key. We say that a sanitizable signature scheme has privately extractable admissible modifications, if there exists a PPT algorithm ExtAdm which performs the following:

$\alpha \leftarrow$ ExtAdm($\mathsf{pk_S}, \mathsf{sk_Z}, \sigma$): The admissible modifications extraction algorithm inputs a signer public key $\mathsf{pk_S}$, a sanitizer secret key $\mathsf{sk_Z}$, and a signature. It outputs a description α of the admissible modifications.

In what follows, we only consider sanitizable signature schemes which have privately extractable admissible modifications.

3.2   Security of Sanitizable Signatures

We require a sanitizable signature scheme to be immutable, strongly accountable, strongly invisible, strongly proof-restrictedly transparent, and unlinkable. Different variations of these properties were defined in the literature [2,6,7,25]. We will recall the definitions below for completeness. Additionally, we define the notions of weak immutability and weak unlinkability, which are achieved by our first construction. Our second construction then upgrades these properties to their regular counterparts.

We remark that (strong) unforgeability and privacy were considered in the literature. It is known that (strong) signer accountability and (strong) sanitizer accountability together imply (strong) unforgeability, while (strong) proof-restricted transparency implies proof-restricted privacy [6,25]. Unlinkability is also shown to imply privacy [7]. We therefore do not consider unforgeability and privacy explicitly.

Immutability. Immutability requires that a malicious sanitizer cannot change inadmissible blocks. That is, an adversary should not be able to produce a forgery ($\mathsf{pk_Z^*}, m^*, \sigma^*$), such that m^* cannot be produced by any admissible modifications delegated to $\mathsf{pk_Z^*}$. Note that the set of admissible modifications of a signature is bound to (the public key of) the sanitizer to which the signature is issued. We also consider a relaxed notion called weak immutability, where a forgery is not considered valid if m^* can be produced by a modification which is admissible for *some* (not necessarily $\mathsf{pk_Z^*}$) sanitizers.

Definition 7 (Immutability [6]). *A sanitizable signature scheme Π is said to be* immutable *if for all PPT adversaries $\mathcal{A}$, the probability that the experiment* $\Pr\left[\mathsf{ExpImmutability}_{\mathcal{A},\Pi}(1^\lambda) = 1\right] \leq \mathsf{negl}(\lambda)$ *where* $\mathsf{ExpImmutability}_{\mathcal{A},\Pi}(1^\lambda)$ *is defined in Fig. 3. Additionally, we say that Π is* weakly immutable *if, in the experiment* $\mathsf{wExpImmutability}_{\mathcal{A},\Pi}(1^\lambda)$, *the condition* $\boxed{\mathsf{pk_Z^*} = \mathsf{pk}_{Z,i}}$ *in the dashed box is dropped.*

Strong Transparency. Transparency means that sanitized signatures look like non-sanitized signatures. Rigorously speaking, transparency cannot be achieved if one is given oracle access to a prove oracle, which distinguishes sanitized signatures from fresh signatures. A relaxed notion, known as proof-restricted transparency is thus considered, which requires that one cannot decide whether a signature is sanitized or fresh, without the help of the prove oracle.

Definition 8 (Strong (Proof-Restricted) Transparency [25]**).** *A sanitizable signature scheme Π is* strongly proof-restrictedly transparent *if for all PPT adversaries $\mathcal{A}$,*

$$\left| \Pr\left[\mathsf{ExpTransparency}^0_{\mathcal{A},\Pi}(1^\lambda) = 1 \right] - \Pr\left[\mathsf{ExpTransparency}^1_{\mathcal{A},\Pi}(1^\lambda) = 1 \right] \right| \leq \mathsf{negl}(\lambda)$$

where $\mathsf{ExpTransparency}^b_{\mathcal{A},\Pi}(1^\lambda)$ is defined in Fig. 3. If

$$\Pr\left[\mathsf{ExpTransparency}^0_{\mathcal{A},\Pi}(1^\lambda) = 1 \right] = \Pr\left[\mathsf{ExpTransparency}^1_{\mathcal{A},\Pi}(1^\lambda) = 1 \right]$$

then we say Π is perfectly strongly proof-restrictedly transparent. *Furthermore, if the step $\mathcal{Q} = \mathcal{Q} \| (\delta(m), \sigma')$ in the $\mathsf{Sign/SanO}_b$ oracle (highlighted in the dashed box) is dropped, so that $\mathcal{Q}$ remains empty throughout the experiment, then we simply say Π is* perfectly strongly transparent.

Strong Accountability. This property demands that the origin of a (possibly sanitized) signature should be undeniable by the signer.

Definition 9 (Strong Sanitizer-Accountability [25]**).** *A sanitizable signature scheme Π is* strongly sanitizer-accountable *if for all PPT adversaries $\mathcal{A}$,*

$$\Pr\left[\mathsf{ExpSanAcc}_{\mathcal{A},\Pi}(1^\lambda) = 1 \right] \leq \mathsf{negl}(\lambda)$$

where $\mathsf{ExpSanAcc}_{\mathcal{A},\Pi}(1^\lambda)$ is defined in Fig. 3.

Definition 10 (Strong Signer-Accountability [25]**).** *A sanitizable signature scheme Π is* strongly signer-accountable *if for all PPT adversaries $\mathcal{A}$,*

$$\Pr\left[\mathsf{ExpSigAcc}_{\mathcal{A},\Pi}(1^\lambda) = 1 \right] \leq \mathsf{negl}(\lambda)$$

where $\mathsf{ExpSigAcc}_{\mathcal{A},\Pi}(1^\lambda)$ is defined in Fig. 3.

Invisibility. Invisibility requires that the admissible modifications of a signature are hidden from an external observer.

Definition 11 (Strong Invisibility [2]**).** *A sanitizable signature scheme Π is* strongly invisible *if for all PPT adversaries $\mathcal{A}$,*

$$\left| \Pr\left[\mathsf{ExpInvisibility}^0_{\mathcal{A},\Pi}(1^\lambda) = 1 \right] - \Pr\left[\mathsf{ExpInvisibility}^1_{\mathcal{A},\Pi}(1^\lambda) = 1 \right] \right| \leq \mathsf{negl}(\lambda)$$

where $\mathsf{ExpInvisibility}^b_{\mathcal{A},\Pi}(1^\lambda)$ is defined in Fig. 3.

Unlinkability. Unlinkability means that one cannot decide the source of a given sanitized signature, unless it is revealed trivially by the message. The notion is modeled by considering an experiment where the adversary is given a "left-or-right sanitize" oracle $\mathsf{LoRSanitO}$ which, on input two signatures, sanitizes one of them and returns the resulting signature. We also consider a relaxed notion called weak unlinkability, where the adversary is only allowed to query $\mathsf{LoRSanitO}$ on honestly generated signatures.

Definition 12 (Weak Unlinkability). *A sanitizable signature scheme* SS *is weakly unlinkable if for all PPT adversaries* $\mathcal{A}$,

$$\left| \Pr\left[\mathsf{wExpUnlink}^0_{\mathcal{A},\mathsf{SS}}(1^\lambda) = 1 \right] - \Pr\left[\mathsf{wExpUnlink}^1_{\mathcal{A},\mathsf{SS}}(1^\lambda) = 1 \right] \right| \leq \mathsf{negl}(\lambda)$$

where $\mathsf{wExpUnlink}^b_{\mathcal{A},\mathsf{SS}}(1^\lambda)$ *is defined in Fig. 3.*

Definition 13 (Unlinkability [6]). *A sanitizable signature scheme* SS *is unlinkable if for all PPT adversaries* $\mathcal{A}$,

$$\left| \Pr\left[\mathsf{ExpUnlink}^0_{\mathcal{A},\mathsf{SS}}(1^\lambda) = 1 \right] - \Pr\left[\mathsf{ExpUnlink}^1_{\mathcal{A},\mathsf{SS}}(1^\lambda) = 1 \right] \right| \leq \mathsf{negl}(\lambda)$$

where $\mathsf{ExpUnlink}^b_{\mathcal{A},\mathsf{SS}}(1^\lambda)$ *is defined in Fig. 3.*

4 Construction

We propose a two-step construction of sanitizable signatures with immutability, strong accountability, strong proof-restricted transparency, strong invisibility, and unlinkability. In the first step, using equivalence class signatures and other basic primitives, we construct a scheme with weak immutability, perfect strong transparency, strong invisibility, and weak unlinkability. This scheme does not achieve accountability. Next, we show how one can transform any schemes with these properties one with all desirable properties, using verifiable ring signatures.

4.1 Construction I: Achieving Unlinkability and Invisibility

Let $\ell > 1$ be an integer. Let EQS be an equivalence class signature scheme, H : $\{0,1\}^* \to \mathbb{G}_2$ be a hash function (to be modeled as a random oracle), and PKE be a public-key encryption scheme. We present in Fig. 4 a construction of sanitizable signatures Π_1. The construction satisfies weak immutability, strong invisibility, perfect strong transparency, and weak unlinkability, but not accountability.

Informally, the signer issues signatures as follows. On input a message $m = m_1 \| \ldots \| m_\ell$, the signer samples ℓ fresh BLS-like public and secret keys, which are used to sign the ℓ messages. Concretely, the i-th public key consists of a tuple $(X_i, Y_i) \in \mathbb{G}_1^2$ with $Y_i = X_i^{y_i}$ for some $y_i \in \mathbb{Z}_q$, and the secret key is y_i. It then signs the vectors $\bar{X} = (X_1, \ldots, X_\ell)$ and $\bar{Y} = (Y_1, \ldots, Y_\ell)$ using EQS. Next, in the same way as in [2], it encrypts the BLS-like secret keys y_i corresponding to the admissible message blocks using the PKE public key of the sanitizer. Finally, it outputs the signature which consists of two EQS signatures, ℓ BLS-like signatures and public keys, and a PKE ciphertext.

To sanitize, the sanitizer decrypts the PKE ciphertext and obtains the BLS-like secret keys corresponding to the admissible blocks, which are then used to sign the corresponding modified messages. Using the homomorphic property of the BLS-like scheme, the sanitizer can rerandomize $\bar{X}$ and $\bar{Y}$ to $\bar{X}^r$ and $\bar{Y}^{r \cdot s}$ respectively, and rerandomize the signatures accordingly so that they are compatible with the new public keys. Using the signature adaptation properties of

$\underline{\mathsf{Setup}(1^\lambda, 1^\ell)}$

$(\mathbb{G}_1, \mathbb{G}_2, \mathbb{G}_T, G_1, G_2, G_T, e, q) \leftarrow \mathsf{BGGen}(1^\lambda)$

$\mathcal{BG} := (\mathbb{G}_1, \mathbb{G}_2, \mathbb{G}_T, G_1, G_2, G_T, e, q)$

return $\mathsf{pp} := (\mathcal{BG}, 1^\lambda, 1^\ell)$

$\underline{\mathsf{KGen}_S(\mathsf{pp})}$

return $(\mathsf{pk}_S, \mathsf{sk}_S) \leftarrow \mathsf{EQS.KGen}(\mathcal{BG}, 1^\ell)$

$\underline{\mathsf{KGen}_Z(\mathsf{pp})}$

return $(\mathsf{pk}_Z, \mathsf{sk}_Z) \leftarrow \mathsf{PKE.KGen}(1^\lambda)$

$\underline{\mathsf{Sign}(\mathsf{sk}_S, \mathsf{pk}_Z, m, \alpha)}$

if $|\alpha| \neq \ell$ **then return** $\bot$

$x_i, y_i \leftarrow \mathbb{Z}_q^*, \forall i \in [\ell]$

$X_i := G_1^{x_i}, Y_i := X_i^{y_i}, \forall i \in [\ell]$

$\mu \leftarrow \mathsf{EQS.Sign}(\mathsf{sk}_S, (X_1, \ldots, X_\ell))$

$\eta \leftarrow \mathsf{EQS.Sign}(\mathsf{sk}_S, (Y_1, \ldots, Y_\ell))$

$\sigma_i := \mathsf{H}(i\|m_i)^{y_i}, \forall i \in [\ell]$

$\zeta_i := \begin{cases} y_i & i \in \alpha \\ 0 & \text{otherwise} \end{cases}, \forall i \in [\ell]$

$c \leftarrow \mathsf{PKE.Enc}(\mathsf{pk}_Z, (\alpha, \{\zeta_i\}_{i \in [\ell]}))$

$\sigma := (\mu, \eta, \{\sigma_i, X_i, Y_i\}_{i=1}^\ell, c)$

return σ

$\underline{\mathsf{Verify}(\mathsf{pk}_S, \mathsf{pk}_Z, m, \sigma)}$

$b_{-2} := (\forall k \in [\ell], Y_k \neq G_1)$

$b_{-1} := \mathsf{EQS.Vf}(\mathsf{pk}_S, (X_1, \ldots, X_\ell), \mu)$

$b_0 := \mathsf{EQS.Vf}(\mathsf{pk}_S, (Y_1, \ldots, Y_\ell), \eta)$

$b_i := (e(X_i, \sigma_i) = e(Y_i, \mathsf{H}(i\|m_i))), \forall i \in [\ell]$

return $\displaystyle\bigcap_{i=-2}^\ell b_i$

$\underline{\mathsf{San}(\mathsf{pk}_S, \mathsf{sk}_Z, m, \delta, \sigma)}$

$(\alpha, \{\zeta_i\}_{i \in [\ell]}) \leftarrow \mathsf{PKE.Dec}(\mathsf{sk}_Z, c)$

if $\delta \not\subseteq \alpha$ **then return** $\bot$

$m' := \delta(m)$

$r, s \leftarrow \mathbb{Z}_q^*$

$(X_1', \ldots, X_\ell') := (X_1, \ldots, X_\ell)^r$

$(Y_1', \ldots, Y_\ell') := (Y_1, \ldots, Y_\ell)^{r \cdot s}$

$\bar{X} := (X_1, \ldots, X_\ell)$

$\bar{Y} := (Y_1, \ldots, Y_\ell)$

$\mu' \leftarrow \mathsf{EQS.ChgRep}(\mathsf{pk}_S, \bar{X}, \mu, r)$

$\eta' \leftarrow \mathsf{EQS.ChgRep}(\mathsf{pk}_S, \bar{Y}, \eta, s)$

foreach $i \in [\ell]$ **do**

$\quad \zeta_i' := s \cdot \zeta_i$

$\quad \sigma_i' := \begin{cases} \mathsf{H}(i\|m_i')^{\zeta_i'} & i \in \alpha \\ \sigma_i^s & \text{otherwise} \end{cases}$

endfor

$c' \leftarrow \mathsf{PKE.Enc}(\mathsf{pk}_Z, (\alpha, \{\zeta_i'\}_{i \in [\ell]}))$

$\sigma' := (\mu', \eta', \{\sigma_i', X_i', Y_i'\}_{i=1}^\ell, c')$

return σ'

$\underline{\mathsf{ExtAdm}(\mathsf{pk}_S, \mathsf{sk}_Z, \sigma)}$

$\tau \leftarrow \mathsf{PKE.Dec}(\mathsf{sk}_Z, c)$

parse τ **as** $(\alpha, \{\zeta_i\}_{i \in [\ell]})$

return α

Fig. 4. Construction of weak sanitizable signatures. Prove and Judge always output ϵ (the empty string) and S (the signer) respectively, and are omitted.

EQS, it can also obtain fresh-looking EQS signatures on $\bar{X}^r$ and $\bar{Y}^{r \cdot s}$ respectively. Finally, the sanitizer re-encrypts the new BLS-like secret keys, and outputs the signature.

Since we do not aim to provide accountability, the prove algorithm always returns the empty string ϵ and the judge algorithm always outputs S. The correctness of Π_1 follows trivially from the correctness of the building blocks. Below, we state our main theorem and we defer its proof to Sect. 5.

Theorem 1. *Let $q > 2^\lambda$. If EQS is EUF-CMA-secure, then Π_1 is weakly immutable in the generic group and random oracle model. If PKE is IND-CCA-secure, then Π_1 is strongly invisible. If EQS perfectly adapts signatures, then Π_1 is perfectly strongly transparent (and hence also perfectly strongly proof-restrictedly transparent). If the equivalence relation $\mathcal{R}$ is class-hiding, EQS perfectly adapt signatures, and PKE is correct and is IND-CCA-secure, then Π_1 is weakly unlinkable in the generic group random oracle model.*

Finally, we remark that it is trivial to extend the construction to the multi-sanitizer setting by encrypting the (possibly different subsets of) BLS-like keys for different sanitizers.

4.2   Construction II: Generic Transformation for Accountability

In this section, we show a generic transformation (Fig. 5), from any weakly immutable, non-accountable, strongly invisible, strongly proof-restricted transparent, and weakly unlinkable schemes Π_1, to an immutable, strongly accountable, strongly invisible, strongly proof-restricted transparent, and unlinkable scheme Π_2, using a verifiable ring signature scheme VRS.

An overview of the transform follows. The signer signs the public key of the sanitizer and the message in σ_{SS} using Π_1, then signs σ_{SS} in σ_{VRS} using VRS, where the ring contains the public key of the signer and the public key of the sanitizer. The signer outputs the signature $\sigma = (\sigma_{SS}, \sigma_{VRS})$. To sanitize, the sanitizer sanitizes σ_{SS} using Π_1 to produce σ'_{SS}, then signs σ'_{SS} in σ'_{VRS} using VRS. The sanitized signature is $\sigma' = (\sigma'_{SS}, \sigma'_{VRS})$. To verify any signature $\sigma = (\sigma_{SS}, \sigma_{VRS})$, the verifier uses the verification algorithm of Π_1 on σ_{SS} and the verification algorithm of VRS on σ_{VRS}. To prove that a signature $\sigma' = (\sigma'_{SS}, \sigma'_{VRS})$ is sanitized, the signer proves that he did not generate σ'_{VRS} using the prove algorithm of VRS, which gives accountability.

Next, we sketch why the other security properties are preserved. For conciseness, we omit the qualitative attributes such as *strong* and *proof-restricted* in the following discussion. First, since Π_1 is weakly immutable, the sanitizer is not able to forge the part σ'_{SS} of a sanitized signature for a non-admissible message nor changing the sanitizer public key (which is signed as a message of Π_1). This implies that the resulting scheme is immutable. Next, since Π_1 is transparent, one cannot guess whether a signature is sanitized or not from the part σ_{SS}. On the other hand, since VRS is anonymous, one cannot guess whether the part σ_{VRS} was created by the signer or by the sanitizer. Combining both properties,

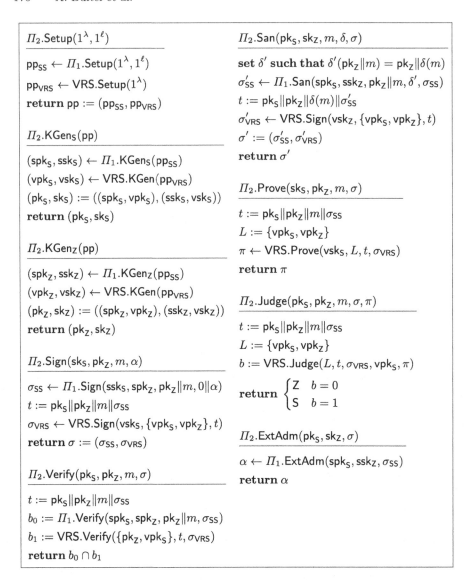

$\Pi_2.\mathsf{Setup}(1^\lambda, 1^\ell)$

$\mathsf{pp}_{\mathsf{SS}} \leftarrow \Pi_1.\mathsf{Setup}(1^\lambda, 1^\ell)$
$\mathsf{pp}_{\mathsf{VRS}} \leftarrow \mathsf{VRS}.\mathsf{Setup}(1^\lambda)$
return $\mathsf{pp} := (\mathsf{pp}_{\mathsf{SS}}, \mathsf{pp}_{\mathsf{VRS}})$

$\Pi_2.\mathsf{KGen}_{\mathsf{S}}(\mathsf{pp})$

$(\mathsf{spk}_{\mathsf{S}}, \mathsf{ssk}_{\mathsf{S}}) \leftarrow \Pi_1.\mathsf{KGen}_{\mathsf{S}}(\mathsf{pp}_{\mathsf{SS}})$
$(\mathsf{vpk}_{\mathsf{S}}, \mathsf{vsk}_{\mathsf{S}}) \leftarrow \mathsf{VRS}.\mathsf{KGen}(\mathsf{pp}_{\mathsf{VRS}})$
$(\mathsf{pk}_{\mathsf{S}}, \mathsf{sk}_{\mathsf{S}}) := ((\mathsf{spk}_{\mathsf{S}}, \mathsf{vpk}_{\mathsf{S}}), (\mathsf{ssk}_{\mathsf{S}}, \mathsf{vsk}_{\mathsf{S}}))$
return $(\mathsf{pk}_{\mathsf{S}}, \mathsf{sk}_{\mathsf{S}})$

$\Pi_2.\mathsf{KGen}_{\mathsf{Z}}(\mathsf{pp})$

$(\mathsf{spk}_{\mathsf{Z}}, \mathsf{ssk}_{\mathsf{Z}}) \leftarrow \Pi_1.\mathsf{KGen}_{\mathsf{Z}}(\mathsf{pp}_{\mathsf{SS}})$
$(\mathsf{vpk}_{\mathsf{Z}}, \mathsf{vsk}_{\mathsf{Z}}) \leftarrow \mathsf{VRS}.\mathsf{KGen}(\mathsf{pp}_{\mathsf{VRS}})$
$(\mathsf{pk}_{\mathsf{Z}}, \mathsf{sk}_{\mathsf{Z}}) := ((\mathsf{spk}_{\mathsf{Z}}, \mathsf{vpk}_{\mathsf{Z}}), (\mathsf{ssk}_{\mathsf{Z}}, \mathsf{vsk}_{\mathsf{Z}}))$
return $(\mathsf{pk}_{\mathsf{Z}}, \mathsf{sk}_{\mathsf{Z}})$

$\Pi_2.\mathsf{Sign}(\mathsf{sk}_{\mathsf{S}}, \mathsf{pk}_{\mathsf{Z}}, m, \alpha)$

$\sigma_{\mathsf{SS}} \leftarrow \Pi_1.\mathsf{Sign}(\mathsf{ssk}_{\mathsf{S}}, \mathsf{spk}_{\mathsf{Z}}, \mathsf{pk}_{\mathsf{Z}}\|m, 0\|\alpha)$
$t := \mathsf{pk}_{\mathsf{S}}\|\mathsf{pk}_{\mathsf{Z}}\|m\|\sigma_{\mathsf{SS}}$
$\sigma_{\mathsf{VRS}} \leftarrow \mathsf{VRS}.\mathsf{Sign}(\mathsf{vsk}_{\mathsf{S}}, \{\mathsf{vpk}_{\mathsf{S}}, \mathsf{vpk}_{\mathsf{Z}}\}, t)$
return $\sigma := (\sigma_{\mathsf{SS}}, \sigma_{\mathsf{VRS}})$

$\Pi_2.\mathsf{Verify}(\mathsf{pk}_{\mathsf{S}}, \mathsf{pk}_{\mathsf{Z}}, m, \sigma)$

$t := \mathsf{pk}_{\mathsf{S}}\|\mathsf{pk}_{\mathsf{Z}}\|m\|\sigma_{\mathsf{SS}}$
$b_0 := \Pi_1.\mathsf{Verify}(\mathsf{spk}_{\mathsf{S}}, \mathsf{spk}_{\mathsf{Z}}, \mathsf{pk}_{\mathsf{Z}}\|m, \sigma_{\mathsf{SS}})$
$b_1 := \mathsf{VRS}.\mathsf{Verify}(\{\mathsf{pk}_{\mathsf{Z}}, \mathsf{vpk}_{\mathsf{S}}\}, t, \sigma_{\mathsf{VRS}})$
return $b_0 \cap b_1$

$\Pi_2.\mathsf{San}(\mathsf{pk}_{\mathsf{S}}, \mathsf{sk}_{\mathsf{Z}}, m, \delta, \sigma)$

set δ' **such that** $\delta'(\mathsf{pk}_{\mathsf{Z}}\|m) = \mathsf{pk}_{\mathsf{Z}}\|\delta(m)$
$\sigma'_{\mathsf{SS}} \leftarrow \Pi_1.\mathsf{San}(\mathsf{spk}_{\mathsf{S}}, \mathsf{ssk}_{\mathsf{Z}}, \mathsf{pk}_{\mathsf{Z}}\|m, \delta', \sigma_{\mathsf{SS}})$
$t := \mathsf{pk}_{\mathsf{S}}\|\mathsf{pk}_{\mathsf{Z}}\|\delta(m)\|\sigma'_{\mathsf{SS}}$
$\sigma'_{\mathsf{VRS}} \leftarrow \mathsf{VRS}.\mathsf{Sign}(\mathsf{vsk}_{\mathsf{Z}}, \{\mathsf{vpk}_{\mathsf{S}}, \mathsf{vpk}_{\mathsf{Z}}\}, t)$
$\sigma' := (\sigma'_{\mathsf{SS}}, \sigma'_{\mathsf{VRS}})$
return σ'

$\Pi_2.\mathsf{Prove}(\mathsf{sk}_{\mathsf{S}}, \mathsf{pk}_{\mathsf{Z}}, m, \sigma)$

$t := \mathsf{pk}_{\mathsf{S}}\|\mathsf{pk}_{\mathsf{Z}}\|m\|\sigma_{\mathsf{SS}}$
$L := \{\mathsf{vpk}_{\mathsf{S}}, \mathsf{vpk}_{\mathsf{Z}}\}$
$\pi \leftarrow \mathsf{VRS}.\mathsf{Prove}(\mathsf{vsk}_{\mathsf{S}}, L, t, \sigma_{\mathsf{VRS}})$
return π

$\Pi_2.\mathsf{Judge}(\mathsf{pk}_{\mathsf{S}}, \mathsf{pk}_{\mathsf{Z}}, m, \sigma, \pi)$

$t := \mathsf{pk}_{\mathsf{S}}\|\mathsf{pk}_{\mathsf{Z}}\|m\|\sigma_{\mathsf{SS}}$
$L := \{\mathsf{vpk}_{\mathsf{S}}, \mathsf{vpk}_{\mathsf{Z}}\}$
$b := \mathsf{VRS}.\mathsf{Judge}(L, t, \sigma_{\mathsf{VRS}}, \mathsf{vpk}_{\mathsf{S}}, \pi)$
return $\begin{cases} \mathsf{Z} & b = 0 \\ \mathsf{S} & b = 1 \end{cases}$

$\Pi_2.\mathsf{ExtAdm}(\mathsf{pk}_{\mathsf{S}}, \mathsf{sk}_{\mathsf{Z}}, \sigma)$

$\alpha \leftarrow \Pi_1.\mathsf{ExtAdm}(\mathsf{spk}_{\mathsf{S}}, \mathsf{ssk}_{\mathsf{Z}}, \sigma_{\mathsf{SS}})$
return α

Fig. 5. Generic transformation from weak to fully-fledged sanitizable signatures.

we conclude that one cannot guess whether the signature was sanitized or not, *i.e.*, Π_2 is transparent. Thirdly, Π_1 is invisible, so the part σ_{SS} hides all information about the possible modifications of the message. Moreover, The signature σ_{VRS} contains no information about the modifiable parts of the message. This implies that Π_2 is invisible. Finally, Π_1 is unlinkable, so the first part σ'_{SS} of a sanitized signature hides any information about the original signature, and the second part σ'_{VRS} does not depend on the original signature, so our resulting scheme Π_2 is also unlinkable. Note that Π_1 is *weakly* unlinkable in the sense that it is no longer secure if the adversary is allowed to send fresh signatures to the oracle LoRSanit$\mathcal{O}$. This does not impact the security of Π_2, because σ_{SS} is signed in σ_{VRS}, so to produce a fresh signature $(\sigma'_{SS}, \sigma'_{VRS})$, the adversary should be able to forge σ'_{VRS}, which is supposed to be hard under the hypothesis that the VRS scheme is unforgeable.

The correctness of Π_2 follows trivially from the correctness of Π_1 and VRS. Below, we state the formal security results for the construction. Due to space constraints, we refer to the full version of this work for the formal security proofs.

Theorem 2. *If Π_1 is weakly immutable, then Π_2 is immutable. If Π_1 is weakly unlinkable, and VRS is strongly unforgeable, then Π_2 is unlinkable. If Π_1 is strongly invisible then Π_2 is strongly invisible. If VRS is strongly accountable, then Π_2 is strongly signer accountable. If VRS is strongly non-seizable, then Π_2 is strongly sanitizer accountable. If VRS is anonymous and Π_1 is strongly proof-restrictedly transparent, then Π_2 is strongly proof-restrictedly transparent.*

We remark that verifiable ring signatures can be constructed generically from linkable ring signatures [27], which in turn can be generically constructed from unique ring signatures [18]. It is also possible to use any stronger primitive such as traceable [21] or accountable [35] ring signatures, as long as the signers are accountable. Furthermore, the transform can be easily extended to a multi-sanitizer setting by signing with respect to a ring which consists of the signer and multiple sanitizers. Depending on the variant of ring signatures used, we obtain different flavors of accountability. As the implications are straightforward, we do not elaborate further.

5 Security Proof for Construction I

The following proof uses the generic group model abstraction of Shoup [33] and we refer the reader to [3] for a comprehensive introduction to the bilinear group model. Here we state the central lemma useful for proving facts about generic attackers.

Lemma 2 (Schwartz-Zippel). *Let $F(X_1, \ldots, X_m)$ be a non-zero polynomial of degree $d \geq 0$ over a field $\mathbb{F}$. Then the probability that $F(x_1, \ldots, x_m) = 0$ for randomly chosen values $(x_1, \ldots, x_m)$ in $\mathbb{F}^n$ is bounded from above by $\frac{d}{|\mathbb{F}|}$.*

5.1 Weak Immutability

Proof (Weak Immutability). To prove that Π_1 is weakly immutable, we first show the generic hardness of the following problem.

Lemma 3. *Let* $(\mathbb{G}_1, \mathbb{G}_2, \mathbb{G}_T, G_1, G_2, G_T, e, q) \leftarrow \mathsf{BGGen}(1^\lambda)$ *with* $q > 2^\lambda$, *and* $a, b, c \leftarrow \mathbb{Z}_q$. *For all generic group adversary* $\mathcal{A}$, *the probability that* $\mathcal{A}$ *on input* $(G_1, G_1^a, G_1^b, G_2, G_2^b, G_2^c)$ *outputs* $(G_1^u, G_1^v, G_1^x, G_1^y, G_2^z)$ *such that*

$$
\begin{cases}
au - x = 0 \\
bv - y = 0 \\
cy - xz = 0 \\
v \neq 0
\end{cases}
$$

is negligible.

Proof. Let $(G_1^u, G_1^v, G_1^x, G_1^y, G_2^z)$ be the output of $\mathcal{A}$. Since $\mathcal{A}$ is generic, it holds that

$$
\begin{aligned}
u &= u_1 + u_a a + u_b b \\
v &= v_1 + v_a a + v_b b \\
x &= x_1 + x_a a + x_b b \\
y &= y_1 + y_a a + y_b b \\
z &= z_1 + z_b b + z_c c
\end{aligned}
$$

for some coefficients $u_1, u_a, u_b, v_1, v_a, v_b, x_1, x_a, x_b, y_1, y_a, y_b, z_1, z_b, z_c \in \mathbb{Z}_q$. By the relation $au - x = 0$, we have $-x_1 + (u_1 - x_a)a - x_b b + u_a a^2 + u_b ab = 0$. Note that $f(A, B) := -x_1 + (u_1 - x_a)A - x_b B + u_a A^2 + u_b AB$ is a quadratic polynomial in the variables A and B. Suppose f is not a zero polynomial, by the Schwartz-Zippel lemma (Lemma 2), for $a, b \leftarrow \mathbb{Z}_q$, the probability that $f(a, b) = 0$ is upper bounded by $2/q < 2^{1-\lambda}$ which is negligible. Therefore we can assume that f is always zero. In particular, we have $x_1 = x_b = 0$. Similarly, by examining the relation $bv - y = 0$, we can assume that $v_1 = y_b$, and $y_1 = y_a = 0$. We can therefore write $x = x_a a$ and $y = y_b b$. Next, we examine the relation $cy - xz = 0$, which implies

$$
y_b bc - x_a z_1 a - x_a z_b ab - x_a z_c ac = 0.
$$

Using the Schwartz-Zippel lemma again, we can assume that $y_b = 0$. However, this means that $v = v_1 = y_b = 0$, which contradicts with the fourth relation $v \neq 0$. □

Now, suppose there exists a generic group adversary $\mathcal{A}$ against the weak immutability of Π_1. We construct a generic group adversary $\mathcal{C}$ which solves the problem defined in Lemma 3. $\mathcal{C}$ receives as challenge $(G_1, G_1^a, G_1^b, G_2, G_2^c)$ from its challenger. It then simulates the ExpImmutability experiment for $\mathcal{A}$ by setting the public parameters and the signer keys honestly. Without loss of generality, assume that $\mathcal{A}$ makes $Q_1 = \mathsf{poly}(\lambda)$ signing oracle queries and $Q_2 = \mathsf{poly}(\lambda)$ random oracle queries for $\mathsf{H}()$. $\mathcal{C}$ additionally samples $i^\dagger, j^\dagger \leftarrow [Q_1]$ as a guess of which Sign oracle query $\mathcal{A}$ will attack against, $k^\dagger \leftarrow [\ell]$ as the index of the inadmissible block that will be modified in the forgery message, $l^\dagger \leftarrow [Q_2]$ as a guess of which $\mathsf{H}()$ oracle query $\mathcal{A}$ will include as the inadmissible modification in the forgery message.

Answering Random Oracle Queries. Upon receiving (k_l, m_l) as the l-th distinct query to the H() oracle, if $l \neq l^\dagger$, $\mathcal{C}$ answers the query by picking $t_l \leftarrow \mathbb{Z}_q^*$ and return $h_l := G_2^{t_l} \in \mathbb{G}_2$ to $\mathcal{A}$. If $l = l^\dagger$, then $\mathcal{C}$ sets $h_l = G_2^c$ where G_2^c was received as a challenge as described above. If (k_l, m_l) was a message that was queried previously, then reply with the same response as before.

Answering Sign Oracle Queries. Upon receiving $(\mathsf{pk}_{\mathsf{Z}}, m_i, \alpha_i)$ as the i-th query to the $\mathsf{Sign}\mathcal{O}$ oracle, if $i \neq i^\dagger$ and $i \neq j^\dagger$, $\mathcal{C}$ answers the query honestly by running the procedures as defined in the $\mathsf{Sign}\mathcal{O}$ oracle.

In the case $i = i^\dagger$ or $i = j^\dagger$, $\mathcal{C}$ generates the signature honestly except for the following changes:

1. If $i = i^\dagger$, then $\mathcal{C}$ picks the elements $X_{i^\dagger,1}, \ldots, X_{i^\dagger,\ell}$ as follows. $\mathcal{C}$ picks $X_{i^\dagger,k^\dagger} = G_1^a$ which it had received from its challenger in the beginning. For all other $k \in [\ell] \setminus \{k^\dagger\}$, $\mathcal{C}$ generates the X_k honestly by picking $x_{i^\dagger,k} \leftarrow \mathbb{Z}_q^*$ and setting $X_{i^\dagger,k} = G_1^{x_{i^\dagger,k}}$ (as done in the $\mathsf{Sign}\mathcal{O}$ oracle). The rest of the signature is generated as in the $\mathsf{Sign}\mathcal{O}$ oracle.

2. Suppose $i = j^\dagger$. If $k^\dagger \in \alpha_{j^\dagger}$, or $(k^\dagger, m_{j^\dagger,k^\dagger}) = (k_{l^\dagger}, m_{l^\dagger})$, then abort. Otherwise, let $t^\dagger$ be such that $H(k^\dagger \| m_{j^\dagger,k^\dagger}) = G_2^{t^\dagger}$. $\mathcal{C}$ first generates $X_{i^\dagger,1}, \ldots, X_{i^\dagger,\ell}$ by picking $x_{j^\dagger,k} \leftarrow \mathbb{Z}_q^*$ and setting $X_{j^\dagger,k} := G_1^{x_{j^\dagger,k}}$ for all $k \in [\ell]$. Then $\mathcal{C}$ picks the elements $Y_{i^\dagger,1}, \ldots, Y_{i^\dagger,\ell}$ as follows. $\mathcal{C}$ picks $Y_{j^\dagger,k^\dagger} = G_1^b$ which it had received from its challenger in the beginning. It then generates $\sigma_{j^\dagger,k^\dagger}$ as $(G_2^b)^{\frac{t^\dagger}{x_{j^\dagger,k^\dagger}}}$. For all other $k \neq k^\dagger$, $\mathcal{C}$ generates the $Y_{j^\dagger,k}$ and the rest of the signature honestly as done in the $\mathsf{Sign}\mathcal{O}$ oracle. Note that as we assume $k^\dagger \notin \alpha_{j^\dagger}$ in this case, the value $y_{j^\dagger,k^\dagger}$ is not needed to generate the signature. Therefore the signature can be simulated faithfully.

Answering Prove Oracle Queries. The Prove oracle is trivially simulatable since the Prove algorithm always returns ϵ.

Clearly, assuming that $\mathcal{C}$ did not abort, $\mathcal{C}$ simulates the wExpImmutability experiment for $\mathcal{A}$ faithfully. Eventually, $\mathcal{A}$ outputs $(\mathsf{pk}_{\mathsf{Z}}^*, m^*, \sigma^*)$ as a forgery such that $\mathsf{Verify}(\mathsf{pk}_{\mathsf{S}}^\dagger, \mathsf{pk}_{\mathsf{Z}}^*, m^*, \sigma^*) = 1$, and $m_k^* \neq m_{i,k}$ for some i, k such that $k \notin \alpha_i$. Since $Q_1, \ell \in \mathsf{poly}(\lambda)$, with non-negligible probability it holds that $m_{k^\dagger}^* \neq m_{j^\dagger,k^\dagger}$ and $k^\dagger \notin \alpha_{j^\dagger}$. Moreover, since $Q_2 \in \mathsf{poly}(\lambda)$, with non-negligible probability it holds that $(k^\dagger, m_{k^\dagger}^*) = (k_{l^\dagger}, m_{l^\dagger})$. If that is the case, then the abort conditions in the above procedures of answering sign oracle queries are never triggered.

Parse σ^* as $(\mu^*, \eta^*, \{\sigma_j^*, X_j^*, Y_j^*\}_{j=1}^\ell, c^*)$. By the EUF-CMA-security of EQS, with overwhelming probability we have that $[X_1^*, \ldots, X_\ell^*]_{\mathcal{R}} = [X_{i^*,1}, \ldots, X_{i^*,\ell}]_{\mathcal{R}}$ for some i^*, and $[Y_1^*, \ldots, Y_\ell^*]_{\mathcal{R}} = [Y_{j^*,1}, \ldots, Y_{j^*,\ell}]_{\mathcal{R}}$ for some j^* (otherwise we can construct an adversary against the EUF-CMA-security of EQS by simply outputting μ or η). Therefore, there exists $r, s \in \mathbb{Z}_q$ such that $(X_{i^*,1}, \ldots, X_{i^*,\ell})^r = (X_1^*, \ldots, X_\ell^*)$ and $(Y_{j^*,1}, \ldots, Y_{j^*,\ell})^{r \cdot s} = (Y_1^*, \ldots, Y_\ell^*)$.

Since $Q_1 \in \mathsf{poly}(\lambda)$, it happens with non-negligible probability that $(i^\dagger, j^\dagger) = (i^*, j^*)$. Suppose this is the case. Let k' be arbitrary with $k' \neq k^\dagger$. $\mathcal{C}$ extracts G_1^r and G_1^{rs} by computing

$$(X_{k'}^*)^{\frac{1}{x_{i^*,k'}}} = G_1^{r \cdot (x_{i^*,k'}) \cdot \frac{1}{x_{i^*,k'}}} = G_1^r$$

$$(Y_{k'}^*)^{\frac{1}{(x_{j^*,k'}) \cdot (y_{j^*,k'})}} = (G_1^{r \cdot s})^{\frac{(x_{j^*,k'}) \cdot (y_{j^*,k'})}{(x_{j^*,k'}) \cdot (y_{j^*,k'})}} = G_1^{r \cdot s}.$$

Since $\mathsf{Verify}(\mathsf{pk_S}, \mathsf{pk_Z^*}, m^*, \sigma^*) = 1$, this implies that $Y_{k^\dagger}^* = G_1^{r \cdot s \cdot b} \neq G_1$. This means that $r \cdot s \neq 0$. Furthermore, we have

$$e(X_{k^\dagger}^*, \sigma_{k^\dagger}^*) = e(Y_{k^\dagger}^*, \mathsf{H}(k^\dagger \| m_{k^\dagger}^*))$$

$$e(X_{i^\dagger,k^\dagger}^r, \sigma_{k^\dagger}^*) = e(Y_{j^\dagger,k^\dagger}^{r \cdot s}, G_2^c)$$

$$e(G_1^{r \cdot a}, \sigma_{k^\dagger}^*) = e(G_1^{r \cdot s \cdot b}, G_2^c)$$

$$\sigma_{k^\dagger}^* = G_2^{\frac{s \cdot b \cdot c}{a}}$$

Now, set $\mathcal{C}$ outputs $(G_1^u, G_1^v, G_1^x, G_1^y, G_2^z) := (G_1^r, G_1^{r \cdot s}, G_1^{r \cdot a}, G_1^{r \cdot s \cdot b}, G_2^{\frac{s \cdot b \cdot c}{a}})$. By a routine calculation, one can verify that $au - x = 0$, $bv - y = 0$, $cy - xz = 0$ and $v \neq 0$. Since $\mathcal{A}$ only performs generic group operations, so does $\mathcal{C}$, which contradicts with Lemma 3.   □

5.2   Strong Invisibility

Proof (Strong Invisibility). We prove strong invisibility by hybrid argument. We define an intermediate experiment Hyb^b which is identical to $\mathsf{ExpInvisibility}_{\mathcal{A},\Pi}^b(1^\lambda)$ for both $b \in \{0,1\}$, except for the following changes: When answering $\mathsf{LoRAdm}\mathcal{O}_b$ oracle queries, the challenger signs with respect to the policy $\alpha_0 \circ \alpha_1$ instead of α_b. We argue that, in the view of the adversary, the experiments Hyb^b and $\mathsf{ExpInvisibility}_{\mathcal{A},\Pi}^b(1^\lambda)$ are computationally indistinguishable for $b \in \{0,1\}$. Suppose that is the case, since obviously Hyb^0 is functionally equivalent to Hyb^1, it holds that $\mathsf{ExpInvisibility}_{\mathcal{A},\Pi}^0(1^\lambda)$ is computationally indistinguishable to $\mathsf{ExpInvisibility}_{\mathcal{A},\Pi}^1(1^\lambda)$.

Before proving the claim above, we state two key observations. First, note that the signatures returned by the $\mathsf{LoRAdm}\mathcal{O}_b$ oracle in the all experiments are identically distributed if $\mathsf{pk_Z} \neq \mathsf{pk_Z^\dagger}$ (since now it must hold that $\alpha_0 = \alpha_1$ for the oracle to not abort). In the case $\mathsf{pk_Z} = \mathsf{pk_Z^\dagger}$, the signatures returned by the oracle are almost identically distributed, except for the ciphertext c. In particular, in the experiment $\mathsf{ExpInvisibility}_{\mathcal{A},\Pi}^b(1^\lambda)$, the ciphertext is an encryption of the message $(\alpha_b, \{\zeta_{b,i}\}_{i=0}^\ell)$, where $\zeta_{b,i} = x_i$ for all $i \in \alpha_b$, and is zero otherwise. On the other hand, in Hyb^b, the ciphertext is an encryption of the message $(\alpha_0 \circ \alpha_1, \{\zeta_{b,i}\}_{i=0}^\ell)$, where $\zeta_{b,i} = x_i$ for all $i \in \alpha_0 \circ \alpha_1$, and is zero otherwise.

The second observation is that, due to the restriction imposed on the $\mathsf{San}\mathcal{O}'$ oracle, the values x_i for all $i \in (\alpha_b - (\alpha_0 \circ \alpha_1))$ are never used in any experiments.

With the above observations, we show how one can construct an algorithm $\mathcal{C}$, which breaks the IND-CCA-security of PKE, using a distinguisher which distinguishes Hyb^b from $\mathsf{ExpInvisibility}^b_{\mathcal{A},\Pi}(1^\lambda)$. $\mathcal{C}$ receives a public key $\mathsf{pk}_{\mathsf{PKE}}$ from the IND-CCA challenger, and acts as the challenger of either the experiment $\mathsf{ExpInvisibility}^b_{\mathcal{A},\Pi}(1^\lambda)$ or Hyb^b by setting $\mathsf{pk}^\dagger_Z := \mathsf{pk}_{\mathsf{PKE}}$ and generating other keys honestly.

Let $(\mathsf{pk}_Z, m_j, \alpha_{j,0}, \alpha_{j,1})$ be the j-th query to the $\mathsf{LoRAdmO}_b$ oracle. $\mathcal{C}$ answers the query honestly if $\mathsf{pk}_Z \neq \mathsf{pk}^\dagger_Z$. In the case where $\mathsf{pk}_Z = \mathsf{pk}^\dagger_Z$, $\mathcal{C}$ generates the ciphertext c_j in the following way. It samples $y_{j,i} \leftarrow_\$ \mathbb{Z}^*_q$ for all $i \in [\ell]$, and prepares

$$\zeta_{b,j,i} := \begin{cases} y_{j,i} & i \in \alpha_{j,b} \\ 0 & \text{otherwise} \end{cases}, \ \forall i \in [\ell] \qquad \zeta'_{b,j,i} := \begin{cases} y_{j,i} & i \in \alpha_{j,0} \circ \alpha_{j,1} \\ 0 & \text{otherwise} \end{cases}, \ \forall i \in [\ell]$$

$$\tau_{b,j} := (\alpha_{j,b}, \{\zeta_{b,j,i}\}^\ell_{i=1}) \qquad\qquad \tau'_{b,j} := (\alpha_{j,0} \circ \alpha_{j,1}, \{\zeta'_{b,j,i}\}^\ell_{i=1})$$

and queries the EncO_b oracle provided by the IND-CCA challenger on $(\tau_{b,j}, \tau'_{b,j})$ and receive c_j. $\mathcal{C}$ generates the rest of the signature honestly.

Upon receiving a query $(\mathsf{pk}_S, m, \delta, \sigma)$ to the $\mathsf{SanO'}$ oracle, $\mathcal{C}$ parses σ as $(\mu, \eta, \{\sigma_i, X_i, Y_i\}^\ell_{i=1}, c)$ and checks if $c = c_j$ for some j. If so, it uses $\{y_{j,i}\}_{i \in \alpha_{j,0} \cap \alpha_{j,1}}$ to answer the oracle query. If not, it queries the DecO oracle provided by the IND-CCA challenger on c, receives $\tau = (\alpha, \{\zeta_i\}_{i \in \ell})$, and uses it to answer the oracle query.

Clearly, depending on the choice of the IND-CCA challenger, our adversary simulates either the experiment $\mathsf{ExpsInvis}^b_{\Pi,\mathcal{A}}(1^\lambda)$ or Hyb^b faithfully. Therefore, if there exists a distinguisher which distinguishes the two experiments with a certain probability, then our adversary can guess the choice of the IND-CCA challenger with the same probability. $\qquad\qquad\square$

5.3 Perfect Strong Transparency

Proof (Perfect Strong Transparency). We show that the construction is perfectly strongly transparent through hybrid argument. First, observe that the Prove algorithm, and hence also the ProveO oracle, always returns the empty string ϵ, it is safe to drop the step $Q = Q \| (\delta(m), \sigma')$ in the Sign/SanO_b oracle.

Now, let $Q = \mathrm{poly}(\lambda)$ be the number of queries that the adversary $\mathcal{A}$ make to the Sign/SanO_b oracle. We define the hybrids $\mathsf{Hyb}_0, \ldots, \mathsf{Hyb}_q$ as follows. The hybrid Hyb_0 is identical to $\mathsf{ExpTrans}^0_{\Pi,\mathcal{A}}(1^\lambda)$. For $j \in [Q]$, Hyb_j is almost identical to Hyb_{j-1}, except that in the former the j-th query to the Sign/SanO_b is answered as in $\mathsf{ExpTrans}^1_{\Pi,\mathcal{A}}(1^\lambda)$. That is, the first j signatures returned by Sign/SanO_b are sanitized, while the last $Q - j$ signatures are freshly signed. Note that Hyb_Q is identical to $\mathsf{ExpTrans}^1_{\Pi,\mathcal{A}}(1^\lambda)$. Obviously, if $\Pr[\mathsf{Hyb}_{j-1} = 1] = \Pr[\mathsf{Hyb}_j = 1]$ for all $j \in [Q]$, then $\Pr[\mathsf{ExpTrans}^0_{\Pi,\mathcal{A}}(1^\lambda) = 1] = \Pr[\mathsf{ExpTrans}^1_{\Pi,\mathcal{A}}(1^\lambda) = 1]$.

Fix $j \in [Q]$. In the following, we show that $\Pr[\mathsf{Hyb}_{j-1} = 1] = \Pr[\mathsf{Hyb}_j = 1]$. Let (m, δ, α) be the j-th query of $\mathcal{A}$ to the Sign/SanO_b oracle. If $\delta \notin \alpha$, then the oracle returns $\perp$ in both experiments and thus the equality holds trivially. Otherwise, let $m' := \delta(m)$, and let σ' be the response. In Hyb_{j-1}, the signature σ' is drawn from a distribution $\mathcal{D}$ where

$$\mathcal{D} := \left\{ \sigma : \begin{array}{l} x_i, y_i \leftarrow \mathbb{Z}_q^*, \ X_i := G_1^{x_i}, \ Y_i := X_i^{y_i}, \ \forall i \in [\ell] \\ \mu \leftarrow \mathsf{EQS.Sign}(\mathsf{sk}_S^\dagger, (X_1, \dots, X_\ell)) \\ \eta \leftarrow \mathsf{EQS.Sign}(\mathsf{sk}_S^\dagger, (Y_1, \dots, Y_\ell)) \\ \sigma_i \leftarrow \mathsf{H}(i \| m_i')^{y_i}, \ \forall i \in [\ell] \\ \zeta_i := \begin{cases} y_i & i \in \alpha \\ 0 & \text{otherwise} \end{cases}, \ \forall i \in [0, \ell] \\ \tau := (\alpha, \{\zeta_i\}_{i \in [\ell]}) \\ c \leftarrow \mathsf{PKE.Enc}(\mathsf{pk}_Z^\dagger, \tau) \\ \sigma := (\mu, \eta, \{\sigma_i, X_i, Y_i\}_{i=1}^\ell, c) \end{array} \right\}.$$

Replacing x_i and y_i with $r \cdot x_i$ and $s \cdot y_i$ respectively for some $r, s \leftarrow \mathbb{Z}_q^*$, we obtain a distribution $\mathcal{D}' = \mathcal{D}$ where

$$\mathcal{D}' := \left\{ \sigma : \begin{array}{l} r, s \leftarrow \mathbb{Z}_q^* \\ x_i, y_i \leftarrow \mathbb{Z}_q^*, \ X_i := G_1^{x_i}, \ Y_i := X_i^{y_i}, \ \forall i \in [\ell] \\ \mu \leftarrow \mathsf{EQS.Sign}(\mathsf{sk}_S^\dagger, (X_1, \dots, X_\ell)^r) \\ \eta \leftarrow \mathsf{EQS.Sign}(\mathsf{sk}_S^\dagger, (Y_1, \dots, Y_\ell)^{r \cdot s}) \\ \sigma_i \leftarrow \mathsf{H}(i \| m_i')^{s \cdot y_i}, \ \forall i \in [\ell] \\ \zeta_i := \begin{cases} s \cdot y_i & i \in \alpha \\ 0 & \text{otherwise} \end{cases}, \ \forall i \in [\ell] \\ \tau := (\alpha, \{\zeta_i\}_{i \in [\ell]}) \\ c \leftarrow \mathsf{PKE.Enc}(\mathsf{pk}_Z^\dagger, \tau) \\ \sigma := (\mu, \eta, \{\sigma_i, X_i^r, Y_i^{r \cdot s}\}_{i=1}^\ell, c) \end{array} \right\}.$$

By the perfect adaption of EQS, the distribution of $\mathsf{EQS.Sign}(\mathsf{sk}_S^\dagger, (X_1, \dots, X_\ell)^r)$ and $\mathsf{EQS.Sign}(\mathsf{sk}_S^\dagger, (Y_1, \dots, Y_\ell)^{r \cdot s})$ is identical to that of $\mathsf{ChgRep}(\mathsf{pk}_S^\dagger, (X_1, \dots, X_\ell), \mu', r)$ and $\mathsf{ChgRep}(\mathsf{pk}_S^\dagger, (Y_1, \dots, Y_\ell), \eta', r \cdot s)$, where $\mu' \leftarrow \mathsf{EQS.Sign}(\mathsf{sk}_S^\dagger, (X_1, \dots, X_\ell))$ and $\eta' \leftarrow \mathsf{EQS.Sign}(\mathsf{sk}_S^\dagger, (Y_1, \dots, Y_\ell))$. Therefore, we obtain a distribution $\mathcal{D}'' = \mathcal{D}'$ with

$$\mathcal{D}'' := \left\{ \sigma : \begin{array}{l} r, s \leftarrow \mathbb{Z}_q^* \\ x_i, y_i \leftarrow \mathbb{Z}_q^*, \ X_i := G_1^{x_i}, \ Y_i := X_i^{y_i}, \ \forall i \in [\ell] \\ \mu' \leftarrow \mathsf{EQS.Sign}(\mathsf{sk}_S^\dagger, (X_1, \dots, X_\ell)) \\ \eta' \leftarrow \mathsf{EQS.Sign}(\mathsf{sk}_S^\dagger, (Y_1, \dots, Y_\ell)) \\ \mu \leftarrow \mathsf{ChgRep}(\mathsf{pk}_S^\dagger, (X_1, \dots, X_\ell), \mu', r) \\ \eta \leftarrow \mathsf{ChgRep}(\mathsf{pk}_S^\dagger, (Y_1, \dots, Y_\ell), \eta', r \cdot s) \\ \sigma_i \leftarrow \mathsf{H}(i \| m_i')^{s \cdot y_i}, \ \forall i \in [\ell] \\ \zeta_i := \begin{cases} s \cdot y_i & i \in \alpha \\ 0 & \text{otherwise} \end{cases}, \ \forall i \in [\ell] \\ \tau := (\alpha, \{\zeta_i\}_{i \in [\ell]}) \\ c \leftarrow \mathsf{PKE.Enc}(\mathsf{pk}_Z^\dagger, \tau) \\ \sigma := (\mu, \eta, \{\sigma_i, X_i^r, Y_i^{r \cdot s}\}_{i=1}^\ell, c) \end{array} \right\}.$$

Note that in Hyb_j, the signature σ' is drawn exactly from $\mathcal{D}''$. Therefore we can conclude that Hyb_{j-1} and Hyb_j are functionally equivalent. $\qquad\qquad\square$

5.4   Weak Unlinkability

Proof (Weak Unlinkability). To show that the experiments $\mathsf{wExpUnlink}_{\Pi,\mathcal{A}}^b(1^\lambda)$, where $b \in \{0,1\}$, are computationally indistinguishable in the view of the adversary we define the following sequence of hybrids.

Hyb_0^b : Defined as $\mathsf{wExpUnlink}_{\Pi,\mathcal{A}}^b(1^\lambda)$.

Hyb_1^b : Defined as Hyb_0^b, except that an additional list $\tilde{L}$ is initialized empty at the beginning of the experiment. Then, when a ciphertext $c \leftarrow \mathsf{PKE.Enc}(\mathsf{pk}_Z^\dagger, \tau)$ is generated in the subroutine Sign of the oracle Sign$\mathcal{O}$, a new entry $(c, \tau, \{x_i, y_i\}_{i\in[\ell]})$ is added to $\tilde{L}$. The wLoRSanit oracle runs the following modified version of the subroutine $\tilde{\mathsf{San}}$: On input a certain $\tilde{c}$, it first checks whether there is an entry $(\tilde{c}, \tilde{\tau}, \{\tilde{x}_i, \tilde{y}_i\}_{i\in[\ell]})$ in $\tilde{L}$ and, if so, proceeds by setting $\tau = \tilde{\tau}$. Otherwise the algorithm aborts.

Hyb_2^b : Defined as Hyb_1^b, except that the ciphertext c is computed as $c \leftarrow \mathsf{PKE.Enc}(\mathsf{pk}_Z^\dagger, (\alpha, 0^\ell))$ in the Sign$\mathcal{O}$ oracle. The suboutine $\tilde{\mathsf{San}}$ also computes $c' \leftarrow \mathsf{PKE.Enc}(\mathsf{pk}_Z^\dagger, (\alpha, 0^\ell))$.

Hyb_3^b : Defined as Hyb_2^b, except that the subroutine $\tilde{\mathsf{San}}$ is modified to compute the signatures μ' and η' as $\mu' \leftarrow \mathsf{EQS.Sign}(\mathsf{sk}_S^\dagger, (X_1', \dots, X_\ell'))$ and $\eta' \leftarrow \mathsf{EQS.Sign}(\mathsf{sk}_S^\dagger, (Y_1', \dots, Y_\ell'))$, respectively.

Hyb_4^b : Defined as Hyb_3^b, except that the subroutine $\tilde{\mathsf{San}}$ samples a fresh tuple $(Z_1, \dots, Z_\ell) \leftarrow \mathbb{G}_1^\ell$ is sampled and $(X_1', \dots, X_\ell') := (Z_1, \dots, Z_\ell)$ and $(Y_1', \dots, Y_\ell') := (Z_1^{\tilde{y}_1}, \dots, Z_\ell^{\tilde{y}_\ell})^s$.

Hyb_5^b : Defined as Hyb_4^b, except that the subroutine $\tilde{\mathsf{San}}$ samples a tuple $(w_1, \dots, w_\ell) \leftarrow \mathbb{Z}_q^\ell$ and computes σ_i' as $\mathsf{H}(m_i')^{w_i}$ and $(Y_1', \dots, Y_\ell')$ as $(Z_1^{w_1}, \dots, Z_\ell^{w_\ell})$.

Observe that in the experiment Hyb_5^b the output of the wLoRSanit oracle in Hyb_5^b is completely decorrelated from the random coin b. It follows that for all PPT adversaries we have that

$$\left| \Pr\left[\mathsf{Hyb}_5^0 = 1\right] - \Pr\left[\mathsf{Hyb}_5^1 = 1\right] \right| \leq \mathsf{negl}(\lambda).$$

We now proceed by showing the indistinguishability of each pair of hybrids.

Lemma 4. *Suppose* PKE *is correct. Then for all PPT* $\mathcal{A}$ *and* $b \in \{0,1\}$ *it holds that*

$$\left| \Pr\left[\mathsf{Hyb}_0^b = 1\right] - \Pr\left[\mathsf{Hyb}_1^b = 1\right] \right| \leq \mathsf{negl}(\lambda).$$

Proof (of Lemma 4). The experiments differ in the fact that in Hyb_1^b the LoRSanit oracle aborts when queried on some $\tilde{c}$ such that no entry $(\tilde{c}, \cdot)$ is present in $\tilde{L}$. This implies that $\tilde{c}$ was not produced by the signing oracle Sign$\mathcal{O}$, therefore also Hyb_0^b aborts on the same input. The indistinguishability follows by the correctness of the encryption scheme. $\qquad\qquad\square$

Lemma 5. *Suppose* PKE *is IND-CCA secure. Then for all PPT $\mathcal{A}$ and $b \in \{0,1\}$,*

$$\left| \Pr\left[\mathsf{Hyb}_1^b = 1 \right] - \Pr\left[\mathsf{Hyb}_2^b = \right] \right| \le \mathsf{negl}(\lambda).$$

Proof (of Lemma 5). The lemma follows by a simple reduction to the (multiple-message) CCA-security of the encryption scheme. On input a public key $\mathsf{pk}_{\tilde{z}}^\dagger$, the reduction computes c by querying the challenger on $(\tau, (\alpha, 0^\ell))$ and plugging in the corresponding ciphertext c^*. The ciphertext c' is computed analogously. The oracle SanO is simulated by passing the input ciphertexts $\tilde{c}$ to the decryption oracle and setting τ to be the corresponding output. It is easy to show that in the one case the reduction perfectly simulates the distributions of Hyb_1^b and in the other case it is identical to Hyb_2^b. By the CCA-security of the encryption scheme the claim follows. □

Lemma 6. *If* EQS *perfectly adapts signatures, then for all PPT $\mathcal{A}$ and $b \in \{0,1\}$,*

$$\left| \Pr\left[\mathsf{Hyb}_2^b = 1 \right] - \Pr\left[\mathsf{Hyb}_3^b = 1 \right] \right| = 0.$$

Proof (of Lemma 6). Trivial. □

Lemma 7. *Let $q > 2^\lambda$. For all generic group adversary $\mathcal{A}$ and $b \in \{0,1\}$ it holds that*

$$\left| \Pr\left[\mathsf{Hyb}_3^b = 1 \right] - \Pr\left[\mathsf{Hyb}_4^b = 1 \right] \right| \le \mathsf{negl}(\lambda).$$

Proof (of Lemma 7). First observe that in Hyb_4^b (with a slight notation abuse)

$$(Y_1', \ldots, Y_\ell') = (Z_1^{\tilde{y}_1}, \ldots, Z_\ell^{\tilde{y}_\ell})^s = (X_1', \ldots, X_\ell')^{s(\tilde{y}_1, \ldots, \tilde{y}_\ell)}$$

whereas in Hyb_3^b

$$(Y_1', \ldots, Y_\ell') = (Y_1, \ldots, Y_\ell)^{r \cdot s} = (X_1^{\tilde{y}_1}, \ldots, X_\ell^{\tilde{y}_\ell})^{r \cdot s} = (X_1', \ldots, X_\ell')^{s(\tilde{y}_1, \ldots, \tilde{y}_\ell)}.$$

Therefore if the tuple $(X_1', \ldots, X_\ell')$ has the same distribution in both experiments the indistinguishability follows. It remains to show that

$$\left(G_1, \frac{X_1, \ldots, X_\ell}{Z_1, \ldots, Z_\ell} \right) \approx \left(G_1, \frac{X_1, \ldots, X_\ell}{X_1^r, \ldots, X_\ell^r} \right)$$

over the random choice of $(Z_1, \ldots, Z_\ell, r)$. It is easy to show that the two distributions are indistinguishable by the hardness of the decisional Diffie-Hellman problem [14]. For completeness, and as a warm-up for the proof of the next lemma, we show that this holds in the generic group model. For ease of exposition, we denote symbolically $X_k := G_1^{x_k}$ and $Z_k := G_1^{z_k}$ for all $k \in [\ell]$. For the left distribution we can rewrite all equations that the adversary learns as symbolic degree 1 polynomials

$$\mathfrak{x}_1 x_1 + \ldots + \mathfrak{x}_\ell x_\ell + \mathfrak{z}_1 z_1 + \ldots + \mathfrak{z}_\ell z_\ell + \mathfrak{c} = 0$$

for some coefficients $(\mathfrak{x}_1, \ldots, \mathfrak{x}_\ell, \mathfrak{z}_1, \ldots, \mathfrak{z}_\ell, \mathfrak{c})$. For the right distributions we have

$$\mathfrak{x}_1 x_1 + \ldots + \mathfrak{x}_\ell x_\ell + \mathfrak{z}_1 x_1 r + \ldots + \mathfrak{z}_\ell x_\ell r + \mathfrak{c} = 0.$$

Since $(x_1, \ldots, x_\ell)$ and $(z_1, \ldots, z_\ell)$ are uniformly chosen, by Lemma 2 all coefficients in the left distribution must be 0 with all but negligible probability. The same holds for the right distribution, since r is uniformly sampled. It follows that a generic adversary cannot learn any non-trivial relation when it is given either the left or the right distribution. Therefore the left and right distributions look identical.   □

Lemma 8. *Let $q > 2^\lambda$. For all generic group adversary $\mathcal{A}$ and $b \in \{0,1\}$ it holds that*

$$\left| \Pr\left[\mathsf{Hyb}_4^b = 1 \right] - \Pr\left[\mathsf{Hyb}_5^b = 1 \right] \right| \leq \mathsf{negl}(\lambda).$$

Proof (of Lemma 8). The two experiments differ in the way the variables $(Y_1', \ldots, Y_\ell')$ and $(\sigma_1', \ldots, \sigma_\ell')$ are computed. Suppose that $\mathsf{H}(i\|m_i)$ and $\mathsf{H}(i\|m_i')$ are programed to $G_2^{t_i^0}$ and $G_2^{t_i^1}$ respectively, where $(t_1^0, t_1^1, \ldots, t_\ell^0, t_\ell^1)$ is a randomly sampled vector in $\mathbb{Z}_q^{2\ell}$. The indistinguishability of the two hybrids reduces to arguing about the proximity of the following distributions

$$
\begin{pmatrix}
& G_1^{y_1}, & \cdots, & G_1^{y_\ell}, & \\
G_1, & G_1^{z_1}, & \cdots, & G_1^{z_\ell}, & \\
& G_1^{sy_1 z_1}, & \cdots, & G_1^{sy_\ell z_\ell}, & \\
& G_2^{t_1^0 y_1}, & \cdots, & G_2^{t_\ell^0 y_\ell}, & \\
G_2, & G_2^{st_1^1 y_1}, & \cdots, & G_2^{st_\ell^1 y_\ell}, & \\
& G_2^{t_1^0}, & \cdots, & G_2^{t_\ell^0}, & \\
& G_2^{t_1^1}, & \cdots, & G_2^{t_\ell^1} &
\end{pmatrix}
\approx
\begin{pmatrix}
& G_1^{y_1}, & \cdots, & G_1^{y_\ell}, & \\
G_1, & G_1^{z_1}, & \cdots, & G_1^{z_\ell}, & \\
& G_1^{w_1 z_1}, & \cdots, & G_1^{w_\ell z_\ell}, & \\
& G_2^{t_1^0 y_1}, & \cdots, & G_2^{t_\ell^0 y_\ell}, & \\
G_2, & G_2^{t_1^1 w_1}, & \cdots, & G_2^{t_\ell^1 w_\ell}, & \\
& G_2^{t_1^0}, & \cdots, & G_2^{t_\ell^0}, & \\
& G_2^{t_1^1}, & \cdots, & G_2^{t_\ell^1} &
\end{pmatrix}
$$

where the LHS corresponds to the distributions in Hyb_4^b and the RHS corresponds to the distributions in Hyb_5^b. Note that all non-trivial relations that the generic attacker can learn are restricted to certain polynomials of degree at most 2. For illustration, we can symbolically write the relations obtained from the RHS as

$$\sum_{i \in [\ell], j \in [\ell]} \mathfrak{a}_{i,j} \left(t_i^1 w_i \cdot w_j z_j \right) \qquad + \sum_{i \in [\ell], j \in [\ell]} \mathfrak{b}_{i,j} \left(t_i^1 w_i \cdot y_j \right)$$

$$+ \sum_{i \in [\ell], j \in [\ell]} \mathfrak{c}_{i,j} \left(t_i^0 y_i \cdot w_j z_j \right) \qquad + \sum_{i \in [\ell], j \in [\ell]} \mathfrak{d}_{i,j} \left(t_i^0 y_i \cdot y_j \right)$$

$$+ \sum_{i \in [\ell], j \in [\ell], b \in \{0,1\}} \mathfrak{e}_{i,j}^b \left(t_i^b \cdot w_j z_j \right) \qquad + \sum_{i \in [\ell], j \in [\ell], b \in \{0,1\}} \mathfrak{f}_{i,j}^b \left(t_i^b \cdot y_j \right)$$

$$+ \sum_{i \in [\ell], j \in [\ell]} \mathfrak{g}_{i,j} \left(t_i^1 w_i \cdot z_j \right) \qquad + \sum_{i \in [\ell]} \mathfrak{h}_i \left(t_i^1 w_i \right)$$

$$+ \sum_{i\in[\ell],j\in[\ell]} \mathfrak{i}_{i,j} \left(t_1^0 y_i \cdot z_j\right) \qquad + \sum_{i\in[\ell]} \mathfrak{j}_i \left(t_1^0 y_i\right)$$

$$+ \sum_{i\in[\ell],j\in[\ell],b\in\{0,1\}} \mathfrak{k}_{i,j}^b \left(t_i^b \cdot z_j\right) \qquad + \sum_{i\in[\ell],b\in\{0,1\}} \mathfrak{l}_i^b \left(t_i^b\right)$$

$$+ \sum_{i\in[\ell]} \mathfrak{m}_i(y_i) \qquad + \sum_{i\in[\ell]} \mathfrak{n}_i(z_i)$$

$$+ \sum_{i\in[\ell]} \mathfrak{o}_i(w_i z_i) \qquad +\mathfrak{p}$$

$$= 0.$$

whereas for the LHS the equation is identical except that all occurrences of w_i and w_j are replaced with $y_i \cdot s$ and $y_j \cdot s$, respectively. Since all variables are uniformly distributed, by Lemma 2 we have that the coefficient of each unique monomial must be 0 with all but negligible probability. It is left to argue that each non-trivial relation obtained on the RHS imply also a corresponding non-trivial relation on the LHS, and viceversa. By inspection we isolate the pairs

$$\left(\sum_{i\in[\ell],j\in[\ell],b\in\{0,1\}} \mathfrak{e}_{i,j}^b \left(t_i^b \cdot w_j z_j\right), \sum_{i\in[\ell],j\in[\ell]} \mathfrak{g}_{i,j} \left(t_i^1 w_i \cdot z_j\right) \right)$$

and

$$\left(\sum_{i\in[\ell],j\in[\ell],b\in\{0,1\}} \mathfrak{f}_{i,j}^b \left(t_i^b \cdot y_j\right), \sum_{i\in[\ell]} \mathfrak{j}_i(t_i^0 y_i) \right)$$

that have potentially common monomials. For the latter case it is enough to observe that the monomials are identical for both the LHS and the RHS distributions as they are independent of w_i and s for all $i \in [\ell]$. Therefore if

$$\sum_{i\in[\ell],j\in[\ell],b\in\{0,1\}} \mathfrak{f}_{i,j}(t_i^b \cdot y_j) + \sum_{i\in[\ell]} \mathfrak{j}_i(t_i^0 y_i) = 0$$

in the RHS then so it does in the LHS, and vice versa. For the former case we have that collisions occur only when $i = j$ and $b = 1$, as otherwise the monomials are distinct and therefore any non trivial set of coefficients will not cancel out (with very high probability). Setting $i = j$ and $b = 1$, for the RHS we have the following constraint

$$\sum_{i\in[\ell]} \mathfrak{e}_{i,i}^1 \left(t_i^1 w_i z_i\right) + \sum_{i\in[\ell]} \mathfrak{g}_{i,i} \left(t_i^1 w_i z_i\right) = 0$$

which implies that, with overwhelming probability, for all $i \in [\ell]$ it holds that $\mathfrak{e}_{i,i}^1 = -\mathfrak{g}_{i,i}$. Applying this constraint to the LHS we obtain a corresponding non-trivial relation

$$\sum_{i\in[\ell]} \mathfrak{e}_{i,i}^1 \left(st_i^1 y_i z_i\right) + \sum_{i\in[\ell]} \mathfrak{g}_{i,i} \left(st_i^1 y_i z_i\right) = 0.$$

The reverse direction holds with an identical argument. Since there is a bijection between the non-trivial relations on the LHS and those on the RHS, we can conclude that the view of $\mathcal{A}$ in the two cases are indistinguishable.   □

Acknowledgments. This work is a result of the collaborative research project PROMISE (16KIS0763) by the German Federal Ministry of Education and Research (BMBF). FAU authors were also supported by the German research foundation (DFG) through the collaborative research center 1223, and by the state of Bavaria at the Nuremberg Campus of Technology (NCT). NCT is a research cooperation between the Friedrich-Alexander-Universität Erlangen-Nürnberg (FAU) and the Technische Hochschule Nürnberg Georg Simon Ohm (THN).

References

1. Ateniese, G., Chou, D.H., de Medeiros, B., Tsudik, G.: Sanitizable signatures. In: di Vimercati, S.C., Syverson, P., Gollmann, D. (eds.) ESORICS 2005. LNCS, vol. 3679, pp. 159–177. Springer, Heidelberg (2005). https://doi.org/10.1007/11555827_10

2. Beck, M.T., et al.: Practical strongly invisible and strongly accountable sanitizable signatures. In: Pieprzyk, J., Suriadi, S. (eds.) ACISP 2017, Part I. LNCS, vol. 10342, pp. 437–452. Springer, Cham (2017). https://doi.org/10.1007/978-3-319-60055-0_23

3. Boneh, D., Boyen, X.: Efficient selective-ID secure identity-based encryption without random oracles. In: Cachin, C., Camenisch, J.L. (eds.) EUROCRYPT 2004. LNCS, vol. 3027, pp. 223–238. Springer, Heidelberg (2004). https://doi.org/10.1007/978-3-540-24676-3_14

4. Boneh, D., Lynn, B., Shacham, H.: Short signatures from the Weil pairing. In: Boyd, C. (ed.) ASIACRYPT 2001. LNCS, vol. 2248, pp. 514–532. Springer, Heidelberg (2001). https://doi.org/10.1007/3-540-45682-1_30

5. Brzuska, C., et al.: Redactable signatures for tree-structured data: definitions and constructions. In: Zhou, J., Yung, M. (eds.) ACNS 2010. LNCS, vol. 6123, pp. 87–104. Springer, Heidelberg (2010). https://doi.org/10.1007/978-3-642-13708-2_6

6. Brzuska, C., et al.: Security of sanitizable signatures revisited. In: Jarecki, S., Tsudik, G. (eds.) PKC 2009. LNCS, vol. 5443, pp. 317–336. Springer, Heidelberg (2009). https://doi.org/10.1007/978-3-642-00468-1_18

7. Brzuska, C., Fischlin, M., Lehmann, A., Schröder, D.: Unlinkability of sanitizable signatures. In: Nguyen, P.Q., Pointcheval, D. (eds.) PKC 2010. LNCS, vol. 6056, pp. 444–461. Springer, Heidelberg (2010). https://doi.org/10.1007/978-3-642-13013-7_26

8. Brzuska, C., Pöhls, H.C., Samelin, K.: Non-interactive public accountability for sanitizable signatures. In: De Capitani di Vimercati, S., Mitchell, C. (eds.) EuroPKI 2012. LNCS, vol. 7868, pp. 178–193. Springer, Heidelberg (2013). https://doi.org/10.1007/978-3-642-40012-4_12

9. Bultel, X., Lafourcade, P.: Unlinkable and strongly accountable sanitizable signatures from verifiable ring signatures. In: Capkun, S., Chow, S.S.M. (eds.) CANS 2017. LNCS, vol. 11261, pp. 203–226. Springer, Cham (2018). https://doi.org/10.1007/978-3-030-02641-7_10

10. Camenisch, J., Derler, D., Krenn, S., Pöhls, H.C., Samelin, K., Slamanig, D.: Chameleon-hashes with ephemeral trapdoors. In: Fehr, S. (ed.) PKC 2017, Part II. LNCS, vol. 10175, pp. 152–182. Springer, Heidelberg (2017). https://doi.org/10.1007/978-3-662-54388-7_6
11. Canard, S., Jambert, A.: On extended sanitizable signature schemes. In: Pieprzyk, J. (ed.) CT-RSA 2010. LNCS, vol. 5985, pp. 179–194. Springer, Heidelberg (2010). https://doi.org/10.1007/978-3-642-11925-5_13
12. Canard, S., Jambert, A., Lescuyer, R.: Sanitizable signatures with several signers and sanitizers. In: Mitrokotsa, A., Vaudenay, S. (eds.) AFRICACRYPT 2012. LNCS, vol. 7374, pp. 35–52. Springer, Heidelberg (2012). https://doi.org/10.1007/978-3-642-31410-0_3
13. Derler, D., Pöhls, H.C., Samelin, K., Slamanig, D.: A general framework for redactable signatures and new constructions. In: Kwon, S., Yun, A. (eds.) ICISC 2015. LNCS, vol. 9558, pp. 3–19. Springer, Cham (2016). https://doi.org/10.1007/978-3-319-30840-1_1
14. Diffie, W., Hellman, M.E.: New directions in cryptography. IEEE Trans. Inf. Theory **22**(6), 644–654 (1976)
15. ElGamal, T.: A public key cryptosystem and a signature scheme based on discrete logarithms. In: Blakley, G.R., Chaum, D. (eds.) CRYPTO 1984. LNCS, vol. 196, pp. 10–18. Springer, Heidelberg (1985). https://doi.org/10.1007/3-540-39568-7_2
16. Fischlin, M., Harasser, P.: Invisible sanitizable signatures and public-key encryption are equivalent. Cryptology ePrint Archive, Report 2018/337 (2018). https://eprint.iacr.org/2018/337
17. Fleischhacker, N., Krupp, J., Malavolta, G., Schneider, J., Schröder, D., Simkin, M.: Efficient unlinkable sanitizable signatures from signatures with re-randomizable keys. In: Cheng, C.-M., Chung, K.-M., Persiano, G., Yang, B.-Y. (eds.) PKC 2016, Part I. LNCS, vol. 9614, pp. 301–330. Springer, Heidelberg (2016). https://doi.org/10.1007/978-3-662-49384-7_12
18. Franklin, M., Zhang, H.: A framework for unique ring signatures. Cryptology ePrint Archive, Report 2012/577 (2012). http://eprint.iacr.org/2012/577
19. Fuchsbauer, G., Hanser, C., Slamanig, D.: Structure-preserving signatures on equivalence classes and constant-size anonymous credentials, February 2018
20. Fujisaki, E., Okamoto, T.: Secure integration of asymmetric and symmetric encryption schemes. J. Cryptol. **26**(1), 80–101 (2013)
21. Fujisaki, E., Suzuki, K.: Traceable ring signature. In: Okamoto, T., Wang, X. (eds.) PKC 2007. LNCS, vol. 4450, pp. 181–200. Springer, Heidelberg (2007). https://doi.org/10.1007/978-3-540-71677-8_13
22. Hanser, C., Slamanig, D.: Structure-preserving signatures on equivalence classes and their application to anonymous credentials. In: Sarkar, P., Iwata, T. (eds.) ASIACRYPT 2014, Part I. LNCS, vol. 8873, pp. 491–511. Springer, Heidelberg (2014). https://doi.org/10.1007/978-3-662-45611-8_26
23. Johnson, R., Walsh, L., Lamb, M.: Homomorphic signatures for digital photographs. In: Danezis, G. (ed.) FC 2011. LNCS, vol. 7035, pp. 141–157. Springer, Heidelberg (2012). https://doi.org/10.1007/978-3-642-27576-0_12
24. Johnson, R., Molnar, D., Song, D., Wagner, D.: Homomorphic signature schemes. In: Preneel, B. (ed.) CT-RSA 2002. LNCS, vol. 2271, pp. 244–262. Springer, Heidelberg (2002). https://doi.org/10.1007/3-540-45760-7_17
25. Krenn, S., Samelin, K., Sommer, D.: Stronger security for sanitizable signatures. In: Garcia-Alfaro, J., Navarro-Arribas, G., Aldini, A., Martinelli, F., Suri, N. (eds.) DPM/QASA-2015. LNCS, vol. 9481, pp. 100–117. Springer, Cham (2016). https://doi.org/10.1007/978-3-319-29883-2_7

26. Lai, R.W.F., Zhang, T., Chow, S.S.M., Schröder, D.: Efficient sanitizable signatures without random oracles. In: Askoxylakis, I., Ioannidis, S., Katsikas, S., Meadows, C. (eds.) ESORICS 2016, Part I. LNCS, vol. 9878, pp. 363–380. Springer, Cham (2016). https://doi.org/10.1007/978-3-319-45744-4_18

27. Liu, J.K., Wei, V.K., Wong, D.S.: Linkable spontaneous anonymous group signature for ad hoc groups (extended abstract). In: Wang, H., Pieprzyk, J., Varadharajan, V. (eds.) ACISP 2004. LNCS, vol. 3108, pp. 325–335. Springer, Heidelberg (2004). https://doi.org/10.1007/978-3-540-27800-9_28

28. Lu, J., Wang, X.: Verifiable ring signature (2003)

29. Miyazaki, K., Hanaoka, G., Imai, H.: Invisibly sanitizable digital signature scheme. IEICE Trans. Fundam. Electron. Commun. Comput. Sci. **91**, 392–402 (2008)

30. Okamoto, T., Tada, M., Okamoto, E.: Extended proxy signatures for smart cards. In: Mambo, M., Zheng, Y. (eds.) ISW 1999. LNCS, vol. 1729, pp. 247–258. Springer, Heidelberg (1999). https://doi.org/10.1007/3-540-47790-X_21

31. Pöhls, H.C., Samelin, K.: On updatable redactable signatures. In: Boureanu, I., Owesarski, P., Vaudenay, S. (eds.) ACNS 2014. LNCS, vol. 8479, pp. 457–475. Springer, Cham (2014). https://doi.org/10.1007/978-3-319-07536-5_27

32. Shim, K.-A.: An identity-based proxy signature scheme from pairings. In: Ning, P., Qing, S., Li, N. (eds.) ICICS 2006. LNCS, vol. 4307, pp. 60–71. Springer, Heidelberg (2006). https://doi.org/10.1007/11935308_5

33. Shoup, V.: Lower bounds for discrete logarithms and related problems. In: Fumy, W. (ed.) EUROCRYPT 1997. LNCS, vol. 1233, pp. 256–266. Springer, Heidelberg (1997). https://doi.org/10.1007/3-540-69053-0_18

34. Wang, H., Pieprzyk, J.: Efficient one-time proxy signatures. In: Laih, C.-S. (ed.) ASIACRYPT 2003. LNCS, vol. 2894, pp. 507–522. Springer, Heidelberg (2003). https://doi.org/10.1007/978-3-540-40061-5_32

35. Xu, S., Yung, M.: Accountable ring signatures: a smart card approach. In: Quisquater, J.J., Paradinas, P., Deswarte, Y., El Kalam, A.A. (eds.) Smart Card Research and Advanced Applications VI. IFIPAICT, vol. 153, pp. 271–286. Springer, Boston (2004). https://doi.org/10.1007/1-4020-8147-2_18

Group Signatures with Selective Linkability

Lydia Garms[1(✉)] and Anja Lehmann[2]

[1] Royal Holloway, University of London, Egham, UK
Lydia.Garms.2015@live.rhul.ac.uk
[2] IBM Research - Zurich, Rüschlikon, Switzerland
anj@zurich.ibm.com

Abstract. Group signatures allow members of a group to anonymously produce signatures on behalf of the group. They are an important building block for privacy-enhancing applications, e.g., enabling user data to be collected in authenticated form while preserving the user's privacy. The linkability between the signatures thereby plays a crucial role for balancing utility and privacy: knowing the correlation of events significantly increases the utility of the data but also severely harms the user's privacy. Therefore group signatures are unlinkable per default, but either support linking or identity escrow through a dedicated central party or offer user-controlled linkability. However, both approaches have significant limitations. The former relies on a fully trusted entity and reveals too much information, and the latter requires exact knowledge of the needed linkability at the moment when the signatures are created. However, often the exact purpose of the data might not be clear at the point of data collection. In fact, data collectors tend to gather large amounts of data at first, but will need linkability only for selected, small subsets of the data. We introduce a new type of group signature that provides a more flexible and privacy-friendly access to such selective linkability. When created, all signatures are fully unlinkable. Only when strictly needed or desired, should the required pieces be made linkable with the help of a central entity. For privacy, this linkability is established in an oblivious and non-transitive manner. We formally define the requirements for this new type of group signatures and provide an efficient instantiation that provably satisfies these requirements under discrete-logarithm based assumptions.

1 Introduction

Group signatures are a powerful and well-studied primitive that allow members of a group to sign messages on behalf of the group in an anonymous way [2,4,9, 10,21,22,28,32–34]. That is, a verifier of a group signature is assured that it was signed by a valid member of the group, but it does not learn anything about the identity of the signer, or even whether two signatures stem from the same user.

L. Garms—Work done as an intern at IBM Research – Zurich.

D. Lin and K. Sako (Eds.): PKC 2019, LNCS 11442, pp. 190–220, 2019.
https://doi.org/10.1007/978-3-030-17253-4_7

This makes group signatures highly suited whenever data is collected that needs to be authenticated while, at the same time, the privacy of the data sources must be respected and preserved. In particular when data is collected from users, the protection of their privacy is of crucial importance, and sees increased attention due to the recently introduced General Data Protection Regulation (GDPR) [1], Europe's new privacy regulation. In fact, the GDPR creates strong incentives for data collectors to thoroughly protect users' data and implement the principle of data minimization, as data breaches are fined with up to 4% of an enterprises annual turnover.

When aiming to implement such techniques for privacy and data protection, one needs to find a good balance with utility though: data gets collected in order to be analysed and to generate new insights. For these processes it is usually necessary to know the correlation among different data events, as they carry a crucial part of the information. For instance, when a group of users measure and upload their blood pressure via wearable activity trackers, several high value measurements are not critical when they are distributed over many participants, but might be alarming when originating from a single user.

Often the exact purpose of the data might not be clear at the point of data collection. In fact, given the rapid advancements in machine learning and the ubiquitously available and cheap storage, data collectors tend to gather large amounts of data at first, and will only use small subsets for particular applications as they arise. A famous example are the Google Street View cars that inadvertently recorded public Wi-Fi data like SSID information, which later got used to improve Google's location services.

Ideally, the data should be collected and stored in authenticated and unlinkable form, and only the particular subsets that are needed later on should be correlated in a controlled and flexible manner.

Linkability in Group Signatures. To address the tension between privacy and utility, group signatures often have built-in measures that control linkability of otherwise anonymously authenticated information. Interestingly, despite the long line of work on this subject, none of the solutions provides the functionality to cater for the flexibility needed in practice: They either recover linkablity in a privacy-invasive way or offer control only in a static manner.

Group Signatures with Opening. Standard group signatures [4,5,9,10,22,34] guarantee full unlinkability of signatures, except to the group manager (or dedicated opening authority) that owns a so-called *opening* key. The opening key allows the group manager, when given a signature, to recover the signer's identity. Originally, the opening was intended to prevent abuse of anonymity, and rather meant to be used in extreme situations. Clearly, the opening capability can also be leveraged to determine the linkability of various data events, but at high costs for privacy: every request for linkability will recover the full identity of the signer, and the central group manager learns the (signed) data of the data collectors and their correlation.

Group Signatures with Controlled Linkability. A more suitable solution are group signatures with controlled linkability [29,30,37]. In these schemes, signatures are unlinkable except to a dedicated linking authority with a secret key: on input two signatures it tells whether they stem from the same user or not. This is much better then revealing the identity of the user, but still relies on a *fully trusted* entity that will learn the collectors' signed data. Further, this approach does not scale well for applications where a data collector is interested in the correlations within a large data set. To link a data set of n signed entries, each pair of signatures would have to be compared, which would require $n(n-1)/2$ requests to the linking authority. Another related concept are *traceable* group signatures [31] where a dedicated entity can generate a tracing trapdoor for each user which allows to trace this user's signatures. This approach is not suitable for our use case of controlled data linkage either, as it requires knowledge of the users' identities behind the anonymous group signatures or trapdoors for *all* users, and also needs every signature to be tested for every trapdoor.

Group Signatures with User-Controlled Linkability. Finally, schemes with user-controlled linkability exist, mostly in the context of Direct Anonymous Attestation (DAA) [6,11,12,14,15] or anonymous credentials [19,35]. For linkability, a so-called *basename* is chosen alongside the message and all signatures with the same basename can easily be linked, but signatures for different basenames remain unlinkable. In contrast to solutions with opening or linking authorities, the linkability here can be publicly verified: a signature in such schemes contains a *pseudonym* that is deterministically derived from the user's secret key and the basename. Thus, the user re-uses the same pseudonym whenever he wants to be linkable. On the downside, this linkage is immediate and static. That is, the users have to choose at the beginning whether they want to disclose their data in a fully unlinkable manner, or linked w.r.t. a context-specific pseudonym. There is no option to selectively correlate the data after it has been disclosed. Therefore, users, or rather the data collectors allowing the use of such protocols, will hesitate to choose the option of unlinkability, as they fear to lose too much information by the irreversible decorrelation.

Our Contributions. In this work we overcome the aforementioned limitations by introducing a new type of group signatures that allows for flexible and selective linkability. We achieve that functionality by combining ideas from the different approaches discussed above: Group signatures are associated with pseudonyms, but pseudonyms are all *unlinkable per default*. Only when needed, a set of signatures – or rather the pseudonyms – can be linked in an efficient manner through a central entity, the *converter*. The converter receives a batch of pseudonymous data and transforms them into a consistent representation, meaning that all pseudonyms stemming from the same user will be converted into the same value. To preserve the privacy of the users and their data, the converter correlates the data in a fully blind way, i.e., not learning anything about the pseudonyms he transforms. We term these new form of group signatures CLS, which stands for convertably linkable (group) signatures.

Security and Privacy for CLS. A crucial property that we want from pseudonym conversions is that they establish linkability only strictly within the queried data, i.e., linked pseudonyms from different queries should not be transitive. Otherwise, different re-linked data sets with overlapping input data could be pieced together, thereby gradually eroding the user's privacy. Aiming for such *non-transitivity* has an immediate impact on the overall setting: we need to channel both, the pseudonyms and messages, blindly through the converter, as transforming pseudonyms without the messages would require linkability between the in- and outputs of the conversion query, which in turn allows to correlate outputs from different queries.

We formally define the security of CLS through a number of security games, strongly inspired by the existing work on group signatures and DAA [4,5,15]. That is, we want signatures to be fully *anonymous* and unlinkable bearing in mind the information that is revealed through the selective linkability. We discuss that the classic anonymity notion adapted to our setting won't suffice, as it cannot guarantee the desired *non-transitivity*. In fact, capturing the achievable privacy and non-transitivity property in the presence of adaptive conversion queries was one of the core challenges of this work, and we formalize this property through a simulation-based definition. If the converter is corrupt, then unlinkability of signatures no longer holds, but the adversary should neither be able to trace signatures to a particular user, nor harm the obliviousness of queries which is captured in the *conversion blindness* and *join anonymity* properties. The guarantees in terms of unforgeability are captured through *non-frameability* and *traceability* requirements. The former says that corrupt users should not be able to impersonate honest users, and the latter guarantees that the power of an adversary should be bounded by the number of corrupt users he controls.

From a corruption point of view, we assume the data collector to be at most honest-but-curious towards the converter, i.e., even a corrupt data collector will only query pseudonym-message pairs that it has received along with a valid signature. We consider this a reasonable assumption, as data collectors that will use such a CLS scheme do so in order to implement the principle of data minimization on their own premises, and don't have an incentive to cheat themselves.

Efficient Instantiation. We propose an efficient construction of such CLS schemes, following the classical sign-and-encrypt paradigm that underlies most group signatures. Roughly, we use BBS+ signatures [3] for attesting group membership, i.e., a user will blindly receive a BBS+ signature from the group issuer on a secret key y chosen afresh by the user. To sign a message m on behalf of the group, the user computes a signature-proof-of-knowledge (SPK) for m where he proves knowledge of such an issuer's signature on its secret key and also encrypts it's user key (or rather its "public key" version h^y) under the converter's public key. The ciphertext that encrypts h^y serves as the pseudonym nym.

When the converter is asked to recover the correlations for a set of k pseudonym-message pairs $(nym_1, m_1), \ldots (nym_k, m_k)$, it blindly decrypts each pseudonym and blindly raises the result to the power of r which is chosen fresh for every conversion query, but used consistently within. That is, all pseudonyms belonging to the same user will be mapped to the same query-specific DDH tuple h^{yr} which allows for linkage of data within the query, but guarantees that converted pseudonyms remain unlinkable across queries. To achieve obliviousness and non-transitivity of conversions, we encrypt all pseudonyms and messages with a re-randomisable (homomorphic) encryption scheme under the blinding key of the data collector. The re-randomisation is applied by the converter before he returns the transformed values, which ensures that the data collector cannot link the original and the converted pseudonyms by any cryptographic value. Clearly, if the associated messages are unique, then the data collector can link in- and outputs anyway, but our scheme should not introduce any additional linkage. Given that the pseudonyms are encryptions under the converter's public key, we need to add the second layer of encryption in a way that it doesn't interfere with the capabilities of the inner ciphertext. Using a nested form of ElGamal encryption [23] gives us these properties as well as the needed re-randomisability.

Finally, we prove that our instantiation satisfies the desired security and privacy requirements under the DDH, q-SDH and DCR assumption in the random oracle model. Our construction relies on type-3 pairings and performs most of the work in $\mathbb{G}_1$ which comes with significant efficiency benefits. In fact, we show that our construction is reasonably efficient considering the increased flexibility when establising the linkability in such a selective and controlled manner.

Other Related Work. A number of results exist that establish convertible pseudonyms in the setting of distributed databases and have inspired our work. Therein, the data gets created and maintained in a distributed manner. For privacy, related data is stored under different, database-specific pseudonyms that are seemingly unlinkable and can only be correlated by a central entity that controls the data flow. While the initial approach by Galindo and Verheul [26] required the converter to be a trusted third party, Camenisch and Lehmann [17, 18] later showed how the converter can operate in an oblivious manner. However, none of these solutions supports *authenticated* data collection and [26] and [17] even let the (trusted) converter establish all pseudonyms. The pseudonym system in [18] bootstraps pseudonyms in a blind way from a user secret, but for every new pseudonym that requires the user, converter and targeted data base to engage in an interactive protocol. Clearly, this is not practical for a setting where users frequently want to upload data. Further, all schemes re-use the same pseudonym for a user within a database, whereas our solution creates fresh and unlinkable pseudonyms for every new data item.

2   Preliminaries

This section presents all building blocks and assumptions that are needed for our CLS construction. We use ElGamal encryption as re-randomisable and homomorphic encryption scheme that is chosen plaintext secure, BBS+ signatures [3], and standard proof protocols.

Bilinear Maps & q-SDH Assumption. Let $\mathbb{G}_1$, $\mathbb{G}_2$, $\mathbb{G}_T$ be cyclic groups of prime order p. A map $e : \mathbb{G}_1 \times \mathbb{G}_2 \to \mathbb{G}_T$ must satisfy the following conditions: *bilinearity*, i.e., $e(g_1^x, g_2^y) = e(g_1, g_2)^{xy}$; *non-degeneracy*, i.e., for all generators $g_1 \in \mathbb{G}_1$ and $g_2 \in \mathbb{G}_2$, $e(g_1, g_2)$ generates $\mathbb{G}_T$; and *efficiency*, i.e., there exists an efficient algorithm $\mathcal{G}(1^\tau)$ that outputs a bilinear group $(p, \mathbb{G}_1, \mathbb{G}_2, \mathbb{G}_T, e, g_1, g_2)$, and an efficient algorithm to compute $e(a, b)$ for all $a \in \mathbb{G}_1$, $b \in \mathbb{G}_2$.

We use type-3 pairings [25] in this work, i.e., we do not assume $\mathbb{G}_1 = \mathbb{G}_2$ or the existence of an isomorphism between both groups in our scheme and security proofs. The advantage of type-3 pairings is that they enjoy the most efficient curves.

q-Strong Diffie Hellman Assumption (q-SDH). There are two versions of the q-Strong Diffie Hellman Assumption. The first version, given by Boneh and Boyen in [7], is defined in a type-1 or type-2 pairing setting. We use their second version of that definition that supports type-3 pairings and was stated in the journal version of their paper [8].

Given $(g_1, g_1^\chi, g_1^{(\chi)^2}, ..., g_1^{(\chi)^q}, g_2, g_2^\chi)$ such that $g_1 \in \mathbb{G}_1, g_2 \in \mathbb{G}_2$, output $(g_1^{\frac{1}{\chi+x}}, x) \in \mathbb{G}_1 \times \mathbb{Z}_p \backslash \{-\chi\}$.

BBS+ Signatures. Our scheme will make use of BBS+ signatures given by Au et al. [3], and inspired by BBS group signatures introduced in [9].

Key Generation: Take $(h_1, h_2) \leftarrow_\$ \mathbb{G}_1^2$, $x \leftarrow_\$ \mathbb{Z}_p^*$, $w \leftarrow g_2^x$, and set $sk = x$ and $pk = (w, h_1, h_2)$.

Signature: On input a message $m \in \mathbb{Z}_p$ and secret key x, pick $e, s \leftarrow_\$ \mathbb{Z}_p$ and compute $A \leftarrow (g_1 h_1^s h_2^m)^{\frac{1}{e+x}}$. Output signature $\sigma \leftarrow (A, e, s)$.

Verification: On input a public key $(w, h_1, h_2) \in \mathbb{G}_2 \times \mathbb{G}_1^2$, message $m \in \mathbb{Z}_p$, and purported signature $(A, e, s) \in \mathbb{G}_1 \times \mathbb{Z}_p^2$, check $e(A, wg_2^e) = e(g_1 h_1^s h_2^m, g_2)$.

When proving the unforgability of our scheme (called traceability in our setting), we will make use of techniques from [14] which prove the unforgeability of BBS+ signatures in the type-3 setting. Originally, Au et al. [3], proved the BBS+ signature secure under the first version of the q-SDH assumption given in [7], making use of the isomorphism between the groups in the security proof.

Re-randomisable ElGamal Encryption. We use the ElGamal encryption scheme [23] with public parameters $(\mathbb{G}_1, g, p)$, such that the DDH problem is hard with respect to τ, i.e p is a τ bit prime.

Key Generation: Choose $sk \leftarrow_\$ \mathbb{Z}_p^*$, $pk \leftarrow g^{sk}$, and output (pk, sk).

Encryption: On input (pk, m), choose $r \leftarrow_\$ \mathbb{Z}_p^*$, and output $c \leftarrow (g^r, pk^r m)$.

Decryption: On input $(sk, (c_1, c_2))$, output $m \leftarrow c_2 c_1^{-sk}$.

ElGamal encryption is chosen-plaintext secure under the DDH assumption. In our construction, we will use the *homomorphic* property of ElGamal, i.e., if $C_1 \in \mathsf{Enc}(pk, m_1)$, and $C_2 \in \mathsf{Enc}(pk, m_2)$, then $C_1 \odot C_2 \in \mathsf{Enc}(pk, m_1 \cdot m_2)$.

We further use that ElGamal ciphertexts $c = \mathsf{Enc}(pk, m)$ are *publicly re-randomisable* in the sense that a re-randomised version c' of c looks indistinguishable from a fresh encryption of the underlying plaintext m. The following procedure clearly satisfies this:

Re-randomisation: On input $(pk, (c_1, c_2))$, get $r' \leftarrow_\$ \mathbb{Z}_p^*$ and output $(c_1 g^{r'}, c_2 pk^{r'})$.

2.1 Proof Protocols

We follow the notation defined in [16] when referring to zero-knowledge proofs of knowledge of discrete logarithms. For example $\mathsf{PK}\{(a, b, c) : y = g^a h^b \wedge \tilde{y} = \tilde{g}^a \tilde{h}^c\}$ denotes a zero knowledge proof of knowledge of integers a, b and c such that $y = g^a h^b$ and $\tilde{y} = \tilde{g}^a \tilde{h}^c$ hold. SPK denotes a signature proof of knowledge, that is a non-interactive transformation of a proof PK, e.g., using the Fiat-Shamir heuristic [24] in the random oracle. Using the Fiat-Shamir heuristic, the witness can be extracted from these proofs by rewinding the prover and programming the random oracle. Alternatively, these proofs can be extended to be online-extractable, by verifiably encrypting the witness to a public key defined in the common reference string. Clearly this requires a trusted common reference string. We underline the values that we need to be online-extractable in our proofs.

We require the proof system to be *simulation-sound* and *zero-knowledge*. The latter roughly says that there must exist a simulator that can generate simulated proofs which are indistinguishable from real proofs from the view of the adversary. The simulation-soundness is a strengthened version of normal soundness and guarantees that an adversary, even after having seen simulated proofs of false statements of his choice, cannot produce a valid proof of a false statement himself.

3 Definition & Security Model for CLS

In this section we first introduce the syntax and generic functionality of CLS and then present the desirable security and privacy properties for such schemes.

The following entities are involved in an CLS scheme: an issuer $\mathcal{I}$, a set of users $\mathcal{U} = \{uid_i\}$, a Verifier $\mathcal{V}$ and a converter $\mathcal{C}$. The issuer $\mathcal{I}$ is the central entity that allows users to join the group. Once joined, a user can then sign on behalf of the group in a pseudonymous way. That is, a verifier $\mathcal{V}$ can test the validity of a signature w.r.t the group's public key but does not learn any information about the particular user that created the signature. Most importantly, we want the pseudonymously signed data to be linkable in a controlled yet blind manner. Such selected linkability can be requested through the converter $\mathcal{C}$ that can blindly transform tuples of pseudonym-message pairs into a consistent representation.

3.1   Syntax of CLS

Our notation closely follows the definitional framework for dynamic group signatures given in [5]. We stress that our algorithms (and security notions) are flexible enough to cover settings where multiple verifiers and converters exist. For the sake of simplicity, however, we focus on the setting where there is only one entity each.

Definition 1 (CLS). *A convertably linkable group signature scheme CLS consists of the following algorithms:*

Setup & Key Generation. We model key generation individually per party, and refer to (param, ipk, cpk) as the group public key gpk.

Setup(1^τ) → **param:** on input a security parameter 1^τ, outputs param, the public parameters for the scheme.

IKGen(**param**) → (ipk, isk): performed by the issuer $\mathcal{I}$, outputs the issuer secret key isk, and the issuing public key ipk.

CKGen(**param**) → (cpk, csk): performed by the Converter $\mathcal{C}$, outputs the converter secret key csk, and the converter public key cpk.

BKGen(**param**) → (bpk, bsk): performed by the verifier $\mathcal{V}^1$, outputs a blinding secret key, bsk, and blinding public key, bpk. As the key is only used for blinding purposes, (bpk, bsk) can be ephemeral. We write $\mathcal{BPK}$ as the public key space induced by BKGen.

Join, Sign & Verify. As in standard dynamic group signatures we have a dedicated join procedure that a user has to complete with the issuer. All users that have successfully joined the group can then create pseudonymous signatures on behalf of the group, i.e., that verify w.r.t. the group public key bpk. For ease of expression we treat the pseudonym nym as a dedicated part of the signature.

⟨**Join**(gpk), **Issue**(isk, gpk)⟩: a user uid joins the group by engaging in a interactive protocol with the Issuer $\mathcal{I}$. The user uid and Issuer $\mathcal{I}$ perform algorithms Join and Issue respectively. These are input a state and an incoming message respectively, and output an updated state, an outgoing message, and a decision, either cont, accept, or reject. The initial input to Join is the group public key, gpk, whereas the initial input to Issue is the issuer secret key, isk, and the issuer public key ipk. If the user uid accepts, Join has a private output of $\mathbf{gsk}[uid]$.

Sign($gpk, \mathbf{gsk}[uid], m$) → ($nym, \sigma$): performed by the user with identifier uid, with input the group public key gpk, the user's secret key $\mathbf{gsk}[uid]$, and a message m. Outputs a pseudonym nym and signature σ.

Verify(gpk, m, nym, σ) → {0, 1}: performed by the Verifier $\mathcal{V}$. Outputs 1 if σ is a valid signature on m for pseudonym nym under the group public key gpk, and 0 otherwise.

---

[1] For sake of simplicity we state the algorithms for the setting where the requester and receiver of conversions is the same party, namely the verifier. However, our algorithms work in a public key setting to facilitate more general settings as well.

Blind Conversion. Finally, we want our pseudonymous group signatures to be blindly convertable. Thus, we introduce a dedicated Blind and Unblind procedure for the verifier and a Convert algorithm that requires the converter's secret key. The latter transforms the unlinkable pseudonyms in a consistent manner, i.e., outputting converted pseudonyms that are consistent whenever the input pseudonyms belong to the same user.

Blind$(gpk, bpk, (nym, m)) \rightarrow (cnym, c)$: performed by the verifier $\mathcal{V}$ on input a pseudonym-message pair(nym, m) and blinding public key bpk, group public key gpk. Outputs a blinded pseudonym and message.

Convert$(gpk, csk, bpk, \{(cnym_i, c_i)\}_k) \rightarrow \{(\overline{cnym}_i, \overline{c}_i)\}_k$: performed by the converter $\mathcal{C}$, on input k blinded pseudonym-message tuples $\{(cnym_i, c_i)\}_k = ((cnym_1, c_1), ..., (cnym_k, c_k))$, and the public blinding key bpk used. Outputs converted pseudonyms $\{(\overline{cnym}_i, \overline{c}_i)\}_k = ((\overline{cnym}_1, \overline{c}_1), ..., (\overline{cnym}_k, \overline{c}_k))$

Unblind$(bsk, (\overline{cnym}, \overline{c})) \rightarrow (\overline{nym}, \overline{m})$: performed by the Verifier $\mathcal{V}$ on input a converted pseudonym-message tuple, and the blinding secret key bsk. Outputs an unblinded converted pseudonym-message tuple $(\overline{nym}, \overline{m})$.

We sometimes make the randomness r used in these algorithms explicit, and e.g. write Blind$(gpk, bpk, (nym, m); r)$.

3.2 Security Properties

We want that CLS schemes enjoy roughly the same security and privacy properties as group signatures when taking the added linkability into account. Defining these properties when pseudonyms can be *selectively* and *adaptively* converted is very challenging, though, as it requires a lot of care to avoid trivial wins while keeping the adversary as powerful as possible.

In a nutshell, we require the following guarantees from convertably linkable group signatures, where *(join) anonymity* and *non-transitivity* capture the privacy-related properties and *non-frameability* and *traceability* formalize the desired unforgeability.

(Join) Anonymity: Pseudonymous signatures should be unlinkable and untraceable (to a join session) even when the issuer and verifier are corrupt. When the converter is honest, unlinkability holds for all signatures for which the associated pseudonyms have not been explicitly linked through a conversion request. If the converter is corrupt and also controlled by the adversary, unlinkability is no longer possible, yet the anonymity of joins must remain.

Non-transitivity: Converted pseudonyms should be non-transitive, i.e., the verifier should not be able to link the outputs of different convert queries. Otherwise, a corrupt verifier would be able to gradually link together all pseudonyms that have ever been queried to the converter.

Conversion Blindness: The converter learns nothing about the pseudonyms (and messages) it receives and the transformed pseudonyms it computes.

Non-frameability: An adversary controlling the issuer and some corrupt users, should not be able to impersonate other honest users, i.e., create pseudonymous signatures that would be linked to a pseudonym of an honest user.

Traceability: An adversary should not be able to create more signatures that remain unlinkable in a conversion than he controls corrupt users.

Clearly, any re-linked subset of the originally anonymous data increases the risk of re-identification. Thus, the converter could enforce some form of access control to the re-linked data, e.g., only converting a certain amount of pseudonyms at once. The non-transitivity requirement then ensures that a corrupt verifier cannot further aggregate the individually learned data. We stress that our security properties only formalize the achievable privacy for the pseudonyms and signatures. They do not *and cannot* capture information leakage through the messages that the users sign. This is the case for all group signatures though, and not special to our setting.

Oracles & State. The security notions we formalize in the following make use a number of oracles which keep joint state, e.g., keeping track of queries and the set of corrupted parties. We present the detailed description of all oracles in Fig. 1 and an overview of them and their maintained records below.

ADDU (join of honest user & honest issuer) Creates a new honest user for *uid* and internally runs a join protocol between the honest user and honest issuer. At the end, the honest user's secret key **gsk**[*uid*] is generated and from then on signing queries for *uid* will be allowed.

SNDU (join of honest user & corrupt issuer) Creates a new honest user for *uid* and runs the join protocol on behalf of *uid* with the corrupt issuer. If the join session completes, the oracle will store the user's secret key **gsk**[*uid*].

SNDI (join of corrupt user & honest issuer) Runs the join protocol on behalf of the honest issuer with corrupt users. For joins of honest users, the ADDU oracle must be used.

SIGN This oracle returns signatures for honest users that have successfully joined (via ADDU or SNDU, depending on the game).

CONVERT The oracle returns a set of converted pseudonyms along with their messages. To model that conversion is triggered by an at most honest-but-curious verifier, we request $\mathcal{V}$ to provide the unblinded set of pseudonyms along with signatures. The conversion will only be done when all signatures are valid. The oracle then internally blinds the pseudonym-message pairs and returns the blinded input, the randomness used for the blinding along with the converted output. When this oracle is used in the anonymity game, it further checks that the input does not allow the adversary to trivially win by converting the challenge pseudonym together with pseudonyms from either of the challenge users.

All oracles have access to the following records maintained as global state:

HUL List of *uid*'s of honest users, initially set to $\varnothing$. New honest users can be added by queries to the ADDU oracle (when the issuer is honest) or SNDU oracle (when the issuer is corrupt).

CUL List of corrupt users that have (requested) to join the group. Initially set to $\varnothing$, new corrupt users can be added through the SNDI oracle if the issuer is honest. If the issuer is corrupt, we do not keep track of corrupt users.

SL List of (uid, m, nym, σ) tuples requested from the SIGN oracle.

Helper Algorithms. We introduce two additional algorithms for notational simplicity in our security games: Identify and UnLink. Roughly, Identify allows to

---

ADDU(uid)

---

if $uid \in$ HUL $\cup$ CUL   return $\perp$

HUL $\leftarrow$ HUL $\cup$ $\{uid\}$, $\mathbf{gsk}[uid] \leftarrow \perp$

$\mathbf{dec}^{uid} \leftarrow$ cont, $\mathrm{st}_{\mathsf{Join}}^{uid} \leftarrow gpk$

$\mathrm{st}_{\mathsf{Issue}}^{uid} \leftarrow (isk, gpk)$

$(\mathrm{st}_{\mathsf{Join}}^{uid}, M_{\mathsf{Issue}}, \mathbf{dec}^{uid}) \leftarrow$ Join($\mathrm{st}_{\mathsf{Join}}^{uid}, \perp$)

while $\mathbf{dec}^{uid}$ = cont

  $(\mathrm{st}_{\mathsf{Issue}}^{uid}, M_{\mathsf{Join}}, \mathbf{dec}^{uid}) \leftarrow$ Issue($\mathrm{st}_{\mathsf{Issue}}^{uid}, M_{\mathsf{Issue}}$)

  $(\mathrm{st}_{\mathsf{Join}}^{uid}, M_{\mathsf{Issue}}, \mathbf{dec}^{uid}) \leftarrow$ Join($\mathrm{st}_{\mathsf{Join}}^{uid}, M_{\mathsf{Join}}$)

if $\mathbf{dec}^{uid}$ = accept $\mathbf{gsk}[uid] \leftarrow \mathrm{st}_{\mathsf{Join}}^{uid}$

return accept

SIGN(uid, m)

---

if $uid \notin$ HUL or $\mathbf{gsk}[uid] = \perp$

  return $\perp$

$(nym, \sigma) \leftarrow$ Sign($gpk, \mathbf{gsk}[uid], m$)

SL $\leftarrow$ SL $\cup$ $\{(uid, m, nym, \sigma)\}$

return (σ, nym)

SNDI(uid, M_{in})

---

if $uid \in$ HUL   return $\perp$

if $uid \notin$ CUL

  CUL $\leftarrow$ CUL $\cup$ $\{uid\}$

  $dec^{uid} \leftarrow$ cont

if $dec^{uid} \neq$ cont   **return** $\perp$

if undefined $\mathrm{st}_{\mathsf{Issue}}^{uid} \leftarrow (isk, gpk)$

$(\mathrm{st}_{\mathsf{Issue}}^{uid}, M_{\mathsf{out}}, \mathbf{dec}^{uid}) \leftarrow$ Issue($\mathrm{st}_{\mathsf{Issue}}^{uid}, M_{\mathsf{in}}$)

return $(M_{\mathsf{out}}, \mathbf{dec}^{uid})$

SNDU(uid, M_{in})

---

if $uid \in$ CUL   return $\perp$

if $uid \notin$ HUL

  HUL $\leftarrow$ HUL $\cup$ $\{uid\}$

  $\mathbf{gsk}[uid] \leftarrow \perp$, $M_{\mathsf{in}} \leftarrow \perp$, $\mathbf{dec}^{uid} \leftarrow$ cont

if $\mathbf{dec}^{uid} \neq$ cont   **return** $\perp$

if $\mathrm{st}_{\mathsf{Join}}^{uid}$ undefined $\mathrm{st}_{\mathsf{Join}}^{uid} \leftarrow gpk$

$(\mathrm{st}_{\mathsf{Join}}^{uid}, M_{\mathsf{Out}}, \mathbf{dec}^{uid}) \leftarrow$ Join($\mathrm{st}_{\mathsf{Join}}^{uid}, M_{\mathsf{in}}$)

if $\mathbf{dec}^{uid}$ = accept $\mathbf{gsk}[uid] \leftarrow \mathrm{st}_{\mathsf{Join}}^{uid}$

return $(M_{\mathsf{Out}}, \mathbf{dec}^{uid})$

CONVERT($(nym_1, m_1, \sigma_1), \ldots, (nym_k, m_k, \sigma_k), bpk$)

---

if $\exists i \in [1, k]$ s.t. Verify($gpk, m_i, nym_i, \sigma_i$) = 0   **return** $\perp$

if $bpk \notin \mathcal{BPK}$ **return** $\perp$

if $\exists i$ s.t. $nym_i = nym^*$ and $\exists j \neq i$ s.t. Identify(uid_d^*, nym_j) = 1 for $d \in \{0, 1\}$

  return $\perp$

else compute $(cnym_i, c_i) \leftarrow$ Blind($gpk, bpk, (nym_i, m_i); r_i$) for $i = 1, \ldots, k$

  and $\{(\overline{cnym}_i, \overline{c}_i)\}_k \leftarrow$ Convert($gpk, csk, bpk, \{(cnym_i, c_i)\}_k$)

return $(\{(cnym_i, c_i)\}_k, \{(\overline{cnym}_i, \overline{c}_i)\}_k, r_1, \ldots, r_k)$

Fig. 1. Oracles used in our security games

test whether a pseudonym belongs to a certain *uid* by exploiting the converta-
bility of pseudonyms. That is, we create a second signature for **gsk**[*uid*] and use
the converter's secret key to test whether both are linked. If so, Identify returns
1. This algorithm already uses our second helper algorithm UnLink internally,
which takes a list of (correctly formed) pseudonym-message pairs and returns 1
if they are all unlinkable and 0 otherwise.

Identify(gpk, csk, uid, m, nym)

$(nym', \sigma') \leftarrow$ Sign($gpk,$ **gsk**[*uid*], 0)
if UnLink($gpk, csk, ((nym, m), (nym', 0))) = 0$ **return** 1
else return 0

UnLink($gpk, csk, ((nym_1, m_1), ..., (nym_k, m_k))$)

$(bpk, bsk) \leftarrow$ BKGen(param)
$\forall i \in [1, k]$ $(cnym_i, c_i) \leftarrow$ Blind($gpk, bpk, (nym_i, m_i)$)
$\{(\overline{cnym}_i, \overline{c}_i)\}_k \leftarrow$ Convert($gpk, csk, bpk, \{(cnym_i, c_i)\}_k$)
$\forall i \in [1, k]$ $(\overline{nym}_i, \overline{m}_i) \leftarrow$ Unblind($bsk, (\overline{cnym}_i, \overline{c}_i)$)
if $\exists(i, j)$ with $i \neq j$ s.t. $\overline{nym}_i = \overline{nym}_j$ **return** 0
else return 1

For even more simplicity we often omit the keys for the algorithms (as they
are clear from the context). That is, we write Identify(uid, nym) which will indicate whether the pseudonym nym belongs to the user with identity uid or not.
Likewise we write UnLink($nym_1, \ldots, nym_k$) to test whether all pseudonyms are
uncorrelated or not.

Correctness. CLS signatures should be correct and consistent when being
produced by honest parties. More precisely, we formulate correctness via three
requirements: *Correctness of sign* guarantees that signatures formed using the
Sign algorithm with a user secret key generated honestly will verify correctly.
Correctness of conversion guarantees that after blinding, converting and then
unblinding correctly, the output will be correctly linked messages/pseudonyms.
Consistency is a stronger variant of conversion-correctness and requires that the
correlations of pseudonyms established through the conversion procedure must
be consistent across queries. More precisely, if a conversion query reveals that
two pseudonym nym_1 and nym_2 are linked, and another one that nym_2 and
nym_3 are linked, then it must also hold that a conversion query for nym_1 and
nym_3 returns linked pseudonyms. We require that this property even holds for
maliciously formed pseudonyms, which will be a helpful property in some of
our security proofs. For space reasons, the detailed correctness definitions are
deferred to the full paper [27].

Anonymity *(Corrupt Issuer & Verifier).* This security requirement captures the desired anonymity properties when both the issuer and verifier are
corrupt. Just as in conventional group signatures, we want that the signatures

of honest users are unlinkable and cannot be traced back to a user's join session with the corrupt issuer. To model this property, we let the adversary output uid's of two honest users together with a message and return a challenge (nym^*, σ^*) that is created either by user uid_0 or uid_1. For anonymity, the adversary should not be able to determine the user's identity better than by guessing.

In our setting, this property must hold when the corrupt verifier has access to the conversion oracle where it can obtain linked subsets of the pseudonymous data. To avoid trivial wins, the adversary is not allowed to make conversion queries that link the challenge pseudonym nym^* to another pseudonym belonging to one of the two honest challenge users.

Definition 2 (Anonymity). *A CLS scheme satisfies anonymity if for all polynomial time adversaries $\mathcal{A}$ the following advantage is negligible in τ:*

$$\left| \Pr[\mathbf{Exp}_{\mathcal{A},CLS}^{anon-0}(\tau) = 1] - \Pr[\mathbf{Exp}_{\mathcal{A},CLS}^{anon-1}(\tau) = 1] \right|.$$

Experiment: $\mathbf{Exp}_{\mathcal{A},CLS}^{anon-b}(\tau)$

param $\leftarrow$ Setup(1^τ), $(ipk, isk) \leftarrow$ IKGen(param), $(cpk, csk) \leftarrow$ CKGen(param)

$gpk \leftarrow$ (param, ipk, cpk), HUL, CUL, SL $\leftarrow \varnothing$

$(uid_0^*, uid_1^*, m^*, st) \leftarrow \mathcal{A}^{\text{SNDU,SIGN,CONVERT}}$(choose, gpk, isk)

if $uid_0^* \notin$ HUL or $\mathbf{gsk}[uid_0^*] = \perp$ or $uid_1^* \notin$ HUL or $\mathbf{gsk}[uid_1^*] = \perp$ **return** 0

$(nym^*, \sigma^*) \leftarrow$ Sign($gpk, \mathbf{gsk}[uid_b^*], m^*$)

$b^* \leftarrow \mathcal{A}^{\text{SNDU,SIGN,CONVERT}}$(guess, st, nym^*, σ^*)

return b^*

Non-transitivity *(Corrupt Issuer & Verifier)*. The second privacy-related property we want to guarantee when both the issuer and verifier are corrupt, is the strict non-transitivity of conversions. This ensures that the outputs of separate convert queries cannot be linked together, further than what is already possible due the messages queried. For example if $\overline{nym}_1$ and $\overline{nym}_2$ are outputs by two separate convert queries, the adversary should not be able to decide whether they were derived from the same pseudonym or not. Otherwise the verifier could gradually build lists of linked pseudonyms, adding to these during every convert query and eventually recover the linkability among all pseudonymous signatures.

To model non-transitivity of conversions we use a simulation-based approach, requiring the indistinguishability of an ideal and a real world. In the real world, all convert queries are handled normally through the CONVERT oracle defined in Fig. 1. Whereas in the ideal world, the converted pseudonyms are produced by a simulator SIM through the CONVSIM oracle defined below. For a conversion request of input $(nym_1, m_1, \sigma_1), \ldots, (nym_k, m_k, \sigma_k)$ the simulator will only learn which of the messages belong together, i.e., are associated to pseudonyms that belong to the same user uid. For *honest* users this can be looked up through the records of the signing oracle that stores tuples $(uid, m_i, nym_i, \sigma_i)$ for each signing query. Thus, we let the simulator mimic the conversion output for all pseudonyms stemming form honest users, and convert pseudonyms from corrupt users normally (as there is no privacy to guarantee for them anyway). Finally, the

CONVSIM oracle outputs a random shuffle of the correctly converted pseudonyms of corrupt users, and the simulated ones for honest users. As mentioned before, we assume the verifier to be honest-but-curious, which we enforce by requesting the adversary to output valid signatures along with the pseudonyms to be converted and handle the blinding step within the conversion oracle.

Definition 3 (Non-transitivity). *A CLS scheme satisfies non-transitivity if for all polynomial time adversaries $\mathcal{A}$ there exists an efficient simulator SIM such that the following advantage is negligible in τ:*

$$\left| \Pr[\mathbf{Exp}_{\mathcal{A},CLS}^{nontrans-0}(\tau) = 1] - \Pr[\mathbf{Exp}_{\mathcal{A},CLS}^{nontrans-1}(\tau) = 1] \right|.$$

Experiment: $\mathbf{Exp}_{\mathcal{A},CLS}^{nontrans-b}(\tau)$

param $\leftarrow$ Setup(1^τ), $(ipk, isk) \leftarrow$ IKGen(param), $(cpk, csk) \leftarrow$ CKGen(param)

$gpk \leftarrow$ (param, ipk, cpk), HUL, CUL, SL $\leftarrow \varnothing$

$b^* \leftarrow \mathcal{A}^{\text{SNDU,SIGN,CONVX}}$(guess, gpk, isk)

 where the oracle CONVX works as follows:

  if $b = 0$ (real world) **then** CONVX is the standard CONVERT oracle

  if $b = 1$ (ideal world) **then** CONVX is the simulated CONVSIM oracle

 return b^*

CONVSIM$((nym_1, m_1, \sigma_1), \ldots, (nym_k, m_k, \sigma_k), bpk)$

---

if $\exists i \in [1, k]$ s.t. Verify($gpk, m_i, nym_i, \sigma_i$) = 0 or $bpk \notin \mathcal{BPK}$ **return** $\perp$

Set CL $\leftarrow \varnothing$

Compute $(cnym_i, c_i) \leftarrow$ Blind($gpk, bpk, (nym_i, m_i); r_i$) for $i = 1, \ldots, k$

$\forall i \in [1, k]$ // determine message clusters L_{uid} for honest users and list CL of corrupt pseudonyms

 if $(uid, m_i, nym_i, \sigma_i) \in$ SL // pseudonyms from honest users

  if L_{uid} does not exist, create $\mathsf{L}_{uid} \leftarrow \{m_i\}$ **else** set $\mathsf{L}_{uid} \leftarrow \mathsf{L}_{uid} \cup \{m_i\}$

 else CL $\leftarrow$ CL $\cup \{(c_i, cnym_i)\}$ // pseudonyms from corrupt users

$\{(\overline{cnym}_i, \overline{c}_i)\}_{i=1,\ldots,k'} \leftarrow$ Convert(gpk, csk, bpk, CL) for $k' \leftarrow |$CL$|$ // normally convert corrupt nyms

Let $\mathsf{L}_{uid_1}, \ldots \mathsf{L}_{uid_{k''}}$ be the non-empty message clusters created above

$\{(\overline{cnym}_i, \overline{c}_i)\}_{i=k'+1,\ldots k} \leftarrow$ SIM($gpk, bpk, \mathsf{L}_{uid_1}, \ldots \mathsf{L}_{uid_{k''}}$) // simulate conversion for honest nyms

Let $\{(\overline{cnym}'_i, \overline{c}'_i)\}_{i=1,\ldots k}$ be a random permutation of $\{(\overline{cnym}_i, \overline{c}_i)\}_{i=1,\ldots k}$

return $(\{(cnym_i, c_i, r_i)\}_{i=1,\ldots,k}, \{(\overline{cnym}'_i, \overline{c}'_i)\}_{i=1,\ldots k}, r_1, \ldots, r_k)$

Anonymity vs. Non-transitivity. Note that non-transitivity is not covered by the anonymity notion defined before: A scheme that satisfies anonymity could output the converted pseudonyms in the exact same order as the input ones, allowing trivial linkage between the in- and output of each conversion request. Thus, whenever the same pseudonym is used as input to several conversion queries, this would enable the linkability of the transformed pseudonyms across the different conversions, which is exactly what non-transitivity aims to avoid. On the first glance, it might seem odd that having transitive conversions does not harm our anonymity property. However, transitivity is only useful when *several* pseudonyms belonging to the same user appear in each conversion request with one pseudonym being re-used in all these sessions. In the anonymity game, the challenge pseudonym is not allowed to be used in combination with any other pseudonym stemming from either of the challenge users (as this would make the definition unachievable), and thus the transitivity of conversions can not be exploited.

Conversion Blindness *(Corrupt Issuer & Converter).* A crucial property of our signatures is that they can be converted in an oblivious manner, i.e., without the converter learning anything about the pseudonyms or messages it converts. In particular, this blindness property ensures the unlinkability of blinded inputs across several conversion requests. Conversion blindness should hold if both the issuer and converter are corrupt, but the verifier is honest. We formalize this property in a classic indistinguishability style: the adversary outputs two tuples of pseudonym-message pairs and receives a blinded version of either of them. Given that blinding of pseudonyms is a public-key operation we don't need an additional blinding oracle. In fact, we don't give the adversary *any* oracle access at all in this game. He already corrupts the issuer and converter, and this property does not distinguish between honest and corrupt users, thus we simply assume that the adversary has full control over all users as well.

Definition 4 (Conversion Blindness). *A CLS scheme satisfies conversion blindness if: for all polynomial time adversaries $\mathcal{A}$ the following advantage is negligible in τ:*

$$\left| \Pr[\mathbf{Exp}_{\mathcal{A},CLS}^{blind-conv-0}(\tau) = 1] - \Pr[\mathbf{Exp}_{\mathcal{A},CLS}^{blind-conv-1}(\tau) = 1] \right|.$$

Experiment: $\mathbf{Exp}_{\mathcal{A},CLS}^{blind-conv-b}(\tau)$

$param \leftarrow \mathsf{Setup}(1^\tau), (ipk, isk) \leftarrow \mathsf{IKGen}(param), (cpk, csk) \leftarrow \mathsf{CKGen}(param)$

$gpk \leftarrow (param, ipk, cpk), (bpk, bsk) \leftarrow \mathsf{BKGen}(param)$

$(st, (nym_0, m_0), (nym_1, m_1)) \leftarrow \mathcal{A}(\mathsf{choose}, gpk, isk, csk, bpk)$

$(cnym^*, c^*) \leftarrow \mathsf{Blind}(gpk, bpk, (nym_b, m_b))$

$b^* \leftarrow \mathcal{A}(\mathsf{guess}, st, cnym^*, c^*)$

return b^*

Join Anonymity *(Corrupt Issuer & Converter & Verifier).* The final privacy related property we require from a CLS is the anonymity of joins even if *all* central entities are corrupt. Here the challenge is that the adversary, controlling the issuer, converter and verifier, should not be able to link signatures of an honest user back to a particular join session. This is the best one can hope for in this corruption setting as unlinkability of signatures (as guaranteed by our anonymity property) is no longer possible: the corrupt converter can simply convert all signatures/pseudonyms into a consistent representation. Such a property does not exist in conventional group signatures, as therein a corrupt opener can always reveals the join identity. In our setting, signatures can only be linked instead of being opened and thus anonymity of the join procedure can and should be preserved.

To model this property we let the adversary output two identities of honest users uid_0, uid_1 that have successfully joined. We then give the adversary access to a signing oracle for one them. This is done by adding the challenge user uid^* (where uid^* stands for a dummy handle) to the list of honest users HUL with user secret key $\mathbf{gsk}[uid_b]$. Thus, in the second stage of the game, the adversary can invoke the SIGN oracle on uid^* to receive signatures of messages of his choice for the challenge user. The adversary wins if he can determine the bit b better than by guessing. To avoid trivial wins, the adversary is not allowed to see any signature directly from uid_0 or uid_1.

Definition 5 (Join Anonymity). *A CLS scheme satisfies join anonymity if: for all polynomial time adversaries $\mathcal{A}$ the following advantage is negligible in τ:*

$$\left| \Pr[\mathsf{Exp}_{\mathcal{A},CLS}^{anon-join-0}(\tau) = 1] - \Pr[\mathsf{Exp}_{\mathcal{A},CLS}^{anon-join-1}(\tau) = 1] \right|.$$

Experiment: $\mathsf{Exp}_{\mathcal{A},CLS}^{anon-join-b}(\tau)$

$param \leftarrow \mathsf{Setup}(1^\tau), (ipk, isk) \leftarrow \mathsf{IKGen}(param), (cpk, csk) \leftarrow \mathsf{CKGen}(param)$

$gpk \leftarrow (param, ipk, cpk), \mathsf{HUL}, \mathsf{CUL}, \mathsf{SL} \leftarrow \varnothing$

$(st, uid_0, uid_1) \leftarrow \mathcal{A}^{\mathsf{SNDU,SIGN}}(\mathsf{choose}, gpk, isk, csk)$

if uid_0 or $uid_1 \notin \mathsf{HUL}$ or $\mathbf{gsk}[uid_0] = \perp$ or $\mathbf{gsk}[uid_1] = \perp$ return $\perp$

Choose $uid^*, \mathsf{HUL} \leftarrow \mathsf{HUL} \cup \{uid^*\}, \mathbf{gsk}[uid^*] \leftarrow \mathbf{gsk}[uid_b]$

$b^* \leftarrow \mathcal{A}^{\mathsf{SNDU,SIGN}}(\mathsf{guess}, st, uid^*)$

return b^* if $(uid_d, *) \notin \mathsf{SL}$ for $d = 0, 1$ else return 0

Non-frameability *(Corrupt Issuer & Converter & User).* This notion captures the desired unforgeability properties when the issuer, converter and some of the users are corrupt, and requires that an adversary should not be able to impersonate an honest user. Our definition is very similar to the non-frameability definitions in standard group signature or DAA schemes [4–6]. Roughly, the only part we have to change is how we detect that an honest user has been framed. In group signatures, non-frameability exploits the presence of the group manager that can open signatures and requests that an adversary cannot produce signatures that will open to an honest user who hasn't created said signature. Here we have the converter instead of the group manager (or dedicated opening authority), and thus express non-frameability through the linkage that is created in a conversion. More precisely, an adversary should not be able to produce a valid signature (nym^*, σ^*) that within a conversion request would falsely link to a signature of an honest user. For generality (and sake of brevity), we use our helper function Identify that we introduced at the beginning of this section to express that the adversary's signature should not be recognized as a signature of an honest user.

Definition 6 (Non-frameability). *A CLS scheme satisfies non-frameability if for all polynomial time adversaries $\mathcal{A}$, the advantage $\Pr[\mathsf{Exp}_{\mathcal{A},CLS}^{nonframe}(\tau) = 1]$ is negligible in τ.*

Experiment: $\mathbf{Exp}_{\mathcal{A},\mathsf{CLS}}^{nonframe}(\tau)$

---

param $\leftarrow$ Setup(1^τ), $(ipk, isk) \leftarrow$ IKGen(param), $(cpk, csk) \leftarrow$ CKGen(param)

$gpk \leftarrow (\text{param}, ipk, cpk)$, HUL, CUL, SL $\leftarrow \varnothing$

$(uid, m^*, nym^*, \sigma^*) \leftarrow \mathcal{A}^{\mathsf{SNDU,SIGN}}(gpk, isk, csk)$

return 1 **if** all of the following conditions are satisfied:

Verify$(gpk, m^*, nym^*, \sigma^*) = 1$ and

Identify$(uid, m^*, nym^*) = 1$ where $uid \in$ HUL and

$(uid, m^*, nym^*, \sigma^*) \notin$ SL

Traceability _(Corrupt Converter & User)_. Our final requirement formalizes the unforgeability properties when only the converter and some users are corrupt. In this setting, an adversary should not be able to output more pseudonymous signatures that remain unlinkable in a conversion than the number of users it has corrupted. This is again an adaptation of the existing traceability notions for group signatures with an opening authority [4,5] or user-controlled linkability [6]. Interestingly, in the latter work (that is closer to our setting than standard group signatures), two traceability notions where introduced: While one is similar in spirit to our notion, a second property guarantees that all signatures of corrupt users can be traced back to the exact signing key that the corrupt user has established in the join protocol with the honest issuer. This seems a bit of an odd requirement, as it is not noticeable in the real world. In fact, we do not limit the strategy of the adversary in that way and only require his power to be bounded by the amount of corrupt users he controls.

Our definition stated below uses our helper algorithm UnLink that we introduced at the beginning of this section and that internally uses the Convert algorithm to detect whether pseudonyms are unlinkable or not. Note that UnLink returns 1 only if _all_ inputs are mutually unlinkable, i.e., there is not a single tuple of input pseudonyms that got converted to the same value.

Definition 7 (Traceability). _A CLS scheme satisfies traceability if for all poly-time adversaries_ $\mathcal{A}$ _the advantage_ $\Pr[\mathbf{Exp}_{\mathcal{A},\mathsf{CLS}}^{trace}(\tau) = 1]$ _is negligible in_ τ.

Experiment: $\mathbf{Exp}_{\mathcal{A},\mathsf{CLS}}^{trace}(\tau)$

---

param $\leftarrow$ Setup(1^τ), $(ipk, isk) \leftarrow$ IKGen(param), $(cpk, csk) \leftarrow$ CKGen(param)

$gpk \leftarrow (\text{param}, ipk, cpk)$, HUL, CUL, SL $\leftarrow \varnothing$

$((m_1, nym_1, \sigma_1), ..., (m_k, nym_k, \sigma_k)) \leftarrow \mathcal{A}^{\mathsf{ADDU,SNDI,SIGN}}(gpk, csk)$

return 1 **if** all of the following conditions are satisfied:

$\forall j \in [1, k] :$ Verify$(gpk, m_j, nym_j, \sigma_j) = 1$ and $(*, m_j, nym_j, \sigma_j) \notin$ SL and

$k > |\mathsf{CUL}|$ and

UnLink$(gpk, csk, ((nym_1, m_1), ..., (nym_k, m_k))) = 1$

4   Our CLS Construction

We now present our construction that securely realizes such CLS group signatures. Our scheme follows the classical sign-and-encrypt paradigm: we use BBS+ signatures [3] for attesting group membership, i.e., a user will blindly receive a BBS+ signature from the group issuer on the user's secret key y. To sign a message m on behalf of the group, the user computes a SPK for m where he proves knowledge of a BBS+ signature on y and also encrypts h^y under the converter's public key. The ElGamal ciphertext that encrypts h^y serves as the associated pseudonym nym.

To blind a set of k pseudonym-message pairs $(nym_1, m_1), \ldots (nym_k, m_k)$ for conversion, the verifier encrypts each value under its own ElGamal public key. As the pseudonyms are already ElGamal ciphertexts themselves, this results in a nested double-encryption of h^y being encrypted under both keys. The converter then decrypts the "inner" part of the ciphertext and blindly raises the result to a random value r. This r is chosen fresh for every conversion query, but used consistently within. That is, all pseudonyms belonging to the same user will be mapped to the same query-specific DDH tuple h^{yr}. Finally, the converter re-randomises all ciphertexts and shuffles them to destroy any linkage between the in- and output tuples—this is crucial for achieving the desired non-transitivity property. The verifier then simply decrypts the received tuples and can link correlated data via the converted pseudonyms $\overline{cnym}_i$.

4.1   Detailed Description of CLS–DDH

Setup & Key Generation. We use a bilinear group $(p, \mathbb{G}_1, \mathbb{G}_2, \mathbb{G}_T, e, g_1, g_2)$ with g_1 and g_2 being generators of $\mathbb{G}_1$ and $\mathbb{G}_2$ respectively. Further, we need four additional generators g, h and h_1, h_2 in $\mathbb{G}_1$, where h_1, h_2 are used for the BBS+ part, and g, h will be used for the ElGamal encryption.

$\mathsf{Setup}(1^\tau)$

$(p, \mathbb{G}_1, \mathbb{G}_2, \mathbb{G}_T, e, g_1, g_2) \leftarrow \mathcal{G}(1^\tau), g, h, h_1, h_2 \leftarrow_\$ \mathbb{G}_1$

return param $\leftarrow (\mathbb{G}_1, \mathbb{G}_2, \mathbb{G}_T, p, e, g_1, g_2, g, h, h_1, h_2)$

$\mathsf{IKGen}(\text{param})$	$\mathsf{CKGen}(\text{param})$	$\mathsf{BKGen}(\text{param})$
$isk \leftarrow_\$ \mathbb{Z}_p^*, ipk \leftarrow g_2^{isk}$	$csk \leftarrow_\$ \mathbb{Z}_p^*, cpk \leftarrow g^{csk}$	$bsk \leftarrow_\$ \mathbb{Z}_p^*, bpk \leftarrow g^{bsk}$
return (ipk, isk)	**return** (cpk, csk)	**return** (bpk, bsk)

Join. To join the group, users perform an interactive protocol with the issuer to obtain their user secret key and group credential. Roughly, the **gsk**[uid] of a user consists of a secret key $y \in \mathbb{Z}_p^*$ and a BBS+ signature (A, x, s) of $\mathcal{I}$ on y, where $A = (g_1 h_1^y h_2^s)^{1/(isk+x)}$. The detailed protocol of $\langle \mathsf{Join}(gpk), \mathsf{Issue}(isk, gpk) \rangle$ is given in Fig. 2.

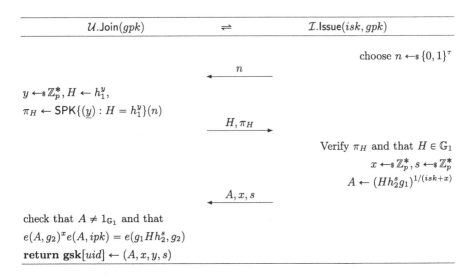

Fig. 2. Join protocol of our CLS–DDH construction.

Sign & Verify. To sign a message m under $\mathbf{gsk}[uid] = (A, x, y, s)$, the user proves knowledge of a BBS+ credential (A, x, s) on its secret key y and also encrypts h^y under the converter's public key cpk. The proof π then proves knowledge of the BBS+ credential and asserts that the encryption contains the same value y. From π we only need the value y to be online extractable. We use the improved SPK from Camenisch et al. [14] who have shown how to move most of the work from $\mathbb{G}_T$ to $\mathbb{G}_1$ and thus yield a much faster instantiation than the original proof by Au et al. [3]. For verification, one verifies the proof π and some correctness properties of the re-randomised versions of A that are sent along with the proof. In more detail, Sign and Verify are defined as follows:

Sign($gpk, \mathbf{gsk}[uid], m$)

---

parse $\mathbf{gsk}[uid] = (A, x, y, s)$, $gpk = (ipk, cpk)$

$\alpha \leftarrow_\$ \mathbb{Z}_p^*$, $nym_1 \leftarrow g^\alpha$, $nym_2 \leftarrow cpk^\alpha h^y$, $r_1, r_2, r_3 \leftarrow_\$ \mathbb{Z}_p^*$,

$A' \leftarrow A^{r_1}, \hat{A} \leftarrow A'^{-x}(g_1 h_1^y h_2^s)^{r_1}, d \leftarrow (g_1 h_1^y h_2^s)^{r_1} h_2^{-r_2}, r_3 \leftarrow r_1^{-1}, s' \leftarrow s - r_2 r_3$

$\pi \leftarrow \mathsf{SPK}\{(x, y, r_2, r_3, s', \alpha) : nym_1 = g^\alpha \wedge nym_2 = cpk^\alpha h^y$

$\qquad \wedge \hat{A}/d = A'^{-x} h_2^{r_2} \wedge g_1 h_1^y = d^{r_3} h_2^{-s'}\}(m)$

$\sigma \leftarrow (A', \hat{A}, d, \pi), nym \leftarrow (nym_1, nym_2)$

return (nym, σ)

Verify(gpk, m, nym, σ)

---

parse $\sigma = (A', \hat{A}, d, \pi)$

return 1 if $A' \neq 1_{\mathbb{G}_1}, e(A', ipk) = e(\hat{A}, g_2)$,

and π holds for $A', \hat{A}, d, nym, m$ w.r.t. gpk

Blind Conversions. When the verifier wants to learn which of the pseudonymously received messages belong together, it sends a batch of pseudonym-message pairs in blinded form to the converter. That is, it encrypts the messages and pseudonyms using ElGamal encryption. The pseudonyms are ElGamal ciphertexts itself and we roughly wrap them in another encryption layer. The converter then blindly decrypts the pseudonyms, i.e., decrypts the "inner" part of the ciphertext, which yields h^y encrypted under the verifiers blinding key bpk. To ensure non-transitivity, i.e., restrict the linkage of pseudonyms to hold only within the queried batch, the converter blindly raises the encrypted h^y to a random exponent r. This value is chosen afresh for every batch but used consistently within the query, i.e., all pseudonyms that belong to the same user with secret key y will be mapped consistently to h^{yr}. To ensure that the ciphertexts and their order cannot leak any additional information, we let the converter re-randomize and shuffle all ciphertexts before he returns them to the verifier. Both the verifier and the converter are assumed to be at most honest-but-curious, and so proofs that they have performed Blind and Convert correctly are not needed.

Blind(gpk, bpk, nym, m)

---

parse $gpk = (ipk, cpk)$, $nym = (nym_1, nym_2)$

$\alpha, \beta, \gamma \leftarrow_\$ \mathbb{Z}_p^*$

$cnym_1 \leftarrow nym_1 g^\beta$, $cnym_2 \leftarrow g^\alpha$, $cnym_3 \leftarrow nym_2 cpk^\beta bpk^\alpha$

$c_1 \leftarrow g^\gamma, c_2 \leftarrow bpk^\gamma m$

$cnym \leftarrow (cnym_1, cnym_2, cnym_3)$, $c \leftarrow (c_1, c_2)$

return $(cnym, c)$

Convert$(gpk, csk, bpk, ((cnym_1, c_1), ..., (cnym_k, c_k)))$

---

parse $cnym_i = (cnym_{i,1}, cnym_{i,2}, cnym_{i,3})$, $c_i \leftarrow (c_{i,1}, c_{i,2})$, $r \leftarrow_\$ \mathbb{Z}_p^*$

for $i = 1, \ldots k$:

$\quad cnym'_{i,1} \leftarrow cnym^r_{i,2}$, $cnym'_{i,2} \leftarrow (cnym_{i,3} cnym_{i,1}^{-csk})^r$ // decrypt nym and raise to r

$\quad r_1, r_2 \leftarrow_\$ \mathbb{Z}_p^*$ // re-randomize all ciphertexts

$\quad cnym''_{i,1} \leftarrow cnym'_{i,1} g^{r_1}$, $cnym''_{i,2} \leftarrow cnym'_{i,2} bpk^{r_1}$

$\quad c'_{i,1} \leftarrow c_{i,1} g^{r_2}$, $c'_{i,2} \leftarrow c_{i,2} bpk^{r_2}$

choose random permutation Π, **for** $i = 1, \ldots, k$: $(\overline{cnym}_i, \overline{c}_i) \leftarrow (cnym''_{\Pi(i)}, c'_{\Pi(i)})$

return $((\overline{cnym}_1, \overline{c}_1), ..., (\overline{cnym}_k, \overline{c}_k))$

Unblind$(bsk, (\overline{cnym}, \overline{c}))$

---

parse $\overline{cnym} = (\overline{cnym}_1, \overline{cnym}_2)$, $\overline{c} \leftarrow (\overline{c}_1, \overline{c}_2)$

$\overline{nym} \leftarrow \overline{cnym}_2 \overline{cnym}_1^{-bsk}$, $m \leftarrow \overline{c}_2 \overline{c}_1^{-bsk}$

return $(\overline{nym}, m)$

4.2   Security of CLS–DDH

We now show that our scheme satisfies all security properties defined in Sect. 3. More precisely, we show that the following theorem holds (using the type-3 pairing version of the q-SDH assumption given in [8]).

Theorem 1. *The CLS–DDH construction presented in Sect. 4.1 is a secure CLS as defined in Sect. 3 if the DDH assumption holds in $\mathbb{G}_1$, the q-SDH assumption holds, and the SPK is simulation-sound, zero-knowledge and online extractable (for the underlined values).*

In the following we focus on the proof of non-transitivity which was the most challenging property to define and prove. For the other properties we provide short proof sketches and refer for the detailed proofs to the full paper [27].

Lemma 1. *The CLS–DDH construction presented in Sect. 4.1 satisfies **anonymity** if the DDH assumption holds in $\mathbb{G}_1$, and the SPK is unbounded simulation-sound, zero knowledge and online extractable (for the underlined values).*

Proof (sketch). Roughly, anonymity follows from the unlinkability property of BBS+ signatures, the CPA-security from ElGamal (used to compute the pseudo-nyms under cpk), and the DDH assumption (for showing that the conversion doesn't leak any information). Recall that in this setting, the converter is honest, i.e., $\mathcal{A}$ does not know csk but is given access to the CONVERT oracle. Thus, the surprising part might be that CPA encryption is sufficient, despite the converter having to decrypt the blinded pseudonyms. However, in the security proof we can simulate decryption queries by computing the converted pseudonyms from scratch and returning fresh encryptions of them (under bpk) to the adversary. That is, here we use that the convert algorithm returns *re-randomised* cipher-texts which, for ElGamal encryption, are distributed as fresh encryptions. To recover the plaintext, i.e., h^y that needs to be encrypted under bpk, we either look up h^y from our internal records (when the pseudonyms stem from honest users) or extract y from π (when the pseudonym belongs to a corrupt user). Thus, for each tuple (m_i, nym_i, σ_i) sent to the CONVERT we check if an entry $(uid_i, m_i, nym_i, \sigma_i)$ in the list of created signatures SL exist, and if so we look up the h^{y_i} value we have chosen when mimicking the join protocol for this honest user uid_i. For computing the converted pseudonyms, we then simply compute $\overline{cnym}_i = \mathsf{Enc}(bpk, h^{y_i r})$ for a fresh r. Note that in the case of pseudonyms from corrupt users it is not sufficient to extract just h^y, which would be much more efficient than extracting y: When we have to embed a DDH challenge in the converted output, we won't be privy of the converter's exponent r that is supposed to be used in all converted pseudonyms $h^{y_i r}$. Knowing y we can simply compute R^y for $R = g^r$ being a part of the DDH challenge.   □

Lemma 2. *The CLS–DDH construction presented in Sect. 4.1 satisfies **non-transitivity** if the DDH assumption holds in $\mathbb{G}_1$, and the SPK is unbounded simulation-sound, zero knowledge and online extractable (for the underlined value).*

Proof. For proving non-transitivity, we have to show that there exists an efficient simulator SIM that makes the real and simulated game indistinguishable. We start by describing the simulator and then explain why the real and simulated conversion oracles CONVERT and CONVSIM are indistinguishable.

$$\underline{\mathsf{SIM}(gpk, bpk, \mathsf{L}_{uid_1}, \dots \mathsf{L}_{uid_{k'}})}$$

$l \leftarrow 0, \forall j \in [1, k']$

$\quad nym' \leftarrow_\$ \mathbb{G}_1; \forall m \in L_{uid_j}$

$\qquad l \leftarrow l + 1, (\overline{cnym}_l, \overline{c}_l) \leftarrow \mathsf{Blind}(gpk, bpk, (nym', m))$

return $((\overline{cnym}_1, \overline{c}_1), \dots (\overline{cnym}_l, \overline{c}_l))$

We assume that an adversary $\mathcal{A}$ exists, that makes q queries to the SNDU oracle for distinct user identifiers, that guesses b correctly in the non-transitivity game with SIM given above and wins with probability $\epsilon + 1/2$.

We will stepwise make the real-world (b=0) and the simulated world (b=1) equivalent, using a sequence of Games $\mathcal{H}_j$ for $j = 0, \dots, q$. The idea is that in Game $\mathcal{H}_j$ we will not use simulated conversions for all users $uid_1, \dots, uid_j$ in order of when they were queried to SNDU. More precisely, we define Game $\mathcal{H}_j$ to be as given in Fig. 3 with all other oracles identical to in the non-transitivity experiment. Let S_j be the event that $\mathcal{A}$ guesses b correctly in Game $\mathcal{H}_j$, with the simulator given above. Game $\mathcal{H}_j$ keeps track of the queries to SNDU, adding the first j queries uid to a set UL. Then during queries to CONVSIM, if a signature of a user in UL is queried, these are treated in the same way as pseudonyms for corrupted users, i.e., they are normally converted using the Convert algorithm.

Game $\mathcal{H}_0$ is identical to the non-transitivity game, because UL is empty. Therefore, $\Pr[S_0] = \epsilon + 1/2$. In Game $\mathcal{H}_q$, UL contains all honest users, and so the CONVSIM oracle is now identical to the CONVERT oracle, and inputs to the adversary are now independent of b, therefore $\Pr[S_q] = 1/2$.

We now show that if an adversary can distinguish Games $\mathcal{H}_j$ and $\mathcal{H}_{j+1}$, we can turn this into a distinguisher $\mathcal{D}_j$ that can break the DDH assumption. We describe the reduction and the additional simulation that is needed therein in Figs. 4 and 5.

We now argue that when a DDH tuple (D_1, D_2, D_3, D_4) is input to $\mathcal{D}_j$, the inputs to $\mathcal{A}$ are distributed identically to in Game $\mathcal{H}_{j+1}$; when a DDH tuple is not input, the inputs to $\mathcal{A}$ are distributed identically to in Game $\mathcal{H}_j$. That is for $D_1 = h, D_2 = h^a, D_3 = h^b, D_4 = h^c$, the oracles provided by $\mathcal{D}_j$ will be exactly as in $\mathcal{H}_{j+1}$ when $c = ab$, and as in $\mathcal{H}_j$ otherwise.

First, note that gpk, csk, isk are distributed identically as to the non-transitivity game, as χ is chosen randomly and independently when setting $h_1 \leftarrow h^\chi$.

Simulating the SNDU Oracle. The SNDU oracle only differs from the oracle in the non-transitivity experiment during the $(j + 1)$-th query by embedding D_2 of the DDH challenger into the user's "public key" H using knowledge of χ. Clearly, H is distributed identically as when computed normally, and π_H can be

---

Game $\mathcal{H}_j$

$t \leftarrow 0, b \leftarrow_\$ \{0,1\}, \text{param} \leftarrow \text{Setup}(1^\tau)$

$\text{HUL, CUL, SL} \leftarrow \varnothing$

$(ipk, isk) \leftarrow \text{IKGen}(\text{param}), (cpk, csk) \leftarrow \text{CKGen}(\text{param})$

$gpk \leftarrow (\text{param}, ipk, cpk), b^* \leftarrow \mathcal{A}^{\text{SNDU,SIGN,CONVX}}(\text{guess}, gpk, isk)$

return b^*

$\text{SNDU}(uid, M_{\text{in}})$

---

if $uid \notin \text{HUL}, t \leftarrow t+1, \text{if } t \leqslant j \quad \text{UL} \leftarrow \text{UL} \cup \{uid\}$

Continue from line 5 of standard SNDU oracle

$\text{CONVSIM}((nym_1, m_1, \sigma_1), \ldots, (nym_k, m_k, \sigma_k), bpk)$

---

if $\exists i \in [1,k]$ s.t. $\text{Verify}(gpk, m_i, nym_i, \sigma_i) = 0$ or $bpk \notin \mathcal{BPK}$ **return** $\perp$

Set $\text{CL} \leftarrow \varnothing$

Compute $(cnym_i, c_i) \leftarrow \text{Blind}(gpk, bpk, (nym_i, m_i); r_i)$ for $i = 1, \ldots, k$

$\forall i \in [1, k]$

    if $(uid, m_i, nym_i, \sigma_i) \in \text{SL}$

        if L_{uid} does not exist, create $\text{L}_{uid} \leftarrow \{m_i\}, \text{CL}_{uid} \leftarrow \{(c_i, cnym_i)\}$

        else set $\text{L}_{uid} \leftarrow \text{L}_{uid} \cup \{m_i\}, \text{CL}_{uid} \leftarrow \text{CL}_{uid} \cup \{(c_i, cnym_i)\}$

    else $\text{CL} \leftarrow \text{CL} \cup \{(c_i, cnym_i)\}$

$\{(\overline{cnym}_i, \bar{c}_i)\}_{i=1,\ldots k'} \leftarrow \text{Convert}(gpk, csk, bpk, \text{CL} \cup \bigcup_{uid \in \text{UL}} \text{CL}_{uid})$

for $k' \leftarrow |\text{CL} \cup \bigcup_{uid \in \text{UL}} \text{CL}_{uid}|$

let $\text{L}_{uid_1}, \ldots \text{L}_{uid_{k''}}$ be the non-empty message clusters created above

Let $\text{NUL} \leftarrow \{uid_1, \ldots uid_{k''}\} \backslash \text{UL}$

$\{(\overline{cnym}_i, \bar{c}_i)\}_{i=k'+1,\ldots k} \leftarrow \text{SIM}(gpk, bpk, \bigcup_{uid \in \text{NUL}} \text{L}_{uid})$

Choose random permutation $\Pi; \forall i \in [1, k]$ $(\overline{cnym}'_i, \bar{c}'_i) \leftarrow (\overline{cnym}_{\Pi(i)}, \bar{c}_{\Pi(i)})$

return $(\{(cnym_i, c_i, r_i)\}_{i=1,\ldots,k}, \{(\overline{cnym}'_i, \bar{c}'_i)\}_{i=1,\ldots k}, r_1, \ldots, r_k)$

Fig. 3. Description of Game $\mathcal{H}_j$ and the changes to the SNDU and CONVSIM oracles.

simulated due to the zero-knowledge property of the proof system. Note that y is not defined for this honest user, but this is not output to $\mathcal{A}$, or used in the next stage of the protocol.

Simulating the SIGN Oracle. The SIGN oracle is identical to the oracle in the non-transitivity experiment, when $uid \neq uid'$ is queried. When uid' is queried, we simply encrypt D_2 instead of h^y.

This is consistent with SNDU, as $H = D_2^x$. Further, A', d' are chosen randomly and independently, and $\hat{A} = A'^{isk}$ and so these are distributed identically

---

$\mathcal{D}_j(D_1, D_2, D_3, D_4)$

$t \leftarrow 0, b, \leftarrow_\$ \{0,1\}, h \leftarrow D_1, \chi \leftarrow_\$ \mathbb{Z}_p^*, h_1 \leftarrow h^\chi$

Finish computing gpk, csk, isk as in Setup, IKGen, CKGen

HUL, CUL, SL $\leftarrow \varnothing$

$b^* \leftarrow \mathcal{A}^{\text{SNDU,SIGN,CONVX}}(\text{guess}, gpk, isk)$

return b^*

SNDU(uid, n)

---

if $uid \notin$ HUL, $t \leftarrow t + 1$, if $t \leqslant j$ UL $\leftarrow$ UL $\cup$ $\{uid\}$

   HUL $\leftarrow$ HUL $\cup$ $\{uid\}$, $\mathbf{gsk}[uid] \leftarrow \perp, M_{\text{in}} \leftarrow \perp, \mathbf{dec}^{uid} \leftarrow$ cont

   if $t = j + 1$ $uid' \leftarrow uid, H \leftarrow D_2^\chi$ simulate π_H with $H, n, st_{uid} \leftarrow (\perp, H, \pi_H)$

     return $((H, \pi_H), \text{cont})$

Continue from line 5 of standard SNDU oracle

SIGN(uid, m)

---

if $uid \neq uid'$ perform SIGN oracle from Anonymity experiment

else $\alpha, \beta \leftarrow_\$ \mathbb{Z}_p^*, nym_1 \leftarrow g^\alpha, nym_2 \leftarrow cpk^\alpha D_2$

$A', d \leftarrow_\$ \mathbb{Z}_p^*, \hat{A} \leftarrow A'^{isk}$

Simulate π with $A', \hat{A}, d, nym_1, nym_2, m$

$\sigma \leftarrow (A', \hat{A}, d, \pi)$ return $((nym_1, nym_2), \sigma)$

Fig. 4. Oracles for $\mathcal{D}_j$ our distinguishing algorithm for the DDH problem. The CONVERT oracle remains unchanged, and the CONVSIM oracle using the DDH challenge is given in Fig. 4.

to in Sign. The SPK π can be simulated due to the zero knowledge property of the proof system.

Simulating the CONVSIM Oracle. What remains to be shown is that the CONVSIM oracle created by $\mathcal{D}_j$ either behaves identical to the CONVSIM oracle in Game $\mathcal{H}_j$ or as in $\mathcal{H}_{j+1}$, depending on whether its input was a DDH tuple or not. We know that $D_3 = h^{\tilde{r}}$ for some $\tilde{r}$ and thus it must hold that $D_3^{yr} = h^{\tilde{r}ry}$. Finally, we derive $\overline{cnym}$ by encrypting D_3^{yr} from scratch under bpk, which is not noticeable to the adversary due to the re-randomisation that is applied in the conversion algorithm.

If (D_1, D_2, D_3, D_4) is a DDH tuple, then $D_4^r = h^{\tilde{r}r\tilde{y}}$. Therefore as $\tilde{y} = y_{uid'}$, the inputs to $\mathcal{A}$ are also distributed identically to in Game $\mathcal{H}_{j+1}$. Whereas if (D_1, D_2, D_3, D_4) is *not* a DDH tuple, then D_4^r, is distributed identically to nym', which was chosen randomly and independently. Therefore the inputs to $\mathcal{A}$ are distributed identically to in Game $\mathcal{H}_j$.

Reduction to the DDH problem. Therefore the probability that $\mathcal{D}_j$ outputs 1 if it was given a valid DDH tuple as input is $\Pr[S_{j+1}]$, and $\Pr[S_j]$ is the probability

---

$\mathsf{CONVSIM}((nym_1, m_1, \sigma_1), \ldots, (nym_k, m_k, \sigma_k), bpk)$

---

if $\exists i \in [1, k]$ s.t. $\mathsf{Verify}(gpk, m_i, nym_i, \sigma_i) = 0$ or $bpk \notin \mathcal{BPK}$ **return** $\perp$

Set $\mathsf{CL} \leftarrow \emptyset, r \leftarrow_{\$} \mathbb{Z}_p^*$

Compute $(cnym_i, c_i) \leftarrow \mathsf{Blind}(gpk, bpk, (nym_i, m_i); r_i)$ for $i = 1, \ldots, k$

$\forall i \in [1, k]$

    if $(uid, m_i, nym_i, \sigma_i) \in \mathsf{SL}$

        if L_{uid} does not exist $\mathsf{L}_{uid} \leftarrow \{m_i\}, \mathsf{CL}_{uid} \leftarrow \{(m_i, y_{uid})\}$

        else $L_{uid} \leftarrow \mathsf{L}_{uid} \cup \{m_i\}, \mathsf{CL}_{uid} \leftarrow \mathsf{CL}_{uid} \cup \{(m_i, y_{uid})\}$

    else Extract y_i from $\sigma_i, \mathsf{CL} \leftarrow \mathsf{CL} \cup \{(m_i, y_i)\}$

let $\mathsf{L}_{uid_1}, \ldots \mathsf{L}_{uid_{k''}}$ be the non-empty message clusters created above

$n \leftarrow 0;\quad \forall (m, y) \in \mathsf{CL} \cup \bigcup_{uid \in \mathsf{UL}} \mathsf{CL}_{uid}$

    $n \leftarrow n + 1, (\overline{cnym}_n, \overline{c}_n) \leftarrow \mathsf{Blind}(gpk, bpk, (D_3^{yr}, m))$

if $\mathsf{L}_{uid'}$ exists $\forall m \in L_{uid'}$

    $n \leftarrow n + 1, (\overline{cnym}_n, \overline{c}_n) \leftarrow \mathsf{Blind}(gpk, bpk, (D_4^r, m))$

$\{(\overline{cnym}_i, \overline{c}_i)\}_{i=n+1, \ldots k} \leftarrow \mathsf{SIM}(gpk, bpk, \bigcup_{uid \in \mathsf{NUL}, uid \neq uid'} L_{uid})$

Choose random permutation $\Pi; \forall i \in [1, k]\quad (\overline{cnym}'_i, \overline{c}'_i) \leftarrow (\overline{cnym}_{\Pi(i)}, \overline{c}_{\Pi(i)})$

return $(\{(cnym_i, c_i, r_i)\}_{i=1, \ldots, k}, \{(\overline{cnym}'_i, \overline{c}'_i)\}_{i=1, \ldots k}, r_1, \ldots, r_k)$

Fig. 5. The $\mathsf{CONVSIM}$ oracle used by distinguisher $\mathcal{D}_j$ given in Fig. 5. To avoid confusion, we write uid' to refer to the $j + 1$-th user that has joined the group (and for which $\mathcal{D}_j$ embedded the DDH challenge).

that $\mathcal{D}_j$ outputs 1 when the input was not a DDH tuple. The advantage of $\mathcal{D}_j$ is then $|\Pr[S_j] - \Pr[S_{j+1}]|$, therefore $|\Pr[S_j] - \Pr[S_{j+1}]| = \epsilon_{\mathsf{DDH}}$.

Overall, for our sequence of games $\mathcal{H}_0$ to $\mathcal{H}_q$ it holds that $|\Pr[S_0] - \Pr[S_q]| \leqslant q\epsilon_{\mathsf{DDH}}$ and thus $\epsilon \leqslant q\epsilon_{\mathsf{DDH}}$ is negligible. This concludes our proof that the CLS–DDH construction satisfies non-transitivity. $\square$

Lemma 3. *The CLS–DDH construction presented in Sect. 4.1 satisfies **conversion blindness** if the DDH assumption holds in $\mathbb{G}_1$.*

Proof (sketch). Given that all a corrupt converter sees are ElGamal ciphertexts that are encrypted under a key bpk for which bsk is not known to the adversary, the proof for conversion blindness is a straightforward reduction to the CPA-security of ElGamal which holds under the DDH assumption. $\square$

Lemma 4. *The CLS–DDH construction presented in Sect. 4.1 satisfies **join anonymity** if the DDH assumption holds in $\mathbb{G}_1$, and the SPK is zero knowledge.*

Proof (sketch). For proving that adversary $\mathcal{A}$ cannot break the join anonymity of our CLS–DDH construction we have to show that it is infeasible to link a join session of an honest user to the user's signatures. In this setting the adversary controls both the converter and issuer. The only value the corrupt issuer learns during the join protocol from an honest user is $H = h_1^y$ for the user's secret y and π_H, the proof of knowledge of y. When receiving signatures from the user, the adversary can use the converter's secret key to recover h^y from nym and also sees π, the proof-of-knowledge of a BBS+ signature on y. By the zero-knowledge property of the proof system, neither π nor π_H leak any information about y. It is easy to see that an adversary that can link h_1^y and h^y for the independent generators h_1 and h can be turned into an adversary breaking the DDH assumption. $\square$

Lemma 5. *The CLS–DDH construction presented in Sect. 4.1 satisfies **non-frameability** if the DL assumption holds in $\mathbb{G}_1$, and the SPK is simulation-sound and zero knowledge.*

Proof (sketch). If an adversary $\mathcal{A}$ exists that can break the non-frameability of our CLS–DDH scheme, then we can build an adversary $\mathcal{A}'$ that breaks the discrete logarithm assumption. Recall that non-frameability ensures that an adversary should not be able to create a valid signature that Convert will falsely link to signatures of an honest user. In the proof we embed re-randomized versions of a DL challenge $D = h^y$ in the join protocol for all users, i.e., using D^r instead of H when receiving the BBS+ signature from the corrupt issuer. We also set the public parameters such that $h_1 = h^z$ for a random exponent z. For signature queries we use the knowledge of z to compute proper looking pseudonyms, and then mimic the SPK by choosing A', d' randomly, setting $\hat{A} \leftarrow A'^{risk}$, and simulating π. If the adversary outputs his forgery (nym^*, σ^*, m) we extract y from π^* contained in σ^*. Clearly, this also relies on the simulation soundness and zero-knowledge property of the proof system. $\square$

Lemma 6. *The CLS–DDH construction presented in Sect. 4.1 satisfies **traceability** if the q-SDH assumption holds, and the SPK is simulation-sound, zero knowledge and online extractable.*

Proof (sketch). We show that if an adversary $\mathcal{A}$ can break traceability for the CLS–DDH construction then we can build an adversary $\mathcal{A}'$ that breaks the q-SDH assumption. Roughly, to win the traceability game the adversary must be able to create more signatures that remain unlinkable in Convert than users he controls, which requires $\mathcal{A}$ to forge BBS+ signatures. Our proof closely follows the revised proof of the unforgeability of BBS+ signatures given in [14]. Note that this uses the newer version of the q-SDH assumption [8] that supports type-3 pairings, which in turn allows to prove the unforgeability of BBS+ signatures in the type-3 pairing setting. $\square$

4.3 Instantiation of SPK and Efficiency

We now discuss how to securely instantiate the online-extractable SPK's used in our CLS–DDH construction and state the computational cost and lengths of signatures and pseudonyms.

Instantiation of SPK's. We have two non-interactive zero-knowledge proofs of knowledge in our scheme: π_H used in the join protocol for proving knowledge of y in $H = h_1^y$, and π proving knowledge of a BBS+ signature on y and that nym encrypts the same y. In both cases we need the witness y to be online extractable. For this, we additionally encrypt y under a public key that needs to be added to param (and to which in security proof we will know the secret key for), and extend π and π_H to prove that the additional encryption contains the same y that is used in the rest of the proof. For the verifiable encryption of y we use Paillier encryption [20], that is secure under the DCR assumption [36].

For transforming interactive into non-interactive zero-knowledge proofs we rely on the Fiat-Shamir heuristic that ensures security in the random oracle model. Due to this, we can now state Corollary 1.

Corollary 1. *The CLS–DDH construction presented in Sect. 4.1, with the SPK instantiated as above, is a secure CLS as defined in Sect. 3 under the DDH, q-SDH and DCR assumption in the random oracle model.*

Computational Cost. We give the operations required for the entities involved in the scheme in the table below. We denote k exponentiation in group $\mathbb{G}_i$ by $k\mathsf{exp}_{\mathbb{G}_i}$, k hash function calls by $k\mathsf{hash}$, and k pairing operations by $k\mathsf{pair}$. We denote k exponentiations in $\mathbb{Z}_{n^2}^*$ due to the Paillier encryption used, by $k\mathsf{exp}_{\mathbb{Z}_{n^2}^*}$.

Entity	Algorithm	Computational Cost
User	Sign	$16\mathsf{exp}_{\mathbb{G}_1} + 15\mathsf{exp}_{\mathbb{Z}_{n^2}} + 1\mathsf{hash}$
Verifier	Verify	$12\mathsf{exp}_{\mathbb{G}_1} + 11\mathsf{exp}_{\mathbb{Z}_{n^2}} + 1\mathsf{hash} + 2\mathsf{pair}$
	Blind	$6\mathsf{exp}_{\mathbb{G}_1}$
	Unblind	$2\mathsf{exp}_{\mathbb{G}_1}$
Converter	Convert(k pseudonyms input)	$7k\mathsf{exp}_{\mathbb{G}_1}$

Pseudonym & Signature Length. We give the sizes of pseudonyms and signatures in terms of the amount of group elements below. We denote the length required to represent k elements in $\mathbb{G}_1$ as $k\mathbb{G}_1$, k outputs of a hash function as kH, and k elements in $\mathbb{Z}_{n^2}^*$, due to the Paillier encryption used, as $k\mathbb{Z}_{n^2}^*$.

Pseudonym				Signature
Original	Blinded	Converted	Unblinded Converted	
nym	$cnym$	$\overline{cnym}$	$\overline{nym}$	σ
$2\mathbb{G}_1$	$3\mathbb{G}_1$	$2\mathbb{G}_1$	$1\mathbb{G}_1$	$3\mathbb{G}_1\ 6\mathbb{Z}_p\ 1H\ 6\mathbb{Z}_{n^2}^*$

5   Conclusion and Future Work

In this work we have introduced a new form of group signatures that support flexible and controlled linkability: data can be collected in authenticated and fully unlinkable form, whilst still allow the data to be obliviously relinked by queries to a central entity. We have formalized the required security properties in a dynamic model, i.e., users are able to join the scheme, and proposed an efficient scheme that satisfies these requirement under discrete logarithm and Paillier assumptions in the random oracle model.

There are a number of open problem we consider to be interesting avenues for future work: Compared with the anonymity requirements of conventional *dynamic* group signatures, our anonymity notions are somewhat weaker as we do not allow the adversary to corrupt the two challenge users after it received the challenge signature. This means that our privacy related requirements do not yield *forward anonymity*. Given the conversion functionality that is inherent in our setting, achieving such stronger notion seems challenging, if not even impossible. In fact, for the related problem of group signatures with user-controlled linkability with signature-based revocation, forward anonymity has not been achieved by any of the existing schemes either.

Another direction for further work would be to investigate how to achieve security against fully malicious verifiers. On a high level, this will require to forward blinded versions of the users' signatures to the converter, allowing him to check the validity of the blinded inputs. The challenge is to do this while preserving the converter's capability to blindly decrypt and transform the inputs.

In a similar vein, we have considered the verifier to be both the data collector and data processor so far. However, our blind and unblind algorithms already cater for a more flexible setting, as they are specified in the public-key setting. That is, the verifier could blind and push the data to be linked towards a dedicated data processor holding the secret unblinding key. This has the advantage that data storage and processing can be strictly separated. For such a setting it might be desirable to preserve the authenticity of the data throughout the process, i.e., the blind conversion must also take the signatures as input and transform them into valid signatures for the re-linked pseudonyms.

Acknowledgments. The first author is supported by the UK Government as part of the CDT in Cyber Security program at Royal Holloway University of London (EP/K035584/1). The second author was supported by the European Union's Horizon 2020 research and innovation program under Grant Agreement Number 768953 (ICT4CART).

References

1. EU general data protection regulation. https://gdpr-info.eu
2. Ateniese, G., Camenisch, J., Joye, M., Tsudik, G.: A practical and provably secure coalition-resistant group signature scheme. In: Bellare, M. (ed.) CRYPTO 2000. LNCS, vol. 1880, pp. 255–270. Springer, Heidelberg (2000). https://doi.org/10.1007/3-540-44598-6_16

3. Au, M.H., Susilo, W., Mu, Y.: Constant-size dynamic k-TAA. In: De Prisco, R., Yung, M. (eds.) SCN 2006. LNCS, vol. 4116, pp. 111–125. Springer, Heidelberg (2006). https://doi.org/10.1007/11832072_8

4. Bellare, M., Micciancio, D., Warinschi, B.: Foundations of group signatures: formal definitions, simplified requirements, and a construction based on general assumptions. In: Biham, E. (ed.) EUROCRYPT 2003. LNCS, vol. 2656, pp. 614–629. Springer, Heidelberg (2003). https://doi.org/10.1007/3-540-39200-9_38

5. Bellare, M., Shi, H., Zhang, C.: Foundations of group signatures: the case of dynamic groups. In: Menezes, A. (ed.) CT-RSA 2005. LNCS, vol. 3376, pp. 136–153. Springer, Heidelberg (2005). https://doi.org/10.1007/978-3-540-30574-3_11

6. Bernhard, D., Fuchsbauer, G., Ghadafi, E., Smart, N.P., Warinschi, B.: Anonymous attestation with user-controlled linkability. Int. J. Inf. Secur. **12**(3), 219–249 (2013)

7. Boneh, D., Boyen, X.: Short signatures without random oracles. In: Cachin and Camenisch [13], pp. 56–73

8. Boneh, D., Boyen, X.: Short signatures without random oracles and the SDH assumption in bilinear groups. J. Cryptol. **21**(2), 149–177 (2008)

9. Boneh, D., Boyen, X., Shacham, H.: Short group signatures. In: Franklin, M. (ed.) CRYPTO 2004. LNCS, vol. 3152, pp. 41–55. Springer, Heidelberg (2004). https://doi.org/10.1007/978-3-540-28628-8_3

10. Bootle, J., Cerulli, A., Chaidos, P., Ghadafi, E., Groth, J.: Foundations of fully dynamic group signatures. In: Manulis, M., Sadeghi, A.-R., Schneider, S. (eds.) ACNS 2016. LNCS, vol. 9696, pp. 117–136. Springer, Cham (2016). https://doi.org/10.1007/978-3-319-39555-5_7

11. Brickell, E.F., Camenisch, J., Chen, L.: Direct anonymous attestation. In: Atluri, V., Pfitzmann, B., McDaniel, P. (eds.) ACM CCS 2004, pp. 132–145. ACM Press, October 2004

12. Brickell, E., Li, J.: A pairing-based DAA scheme further reducing TPM resources. In: Acquisti, A., Smith, S.W., Sadeghi, A.-R. (eds.) Trust 2010. LNCS, vol. 6101, pp. 181–195. Springer, Heidelberg (2010). https://doi.org/10.1007/978-3-642-13869-0_12

13. Cachin, C., Camenisch, J.L. (eds.): EUROCRYPT 2004. LNCS, vol. 3027. Springer, Heidelberg (2004). https://doi.org/10.1007/b97182

14. Camenisch, J., Drijvers, M., Lehmann, A.: Anonymous attestation using the strong Diffie Hellman assumption revisited. In: Franz, M., Papadimitratos, P. (eds.) Trust 2016. LNCS, vol. 9824, pp. 1–20. Springer, Cham (2016). https://doi.org/10.1007/978-3-319-45572-3_1

15. Camenisch, J., Drijvers, M., Lehmann, A.: Universally composable direct anonymous attestation. In: Cheng, C.-M., Chung, K.-M., Persiano, G., Yang, B.-Y. (eds.) PKC 2016. LNCS, vol. 9615, pp. 234–264. Springer, Heidelberg (2016). https://doi.org/10.1007/978-3-662-49387-8_10

16. Camenisch, J., Kiayias, A., Yung, M.: On the portability of generalized schnorr proofs. In: Joux, A. (ed.) EUROCRYPT 2009. LNCS, vol. 5479, pp. 425–442. Springer, Heidelberg (2009). https://doi.org/10.1007/978-3-642-01001-9_25

17. Camenisch, J., Lehmann, A.: (Un)linkable pseudonyms for governmental databases. In: Ray, I., Li, N., Kruegel, C. (eds.) ACM CCS 2015, pp. 1467–1479. ACM Press, October 2015

18. Camenisch, J., Lehmann, A.: Privacy-preserving user-auditable pseudonym systems. In: 2017 IEEE European Symposium on Security and Privacy (EuroS&P), pp. 269–284. IEEE (2017)

19. Camenisch, J., Lysyanskaya, A.: An efficient system for non-transferable anonymous credentials with optional anonymity revocation. In: Pfitzmann, B. (ed.) EUROCRYPT 2001. LNCS, vol. 2045, pp. 93–118. Springer, Heidelberg (2001). https://doi.org/10.1007/3-540-44987-6_7
20. Camenisch, J., Shoup, V.: Practical verifiable encryption and decryption of discrete logarithms. In: Boneh, D. (ed.) CRYPTO 2003. LNCS, vol. 2729, pp. 126–144. Springer, Heidelberg (2003). https://doi.org/10.1007/978-3-540-45146-4_8
21. Camenisch, J., Stadler, M.: Efficient group signature schemes for large groups (extended abstract). In: Kaliski Jr., B.S. (ed.) CRYPTO 1997. LNCS, vol. 1294, pp. 410–424. Springer, Heidelberg (1997). https://doi.org/10.1007/BFb0052252
22. Chaum, D.: Some weaknesses of "weaknesses of undeniable signatures" (rump session). In: Davies, D.W. (ed.) EUROCRYPT 1991. LNCS, vol. 547, pp. 554–556. Springer, Heidelberg (1991). https://doi.org/10.1007/3-540-46416-6_54
23. ElGamal, T.: On computing logarithms over finite fields. In: Williams, H.C. (ed.) CRYPTO 1985. LNCS, vol. 218, pp. 396–402. Springer, Heidelberg (1986). https://doi.org/10.1007/3-540-39799-X_28
24. Fiat, A., Shamir, A.: How to prove yourself: practical solutions to identification and signature problems. In: Odlyzko, A.M. (ed.) CRYPTO 1986. LNCS, vol. 263, pp. 186–194. Springer, Heidelberg (1987). https://doi.org/10.1007/3-540-47721-7_12
25. Galbraith, S.D., Paterson, K.G., Smart, N.P.: Pairings for cryptographers. Discrete Appl. Math. 156(16), 3113–3121 (2008)
26. Galindo, D., Verheul, E.R.: Microdata sharing via pseudonymization. Joint UNECE/Eurostat work session on statistical data confidentiality (2007)
27. Garms, L., Lehmann, A.: Group signatures with selective linkability (2019). https://eprint.iacr.org/2019/027
28. Groth, J.: Fully anonymous group signatures without random oracles. In: Kurosawa, K. (ed.) ASIACRYPT 2007. LNCS, vol. 4833, pp. 164–180. Springer, Heidelberg (2007). https://doi.org/10.1007/978-3-540-76900-2_10
29. Hwang, J.Y., Lee, S., Chung, B.H., Cho, H.S., Nyang, D.: Short group signatures with controllable linkability. In: 2011 Workshop on Lightweight Security & Privacy: Devices, Protocols and Applications (LightSec), pp. 44–52. IEEE (2011)
30. Hwang, J.Y., Lee, S., Chung, B.H., Cho, H.S., Nyang, D.: Group signatures with controllable linkability for dynamic membership. Inf. Sci. 222, 761–778 (2013)
31. Kiayias, A., Tsiounis, Y., Yung, M.: Traceable signatures. In: Cachin and Camenisch [13], pp. 571–589
32. Kiayias, A., Yung, M.: Group signatures with efficient concurrent join. In: Cramer, R. (ed.) EUROCRYPT 2005. LNCS, vol. 3494, pp. 198–214. Springer, Heidelberg (2005). https://doi.org/10.1007/11426639_12
33. Libert, B., Ling, S., Nguyen, K., Wang, H.: Zero-knowledge arguments for lattice-based accumulators: logarithmic-size ring signatures and group signatures without trapdoors. In: Fischlin, M., Coron, J.-S. (eds.) EUROCRYPT 2016. LNCS, vol. 9666, pp. 1–31. Springer, Heidelberg (2016). https://doi.org/10.1007/978-3-662-49896-5_1
34. Libert, B., Peters, T., Yung, M.: Scalable group signatures with revocation. In: Pointcheval, D., Johansson, T. (eds.) EUROCRYPT 2012. LNCS, vol. 7237, pp. 609–627. Springer, Heidelberg (2012). https://doi.org/10.1007/978-3-642-29011-4_36
35. Lysyanskaya, A., Rivest, R.L., Sahai, A., Wolf, S.: Pseudonym systems. In: Heys, H., Adams, C. (eds.) SAC 1999. LNCS, vol. 1758, pp. 184–199. Springer, Heidelberg (2000). https://doi.org/10.1007/3-540-46513-8_14

36. Paillier, P.: Public-key cryptosystems based on composite degree residuosity classes. In: Stern, J. (ed.) EUROCRYPT 1999. LNCS, vol. 1592, pp. 223–238. Springer, Heidelberg (1999). https://doi.org/10.1007/3-540-48910-X_16
37. Slamanig, D., Spreitzer, R., Unterluggauer, T.: Adding controllable linkability to pairing-based group signatures for free. In: Chow, S.S.M., Camenisch, J., Hui, L.C.K., Yiu, S.M. (eds.) ISC 2014. LNCS, vol. 8783, pp. 388–400. Springer, Cham (2014). https://doi.org/10.1007/978-3-319-13257-0_23

Let a Non-barking Watchdog Bite: Cliptographic Signatures with an Offline Watchdog

Sherman S. M. Chow[1], Alexander Russell[2], Qiang Tang[3], Moti Yung[4,5], Yongjun Zhao[1(✉)], and Hong-Sheng Zhou[6]

[1] Chinese University of Hong Kong, Shatin, Hong Kong
{sherman,yjzhao}@ie.cuhk.edu.hk
[2] University of Connecticut, Storrs, USA
acr@cse.uconn.edu
[3] New Jersey Institute of Technology, Newark, USA
qiang@njit.edu
[4] Google Inc., New York, USA
[5] Columbia University, New York, USA
moti@cs.columbia.edu
[6] Virginia Commonwealth University, Richmond, USA
hszhou@vcu.edu

Abstract. We study how to construct secure digital signature schemes in the presence of kleptographic attacks. Our work utilizes an offline watchdog to clip the power of subversions via only one-time black-box testing of the implementation. Previous results essentially rely on an online watchdog which requires the collection of all communicating transcripts (or active re-randomization of messages).

We first give a simple but generic construction, without random oracles, in the partial-subversion model in which key generation and signing algorithms can be subverted. Then, we give the first digital signature scheme in the complete-subversion model in which all cryptographic algorithms can be subverted. This construction is based on the full-domain hash. Along the way, we enhance the recent result of Russell *et al.* (CRYPTO 2018) about correcting a subverted random oracle.

Keywords: Signatures · Subversion resilience · Offline watchdog

S. S. M. Chow—Supported by GRF (CUHK 14210217) of the Research Grants Council, Hong Kong.
A. Russell—Supported in part by NSF award 1801487.
Q. Tang—Supported in part by NSF award 1801492.
H.-S. Zhou—Supported in part by NSF award 1801470.

D. Lin and K. Sako (Eds.): PKC 2019, LNCS 11442, pp. 221–251, 2019.
https://doi.org/10.1007/978-3-030-17253-4_8

1   Introduction

Modern cryptography has been spectacularly successful. We have already seen a flurry of cryptographic tools with versatile functionalities and rigorous security analyses. Yet, the formal security guarantees come with an implicit caveat – they only hold if the implementations faithfully realize the specifications the formal security proof is analyzing. Our experiences tell us that implementation can be tricky. Programming bugs may go undetected and subtle errors can make the implementation faulty. Apart from unintended blunders which may spoil the security guarantee, implementations of cryptographic algorithms can be subverted with *fully adversarial implementations* which look correct even under fairly intensive (black-box) testing. Such kind of subversion, or in general, *kleptographic* attack [27,28], is not just a pathological concern, but has been understood as a real threat since the Snowden revelations [22]. Concretely speaking, whenever a "third-party" software library or hardware device is relied upon by a bigger cryptographic system, it is hard to assert its security even if the said cryptographic system is "provably secure" in the traditional sense.

At a high level, kleptography considers a "proud-but-curious" adversary whose goal is to break the security of a certain cryptographic primitive by supplying a malformed implementation of it without being detected. Under such a setting, the adversary has many viable attack strategies. For example, the malicious implementation of a signature verification algorithm may always return "1" when seeing a certain hard-coded string[1]. For another example, the subverted randomized (*e.g.*, encryption) algorithm may leak secret information via a steganographic channel [4,23]. These general and powerful attack strategies are undetectable under offline black-box testing. Given these attacks, it is not surprising that all existing defense mechanisms rely on extra trust assumptions, such as trusted online reverse firewall [10,16,21], trusted key generation algorithm [2,5], trusted initialization [17], *etc.*

Recently, Russell *et al.* [23] proposed a framework (called cliptography) for systematically studying how to secure cryptographic primitives in the presence of kleptographic attacks, *i.e.*, how to clip the power of kleptographic attacks. The framework is characterized by three parties: an adversary, who may provide potentially subverted implementations of cryptographic algorithms; a "watchdog", who either certifies or rejects the implementations by subjecting them to (black-box) interrogation according to the genuine specification of the algorithms; and a challenger, who plays with the adversary in a conventional security game, but now using the potentially subverted implementations. This framework is capable of capturing a wide range of subversion capabilities and defense mechanisms.

---

[1] This can be viewed as applying the input-triggered attack [13] to signature schemes.

- **Online watchdog vs. offline watchdog.** We can define two flavors of watchdogs, depending on the information given to it. The strong (and less attractive) model of *online watchdog* [23] is provided with access to the full transcript of the challenger-adversary security game. It could be valuable for establishing feasibility results, but in practice, it is not easy to instantiate such a watchdog, as it has to piggyback on the implementations, collecting all communication transcripts to detect abnormal inputs, and "barking" all the time. The weaker (and perhaps more attractive) model is the *offline watchdog* model [23,25]. The watchdog simply interrogates the supplied implementations, comparing them with the specification of the primitives, and declares them to be "fit" or "unfit." In other words, the watchdog only needs to "bark" once, and then it can go offline afterward.

- **Partial subversion vs. complete subversion.** The adversary may be more interested in subverting certain cryptographic algorithms than the others. For instance, if the attack goal is to learn the secret signing key, the attacker will be less interested in subverting the verification algorithm than the signing algorithm, since the verification result can only carry 1-bit of information and it is likely to be kept locally. It is thus still worthy to consider the *partial-subversion* model, in which some algorithms can be explicitly excluded from subversion in the security game. Some subversion defense methods are established in this model, *e.g.*, honest key generation algorithm and honest verification algorithm of a digital signature scheme [2]. The cliptography framework by Russell *et al.* [23] can easily capture partial subversion by letting the challenger run the genuine algorithm in the security game. Of course, it is of great importance to consider a more powerful adversary who can launch a *complete subversion* which subverts *all* the relevant cryptographic elements of a scheme [23] (excluding the computing base).

- **Trusted computing base.** Note that the complete-subversion model above only refers to the *functional components*, *i.e.*, the cryptographic algorithms, which should be distinguished from the user computing base for basic operations such as $\oplus$, $=$, "reassembly", *etc.* The trusted computing base for (some of) these operations is provided by the architecture, which is normally not under the control of the cryptography implementation/library provider.

  Russell *et al.* [23,25] recently proposed the split-program strategy for immunizing kleptographic attacks on randomized algorithms. The idea of this non-black-box technique is to decompose the algorithm into a *constant* number of smaller components. The adversary can still provide subverted implementations of *all* these components but the challenger will faithfully *amalgamate* these components into a fully functional implementation, which will be used in the security game. Note that all components are still subject to black-box interrogation by the (online/offline) watchdog. Such non-black-box testing and trusted amalgamation can be captured by simply providing specifications of all small components of the algorithm to the watchdog.

Current Status of Subversion-Resistant Signatures. To the best of our knowledge, only three previous works considered subversion-resistant signature schemes. The work by Ateniese *et al.* [2] not only relies on a priori "verifiability" condition which essentially requires an online watchdog to instantiate, but also assumes trusted key generation algorithm (or requires a trusted online "reverse firewall"). The result of Russell *et al.* [23], despite in the complete-subversion model, (explicitly) requires an online watchdog too. Fischlin and Mazaheri [17] recently proposed a new defense mechanism called "self-guarding" which requires users to have a trusted initialization phase to generate genuine message signature pairs for randomly chosen messages. We continue the pursuit of reducing the trust assumption needed for subversion-resistant signature schemes.

1.1 Our Contributions

We investigate subversion-resistant EUF-CMA-secure (simply put, cliptographic) digital signature schemes in the above framework with only an offline watchdog.

A Simple Generic Construction in the Partial-Subversion Model. We start with a simple construction which works for any existing signature schemes. So, one can just apply a simple "patch", or install a "small" (due to its simplicity) add-on without changing the underlying system. Note that for this generic construction, the verification algorithm is still trusted.

How Difficult Is Our Problem? First, note that the *key generation* can be handled by the recent double-splitting technique [25]. The main difficulty appears in the Sign algorithm. Recall that one potential catastrophe of a subverted signing algorithm is the revelation of the secret key. It is relatively easier to discover such a subversion if the secret key is blatantly output as the "signature". A more sophisticated kleptographic attacker will hide this secret. When the signing algorithm is randomized, it provides a convenient subliminal channel. A natural preventative measure is to use clean randomness to re-randomize the signatures (if they are publicly re-randomizable), with the existence of a cryptographic reverse firewall [21]. Alternatively, a *unique* signature scheme, in which there is only one valid signature for each message, simply does not feature any subliminal channel. These explain in a high-level way the feasibility results of Ateniese *et al.* [2]. Nevertheless, many signature schemes, especially those efficient ones with security proven in the standard model, are randomized (*e.g.* [8]). So our first question is: can we upgrade the signing algorithm of a probabilistic signature scheme?

Our Generic Construction. A general defense against input-triggered attacks [13] is to mandate that the subverted implementation only takes a random message. Russell *et al.* [25] construct subversion-resistant encryption schemes in the offline-watchdog model with this idea. The encryption algorithm invokes two instances of encryption, one encrypting $u \oplus m$ and the other encrypting u. Adopting this strategy naïvely in the context of signature signing does not work. The scheme $\mathsf{Sign}_{\mathrm{SPEC}}(\mathsf{sk}, m) = (\mathsf{Sign}'_{\mathrm{SPEC}}(\mathsf{sk}, u), \mathsf{Sign}'_{\mathrm{SPEC}}(\mathsf{sk}, u \oplus m), u)$ is trivially forgeable.

We fixed this forgeable scheme by two techniques: (i) Domain-separation: We append different special symbols to the inputs in the two invocations, so that the output of the first invocation cannot be interpreted as the second one (and vice versa); (ii) One-time random tag: We also need to make sure that no one can mix-and-match (the components of) signatures for different messages to create new forgeries. To do so, we further include a random tag r that binds the two signature components together, also making sure that they are one-use only. We note that the domain-separation technique has been used in other contexts, such as random oracle instantiation. Similar one-time random tag structure has also appeared in the context of structure-preserving signature [1], but their work does not randomize the message to be signed.

Moreover, to handle the subliminal channel attack due to biased randomness, we decouple the randomness generation from the randomized algorithm [25]. The randomness generation can be further handled via the double-splitting technique, while the deterministic counterpart for signing can be safeguarded by only an offline watchdog as we feed only uniform messages as input.

FDH-Based Construction in the Complete-Subversion Model. Our main contribution is a secure signature scheme in the complete-subversion model which further handles the subverted verification algorithm.[2] This is the first signature scheme that achieves such security goals. The simple generic construction above cannot handle subversion of verification algorithm. Indeed, it is not clear how to generically apply the randomization strategy to the potentially adversarial inputs to be fed to the verification (*i.e.*, the message m and the signature σ), such that the signature verification algorithm still works on these randomized inputs, without jeopardizing the unforgeability of the signature scheme.

Our second construction hence does not take the generic randomization approach, but instead handles the classical full-domain hash (FDH) [7,11] paradigm. In this paradigm, the signing algorithm first hashes the message and then inverts the hashed value via a trapdoor one-way permutation. The adversary is supposed to provide the implementation of each algorithm: $\mathsf{KG}_{\mathrm{IMPL}}$, $\mathsf{Sign}_{\mathrm{IMPL}}$, $\mathsf{Verify}_{\mathrm{IMPL}}$ and also the implementation of the hash h_{IMPL}.

First, we note that the *key generation* can be handled the same way as our generic transformation above applying the recent double-splitting technique [25].

Regarding the *hash function*, we utilize the recent work of Russell *et al.* [26], which provides a simple construction that can correct a subverted random oracle, such that the resulting function will be as good as an ideal random function. The construction requires some public randomness that is generated after the implementation of the hash is supplied. To apply their theorems [26], and ensure that the "corrected" hash can be considered to be a random oracle, we need to ensure (i) the subversion disagrees on its specification only at a negligible

---

[2] As elaborated above, the trusted computing base including operations like "⊕" and "=" are still in place. They are actually necessary due to the known (simple) trigger attacks [13] assuming only an offline watchdog. Our goal is to reduce the number of trusted functional components, and keep the remaining as simple as possible, *e.g.*, without any trusted large group operations.

fraction; (ii) there is randomness that can be generated and published after the malicious implementations are supplied; (iii) "interpret" their "replacement lemma" [26] such that it is suitable for our application. Point (iii) is more complex than it looks, especially when all the other algorithms are subverted. See below.

It is challenging to deal with the *signing algorithm*. To avoid the signing implementation to leak the secret triggered by some hidden input, we will apply the "corrected" random oracle [26] to the message before passing it into the evaluation function of the underlying one-way permutation. The adversary is required to provide the implementation of the inversion function, and the implementation of the hash, separately, to enforce the actual inputs to the implementation of inversion function are $\mathsf{sk}, \tilde{h}_R(m)$, which are generated by a known distribution.

However, we remark that simply viewing $\tilde{h}_R$ as a good random oracle $g(\cdot)$ (trivially applying the replacement lemma [26]) is still problematic. As the subverted $\mathsf{Inv}_{\mathrm{IMPL}}$ could simply use $g(z)$ as the backdoor and output the secret key sk directly when z appears in a signing query (*i.e.*, $\mathsf{Sign}_{\mathrm{IMPL}}(\mathsf{sk}, z) = \mathsf{Inv}_{\mathrm{IMPL}}(\mathsf{sk}, g(z)) = \mathsf{sk}$).

The problem here is that the adversary can query random oracle when generating the implementations and plant the trigger accordingly. To defend against such attack, we have to disable the adversary from making useful random oracle queries during the implementation-generation phase. Observe that if we have some randomness R generated after $\mathsf{Sign}_{\mathrm{IMPL}}$ is provided, and R is involved in the "encoding" of the message before sending to $\mathsf{Inv}_{\mathrm{IMPL}}$, then the above problem could be mitigated. Luckily, the correction function from [26] already involves randomness generated after the time that implementations are provided. What we need to adapt here is to derive a "stronger replacement theorem" that the correction function of [26] is actually "as good as" (in the sense of indifferentiability) a *keyed* hash (where, the key could be public, but sampled after the implementation is provided). See Sect. 4.3 for details.

Finally, it is also tricky to deal with the *verification algorithm*. Suppose the implementation of the verification takes input public key pk and a message-signature pair (m, σ), and outputs 0 or 1 to decide whether the signature is valid. The input-triggered attack again can be applied here in a way that, for some randomly chosen message m^*, $\mathsf{Verify}_{\mathrm{IMPL}}(\cdot, m^*, \cdot)$ always outputs 1. Opening up the verification functionality of the full-domain hash signature, it is actually to check whether evaluating the signature equals to the ("corrected") hash of the message. We propose to do such canonical verification explicitly, that the equality operation (and the "corrected" hash) will be done by the user. The adversary will provide the implementation of the evaluation function. This simple decomposition of the verification functionality changes the task of the adversarial implementation from targeting one bit to predicting a random value, which is the output of the "corrected" hash. We remark here that, as above, the use of the public randomness is also critical to prevent the adversary from making useful random oracle queries during the manufacturing phase of $\mathsf{Verify}_{\mathrm{IMPL}}$.

There still exists a subtler attack, that the attacker might use the trigger signature material σ^* to directly carry the information of $h_R(m^*)$. This has to be resolved by strictly restricting the length of σ^* and doing a length check. As σ^* first needs to carry certain trigger information which is independent of the output of $h_R(m^*)$, this thus burns the information needed for a precise prediction of the value of $h_R(m^*)$.

1.2 Related Works

Kleptography introduced by Young and Yung [27,28] primarily highlighted the possibility of subverting key generation and left open the problem of defending against such subversion. A recent line of work of Russell *et al.* [23,25,26] has initiated a systematic study of cliptography about defending against kleptographic attacks by redesigning the specification and leveraging architectural tools. In particular, they provided a subversion-resistant digital signature, assuming an online watchdog [23].

Also recently, new attacks and defense mechanisms in the kleptographic setting keep appearing. In particular, Bellare *et al.* [5] studied subverted randomized encryption algorithms, building a steganographic channel that leaks secrets bit by bit. Indeed, subliminal channel attacks turn out to be the major obstacle in this area, and have been further explored by Ateniese *et al.* [2], Bellare *et al.* [3,4], Degabriele *et al.* [13], Dodis *et al.* [15], and Liu *et al.* [19]. A common feature of these works [3–5,13] is to adopt *deterministic* algorithms and to assume honest key generation to defend against subliminal channel attacks.

Furthermore, these works do not rely merely on testing. In fact, most require an a priori "decryptability" condition which demands that every message encrypted using the implementation should be decrypted correctly using the specification. A notable exception is the work of Degabriele *et al.* [13]. However, it relies on an online watchdog that possesses access to the actual challenger-adversary communication transcript (including the internal state of the challenger).

Another research line [10,16,21] considered defense mechanisms with a "reverse firewall" that faithfully "re-randomizes" incoming and outgoing communication. On one hand, this model is attractive as it may permit quite general feasibility results. On the other hand, it relies on an independent component which is a source of trusted randomness (which generalized the "trusted warden" [14] used to eliminate subliminal channels in authentication protocols) and "re-randomizable" structure of the underlying algorithms.

Recently, Fischlin and Mazaheri [17] proposed a new defense mechanism called "self-guarding", which assumes that a genuine version of the cryptographic implementations is available before they get substituted. The self-guarding primitive then leverages information gathered using that genuine implementation at the initial phase to re-randomize potentially malicious inputs like the reverse firewall approach (assuming trusted basic operations like exclusive-or or group operation). They constructed several self-guarding primitives including digital signature schemes. Besides the trusted "setup", their signature construction comes at a price that verification/signing key size and signature size all inflate by a factor of $O(\lambda)$ where λ is the security parameter.

Finally, also motivated by the doubt on the implementation, cryptographers (*e.g.*, [18,29]) studied combiners of cryptographic primitives such that as long there exists one component primitive is secure, even if it is not known which one is that, the combined primitive remains secure.

Organization. In Sect. 2, we define the security for subversion-resistant digital signature. In Sect. 3, we give our first construction – a simple and generic scheme in the partial-subversion model; in Sect. 4, we give our second construction – an FDH-based signature scheme in the complete-subversion model. Both constructions use only an offline watchdog. Finally, the crooked indifferentiability model can be found at Appendix A.

2   Definition of Subversion-Resistant Signatures

First, we recall the definition of subversion-resistant signatures [23]. Its goal is fairly simple: the security of the digital signature scheme – unforgeability – should be preserved even one uses the malicious implementations supplied by the adversary, as long as the adversarial implementation is not detected. The detection is done by a trusted entity called watchdog who has the specification of the algorithms and it will interrogate (via oracle accesses of) the implementation to see whether it is consistent with the specification. The subversion-resistant signature game is defined as the classical unforgeability game, except that the challenger will use the *implementations supplied by the adversary* instead of the specification of the algorithms. In particular, the challenger runs the key generation algorithm $\mathsf{KG}_{\mathrm{IMPL}}$ to generate the challenged signing key and verification key, uses the signing functionality $\mathsf{Sign}_{\mathrm{IMPL}}$ to answer signing queries and use the implementation of verification functionality $\mathsf{Verify}_{\mathrm{IMPL}}$ to verify the final forgery that the adversary made. Definition 1 formalizes the high-level description above. It can be viewed as a special case of the cliptographic game [23, Definition 2] under the context of digital signature schemes.

Definition 1. *A specification $\Pi_{\mathrm{SPEC}} = (\mathsf{KG}_{\mathrm{SPEC}}, \mathsf{Sign}_{\mathrm{SPEC}}, \mathsf{Verify}_{\mathrm{SPEC}})$ for a digital signature scheme Π is* **subversion-resistant** *in the offline-watchdog model, if there exists a probabilistic polynomial-time (PPT) watchdog $\mathcal{W}$, s.t., for any PPT adversary $\mathcal{A}$ playing the security game (Fig. 1) with the challenger $\mathcal{C}$, either the* advantage *of the adversary $\mathcal{A}$ in the security game $\mathbf{Adv}_{\mathcal{A}}(1^\lambda) = \Pr[b_{\mathcal{C}} = 1]$ is negligible, or the* detection probability $\mathbf{Det}_{\mathcal{W},\mathcal{A}}(1^\lambda)$ *of the watchdog $\mathcal{W}$ with respect to $\mathcal{A}$ is non-negligible. Here, $\mathbf{Det}_{\mathcal{W},\mathcal{A}}(1^\lambda)$ is defined by*

$$\left| \Pr[\mathcal{W}^{\mathsf{KG}_{\mathrm{IMPL}},\mathsf{Sign}_{\mathrm{IMPL}},\mathsf{Verify}_{\mathrm{IMPL}}}(1^\lambda) = 1] - \Pr[\mathcal{W}^{\mathsf{KG}_{\mathrm{SPEC}},\mathsf{Sign}_{\mathrm{SPEC}},\mathsf{Verify}_{\mathrm{SPEC}}}(1^\lambda) = 1] \right|.$$

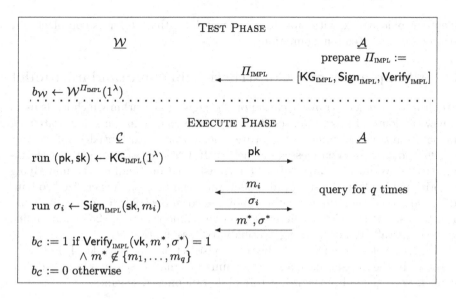

Fig. 1. Subversion-resistant signature game in the offline-watchdog model

As discussed earlier in Sect. 1, depending on the watchdog power, there could be different variants of the above model. The most realistic watchdog only performs one-time testing, which is called an offline watchdog. In practice, an offline watchdog can be some industrial labs or security experts. We can also consider a more stringent *online* watchdog that additionally checks all communication transcripts between the challenger and the adversary. The online-watchdog model has been explicitly considered under the context of digital signatures [23]. Clearly, an online watchdog is much powerful and makes the design of subversion-resistant scheme easier, but it is also more costly to realize an online watchdog. An online watchdog has to piggyback on the implementation and actively monitor all communications of an implementation.

Unfortunately, with only an offline watchdog, it is impossible to achieve unforgeability in the kleptographic setting [2], even if only the Sign algorithm is subverted. To see, recall the input-triggered attack mentioned above: the subverted signing algorithm $\mathsf{Sign}_{\mathrm{IMPL}}$ simply outputs the secret key when signing on a hard-coded trigger message m which is selected uniformly by the adversary. It is obvious that the adversary can make one single signing query to totally break the unforgeability. Previous work [23] got around this by introducing an online watchdog. Another work [2] introduced a "verifiability" assumption – any signature generated by the malicious signing implementation should be verified by the genuine Verify algorithm. This verifiability assumption can only be ensured with an online watchdog. This impossibility holds when the implementation is used as a black box, without doing any post-processing. We will show below that if the user can do some basic operation, *e.g.*, equality check and "$\oplus$", then it is possible to construct a digital signature scheme secure against the powerful kleptographic attack, with only an offline watchdog that performs non-black-box testing (*i.e.*, trusted amalgamation).

3   A Simple Generic Construction in the Standard Model

We propose a generic transformation on the signing algorithm which leads us to a new randomized subversion-resistant signature scheme in the offline-watchdog model from any deterministic signature scheme that is existentially unforgeable against adaptive chosen-message attack (EUF-CMA, *cf.*, Definition 8) (assuming trusted verification and "$\oplus$"). Our transformation (modulo the underlying algorithms) holds in the standard model[3], and can be easily generalized to handle randomized signatures as well. As discussed in Sect. 2, previous subversion-resistant signature schemes either rely on an online watchdog [23], or an online reverse firewall [10], or a strong "verifiability" assumption [2].

Figure 2 below formally describes our construction. For the sake of simplicity, we describe the transformation for deterministic signature schemes first, and then show how to generalize the result to handle randomized schemes.

Key Generation. We handle the key generation by adopting the recently proposed double-splitting technique [25, Theorem 3.5], which we recall in Appendix B. This guarantees that the implementation of a carefully designed specification of key generation can be used as good as the specification, as long as the randomness generation algorithm is executed independently. We refer to [25] for details. Our result can be lifted to allow malicious key generation by directly applying the existing technique [25].

Sign. We augment the specification of the signing algorithm $\mathsf{dSign}_{\mathrm{SPEC}}$ with a random tag generator $\mathsf{RG}_{\mathrm{SPEC}}$ and a random message generator $\mathsf{MG}_{\mathrm{SPEC}}$, *i.e.*, $\mathsf{Sign}_{\mathrm{SPEC}} = (\mathsf{RG}_{\mathrm{SPEC}}, \mathsf{MG}_{\mathrm{SPEC}}, \mathsf{dSign}_{\mathrm{SPEC}})$. $\mathsf{RG}_{\mathrm{SPEC}}$ and $\mathsf{MG}_{\mathrm{SPEC}}$ are merely for generating uniformly random tags and messages of a certain length. Therefore, they can also be handled[4] by the double-splitting technique [25, Theorem 3.4], similar to the key generation algorithm. To sign a message m, the user first runs $\mathsf{MG}_{\mathrm{IMPL}}$ (the implementation) to sample a random message u, and compute a message $m' = u \oplus m$. The user also runs $\mathsf{RG}_{\mathrm{IMPL}}$ to generate a random tag r from some super-polynomial-size domain. The user will call $\mathsf{dSign}_{\mathrm{IMPL}}$ twice to sign two distinct messages $m_1 = (r||u||\text{"1"})$ and $m_2 = (r||m'||\text{"2"}) = (r||u \oplus m||\text{"2"})$, where "1" and "2" are two special symbols. The ultimate output of the signing algorithm is $\sigma = (r, u, \sigma_1, \sigma_2)$ where σ_1, σ_2 are the corresponding output of the two invocations of $\mathsf{dSign}_{\mathrm{IMPL}}$.

Verify. Verification works straightforwardly: parse σ as $(r, u, \sigma_1, \sigma_2)$, compute $m' = u \oplus m$, compose m_1 and m_2 (using trusted "$\oplus$"), and verify σ_1 and σ_2.

---

[3] In the full version [24] of [25], the authors discussed how to achieve subversion-resistant randomness generation in the standard model, at the cost of efficiency. See Appendix B and [24] for details.

[4] $\mathsf{RG}_{\mathrm{SPEC}}$ and $\mathsf{MG}_{\mathrm{SPEC}}$ will be split into three pieces exactly in Fig. 14.

Given an EUF-CMA-secure deterministic signature $SS'_{\text{SPEC}} := (\text{KGen}'_{\text{SPEC}}, \text{dSign}'_{\text{SPEC}},$ $\text{Verify}'_{\text{SPEC}})$, and assuming trusted "$\oplus$", our subversion-resistant signature scheme $SS_{\text{SPEC}} := (\text{KGen}_{\text{SPEC}}, \text{Sign}_{\text{SPEC}}, \text{Verify}_{\text{SPEC}})$ is defined below:

- Key generation: $(\text{pk}, \text{sk}) \leftarrow \text{KGen}_{\text{SPEC}}(\lambda)$, where $\text{KGen}_{\text{SPEC}}(\lambda)$ is the stego-free version of $\text{KGen}'_{\text{SPEC}}$ in the trusted-amalgamation model (see Theorem 5 [25, Theorem 3.5] in Appendix B).
- Sign: $\sigma \leftarrow \text{Sign}_{\text{IMPL}}(\text{pk}, \text{sk}, m)$, where $\text{Sign}_{\text{SPEC}}(\text{pk}, \text{sk}, m)$ is given by:
  sample uniformly random string and message $r \leftarrow \text{RG}_{\text{SPEC}}(1^\lambda)$, $u \leftarrow \text{MG}_{\text{SPEC}}(1^\lambda)$, where RG_{SPEC} and MG_{SPEC} are stego-free randomness generation algorithms (see Theorem 4 [25, Theorem 3.4] in Appendix B);
  compute $\sigma_1 \leftarrow \text{dSign}'_{\text{SPEC}}(\text{sk}, (r||u||\text{"1"}))$ and $\sigma_2 \leftarrow \text{dSign}'_{\text{SPEC}}(\text{sk}, (r||u \oplus m||\text{"2"}))$;
  output $\sigma = (r, u, \sigma_1, \sigma_2)$.
- Verification: $b \leftarrow \text{Verify}_{\text{SPEC}}(\text{pk}, m, \sigma)$, where $\text{Verify}_{\text{SPEC}}$ is given by:
  parse the input σ as $(r, u, \sigma_1, \sigma_2)$;
  run $\text{Verify}'_{\text{SPEC}}(\text{pk}, (r||u||\text{"1"}), \sigma_1)$ and $\text{Verify}'_{\text{SPEC}}(\text{pk}, (r||u \oplus m||\text{"2"}), \sigma_2)$;
  return 1 if and only if both verifications succeed.

Fig. 2. Subversion-resistant signature scheme SS_{SPEC} in the offline-watchdog model

Before detailing the security analysis, we briefly explain how our design ensures security. First, KG_{SPEC} is subversion resistant because we are directly applying the result in [25] (also see Theorem 5). Second, the $\text{Sign}_{\text{SPEC}}$ algorithm is subversion resistant because by design the input to $\text{dSign}'_{\text{SPEC}}$ comes from a public (uniform) distribution. A simple watchdog can further guarantee that $\text{dSign}_{\text{IMPL}}$ is consistent with the specification when the output is sampled from $\mathcal{SK} \times \mathcal{R} \times \mathcal{M} \times \{\text{"1"}, \text{"2"}\}$, where $\mathcal{SK}$ denotes the space of signing keys, $\mathcal{R}$ denotes the super-polynomial-size tag space, and $\mathcal{M}$ denotes the message space. Third, the special symbols ("1" and "2") and the random tag r ensure EUF-CMA-security as follows: (1) the two special symbols separate the input domain so that the output of the first invocation of $\text{dSign}'_{\text{SPEC}}$ (with "1" appended) cannot be the output of the second invocation (with "2" appended) for a forgery of $\text{Sign}_{\text{SPEC}}$, and vice versa; (2) the random tag r drawn from a super-polynomial-size domain makes sure that the signature $\sigma = (\sigma_1, \sigma_2)$ for some message m is one-use only: the adversary cannot mix-and-match different signatures to create new forgeries.

Theorem 1. *For any* EUF-CMA-*secure deterministic digital signature scheme* SS'_{SPEC}, *the specification* SS_{SPEC} *described in Fig. 2 is subversion resistant in the trusted-amalgamation model, assuming a trusted "$\oplus$" operation and trusted the verification algorithm, and* RG_{SPEC} *outputs uniformly random tag from some super-polynomial-size domain.*

Proof. The watchdog for SS_{SPEC} is a combination of the watchdogs of the underlying components, including watchdogs for key generation (KG_{SPEC}), random tag generation (RG_{SPEC}), random message generation (MG_{SPEC}). There is also a watchdog that makes sure $\text{dSign}_{\text{IMPL}}$ is consistent with the specification on inputs

challenger to obtain u_i generated either by $\mathsf{MG}_{\mathrm{IMPL}}$ or by $\mathsf{MG}_{\mathrm{SPEC}}$, and uses u_i to compute appropriate responses for $\mathcal{A}$ using implementations provided by $\mathcal{A}$. Finally, $\mathcal{B}$ outputs whatever $\mathcal{A}$ outputs. It is easy to see that the simulation is perfect, and the advantage of $\mathcal{B}$ is the same as the advantage of $\mathcal{A}$. The second inequality follows the same argument. $\qquad\square$

Game-4. G_4 is the same as G_3 except $\mathsf{dSign}'_{\mathrm{IMPL}}$ is replaced by $\mathsf{dSign}'_{\mathrm{SPEC}}$. Note that in G_4, all the implementations have been replaced by their genuine specifications.

Lemma 3. $|\mathbf{Adv}_{\mathcal{A}}^{G_4} - \mathbf{Adv}_{\mathcal{A}}^{G_3}| \leq \mathsf{negl}(\lambda)$.

Proof. This again follows from Theorem 5 using a similar argument as in Lemma 1. Note that the inputs to dSign' are drawn from public distributions (either $\mathcal{SK} \times \mathcal{R} \times \mathcal{M} \times \{\text{"1"}\}$ or $\mathcal{SK} \times \mathcal{R} \times \mathcal{M} \times \{\text{"2"}\}$). $\qquad\square$

Finally, we need to show that $\mathbf{Adv}_{\mathcal{A}}^{G_4}$ is indeed negligible, which is equivalent to showing that $\mathcal{SS}_{\mathrm{SPEC}}$ is indeed an EUF-CMA-secure signature scheme. To this end, we design a simple reduction algorithm reducing the EUF-CMA-security of $\mathsf{Sign}_{\mathrm{SPEC}}$ to that of $\mathsf{dSign}'_{\mathrm{SPEC}}$. Suppose there is an adversary $\mathcal{A}$ that breaks EUF-CMA-security of $\mathsf{Sign}_{\mathrm{SPEC}}$, we design an adversary $\mathcal{B}$ that breaks $\mathsf{dSign}'_{\mathrm{SPEC}}$. For any signing query m, $\mathcal{B}$ randomly chooses (r, u), and submits signing queries $(r||u||\text{"1"})$ and $(r||u \oplus m||\text{"2"})$ to the oracle $\mathcal{O}^{\mathsf{dSign}'_{\mathrm{SPEC}}}(\cdot)$. $\mathcal{B}$ locally maintains a list of records in the form $(r, u, m, \sigma_1, \sigma_2)$ where σ_1, σ_2 are the responses from $\mathcal{O}^{\mathsf{dSign}'_{\mathrm{SPEC}}}(\cdot)$, and forwards $\sigma = (r, u, \sigma_1, \sigma_2)$ to $\mathcal{A}$. Eventually $\mathcal{A}$ outputs a forgery (σ^*, m^*), where $\sigma^* = (r^*, u^*, \sigma_1^*, \sigma_2^*)$, with non-negligible probability.

To see how $\mathcal{B}$ can extract a valid forgery for $\mathsf{dSign}'_{\mathrm{SPEC}}$ from $\mathcal{A}$'s forgery (σ^*, m^*), notice that by (σ^*, m^*) being a valid forgery for $\mathsf{Sign}_{\mathrm{SPEC}}$, it means that both $(\sigma_1^*, (r^*||u^*||\text{"1"}))$ and $(\sigma_2^*, (r^*||u^* \oplus m^*||\text{"2"}))$ are valid message-signature pairs for $\mathsf{dSign}'_{\mathrm{SPEC}}$, and that $\mathcal{A}$ has never queried the signing oracle for m^*. The latter indicates that $\mathcal{B}$'s local list does not contain any entry in the form $(\cdot, \cdot, m^*, \cdot, \cdot)$. We discuss several cases:

1. Tag r^* does not appear in any entries of $\mathcal{B}$'s record: Both $(\sigma_1^*, (r^*||u^*||\text{"1"}))$ and $(\sigma_2^*, (r^*||u^* \oplus m^*||\text{"2"}))$ are valid forgeries for $\mathsf{dSign}'_{\mathrm{SPEC}}$;
2. Tag r^* exists in some records in the form $(r^*, u, \cdot, \cdot, \cdot)$: By our assumption that the tags are supposed to be drawn from a super-polynomial-size space, with overwhelming probability all the tags in $\mathcal{B}$'s record are unique. Without loss of generality, assume that this unique record is $(r^*, u, m, \sigma_1, \sigma_2)$. That means $(r^*||u||\text{"1"})$ and $(r^*||u \oplus m||\text{"2"})$ are the only queries sent to $\mathcal{O}^{\mathsf{dSign}'_{\mathrm{SPEC}}}(\cdot)$ which begin with tag r^*. If $u^* \neq u$, then $(\sigma_1^*, (r^*||u^*||\text{"1"}))$ must be a valid forgery for $\mathsf{dSign}'_{\mathrm{SPEC}}$;
3. r^* and u^* appear in a unique entry of the form $(r^*, u^*, m, \sigma_1, \sigma_2)$: Using the same argument above, $(r^*||u^*||\text{"1"})$ and $(r^*||u^* \oplus m||\text{"2"})$ are the only queries sent to $\mathcal{O}^{\mathsf{dSign}'_{\mathrm{SPEC}}}(\cdot)$ which begin with tag r^*. It must hold that $m^* \neq m$. Otherwise, $\mathcal{A}$ must have asked for a signature for m^* from $\mathcal{B}$. Given that $m^* \neq m$, $(\sigma_2^*, (r^*||u^* \oplus m^*||\text{"2"}))$ must be a valid forgery for $\mathsf{dSign}'_{\mathrm{SPEC}}$.

By our assumption that $\mathsf{dSign}'_{\text{SPEC}}$ is EUF-CMA-secure, $\mathbf{Adv}_{\mathcal{A}}^{G_4}$ is negligible. Putting all the lemmas above together, we complete our proof. □

It is straightforward to generalize Theorem 1 to handle randomized signatures. Basically, the randomized signing algorithm $\mathsf{rSign}_{\text{SPEC}}(\mathsf{sk}, m)$ needs to be split into two components $\mathsf{RG}'_{\text{SPEC}}(1^\lambda)$ and $\mathsf{dSign}_{\text{SPEC}}(r; (\mathsf{sk}, m))$. $\mathsf{RG}'_{\text{SPEC}}$ generates uniform randomness needed by $\mathsf{rSign}_{\text{SPEC}}$, and $\mathsf{dSign}_{\text{SPEC}}$ is a deterministic algorithm, so that for all sk, m, it holds that $\mathsf{rSign}_{\text{SPEC}}(\mathsf{sk}, m) = \mathsf{dSign}_{\text{SPEC}}(\mathsf{RG}'_{\text{SPEC}}(1^\lambda); (\mathsf{sk}, m))$. Both $\mathsf{RG}'_{\text{SPEC}}$ and $\mathsf{dSign}_{\text{SPEC}}$ can be made subversion-resistant easily. The security proof above only needs to be augmented with an additional hybrid game that replaces $\mathsf{RG}'_{\text{IMPL}}$ with $\mathsf{RG}'_{\text{SPEC}}$.

Corollary 1. *For any* EUF-CMA-*secure (randomized) digital signature scheme* $\mathcal{SS}'_{\text{SPEC}}$, *the specification* $\mathcal{SS}_{\text{SPEC}}$ *described above is subversion-resistant in the trusted-amalgamation model, assuming a trusted "$\oplus$" operation and trusted verification algorithm, and* $\mathsf{RG}_{\text{SPEC}}$ *outputs uniformly random tag from some super-polynomial-size domain.*

4 FDH-Based Signatures Under Complete Subversion

Now we describe our second construction of signature scheme which only requires an offline watchdog when all cryptographic algorithms ($\mathsf{KG}, \mathsf{Sign}, \mathsf{Verify}$) and the hash functions are subjected to subversion. Our scheme follows the full-domain hash [7,11] paradigm, one of the most classical applications of random oracles.

4.1 High-Level Ideas

In an FDH-based signature scheme, the signing algorithm first hashes the message and then inverts the hashed value using a trapdoor one-way permutation. Suppose the adversary can subvert the implementation of each algorithm: $\mathsf{KG}_{\text{IMPL}}, \mathsf{Sign}_{\text{IMPL}}, \mathsf{Verify}_{\text{IMPL}}$ and also the implementation of the hash h_{IMPL}. Several natural questions arise. Let us examine the algorithms one by one.

As discussed in the introduction, we will handle those algorithms one by one. Here we elaborate a bit more. The intuition for defending against the trigger is that the Sign algorithm cannot be fed with a random message. Without the trusted re-randomization, our idea is to hash the message. While hashing alone does not resolve the problem as the trigger can be trivially propagated through the hash. One simple observation is to hash the message together with some random element that is not known to the attacker, *e.g.*, public-key material. Now, this naturally leads us to consider hash subversion.

Fortunately, Russell *et al.* [26] provided a simple construction that can correct a subverted random oracle, such that the resulting function will be as good as an ideal random function. To apply their theorems [26], we need to ensure (i) the subversion disagrees with its specification only at a negligible fraction; (ii) there is randomness that can be generated and published after the malicious implementations are supplied; (iii) interpret the "replacement" lemma to be suitable for our application. Requirement (i) is easy and repeatedly used in the cliptography literature [23,25]. As the hash function is a deterministic function, the offline watchdog can simply evaluate the implementation and compare with the output of the specification. For (ii), observe that the implementation of key generation $\mathsf{KG}_{\mathrm{IMPL}}$ will produce a public key, which should be unpredictable to the adversary (otherwise, the watchdog can keep sampling to find a collision to differentiate $\mathsf{KG}_{\mathrm{IMPL}}$ from $\mathsf{KG}_{\mathrm{SPEC}}$). It follows that if $\mathsf{KG}_{\mathrm{IMPL}}$ can be treated as honestly generated (see above), we can extend the key generation to also output some randomness R which will be part of the public key. Requirement (iii) is a bit subtler. Simply replacing the corrected hash with a trusted random oracle is not enough. See the next point of subverting $\mathsf{Sign}_{\mathrm{IMPL}}$ and Sect. 4.3 below.

The traditional implementation of the verification takes input public key pk and a message-signature pair (m, σ), and outputs 0 or 1 to decide whether the signature is valid. The input-triggered attack can be applied here easily. $\mathsf{Verify}_{\mathrm{IMPL}}(\cdot, m^*, \cdot)$ can just always outputs 1 for some randomly chosen message m^* (or a special signature element σ^*). In the full-domain hash, opening up the verification functionality, it is actually to check whether evaluating the signature is equal to the ("corrected") hash of the message. We first propose to do such a canonical verification explicitly, that the equality operation will be done by the user. The adversary will provide the implementation of the evaluation function of the one-way permutation. This simple decomposition of the verification functionality changes the task of the adversarial implementation from targeting one bit to predicting a random value, which is the output of the "corrected" hash. We remark here that, same as above, the use of the public randomness is also important for preventing the adversary from making useful random oracle queries during the manufacturing phase of $\mathsf{Verify}_{\mathrm{IMPL}}$.

There still exists a subtler attack, that the attacker might use the trigger signature material σ^* to directly carry the information of $h_R(m^*)$. Such kind of attack looks like the "big brother" $\mathcal{A}$ is communicating directly to the "little brother" – the subverted implementation for action items. This has to be resolved by strictly restricting the length of σ^* and doing a length check. We note that in the setting of FDH, since we use trapdoor one-way *permutation*, thus the length is tight, and the simple length checking already works. See the proof of Lemma 7.

4.2 Our Subversion-Resistant FDH-Based Signature Scheme in the Offline-Watchdog Model

Given a trapdoor one-way permutation, with specification denoted by $\mathcal{F}_{\mathrm{SPEC}} := (\mathsf{KG}^{\mathcal{F}}_{\mathrm{SPEC}}, \mathsf{Eval}^{\mathcal{F}}_{\mathrm{SPEC}}, \mathsf{Inv}^{\mathcal{F}}_{\mathrm{SPEC}})$, and a public hash function (or a family of hash functions for consistency) with specification $\left\{ h_i : \{0,1\}^* \to \{0,1\}^n \right\}_{i=0,\ldots,\ell}$, where we assume the message space is $\mathcal{M} = \{0,1\}^n$; we construct a subversion-resistant signature scheme $\mathcal{SS}$ with specification $\mathcal{SS}_{\mathrm{SPEC}} := (\mathsf{KG}^{\mathcal{SS}}_{\mathrm{SPEC}}, \mathsf{Sign}^{\mathcal{SS}}_{\mathrm{SPEC}}, \mathsf{Verify}^{\mathcal{SS}}_{\mathrm{SPEC}})$.

Note that the family of $\{h_i\}_{i=1}^{\ell}$ may be simply derived from one hash using different indices, *e.g.*, $\forall x, h_i(x) = h(i, x)$, where $i = 1, \ldots, \ell = 3n + 1$.

- Key generation: $(\mathsf{pk}, \mathsf{sk}) \leftarrow \mathsf{KG}^{\mathcal{SS}}_{\mathrm{SPEC}}(\lambda)$, where $\mathsf{KG}^{\mathcal{SS}}_{\mathrm{SPEC}}$[5] is given by:
  The algorithm generates $(f, td_f) \leftarrow \mathsf{KG}^{\mathcal{F}}_{\mathrm{SPEC}}(\lambda)$, and $R := r_1, \ldots, r_\ell \leftarrow \{0,1\}^{n\ell}$.

  The algorithm sets $\mathsf{pk} := (f, R)$ and $\mathsf{sk} := td_f$;

- Sign: $\sigma \leftarrow \mathsf{Sign}^{\mathcal{SS}}_{\mathrm{SPEC}}(\mathsf{pk}, \mathsf{sk}, m)$, where $\mathsf{Sign}^{\mathcal{SS}}_{\mathrm{SPEC}} := (\{h_i\}^\ell_{i=0}, \mathsf{Inv}_{\mathrm{SPEC}})$ is given by:

  Upon receiving message m, the algorithm first computes $\tilde{m} = h_R(m) = h_0\left(\bigoplus^\ell_{i=1} h_i(m \oplus r_i)\right)$, and then generate the signature as $\sigma = \mathsf{Inv}^{\mathcal{F}}_{\mathrm{SPEC}}(\mathsf{sk}, \tilde{m})$.

  $\mathsf{Sign}_{\mathrm{SPEC}} := (\{h_i\}^\ell_{i=1}, \mathsf{Inv}_{\mathrm{SPEC}})$ means, explicitly, the adversary should follow this decomposition, and provide implementations of $\{\tilde{h}_i\}^\ell_{i=1}$ and $\mathsf{Inv}_{\mathrm{IMPL}}$ individually.

- Verification: $b \leftarrow \mathsf{Verify}^{\mathcal{SS}}_{\mathrm{SPEC}}(\mathsf{pk}, m, \sigma)$, where $\mathsf{Verify}^{\mathcal{SS}}_{\mathrm{SPEC}} := (\{h_i\}^\ell_{i=1}, \mathsf{Eval}_{\mathrm{SPEC}})$ is given by:

  Upon receiving message-signature pair (m, σ) and a public key pk, the algorithm only proceeds if the length of σ^* is correct (equals to the hash output length n), it then computes $\tilde{m} = h_R(m) = h_0\left(\bigoplus^\ell_{i=1} h_i(m \oplus r_i)\right)$, if $\mathsf{Eval}^{\mathcal{SS}}_{\mathrm{SPEC}}(\mathsf{pk}, \sigma) = \tilde{m}$, set $b := 1$; otherwise, set $b := 0$. Here, $\mathsf{pk} = (f, R)$.

  Likewise, $\mathsf{Verify}^{\mathcal{SS}}_{\mathrm{SPEC}} := (\{h_i\}^\ell_{i=1}, \mathsf{Eval}_{\mathrm{SPEC}})$ means that for Verify the adversary should supply the implementation of $\mathsf{Eval}_{\mathrm{IMPL}}$ (while $\{h_i\}$ can be reused).

4.3   How to Use the Replacement Theorem [26]

To prepare us for the security proof, we first strengthen the previous result about correcting random oracle. Let us recall the replacement theorem [26] for establishing that a corrected random oracle is as good as a truly random function when used in larger systems.

General Replacement with Crooked Indifferentiability. Security-preserving replacement has been shown in the indifferentiability framework [20]: if $C^{\mathcal{G}}$ is indifferentiable from $\mathcal{F}$, then $C^{\mathcal{G}}$ can replace $\mathcal{F}$ in any cryptosystem, and the resulting cryptosystem in the $\mathcal{G}$ model is at least as secure as that in the $\mathcal{F}$ model. It has been shown [26] that the replacement property can also hold in the *crooked indifferentiability* framework (see Appendix A.2 and [26] for a detailed definition).

   To model "as secure" (when correcting a subverted object) when used in larger systems (see illustration in Fig. 3 excluding R), consider an ideal primitive $\mathcal{G}$, we can define the $\mathcal{G}$-crooked-environment $\widehat{\mathcal{E}}$ as follows: Initially, the crooked environment $\widehat{\mathcal{E}}$ manufactures and then publishes a subverted implementation

---

[5] We remark here that the $\mathsf{KG}^{\mathcal{SS}}_{\mathrm{SPEC}}$ algorithm will be split into four pieces exactly as [25].

of $\mathcal{G}$, denoted by $\tilde{\mathcal{G}}$. Then $\widehat{\mathcal{E}}$ runs the attacker $\mathcal{A}$, and the cryptosystem $\mathcal{P}$ is developed. In the $\mathcal{G}$ model, cryptosystem $\mathcal{P}$ has oracle accesses to C whereas attacker $\mathcal{A}$ has oracle accesses to $\mathcal{G}$; note that, C has oracle accesses to $\tilde{\mathcal{G}}$, not directly to $\mathcal{G}$. In the $\mathcal{F}$ model, both $\mathcal{P}$ and $\mathcal{A}$ have oracle accesses to $\mathcal{F}$. Finally, the crooked environment $\widehat{\mathcal{E}}$ returns a binary decision output. It was shown [26] that if a construction C is $\mathcal{G}$-crooked indifferentiable with another object $\mathcal{F}$, $C^{\mathcal{G}}$ would be as secure as $\mathcal{F}$ when used in any larger system $\mathcal{P}$.

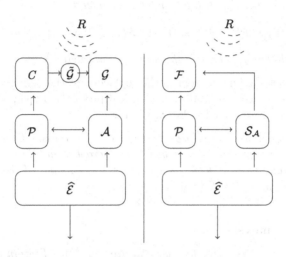

Fig. 3. Environment $\widehat{\mathcal{E}}$ interacts with cryptosystem $\mathcal{P}$ and Attacker $\mathcal{A}$: In the $\mathcal{G}$ model (left), $\mathcal{P}$ has oracle accesses to C whereas $\mathcal{A}$ has oracle accesses to $\mathcal{G}$; the algorithm C has oracle accesses to the subverted $\tilde{\mathcal{G}}$. In the $\mathcal{F}$ model, both $\mathcal{P}$ and $\mathcal{S}_{\mathcal{A}}$ have oracle accesses to $\mathcal{F}$.

*An **Easier-to-Use Interpretation** for Correcting Subverted Random Oracles.* Using the definition and the theorem as is, however, will cause some trouble when applying the result of correcting a subverted random oracle, especially when plugging it to a larger system. We first reflect the public randomness generated after implementation is provided more explicitly in the model. Moreover, we also need to adjust the "ideal world" a little bit so that the targeted ideal object (in particular, a random oracle here) is also utilizing such public randomness, which yields a slightly stronger object of (ideal) *keyed* hash. These two adjustments will be critical for the application to our FDH construction.

For simplicity, we focus only on random oracles here. Consider a random oracle $\mathcal{G}$, we augment the $\mathcal{G}$-crooked-environment $\widehat{\mathcal{E}}$ as follows: Initially, the crooked environment $\widehat{\mathcal{E}}$ deploys the attacker $\mathcal{A}$ to query $\mathcal{G}$ for some preprocessing. It follows immediately $\widehat{\mathcal{E}}$ deploys the crooked implementation $\tilde{\mathcal{G}}$ and the cryptosystem $\mathcal{P}$ (which itself could be malicious or containing subverted components). Some randomness R is then drawn and published, which is utilized by construction C. On the other hand, in the world using random oracle $\mathcal{F}$, originally after R is generated, $\mathcal{F}(\cdot)$ becomes $\mathcal{F}(R, \cdot)$ (with the first half of inputs fixed by a randomly selected R). The interactions among $\mathcal{A}, \mathcal{P}, \mathcal{E}$ and the rest of the definition of "as secure" remain the same. See Fig. 3.

Definition 2. *Consider random oracles $\mathcal{G}$ and $\mathcal{F}$ (both with variable input length). A cryptosystem $\mathcal{P}$ is said to be at least as secure in the augmented $\mathcal{G}$-crooked model with algorithm C as in the $\mathcal{F}$ model, if for any augmented $\mathcal{G}$-crooked-environment $\widehat{\mathcal{E}}$ and any attacker $\mathcal{A}$ in the augmented $\mathcal{G}$-crooked model, there exists an attacker $\mathcal{S}_\mathcal{A}$ in the $\mathcal{F}$ model, such that:*

$$\Pr[\widehat{\mathcal{E}}(\mathcal{P}^{C^{\mathcal{G}}}, \mathcal{A}^{\mathcal{G}}) = 1] - \Pr[\widehat{\mathcal{E}}(\mathcal{P}^{\mathcal{F}}, \mathcal{S}_\mathcal{A}^{\mathcal{F}}) = 1] \le \epsilon.$$

where ϵ is a negligible function of the security parameter λ.

We can prove a similar theorem as the replacement theorem [26] for the augmented definition (with essentially an identical proof technique, see the dashed frames in Fig. 4 and we refer to [26] for details).

Corollary 2. *Let $\mathcal{P}$ be a cryptosystem with oracle accesses to a random oracle $\mathcal{F}$. Let C be an algorithm such that $C^{\mathcal{G}}$ is $\mathcal{G}$-crooked-indifferentiable from $\mathcal{F}$. Then cryptosystem $\mathcal{P}$ is at least as secure in the augmented $\mathcal{G}$-crooked model with algorithm C as in the $\mathcal{F}$ model.*

4.4 Security Analysis

Theorem 2. *If $\mathcal{F}_{\mathrm{SPEC}}$ is a trapdoor permutation, the specification of $\{h_i\}_{i=0,\dots,\ell}$ are random oracles, then the signature scheme $\mathcal{SS}$ with specification $\mathcal{SS}_{\mathrm{SPEC}}$ constructed above is subversion resistant with an offline watchdog, assuming the "$\oplus$" and "$=$" operations are honestly carried out (and execute the pieces independently as [25]).*

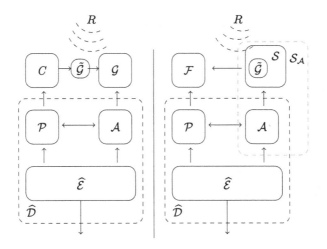

Fig. 4. Construction of attacker $\mathcal{S}_\mathcal{A}$ from attacker $\mathcal{A}$ and simulator $\mathcal{S}$

Proof. First, to simplify the presentation of the analysis in the cliptographic setting, we ignore the checking phase of the offline watchdog in the game transitions, while taking the simple guarantees such as deterministic function will be correct on an overwhelming portion of inputs as the condition. The security can then be seen simply by walking through the sequence of game hopping over games G_i's (closer to the usual case). Let the advantage of adversary $\mathcal{A}$ in game G_i be $\mathbf{Adv}_{\mathcal{A}}^{G_i}$.

Game-0. G_0 is exactly the same security game as defined in Definition 1 (the execute phase with the challenger $\mathcal{C}$ using implementations provided by the adversary $\mathcal{A}$) instantiating with our construction described in Sect. 4.2. See Fig. 5.

Game-1. G_1 is identical to G_0 except that the key generation implementation $\mathsf{KG}_{\mathrm{IMPL}}$ is substituted with its specification $\mathsf{KG}_{\mathrm{SPEC}}$. See Fig. 6.

Lemma 4. $|\mathbf{Adv}_{\mathcal{A}}^{G_0} - \mathbf{Adv}_{\mathcal{A}}^{G_1}| \leq \mathsf{negl}(\lambda)$.

Proof. The proof is identical to the one for Lemma 1. □

Game-2. G_2 is identical to G_1 except that the message encoding function using corrected hash $\tilde{h}_R(\cdot)$ is replaced with a truly random g parameterized by R, *i.e.*, $g(R, \cdot)$. See Fig. 7.

Lemma 5. $|\mathbf{Adv}_{\mathcal{A}}^{G_1} - \mathbf{Adv}_{\mathcal{A}}^{G_2}| \leq \mathsf{negl}(\lambda)$.

Proof. This follows directly from Corollary 2 that the corrected function using subverted random oracle $\tilde{h}_R(\cdot)$ can be replaced with a truly random function g indexed by the randomness R which is generated after.

We can simply view the augmented h-crooked environment in the corollary as the actual adversary here in the game, and the larger cryptosystem $\mathcal{P}$ is simply composed of the signature implementations. □

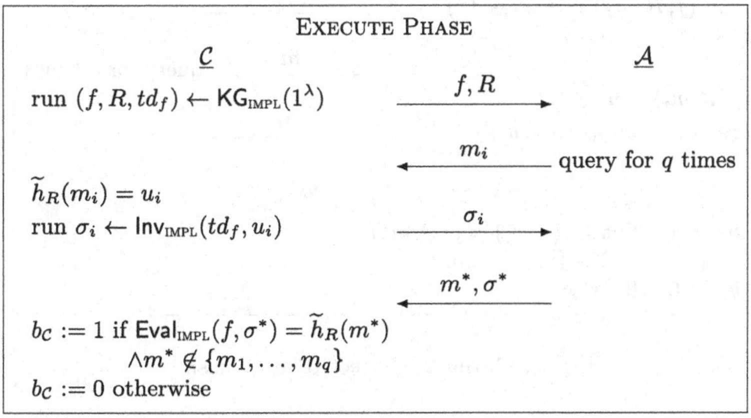

Fig. 5. Game-0: The original cliptographic signature game

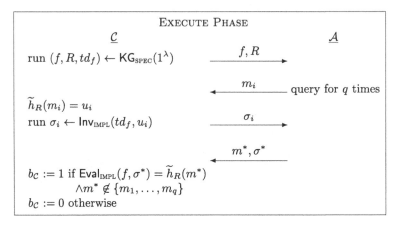

Fig. 6. **Game-1**: Honest key generation

Game-3. G_3 is identical to G_2 except that the implementation of the actual signing function $\mathsf{Inv}_{\mathrm{IMPL}}$ is substituted with its specification $\mathsf{Inv}_{\mathrm{SPEC}}$. See Fig. 8.

Lemma 6. $|\mathbf{Adv}_{\mathcal{A}}^{G_2} - \mathbf{Adv}_{\mathcal{A}}^{G_3}| \leq \mathsf{negl}(\lambda).$

Proof. Now we need to demonstrate that when a keyed hash is used (the key is public but sampled after the implementation of the signing functionality is provided), $\mathsf{Inv}_{\mathrm{SPEC}}$ is actually stego-free in the sense that the adversary cannot distinguish whether she is interacting with $\mathsf{Inv}_{\mathrm{IMPL}}$ or $\mathsf{Inv}_{\mathrm{SPEC}}$, even if she can freely choose potentially triggered inputs.

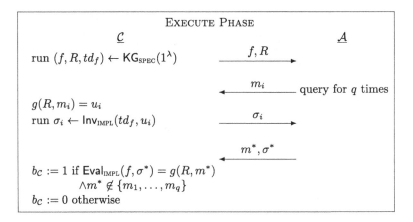

Fig. 7. **Game-2**: Corrected keyed hash

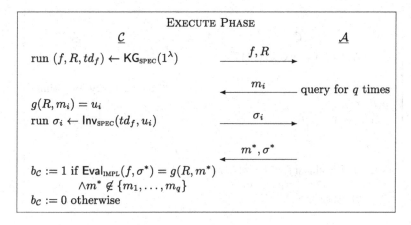

Fig. 8. Game-3: Honest Sign

Let us first look at a simpler challenge game. Consider a random oracle $h : \{0,1\}^* \to \{0,1\}^n$. Suppose an attacker $\mathcal{A}$ makes some q_1 number of queries to h, define a target set $T \subset \{0,1\}^n$ with a polynomially large size q_2, generate uniform randomness R with length λ, and R public. The adversary will try to find an input x such that $h(R,x)$ falls into T. It is not hard to see that $\Pr[h(R,x) \in T] = \frac{q_1 q_2}{2^\lambda}$ which is negligible in λ if the adversary makes one attempt (and remains negligible if $\mathcal{A}$ makes polynomially many attempts).

Now instantiating such statement under our setting: simply using the points that $\mathsf{Inv}_{\mathrm{IMPL}}$ differ from $\mathsf{Inv}_{\mathrm{SPEC}}$ to define such T (the offline watchdog ensures that the "discrepancy set" T has to be exponentially small). Now when the adversary makes a signing query m, it is to find such an input that makes the output of $g(R,m)$ to fall into the target set T. This probability would be negligible. It follows that the output of $\mathsf{Inv}_{\mathrm{IMPL}}$ and $\mathsf{Inv}_{\mathrm{SPEC}}$ when evaluating on $g(R,x)$ will be the same for an overwhelming probability for every x. Thus $\mathsf{Inv}_{\mathrm{IMPL}}$ satisfies the stego-free notion even with an adversarially chosen input x. $\square$

Game-4. G_4 is identical to G_3 except that the implementation of the actual verification function $\mathsf{Eval}_{\mathrm{IMPL}}$ is substituted with its specification $\mathsf{Eval}_{\mathrm{SPEC}}$. Now all the implementations are actually honestly generated, thus G_4 essentially falls back to the classical unforgeability game for FDH signatures. See Fig. 9.

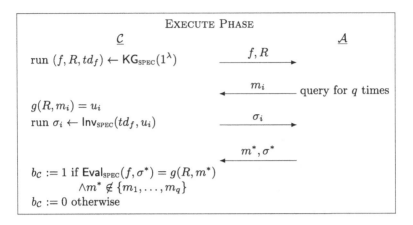

Fig. 9. Game-4: Honest Verify

Lemma 7. $|\mathbf{Adv}_{\mathcal{A}}^{G_3} - \mathbf{Adv}_{\mathcal{A}}^{G_4}| \leq \mathsf{negl}(\lambda)$.

Proof. Now we need to demonstrate that when a keyed hash is used (the key is public but sampled after the implementation of the signing functionality is provided), and a trusted equality test is in place, $\mathsf{Eval}_{\mathrm{IMPL}}$ performs essentially the same as $\mathsf{Eval}_{\mathrm{SPEC}}$ when predicting an output of $g(R, m^*)$.

Suppose $\mathsf{Eval}_{\mathrm{IMPL}}(f, \sigma^*) \neq \mathsf{Eval}_{\mathrm{SPEC}}(f, \sigma^*)$, that means σ^* falls into the set of inputs that $\mathsf{Eval}_{\mathrm{IMPL}}$ and $\mathsf{Eval}_{\mathrm{SPEC}}$ differ. To escape from the watchdog's detection of this inconsistency, those inputs must contain at least $\omega(\lambda)$ bits of entropy about some trigger that $\mathsf{Eval}_{\mathrm{IMPL}}$ can explore to recognize those inputs to deviate from the specification. Otherwise, the watchdog would be able to trivially find such a trigger point. Moreover, that information is independent of $g(R, m^*)$, as R is chosen after $\mathsf{Eval}_{\mathrm{IMPL}}$ was created. On the other hand, since $|\sigma^*| = |g(R, m^*)|$, there are at most $n - \omega(\lambda)$ bits left in σ^* that can contain information about $g(R, m^*)$. While $g(R, m^*)$ is a uniform value in the range of $\mathsf{Eval}_{\mathrm{SPEC}}$, it follows that for any σ^*, $\Pr[\mathsf{Eval}_{\mathrm{IMPL}}(\sigma^*) = g(R, m^*)] = \mathsf{negl}(\lambda)$. □

G_4 is essentially the original FDH security game, thus putting together all those lemmas, we can complete the proof. □

A   The Model: Crooked Indifferentiability

A.1   Preliminary: Indifferentiability

The notion of indifferentiability proposed in the elegant work of Maurer *et al.* [20] has been found very useful for studying the security of hash function and many other primitives. This notion is an extension of the classical notion of indistinguishability, when one or more oracles are publicly available. The indifferentiability notion is originally given in the framework of random systems [20] providing interfaces to other systems. Coron *et al.* [12] demonstrate an equivalent indifferentiability notion but in the framework of Interactive Turing Machines (as in [9]). The indifferentiability formulation in this subsection is essentially taken from Coron *et al.* [12]. In the next subsection, we will introduce our new notion, *crooked indifferentiability*.

Defining Indifferentiability. An ideal primitive is an algorithmic entity which receives inputs from one of the parties and returns its output immediately to the querying party. We now proceed to the definition of indifferentiability [12,20]:

Definition 3 (Indifferentiability [12,20]). *A Turing machine C with oracle accesses to an ideal primitive $\mathcal{G}$ is said to be (t_D, t_S, q, ϵ)-indifferentiable from an ideal primitive $\mathcal{F}$, if there is a simulator S, such that for any distinguisher D, it holds that:*

$$\left| \Pr[D^{C,\mathcal{G}} = 1] - \Pr[D^{\mathcal{F},S} = 1] \right| \le \epsilon.$$

The simulator S has oracle accesses to $\mathcal{F}$ and runs in time at most t_S. The distinguisher D runs in time at most t_D and makes at most q queries. Similarly, $C^{\mathcal{G}}$ is said to be (computationally) indifferentiable from $\mathcal{F}$ if ϵ is a negligible function of the security parameter λ (for polynomially bounded t_D and t_S). See Fig. 10.

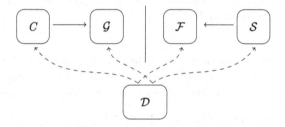

Fig. 10. Indifferentiability: Distinguisher D either interacts with algorithm C and ideal primitive $\mathcal{G}$, or with ideal primitive $\mathcal{F}$ and simulator S. Algorithm C has oracle access to $\mathcal{G}$, while simulator S has oracle access to $\mathcal{F}$.

As illustrated in Fig. 10, the role of the simulator is to simulate the ideal primitive $\mathcal{G}$ so that no distinguisher can tell whether it is interacting with C and $\mathcal{G}$, or with $\mathcal{F}$ and S; in other words, the output of S should look "consistent" with what the distinguisher can obtain from $\mathcal{F}$. Note that the simulator does not see the distinguisher's queries to $\mathcal{F}$; however, it can call $\mathcal{F}$ directly when needed for the simulation.

Replacement. It is shown that [20] if $C^{\mathcal{G}}$ is indifferentiable from $\mathcal{F}$, then $C^{\mathcal{G}}$ can replace $\mathcal{F}$ in any cryptosystem, and the resulting cryptosystem is at least as secure in the $\mathcal{G}$ model as in the $\mathcal{F}$ model.

We use the definition of [20] to specify what it means for a cryptosystem to be at least as secure in the $\mathcal{G}$ model as in the $\mathcal{F}$ model. A cryptosystem is modeled as an Interactive Turing Machine with an interface to an adversary $\mathcal{A}$ and to a public oracle. The cryptosystem is run by an environment $\mathcal{E}$ which provides a binary output and also runs the adversary. In the $\mathcal{G}$ model, cryptosystem $\mathcal{P}$ has oracle access to C whereas attacker $\mathcal{A}$ has oracle access to $\mathcal{G}$. In the $\mathcal{F}$ model, both $\mathcal{P}$ and $\mathcal{A}$ have oracle access to $\mathcal{F}$. The definition is illustrated in Fig. 11.

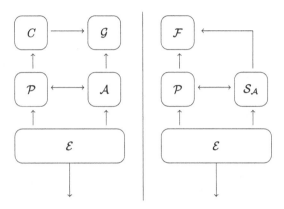

Fig. 11. Environment $\mathcal{E}$ interacts with cryptosystem $\mathcal{P}$ and attacker $\mathcal{A}$: In the $\mathcal{G}$ model (left), $\mathcal{P}$ has oracle access to C whereas $\mathcal{A}$ has oracle access to $\mathcal{G}$. In the $\mathcal{F}$ model, both $\mathcal{P}$ and $\mathcal{S}_\mathcal{A}$ have oracle access to $\mathcal{F}$.

Definition 4. *A cryptosystem is said to be at least as secure in the $\mathcal{G}$ model with algorithm C as in the $\mathcal{F}$ model, if for any environment $\mathcal{E}$ and any attacker $\mathcal{A}$ in the $\mathcal{G}$ model, there exists an attacker $\mathcal{S}_\mathcal{A}$ in the $\mathcal{F}$ model, such that:*

$$\Pr[\mathcal{E}(\mathcal{P}^C, \mathcal{A}^\mathcal{G}) = 1] - \Pr[\mathcal{E}(\mathcal{P}^\mathcal{F}, \mathcal{S}_\mathcal{A}^\mathcal{F}) = 1] \leq \epsilon.$$

where ϵ is a negligible function of the security parameter λ. Similarly, a cryptosystem is said to be computationally at least as secure, etc., if $\mathcal{E}$, $\mathcal{A}$, and $\mathcal{S}_\mathcal{A}$ are polynomial-time in λ.

We have the following security-preserving (replacement) theorem, which says that when an ideal primitive is replaced by an indifferentiable one, the security of the "bigger" cryptosystem remains.

Theorem 3 ([12,20]). *Let $\mathcal{P}$ be a cryptosystem with oracle accesses to an ideal primitive $\mathcal{F}$. Let C be an algorithm such that $C^\mathcal{G}$ is indifferentiable from $\mathcal{F}$. Then cryptosystem $\mathcal{P}$ is at least as secure in the $\mathcal{G}$ model with algorithm C as in the $\mathcal{F}$ model.*

A.2   Crooked Indifferentiability

The ideal primitives that we focus on in this paper are random oracles. A random oracle [6] is an ideal primitive which provides a random output for each new query, and for the identical input queries the same answer will be given. Next, we will formalize a new notion called crooked indifferentiability. Our formalization is for random oracles. We remark that the formalization can be trivially extended for all ideal primitives.

Crooked Indifferentiability for Random Oracles. As mentioned in the Introduction, we are considering to repair a subverted random oracle, such that the corrected construction can be used as good as an unsubverted one. It is thus natural to consider the indifferentiability notion. However, we need to adjust the notion to reflect the subversion and to avoid trivial impossibility. There are two main modifications to the original indifferentiability notion.

1. The deterministic construction will have oracle accesses to the random oracle only via the subverted implementation $\tilde{H}$ but not via the ideal primitive H. This creates lots of difficulty (and even impossibility) for us to develop a suitable construction. For that reason, the construction is allowed to access to trusted but public randomness r.
2. The simulator will also have oracle accesses to the subverted implementation $\tilde{H}$ and also the public randomness r.

The second one is necessary. It is clearly impossible to have an indifferentiability definition with a simulator that has no accesses to $\tilde{H}$, as the distinguisher can simply make query an input such that C will use a value that is modified by $\tilde{H}$ while S has no way to reproduce it. More importantly, we will show below that, the security will still be preserved to replace an ideal random oracle with a construction satisfying our definition (with an augmented simulator). We will prove the security-preserving (*i.e.*, replacement) theorem from [20] and [12] similarly with our adapted notions.

Definition 5 (*H*-crooked indifferentiability). *Consider a distinguisher $\widehat{D}$ and the following multi-phase real execution.*

Initially, the distinguisher $\widehat{D}$ who has oracle accesses to ideal primitive H, publishes a subverted implementation of H, and denotes it by $\tilde{H}$.

Secondly, a uniformly random string r is sampled and published.

Thirdly, a deterministic construction C is developed: the construction C has random string r as input, and has oracle accesses to $\tilde{H}$ (which can be considered as a crooked version of H).

Finally, the distinguisher $\widehat{D}$, after having random string r as input, and oracle accesses to the pair (C, H), returns a decision bit b. Often, we call $\widehat{D}$ the H-crooked-distinguisher.

In addition, consider the corresponding multi-phase ideal execution with the same H-crooked-distinguisher $\widehat{D}$, where ideal primitive $\mathcal{F}$ is provided.

The first two phases are the same (as those in the real execution).

In the third phase, a simulator S will be developed: the simulator has random string r as input, and has oracle accesses to $\tilde{H}$, as well as the ideal primitive $\mathcal{F}$.

In the last phase, the H-crooked-distinguisher $\widehat{D}$, after having random string r as input, and having oracle accesses to an alternative pair $(\mathcal{F}, S)$, returns a decision bit b.

We say that construction C is $(t_{\widehat{\mathcal{D}}}, t_{\mathcal{S}}, q, \epsilon)$-$H$-crooked-indifferentiable from ideal primitive $\mathcal{F}$, if there is a simulator $\mathcal{S}$ so that for any H-crooked-distinguisher $\widehat{\mathcal{D}}$, it satisfies that the real execution and the ideal execution are indistinguishable. Specifically, the following difference should be upper bounded by $\epsilon(\lambda)$:

$$\left| \Pr_{u,r,H}\left[\tilde{H} \leftarrow \widehat{\mathcal{D}} \ : \ \widehat{\mathcal{D}}^{C^{\tilde{H}}(r),H}(\lambda, r) = 1 \right] - \Pr_{u,r,\mathcal{F}}\left[\tilde{H} \leftarrow \widehat{\mathcal{D}} \ : \ \widehat{\mathcal{D}}^{\mathcal{F}, \mathcal{S}^{\tilde{H},\mathcal{F}}(r)}(\lambda, r) = 1 \right] \right|.$$

Here u is the coins of $\widehat{\mathcal{D}}$, $H : \{0,1\}^{\lambda} \rightarrow \{0,1\}^{\lambda}$ and $\mathcal{F} : \{0,1\}^{k} \rightarrow \{0,1\}^{k}$ denote random functions. See Fig. 12 for a detailed illustration of the last phase in both the real and ideal executions.

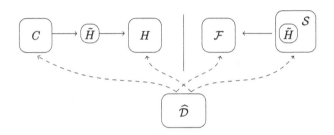

Fig. 12. *H-crooked Indifferentiability: distinguisher $\widehat{\mathcal{D}}$, in the first phase, manufactures and publishes a subverted implementation denoted by $\tilde{H}$, for ideal primitive H; then in the second phase, a random string r is published; after that, in the third phase, algorithm C, and simulator $\mathcal{S}$ are developed; the H-crooked-distinguisher $\widehat{\mathcal{D}}$, in the last phase, either interacting with algorithm C and ideal primitive H, or with ideal primitive $\mathcal{F}$ and simulator $\mathcal{S}$, returns a decision bit. Here, algorithm C has oracle accesses to $\tilde{H}$, while simulator $\mathcal{S}$ has oracle accesses to $\mathcal{F}$ and $\tilde{H}$.*

B   Stego-Free Specifications for Randomness Generation and Randomized Algorithms with Known Input Distribution

We recall the definition of stego-free randomness generation and stego-free randomized algorithms with public input distributions [25], and the general results that yield stego-free specifications for them in the trusted-amalgamation model.

Definition 6 (Stego-free randomness generation [25, Definition 3.1]). *For a randomized algorithm G with specification $\mathsf{G}_{\mathrm{SPEC}}$, we say such specification $\mathsf{G}_{\mathrm{SPEC}}$ is stego-free in the offline-watchdog model, if there exists a PPT watchdog $\mathcal{W}$ so that for any PPT adversary $\mathcal{A}$ playing the game in Fig. 13 with challenger $\mathcal{C}$, at least one of the following conditions hold:*

$$\mathbf{Adv}_{\mathcal{A}} \text{ is negligible or } \mathbf{Det}_{\mathcal{W},\mathcal{A}} \text{ is non-negligible,}$$

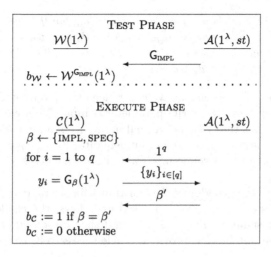

Fig. 13. Stego-freeness game for randomness generation

where $\mathbf{Adv}_{\mathcal{A}}(1^\lambda) = |\Pr[b_\mathcal{C} = 1] - \frac{1}{2}|$ and $\mathbf{Det}_{\mathcal{W},\mathcal{A}}(1^\lambda) = |\Pr[\mathcal{W}^{\mathsf{G}_{\mathrm{IMPL}}}(1^\lambda) = 1] - \Pr[\mathcal{W}^{\mathsf{G}_{\mathrm{SPEC}}}(1^\lambda) = 1]|$.

Theorem 4 ([25, Theorem 3.4]). *Consider randomness generation* RG *with specification* $(\mathsf{RG}^0_{\mathrm{SPEC}}, \mathsf{RG}^1_{\mathrm{SPEC}}, \Phi_{\mathrm{SPEC}})$ *as described below (see Fig. 14):*

- *Given* 1^λ, $\mathsf{RG}^0_{\mathrm{SPEC}}$ *and* $\mathsf{RG}^1_{\mathrm{SPEC}}$ *output uniformly random strings of length* λ;
- Φ_{SPEC} *is a hash function so that* $\Phi_{\mathrm{SPEC}}(w)$ *has length* $\lceil |w|/2 \rceil$;
- *the specification for* $\mathsf{RG}(1^\lambda)$ *is the trusted composition:*
  $\Phi_{\mathrm{SPEC}}(\mathsf{RG}^0_{\mathrm{SPEC}}(1^\lambda), \mathsf{RG}^1_{\mathrm{SPEC}}(1^\lambda))$.

Then $\mathsf{RG}_{\mathrm{SPEC}}$ *is stego-free if* Φ_{SPEC} *is modeled as a random oracle.*

Note that the above theorem only asserts how to purify randomness generation algorithm G in the random oracle model by splitting G into a constant number of components. It is possible to extend the result to the standard model if we are willing to have polynomially many segments. Such result is demonstrated in the full version [24] of [25]. We quote their result as follows:

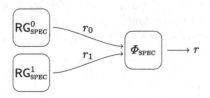

Fig. 14. Subversion-resistant specification for randomness generation

Proposition 1 ([24]). *There exists a specification for the randomness generation that outputs n bits that is stego-free with the trusted amalgamation and $O(n^\epsilon / \log n)$ segments for any constant ϵ. Similar results hold for randomized algorithms with public input distribution.*

The definition and theorems above cover elementary randomness generation algorithms that only takes a security parameter as input. They can be generalized to consider algorithms that take additional inputs from a large domain in which the adversary specifies a randomized input generator IG, which implicitly defines $\mathsf{G}(1^\lambda, \mathsf{IG}(1^\lambda))$. This class of randomized algorithm includes key generation and bit encryption *etc.*

Formally, let G be a randomized algorithm using λ random bits for inputs of length n. The stego-free game is revised as follows: the challenges $\{y_i\}$ are generated by first sampling $m_i \leftarrow \mathsf{IG}(1^\lambda)$, and then obtaining $y_i \leftarrow \mathsf{G}_\beta(1^\lambda, m_i)$ by calling G_β. The watchdog is provided oracle access to IG to test $\mathsf{G}_{\mathrm{IMPL}}$.

Definition 7 (Stego-free randomized algorithm [25, Definition 3.2]). *For a randomized algorithm G, we say the specification $\mathsf{G}_{\mathrm{SPEC}}$ is stego-free in the offline-watchdog model, if there exists an offline PPT watchdog $\mathcal{W}$, for any PPT adversary $\mathcal{A}$ playing the following game in Fig. 15 with challenger $\mathcal{C}$, such that either*

$$\mathbf{Adv}_{\mathcal{A}} \text{ is negligible, or, } \mathbf{Det}_{\mathcal{W},\mathcal{A}} \text{ is non-negligible,}$$

where $\mathbf{Adv}_{\mathcal{A}}(1^\lambda) = |\Pr[b_\mathcal{C} = 1] - \frac{1}{2}|$ and $\mathbf{Det}_{\mathcal{W},\mathcal{A}}(1^\lambda) = |\Pr[\mathcal{W}^{\mathsf{G}_{\mathrm{IMPL}}}(1^\lambda) = 1] - \Pr[\mathcal{W}^{\mathsf{G}_{\mathrm{SPEC}}}(1^\lambda) = 1]|$.

Russell *et al.* [25] established a general transformation yielding a stego-free specification for randomized algorithms with a public input distribution. Consider a randomized algorithm G which uses λ random bits for inputs of length n. Let $(\mathsf{dG}, \mathsf{RG})$ denote the natural specification of G that isolates randomness generation: $\mathsf{RG}(1^\lambda)$ produces λ uniformly random bits and $\mathsf{dG}(r, m)$ is a deterministic algorithm so that for every $m \leftarrow \mathsf{IG}(1^\lambda)$, $\mathsf{G}(m)$ is equal to $\mathsf{dG}(\mathsf{RG}(1^\lambda, m))$ for $n = |m|$. Consider the transformed specification for G of the form $(\mathsf{RG}_0, \mathsf{RG}_1, \Phi, \mathsf{dG})$ where dG is as above. $\mathsf{RG}_0(1^\lambda)$ and $\mathsf{RG}_1(1^\lambda)$ output λ uniform bits, and Φ is a hash function that carries strings of length 2λ to strings of length λ. We have the following theorem:

Theorem 5 ([25, Theorem 3.5]). *For any randomized algorithm G, consider the specification $\mathsf{G}_{\mathrm{SPEC}} := (\mathsf{RG}_{\mathrm{SPEC}}, \mathsf{dG}_{\mathrm{SPEC}})$, where $\mathsf{RG}_{\mathrm{SPEC}}$ and $\mathsf{dG}_{\mathrm{SPEC}}$ are as above. Let $(\mathsf{RG}_{\mathrm{SPEC}}^0, \mathsf{RG}_{\mathrm{SPEC}}^1, \Phi_{\mathrm{SPEC}})$ be the double-split specification of $\mathsf{RG}_{\mathrm{SPEC}}$ as in Fig. 14. $\mathsf{G}_{\mathrm{SPEC}}$ is stego-free with a trusted amalgamation (according to Definition 7). Here Φ_{SPEC} is modeled as a random oracle.*

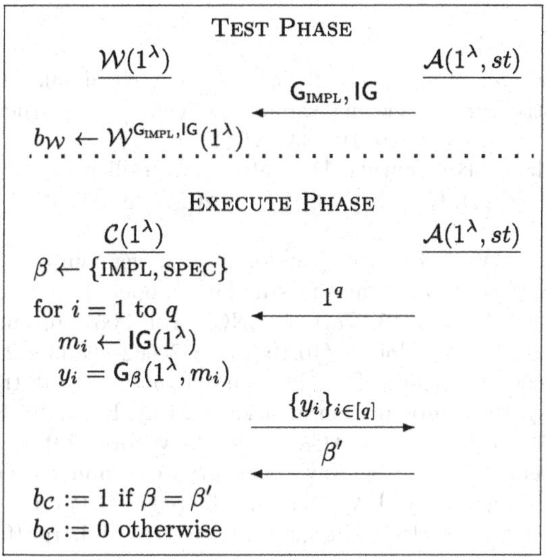

$$
\begin{array}{ll}
& \textsc{Test Phase} \\
\underline{\mathcal{W}(1^\lambda)} & \underline{\mathcal{A}(1^\lambda, st)} \\
& \xleftarrow{\quad \mathsf{G}_{\text{IMPL}}, \mathsf{IG} \quad} \\
b_\mathcal{W} \leftarrow \mathcal{W}^{\mathsf{G}_{\text{IMPL}},\mathsf{IG}}(1^\lambda) &
\end{array}
$$

$$
\begin{array}{ll}
& \textsc{Execute Phase} \\
\underline{\mathcal{C}(1^\lambda)} & \underline{\mathcal{A}(1^\lambda, st)} \\
\beta \leftarrow \{\text{IMPL}, \text{SPEC}\} & \\
\text{for } i = 1 \text{ to } q & \xleftarrow{\quad 1^q \quad} \\
\quad m_i \leftarrow \mathsf{IG}(1^\lambda) & \\
\quad y_i = \mathsf{G}_\beta(1^\lambda, m_i) & \\
& \xrightarrow{\quad \{y_i\}_{i \in [q]} \quad} \\
& \xleftarrow{\quad \beta' \quad} \\
b_\mathcal{C} := 1 \text{ if } \beta = \beta' & \\
b_\mathcal{C} := 0 \text{ otherwise} &
\end{array}
$$

Fig. 15. Stego-freeness game for randomized algorithms with input distribution $\{1^\lambda\} \times \mathsf{IG}$

C Signature Schemes

A signature scheme is a triple of algorithms $\mathcal{SS} = (\mathsf{KGen}, \mathsf{Sign}, \mathsf{Verify})$. The KGen algorithm takes as input the security parameter λ and outputs a pair of verification/signing key $(\mathsf{vk}, \mathsf{sk})$. The Sign algorithm takes as input sk, a message $m \in \mathcal{M}$ (and random coins $r \in \mathcal{R}$ if Sign is probabilistic), and outputs a signature $\sigma \in \Sigma$. The Verify algorithm takes as input vk and a pair (m, σ) and outputs a bit indicating whether the signature is valid for message m under vk.

Definition 8 (Existential unforgeability). *Let $\mathcal{SS} = (\mathsf{KGen}, \mathsf{Sign}, \mathsf{Verify})$ be a signature scheme. We say that $\mathcal{SS}$ is (t, q, ϵ)-existentially unforgeable under adaptive chosen-message attack (EUF-CMA-secure) if for all* PPT *adversaries $\mathcal{A}$ running in time t it holds:*

$$
\Pr\left[
\begin{array}{l}
\mathsf{Verify}(\mathsf{vk}, (m^*, \sigma^*)) = 1 \\
\wedge \; m^* \notin \mathcal{Q}
\end{array}
:
\begin{array}{l}
(\mathsf{vk}, \mathsf{sk}) \leftarrow \mathsf{KGen}(1^\lambda); \\
(m^*, \sigma^*) \leftarrow \mathcal{A}^{\mathsf{Sign}(\mathsf{sk}, \cdot)}(\mathsf{vk})
\end{array}
\right] \le \epsilon
$$

where $\mathcal{Q} = \{m_1, \ldots, m_q\}$ denotes the set of queries to the signing oracle. Whenever $\epsilon(\lambda) = \mathsf{negl}$ and $q = \mathsf{poly}$, we simply say that $\mathcal{SS}$ is EUF-CMA-secure.

References

1. Abe, M., Chase, M., David, B., Kohlweiss, M., Nishimaki, R., Ohkubo, M.: Constant-size structure-preserving signatures: generic constructions and simple assumptions. J. Cryptology **29**(4), 833–878 (2016)
2. Ateniese, G., Magri, B., Venturi, D.: Subversion-resilient signature schemes. In: Ray, I., Li, N., Kruegel, C. (eds.) ACM CCS 2015, pp. 364–375. ACM Press, New York (2015)
3. Bellare, M., Hoang, V.T.: Resisting randomness subversion: fast deterministic and hedged public-key encryption in the standard model. In: Oswald, E., Fischlin, M. (eds.) EUROCRYPT 2015, Part II. LNCS, vol. 9057, pp. 627–656. Springer, Heidelberg (2015). https://doi.org/10.1007/978-3-662-46803-6_21
4. Bellare, M., Jaeger, J., Kane, D.: Mass-surveillance without the state: strongly undetectable algorithm-substitution attacks. In: Ray, I., Li, N., Kruegel, C. (eds.) ACM CCS 2015, pp. 1431–1440. ACM Press, New York (2015)
5. Bellare, M., Paterson, K.G., Rogaway, P.: Security of symmetric encryption against mass surveillance. In: Garay, J.A., Gennaro, R. (eds.) CRYPTO 2014. LNCS, vol. 8616, pp. 1–19. Springer, Heidelberg (2014). https://doi.org/10.1007/978-3-662-44371-2_1
6. Bellare, M., Rogaway, P.: Random oracles are practical: a paradigm for designing efficient protocols. In: Ashby, V. (ed.) ACM CCS 1993, pp. 62–73. ACM Press, New York (1993)
7. Bellare, M., Rogaway, P.: The exact security of digital signatures-how to sign with RSA and Rabin. In: Maurer, U. (ed.) EUROCRYPT 1996. LNCS, vol. 1070, pp. 399–416. Springer, Heidelberg (1996). https://doi.org/10.1007/3-540-68339-9_34
8. Boneh, D., Boyen, X.: Short signatures without random oracles and the SDH assumption in bilinear groups. J. Cryptology **21**(2), 149–177 (2008)
9. Canetti, R.: Universally composable security: a new paradigm for cryptographic protocols. In: 42nd FOCS, pp. 136–145. IEEE Computer Society Press, October 2001
10. Chen, R., Mu, Y., Yang, G., Susilo, W., Guo, F., Zhang, M.: Cryptographic reverse firewall via malleable smooth projective hash functions. In: Cheon, J.H., Takagi, T. (eds.) ASIACRYPT 2016, Part I. LNCS, vol. 10031, pp. 844–876. Springer, Heidelberg (2016). https://doi.org/10.1007/978-3-662-53887-6_31
11. Coron, J.-S.: On the exact security of full domain hash. In: Bellare, M. (ed.) CRYPTO 2000. LNCS, vol. 1880, pp. 229–235. Springer, Heidelberg (2000). https://doi.org/10.1007/3-540-44598-6_14
12. Coron, J.-S., Dodis, Y., Malinaud, C., Puniya, P.: Merkle-Damgård revisited: how to construct a hash function. In: Shoup, V. (ed.) CRYPTO 2005. LNCS, vol. 3621, pp. 430–448. Springer, Heidelberg (2005). https://doi.org/10.1007/11535218_26
13. Degabriele, J.P., Farshim, P., Poettering, B.: A more cautious approach to security against mass surveillance. In: Leander, G. (ed.) FSE 2015. LNCS, vol. 9054, pp. 579–598. Springer, Heidelberg (2015). https://doi.org/10.1007/978-3-662-48116-5_28
14. Desmedt, Y.: Abuses in cryptography and how to fight them. In: Goldwasser, S. (ed.) CRYPTO 1988. LNCS, vol. 403, pp. 375–389. Springer, New York (1990). https://doi.org/10.1007/0-387-34799-2_29
15. Dodis, Y., Ganesh, C., Golovnev, A., Juels, A., Ristenpart, T.: A formal treatment of backdoored pseudorandom generators. In: Oswald, E., Fischlin, M. (eds.) EUROCRYPT 2015, Part I. LNCS, vol. 9056, pp. 101–126. Springer, Heidelberg (2015). https://doi.org/10.1007/978-3-662-46800-5_5

16. Dodis, Y., Mironov, I., Stephens-Davidowitz, N.: Message transmission with reverse firewalls—secure communication on corrupted machines. In: Robshaw, M., Katz, J. (eds.) CRYPTO 2016, Part I. LNCS, vol. 9814, pp. 341–372. Springer, Heidelberg (2016). https://doi.org/10.1007/978-3-662-53018-4_13

17. Fischlin, M., Mazaheri, S.: Self-guarding cryptographic protocols against algorithm substitution attacks. In: 31st IEEE Computer Security Foundations Symposium, CSF 2018, Oxford, United Kingdom, 9–12 July 2018, pp. 76–90 (2018)

18. Giacon, F., Heuer, F., Poettering, B.: KEM combiners. In: Abdalla, M., Dahab, R. (eds.) PKC 2018, Part I. LNCS, vol. 10769, pp. 190–218. Springer, Cham (2018). https://doi.org/10.1007/978-3-319-76578-5_7

19. Liu, C., Chen, R., Wang, Y., Wang, Y.: Asymmetric subversion attacks on signature schemes. In: Susilo, W., Yang, G. (eds.) ACISP 2018. LNCS, vol. 10946, pp. 376–395. Springer, Cham (2018). https://doi.org/10.1007/978-3-319-93638-3_22

20. Maurer, U., Renner, R., Holenstein, C.: Indifferentiability, impossibility results on reductions, and applications to the random oracle methodology. In: Naor, M. (ed.) TCC 2004. LNCS, vol. 2951, pp. 21–39. Springer, Heidelberg (2004). https://doi.org/10.1007/978-3-540-24638-1_2

21. Mironov, I., Stephens-Davidowitz, N.: Cryptographic reverse firewalls. In: Oswald, E., Fischlin, M. (eds.) EUROCRYPT 2015, Part II. LNCS, vol. 9057, pp. 657–686. Springer, Heidelberg (2015). https://doi.org/10.1007/978-3-662-46803-6_22

22. Perlroth, N., Larson, J., Shane, S.: NSA able to foil basic safeguards of privacy on web. The New York Times, September 2013

23. Russell, A., Tang, Q., Yung, M., Zhou, H.-S.: Cliptography: clipping the power of kleptographic attacks. In: Cheon, J.H., Takagi, T. (eds.) ASIACRYPT 2016, Part II. LNCS, vol. 10032, pp. 34–64. Springer, Heidelberg (2016). https://doi.org/10.1007/978-3-662-53890-6_2

24. Russell, A., Tang, Q., Yung, M., Zhou, H.-S.: Destroying steganography via amalgamation: kleptographically CPA secure public key encryption. Cryptology ePrint Archive, Report 2016/530 (2016). http://eprint.iacr.org/2016/530

25. Russell, A., Tang, Q., Yung, M., Zhou, H.-S.: Generic semantic security against a kleptographic adversary. In: Thuraisingham, B.M., Evans, D., Malkin, T., Xu, D. (eds.) ACM CCS 2017, pp. 907–922. ACM Press, New York (2017)

26. Russell, A., Tang, Q., Yung, M., Zhou, H.-S.: Correcting subverted random oracles. In: Shacham, H., Boldyreva, A. (eds.) CRYPTO 2018, Part II. LNCS, vol. 10992, pp. 241–271. Springer, Cham (2018). https://doi.org/10.1007/978-3-319-96881-0_9

27. Young, A., Yung, M.: The dark side of "black-box" cryptography or: should we trust capstone? In: Koblitz, N. (ed.) CRYPTO 1996. LNCS, vol. 1109, pp. 89–103. Springer, Heidelberg (1996). https://doi.org/10.1007/3-540-68697-5_8

28. Young, A., Yung, M.: Kleptography: using cryptography against cryptography. In: Fumy, W. (ed.) EUROCRYPT 1997. LNCS, vol. 1233, pp. 62–74. Springer, Heidelberg (1997). https://doi.org/10.1007/3-540-69053-0_6

29. Zhang, C., Cash, D., Wang, X., Yu, X., Chow, S.S.M.: Combiners for chosen-ciphertext security. In: Dinh, T.N., Thai, M.T. (eds.) COCOON 2016. LNCS, vol. 9797, pp. 257–268. Springer, Cham (2016). https://doi.org/10.1007/978-3-319-42634-1_21

Zero-Knowledge

Zero-Knowledge Elementary Databases with More Expressive Queries

Benoît Libert[1,2], Khoa Nguyen[3], Benjamin Hong Meng Tan[3,4(✉)], and Huaxiong Wang[3]

[1] CNRS, Laboratoire LIP, Lyon, France
[2] ENS de Lyon, Laboratoire LIP (U. Lyon, CNRS, ENSL, Inria, UCBL), Lyon, France
[3] School of Physical and Mathematical Sciences, Nanyang Technological University, Singapore, Singapore
benjamin-tan@i2r.a-star.edu.sg
[4] Institute for Infocomm Research, A*STAR, Singapore, Singapore

Abstract. Zero-knowledge elementary databases (ZK-EDBs) are cryptographic schemes that allow a prover to commit to a set D of key-value pairs so as to be able to prove statements such as "x belongs to the support of D and $D(x) = y$" or "x is not in the support of D". Importantly, proofs should leak no information beyond the proven statement and even the size of D should remain private. Chase *et al.* (Eurocrypt'05) showed that ZK-EDBs are implied by a special flavor of non-interactive commitment, called *mercurial commitment*, which enables efficient instantiations based on standard number theoretic assumptions. On the other hand, the resulting ZK-EDBs are only known to support proofs for simple statements like (non-)membership and value assignments. In this paper, we show that mercurial commitments actually enable significantly richer queries. We show that, modulo an additional security property met by all known efficient constructions, they actually enable range queries over keys and values – even for ranges of super-polynomial size – as well as membership/non-membership queries over the space of values. Beyond that, we exploit the range queries to realize richer queries such as k-nearest neighbors and revealing the k smallest or largest records within a given range. In addition, we provide a new realization of trapdoor mercurial commitment from standard lattice assumptions, thus obtaining the most expressive quantum-safe ZK-EDB construction so far.

Keywords: Zero-knowledge databases · Expressive queries · Lattice-based commitments

1 Introduction

Zero-knowledge sets (ZKS), as introduced by Micali, Rabin and Kilian [21], allow a prover P to commit to a finite set S without revealing its size. The commitment is generated such that the prover can efficiently and non-interactively prove

© International Association for Cryptologic Research 2019
D. Lin and K. Sako (Eds.): PKC 2019, LNCS 11442, pp. 255–285, 2019.
https://doi.org/10.1007/978-3-030-17253-4_9

the membership or non-membership of certain elements x in the committed set S. The zero-knowledge property mandates that proofs reveal no information beyond the truth of the statement: even its cardinality should remain hidden. The soundness property captures the prover's inability to prove contradictory statements "$x \in S$" and "$x \notin S$" about the same S.

Zero-knowledge elementary databases (ZK-EDBs) generalize the notion of zero-knowledge sets to elementary databases (EDBs). An EDB D is a partial function: a set of key-value pairs (x, y) where each key x of the universe occurs at most once and thus takes at most one value $y = D(x)$. For syntactic reasons, keys x not in D are assigned $D(x) = \bot$. Each query x obtains a response $D(x)$ and a proof of its correctness. Again, proofs should reveal no information beyond the value $D(x)$: particularly the number of records in D. Here, soundness requires the infeasibility of proving two distinct values y, y' for any given x. Micali *et al.* [21] described an elegant construction of ZK-EDB based on the discrete logarithm assumption, which was generalized by Chase *et al.* [5,6] to a general design of ZK-EDBs from a lower-level primitive called *mercurial commitment*.

In short, mercurial commitments are commitment schemes which generate commitments in either a hard or soft mode. The former satisfies the usual binding property while the latter allows the sender to create dummy commitments that do not commit the sender to any message. The ZK-EDB constructions of [5,6,21] combine mercurial commitments with a Merkle tree [20], where each internal node contains a mercurial commitment to its two children. The existence of dummy commitments is exactly what allows the sender to commit to the database in polynomial time without revealing its size. The latter is hidden by having a super-polynomial upper bound on the number of leaves in the Merkle tree. Each leaf is assigned to a key x and contains a real commitment to the value $y = D(x)$ and every internal node contains a commitment to its two children. By storing a dummy commitment at the root of each empty subtree, the sender is able to commit to the entire $D = \{(x, y)\}$ in polynomial time.

While efficient and based on standard assumptions, the ZK-EDB realizations of [5,6,21] have relatively limited expressivity; only simple statements like "x does not belong in D" or "x is in D with value $y = D(x)$" can be proved. In this paper, we show that mercurial commitments actually enable proofs of more involved statements like range queries over keys and values as well as k-nearest neighbour and k-minimum/maximum queries. As special cases, our techniques make it possible to prove membership or non-membership over values, which was not known to be possible without revealing the database size.

OUR CONTRIBUTION. In this paper, we investigate the extent to which expressive queries can be proven with efficient ZK-EDB protocols from mercurial commitments. We extend the constructions of [5,6,21] to allow the prover to convincingly answer queries of the form "Give me all database records $(x, y) \in D$ whose keys x lie within the range $[a_x, b_x]$". For any $[a_x, b_x]$ of super-polynomial length, we show that a simple tweak in mercurial commitments allows efficient, polynomial-sized proofs of correctness of the response without leaking the database size.

In a second step, we extend this technique so as to handle range queries over values. Namely, for a super-polynomially large interval $[a_y, b_y]$, we allow the prover to answer queries "Send me all records $(x, y) \in D$ with values y in the interval $[a_y, b_y]$". Again, we can prove correctness of the response in zero-knowledge with a polynomial-size proof. As a special case of range queries over values, we can prove statements like "No key x of the database is assigned the value y" or "y occurs in D and the corresponding set of keys is $D^{-1}(y)$". We note that previous ZK-EDB protocols [5,6,21] were unable to handle such statements while hiding the database size: the only way to prove that no record of the form $(*, y)$ exists was to prove inequalities $y_i \neq y$ for all records (x_i, y_i).

In a third step, we also handle range queries over records. Namely, each query consists of a "narrow" rectangle $[a_x, b_x] \times [a_y, b_y]$ and the response consists of all records (x, y) such that $x \in [a_x, b_x]$ and $y \in [a_y, b_y]$. Here, we can handle rectangles of polynomial width $[a_y, b_y]$ and super-polynomial height $[a_x, b_x]$ with a proof size which is linear in the size of $[a_y, b_y]$ and the number of records in $[a_x, b_x] \times [a_y, b_y]$. However, the proof length does not depend on $(b_x - a_x)$, allowing it to be very large. As a special case $[x, x] \times [y, y]$ of range query over records, we can efficiently prove that specific records (x, y) do not belong to D, which amounts to saying "if x is in D at all, the corresponding value is not y". In the full version of this paper, we apply range queries to enable more interesting queries such as k-nearest neighbour and k-minimim/maximum. In the following, we refer to ZK-EDB protocols supporting such richer queries as "Zero-knowledge expressive elementary database" (ZK-EEDB).

We insist on building ZK-EEDBs without interaction or random oracles: as in [5,6,21], only a common reference string is assumed, which is necessary for NIZK proofs in the standard model anyway [1]. Our constructions are instantiable with existing mercurial commitments based on standard number theoretic assumptions. We identify a new equivocation property of mercurial commitments which is actually present in a generic construction of trapdoor mercurial commitment from Σ-protocols due to Catalano et $al.$ [2]. Since the number theoretic constructions of [5,6,21] can be seen as instantiations of the general construction of [2], this immediately provides us with ZK-EEDBs based on the discrete logarithm and factoring/RSA assumptions. In addition, we provide a new construction of trapdoor mercurial commitment (TMC) based on a well-studied assumption in standard (i.e., non-ideal) lattices. Our new lattice-based TMC is a direct construction, which is not implied by the generic construction of [2]; rather, it draws inspiration from [21]. In non-ideal lattices, it performs better than TMC schemes implied by [2] under the same assumptions.

OUR TECHNIQUES. Our setting involves a database owner who publishes a short string com_D that commits him to a particular database D consisting of records, which are key-value pairs $(x, D(x))$, where $x, D(x) \in [0, 2^\ell)$. The prover is required to answer queries and prove that the response is consistent with the committed database D in zero-knowledge, including not revealing how many keys x are in the support $[D]$ of D. For this purpose, we follow the approach of using mercurial commitments [5,6].

In mercurial commitments, the binding property is relaxed by allowing the committer to softly open a commitment and say "The commitment opens to this message if it can be opened at all". During the commitment phase, the sender can either create a hard commitment, which can be hard/soft-opened to a unique message, or a soft commitment, which it can soft-open to any message. Unlike soft commitments, hard commitments can be opened both in the soft and the hard way, but soft openings can never contradict hard ones. Besides, hard and soft commitments should be computationally indistinguishable.

When a Merkle tree has a super-polynomial number of leaves, the prover has to store a soft commitment at the root of each empty sub-tree in order to commit to an EDB in polynomial time. In order to prove that some key is not in the database, the prover can soft-open all soft commitments on the path that connects the corresponding leaf to the root while generating the missing soft commitments at the time of proving non-membership.

When it comes to generating a proof for a range query $[a_x, b_x]$ over keys, the difficulty is to find a way to convince a verifier that no key of $[a_x, b_x]$ was omitted in the response. If $[a_x, b_x]$ is super-polynomially large, we cannot generate proofs of non-membership for all elements of $[a_x, b_x]$ that are not in the support $[D]$ of D. Our solution to this problem is to rely on the Subset Cover framework of Naor, Naor and Lotspiech [25] and find the smallest set of nodes $\mathcal{P}$ that contains an ancestor of all leaves $[a_x, b_x] \setminus [D]$ and no ancestor of those in $[a_x, b_x] \cap [D]$. For each node $x \in \mathcal{P}$, we can have the prover convince the verifier that the soft commitment associated to x (which is created if it did not exist yet and authenticated via a path from x to the root) is really a soft commitment, by revealing the soft-commitment coins. For the sake of proving the zero-knowledge property, we need that the simulator be able to create fake commitments which can be subsequently equivocated by revealing fake hard/soft openings or pretending that they were soft commitments. For this purpose, we thus define a new equivocation property of mercurial commitments by requiring that fake commitments be not only equivocable as defined by prior works [2], but also "explainable" as soft commitments by using a trapdoor to compute plausible soft commitment coins. Fortunately, all known trapdoor mercurial commitments based on standard assumptions [2,5] satisfy this additional equivocation property. By using the Complete Subtree technique of Naor $et\ al.$ [25], we are able to prove range queries $[a_x, b_x]$ in zero-knowledge with proofs of size $O(\ell \cdot |\mathfrak{R}| \cdot \log(b_x - a_x))$, where $\mathfrak{R} = [a_x, b_x] \cap [D]$ and ℓ is the height of the Merkle tree.

In order to handle range queries over values, our idea is to have the prover commit to D by generating two Merkle trees. While the first one is computed in the same way as in ordinary ZK-EDBs, the second tree is used as a "reversed database" D^{-1}: namely, the keys of D^{-1} are the values y of D and their values are ZKS commitments to all the keys $x \in D^{-1}(y)$ such that $(x, y) \in D$. The reversed database D^{-1} thus uses nested Merkle trees in that each leaf y of D^{-1} may be assigned a value $com_{D_y^{-1}}$, which is itself a size-hiding Merkle tree commitment whose non-empty leaves contain the keys x of D that map to y. Of course, we need to prevent the prover from cheating by using inconsistent Merkle trees in the two commitments com_D and com_{D-1}. To this end, we thus have proofs of membership consist of authentication paths in the two Merkle trees. By doing so, we can show that no dishonest prover can prove contradictory statements without breaking the binding property of the mercurial commitment scheme. Our NIZK proofs for range queries readily carry over to prove the correctness of responses to range queries over values $[a_y, b_y]$. In particular, it yields a simple method of proving that a given value is not reached by the partial function D.

Our lattice-based trapdoor mercurial commitment is statistically hiding and computationally binding under the Short-Integer-Solution (SIS) assumption [24]. It builds on the lattice-based trapdoor commitment (KTX) of Kawachi et al. [16] and Micciancio-Peikert trapdoors [22]. While partially inspired by the discrete-log-based construction of [5], it is a direct construction with large message space which is *not* implied by the generic constructions of [2,5,6].

Intuitively, we generate two public matrices $\mathbf{A}_0, \mathbf{A}_1$, the former to be applied to messages and the latter to determine the mode of the commitment. When producing a commitment to some message, using a random matrix $\mathbf{R}$, we first compute a matrix $\mathbf{B} = [\mathbf{A}_1 \mid \mathbf{B}_1]$, where $\mathbf{B}_1 = \mathbf{A}_1\mathbf{R}$ (resp. $\mathbf{B}_1 = \mathbf{G} - \mathbf{A}_1\mathbf{R}$) if the commitment is a hard (resp. soft) one. The pair $\mathbf{A}_0, \mathbf{B}$ can be considered the public key of an instance of the KTX commitment scheme, with an associated trapdoor for $\mathbf{B}$ if the mercurial commitment is a soft one.

A mercurial commitment to a message, $\boldsymbol{\mu}$, is a commitment, "public key" pair, $\mathbf{C} = (\mathbf{c} = \mathbf{A}\boldsymbol{\mu} + \mathbf{Br}, \mathbf{B}_1)$ for some commitment randomness $\mathbf{r}$. The two flavors of openings are straightforward: Soft openings to $\boldsymbol{\mu}$ are simply openings of $\mathbf{c}$ to $\boldsymbol{\mu}$ with the associated "public key" $\mathbf{A}_0, \mathbf{B} = [\mathbf{A} \mid \mathbf{B}_1]$. Hard openings, on the other hand, have an additional step of showing that $\mathbf{B}_1 = \mathbf{A}_1\mathbf{R}$ for some $\mathbf{R}$, essentially demonstrating that the "public key" does not have an embedded trapdoor.

Catalano et al. [2, Section 5] built a TMC scheme with large message space from any trapdoor commitment where a Σ-protocol allows proving knowledge of an opening to 0. For this purpose, the Σ-protocol is required to have a large challenge space, which becomes the message space of the TMC scheme. In the lattice setting, the only known Σ-protocols [19] with large challenge space operate over ideal lattices and thus require less standard assumptions than non-ideal lattices. Moreover, their honest-verifier zero-knowledge property relies on the prover performing rejection sampling and outputting a simulated transcript only with some probability, say $1/c$, for some constant c. Since the TMC scheme of [2, Section 5] generates hard commitments by running the HVZK simulator of the underlying Σ-protocol, the hard-committer can only produce a properly distributed hard commitment after c attempts on average. Our TMC scheme eliminates the need for several attempts and only requires one attempt to generate a hard commitment.

RELATED WORK. Ostrovsky, Rackoff and Smith [28] described protocols handling orthogonal multi-dimensional range queries for committed databases allowing for d-dimensional key spaces. While their protocols extend to provide privacy by means of zero-knowledge proofs, they do not hide the database size.

Chase *et al.* [5,6] and Catalano *et al.* [2] described size-hiding constructions of ZK-EDBs under general assumptions. In particular, Catalano, Dodis and Visconti [2] gave simplified security definitions for (trapdoor) mercurial commitments and showed how to obtain them from one-way functions in the shared random string model.

An EDB D is a partial function: a set of key-value pairs (x, y) where each key x of the universe occurs at most once and thus takes at most one value $y = D(x)$.

Liskov [18] considered the notion of updatable zero-knowledge databases in the random oracle model. Prabhakaran and Xue [31] put forth the similar notion of statistically hiding sets, which allows for more efficient constructions. For the sake of efficiency, Kate *et al.* [15] considered quasi-database commitments which do not aim at hiding the database size. Catalano, Fiore and Messina [4] suggested a technique for compressing proofs of non-membership in ZK-EDB protocols. Libert and Yung [17] extended their idea to compress both proofs of membership and non-membership, while Catalano and Fiore [3] achieved similar proof compressions under more standard number theoretic assumptions.

An orthogonal line of work investigated the feasibility of stronger definitions in size-hiding database commitments. Gennaro and Micali [9] formalized the notion of independent ZK-EDBs, which prevents adversaries from correlating their committed databases to those of honest committers. In the plain model, Chase and Visconti [7] considered zero-knowledge protocols providing stronger simulation-based security at the expense of an interactive commitment phase.

The aforementioned constructions all relate to elementary databases. Ghosh *et al.* [11] formalized the notion of zero-knowledge lists. In the random oracle model, they gave size-hiding protocols where the prover can demonstrate the order in which elements appear in a committed list. Goyal *et al.* [13] gave black-box constructions of size-hiding database commitments supporting more general queries. Their goal is orthogonal to ours as they rely on the "MPC-in-the-head" technique [14] to obtain black-box constructions using interaction. Here, we aim at non-interactive constructions in the standard model from standard assumptions, although we restrict ourselves to range queries.

We also mention a large body of work devoted to authenticated data structures [12,26,27,29,30,32]. We insist that these result address a different problem than ours as they stand in the three party setting. Namely, in order to achieve a better efficiency, they assume that the committer is a honest database owner that always faithfully computes commitments whereas proofs are generated by an untrusted server. While reasonable in some applications (e.g., certificate revocation with a trusted certification authority [26]), the assumption of a honest committer is too much to ask for in other settings. With a pricing database, for example, it is desirable to have guarantees against price discrimination by the database owner. For this reason, we focus on the two-party setting which is usually more challenging and results in less efficient schemes. Our protocols are indeed less efficient than the range queries of Ghosh *et al.* [12] – which, to our knowledge, is the best size-hiding construction handling range queries in the three-party setting – but they do not assume a trusted committer.

2   Preliminaries

NOTATIONS. In our notations, λ always stands for the security parameter. Let ϵ denote the empty string. For $x \in \{0,1\}^{\ell}$, let x' be the binary string that is equal to x except with the final bit flipped and $x0$ be ($x1$ respectively) the string of length $\ell + 1$ with 0 (1 respectively) appended to x. Besides that, we denote the string consisting of the first i bits of x with $x|_i$. For a string of length ℓ, $x|_0 = \epsilon$ and $x|_{\ell} = x$. For a set $\mathcal{S}$, $U(\mathcal{S})$ denotes the uniform distribution over $\mathcal{S}$ and $x \leftarrow U(\mathcal{S})$ means that element x is sampled from the distribution $U(\mathcal{S})$.

For another elementary database $\mathsf{D} = \{(x, \mathsf{D}(x))\} \subset [0, 2^{\ell}) \times [0, 2^{\ell})$, a set of key-value pairs, let $[\mathsf{D}]$ denote the set of keys $x \in [0, 2^{\ell})$ such that there exists a $y \in [0, 2^{\ell})$ with $(x, y) \in \mathsf{D}$. We write $\mathsf{D}(x) = \perp$ to indicate that there exists no $y \in [0, 2^{\ell})$ such that $(x, y) \in \mathsf{D}$. We write $x \in \mathsf{D}$ to say that $(x, \mathsf{D}(x)) \in \mathsf{D}$ for some $\mathsf{D}(x) \in [0, 2^{\ell})$, if there is no ambiguity. For a range $\mathfrak{R} = [a_x, b_x] \times [a_y, b_y]$, we use $[\mathfrak{R}]$ to denote $[a_x, b_x]$.

2.1   Trapdoor Mercurial Commitments

Informally, trapdoor mercurial commitments (TMC) are commitment schemes with two flavors of commitments and openings: hard and soft. Hard commitments are like regular commitments to a message M and can only be hard-and soft-opened to M. Hard openings are like regular openings for hard commitments. Soft commitments commit to no particular message and cannot be hard-opened at all but can be soft-opened to any message. Soft openings tease that a commitment potentially opens to some message M, and corresponds to the statement "if this commitment can be hard-opened at all, it can only be to M". Following the definitions proposed by Catalano, Dodis and Visconti [2], TMC consists of ten PPT algorithms, (Setup, $\mathbb{H}$Commit, $\mathbb{H}$Open, $\mathbb{H}$Verify, $\mathbb{S}$Commit, $\mathbb{S}$Open, $\mathbb{S}$Verify, MFake, $\mathbb{H}$Equivocate, $\mathbb{S}$Equivocate).

- $(mpk, msk) \leftarrow \mathsf{Setup}(1^{\lambda})$: Taking security parameter λ as input, outputs a public mercurial commitment key mpk and secret mercurial trapdoor msk.
- $C \leftarrow \mathbb{H}\mathsf{Commit}(mpk, M; R)$: Taking public key mpk, message M and random coins R as inputs, outputs a hard commitment C for M.
- $\pi \leftarrow \mathbb{H}\mathsf{Open}(mpk, M; R)$: Taking public key mpk, message M and random coins R as inputs, outputs a hard opening π for C of M.
- $\mathbb{H}\mathsf{Verify}(mpk, M, C, \pi)$: Taking public key mpk, message M, commitment C and hard opening π as inputs, accepts if π proves that C is a valid hard commitment to M and rejects otherwise.
- $C \leftarrow \mathbb{S}\mathsf{Commit}(mpk; R)$: Taking public key mpk and random coins R as inputs, output a soft commitment C to no message in particular.
- $\tau \leftarrow \mathbb{S}\mathsf{Open}(mpk, M, \mathsf{flag}; R)$: Given mpk, M, a flag flag and random coins R, if $\mathsf{flag} = \mathbb{H}$, output soft opening τ "associated" to hard commitment $C = \mathbb{H}\mathsf{Commit}(mpk, M; R)$. Otherwise, $\mathsf{flag} = \mathbb{S}$ and τ is a soft opening "associated" to the soft commitment $C = \mathbb{S}\mathsf{Commit}(mpk; R)$ for message M.

- $\mathbb{S}$Verify(mpk, M, C, τ): Taking public key mpk, message M, commitment C and soft opening τ, accepts if C can be potentially hard opened to M in the future and rejects otherwise.
- $C \leftarrow$ MFake($msk; R$): Taking secret key msk and random coins R as inputs, outputs a "fake" commitment C that are initially not tied to any message.
- $\pi \leftarrow \mathbb{H}$Equivocate($msk, M; R$): Taking secret key msk, message M and random coins R, outputs a supposedly valid hard opening π (hard-fake) of the fake commitment $C =$ MFake($msk; R$) to M.
- $\tau \leftarrow \mathbb{S}$Equivocate($msk, M; R$): Taking secret key msk, message M and random coins R, outputs a supposedly valid soft opening τ (soft-fake) of the fake commitment $C =$ MFake($msk; R$).

Remark 1. In many cases, including all currently known constructions, the soft opening of a hard commitment is a proper part of the hard opening to the same message. Therefore, $\mathbb{S}$Verify performs a proper subset of the tests done by $\mathbb{H}$Verify. Such trapdoor mercurial commitment schemes are called *proper*.

Correctness. Trapdoor mercurial commitments are *correct* if, with overwhelming probability, for all $(mpk, msk) \leftarrow$ Setup(1^λ), and message space $\mathcal{M}$

- Hard commitments: For all messages $M \in \mathcal{M}$ and for all random coins R, if $C = \mathbb{H}$Commit($mpk, M; R$), then
  1. for all $\tau \leftarrow \mathbb{S}$Open($mpk, M, \mathbb{H}; R$), $\mathbb{S}$Verify(mpk, M, C, τ) accepts.
  2. for all $\pi \leftarrow \mathbb{H}$Open($mpk, M; R$), $\mathbb{H}$Verify(mpk, M, C, π) accepts.
- Soft commitments: For all coins R, if $C \leftarrow \mathbb{S}$Commit($mpk; R$), then for all $M \in \mathcal{M}$ and $\tau \leftarrow \mathbb{S}$Open($mpk, M, \mathbb{S}; R$), $\mathbb{S}$Verify(mpk, M, C, τ) accepts.
- Equivocations: For all random coins R, if $C \leftarrow$ MFake($msk; R$), then for all $M \in \mathcal{M}$, the following conditions are satisfied w.h.p.
  1. If $\pi \leftarrow \mathbb{H}$Equivocate($msk, M; R$), $\mathbb{H}$Verify(mpk, M, C, π) accepts.
  2. If $\tau \leftarrow \mathbb{S}$Equivocate($msk, M; R$), $\mathbb{S}$Verify(mpk, M, C, τ) accepts.
  3. If $R' \leftarrow$ FakeExplain(msk, R), we have $C = \mathbb{S}$Commit($mpk; R'$).

Security. The security properties are similar to trapdoor commitments, *binding*, *hiding* and *equivocation*, except they are modified to accommodate the two different flavors of commitments and openings.

- *Mercurial-binding*: Given mpk, no PPT adversary $\mathcal{A}$ can find C, M, π, M', π' (respectively C, M, τ, M', π') such that π (respectively τ) is a valid hard (respectively soft) opening of C to M and π' is a valid hard opening of C to $M \neq M'$.
- *Mercurial-hiding*: No PPT adversary $\mathcal{A}$, given mpk, can find a message $M \in \mathcal{M}$ where it can distinguish a random hard commitment/soft opening tuple $(M, \mathbb{H}$Commit($mpk, M; R$), $\mathbb{S}$Open($mpk, M, \mathbb{H}; R$)) from a random soft commitment/soft opening tuple $(M, \mathbb{S}$Commit($mpk; R$), $\mathbb{S}$Open($mpk, M, \mathbb{S}; R$)).

In particular, the mercurial-binding property implies that $\mathcal{A}$ cannot find C which can be soft-opened or hard-opened to one message and then hard-opened to another: a soft opening can never disagree with a hard opening. This also implies the infeasibility of hard opening a commitment C to some message and simultaneously explain it as a soft commitment.

Catalano *et al.* [2] formalized the hiding properties of trapdoor mercurial commitments with several equivocation properties. They require the existence of an algorithm producing fake commitments which can be equivocated in a hard and soft way using a trapdoor. Even if the trapdoor is public, it should be infeasible to distinguish fake commitments and their equivocations into hard (resp. soft) commitments from hard (resp. soft) commitments and their hard (resp. soft) openings. On top of these three equivocation properties, we introduce a 4-th property called Soft-Explain equivocation (or SE equivocation for short). Namely, the trapdoor msk should make it possible to explain a fake commitment by outputting plausible random coins that explain it as a soft commitment.

- *Equivocation*: There are three related conditions for equivocation that have to be satisfied by mercurial commitments. Each is defined by a pair of games, one real and one ideal, and no PPT adversary A can distinguish between them, even if the trapdoor key msk is given at the beginning of each game, real or ideal. In all games R denotes a set of random coins sampled from the appropriate distribution.
  - *HH Equivocation*: The real game has $\mathcal{A}$ choose a message $M \in \mathcal{M}$ and receive $(M, \mathbb{H}\mathsf{Commit}(mpk, M; R), \mathbb{H}\mathsf{Open}(mpk, M; R))$ while the ideal game has $\mathcal{A}$ choose a message $M \in \mathcal{M}$ and obtain the tuple $(M, \mathsf{MFake}(msk; R), \mathbb{H}\mathsf{Equivocate}(msk, M; R))$.
  - *HS Equivocation*: The real game has $\mathcal{A}$ choose a message $M \in \mathcal{M}$ and receive $(M, \mathbb{H}\mathsf{Commit}(mpk, M; R), \mathbb{S}\mathsf{Open}(mpk, M; R))$ while the ideal game has $\mathcal{A}$ choose a message $M \in \mathcal{M}$ and obtain the tuple $(M, \mathsf{MFake}(msk; R), \mathbb{S}\mathsf{Equivocate}(msk, M; R))$.
  - *SS Equivocation*: The real game has $\mathcal{A}$ first get $C = \mathbb{S}\mathsf{Commit}(mpk; R)$, then choose $M \in \mathcal{M}$ and finally receive $\mathbb{S}\mathsf{Open}(mpk, M, \mathbb{S}; R)$ while the ideal game has $\mathcal{A}$ first get $C = \mathsf{MFake}(msk; R)$, then choose $M \in \mathcal{M}$ and receive $\mathbb{S}\mathsf{Equivocate}(msk, M; R)$.

Remark 2. As noted by Catalano *et al.* [2], HS and SS equivocation implies mercurial-hiding. In addition, for proper mercurial commitments, HH equivocation implies HS equivocation. So it suffices to verify HH and SS equivocations and mercurial-binding for the security of any proper mercurial commitment scheme.

2.2 Merkle Trees

Let $\mathcal{T}_\ell$ denote a full and complete binary tree of depth ℓ, with the depth of the root defined as 0 and leaves ℓ. Nodes at depth $i > 0$ are labeled with i-bit binary strings corresponding to the i-bit binary decomposition of 0 to $2^i - 1$. Let $[a, b], [a, b)$ denote the set $\{a, a + 1, \ldots, b - 1, b\}$ and $\{a, a + 1, \ldots, b - 1\}$ respectively. For any node x in the tree $\mathcal{T}_\ell$, we let x' mean its sibling in the tree. We call the canonical covering of $[a, b]$, $\mathcal{P}_{[a,b]}$, the unique minimal set of nodes of $\mathcal{T}_\ell$ such that each node in $[a, b]$ is the descendant of some node in $\mathcal{P}_{[a,b]}$ and for every node in $x \in \mathcal{P}_{[a,b]}$, the subtree rooted at x has leaves that are all within $[a, b]$.

Zero-Knowledge Elementary Databases and Sets. Proposed by Micali, Rabin and Kilian [21], zero-knowledge elementary databases (ZK-EDB) and sets (ZKS) enable efficient answers to membership queries in zero-knowldege. ZK-EDB is a scheme that allows one to commit to a secret database D of records and non-interactively produce proofs of (non-)membership. Membership queries on D committed in com_D take a key x as input and expect an answer $(x, D(x))$ which is the record in D corresponding to the key x if $x \in$ D. In particular, zero-knowledge sets are ZK-EDBs where $D(x) = 1$ if $x \in$ D.

Formally, a ZK-EDB has four algorithms (Init, ComDB, ProveQ, VerifyQ),

- $(crs, tk) \leftarrow$ Init(1^λ): Taking security parameter λ as input, generates and outputs common reference string (CRS) crs and trapdoor information tk.
- $(com, \Delta) \leftarrow$ ComDB(crs, D): Taking the CRS crs and database D as inputs, outputs a commitment of D, com, and opening information Δ.
- $\Pi_x \leftarrow$ ProveQ$(crs, (com, \Delta), x)$: Taking the CRS crs, database commitment and opening information (com, Δ) and key x as inputs, outputs a proof Π_x of either $x \in$ D or $x \notin$ D.
- $y \leftarrow$ VerifyQ(crs, com, x, Π_x): Taking the CRS crs, database commitment com, key x and proof Π_x as inputs, outputs y where

$$y = \begin{cases} D(x), & \text{if } x \in [D]; \\ \bot, & \text{if } x \notin [D]; \\ bad, & \text{if it otherwise believes that the prover is cheating.} \end{cases}$$

Security. The three security properties of ZK-EDB are *completeness, soundness* and *zero-knowledge*. The first one requires that honestly generated proofs always satisfy verification with VerifyQ. Soundness mandates that provers be unable to produce a key x and successful proofs Π_x, Π_x' such that they do not verify to the same value y. Finally, zero-knowledge implies that each proof Π_x only reveals the value $D(x)$ and nothing else about D.

Merkle Trees from Trapdoor Mercurial Commitments. Although Micali *et al.* constructed ZKS and ZK-EDB specifically from number-theoretic assumptions, Chase *et al.* [5,6] introduced the TMC primitive and showed that ZKS and ZK-EDB are simply Merkle trees built with TMC. The key to their size-hiding property is that TMC allows a committer compute portions of the Merkle tree that do not contain database elements only when required in proofs.

We detail four algorithms, BuildTree, $\mathbb{H}$OpenPath, $\mathbb{S}$OpenPath and VerifyPath, which we will use in Sects. 3 and 4. These algorithms encapsulate the construction of a ZK-EDB scheme from TMC in [5,6]: ComDB corresponds to BuildTree, ProveQ to $\mathbb{H}$OpenPath and $\mathbb{S}$OpenPath based on the value $D(x)$ and VerifyQ to VerifyPath. Let λ be a security parameter, $(crs, tk) \leftarrow$ Setup(1^λ) and a database $D = \{(x, D(x)) \mid (x, D(x)) \in [0, 2^\ell) \times [0, 2^\ell)\}$.

- $(com, \Delta) \leftarrow \mathsf{BuildTree}(crs, \mathsf{D})$: Taking as inputs CRS crs and database D, build a Merkle tree of depth ℓ, indexed by strings in $\bigcup_{i=0}^{\ell} \{0,1\}^i$, as follows:
  1. For each leaf $j \in \{0,1\}^\ell$ with $\mathsf{D}(j) \neq \bot$, $C_j = \mathbb{H}\mathsf{Commit}(crs, \mathsf{D}(j); R_j)$. For every leaf j with its sibling $j' \in \mathsf{D}$ but $j \notin \mathsf{D}$, set $C_j = \mathbb{S}\mathsf{Commit}(crs; R_j)$. For all other leaves j, set $C_j = nil$.
  2. At depth i from $\ell - 1$ to 0 and each $\rho \in \{0,1\}^i$, define C_ρ as follows. For all ρ such that $C_{\rho 0}, C_{\rho 1} \neq nil$, set $C_\rho = \mathbb{H}\mathsf{Commit}(crs, (C_{\rho 0}, C_{\rho 1}); R_\rho)$. For all ρ such that C_ρ was defined but not $C_{\rho'}$, $C_{\rho'} = \mathbb{S}\mathsf{Commit}(crs; R_{\rho'})$. For any other string $\rho \in \{0,1\}^i$, set $C_\rho = nil$.
  3. After the end of Step 2, if the value at the root $C_\epsilon = nil$, meaning $\{C_j\} = \emptyset$, then set $C_\epsilon = \mathbb{S}\mathsf{Commit}(crs; R_\epsilon)$.

  Output $com = C_\epsilon$ and $\Delta = \{R_j\}$, the set of random coins for all commitments computed in the steps above.
- $\Pi_z \leftarrow \mathbb{H}\mathsf{OpenPath}(crs, (com, \Delta), z)$: Given crs, a database commitment com and the opening information Δ for a database D and a key $z \in \mathsf{D}$, define the hard authentication path for $z \in \mathsf{D}$ as the set of hard openings for nodes in indices $z = z|_\ell, z|_{\ell-1}, \ldots, z|_1$ which form a path from z to the root $\epsilon = z|_0$. Proceed to decommit all the nodes on the path as follows:
  1. Compute $\pi_z \leftarrow \mathbb{H}\mathsf{Open}(crs, (z, \mathsf{D}(z)); R_z)$.
  2. At each depth j from $\ell - 1$ to 0, compute the hard opening for $C_{z|_j}$ to $(C_{z|_j 0}, C_{z|_j 1})$, $\pi_{z|_j} \leftarrow \mathbb{H}\mathsf{Open}(crs, (C_{z|_j 0}, C_{z|_j 1}); R_{z|_j})$.

  Output $\Pi_z = (\mathsf{D}(z), \{C_{z|_j}, C_{(z|_j)'}\}_{1 \le j \le \ell}, \{\pi_{z|_j}\}_{0 \le j \le \ell})$.
- $\Pi_z \leftarrow \mathbb{S}\mathsf{OpenPath}(crs, (com, \Delta), z)$: Taking as inputs CRS crs, database commitment com and opening information Δ for a database D and a key $z \in \mathsf{D}$, define the soft authentication path for $z \notin \mathsf{D}$ as the set of soft openings for nodes at indices $z = z|_\ell, z|_{\ell-1}, \ldots, z|_1$ which form a path from z to the root $\epsilon = z|_0$. Let h be the largest value such that $C_{z|_h} \neq nil$.
  1. If the complete path does not exist, i.e., $C_z = nil$, fill it out to leaf z:
     a. Compute $C_z = \mathbb{S}\mathsf{Commit}(crs; R_z)$, $C_{z'} = \mathbb{S}\mathsf{Commit}(crs; R_{z'})$.
     b. At depth j from $\ell - 1$ to $h + 1$, compute $C_{z|_j} = \mathbb{S}\mathsf{Commit}(crs; R_{z|_j})$ and $C_{(z|_j)'} = \mathbb{S}\mathsf{Commit}(crs; R_{(z|_j)'})$.
  2. Otherwise, $C_z = \mathbb{S}\mathsf{Commit}(crs; R_z)$ and we proceed to the next step.
  3. Produce soft openings to nodes along the path from leaf z to the root.
     a. Compute $\tau_z = \mathbb{S}\mathsf{Open}(crs, \bot, \mathbb{S}; R_z)$, soft opening of C_z to $\bot$.
     b. At depth j from $\ell - 1$ to $h + 1$, compute soft openings of $C_{z|_j}$ to their children, $\tau_{z|_j} = \mathbb{S}\mathsf{Open}(crs, (C_{z|_j 0}, C_{z|_j 1}), \mathbb{S}; R_{z|_j})$.
     c. For j from h to 1, compute $\tau_{z|_h} = \mathbb{S}\mathsf{Open}(crs, (C_{z|_h 0}, C_{z|_h 1}), \mathbb{H}; R_{z|_h})$.
     d. If $C_\epsilon = \mathbb{S}\mathsf{Commit}(crs; R_\epsilon)$, set $\tau_\epsilon = \mathbb{S}\mathsf{Open}(crs, (C_{z|_0}, C_{z|_1}), \mathbb{S}; R_\epsilon)$. Otherwise, $\tau_\epsilon = \mathbb{S}\mathsf{Open}(crs, (C_{z|_0}, C_{z|_1}), \mathbb{H}; R_\epsilon)$

  Output $\Pi_z = (\bot, \{C_{z|_j}, C_{(z|_j)'}\}_{1 \le j \le \ell}, \{\tau_{z|_j}\}_{0 \le j \le \ell})$. Also, add any random coins used when a path is filled out to Δ for use with later proofs.

- $ans \leftarrow$ VerifyPath(crs, com, z, Π_z): Taking as inputs CRS crs, database commitment com, key z and proof Π_z, check the proof which has two possible forms:
  - $\mathsf{D}(z) \neq \perp$: $\Pi_z = (\mathsf{D}(z), \{C_{z|_j}, C_{(z|_j)'}\}_{1 \leq j \leq \ell}, \{\pi_{z|_j}\}_{0 \leq j \leq \ell})$.
    1. Run $\mathbb{H}$Verify$(crs, \mathsf{D}(z), C_z, \pi_z)$ and set $ans = bad$ if it rejects.
    2. Otherwise, for j from $\ell - 1$ to 0, run $\mathbb{H}$Verify$(crs, (C_{z|_j 0}, C_{z_j 1}, \pi_{z|_j})$ and set $ans = bad$ if any of them reject.

    If $ans \neq bad$, then set and output $ans = \mathsf{D}(z)$.
  - $\mathsf{D}(z) = \perp$: $\Pi_z = (\perp, \tau_z, \{C_{z|_j}, C_{(z|_j)'}\}_{1 \leq j \leq \ell}, \{\tau_{z|_j}\}_{0 \leq j \leq \ell})$.
    1. Run $\mathbb{S}$Verify$(crs, \perp, C_z, \tau_z)$ and set $ans = bad$ if it does not accept.
    2. Otherwise, for j from $\ell - 1$ to 0, run $\mathbb{S}$Verify$(crs, (C_{z|_j 0}, C_{z_j 1}, \tau_{z|_j})$ and set $ans = bad$ if any of them do not accept.

    If $ans \neq bad$, then set and output $ans = \perp$.

Complete Subtree Method. We recall the complete subtree method proposed by Naor, Naor and Lotspiech [25], which is one of the algorithms in the subset-cover framework. This technique is also used by Ghosh et al. [12] to obtain one-dimensional range queries in the three party setting. This work, on the other hand, is in the two party setting which is more challenging to realize.

For a full and complete binary tree of depth ℓ, $\mathcal{T}_\ell$, with nodes indexed by binary strings of length up to ℓ. Every node x of $\mathcal{T}_\ell$ defines a subset $\mathcal{S}_x$ of leaves, those in the full and complete subtree rooted at x. Conversely, for a given set of leaves $\mathcal{R}$, a directed Steiner Tree, denoted by $ST(\mathcal{R})$ in $\mathcal{T}_\ell$, is induced. $ST(\mathcal{R})$ is the minimal subtree (rooted at ϵ) of $\mathcal{T}_\ell$ that connects all the leaves in $\mathcal{R}$. Let $\mathcal{P} = \{p_1, \ldots, p_m\}$ be the set of nodes that are adjacent to nodes of outdegree one in $ST(\mathcal{R})$, which is the canonical covering of $[0, 2^\ell) \backslash \mathcal{R}$. Naor, Naor and Lotspiech [25] found that the size of $\mathcal{P}$ is upper-bounded by $|\mathcal{R}| \log(2^\ell / |\mathcal{R}|)$.

2.3 Background on Lattices

Lattices. Let n, m, and $q \geq 2$ be integers. For matrix $\mathbf{A} \in \mathbb{Z}_q^{n \times m}$, define the m-dimensional lattice:

$$\Lambda^{\perp}(\mathbf{A}) = \{\mathbf{x} \in \mathbb{Z}^m : \mathbf{A} \cdot \mathbf{x} = \mathbf{0} \bmod q\} \subseteq \mathbb{Z}^m.$$

For any $\mathbf{u}$ in the image of $\mathbf{A}$, define $\Lambda^{\mathbf{u}}(\mathbf{A}) = \{\mathbf{x} \in \mathbb{Z}^m : \mathbf{A} \cdot \mathbf{x} = \mathbf{u} \bmod q\}$.

Definition 1 ($\mathsf{SIS}_{n,m,q,\beta}$). *Given a uniformly random matrix $\mathbf{A} \in \mathbb{Z}_q^{n \times m}$, find a non-zero vector $\mathbf{v} \in \Lambda^{\perp}(\mathbf{A})$ such that $\|\mathbf{v}\| \leq \beta$.*

If $m, \beta \in \mathsf{poly}(n)$ and $q > \beta \cdot \omega(\sqrt{n \log n})$, then the $\mathsf{SIS}_{n,m,q,\beta}$ problem is at least as hard as lattice problem SIVP_γ for some $\gamma = \beta \cdot \widetilde{\mathcal{O}}(\sqrt{n})$ (see, e.g., [10,23]).

Gaussian Distributions. For integer $m > 0$, let $D_{\mathbb{Z}^m, \sigma}$ be the discrete Gaussian distribution over $\mathbb{Z}^m$ with parameter $\sigma > 0$. In the following lemmas, we review several well-known facts from [10].

Lemma 1. *We have $\Pr\left[\|\mathbf{r}\| > \sigma \sqrt{m} \mid \mathbf{r} \hookleftarrow D_{\mathbb{Z}^m, \sigma} \right] \leq 2^{-m}$.*

Lemma 2. *Let n be a positive integer, q be a prime, $m \geq 2n \log q$ and $\sigma = \Omega(\sqrt{n \log q \log n})$. Then, for a uniformly random $\mathbf{A} \in \mathbb{Z}_q^{n \times m}$ and for $\mathbf{r} \hookleftarrow D_{\mathbb{Z}^m, \sigma}$, the distribution of $\mathbf{u} = \mathbf{A} \cdot \mathbf{r} \bmod q$ is statistically close to uniform over $\mathbb{Z}_q^n$. Moreover, the conditional distribution of $\mathbf{r}$ given $\mathbf{u}$ is $D_{\Lambda^{\mathbf{u}}(\mathbf{A}), \sigma}$.*

Lemma 3. *For $\sigma \geq \widetilde{\mathcal{O}}(\sqrt{m})$, the min-entropy of $D_{\mathbb{Z}^m, \sigma}$ is at least $m - 1$.*

When sampling a matrix $\mathbf{R} = [\mathbf{r}_1 \mid \cdots \mid \mathbf{r}_w] \in \mathbb{Z}^{m \times w}$, where $\mathbf{r}_i \hookleftarrow D_{\mathbb{Z}^m, \sigma}$ for all $i = 1, \ldots, w$, we will use the notation $\mathbf{R} \hookleftarrow D_{\mathbb{Z}^{m \times w}, \sigma}$.

Trapdoors for Lattices. We will employ the lattice trapdoors introduced by Micciancio and Peikert [22]. For any positive integer k, let $\mathbf{I}_k$ denote the identity matrix of order k. Let n be a positive integer, $q \in \mathsf{poly}(n)$ be a modulus and $w = n\lceil \log q \rceil$. Define the gadget matrix $\mathbf{G} = \mathbf{I}_n \otimes (1, 2, \ldots, 2^{\lceil \log q \rceil - 1}) \in \mathbb{Z}_q^{n \times w}$.

Let $m = \bar{m} + w$, for some $\bar{m} > w$. A trapdoor for matrix $\mathbf{A} \in \mathbb{Z}_q^{n \times m}$ is a matrix $\mathbf{R} \in \mathbb{Z}^{\bar{m} \times w}$ such that $\mathbf{A} \begin{bmatrix} \mathbf{R} \\ \mathbf{I}_w \end{bmatrix} = \mathbf{G}$. In particular, if $\mathbf{A} = [\bar{\mathbf{A}} \mid \mathbf{G} - \bar{\mathbf{A}} \cdot \mathbf{R}]$, where $\bar{\mathbf{A}} \in \mathbb{Z}_q^{n \times \bar{m}}$, then $\mathbf{R}$ is a trapdoor for $\mathbf{A}$.

Lemma 4 ([22]). *Let $n, q, w, \bar{m}, m$ be as above. Then, there exists a PPT algorithm $\mathsf{TrapGen}(n, m, q)$ that outputs a matrix $\mathbf{A} \in \mathbb{Z}_q^{n \times m}$ together with a trapdoor $\mathbf{R} \in \mathbb{Z}^{\bar{m} \times w}$, such that the distribution of $\mathbf{A}$ is statistically close to uniform.*

Moreover, for any $\mathbf{u} \in \mathbb{Z}_q^n$ and $\sigma = \Omega(\sqrt{n \log q \log n})$, there exists a PPT algorithm $\mathsf{SampleD}(\mathbf{R}, \mathbf{A}, \mathbf{u}, \sigma)$ that outputs $\mathbf{r} \in \mathbb{Z}^m$ sampled from a distribution statistically close to $D_{\Lambda^{\mathbf{u}}(\mathbf{A}), \sigma}$.

As shown by Micciancio and Peikert, a trapdoor for matrix $\mathbf{A} \in \mathbb{Z}_q^{n \times m}$ can be efficiently extended into a trapdoor for any matrix $\mathbf{B} \in \mathbb{Z}_q^{n \times (m+w)}$ of the form $\mathbf{B} = [\mathbf{A} \mid \mathbf{A}']$, where matrix $\mathbf{A}' \in \mathbb{Z}_q^{n \times w}$.

3 Zero-Knowledge Expressive Elementary Database from Trapdoor Mercurial Commitments

We construct a new flavor of size-hiding zero-knowledge database, called zero-knowledge expressive elementary database (ZK-EEDB). It allows databases D to be secretly committed in a public digest and several queries on D to be efficiently answered in zero-knowledge. The databases supported by ZK-EEDB are sets of records, which are key-value pairs $(x, \mathsf{D}(x)) \in [0, 2^\ell) \times [0, 2^\ell)$ and the queries supported by ZK-EEDB include queries over keys and values.

Besides membership over keys which was previously considered by Micali, Rabin and Kilian [21] in zero-knowledge elementary database, ZK-EEDB enables range queries over records of D, generalizing range queries over keys and values. We introduce the ability to generate proofs of correctness for answers to range queries over values in zero-knowledge with ZK-EEDB. The membership query over values, in this work, is the query which, given y, asks for the set $\mathsf{D}^{-1}(y) = \{x_i \mid x_i \in [\mathsf{D}]$ such that $\mathsf{D}(x_i) = y\}$. A range query over values is membership extended to a range of values $[a_y, b_y]$. From our techniques, we gain the ability to prove correctness of answers to range queries over records that is efficient for any super-polynomial range of keys.

First, we introduce new notations for values of a database D and the query types considered in ZK-EEDB. Following that, ZK-EEDB is formally defined and its security properties detailed. Then, we describe our techniques that enable efficient range queries over records of a database D. Finally, we end the section with a construction with TMC.

A Database of Values, D^{-1}. In this work, we consider queries over values of a database D in addition to queries over its keys. To achieve it efficiently, we use an alternate view of D, called D^{-1}, which is essentially a "reversed directory": namely, D^{-1} is the set $\{(y, D^{-1}(y)) \mid y \in [0, 2^\ell)\}$, where $D^{-1}(y) = \{x \mid x \in D \text{ and } D(x) = y\}$. The key-space of the database D^{-1} is thus the value-space of D and each key $y \in [D^{-1}]$ has a value $D^{-1}(y)$, which is the set of keys $x \in [D]$ that are assigned the value y (i.e., $D(x) = y$).

Queries in ZK-EEDB. Note that the answer to any query should come with a proof of correctness. We now describe a specific kind of query supported by our ZK-EEDB primitive which actually captures a total of six different queries.

- Range (Record) queries: Given a range $\mathfrak{R} = [a_x, b_x] \times [a_y, b_y] \subset [0, 2^\ell) \times [0, 2^\ell)$, they return the set $\mathcal{L}$ of records such that $\mathcal{L} = D \cap ([a_x, b_x] \times [a_y, b_y])$.
  - For general $\mathfrak{R} = [a_x, b_x] \times [a_y, b_y]$, $[a_x, b_x]$ can be super-polynomial in ℓ.
  - Range queries over values (resp. keys) correspond to the input range $[0, 2^\ell) \times [a_y, b_y]$ (resp. $[a_x, b_x] \times [0, 2^\ell)$). For such queries, the interval $[a_y, b_y]$ (resp. $[a_x, b_x]$) can be super-polynomial or even exponential in ℓ.
  - Membership queries over records (resp. values and keys) correspond to the input range $[x, x] \times [y, y]$ (resp. $[0, 2^\ell) \times [y, y]$ and $[x, x] \times [0, 2^\ell)$).

3.1 Zero-Knowledge Expressive Elementary Database

ZK-EEDB has four algorithms: Init, ComDB, ProveRQ, VerifyRQ.

- $(crs, tk) \leftarrow \text{Init}(1^\lambda)$: Takes as input security parameter λ and outputs a common reference string (CRS) crs and trapdoor key tk.
- $(com, \Delta) \leftarrow \text{ComDB}(crs, D)$: Takes in crs and a database $D = \{(x, D(x))\}$. It returns a commitment com to D and a decommitment information Δ.
- $\Pi_\mathfrak{R} \leftarrow \text{ProveRQ}(crs, (com, \Delta), \mathfrak{R})$: Inputs crs, a database commitment and decommitment information (com, Δ) and a range $\mathfrak{R}$. It returns a proof of correctness $\Pi_\mathfrak{R}$ of the range query with input range $\mathfrak{R} \subset [0, 2^\ell) \times [0, 2^\ell)$.
- $\mathcal{L} \leftarrow \text{VerifyRQ}(crs, com, \mathfrak{R}, \Pi_\mathfrak{R})$: Inputs crs, a database commitment com, a range $\mathfrak{R} \subset [0, 2^\ell) \times [0, 2^\ell)$ and a purported proof $\Pi_\mathfrak{R}$. It returns

$$z = \begin{cases} D \cap \mathfrak{R}, & \text{if the proof is correct;} \\ bad, & \text{if the proof is deemed invalid.} \end{cases}$$

We consider the same properties as in standard ZK-EDB protocols: namely, *completeness, soundness* and *zero-knowledge*, adapted to support the more expressive queries in ZK-EEDB. Correctness mandates that, for any query, correctly computed proofs satisfy the verification algorithm. Zero-knowledge requires that there exist an efficient simulator which is only granted oracle access to the database and outputs proofs for queries that are indistinguishable from those produced by a real prover using the real database as a witness. Soundness requires that no contradictory statements about the committed database can be proven by the adversary. Informally speaking, no PPT adversary can find two ranges $\mathfrak{R}, \mathfrak{R}'$ and proofs Π, Π' for which there exists a record $(x, y) \in \mathfrak{R} \cap \mathfrak{R}'$ that is in the answer to the first query but not the second. Formally, we have

- *Completeness*: For all databases D and all keys x, we have
  $\Pr[crs \leftarrow \mathsf{Init}(1^\lambda);\ (com, \Delta) \leftarrow \mathsf{ComDB}(crs, \mathsf{D});$

  $\quad \Pi_{\mathfrak{R}} \leftarrow \mathsf{ProveRQ}(crs, (com, \Delta), \mathfrak{R});$

  $\quad \mathsf{VerifyRQ}(crs, com, \mathfrak{R}, \Pi_{\mathfrak{R}}) \neq bad] = 1 - \nu(\lambda),$
  for some negligible function $\nu(\cdot)$.
- *Soundness*: For any PPT algorithm P′, the probability
  $\Pr[crs \leftarrow \mathsf{Init}(1^\lambda);\ (com, \mathfrak{R}, \Pi, \mathfrak{R}', \Pi') \leftarrow \mathsf{P}'(crs);$

  $\quad (\mathsf{VerifyRQ}(crs, com, \mathfrak{R}, \Pi) = \mathcal{L} \neq bad)$

  $\quad \wedge\ (\mathsf{VerifyRQ}(crs, com, \mathfrak{R}', \Pi') = \mathcal{L}' \neq bad)$

  $\quad \wedge\ (\exists (x, y) \in \mathfrak{R} \cap \mathfrak{R}' \text{ s.t. } ((x, y) \in \mathcal{L}) \wedge ((x, y) \notin \mathcal{L}')],$
  is bounded by $\nu(\lambda)$, for some negligible function $\nu(\cdot)$.
- *Zero-Knowledge*: For any PPT adversary $\mathcal{A}$ and any efficiently computable database D, there exists an efficient simulator consisting of a triple of algorithms $(\mathsf{SInit}, \mathsf{SCom}, \mathsf{SProveQ}^{\mathsf{D}})$ such that the outputs of the following two experiment outputs are indistinguishable:
  Real experiment:
  1. Let $crs \leftarrow \mathsf{Init}(1^\lambda), (com, \Delta) \leftarrow \mathsf{ComDB}(crs, \mathsf{D})$ and $s_0 = \Pi_0 = \varepsilon$.
  2. For $1 \leq i \leq n$, we have $(\mathfrak{R}_i, s_i) \leftarrow \mathcal{A}(crs, com, \Pi_0, \ldots, \Pi_{i-1}, s_{i-1})$ and $\mathcal{A}$ gets a real proof $\Pi_i = \mathsf{ProveRQ}(crs, (com, \Delta), \mathfrak{R}_i)$.
  The experiment outputs $(crs, \mathfrak{R}_1, \Pi_1, \ldots, \mathfrak{R}_n, \Pi_n)$.
  Ideal experiment:
  1. Let $(crs', st_0) \leftarrow \mathsf{SInit}(1^\lambda), (com', st_1) \leftarrow \mathsf{SCom}(st_0)$ and $s_0 = \Pi_0' = \varepsilon$.
  2. For $1 \leq i \leq n$, we have $(\mathfrak{R}_i, s_i) \leftarrow \mathcal{A}(crs', com', \Pi_0', \ldots, \Pi_{i-1}', s_{i-1})$ and $\mathcal{A}$ gets a simulated proof $\Pi_i' \leftarrow \mathsf{SProveRQ}^{\mathsf{D}}(crs', st_1, \mathfrak{R}_i)$.
  The experiment outputs $(crs', \mathfrak{R}_1, \Pi_1', \ldots, \mathfrak{R}_n, \Pi_n')$.

In the ideal experiment, $\mathsf{SProveQ}^{\mathsf{D}}$ is an oracle that is allowed to invoke a database oracle D and receive the set of records $\mathsf{D} \cap \mathfrak{R}$ for any range $\mathfrak{R} = [a_x, b_x] \times [a_y, b_y]$ chosen by the adversary.

Here, a few comments about our security definitions are in order. We recall that, in size-hiding database commitments, the commitment *must* be shorter than the database since, otherwise, an upper bound on the database size is leaked. This naturally leads us to use statistically-hiding commitments, where we cannot properly speak of the "content" of a commitment since valid openings exist for any database. What matters is thus what the adversary is able to prove about the commitments it generates. In non-interactive size-hiding database commitments (at least under falsifiable assumptions), soundness can only be defined by preventing proofs for conflicting statements. In standard ZK-EDBs, it means one cannot prove distinct values for any key in a committed DB. For ZK-EEDBs, we extend it to range queries which are akin to batch queries. Our definition of soundness is thus adjusted to account for the answer being a set of records instead a value.

In the definitions of Ostrovsky *et al.* [28], soundness includes that, for any valid proofs produced by the prover, there exists a valid database compatible with the proven statements. This property is straightforward to show in our scheme and can be added to our model. Furthermore, although range queries can admit exponentially large ranges, it is still necessary to hide database size to maintain the zero-knowledge property of ZK-EEDB, which requires that verifiers leak nothing beyond the statements involved in all queries.

3.2 A Construction of ZK-EEDB from TMC: Initialization and Commitment Generation

In this section, we describe how to initialize a ZK-EEDB instance and commit to a database D by exploiting two size-hiding trees. Details of the proof generation and verification for ZK-EEDB queries are deferred to Sect. 4.

ZK-EEDB Database Commitments from TMC. To construct ZK-EEDBs, our idea is to use two Merkle trees to commit to the database D, each in a different representation. While ordinary ZK-EDBs consist of a single Merkle tree, ZK-EEDB relies on two size-hiding trees: (i) A (key) Merkle tree of height ℓ, which commits to a value $D(x)$ at each leaf $x \in [D]$; (ii) A (value) Merkle tree also of height ℓ that is two-tiered: each leaf y stores a commitment to the root value of a size-hiding Merkle tree that accumulates D_y^{-1}. Here, $D_y^{-1} = \{(x, 1) \mid (x, y) \in D\}$ is a zero-knowledge set encoded as a ZK-EDB with keys x and value 1 if and only if $(x, y) \in D$.

The value Merkle tree can be seen as a commitment to the reversed database $D_{com}^{-1} = \{(y, com_{D_y^{-1}}) \mid D^{-1}(y) \neq \emptyset\}$. Although defined differently earlier, we use D^{-1} from here on to denote D_{com}^{-1}. This is the main technique enabling efficient queries over values and records: Soft-opening paths in the value Merkle tree allow us to efficiently prove statements about non-membership of a value y (i.e., D contains no record of the form $(*, y)$). In existing single-tree-based constructions of ZK-EDBs, such queries are simply impossible to prove in zero-knowledge as each key must be separately proven to not have $D(x) = y$ (which betrays the database size and is highly inefficient). However, in ZK-EEDB, the root value of the Merkle tree that accumulates D_y^{-1} is simply revealed to be empty by explaining the value stored at the leaf y in the value Merkle tree is a soft commitment C_y and showing a soft authentication path from y to the root.

With two commitments to the same database under different representations, we need to add checks to enforce that the two Merkle trees are consistent with each other. Whenever a record is proven to be in D via com_D and the first Merkle tree, the same record is also proven to be correctly committed in $com_{D^{-1}}$ using the second Merkle tree. This prevents malicious provers from proving contradictory statements as both commitments have to agree at any record that has been proven to be in D. We insist that a cheating prover cannot win by using inconsistent databases in the two trees since, even by doing so, it will remain unable to prove contradictory statements without breaking the binding properties of the underlying mercurial commitment.

We now describe the initialization and commitment algorithms, Init and ComDB for ZK-EEDB from the TMC scheme, TMC.

- $(crs, tk) \leftarrow \mathsf{Init}(1^\lambda)$: compute and return $(crs, tk) \leftarrow \mathsf{TMC.Setup}(1^\lambda)$.
- $(com, \Delta) \leftarrow \mathsf{ComDB}(crs, D)$:
  1. Compute $(com_D, \Delta_D) \leftarrow \mathsf{BuildTree}(crs, D)$.
  2. For every y with $D^{-1}(y) \neq \emptyset$, compute commitments of D_y^{-1} by running $(com_{D_y^{-1}}, \Delta_{D_y^{-1}}) \leftarrow \mathsf{BuildTree}(crs, D_y^{-1})$.
  3. Compute $(com_{D^{-1}}, \Delta_{D^{-1}})$ with $\mathsf{BuildTree}(crs, D^{-1})$.

Return $(com = (com_D, com_{D^{-1}}), \Delta = (\Delta_D, \{com_{D_y^{-1}}\}_{y \in [D^{-1}]}, \Delta_{D^{-1}}))$.

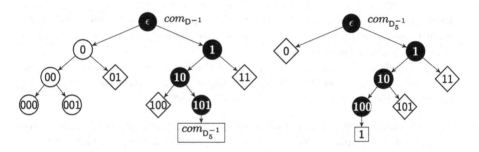

Fig. 1. The value Merkle tree in ZK-EEDB with authentication paths for $(4, 5) \in D$.

4 Queries in ZK-EEDB

We first show how to prove correctness for answers to range queries in zero-knowledge for some database D committed with a Merkle tree and TMC scheme. Then, we apply the techniques to construct the ProveRQ and VerifyRQ algorithms in ZK-EEDB. Let the TMC scheme used, TMC, be implicit in the algorithms.

4.1 Range Queries with a Single Merkle Tree

For a single Merkle tree, a range query is an interval $[a, b] \subseteq [0, 2^\ell)$ of keys. Our range query proofs uses two key ideas: Steiner trees and a set of novel explanation algorithms. We can split the leaves in $[a, b]$ into two sets, $\mathcal{R} \subseteq [D]$ with values in D, and the others, $[a,b]\backslash\mathcal{R}$. Proving correctness for $[a,b]$ means showing that every $x \in \mathcal{R}$ is a member of [D] and the remaining keys $[a,b]\backslash\mathcal{R}$ are not.

The Steiner tree characterizes the minimum set of nodes that have to be hard-opened to form the authentication paths for every leaf in $\mathcal{R}$. At the same time, it defines a polynomial-sized covering set for the remaining keys $[a,b]\backslash\mathcal{R}$. Then, the explanation algorithms are used to reveal that the covering set consists of soft commitments, so no hard authentication paths can be built from leaves in $[a,b]\backslash\mathcal{R}$ to the root of the Merkle tree.

Explanations for Trapdoor Mercurial Commitments. For our purposes, we introduce three new algorithms Explain, EVerify, FakeExplain to the syntax of TMC schemes. These algorithms reveal and verify that a commitment is a soft commitment and produce a "fake" proof that a fake commitment is a soft commitment. Explain is used by the prover when producing range proofs, EVerify is used by the verifier when checking if proofs are correct and FakeExplain is used by the simulator from the zero-knowledge property.

Note that Catalano *et al.* [2]'s construction of TMCs, and thus all known TMC schemes, can be easily adapted to support the three new algorithms introduced in this work. This is given in the full version of this work.

- $R \leftarrow$ Explain($mpk; R$): On input of the public commitment key mpk and random coin R such that $C = \mathbb{S}\mathsf{Commit}(mpk; R)$, it outputs the random coin R that explains C as a soft commitment.
- EVerify(mpk, C, R): On input of the public commitment key mpk, a commitment C and random coins R, it accepts if R is deemed as convincing evidence that C is a soft commitment.
- $R' \leftarrow$ FakeExplain($msk; R$): On input of the public commitment key mpk and random coins R such that $C = \mathsf{MFake}(mpk; R)$, this algorithm outputs random coins R' such that $C = \mathbb{S}\mathsf{Commit}(mpk; R')$.

It is straightforward to see that EVerify will only accept if the inputs are soft commitment, explanation or fake commitment, fake explanation pairs. If an adversary can produce explanations for some hard commitment that EVerify accepts, then mercurial binding is broken: The explanation can be adapted to produce soft-openings to any message like fake commitments which contradicts the mercurial binding property that hard commitments can only be hard-/soft-opened to a unique message.

With these three new algorithms, we require an additional equivocation property, *soft-explain* (SE) equivocation, for the security of TMC schemes.

- *SE Equivocation*: The real game provides $\mathcal{A}$ with a soft commitment $C = \mathbb{S}\mathsf{Commit}(mpk; R)$ and the corresponding random coins R. The ideal game provides $\mathcal{A}$ with a fake commitment $C = \mathsf{MFake}(msk; R)$ and a fake explanation $R' \leftarrow$ FakeExplain($msk; R$) of C as a soft commitment.

Optimized Proof of Membership for an Interval. A naive method to prove membership of a set of keys of D lying in some interval $[a,b]$, $\mathcal{R}$, is to return $|\mathcal{R}|$ many hard authentication paths. This is sub-optimal as there are duplicated hard openings as authentication paths merge closer to the root of the Merkle tree. We show how the Steiner tree yields the optimal set of hard openings.

For a set of leaves $\mathcal{R} \subseteq [\mathsf{D}] \cap [a, b]$, let $ST(\mathcal{R})$ be the Steiner tree of $\mathcal{R}$, the minimal subtree connecting the leaves of $\mathcal{R}$ to the root. We use $ST(\mathcal{R})_j$ to mean the set of nodes in $ST(\mathcal{R})$ at depth j. We define the authentication Steiner tree of $\mathcal{R}$, $\Pi_{\mathcal{R}}$, as the set of hard openings for each node in $ST(\mathcal{R})$: namely, hard openings π_x to $\mathsf{D}(x)$ for each leaf $x \in \mathcal{R}$, and π_y to $(C_y, C_{y'})$ for each internal node $y \in ST(\mathcal{R}) \backslash \mathcal{R}$. By definition, hard authentication paths for all $x \in \mathcal{R}$ are in $\Pi_{\mathcal{R}}$ above which has $\mathcal{O}(|\mathcal{R}| \cdot \ell)$ nodes. The mechanism and its verification is formalized in $\mathbb{H}\mathsf{OpenST}$ and $\mathsf{VerifyST}$ with $(com, \Delta) \leftarrow \mathsf{BuildTree}(crs, \mathsf{D})$.

- $\Pi_{\mathcal{R}} \leftarrow \mathbb{H}\mathsf{OpenST}(crs, (com, \Delta), \mathcal{R})$: With inputs CRS crs, database commitment com, decommitment information Δ and set $\mathcal{R} \subseteq [\mathsf{D}]$, return $\Pi_{\mathcal{R}}$ as follows:
  1. For each leaf $x \in \mathcal{R}$, compute $\pi_x \leftarrow \mathbb{H}\mathsf{Open}(crs, \mathsf{D}(x); R_x)$.
  2. For j from $\ell - 1$ to 0 and $z \in ST(\mathcal{R})_j$, the set of nodes in $ST(\mathcal{R})$ at depth j, compute $\pi_z \leftarrow \mathbb{H}\mathsf{Open}(crs, (C_{z0}, C_{z1}); R_z)$.

  Set $\Pi_{\mathcal{R}} = (\{(x, \mathsf{D}(x)), \pi_x\}_{x \in \mathcal{R}}, \{C_z, C_{z'}, \pi_z\}_{z \in ST(\mathcal{R}) \backslash \mathcal{R}})$.

- $\mathcal{L} \leftarrow \mathsf{VerifyST}(crs, com, \mathcal{R}, \Pi_{\mathcal{R}})$: With inputs CRS crs, database commitment com, set $\mathcal{R}$,
  1. For each leaf $x \in \mathcal{R}$, compute $\mathbb{H}\mathsf{Verify}(crs, \mathsf{D}(x), C_x, \pi_x)$ and continue if all verifications accept. Otherwise, set and output $\mathcal{L} = bad$.
  2. For j from $\ell - 1$ to 0 and $z \in ST(\mathcal{R})_j$, the set of nodes in $ST(\mathcal{R})$ at depth j, compute $\mathbb{H}\mathsf{Verify}(crs, (C_{z0}, C_{z1}), C_z, \pi_z)$ and continue if all verifications accept. Otherwise, set and output $\mathcal{L} = bad$.

  Return $\mathcal{L} = \mathcal{R}$ if $\mathcal{L} \neq bad$.

Proof of Non-membership for an Interval. With the authentication Steiner tree for $\mathcal{R}$ proving that keys $x \in \mathcal{R}$ are in $[\mathsf{D}]$, we need to show that the other keys in $[a, b] \backslash \mathcal{R}$ do not appear in D. This is achieved with a crucial observation: If an internal node y' is a soft commitment or nil, then no descendant of y' has a valid hard authentication path and cannot be in $[\mathsf{D}]$. So, we use $\mathsf{Explain}$ to prove that no leaves in $[a, b] \backslash \mathcal{R}$ have a hard authentication path to the root. In particular, if $\mathcal{P}$ is the canonical covering of $[a, b] \backslash \mathcal{R}$, we have $C_x = nil$ or $\mathbb{S}\mathsf{Commit}(mpk; R_x)$ for any node $x \in \mathcal{P}$ after $\mathsf{BuildTree}(crs, \mathsf{D})$.

The values C_z of $z \in \mathcal{P}$ are explained as soft commitments to show that the leaves $[a, b] \backslash \mathcal{R}$ cannot be involved in a proof of membership. With $\mathcal{R} = \{x_1, \ldots, x_m\}$. The canonical coverings of intervals $[a, x_1 - 1]$ and $[x_m + 1, b]$ may not be siblings of nodes in $ST(\mathcal{R})$ but descendants instead. In those cases, we compute soft authentication paths from these canonical coverings to the ancestors which are siblings of some nodes in $ST(\mathcal{R})$. Those $z \in \mathcal{P}$ whose siblings z' are in $ST(\mathcal{R})$ do not need additional proof elements. The entire process adds $\mathcal{O}(|\mathcal{R}| \cdot \log((b - a)/|\mathcal{R}|))$ nodes which is only a constant factor larger than $|ST(\mathcal{R})| = |\mathcal{R}| \cdot \ell$. Thus, the entire range proof has size $\mathcal{O}(|\mathcal{R}| \cdot \ell)$, independent of the length of the input interval and allows for exponentially large inputs.

274   B. Libert et al.

– $\Pi_{[a,b]} \leftarrow \mathsf{OpenI}(crs, (com, \Delta), [a,b])$: If $a = b$, prove membership of a with $\mathbb{H}\mathsf{OpenPath}$ and non-membership with $\mathbb{S}\mathsf{OpenPath}$. Otherwise proceed as follows. Let $\mathcal{R}$ be the set of keys in $[\mathsf{D}] \cap [a,b]$.

- If $\mathcal{R} = \emptyset$, set $\Pi_{[a,b],\mathcal{R}} = nil$ and let $\mathcal{P}$ be the canonical covering of the leaves in $[a,b]$. For each $x \in \mathcal{P}$:
  1. Compute $C_q \leftarrow \mathbb{S}\mathsf{Commit}(crs; R_q)$ if $C_q = nil$ for $q = x, x'$.
  2. Compute $R_x \leftarrow \mathsf{Explain}(crs, C_x; R_x)$.
  3. For i from $|x| - 1$ to 0, compute $C_q \leftarrow \mathbb{S}\mathsf{Commit}(crs; R_{x|_i})$ if either of $q = x|_i, (x|_i)'$ has not been computed previously. Then, compute $\tau_{x|_i} \leftarrow \mathbb{S}\mathsf{Open}(crs, (C_{x|_i 0}, C_{x|_i 1}); R_{x|_i})$.
  Set $\Pi_{[a,b],\mathcal{P}} = \{R_x, \{C_{x|_i 0}, C_{x|_i 1}, \tau_{x|_i}\}_{0 \le i \le |x|-1}\}_{x \in \mathcal{P}}$, proofs that C_x is a soft commitment and committed to com for $x \in \mathcal{P}$.
- Otherwise, $\mathcal{R} \ne \emptyset$ and compute the authentication Steiner tree of $\mathcal{R}$, $\Pi_{[a,b],\mathcal{R}} \leftarrow \mathbb{H}\mathsf{OpenST}(crs, (com, \Delta), \mathcal{R})$.
  1. (*Explain canonical covering.*) Let $\mathcal{P}$ be the canonical covering of the keys in $[a,b] \backslash \mathcal{R}$, for $x \in \mathcal{P}$, compute $R_x \leftarrow \mathsf{Explain}(crs, C_x; R_x)$
  2. (*Prove connection to $ST(\mathcal{R})$.*) If $x' \notin ST(\mathcal{R})$, let h_x be such that $x|_{h_x} = y'$ for some $y \in ST(\mathcal{R})$. For i from $|x| - 1$ to h_x, compute $\tau_{x|_i} \leftarrow \mathbb{S}\mathsf{Open}(crs, (C_{x|_i 0}, C_{x|_i 1}); R_{x|_i})$.
  Set $\Pi_{[a,b],\mathcal{P}} = \{R_x, \{C_{x|_i 0}, C_{x|_i 1}, \tau_{x|_i}\}_{h_x \le i \le |x|-1}\}_{x \in \mathcal{P}}$, proving C_x are soft commitments and their paths to com meet $ST(\mathcal{R})$ for $x \in \mathcal{P}_{[a,b]}$.
Output $\Pi_{[a,b]} = (\Pi_{[a,b],\mathcal{P}}, \Pi_{[a,b],\mathcal{R}})$ and add the randomness of any commitments computed to Δ.

– $\mathcal{L} \leftarrow \mathsf{VerifyI}(crs, com, \mathfrak{R}, \Pi_{[a,b]})$: If $a = b$, $\Pi_{[a,b]} = \Pi_a$ and compute $y \leftarrow \mathsf{VerifyPath}(crs, com, a, \Pi_a)$. Set $\mathcal{L}' = \{(a, y)\}$ if $y \notin \{\bot, bad\}$ and $\mathcal{L}' = \emptyset$ if $y = \bot$. If $a \ne b$, let the proof $\Pi_{[a,b]} = (\Pi_{[a,b],\mathcal{P}}, \Pi_{[a,b],\mathcal{R}})$, where $\mathcal{R}$ denotes the set of keys returned. Set $\mathcal{L}' = \emptyset$ and proceed as follows.

- If $\mathcal{R} = \emptyset$, $\Pi_{[a,b],\mathcal{R}} = nil$, $\Pi_{[a,b],\mathcal{P}} = \{R_x, \{C_{x|_i 0}, C_{x|_i 1}, \tau_{x|_i}\}_{0 \le i \le |x|-1}\}_{x \in \mathcal{P}}$. For each $x \in \mathcal{P}$, where $\mathcal{P}$ is the canonical covering of $[a,b]$:
  a. Compute $\mathsf{EVerify}(crs, C_x, R_x)$ to check that C_x is a soft commitment. Set $y = bad$ if it is not.
  b. For i from $|x| - 1$ to 0, compute $\mathbb{S}\mathsf{Verify}(crs, (C_{x|_i 0}, C_{x|_i 1}), C_x, \tau_x)$ and set $y = bad$ if any verification fails.
- Otherwise, $(\Pi_{[a,b],\mathcal{R}} = (\{(x, \mathsf{D}(x)), \pi_x\}_{x \in \mathcal{R}}, \{C_z, C_{z'}, \pi_z\}_{z \in ST(\mathcal{R}) \backslash \mathcal{R}})$ and $\Pi_{[a,b],\mathcal{P}} = \{R_x, \{C_{x|_i 0}, C_{x|_i 1}, \tau_{x|_i}\}_{h_x \le i \le |x|-1}\}_{x \in \mathcal{P}}$.
  1. Compute $\mathcal{L}' \leftarrow \mathsf{VerifyST}(crs, com, \mathcal{R}, \Pi_{[a,b],\mathcal{R}})$ to check the authentication Steiner tree.
  2. (*Check canonical covering of $[a,b] \backslash \mathcal{R}$.*) Let $\mathcal{P}$ be the canonical covering of the keys in $[a,b] \backslash \mathcal{R}$. For each $x \in \mathcal{P}$:
     a. Compute $\mathsf{EVerify}(crs, C_x, R_x)$ and set $y = bad$ if it fails.
     b. For i from $|x| - 1$ to h_x, compute $\mathbb{S}\mathsf{Verify}(crs, (C_{x0}, C_{x1}), \tau_x)$ and set $y = bad$ if any verification fails.
If $\mathcal{L}'$ and $y \ne bad$, set and output $\mathcal{L} = \mathcal{L}'$.

4.2   Range Queries over Records in ZK-EEDB

Let $(crs, tk) \leftarrow \mathsf{Init}(1^\lambda)$ and $(com, \Delta) \leftarrow \mathsf{ComDB}(crs, \mathsf{D})$ be the ZK-EEDB commitment and decommitment information of a database D and consider an arbitrary range $\mathfrak{R} = [a_x, b_x] \times [a_y, b_y]$. Correctness of its answer is proved in zero-knowledge with several membership and range proofs in the Merkle trees built in ComDB. Due to space constraints, we sketch the algorithms for range proof generation and verification and defer its formal description the full version of this work.

ProveRQ. The value Merkle tree can be seen as a two-tiered size-hiding commitment to D, by storing commitments to $\mathsf{D}^{-1}(y)$ for every possible value in the universe $y \in [0, 2^\ell)$. Proofs of membership of a record (x, y) on the value Merkle tree would comprise of two parts. First, the committer proves that the value at some leaf x is a hard commitment to 1 in the commitment $com_{\mathsf{D}_y^{-1}}$. This shows that the record (x, y) is in some database committed in some commitment $com_{\mathsf{D}_y^{-1}}$, which we next prove to be the commitment to D_y^{-1}. We achieve this by proving that $com_{\mathsf{D}_y^{-1}}$ is committed in the value at leaf y in the ZK-EEDB commitment of the value Merkle tree, $com_{\mathsf{D}^{-1}}$.

Moving into the sketch of the algorithm, we begin with the most straightforward case: range queries over keys with $\mathfrak{R} = [a_x, b_x] \times [0, 2^\ell)$. For this, we simply use OpenI to prove (non-)membership of all keys in $[a_x, b_x]$ of the key Merkle tree. Then, for consistency, we prove that each record $(x, \mathsf{D}(x))$ is committed in the value Merkle tree as well. Next, for range queries over values with range $[0, 2^\ell) \times [a_y, b_y]$, the procedure is similar. We use OpenI on the first tier of the value Merkle tree with the interval $[a_y, b_y]$, which proves that some values do not occur in D and the remaining values store commitments to some non-empty D_y^{-1}. After that, we simply reveal the entire Merkle tree for each non-empty D_y^{-1} with OpenI on the interval $[0, 2^\ell)$. Finally, for consistency, we generate the hard authentication path from leaf x to the root of the key Merkle tree for each record (x, y) that is shown to be in D from the value Merkle tree.

Finally, we describe the proof generation for range queries over records with $\mathfrak{R} = [a_x, b_y] \times [a_y, b_y]$. We start in the first tier of the value Merkle tree, and prove that $com_{\mathsf{D}_y^{-1}}$ is the commitment to D_y^{-1} for each $y \in [a_y, b_y]$; a hard (resp. soft) authentication path from y to the root of the value Merkle tree is generated for those that are non-empty (resp. empty) in $[a_x, b_x]$. Then, for each $y \in \mathsf{D}_y^{-1}$, we use OpenI to prove (non-)membership of all the keys in the interval $[a_x, b_x]$. Consistency is proven in the same way as range queries over values.

VerifyRQ. To verify range proofs, we verify proofs for the key and value Merkle tree separately for the set of records $\mathcal{L}$ returned. For the key Merkle tree, the process is straightforward; we either verify a (non-)membership proof for an interval $[a_x, b_x]$ in range queries over keys or a set of hard authentication paths in the other two range queries. Proofs for the value Merkle tree consists of verifying that records are committed in some commitments which purport to be of D_y^{-1}. These supposed commitments of D_y^{-1} are then verified to be what they are by checking that they are committed in $com_{D^{-1}}$. Proofs fail verification if any of the sub-proofs are incorrect.

For range queries over keys, honestly computed range proofs Π contain a (non-)membership proof for all keys $x \in [a_x, b_x]$ which we verify with VerifyI. Then, for consistency, Π also contains individual hard authentication paths for each record $(x, D(x)) \in \mathcal{L}$ from leaf x to a claimed commitment of $D^{-1}(D(x))$ and hard authentication path from leaf $D(x)$ to the root of the value Merkle tree whose value is $com_{D^{-1}}$. These are verified with the authentication path verification algorithm VerifyPath.

Let $\mathcal{L}$ denote the set of records returned by the prover and Π be the range proof. For range queries over values, the set $\mathcal{L}$ can be partitioned into $\mathcal{L} = \bigcup_{y \in \mathcal{V}} \{(x_i, D(x_i) = y)\}$, where $\mathcal{V}$ is the set of unique values that occur in $\mathcal{L}$. Then, we only need to verify (non-)membership proofs for all keys in $D^{-1}(y)$ for $y \in \mathcal{V}$, to check that the records returned are correctly commited in some claimed commitment of $D^{-1}(y)$. Finally, we verify (non-)membership proofs for the interval $y \in [a_y, b_y]$ of the value Merkle tree using VerifyI to check that the claimed commitments to D_y^{-1} for $y \in [a_y, b_y]$ are valid and the remaining D_y^{-1}'s are empty. Consistency checks are straightforward, each record returned is checked to have a valid hard authentication path in Π with VerifyPath.

Lastly, for range queries over records, consistency checks are identical to range queries over values and so we focus on the differences in the value Merkle tree. Instead of checking only $y \in \mathcal{V}$, we have to do verify the (non-)membership proof for the interval $[a_x, b_x]$ with the claimed $com_{D_y^{-1}}$ for every $y \in [a_y, b_y]$. This is done with VerifyI. Finally, we check that the claimed commitments to D_y^{-1} are correctly committed with valid hard or soft authentication paths, for every $y \in [a_y, b_y]$, to the root of the value Merkle tree whose value is $com_{D^{-1}}$.

Proof Sizes. There are three cases with different input ranges $\mathfrak{R}$ and proof sizes, which is taken to be the number of nodes to open or explain. Let $\mathcal{L}$ denote the answer to the range query with input $\mathfrak{R} = [a_x, b_x] \times [a_y, b_y]$.

First, the general case where $[a_x, b_x]$ and $[a_y, b_y]$ are not $[0, 2^\ell)$. We partition $\mathcal{L} = \bigcup_{y \in [a_y, b_y]} \mathcal{L}_y$ based on the value of the record. The proof consists of $(b_y - a_y)$ authentication paths in the value Merkle tree, the same number of authentication Steiner trees, one in every Merkle tree with root value $com_{D_y^{-1}}$ for $y \in [a_y, b_y]$ and finally $|\mathcal{L}|$ authentication paths in the key Merkle tree. The Steiner trees and paths would have $\mathcal{O}(|\mathcal{L}_y|\ell)$ and ℓ nodes each respectively. This brings the total proof size to $\mathcal{O}(((b_y - a_y)(1 + K) + |\mathcal{L}|)\ell)$ nodes, where $K = \max_{y \in [a_y, b_y]} |\mathcal{L}_y|$.

Next, we consider range queries over values with $\mathfrak{R} = [0, 2^\ell) \times [a_y, b_y]$. Let $\mathcal{V}$ be the set of distinct values in the answer set $\mathcal{L}$, which we partition into disjoint subsets based on the value of the record, i.e., $\mathcal{L} = \bigcup_{y \in \mathcal{V}} \mathcal{L}_y$. Since the only difference between this and the general case is that use OpenI, we have only one authentication Steiner tree for the value Merkle tree and $|\mathcal{V}|$ many Steiner trees for each D_y^{-1} with $y \in \mathcal{V}$. Therefore, the proof size for this case is $\mathcal{O}((|\mathcal{L}| + |\mathcal{V}|(1 + K))\ell)$ with $K = \max_{y \in \mathcal{V}} |\mathcal{L}_y|$.

Lastly, for range queries over keys with $\mathfrak{R} = [a_x, b_x] \times [0, 2^\ell)$, the proof consists of the authentication Steiner tree of $\mathcal{L}$ in the key Merkle tree and $\mathcal{O}(|\mathcal{L}|$

authentication paths in the Merkle tree and some set of Merkle trees with root value $com_{D_y^{-1}}$ where $(x,y) \in \mathcal{L}$. In total, the proof size is $\mathcal{O}(|\mathcal{L}|\ell)$.

Overall, ProveRQ supports super-polynomial intervals $[a_x, b_x]$ over the key-space for any query and value-space for range queries over values. For range queries over records, only polynomial length intervals $[a_y, b_y]$ are supported.

4.3 Security of the ZK-EEDB Construction

Recall that ZK-EEDB has three properties, correctness, soundness and zero-knowledge. Correctness can be verified from the construction of ZK-EEDB easily.

Theorem 1. *The ZK-EEDB resulting from this construction is sound if the TMC scheme is mercurial-binding.*

Proof. Suppose that the adversary can produce two contradicting range queries with valid proofs, $\mathfrak{R}, \Pi$ and $\mathfrak{R}', \Pi'$. There must exist a record $(x,y) \in \mathfrak{R} \cap \mathfrak{R}'$ in $\mathcal{L} = \text{VerifyRQ}(crs, com, \mathfrak{R}, \Pi)$ but not $\mathcal{L}' = \text{VerifyRQ}(crs, com, \mathfrak{R}', \Pi')$. There are two cases in this situation: (i) There exists another record $(x,y') \in \mathcal{L}'$ such that $y' \neq y$; (ii) There exists no $y' \in [0, 2^\ell)$ such that $(x,y') \in \mathcal{L}'$.

In case (i), both (x,y) and (x,y') have valid proofs that they are committed in com_D. This means that Π and Π' contain two valid hard decommitments to distinct values in two distinct authentication paths for the leaf x of the Merkle tree of com_D. This breaks the mecurial-binding property of the TMC scheme in the same way as in the proof of the soundness property in ordinary ZK-EDBs.

In case (ii), there exists no record with key x in $\mathcal{L}'$. This implies that Π' contains a proof that $(x,1) \notin D_y^{-1}$ and therefore $x \notin D^{-1}(y)$. However, Π does contain a proof that $(x,1) \in D_y^{-1}$, leading to a contradiction between Π and Π'.

For this to happen, the first possibility is that the two proofs differ in their commitments $com_{D^{-1}}$ of $D^{-1}(y)$. If so, the value at leaf y of the Merkle tree of $com_{D^{-1}}$ has a valid hard opening to one value in Π while in Π', the value at the leaf or some node along its path to the root is either explained as a soft commitment or soft-opened to a message contradicting the hard opening. This contradicts the mercurial-binding property of the TMC scheme, which says that a mercurial commitment cannot be soft-opened to one message and hard-opened to a different one. The second possibility is that the commitments $com_{D_y^{-1}}$ are identical in both Π and Π' but the two proofs depart within the Merkle tree with root value $com_{D_y^{-1}}$. Since Π proves that $(x,1) \in D_y^{-1}$, it contains a hard authentication path from leaf x to the root. However, Π' proves that $(x,1) \notin D_y^{-1}$, meaning either: (a) The value at leaf x is a soft commitment; (b) Some node along the path from leaf x to the root is explained as a soft commitment in Π'. Either way, Π shows that the value at some node is a hard commitment whereas Π' shows that otherwise, the value at the same node either explained as a soft commitment or soft-opened to a message that contradicts the hard opening in Π. As before, this contradicts the mercurial-binding property of the TMC scheme.

Theorem 2. *The ZK-EEDB resulting from this construction satisfies the zero-knowledge property if the TMC scheme satisfies the four equivocation properties.*

Proof. The zero-knowledge property follows from the equivocation properties enabled by the trapdoor in the TMC scheme. The ZK-EEDB simulator (SInit, SCom, SProveRQ^D), which is constructed below, is similar to the ZK-EDB simulator. However, a key change is that SProveRQ^D additionally uses FakeExplain. To simulate range proofs, FakeExplain allows explaining fake commitments as soft commitments when some subtrees have to be proved empty.

- $(crs', st_0) \leftarrow$ SInit(1^λ): Run $(crs, tk) \leftarrow$ Init(1^λ) and output the common reference string and simulator state $(crs' = crs, st_0 = tk)$.
- $(com', st_1) \leftarrow$ SCom(st_0): Compute $com'_D \leftarrow$ MFake($crs'; R_0$) and $com'_{D^{-1}} \leftarrow$ MFake($crs'; R_1$) and output $(com' = (com'_D, com'_{D^{-1}}), st_1 = (R, tk))$.
- $\Pi' \leftarrow$ SProveRQ^D($crs', st_1, \mathfrak{R} = [a_x, b_x] \times [a_y, b_y]$): Obtain the set $\mathcal{S} = D \cap \mathfrak{R}$ by querying the database oracle and let $\mathcal{S}' \in st_1$ contain the commitments and proofs that were computed in previous queries. We denote with $\mathcal{S}_{D^{-1}}$, the set of distinct values in $\mathcal{S}$. Then, let $[\mathcal{S}]_{D_y^{-1}}$ be the set of keys in $[\mathcal{S}]$ whose values in D are y. Compute Π' as follows:

  1. The answer defines several Steiner trees and paths that are needed to prove the correctness of the answer to the adversary.
     a. If $[a_y, b_y] = [0, 2^\ell)$, then $\mathcal{S}$ induces an authentication Steiner tree, $ST([\mathcal{S}])$ in the Merkle tree of com'_D and $|\mathcal{S}|$ many authentication paths, $\mathcal{L}$ and $\mathcal{L}_y$, in the Merkle trees of $com'_{D^{-1}}$ and $com'_{D_y^{-1}}$ for $y \in \mathcal{S}_{D^{-1}}$ respectively.
     b. If $[a_x, b_x] = [0, 2^\ell)$, then $\mathcal{S}_{D^{-1}}$ defines an authentication Steiner tree, $ST(\mathcal{S}_{D^{-1}})$ in the Merkle tree of $com'_{D^{-1}}$ and similar Steiner trees $ST([\mathcal{S}]_y)$ in the Merkle trees of $com'_{D_y^{-1}}$ for $y \in \mathcal{S}_{D^{-1}}$. Finally, $[\mathcal{S}]$ defines $|[\mathcal{S}]|$ many authentication paths $\mathcal{L}$ in the Merkle tree of com'_D.
     c. If neither $[a_x, b_x]$ not $[a_y, b_y]$ are $[0, 2^\ell)$, then $\mathcal{S}_{D^{-1}}$ defines $|ST(\mathcal{S}_{D^{-1}})|$ paths, $\mathcal{L}$ in the Merkle tree of $com'_{D^{-1}}$ and Steiner trees $ST([\mathcal{S}]_y)$ in the Merkle trees of $com'_{D_y^{-1}}$ for $y \in \mathcal{S}_{D^{-1}}$. $[\mathcal{S}]$ also defines an authentication Steiner tree $ST([\mathcal{S}])$ in the Merkle tree of com'_D.
  2. For each range type, let $\mathcal{N}$ be the set of nodes in the trees and paths induced by the answer $D \cap \mathfrak{R}$. Then, for every node $x \in \mathcal{N} \setminus \mathcal{S}'$, compute fake commitments $C_x \leftarrow$ MFake($crs; R_x$).
  3. For the fake commitments created in Step 2 and their parents, compute appropriate hard and soft decommitments and explanations using ℍEquivocate, 𝕊Equivocate and FakeExplain to simulate an honest proof.
  4. Add the fake commitments, hard and soft decommitments and explanations computed in Steps 1 and 2 to the state st_1.

The output of the simulator is indistinguishable from that of an honest prover because of the equivocation properties of the TMC scheme used. There are two types of outputs from the simulator, the CRS from initialization and fake commitments, decommitments and explanations in proofs to queries from the adversary. The simulated CRS is indistinguishable from a real CRS one as both are trapdoor mercurial commitment keys. From the four equivocation properties of the TMC scheme, the joint distribution of fake commitments and their hard/soft equivocations or explanations are statistically indistinguishable from hard/soft commitments and their hard/soft openings or explanations. $\qquad\square$

5 Lattice Instantiations

5.1 A Trapdoor Mercurial Commitment from Standard Lattices

Let $\lambda \in \mathbb{N}$ be a security parameter. The scheme works with message space $\mathcal{M} = \{0, 1\}^l$, where $l \in \mathsf{poly}(\lambda)$. For a dimension $n = \mathcal{O}(\lambda)$ and prime modulus $q = \widetilde{\mathcal{O}}(l \cdot n^2 + n^4)$, let $w = n\lceil \log q \rceil$, $\bar{m} = 2n\lceil \log q \rceil$ and $m = \bar{m} + w$. Choose a Gaussian parameter $\sigma = \Omega(\sqrt{n \log q \log n})$.

- $(mpk, msk) \leftarrow \mathsf{Setup}(1^\lambda)$: Choose a matrix $\mathbf{A}_0 \hookleftarrow U(\mathbb{Z}_q^{n \times l})$. Run algorithm $\mathsf{TrapGen}(n, m, q)$ (Lemma 4) to generate a pair $(\mathbf{A}_1, \mathbf{T})$, where $\mathbf{A}_1 \in \mathbb{Z}_q^{n \times m}$ is statistically close to uniform and $\mathbf{T} \in \mathbb{Z}^{\bar{m} \times w}$ is its trapdoor.
  Output $mpk = (\mathbf{A}_0, \mathbf{A}_1)$ and $msk = \mathbf{T}$.
- $\mathbf{C} \leftarrow \mathbb{H}\mathsf{Commit}(mpk, \boldsymbol{\mu}; (\mathbf{R}, \mathbf{r}))$: Given a message $\boldsymbol{\mu} \in \{0, 1\}^l$ and randomness $\mathbf{R} \hookleftarrow D_{\mathbb{Z}^{m \times w}, \sigma}$ and $\mathbf{r} \hookleftarrow D_{\mathbb{Z}^{m+w}, \sigma}$, define $\mathbf{B} = [\mathbf{A}_1 \mid \mathbf{B}_1] \in \mathbb{Z}_q^{n \times (m+w)}$, where $\mathbf{B}_1 = \mathbf{A}_1 \cdot \mathbf{R} \in \mathbb{Z}_q^{n \times w}$. Then, compute $\mathbf{c} = \mathbf{A}_0 \cdot \boldsymbol{\mu} + \mathbf{B} \cdot \mathbf{r} \in \mathbb{Z}_q^n$ and output the hard commitment $\mathbf{C} = (\mathbf{c}, \mathbf{B}_1) \in \mathbb{Z}_q^n \times \mathbb{Z}_q^{n \times w}$.
- $\pi \leftarrow \mathbb{H}\mathsf{Open}(mpk, \boldsymbol{\mu}; (\mathbf{R}, \mathbf{r})$: Output $\pi = (\mathbf{R}, \mathbf{r}) \in \mathbb{Z}^{m \times w} \times \mathbb{Z}^{m+w}$.
- $\mathbb{H}\mathsf{Verify}(mpk, \boldsymbol{\mu}, \mathbf{C}, \pi)$: Given a commitment $\mathbf{C} = (\mathbf{c}, \mathbf{B}_1) \in \mathbb{Z}_q^n \times \mathbb{Z}_q^{n \times w}$ and a purported hard opening $\pi = (\mathbf{R}, \mathbf{r})$, proceed as follows.
  1. Return 0 if $\mathbf{R} = [\mathbf{r}_1 \mid \ldots \mid \mathbf{r}_w]$ has a column such that $\|\mathbf{r}_i\| > \sigma\sqrt{m}$ or if $\|\mathbf{r}\| > \sigma\sqrt{m+w}$.
  2. Let $\mathbf{B} = [\mathbf{A}_1 \mid \mathbf{B}_1] \in \mathbb{Z}_q^{n \times (m+w)}$. Return 1 if $\mathbf{B}_1 = \mathbf{A}_1 \cdot \mathbf{R}$ and $\mathbf{c} = \mathbf{A}_0 \cdot \boldsymbol{\mu} + \mathbf{B} \cdot \mathbf{r}$.
- $\mathbf{C} \leftarrow \mathbb{S}\mathsf{Commit}(mpk; (\mathbf{R}, \mathbf{r}))$: Given $\mathbf{R} \hookleftarrow D_{\mathbb{Z}^{m \times w}, \sigma}$ and $\mathbf{r} \hookleftarrow D_{\mathbb{Z}^{m+w}, \sigma}$, compute the matrix $\mathbf{B} = [\mathbf{A}_1 \mid \mathbf{G} - \mathbf{A}_1 \cdot \mathbf{R}] \in \mathbb{Z}_q^{n \times (m+w)}$ and $\mathbf{c} = \mathbf{B} \cdot \mathbf{r} \in \mathbb{Z}_q^n$. Output $\mathbf{C} = (\mathbf{c}, \mathbf{B}_1) \in \mathbb{Z}_q^n \times \mathbb{Z}_q^{n \times w}$, where $\mathbf{B}_1 = \mathbf{G} - \mathbf{A}_1 \cdot \mathbf{R}$. Note that matrix $\mathbf{R}$ is a trapdoor for $\mathbf{B}$.
- $\tau \leftarrow \mathbb{S}\mathsf{Open}(mpk, \boldsymbol{\mu}, \mathsf{flag}; (\mathbf{R}, \mathbf{r}))$:
  - If $\mathsf{flag} = \mathbb{S}$, we must have $\mathbf{C} = (\mathbf{c}, \mathbf{B}_1) = (\mathbf{B} \cdot \mathbf{r}, \mathbf{G} - \mathbf{A}_1 \cdot \mathbf{R})$. Compute $\mathbf{c}' = \mathbf{c} - \mathbf{A}_0 \cdot \boldsymbol{\mu}$ and sample $\mathbf{r}' \leftarrow \mathsf{SampleD}(\mathbf{R}, \mathbf{B}, \mathbf{c}', \sigma)$ (Lemma 4).
    Then, output $\tau = \mathbf{r}' \in \mathbb{Z}^{m+w}$, which satisfies $\mathbf{c} = \mathbf{A}_0 \cdot \boldsymbol{\mu} + \mathbf{B} \cdot \mathbf{r}'$ and $\|\mathbf{r}'\| \le \sigma\sqrt{m+w}$ with overwhelming probability (Lemma 1).
  - If $\mathsf{flag} = \mathbb{H}$, output $\tau = \mathbf{r} \in \mathbb{Z}^{m+w}$.
- $\mathbb{S}\mathsf{Verify}(mpk, \boldsymbol{\mu}, \mathbf{C}, \tau)$: Let $\mathbf{C} = (\mathbf{c}, \mathbf{B}_1) \in \mathbb{Z}_q^n \times \mathbb{Z}_q^{n \times w}$ and $\tau = \mathbf{r} \in \mathbb{Z}^{m+w}$ and define $\mathbf{B} = [\mathbf{A}_1 \mid \mathbf{B}_1] \in \mathbb{Z}_q^{n \times (m+w)}$. Return 1 if $\mathbf{c} = \mathbf{A}_0 \cdot \boldsymbol{\mu} + \mathbf{B} \cdot \mathbf{r}$ and $\|\mathbf{r}\| \le \sigma\sqrt{m+w}$. Otherwise, return 0.

- $\mathbf{C} \leftarrow \mathsf{MFake}(mpk; (\mathbf{R}, \mathbf{r}))$: Given $\mathbf{R} \hookleftarrow D_{\mathbb{Z}^{m \times w}, \sigma}$ and $\mathbf{r} \hookleftarrow D_{\mathbb{Z}^{m+w}, \sigma}$, compute $\mathbf{B} = [\mathbf{A}_1 \mid \mathbf{B}_1] \in \mathbb{Z}_q^{n \times (m+w)}$, where $\mathbf{B}_1 = \mathbf{A}_1 \cdot \mathbf{R}$, and compute $\mathbf{c} = \mathbf{B} \cdot \mathbf{r}$. Output $\mathbf{C} = (\mathbf{c}, \mathbf{B}_1)$.
- $\pi \leftarrow \mathbb{H}\mathsf{Equivocate}(msk, \boldsymbol{\mu}; (\mathbf{R}, \mathbf{r}))$: Let $msk = \mathbf{T} \in \mathbb{Z}^{\bar{m} \times w}$ and let the fake commitment be $\mathbf{C} = (\mathbf{c}, \mathbf{B}_1) = (\mathbf{B} \cdot \mathbf{r}, \mathbf{A}_1 \cdot \mathbf{R})$, where $\mathbf{B} = [\mathbf{A}_1 \mid \mathbf{A}_1 \cdot \mathbf{R}]$. Compute $\mathbf{c}' = \mathbf{c} - \mathbf{A}_0 \cdot \boldsymbol{\mu}$. Then, extend $\mathbf{T}$ into a trapdoor $\mathbf{T_B}$ for the matrix $\mathbf{B} = [\mathbf{A}_1 \mid \mathbf{A}_1 \cdot \mathbf{R}]$ and sample $\mathbf{r}' \leftarrow \mathsf{SampleD}(\mathbf{T_B}, \mathbf{B}, \mathbf{c}', \sigma)$. Output $\pi = (\mathbf{R}, \mathbf{r}') \in \mathbb{Z}^{m \times w} \times \mathbb{Z}^{m+w}$.
- $\tau \leftarrow \mathbb{S}\mathsf{Equivocate}(msk, \boldsymbol{\mu}; (\mathbf{R}, \mathbf{r}))$: Let $msk = \mathbf{T} \in \mathbb{Z}^{\bar{m} \times w}$ and let the fake commitment be $\mathbf{C} = (\mathbf{c}, \mathbf{B}_1) = (\mathbf{B} \cdot \mathbf{r}, \mathbf{A}_1 \cdot \mathbf{R})$, where $\mathbf{B} = [\mathbf{A}_1 \mid \mathbf{A}_1 \cdot \mathbf{R}]$. Compute $\mathbf{c}' = \mathbf{c} - \mathbf{A}_0 \cdot \boldsymbol{\mu}$. Then, extend $\mathbf{T}$ into a trapdoor $\mathbf{T_B}$ for the matrix $\mathbf{B} = [\mathbf{A}_1 \mid \mathbf{A}_1 \cdot \mathbf{R}]$ and sample $\mathbf{r}' \leftarrow \mathsf{SampleD}(\mathbf{T_B}, \mathbf{B}, \mathbf{c}', \sigma)$. Output $\tau = \mathbf{r}' \in \mathbb{Z}^{m+w}$.
- $(\mathbf{R}', \mathbf{r}') \leftarrow \mathsf{FakeExplain}(msk; (\mathbf{R}, \mathbf{r}))$: Given $msk = \mathbf{T} \in \mathbb{Z}^{\bar{m} \times w}$ together with a Gaussian matrix $\mathbf{R} = [\mathbf{r}_1 \mid \ldots \mid \mathbf{r}_w] \hookleftarrow D_{\mathbb{Z}^{m \times w}, \sigma}$ and a vector $\mathbf{r} \hookleftarrow D_{\mathbb{Z}^{m+w}, \sigma}$ such that $\mathbf{C} = (\mathbf{c}, \mathbf{B}_1) = (\mathbf{B} \cdot \mathbf{r}, \mathbf{A}_1 \cdot \mathbf{R})$ is a fake commitment, set $\mathbf{r}' = \mathbf{r}$ and use the trapdoor $\mathbf{T}$ for $\mathbf{A}_1$ to sample a small-norm $\mathbf{R}' = [\mathbf{r}_1' \mid \ldots \mid \mathbf{r}_w']$ such that $\mathbf{A}_1 \cdot \mathbf{R}' = \mathbf{G} - \mathbf{A}_1 \cdot \mathbf{R}$. To do this, let $\mathbf{G} = [\mathbf{g}_1 \mid \ldots \mid \mathbf{g}_w]$, and for each $i \in [w]$, sample $\mathbf{r}_i' \leftarrow \mathsf{SampleD}(\mathbf{T}, \mathbf{A}_1, \mathbf{g}_i - \mathbf{A}_1 \cdot \mathbf{r}_i)$. Then, output $(\mathbf{R}', \mathbf{r}')$ which satisfy $\mathbf{C} = (\mathbf{c}, \mathbf{B}_1) = (\mathbf{B} \cdot \mathbf{r}', \mathbf{G} - \mathbf{A}_1 \cdot \mathbf{R}')$.

5.2   Analysis

We prove that the trapdoor mercurial commitment scheme described in Sect. 5.1 satisfies the correctness and security properties defined in Sect. 2.1.

Correctness. By Lemma 1, with overwhelming probability, samples from discrete Gaussian distributions $D_{\mathbb{Z}^m, \sigma}$ and $D_{\mathbb{Z}^{m+w}, \sigma}$ have their Euclidean norms bounded by $\sigma\sqrt{m}$ and $\sigma\sqrt{m+w}$, respectively. Moreover, the outputs of $\mathsf{SampleD}$ are statistically close to discrete Gaussian samples, by Lemma 4. Therefore, if proofs π and τ are generated as in Sect. 5.1, then they should pass the verifications for Euclidean norms performed by algorithms $\mathbb{H}\mathsf{Verify}$ and $\mathbb{S}\mathsf{Verify}$. Note further that the equations modulo q verified by these algorithms must hold by construction. As a result, the scheme is correct with overwhelming probability.

Security. In the following lemmas, we show that the proposed scheme satisfies mercurial-binding under the SIS assumption, and HH, HS, SS and SE equivocation in the statistical sense.

Lemma 5. *The scheme is mercurial-binding under the* $\mathsf{SIS}_{n,m,q,\beta}$ *assumption, with* $\beta = \sigma \cdot (l\sqrt{\bar{m}} + \sqrt{\sigma m \bar{m}(\sigma^2 w^3 + 2m)})$.

Proof. Since the scheme is a proper mercurial commitment (i.e., hard openings contain their corresponding soft opening as a proper subset), we only need to consider the hard-soft case. Towards a contradiction, let us assume that the adversary can come up with a commitment $\mathbf{C} = (\mathbf{c}, \mathbf{B}_1) \in \mathbb{Z}_q^n \times \mathbb{Z}_q^{n \times w}$ which it can hard-open to a message $\boldsymbol{\mu}$ and soft-opened to a different message $\boldsymbol{\mu}'$. This means that the adversary can output $(\boldsymbol{\mu}, \mathbf{R}, \mathbf{r}) \in \{0,1\}^l \times \mathbb{Z}^{m \times w} \times \mathbb{Z}^{m+w}$ and $(\boldsymbol{\mu}', \mathbf{r}') \in \{0,1\}^l \times \mathbb{Z}^{m+w}$ such that $\mathbf{B}_1 = \mathbf{A}_1 \cdot \mathbf{R}$ and

$$\mathbf{c} = \mathbf{A}_0 \cdot \boldsymbol{\mu} + [\mathbf{A}_1 \mid \mathbf{A}_1 \cdot \mathbf{R}] \cdot \mathbf{r} = \mathbf{A}_0 \cdot \boldsymbol{\mu}' + [\mathbf{A}_1 \mid \mathbf{A}_1 \cdot \mathbf{R}] \cdot \mathbf{r}'. \tag{1}$$

Assuming that such a mercurial-binding adversary $\mathcal{A}$ exists, we can build a $\mathsf{SIS}_{n,m,q,\beta}$ solver $\mathcal{B}$ which takes as input a $\mathsf{SIS}_{n,m,q,\beta}$ instance $\mathbf{A} \in \mathbb{Z}_q^{n \times \bar{m}}$ and finds a non-zero vector $\mathbf{v}^\star \in \mathbb{Z}^{\bar{m}}$ of $\Lambda^\perp(\mathbf{A})$ such that $\|\mathbf{v}^\star\| \leq \beta$. To this end, $\mathcal{B}$ samples $\mathbf{R}_0 \hookleftarrow D_{\mathbb{Z},\sigma}^{\bar{m} \times l}$, $\mathbf{R}_1 \hookleftarrow D_{\mathbb{Z},\sigma}^{\bar{m} \times m}$ and defines

$$\mathbf{A}_0 = \mathbf{A} \cdot \mathbf{R}_0 \in \mathbb{Z}_q^{n \times l}, \qquad \mathbf{A}_1 = \mathbf{A} \cdot \mathbf{R}_1 \in \mathbb{Z}_q^{n \times m}.$$

Note that, by Lemma 2, matrices $\mathbf{A}_0$ and $\mathbf{A}_1$ are statistically close to the distributions $U(\mathbb{Z}_q^{n \times l})$ and $U(\mathbb{Z}_q^{n \times m})$, respectively. The adversary $\mathcal{A}$ is given $mpk = (\mathbf{A}_0, \mathbf{A}_1)$ and, assuming that it can output $(\boldsymbol{\mu}, \mathbf{R}, \mathbf{r})$ and $(\boldsymbol{\mu}', \mathbf{r}')$ satisfying (1) for distinct $\boldsymbol{\mu} \neq \boldsymbol{\mu}'$, we have

$$\mathbf{A}_0 \cdot (\boldsymbol{\mu} - \boldsymbol{\mu}')) = \mathbf{A}_1 \cdot [\mathbf{I}_m \mid \mathbf{R}] \cdot (\mathbf{r}' - \mathbf{r}) \mod q.$$

This implies that

$$\mathbf{v}^\star = \mathbf{R}_0 \cdot (\boldsymbol{\mu} - \boldsymbol{\mu}') + \mathbf{R}_1 \cdot [\mathbf{I}_m \mid \mathbf{R}] \cdot (\mathbf{r} - \mathbf{r}') \in \mathbb{Z}^{\bar{m}} \tag{2}$$

is a short vector of $\Lambda^\perp(\mathbf{A})$ with norm $\|\mathbf{v}^\star\| \leq \sigma \cdot (l\sqrt{\bar{m}} + \sqrt{\sigma m \bar{m}(\sigma^2 w^3 + 2m)})$. Moreover, we claim that it is non-zero with overwhelming probability. Indeed, $(\boldsymbol{\mu} - \boldsymbol{\mu}') \in \{-1, 0, 1\}^l$ has at least one non-zero coordinate by hypothesis. Given that the columns of $\mathbf{R}_0$ have at least $\Omega(n)$ bits of min-entropy conditionally on $\mathbf{A}_0 = \mathbf{A} \cdot \mathbf{R}_0$ (by Lemmas 2 and 3), the product $\mathbf{R}_0 \cdot (\boldsymbol{\mu} - \boldsymbol{\mu}')$ is a linear combination (with coefficients in $\{-1, 0, 1\}$) of the columns of $\mathbf{R}_0$ which contains a completely unpredictable term. Hence, the right-hand-side member of (2) can only cancel over $\mathbb{Z}^{\bar{m}}$ with negligible probability.   □

Lemma 6. *The scheme provides HH, HS, SS and SE equivocation in the statistical sense.*

Proof. For any message $\boldsymbol{\mu}$, we show that the distribution of fake commitments and their hard equivocations to $\boldsymbol{\mu}$ is statistically close to that of hard commitments and their hard openings to $\boldsymbol{\mu}$.

We note that $\mathbf{B}_1$ is generated in the same way in both fake and hard commitments. Moreover, since $\mathbf{A}_1$ is statistically uniform over $\mathbb{Z}_q^{n \times m}$, Lemma 2 implies that the distribution $\{(\mathbf{A}_1, \mathbf{B}_1) = (\mathbf{A}_1, \mathbf{A}_1 \cdot \mathbf{R}) \mid \mathbf{R} \hookleftarrow D_{\mathbb{Z}^{m \times w}, \sigma}\}$ is statistically close to the distribution $U(\mathbb{Z}_q^{n \times m}) \times U(\mathbb{Z}_q^{n \times w})$, meaning $\mathbf{B} \sim U(\mathbb{Z}_q^{n \times (m+w)})$ in both hard and fake commitments. By Lemma 2, we find that the distribution of fake commitments $(\mathbf{c}, \mathbf{B}_1)$, which is given by $\{([\mathbf{A}_1 \mid \mathbf{B}_1] \cdot \mathbf{r}, \mathbf{B}_1) \mid \mathbf{r} \hookleftarrow D_{\mathbb{Z}^{m+w}, \sigma}\}$, is in turn statistically close to $U(\mathbb{Z}_q^n) \times U(\mathbb{Z}_q^{n \times (m+w)})$. This implies that the distribution of fake commitments remains statistically unchanged if we compute $\mathbf{c}$ as $\mathbf{c} = \mathbf{A} \cdot \boldsymbol{\mu} + \mathbf{B} \cdot \mathbf{r}$ instead of $\mathbf{c} = \mathbf{B} \cdot \mathbf{r}$. We call ideal$_1$ this modification of the ideal experiment. Moreover, by Lemma 2 again, we know that, for any statistically uniform matrix $\mathbf{A} \sim U(\mathbb{Z}_q^{n \times (m+w)})$, the distribution

$$\left\{(\mathbf{A}, \mathbf{A} \cdot \mathbf{r}, \mathbf{r}) \in \mathbb{Z}_q^{n \times (m+w)} \times \mathbb{Z}_q^n \times \mathbb{Z}^{m+w} \mid \mathbf{r} \hookleftarrow D_{\mathbb{Z}^{m+w}, \sigma}\right\} \tag{3}$$

is statistically close to

$$\left\{(\mathbf{A}, \mathbf{u}, \mathbf{r}) \in \mathbb{Z}_q^{n \times (m+w)} \times \mathbb{Z}_q^n \times \mathbb{Z}^{m+w} \mid \mathbf{u} \hookleftarrow U(\mathbb{Z}_q^n), \mathbf{r} \hookleftarrow D_{\Lambda^{\mathbf{u}}(\mathbf{A}), \sigma}\right\}. \tag{4}$$

Consequently, we can modify ideal_1 by changing the way to equivocate the fake commitment. Instead of using extending $\mathbf{T}$ into a trapdoor for $\mathbf{B} = [\mathbf{A}_1 \mid \mathbf{B}_1]$ and using it to sample $\mathbf{r}$ in a coset of the lattice $\Lambda^{\perp}(\mathbf{B})$, we just reveal the vector $\mathbf{r} \hookleftarrow D_{\mathbb{Z}^{m+w}, \sigma}$ that was used to compute $\mathbf{c} = \mathbf{A} \cdot \boldsymbol{\mu} + \mathbf{B} \cdot \mathbf{r}$. If we call this experiment ideal_2, we find it statistically indistinguishable from the ideal experiment thanks to the statistical closeness of (3) and (4). We observe that ideal_2 is nothing but the real HH equivocation experiment since $\mathbf{B}_1$ is generated in the same way in both experiments. This shows the HH equivocation property. The HS and SS equivocation properties can be shown in a completely similar way.

As for the SE equivocation property, it follows from two observations. First, Lemma 2 implies that the distributions

$$D_{\mathsf{fake}} := \left\{\mathbf{A}_1 \cdot \mathbf{R} \mid \mathbf{R} \hookleftarrow D_{\mathbb{Z}^{m \times w}, \sigma}\right\}, \quad D_{\mathsf{soft}} := \left\{\mathbf{G} - \mathbf{A}_1 \cdot \mathbf{R}' \mid \mathbf{R}' \hookleftarrow D_{\mathbb{Z}^{m \times w}, \sigma}\right\}$$

are both statistically close to $U(\mathbb{Z}_q^{n \times w})$. Hence, the adversary's view remains statistically the same if we generate fake commitments by sampling $\mathbf{B}_1$ from D_{soft} instead of D_{fake} in the ideal experiment. Moreover, since distributions (3) and (4) are statistically close, $\mathcal{A}$'s view remains statistically the same after modification. instead of using the trapdoor $\mathbf{T}$ of $\Lambda^{\perp}(\mathbf{A}_1)$, we reveal the Gaussian matrix $\mathbf{R}'$, used to get $\mathbf{B}_1 = \mathbf{G} - \mathbf{A}_1 \cdot \mathbf{R}'$ after sampling $\mathbf{R}' \hookleftarrow D_{\mathbb{Z}^{m \times w}, \sigma}$. With this, the result is identical to the real game, proving the SE property.   □

5.3 Remarks

The scheme from Sect. 5.1 produces commitments of the form $\mathbf{C} = (\mathbf{c}, \mathbf{B}_1) \in \mathbb{Z}_q^n \times \mathbb{Z}_q^{n \times w}$, and thus, have length $k = n(w+1)\lceil \log q \rceil$ bits. Its message space is $\mathcal{M} = \{0, 1\}^l$, where l can vary depending on the context.

The scheme leads to a lattice-based ZK-EEDB system, following the constructions of Sects. 3 and 4. In this system, the following 4 different message lengths, $\{l_1, l_2, l_3, l_4\}$, are considered.

1. At leaves of the first tree, we commit to values of bit-length $l_1 = \ell$.
2. At non-leaf nodes in both trees, since we commit to 2 commitment strings, we work with message length $l_2 = 2k$.
3. At leaves of the second tree, we store commitments to $\mathsf{D}^{-1}(y)$, which is a commitment string of bit-length $l_3 = k$.
4. When building a commitment of $\mathsf{D}_y^{-1} = \{(x, 1) \mid (x, y) \in \mathsf{D}\}$, we also work with message length $l_4 = 1$.

To handle these message lengths, we need only adjust the number of columns in $\mathbf{A}_0 \in \mathbb{Z}_q^{n \times l}$, with $l = \max\{l_1, l_2, l_3, l_4\}$. For each $i \in [4]$, we use $\mathbf{A}_{0,i} \in \mathbb{Z}_q^{n \times l_i}$, the matrix that is the first l_i columns of $\mathbf{A}_0$, to commit to a length-l_i message.

A description of an authentication path with its commitment strings requires $\zeta = \mathcal{O}(l \cdot k)$ bits, which is $\widetilde{\mathcal{O}}(\lambda^3)$ when $l = \mathcal{O}(\lambda)$. Fortunately, this can be greatly reduced if the TMC scheme is adapted to the ring setting. As shown by Micciancio and Peikert [22] and later by Ducas and Micciancio [8], with appropriate choice of parameters, all the lattice-based cryptographic ingredients of Sect. 2.3 can be adapted to the ring setting. This lets us use $w = \mathcal{O}(\log q)$ (instead of $w = \mathcal{O}(n \log q)$), thereby reducing the commitment size and ζ by a factor of $\mathcal{O}(\lambda)$. We refer to the full version of this work for the details.

Acknowledgements. Part of this research was funded by Singapore Ministry of Education under Research Grant MOE2016-T2-2-014(S). Another part was funded by BPI-France in the context of the national project RISQ (P141580). This work was also supported in part by the European Union PROMETHEUS project (Horizon 2020 Research and Innovation Program, grant 780701). Khoa Nguyen was also supported by the Gopalakrishnan – NTU Presidential Postdoctoral Fellowship 2018. Huaxiong Wang was also supported by the National Research Foundation, Prime Minister's Office, Singapore under its Strategic Capability Research Centres Funding Initiative.

References

1. Blum, M., Feldman, P., Micali, S.: Non-interactive zero-knowledge and its applications. In: STOC, pp. 103–112. ACM (1988)
2. Catalano, D., Dodis, Y., Visconti, I.: Mercurial commitments: minimal assumptions and efficient constructions. In: Halevi, S., Rabin, T. (eds.) TCC 2006. LNCS, vol. 3876, pp. 120–144. Springer, Heidelberg (2006). https://doi.org/10.1007/11681878_7
3. Catalano, D., Fiore, D.: Vector commitments and their applications. In: Kurosawa, K., Hanaoka, G. (eds.) PKC 2013. LNCS, vol. 7778, pp. 55–72. Springer, Heidelberg (2013). https://doi.org/10.1007/978-3-642-36362-7_5
4. Catalano, D., Fiore, D., Messina, M.: Zero-knowledge sets with short proofs. In: Smart, N. (ed.) EUROCRYPT 2008. LNCS, vol. 4965, pp. 433–450. Springer, Heidelberg (2008). https://doi.org/10.1007/978-3-540-78967-3_25
5. Chase, M., Healy, A., Lysyanskaya, A., Malkin, T., Reyzin, L.: Mercurial commitments with applications to zero-knowledge sets. In: Cramer, R. (ed.) EUROCRYPT 2005. LNCS, vol. 3494, pp. 422–439. Springer, Heidelberg (2005). https://doi.org/10.1007/11426639_25
6. Chase, M., Healy, A., Lysyanskaya, A., Malkin, T., Reyzin, L.: Mercurial commitments with applications to zero-knowledge sets. J. Cryptology **26**(2), 251–279 (2013)
7. Chase, M., Visconti, I.: Secure database commitments and universal arguments of quasi knowledge. In: Safavi-Naini, R., Canetti, R. (eds.) CRYPTO 2012. LNCS, vol. 7417, pp. 236–254. Springer, Heidelberg (2012). https://doi.org/10.1007/978-3-642-32009-5_15
8. Ducas, L., Micciancio, D.: Improved short lattice signatures in the standard model. In: Garay, J.A., Gennaro, R. (eds.) CRYPTO 2014. LNCS, vol. 8616, pp. 335–352. Springer, Heidelberg (2014). https://doi.org/10.1007/978-3-662-44371-2_19

9. Gennaro, R., Micali, S.: Independent zero-knowledge sets. In: Bugliesi, M., Preneel, B., Sassone, V., Wegener, I. (eds.) ICALP 2006. LNCS, vol. 4052, pp. 34–45. Springer, Heidelberg (2006). https://doi.org/10.1007/11787006_4

10. Gentry, C., Peikert, C., Vaikuntanathan, V.: Trapdoors for hard lattices and new cryptographic constructions. In: STOC 2008 (2008)

11. Ghosh, E., Ohrimenko, O., Tamassia, R.: Verifiable order queries and order statistics on a list in zero-knowledge. In: ACNS (2015)

12. Ghosh, E., Ohrimenko, O., Tamassia, R.: Efficient verifiable range and closest point queries in zero-knowledge. PoPETs **2016**(4), 373–388 (2016)

13. Goyal, V., Ostrovsky, R., Scafuro, A., Visconti, I.: Black-box non-black-box zero knowledge. In: STOC (2014)

14. Ishai, Y., Kushilevitz, E., Ostrovksy, R., Sahai, A.: Zero-knowledge from secure multiparty computation. In: STOC (2007)

15. Kate, A., Zaverucha, G.M., Goldberg, I.: Constant-size commitments to polynomials and their applications. In: Abe, M. (ed.) ASIACRYPT 2010. LNCS, vol. 6477, pp. 177–194. Springer, Heidelberg (2010). https://doi.org/10.1007/978-3-642-17373-8_11

16. Kawachi, A., Tanaka, K., Xagawa, K.: Concurrently secure identification schemes based on the worst-case hardness of lattice problems. In: Pieprzyk, J. (ed.) ASIACRYPT 2008. LNCS, vol. 5350, pp. 372–389. Springer, Heidelberg (2008). https://doi.org/10.1007/978-3-540-89255-7_23

17. Libert, B., Yung, M.: Concise mercurial vector commitments and independent zero-knowledge sets with short proofs. In: Micciancio, D. (ed.) TCC 2010. LNCS, vol. 5978, pp. 499–517. Springer, Heidelberg (2010). https://doi.org/10.1007/978-3-642-11799-2_30

18. Liskov, M.: Updatable zero-knowledge databases. In: Roy, B. (ed.) ASIACRYPT 2005. LNCS, vol. 3788, pp. 174–198. Springer, Heidelberg (2005). https://doi.org/10.1007/11593447_10

19. Lyubashevsky, V.: Fiat-shamir with aborts: applications to lattice and factoring-based signatures. In: Matsui, M. (ed.) ASIACRYPT 2009. LNCS, vol. 5912, pp. 598–616. Springer, Heidelberg (2009). https://doi.org/10.1007/978-3-642-10366-7_35

20. Merkle, R.C.: A certified digital signature. In: Brassard, G. (ed.) CRYPTO 1989. LNCS, vol. 435, pp. 218–238. Springer, New York (1990). https://doi.org/10.1007/0-387-34805-0_21

21. Micali, S., Rabin, M.O., Kilian, J.: Zero-knowledge sets. In: 44th FOCS (2003)

22. Micciancio, D., Peikert, C.: Trapdoors for lattices: simpler, tighter, faster, smaller. In: Pointcheval, D., Johansson, T. (eds.) EUROCRYPT 2012. LNCS, vol. 7237, pp. 700–718. Springer, Heidelberg (2012). https://doi.org/10.1007/978-3-642-29011-4_41

23. Micciancio, D., Peikert, C.: Hardness of SIS and LWE with small parameters. In: Canetti, R., Garay, J.A. (eds.) CRYPTO 2013. LNCS, vol. 8042, pp. 21–39. Springer, Heidelberg (2013). https://doi.org/10.1007/978-3-642-40041-4_2

24. Micciancio, D., Regev, O.: Worst-case to average-case reductions based on gaussian measures. SIAM J. Comput. **37**(1), 267–302 (2007)

25. Naor, D., Naor, M., Lotspiech, J.: Revocation and tracing schemes for stateless receivers. In: Kilian, J. (ed.) CRYPTO 2001. LNCS, vol. 2139, pp. 41–62. Springer, Heidelberg (2001). https://doi.org/10.1007/3-540-44647-8_3

26. Naor, M., Nissim, K.: Certificate revocation and certificate update. In: 7th USENIX Security Symposium (1998)

27. Naor, M., Ziv, A.: Primary-secondary-resolver membership proof systems. In: Dodis, Y., Nielsen, J.B. (eds.) TCC 2015. LNCS, vol. 9015, pp. 199–228. Springer, Heidelberg (2015). https://doi.org/10.1007/978-3-662-46497-7_8

28. Ostrovsky, R., Rackoff, C., Smith, A.: Efficient consistency proofs for generalized queries on a committed database. In: Díaz, J., Karhumäki, J., Lepistö, A., Sannella, D. (eds.) ICALP 2004. LNCS, vol. 3142, pp. 1041–1053. Springer, Heidelberg (2004). https://doi.org/10.1007/978-3-540-27836-8_87

29. Papadopoulos, D., Papadopoulos, S., Triandopoulos, N.: Taking authenticated range queries to arbitrary dimensions. In: ACM-CCS (2014)

30. Papamanthou, C., Tamassia, R., Triandopoulos, N.: Optimal verification of operations on dynamic sets. In: Rogaway, P. (ed.) CRYPTO 2011. LNCS, vol. 6841, pp. 91–110. Springer, Heidelberg (2011). https://doi.org/10.1007/978-3-642-22792-9_6

31. Prabhakaran, M., Xue, R.: Statistically hiding sets. In: Fischlin, M. (ed.) CT-RSA 2009. LNCS, vol. 5473, pp. 100–116. Springer, Heidelberg (2009). https://doi.org/10.1007/978-3-642-00862-7_7

32. Tamassia, R.: Authenticated data structures. In: Di Battista, G., Zwick, U. (eds.) ESA 2003. LNCS, vol. 2832, pp. 2–5. Springer, Heidelberg (2003). https://doi.org/10.1007/978-3-540-39658-1_2

Efficient Non-Interactive Zero-Knowledge Proofs in Cross-Domains Without Trusted Setup

Michael Backes[1], Lucjan Hanzlik[1,2], Amir Herzberg[3,4], Aniket Kate[5], and Ivan Pryvalov[1(✉)]

[1] CISPA Helmholtz Center for Information Security, Saarbrücken, Germany
{backes,ivan.pryvalov}@cispa.saarland
[2] Stanford University, Stanford, USA
lucjan.hanzlik@stanford.edu
[3] University of Connecticut, Storrs, USA
amir.herzberg@uconn.edu
[4] Bar Ilan University, Ramat Gan, Israel
[5] Purdue University, West Lafayette, USA
aniket@purdue.edu

Abstract. With the recent emergence of efficient zero-knowledge (ZK) proofs for general circuits, while efficient zero-knowledge proofs of algebraic statements have existed for decades, a natural challenge arose to combine algebraic and non-algebraic statements. Chase et al. (CRYPTO 2016) proposed an interactive ZK proof system for this cross-domain problem. As a use case they show that their system can be used to prove knowledge of a RSA/DSA signature on a message m with respect to a publicly known Pedersen commitment $g^m h^r$. One drawback of their system is that it requires interaction between the prover and the verifier. This is due to the interactive nature of garbled circuits, which are used in their construction. Subsequently, Agrawal et al. (CRYPTO 2018) proposed an efficient non-interactive ZK (NIZK) proof system for cross-domains based on SNARKs, which however require a trusted setup assumption.

In this paper, we propose a NIZK proof system for cross-domains that requires no trusted setup and is efficient both for the prover and the verifier. Our system constitutes a combination of Schnorr based ZK proofs and ZK proofs for general circuits by Giacomelli et al. (USENIX 2016). The proof size and the running time of our system are comparable to the approach by Chase et al. Compared to Bulletproofs (SP 2018), a recent NIZK proofs system on committed inputs, our techniques achieve asymptotically better performance on prover and verifier, thus presenting a different trade-off between the proof size and the running time.

1 Introduction

Zero-knowledge (ZK) proofs, introduced by Goldwasser, Micali, and Rackoff [25], are one of the central cryptographic building blocks, which allow a prover to

© International Association for Cryptologic Research 2019
D. Lin and K. Sako (Eds.): PKC 2019, LNCS 11442, pp. 286–313, 2019.
https://doi.org/10.1007/978-3-030-17253-4_10

convince a verifier that a statement is true without revealing any other information. Goldreich, Micali, and Wigderson showed that ZK proofs for NP-languages are possible [24], which opened up a number of new research directions in cryptography.

Zero-knowledge proof systems are an essential building block used in many privacy-preserving systems, e.g. anonymous credential systems [12] and voting protocols [7,26]. Unfortunately, only a few systems have been used in practice. The main reason is that ZK proofs for general statements are usually inefficient. Thus, the research focus switched from general statements to interesting subclasses. In particular, a prover can efficiently prove knowledge of discrete logarithms in groups of known [18,34] and unknown [6,14] order. Those proofs were extended to allow other statements, e.g., equivalence of discrete logarithms, or knowledge of representation. The main advantage was that using the Fiat-Shamir transformation [21] one can make those systems non-interactive (NIZK), i.e. no interaction between the prover and the verifier is necessary to generate the proof, and transform honest-verifier ZK protocols into full ZK. Groth and Sahai [20,28] further extended the class of efficient NIZK proofs to statements about pairing product equations. The common factor of those proofs is that they are restricted to algebraic groups and cannot be efficiently used to prove statements about non-algebraic structures, e.g., the SHA hash function or the AES encryption scheme.

The problem of efficient interactive ZK proofs for non-algebraic statements was solved by Jawurek et al. [30]. Their system allows to efficiently prove statements of the following form: "The prover knows an input x such that $y = SHA(x)$ for some public y". Unfortunately, one cannot apply the Fiat-Shamir transformation to make those proofs non-interactive. The system is based on garbled circuits [37], which are private coin protocols, which in turn makes the system inherently interactive. Giacomelli et al. [23] addressed this limitation and introduced ZKBoo, a non-interactive proof system for arithmetic circuits, based on the "MPC-in-the-head" technique [29]. In their system, the proof size depends linearly on the number of gates, input and output wires. This work was further improved by Chase et al. [16] with the introduction of the ZKB++ system. The authors were able to reduce the proof size by a constant factor and addressed post-quantum security of the construction. Ames et al. [4] proposed Ligero, a NIZK proof system based on the "MPC-in-the-head" technique, which has the proof size proportional to the square root of the verification circuit size.

An interesting line of research present succinct non-interactive zero-knowledge proofs (SNARKs) [9,22,27]. They allow compact proofs and very efficient verification, but require a complex trusted setup and the prover has to perform a number of public key operations (i.e. modular exponentiations or equivalently elliptic curve point multiplications) proportional to the circuit size. The setup algorithm can be executed by a trusted party or by the participants of the system using multi-party computation (MPC).

While there exist efficient proofs for algebraic and non-algebraic statements, it became a natural challenge to combine both worlds and create a proof system that would work efficiently in both, algebraic and non-algebraic, domains. Obviously, one can implement algebraic structure directly using non-algebraic statements by defining all group operations as functions. This approach introduces a significant overhead in size of the proven statement, which increases the size of the proof and the number of required computations. As noted by [3], depending on the group size, the circuit for computing a single exponentiation could be *thousands or millions* of gates. Alternatively, one can implement arithmetic circuit directly using algebraic statements by treating each gate in a circuit as an algebraic function and proving relations between gates. The prover's/verifier's work and the proof size would be linear in the number of gates, and in case of hash functions or block ciphers it could be *tens of thousands* of public key operations and group elements.

The first attempt to efficiently solve this cross-domain problem was the Crypto'16 work by Chase et al. [17]. Their system can be used e.g. to prove that a given algebraic commitment (e.g. Pedersen commitment) C is a commitment to x, where $F(x) = 1$ and F is expressed as a boolean circuit. The authors show that an efficient proof system for this statement can be used as a building block to construct more efficient proofs of knowledge of a signature and a committed message for RSA-FDH, DSA and EC-DSA signatures. Their system can be extended to a scenario, where we have k commitments to $x_1, \ldots, x_k$ and the input x is the concatenation $x_1 || \ldots || x_k$ of values in those commitments.

Chase et al. propose two constructions of their proof system. For the first the number of public key operations is linear in the size of x and that of symmetric key operations is proportional to the number F_g of gates in F. The second construction reduced the number of public key operations to a number linear in the security parameter λ, but this comes at a cost of additional symmetric key operations which are proportional to $F_g + |x| \cdot \lambda$. Unfortunately, their approach is based on the ZK proofs from [30] and the proof system is therefore interactive by nature.

Bünz et al. [11] presented at S&P'18 efficient NIZK range proofs called Bulletproofs. Those proofs can also be used for proving statements expressed as arithmetic circuits with algebraically committed inputs. The proof technique relies on discrete log assumptions and the Fiat-Shamir transformation. While Bulletproofs produce relatively short proofs, the prover's work is still expensive, specifically, the prover has to perform a number of public key operations linear in the circuit size.

At Crypto'18, Agrawal, Ganesh, and Mohassel [3] presented non-interactive zero-knowledge proofs for composite statements. Whereas the authors addressed the same problem of constructing zero-knowledge proofs in cross-domains, theirs and our proposals differ in the underlying cryptographic blocks that handle the arithmetic part of the proof system. Specifically, their proofs are based on Σ-protocols and SNARKs [22]. As already noted, SNARKs allow for short proofs and fast verification of arithmetic statements, however they require a trusted setup for generating the common reference string (CRS) for a particular circuit F. Typically, the CRS needs to be regenerated for a different circuit F'. This is not desirable in some applications such as ZCash, where an expensive MPC protocol has to be run to generate a CRS [2].

Our Contribution. In this work, we present an efficient (both for the prover and the verifier) non-interactive zero-knowledge proof system for cross-domains that requires no trusted setup assumption. Our system uses ZKB++ [16] as a building block, which is based on a technique called "MPC-in-the-head" [29]. The idea is that the prover represents the circuit F as a multi-party computation (MPC) and generates three shares $x_1 \oplus x_2 \oplus x_3 = x$, where x is the original input of the prover. The prover then performs the MPC computation using the values x_1, x_2, x_3 and given a challenge $e \in \{1, 2, 3\}$ returns the view of computations performed with inputs x_e and x_{e+1}. Executing these steps a number of times decreases the soundness error of the proof. What is more, we can apply the Fiat-Shamir transformation and allow the prover to compute this challenge itself, making the system non-interactive.

We extend this idea to allow algebraic statements. To illustrate our solution let us consider a simple example where the prover publishes $y = SHA(x)$ and a Pedersen commitment $C = g^x \cdot h^r$. In this case, the prover wants to convince the verifier that he knows x. To do so, he performs the "MPC-in-the-head" as in ZKB++ and computes Pedersen commitments to all bits of the values x_1, x_2, x_3. Upon receiving a challenge $e \in \{1, 2, 3\}$, additionally to the views of the MPC the prover opens all commitments to the bits of x_e and x_{e+1}. Finally, to bind the "MPC-in-the-head" part to the Pedersen commitment C, the prover computes commitments to the bits of the value $x_e \oplus x_{e+1} \oplus x_{e+2}$ and proves that these commitments contain the binary representation of the same value that is in C. As in ZKB++, this extended system has to be executed several times in order to decrease the probability of the prover cheating the verifier. However, in contrast to [17] we can apply the Fiat-Shamir transformation to get a NIZK system.

The number of public key operations in our system is proportional to $|x| \cdot \lambda$. This follows directly from the way we combine both domains. Each round we have to prove that the commitments to the bits of $x_e \oplus x_{e+1} \oplus x_{e+2}$ are the binary representation of x. We solve this obstacle by committing to full values of the ZKB++ share and not to its bits and show that we can still compute the XOR value of them because 2 out of 3 values are revealed by the ZKB++ protocol. This unique technique allows us to further decrease the number of public key operations to $O(|x| + \lambda)$.

The contribution of this paper can be summarized as follows. We are the first to present an efficient (both for the prover and the verifier) non-interactive zero-knowledge (NIZK) proof system for algebraic and non-algebraic domains (cross-domains) that requires no trusted setup. The solution is based on a combination of ZKBoo [16,23] with standard Schnorr based proofs [15,34]. Using our techniques, we obtain the efficient non-interactive proof of knowledge (proof of possession) of DSA/RSA signatures, without revealing the signature itself.

Applications. A straightforward application of zero-knowledge proofs in cross-domains are anonymous credentials. Chase et al. [17] observed that many existing credential systems [5,8,10,12,13] rely on signature schemes that are tailored in a specific way to provide the desired properties of the system. The user proves that he knows a value x and a signature under this value. Using zero-knowledge proofs in cross-domains allows to use standard signature schemes like RSA-FDH or DSA for which there exist no efficient proof system in the standard algebraic setting. In contrast to the system by Chase et al. our proofs are non-interactive, which means that they can be used to construct round-optimal anonymous credential systems. This implies that using our techniques, one can create concurrently secure systems based on RSA and DSA signatures.

Another application of NIZK in cross-domains, mentioned in [3], are proofs of solvency for Bitcoin exchanges. In this scenario, an exchange wants to prove to its customers that it is solvent, i.e. that it has enough Bitcoins to cover its liabilities. To this end, the exchange would need to prove the control over some Bitcoin addresses. A certain Bitcoin address is a 160-bit hash of a public ECDSA key [1]. The corresponding proof is a proof of knowledge x such that $H(g^x) = y$, where H is a hash-function such as SHA-256. Here, only y is public, and the exchange would like to keep its public key part g^x hidden, otherwise an adversary could track the movement of exchanges associated with its public key. Since the Bitcoin network does not require a trusted setup assumption, proofs of solvency based on the approach by [3] would require a trusted CRS generation to be done. On the other hand, since our techniques do not require any trusted setup assumption, they can be used directly to prove solvency for Bitcoin exchanges. The proof system would additionally include a proof of equality of discrete logarithm of a committed value and another committed value. More specifically, a prover would need to prove knowledge of x such that $H(g^x) = y$ for some public y. Here the input to the circuit H is g^x. The prover has to commit to g^x as Com_{g^x} and to x as Com_x and use the proof of equality of discrete logarithm of a committed value and another committed value, for which we refer to [17].

Note that ours and the proof system by Chase et al. [17] or any other system cannot be post-quantum secure if the underlying security assumptions in the algebraic domain (integer factorization, discrete logarithms) can be broken by a quantum adversary [35].

Comparison with Existing Techniques. We compare ours and prior work on zero-knowledge proofs in cross-domains in Table 1. We discuss the efficiency of the constructions based on a circuit F and a committed input x. For the algebraic part of the proof system, Σ-protocols are used in all ZK proof systems presented in the table. Σ-protocols require a constant number of public-key operations for a single algebraic statement and do not require any trusted setup assumption. The approach by Chase et al. [17] is the only interactive protocol in the table. In their first construction, the arithmetic part of the proof system is based on garbled circuits, whose prover's/verifier's cost amounts to $O(|F|)$ of symmetric-key operations. The number of public key operations is linear in the input size $|x|$. In the second construction, Chase et al. achieve the number of public key operations independent of $|x|$ at the cost of increasing the circuit that has to be garbled. Various techniques to reduce computation, communication, memory requirements of garbled circuits are available, e.g. [32,36,38]; in [31] XOR-gates can be garbled essentially at no cost. In Bulletproofs [11], the prover has to perform a constant number of public key operations for each multiplication gate of the circuit, while the verifier is more efficient due to the multi-exponentiation trick. The proof size in Bulletproofs is logarithmic in the number of multiplication gates in the arithmetic circuit for verifying the witness. The approach by Agrawal et al. [3], which is based on SNARKs, is the only protocol that requires a trusted setup assumption and produces constant proofs. Verifier's work does not depend on the circuit size, and the number of public key operations is linear in the input size. Prover's work requires a number of public key operations linear in the circuit size. We analyze efficiency of our Construction 2. As we show in Sect. 3.4, it requires $O(|x| + \lambda)$ public key operations, while the number of symmetric-key operations is $O(|F| \cdot \lambda)$, since ZKB++ protocol has to be repeated to reduce the soundness error to a negligible value. Proof size is dominated by ZKB++ and amounts to $O((|F|\lambda + |x|)\lambda)$.

Table 1. Comparison of ZK proof systems in cross-domains for a circuit F with an algebraically committed input x, where $|F|$ denotes the circuit size, $|x|$ the number of input bits. We denote by λ the security parameter, by pub a public-key operation, by sym a symmetric-key operation.

	Non-inter-active	Without trusted setup	Prover's work	Verifier's work	Communication/ Proof size
CGM16 [17] Constr.1	No	Yes	$O(|x| \cdot \text{pub} + |F| \cdot \text{sym})$	$O(|x| \cdot \text{pub} + |F| \cdot \text{sym})$	$O((|F| + |x|)\lambda)$
CGM16 [17] Constr.2	No	Yes	$O(\lambda \cdot \text{pub} + (|F| + |x|\lambda) \cdot \text{sym})$	$O(\lambda \cdot \text{pub} + (|F| + |x|\lambda) \cdot \text{sym})$	$O((|F| + |x|\lambda)\lambda)$
BBB+18 [11]	Yes	Yes	$O(|F| \cdot \text{pub})$	$O(\frac{|F|}{\log(|F|)} \cdot \text{pub})$	$O(\log(|F|)\lambda)$
AGM18 [3]	Yes	No	$O((|F| + \lambda) \cdot \text{pub})$	$O((|x| + \lambda) \cdot \text{pub})$	$O(\lambda)$
This work	Yes	Yes	$O((|x| + \lambda) \cdot \text{pub} + (|F| \cdot \lambda) \cdot \text{sym})$	$O((|x| + \lambda) \cdot \text{pub} + (|F| \cdot \lambda) \cdot \text{sym})$	$O((|F|\lambda + |x|)\lambda)$

Paper Outline. The rest of the paper is organized as follows. Section 2 contains preliminaries. In Sect. 3, we develop our solution for NIZK proofs in cross-domains. The section starts with the problem statement for NIZK proofs in cross-domains. Then, in Sect. 3.1 we present our first attempt cross-domain NIZK proof system based on ZKB++ followed by its security analysis. Next, in Sect. 3.2 we present an improved version and its security analysis. Finally, in Sect. 3.3 we describe the optimization technique to reduce the number of public key operations and in Sect. 3.4 we perform efficiency analysis of our constructions. In Sect. 4, we complement NIZK proofs in cross-domains to allow OR-proofs. Section 5 concludes.

2 Preliminaries

In this section we recall the notions of commitment schemes, zero-knowledge and Σ-protocols. We also recall the details of the ZKBoo protocol introduced by Giacomelli et al. [23].

2.1 Homomorphic Commitment Schemes

Let us by $\mathcal{M}_{ck}$ denote the message space of the commitment scheme and by $\mathcal{OI}_{ck}$ the space of opening information (also called randomness).

Definition 1 (Commitment Scheme). *A commitment scheme consists of the following PPT algorithms* (Gen, Com, Open)*:*

Gen(λ)**:** *on input security parameter λ, this algorithm outputs a commitment key* ck*, which is an implicit input for the below algorithms.*
Com(m, r)**:** *on input message m and opening information r, this deterministic algorithm outputs a commitment C_m.*
Open(C_m, m, r)**:** *on input commitment C_m, message m and opening information r, this algorithm outputs a bit $\{0, 1\}$.*

Definition 2 (Perfect Hiding). *A commitment scheme is perfectly hiding, if for all adversaries $\mathcal{A}$ we have:*

$$\Pr[ck \leftarrow \mathsf{Gen}(\lambda), (m_0, m_1, \mathsf{st}) \leftarrow \mathcal{A}(ck), r \xleftarrow{\$} \mathcal{OI}_{ck}, C \leftarrow \mathsf{Com}(m_0, r) : \mathcal{A}(\mathsf{st}, C) = 1] =$$
$$\Pr[ck \leftarrow \mathsf{Gen}(\lambda), (m_0, m_1, \mathsf{st}) \leftarrow \mathcal{A}(ck), r \xleftarrow{\$} \mathcal{OI}_{ck}, C \leftarrow \mathsf{Com}(m_1, r) : \mathcal{A}(\mathsf{st}, C) = 1].$$

Definition 3 (Computational Binding). *A commitment scheme is computationally binding, if for all PPT adversaries $\mathcal{A}$ we have:*

$$|\Pr[(ck) \leftarrow \mathsf{Gen}(\lambda), (m_0, r_0, m_1, r_1) \leftarrow \mathcal{A}(ck) : m_0 \neq m_1 \wedge$$
$$\mathsf{Com}(m_0, r_0) = \mathsf{Com}(m_1, r_1)]| \leq \mathsf{Adv}_{\mathcal{A}}^{\mathsf{binding}}(\lambda),$$

where we require that $m_0, m_1 \in \mathcal{M}_{ck}$, $r_0, r_1 \in \mathcal{OI}_{ck}$ and $\mathsf{Adv}_{\mathcal{A}}^{\mathsf{binding}}(\lambda)$ is negligible in the security parameter λ.

Definition 4 (Equivocality). *A commitment scheme is equivocal, if there exists an algorithm* Eval *and an alternative* Gen$'$ *algorithm that additionally to the commitment key* ck *returns a trapdoor τ such that given a commitment $C = \mathsf{Com}(m, r)$ we have $C = \mathsf{Com}(m', \mathsf{Eval}(\tau, m', (C, m, r)))$ for any message m', i.e.* Eval *can be used to compute the randomness to open C to an arbitrary value.*

Moreover, we assume that there exists an efficient extraction algorithm Extr$_{ck}$ *that given two openings of the same commitment, i.e. (m_1, r_1, m_2, r_2) where $\mathsf{Com}(m_1, r_1) = \mathsf{Com}(m_2, r_2)$ and $m_1 \neq m_2$, returns the trapdoor τ.*

We require that a commitment scheme is binding, hiding and equivocal. Additionally, in this paper we assume that the used commitment scheme has the following homomorphic property: for all $m_1, m_2 \in \mathcal{M}_{ck}$ and $r_1, r_2 \in \mathcal{OI}_{ck}$ we have: $\mathsf{Com}(m_1, r_1) \cdot \mathsf{Com}(m_2, r_2) = \mathsf{Com}(m_3, r_3)$, where $m_3 = m_1 + m_2$ and $r_3 = r_1 + r_2$. This homomorphism allows us to introduce multiplication by a known scalar, i.e. given $C = \mathsf{Com}(m, r)$ we can compute $C' = [k]C = \mathsf{Com}(k \cdot m, k \cdot r)$, where by $[k]C$ we denote multiplication of commitment C by a public scalar k. What is more, for a given commitment $C_b = \mathsf{Com}(b, r)$ to a bit b, we can easily compute the exclusive-or on this hidden value with a known bit α. If $\alpha = 0$, we leave C unchanged, otherwise, if $\alpha = 1$, we compute $C_{b \oplus \alpha} = C_1 / C_b = \mathsf{Com}(1 - b, -r)$, where $C_1 = \mathsf{Com}(1, 0)$ is formally a commitment to 1 with no randomness (instead of sampling it, it is set to 0). Note that for commitments $C_x = \mathsf{Com}(x, r) = \prod_{i \in [0, |x|-1]} [2^i] C_{x[i]} = \prod_{i \in [0, |x|-1]} [2^i] \mathsf{Com}(x[i], r_{x[i]})$, where $x[i]$ is the i-th bit of x, we can compute a commitment $C_{x \oplus \alpha}$ for a known α. To do so, we apply the above technique bitwise, i.e. to commitments $C_{x[i]}$ and using the new values we then compute the commitment $C_{x \oplus \alpha}$. Notice, that this operation changes the opening information, which is now $\sum_{i \in [0, |x|-1]} (-1)^{\alpha[i]} r_{x[i]}$, i.e. $C_{x \oplus \alpha} = \mathsf{Com}(x \oplus \alpha, \sum_{i \in [0, |x|-1]} (-1)^{\alpha[i]} r_{x[i]})$.

An example of a scheme that has those properties is the one introduced by Pedersen [33]. There, given a commitment key $ck = (g, h, q, p)$, a message $m \in \mathbb{Z}_q$ and an opening information $r \in \mathbb{Z}_q^*$ the commitment is of the form $\mathsf{Com}(m, r) = g^m \cdot h^r \mod p$. Multiplying two commitments $\mathsf{Com}(m_1, r_1) \cdot \mathsf{Com}(m_2, r_2)$ we get $g^{m_1 + m_2} h^{r_1 + r_2}$, which is a commitment to message $m_1 + m_2 \mod q$ with opening information $r_1 + r_2 \mod q$, as required. Note that the commitment scheme is also equivocal and that there exists an extraction algorithm Extr_{ck} (to this end, one simply needs to choose public parameters g, h with a known discrete logarithm).

2.2 Zero-Knowledge Proofs

Let $\mathcal{R} \subset \{0, 1\}^* \times \{0, 1\}^*$ be an efficiently computable binary relation, for which $\mathcal{R}(x, w) = 1 \iff (x, w) \in \mathcal{R}$. We call x a statement and w a witness. A very simple example of such a relation is $\mathcal{R} = \{(x, w) : x = SHA(w)\}$, where we are given a SHA value as part of the statement and the preimage is part of the witness. Obviously, given both values we can easily verify that $\mathcal{R}(x, w) = 1$ by computing the SHA value on w and comparing it with x. We will assume that $|w| \leq \mathsf{poly}(|x|)$, which means that the witness length should be polynomial in the statement length. We will denote by $L_{\mathcal{R}}$ the language consisting of true statements in $\mathcal{R}$, i.e. $L_{\mathcal{R}} = \{x | \exists w : (x, w) \in \mathcal{R}\}$.

We call a cryptographic protocol between two PPT parties, the prover $\mathcal{P}$ and the verifier $\mathcal{V}$ an *argument* for language $L_{\mathcal{R}}$ if it has the following properties. Using communication $\mathcal{P}$ wants to convince $\mathcal{V}$ that $x \in L_{\mathcal{R}}$, where x is a publicly known statement. Obviously, the prover has some extra private input, e.g. he knows a witness for which $\mathcal{R}(x, w) = 1$.

At the end of the protocol the verifier outputs accept if he is convinced and reject otherwise. The protocol is *complete* if for all $x \in L_{\mathcal{R}}$ an honest prover always convinces an honest verifier. We also require that if $x \notin L_\mathcal{R}$, then a cheating prover has only a small chance ϵ (called *soundness error*) to convince an honest verifier. This property should hold for all possible statements not in the language, i.e. for all $x \notin L_\mathcal{R}$ we have $\Pr[\mathcal{V}(x) = \text{accept}] \leq \epsilon$. Finally, we require a property called *zero-knowledge* (ZK). Informally, this means that whatever strategy a verifier follows, he learns nothing besides whether $x \in L_\mathcal{R}$. It follows that he cannot get any information about the private input of the prover. A weaker notion of ZK is called honest-verifier ZK (HVZK). Zero-knowledge property in this case holds only for a verifier, who does not deviate from the protocol.

A special case of such arguments are Σ-protocols, which follow a specific communication pattern similar to the letter Σ. In the rest of the paper we will only consider this type of protocols.

Definition 5 (Σ-Protocol). *A protocol $\Pi_\mathcal{R}$ between a prover $\mathcal{P}$ and a verifier $\mathcal{V}$ is a Σ-protocol for relation $\mathcal{R}$ if:*

- *The protocol consists of three phases:*
  1. *(Commit) $\mathcal{P}$ sends a message a to $\mathcal{V}$,*
  2. *(Challenge) $\mathcal{V}$ picks a random e and sends it to $\mathcal{P}$,*
  3. *(Response) $\mathcal{P}$ sends a second message z to $\mathcal{V}$.*
- *$\Pi_\mathcal{R}$ is complete - if both parties are honest, then for all $x \in L_\mathcal{R}$ we have $\Pr[(\mathcal{P}, \mathcal{V})(x) = 1] = 1$.*
- *$\Pi_\mathcal{R}$ is s-special sound - for any x and any set of s accepting conversations $T = \{(a, e_i, z_i)\}_{i \in \{1,\ldots,s\}}$, where $e_i \neq e_j$ if $i \neq j$, there exists an efficient algorithm Extr that on input T outputs w such that $\mathcal{R}(x, w) = 1$.*
- *$\Pi_\mathcal{R}$ is a special honest-verifier ZK (HVZK) - there exists a PPT simulator $\mathcal{SIM}$ such that on input $x \in L_\mathcal{R}$ outputs a triple (a', e, z') with the same probability distribution of real conversations (a, e, z) of the protocol.*

The last property ensures only that Σ-protocols are ZK if the verifier is honest and does not base his challenge e on the first message of the prover. Σ-protocols have found many applications in the design of efficient identification and signature schemes. The main advantage of using those protocols is that using the Fiat-Shamir transformation [21], they can be made non-interactive in the random oracle model. What is more, using this technique the protocol is ZK even if the verifier is dishonest. Note that if the challenge e is chosen from a set of cardinality c, then s-special soundness implies that the soundness error is $(s-1)/c$.

Notation. Given two commitments $C_x = \mathsf{Com}(x, r_x)$ and $C_y = \mathsf{Com}(y, r_y)$ we will denote by $\mathcal{P}\{(C_x \equiv C_y)\}$ the prover's part and by $\mathcal{V}\{(C_x \equiv C_y)\}$ the verifier's part of a Σ-protocol, where the prover tries to convince the verifier that it knows openings (x, r_x) and (y, r_y) of public commitments C_x and C_y, respectively, such that $x = y$. There exist very efficient Σ-protocols for the above mentioned Pedersen commitments. In such a case, the witness is composed of the committed value x and the opening informations r_x and r_y. We may sometimes append the notation to denote a subroutine algorithm such as *Commit*,

Response, or *Reconstruct*. The *Commit* subroutine has a special output notation. We denote by (st, a) the result of *Commit* execution, where st denotes an
internal state and a the output.

Notation for a Bit Commitment. We will also use this notion for a spe-
cial case, where the prover wants to show that the value committed in $C_x = \mathsf{Com}(x, r_x)$ is a bit, i.e. $x \in \{0, 1\}$. We will use $\mathcal{P}\{(C_x \equiv C_0) \vee (C_x \equiv C_1)\}$
to denote this special case. Note that we do not necessarily require the use of
commitments to values 0 (C_0) and 1 (C_1), as there exist more efficient realizations, i.e. given a commitment $C = g^x \cdot h^r$ the prover simply shows that it
knows the discrete logarithm of C or C/g to the base of h, and therefore C_0
and C_1 may be omitted. Moreover, we will use $\prod_{i=0}^{|x|-1} C_{2^i \cdot x[i]} = \mathsf{Com}(x, r)$ to
denote a commitment to x, where $x = \sum_{i=0}^{|x|-1} 2^i x[i]$, $r = \sum_{i=0}^{|x|-1} 2^i r_{x[i]}$, and
$C_{x[i]} = \mathsf{Com}(x[i], r_{x[i]})$.

2.3   ZKBoo/ZKB++

Giacomelli et al. [23] proposed ZKBoo, an efficient Σ-protocol based on the idea
"MPC-in-the-head" [29]. Subsequently, Chase et al. [16] presented ZKB++, the
successor of ZKBoo, which has more compact proofs. As both versions of the
protocols differ primarily in technical aspects, our techniques can be applied to
either version. The main advantage of this system over the one by Jawurek et al.
[30] is that it can be made non-interactive using the Fiat-Shamir transformation.

ZKBoo/ZKB++ work for arithmetic functions F with prover's input x and
the verifier holding no private input. Let y denote the output of function, i.e.
$y = F(x)$. To create such a zero-knowledge proof of x, the prover splits the input
into 3 shares (x_1, x_2, x_3) and for each pair x_i, x_{i+1} runs the function $F'(x_i, x_{i+1})$
to obtain y_i. F' is constructed in such a way that the correctness property of
ZKBoo/ZKB++ ensures $y_1 \oplus y_2 \oplus y_3 = y$. The prover commits to all three
views. The verifier sends a challenge $e \in \{1, 2, 3\}$, which can be replaced by the
output of the random oracle applied on appropriate inputs. The prover opens
input shares (x_e, x_{e+1}) and the randomness used in computing $F'(x_e, x_{e+1})$ in
the corresponding two views. The verifier then checks whether y_e was correctly
computed or not. Another property of F' is that two out of three views leak no
information about the input x (the property is called 2-privacy; for more details
we refer to Definition 3 in [23]). The protocol is 3-special sound and the soundness
error of the protocol is $2/3$. Therefore, to reduce the soundness error to a negligible value the prover runs multiple independent rounds of ZKBoo/ZKB++
protocol. In Fig. 5 in Appendix we present the non-interactive version of the
ZKB++ protocol.

3   Combining ZKB++ with Algebraic Commitments

In this section we present our main contribution: a Σ-protocol for statements in cross-domains. Throughout this paper we will consider the following statement as the main building block that can be composed to create proofs for more general statements.

Statement 1. *Prove that there exists x such that $F(x) = 1$ and x is committed to C_x, where x is a $|x|$-bit number, F is an arithmetic circuit, and the commitment scheme is based on the group structure of order larger than $2^{|x|}$ and allows some homomorphic operations.*

The naive approach to prove this statement is just to implement all algebraic operations as a part of the circuit F and execute the ZKB++ protocol. However, Chase et al. [17] already noticed that expressing modular exponentiation in a boolean circuit would be computationally too expensive and fairly inefficient. In particular, since the number of gates increases non-linearly in the size of the input, this also means that the proof size increases at the same rate and so does the time required to compute the proof. As we will show, there exists a more efficient way of realizing this kind of proofs.

3.1   Our Technique - First Approach

We propose the following technique, in which we take advantage of:

(1) the fact that the ZKB++ protocol is a Σ-protocol,
(2) the additive sharing of the prover's input x in the group $\mathbb{Z}_2$ in ZKB++,
(3) that Σ-protocols can be executed in parallel,
(4) a multiplicatively homomorphic commitment scheme in the group $\mathbb{Z}_q$; for simplicity we assume that $2^{|x|} < q$, the other case is addressed in Sect. 3.3.

The overall idea is to combine a ZKB++ round with zero-knowledge proofs that input bits of x are bound to the public commitment. This part involves ZK proofs for all individual bits of the ZKB++ input and the three exclusive-or based bit shares. In particular, we prove that the exclusive-or value of those shares is given in a commitment and is equal to the bit representation of x. We then prove that values in the commitments match the real shares by giving opening information for 2 out of 3 commitments, depending on the shares revealed by ZKB++. More details can be found in Construction 1.

Construction 1 (Cross-ZKB++ First Attempt). *Let $x[i]$ denote the i-th bit of input x, i.e. $x = (\dots, x[1], x[0])$. In the following, we describe necessary steps to add to the ZKB++ protocol (Fig. 5) in order to realize the connection between the input bits $(\dots, x[1], x[0])$ of the function F and the public commitment C_x, as defined in Statement 1.*

- *(Commit Phase)—The prover follows the steps specified by the ZKB++ protocol. Then, for each bit i of input x the prover commits to $x[i]$ and to the respective input shares $x[i]_1, x[i]_2, x[i]_3$ and gets $C_{x[i]}, C_{x[i]_1}, C_{x[i]_2}, C_{x[i]_3}$. Again, for each bit i the prover executes the commit phase of a Σ-protocol (with challenge space $\{1, 2, 3\}$) for the following algebraic statement:*

$$\mathcal{P}\{((C_{x[i]} \equiv C_0) \vee (C_{x[i]} \equiv C_1)) \wedge (\prod_{i \in [0, |x|-1]} C_{2^i \cdot x[i]} \equiv C_x) \wedge \tag{1}$$
$$((C_{x[i]_1} \cdot C_{x[i]_2} \cdot C_{x[i]_3} \equiv C_{x[i]}) \vee (C_{x[i]_1} \cdot C_{x[i]_2} \cdot C_{x[i]_3} \equiv C_{2+x[i]}))\}.$$

  The prover sends commitments $\{C_{x[i]}, C_{x[i]_1}, C_{x[i]_2}, C_{x[i]_3}\}_{i \in [0, |x|-1]}$, and the commitments from the ZKB++ protocol and the Σ-protocol to prove the statement Eq. (1) to the verifier.
- *(Challenge Phase)—The verifier sends the challenge $e \in \{1, 2, 3\}$.*
- *(Response Phase)—The prover executes the last phase of the ZKB++ and the other proofs, and sends the result to the verifier. Additionally, he sends the opening information for commitments $C_{x[i]_e}, C_{x[i]_{e+1}}$, for all $i \in [0, |x| - 1]$.*

To verify the result the verifier follows the steps specified by the ZKB++ protocol and additionally performs the following checks: reject if the opening is wrong or the bits of the shares don't match the bits in the ZKB++ views, or if any of the additional algebraic proofs is invalid.

We present in Figs. 1 and 2 the detailed description of Construction 1, instantiated with t rounds of ZKB++ and made non-interactive using the Fiat-Shamir transformation.

Note that the proof system Eq. (1) does not explicitly enforce $C_{x[i]_1}, C_{x[i]_2}, C_{x[i]_3}$ to be commitments to bits. However, as we show in the proof of Theorem 1, it is the case.

Security Analysis

Lemma 1. *Assuming the ZKB++ protocol is complete, the Σ-protocols for the algebraic statements are complete and the used commitment scheme is homomorphic, then Construction 1 is a complete Σ-protocol for the statement in Problem 1.*

Proof. Follows by inspection.   □

Theorem 1. *Assuming the ZKB++ protocol is 3-special sound, the Σ-protocols for the algebraic statements are 2-special sound and the used commitment scheme is homomorphic and equivocal, then Construction 1 is a 3-special sound Σ-protocol for Statement 1.*

Proof. We will prove this theorem by constructing an efficient algorithm Extr_{Cross} that using 3 accepting tuples (a, e_1, z_1), (a, e_2, z_2) and (a, e_3, z_3) can compute $w^* = (x^*, r^*)$, such that $F(x^*) = 1$ and $C_x = \mathsf{Com}(x^*, r^*)$, which is a valid witness for the proven statement.

$\underline{p \leftarrow \mathsf{Prove}(x, C_x = \mathsf{Com}(x, r))}$

1 :   // (*Commit* step)

2 : $(st_\zeta, a_\zeta) \leftarrow \mathsf{ZKB}_F.Commit(x)$

3 :   **foreach** $i \in [0, |x| - 1]$ **do**

4 : $C_{x[i]} = \mathsf{Com}(x[i], r_i)$

5 :   **foreach** $\rho \in [1, t]$ **do**

6 :   Extract shares $x[i]_1^{(\rho)}, x[i]_2^{(\rho)}, x[i]_3^{(\rho)}$ from st_ζ

7 : $C_{x[i]_1^{(\rho)}} = \mathsf{Com}(x[i]_1^{(\rho)}, r_{x[i]_1^{(\rho)}})$

8 : $C_{x[i]_2^{(\rho)}} = \mathsf{Com}(x[i]_2^{(\rho)}, r_{x[i]_2^{(\rho)}})$

9 : $C_{x[i]_3^{(\rho)}} = \mathsf{Com}(x[i]_3^{(\rho)}, r_{x[i]_3^{(\rho)}})$

10 : $(st_x, a_x) \leftarrow \mathcal{P}\{\prod_{i \in [0, |x|-1]} C_{2^i \cdot x[i]} \equiv C_x\}.Commit(x, \sum_{i=0}^{|x|-1} 2^i \cdot r_i, r)$

11 :   **foreach** $i \in [0, |x| - 1]$ **do**

12 : $(st_{x[i]}, a_{x[i]}) \leftarrow \mathcal{P}\{(C_{x[i]} \equiv C_0) \vee (C_{x[i]} \equiv C_1)\}.Commit(x[i], r_i)$

13 :   **foreach** $\rho \in [1, t]$ **do**

14 : $C_{x[i]^{(\rho)}} = C_{x[i]_1^{(\rho)}} \cdot C_{x[i]_2^{(\rho)}} \cdot C_{x[i]_3^{(\rho)}}$

15 : $(st_{x[i]^{(\rho)}}, a_{x[i]^{(\rho)}}) \leftarrow \mathcal{P}\{(C_{x[i]^{(\rho)}} \equiv C_{x[i]}) \vee (C_{x[i]^{(\rho)}} \equiv C_{2+x[i]})\}.Commit($

16 : $x[i]_1^{(\rho)} + x[i]_2^{(\rho)} + x[i]_3^{(\rho)}, r_{x[i]_1^{(\rho)}} + r_{x[i]_2^{(\rho)}} + r_{x[i]_3^{(\rho)}}, r_i)$

17 :   // output of (*Commit* step)

18 : $a = (a_\zeta, (C_{x[i]})_{|x|}, (C_{x[i]_1^{(\rho)}})_{|x| \cdot t}, (C_{x[i]_2^{(\rho)}})_{|x| \cdot t}, (C_{x[i]_3^{(\rho)}})_{|x| \cdot t},$

19 : $a_x, (a_{x[i]})_{|x|}, (a_{x[i]^{(\rho)}})_{|x| \cdot t})$

20 :   // (*Challenge* step)

21 : $e \leftarrow H(a)$

22 :   // (*Response* step)

23 : $\mathbf{r}_\zeta \leftarrow \mathsf{ZKB}_F.Response(e, st_\zeta)$

24 : $\mathbf{r}_x \leftarrow \mathcal{P}\{\prod_{i \in [0, |x|-1]} C_{2^i \cdot x[i]} \equiv C_x\}.Response(e, st_x)$

25 :   **foreach** $i \in [0, |x| - 1]$ **do**

26 : $\mathbf{r}_{x[i]} \leftarrow \mathcal{P}\{(C_{x[i]} \equiv C_0) \vee (C_{x[i]} \equiv C_1)\}.Response(e, st_{x[i]})$

27 :   **foreach** $\rho \in [1, t]$ **do**

28 : $\mathbf{r}_{x[i]^{(\rho)}} \leftarrow \mathcal{P}\{(C_{x[i]^{(\rho)}} \equiv C_{x[i]}) \vee (C_{x[i]^{(\rho)}} \equiv C_{2+x[i]})\}.Response(e, st_{x[i]^{(\rho)}})$

29 :   **return** $(e, a, \mathbf{r}_\zeta, \mathbf{r}_x, (\mathbf{r}_{x[i]})_{|x|}, (\mathbf{r}_{x[i]^{(\rho)}})_{|x| \cdot t},$

30 : $(x[i]_e^{(\rho)}, r_{x[i]_e^{(\rho)}})_{|x| \cdot t}, (x[i]_{e+1}^{(\rho)}, r_{x[i]_{e+1}^{(\rho)}})_{|x| \cdot t})$

Fig. 1. Description of Cross-ZKB++ (First Attempt) Prove algorithm for function $F(x) = 1$ with a committed input $C_x = \mathsf{Com}(x, r)$, made non-interactive using the Fiat-Shamir transformation and with t rounds of ZKB++.

$\{Reject, Accept\} \leftarrow \mathsf{Verify}(C_x, p)$

1: // *Reconstruct* step

2: Parse p as $(e, a, \mathbf{r}_\zeta, \mathbf{r}_x, (\mathbf{r}_{x[i]})_{|x|}, (\mathbf{r}_{x[i]^{(\rho)}})_{|x| \cdot t},$

3: $\qquad (x[i]_e^{(\rho)}, r_{x[i]_e^{(\rho)}})_{|x| \cdot t}, (x[i]_{e+1}^{(\rho)}, r_{x[i]_{e+1}^{(\rho)}})_{|x| \cdot t})$

4: Parse a as $(a_\zeta, (C_{x[i]})_{|x|}, (C_{x[i]_1^{(\rho)}})_{|x| \cdot t}, (C_{x[i]_2^{(\rho)}})_{|x| \cdot t}, (C_{x[i]_3^{(\rho)}})_{|x| \cdot t},$

5: $\qquad a_x, (a_{x[i]})_{|x|}, (a_{x[i]^{(\rho)}})_{|x| \cdot t})$

6: **foreach** $i \in [0, |x| - 1]$ **do**

7: $\quad$ **foreach** $\rho \in [1, t]$ **do**

8: $\qquad Reject$ if $C_{x[i]_e^{(\rho)}} \neq \mathsf{Com}(x[i]_e^{(\rho)}, r_{x[i]_e^{(\rho)}})$ or $C_{x[i]_{e+1}^{(\rho)}} \neq \mathsf{Com}(x[i]_{e+1}^{(\rho)}, r_{x[i]_{e+1}^{(\rho)}})$

9: $(st_\zeta', a_\zeta') \leftarrow \mathsf{ZKB}_F.Reconstruct(e, \mathbf{r}_\zeta)$

10: $Reject$ if $(x_e^{(\rho)})_t, (x_{e+1}^{(\rho)})_t$ do not match respective values in st_ζ'

11: $a_x' \leftarrow \mathcal{V}\{\prod_{i \in [0, |x|-1]} C_{2^i \cdot x[i]} \equiv C_x\}.Reconstruct(e, \mathbf{r}_x)$

12: **foreach** $i \in [0, |x| - 1]$ **do**

13: $\quad a_{x[i]}' \leftarrow \mathcal{V}\{(C_{x[i]} \equiv C_0) \vee (C_{x[i]} \equiv C_1)\}.Reconstruct(e, \mathbf{r}_{x[i]})$

14: $\quad$ **foreach** $\rho \in [1, t]$ **do**

15: $\qquad C_{x[i]^{(\rho)}} = C_{x[i]_1^{(\rho)}} \cdot C_{x[i]_2^{(\rho)}} \cdot C_{x[i]_3^{(\rho)}}$

16: $\qquad a_{x[i]^{(\rho)}}' \leftarrow \mathcal{V}\{(C_{x[i]^{(\rho)}} \equiv C_{x[i]}) \vee (C_{x[i]^{(\rho)}} \equiv C_{2+x[i]})\}.Reconstruct(e, \mathbf{r}_{x[i]^{(\rho)}})$

17: $a' = (a_\zeta', (C_{x[i]})_{|x|}, (C_{x[i]_1^{(\rho)}})_{|x| \cdot t}, (C_{x[i]_2^{(\rho)}})_{|x| \cdot t}, (C_{x[i]_3^{(\rho)}})_{|x| \cdot t},$

18: $\qquad a_x', (a_{x[i]}')_{|x|}, (a_{x[i]^{(\rho)}}')_{|x| \cdot t})$

19: $e' \leftarrow H(a')$

20: $Accept$ if $e' = e$, otherwise $Reject$.

Fig. 2. Description of Cross-ZKB++ (First Attempt) Verify algorithm for function $F(x) = 1$ with a committed input $C_x = \mathsf{Com}(x, r)$, made non-interactive using the Fiat-Shamir transformation and with t rounds of ZKB++.

The algorithm works as follows:

1. First it uses the 3-special soundness of the ZKB++ protocol to extract a value x_{ZKB} for which $F(x_{ZKB}) = 1$.
2. It uses the 2-special soundness of the Σ-protocols for the algebraic statements to extract the values $x[i]$, for all $i \in [0, |x| - 1]$, and the corresponding opening information $r_{x[i]}$.

We now show the rest of his steps. Without loss of generality, let us assume that $e_1 = 1$, $e_2 = 2$ and $e_3 = 3$. For all $i \in [0, |x|-1]$ let $w_2 = (x, r, x[i], r_{x[i]}, x[i]_1, r_{x[i]_1}, x[i]_2, r_{x[i]_2}, x[i]_3, r_{x[i]_3})$ be the witness extracted in step 2 and $w_1 = (x_{ZKB})$ be the witness extracted in step 1. Moreover, for $i \in \{1, 2, 3\}$ let $r_{x[i]_{e_i}}$ and

$r_{x[i]_{e_i+1}}$ be the opening information to commitments $C_{x[i]_{e_i}}$ and $C_{x[i]_{e_i+1}}$, where we know that $C_{x[i]_{e_i}} = \mathsf{Com}(x[i]_{e_i}, r_{x[i]_{e_i}})$ and $C_{x[i]_{e_i+1}} = \mathsf{Com}(x[i]_{e_i+1}, r_{x[i]_{e_i+1}})$.

We now turn to the following observation. If at some point the algorithm Extr_{Cross} encounters two different opening information to one commitment, i.e. $\mathsf{Com}(a,b) = \mathsf{Com}(c,d)$ it can use (a,b,c,d) to compute the equivocal trapdoor and open any commitment to an arbitrarily value. In particular, it can use this trapdoor to open commitment C_x to the value x_{ZKB}, i.e. in case $x \neq x_{ZKB}$ we can use (x,r) and the equivocal trapdoor to compute $x^* = x_{ZKB}$ and the corresponding r^* such that $C_x = \mathsf{Com}(x^*, r^*)$, which would constitute a valid witness w^*.

We now proceed with the proof and notice that due to the verification done by the verifier and the extracted witness w_2, we know that

$$C_{x[i]_1} = \mathsf{Com}(x[i]_1, r_{x[i]_1}) = \mathsf{Com}(x[i]_{e_1}, r_{x[i]_{e_1}}) = \mathsf{Com}(x[i]_{e_3+1}, r_{x[i]_{e_3+1}}),$$
$$C_{x[i]_2} = \mathsf{Com}(x[i]_2, r_{x[i]_2}) = \mathsf{Com}(x[i]_{e_2}, r_{x[i]_{e_2}}) = \mathsf{Com}(x[i]_{e_1+1}, r_{x[i]_{e_1+1}}),$$
$$C_{x[i]_3} = \mathsf{Com}(x[i]_3, r_{x[i]_3}) = \mathsf{Com}(x[i]_{e_3}, r_{x[i]_{e_3}}) = \mathsf{Com}(x[i]_{e_2+1}, r_{x[i]_{e_2+1}}),$$

and that for $i \in \{1,2,3\}$ $x[i]_{e_i}$ are bits that correspond to disclosed views in the ZKB++ protocol. Thus, it follows that $x[i]_1 = x[i]_{e_1}$, $x[i]_2 = x[i]_{e_2}$ and $x[i]_3 = x[i]_{e_3}$ and in particular that $x_{ZKB}[i] = x[i]_1 \oplus x[i]_2 \oplus x[i]_3$ for all $i \in [0, |x|-1]$.

We will now argue that because of the soundness of the proof system used in step 2, for all $i \in [0, |x|-1]$ we have $x[i] = x[i]_1 \oplus x[i]_2 \oplus x[i]_3 = x_{ZKB}[i]$. Let us take a look at the following table.

$x[i]_1$	$x[i]_2$	$x[i]_3$	$x[i]_1 + x[i]_2 + x[i]_3$	$x[i]_1 + x[i]_2 + x[i]_3 - 2$	$x[i]_1 \oplus x[i]_2 \oplus x[i]_3$
0	0	0	0	-2	0
0	0	1	1	-1	1
0	1	0	1	-1	1
0	1	1	2	0	0
1	0	0	1	-1	1
1	0	1	2	0	0
1	1	0	2	0	0
1	1	1	3	1	1

The two rows $x[i]_1 + x[i]_2 + x[i]_3$ and $x[i]_1 + x[i]_2 + x[i]_3 - 2$ correspond to the value that the commitment $C_{x[i]} = \mathsf{Com}(x[i], r_{x[i]})$ can be opened to. However, due to the fact that the statement contains the additional constraint that the commitment opens to a bit, we conclude that for $(x[i], r_{x[i]})$ we have $x[i] = x_{ZKB}[i]$ (we used the coloured background to highlight the only way that witness w_2 can be correct).

Finally, we know that since the witness w_2 is correct, it follows that:

$$\sum_{i \in [0,|x|-1]} 2^i \cdot x[i] = x.$$

However, since $x[i]$ is the i-th bit of x_{ZKB} this means that $x_{ZKB} = x$ and the Extr$_{Cross}$ can return $w^* = (x^*, r^*) = (x_{ZKB}, \sum_{i \in [0,|x|-1]} 2^i \cdot r_{x[i]})$, which is a valid opening for C_x, where $F(x^*) = 1$.

We conclude that the values returned by Extr$_{Cross}$ are a valid witness for Statement 1.   □

Theorem 2. *Assuming the ZKB++ protocol and the Σ-protocols for the algebraic statements are HVZK and the commitment scheme is perfectly hiding, then Construction 1 is a HVZK Σ-protocol for Statement 1.*

Proof. We will show how to construct a simulator $\mathcal{SIM}$ that on input in Statement 1, outputs a transcript (a, e, z). The simulator works as follows:

- It runs the simulator for ZKB++ receiving a transcript (a', e, z'), where z' contains all the bits $x[i]_e$ and $x[i]_{e+1}$. $\mathcal{SIM}$ chooses open information $r_{x[i]_e}$, $r_{x[i]_{e+1}}$ and computes commitments $C_{x[i]_e} = \text{Com}(x[i]_e, r_{x[i]_e})$, $C_{x[i]_{e+1}} = \text{Com}(x[i]_{e+1}, r_{x[i]_{e+1}})$. Note that the openings $r_{x[i]_e}, r_{x[i]_{e+1}}$ are part of the response z. Commitment to the bits $x[i]$ and the bits $x[i]_{e+2}$ are not opened, so the simulator can compute $C_{x[i]}$ and $C_{x[i]_{e+2}}$ as commitments to zero.
- $\mathcal{SIM}$ runs the simulator for the Σ-protocol for the algebraic statements receiving (a'', e'', z''). Note that since this simulator should work for all possible challenges, there is a non-negligible probability that $e'' = e$. Otherwise, $\mathcal{SIM}$ just restarts it.
- Finally, $\mathcal{SIM}$ sets $a = (a', a'', \{C_{x[i]}, C_{x[i]_1}, C_{x[i]_2}, C_{x[i]_3}\}_{i \in [0,|x|-1]})$ and $z = (z', z'', \{r_{x[i]_e}, r_{x[i]_{e+1}}\}_{i \in [0,|x|-1]})$

Since all the simulators used by $\mathcal{SIM}$ generate valid transcripts it remains to show that the commitments $C_{x[i]}$ and $C_{x[i]_{e+2}}$ generated by $\mathcal{SIM}$ are indistinguishable from values in real transcripts. However, this follows directly by the perfectly hiding property of the commitment scheme.   □

Lemma 2. *The soundness error of the Σ-protocol presented in Construction 1 is $2/3$ and it has to be executed $\lambda/(\log_2(3) - 1)$ times/rounds to achieve a soundness error of $2^{-\lambda}$.*

Proof. The soundness error is implied directly from 3-special soundness of the protocol (Theorem 1) and the challenge space of cardinality 3. The number of rounds, let us denote it t, is simply the solution of equation $(2/3)^t = 2^{-\lambda}$.   □

3.2 Improved Version

The main disadvantage of Construction 1 is that we have to compute $O(|x| \cdot t)$ commitments, which influences the number of public key operations we have to additionally compute. The $|x|$ factor is present because for each round $\rho \in [1, t]$ the relation $x[i]_1^{(\rho)} \oplus x[i]_2^{(\rho)} \oplus x[i]_3^{(\rho)} = x[i]^{(\rho)}$ is expressed as a conjunction of two possible statements and we commit to the bits of the input x in every round. In the following, we optimize Construction 1 to increase efficiency by decreasing the number of commitment to $O(|x| + t)$.

Firstly, we notice that we can use the same commitments to bits of x for every round that we repeat the protocol and instead of committing to the bits of the ZKB++ shares we actually compute commitment to the whole values, saving a lot of computations. Note that this idea will only work if the input to ZKB++ is smaller that the order of the algebraic group that we use, otherwise the bitwise exclusive-or of those values will not constitute a accepting input to the ZKB++ circuit (i.e. $x_1 \oplus x_2 \oplus x_3$ is not always equal to $(x_1 \mod q) \oplus (x_2 \mod q) \oplus (x_3 \mod q)$). However, in the next subsection we show how to make the protocol work for ZKB++ input without a size constraint.

Secondly, the bits $x[i]^{(\rho)}_{e(\rho)}$ and $x[i]^{(\rho)}_{e(\rho)+1}$ are revealed in the response step of the ZKB++ protocol (Fig. 5). Based on this observation, we can change the relation

$$x[i]^{(\rho)}_1 \oplus x[i]^{(\rho)}_2 \oplus x[i]^{(\rho)}_3 = x[i]$$

and express the third share using the hidden value x, i.e.

$$x[i]^{(\rho)}_{e(\rho)+2} = x[i] \oplus (x[i]^{(\rho)}_{e(\rho)} \oplus x[i]^{(\rho)}_{e(\rho)+1}).$$

We now take into account that this relation is constructed for known bits and that we can express $C_{a\oplus\alpha}$ for a given C_a and α using homomorphic properties of the commitment scheme. Thus, we can actually compute a commitment to $x[i]^{(\rho)}_{e(\rho)+2}$ using the commitments to bits of x and the revealed bits of values $x[i]^{(\rho)}_{e(\rho)}$ and $x[i]^{(\rho)}_{e(\rho)+1}$. We use this commitment to bind the value $x[i]^{(\rho)}_1 \oplus x[i]^{(\rho)}_2 \oplus x[i]^{(\rho)}_3$ with the value x inside the commitment C_x.

In Construction 2 we describe those ideas in more detail. We will show a single round of the protocol, which only has a soundness error of 2/3 but below present the idea how decrease the soundness error efficiently. Our protocol is divided into four essential steps:

1. committing to bits of x,
2. proving using a Schnorr based Σ-protocol that those commitments contain a bit,
3. a ZKB++ proof that there exists a x_{ZKB} such that $F(x_{ZKB}) = 1$, and
4. constant number of commitments $C_{x_1}, C_{x_2}, C_{x_3}$, which ensure $x = x_{ZKB}$.

Thus, if one would run the protocol many times, this still would require the computation of $O(|x| \cdot t)$ commitments.

We solve this problem by taking advantage of the fact that Schnorr based Σ-protocols can use a larger challenge space that decreases the soundness error without repeating the protocol. Unfortunately, this does not apply for the ZKB++ part and for this to work we have to use a special kind of challenge. Let $e_1, \ldots, e_\rho$ be the challenges used for the ρ runs of the ZKB++ protocol, then we can use e.g. $e_\Sigma = \sum_{i \in [0,\rho-1]} 3^i \cdot e_{i+1}$ in step 2. In other words, we execute the first two steps once using the challenge e_Σ and simultaneously run the last two steps ρ-times, where each ZKB++ execution challenged respectively using $e_1, \ldots, e_\rho$.

This simple trick allows us to increase the efficiency of the proof. Now the prover only has to compute a constant number of commitments per round and commit to the bits of the input x only once.

Construction 2 (Cross-ZKB++). *In the following, we describe necessary steps to add to the ZKB++ protocol (Fig. 5) in order to realize the connection between the input bits $x = (\ldots, x[1], x[0])$ to the function F, where $x < q$ and the public commitment C_x in group of order q, as defined in Statement 1.*

- *(Commit Phase)—The prover executes the commit step of the ZKB++ protocol using input x, where $C_x = \text{Com}(x, r)$. The prover chooses random opening informations $r_1, \ldots r_{|x|-1}$ and commits to the bits $x[i]$ by computing:*

$$C_{x[i]} = \text{Com}(x[i], r_i), \text{ for } i \in [1, |x| - 1].$$

To compute the remaining commitment he uses the opening information $r_0 = r - \sum_{i \in [1, |x|-1]} 2^i \cdot r_i$. Note that because of the homomorphic properties of the commitment scheme this means that $C_x = \prod_{i \in [0, |x|-1]} [2^i] C_{x[i]} = \text{Com}(2^i \cdot x[i], 2^i \cdot r_i)$. For each bit i of input x the prover executes the commit step of a Σ-protocol for the following algebraic statement:

$$\mathcal{P}\{(C_{x[i]} \equiv C_0) \vee (C_{x[i]} \equiv C_1)\}. \tag{2}$$

The next step is also different. In this protocol we commit to the full values of the respective input shares x_1, x_2, x_3 and get $C_{x_1}, C_{x_2}, C_{x_3}$, where $C_{x_1} = \text{Com}(x_1, r_{x_1})$, $C_{x_2} = \text{Com}(x_2, r_{x_2})$, $C_{x_3} = \text{Com}(x_3, r_{x_3})$. The prover sends commitments $\{C_{x[i]}\}_{i \in [0, |x|-1]}$, $C_{x_1}, C_{x_2}, C_{x_3}$ and the commitments from the ZKB++ protocol and the Σ-protocol Eq. (2) to the verifier.
- *(Challenge Phase)—The verifier sends the challenge $e \in \{1, 2, 3\}$ to the prover.*
- *(Response Phase)—The prover executes the response step for ZKB++, the Σ-protocol and sends the result to the verifier. Knowing e, the prover computes $\alpha = x_e \oplus x_{e+1}$, where by $\alpha[i]$ we will denote its i-th bit. Using the homomorphic exclusive-or described in Subsect. 2.1, he then computes the commitment*

$$C_z = \prod_{i \in [0, |x|-1]} [2^i] C_{x[i] \oplus \alpha[i]},$$

which is

$$\text{Com}(x_{e+2}, \sum_{i \in [0, |x|-1]} (-1)^{\alpha[i]} r_{x[i]}).$$

Finally, the prover sends the opening information $r_{x_e}, r_{x_{e+1}}$ for commitments $C_{x_e}, C_{x_{e+1}}$ and value $r_z = r_{x_{e+2}} - \prod_{i \in [0, |x|-1]} (-1)^{\alpha[i]} r_{x[i]}$.

To verify the result the verifier follows the steps specified by the ZKB++ protocol and additionally performs the following checks: reject if the opening is wrong or the shares in the commitments do not match the ones in the ZKB++

views, or if any of the additional algebraic proofs is invalid. The verifier aborts
if $C_x \neq \prod_{i \in [0, |x|-1]} [2^i] C_{x[i]}$. Knowing the shares x_e, x_{e+1} and the openings r_{x_e},
$r_{x_{e+1}}$, the verifier also computes $C_z = \prod_{i \in [0, |x|-1]} [2^i] C_{x[i] \oplus \alpha_i}$ and checks that
$C_z \cdot \mathsf{Com}(0, r_z) = C_{x_{e+2}}$.

We present in Figs. 3 and 4 the detailed description of Construction 2, instantiated with t rounds of ZKB++ and made non-interactive using the Fiat-Shamir transformation.

Security Analysis

Lemma 3. *Assuming the ZKB++ protocol is complete, the Σ-protocols for the algebraic statements are complete and the used commitment scheme is homomorphic, then Construction 2 is a complete Σ-protocol for the statement in Problem 1.*

Proof. Follows by inspection.   □

Theorem 3. *Assuming the ZKB++ protocol is 3-special sound the used Σ-protocols are 2-special sound and the used commitment scheme is homomorphic and equivocal, then Construction 2 is a 3-special sound Σ-protocol for Problem 1.*

Proof. As in the proof of Theorem 1 we will construct an efficient algorithm Extr_{Cross} that using 3 accepting tuples (a, e_1, z_1), (a, e_2, z_2) and (a, e_3, z_3) can compute a witness that the statement is true. The extraction algorithm will return a value x and an opening information r such that $F(x) = 1$ and $C_x = \mathsf{Com}(x, r)$, which is a valid witness for the proven statement. We will now describe the idea behind the algorithm Extr_{Cross}, which is as follows:

- First it uses the 3-special soundness of the ZKB++ protocol to extract a value x_{ZKB} for which $F(x_{ZKB}) = 1$.
- It uses the 2-special soundness of the proof system for Eq. (2) to extract the bits $x[i]$, for all $i \in [0, |x| - 1]$, and the opening information $r_{x[i]}$.
- It computes r_{ZKB}, as described below, and returns $(x^*, r^*) = (x_{ZKB}, r_{ZKB})$ as a valid witness.

We will now show how Extr_{Cross} computes witness $w^* = (x^*, r^*)$ and that the returned values are valid. Let $w_2 = (\{x[i], r_{x[i]}\}_{i \in [0, |x|-1]})$ be the witness extracted in step 2 and $w_1 = (x_{ZKB})$ be the witness extracted in step 1. Moreover, let r_{x_e} and $r_{x_{e+1}}$ be the opening information to commitments $C_{x_{e_1}}$, $C_{x_{e_2}}$ and $C_{x_{e_3}}$, where we know that $C_{x_{e_1}} = \mathsf{Com}(x_{e_1}, r_{x_{e_1}})$, $C_{x_{e_2}} = \mathsf{Com}(x_{e_2}, r_{x_{e_2}})$ and $C_{x_{e_3}} = \mathsf{Com}(x_{e_3}, r_{x_{e_3}})$.

Again we observe that if the algorithm Extr_{Cross} encounters two different opening information to one commitment the equivocal trapdoor can be used to open the commitment C_x to the value $w_1 = x_{ZKB}$.

$p \leftarrow \mathsf{Prove}(x, C_x = \mathsf{Com}(x, r))$

1 :   // (*Commit* step)

2 : $(st_\varsigma, a_\varsigma) \leftarrow \mathsf{ZKB}_F.Commit(x)$

3 :   **foreach** $i \in [1, |x| - 1]$ **do**

4 : $C_{x[i]} = \mathsf{Com}(x[i], r_i)$

5 : $r_0 = r - \displaystyle\sum_{i \in [1, |x|-1]} 2^i \cdot r_i$

6 : $C_{x[0]} = \mathsf{Com}(x[0], r_0)$

7 :   **foreach** $i \in [0, |x| - 1]$ **do**

8 : $(st_{x[i]}, a_{x[i]}) \leftarrow \mathcal{P}\{(C_{x[i]} \equiv C_0) \vee (C_{x[i]} \equiv C_1)\}.Commit(x[i], r_i)$

9 :   **foreach** $\rho \in [1, t]$ **do**

10 :   Extract shares $x_1^{(\rho)}, x_2^{(\rho)}, x_3^{(\rho)}$ from st_ς

11 : $C_{x_1^{(\rho)}} = \mathsf{Com}(x_1^{(\rho)}, r_{x_1^{(\rho)}}), C_{x_2^{(\rho)}} = \mathsf{Com}(x_2^{(\rho)}, r_{x_2^{(\rho)}}), C_{x_3^{(\rho)}} = \mathsf{Com}(x_3^{(\rho)}, r_{x_3^{(\rho)}})$

12 : $a = (a_\varsigma, (C_{x[i]})_{|x|}, (a_{x[i]})_{|x|}, (C_{x_1^{(\rho)}})_t, (C_{x_2^{(\rho)}})_t, (C_{x_3^{(\rho)}})_t)$ // output of (Commit step)

13 :   // (*Challenge* step)

14 : $e \leftarrow H(a)$

15 :   // (*Response* step)

16 : $\mathbf{r}_\varsigma \leftarrow \mathsf{ZKB}_F.Response(e, st_\varsigma)$

17 :   **foreach** $i \in [0, |x| - 1]$ **do**

18 : $\mathbf{r}_{x[i]} \leftarrow \mathcal{P}\{(C_{x[i]} \equiv C_0) \vee (C_{x[i]} \equiv C_1)\}.Response(e, st_{x[i]})$

19 :   **foreach** $\rho \in [1, t]$ **do**

20 : $\alpha^{(\rho)} = x_e^{(\rho)} \oplus x_{e+1}^{(\rho)}$

21 : $C_z^{(\rho)} = \displaystyle\prod_{i \in [0, |x|-1]} [2^i] C_{x[i] \oplus \alpha^{(\rho)}[i]}$

22 : $r_z^{(\rho)} = r_{x_{e+2}^{(\rho)}} - \displaystyle\prod_{i \in [0, |x|-1]} (-1)^{\alpha[i]} r_{x[i]}$

23 :   **return** $(e, a, \mathbf{r}_\varsigma, (\mathbf{r}_{x[i]})_{|x|}, (x_e^{(\rho)}, r_{x_e^{(\rho)}})_t, (x_{e+1}^{(\rho)}, r_{x_{e+1}^{(\rho)}})_t, (r_z^{(\rho)})_t)$

Fig. 3. Description of Cross-ZKB++ Prove algorithm for function $F(x) = 1$ with a committed input $C_x = \mathsf{Com}(x, r)$, made non-interactive using the Fiat-Shamir transformation and with t rounds of ZKB++.

We now proceed with the proof and notice that since all the tuples are accepting, we conclude that the openings of the commitments $C_{x_1}, C_{x_2}, C_{x_3}$ are valid. This is the case because we have valid openings $(x_{e_1}, r_{x_{e_1}}), (x_{e_2}, r_{x_{e_2}}), (x_{e_3}, r_{x_{e_3}})$. It follows that the binary representations of x_1, x_2, x_3 correspond to the correct input of the ZKB++ protocol and we have $x_{ZKB} = x_1 \oplus x_2 \oplus x_3$. Note that this is only true because x_{ZKB} is shorter that the order of the used group. Moreover, we know that by construction:

$\{Reject, Accept\} \leftarrow \mathsf{Verify}(C_x, p)$

1:    // *Reconstruct* step

2:    Parse p as $(e, a, \mathbf{r}_\zeta, (\mathbf{r}_{x[i]})_{|x|}, (x_e^{(\rho)}, r_{x_e^{(\rho)}})_t, (x_{e+1}^{(\rho)}, r_{x_{e+1}^{(\rho)}})_t, (r_z^{(\rho)})_t)$

3:    Parse a as $(a_\zeta, (C_{x[i]})_{|x|}, (a_{x[i]})_{|x|}, (C_{x_1^{(\rho)}})_t, (C_{x_2^{(\rho)}})_t, (C_{x_3^{(\rho)}})_t)$

4:    *Reject* if $C_x \neq \prod_{i \in [0,|x|-1]} [2^i] C_{x[i]}$

5:    **foreach** $\rho \in [1, t]$ **do**

6:      *Reject* if $C_{x_e^{(\rho)}} \neq \mathsf{Com}(x_e^{(\rho)}, r_{x_e^{(\rho)}})$ or $C_{x_{e+1}^{(\rho)}} \neq \mathsf{Com}(x_{e+1}^{(\rho)}, r_{x_{e+1}^{(\rho)}})$

7:      $\alpha^{(\rho)} = x_e^{(\rho)} \oplus x_{e+1}^{(\rho)}$

8:      $C_z^{(\rho)} = \prod_{i \in [0,|x|-1]} [2^i] C_{x[i] \oplus \alpha^{(\rho)}[i]}$

9:      *Reject* if $C_z^{(\rho)} \cdot \mathsf{Com}(0, r_z^{(\rho)}) \neq C_{x_{e+2}^{(\rho)}}$

10:    $(st_\zeta', a_\zeta') \leftarrow \mathsf{ZKB}_F.Reconstruct(e, \mathbf{r}_\zeta)$

11:    *Reject* if $(x_e^{(\rho)})_t, (x_{e+1}^{(\rho)})_t$ do not match respective values in st_ζ'

12:    **foreach** $i \in [0, |x|-1]$ **do**

13:      $a_{x[i]}' \leftarrow \mathcal{V}\{(C_{x[i]} \equiv C_0) \vee (C_{x[i]} \equiv C_1)\}.Reconstruct(e, \mathbf{r}_{x[i]})$

14:    $a' = (a_\zeta', (C_{x[i]})_{|x|}, (a_{x[i]}')_{|x|}, (C_{x_1^{(\rho)}})_t, (C_{x_2^{(\rho)}})_t, (C_{x_3^{(\rho)}})_t)$

15:    $e' \leftarrow H(a')$

16:    *Accept* if $e' = e$, otherwise *Reject*.

Fig. 4. Description of Cross-ZKB++ Verify algorithm for function $F(x) = 1$ with a committed input $C_x = \mathsf{Com}(x, r)$, made non-interactive using the Fiat-Shamir transformation and with t rounds of ZKB++.

$$C_x = \prod_{i \in [0,|x|-1]} [2^i] \mathsf{Com}(x[i], r_{x[i]}),$$

and that $x[i]$ are bits.

Let $e = e_1$, the Extr_{Cross} computes commitment $C_z = \prod_{i \in [0,|x|-1]} [2^i] C_{x[i] \oplus \alpha_i}$, where $\alpha = x_e \oplus x_{e+1}$. Since we know that for e_1 we receive an accepting state, we know that $C_z \cdot \mathsf{Com}(0, r_z) = C_{x_{e+2}} = \mathsf{Com}(x_{e+2}, r_{x_{e+2}})$. This basically means that Extr_{Cross} can open C_z to x_{e+2} using randomness $r_{x_{e+2}} - r_z$. We now distinguish two cases:

1. the openings of C_z and $C_{x_{e+2}}$ are different, i.e. this means that

$$\sum_{i \in [0,|x|-1]} 2^i (x[i] \oplus \alpha_i) \neq x_{e+2},$$

2. the openings of C_z and $C_{x_{e+2}}$ are the same.

In the first case we notice that Extr_{Cross} knows openings of the commitment C_z to two different values. Thus, it can use an extractor Extr_{ck} to compute the equivocality trapdoor for the commitment scheme and compute r_{ZKB} as $\mathsf{Eval}(\tau, x_{ZKB}, (C_x, \sum_{i\in[0,|x|-1]} 2^i x[i], \sum_{i\in[0,|x|-1]} 2^i r_{x[i]}))$. In other words, the extraction algorithm Extr_{Cross} uses the trapdoor to open the commitment from the statement to the value x_{ZKB} for which $F(x_{ZKB}) = 1$. This means that the returned values are a valid witness for the proven statement. In the second case we know that:

$$\sum_{i\in[0,|x|-1]} 2^i (x[i] \oplus \alpha_i) = x_{e+2}.$$

This means that $r^* = \sum_{i\in[0,|x|-1]} 2^i r_{x[i]}$ is an opening of the commitment C_x to a value x' for which we know that $x' \oplus x_e \oplus x_{e+1} = x_{e+2}$. It follows that $x' = x_e \oplus x_{e+1} \oplus x_{e+2} = x_{ZKB}$. Thus, in this case Extr_{Cross} can also return $w^* = (x_{ZKB}, r^*)$, which ends the proof. $\square$

Theorem 4. *Assuming the ZKB++ protocol is HVZK and the commitment scheme is perfectly hiding, then Construction 2 is a HVZK Σ-protocol for Statement 1.*

Proof. We will show how to construct a simulator $\mathcal{SIM}$ that on input of a statement as in Statement 1 with commitment C_x, outputs a transcript (a, e, z). The simulator works as follows:

- It runs the simulator for ZKB++ receiving a transcript (a', e, z'), where z' contains the shares x_e and x_{e+1}.
- $\mathcal{SIM}$ chooses randomness r_{x_e}, $r_{x_{e+1}}$ and computes commitments $C_{x_e} = \mathsf{Com}(x_e, r_{x_e})$, $C_{x[i]_{e+1}} = \mathsf{Com}(x_{e+1}, r_{x_{e+1}})$. Note that the openings for those commitments are part of the response z. Commitments to the bits of $x[i]$ and to x_{e+2} are not opened, so the simulator can compute the commitments $C_{x[i]}$ and $C_{x_{e+2}}$ as follows.
- For $i \in [1, |x| - 1]$ it computes commitments $C_{x[i]}$ as commitments to 0. For $j = 0$ it uses the homomorphic properties of the commitment scheme to compute $C_{x[j]}$ such that $C_x = \prod_{i=0}^{|x|-1} [2^i] C_{x[i]}$.
- It then chooses a randomness r_z and computes

$$C_{x_{e+2}} = \prod_{i\in[0,|x|-1]} C_{2^i \cdot (x[i] \oplus x_e[i] \oplus x_{e+1}[i])} \cdot \mathsf{Com}(0, -(r_z)).$$

- $\mathcal{SIM}$ runs the simulator for the Σ-protocol for the algebraic statement receiving (a'', e'', z''). Note that since this simulator should work for all possible challenges, there is a non-negligible probability that $e'' = e$. Otherwise, $\mathcal{SIM}$ just restarts it.
- Finally, $\mathcal{SIM}$ sets $a = (a', a'', C_{x_1}, C_{x_2}, C_{x_3}, \{C_{x[i]}\}_{i\in[0,|x|-1]})$ and $z = (z', z'', r_{x_e}, r_{x_{e+1}}, r_z)$

$\square$

Lemma 4. *The soundness error of the Σ-protocol presented in Construction 2 is $2/3$.*

Proof. It is implied directly from 3-special soundness of the protocol (Theorem 3) and the challenge space of cardinality 3.   □

3.3   Optimization for Large Input Space

We now show how to reduce the number of public key operations to be proportional to the message space of the commitment scheme and independent of the input size of the function F, which is desirable when the input to the ZKB++ circuit is large and required if we want to use Construction 2 for such circuits. This optimization will utilize the properties of modular arithmetics.

Let $F(m) = 1$ be a function that has to be proven in the cross-domains, and let $m \geq q$ where $[0, q-1]$ is the message space of the commitment scheme. The prover proceeds as follows. Instead of committing to m, it commits to $C = \mathsf{Com}_q(m')$, where m' satisfies $m' < q$ and $m = k \cdot q + m'$ and proves the relation between m and m' as part of F. Let the original cross-domain statement be described as: $\mathcal{P}\{m : (F(m) = 1) \wedge (C_m = \mathsf{Com}_q(m, r))\}$. Then the optimized version is defined as:

$$\mathcal{P}\{m, m', k : (F_{opt}(m, m', k, q) = 1) \wedge C_m = \mathsf{Com}_q(m', r)\},$$

where
$$F_{opt}(m, m', k, q) = (F(m) = 1 \wedge (m = m' + k \cdot q)).$$

It is easy to see that C_m can be opened either to m, or to m', as both values are equal modulo q. Furthermore, the prover indeed proves that m and m' are equal modulo q. Finally, the prover proves that m' is the value committed to in C_m.

This solution requires us to create an arithmetic circuit as part of the statement proven by ZKB++. Fortunately, this is a standard integer multiplication circuit of a number $k < |x|$ and $q = O(\lambda)$. We can view such a multiplication as the addition of q, k-bit numbers. Since adding two k-bit numbers can be done using $O(k)$ gates, it follows that this multiplication can be done using $O(k \cdot q)$ gates, which is also $O(|x| \cdot \lambda)$. In particular, we have that this can be done using $O(|F| \cdot \lambda)$ gates, because $|x| < |F|$. Thus, the asymptotic number of symmetric operations remains the same and we only introduce a slight overhead using this technique.

3.4   Efficiency

We will discuss the computation overhead and increase in the proof size of our techniques. We will compare both constructions for Statement 1 and focus only on public key operations, i.e. exponentiations and multiplications in the used group $\mathbb{G}$ of order q, where $\ell q = \log q$. Let us assume that we run both protocols ρ times for input x and that we use Pedersen commitments. Moreover, we will by ℓ_{ZKB} denote the proof size of the ZKB++ protocol, by ℓ_Σ the proof size of the Σ-protocol for Eq. (1) and by $\ell_\mathbb{G}$ the size of group elements.

In such a case the proof size of Construction 1 is $\rho \cdot (\ell_{ZKB} + \ell_\Sigma + 4 \cdot |x| \cdot \ell_{\mathbb{G}} + 2 \cdot |x| \cdot \ell q)$, which asymptotically is $O(|x| \cdot \rho)$. Construction 2 was introduced to decrease this by depending less on Σ-protocols for algebraic statements and using the homomorphic properties of the commitment scheme. When executed in parallel, the proof size is $\rho \cdot (\ell_{ZKB} + (3 \cdot |x| + 3) \cdot \ell_{\mathbb{G}} + 2 \cdot |x| \cdot \ell q + 3 \cdot \ell q)$, which is better but still $O(|x| \cdot \rho)$. Fortunately, we have shown that certain parts of the computations can be reused throughout every round. Therefore, for an optimized version of Construction 2 we end up with a proof size of $\rho \cdot (\ell_{ZKB} + 3 \cdot \ell_{\mathbb{G}} + 3 \cdot \ell q) + |x| \cdot (3 \cdot \ell_{\mathbb{G}} + 2 \cdot \ell q)$, which is $O(|x| + \rho)$.

To compute the proof in Construction 1 we have to compute $4 \cdot \rho \cdot |x|$ commitments and compute the proof for statement Eq. (1), which strongly depends on the instantiation but it requires at least $O(\rho \cdot |x|)$ exponentiations. Computing commitments to bits costs one exponentiation and one multiplication. In the end, for this construction we require $O(\rho \cdot |x|)$ exponentiations. In case of Construction 2 we have to compute $|x| \cdot (3 \cdot \ell_{\mathbb{G}}) + \rho \cdot 3 \cdot \ell_{\mathbb{G}}$ commitments and $2 \cdot |x|$ exponentiations for the proof for statement Eq. (2). We also have to compute the commitment C_z, which requires us to compute $|x| \cdot \rho$ multiplications in $\mathbb{G}$. Given the fact, that we assumed that $|x|$ is of the size of $\log q$ it follows that the cost of those multiplications is comparable with ρ exponentiations in $\mathbb{G}$. It follows, that for this construction we require only $O(|x| + \rho)$ exponentiations.

4   NIZK OR-proofs in Cross-Domains

Proofs of partial knowledge [19], also known as OR-proofs, allow to efficiently prove only a part of a statement, without revealing, which part has been proven. Below we show how to prove the most simple OR-statement in cross-domains, which can be used as a basis for proving more complex statements.

Statement 2. *Prove knowledge of x_1 s.t. $F(x_1) = 1$ or knowledge of x_2 such that $y = g^{x_2}$, where F is an arithmetic circuit.*

We are going to use ZKB++ for proving the first part and the standard Schnorr proof for the second part. Since the both parts of the proof system are Σ-protocols, a challenge e will be "distributed" between these parts as $e = e_1 + e_2$. Assume $e_1 \in \mathbb{Z}_p$ and $e_2 \in \mathbb{Z}_q$, where $p > q$. The prover generates e_1 or e_2 and derives the remaining element based on e. Both e_1 and e_2 should have the same distribution regardless of the part that is being proved. Depending on which part is being proved, we proceed as follows. Given $e \in \mathbb{Z}_p$, to prove the first part the prover picks $e_2 \leftarrow_R \mathbb{Z}_q$ and computes $e_1 = e - k \cdot e_2$, where $k = \lfloor p/q \rfloor$. Given $e \in \mathbb{Z}_p$, to prove the second part the prover picks $e_1 \leftarrow_R \mathbb{Z}_p$ and computes $e_2' = e - e_1 \in \mathbb{Z}_p$. To preserve the distribution of e_2, the prover performs rejection sampling: it further computes the largest p' that satisfies $p' = k \cdot q \leq p$ for integer k and rejects and regenerates e_1 if $e_1 > \mathbb{Z}_{p'}$, otherwise $e_2 \leftarrow e_2' (\mathrm{mod}\ q)$. It is easy to see that the probability of rejection is at most $1/2$, and e_1 and e_2 are distributed identically regardless of which part has been proven.

Remark 1. If $p \gg q$, it suffices to stay in $\mathbb{Z}_p$ and convert an element from $\mathbb{Z}_p$ to $\mathbb{Z}_q$ by taking its residue.

The prover knows x to a public function F, such that $y = F(x)$, where y is public. t denotes the number of (parallel) rounds.

$p \leftarrow Prove(x)$

1. (Commit step) For each round $\rho \in [1,t]$: Sample random tapes $k_1^{(\rho)}$, $k_2^{(\rho)}$, $k_3^{(\rho)}$ and simulate the MPC protocol to get an output view $\mathsf{View}_j^{(\rho)}$ and output share $y_j^{(\rho)}$.

$$(x_1^{(\rho)}, x_2^{(\rho)}, x_3^{(\rho)}) \leftarrow \mathsf{Share}(x, k_1^{(\rho)}, k_2^{(\rho)}, k_3^{(\rho)})$$
$$= (G(k_1^{(\rho)}), G(k_2^{(\rho)}), x \oplus G(k_1^{(\rho)}) \oplus G(k_2^{(\rho)}))$$
$$\mathsf{View}_j^{(\rho)} \leftarrow \mathsf{Upd}(...\mathsf{Upd}(x_j^{(\rho)}, x_{j+1}^{(\rho)}, k_j^{(\rho)}, k_{j+1}^{(\rho)})...)$$
$$y_j^{(\rho)} \leftarrow \mathsf{Output}(\mathsf{View}_j^{(\rho)})$$

   Commit $D_j^{(\rho)} \leftarrow H'(k_j^{(\rho)}, \mathsf{View}_j^{(\rho)})$, let $a^{(\rho)} = (y_1^{(\rho)}, y_2^{(\rho)}, y_3^{(\rho)}, D_1^{(\rho)}, D_2^{(\rho)}, D_3^{(\rho)})$ and let $a = a^{(1)}, \dots, a^{(t)}$ be the output of this step.
2. Compute the challenge: $e \leftarrow H(a)$. Interpret e such that for $\rho \in [1,t]$, $e^{(\rho)} \in \{1,2,3\}$.
3. (Response step) For each round $\rho \in [1,t]$: let $b^{(\rho)} = (y_{e(\rho)+2}^{(\rho)}, D_{e(\rho)+2}^{(\rho)})$ and set $z^{(\rho)} \leftarrow (\mathsf{View}_{e(\rho)+1}^{(\rho)}, k_{e(\rho)}^{(\rho)}, k_{e(\rho)+1}^{(\rho)})$. If $e^{(\rho)} \neq 1$, add $x_3^{(\rho)}$ to $z^{(\rho)}$. Let $\mathbf{r} \leftarrow [(b^{(1)}, z^{(1)}), \dots, (b^{(t)}, z^{(t)})]$ be the output of this step.
4. Output $p \leftarrow [e, \mathbf{r}]$.

$b \leftarrow Verify(y, p)$:

1. (Reconstruct step) For each round $\rho \in [1,t]$: Run the MPC protocol to reconstruct the views. In particular: compute $x_{e(\rho)}^{(\rho)}, x_{e(\rho)+1}^{(\rho)}$ using $z^{(\rho)}$ as part of $\mathbf{r}$ of p in one of the following ways: $x_1^{(\rho)} \leftarrow G(k_1^{(\rho)})$, $x_2^{(\rho)} \leftarrow G(k_2^{(\rho)})$, or $x_3^{(\rho)}$ given as part of $z_{(\rho)}$.
   Obtain $\mathsf{View}_{e(\rho)+1}^{(\rho)}$ from $z_{(\rho)}$ and compute
$$\mathsf{View}_e^{(\rho)} \leftarrow \mathsf{Upd}(...\mathsf{Upd}(x_j^{(\rho)}, x_{j+1}^{(\rho)}, k_j^{(\rho)}, k_{j+1}^{(\rho)})...), \quad y_{e(\rho)}^{(\rho)} \leftarrow \mathsf{Output}(\mathsf{View}_{e(\rho)}^{(\rho)}),$$
$$y_{e(\rho)+1}^{(\rho)} \leftarrow \mathsf{Output}(\mathsf{View}_{e(\rho)+1}^{(i)}), \quad y_{e(\rho)+2}^{(i)} \leftarrow y \oplus y_{e(\rho)}^{(i)} \oplus y_{e(\rho)+1}^{(i)}.$$
   Compute the commitments for views $\mathsf{View}_{e(\rho)}^{(\rho)}$ and $\mathsf{View}_{e(\rho)}^{(\rho+1)}$. For $j \in \{e^{(\rho)}, e^{(\rho)}+1\}$:
$$D_j^{(\rho)} \leftarrow H'(k_j^{(\rho)}, \mathsf{View}_j^{(\rho)}).$$
   Let $a'^{(\rho)} = (y_1^{(\rho)}, y_2^{(\rho)}, y_3^{(\rho)}, D_1^{(\rho)}, D_2^{(\rho)}, D_3^{(\rho)})$ and note that $y_{e(\rho)+2}^{(\rho)}$ and $D_{e(\rho)+2}^{(\rho)}$ are part of $z_{(\rho)}$. Let $a' = (a'^{(1)}, \dots, a'^{(t)})$ be the output of this step.
2. Compute the challenge: $e' \leftarrow H(a')$. If $e' = e$, output Accept, otherwise output Reject.

Fig. 5. Non-interactive ZKB++ [16].

5   Conclusion

Zero-knowledge proofs are an essential component in various protocols, including payment, electronic voting, anonymous credential systems. Proofs based on algebraic groups and for arithmetic circuits represent two different domains. In this work, we presented an efficient Σ-protocol in cross-domains, which can be used to prove the possession of standard RSA/DSA signatures. Moreover, the protocol can be executed non-interactively using the Fiat-Shamir transformation. It follows, that our results can be applied to build round-optimal and concurrent-secure anonymous credentials based on standard signature schemes. Our techniques are especially beneficial when applied for large circuits and when the prover's running time is critical. As future work, it would be interesting to explore whether the approach by Ames et al. [4] can be used to achieve yet more efficient and compact NIZK proofs in cross-domains.

Acknowledgements. We would like to thank the anonymous reviewers for their valuable comments. This work was supported by the German Research Foundation (DFG) through funding for the project Methoden und Instrumente zum Verständnis und zur Kontrolle von Datenschutz (SFB1223/1) and by the German Federal Ministry of Education and Research (BMBF) through funding for CISPA and the CISPA-Stanford Center for Cybersecurity (FKZ: 16KIS0762).

References

1. Technical background of version 1 bitcoin addresses. https://en.bitcoin.it/wiki/Technical_background_of_version_1_Bitcoin_addresses. Accessed 9 Oct 2018
2. Zcash parameter generation. https://z.cash/technology/paramgen.html. Accessed 8 Oct 2018
3. Agrawal, S., Ganesh, C., Mohassel, P.: Non-interactive zero-knowledge proofs for composite statements. In: Shacham, H., Boldyreva, A. (eds.) CRYPTO 2018. LNCS, vol. 10993, pp. 643–673. Springer, Cham (2018). https://doi.org/10.1007/978-3-319-96878-0_22
4. Ames, S., Hazay, C., Ishai, Y., Venkitasubramaniam, M.: Ligero: lightweight sublinear arguments without a trusted setup. In: Proceedings of the 2017 ACM SIGSAC Conference on Computer and Communications Security, pp. 2087–2104. ACM (2017)
5. Baldimtsi, F., Lysyanskaya, A.: Anonymous credentials light. In: Proceedings of the 2013 ACM SIGSAC Conference on Computer & Communications Security, pp. 1087–1098. ACM (2013)
6. Bangerter, E., Camenisch, J., Maurer, U.: Efficient proofs of knowledge of discrete logarithms and representations in groups with hidden order. In: Vaudenay, S. (ed.) PKC 2005. LNCS, vol. 3386, pp. 154–171. Springer, Heidelberg (2005). https://doi.org/10.1007/978-3-540-30580-4_11
7. Bayer, S., Groth, J.: Efficient zero-knowledge argument for correctness of a shuffle. In: Pointcheval, D., Johansson, T. (eds.) EUROCRYPT 2012. LNCS, vol. 7237, pp. 263–280. Springer, Heidelberg (2012). https://doi.org/10.1007/978-3-642-29011-4_17

8. Belenkiy, M., Chase, M., Kohlweiss, M., Lysyanskaya, A.: P-signatures and non-interactive anonymous credentials. In: Canetti, R. (ed.) TCC 2008. LNCS, vol. 4948, pp. 356–374. Springer, Heidelberg (2008). https://doi.org/10.1007/978-3-540-78524-8_20
9. Ben-Sasson, E., Chiesa, A., Genkin, D., Tromer, E., Virza, M.: SNARKs for C: verifying program executions succinctly and in zero knowledge. In: Canetti, R., Garay, J.A. (eds.) CRYPTO 2013. LNCS, vol. 8043, pp. 90–108. Springer, Heidelberg (2013). https://doi.org/10.1007/978-3-642-40084-1_6
10. Brands, S.A.: Rethinking Public Key Infrastructures and Digital Certificates: Building in Privacy. MIT Press, Cambridge (2000)
11. Bünz, B., Bootle, J., Boneh, D., Poelstra, A., Wuille, P., Maxwell, G.: Bulletproofs: short proofs for confidential transactions and more. In: IEEE Symposium on Security and Privacy (SP), pp. 319–338. IEEE (2018)
12. Camenisch, J., Lysyanskaya, A.: An efficient system for non-transferable anonymous credentials with optional anonymity revocation. In: Pfitzmann, B. (ed.) EUROCRYPT 2001. LNCS, vol. 2045, pp. 93–118. Springer, Heidelberg (2001). https://doi.org/10.1007/3-540-44987-6_7
13. Camenisch, J., Lysyanskaya, A.: Signature schemes and anonymous credentials from bilinear maps. In: Franklin, M. (ed.) CRYPTO 2004. LNCS, vol. 3152, pp. 56–72. Springer, Heidelberg (2004). https://doi.org/10.1007/978-3-540-28628-8_4
14. Camenisch, J., Stadler, M.: Efficient group signature schemes for large groups. In: Kaliski, B.S. (ed.) CRYPTO 1997. LNCS, vol. 1294, pp. 410–424. Springer, Heidelberg (1997). https://doi.org/10.1007/BFb0052252
15. Camenisch, J., Stadler, M.: Proof systems for general statements about discrete logarithms. Technical report, ETH Zurich, Institut für Theoretische Informatik (1997)
16. Chase, M., et al.: Post-quantum zero-knowledge and signatures from symmetric-key primitives. In: Proceedings of the 2017 ACM SIGSAC Conference on Computer and Communications Security, pp. 1825–1842. ACM (2017)
17. Chase, M., Ganesh, C., Mohassel, P.: Efficient zero-knowledge proof of algebraic and non-algebraic statements with applications to privacy preserving credentials. In: Robshaw, M., Katz, J. (eds.) CRYPTO 2016. LNCS, vol. 9816, pp. 499–530. Springer, Heidelberg (2016). https://doi.org/10.1007/978-3-662-53015-3_18
18. Chaum, D., Evertse, J.-H., van de Graaf, J., Peralta, R.: Demonstrating possession of a discrete logarithm without revealing it. In: Odlyzko, A.M. (ed.) CRYPTO 1986. LNCS, vol. 263, pp. 200–212. Springer, Heidelberg (1987). https://doi.org/10.1007/3-540-47721-7_14
19. Cramer, R., Damgård, I., Schoenmakers, B.: Proofs of partial knowledge and simplified design of witness hiding protocols. In: Desmedt, Y.G. (ed.) CRYPTO 1994. LNCS, vol. 839, pp. 174–187. Springer, Heidelberg (1994). https://doi.org/10.1007/3-540-48658-5_19
20. Escala, A., Groth, J.: Fine-tuning Groth-Sahai proofs. In: Krawczyk, H. (ed.) PKC 2014. LNCS, vol. 8383, pp. 630–649. Springer, Heidelberg (2014). https://doi.org/10.1007/978-3-642-54631-0_36
21. Fiat, A., Shamir, A.: How to prove yourself: practical solutions to identification and signature problems. In: Odlyzko, A.M. (ed.) CRYPTO 1986. LNCS, vol. 263, pp. 186–194. Springer, Heidelberg (1987). https://doi.org/10.1007/3-540-47721-7_12
22. Gennaro, R., Gentry, C., Parno, B., Raykova, M.: Quadratic span programs and succinct NIZKs without PCPs. In: Johansson, T., Nguyen, P.Q. (eds.) EUROCRYPT 2013. LNCS, vol. 7881, pp. 626–645. Springer, Heidelberg (2013). https://doi.org/10.1007/978-3-642-38348-9_37

23. Giacomelli, I., Madsen, J., Orlandi, C.: ZKBoo: faster zero-knowledge for boolean circuits. In: USENIX Security Symposium, pp. 1069–1083 (2016)
24. Goldreich, O., Micali, S., Wigderson, A.: How to prove all NP statements in zero-knowledge and a methodology of cryptographic protocol design (extended abstract). In: Odlyzko, A.M. (ed.) CRYPTO 1986. LNCS, vol. 263, pp. 171–185. Springer, Heidelberg (1987). https://doi.org/10.1007/3-540-47721-7_11
25. Goldwasser, S., Micali, S., Rackoff, C.: The knowledge complexity of interactive proof systems. SIAM J. Comput. 18(1), 186–208 (1989)
26. Groth, J.: Non-interactive zero-knowledge arguments for voting. In: Ioannidis, J., Keromytis, A., Yung, M. (eds.) ACNS 2005. LNCS, vol. 3531, pp. 467–482. Springer, Heidelberg (2005). https://doi.org/10.1007/11496137_32
27. Groth, J.: Short pairing-based non-interactive zero-knowledge arguments. In: Abe, M. (ed.) ASIACRYPT 2010. LNCS, vol. 6477, pp. 321–340. Springer, Heidelberg (2010). https://doi.org/10.1007/978-3-642-17373-8_19
28. Groth, J., Sahai, A.: Efficient non-interactive proof systems for bilinear groups. In: Smart, N. (ed.) EUROCRYPT 2008. LNCS, vol. 4965, pp. 415–432. Springer, Heidelberg (2008). https://doi.org/10.1007/978-3-540-78967-3_24
29. Ishai, Y., Kushilevitz, E., Ostrovsky, R., Sahai, A.: Zero-knowledge from secure multiparty computation. In: Proceedings of the Thirty-Ninth Annual ACM Symposium on Theory of Computing, pp. 21–30. ACM (2007)
30. Jawurek, M., Kerschbaum, F., Orlandi, C.: Zero-knowledge using garbled circuits: how to prove non-algebraic statements efficiently. In: Proceedings of the 2013 ACM SIGSAC Conference on Computer & Communications Security, pp. 955–966. ACM (2013)
31. Kolesnikov, V., Schneider, T.: Improved garbled circuit: free XOR gates and applications. In: Aceto, L., Damgård, I., Goldberg, L.A., Halldórsson, M.M., Ingólfsdóttir, A., Walukiewicz, I. (eds.) ICALP 2008. LNCS, vol. 5126, pp. 486–498. Springer, Heidelberg (2008). https://doi.org/10.1007/978-3-540-70583-3_40
32. Naor, M., Pinkas, B., Sumner, R.: Privacy preserving auctions and mechanism design. In: Proceedings of the 1st ACM Conference on Electronic Commerce, pp. 129–139. ACM (1999)
33. Pedersen, T.P.: Non-interactive and information-theoretic secure verifiable secret sharing. In: Feigenbaum, J. (ed.) CRYPTO 1991. LNCS, vol. 576, pp. 129–140. Springer, Heidelberg (1992). https://doi.org/10.1007/3-540-46766-1_9
34. Schnorr, C.P.: Efficient signature generation by smart cards. J. Cryptology 4(3), 161–174 (1991)
35. Shor, P.W.: Algorithms for quantum computation: discrete logarithms and factoring. In: Proceedings of the 35th Annual Symposium on Foundations of Computer Science, pp. 124–134. IEEE (1994)
36. Songhori, E.M., Hussain, S.U., Sadeghi, A.R., Schneider, T., Koushanfar, F.: TinyGarble: highly compressed and scalable sequential garbled circuits. In: 2015 IEEE Symposium on Security and Privacy (SP), pp. 411–428. IEEE (2015)
37. Yao, A.C.C.: How to generate and exchange secrets. In: Proceedings of the 27th Annual Symposium on Foundations of Computer Science, pp. 162–167. IEEE (1986)
38. Zahur, S., Rosulek, M., Evans, D.: Two halves make a whole. In: Oswald, E., Fischlin, M. (eds.) EUROCRYPT 2015. LNCS, vol. 9057, pp. 220–250. Springer, Heidelberg (2015). https://doi.org/10.1007/978-3-662-46803-6_8

Shorter Quadratic QA-NIZK Proofs

Vanesa Daza[1]([✉]), Alonso González[2], Zaira Pindado[1], Carla Ràfols[1],
and Javier Silva[1]

[1] Universitat Pompeu Fabra, Barcelona, Spain
vanesa.daza@upf.edu
[2] ENS de Lyon, Laboratoire LIP (U. Lyon, CNRS, ENSL, Inria, UCBL),
Lyon, France

Abstract. Despite recent advances in the area of pairing-friendly Non-Interactive Zero-Knowledge proofs, there have not been many efficiency improvements in constructing arguments of satisfiability of quadratic (and larger degree) equations since the publication of the Groth-Sahai proof system (JoC'12). In this work, we address the problem of aggregating such proofs using techniques derived from the interactive setting and recent constructions of SNARKs. For certain types of quadratic equations, this problem was investigated before by González et al. (ASIACRYPT'15). Compared to their result, we reduce the proof size by approximately 50% and the common reference string from quadratic to linear, at the price of using less standard computational assumptions. A theoretical motivation for our work is to investigate how efficient NIZK proofs based on falsifiable assumptions can be. On the practical side, quadratic equations appear naturally in several cryptographic schemes like shuffle and range arguments.

1 Introduction

NIZK in Bilinear Groups. Non-Interactive Zero-Knowledge Proofs allow to convince any party of the truth of a statement without revealing any other information. They are a very useful building block in the construction of cryptographic protocols. Since the first pairing-friendly NIZK proof system of Groth, Ostrovsky and Sahai [19] many different constructions have emerged in different models and under different assumptions, for various types of statements. Compared to a plain discrete logarithm setting, bilinear groups have a rich structure which is specially amenable to construct NIZK proofs.

Among this variety of results, there are three particularly interesting families with different advantages in terms of generality, efficiency or strength of the assumptions. On the one hand, there is a line of research initiated by Groth,

A. González—Supported in part by the French ANR ALAMBIC project (ANR-16-CE39-0006).

J. Silva—Supported by a PhD formation grant from the Spanish government, co-financed by the ESF (Ayudas para contratos predoctorales para la formación de doctores 2016).

© International Association for Cryptologic Research 2019
D. Lin and K. Sako (Eds.): PKC 2019, LNCS 11442, pp. 314–343, 2019.
https://doi.org/10.1007/978-3-030-17253-4_11

Ostrovsky and Sahai [19] and which culminated in the Groth-Sahai proof system [21]. The latter result provides relatively efficient proofs for proving satisfiability of several types of quadratic equations in bilinear groups based on standard assumptions. Although several works have tried to improve the efficiency of Groth-Sahai proofs [8,30], for many equation types they still remain the best alternative based on falsifiable assumptions.

Another family of results are the constructions of quasi-adaptive NIZK (QA-NIZK) arguments, initiated by Jutla and Roy [22] and leading to very efficient proofs of very concrete statements. Most notably, given a bilinear group $gk := (p, \mathbb{G}_1, \mathbb{G}_2, \mathbb{G}_T, e, \mathcal{P}_1, \mathcal{P}_2)$, proving membership in linear spaces in $\mathbb{G}_1^m$ or $\mathbb{G}_2^m$, for some $m \in \mathbb{N}$, requires only one group element [23,24]. The power of the quasi-adaptive notion of zero-knowledge allows to specialize the common reference string to the language one is proving membership in, trading generality for efficiency under very weak computational assumptions. Other works have constructed proofs for different languages in the QA-NIZK setting, like the proof for bilateral spaces (linear spaces in $\mathbb{G}_1^m \times \mathbb{G}_2^n$) [14], or, beyond linear spaces, the language of vector commitments to integers opening to a boolean vector [14] or shuffles and range proofs [15].

Finally, in the last few years, an extremely successful line of research has constructed succinct non-interactive arguments of knowledge (zk-SNARKs) [7, 11,16,17,27] for NP complete languages, which are not only constant-size (independent of the witness size) but which are also very efficient in a concrete sense. One of the main downsides of SNARKs is that their security relies on knowledge of exponent assumptions, a very strong type of assumptions classified as non-falsifiable [29]. However, one cannot achieve succinctness (proofs essentially independent of the size of the statement being proved and its witness) and security based on falsifiable assumptions at the same time, as per the impossibility result by Gentry and Wichs [12].

Commit-and-Prove. In a broad sense, we can think of many of the results in these three families as commit-and-prove schemes [5]. This is very clear for the Groth-Sahai proof system, which has even been recast in the commit-and-prove formalism by Escala and Groth [8]. This is probably less obvious for some results in the QA-NIZK setting. However, as noted already in the first QA-NIZK construction of membership in linear spaces [22], in these cases one can often think of the statement as a commitment to the witness. For instance, in the case of proving that a vector y in the exponent is in the linear span of the columns of some matrix $\mathbf{A}$, this means that $y = \mathbf{A}w$ and we can think of y as a commitment to w. Finally, in the case of many SNARK constructions, e.g. [7] the commitment is usually a "knowledge commitment"—from which the witness is extracted in the soundness proof using knowledge assumptions—while the rest can be considered the "proof".

With this idea in mind, it is interesting to compare these three approaches for constructing proofs of satisfiability of d equations in n variables in bilinear groups in terms of proof size. We observe that for linear equations, while the original Groth-Sahai proof system required $O(n)$ group elements for the commit step and $O(d)$ for the "prove" one, recent works have shown how to aggregate the proof in the quasi-adaptive setting [14,23], reducing the "prove" step to $O(1)$ in many cases. For quadratic equations in the other hand, we summarize the three different approaches in Table 1.

Table 1. Three different approaches for proving quadratic equations in bilinear groups. For concreteness, assume that one wants to prove that a set of values $x_1, \ldots, x_n$ form a bitstring, that is, satisfiability of $x_i(x_i - 1) = 0$.

Construction	Assumption	Commitment size	Proof size	CRS size
Groth-Sahai [19]	Falsifiable	$O(n)$	$O(n)$	$O(1)$
QA-NIZK [14]	Falsifiable	$O(n)$	$10|\mathbb{G}_1| + 10|\mathbb{G}_2|$	$O(n^2)$
SNARKs [7]	Non-falsifiable	$|\mathbb{G}_1| + |\mathbb{G}_2|$	$2|\mathbb{G}_1|$	$O(n)$

Motivation. Quadratic equations are much more powerful than linear ones. In particular, they allow to prove boolean Circuit Sat, but they are also important to prove other statements like range, shuffle proofs or validity of an encrypted vote. While for proving statements about large circuits non-falsifiable assumptions are necessary to get around impossibility results, it would be desirable to eliminate them in less demanding settings, to understand better what the security claims mean in a concrete sense. As in the QA-NIZK arguments for linear spaces, there are even natural situations in which the statement is already "an encrypted witness", and it seems unnatural to use the full power of knowledge of exponent assumptions in these cases (for instance, in the case of vote validity).

In summary, it is worth investigating efficiency improvements for quadratic equations under falsifiable assumptions. In particular, aggregating the "prove" step would be an important step towards this goal. The techniques for the linear case do not apply to the quadratic one, and we are only aware of one result in aggregating the proof of quadratic equations, namely the bitstring argument of González et al. [14] for proving that a set of commitments to integers opens to boolean values. There is a large concrete gap between this result and the others in the non-falsifiable setting both in terms of the size of the proof and the common reference string. Thus, it is natural to ask if it is possible to reduce the gap and improve on this result importing techniques from SNARKs in the falsifiable setting.

1.1 Our Results

We introduce new techniques to aggregate proofs of quadratic equations. First, in Sect. 3.1, we construct a proof system for proving that d equations of the type $X_i(X_i - 2) = 0$ are satisfied, where X_i is an affine combination of some $a_1, \ldots, a_n$. The size of the proof is constant and the set of commitments to the variables is of size linear in n, and the size of the CRS is linear in d. The prover computes a number of exponentiations linear in $n + d$, while the verifier computes a number of pairings linear in d. Our proof system is perfect zero-knowledge and computationally sound under a variant of the so-called target strong Diffie-Hellman assumption. These assumptions belong to the broader class of q-assumptions, where each instance of the problem is of size proportional to some integer q, which in our case is the number of equations. In particular, the bitstring language of [14] can be formulated as such a system of equations. In Sect. 3.2 we discuss as a particular case an argument for unit vector, and argue how to modify our general proof system so that it can be proven sound under static assumptions (the full details are in the full version). A typical application of membership in these languages is for computing disjunctions of statements such as "the committed verification key is equal to $\mathcal{V}_1$, or $\mathcal{V}_2$, ..., or $\mathcal{V}_m$", which might be expressed as $vk = \sum_{i=1}^{m} b_i \mathcal{V}_i, b_i \in \{0, 1\}$ and $(b_1, \ldots, b_m)$ is a unit vector.

Next, in Sect. 4, we generalize the previous argument to prove that d equations of the type $(X_i - z_1)(X_i - z_2) \ldots (X_i - z_m) = 0$ are satisfied, where X_i is an affine combination of the variables $a_1, \ldots, a_n$. For this we combine techniques from the interactive setting of [4] for proving set membership in a set of size m of $\mathbb{Z}_p$ with ideas from Sect. 3.1 and from quasi-adaptive aggregation [23]. In the full version, we illustrate how to use this for improved range proofs in bilinear groups under falsifiable assumptions.

Finally, in Sect. 5 we discuss two approaches to construct shuffle arguments. They are the most efficient in terms of proof size in the common reference string model under falsifiable assumptions in bilinear groups (comparing favorably even to the best constructions in the generic bilinear group model [10]), but they have large public parameters (quadratic in the shuffle size) (Tables 2 and 3).

Table 2. The table shows the proof sizes (not including commitments) and CRS sizes of our constructions. We consider d variables and n equations, and m is the size of the set from the set membership proof. The Assumptions 6, 7 and 8 are new.

	Language	Proof size	CRS size	Assumption
Section 3.1	Quadratic equations	$4\|\mathbb{G}_1\| + 6\|\mathbb{G}_2\|$	$(d + O(1))\|\mathbb{G}_1\|$ $+ (d + 3n + O(1))\|\mathbb{G}_2\|$	q-STSDH (7)
Section 3.2	Unit vector	$6\|\mathbb{G}_1\| + 6\|\mathbb{G}_2\|$	$(4(n + 1) + O(1))\|\mathbb{G}_1\|$ $+ (5(n + 1) + O(1))\|\mathbb{G}_2\|$	1-STSDH (7)
Section 4.2	Set Membership	$6\|\mathbb{G}_1\| + 6\|\mathbb{G}_2\|$	$(mn + 2n + 3m + O(1))\|\mathbb{G}_1\|$ $+ (5mn + O(1))\|\mathbb{G}_2\|$	$\mathcal{Z}$-GSDH (6), q-QTSDH (8)

Table 3. Comparison of our shuffle arguments with state-of-the-art arguments. Note that PPA stands for the Pairing Permutation Assumption and SPA for the Simultaneous Pairing Assumption.

	Proof size	CRS size	Assumption
[18]	$15n + 246$	$2n + 8$	PPA, SPA, DLIN
[10]	$(4n - 1)\|\mathbb{G}_1\| + (3n + 1)\|\mathbb{G}_2\|$	$O(n)(\|\mathbb{G}_1\| + \|\mathbb{G}_2\|)$	Bilinear generic group model
[15]	$(4n + 17)\|\mathbb{G}_1\| + 14\|\mathbb{G}_2\|$	$O(n^2)\|\mathbb{G}_1\| + O(n)\|\mathbb{G}_2\|$	SXDH, SSDP [15]
Section 5.1	$(4n + 11)\|\mathbb{G}_1\| + 8\|\mathbb{G}_2\|$	$O(n^2)\|\mathbb{G}_1\| + O(n)\|\mathbb{G}_2\|$	SXDH, 1-STSDH (7)
Section 5.2	$(2n + 11)\|\mathbb{G}_1\| + 8\|\mathbb{G}_2\|$	$O(n^2)(\|\mathbb{G}_1\| + \|\mathbb{G}_2\|)$	SXDH, n-QTSDH (7)

1.2   Our Techniques

Let $\mathbb{G}_1, \mathbb{G}_2, \mathbb{G}_T$ be groups of prime order p and let $e : \mathbb{G}_1 \times \mathbb{G}_2 \to \mathbb{G}_T$ be a bilinear map. Both SNARKs and our schemes can be seen as "commit-and-prove" schemes [8]: in the first step we commit to the solution of the equations. In the case of SNARKs, the knowledge assumption allows to extract the solutions from a constant-size commitment during the soundness proof, but we are trying to avoid using these assumptions, so we require perfectly binding commitments for each element of the solution. The second step is a proof of the opening of the commitments verifying the equations.

Let $r_1, \ldots, r_d \in \mathbb{Z}_p$. The "prove" part is handled with a polynomial aggregation technique in which satisfiability of a set of d equations is encoded into a polynomial $p(X)$ such that $p(r_j) = 0$ if and only if the jth equation is satisfied. To prove that d equations are satisfied, one needs to prove that $p(X)$ is divisible by $\prod_{j=1}^{d}(X - r_j)$. The key to succinctness is that the divisibility condition is only checked at a secret point s chosen by the trusted party who generates the CRS. This preserves soundness as long as the prover only knows s (or powers thereof) in $\mathbb{G}_1$ or $\mathbb{G}_2$, but not its discrete logarithm.

In the soundness proof, the witness is extracted from the knowledge commitment, and then used to find some r_j such that $p(r_j) \neq 0$ and compute auxiliary information which, together with the proof, allows to break a hard problem, e.g. the q-Target Strong Diffie-Hellman Assumption in [7]. Under non-falsifiable assumptions the commitments, even if perfectly binding, can be only opened in the source groups, instead of in $\mathbb{Z}_p$. This has an impact on the soundness proof, as it is not possible to eliminate some terms in the proof to find a solution to the q-TSDH assumption, so we need to consider a more flexible assumption. Furthermore, since the solutions define the coefficients of polynomial $p(X)$, our access to this polynomial is much more limited.

For our set-membership proof we start from the following insight: the satisfiability of equation $b(b - 1) = 0$ can be proven showing knowledge of a signature for b if only signatures for 0 or 1 are known. This approach can be easily extended for larger sets of solutions as done by Camenisch et al. [4]. To express the validity of many signature and message pairs, we again encode the signature verification equations as a problem of divisibility of polynomials.

This requires the signature verification to be expressible as a set of quadratic equations. While structure preserving signatures clearly solve this problem, it is overkill, since we only need unforgeability against static queries. Further, even the generic group construction of [17] requires at least 3 group elements. We choose basic Boneh-Boyen signatures since each signature consists of only one group element. Our argument needs to solve other technical difficulties which are explained in more detail in Sect. 4.

1.3 Related Works

The recent line of research in SNARKs started with [16], in which the first sub-linear arguments without random oracles were presented, but with CRS of quadratic size. Subsequent works have defined alternative models for the encoding of the circuit [7,11,17,26], reducing the CRS size to linear and obtaining smaller proofs, going as small as 3 group elements in the case of [17]. In particular, our encodings are based on those of [7,11].

When considering falsifiable assumptions, one classic way to prove quadratic equations in the non-interactive setting makes use of Groth-Sahai proofs [20], which are quite efficient and can be aggregated to obtain a constant-size proof of many equations.

In this work, we also use techniques from QA-NIZK proofs. This model was introduced in [22] to build proofs of membership in linear subspaces over $\mathbb{G}_1$ or $\mathbb{G}_2$. It was later improved to make proofs constant-size (independent of the size of the witness) [23–25] and adapted to the asymmetric setting [14]. Although introduced initially to build proofs of linear equations, the QA-NIZK setting has also been used to build the first constant-size aggregated proofs of some quadratic equations under standard assumptions [14], in particular the proof that a set of commitments open to bits.

The usage of signatures for proving membership in a set dates back to the work of Camenisch et al. [4] in the interactive setting, and in the non-interactive setting by Rial et al. [31]. Both works achieve constant-size proofs but without aggregation (i.e. proving n instances requires $O(n)$ communication). Set membership proofs were also recently investigated by Bootle and Groth [3] in the interactive setting. They construct proofs logarithmic in the size of the set and aggregate n instances with a multiplicative overhead of $O(\sqrt{n})$. In the non-interactive setting, González et al. constructed set membership proofs of size linear in the size of the set and aggregated many instances without any overhead [15].

1.4 Organization

In Sect. 2 we establish the assumptions required for our proofs, present the relevant security definitions and recall the subschemes that we will make use of, namely ElGamal encryption, Boneh-Boyen signatures, Groth-Sahai proofs and proofs of membership in linear spaces. In Sect. 3, we present our proof system for satisfiability of quadratic equations. In Sect. 4 we present an aggregated argument to prove membership in a set of $\mathbb{Z}_p$. In Sect. 5 we discuss new approaches to construct shuffle arguments. In the full version, we give an argument to prove that a commitment opens to a unit vector which can be proven secure based on a static assumption. We also discuss the application of the set membership argument in $\mathbb{Z}_p$ to range proof.

2   Preliminaries

2.1   Bilinear Groups and Implicit Notation

Let $\mathcal{G}$ be some probabilistic polynomial time algorithm which on input 1^λ, where λ is the security parameter, returns the *group key* which is the description of an asymmetric bilinear group $gk := (p, \mathbb{G}_1, \mathbb{G}_2, \mathbb{G}_T, e, \mathcal{P}_1, \mathcal{P}_2)$, where $\mathbb{G}_1, \mathbb{G}_2$ and $\mathbb{G}_T$ are additive groups of prime order p, the elements $\mathcal{P}_1, \mathcal{P}_2$ are generators of $\mathbb{G}_1, \mathbb{G}_2$ respectively, $e : \mathbb{G}_1 \times \mathbb{G}_2 \to \mathbb{G}_T$ is an efficiently computable, non-degenerate bilinear map, and there is no efficiently computable isomorphism between $\mathbb{G}_1$ and $\mathbb{G}_2$.

Elements in $\mathbb{G}_\gamma$ are denoted implicitly as $[a]_\gamma := a\mathcal{P}_\gamma$, where $\gamma \in \{1, 2, T\}$ and $\mathcal{P}_T := e(\mathcal{P}_1, \mathcal{P}_2)$. For simplicity, we often write $[a]_{1,2}$ for the pair $[a]_1, [a]_2$. The pairing operation will be written as a product $\cdot$, that is $[a]_1 \cdot [b]_2 = [a]_1[b]_2 = e([a]_1, [b]_2) = [ab]_T$. Vectors and matrices are denoted in boldface. Given a matrix $\mathbf{T} = (t_{i,j})$, $[\mathbf{T}]_\gamma$ is the natural embedding of $\mathbf{T}$ in $\mathbb{G}_\gamma$, that is, the matrix whose (i,j)th entry is $t_{i,j}\mathcal{P}_\gamma$. We denote by $|\mathbb{G}_\gamma|$ the bit-size of the elements of $\mathbb{G}_\gamma$.

$\mathbf{I}_n$ refers to the identity matrix in $\mathbb{Z}_p^{n \times n}$, $\mathbf{0}_{m \times n}$ refers to the all-zero matrix in $\mathbb{Z}_p^{m \times n}$, and $\boldsymbol{e}_i^n$ the ith element of the canonical basis of $\mathbb{Z}_p^n$ (simply $\mathbf{I}$, $\mathbf{0}$, and $\boldsymbol{e}_i$, respectively, if n, m are clear from the context).

Given a set $\mathcal{R} = \{r_1, \ldots, r_d\} \subset \mathbb{Z}_p$, we denote by $\ell_i(X) = \prod_{j \neq i} \dfrac{(X - r_i)}{(r_j - r_i)}$ the ith Lagrange interpolation polynomial associated to $\mathcal{R}$.

2.2   Hardness Assumptions

Definition 1. *Let $\ell, k \in \mathbb{N}$. We call $\mathcal{D}_{\ell,k}$ a matrix distribution if it outputs (in PPT time, with overwhelming probability) matrices in $\mathbb{Z}_p^{\ell \times k}$. We define $\mathcal{D}_k := \mathcal{D}_{k+1,k}$.*

The following applies for $\mathbb{G}_\gamma$, where $\gamma \in \{1, 2\}$.

Assumption 1 (Matrix Decisional Diffie-Hellman Assumption in $\mathbb{G}_\gamma$ [9]). *For all non-uniform PPT adversaries $\mathcal{A}$,*

$$|\Pr[\mathcal{A}(gk, [\mathbf{A}]_\gamma, [\mathbf{Aw}]_\gamma) = 1] - \Pr[\mathcal{A}(gk, [\mathbf{A}]_\gamma, [\boldsymbol{z}]_\gamma) = 1]| \approx 0,$$

where the probability is taken over $gk \leftarrow \mathcal{G}(1^\lambda)$, $\mathbf{A} \leftarrow \mathcal{D}_{\ell,k}$, $\boldsymbol{w} \leftarrow \mathbb{Z}_p^k$, $[\boldsymbol{z}]_\gamma \leftarrow \mathbb{G}_\gamma^\ell$ and the coin tosses of adversary $\mathcal{A}$.

Intuitively, the $\mathcal{D}_{\ell,k}$-MDDH assumption means that it is hard to decide whether a vector is in the image space of a matrix or it is a random vector, where the matrix is drawn from $\mathcal{D}_{\ell,k}$. In this paper we will refer to the following matrix distributions:

$$\mathcal{L}_k : \mathbf{A} = \begin{pmatrix} a_1 & 0 & \dots & 0 \\ 0 & a_2 & \dots & 0 \\ \vdots & & \ddots & \vdots \\ 0 & 0 & \dots & a_k \\ 1 & 1 & \dots & 1 \end{pmatrix}, \qquad \mathcal{U}_{\ell,k} : \mathbf{A} = \begin{pmatrix} a_{1,1} & \dots & a_{1,k} \\ \vdots & \ddots & \vdots \\ a_{\ell,1} & \dots & a_{\ell,k} \end{pmatrix},$$

where $a_i, a_{i,j} \leftarrow \mathbb{Z}_p$. The $\mathcal{L}_k$-MDDH Assumption is the k-linear family of Decisional Assumptions and corresponds to the Decisional Diffie-Hellman (DDH) Assumption in $\mathbb{G}_\gamma$ when $k = 1$. The SXDH Assumption states that DDH holds in $\mathbb{G}_\gamma$ for all $\gamma \in \{1, 2\}$. The $\mathcal{U}_{\ell,k}$-MDDH assumption is the *Uniform* Assumption and is the weakest of all matrix assumptions of size $\ell \times k$.

Additionally, we will be using the following family of computational assumptions:

Assumption 2 (Kernel Diffie-Hellman Assumption in $\mathbb{G}_\gamma$ [28]). *For all non-uniform PPT adversaries $\mathcal{A}$:*

$$\Pr\left[[\boldsymbol{x}]_{3-\gamma} \leftarrow \mathcal{A}(gk, [\mathbf{A}]_\gamma) : \boldsymbol{x} \neq \boldsymbol{0} \wedge \boldsymbol{x}^\top \mathbf{A} = \boldsymbol{0} \right] \approx 0,$$

where the probability is taken over $gk \leftarrow \mathcal{G}(1^\lambda)$, $\mathbf{A} \leftarrow \mathcal{D}_{\ell,k}$ and the coin tosses of adversary $\mathcal{A}$.

The $\mathcal{D}_{\ell,k}$-KerMDH$_{\mathbb{G}_\gamma}$ Assumption is not stronger than the $\mathcal{D}_{\ell,k}$-MDDH$_{\mathbb{G}_\gamma}$ Assumption, since a solution to the former allows to decide membership in $\mathbf{Im}([\mathbf{A}]_\gamma)$. In asymmetric bilinear groups, there is a natural variant of this assumption.

Assumption 3 (Split Kernel Diffie-Hellman Assumption [14]). *For all non-uniform PPT adversaries $\mathcal{A}$:*

$$\Pr\left[[\boldsymbol{r}]_1, [\boldsymbol{s}]_2 \leftarrow \mathcal{A}(gk, [\mathbf{A}]_{1,2}) : \boldsymbol{r} \neq \boldsymbol{s} \wedge \boldsymbol{r}^\top \mathbf{A} = \boldsymbol{s}^\top \mathbf{A} \right] \approx 0,$$

where the probability is taken over $gk \leftarrow \mathcal{G}(1^\lambda)$, $\mathbf{A} \leftarrow \mathcal{D}_{\ell,k}$ and the coin tosses of adversary $\mathcal{A}$.

While the Kernel Diffie-Hellman Assumption says one cannot find a non-zero vector in one of the groups which is in the co-kernel of $\mathbf{A}$, the split assumption says one cannot find different vectors in $\mathbb{G}_1^\ell \times \mathbb{G}_2^\ell$ such that the difference of the vector of their discrete logarithms is in the co-kernel of $\mathbf{A}$. As a particular case, [14] considers the *Split Simultaneous Double Pairing Assumption in* $\mathbb{G}_1, \mathbb{G}_2$ (SSDP) which is the $\mathcal{RL}_2$-SKerMDH Assumption, where $\mathcal{RL}_2$ is the distribution which results of sampling a matrix from $\mathcal{L}_2$ and replacing the last row by random elements.

***q*-Assumptions.** We first recall the q-Strong Diffie-Hellman and q-Target Strong Diffie-Hellman assumptions, which essentially tell us that inversion is hard in the exponent, even when given q powers of the element to invert.

Assumption 4 (q-Strong Diffie Hellman Assumption in $\mathbb{G}_\gamma$, q-SDH [2]). *For all non-uniform PPT adversaries $\mathcal{A}$:*

$$\Pr\left[\left(r,[\nu]_\gamma\right) \leftarrow \mathcal{A}(gk,\{[s^i]_\gamma\}_{i=1}^q) : \nu = \frac{1}{s-r}\right] \approx 0,$$

where the probability is taken over $gk \leftarrow \mathcal{G}(1^\lambda)$, $s \leftarrow \mathbb{Z}_p$ and the coin tosses of adversary $\mathcal{A}$.

Assumption 5 (q-Target Strong Diffie-Hellman Assumption, q-TSDH [1]). *For all non-uniform PPT adversaries $\mathcal{A}$:*

$$\Pr\left[(r,[\nu]_T) \leftarrow \mathcal{A}(gk,\{[s^i]_{1,2}\}_{i=1}^q) : \nu = \frac{1}{s-r}\right] \approx 0,$$

where the probability is taken over $gk \leftarrow \mathcal{G}(1^\lambda)$, $s \leftarrow \mathbb{Z}_p$ and the coin tosses of adversary $\mathcal{A}$.

The soundness proofs of our schemes will rely on the following variations of the two assumptions above.

Assumption 6 ($\mathcal{Z}$-Group Strong DH Assumption in $\mathbb{G}_\gamma$, $\mathcal{Z}$-GSDH). *Let $\mathcal{Z} \subset \mathbb{Z}_p$ such that $\#\mathcal{Z} = q$. For all non-uniform PPT adversaries $\mathcal{A}$:*

$$\Pr\left[([z_1]_1,[z_2]_\gamma,[\nu]_2) \leftarrow \mathcal{A}\left(gk,\mathcal{Z},[\varepsilon]_{1,2},\{[s^i]_{1,2}\}_{i=1}^q\right) : \begin{array}{c} z_1 \notin \mathcal{Z} \wedge z_2 = \varepsilon z_1 \\ \nu = \frac{\prod_{z\in\mathcal{Z}}(s-z)}{s-z_1} \end{array}\right] \approx 0,$$

where the probability is taken over $gk \leftarrow \mathcal{G}(1^\lambda)$, $s,\varepsilon \leftarrow \mathbb{Z}_p$ and the coin tosses of adversary $\mathcal{A}$.

The name is motivated by the fact that it is a variant of the q-SDH Assumption in which the adversary must only give $[z_1]_1$ in the group $\mathbb{G}_1$, instead of giving it in $\mathbb{Z}_p$ as in the q-SDH Assumption.

Assumption 7 (q-Square TSDH Assumption, q-STSDH). *For all non-uniform PPT adversaries $\mathcal{A}$:*

$$\Pr\left[(r,[\beta_1]_1,[\beta_2]_2,[\nu]_T) \leftarrow \mathcal{A}\left(gk,[\varepsilon]_2,\{[s^i]_{1,2}\}_{i=1}^q\right) : \begin{array}{c} \beta_1 \neq \pm 1 \\ \beta_2 = \varepsilon\beta_1 \wedge \nu = \frac{\beta_1^2-1}{s-r} \end{array}\right] \approx 0,$$

where the probability is taken over $gk \leftarrow \mathcal{G}(1^\lambda)$, $s,\varepsilon \leftarrow \mathbb{Z}_p$ and the coin tosses of adversary $\mathcal{A}$.

Note that the challenger knows ε, s, so this assumption is falsifiable. Indeed, upon receiving $(r,[\beta_1]_1,[\beta_2]_2,[\nu]_T)$, the challenger verifies that $[\beta_1]_1 \neq [\pm 1]_1$, $e([1]_1,[\beta_2]_2) = e(\varepsilon[\beta_1]_1,[1]_2)$, and $\varepsilon(s-r)[\nu]_T = e([\beta_1]_1,[\beta_2]_2) - e([\varepsilon]_1,[1]_2)$. A similar argument can be made for the other assumptions in this section.

Assumption 8 (q-Quadratic TSDH Assumption, q-QTSDH). *For all non-uniform PPT adversaries $\mathcal{A}$:*

$$
\Pr\left[
\begin{array}{c}
\left(r, [\beta_1]_1, [\beta_2]_1, [\tilde{\beta}_1]_2, [\tilde{\beta}_2]_2, [\nu]_T \right) \leftarrow \mathcal{A}\left(gk, [\varepsilon]_{1,2}, \{[s^i]_{1,2}\}_{i=1}^q \right) : \\
\beta_1 \tilde{\beta}_1 \neq 1 \\
\beta_2 = \varepsilon\beta_1 \wedge \tilde{\beta}_2 = \varepsilon\tilde{\beta}_1 \wedge \nu = \frac{\beta_1 \tilde{\beta}_1 - 1}{s - r}
\end{array}
\right] \approx 0,
$$

where the probability is taken over $gk \leftarrow \mathcal{G}(1^\lambda)$, $s, \varepsilon \leftarrow \mathbb{Z}_p$ and the coin tosses of adversary $\mathcal{A}$.

2.3 Building Blocks

ElGamal Encryption. We denote by $\mathsf{Enc}_{[\mathsf{sk}]}(\mathsf{m}, r)$ the lifted ElGamal encryption of message m with randomness r and public key $[\mathsf{sk}]$. Using implicit group notation, ElGamal encryption is as follows:

$$
\begin{bmatrix} c_1 \\ c_2 \end{bmatrix} = \mathsf{Enc}_{[\mathsf{sk}]}(\mathsf{m}, r) = \mathsf{m}[e_2] + r\begin{bmatrix} 1 \\ \mathsf{sk} \end{bmatrix},
$$

where if one knows the secret key sk in $\mathbb{Z}_p$, then one can recover the message in $\mathbb{G}$ by computing $[c_2] - \mathsf{sk}[c_1] = [\mathsf{m}]$. ElGamal encryption is semantically secure under the DDH assumption. It can be seen as a commitment scheme, in which case it is perfectly binding and computationally hiding under the DDH assumption, and in fact this is how we will use it in our schemes.

Boneh-Boyen Signatures [2]. We briefly recall Boneh-Boyen signatures. Let $\mathbb{G}_1, \mathbb{G}_2, \mathbb{G}_T, e : \mathbb{G}_1 \times \mathbb{G}_2 \to \mathbb{G}_T$ be a bilinear group. Messages are elements of $\mathbb{Z}_p$, and signatures are elements of $\mathbb{G}_2$. The secret key is $\mathsf{sk} \in \mathbb{Z}_p$, and the public key (verification key) is $[\mathsf{sk}]_1 \in \mathbb{G}_1$. To sign a message $x \in \mathbb{Z}_p$, the signer computes

$$
[\sigma]_2 = \left[\frac{1}{\mathsf{sk} - x} \right]_2.
$$

The verifier accepts the signature if the equation $e([\mathsf{sk}]_1 - [x]_1, [\sigma]_2) = [1]_T$ holds. Boneh-Boyen signatures are existentially unforgeable under the q-SDH assumption.

Dual-Mode Commitments and Groth-Sahai Proofs [20]. Groth-Sahai proofs allow to prove satisfiability of quadratic equations in bilinear groups in the non-interactive setting. More precisely, Groth-Sahai proofs deal with equations of the form

$$
\sum_{j=1}^{m_y} a_j \mathsf{y}_j + \sum_{i=1}^{m_x} b_i \mathsf{x}_i + \sum_{i,j=1}^{m_x, m_y} \gamma_{i,j} \mathsf{x}_i \mathsf{y}_j = t,
$$

in which the set of variables is divided into two disjoint subsets $\mathsf{X} = \{\mathsf{x}_1, \ldots, \mathsf{x}_{m_x}\}$ and $\mathsf{Y} = \{\mathsf{y}_1, \ldots, \mathsf{y}_{m_y}\}$, and depending on the type of equation $\mathsf{X}, \mathsf{Y} \subset \mathbb{Z}_p$

(quadratic equations in $\mathbb{Z}_p$), $\mathsf{X} \subset \mathbb{Z}_p, \mathsf{Y} \subset \mathbb{G}_\gamma$ (multi-exponentiation equations in $\mathbb{G}_\gamma$) for $\gamma \in \{1, 2\}$ or $\mathsf{X} \subset \mathbb{G}_1$ and $\mathsf{Y} \subset \mathbb{G}_2$ (pairing product equations). Here the product means a bilinear operation which is multiplication in $\mathbb{Z}_p$, exponentiation or the pairing operation.

The scheme can be seen as a commit-and-prove scheme [8], where in the first step the prover gives commitments to the solutions, and in the second provides a proof that these commitments verify the corresponding equation. In particular, the commitments used are *dual-mode commitments*, that is, commitments that can be either perfectly binding or perfectly hiding, and we can switch from one to the other with an indistinguishable change of security game. More precisely, Groth-Sahai commitments to field elements $z \in \mathbb{Z}_p$ and group elements $[z] \in \mathbb{G}$ are, respectively:

$$\mathsf{Com}(z; w) = z\,[\boldsymbol{u}] + w[\boldsymbol{u}_1], \qquad \mathsf{Com}([z]; w_1, w_2) = \begin{bmatrix} 0 \\ z \end{bmatrix} + w_1[\boldsymbol{u}_1] + w_2[\boldsymbol{u}_2],$$

where $[\boldsymbol{u}], [\boldsymbol{u}_1], [\boldsymbol{u}_2]$ are vectors in $\mathbb{G}^2$ given in the commitment key, and their definitions depend on whether we want the commitments to be perfectly binding or perfectly hiding.

Groth-Sahai proofs are sound, witness-indistinguishable and, in many cases, zero-knowledge. More precisely, the proof is always zero-knowledge for quadratic equations in $\mathbb{Z}_p$ and multi-exponentiation equations, and also for pairing product equations provided that $t = 1$.

QA-NIZK Arguments of Membership in Linear Spaces [22]. We describe some languages for which there exist constant-size QA-NIZK arguments of membership which will be used as building blocks in our constructions. These languages are (i) linear subspaces of $\mathbb{G}_\gamma^m$, $\gamma \in \{1, 2\}$ [23,24], and (ii) bilateral linear subspaces, that is, linear subspaces of $\mathbb{G}_1^m \times \mathbb{G}_2^n$ [14]. For $\gamma \in \{1, 2\}$,

$$\mathcal{L}_{[\mathbf{M}]_\gamma} := \{[\boldsymbol{x}]_\gamma \in \mathbb{G}_\gamma^n : \exists \boldsymbol{w} \in \mathbb{Z}_q^t,\ \boldsymbol{x} = \mathbf{M}\boldsymbol{w}\}, \tag{i}$$

$$\mathcal{L}_{[\mathbf{M}]_1, [\mathbf{N}]_2} := \{([\boldsymbol{x}]_1, [\boldsymbol{y}]_2) \in \mathbb{G}_1^m \times \mathbb{G}_2^n : \exists \boldsymbol{w} \in \mathbb{Z}_q^t,\ \boldsymbol{x} = \mathbf{M}\boldsymbol{w},\ \boldsymbol{y} = \mathbf{N}\boldsymbol{w}\}, \text{(ii)}$$

We use LS (BLS) to designate (bilateral) linear subspace proof systems for the languages $\mathcal{L}_{[\mathbf{M}]_\gamma}$ ($\mathcal{L}_{[\mathbf{M}]_1, [\mathbf{N}]_2}$). These proof systems verify strong soundness, which essentially means that they are sound even when the discrete logarithm of the matrices is given. This property is formally defined in González et al. [14].

Case (i) can be instantiated based on the Kernel Diffie-Hellman Assumption 2, and the proof has size $|\mathbb{G}_\gamma|$, whereas (ii) can be based on the Split Kernel Diffie-Hellman Assumption 3, and the proof has size $2|\mathbb{G}_1| + 2|\mathbb{G}_2|$.

3   Proving Satisfiability of Quadratic Equations

In this section we present a scheme in which soundness is based on the q-STSDH Assumption.

3.1   Arguments for Quadratic Equations from q-Assumptions

Intuition. Given $n, d \in \mathbb{N}$, the number of variables and equations, respectively, we build a proof system for the family of languages

$$
\mathcal{L}_{\text{quad},ck} = \left\{ ([c]_1, \mathbf{V}, \boldsymbol{b}) \in \mathbb{G}_1^{2n} \times \mathbb{Z}_p^{n \times d} \times \mathbb{Z}_p^d \left| \begin{array}{l} \exists \boldsymbol{a}, \boldsymbol{w} \in \mathbb{Z}_p^n \text{ s.t} \\ [c]_1 = \mathsf{Com}_{ck}(\boldsymbol{a}, \boldsymbol{w}) \text{ and} \\ \{\boldsymbol{a}^\top \boldsymbol{v}_j + b_j\}_{j=1}^d \in \{0, 2\} \end{array} \right. \right\}
$$

where $[c]_1 = \mathsf{Com}_{ck}(\boldsymbol{a}, \boldsymbol{w})$ is a vector of ElGamal encryptions. This generalizes to any other perfectly binding commitment of the form $[c]_1 = \mathsf{Com}_{ck}(\boldsymbol{a}; \boldsymbol{w}) = [\mathbf{U}_1 \boldsymbol{a} + \mathbf{U}_2 \boldsymbol{w}]_1$ for $ck = ([\mathbf{U}_1]_1, [\mathbf{U}_2]_1)$, and $[\mathbf{U}_1]_1, [\mathbf{U}_2]_1$ are from a witness sampleable distribution.

We follow the approach of Danezis et al. [7] and encode the equations

$$
\boldsymbol{a}^\top \boldsymbol{v}_j + b_j \in \{0, 2\}
$$

into a *Square Span Program (SSP)*: we construct $n + 1$ polynomials $v_0(X), \ldots, v_n(X)$ and a target polynomial $t(X)$, where $\deg(v_i) < \deg(t) = d$ for all $i \in \{0, \ldots, n\}$. This codification asserts that a witness $\boldsymbol{a}$ satisfies the set of equations if and only if $t(X)$ divides $p(X)$, where

$$
p(X) = \left(v_0(X) + \sum_{i=1}^n a_i v_i(X) \right)^2 - 1.
$$

The polynomials $v_i(X)$, $i \in \{1, \ldots, n\}$, are defined as the interpolation polynomials of the coefficients v_{ij} of $\mathbf{V}$ at $r_1, \ldots, r_d$, which are fixed, arbitrary, pairwise different points of $\mathbb{Z}_p$. Similarly, $v_0(X)$ is the interpolation polynomial of $b_j - 1$ at the same points. That is, if $\boldsymbol{v}_j$ is the jth column of $\mathbf{V}$,

$$
\boldsymbol{a}^\top \boldsymbol{v}_j + b_j - 1 = \sum_{i=1}^n a_i v_{ij} + b_j - 1 = \sum_{i=1}^n a_i v_i(r_j) + v_0(r_j).
$$

Note that the statement $Z \in \{0, 2\}$ is equivalent to $(Z-1)^2 - 1 = 0$ and hence, the polynomial $p(X)$ interpolates the left side of this equation in $r_1, \ldots, r_d$ when Z is replaced by $\boldsymbol{a}^\top \boldsymbol{v}_j + b_j - 1$ for each $j \in \{1, \ldots, d\}$. The target polynomial $t(X) = \prod_{i=1}^d (X - r_i)$ is 0 at $r_1, \ldots, r_d$ and therefore encodes the right sides. This codification gives us the equivalence: the equations hold if and only if $t(X)$ divides $p(X)$.

Danezis et al. constructed a SNARK for this statement, "$t(X)$ divides $p(X)$", which is very efficient because it just checks that the divisibility relation holds at a single secret point $s \in \mathbb{Z}_p$ whose powers $[s]_1, [s]_2, \ldots, [s^d]_1, [s^d]_2$ are published in the CRS. That is, the proof essentially shows "in the exponent" that

$$
p(s) = h(s)t(s),
$$

where $h(X) = p(X)/t(X)$. When all the equations hold, $h(X)$ is a polynomial and the evaluation at s can be constructed as a linear combination of the powers of s in the CRS. When some equation does not hold, $h(X)$ is a rational function, and its evaluation at s is no longer efficiently computable from the CRS. The actual proof system has some additional randomization elements to achieve Zero-Knowledge, but its soundness follows from this argument.

In the scheme of Danezis et al., the prover outputs a perfectly hiding commitment to the witness. In the soundness proof, one uses a knowledge of exponent assumption to extract the witness in $\mathbb{Z}_p^n$ from the commitment. The witness is used to derive a reduction from breaking soundness to the d-TSDH Assumption. More precisely, it follows from the SSP characterization that if the equation with index j^* does not hold, then $p(X) = q(X)(X - r_{j^*}) + b$, for some $b \neq 0$. From the extracted value of the witness $\boldsymbol{a}$ one can identify at least one such j^* and also recover the coefficients of $q(X)$ and the value b in $\mathbb{Z}_p$. From the verification equation, the reduction can obtain

$$\left[\frac{p(s)}{s - r_{j^*}}\right]_T = \left[q(s) + \frac{b}{s - r_{j^*}}\right]_T \tag{1}$$

and using $b, q(s)$ derive $\left[\dfrac{1}{s - r_{j^*}}\right]_T$.

In other words, there are two ways in which the Danezis et al.'s scheme (as well as most other SNARKs) use knowledge assumptions: (a) extracting vectors of committed values from one single group element (beyond what is information-theoretically possible), and (b) extract in the base field, so computing discrete logarithms. Our goal is to avoid knowledge of exponent assumptions, so to circumvent (a) we change the scheme to include perfectly binding commitments to the witness. However, we still have to deal with (b), as our commitments to $\boldsymbol{a}$ can only be opened to $[\boldsymbol{a}]_\gamma \in \mathbb{G}_\gamma$. Therefore, we are no longer able to compute $[q(s)]_T$ since it requires to compute terms of the form $[a_i a_j s^k]_T$ from $[a_i]_1, [a_j]_2$ and powers of s in one of the groups, in any case it would be a multiplication of three group elements.

At this point, we would like to be able to include in the proof a commitment that allows the reduction to extract $q(s)$, but the fact that $q(s)$ is "quadratic" in the witness makes this difficult. For this reason, we factor $q(X)$ into two polynomials $q_1(X)$ and $q_2(X)$. In the soundness game we will program the CRS[1] to depend on an index j^* and let the prover compute binding commitment to $[q_2(s)]_2$, while $[q_1(s)]_1$ can be directly computed from the proof. From these factors we are able to compute $[q(s)]_T$. However, extracting b in $\mathbb{Z}_p$ to obtain a reduction to the q-TSDH problem seems difficult, so we will rely on a more flexible security assumption where we do not need to remove b. The idea of the new assumption is to give the adversary powers of s in the source groups and ask the adversary to output

$$\left(r_{j^*}, [\beta]_1, \left[\frac{b}{s - r_{j^*}}\right]_T\right), \quad \text{where } \beta^2 - 1 = b.$$

---

[1] This is why we lose a factor $1/d$ in the soundness reduction.

However, this is not a hard problem, as the adversary can set b as a combination of $s - r_{j*}$ to achieve elimination of the denominator in $\frac{b}{s-r_{j*}}$. For example, if an adversary sets $\beta = s - r_{j*} + 1$, it can compute a valid solution as $(r_{j*}, [\beta]_1, [s - r_{j*} + 2]_T)$. To prevent this type of attacks from happening, we add an element $[\varepsilon]_2 \in \mathbb{G}_2$ to the challenge, and ask the adversary to output $[\varepsilon\beta]_2$ too, so that β cannot be set as a function of s (since the adversary will not be able to compute εs in $\mathbb{G}_2$). We call the modified assumption the q-STSDH, which is proven to be generically secure (see full version). Further, it can be easily checked that the assumption is falsifiable as we note in Sect. 2.2. To make sure that we can extract $[\varepsilon\beta]_2$ from the prover's output and also that the rest of the elements of the proof are of the right form, we will require the prover to show that its output is in a given linear space.

Scheme Description. Given $n, d \in \mathbb{N}$ we construct a QA-NIZK argument for the language $\mathcal{L}_{\text{quad},ck}$.

Setup.

- Algorithm $\mathsf{K}_0(gk, n, d)$ samples $ck = [u]_1 \leftarrow \mathcal{L}_1$. A commitment $\mathsf{Com}_{ck}(a; w)$ is the concatenation of $\mathsf{Enc}_{ck}(a_i; w_i) = [a_i e_2 + w_i u]_1$. That is, $\mathsf{Com}_{ck}(a; w) = [\mathbf{U}_1 a + \mathbf{U}_2 w]_1$, where $\mathbf{U}_1, \mathbf{U}_2$ are $2n \times n$ matrices such that $\mathbf{U}_1$ has e_2 in the diagonal and $[\mathbf{U}_2]_1$ has u in the diagonal.
- Algorithm $\mathsf{K}_1(gk, ck, n, d)$ picks $s \leftarrow \mathbb{Z}_p$, $\left\{\hat{\phi}_i\right\}_{i\in\{1,\dots,n+1\}} \leftarrow \mathbb{Z}_p^3$, $\mathbf{Q}_2 \leftarrow \mathcal{U}_{3,3}$ and generates also the CRS for proving membership in bilateral linear spaces of Sect. 2, BLS.CRS, for the linear spaces generated by the matrices:

$$[\mathbf{M}]_1 = \begin{bmatrix} e_2 & & & u & & & \\ & \ddots & & & \ddots & & \mathbf{0} \\ & & e_2 & & & u & \\ v_1(s) & \dots & v_n(s) & \mathbf{0} & & t(s) & 0 \end{bmatrix}_1 \in \mathbb{G}_1^{(2n+1)\times(2n+4)},$$

$$[\mathbf{N}]_2 = \begin{bmatrix} v_1(s) & \dots & v_n(s) & & \mathbf{0} & t(s) & 0 \\ \hat{\phi}_1 & \dots & \hat{\phi}_n & & & \hat{\phi}_{n+1} & \mathbf{Q}_2 \end{bmatrix}_2 \in \mathbb{G}_2^{4\times(2n+4)}.$$

The CRS includes the elements

$$\left(gk, ck, \left\{[s^i]_{1,2}\right\}_{i\in\{1,\dots,d\}}, \left\{[\hat{\phi}_i]_2\right\}_{i\in\{1,\dots,n+1\}}, [\mathbf{Q}_2]_2, \mathsf{BLS.CRS} \right).$$

Prover. The prover P with input $(\mathsf{CRS}, [c]_1, \mathbf{V}, b, a)$ picks $\delta \leftarrow \mathbb{Z}_p, r_{q.2} \leftarrow \mathbb{Z}_p^3$ and defines the polynomial

$$p(X) = \left(v_0(X) + \sum_{i=1}^{n} a_i v_i(X) + \delta t(X) \right)^2 - 1 \in \mathbb{Z}_p[X],$$

where each $v_i(X)$, for $i \in \{1, \ldots, n\}$, is the interpolation polynomial of the components v_{ij} of $\mathbf{V}$ at points r_j, for $j \in \{1, \ldots, d\}$, and $v_0(X)$ is the interpolation polynomial of $b_j - 1$ at the same points. It then computes $h(X) = \frac{p(X)}{t(X)}$, which is a polynomial in $\mathbb{Z}_p[X]$ because $\boldsymbol{a}$ satisfies the equations, and the following elements:

$$[V]_1 = [\textstyle\sum_{i=1}^{n} a_i v_i(s) + \delta t(s)]_1 \quad [V]_2 = [\textstyle\sum_{i=1}^{n} a_i v_i(s) + \delta t(s)]_2$$

$$[H]_1 = [h(s)]_1 \qquad\qquad [\boldsymbol{q}_2]_2 = \left[\textstyle\sum_{i=1}^{n} a_i \hat{\phi}_i + \delta \hat{\phi}_{n+1} + \mathbf{Q}_2 \boldsymbol{r}_{q.2} \right]_2.$$

The prover can compute all these elements as linear combinations of the powers of s in the CRS. The prover also computes a BLS proof ψ of

$$([\boldsymbol{c}]_1, [V]_1, [V]_2, [\boldsymbol{q}_2]_2)^\top \in \mathbf{Im} \left(\begin{matrix} [\mathbf{M}]_1 \\ [\mathbf{N}]_2 \end{matrix} \right)$$

with witness $(\boldsymbol{a}, \boldsymbol{w}, \delta, \boldsymbol{r}_{q.2})^\top \in \mathbb{Z}_p^{2n+4}$.

Finally, it sends the proof π to the verifier, where $\pi := \left([H]_1, [V]_{1,2}, \right.$ $\left. [\boldsymbol{q}_2]_2, \psi \right).$

Verifier. The verifier V with input $(\mathrm{CRS}, [\boldsymbol{c}]_1, \mathbf{V}, \boldsymbol{b}, \pi)$ checks whether the equation

$$e([v_0(s) + V]_1, [v_0(s) + V]_2) - [1]_T = e([H]_1, [t(s)]_2) \qquad (2)$$

holds and $\mathsf{BLS.verify}(\psi) = 1$. If both conditions hold, it returns 1, else it returns 0.

Completeness. This property is based on the perfect completeness of membership in bilateral spaces, and the observation that the left hand side of the verification equation is $e\left([v_0(s) + V]_1, [v_0(s) + V]_2\right) - [1]_T = \left[(v_0(s) + V)^2 - 1\right]_T = [p(s)]_T$, and the right hand side is $e\left([H]_1, [t(s)]_2\right) = e\left([h(s)]_1, [t(s)]_2\right) = [p(s)]_T.$

Soundness. We introduce a technical lemma that we will use in the following to prove the soundness of the scheme.

Lemma 1. *Let $v(X)$ be a polynomial in $\mathbb{Z}_p[X]$. For any $r \in \mathbb{Z}_p$, we define $q_2(X)$ and β as the quotient and remainder, respectively, of the polynomial division of $v(X)$ by $X - r$, i.e. $v(X) = q_2(X)(X - r) + \beta$. If $p(X) = v(X)^2 - 1$, then*

$$p(X) = (v(X) + \beta)\, q_2(X)(X - r) + \beta^2 - 1.$$

Proof. By definition, $p(X) = v(X)^2 - 1$, if we expand this expression using the definition of $q_2(X)$ we have:

$$\begin{aligned} p(X) &= v(X)\left(q_2(X)(X - r) + \beta\right) - 1 = v(X)q_2(X)(X - r) + v(X)\beta - 1 \\ &= v(X)q_2(X)(X - r) + q_2(X)(X - r)\beta + \beta^2 - 1 \\ &= (v(X) + \beta)q_2(X)(X - r) + \beta^2 - 1. \end{aligned}$$ $\qquad \square$

Theorem 1. *Let* $\mathsf{Adv}_{Sound}(\mathcal{A})$ *be the advantage of any PPT adversary* $\mathcal{A}$ *against the soundness of the scheme. There exist PPT adversaries* $\mathcal{B}_1, \mathcal{B}_3$ *against the* $\mathcal{L}_1$-$\mathsf{MDDH}_{\mathbb{G}_2}$ *and* d-STSDH *Assumptions, respectively, and an adversary* $\mathcal{B}_2$ *against strong soundness of the* BLS *proof such that*

$$\mathsf{Adv}_{Sound}(\mathcal{A}) \leq d\Big(2\mathsf{Adv}_{\mathcal{L}_1\text{-}\mathsf{MDDH},\mathbb{G}_2}(\mathcal{B}_1) + \mathsf{Adv}_{\mathsf{BLS}}(\mathcal{B}_2) + \mathsf{Adv}_{d\text{-}\mathsf{STSDH}}(\mathcal{B}_3)\Big).$$

Proof. In order to prove soundness we will prove indistinguishability of the following games.

- Real: This is the real soundness game. The output is 1 if the adversary produces a false accepting proof, i.e. if there is some equation $\boldsymbol{a}^\top \boldsymbol{v}_i + b_i \notin \{0, 2\}$ and the verifier accepts the proof.
- Game_0: This game is identical to the previous one, except that the commitment key $\boldsymbol{u}$ is chosen by the game.
- Game_1: This game is identical to the previous one, except that some $j^* \leftarrow \{1, \ldots, d\}$ is chosen and the game aborts if $\boldsymbol{a}$ satisfies the j^*-th equation, i.e. $[\boldsymbol{a}]_1^\top \boldsymbol{v}_{j^*} + [b_{j^*}]_1 \in \{[0]_1, [2]_1\}$.
- Game_2: For $r = r_{j^*}$ and $i \in \{1, \ldots, n+1\}$ let $\alpha_i(X)$ and β_i be the quotient and the reminder of the polynomial division of $v_i(X)$ by $X - r_{j^*}$ if $i \in \{1, \ldots, n\}$, and of $t(X)$ by $X - r_{j^*}$ if $i = n + 1$. This game is identical to the previous one, except that $\mathbf{Q}_2$ is now a uniformly random matrix conditioned on having rank 1, and each $\big[\hat{\boldsymbol{\phi}}_i\big]_2$ is changed to

$$\big[\hat{\boldsymbol{\phi}}_i\big]_2 = [\alpha_i(s)]_2 \boldsymbol{e}_2 + \beta_i[\varepsilon]_2 \boldsymbol{e}_3 + [\mathbf{Q}_2]_2 \boldsymbol{r}_i,$$

where $\varepsilon \leftarrow \mathbb{Z}_p$, $\boldsymbol{r}_i \leftarrow \mathbb{Z}_p^3$ and $\boldsymbol{e}_i$ is the ith vector of the canonical basis of $\mathbb{Z}_p^3$.

Obviously, the games Real and Game_0 are indistinguishable.

Lemma 2. $Pr[\mathsf{Game}_0(\mathcal{A}) = 1] \leq d \cdot Pr[\mathsf{Game}_1(\mathcal{A}) = 1].$

Proof. If $\mathcal{A}$ breaks soundness, at least one equation does not hold. Thus the challenger has at least a probability of $\frac{1}{d}$ of guessing this equation. □

Lemma 3. *There exists a* $\mathcal{L}_1$-$\mathsf{MDDH}_{\mathbb{G}_2}$ *adversary* $\mathcal{B}_1$ *such that*

$$|Pr[\mathsf{Game}_1(\mathcal{A}) = 1] - Pr[\mathsf{Game}_2(\mathcal{A}) = 1]| \leq 2Adv_{\mathcal{L}_1\text{-}\mathsf{MDDH},\mathbb{G}_2}(\mathcal{B}_1).$$

We use a direct application of the rank problem, which is reducible to MDDH, to prove the above Lemma. See the full version for the details.

Lemma 4. *There exists an adversary* $\mathcal{B}_2$ *against the strong soundness of the* BLS *proof and a* d-STSDH *adversary* $\mathcal{B}_3$ *such that*

$$Pr[\mathsf{Game}_3(\mathcal{A}) = 1] \leq \mathsf{Adv}_{\mathsf{BLS}}(\mathcal{B}_2) + \mathsf{Adv}_{d\text{-}\mathsf{STSDH}}(\mathcal{B}_3).$$

Proof. For any adversary which breaks soundness $\mathcal{A}$, let E be the event that $([c]_1, [V]_1, [V]_2, [q_2]_2)^\top \in \mathbf{Im}\left(\begin{bmatrix}\mathbf{M}\end{bmatrix}_1 \\ [\mathbf{N}]_2\right)$ of Sect. 2 and $\overline{E}$ be the complementary event. Obviously,

$$\Pr[\mathsf{Game}_3(\mathcal{A}) = 1] \leq \Pr[\mathsf{Game}_3(\mathcal{A}) = 1|E] + \Pr[\mathsf{Game}_3(\mathcal{A}) = 1|\overline{E}]. \quad (3)$$

We can bound the second summand by the advantage of an adversary $\mathcal{B}_2$ against the strong soundness of BLS. Such an adversary receives $[\mathbf{M}]_1, [\mathbf{N}]_2$ sampled according to the distribution specified by Game_3 and the witness that proves that $\mathbf{M}, \mathbf{N}$ are sampled according to this distribution, which is s (see strong soundness, defined in full version). It also generates the BLS.CRS, and the rest of the CRS is chosen in the usual way. Adversary $\mathcal{B}_2$ can use the output of $\mathcal{A}$ to break the soundness of BLS in a straightforward way.

In the following, we bound the first term of the sum in Eq. (3) by constructing an adversary $\mathcal{B}_3$ which breaks the d-STSDH Assumption in the case that E happens. Note that in this case there exists a witness $(a, w, \delta, r_{q.2})^\top$ of membership in $\mathbf{Im}\left(\begin{bmatrix}\mathbf{M}\end{bmatrix}_1 \\ [\mathbf{N}]_2\right)$. Further, this witness is partially unique, because $[c]_1$ is a perfectly binding commitment, so a, w, δ are uniquely determined, and in particular this uniquely determines the polynomial $p(X)$.

We now describe the full reduction. Adversary $\mathcal{B}_3$ receives a challenge of the d-STSDH Assumption and plugs it in the CRS. The rest of the elements are chosen by adversary $\mathcal{B}_3$ with the distribution specified by the game. The CRS is then sent to the soundness adversary $\mathcal{A}$, who eventually outputs π for the corresponding $[c]_1$.

Adversary $\mathcal{B}_3$ extracts $[a]_1 \in \mathbb{G}_1$ from the knowledge of $u \in \mathbb{Z}_p^2$ and aborts if the j^*-th equation is satisfied. By definition $e([v_0(s) + V]_1, [v_0(s) + V]_2) - [1]_T = [p(s)]_T$. If we divide both sides of the verification equation (2) by $s - r_{j^*}$,

$$\left[\frac{p(s)}{s - r_{j^*}}\right]_T = e\left([H]_1, \left[\frac{t(s)}{s - r_{j^*}}\right]_2\right) = e\left([H]_1, \left[\prod_{i \neq j^*}(s - r_i)\right]_2\right), \quad (4)$$

so the adversary $\mathcal{B}_3$ can compute $\left[\dfrac{p(s)}{s - r_{j^*}}\right]_T$ from $[H]_1$ and the powers of $[s]_{1,2}$ in the CRS. On the other hand, if we apply Lemma 1 to $p(X)$, we have

$$\left[\frac{p(s)}{s - r_{j^*}}\right]_T = \left[(v(s) + \beta)q_2(s) + \frac{\beta^2 - 1}{s - r_{j^*}}\right]_T, \quad (5)$$

and we have $\beta^2 - 1 \neq 0$ (otherwise the j^*-th equation is satisfied, in which case the game aborts). We describe in the following how $\mathcal{B}_3$ can compute right side of (5) and the elements to break the d-STSDH Assumption.

$\mathcal{B}_3$ can compute $[\beta]_1 = \sum_{i=0}^n [a_i]_1 \beta_i$ and also $[v(s) + \beta]_1 = [V]_1 + [\beta]_1$, because it knows $[V]_1$ from the proof π and the extracted values $[a_i]_1$, and β_i are the reminders of dividing $v_i(X)$ by $X - r_{j^*}$.

Since $\mathcal{B}_3$ sampled $\mathbf{Q}_2$ itself, it can recover $[q_2(s)]_2$ and $[\varepsilon\beta]_2$ from $[\mathbf{q}_2]_2$ because it can compute two vectors $\mathbf{v}_2, \mathbf{v}_3 \in \mathbb{Z}_p^3$ such that $\mathbf{v}_i^\top[\mathbf{Q}_2]_2 = \mathbf{0}$, $\mathbf{v}_i^\top \mathbf{e}_j = 0$ if $i \neq j$ and $\mathbf{v}_i^\top \mathbf{e}_j = 1$ if $i = j$. $\mathcal{B}_3$ multiplies these vectors by $\mathbf{q}_2$ (which is correctly computed, because E holds), resulting in:

$$\mathbf{v}_2^\top[\mathbf{q}_2]_2 = \left[\mathbf{v}_2^\top \sum_{i=1}^{n+1} a_i \left(\alpha_i(s)\mathbf{e}_2 + \beta_i \varepsilon \mathbf{e}_3 + \mathbf{Q}_2 \mathbf{r}_i\right) + \mathbf{v}_2^\top \mathbf{Q}_2 \mathbf{r}_{q.2}\right]_2 = \left[\sum_{i=1}^{n+1} a_i \alpha_i(s)\right]_2,$$

$$\mathbf{v}_3^\top[\mathbf{q}_2]_2 = \left[\sum_{i=1}^{n+1} a_i \beta_i \varepsilon\right]_2.$$

From these values, $\mathcal{B}_3$ can compute $[q_2(s)]_2$ and $[\varepsilon\beta]_2$ by adding $[\alpha_0(s)]_2$ and $\beta_0[\varepsilon]_2$ to the above extracted elements, respectively:

$$\left[\alpha_0(s) + \sum_{i=1}^{n+1} a_i \alpha_i(s)\right]_2 = [q_2(s)]_2, \qquad \beta_0[\varepsilon]_2 + \left[\varepsilon \sum_{i=1}^{n+1} a_i \beta_i\right]_2 = [\varepsilon\beta]_2.$$

From these values and $[v(s) + \beta]_2$, computed above, $\mathcal{B}$ can derive $[(v(s) + \beta)q_2(s)]_T$ as $e([v(s)+\beta]_1, [q_2(s)]_2)$, and from Eq. (5) recover $\left[\dfrac{\beta^2 - 1}{s - r_{j*}}\right]_T$.

Finally, $\mathcal{B}_3$ returns $\left(r_{j*}, [\beta]_1, [\varepsilon\beta]_2, \left[\dfrac{\beta^2 - 1}{s - r_{j*}}\right]_T\right)$, breaking the d-STSDH Assumption. $\qquad\square$

Zero-Knowledge. We describe the simulation algorithm $(\mathsf{S}_1, \mathsf{S}_2)$. $\mathsf{S}_1(gk)$ outputs $(\mathrm{CRS}, \tau = \{s\}, \tau_{\mathsf{BLS}})$, the common reference string computed in the usual way plus the simulation trapdoor $s \in \mathbb{Z}_p$ and the simulation trapdoor of the bilateral spaces membership proof.

Simulator $\mathsf{S}_2(\mathrm{CRS}, [c]_1, \tau, \tau_{\mathsf{BLS}})$: This algorithm samples $V^S \in \mathbb{Z}_p$, $\left[q_2^S\right]_2 \leftarrow \mathbb{G}_2^3$, and defines:

$$[H^S]_1 = \left[\frac{(V^S)^2 - 1}{t(s)}\right]_1.$$

S also constructs $\psi^S \leftarrow \mathsf{BLS.simulator}(\mathrm{CRS}, [c]_1, [V^S]_1, [V^S]_2, [q_2^S]_2, \tau_{\mathsf{BLS}})$. The algorithm outputs $\pi := ([c]_1, [V^S]_1, [V^S]_2, [q_2^S]_2, \psi^S)$.

Theorem 2. *The scheme above is Perfect Zero-Knowledge.*

Proof. The key idea behind the proof is that all its the elements can be seen as perfectly hiding commitments to $\mathbf{a}$, where $\mathbf{a}$ is the opening of $[c]_1$. For any V^S and any $\mathbf{a}$, there always exists a compatible δ. Further, since $\mathbf{Q}_2$ has full rank, $[q_2^S]_2$ is compatible with any values $\mathbf{a}, \delta$. $[H^S]_1$ is uniquely determined by V^S and rest of the elements of the CRS. Finally, perfect zero-knowledge follows from the perfect zero-knowledge property of the bilateral space membership proof. $\qquad\square$

3.2   Unit Vector from Static Assumptions

In our argument for aggregating quadratic equations, we obtain succinctness following the usual polynomial aggregation technique used in most SNARK constructions (e.g. [7,11]), namely, the set of interpolation points $r_1, \ldots, r_d \in \mathbb{Z}_p$ is public, while the evaluation point s is only known in the exponent. We can consider a dual approach in which $s \in \mathbb{Z}_p$ is public but $r_1, \ldots r_d$ are in the exponent. We observe that this leads to a trade-off between the type of assumption (q-type vs. static) and size of the CRS (linear vs. quadratic). The second construction reminds us the beginnings of SNARKs, where the CRS was quadratic in the circuit size. The construction is still interesting for proving that a set of n binding commitments to integers open to n binary values $(b_1, \ldots, b_n) \in \{0,1\}^n$ such that $\sum b_i = 1$. In this case, a simple modification of the proof system of Sect. 3.1 leads to a scheme with computational soundness based on static assumptions and linear CRS. The full scheme and its security proof are presented in full version. The unit vector argument can be used, for instance, to improve the constructions of the best pairing-based constructions of ring signature schemes without random oracles and based on falsifiable assumptions [6,13]. It also leads to a shuffle argument, described in Sect. 5.1.

4   Aggregated Set Membership Arguments

In the construction of Sect. 3.1, if $\mathbf{V}$ is the identity matrix and $\boldsymbol{b} = \boldsymbol{0}$, the equations $\boldsymbol{a}\mathbf{V} + \boldsymbol{b} \in \{0,2\}^d$ just prove that each $a_i \in \{0,2\}$. In this section we consider a generalization and build a proof system which proves that some perfectly binding commitments open to $a_i \in \mathcal{Z} = \{z_1, \ldots, z_m\} \subset \mathbb{Z}_p$. The proof is constant-size and uses the Boneh-Boyen signature scheme (the basic scheme from [2, Sect. 4.3]) together with a technique to aggregate quadratic equations similar to the one of Sect. 3.1 and inspired by the quadratic span programs of Gennaro et al. [11].

First, in Sect. 4.1, we describe how to construct an argument of membership for a single $a \in \mathcal{Z}$ and then in Sect. 4.2 we show how to aggregate the argument. In the full version we show how to apply these ideas to construct a range proof.

4.1   Non-aggregated Set Membership Argument

Intuition. We build a constant-size proof of membership for polynomially-large sets in $\mathbb{Z}_p$ with linear CRS. The idea is to give in the common reference string Boneh-Boyen signatures to each element of the set. The proof of membership is just a proof of knowledge of a valid signature. Recall that $[\sigma]_2$ is a valid signature for x if and only if

$$e([\mathsf{sk} - x]_1, [\sigma]_2) - [1]_T = [0]_T.$$

The statement $x \in \mathcal{Z}$ is proven committing to x and to $[\sigma]_2 = \left[\frac{1}{\mathsf{sk}-x}\right]_2$, and giving a Groth-Sahai proof for the satisfiability of the verification equation.

The problem with this approach is that it is not possible to extract $x \in \mathbb{Z}_p$ from its Groth-Sahai commitment, but only $[x]_1 \in \mathbb{G}_1$. Therefore, it is not clear how to reduce soundness to the EUF-CMA security of Boneh-Boyen, as the reduction can only output a "relaxed form" of forgery $([x]_1, [\sigma]_2)$, for some $x \notin \mathcal{Z}$, instead of $(x, [\sigma]_2)$.[2]

It turns out that Boneh-Boyen signatures are not unforgeable when purported forgeries are pairs of the form $([x]_1, [\sigma]_2)$. The problem is that $[x]_1$ may be dependent of sk, whereas this is impossible when $x \in \mathbb{Z}_p$ must be given. Indeed, for any message of the form $[\mathsf{sk} - x]_1$ one might compute a forgery as $[1/x]_2$.

To solve this issue, we force the prover to commit to $[\varepsilon x]_1$, where the discrete logarithm of $[\varepsilon]_1$ remains hidden. Since $[\mathsf{sk} \cdot \varepsilon]_1$ is not given, the adversary cannot choose x to be a function of sk.

Scheme Description. We give a proof of membership in $\mathcal{Z} = \{z_1, \ldots, z_m\} \subset \mathbb{Z}_p$. More precisely, we build a proof for the family of languages:

$$\mathcal{L}_{\mathsf{memb}, \mathcal{Z}, ck} := \{[c]_1 \in \mathbb{G}_1^2 \mid \exists w \in \mathbb{Z}_p \text{ s.t. } [c]_1 = \mathsf{Com}_{ck}(x; w) \text{ and } x \in \mathcal{Z}\}.$$

Setup. Parameters for the Boneh-Boyen signatures are generated. Choose $\varepsilon \leftarrow \mathbb{Z}_p$. The CRS contains $[\varepsilon]_2$, signatures $[\sigma_j]_2 = \left[\frac{1}{\mathsf{sk}-z_j}\right]_2$ of each $z_j \in \mathcal{Z}$, and the Groth-Sahai CRS. The simulation trapdoor is ε and the GS simulation trapdoor for equations which are right-simulatable[3].

Prover. If $x \in \mathcal{Z}$, then there is some pair $([y]_2, [\sigma]_2)$, where $[\sigma]_2$ is in the CRS, such that

$$e([\mathsf{sk}]_1 - [x]_1, [\sigma]_2) = [1]_T \quad \text{and} \quad [y]_2 = x[\varepsilon]_2.$$

The prover produces a Groth-Sahai proof of the equations:

$$e([\mathsf{sk}]_1 - [X]_1, [\Sigma]_2) = [1]_T \quad \text{and} \quad [Y]_2 = X[\varepsilon]_2$$

where X, Y, Σ are the variables.

Verifier. Accept if and only if both proofs are valid.

Theorem 3. *The argument above is computationally quasi-adaptively sound under the $\mathcal{Z}$-GSDH Assumption in $\mathbb{G}_2$ and the soundness of Groth-Sahai proofs.*

Proof. We construct an adversary $\mathcal{B}$ against the $\mathcal{Z}$-GSDH assumption, which receives $gk := (p, \mathbb{G}_1, \mathbb{G}_2, \mathbb{G}_T, e, \mathcal{P}_1, \mathcal{P}_2)$ together with $[\varepsilon]_{1,2}$ and $\{[s^i]_{1,2}\}_{i=1}^m$ from

---

[2] An alternative is of course to commit to x bit-by-bit to make it extractable, but it is completely impractical.

[3] See Ràfols [30]. These are statements for which only the commitments in $\mathbb{G}_2$ need to be perfectly hiding and where it is sufficient to get the simulation trapdoor to equivocate commitments in $\mathbb{G}_2$.

the challenger. The adversary defines a new generator for $\mathbb{G}_2$, $\overline{\mathcal{P}}_2 = [\prod_{i=1}^{m}(s - z_i)]_2$, defines a new group key $\overline{gk} := (p, \mathbb{G}_1, \mathbb{G}_2, \mathbb{G}_T, e, \mathcal{P}_1, \overline{\mathcal{P}}_2)$, and defines $[\mathsf{sk}]_1 = [s]_1$. Note that we use implicit notation with respect to $\mathcal{P}_1, \mathcal{P}_2$ and not with respect to the new generators.

The adversary can now build the signatures

$$\left(z_j[\varepsilon]_2, \left[\prod_{\substack{i=1 \\ i \neq j}}^{m}(s - z_i) \right]_2 \right) = \left(z_j[\varepsilon]_2, \frac{1}{\mathsf{sk} - z_j}\overline{\mathcal{P}}_2 \right)$$

which are valid with respect to the group key $\overline{gk}$.

Let $\mathcal{A}$ be an adversary against our set membership proof. Adversary $\mathcal{B}$ runs $\mathcal{A}$ with the new group key $\overline{gk}$, Groth-Sahai commitment keys for which it knows the discrete logarithm (in order to open commitments), and signatures $([\sigma_1]_2, \ldots, [\sigma_m]_2)$. Suppose that $\mathcal{A}$ wins by producing an accepting proof for some $x \notin \mathcal{Z}$. From the adversary's proof and committed values one can extract $[x]_1$ and $([y^*]_2, [\sigma^*]_2)$ and, from perfect soundness of Groth-Sahai proofs, it follows that

$$e([\mathsf{sk}]_1 - [x]_1, [\sigma^*]_2) = e(\mathcal{P}_1, \overline{\mathcal{P}}_2) \quad \text{and} \quad [y^*]_2 = x[\varepsilon]_2.$$

This implies that $[\sigma^*]_2 = \left[\frac{\prod_{j=1}^{m}(\mathsf{sk}-z_j)}{\mathsf{sk}-x} \right]_2$, and hence $([x]_1, [y^*]_2, [\sigma^*]_2)$ is a solution to the $\mathcal{Z}$-GSDH problem. □

Theorem 4. *The argument above is composable zero-knowledge under the composable zero-knowledge property of Groth-Sahai proofs.*

Proof. The proof simulator uses the Groth-Sahai trapdoor and ε to simulate the Groth-Sahai proof of both equations (note that even though the commitment $[c]_1$ is part of the statement, both equations are right-simulatable when ε is known). □

4.2 Aggregated Set Membership Argument

Let $\mathcal{Z} \subset \mathbb{Z}_p$, $m = |\mathcal{Z}|$, and $n \in \mathbb{N}$. We construct a QA-NIZK argument for the following language

$$\mathcal{L}_{\mathsf{memb}, \mathcal{Z}, ck} := \left\{ [c]_1 \in \mathbb{G}_1^{2n} \; \middle| \; \begin{array}{l} \exists w \in \mathbb{Z}_p^n \text{ s.t. } [c]_1 = \mathsf{Com}_{ck}(x; w) \\ \text{and } x_1, \ldots, x_n \in \mathcal{Z} \end{array} \right\},$$

where $[c]_1 = \mathsf{Com}_{ck}(x; w)$ is a vector of ElGamal encryptions. The generalization to other perfectly binding commitments is straightforward.

Intuition. To express the validity of n signature and message pairs, we construct polynomials $v(X), y(X)$, which encode the set of n verification equations for the Boneh-Boyen signatures. Given the set $\mathcal{R} = \{r_1, \ldots, r_n\} \subset \mathbb{Z}_p$, recall that we denote as $\ell_i(X)$ the ith Lagrange interpolation polynomial associated to $\mathcal{R}$.

We define $v_0(X)$ as the constant polynomial $v_0(X) = \mathsf{sk}$, and $t(X) = \prod_{r_j \in \mathcal{R}}(X - r_j)$. The set of polynomials $v_0(X), \{\ell_i(X)\}_{i=0}^n, t(X)$ accepts $x_1, \ldots, x_n$ if and only if $t(X)$ divides $(v_0(X) - v(X))y(X) - 1$, where

$$v(X) = \sum_{j=1}^{n} x_i \ell_i(X), \qquad y(X) = \sum_{i=1}^{m} \sigma_{k(i)} \ell_i(X),$$

and $\sigma_{k(i)}$ is the signature of some $z_{k(i)}$ such that $x_i = z_{k(i)}$.

That is, at any point $r_j \in \mathcal{R}$, if $x_j = v(r_j)$, then $y(r_j)$ is a valid signature of x_j. This follows from

$$(v_0(X) - v(X))y(X) - 1 = h(X)t(X) \text{ for some polynomial } h(X)$$
$$\implies (v_0(r_j) - v(r_j))y(r_j) - 1 = 0 \iff (\mathsf{sk} - x_j)y(r_j) - 1 = 0.$$

In particular, if $j \in [n]$ is such that $x_j \notin \mathcal{Z}$, then $y(r_j)$ is a forgery for x_j. For simplicity, in this exposition we ignore the issue mentioned in previous section about commitment extractability, but this is taken into account in the argument.

Note that to compute $y(X)$ given $\ell_i(X)$ in some source group, the prover would need to know the discrete logarithm of the signatures. To render the interpolation polynomials efficiently computable, we include in the CRS the terms $[\sigma_i s^j]_2$, where $\sigma_i = \frac{1}{\mathsf{sk} - z_i}$, for all $i \in \{1, \ldots, m\}, j \in \{1, \ldots, n\}$, and all other values which require the signature's discrete logarithm. Consequently, our CRS is of size $O(nm)$.

A direct instantiation of techniques from Sect. 3.1 requires perfectly binding commitments to each of the signatures and hence, a proof of size linear in the number of statements. But it turns out that perfectly binding commitments to signatures are not necessary for proving membership in $\mathcal{Z}$. To achieve this, we use a trick similar to Sect. 3.1. We program the CRS in order to extract a valid signature for x_{j^*}, for a random $j^* \in \{1, \ldots, n\}$, in such a way that the adversary might only detect the change in the CRS with negligible probability.

Scheme Description. Given $m, n \in \mathbb{N}$ and a set $\mathcal{Z} \subset \mathbb{Z}_p, |\mathcal{Z}| = m$, we construct a QA-NIZK argument for the language $\mathcal{L}_{\mathsf{memb}, \mathcal{Z}, ck}$.

Setup.

- Algorithm $\mathsf{K}_0(gk)$ sets $ck = [\boldsymbol{u}]_1 \leftarrow \mathcal{L}_1$.
- Algorithm $\mathsf{K}_1(gk, ck)$ picks $s \leftarrow \mathbb{Z}_p, \left\{\phi_i, \hat{\phi}_i\right\}_{i \in \{1, \ldots, n+1\}} \leftarrow \mathbb{Z}_p^3 \times \mathbb{Z}_p^4, \mathbf{Q}_1 \leftarrow \mathcal{U}_{3,3}, \mathbf{Q}_2 \leftarrow \mathcal{U}_{4,4}$, picks a Boneh-Boyen secret key $\mathsf{sk} \leftarrow \mathbb{Z}_p$, generates signatures $[\sigma_1]_2, \ldots, [\sigma_m]_2$ for each element in $\mathcal{Z}$ and generates also crs_{Π_1} and crs_{Π_2}

for proving membership in the linear spaces generated, respectively, by the matrices $\mathbf{M}, \mathbf{N}$, where:

$$[\mathbf{M}]_1 = \begin{bmatrix} e_2 & & & u & & & \\ & \ddots & & & \ddots & & \mathbf{0} \\ & & e_2 & & u & & \\ \hline \ell_1(s) \ldots \ell_n(s) & & & \mathbf{0} & & t(s) & \mathbf{0} \\ \phi_1 & \cdots & \phi_n & & & \phi_{n+1} & \mathbf{Q}_1 \end{bmatrix}_1 \in \mathbb{G}_1^{(2n+4)\times(2n+4)},$$

$$[\mathbf{N}]_2 = \begin{bmatrix} \sigma_1\ell_1(s) & \sigma_1\ell_2(s) & \cdots & \sigma_m\ell_n(s) & t(s) & \mathbf{0} \\ \sigma_1\hat{\phi}_1 & \sigma_1\hat{\phi}_2 & \cdots & \sigma_m\hat{\phi}_n & \hat{\phi}_{n+1} & \mathbf{Q}_2 \end{bmatrix}_2 \in \mathbb{G}_2^{5\times(nm+5)}.$$

The CRS includes the elements

$$\left(gk, ck, \left\{ [s^j]_1, [\mathsf{sk}s^j]_1, [\sigma_i s^j]_{1,2}, [\phi_i]_1, [\sigma_i\hat{\phi}_j]_2 \right\}_{i\in\{1,\ldots,m\},j\in\{1,\ldots,n\}}, [\phi_{n+1}]_1, [\hat{\phi}_{n+1}]_2, \right.$$
$$\left. [\mathbf{Q}_1]_1, [\mathbf{Q}_2]_2, \mathsf{crs}_{\Pi_1}, \mathsf{crs}_{\Pi_2} \right).$$

Prover. The prover $\mathsf{P}(\mathsf{CRS}, [c]_1, x, w)$ picks $\delta_v, \delta_y \leftarrow \mathbb{Z}_p, r_{q.1} \leftarrow \mathbb{Z}_p^3, r_{q.2} \leftarrow \mathbb{Z}_p^4$ and defines the polynomials

$$v(X) = \sum_{i=1}^n x_i\ell_i(X) + \delta_v t(X), \qquad y(X) = \sum_{i=1}^n \sigma_{k(i)}\ell_i(X) + \delta_y t(X)$$
$$h(X) = \frac{(v_0(X) - v(X))y(X) - 1}{t(X)}$$

where $v_0(r_j) = \mathsf{sk}$, for all $j \in \{1, \ldots, n\}$, $t(X) = \prod_{r\in\mathcal{R}}(X - r)$ and $\ell_i(X)$ is the ith Lagrangian interpolation polynomial associated to $\mathcal{R}$. By definition of the language, each x_i is equal to $z_{k(i)}$, for some $k(i) \in \{1, \ldots, m\}$.

The prover computes the following elements:

$$[H]_1 = [h(s)]_1$$
$$[V]_1 = [v(s)]_1 \qquad [q_1]_1 = \left[\sum_{i=1}^n x_i\phi_i + \delta_v\phi_{n+1} + \mathbf{Q}_1 r_{q.1}\right]_1$$
$$[Y]_2 = [y(s)]_2 \qquad [q_2]_2 = \left[\sum_{i=1}^n \sigma_{k(i)}\hat{\phi}_i + \delta_y\hat{\phi}_{n+1} + \mathbf{Q}_2 r_{q.2}\right]_2.$$

The prover also computes two LS proofs

$$\psi_1 \leftarrow \Pi_1.\mathsf{LS.prove}\left(\mathsf{crs}_{\Pi_1}, \begin{bmatrix} c \\ V \\ q_1 \end{bmatrix}_1, \begin{pmatrix} x \\ w \\ \delta_v \\ r_{q.1} \end{pmatrix}\right), \psi_2 \leftarrow \Pi_2.\mathsf{LS.prove}\left(\mathsf{crs}_{\Pi_2}, \begin{bmatrix} Y \\ q_2 \end{bmatrix}_2, \begin{pmatrix} y \\ \delta_y \\ r_{q.2} \end{pmatrix}\right),$$

where $y = (y_{1,1}, y_{1,2}, \ldots, y_{n,m})$ and $y_{i,j}$ is equal to 1 if $i = k(j)$ and 0 otherwise. Finally, it sends the proof π to the verifier, where

$$\pi := ([H]_1, [V]_1, [Y]_2, [q_1]_1, [q_2]_2, \psi_1, \psi_2).$$

Verifier. The verifier $V(\text{CRS}, \pi)$ checks whether the equation

$$e([H]_1, [t(s)]_2) = e([v_0(s)]_1 - [V]_1, [Y]_2) - [1]_T \text{ holds, and}$$

$$\Pi_1.\text{LS.verify}\left(\text{crs}_{\Pi_1}, \begin{bmatrix} c \\ V \\ q_1 \end{bmatrix}_1, \psi_1\right) = 1, \quad \Pi_2.\text{LS.verify}\left(\text{crs}_{\Pi_2}, \begin{bmatrix} Y \\ q_2 \end{bmatrix}_2, \psi_2\right) = 1.$$

If all of these conditions hold, it returns 1, else 0.

Completeness. If $x_1, \ldots, x_n \in \mathcal{Z}$ then $(v_0(r_j) - v(r_j))y(r_j) - 1 = (x_{k(j)} + \text{sk})\sigma_{k(j)} - 1 = 0$ for all j, and thus $(v_0(X) - v(X))y(X) = 1 \mod t(X)$. This implies that $h(X)$ is a well defined polynomial in $\mathbb{Z}_p[X]$ such that $e([h(s)]_1, [t(s)]_2) = e([v_0(s) - v(s)]_1, [y(s)]_2) - [1]_T$. It is easy to check that

$$\begin{pmatrix} c \\ V \\ q_1 \end{pmatrix} = \mathbf{M} \begin{pmatrix} x \\ w \\ \delta_v \\ r_{q.1} \end{pmatrix} \text{ and } \begin{pmatrix} Y \\ q_2 \end{pmatrix} = \mathbf{N} \begin{pmatrix} y \\ \delta_y \\ r_{q.2} \end{pmatrix},$$

where $y = (y_{1,1}, \ldots, y_{m,n})$, and therefore ψ_1, ψ_2 are valid proofs.

Soundness

Theorem 5. *Let $\text{Adv}_{PS}(\mathcal{A})$ be the advantage of a PPT adversary $\mathcal{A}$ against the soundness of the scheme. There exist PPT adversaries $\mathcal{B}_1, \mathcal{B}_2, \mathcal{B}_{3,1}, \mathcal{B}_{3,2}, \mathcal{B}_4, \mathcal{B}_5$ such that*

$$\text{Adv}_{PS}(\mathcal{A}) \leq n \, (\, 2\text{Adv}_{\mathcal{L}_1\text{-MDDH},\mathbb{G}_1}(\mathcal{B}_1) + 3\text{Adv}_{\mathcal{L}_1\text{-MDDH},\mathbb{G}_2}(\mathcal{B}_2) + \text{Adv}_{\text{LS},\Pi_1}(\mathcal{B}_{3,1})$$
$$+ \text{Adv}_{\text{LS},\Pi_2}(\mathcal{B}_{3,2}) + \text{Adv}_{\mathcal{Z}\text{-GSDH},\mathbb{G}_1}(\mathcal{B}_4) + \text{Adv}_{n\text{-QTSDH}}(\mathcal{B}_5)) \, .$$

Proof. In order to prove soundness we will prove indistinguishability of the following games.

- Real: This is the real soundness game. The output is 1 if the adversary produces a false accepting proof, i.e. if there is some $x_i \notin \mathcal{Z}$ and the verifier accepts the proof.
- Game$_0$: This game is identical to the previous one, except that the commitment key u is chosen by the game in order to extract $[x]_1$ from $[c]_1$.
- Game$_1$: This game is identical to the previous one, except that some $j^* \leftarrow \{1, \ldots, n\}$ is chosen and the game aborts if the extracted value $[x]_1$ is such that $[x_{j^*}]_1 \in [\mathcal{Z}]_1$.
- Game$_2$: For $i = 1, \ldots, n$, let $\alpha_i(X)$ and β_i be the quotient and the reminder, respectively, of dividing $\ell_i(X)$ by $X - r_{j^*}$. Let $\alpha_{n+1}(X)$ and β_{n+1} be the quotient and the reminder of dividing $t(X)$ by $X - r_{j^*}$. This game is identical to the previous one, except that $\mathbf{Q}_1$ is now a uniformly random matrix conditioned on having rank 1, and for $i = 1, \ldots, n+1$, $[\phi_i]_1$ is changed to

$$[\phi_i]_1 = [\alpha_i(s)]_1 e_2^3 + \beta_i[\varepsilon]_1 e_3^3 + [\mathbf{Q}_1]_1 r_i,$$

where e_j^3 is the jth vector of the canonical basis of $\mathbb{Z}_p^3$, $r_i \leftarrow \mathbb{Z}_p^3$, $\varepsilon \leftarrow \mathbb{Z}_p$.

- Game$_3$: Let $\alpha_i(X)$ and β_i be defined as above. This game is identical to the previous one, except that $\mathbf{Q}_2$ is now a uniformly random matrix conditioned on having rank 1, and each $\left[\hat{\phi}_i\right]_2$ is now defined as

$$\left[\hat{\phi}_i\right]_2 = [\alpha_i(s)]_2 e_2^4 + [\beta_i]_2 e_3^4 + \beta_i[\varepsilon]_2 e_4^4 + [\mathbf{Q}_2]_2 \tilde{r}_i,$$

where e_j^4 is the jth vector of the canonical basis of $\mathbb{Z}_p^4$, $\tilde{r}_i \leftarrow \mathbb{Z}_p^4$ and $\varepsilon \leftarrow \mathbb{Z}_p$ is the same value used in the definition of $[\phi_i]_1$.

Obviously, the games Real and Game$_0$ are indistinguishable. The proofs of indistinguishablility of Game$_1$, Game$_2$ and Game$_2$, Game$_3$ are the same as their analogues in Sect. 3.1, which can be found in the full version. We proceed to prove that in Game$_3$ the adversary wins only with negligible probability.

Lemma 5. *There exists adversaries $\mathcal{B}_{3,i}$ against the soundness of Π_i.LS, an adversary $\mathcal{B}_4$ against $\mathcal{Z}$-GSDH in $\mathbb{G}_1$, and an adversary $\mathcal{B}_5$ against n-QTSDH such that*

$$Pr[\mathsf{Game}_3(\mathcal{A}) = 1] \leq \mathsf{Adv}_{\mathsf{LS}}(\mathcal{B}_{3,1}) + \mathsf{Adv}_{\mathsf{LS}}(\mathcal{B}_{3,2}) + \mathsf{Adv}_{n\text{-QTSDH}}(\mathcal{B}_4) + \mathsf{Adv}_{\mathcal{Z}\text{-GSDH},\mathbb{G}_1}(\mathcal{B}_5).$$

Proof. Let E_1 be the event where $(\boldsymbol{c}, V, \boldsymbol{q}_1)$ is not in the image of $\mathbf{M}$, E_2 the event that $(Y, \boldsymbol{q}_2)$ is not in the image of $\mathbf{N}$, and $E_3 = \overline{E_1 \cup E_2}$. Then

$$\Pr[\mathsf{Game}_3(\mathcal{A}) = 1] \leq \Pr[\mathsf{Game}_3(\mathcal{A}) = 1|E_1] + \Pr[\mathsf{Game}_3(\mathcal{A}) = 1|E_2] + \\ + \Pr[\mathsf{Game}_3(\mathcal{A}) = 1|E_3], \tag{6}$$

and, clearly,

$$\Pr[\mathsf{Game}_3(\mathcal{A}) = 1|E_1] + \Pr[\mathsf{Game}_3(\mathcal{A}) = 1|E_2] \leq \mathsf{Adv}_{\Pi_1.\mathsf{LS}}(\mathcal{B}_{3,1}) + \mathsf{Adv}_{\Pi_2.\mathsf{LS}}(\mathcal{B}_{3,2}).$$

We now proceed to bound $\Pr[\mathsf{Game}_3(\mathcal{A}) = 1|E_3]$. Conditioned on E_3, there exist some $\boldsymbol{x}^\dagger, \boldsymbol{w}, \delta_v, \boldsymbol{r}_{q.1}$ and $\boldsymbol{y}^\dagger, \delta_y, \boldsymbol{r}_{q.2}$ such that $(\boldsymbol{c}, V, \boldsymbol{q}_1)^\top = \mathbf{M}(\boldsymbol{x}^\dagger, \boldsymbol{w}, \delta_v, \boldsymbol{r}_{q.1})^\top$ and $(Y, \boldsymbol{q}_2)^\top = \mathbf{N}(\boldsymbol{y}^\dagger, \delta_y, \boldsymbol{r}_{q.2})^\top$. Given that $\boldsymbol{c}$ is perfectly binding, it must be that $\boldsymbol{x} = \boldsymbol{x}^\dagger$. It follows that $V = \sum_{i=1}^n x_i \ell_i(s) + \delta_v t(s) = v(s)$ and $Y = y^\dagger(s)$ for some polynomial $y^\dagger(X) = \sum_{i=1}^n \sum_{j=1}^m y_{i,j}^\dagger \sigma_i \ell_i(X) + \delta_y t(X)$. Further, except with probability $1/q$, each e_j^i is linearly independent of the columns of $[\mathbf{Q}_1]_1, [\mathbf{Q}_2]_2$, so one can extract from $[\boldsymbol{q}_1]_1$ (resp. $[\boldsymbol{q}_2]_2$) the coefficients of these vectors in its expression in terms of $[\mathbf{Q}_1]_1, e_2^3, e_3^3$ (resp. $[\mathbf{Q}_2]_2, e_2^4, e_3^4, e_4^4$), which are:

$$\begin{bmatrix} \sum_{i=1}^{n+1} x_i \alpha_i(s) \\ \sum_{i=1}^{n+1} x_i \beta_i \varepsilon \end{bmatrix}_1 = \begin{bmatrix} \alpha(s) \\ \beta\varepsilon \end{bmatrix}_1 \text{ and } \begin{bmatrix} \sum_{i,j=1}^{m,n} y_{i,j}^\dagger \sigma_i \tilde{\alpha}_j(s) + \delta_y \tilde{\alpha}_{n+1}(s) \\ \sum_{i,j=1}^{m,n} y_{i,j}^\dagger \sigma_i \tilde{\beta}_j + \delta_y \tilde{\beta}_{n+1} \\ \sum_{i,j=1}^{m,n} y_{i,j}^\dagger \sigma_i \tilde{\beta}_j \varepsilon + \delta_y \tilde{\beta}_{n+1} \varepsilon \end{bmatrix}_2 = \begin{bmatrix} \tilde{\alpha}(s) \\ \tilde{\beta} \\ \tilde{\beta}\varepsilon \end{bmatrix}_2$$

where $x_{n+1} = \delta_v$ and $\alpha(X), \tilde{\alpha}(X)$ are the quotients and $\beta, \tilde{\beta}$ are the reminders of dividing, respectively, $v(X)$ and $y(X)$ by $X - r_{j^*}$.

If we divide both sides of the verification equation by $(s - r_{j^*})$, and we denote by $\alpha_0(s), \beta_0$ we get that

$$e\left([H]_1, \left[\frac{t(s)}{s - r_{j^*}}\right]_2\right) = \frac{1}{s - r_{j^*}}(e([v_0(s)]_1 - [v(s)]_1, [y(s)]_2) - [1]_T)$$

$$= \frac{1}{s - r_{j^*}} \Big[(v_0(s) - v(s))(\tilde{\alpha}(s)(s - r_{j^*}) + \tilde{\beta}) - 1\Big]_T$$

$$= [(v_0(s) - v(s))\tilde{\alpha}(s) + \alpha(s)\tilde{\beta}]_T + \left[\frac{(v_0(s) - \beta)\tilde{\beta} - 1}{s - r_{j^*}}\right]_T$$

Note that $\beta = v(r_{j^*}) = x_{j^*}, v_0(s) = \mathsf{sk}$ and thus if $(v_0(s) - \beta)\tilde{\beta} - 1 = 0$, then $\tilde{\beta}$ is a valid signature for x_{j^*}.

Let E_4 the event $(v_0(s) - \beta)\tilde{\beta} - 1 = 0$ and thus $\Pr[\mathsf{Game}_4(\mathcal{A}) = 1|E_3] \leq \Pr[\mathsf{Game}_4(\mathcal{A}) = 1|E_4 \cap E_3] + \Pr[\mathsf{Game}_4(\mathcal{A}) = 1|\overline{E_4} \cap E_3]$.

We build an adversary $\mathcal{B}_4$ against Assumption 6 which receives $gk, \{[\mathsf{sk}^i]_1, [\mathsf{sk}^i]_2\}_{i\in[m]}, [\varepsilon]_{1,2}$. Essentially, the adversary works as the one described in Sect. 4.1 for the (non-aggregated) set membership argument. It simulates $\mathsf{Game}_4(\mathcal{A})$ computing all the discrete logarithms of the CRS itself, except for the Boneh-Boyen secret key, $[\varepsilon]_{1,2}$, and the signatures in the CRS are computed as in Sect. 4.1. When $\mathcal{A}$ outputs $[q_1]_1, [q_2]_2$, $\mathcal{B}_4$ extracts $[\beta\varepsilon]_1, [\tilde{\beta}]_2$ and returns $([x_{j^*}]_1, [\beta\varepsilon]_1, [\tilde{\beta}]_2)$. In the case E_4, we have already argued that $\tilde{\beta}$ is a valid signature for x_{j^*}, and in this game $x_{j^*} \notin S$. We conclude that $\Pr[\mathsf{Game}_4(\mathcal{A}) = 1|E_4 \cap E_3] \leq \mathsf{Adv}_{\mathcal{Z}\text{-}\mathbf{GSDH},\mathbb{G}_1}(\mathcal{B}_4)$.

We also construct $\mathcal{B}_5$ an adversary against Assumption 8. It receives as input $[\varepsilon]_1, [\varepsilon]_2, [s]_1, [s]_2, \ldots, [s^d]_1[s^d]_2$ and it starts a simulation of $\mathsf{Game}_4(\mathcal{A})$, by sampling honestly the rest of the elements of the CRS. Finally, $\mathcal{A}$ outputs $[V]_1, [Y]_2, [q_1]_1, [q_2]_2$ as part of the purported proof for $[c]_1$. We will see in the following how $\mathcal{B}_4$ computes $[\nu]_T := \left[\frac{(v_0(s) - \beta)\tilde{\beta} - 1}{s - r_{j^*}}\right]_T$ and returns $([v_0(s) - \beta]_1, [(v_0(s) - \beta)\varepsilon]_1, [\tilde{\beta}]_2, [\tilde{\beta}\varepsilon]_2, [\nu]_T)$, with $(v_0(s) - \beta)\tilde{\beta} - 1 \neq 0$, breaking Assumption 8.

The values $[\tilde{\alpha}(s)]_2, [\tilde{\beta}]_2$ and $[\tilde{\beta}\varepsilon]_2$ are extracted from $[q_2]_2$, while $[\alpha(s)]_1, [\beta\varepsilon]_1$ are extracted from $[q_1]_1$, $[\beta]_1 = [x_{j^*}]_1$ is extracted from $[c]_1$, $\beta_0 = \mathsf{sk}$, and $[v_0(s)\varepsilon]_1 = \mathsf{sk}[\varepsilon]_1$ can be computed by $\mathcal{B}_5$ because it sampled sk. The value $[\nu]_T$ is computed as

$$[\nu]_T := e\left([H]_1, \left[\frac{t(s)}{s - r_{j^*}}\right]_2\right) - e([v_0(s)]_1 - [V]_1, [\tilde{\alpha}(s)]_2) - e\left([\alpha(s)]_1, [\tilde{\beta}]_2\right).$$

Zero-Knowledge. The proof of perfect zero-knowledge is essentially the same as for Theorem 2. Note that $[V]_1, [Y]_2, [q_1]_1, [q_2]_2$ are independent of x, while $[H]_1$ is the unique solution to the verification equation. Perfect zero-knowledge of the argument of membership in linear spaces implies that the proofs ψ_1, ψ_2 can be simulated with the same distribution as honest proofs.

5   Shuffle Arguments

From our results, we can construct two different shuffle arguments in the CRS model under falsifiable assumptions. They both follow the basic template of the shuffle argument of [15]. Let $[c_1]_2, [c_2]_2$ be two vectors of n ciphertexts which open to vectors of plaintexts $[m_1]_2, [m_2]_2$, respectively, and we want to prove that m_2 is a permutation of m_1. The shuffle argument of [15] consists of the following steps. The CRS includes a vector of group elements $[z]_1 = ([z_1]_1, \ldots, [z_n]_1)$ sampled uniformly and independently. The prover chooses a permutation $[x]_1 = ([x_1]_1, \ldots, [x_n]_1)$ of $[z]_1$ and proves: (1) $x_i \in \mathcal{Z} = \{z_1, \ldots, z_n\}$ for all $i \in \{1, \ldots, n\}$, (2) $\sum x_i = \sum z_i$ and (3) $\sum z_i m_{1,i} = \sum x_i m_{2,i}$.

The first two steps force x to be a permutation of z: if all $x_i \in \mathcal{Z}$ and their sum equals the sum of all the elements in $\mathcal{Z}$ and x is not a permutation, the prover has found a non-trivial combination of elements of $\mathcal{Z}$ which is 0, which is a type of kernel problem. The last step links this fact with m_2 being a permutation of m_1.

In both our constructions and in the original argument of [15], Steps (2) and (3) are handled with the following Groth-Sahai equations, in which upper-case letters are variables for which the prover has provided commitments: (2) $\sum [X_i]_1 = \sum [z_i]_1$ and (3) $\sum e([z_i]_1, [M_{1,i}]_2) = \sum e([X_i]_1, [M_{2,i}]_2)$.

We next specify two different ways of proving Step 1, which results in two different constructions with different performance.

5.1   Unit Vector Argument

The first approach is the closest to the work of González et al. [15]. There, Step 1 is rewritten as proving that $x = z^\top B$, for a matrix $B = (b_1 | \ldots | b_n) \in \{0,1\}^{n^2}$, where the b_i are unitary vectors (not necessarily different, as this is handled by step 2). The approach of [15] is to adopt a commit-and-prove strategy using arguments for linear spaces and the bitstring argument of [14]. The 'prove' part is constant-size, but the 'commit' part is a priori quadratic, as we would need to commit to each entry of the matrix B.

To overcome this and obtain linear complexity, they switch to shrinking commitments to each row b_i^* of B, which take only two elements each. Obviously these commitments cannot be perfectly binding, and this fact interferes with the extraction step in soundness proof. However, a key step in their argument is that they set these commitments in a way that one single coordinate j^* (which remains unknown to the adversary) is perfectly binding. Thus the corresponding column is uniquely determined and can be extracted in the proof. From here, it is concluded that an adversary cannot cheat in the j^*-th ciphertext, and since j^* is unknown to the adversary, general soundness is reduced to this case with a tightness loss of $1/n$. Note that this is on top of the factor $1/n$ from the bitstring argument, resulting in a soundness loss of $1/n^2$.

We observe that we can plug our unit vector argument instead of the one from [14], modified to accept shrinking commitments to each of the rows of B as those in [15]. We include an additional game at the beginning of the soundness proof of the unit vector argument, in which we choose a random coordinate and abort if the corresponding commitment is not in the language. From here on the proof works as in unit vector presented in the full version. This proof inherits the disadvantages of [15], namely the quadratic CRS and the tightness loss in the security reduction, but we improve the proof size from $(4n + 17)|\mathbb{G}_1| + 14|\mathbb{G}_2|$ to $(4n + 11)|\mathbb{G}_1| + 8|\mathbb{G}_2|$ and our proof still uses falsifiable and static assumptions.

5.2 Argument of Membership in a Set of Group Elements

Another approach to Step 1, instead of the aggregated unit vector proofs, is to prove directly membership in a subset $\mathcal{Z} = \{[z_1]_1, \ldots, [z_n]_1\} \subset \mathbb{G}_1$. Note that the set is witness sampleable and in particular, the discrete logarithms might be known when generating the CRS. More precisely, we want to construct an argument for the language

$$\mathcal{L}_{\text{memb-group}, \mathcal{Z}, ck} := \left\{ [c]_1 \in \mathbb{G}_1^2 \mid \exists w \in \mathbb{Z}_p \text{ s.t. } [c]_1 = \mathsf{Com}_{ck}([x]_1; w) \text{ and } [x]_1 \in \mathcal{Z} \right\},$$

and for efficiency, the proof should be aggregated. This can be achieved by modifying the aggregated membership in a subset of $\mathbb{Z}_p$ from Sect. 4.2. Note that there we had $x \in \mathbb{Z}_p$, and this was necessary to produce the proof, so to ensure completeness when the prover knows only $[x]_1 \in \mathcal{Z} \subset \mathbb{G}_1$, we provide additional elements in the CRS. This is possible because the set is witness sampleable. More precisely, x was involved in the definition of the terms

$$[V]_1 = [v(s)]_1, \qquad \text{where } v(X) = \sum_{i=1}^{n} x_i \ell_i(X) + \delta_v t(X),$$

$$[q_1]_1 = \left[\sum_{i=1}^{n} x_i \phi_i + \delta_v \phi_{n+1} + \mathbf{Q}_1 r_{q.1} \right]_1,$$

so we include the elements $\{[z_i \ell_j(s)]_1, [z_i \phi_j]_1\}_{i,j \in \{1,\ldots,n\}}$ in the CRS. The proof works exactly the same, as the reduction could only open the commitments in the group.

We can use this to prove Step 1 of the shuffle argument above. In this case, the CRS size is still quadratic in the number of ciphertexts, but we avoid losing the second factor $1/n$ in the reduction, and the proof consists only of the commitments to $[x_i]_1$ and a constant number of elements. More precisely, the proof size is $(2n + 11)|\mathbb{G}_1| + 8|\mathbb{G}_2|$.

References

1. Boneh, D., Boyen, X.: Secure identity based encryption without random oracles. In: Franklin, M. (ed.) CRYPTO 2004. LNCS, vol. 3152, pp. 443–459. Springer, Heidelberg (2004). https://doi.org/10.1007/978-3-540-28628-8_27
2. Boneh, D., Boyen, X.: Short signatures without random oracles and the SDH assumption in bilinear groups. J. Cryptology **21**(2), 149–177 (2008)

3. Bootle, J., Groth, J.: Efficient batch zero-knowledge arguments for low degree polynomials. In: Abdalla, M., Dahab, R. (eds.) PKC 2018. LNCS, vol. 10770, pp. 561–588. Springer, Cham (2018). https://doi.org/10.1007/978-3-319-76581-5_19

4. Camenisch, J., Chaabouni, R., Shelat, A.: Efficient protocols for set membership and range proofs. In: Pieprzyk, J. (ed.) ASIACRYPT 2008. LNCS, vol. 5350, pp. 234–252. Springer, Heidelberg (2008). https://doi.org/10.1007/978-3-540-89255-7_15

5. Canetti, R., Lindell, Y., Ostrovsky, R., Sahai, A.: Universally composable two-party and multi-party secure computation. In: 34th ACM STOC, pp. 494–503. ACM Press, May 2002

6. Chandran, N., Groth, J., Sahai, A.: Ring signatures of sub-linear size without random oracles. In: Arge, L., Cachin, C., Jurdziński, T., Tarlecki, A. (eds.) ICALP 2007. LNCS, vol. 4596, pp. 423–434. Springer, Heidelberg (2007). https://doi.org/10.1007/978-3-540-73420-8_38

7. Danezis, G., Fournet, C., Groth, J., Kohlweiss, M.: Square span programs with applications to succinct NIZK arguments. In: Sarkar, P., Iwata, T. (eds.) ASIACRYPT 2014, Part I. LNCS, vol. 8873, pp. 532–550. Springer, Heidelberg (2014). https://doi.org/10.1007/978-3-662-45611-8_28

8. Escala, A., Groth, J.: Fine-tuning Groth-Sahai proofs. In: Krawczyk, H. (ed.) PKC 2014. LNCS, vol. 8383, pp. 630–649. Springer, Heidelberg (2014). https://doi.org/10.1007/978-3-642-54631-0_36

9. Escala, A., Herold, G., Kiltz, E., Ràfols, C., Villar, J.: An algebraic framework for Diffie-Hellman assumptions. In: Canetti, R., Garay, J.A. (eds.) CRYPTO 2013, Part II. LNCS, vol. 8043, pp. 129–147. Springer, Heidelberg (2013). https://doi.org/10.1007/978-3-642-40084-1_8

10. Fauzi, P., Lipmaa, H., Siim, J., Zając, M.: An efficient pairing-based shuffle argument. In: Takagi, T., Peyrin, T. (eds.) ASIACRYPT 2017, Part II. LNCS, vol. 10625, pp. 97–127. Springer, Cham (2017). https://doi.org/10.1007/978-3-319-70697-9_4

11. Gennaro, R., Gentry, C., Parno, B., Raykova, M.: Quadratic span programs and succinct NIZKs without PCPs. In: Johansson, T., Nguyen, P.Q. (eds.) EUROCRYPT 2013. LNCS, vol. 7881, pp. 626–645. Springer, Heidelberg (2013). https://doi.org/10.1007/978-3-642-38348-9_37

12. Gentry, C., Wichs, D.: Separating succinct non-interactive arguments from all falsifiable assumptions. In: Fortnow, L., Vadhan, S.P. (eds.) 43rd ACM STOC, pp. 99–108. ACM Press, June 2011

13. González, A.: A ring signature of size $O(\sqrt[3]{n})$ without random oracles. Cryptology ePrint Archive, Report 2017/905 (2017). http://eprint.iacr.org/2017/905

14. González, A., Hevia, A., Ràfols, C.: QA-NIZK arguments in asymmetric groups: new tools and new constructions. In: Iwata, T., Cheon, J.H. (eds.) ASIACRYPT 2015, Part I. LNCS, vol. 9452, pp. 605–629. Springer, Heidelberg (2015). https://doi.org/10.1007/978-3-662-48797-6_25

15. González, A., Ráfols, C.: New techniques for non-interactive shuffle and range arguments. In: Manulis, M., Sadeghi, A.-R., Schneider, S. (eds.) ACNS 2016. LNCS, vol. 9696, pp. 427–444. Springer, Cham (2016). https://doi.org/10.1007/978-3-319-39555-5_23

16. Groth, J.: Short pairing-based non-interactive zero-knowledge arguments. In: Abe, M. (ed.) ASIACRYPT 2010. LNCS, vol. 6477, pp. 321–340. Springer, Heidelberg (2010). https://doi.org/10.1007/978-3-642-17373-8_19

17. Groth, J.: On the size of pairing-based non-interactive arguments. In: Fischlin, M.,
    Coron, J.-S. (eds.) EUROCRYPT 2016, Part II. LNCS, vol. 9666, pp. 305–326.
    Springer, Heidelberg (2016). https://doi.org/10.1007/978-3-662-49896-5_11
18. Groth, J., Lu, S.: A non-interactive shuffle with pairing based verifiability. In:
    Kurosawa, K. (ed.) ASIACRYPT 2007. LNCS, vol. 4833, pp. 51–67. Springer,
    Heidelberg (2007). https://doi.org/10.1007/978-3-540-76900-2_4
19. Groth, J., Ostrovsky, R., Sahai, A.: New techniques for noninteractive zero-
    knowledge. J. ACM **59**(3), 11 (2012)
20. Groth, J., Sahai, A.: Efficient non-interactive proof systems for bilinear groups.
    In: Smart, N. (ed.) EUROCRYPT 2008. LNCS, vol. 4965, pp. 415–432. Springer,
    Heidelberg (2008). https://doi.org/10.1007/978-3-540-78967-3_24
21. Groth, J., Sahai, A.: Efficient noninteractive proof systems for bilinear groups.
    SIAM J. Comput. **41**(5), 1193–1232 (2012)
22. Jutla, C.S., Roy, A.: Shorter quasi-adaptive NIZK proofs for linear subspaces. In:
    Sako, K., Sarkar, P. (eds.) ASIACRYPT 2013, Part I. LNCS, vol. 8269, pp. 1–20.
    Springer, Heidelberg (2013). https://doi.org/10.1007/978-3-642-42033-7_1
23. Jutla, C.S., Roy, A.: Switching lemma for bilinear tests and constant-size NIZK
    proofs for linear subspaces. In: Garay, J.A., Gennaro, R. (eds.) CRYPTO 2014,
    Part II. LNCS, vol. 8617, pp. 295–312. Springer, Heidelberg (2014). https://doi.
    org/10.1007/978-3-662-44381-1_17
24. Kiltz, E., Wee, H.: Quasi-adaptive NIZK for linear subspaces revisited. In: Oswald,
    E., Fischlin, M. (eds.) EUROCRYPT 2015, Part II. LNCS, vol. 9057, pp. 101–128.
    Springer, Heidelberg (2015). https://doi.org/10.1007/978-3-662-46803-6_4
25. Libert, B., Peters, T., Joye, M., Yung, M.: Non-malleability from malleability:
    simulation-sound quasi-adaptive NIZK proofs and CCA2-secure encryption from
    homomorphic signatures. In: Nguyen, P.Q., Oswald, E. (eds.) EUROCRYPT 2014.
    LNCS, vol. 8441, pp. 514–532. Springer, Heidelberg (2014). https://doi.org/10.
    1007/978-3-642-55220-5_29
26. Lipmaa, H.: Progression-free sets and sublinear pairing-based non-interactive zero-
    knowledge arguments. In: Cramer, R. (ed.) TCC 2012. LNCS, vol. 7194, pp. 169–
    189. Springer, Heidelberg (2012). https://doi.org/10.1007/978-3-642-28914-9_10
27. Lipmaa, H.: Succinct non-interactive zero knowledge arguments from span pro-
    grams and linear error-correcting codes. In: Sako, K., Sarkar, P. (eds.) ASI-
    ACRYPT 2013, Part I. LNCS, vol. 8269, pp. 41–60. Springer, Heidelberg (2013).
    https://doi.org/10.1007/978-3-642-42033-7_3
28. Morillo, P., Ràfols, C., Villar, J.L.: The kernel matrix Diffie-Hellman assumption.
    In: Cheon, J.H., Takagi, T. (eds.) ASIACRYPT 2016, Part I. LNCS, vol. 10031, pp.
    729–758. Springer, Heidelberg (2016). https://doi.org/10.1007/978-3-662-53887-
    6_27
29. Naor, M.: On cryptographic assumptions and challenges (invited talk). In: Boneh,
    D. (ed.) CRYPTO 2003. LNCS, vol. 2729, pp. 96–109. Springer, Heidelberg (2003).
    https://doi.org/10.1007/978-3-540-45146-4_6
30. Ràfols, C.: Stretching Groth-Sahai: NIZK proofs of partial satisfiability. In: Dodis,
    Y., Nielsen, J.B. (eds.) TCC 2015, Part II. LNCS, vol. 9015, pp. 247–276. Springer,
    Heidelberg (2015). https://doi.org/10.1007/978-3-662-46497-7_10
31. Rial, A., Kohlweiss, M., Preneel, B.: Universally composable adaptive priced obliv-
    ious transfer. In: Shacham, H., Waters, B. (eds.) Pairing 2009. LNCS, vol. 5671, pp.
    231–247. Springer, Heidelberg (2009). https://doi.org/10.1007/978-3-642-03298-
    1_15

Short Discrete Log Proofs for FHE and Ring-LWE Ciphertexts

Rafael del Pino[1]([✉]), Vadim Lyubashevsky[2], and Gregor Seiler[2,3]

[1] ENS Paris, Paris, France
Rafael.Del.Pino@ens.fr
[2] IBM Research – Zurich, Zurich, Switzerland
[3] ETH Zurich, Zurich, Switzerland

Abstract. In applications of fully-homomorphic encryption (FHE) that involve computation on encryptions produced by several users, it is important that each user proves that her input is indeed well-formed. This may simply mean that the inputs are valid FHE ciphertexts or, more generally, that the plaintexts m additionally satisfy $f(m) = 1$ for some public function f. The most efficient FHE schemes are based on the hardness of the Ring-LWE problem and so a natural solution would be to use lattice-based zero-knowledge proofs for proving properties about the ciphertext. Such methods, however, require larger-than-necessary parameters and result in rather long proofs, especially when proving general relationships.

In this paper, we show that one can get much shorter proofs (roughly 1.25 KB) by first creating a Pedersen commitment from the vector corresponding to the randomness and plaintext of the FHE ciphertext. To prove validity of the ciphertext, one can then prove that this commitment is indeed to the message and randomness and these values are in the correct range. Our protocol utilizes a connection between polynomial operations in the lattice scheme and inner product proofs for Pedersen commitments of Bünz et al. (S&P 2018). Furthermore, our proof of equality between the ciphertext and the commitment is very amenable to amortization – proving the equivalence of k ciphertext/commitment pairs only requires an additive factor of $O(\log k)$ extra space than for one such proof. For proving additional properties of the plaintext(s), one can then directly use the logarithmic-space proofs of Bootle et al. (Eurocrypt 2016) and Bünz et al. (IEEE S&P 2018) for proving arbitrary relations of discrete log commitment.

Our technique is not restricted to FHE ciphertexts and can be applied to proving many other relations that arise in lattice-based cryptography. For example, we can create very efficient verifiable encryption/decryption schemes with short proofs in which confidentiality is based on the hardness of Ring-LWE while the soundness is based on the discrete logarithm problem. While such proofs are not fully post-quantum, they are adequate in scenarios where secrecy needs to be future-proofed, but one only needs to be convinced of the validity of the proof in the pre-quantum era.

R. del Pino—Work done while at IBM Research – Zurich, Switzerland.

D. Lin and K. Sako (Eds.): PKC 2019, LNCS 11442, pp. 344–373, 2019.
https://doi.org/10.1007/978-3-030-17253-4_12

We furthermore show that our zero-knowledge protocol can be easily modified to have the property that breaking soundness implies solving discrete log in a short amount of time. Since building quantum computers capable of solving discrete logarithm in seconds requires overcoming many more fundamental challenges, such proofs may even remain valid in the post-quantum era.

1   Introduction

Fully-homomorphic encryption (FHE) allows for evaluations of arbitrary functions over encrypted data. The traditional application of this primitive is outsourcing – a user encrypts his data and sends it to a server who performs the (intensive) computation and returns back the encrypted result. In this scenario, the user is the only one affected by the outcome of the computation, and so it is not necessary for him to prove that his ciphertexts he submitted to the server are properly formed.

There are other applications of FHE, however, that involve computations on ciphertexts submitted by several users [LTV12, MW16, PS16]. For example, multi-key FHE allows the server to compute over ciphertexts encrypted under different keys and produce a result that can then be jointly decrypted by the participating parties. One can also use FHE in a "distributed ledger" (e.g. [ABB+18]) setting where users can submit ciphertexts encrypted under some particular public key and a computation can be performed by anyone on behalf of the holder of the secret key to produce an encrypted output. This is useful in scenarios where certain entities (the holder of the secret key in our example) wish to perform only a limited amount of computation.

For the above scenarios where more than one user is involved, it is important that each party provides a zero-knowledge proof that his input is a valid FHE ciphertext – otherwise the final output may, unknowingly to anyone else, be constructed from invalid data. It may furthermore be necessary to prove that the encrypted message satisfies certain additional properties dictated by the protocol. For encryptions based on the discrete logarithm problem, such proofs can be very efficiently constructed for certain relations using techniques in [CS03] and for general circuits using the more recent *logarithmic space* proofs for discrete logarithms [BCC+16, BBB+17]. FHE schemes, on the other hand, are constructed from LWE (or LWE-like) encryption schemes (e.g. [BGV12]), which unfortunately do not enjoy such practical proofs. For example, the most efficient verifiable encryption scheme for Ring-LWE [LN17] ciphertexts only handles linear relations $\mathbf{B}\vec{m} = \vec{t}$ and gives proofs of knowledge of an $\vec{m}'$ satisfying $\mathbf{B}\vec{m}' = c \cdot \vec{t}$, where c is some polynomial with small coefficients. This is satisfactory in some scenarios (see [LN17] for examples), but is not general enough for many other applications. Obtaining proofs without the polynomial c even for simple relations would make the proof sizes on the order of megabytes (cf. [LLNW18]).

In this work, we take a different approach for creating such proofs. An FHE (or more generally, a Ring-LWE) ciphertext can be written as

$$\mathbf{A}\vec{\mathbf{s}} = \vec{\mathbf{t}} \tag{1}$$

where $\mathbf{A}$ is the public key, $\vec{\mathbf{t}}$ is the ciphertext, and $\vec{\mathbf{s}}$ consists of the randomness and the message. All operations are performed over some polynomial ring $\mathcal{R}_q = \mathbb{Z}_q[X]/(\mathbf{f})$ for some integer q and a monic, irreducible polynomial $\mathbf{f} \in \mathbb{Z}[X]$ of degree d.

The main result of the current work is an efficient protocol for proving knowledge of $\vec{\mathbf{s}}$ with small coefficients in the above equation. Our strategy is to first create a joint Pedersen commitment $t = \mathrm{Com}(\vec{\mathbf{s}})$ to all the coefficients in $\vec{\mathbf{s}}$, and prove in zero-knowledge that these coefficients, when interpreted as a polynomial vector $\vec{\mathbf{s}}$, satisfy (1). At the same time, the proof will also show that the coefficients of $\vec{\mathbf{s}}$ are in the required range for valid Ring-LWE ciphertexts. Moreover, if we have many Ring-LWE ciphertexts $\vec{\mathbf{t}}_1, \ldots, \vec{\mathbf{t}}_k$, then the size of our proof is only approximately an *additive factor* of $O(\log k)$ larger than the proof for one equation in (1).

Once we have a Pedersen commitment of the coefficients of $\vec{\mathbf{s}}$, we can additionally use the aforementioned very efficient zero-knowledge proofs for discrete logarithm commitments [BCC+16, BBB+17] to prove arbitrary properties of the plain-text contained in $\vec{\mathbf{s}}$. This gives us a verifiable encryption scheme (and also a verifiable decryption scheme) for Ring-LWE ciphertexts (see Sect. 1.5). As an example of the proof size, a proof of ciphertext validity of a Ring-LWE encryption scheme in (9) requires only 1.25 KB.

1.1   Post-quantum Security

One of the side advantages of FHE based on Ring-LWE is that the encryption scheme remains secure against quantum attacks (assuming that the Ring-LWE problem is post-quantum secure). Since Pedersen commitments are statistically-hiding and all the proofs are statistical zero-knowledge, the secrecy of the ciphertext and the Pedersen commitment is still based on just Ring-LWE. The soundness of the proofs, however, is based on the hardness of the discrete log problem and is therefore not post-quantum.

Having the soundness of the proof not be post-quantum is still, for many scenarios, acceptable even if we do foresee quantum computers appearing in the future. For example, all proofs created until quantum computers capable of breaking discrete log actually appear would still be valid. Furthermore, the protocol can be easily altered to force the prover to create his Pedersen commitment and the zero-knowledge proof with "fresh" randomly-chosen generators and complete his proof in a specified amount of time.[1] Breaking the soundness

---

[1] If the proof is to be made non-interactive, the randomness for creating the generators could come from some public randomness beacons (e.g. the NIST randomness beacon).

of this proof system would thus require solving the discrete log problem using a quantum computer within a prescribed (e.g. several seconds) time interval.

While building a quantum computer capable of breaking cryptographic problems presents a very substantial scientific and engineering challenge, building one that is capable of solving such problems in *seconds* is a potentially significantly harder problem. For a 2048-bit number, under some reasonable assumptions on the error rate and the speed of each gate computation on a superconducting platform, this would take around 27 h and a billion physical qubits [FMMC12]. A trapped-ion based computer with very low error rate would need 110 days to perform the same operation [LWF+17]. One can sometimes decrease the running time by utilizing more qubits, but there are several other roadblocks that would keep the computation time from decreasing beyond certain barriers (c.f. [Gid18] for a discussion). While it is too early to guess when (or if) it will be possible to run Shor's algorithm in under a minute, it certainly appears to be a problem that will require overcoming many more fundamental challenges even after a "basic" fault-tolerant universal quantum computer is built.

1.2 Other Applications

Our general result gives a way to prove knowledge that the secret $\vec{s}$ in the linear equation (1) is the same as in the commitment $\mathrm{Com}(\vec{s})$, where $\mathrm{Com}(\cdot)$ is a Pedersen commitment to the individual coefficients of $\vec{s}$. Because (1) is quite generic, it can be used to represent many relations throughout lattice cryptography. For example, ciphertexts, commitments, public keys in encryption/signature schemes, etc. are all of this form. One can therefore apply our protocol as a first step in a larger protocol that needs to prove something about the secret $\vec{s}$. For example, verifiable encryption and decryption schemes (where the prover or decryptor needs to prove that the plaintext m satisfies $f(m) = 1$ for some public function f) has many applications (c.f. [CS03]) and such schemes that retain the post-quantum secrecy of the ciphertext can thus be built using our techniques. We sketch the construction in Sect. 1.5 and note that proving validity of FHE ciphertexts is just a special case of verifiable encryption.

1.3 Previous Related Work

A connection between Ring-LWE and discrete log commitments has been previously explored by Benhamouda et al. [BCK+14]. The construction in the current paper is completely different and enjoys significant advantages (both theoretical and practical) over the aforementioned prior work. Firstly, the modulus q in (1) has to be the same as the group size underlying the discrete log commitment for the proof in [BCK+14] – and taking $q \approx 2^{256}$ would require making the Ring-LWE/FHE scheme significantly less efficient than it needs to be (typical sizes of q are $\approx 2^{30}$). Secondly, the protocol in [BCK+14] requires a separate Pedersen commitment for every coefficient of $\vec{s}$ rather than one commitment for all the coefficients of $\vec{s}$. Thirdly, the proof is a Σ-protocol with soundness error $1/d$ (where n is the degree of $\mathbf{f}$) and so needs to be repeated around a dozen times. While [BCK+14] did not provide concrete parameters, we would estimate that our proofs would be shorter by 2–3 orders of magnitude. And additionally, our current proof can be amortized for proving k equations as in (1) while only incurring an $O(\log k)$ additive overhead.

Our work can also be seen as complementary to that of Fiore, Gennaro, and Pastro [FGP14] where they give a succinct proof that the evaluation in the FHE scheme was performed correctly for certain types of functions.

1.4   High Level Overview of the Protocol

Our general proof is for k copies of (1) – in other words a proof of a matrix $\mathbf{S} \in \mathcal{R}_q^{m \times k}$ with bounded coefficients such that

$$\mathbf{AS} = \mathbf{T} \bmod (\mathbf{f}, q). \tag{2}$$

We will explicitly write out which modular reductions occur as it will change throughout the protocol.

In this overview, we will sketch the proof of a simpler version of (2), which is just a Ring-LWE/Ring-SIS equation

$$\sum_{i=1}^{m} \mathbf{a}_i \mathbf{s}_i = \mathbf{t} \bmod (\mathbf{f}, q) \tag{3}$$

where $\mathbf{a}_i, \mathbf{t}, \mathbf{s}_i \in \mathcal{R}_q$ and the coefficients of $\mathbf{s}_i$ have absolute value less than B. Afterwards, we will explain how this can be extended to the full proof of (2). Let G be a group of size $p \leq 2^{256}$ in which the discrete problem is hard.

The prover first rewrites (3) so that it is entirely over the ring $\mathbb{Z}[X]$ – i.e. there are no reductions modulo q and $\mathbf{f}$:

$$\sum_{i=1}^{m} \mathbf{a}_i \mathbf{s}_i = \mathbf{t} - \mathbf{r}_1 \cdot q - \mathbf{r}_2 \cdot \mathbf{f}. \tag{4}$$

The polynomials $\mathbf{r}_1$ and $\mathbf{r}_2$ are not unique, but we would like them to simultaneously have small coefficients and be of small degree. We show that $\mathbf{r}_1$ can be of degree $2(d-1)$ and have coefficients of absolute value at most $\frac{d}{2}(Bm + \|\mathbf{f}\|_\infty)$, while $\mathbf{r}_2$ can have degree $d-2$ with coefficients having absolute value at most $\frac{1}{2}(q-1)$.

The prover creates a Pedersen commitment $t = \text{Com}(\mathbf{s}_1, \dots, \mathbf{s}_m, \mathbf{r}_1, \mathbf{r}_2) \in G$ where each integer coefficient of $\mathbf{s}_i$ and $\mathbf{r}_i$ is in the exponent of a different generator g_j.[2] The prover sends t to the verifier.

---

[2] If we would like to achieve post-quantum security based on the assumption that discrete log cannot be solved in a prescribed amount of time, then the g_i should not be known to the prover before the start of the proof. This can be arranged by either having the verifier sending them (or more precisely, send a short seed that expands into the prescribed number of generators) at the start of the protocol or using a randomness beacon in non-interactive proofs.

The verifier chooses a random challenge element $\alpha \in \mathbb{Z}_p$ and sends it to the prover. The prover now needs to give several proofs. In the real protocol, all these will be combined into one proof, but for ease of exposition, we will explain them separately here. The first proof is a range proof $\pi_{s,r}$ from [BBB+17] showing that all the committed values in t are in the correct ranges. The second proof is a proof that (4) evaluated at α holds true over the field $\mathbb{Z}_p$. By the Schwartz-Zippel lemma, this implies that with probability $> 1 - 2d/|G|$, this equation also holds true over the polynomial ring $\mathbb{Z}_p[X]$. Since we have already proven that the coefficients of s_i and r_i are relatively small and we assumed that q is also small (compared to p), we know that if (4) holds true in $\mathbb{Z}_p[X]$, then it also holds over $\mathbb{Z}[X]$ because no reduction modulo p takes place. This will complete the proof. We now just have to prove that (4) evaluated at α holds true mod p.

Define the matrices

$$U = \begin{bmatrix} \mathbf{a}_1(\alpha) \cdots \mathbf{a}_m(\alpha) \ q \ \mathbf{f}(\alpha) \end{bmatrix} \bmod p, \ S = \begin{bmatrix} - \ \mathbf{s}_1 \ - \\ \cdots \\ - \ \mathbf{s}_m \ - \\ - \ \mathbf{r}_1 \ - \\ - \ \mathbf{r}_2 \ - \end{bmatrix}, V = \begin{bmatrix} 1 \\ \alpha \\ \cdots \\ \alpha^{d-1} \end{bmatrix} \bmod p,$$

(5)

where the rows of S consist of the integer coefficients of $\mathbf{s}_i$ and $\mathbf{r}_i$ with the constant coefficient being in the leftmost column row and the coefficients of X^{d-1} being in the rightmost (e.g. if $\mathbf{s}_i = \sum_{j=0}^{d-1} \sigma_j X^j$, then the ith row of S is $[\sigma_0 \ \sigma_1 \cdots \sigma_{d-1}]$. With this notation, observe that the matrix product

$$SV = \begin{bmatrix} \mathbf{s}_1(\alpha) \cdots \mathbf{s}_m(\alpha) \ \mathbf{r}_1(\alpha) \ \mathbf{r}_2(\alpha) \end{bmatrix}^T \bmod p,$$

and so

$$USV = \sum_{i=1}^m \mathbf{a}_i(\alpha)\mathbf{s}_i(\alpha) + \mathbf{r}_1(\alpha)q + \mathbf{r}_2(\alpha)\mathbf{f}(\alpha) \bmod p.$$

Thus if we prove that

$$USV = \mathbf{t}(\alpha) \bmod p, \tag{6}$$

then we will end up proving that (4) evaluated at α is true modulo p. Since U, V and $\mathbf{t}(\alpha)$ are public and we have a commitment to the coefficients of S, we can apply an extension of the inner-products proofs from [BCC+16, BBB+17] to prove our linear relation.[3] To complete the protocol, the prover simply sends $\pi, \pi_{s,r}$ to the verifier and he accepts if all the proofs are correct.

---

[3] The "inner-product" proofs in [BCC+16, BBB+17] show that the vectors committed to in a Pedersen commitment satisfy a linear relation. This can also be extended to matrices.

Combining the Two Proofs. In the real protocol which we describe in Sect. 5, we combine the two proofs $\pi_{s,r}$ and π into one. The reason is that the range proof $\pi_{s,r}$ in [BBB+17] works by writing each coefficient in binary, storing a matrix of these coefficients, and then giving a proof that each coefficient of the decomposition is 0 or 1 (the number of these coefficients then implies the range). Due to the fact that the ranges of the $\mathbf{s}_i$ and $\mathbf{r}_i$ are different, storing these in the same matrix would require us to increase the size of the matrix to accommodate the largest coefficients, which would be wasteful. Thus instead of proving the matrix equation (6), we write these out as a series of appropriate equations (each of varying lengths) where the coefficients of S are in binary and prove those instead. This allows us to do a range proof and the proof of (6) in one step.

We provide explicit details of the above algorithm in Sect. 5. We additionally obtain a tighter security proof of the inner-product proof of [BCC+16, BBB+17] by using a different extraction strategy, described in Sect. 3. In addition, our zero-knowledge range proof is somewhat simpler than the one in [BBB+17] because our range proof is constructed on top of a zero-knowledge inner product proof instead of the original Bulletproof inner product proof which is not zero-knowledge. This allows for not blinding the vectors in the range proof simplifying extraction and saving two rounds of the protocol. The additional complexity in the inner product proof is basically just a Schnorr proof (see Sect. 4). These small improvements may be of independent interest.

Some Observations About the Proof Strategy. The reason that we converted (3) into (4) and then used the Schwartz-Zippel lemma for proving (4) is for reducing the *time* complexity of the proof. An alternate, simpler, procedure for proving (3) would have been the following: first write (3) as

$$\sum_{i=1}^{m} \mathbf{a}_i \mathbf{s}_i = \mathbf{t} + \mathbf{r}_1 q \bmod \mathbf{f}, \tag{7}$$

and create the commitments t_s and t_{r_1} as before. Now, observe that polynomial multiplication $\mathbf{a}_i \mathbf{s}_i$ can be written as a matrix/vector product $\mathbf{As}$, where column j (labeled from 0 to $d-1$) of $\mathbf{A}$ consists of the coefficients of the $d-1$ degree polynomial $\mathbf{a}_i X^j \bmod \mathbf{f}$ and $\mathbf{s}$ is a vector of coefficients of $\mathbf{s}_i$. Thus $\sum_{i=1}^{m} \mathbf{a}_i \mathbf{s}_i$ can be written as a matrix/vector product itself. Then one could directly apply the modified inner-product proof to prove (7) modulo p, which would again imply that this equation holds true over $\mathbb{Z}$ (since the coefficients are all much smaller than p), and so this implies (3).

The main problem with the above approach is that the matrices $\mathbf{A}$ are $d \times d$ matrices, and so the proof of matrix/vector product would require $O(d^2)$ exponentiations (or multiplications in elliptic curve groups) in G. For typical values of $d > 1000$, this operation is quite expensive and could take several minutes even on a reasonably powerful machine. Our proof, on the other hand, takes advantage of the fact that the operations can be interpreted over the ring $\mathbb{Z}_p[X]$ for a very large p and one can then prove polynomial equality via the Schwartz-Zippel lemma. Since polynomial evaluation is an inner-product of d-dimensional vectors, constructing a matrix product proof only requires $O(d)$ exponentiations per evaluation. Note that this is also the reason that our proofs would be much less computationally efficient for proving relations over $\mathbb{Z}$ (i.e. LWE/SIS relations).

Another issue to draw attention to is that the polynomial equations we want to prove are modulo q, whereas the proofs are done modulo a larger p. As mentioned before, the reason for this is that in typical cryptographic applications of the Ring-LWE/Ring-SIS problems (such as FHE), the modulus q is not very large (smaller than 2^{40}). On the other hand, the discrete log commitments must be performed over a much larger-size group. If, however, an application called for the modulus q to be a large prime, then our proof could use $q = p$, and we would never need to switch to working over $\mathbb{Z}[X]$ – we could always work over $\mathbb{Z}_q[X]$ and have no need for the polynomial $\mathbf{r}_1$.

Simultaneously Proving k Polynomial Equations. The proof for proving knowledge of $\mathbf{S}$ satisfying (2) is a straightforward extension of the above-described algorithm with the strategy for the proof being the same. First, we will prove that in the analogue of (4),

$$\mathbf{AS} = \mathbf{T} - q\mathbf{R}_1 - \mathbf{f}\mathbf{R}_2, \tag{8}$$

all the coefficients of $\mathbf{S}, \mathbf{R}_1, \mathbf{R}_2$ are small and then prove that the above equation holds, with high probability, over the ring $\mathbb{Z}_p[X]$ for a very large p. This will imply that (8) also holds over $\mathbb{Z}[X]$, and thus (2) is true. We now describe the protocol in slightly more detail.

The first step of the protocol remains virtually identical with the prover committing to $\mathbf{S}$ and $\mathbf{R}_1, \mathbf{R}_2$. After receiving the challenge α, the prover again wishes to show that the coefficients of $\mathbf{S}, \mathbf{R}_1, \mathbf{R}_2$ are in the appropriate ranges and prove the equality of (8) where each polynomial is evaluated at α.

If we define $I_n \in \mathbb{Z}^{n \times n}$ to be the identity matrix, then one can rewrite what we would like to prove as

$$\begin{bmatrix} \mathbf{A}(\alpha) & qI_n & \mathbf{f}(\alpha)I_n \end{bmatrix} \cdot \begin{bmatrix} \mathbf{S}(\alpha) \\ \mathbf{R}_1(\alpha) \\ \mathbf{R}_2(\alpha) \end{bmatrix} = \mathbf{T}(\alpha) \bmod p.$$

If, for a polynomial $m \times k$ matrix $\mathbf{S}$, we create the $m \times (kd)$ integer matrix $\vec{S}$ by writing each polynomial in $\mathbf{S}$ as a row consisting of its d coefficients (the way that $\mathbf{s}_i$ were expanded in the matrix S in (5)), then we can rewrite the above equation as

$$\begin{bmatrix} \mathbf{A}(\alpha) & qI_n & \mathbf{f}(\alpha)I_n \end{bmatrix} \cdot \begin{bmatrix} \vec{S} \\ \vec{R}_1 \\ \vec{R}_2 \end{bmatrix} \cdot \left(I_k \otimes \begin{bmatrix} 1 \\ \alpha \\ \cdots \\ \alpha^{d-1} \end{bmatrix} \right) = \mathbf{T}(\alpha) \bmod p.$$

Since all the matrices in the above equation except $\begin{bmatrix} \vec{S} \\ \vec{R}_1 \\ \vec{R}_2 \end{bmatrix}$ are public, we can

again apply the modified inner-product proof from [BCC+16,BBB+17] to prove the equality modulo p. And again, as before, our real protocol would combine the range proof and modified inner-product proof into one proof.

1.5 Application to Verifiable Encryption and Decryption for Ring-LWE Ciphertexts

Notice that the first step of our proof involved creating a Pedersen commitment t to the coefficients of $\mathbf{S}$. The rest of the proof then went on to show that the commitment is really to an $\mathbf{S}$ satisfying (2). Since at the end of the protocol, we end up with a Pedersen commitment to $\mathbf{S}$, we can use another SNARK (e.g. one from [BBB+17]) that proves arbitrary relations of its committed values. Thus just proving knowledge of $\mathbf{S}$ naturally gives rise to verifiable encryption and decryption schemes for Ring-LWE encryption, as we sketch below.

In a verifiable encryption scheme, the encryptor produces an encryption of a message m and a ZKPoK that the ciphertext is a valid encryption to m and that $f(m) = 1$ for a public function f. Consider the following "usual" encryption scheme based on Ring-LWE [LPR13]:

The secret key are polynomials $\mathbf{s}, \mathbf{e}$ with small, bounded coefficients and the public key consists of a random polynomial $\mathbf{a} \in \mathcal{R}_q$ and $\mathbf{t} = \mathbf{as} + \mathbf{e} \in \mathcal{R}_q$.

The encryption of a message $\mathbf{m} \in \mathcal{R}_q$, where all coefficients of $\mathbf{m}$ are in the range $[0, p)$, is created as in the below equation, where $\mathbf{r}, \mathbf{e}_1, \mathbf{e}_2$ are polynomials with bounded coefficients.

$$\begin{bmatrix} p\mathbf{a} & p & 0 & 0 \\ p\mathbf{t} & 0 & p & 1 \end{bmatrix} \cdot \begin{bmatrix} \mathbf{r} \\ \mathbf{e}_1 \\ \mathbf{e}_2 \\ \mathbf{m} \end{bmatrix} = \begin{bmatrix} \mathbf{u} \\ \mathbf{v} \end{bmatrix} \tag{9}$$

For a verifiable encryption scheme, we can use our proof system with $\mathbf{A} \in \mathcal{R}_q^{2\times 4}$ and $\mathbf{S} \in \mathcal{R}_q^{4\times 1}$ to create a Pedersen commitment(s) to $\mathbf{S}$ and prove that all the coefficients of $\mathbf{r}, \mathbf{e}_i, \mathbf{m}$ lie within their prescribed bounds and that (9) is satisfied by the commitment(s) representing $\mathbf{S}$. The preceding proves knowledge of the plaintext $\mathbf{m}$ for the ciphertext $\begin{bmatrix} \mathbf{u} \\ \mathbf{v} \end{bmatrix}$.

To decrypt a ciphertext $\begin{bmatrix} \mathbf{u} \\ \mathbf{v} \end{bmatrix}$, the decryptor first computes

$$\mathbf{v} - \mathbf{us} = p(\mathbf{er} + \mathbf{e}_2 - \mathbf{se}_1) + \mathbf{m}. \tag{10}$$

Since all the coefficients of the above equation are small, no reduction modulo q takes place and this equation holds true over $\mathbb{Z}[X]$. Computing $\mathbf{v} - \mathbf{us} \bmod p$ therefore recovers $\mathbf{m}$.

To construct a verifiable decryption scheme, let $\mathbf{g} = \mathbf{er} + \mathbf{e}_2 - \mathbf{se}_1$ from the above equation. Let β be a bound on $\mathbf{g}$ such that no reduction modulo q takes place in (10) and so decryption still works (i.e. β should be less than approximately q/p). Then the decryptor should be able to prove knowledge of $\mathbf{s}, \mathbf{e}, \mathbf{g}, \mathbf{m}$ in the following equation with coefficients of $\mathbf{s}, \mathbf{e}$ having the appropriate bounds and $\mathbf{m}$ having all coefficients in $[0, p)$.

$$\begin{bmatrix} \mathbf{a}\ 1\ 0\ 0 \\ \mathbf{u}\ 0\ p\ 1 \end{bmatrix} \cdot \begin{bmatrix} \mathbf{s} \\ \mathbf{e} \\ \mathbf{g} \\ \mathbf{m} \end{bmatrix} = \begin{bmatrix} \mathbf{t} \\ \mathbf{v} \end{bmatrix}. \tag{11}$$

Proving the above shows that $\mathbf{m}$ is a valid decryption. To show that there is only one possible decryption (i.e. only one possible solution to the above equation), suppose there exist two solutions:

$$\begin{bmatrix} \mathbf{a}\ 1\ 0\ 0 \\ \mathbf{u}\ 0\ p\ 1 \end{bmatrix} \cdot \begin{bmatrix} \mathbf{s} \\ \mathbf{e} \\ \mathbf{g} \\ \mathbf{m} \end{bmatrix} = \begin{bmatrix} \mathbf{t} \\ \mathbf{v} \end{bmatrix} \text{ and } \begin{bmatrix} \mathbf{a}\ 1\ 0\ 0 \\ \mathbf{u}\ 0\ p\ 1 \end{bmatrix} \cdot \begin{bmatrix} \mathbf{s}' \\ \mathbf{e}' \\ \mathbf{g}' \\ \mathbf{m}' \end{bmatrix} = \begin{bmatrix} \mathbf{t} \\ \mathbf{v} \end{bmatrix}. \tag{12}$$

If $\mathbf{s} \neq \mathbf{s}'$, then the first row of (12) implies a non-zero solution to

$$\mathbf{a}(\mathbf{s} - \mathbf{s}') + (\mathbf{e} - \mathbf{e}') = 0.$$

Writing $\mathbf{a}$ as above can either be shown to be impossible either via an information-theoretic argument or via the computational assumption that the Ring-SIS problem [PR06,LM06] is hard.[4]

If $\mathbf{s} = \mathbf{s}'$, then the second row of (12) implies that $p(\mathbf{g} - \mathbf{g}') + (\mathbf{m} - \mathbf{m}') = \mathbf{0}$. Since the coefficients are small enough that no reduction modulo q takes place, the preceding implies that $\mathbf{m} - \mathbf{m}'$ is a multiple of p, which implies that $\mathbf{m} = \mathbf{m}'$ (since the coefficients of $\mathbf{m} - \mathbf{m}'$ are in the range $(-p, p)$.)

1.6 Open Problems

We have shown how linear relations over polynomial rings can have very compact proofs by converting the problem into a form that is compatible with the compact SNARKs in [BCC+16,BBB+17]. While the proofs are small, creating such proofs may require on the order of hundreds of thousands of exponentiations. It would therefore be interesting to see whether one can transform the problem into a form compatible with SNARKS that are less compact but may require fewer operations, such as for example those in [WTS+18]. Since the latter proofs are particularly tailored to parallelizable functions, they may also result in rather efficient proofs for LWE/SIS ciphertexts, and not require one to work over polynomial rings. We leave this direction as an open problem.

---

[4] In general, the polynomial $\mathbf{a}$ is created as $H(seed)$, where H is a cryptographic hash function and the seed is public. It is therefore a valid assumption that $\mathbf{a}$ is random in $\mathcal{R}_q$.

2 Notation

We use bold letters $\mathbf{f}$ for polynomials, arrows for column vectors as in $\vec{v}$, and capital letters A for matrices. Vectors and matrices of polynomials are denoted by bold letters $\vec{\mathbf{v}}$ with arrows and bold capital letters $\mathbf{M}$, respectively. We write $\mathcal{R} = \mathbb{Z}[X]/(\mathbf{f})$ for the ring of integer polynomials modulo a monic irreducible polynomial $\mathbf{f} \in \mathbb{Z}[X]$, $\mathcal{R}_q$ for the quotient ring $\mathcal{R}/q\mathcal{R}$ for some prime q and similarly $\mathbb{Z}_p$ for $\mathbb{Z}/p\mathbb{Z}$.

Let $\vec{v}_1 \in \mathbb{Z}_p^n$ and $\vec{v}_2 \in \mathbb{Z}_p^n$ be two vectors over $\mathbb{Z}_p$. Then we write $\langle \vec{v}_1, \vec{v}_2 \rangle \in \mathbb{Z}_p$, $\vec{v}_1 \circ \vec{v}_2 \in \mathbb{Z}_p^n$ and $\vec{v}_1 \otimes \vec{v}_2 \in \mathbb{Z}_p^{n^2}$ for their inner product, componentwise product and tensor product, respectively.

Norms. The absolute value $|a|$ of an element $a \in \mathbb{Z}_q$ is defined to be the absolute value of the centralized representative in $\{-(q-1)/2, \ldots, (q-1)/2\}$. The infinity norm $\|\mathbf{s}\|_\infty$ of a polynomial $\mathbf{s} \in \mathcal{R}_q$ is the maximum absolute value of all of its coefficients. Likewise, the infinity norm $\|\vec{\mathbf{s}}\|_\infty$ of a vector of polynomials is the maximum over the infinity norms of its coefficient polynomials.

Multi Exponentiations. For a group G of order p, written multiplicatively, and vectors $\vec{g} = (g_1, \ldots, g_n)^T \in G^n$ and $\vec{a} = (a_1, \ldots, a_n)^T \in \mathbb{Z}_p^n$ we use the notation

$$\vec{g}^{\vec{a}} = g_1^{a_1} \ldots g_n^{a_n} \in G.$$

Throughout the paper the group G will be understood to be cyclic of prime order p with hard computational discrete-log problem. A Pedersen multi-commitment over generators $\vec{g} \in G^n, u \in G$ to a vector $\vec{v} \in \mathbb{Z}_p^n$ with randomness $\rho \xleftarrow{\$} \mathbb{Z}_p$ is given by the multi-exponentiation $t = \vec{g}^{\vec{v}} u^\rho$. This is clearly perfectly hiding and computationally binding under the assumption that it is hard to compute a non-trivial discrete-log relation between the generators $\vec{g}, u$. The latter problem is easily seen to be equivalent to the discrete-log problem.

Serializing Matrices to Vectors. We will need to serialize matrices $A \in \mathbb{Z}_p^{n \times m}$ to vectors. For this reason we define functions

$$\text{Serialize} \colon \mathbb{Z}_p^{n \times m} \to \mathbb{Z}_p^{nm}, \ A \mapsto \vec{a}$$

where $\vec{a}$ contains the coefficients of A in row major order. So if $A = (a_{ij})$, $0 \leq i \leq n-1, 0 \leq j \leq m-1$, then $\vec{a} = (a_i)$ with $a_{mi+j} = a_{ij}$. In many programming languages, most notably C, this is how matrices are stored in memory so that Serialize is a non-operation in these languages. We extend Serialize to polynomial matrices over $\mathbb{Z}[X]$ by first expanding each polynomial to its row coefficient vector and then proceeding as before.

Expanding Integers to Their Binary Representation. We will also need to map integers to their binary representation, including negative integers. For this we define the function

$$\text{Binary}_b \colon \{-2^{b-1}, \dots, 2^{b-1} - 1\} \to \{0, 1\}^b, \; z \mapsto \vec{z}$$

that maps a signed b-bit integer to its binary representation using two's complement. More precisely, $\vec{z} = (z_0, \dots, z_{b-1})^T$ is defined by

$$z = z_0 + z_1 2 + \dots + z_{b-2} 2^{b-2} - z_{b-1} 2^{b-1}.$$

Again this representation for signed integers is used by all modern CPU's and Binary is a non-operation. We extend Binary to vectors where Binary is applied to each coefficient individually.

3 Forking Lemma

For proving the security of proof systems based on the Bulletproof technique from [BBB+17] one needs a special forking lemma which shows that it is possible to obtain many accepting transcripts from a prover for challenges that are organized in a large tree. The forking lemma used in the Bulletproof paper goes back to [BCC+16, Lemma 1]. It is only stated in terms asymptotic in the security parameter. Moreover, the tree finding algorithm for computing the tree that is given and analyzed in the proof of the forking lemma does not try to avoid collisions between the challenges. But it is necessary that there are no collision so that the transcripts can be used for extraction. Therefore, in order to compute the success probability of the tree finding algorithm, the collision probability has to be taken into account in addition to the failure probability of the prover. For a 256 bit curve, the collision probability gets quite large for moderately sized trees and as a result of this the reasoning of the forking lemma only applies to provers whose failure probability $1 - \varepsilon$ is small. Concretely, to obtain a tree of accepting transcripts of height μ where every inner node has n children one needs $\varepsilon > n^\mu / 2^{85}$. For example in the case of the Bulletproof inner product proof, where $n = 4$ and $\mu = \log l$ with l the length of the vectors, $\varepsilon > l^2 / 2^{85}$ and the forking lemma only proves the inner product proof to be sound with soundness error 2^{-35} if $l = 2^{25}$, a length easily reached in our application. One would need to repeat the proof four times in order to get below 2^{-128}.

We give a different forking lemma with a different extraction algorithm together with a concrete analysis in this section. Our forking lemma achieves negligible soundness error. It is still non-tight though, which is unavoidable as one needs to obtain $n^\mu = l^{\log n}$ transcripts. We stress that we do not think that this non-tightness in the security proof allows for any actual attacks for 256 bit curves. Let us start by recalling the definition of a tree of accepting transcripts.

Definition 3.1. *Let $\mathcal{P}^*$ be a deterministic prover for a $(2\mu+1)$-move interactive proof protocol where the honest verifier $\mathcal{V}$ sends μ challenges in steps $2, 4, \ldots, 2\mu$. An $(n_1, \ldots, n_\mu)$-tree of accepting transcripts associated with $\mathcal{P}^*$ is a tree of height μ of the following form. Every node in level i, $0 \leq i \leq \mu - 1$, has precisely n_{i+1} children, all nodes except the root are labeled by a challenge and each leaf additionally contains the transcript obtained by interacting with $\mathcal{P}^*$ and sending the challenges in the path from the root to this leaf. Moreover, the challenges in all nodes with the same parent are distinct and $\mathcal{V}$ accepts all transcripts in the leaves.*

Lemma 3.2. *Let $\mathcal{P}^*$ be a deterministic prover for a $(2\mu + 1)$-move interactive proof protocol where the honest verifier $\mathcal{V}$ sends $\mu = \log(l)$ uniformly random challenges from a set $\mathcal{C}$ of size p in steps $2, 4, \ldots, 2\mu$. Then there exists an algorithm TREE-FINDER that, when given rewindable black-box access to $\mathcal{P}^*$, computes an $(n_1, \ldots, n_\mu)$-tree of accepting transcripts with probability at least $1/4$ in expected time at most*

$$O\left(\frac{l^{\log n + \log \alpha} \log l}{\varepsilon}\right) \quad (l \to \infty)$$

for every $\alpha > \left(\frac{1}{1-n/p}\right)^2$ and with $n = \max_{1 \leq i \leq \mu-1} n_i$ under the assumption that $\mathcal{P}^*$ convinces $\mathcal{V}$ with probability $\varepsilon \geq \frac{\alpha^\mu}{\alpha-1} \frac{n_\mu}{p} = \frac{l^{\log \alpha}}{\alpha-1} \frac{n_\mu}{p}$. Running $\mathcal{P}^*$ once is assumed to take unit time.

Proof. We construct TREE-FINDER = TREE-FINDER(1) as a recursive algorithm with TREE-FINDER(i), $i = 1, \ldots, \mu$, interacting with $\mathcal{P}^*$ from the $2i$-th move onward. A naive first approach would be as follows. For $i < \mu$, TREE-FINDER(i) would run $\mathcal{P}^*$ until and including move $2i + 1$ sending a uniformly random challenge $c_i \in \mathcal{C}$ in step $2i$. Then the algorithm would call TREE-FINDER($i + 1$). Afterwards it would rewind $\mathcal{P}^*$ back to just after step $2(i - 1) + 1$ and repeat the process for a total of n_i *different* challenges. So in the second iteration TREE-FINDER(i) would sample a uniform challenge from $\mathcal{C} \setminus \{c_i\}$. The tree-finding algorithm TREE-FINDER(μ) in the last level would send a last challenge c_μ and check whether the interaction with $\mathcal{P}^*$ led to a valid proof, i.e. $\mathcal{V}$ would accept the proof. Then it would repeat for as many last challenges c_μ as needed to get n_μ valid proofs for n_μ different c_μ. The problem with this approach is that in any level for many challenges c_i there might only be very few continuations $c_{i+1}, \ldots, c_\mu$ that lead to valid proofs (or none at all). Hence the tree-finding algorithm might run into dead ends where TREE-FINDER(μ) runs for a very long time or does not terminate at all.

For fixed challenges $c_1, \ldots, c_{i-1}$, let ε_i be the acceptance probability over all uniform continuations $c_i, \ldots, c_\mu$. In particular $\varepsilon_1 = \varepsilon$. Then for some c_i let $\varepsilon_{i+1} = \varepsilon_{i+1}(c_i)$ be the acceptance probability under the additional condition that the i-th challenge is c_i. Now from a standard heavy rows/averaging argument we know $\varepsilon_{i+1} \geq \varepsilon_i/\alpha$, $\alpha > 1$, for at least a fraction of $1 - 1/\alpha$ of the c_i. Therefore our solution to the problem is as follows. After choosing c_i, TREE-FINDER(i)

estimates ε_{i+1} by running $\mathcal{P}^*$ until the end for many continuations $c_{i+1}, \ldots, c_\mu$ and counting the number of valid proofs. Then the tree finding algorithm only continues with c_i if the acceptance probability does not decrease too much by fixing c_i. The complete algorithm is as follows where $1 < \lambda < \sqrt{\alpha}$ and T_i are specified later.

1: **function** TREE-FINDER(i)
2:      Initialize *tree* as a tree containing only an empty root
3:      $\mathcal{C}' = \emptyset$
4:      **while** $|\mathcal{C}'| < n_i$ **do**
5:          **if** $i = \mu$ **then**
6:              Run $\mathcal{P}^*$ until the end using a fresh challenge $c_\mu \xleftarrow{\$} \mathcal{C} \setminus \mathcal{C}'$ and let *tr* be the transcript of the full interactive proof
7:              **if** proof is valid **then**
8:                  Append new leaf (c_μ, tr) to the root of *tree*
9:                  $\mathcal{C}' = \mathcal{C}' \cup \{c_\mu\}$
10:             **end if**
11:         **else**
12:             **repeat**
13:                 Run $\mathcal{P}^*$ up to and including step $2i + 1$ using a fresh challenge $c_i \xleftarrow{\$} \mathcal{C} \setminus \mathcal{C}'$
14:                 $count = 0$
15:                 **for** $j = 1, \ldots, T_i$ **do**
16:                     Run $\mathcal{P}^*$ until the end with fresh challenges $c_{i+1}, \ldots, c_\mu \xleftarrow{\$} \mathcal{C}$
17:                     **if** proof is valid **then**
18:                         $count = count + 1$
19:                     **end if**
20:                     Rewind $\mathcal{P}^*$ back to just after step $2i + 1$
21:                 **end for**
22:                 **if** $count < \lambda T_i \frac{\varepsilon}{\alpha^i}$ **then**
23:                     Rewind $\mathcal{P}^*$ back to just after step $2(i - 1) + 1$
24:                 **end if**
25:             **until** $count >= \lambda T_i \frac{\varepsilon}{\alpha^i}$
26:             $tree' \leftarrow$ TREE-FINDER($i + 1$)
27:             Label root of $tree'$ by c_i and append $tree'$ to the root of *tree*
28:             $\mathcal{C}' = \mathcal{C}' \cup \{c_i\}$
29:         **end if**
30:     **end while**
31:     **return** *tree*
32: **end function**

We analyze the algorithm under the assumption $\varepsilon_i \geq \varepsilon/\alpha^{i-1}$. The challenge c_i is chosen and the acceptance probability $\varepsilon_{i+1} = \varepsilon_{i+1}(c_i)$ estimated during the loop in lines 12–25. We define the following probabilities in one iteration of the loop.

$$p_0 = \Pr\left[count < \lambda T_i \frac{\varepsilon}{\alpha^i}\right],$$

$$p_1 = \Pr\left[count \geq \lambda T_i \frac{\varepsilon}{\alpha^i} \text{ and } \varepsilon_{i+1}(c_i) \geq \frac{\varepsilon}{\alpha^i}\right],$$

$$p_2 = \Pr\left[count \geq \lambda T_i \frac{\varepsilon}{\alpha^i} \text{ and } \varepsilon_{i+1}(c_i) < \frac{\varepsilon}{\alpha^i}\right].$$

So p_0, p_1 and p_2 are the probabilities of continuing the loop, choosing a "good" challenge c_i, and choosing a "bad" challenge, respectively. Note that $p_0 + p_1 + p_2 = 1$. By the heavy rows argument, with probability at least $1 - 1/\sqrt{\alpha} - n/p$, $\varepsilon_{i+1}(c_i) \geq \varepsilon/(\sqrt{\alpha} \cdot \alpha^{i-1})$. Therefore and by the Chernoff bound,

$$p_1 = \Pr\left[count \geq \lambda T_i \frac{\varepsilon}{\alpha^i} \text{ and } \varepsilon_{i+1} \geq \frac{\varepsilon}{\alpha^i}\right]$$

$$\geq \Pr\left[count \geq \lambda T_i \frac{\varepsilon}{\alpha^i} \text{ and } \varepsilon_{i+1} \geq \frac{\varepsilon}{\sqrt{\alpha} \cdot \alpha^{i-1}}\right]$$

$$= \Pr\left[\varepsilon_{i+1} \geq \frac{\varepsilon}{\sqrt{\alpha} \cdot \alpha^{i-1}}\right] \Pr\left[count \geq \lambda T_i \frac{\varepsilon}{\alpha^i} \;\middle|\; \varepsilon_{i+1} \geq \frac{\varepsilon}{\sqrt{\alpha} \cdot \alpha^{i-1}}\right]$$

$$\geq \left(1 - \frac{1}{\sqrt{\alpha}} - \frac{n}{p}\right) \Pr\left[count \geq \lambda T_i \frac{\varepsilon}{\alpha^i} \;\middle|\; \varepsilon_{i+1} \geq \frac{\varepsilon}{\sqrt{\alpha} \cdot \alpha^{i-1}}\right]$$

$$\geq \left(1 - \frac{1}{\sqrt{\alpha}} - \frac{n}{p}\right) \Pr\left[count \geq \frac{\lambda}{\sqrt{\alpha}} T_i \varepsilon_{i+1} \;\middle|\; \varepsilon_{i+1} \geq \frac{\varepsilon}{\sqrt{\alpha} \cdot \alpha^{i-1}}\right]$$

$$\geq \left(1 - \frac{1}{\sqrt{\alpha}} - \frac{n}{p}\right)\left(1 - \Pr\left[count \leq \frac{\lambda}{\sqrt{\alpha}} T_i \varepsilon_{i+1} \;\middle|\; \varepsilon_{i+1} \geq \frac{\varepsilon}{\sqrt{\alpha} \cdot \alpha^{i-1}}\right]\right)$$

$$\geq \left(1 - \frac{1}{\sqrt{\alpha}} - \frac{n}{p}\right)\left(1 - \exp\left(-\frac{(1 - \lambda/\sqrt{\alpha})^2}{2} T_i \varepsilon_{i+1}\right)\right)$$

$$\geq \left(1 - \frac{1}{\sqrt{\alpha}} - \frac{n}{p}\right)\left(1 - \exp\left(-\frac{(\sqrt{\alpha} - \lambda)^2}{2\sqrt{\alpha}} T_i \frac{\varepsilon}{\alpha^i}\right)\right) = p_1'$$

On the other hand we find for p_2,

$$p_2 = \Pr\left[\varepsilon_{i+1} < \frac{\varepsilon}{\alpha^i}\right] \Pr\left[count \geq \lambda T_i \frac{\varepsilon}{\alpha^i} \;\middle|\; \varepsilon_{i+1} < \frac{\varepsilon}{\alpha^i}\right]$$

$$\leq \Pr\left[count \geq (1 + \delta) T_i \varepsilon_{i+1} \;\middle|\; \varepsilon_{i+1} < \frac{\varepsilon}{\alpha^i}\right]$$

$$\leq \exp\left(-\frac{1}{3}\min(\delta, \delta^2)\varepsilon_{i+1} T_i\right)$$

where we have set $\delta > 0$ such that $(1 + \delta)\varepsilon_{i+1} = \lambda\varepsilon/\alpha^i$, i.e. $\delta = \frac{\lambda\varepsilon}{\alpha^i\varepsilon_{i+1}} - 1$. We want to bound $\min(\delta, \delta^2)\varepsilon_{i+1}$ from below. Notice that

$$\delta^2\varepsilon_{i+1} = \frac{\lambda^2\varepsilon^2}{\alpha^{2i}\varepsilon_{i+1}} - \frac{2\lambda\varepsilon}{\alpha^i} + \varepsilon_{i+1}$$

is strictly decreasing on the interval $\varepsilon_{i+1} \in [0, \varepsilon/\alpha^i[$. Hence,

$$\delta^2\varepsilon_{i+1} > \frac{\lambda^2\varepsilon}{\alpha^i} - \frac{2\lambda\varepsilon}{\alpha^i} + \frac{\varepsilon}{\alpha^i} = \frac{\varepsilon}{\alpha^i}(\lambda - 1)^2.$$

Moreover, $\delta\varepsilon_{i+1} > (\lambda - 1)\frac{\varepsilon}{\alpha^i}$ and therefore

$$p_2 < \exp\left(-\frac{(\lambda - 1)^2}{3}T_i\frac{\varepsilon}{\alpha^i}\right) = p_2'.$$

We set λ such that the arguments of the exponential function in p_1' and p_2' are equal; that is,

$$\frac{(\sqrt{\alpha} - \lambda)^2}{2\sqrt{\alpha}} = \frac{(\lambda - 1)^2}{3}.$$

Then $p_1' = (1 - 1/\sqrt{\alpha} - n/p)(1 - p_2')$. With these probabilities we now calculate the probability that the loop ends with a bad c_i. It is given by

$$p_{\text{bad}} = \sum_{j=0}^{\infty} p_0^k p_2 = \frac{p_2}{1 - p_0} = \frac{p_2}{p_1 + p_2} = \frac{1}{1 + p_1/p_2} < \frac{1}{1 + p_1'/p_2'} = \frac{p_2'}{p_1' + p_2'}.$$

The probability that the first-level TREE-FINDER(1) chooses n_1 good challenges c_1 is $(1 - p_{\text{bad}})^{n_1}$. Under this condition our assumption $\varepsilon_2 \geq \varepsilon/\alpha$ is true for the second-level tree finders and they all choose only good challenges with probability $(1 - p_{\text{bad}})^{n_1 n_2}$. Write $N = \sum_{i=1}^{\mu-1}(n_1 \ldots n_i) \leq \sum_{i=1}^{\mu-1} n^i = \frac{n^\mu - n}{n - 1} < n^\mu = (2^{\log n})^\mu = (2^\mu)^{\log n} = l^{\log n}$ for $n = \max_{1 \leq i \leq \mu-1} n_i$. We see that with probability $(1 - p_{\text{bad}})^N$ only good challenges are chosen in the whole execution of the tree-finding algorithm and the assumption is true for all invocations of TREE-FINDER(i). Now, by the Bernoulli inequality,

$$(1 - p_{\text{bad}})^N \geq 1 - Np_{\text{bad}} > 1 - \frac{Np_2'}{p_2' + p_1'}$$

$$= 1 - \frac{Np_2'}{p_2' + (1 - 1/\sqrt{\alpha} - n/p)(1 - p_2')}$$

$$> 1 - \frac{Np_2'}{1 - 1/\sqrt{\alpha} - n/p},$$

which is bigger than $1/2$ if $p_2' \leq (1 - 1/\sqrt{\alpha} - n/p)/(2N)$, which in turn is implied by

$$T_i = \frac{3}{(\lambda - 1)^2}\frac{\alpha^i}{\varepsilon}\ln\left(\frac{2N}{1 - 1/\sqrt{\alpha} - n/p}\right) = O\left(\frac{l^{\log \alpha + \log n}}{\varepsilon}\right) \quad (l \to \infty).$$

The expected number of iterations of the loop in lines $12-25$ under the condition that a good c_i is chosen is

$$\sum_{j=1}^{\infty} j \frac{p_0^{j-1} p_1}{p_1/(1-p_0)} = (1-p_0) \sum_{j=1}^{\infty} j p_0^{j-1}$$

$$= \frac{1}{1-p_0} = \frac{1}{p_1 + p_2}$$

$$< \frac{1}{p_1'} = \frac{1}{(1 - 1/\sqrt{\alpha} - n/p)(1 - p_2')}$$

$$= O(1)$$

and each iteration takes time $T_i + 1$. So with probability at least $1/2$ the conditioned expected runtime of the whole tree finding algorithm is at most

$$t = \sum_{i=1}^{\mu-1} n^i \frac{1}{p_1'}(T_i + 1) + \frac{n^{\mu-1} n_\mu}{\varepsilon/\alpha^{\mu-1} - n_\mu/p}$$

$$< \frac{1}{p_1'} \sum_{i=1}^{\mu-1} n^i T_i + \frac{1}{p_1'} l^{\log n} + \frac{n_\mu}{n} \frac{l^{\log n + \log \alpha}}{\varepsilon}$$

$$= \frac{1}{p_1'} \frac{3}{(\lambda-1)^2} \frac{1}{\alpha n - 1} \ln\left(\frac{2N}{1 - 1/\sqrt{\alpha} - n/p}\right) \frac{l^{\log n + \log \alpha}}{\varepsilon}$$

$$+ \frac{n_\mu}{n} \frac{l^{\log n + \log \alpha}}{\varepsilon} + \frac{1}{p_1'} l^{\log n}$$

$$= O\left(\frac{l^{\log n + \log \alpha} \log l}{\varepsilon}\right).$$

Here we have used $\varepsilon \geq \alpha^\mu n_\mu/((\alpha-1)p)$ which implies $\varepsilon/\alpha^{\mu-1} - n_\mu/p \geq \varepsilon/\alpha^\mu = \varepsilon/l^{\log \alpha}$. When we are not so lucky and some bad challenges are chosen the algorithm might run for a long time but we just limit the runtime to $2t$. Then the probability for obtaining a full n-tree of accepting transcripts is at least $\frac{1}{2}(1 - \frac{1}{2}) = \frac{1}{4}$ since the probability that an algorithm with expected runtime t runs longer than $2t$ is at most $1/2$. Notice that in expected time $8t$ we can obtain an n-tree of accepting transcripts. □

Example. The implied constant in the big-O statement for the runtime of the extractor is readily computed from the formulas in the proof of Lemma 3.2. For example in the case where $p \approx 2^{256}$, $n = 4$, $l = 2^{25}$ and $\alpha = 1.3$, one finds that $\lambda \approx 1.075$ and the implied constant is about 1564.

4   Zero-Knowledge Inner Product Proof

In an inner product proof there is a commitment $t = \vec{g}^{\vec{v}_1} \vec{h}^{\vec{v}_2} u^\rho$ to two vectors whose inner product $x = \langle \vec{v}_1, \vec{v}_2 \rangle$ is publicly known. The goal is to prove knowledge of an opening to t that really fulfills this inner product relation. In this section we give a variant of the Bulletproof inner product proof which differs in that it is zero-knowledge. In the original protocol, after folding the vectors down to just 1-dimensional elements, the prover reveals the opening to the commitment. The main difference of the modified protocol from this section is that instead of revealing the opening it uses a Schnorr-type proof to prove knowledge of an opening in zero-knowledge, in a way that also proves the necessary product relation. With a zero-knowledge inner product proof at hand we can significantly simplify our main protocol compared to the similar Bulletproof range proof from [BBB+17]. For example, our proof is only three round compared to the five rounds of the range proof. The advantage stems from the fact that the secret vectors do not have to be blinded which is the reason for much of the complication in the Bulletproof range proof. We write $\bowtie\!\Pi_{\langle\cdot,\cdot\rangle}(\cdot;\cdot)$ for our inner product proof protocol, which is detailed in Fig. 1.

The length l of the secret vectors $\vec{v}_1$, $\vec{v}_2$ is assumed to be a power of two. In the main protocol from Sect. 5 we need an inner product proof for vectors of arbitrary length but it is trivial to achieve this by just padding the vectors with zeros. If $t = \vec{g}^{\vec{v}_1}\vec{h}^{\vec{v}_2}u^\rho$ is a commitment to two vectors of length l which is not a power of two, we can just interpret this as a commitment to vectors of length $2^{\lceil \log l \rceil}$ over more generators $\vec{g}'$, $\vec{h}'$. Notice that the inner product of the padded vectors stays the same.

Theorem 4.1. *The protocol given in Figs. 1 and 2 is complete, perfectly honest verifier zero-knowledge and generalized special sound under the discrete-log assumption. So there is an extractor $\mathcal{E}$ that, when given rewindable black-box access to a deterministic prover $\mathcal{P}^*$, either outputs an opening $\vec{v}_1^*, \vec{v}_2^* \in \mathbb{Z}_p^l$, $\rho^* \in \mathbb{Z}_p$ of t, i.e. $t = \vec{g}^{\vec{v}_1^*}\vec{h}^{\vec{v}_2^*}u^{\rho^*}$, such that $x = \langle \vec{v}_1^*, \vec{v}_2^* \rangle$, or a non-trivial discrete-log relation between $\vec{g}, \vec{h}, u$ and two auxiliary generators $e, f \in G$. The extractor $\mathcal{E}$ runs in expected time at most $O(l^{2+\log \alpha} \log l/\varepsilon)$ for some $\alpha > 1$, for example $\alpha = 1.3$, when $\mathcal{P}^*$ has acceptance probability $\varepsilon \geq 10\frac{\alpha}{\alpha-1}l^{\log \alpha}/p$. Running $\mathcal{P}^*$ once is assumed to take unit time.*

Proof. The subprotocol without the first move is a $2\mu + 1$ move protocol for $\mu = \log(l) + 1$, which fulfills the prerequisites of the forking lemma given in Lemma 3.2. After sending a uniformly random generator $a = e^b$ of the group G for a uniform $b \in \mathbb{Z}_p$, the extractor $\mathcal{E}$ can thus use TREE-FINDER to obtain a $(4,\ldots,4,5)$-tree of accepting transcripts of this subprotocol. More precisely, with probability at least $1/2$ over the choice of a, the verifier $\mathcal{V}$ will accept with probability at least $\varepsilon/2 \geq \frac{\alpha^\mu}{\alpha-1}n_\mu/p$. Therefore TREE-FINDER will be successful with probability at least $1/8$. If it is not successful, $\mathcal{E}$ restarts.

Consider the 5 accepting transcripts from neighboring leaves with the same parent node. Only the last challenges differ in the transcripts and we have the 5 verification equations

$$(t'')^{c_i} w(w')^{c_i^{-1}} = g^{z_{1,i}} h^{z_{2,i}} a^{c_i^{-1} z_{1,i} z_{2,i}} u^{\tau_i} \tag{13}$$

Prover $\mathcal{P}$	Verifier $\mathcal{V}$
Inputs:	
$\vec{g}, \vec{h} \in G^l; u \in G$	$\vec{g}, \vec{h}, u, t, x$
$\vec{v}_1, \vec{v}_2 \in \mathbb{Z}_p^l; \rho \in \mathbb{Z}_p$	
$t = \vec{g}^{\vec{v}_1} \vec{h}^{\vec{v}_2} u^\rho$	
$x = \langle \vec{v}_1, \vec{v}_2 \rangle$	

$$\xleftarrow{\qquad a \qquad} \qquad a \xleftarrow{\$} G$$

$t' = ta^x$ $\qquad\qquad\qquad\qquad\qquad$ $t' = ta^x$

The parties run $(g, h, t''; v_1, v_2, \rho') = \text{FOLDING}(\vec{g}, \vec{h}, a, u, t'; \vec{v}_1, \vec{v}_2, \rho)$ where the secrets $v_1, v_2, \rho' \in \mathbb{Z}_p$ are such that $t'' = g^{v_1} h^{v_2} a^{v_1 v_2} u^{\rho'}$.

$y_1, y_2, \sigma, \sigma' \xleftarrow{\$} \mathbb{Z}_p$

$w = g^{y_1} h^{y_2} a^{y_1 v_2 + y_2 v_1} u^\sigma$

$w' = a^{y_1 y_2} u^{\sigma'}$ $\qquad \xrightarrow{\quad w, w' \quad}$

$\qquad\qquad\qquad\qquad \xleftarrow{\quad c \quad} \qquad c \xleftarrow{\$} \mathbb{Z}_p^\times$

$z_1 = y_1 + cv_1$

$z_2 = y_2 + cv_2$

$\tau = c\rho' + \sigma + c^{-1}\sigma'$ $\qquad \xrightarrow{\quad z_1, z_2, \tau \quad}$

$\qquad\qquad\qquad\qquad\qquad (t'')^c w (w')^{c^{-1}} \stackrel{?}{=} g^{z_1} h^{z_2} a^{c^{-1} z_1 z_2} u^\tau$

Fig. 1. Zero-knowledge inner product Bulletproof $\bowtie\Pi_{\langle \cdot, \cdot \rangle}(\cdot; \cdot)$. It proves knowledge of an opening to a Pedersen commitment $t = \vec{g}^{\vec{v}_1} \vec{h}^{\vec{v}_2} u^\rho$ such that the vectors $\vec{v}_1$ and $\vec{v}_2$ fulfill an inner product relation $\langle \vec{v}_1, \vec{v}_2 \rangle = x$.

for $i = 1, \ldots, 5$ with distinct $c_i \in \mathbb{Z}_p$. Let $(\lambda_1, \lambda_2, \lambda_3)^T \in \mathbb{Z}_p^3$ be the solution of the linear system

$$\begin{pmatrix} 1 & 1 & 1 \\ c_1 & c_2 & c_3 \\ c_1^{-1} & c_2^{-1} & c_3^{-1} \end{pmatrix} \begin{pmatrix} \lambda_1 \\ \lambda_2 \\ \lambda_3 \end{pmatrix} = \begin{pmatrix} 0 \\ 1 \\ 0 \end{pmatrix}.$$

It exists because it is well-known that the determinant of this Vandermonde matrix is equal to $-(c_1 c_2 c_3)^{-1}(c_1 - c_2)(c_1 - c_3)(c_2 - c_3) \neq 0$. Now raise the first 3 equations in 13 for $i = 1, 2, 3$ to the powers of λ_i and multiply them. This gives

$$t'' = g^{v_1^*} h^{v_2^*} a^{x^*} u^{\tau^*}$$

Prover $\mathcal{P}$ Verifier $\mathcal{V}$

Inputs:

$\vec{g}, \vec{h} \in G^l; a, u \in G$ $\vec{g}, \vec{h}, a, u, t$

$\vec{v}_1, \vec{v}_2 \in \mathbb{Z}_p^l; \rho \in \mathbb{Z}_p$

$t = \vec{g}^{\vec{v}_1} \vec{h}^{\vec{v}_2} a^{\langle \vec{v}_1, \vec{v}_2 \rangle} u^\rho$

Outputs:

$g, h \in G$ g, h, t'

$v_1, v_2, \rho' \in \mathbb{Z}_p$

$t' = g^{v_1} h^{v_2} a^{v_1 v_2} u^{\rho'}$

If $l > 1$, define $l' = \frac{l}{2}$ and write $\vec{g} = \left(\frac{\vec{g}_t}{\vec{g}_b} \right), \vec{h} = \left(\frac{\vec{h}_t}{\vec{h}_b} \right), \vec{v}_i = \left(\frac{\vec{v}_{i,t}}{\vec{v}_{i,b}} \right)$, where $\vec{g}_j, \vec{h}_j, \vec{v}_{i,j} \in G^{l'}$ for $i = 1, 2, j = t, b$. Then,

$$\sigma_{-1}, \sigma_1 \xleftarrow{\$} \mathbb{Z}_p$$

$$t_{-1} = \vec{g}_t^{\vec{v}_{1,b}} \vec{h}_b^{\vec{v}_{2,t}} a^{\langle \vec{v}_{1,b}, \vec{v}_{2,t} \rangle} u^{\sigma_{-1}}$$

$$t_1 = \vec{g}_b^{\vec{v}_{1,t}} \vec{h}_t^{\vec{v}_{2,b}} a^{\langle \vec{v}_{1,t}, \vec{v}_{2,b} \rangle} u^{\sigma_1} \xrightarrow{\quad t_{-1}, t_1 \quad}$$

$$\xleftarrow{\qquad c \qquad} \qquad c \xleftarrow{\$} \mathbb{Z}_p^\times$$

$$\vec{v}_1' = \vec{v}_{1,t} + c^{-1} \vec{v}_{1,b}$$

$$\vec{v}_2' = \vec{v}_{2,t} + c \vec{v}_{2,b}$$

$$\rho'' = c^{-1} \sigma_{-1} + \rho + c \sigma_1$$

and both parties compute $\vec{g}' = \vec{g}_t \circ \vec{g}_b^c$, $\vec{h}' = \vec{h}_t \circ \vec{h}_b^{c^{-1}}$ and $t'' = t_{-1}^{c^{-1}} t t_1^c$. They recursively run $(g, h, t'; v_1, v_2, \rho') = \text{FOLDING}(\vec{g}', \vec{h}', a, u, t''; \vec{v}_1', \vec{v}_2', \rho'')$ where $\mathcal{P}$ knows $\vec{v}_1', \vec{v}_2', \rho''$ such that $t'' = (\vec{g}')^{\vec{v}_1'} (\vec{h}')^{\vec{v}_2'} a^{\langle \vec{v}_1', \vec{v}_2' \rangle} u^{\rho''}$.

Else $g = \vec{g}, h = \vec{h} \in G$, and $\mathcal{P}$ knows $v_1 = \vec{v}_1, v_2 = \vec{v}_2, \rho' = \rho \in \mathbb{Z}_p$, such that $t' = t = g^{v_1} h^{v_2} a^{v_1 v_2} u^{\rho'}$.

Fig. 2. Bulletproof folding protocol $\text{FOLDING}(\vec{g}, \vec{h}, a, u, t; \vec{v}_1, \vec{v}_2, \rho)$. This reduces a Pedersen multi-commitment of the form $t = \vec{g}^{\vec{v}_1} \vec{h}^{\vec{v}_2} a^{\langle \vec{v}_1, \vec{v}_2 \rangle} u^\rho$ to a new commitment $t' = g^{v_1} h^{v_2} a^{v_1 v_2} u^{\rho'}$ with the same (inner) product structure but in dimension 1. Furthermore, given an opening for t' having the correct inner product structure, one can extract an opening for t that also has the inner product structure by using the extractor from the forking lemma (Lemma 3.2).

where for example $v_1^* = \sum_{i=1}^3 \lambda_i z_{1,i}$. In the same manner we can extract openings for w and w',

$$w = g^{y_1^*} h^{y_2^*} a^{x_w^*} u^{\sigma^*},$$
$$w' = g^{(y_1')^*} h^{(y_2')^*} a^{x_{w'}^*} u^{(\sigma')^*}.$$

With these openings to t'', w and w' we can reconstruct the equations in (13) and get

$$(t'')^{c_i} w (w')^{c_i^{-1}}$$
$$= g^{c_i v_1^* + y_1^* + c_i^{-1}(y_1')^*} h^{c_i v_2^* + y_2^* + c_i^{-1}(y_2')^*} a^{c_i x^* + x_w^* + c_i^{-1} x_{w'}^*} u^{c_i \rho^* + \sigma^* + c_i^{-1}(\sigma')^*}$$
$$= g^{z_{1,i}} h^{z_{2,i}} a^{c_i^{-1} z_{1,i} z_{2,i}} u^{\tau_i}.$$

By comparing exponents we either find a non-trivial discrete-log relation between g, h, a, u, which gives a relation between $\vec{g}, \vec{h}, u, e$ since $\mathcal{E}$ knows expressions of g, h, a, u as powers of $\vec{g}, \vec{h}, u, e$. Or we have

$$c_i x^* + x_w^* + c_i^{-1} x_{w'}^* = c_i^{-1} z_{1,i} z_{2,i}$$
$$= c_i^{-1} \left(c_i v_1^* + y_1^* + c_i^{-1}(y_1')^* \right) \left(c_i v_2^* + y_2^* + c_i^{-1}(y_2')^* \right).$$

Multiplying this equation by c_i^3 yields a polynomial of degree 4 which has five roots c_i. Hence it must be the zero polynomial and from the leading coefficient we get $x^* = v_1^* v_2^*$ and thus

$$t'' = g^{v_1^*} h^{v_2^*} a^{v_1^* v_2^*} u^{\tau^*}.$$

The extractor performs this process for all parents in the second-to-last level $\mu - 1 = \log(l)$ of the tree of accepting transcripts. Then, with the same techniques and as is detailed in [BBB+17], the extractor can invert all the $\log(l)$ folding steps and either compute a non-trivial discrete-log relation or an opening $\vec{v}_1, \vec{v}_2, x^*, \rho^*$ of $t' = ta^x$,

$$ta^x = \vec{g}^{\vec{v}_1} \vec{h}^{\vec{v}_2} a^{x^*} u^{\rho^*},$$

such that $x^* = \langle \vec{v}_1, \vec{v}_2 \rangle$. If $x^* = x$ then $\mathcal{E}$ has an opening of t as stated in the theorem. If not, $\mathcal{E}$ starts over from scratch but samples a challenge generator $a' = f^{b'} \in \mathbb{Z}_p$ for the first move. By this $\mathcal{E}$ obtains an opening

$$t(a')^x = \vec{g}^{\vec{v}_1^*} \vec{h}^{\vec{v}_2^*} (a')^{x^{**}} u^{\rho^{**}},$$

and can compute

$$\vec{g}^{\vec{v}_1 - \vec{v}_1^*} \vec{h}^{\vec{v}_2 - \vec{v}_2^*} e^{b(x^* - x)} f^{b'(x^{**} - x)} u^{\rho^* - \rho^{**}} = 1,$$

which is a non-trivial discrete-log relation. Not taking into account the simple arithmetic over $\mathbb{Z}_p$, the expected running time of $\mathcal{E}$ is at most 16 times the expected running time of TREE-FINDER.

We turn to the zero-knowledge property. The first message by the verifier containing the generator a and all the messages in the folding protocol are independently uniformly random. This is because all the cross-terms t_{-1}, t_1 are independently blinded with independently random factors $u^{\sigma_{-1}}$ and u^{σ_1}. So the simulator can just choose $a \xleftarrow{\$} G$ and all messages in the folding protocol uniformly randomly. From these messages the honest verifier computes the generators g, h and the commitment t''. Now it remains to simulate the Schnorr-type protocol at the end for proving knowledge of an opening of t'' that obeys the product relation. This is made possible by how we set up the verification equation. The simulator first samples $c \xleftarrow{\$} \mathbb{Z}_p$, and then $z_1, z_2 \xleftarrow{\$} \mathbb{Z}_p$, which are independent from the previously chosen messages because of y_1 and y_2, respectively. Then he chooses $w' \xleftarrow{\$} G$ which is independent because of the blinding factor $u^{\sigma'}$. Last the simulator samples $\tau \xleftarrow{\$} \mathbb{Z}_p$ which is still uniformly random because of σ. Now $w \in G$ is not independent anymore but instead fully determined by the previous choices and the simulator can compute it correctly as

$$w = (t'')^{-c}(w')^{-c^{-1}}g^{z_1}h^{z_2}a^{c^{-1}z_1z_2}u^{\tau},$$

which clearly makes the verification equation true.

5   The Main Protocol

In this section we present in detail our protocol to prove knowledge of a matrix $\mathbf{S} \in \mathcal{R}_q^{m \times k}$ consisting of short polynomials of infinity norm less than B such that

$$\mathbf{AS} = \mathbf{T} \text{ over } \mathcal{R}_q \tag{14}$$

where $\mathbf{A} \in \mathcal{R}_q^{n \times m}$ and $\mathbf{T} \in \mathcal{R}_q^{n \times k}$ are public.

First, when $\mathbf{A}, \mathbf{S}, \mathbf{T}$ are lifted to matrices over $\mathbb{Z}[X]$, the equation is true modulo q and $\mathbf{f}$. So there are matrices $\mathbf{R}_1, \mathbf{R}_2$ over $\mathbb{Z}[X]$ such that

$$\mathbf{AS} + q\mathbf{R}_1 + \mathbf{f}\mathbf{R}_2 = \mathbf{T} \text{ over } \mathbb{Z}[X]. \tag{15}$$

More precisely, notice that $\mathbf{T} - \mathbf{AS} \in (\mathbb{Z}[X])^{n \times k}$ consists of polynomials of degree at most $2(d-1)$ and infinity norm less than $mdBq/2$ when we use central representatives for coefficients in $\mathbb{Z}_q$. Moreover, $\mathbf{T} - \mathbf{AS}$ is a multiple of $\mathbf{f}$ modulo q. So we can exactly divide $\mathbf{T} - \mathbf{AS}$ by $\mathbf{f}$ over $\mathbb{Z}_q[X]$ to obtain $\mathbf{R}_2$ with polynomials of degree at most $d-2$ and coefficients in $\{-(q-1)/2, \ldots, (q-1)/2\}$. Then, dividing $\mathbf{T} - \mathbf{AS} - \mathbf{f}\mathbf{R}_2$ by q yields $\mathbf{R}_1$ with polynomials of degree at most $2(d-1)$ and infinity norm less than $(mdB + d \|\mathbf{f}\|_{\infty})/2$. Next, for a prime p we have

$$\mathbf{AS} + q\mathbf{R}_1 + \mathbf{f}\mathbf{R}_2 = \mathbf{T} \text{ over } \mathbb{Z}_p[X], \tag{16}$$

and then for an $\alpha \in \mathbb{Z}_p$ the equation

$$\mathbf{A}(\alpha)\mathbf{S}(\alpha) + q\mathbf{R}_1(\alpha) + \mathbf{f}(\alpha)\mathbf{R}_2(\alpha) = \mathbf{T}(\alpha) \text{ over } \mathbb{Z}_p[X]. \tag{17}$$

Conversely, by the Schwartz-Zippel lemma, if Eq. (17) is true for a uniformly random α, then Eq. (16) holds with probability at least $1 - 2(d - 1)/p$. In this case, if $p \geq 2(mdB + d\left\|\mathbf{f}\right\|_{\infty})q$, Eq. (15) is true since no reduction modulo p takes place, and Eq. (14) follows. So in order to prove knowledge of a matrix $\mathbf{S} \in \mathcal{S}_B^{m \times k}$ as in Eq. (14), it suffices to prove knowledge of matrices $\mathbf{S}$, $\mathbf{R}_1$ and $\mathbf{R}_2$ of integer polynomials whose coefficients have absolute value less than B, $B_1 = (mdB + d\left\|\mathbf{f}\right\|_{\infty})/2$ and $B_2 = q/2$, respectively, such that Eq. (17) is true for a uniformly random α.

We describe our strategy for conducting such a proof. If we expand all polynomials in the secret matrices $\mathbf{S}, \mathbf{R}_1, \mathbf{R}_2$ to their coefficient row vectors of dimensions d, $2d - 1$ and $d - 1$, respectively, and hence consider the matrices as integer matrices S, R_1, R_2, then, with $\vec{\alpha}_d = (1, \alpha, \dots, \alpha^{d-1})^T$, we can equivalently write

$$\mathbf{A}(\alpha)S(I_k \otimes \vec{\alpha}_d) + qR_1(I_k \otimes \vec{\alpha}_{2d-1}) + \mathbf{f}(\alpha)R_2(I_k \otimes \vec{\alpha}_{d-1}) = \mathbf{T}(\alpha). \qquad (18)$$

Now a natural strategy would be to produce a Pedersen multi-commitment over a group of order p to the secret matrices S, R_1, R_2. Then one could prove that the matrices fulfill Eq. (18) by reducing them to integers using in the order of $\log(mkd)$ bulletproof folding steps. In addition one would also need to give a range proof that the coefficients of the matrices are sufficiently small. For increased efficiency we combine these proofs in one single proof.

The usual method for range proofs consists of expressing the coefficients by their binary representations so that the range follows from the number of bits used per coefficient. The proof that this representation really only contains bits in $\{0, 1\}$ is most easily done via an inner product proof as in [BBB+17]. Therefore we want to reduce Eq. (18) to an inner product equation which then can be integrated into the range proof. To this end we first multiply from both sides by uniformly random vectors $\vec{\beta} \in \mathbb{Z}_p^k$ and $\vec{\gamma} \in \mathbb{Z}_p^n$, so that

$$\vec{\gamma}^T\mathbf{A}(\alpha)S(\vec{\beta} \otimes \vec{\alpha}_d) + q\vec{\gamma}^T R_1(\vec{\beta} \otimes \vec{\alpha}_{2d-1}) + \mathbf{f}(\alpha)\vec{\gamma}^T R_2(\vec{\beta} \otimes \vec{\alpha}_{d-1}) = \vec{\gamma}^T\mathbf{T}(\alpha)\vec{\beta}.$$

This equation implies Eq. (18) with probability at least $1 - 2/p$. Next we serialize the secret matrices to column vectors $\vec{s} \in \mathbb{Z}^{mkd}$, $\vec{r}_1 \in \mathbb{Z}^{nk(2d-1)}$ and $\vec{r}_2 \in \mathbb{Z}^{nk(d-1)}$ in row-major order. With these the last equation is equivalent to the inner product equation

$$\left\langle \mathbf{A}(\alpha)^T\vec{\gamma} \otimes \vec{\beta} \otimes \vec{\alpha}_d, \vec{s} \right\rangle + \left\langle q\vec{\gamma} \otimes \vec{\beta} \otimes \vec{\alpha}_{2d-1}, \vec{r}_1 \right\rangle + \left\langle \mathbf{f}(\alpha)\vec{\gamma} \otimes \vec{\beta} \otimes \vec{\alpha}_{d-1}, \vec{r}_2 \right\rangle$$
$$= \vec{\gamma}^T\mathbf{T}(\alpha)\vec{\beta}.$$

Finally, we expand each secret vector one more time and replace the coefficients by their binary representation using two's complement for negative numbers. We get

$$\left\langle \mathbf{A}(\alpha)^T \vec{\gamma} \otimes \vec{\beta} \otimes \vec{\alpha}_d \otimes \vec{2}_b, \mathrm{Binary}_b(\vec{s}) \right\rangle$$
$$+ \left\langle q\vec{\gamma} \otimes \vec{\beta} \otimes \vec{\alpha}_{2d-1} \otimes \vec{2}_{b_1}, \mathrm{Binary}_{b_1}(\vec{r}_1) \right\rangle$$
$$+ \left\langle \mathbf{f}(\alpha)\vec{\gamma} \otimes \vec{\beta} \otimes \vec{\alpha}_{d-1} \otimes \vec{2}_{b_2}, \mathrm{Binary}_{b_2}(\vec{r}_2) \right\rangle$$
$$= \vec{\gamma}^T \mathbf{T}(\alpha)\vec{\beta}, \tag{19}$$

where $\vec{2}_b = (1, 2, \dots, 2^{b-2}, -2^{b-1})^T$, $b = \lceil \log(B) \rceil + 1$, $b_1 = \lceil \log(B_1) \rceil + 1 = \lceil \log(mdB + d\|\mathbf{f}\|_\infty) \rceil$ and $b_2 = \lceil \log(B_2) \rceil + 1 = \lceil \log(q) \rceil$. For the sake of clarity in what follows we concatenate the public and secret vectors and define

$$\vec{v} = \mathbf{A}(\alpha)^T \vec{\gamma} \otimes \vec{\beta} \otimes \vec{\alpha}_d \otimes \vec{2}_b \,\|\, q\vec{\gamma} \otimes \vec{\beta} \otimes \vec{\alpha}_{2d-1} \otimes \vec{2}_{b_1} \,\|\, \mathbf{f}(\alpha)\vec{\gamma} \otimes \vec{\beta} \otimes \vec{\alpha}_{d-1} \otimes \vec{2}_{b_2},$$
$$\vec{s}_1 = \mathrm{Binary}_b(\vec{s}) \,\|\, \mathrm{Binary}_{b_1}(\vec{r}_1) \,\|\, \mathrm{Binary}_{b_2}(\vec{r}_2)$$

so that we can write $\langle \vec{v}, \vec{s}_1 \rangle = \vec{\gamma}^T \mathbf{T}(\alpha)\vec{\beta}$.

It remains to prove that the secret vector $\vec{s}_1$ only contains coefficients in $\{0,1\}$. As usual this is done by proving that there is a second vector $\vec{s}_2$, the vector with all bits flipped, such that $\vec{s}_1 \circ \vec{s}_2 = \vec{0}$ and $\vec{s}_1 + \vec{s}_2 = \vec{1}$. The first property holds with probability at least $1 - 1/p$ if $\langle \vec{\varphi}, \vec{s}_1 \circ \vec{s}_2 \rangle = \langle \vec{\varphi} \circ \vec{s}_2, \vec{s}_1 \rangle = 0$ for a uniformly random vector $\vec{\varphi}$. Similarly, the second property follows with overwhelming probability from $\langle \vec{\varphi}, \vec{s}_1 + \vec{s}_2 \rangle = \langle \vec{\varphi}, \vec{s}_1 \rangle + \langle \vec{\varphi} \circ \vec{s}_2, \vec{1} \rangle = \langle \vec{\varphi}, \vec{1} \rangle$. We incorporate both inner product equations into Eq. (19) and arrive at

$$\left\langle \vec{v} + \vec{\varphi} \circ \vec{s}_2 + \psi\vec{\varphi}, \vec{s}_1 + \psi\vec{1} \right\rangle = \vec{\gamma}^T \mathbf{T}(\alpha)\vec{\beta} + \psi \left\langle \vec{v}, \vec{1} \right\rangle + (\psi + \psi^2) \left\langle \vec{\varphi}, \vec{1} \right\rangle$$

where $\psi \in \mathbb{Z}_p$ is another uniformly random field element with the purpose of separating the three inner product equations.

When given a Pedersen multi-commitment to the vectors $\vec{s}_2$ and $\vec{s}_1$ it is easy to compute a commitment to $\vec{v}_1 = \vec{v} + \vec{\varphi} \circ \vec{s}_2 + \psi\vec{\varphi}$ and $\vec{v}_2 = \vec{s}_1 + \psi\vec{1}$. It might be unclear at first how to multiply $\vec{s}_2$ componentwise with $\vec{\varphi}$ inside the multi-commitment, which means each coefficient has to be multiplied by a different value. There is a standard trick to do this. Suppose $\vec{g} \in G^l$ is the vector of generators underlying $\vec{s}_2$. Then we just reinterpret this part of the commitment as a commitment over generators $\vec{g}' = \vec{g}^{\vec{\varphi}^{-1}}$. Since $\vec{g}^{\vec{s}_2} = (\vec{g}^{\vec{\varphi}^{-1}})^{\vec{\varphi} \circ \vec{s}_2} = (\vec{g}')^{\vec{s}_2}$, our original commitment containing $\vec{s}_2$ over $\vec{g}$ thus becomes a commitment containing $\vec{\varphi} \circ \vec{s}_2$ over $\vec{g}'$. Now given the commitment to $\vec{v}_1$ and $\vec{v}_2$ we prove that the inner product of these vectors of dimension $l = mkdb + nk(2d-1)b_1 + nk(d-1)b_2$ is equal to $x = \vec{\gamma}^T \mathbf{T}(\alpha)\vec{\beta} + \psi\langle \vec{v}, \vec{1} \rangle + (\psi + \psi^2)\langle \vec{\varphi}, \vec{1} \rangle$. It follows with overwhelming probability that $\vec{s}_1$ gives rise to a matrix $\mathbf{S} \in \mathcal{R}_q^{m \times k}$ of short polynomials such that $\mathbf{AS} = \mathbf{T}$ over $\mathcal{R}_q$. For the inner product proof we make use of Bulletproofs, which have communication cost logarithmic in l. But in contrast to the range proof in [BBB+17], we do not blind the vectors and instead use a variant of the Bulletproof inner product proof that is zero knowledge. Here one first reduces the vectors to dimension 1 and then uses a zero-knowledge Schnorr-type proof for the one-dimensional base case. See Fig. 3 for the complete protocol and Theorem 5.1 for its security. We state the zero-knowledge inner product Bulletproof in Fig. 1.

Theorem 5.1. *If $p \geq 2(mdB + d\|\mathbf{f}\|_\infty)q$, then the protocol in Fig. 3 is complete, perfectly honest verifier zero-knowledge and generalized special sound under the discrete-log assumption in the sense that there is an extractor $\mathcal{E}$ with the following properties. When given rewindable black-box access to a deterministic prover $\mathcal{P}^*$ that convinces the honest verifier with probability $\varepsilon \geq 100l/p$, $\mathcal{E}$ either outputs a solution $\mathbf{S}^* \in \mathcal{R}_q^{m \times k}$ to $\mathbf{AS}^* = \mathbf{T}$, which consists of polynomials whose coefficients fit in $b = \lceil \log(B) \rceil + 1$ bits, or a non-trivial discrete-log relation between generators of the group G. The extractor $\mathcal{E}$ runs in expected time at most $O(l^{2.4} \log l/\varepsilon)$. Running $\mathcal{P}^*$ once is assumed to take unit time.*

Proof. Completeness is clear from the discussion at the beginning of Sect. 5 and the zero-knowledge property follows immediately from the fact that the inner product proof is honest verifier zero-knowledge; see Theorem 4.1. Let us now prove soundness. The extractor $\mathcal{E}$ runs $\mathcal{P}^*$, sends uniformly random challenges in the second move and then uses the extractor for the inner product proof assuming acceptance probability $\varepsilon/2$ to get an opening for t, c.f. Theorem 4.1. From an averaging argument we know that for at least half of the challenges in the second move the inner product proof π is valid with probability at least $\varepsilon/2$. Then, since $\varepsilon/2 > 10\alpha l^{\log \alpha}/((\alpha-1)p)$ for $\alpha \geq 1.3$, the conditions of Theorem 4.1 are met. So after an expected number of 2 trials we can assume that $\mathcal{E}$ either has a non-trivial discrete-log relation or an opening $\vec{v}_1^*, \vec{v}_2^*, \rho^*$ of t, i.e.

$$t = (\vec{g}')^{\vec{v}_1^*} \vec{h}^{\vec{v}_2^*} u^{\rho^*},$$

such that $\langle \vec{v}_1^*, \vec{v}_2^* \rangle = x$. Since $t = w(\vec{g}')^{\vec{v}+\psi\vec{\varphi}} \vec{h}^\psi$, we get the opening $\vec{\varphi} \circ \vec{s}_2^* = \vec{v}_1^* - \vec{v} - \psi\vec{\varphi}, \vec{s}_1^* = \vec{v}_2^* - \psi\vec{1}, \rho^*$ for w such that

$$\langle \vec{v}, \vec{s}_1^* \rangle + \left\langle \vec{v}, \psi\vec{1} \right\rangle + \langle \vec{\varphi} \circ \vec{s}_2^*, \vec{s}_1^* \rangle + \left\langle \vec{\varphi} \circ \vec{s}_2^*, \psi\vec{1} \right\rangle + \langle \psi\vec{\varphi}, \vec{s}_1^* \rangle + \left\langle \psi\vec{\varphi}, \psi\vec{1} \right\rangle$$

$$= \langle \vec{v}, \vec{s}_1^* \rangle + \langle \vec{\varphi}, \vec{s}_1^* \circ \vec{s}_2^* \rangle + \psi \langle \vec{\varphi}, \vec{s}_1^* + \vec{s}_2^* \rangle + \psi^2 \left\langle \vec{\varphi}, \vec{1} \right\rangle + \psi \left\langle \vec{v}, \vec{1} \right\rangle$$

$$= \vec{\gamma}^T \mathbf{T}(\alpha)\vec{\beta} + \psi \left\langle \vec{v}, \vec{1} \right\rangle + (\psi + \psi^2) \left\langle \vec{\varphi}, \vec{1} \right\rangle.$$

The last equation is equivalent to

$$\langle \vec{v}, \vec{s}_1^* \rangle + \langle \vec{\varphi}, \vec{s}_1^* \circ \vec{s}_2^* \rangle + \psi \left\langle \vec{\varphi}, \vec{s}_1^* + \vec{s}_2^* - \vec{1} \right\rangle = \vec{\gamma}^T \mathbf{T}(\alpha)\vec{\beta},$$

which can be interpreted as a multivariate polynomial P over $\mathbb{Z}_p$ in $n+k+l+2$ variables that evaluates to zero at $(\alpha, \vec{\beta}, \vec{\gamma}, \vec{\varphi}, \psi)$. If the polynomial is the zero polynomial it follows that

$$\vec{s}_1^* \circ \vec{s}_2^* = 0 \text{ and } \vec{s}_1^* + \vec{s}_2^* = \vec{1}$$

so $\vec{s}_1^*$ is a binary vector with entries $s_{1,i}^* \in \{0,1\}$. Write $\mathbf{S}^* \in (\mathbb{Z}[X])^{m \times k}$ for the polynomial matrix in which the coefficient of X^ν, $0 \leq \nu \leq d-1$, of the polynomial in the (i,j)-th entry, $0 \leq i \leq m-1$, $0 \leq j \leq k-1$, is given by

$$s_{1,bdki+bdj+b\nu}^* + s_{1,bdki+bdj+b\nu+1}^* 2 + \cdots + s_{1,bdki+bdj+b\nu+(b-2)}^* 2^{b-2}$$
$$- s_{1,bdki+bdj+b\nu+(b-1)}^* 2^{b-1}.$$

Proceed similarly for $\mathbf{R}_1^*, \mathbf{R}_2^* \in (\mathbb{Z}[X])^{n \times k}$ starting from coefficient $s_{1,bdkm}^*$ and $s_{1,bdkm+b_1(2d-1)kn}^*$ of $\vec{s}_1^*$, respectively. In other words, $\mathbf{S}^*, \mathbf{R}_1^*$ and $\mathbf{R}_2^*$ are such that

$$\text{Binary}_b(\text{Serialize}(\mathbf{S}^*)) \parallel \text{Binary}_{b_1}(\text{Serialize}(\mathbf{R}_1^*)) \parallel \text{Binary}_{b_2}(\text{Serialize}(\mathbf{R}_2^*))$$
$$= \vec{s}_1^*.$$

By construction the polynomials in $\mathbf{S}^*$, $\mathbf{R}_1^*$ and $\mathbf{R}_2^*$ have coefficients that fit in b, b_1 and b_2 bits, respectively. Then, since $\langle \vec{v}, \vec{s}_1^* \rangle = \vec{\gamma}^T \mathbf{T}(\alpha) \vec{\beta}$, it follows by inspection

$$\vec{\gamma}^T \left(\mathbf{AS}^* + q\mathbf{R}_1^* + \mathbf{fR}_2^* - \mathbf{T} \right)(\alpha)\vec{\beta} = 0 \text{ in } \mathbb{Z}_p.$$

The coefficient of X^ν of the polynomial in the (i,j)-th entry of the matrix in the middle corresponds to the coefficient of $\alpha^\nu \beta_j \gamma_i$ of our multivariate polynomial P that we assume to be zero. So,

$$\mathbf{AS}^* + q\mathbf{R}_1^* + \mathbf{fR}_2^* = \mathbf{T} \text{ over } \mathbb{Z}_p[X]$$

but from our assumption on p this equation is even true over $\mathbb{Z}[X]$ and we finally get $\mathbf{AS}^* = \mathbf{T}$ over $\mathcal{R}_q$.

It remains to consider the case where $P \neq 0$. Note that in this case the polynomial is of total degree at most $2d$. Consequently, it can evaluate to zero at no more than $2dp^{n+k+l+1}$ points in $\mathbb{Z}_p^{n+k+l+2}$ (this is just a counting version of the Schwartz-Zippel lemma). Now the extractor $\mathcal{E}$ reruns $\mathcal{P}^*$ but sends a uniform challenge $(\alpha, \vec{\beta}, \vec{\gamma}, \vec{\varphi}, \psi) \in \mathbb{Z}_p^{n+k+l+2}$ from the set of non-roots of P. Then $\mathcal{E}$ again tries to extract from the inner product proof and continues in this fashion until he is successful for a second time. At least for a fraction of $\frac{1}{2} - \frac{2d}{p}$ of the non-roots, the inner product proof is accepted with probability at least $\varepsilon/2$. So after an expected number of roughly 2 trials $\mathcal{E}$ will get a non-trivial discrete-log relation or new multivariate polynomial P' that is zero outside of the small set of roots of our original polynomial P so that P' must be different to P. But then, since P and P' are in one-to-one correspondence to openings of the commitment t, we must have two different openings and can compute a non-trivial discrete-log relation. We see the total expected runtime of $\mathcal{E}$ is at most 4 times the expected runtime of the extractor of the inner product proof. $\square$

5.1   Proof Size

The communication size of our protocol from Fig. 3 is very small. Instead of all the individual challenges in the second move the verifier can just send a short seed that is expanded to the challenges with the help of a XOF. Moreover, in the non-interactive version of the protocol via the Fiat-Shamir transform the challenges are expanded from public information and the first message. So such a non-interactive proof only consists of the first message and the inner product proof of size logarithmic in l. Simple counting shows that one full non-interactive proof consists of $2\lceil \log l \rceil + 3$ group elements and 3 elements of $\mathbb{Z}_p$. If a 256 bit elliptic curve is used for G, then this results in $64\lceil \log l \rceil + 192$ bytes per proof.

Prover $\mathcal{P}$ Verifier $\mathcal{V}$

Inputs:

$\mathbf{A} \in \mathcal{R}_q^{n \times m}, \mathbf{S} \in \mathcal{S}_B^{m \times k}$ $\mathbf{A}, \mathbf{T}, b, b_1, b_2, l, \vec{g}, \vec{h}, u$

$\mathbf{T} = \mathbf{AS} \in \mathcal{R}_q^{n \times k}$

$b = \lceil \log(B) \rceil + 1$

$b_1 = \lceil \log(mdB + d\|\mathbf{f}\|_\infty) \rceil$

$b_2 = \lceil \log(q) \rceil$

$l = mkdb + nk(2d-1)b_1$
$\quad + nk(d-1)b_2$

$\vec{g}, \vec{h} \in G^l, u \in G$

$\mathbf{R}_2 = (\mathbf{T} - \mathbf{AS})/\mathbf{f}$ over $\mathbb{Z}_q[X]$

$\mathbf{R}_1 = (\mathbf{T} - \mathbf{AS} - \mathbf{fR}_2)/q$ over $\mathbb{Z}[X]$

$\vec{s} = \text{Serialize}(\mathbf{S}) \in \mathbb{Z}^{mkd}$

$\vec{r}_1 = \text{Serialize}(\mathbf{R}_1) \in \mathbb{Z}^{nk(2d-1)}$

$\vec{r}_2 = \text{Serialize}(\mathbf{R}_2) \in \mathbb{Z}^{nk(d-1)}$

$\vec{s}_1 = \text{Binary}_b(\vec{s}) \| \text{Binary}_{b_1}(\vec{r}_1)$
$\quad \| \text{Binary}_{b_2}(\vec{r}_2)$

$\vec{s}_2 = \vec{s}_1 + \vec{1} \in \mathbb{Z}_2^l \text{ (XOR)}$

$\rho \xleftarrow{\$} \mathbb{Z}_p$

$w = \vec{g}^{\vec{s}_2} \vec{h}^{\vec{s}_1} u^\rho$

$\xrightarrow{\quad w \quad}$

$\alpha \xleftarrow{\$} \mathbb{Z}_p^\times, \vec{\beta} \xleftarrow{\$} (\mathbb{Z}_p^\times)^k, \vec{\gamma} \xleftarrow{\$} (\mathbb{Z}_p^\times)^n$

$\xleftarrow{\alpha, \vec{\beta}, \vec{\gamma}, \vec{\varphi}, \psi} \quad \vec{\varphi} \xleftarrow{\$} (\mathbb{Z}_p^\times)^l, \psi \xleftarrow{\$} \mathbb{Z}_p^\times$

$\vec{g}' = \vec{g}^{\,-\vec{\varphi}}$ $\vec{g}' = \vec{g}^{\,-\vec{\varphi}}$

$\vec{v} = \mathbf{A}(\alpha)^T \vec{\gamma} \otimes \vec{\beta} \otimes {}^{\to}_d \otimes \vec{2}_b$ $\vec{v} = \mathbf{A}(\alpha)^T \vec{\gamma} \otimes \vec{\beta} \otimes {}^{\to}_d \otimes \vec{2}_b$

$\quad \| q\vec{\gamma} \otimes \vec{\beta} \otimes {}^{\to}_{2d-1} \otimes \vec{2}_{b_1}$ $\quad \| q\vec{\gamma} \otimes \vec{\beta} \otimes {}^{\to}_{2d-1} \otimes \vec{2}_{b_1}$

$\quad \| \mathbf{f}(\alpha)\vec{\gamma} \otimes \vec{\beta} \otimes {}^{\to}_{d\alpha 1} \otimes \vec{2}_{b_2} \in \mathbb{Z}_p^l$ $\quad \| \mathbf{f}(\alpha)\vec{\gamma} \otimes \vec{\beta} \otimes {}^{\to}_{d\alpha 1} \otimes \vec{2}_{b_2}$

$t = w(\vec{g}')^{\vec{v} + \psi\vec{\varphi}} \vec{h}^\psi$ $t = w(\vec{g}')^{\vec{v} + \psi\vec{\varphi}} \vec{h}^\psi$

$\vec{v}_1 = \vec{v} + {}^{\to} \alpha \vec{s}_2 + \psi\vec{\varphi}$

$\vec{v}_2 = \vec{s}_1 + \psi\vec{1}$

$x = \langle \vec{v}_1, \vec{v}_2 \rangle$ $x = \vec{\gamma}^T \mathbf{T}(\alpha)\vec{\beta} + \psi \left\langle \vec{v}, \vec{1} \right\rangle$
$\qquad\qquad\qquad\qquad\qquad\qquad + (\psi + \psi^2)\langle \vec{\varphi}, \vec{1} \rangle \in \mathbb{Z}_p$

The parties run the zero-knowledge inner product proof $\bowtie\Pi_{\langle \cdot, \cdot \rangle}(\vec{g}', \vec{h}, u, t, x; \vec{v}_1, \vec{v}_2, \rho)$
and the verifier $\mathcal{V}$ accepts if he accepts in $\bowtie\Pi_{\langle \cdot, \cdot \rangle}(\cdot; \cdot)$.

Fig. 3. Discrete-log based zero-knowledge proof of knowledge of a short solution to a matrix equation over $\mathcal{R}_q$.

5.2   Number of Exponentiations

Computing multi-exponentiations over G is by far the most time-consuming operation in our main protocol. We count the number of exponentiations to be performed by the prover and verifier in order to estimate the time needed to execute the protocol. The prover computes l exponentiations for $\vec{g}'$, $l+1$ exponentiations for t and only 1 exponentiation for w ($\vec{s}_1$ and $\vec{s}_2$ are binary) plus the exponentiations in the inner product proof. The verifier computes $2l+1$ exponentiations and those from the inner product proof. In the inner product proof the prover has to compute $2 \cdot 2^{\lceil \log l \rceil - i} + 6$ exponentiations in the i-th folding level, $i = 0, \ldots, \lceil \log l \rceil - 1$. This amounts to $4 \cdot 2^{\lceil \log l \rceil} + 6 \lceil \log l \rceil - 4 < 8l + 6 \log l + 2$ exponentiations for the full Bulletproof folding. In addition there are 6 exponentiations needed for the Schnorr-type proof. The verifier performs $4 \lceil \log l \rceil < 4 \log l + 1$ exponentiations for the folding protocol and 6 exponentiations for the verification equation. This can be heavily optimized by delaying exponentiations; see [BBB+17, Section 6.2]. We conclude that the total exponentiation costs for the prover and verifier are less than $10l + 6 \log l + 10$ and $2l + 4 \log l + 10$ exponentiations.

5.3   Example

We return to the example of a verifiable encryption scheme from Sect. 1.5. In the case of verifiable encryption, one has to prove a matrix equation $\mathbf{A}\vec{s} = \vec{t}$ with parameters $n = 2$, $m = 4$, $k = 1$, $B = 4$. For the ring $\mathcal{R}_q$, a common example for encrypting messages that are binary polynomials (c.f. [ADPS16]) is setting $\mathbf{f} = X^{1024} + 1$ and q being a prime of about 13 bits, and $p = 2$. With these parameters we find the length l of the secret vectors $\vec{s}_1$ and $\vec{s}_2$ in the inner product proof to be equal to 100296. It then follows from above that the prover and verifier need to compute about 724986 and 200667 exponentiations to run our protocol for this application. With current CPUs one exponentiation on a 256 bit elliptic curve can be computed in about 35000 cycles (see https://bench. cr.yp.to/results-dh.html), which amounts to roughly 85000 exponentiations per second. So computing one of our proofs should be possible in less than 10 s. This can then be improved by using specialized algorithms for computing multi-exponentiations, in particular Pippenger's algorithm [Pip80]. The size of the proof is 1.25 kbyte.

Acknowledgements. We thank the reviewers for their careful reading of the proofs and useful suggestions. This work was supported in part by the SNSF ERC Transfer Grant CRETP2-166734 FELICITY and H2020 FutureTPM.

References

[ABB+18] Androulaki, E., et al.: Hyperledger fabric: a distributed operating system for permissioned blockchains. CoRR, abs/1801.10228 (2018)

[ADPS16] Alkim, E., Ducas, L., Pöppelmann, T., Schwabe, P.: Post-quantum key exchange - a new hope. In: USENIX, pp. 327–343 (2016)

[BBB+17] Bünz, B., Bootle, J., Boneh, D., Poelstra, A., Wuille, P., Maxwell, G.: Bulletproofs: short proofs for confidential transactions and more. IACR Cryptology ePrint Archive, 2017:1066 (2017)

[BCC+16] Bootle, J., Cerulli, A., Chaidos, P., Groth, J., Petit, C.: Efficient zero-knowledge arguments for arithmetic circuits in the discrete log setting. In: Fischlin, M., Coron, J.-S. (eds.) EUROCRYPT 2016. LNCS, vol. 9666, pp. 327–357. Springer, Heidelberg (2016). https://doi.org/10.1007/978-3-662-49896-5_12

[BCK+14] Benhamouda, F., Camenisch, J., Krenn, S., Lyubashevsky, V., Neven, G.: Better zero-knowledge proofs for lattice encryption and their application to group signatures. In: Sarkar, P., Iwata, T. (eds.) ASIACRYPT 2014. LNCS, vol. 8873, pp. 551–572. Springer, Heidelberg (2014). https://doi.org/10.1007/978-3-662-45611-8_29

[BGV12] Brakerski, Z., Gentry, C., Vaikuntanathan, V.: (Leveled) fully homomorphic encryption without bootstrapping. In: ITCS, pp. 309–325 (2012)

[CS03] Camenisch, J., Shoup, V.: Practical verifiable encryption and decryption of discrete logarithms. In: Boneh, D. (ed.) CRYPTO 2003. LNCS, vol. 2729, pp. 126–144. Springer, Heidelberg (2003). https://doi.org/10.1007/978-3-540-45146-4_8

[FGP14] Fiore, D., Gennaro, R., Pastro, V.: Efficiently verifiable computation on encrypted data. In: Proceedings of the 2014 ACM SIGSAC Conference on Computer and Communications Security, Scottsdale, AZ, USA, 3–7 November 2014, pp. 844–855 (2014)

[FMMC12] Fowler, A.G., Mariantoni, M., Martinis, J.M., Cleland, A.N.: Surface codes: towards practical large-scale quantum computation. Phys. Rev. A **86**, 032324 (2012)

[Gid18] Gidney, C.: Why will quantum computers be slow? (2018). http://algassert.com/post/1800. Accessed 6 Mar 2019

[LLNW18] Libert, B., Ling, S., Nguyen, K., Wang, H.: Lattice-based zero-knowledge arguments for integer relations. In: Shacham, H., Boldyreva, A. (eds.) CRYPTO 2018. LNCS, vol. 10992, pp. 700–732. Springer, Cham (2018). https://doi.org/10.1007/978-3-319-96881-0_24

[LM06] Lyubashevsky, V., Micciancio, D.: Generalized compact knapsacks are collision resistant. In: Bugliesi, M., Preneel, B., Sassone, V., Wegener, I. (eds.) ICALP 2006, Part II. LNCS, vol. 4052, pp. 144–155. Springer, Heidelberg (2006). https://doi.org/10.1007/11787006_13

[LN17] Lyubashevsky, V., Neven, G.: One-shot verifiable encryption from lattices. In: Coron, J.-S., Nielsen, J.B. (eds.) EUROCRYPT 2017. LNCS, vol. 10210, pp. 293–323. Springer, Cham (2017). https://doi.org/10.1007/978-3-319-56620-7_11

[LPR13] Lyubashevsky, V., Peikert, C., Regev, O.: On ideal lattices and learning with errors over rings. J. ACM **60**(6), 43 (2013). Preliminary Version Appeared in EUROCRYPT 2010

[LTV12] López-Alt, A., Tromer, E., Vaikuntanathan, V.: On-the-fly multiparty computation on the cloud via multikey fully homomorphic encryption. In: STOC, pp. 1219–1234 (2012)

[LWF+17] Lekitsch, B., et al.: Blueprint for a microwave trapped ion quantum computer. Sci. Adv. **3**(2), e1601540 (2017)

[MW16] Mukherjee, P., Wichs, D.: Two round multiparty computation via multikey FHE. In: Fischlin, M., Coron, J.-S. (eds.) EUROCRYPT 2016. LNCS, vol. 9666, pp. 735–763. Springer, Heidelberg (2016). https://doi.org/10.1007/978-3-662-49896-5_26

[Pip80] Pippenger, N.: On the evaluation of powers and monomials. SIAM J. Comput. **9**(2), 230–250 (1980)

[PR06] Peikert, C., Rosen, A.: Efficient collision-resistant hashing from worst-case assumptions on cyclic lattices. In: Halevi, S., Rabin, T. (eds.) TCC 2006. LNCS, vol. 3876, pp. 145–166. Springer, Heidelberg (2006). https://doi.org/10.1007/11681878_8

[PS16] Peikert, C., Shiehian, S.: Multi-key FHE from LWE, revisited. In: Hirt, M., Smith, A. (eds.) TCC 2016. LNCS, vol. 9986, pp. 217–238. Springer, Heidelberg (2016). https://doi.org/10.1007/978-3-662-53644-5_9

[WTS+18] Wahby, R.S., Tzialla, I., Shelat, A., Thaler, J., Walfish, M.: Doubly-efficient zkSNARKs without trusted setup. In: Proceedings of the 2018 IEEE Symposium on Security and Privacy, SP 2018, San Francisco, California, USA, 21–23 May 2018, pp. 926–943 (2018)

Publicly Verifiable Proofs
from Blockchains

Alessandra Scafuro[1], Luisa Siniscalchi[2(✉)], and Ivan Visconti[2]

[1] NCSU, Raleigh, USA
ascafur@ncsu.edu
[2] DIEM, University of Salerno, Fisciano, Italy
{lsiniscalchi,visconti}@unisa.it

Abstract. A proof system is publicly verifiable, if anyone, by looking at the transcript of the proof, can be convinced that the corresponding theorem is true. Public verifiability is important in many applications since it allows to compute a proof only once while convincing an unlimited number of verifiers.

Popular interactive proof systems (e.g., Σ-protocols) protect the witness through various properties (e.g., witness indistinguishability (WI) and zero knowledge (ZK)) but typically they are not publicly verifiable since such proofs are convincing only for those verifiers who contributed to the transcripts of the proofs. The only known proof systems that are publicly verifiable rely on a non-interactive (NI) prover, through trust assumptions (e.g., NIZK in the CRS model), heuristic assumptions (e.g., NIZK in the random oracle model), specific number-theoretic assumptions on bilinear groups or relying on obfuscation assumptions (obtaining NIWI with no setups).

In this work we construct publicly verifiable witness-indistinguishable proof systems from any Σ-protocol, based *only* on the existence of a very generic blockchain. The novelty of our approach is in enforcing a non-interactive verification (thus guaranteeing public verifiability) while allowing the prover to be interactive and talk to the blockchain (this allows us to circumvent the need of strong assumptions and setups). This opens interesting directions for the design of cryptographic protocols leveraging on blockchain technology.

1 Introduction

Blockchains are a surprising reality. Bitcoin, Ethereum, Cardano, Ripple, Zcash etc. [3,9,19,45,49] are all examples of permissionless[1] blockchains used to implement a cryptocurrency. Above all, Bitcoin [45] was the first cryptocurrency and

A. Scafuro—Work supported by NSF grant # 1012798.
L. Siniscalchi and I. Visconti—Research supported in part by the European Union's Horizon 2020 research and innovation programme under grant agreement No 780477 (project PRIViLEDGE) and in part by "GNCS - INdAM".

---

[1] In the remaining of the paper we will omit the adjective "permissionless" since this work focuses on the permissionless setting only.

© International Association for Cryptologic Research 2019
D. Lin and K. Sako (Eds.): PKC 2019, LNCS 11442, pp. 374–401, 2019.
https://doi.org/10.1007/978-3-030-17253-4_13

the first decentralized blockchain, and recently has celebrated 10 years of life. From a technical point of view, the robustness achieved by Bitcoin – which is a completely decentralized system developed by the voluntary effort of a large community – has motivated the cryptographic community to study the underlying consensus protocol in order to rigorously define what security properties it actually achieves and under which assumptions on the adversary [1,2,24,46]. Specifically, the works by Garay et al. [24] and Pass et al. [46] identify three properties achieved by the Bitcoin backbone protocol: *consistency*, which means that any two honest parties should share the same view of the blockchain, up to T blocks; *chain growth*, which means that the blockchain, as seen by the honest parties, will grow with a steady rate; and *chain quality*, which states that for any sequence of consecutive blocks, at least a fraction of them are contributed by honest parties. Such security properties have been adopted in all subsequent blockchain designs [2,34,47,48], enforcing the intuition that any blockchain protocol, taken as a black box, must guarantee them.

In this paper, we investigate how to leverage the sole assumption that a blockchain exists to achieve cryptographic tasks that do not seem possible without trust assumptions, heuristic security, strong computational assumptions or specific number-theoretic assumptions.

Publicly Verifiable Witness-Indistinguishable Proofs[2] (of Knowledge). We look at the problem of achieving "privacy-preserving" but still *publicly verifiable* proof systems. In a proof system a prover P wishes to convince a verifier V that a statement $x \in L$ is true, where L is an NP language. A proof system is privacy-preserving if the transcript of the proof somehow protects the privacy of the witness used in the proof, that is, it satisfies a witness hiding/indistinguishability (WH, WI) property [21] or zero-knowledge property [28]. A proof system is *publicly verifiable*, if any one, by looking at the transcript of the proof, can be convinced that the theorem is true. The verification procedure is therefore noninteractive. Public verifiability is useful in many settings where a prover would like to reuse the same proof with many verifiers, or in general when we want the proof to be transferable.

Public verifiability and witness hiding/indistinguishability are two important properties that are easy to achieve separately. To achieve public verifiability, ignoring any protection for the witness, one can simply publish the witness. If instead only witness hiding/indistinguishability is desired, ignoring public verifiability, there is a rich body of literature that explores many constructions, under several assumptions and for various languages. For example, WI proof systems for all NP are known from minimal assumptions [21,23], and various Σ-protocols [17] for specific languages, such as the language of DDH tuples [16,50] are WH/WI[3].

---

[2] In the introduction, informally we will generically use the word "proof" to refer also to *computationally sound* proofs [44].

[3] Every perfect special honest-verifier zero-knowledge (SHVZK) is WI [16]. If a Σ-protocol is computational SHVZK, then it could not enjoy the WI property [11],

Instead, achieving public verifiability *and* witness indistinguishability at the same time, is very non-trivial. In particular, any *interactive* witness indistinguishable proof, is intrinsically not publicly verifiable, since no one, besides the verifier who chooses the messages in the protocol, can be guaranteed that the prover did not know the messages in advance and thus believe in the validity of the proof. If the WI proof system is public coin, one could use the Fiat-Shamir transform [22] and replace the messages of the verifier with the output of the random oracle. However, this is an heuristic assumption that we wish to avoid towards providing publicly verifiable WI proof systems. We also would like to avoid trusted setups that have been widely used to get NIZK [6,13,21,31,38–41]. A relaxed trusted setup was used by [30] where there are multiple common reference strings and a majority of them is required to be honest. While such assumption is more realistic, we notice that the construction of [30] is based on a setup that does not reflect what is available in the real world. Our goal is to end up with publicly verifiable proofs that can be run exploiting a generic blockchain as setup.

The above discussion seemingly suggests that for a WI proof to be publicly verifiable, it must be either non-interactive. The only known non-interactive witness-indistinguishable proof systems without trusted setups and heuristic assumptions are due to:

- Groth, Ostrovsky and Sahai [31], and is based on specific number-theoretic hardness assumptions in bilinear groups. Such a scheme is not a proof of knowledge (for some languages, membership of an instance is trivially checkable by inspection, as for the case of knowledge of one out of two discrete logarithms, and what really matters is to make sure that a succeeding prover always knows a witness proving the truthfulness of the theorem).
- Bitansky and Paneth [5], and is based on indistinguishable obfuscation [26] and one-way permutations. In particular, their construction leverages the existence of witness encryption schemes [27] and the existence of ZAPs [18]. As in [31], the proposed approach does not provide the proof of knowledge property.

This is somewhat unsatisfactory. Given that we have a rich portfolio of interactive WI proof systems (and a large part of it consists of Σ-protocols), under various (weaker) complexity assumptions, optimized for different languages and that provide also proof-size optimizations, we would like to use these systems also when public verifiability is required. In this paper we ask the following question:

Can we construct a publicly-verifiable WI proof system given any Σ-protocol, by leveraging only the existence of a blockchain, and without any additional assumption?

---

however [25] shows that the OR-composition of computational SHVZK Σ-protocols is WI when all involved instances are true.

Goyal and Goyal in [29] proposed to use specific blockchains to construct a non-interactive zero-knowledge proof of knowledge. They do so by assuming the existence of a non-interactive WI proof system in the standard model (therefore inheriting all the limitations discussed above) that they use in conjunction with the assumption that the underlying blockchain is based on a proof-of-stake (PoS) consensus protocol. Their construction crucially leverages the PoS setting, and in addition also imposes other specific requirements on the cryptographic primitives used in the underlying consensus protocol (i.e., they require that the blockchain protocol uses a signature scheme which keys can be used also in a CPA-secure encryption scheme).

Our Contribution. As main contribution of this work we show how to construct a publicly verifiable WI proof systems from any Σ-protocol essentially assuming only the chain quality property of any blockchain[4].

We relax the connection between non-interactiveness and public verifiability by proposing a novel approach which consists in having an execution of a Σ-protocol where the prover is interactive, but the verifier's message is somehow played by the blockchain, making the verification process completely non-interactive for anyone who has access to the blockchain. If the underlying Σ-protocol additionally satisfies the delayed-input property (that is, a prover can compute the first round without knowing the theorem that she will prove, then our proof system allows preprocessing of the first message, and the actual proof can be computed in one-shot, therefore is completely non-interactive (modulo just one round of offline preprocessing done by the prover without knowing which instance will be proven and when). We also discuss the case of on-chain and off-chain verifiability depending on the blocksize supported by the blockchain and the communication efficiency of the underlying Σ-protocol.

Additionally, we observe that our publicly verifiable WI could be used in the construction of [29] to obtain a publicly verifiable ZK proof of knowledge with improved complexity assumptions relying on PoS blockchains. While the above observation might look an interesting improvement over the state-of-the art, more interestingly as additional contribution in this work we discuss some issues in the approach of [29] that can seemingly be addressed only by relying on additional assumptions (possibly implicit in [29] but that we believe it is worthy to make explicit).

1.1 Our Techniques

In order to construct publicly verifiable WI proofs we start with any Σ-protocol [17]. A Σ-protocol is a 3-round public-coin proof system that satisfies special soundness and special honest-verifier zero-knowledge (HVZK) properties, where the first and third round are computed by the prover and the second round

---

[4] The actual assumption is a bit different but is essentially captured by the chain quality property and some natural requirements that are seemingly satisfied by known blockchains.

is a random string sent by the verifier. A transcript (a, c, z) of a Σ-protocol is not publicly verifiable, indeed, due to the special HVZK property, anyone could come up with an accepting transcript by choosing c on its own. Our goal is to compute c in a verifiable manner, *without relying on the random oracle*, but simply leveraging the properties of *any* blockchain.

Challenge 1: Extracting Random Bits from Any Blockchain. Several works [4,7] have investigate the possibility of implementing a publicly verifiable beacon from the bitcoin blockchain. In particular, Bentov, Gabizon and Zuckerman in [4] show that, under stronger assumptions on the adversary (i.e., assuming that the adversary would not too often discard blocks that she computed), it is possible to extract unbiased and publicly verifiable bits from the bitcoin blockchain and thus realize a publicly verifiable beacon. Their result is somehow unsatisfactory for our goals since (1) it is tailored to bitcoin, (2) it makes additional assumptions on the adversary beyond the generic properties of a blockchain.

Our observation is that for our purposes we do not need the strong guarantees required by a publicly verifiable beacon. In particular, we don't need to precisely identify which string is random, we only need to ensure that, within a long string of bits, there exists a subsequence of λ bits that is sufficiently unpredictable to the adversary. In other words, in our setting, we can relax the requirement that the challenge c is a string of λ random bits, and instead consider c to be a much longer string composed by τ substrings $c_1, \ldots, c_\tau$, and the guarantee is that some of the substrings have sufficient min-entropy and are independently generated.

This relaxation allows us to extract enough random bits by essentially only assuming that the blockchain satisfies a property that is very similar to the η-chain quality property defined in [46]. Recall that η-chain quality states that for any K consecutive blocks in any chain held by some honest party, the fraction of blocks that were contributed by honest parties is at least η, with overwhelming probability in K. Our assumption is similar in the sense that we additionally observe that a block generated by an honest party must contain strings with high min-entropy, at the very least for the cryptographic material required to generate a block that must be unpredictable to an adversary (e.g., a wallet identifier used by the miner to cash the reward). More specifically, for each block created by a honest party, we identify a field that contains high min-entropy material (and discard the data concerned the transactions since they could have 0 entropy). We only need to assume that a constant number of blocks in a long enough sequence of blocks are computed by distinct honest parties (or even the same party as long as the special field is computed with independent randomness), then these chunks of the blocks can legitimately be considered as independent sources of randomness. Putting the above things together, we can think of K consecutive blocks as K potential sources of randomness, out of which a constant η (notice that we don't need a constant fraction, but just a constant) are guaranteed to be independent and have high min-entropy.

Our idea is therefore to leverage the above observations along with a multiple-source randomness extractor. The 3-source randomness extractor of Lin [36], given in input 3 high min-entropy independent sources, outputs a λ-bit truly random string. By using the η-chain quality property and the observation we made about honest blocks, our goal is to retrieve 3 honest blocks on which to apply the extractor. Since we don't know which blocks are honest, we will just consider all possible $\binom{K}{3}$ triples of distinct blocks over last K blocks of the blockchain. The η-chain quality guarantees that at least 3 of them are honest. We are guaranteed that there exists a triple of honest block chunks that are independent high min-entropy sources (we stress again, that we will consider only certain strings of the blocks that contain high min-entropy information, we also note that such strings have to be sufficiently long and have sufficient min-entropy for the output of the randomness extractor to be statistically close to uniform). By running the 3-source extractor on input such triple we will obtain a random string.

Are We Done by Just Using ZAPs? Since our approach consists in extracting random bits from the blockchain, one potential shortcut to obtain a publicly verifiable WI proof could consist of using the extracted bits as the first round of a ZAP, therefore requiring that the prover just computes the second round. This solution however comes with several shortcomings that we want to avoid.

First of all, the second round of the ZAP requires computational assumptions that are not necessarily used by the blockchain. For instance, the ZAP of [18] requires doubly-enhanced trapdoor permutations. In our case, we aim at relying on collision-resistant hash functions only.

Second, a ZAP is not a proof of knowledge and therefore is not useful when knowledge of the witness is what really matters. Indeed we will construct a proof of knowledge.

Third, as we observed above, our guarantee is only that 1 out of $\binom{K}{3}$ retrieved strings is random, but we don't know which one. The ZAP of [18] relies on an extremely long random string sent by the verifier. Obtaining such a huge random string (even assuming that we can extract many huge strings so that at least one of them is random), through extraction of random bits from the blocks of current blockchains is not realistic. Because of the above shortcomings, we devised a more elaborated construction that is in spirit much close to available blockchains, avoiding strong additional assumptions.

Challenge 2: Size of the Transcript and Off-Chain Public Verifiability. Given that we are able to extract random[5] bits from the blockchain, our proof system starting from a Σ-protocol and ending with a publicly verifiable WI proof follows naturally the Fiat-Shamir transform, and it works as follows.

The prover computes τ first rounds $a_1, \ldots, a_\tau$ of the Σ-protocol and publishes them on the blockchain $\mathbf{B}$, where $\tau = \binom{K}{3}$. Then, P waits for K new blocks (where K depends on the chain-consistency and chain-quality properties) added to the blockchain after the first message was posted. Let us denote such blocks as $B_1, \ldots, B_K$. The prover obtains challenges $c_1, \ldots, c_\tau$ by evaluating the

---

[5] We stress that we obtain a random string that is an unknown position in a vector of $\binom{K}{3}$ strings.

randomness extractor[6] on τ triples of distinct blocks in the set $\{B_1, \ldots, B_K\}$. Finally, P publishes the third rounds $z_1, \ldots, z_\tau$.

The above approach works only when each message a_i fits in the space allowed for a transaction in a block of the blockchain. This might not be necessarily true for any Σ-protocol. Some Σ-protocols might require a first round that is cubic or more in the security parameter and in the length of the statement, and once concretely instantiated, it might easily lead to a first round of few megabytes (and perhaps gigabytes if the instance is really large, also considering potential NP reductions), which can obviously be beyond what is allowed by a blockchain.

To overcome this problem, we propose to upload the hash of the first message, i.e., $H(\text{sid}|a_1||..||a_\tau)$ for an arbitrarily specified handle sid, on the blockchain. Then each c_i is computed as above, and then the third round would consist in revealing the a_i's and the answer z_i's to the verifier only. We call this the extended transcript. This approach allows public verifiability *off-chain*. That is, the entire proof cannot be downloaded from the blockchain, but must be obtained from another source (either the prover itself or another repository), and this is the standard way non-interactive proofs have always been propagated to be verified. We stress that the verifier here would not contribute in the computation of the transcript, she only needs to see the extended version of the transcript. Thus the proof is still reusable many times and is verifiable non-interactively (i.e., it is publicly verifiable). To choose a collision-resistant hash function H, we leverage the blockchain again. We observe that in all existent blockchains, the blocks are chained using a public collision-resistant hash function, that we can use in our proof system.

If instead a transaction of the blockchain can accommodate an a_i and a z_i of the underlying Σ-protocol, then we even get a better property (i.e., on-chain public verifiability) since the NIWI proof will appear completely in the blockchain and therefore there is no need to think about propagating a proof to reach several verifiers.

Additional Properties. Our publicly verifiable WI proof system achieves also additional properties such as:

- Pre-processing: if the underlying Σ-protocol is delayed input, that is, it allows the prover to compute the first round without knowing the theorem to be proven, then a prover can pre-process the first round, and then simply compute z when necessary. To leverage this property the underlying Σ-protocol must be an adaptive-input WI proof of knowledge. This additional requirement however does not significantly restrict the class of suitable Σ-protocols since there are known transformations that add such properties [10,12].
- Proof of knowledge: if the underlying WI proof system is special sound, then we show that our NIWI is also a proof of knowledge. The idea is that in the reduction, our knowledge extraction can simulate the blockchain to the malicious prover and change the relevant subsequence of the honest blocks

---

[6] More specifically, only some specific parts of the blocks are given as input to the randomness extractor.

(i.e., the cryptographic material bringing high min-entropy) in order to change the output of the randomness extractor and obtain a new challenge.

- Statistical WI PoK: when instantiating our compiler with the LS Σ-protocol [35] and its underlying commitments with a statistically hiding commitment scheme from collision-resistant hash functions, we obtain a statistical WI PoK system. Statistical WI allows to protect the privacy of the secret for ever, even w.r.t. future quantum/unbounded adversaries. The collision-resistant hash function that we use is again the one inferred by the blockchain.

On Achieving Publicly Verifiable Zero Knowledge. A natural next step is to use our publicly verifiable NIWI to construct a publicly verifiable zero-knowledge proof. For example, we could plug our NIWI in the construction provided in [29], that works on any NIWI. This would seemingly produce a NIZK without the strong hardness assumptions (i.e., a NIWI in the standard model required by [29]). We observe, however, that the approach taken in [29] to achieve the zero-knowledge property is affected by some issues that can be apparently tackled only by making additional assumptions on the blockchain protocol that do not seem to be applicable to real-world scenarios. We discuss such issues of the construction of [29] in Sect. 4. In conclusion, achieving publicly verifiable zero knowledge with mild assumptions w.r.t. the most currently used real-world blockchains is an interesting open question.

2 Definitions

Preliminary. We denote the security parameter by λ and use "$||$" as concatenation operator (i.e., if a and b are two strings then by $a||b$ we denote the concatenation of a and b). For a finite set Q, $x \leftarrow Q$ sampling of x from Q with uniform distribution. We use the abbreviation PPT that stays for probabilistic polynomial time. We use poly$(\cdot)$ to indicate a generic polynomial function. A *polynomial-time relation* $\mathcal{R}$ (or *polynomial relation*, in short) is a subset of $\{0,1\}^* \times \{0,1\}^*$ such that membership of (x,w) in $\mathcal{R}$ can be decided in time polynomial in $|x|$. For $(x,w) \in \mathcal{R}$, we call x the *instance* and w a *witness* for x. For a polynomial-time relation $\mathcal{R}$, we define the $\mathcal{NP}$-language $L_\mathcal{R}$ as $L_\mathcal{R} = \{x | \exists\, w : (x,w) \in \mathcal{R}\}$. Analogously, unless otherwise specified, for an $\mathcal{NP}$-language L we denote by $\mathcal{R}$ the corresponding polynomial-time relation (that is, $\mathcal{R}$ is such that $L = L_\mathcal{R}$). We will denote by $\mathcal{P}^{\mathsf{st}}$ a stateful algorithm $\mathcal{P}$ with state st.

Definition 1 (Computational indistinguishability). *Let* $X = \{X_\lambda\}_{\lambda \in \mathbb{N}}$ *and* $Y = \{Y_\lambda\}_{\lambda \in \mathbb{N}}$ *be ensembles, where* X_λ*'s and* Y_λ*'s are probability distribution over* $\{0,1\}^l$, *for same* $l = \mathsf{poly}(\lambda)$. *We say that* $X = \{X_\lambda\}_{\lambda \in \mathbb{N}}$ *and* $Y = \{Y_\lambda\}_{\lambda \in \mathbb{N}}$ *are* computationally indistinguishable, *denoted* $X \approx Y$, *if for every* PPT *distinguisher* $\mathcal{D}$ *there exists a negligible function* ν *such that for sufficiently large* $\lambda \in \mathbb{N}$,

$$\left| \Pr\left[\, t \leftarrow X_\lambda : \mathcal{D}(1^\lambda, t) = 1 \,\right] - \Pr\left[\, t \leftarrow Y_\lambda : \mathcal{D}(1^\lambda, t) = 1 \,\right] \right| < \nu(\lambda).$$

We note that in the usual case where $|X_\lambda| = \Omega(\lambda)$ and λ can be derived from a sample of X_λ, it is possible to omit the auxiliary input 1^λ. In this paper we also use the definition of *Statistical Indistinguishability*. This definition is the same as Definition 1 with the only difference that the distinguisher $\mathcal{D}$ is unbounded. In this case use $X \equiv_s Y$ to denote that two ensembles are statistically indistinguishable.

The definitions of standard tools can be found in Appendix A.

2.1 Blockchain Protocols

The next two sections follow almost verbatim (with some changes) from [29,46]. A blockchain protocol Γ consists of 4 polynomial-time algorithms (UpdateState, GetRecords, Broadcast, GetHash) with the following syntax.

- UpdateState(1^λ, st): It takes as input the security parameter λ, local state st and outputs the updated state st'.
- GetRecords(1^λ, st): It takes as input the security parameter λ and state st. It outputs the longest ordered sequence of valid blocks **B** (or simply blockchain) contained in the state variable, where each block in the chain itself contains an unordered sequence of records messages.
- Broadcast(1^λ, m): It takes as input the security parameter λ and a message m, and broadcasts the message over the network to all nodes executing the blockchain protocol. It does not give any output.
- GetHash(1^λ, **B**): It takes as input a security parameter 1^λ and a blockchain **B**, and outputs the description of a collision-resistant hash function $h(\cdot)$ publicly available in **B**.

As in [24,46] the blockchain protocol is also parameterized by a validity predicate V that captures semantics of any particular blockchain application. We will indicate with Γ^{V} a blockchain protocol Γ that has validate predicate V.

Remark on the Algorithm GetHash. We are assuming that a blockchain protocol Γ makes use of a collision-resistant hash function $h(\cdot)$ to maintain the blockchain structure (i.e., to chain the blocks). We explicitly add this algorithm since the same collision-resistant hash function used to chain blocks will then be used in cryptographic protocols that make use of the blockchain. Our assumption is obviously satisfied by the existing blockchains.

Execution of Γ^{V}. At a very high level, the execution of the protocol Γ^{V} proceeds in rounds that model time steps. Each participant in the protocol runs the UpdateState algorithm to keep track of the current (latest) blockchain state. This corresponds to listening on the broadcast network for messages from other nodes. The GetRecords algorithm is used to extract an ordered sequence of blocks encoded in the blockchain state variable, which is considered as the common public ledger among all the nodes. The Broadcast algorithm is used by a party when she wants to post a new message m on the blockchain. Note that the message m is accepted by the blockchain protocol only if it satisfies the validity predicate V given the current state, (i.e., the current sequence of blocks).

Following prior works [24,33,46], we define the protocol execution following the activation model of the Universal Composability framework of [8] (though like [29] we will not prove UC-security of our results). For any blockchain protocol Γ^V(UpdateState, GetRecords, Broadcast, GetHash), the protocol execution is directed by the environment $\mathcal{Z}(1^\lambda)$ where λ is the security parameter. The environment $\mathcal{Z}$ activates the parties as either honest or corrupt, and is also responsible for providing inputs/records to all parties in each round. All the corrupt parties are controlled by the adversary $\mathcal{A}$ that can corrupt them adaptively after that the execution of Γ^V started. The adversary is also responsible for delivery of all network messages. Honest parties start by executing UpdateState on input 1^λ with an empty local state $\mathsf{st} = \epsilon$.

- In round r, each honest party P_i potentially receives a message(s) m from $\mathcal{Z}$ and potentially receives incoming network messages (delivered by $\mathcal{A}$). It may then perform any computation, broadcast a message (using Broadcast algorithm) to all other parties (which will be delivered by the adversary; see below) and update its local state st_i. It could also attempt to "add" a new block to its chain (e.g., by running the mining procedure).
- $\mathcal{A}$ is responsible for delivering all messages sent by parties (honest or corrupted) to all other parties. $\mathcal{A}$ cannot modify the content of messages broadcast by honest parties, but it may delay or reorder the delivery of a message as long as it eventually delivers all messages within a certain time limit. The identity of the sender is not known to the recipient.
- At any point $\mathcal{Z}$ can communicate with adversary $\mathcal{A}$.

Blockchain Notation. With the notation $\mathbf{B} \preceq \mathbf{B}'$ we will denote that the blockchain $\mathbf{B}$ is a prefix of the blockchain $\mathbf{B}'$. We denote by $\mathbf{B}^{\lceil n}$ the chain resulting from "pruning" the last n blocks in $\mathbf{B}$. In the paper we will consider a block in the blockchain as a string $\mathbf{s}$ and a sub-string of $\mathbf{s}$ as a part of a block (a sub-block).

Let P be a party playing in Γ^V protocol, the view of P consists of the messages received during the execution of Γ^V, along with its randomness and its inputs. Let $\mathsf{Exec}^{\Gamma^V}(\mathcal{A}, \mathcal{H}, \mathcal{Z}, 1^\lambda)$ be the random variable denoting the joint view of all parties in the execution of protocol Γ^V with adversary $\mathcal{A}$ and set of honest parties $\mathcal{H}$ in environment $\mathcal{Z}$. This joint view view fully determines the execution. Let $\Gamma^V_{\mathsf{view}}(\mathcal{A}, \mathcal{H}, \mathcal{Z}, 1^\lambda)$ denote an execution of $\Gamma^V(\mathcal{A}, \mathcal{H}, \mathcal{Z}, 1^\lambda)$ producing view as joint view.

Some Constraints on the Adversary. In order show that a blockchain enjoys some useful properties like chain quality, prior works [24,46] restrict their analysis to compliant executions of Γ^V. Such blockchain implementation assume some restrictions on the power of the adversary. For instance, they require that any broadcasted message is delivered in a maximum number of time steps, as we have specified earlier, or could require secure erasure for honest parties. Those works showed that certain desirable security properties are respected except with negligible probability in any compliant execution. Obviously when in our work we claim results assuming some properties of the blockchain, we are taking into account compliant executions of the underlying blockchain protocol only. The same is done by [29].

Properties of a Γ^V Protocol. The following section is taken verbatim from [29], and the following properties where defined in previous works [24,46].

Chain consistency predicate. Let Consistent be the predicate such that Consistent$^\eta$(view) = 1 iff for all rounds $r \leq \tilde{r}$ and all parties P_i, P_j (potentially the same) in view such that P_i is honest at round r with blockchain **B** and P_j is honest at round $\tilde{r}$ with blockchain $\tilde{\mathbf{B}}$, we have that $\mathbf{B}^{\lceil \eta} \leq \tilde{\mathbf{B}}$.

Definition 2 *(Chain Consistency). A blockchain protocol Γ^V satisfies $n_0(\cdot)$-consistency with adversary $\mathcal{A}$, honest parties $\mathcal{H}$, and environment $\mathcal{Z}$, if there exists a negligible function $\nu(\cdot)$ such that for every $\lambda \in \mathbb{N}$, $\eta > n_0(\cdot)$ the following holds:*

$$\Pr\left[\text{ Consistent}^\eta(\text{view}) = 1 \middle| \text{view} \leftarrow \text{Exec}^{\Gamma^V}(\mathcal{A}, \mathcal{H}, \mathcal{Z}, 1^\lambda) \right] \geq 1 - \nu(\lambda).$$

Chain quality predicate. Let Quality be the predicate such that Quality$^\eta_{\mathcal{A}}$ (view, μ) = 1 iff for all rounds $r \geq \eta$ and all parties P_i in view such that P_i is honest at round r with blockchain **B**, we have that out of η last blocks in **B** at least μ fraction of blocks are "honest".

Note that a block is said to be honest iff it is mined by an honest party.

Definition 3 *(Chain Quality). A blockchain protocol Γ^V satisfies $(\mu(\cdot), n_0(\cdot))$-chain quality with adversary $\mathcal{A}$, honest parties $\mathcal{H}$, and environment $\mathcal{Z}$, if there exists a negligible function $\nu(\cdot)$ such that for every $\lambda \in \mathbb{N}$, $\eta > \eta_0(\lambda)$ the following holds:*

$$\Pr\left[\text{ Quality}^\eta_{\mathcal{A}}(\text{view}, \mu(\lambda)) = 1 \middle| \text{view} \leftarrow \text{Exec}^{\Gamma^V}(\mathcal{A}, \mathcal{H}, \mathcal{Z}, 1^\lambda) \right] \geq 1 - \nu(\lambda).$$

In the rest of the paper we will indicate with $(\mu(\cdot), n_0(\cdot))$ the chain quality parameters of Γ^V.

2.2   Definitions of Publicly Verifiable WI Arguments of Knowledge

Here we define publicly verifiable proofs over a blockchain. The main insight of our definition is that the verification is non-interactive, and the verifier does not need to be a party involved in the blockchain. The prover instead needs to actively interact with the blockchain.

Definition 4. *A pair of stateful* PPT *algorithms* $\Pi = (\mathcal{P}, \mathcal{V})$ *over a blockchain protocol* Γ^{V} *is a publicly verifiable argument system for the* $\mathcal{NP}$-*language* $\mathcal{L}$ *with witness relation* $\mathcal{R}$ *if it satisfies the following properties:*

Completeness. $\forall\ x, w$ *s.t.* $\mathcal{R}(x, w) = 1$, $\forall$ PPT *adversary* $\mathcal{A}$ *and set of honest parties* $\mathcal{H}$ *and environment* $\mathcal{Z}$, *assuming that* $\mathcal{P} \in \mathcal{H}$, *there exist negligible functions* $\nu_1(\cdot)$, $\nu_2(\cdot)$ *such that:*

$$\Pr \left[\mathcal{V}(x, \pi, \mathbf{B}) = 1 \ \vdots \ \begin{array}{c} \mathsf{view} \leftarrow \mathsf{Exec}^{\Gamma^{\mathsf{V}}}(\mathcal{A}, \mathcal{H}, \mathcal{Z}, 1^\lambda) \\ \pi \leftarrow \mathcal{P}^{\mathsf{st}_\mathcal{P}}(x, w) \\ \mathbf{B} = \mathsf{GetRecords}(1^\lambda, \mathsf{st}_j) \end{array} \right] \geq 1 - \nu_1(|x|) - \nu_2(\lambda)$$

where $\mathsf{st}_\mathcal{P}$ *denotes the state of* $\mathcal{P}$ *during the execution* $\Gamma^{\mathsf{V}}_{\mathsf{view}}(\mathcal{A}, \mathcal{H}, \mathcal{Z}, 1^\lambda)$. *The running time of* $\mathcal{P}$ *is polynomial in the size of the blockchain* $\mathbf{B} = \mathsf{GetRecords}(1^\lambda, \mathsf{st}_j)$ *where* st_j *is the state of* $\mathsf{P}_j \in \mathcal{H}$ *at the end of the execution* $\Gamma^{\mathsf{V}}_{\mathsf{view}}(\mathcal{A}, \mathcal{H}, \mathcal{Z}, 1^\lambda)$[7]. *Furthermore* st_j *is the state of an honest party* $\mathsf{P}_j \in \mathcal{H}$ *at the end of the execution* $\Gamma^{\mathsf{V}}_{\mathsf{view}}(\mathcal{A}, \mathcal{H}, \mathcal{Z}, 1^\lambda)$.
If all message of π *are in the blockchain then the proof is* on-chain, *and is* off-chain *otherwise.*

Soundness. $\forall\ x \notin \mathcal{L}$, $\forall$ *stateful* PPT *adversary* $\mathcal{A}$ *and set of honest parties* $\mathcal{H}$ *and environment* $\mathcal{Z}$, *there exist negligible functions* $\nu_1(\cdot)$, $\nu_2(\cdot)$ *such that:*

$$\Pr \left[\mathcal{V}(x, \pi, \mathbf{B}) = 1 \ \vdots \ \begin{array}{c} \mathsf{view} \leftarrow \mathsf{Exec}^{\Gamma^{\mathsf{V}}}(\mathcal{A}, \mathcal{H}, \mathcal{Z}, 1^\lambda) \\ \pi, x \leftarrow \mathcal{A}^{\mathsf{st}_\mathcal{A}} \\ \mathbf{B} = \mathsf{GetRecords}(1^\lambda, \mathsf{st}_j) \end{array} \right] \leq \nu_1(|x|) + \nu_2(\lambda)$$

where $\mathsf{st}_\mathcal{A}$ *denotes the state of* $\mathcal{A}$ *during the execution* $\Gamma^{\mathsf{V}}_{\mathsf{view}}(\mathcal{A}, \mathcal{H}, \mathcal{Z}, 1^\lambda)$. *Furthermore* st_j *is the state of an honest party* $\mathsf{P}_j \in \mathcal{H}$ *at the end of the execution* $\Gamma^{\mathsf{V}}_{\mathsf{view}}(\mathcal{A}, \mathcal{H}, \mathcal{Z}, 1^\lambda)$.

Definition 5. *A public verifiable argument system* $\Pi = (\mathcal{P}, \mathcal{V})$ *over a blockchain protocol* Γ^{V} *for the* $\mathcal{NP}$-*language* $\mathcal{L}$ *with witness relation* $\mathcal{R}$ *is an argument of Knowledge (AoK) if it satisfies the following property.*

Argument of Knowledge (AoK). *There is a stateful* PPT *algorithm* $\mathcal{E}$ *such that for all* x, *any stateful* PPT *adversary* $\mathcal{A}$ *and any set of honest parties* $\mathcal{H}$ *and environment* $\mathcal{Z}$, *there exist negligible functions* $\nu_1(\cdot)$, $\nu_2(\cdot)$ *such that:*

$$\left\{ (\mathsf{view}_\mathcal{A}) : \mathsf{view} \leftarrow \mathsf{Exec}^{\Gamma^{\mathsf{V}}}(\mathcal{A}, \mathcal{H}, \mathcal{Z}, 1^\lambda) \right\} \approx \left\{ (\mathsf{view}_\mathcal{A}) : \mathsf{view} \leftarrow \mathsf{Exec}^{\Gamma^{\mathsf{V}}}(\mathcal{A}, \mathcal{E}, \mathcal{Z}, 1^\lambda) \right\}$$

and

$$\Pr \left[\mathcal{V}(x, \pi, \mathbf{B}) = 0 \vee \mathcal{R}(x, w) = 1 \ \vdots \ \begin{array}{c} \mathsf{view} \leftarrow \mathsf{Exec}^{\Gamma^{\mathsf{V}}}(\mathcal{A}, \mathcal{E}, \mathcal{Z}, 1^\lambda) \\ \mathbf{B} = \mathsf{GetRecords}(1^\lambda, \mathsf{st}_j) \\ w \leftarrow \mathcal{E}(\pi, x), (\pi, x) \leftarrow \mathcal{A}^{\mathsf{st}_\mathcal{A}} \end{array} \right] \geq 1 - \nu_1(|x|) - \nu_2(\lambda)$$

---

[7] Note that after that $\mathcal{P}$ outputs π, the execution of $\Gamma^{\mathsf{V}}_{\mathsf{view}}(\mathcal{A}, \mathcal{H}, \mathcal{Z}, 1^\lambda)$ could still continue even though $\mathsf{st}_\mathcal{P}$ will not change anymore.

where $\mathsf{st}_{\mathcal{A}}$ denotes the state of $\mathcal{A}$ during the execution $\Gamma^{\mathsf{V}}_{\mathsf{view}}(\mathcal{A}, \mathcal{E}, \mathcal{Z}, 1^{\lambda})$ and $\mathsf{view}_{\mathcal{A}}$ is the view of $\mathcal{A}$ in view. Furthermore st_j is the state of an honest party $\mathsf{P}_j \in \mathcal{H}$ at the end of the execution $\Gamma^{\mathsf{V}}_{\mathsf{view}}(\mathcal{A}, \mathcal{H}, \mathcal{Z}, 1^{\lambda})$.

Definition 6. *A publicly verifiable argument system* $\Pi = (\mathcal{P}, \mathcal{V})$ *over a blockchain protocol* Γ^{V} *for the* $\mathcal{NP}$-*language* $\mathcal{L}$ *with witness relation* $\mathcal{R}$ *is witness indistinguishable (WI) if it satisfies the following property:*

$\forall\, x, w_0, w_1$ *s.t.* $\mathcal{R}(x, w_0) = 1$ *and* $\mathcal{R}(x, w_1) = 1$, $\forall$ *stateful* PPT *adversary* $\mathcal{A}$ *and set of honest parties* $\mathcal{H}$ *and environment* $\mathcal{Z}$, *assuming that* $\mathcal{P} \in \mathcal{H}$ *it holds that:*

$$\left\{ (\mathsf{view}_{\mathcal{A}}, \pi) : \mathsf{view} \leftarrow \mathsf{Exec}^{\Gamma^{\mathsf{V}}}(\mathcal{A}, \mathcal{H}, \mathcal{Z}, 1^{\lambda}), \pi \leftarrow \mathcal{P}^{\mathsf{st}_{\mathcal{P}}}(x, w_0) \right\}$$

$$\approx$$

$$\left\{ (\mathsf{view}_{\mathcal{A}}, \pi) : \mathsf{view} \leftarrow \mathsf{Exec}^{\Gamma^{\mathsf{V}}}(\mathcal{A}, \mathcal{H}, \mathcal{Z}, 1^{\lambda}), \pi \leftarrow \mathcal{P}^{\mathsf{st}_{\mathcal{P}}}(x, w_1) \right\}$$

where $\mathsf{st}_{\mathcal{P}}$ *denotes the state of* $\mathcal{P}$ *during the execution* $\Gamma^{\mathsf{V}}_{\mathsf{view}}(\mathcal{A}, \mathcal{H}, \mathcal{Z}, 1^{\lambda})$ *and* $\mathsf{view}_{\mathcal{A}}$[8] *is the view of* $\mathcal{A}$ *in* view.

Definition 7 (Min-Entropy). *Let* X *be a random variable with finite support* $\mathcal{X}$. *The min-entropy* $H_{\infty}(X)$ *of* X *is defined by*

$$H_{\infty}(X) = \min_{x \in \mathcal{X}} \log_2(1/\Pr[X = x]).$$

For $X \in \{0,1\}^n$, we call X a (n, λ)-source, where λ is the min-entropy of X (i.e., $\lambda = H_{\infty}(X)$).

Definition 8 (Honest Block Generation Algorithm). *An honest block-generation algorithm is a randomized* PPT *algorithm* $\mathsf{HB} : \{0,1\}^* \to \{0,1\}^n$, *where* $n = \mathsf{poly}(\lambda)$, *such that there exists a deterministic function* s *such that for all* $x \in \{0,1\}^*$, $v = s(\mathsf{HB}(x))$, $|v| = n$ *it holds that*

$$H_{\infty}(s(\mathsf{HB}(x))) \geq \lambda$$

and therefore $s(\mathsf{HB}(\cdot))$ *is a* (n, λ)-*source.*

Assumption 1. *Let* Γ^{V} *be a blockchain protocol. There exists* $t = \mathsf{poly}(\lambda)$ *such that the probability that a sequence of* t *consecutive blocks in a blockchain* **B** *generated via* Γ^{V} *does not include at least 3 blocks computed by a* HB *is negligible in* λ.

---

[8] Note that $\mathsf{view}_{\mathcal{A}}$ can contain auxiliary inputs from the execution of $\Gamma^{\mathsf{V}}(\mathcal{A}, \mathcal{H}, \mathcal{Z}, 1^{\lambda})$ that could continue after that π is computed.

3   Publicly Verifiable WI AoK

In order to construct an off-chain publicly verifiable non-interactive witness indistinguishable argument of knowledge $\Pi_{\mathsf{wi}} = (\mathcal{P}_{\mathsf{wi}}, \mathcal{V}_{\mathsf{wi}})$ over a blockchain protocol $\Gamma^{\mathsf{V}} = (\mathsf{UpdateState}, \mathsf{GetRecords}, \mathsf{Broadcast}, \mathsf{GetHash})$ for the $\mathcal{NP}$-language $\mathcal{L}^9$ we make use of the following tools:

- A 3-round delayed-input public-coin adaptive-input WI adaptive-input special sound proof system $\Pi_{\Sigma} = (\mathcal{P}_{\Sigma}, \mathcal{V}_{\Sigma})$ for the $\mathcal{NP}$-language $\mathcal{L}$ with instance length ℓ;
- An efficient procedure ExtProc that on input a 3-source randomness extractor $\mathsf{E}_{n,\lambda}$ and a sequence of $t = 3 \cdot q^{10}$ blocks $B_1, \ldots, B_t$ computes the following steps:
  1. Construct a set of sub-blocks (through the function s) adding a sub-block for each block in the sequence $\{B_1, \ldots, B_t\}$.
  2. Evaluate $\mathsf{E}_{n,\lambda}$ on all the possible subsets of 3 elements of the set of sub-blocks.
  3. Output all the $\binom{t}{3}$ evaluations of $\mathsf{E}_{n,\lambda}$.

$\Pi_{\mathsf{wi}} = (\mathcal{P}_{\mathsf{wi}}, \mathcal{V}_{\mathsf{wi}})$ works as follows.

$\mathcal{P}_{\mathsf{wi}}$ on input parameters (ℓ, s, t), an instance x and a witness w s.t. $\mathcal{R}(x, w) = 1$ computes the following steps, where x and w are used in the 7th step.

1. Set $st_{\mathcal{P}} = \epsilon$ and run $st_{\mathcal{P}} = \mathsf{UpdateState}(1^{\lambda}, st_{\mathcal{P}})$.
2. Run $\mathbf{B} = \mathsf{GetRecords}(1^{\lambda}, st_{\mathcal{P}})$, $h(\cdot) = \mathsf{GetHash}(1^{\lambda}, \mathbf{B})$.
3. Let $\tau = \binom{t}{3}$. For $i = 1, \ldots, \tau$: compute $\Sigma_i^1 \leftarrow \mathcal{P}_{\Sigma}(1^{\lambda}, \ell)$.
4. Compute $\alpha \leftarrow h(\Sigma_1^1, || \ldots || \Sigma_{\tau}^1)^{11}$ and post α on the blockchain by running $\mathsf{Broadcast}(1^{\lambda}, \alpha)$.
5. Run $st_{\mathcal{P}} = \mathsf{UpdateState}(1^{\lambda}, st_{\mathcal{P}})$, $\mathbf{B} = \mathsf{GetRecords}(1^{\lambda}, st_{\mathcal{P}})$ and wait until α is posted on the blockchain and further the chain is extended by t blocks.
6. Let B^* be the block of the blockchain $\mathbf{B}$ where the message α is posted and let $B_1, \ldots, B_t$ be the t consecutive blocks of the blockchain $\mathbf{B}$ after B^*. Run $\{\Sigma_i^2\}_{i=1}^{\tau} = \mathsf{ExtProc}(\mathsf{E}_{n,\lambda}, B_1, \ldots, B_t)$.
7. For $i = 1, \ldots, \tau$ compute $\Sigma_i^3 \leftarrow \mathcal{P}_{\Sigma}(\Sigma_i^2, x, w)$.
8. Run $st_{\mathcal{P}} = \mathsf{UpdateState}(1^{\lambda}, st_{\mathcal{P}})$ and $\mathbf{B}' = \mathsf{GetRecords}(1^{\lambda}, st_{\mathcal{P}})$.
9. Set $\pi = (x, \alpha, \{\Sigma_i^1, \Sigma_i^2, \Sigma_i^3\}_{i=1}^{\tau}, \mathbf{B}')$ and output π.

$\mathcal{V}_{\mathsf{wi}}$ on input the statement x, $\pi = (\alpha, \{\Sigma_i^1, \Sigma_i^2, \Sigma_i^3\}_{i=1}^{\tau}, \mathbf{B}')$, and a blockchain $\tilde{\mathbf{B}}$ works as follows. If the message α is not posted on the blockchain $\mathbf{B}'$ then $\mathcal{V}_{\mathsf{wi}}$ outputs 0 otherwise she continues with the following steps.

---

[9] We remark that our results require that Assumption 1 is not violated.
[10] q is s.t. $q \geq n_0(\lambda)$ where $(\mu(\cdot), n_0(\cdot))$ are the chain quality parameters of Γ^{V}.
[11] The hash value of the string $\Sigma_1^1, || \ldots || \Sigma_{\tau}^1$ is computed through a Merkle Tree [43], therefore α corresponds to the root of a Merkle Tree.

Let B^* be the block of the blockchain $\mathbf{B}'$ where the message α is posted. Let $B_1, \ldots, B_t$ be t blocks of the blockchain $\mathbf{B}'$ after B^*. $\mathcal{V}_{\mathsf{wi}}$ computes $\mathsf{h}(\cdot) = \mathsf{GetHash}(1^\lambda, \mathbf{B}')$, $\{\Sigma_i^2\}_{i=1}^\tau = \mathsf{ExtProc}(\mathsf{E}_{n,\lambda}, B_1, \ldots, B_t)$ and outputs 1 if the following conditions are satisfied:

1. $\mathbf{B}' \leq \tilde{\mathbf{B}}$;
2. $\alpha = \mathsf{h}(\Sigma_1^1 || \ldots || \Sigma_\tau^1)$;
3. $\mathcal{V}_\Sigma(x, \Sigma_i^1, \Sigma_i^2, \Sigma_i^3) = 1$ for $i = 1, \ldots, \tau$.

Theorem 1. *Under Assumption 1 and assuming the existence of one-to-one one-way functions[12], $\Pi_{\mathsf{wi}} = (\mathcal{P}_{\mathsf{wi}}, \mathcal{V}_{\mathsf{wi}})$ is a publicly verifiable off-chain adaptive-input witness-indistinguishable argument of knowledge over a blockchain protocol $\Gamma^\mathsf{V} = (\mathsf{UpdateState}, \mathsf{GetRecords}, \mathsf{Broadcast}, \mathsf{GetHash})$ for $\mathcal{NP}$.*

Completeness. Completeness follows by the chain consistency of Γ^V, the completeness of Π_Σ and the definitions of $\mathsf{h}, \mathsf{E}_{n,\lambda}$. We note that a candidate to instantiate $\Pi_\Sigma = (\mathcal{P}_\Sigma, \mathcal{V}_\Sigma)$ is the construction of [20] that is delayed-input, and adaptive-input secure in the variant of [10].

A Note on the Delayed-Input Property of Π_{wi}. Fixing any x, w, s.t. $\mathcal{R}(x, w) = 1$, we note that $\mathcal{P}_{\mathsf{wi}}$ is using x, w just to compute the 7th step of Π_{wi}. Therefore, Π_{wi} can compute the first 6 steps of Π_{wi} as a preprocessing phase, without knowing x or w (just the size is required). Then when (in any point in the future) x, w will be available $\mathcal{P}_{\mathsf{wi}}$ computes the last 3 steps of Π_{wi}.

We also want to point out that Theorem 1 holds even when there is no delayed-input property, therefore for any WI Σ-protocol, however in this case x, w are needed by $\mathcal{P}_{\mathsf{wi}}$ already when she computes the 1st step of Π_{wi}.

Adaptive-Input Witness Indistinguishability. In order to show that Π_{wi} enjoys the witness indistinguishability property we will consider the following 2 hybrid experiments.

Let $H_0(\lambda)$ be defined as the execution of Π_{wi}, where $\mathcal{P}_{\mathsf{wi}}$ uses the witness w_0. Let $H_1(\lambda)$ be defined as the execution of Π_{wi}, where $\mathcal{P}_{\mathsf{wi}}$ uses the witness w_1. Let $\mathcal{A}$ be the adversary as defined in Definition 6. The output of each experiment is the pair $(\pi, \mathsf{view}_\mathcal{A})$, where π is the transcript of Π_{wi} computed in the experiment and $\mathsf{view}_\mathcal{A}$ is the view of $\mathcal{A}$ in the experiment.

Claim 1. *For every x, w_0, w_1 s.t. $\mathcal{R}(x, w_0) = 1$ and $\mathcal{R}(x, w_1) = 1$ chosen adaptively by $\mathcal{A}$ it holds that $H_0(\lambda) \approx H_1(\lambda)$.*

Proof. Suppose by contradiction the above claim does not hold, then it is possible to construct a malicious verifier $\mathcal{V}_\Sigma^*$ that breaks the adaptive-input WI property of Π_Σ. Let $\mathcal{CH}$ be the challenger of adaptive WI game of Π_Σ. $\mathcal{V}_\Sigma^*$ will interact as a proxy between $\mathcal{CH}$ and $\mathcal{A}$ for the messages $\{\Sigma_i^1, \Sigma_i^3\}_{i=1}^\tau$ and she will compute

---

[12] The need of one-to-one one-way functions will be removed by Corollary 1. Theorem 1 also needs the existence of CRHFs, but as specified earlier we are assuming that a blockchain protocol along with a genesis block already specifies a CRHF.

all other messages following $\mathcal{P}_{wi}$ of H_0 (of H_1). In the end of the interaction $\mathcal{V}_{\Sigma}^*$ will output the output of $\mathcal{A}$.

In more details, $\mathcal{V}_{\Sigma}^*$ receives $\{\tilde{\Sigma}_i^1\}_{i=1}^\tau$ from $\mathcal{CH}$ and sets $\Sigma_i^1 = \tilde{\Sigma}_i^1$ for $i = \{1,\ldots,\tau\}$, then to compute the other steps of Π_{wi}, until Step 7, she acts as $\mathcal{P}_{wi}$ of H_0 (of H_1). In particular in Step 6 $\mathcal{V}_{\Sigma}^*$ computes $\{\Sigma_i^2\}_{i=1}^\tau$ as $\mathcal{P}_{wi}$ of H_0 (of H_1) does. $\mathcal{V}_{\Sigma}^*$ sends $\{\Sigma_i^2\}_{i=1}^\tau$ to $\mathcal{CH}$ along with x, w_0, w_1 obtained from $\mathcal{A}$. $\mathcal{V}_{\Sigma}^*$ receives $\{\tilde{\Sigma}_i^3\}_{i=1}^\tau$ from $\mathcal{CH}$ and sets $\Sigma_i^3 = \tilde{\Sigma}_i^3$ for $i = \{1,\ldots,\tau\}$, $\mathcal{V}_{\Sigma}^*$ completes the computations of π precisely as $\mathcal{P}_{wi}$ does in both H_0 and H_1. At the end of the execution $\mathcal{V}_{\Sigma}^*$ outputs what $\mathcal{A}$ outputs. The proof is concluded observing that if $\mathcal{CH}$ uses the witness w_0 to compute $\{\tilde{\Sigma}_i^3\}_{i=1}^\tau$ then the reduction is distributed as H_0. Instead if $\mathcal{CH}$ uses the witness w_1 to compute $\{\tilde{\Sigma}_i^3\}_{i=1}^\tau$ then the reduction is distributed as H_1.

From Claim 1 we can conclude that $H_0(\lambda) \approx H_1(\lambda)$.

High-Level Overview of the Proof of Adaptive-Input Soundness. Assume by contradiction that there exists $\mathcal{P}^*$ that produces with probability non-negligible p an accepting π of Π_{wi} w.r.t. $x \notin L$, where x is adaptively chosen by $\mathcal{P}^*$.

The proof will proceeds in 3 steps:

(1) We will describe an efficient procedure Proc that internally executes $\Gamma^V(\mathcal{P}^*, \mathcal{H}, \mathcal{Z}, 1^\lambda)$. Proc will use a specific rewinding strategy.
(2) We will prove that with non-negligible probability Proc outputs $(x, \Sigma_y^1, \Sigma_y^2, \Sigma_y^3), (\tilde{x}, \tilde{\Sigma}_y^1, \tilde{\Sigma}_y^2, \tilde{\Sigma}_y^3)$ s.t. $\Sigma_y^1 = \tilde{\Sigma}_y^1$ and $\Sigma_y^2 \neq \tilde{\Sigma}_y^2$.
(3) We will use the output of Proc to reach a contradiction. In more details, we note that by the adaptive-input soundness of Π_{Σ} there exists an algorithm that on input $(x, \Sigma_y^1, \Sigma_y^2, \Sigma_y^3)$ and $(\tilde{x}, \Sigma_y^1, \tilde{\Sigma}_y^2, \tilde{\Sigma}_y^3)$ in polynomial time outputs $w, \tilde{w}$ s.t. $\mathcal{R}(x, w) = 1$ and $\mathcal{R}(\tilde{x}, \tilde{w}) = 1$. Therefore we reach a contradiction since we were assuming that $x \notin \mathcal{L}$.

Adaptive-Input Soundness. We will now proceed more formally. Assume by contradiction that there exists $\mathcal{P}^*$ that produces with probability non-negligible p an accepting π of Π_{wi} w.r.t. $x \notin L$, where x is adaptively chosen by $\mathcal{P}^*$.

Let us fix $y \in \{1,\ldots,\tau\}$ and consider the following experiment Proc(y). Proc(y):

1. Sample at random a long enough string ω and execute $\Gamma^V(\mathcal{P}^*, \mathcal{H}, \mathcal{Z}, 1^\lambda)$ emulating all the honest parties $\mathcal{H}$ using different substrings of ω as randomnesses.
2. If $\mathcal{P}^*$ sends x and an accepting $\pi = (\alpha, \{\Sigma_i^1, \Sigma_i^2, \Sigma_i^3\}_{i=1}^\tau, \mathbf{B})$ w.r.t x compute step 3 and abort otherwise.
3. Let $\tilde{\mathbf{B}}$ be the blockchain that is defined by the state of some honest party after that the message α is posted by $\mathcal{P}^*$, and let B^* be the block in $\tilde{\mathbf{B}}$ where this message is posted.s that participate in the execution of Γ only after the block B^*. Rewind the execution of $\Gamma^V(\mathcal{P}^*, \mathcal{H}, \mathcal{Z}, 1^\lambda)$ just after the block B^* is created.
4. Sample at random a long enough string ω' and continue the execution of $\Gamma^V(\mathcal{P}^*, \mathcal{H}, \mathcal{Z}, 1^\lambda)$ emulating all the honest parties $\mathcal{H}$ using different substrings of ω' as randomnesses.

5. If $\mathcal{P}^\star$ sends $\tilde{x}$ and an accepting $\tilde{\pi} = (\tilde{\alpha}, \{\tilde{\Sigma}_i^1, \tilde{\Sigma}_i^2, \tilde{\Sigma}_i^3\}_{i=1}^\tau, \mathbf{B})$ w.r.t. $\tilde{x}$ compute the following steps and `abort` otherwise.

  5.1. If $(\tilde{\Sigma}_y^1 \neq \Sigma_y^1)$ stop and output $(\tilde{\Sigma}_1^1, ||\ldots ||\tilde{\Sigma}_y^1||\ldots ||\tilde{\Sigma}_\tau^1, \Sigma_1^1, ||\ldots ||\Sigma_y^1||\ldots ||\Sigma_\tau^1)$.

  5.2. If $(\tilde{\Sigma}_y^2 \neq \Sigma_y^2)$ stop and output $(x, \Sigma_y^1, \Sigma_y^2, \Sigma_y^3)$, $(\tilde{x}, \Sigma_y^1, \tilde{\Sigma}_y^2, \tilde{\Sigma}_y^3)$.

  5.3. If $(\tilde{\Sigma}_y^2 = \Sigma_y^2)$ stop and output 0.

Claim 2. The probability that `Proc` obtains from $\mathcal{P}^\star$ two accepting transcripts $\pi, \tilde{\pi}$ of Π_{wi} respectively in Step 2 and in Step 5 is at least p^2.

We note that the views defined by $\mathsf{Exec}^{\Gamma^V}(\mathcal{P}^\star, \mathcal{H}, \mathcal{Z}, 1^\lambda)$ before and after a rewind are statistically close because the procedure `Proc` acts in the same way after and before a rewind, using just a different randomness for emulating the honest parties. Therefore the view of $\mathcal{P}^\star$ before a rewind is statistically close to the view of $\mathcal{P}^\star$ after a rewind. Since, before step 3 we are assuming (by contradiction) that $\mathcal{P}^\star$ will compute an accepting π of Π_{wi} w.r.t. $x \notin \mathcal{L}$ with non-negligible probability p, after a rewind $\mathcal{P}^\star$ will do the same with the same probability. From the above arguments we can conclude that the claim holds.

Claim 3. For every $y \in \{1, ..., \tau\}$ if `Proc`(y) receives an accepting $\tilde{\pi}$ in Step 5, then `Proc`(y) outputs 0 with negligible probability.

Let $B_1, ..., B_t$ be the blocks used by $\mathcal{P}^\star$ to run $\{\Sigma_i^2\}_{i=1}^\tau = \mathsf{ExecProc}$ $(\mathsf{E}_{n,\lambda}, B_1, ..., B_t)$. From Assumption 1 it follows that at least 3 independent sub-blocks have enough[13] min-entropy. Therefore at least one 2nd round of Π_Σ obtained by `ExecProc` is distributed statistically close to the uniform distribution over $\{0,1\}^\lambda$. Let us call this 2nd round of Π_Σ the *good challenge*. It also follows from Assumption 1 that this min-entropy comes from the randomnesses used to run `HB` by honest parties. Let us call the independent sub-blocks with enough min-entropy the *good sub-blocks*. Note that the procedure `Proc` after a rewind changes the randomness used by the honest parties and thus from the definition of $\mathsf{E}_{n,\lambda}$ the *good challenge* produced by `ExecProc` will change before and after the rewind with overwhelming probability.

Claim 4. For every $y \in \{1, ..., \tau\}$ if `Proc`(y) receives an accepting $\tilde{\pi}$ in Step 5, then `Proc`(y) outputs $(\tilde{\Sigma}_1^1, ||\ldots ||\tilde{\Sigma}_y^1||\ldots ||\tilde{\Sigma}_\tau^1, \Sigma_1^1, ||\ldots ||\Sigma_y^1||\ldots ||\Sigma_\tau^1)$ s.t. $(\tilde{\Sigma}_y^1 \neq \Sigma_y^1)$ with negligible probability.

Suppose that the claim does not hold. We will show a PPT $\mathcal{A}_h$ that breaks the collision resistance of $h(\cdot)$. $\mathcal{A}_h$ chooses y at random from $\{1, ..., \tau\}$ and follows the steps of `Proc`(y). $\mathcal{A}_h$ outputs what `Proc`(y) outputs.

From Claim 3 it follows that if `Proc`(y) receives an accepting $\tilde{\pi}$ in Step 5 it outputs 0 with negligible probability, therefore $\mathcal{P}^\star$ produces two accepting proofs π and $\tilde{\pi}$ that contain two accepting transcripts of Π_Σ, namely $(x, \Sigma_y^1, \Sigma_y^2, \Sigma_y^3)$

---

[13] From Assumption 1, it follows that there are at least λ bits of min-entropy in each of the 3 sub-blocks.

and $(\tilde{x}, \Sigma_y^1, \tilde{\Sigma}_y^2, \tilde{\Sigma}_y^3)$. These two accepting transcripts of Π_Σ (by contradiction) differ also in the first round, but $\tilde{\Sigma}_y^1, \Sigma_y^1$ are s.t. $\mathsf{h}(\tilde{\Sigma}_1^1, \| \ldots \| \tilde{\Sigma}_y^1 \| \ldots \| \tilde{\Sigma}_\tau^1) = \mathsf{h}(\Sigma_1^1, \| \ldots \| \Sigma_y^1 \| \ldots \| \Sigma_\tau^1)$ since both π and $\tilde{\pi}$ are accepting. We can conclude that $\mathcal{A}_\mathsf{h}$ succeeds to find a collision for $\mathsf{h}(\cdot)$ with non-negligible probability.

From Claims 2, 3, 4 it follows that $\mathtt{Proc}$ outputs $(x, \Sigma_y^1, \Sigma_y^2, \Sigma_y^3)$, $(\tilde{x}, \Sigma_y^1, \tilde{\Sigma}_y^2, \tilde{\Sigma}_y^3)$ with probability at least p^2 therefore, due to the adaptive-input soundness of Π_Σ, using $(x, \Sigma_y^1, \Sigma_y^2, \Sigma_y^3)$ and $(\tilde{x}, \Sigma_y^1, \tilde{\Sigma}_y^2, \tilde{\Sigma}_y^3)$ it is possible to compute and extract $w, \tilde{w}$ s.t. $\mathcal{R}(x, w) = 1$ and $\mathcal{R}(\tilde{x}, \tilde{w}) = 1$. Therefore we reach a contradiction since we were assuming that $x \notin L$.

AoK. Let $\mathcal{P}^\star$ be an adversary that with non-negligible probability produces an accepting π of Π_wi w.r.t. x, where x is adaptively chosen by $\mathcal{P}^\star$. Then, we show an extractor $\mathcal{E}$ that with oracle access to $\mathcal{P}^\star$ in expected polynomial time outputs w s.t. $\mathcal{R}(x, w) = 1$.

$\mathcal{E}$ works as follows. $\mathcal{E}$ runs the firs 2 steps of $\mathtt{Proc}$ and if it obtains a first accepting transcript of Π_wi w.r.t. x, then it rewinds $\mathcal{P}^\star$ until it obtains a second accepting transcript of Π_wi, or a specific bound on the number of attempts is reached. $\mathcal{E}$ applies the same rewinding procedure described in steps 3 and 4 of $\mathtt{Proc}$.

Let us denote as colliding transcripts, two transcripts $(\Sigma^1, \Sigma^2, \Sigma^3)$ and $(\tilde{\Sigma}^1, \tilde{\Sigma}^2, \tilde{\Sigma}^3)$ of Π_Σ w.r.t. x and $\tilde{x}$, s.t. $\Sigma^1 = \tilde{\Sigma}_1$ and $\Sigma^2 \neq \tilde{\Sigma}_2$. We make the following observations:

Obs. (1) If in one of the rewinds $\mathcal{P}^\star$ gives a second accepting transcripts of Π_wi then from Claims 2, 3, 4 it follows that $\mathcal{E}$ obtains two colliding transcripts of Π_Σ.

Obs. (2) If $\mathcal{E}$ is able to obtain from $\mathcal{P}^\star$ two colliding transcripts of Π_Σ for statements $x, \tilde{x}$ then $\mathcal{E}$ runs the extractor of Π_Σ and obtains in polynomial time $w, \tilde{w}$ s.t. $\mathcal{R}(x, w) = 1$ and $\mathcal{R}(\tilde{x}, \tilde{w}) = 1$.

Obs. (3) For the same arguments exposed in Claim 2 in each rewind the view of $\mathcal{P}^\star$ before a rewind is statistically close to the view of $\mathcal{P}^\star$ after a rewind.

Therefore from standard arguments it follows that in expected polynomial time $\mathcal{E}$ outputs w s.t. $\mathcal{R}(x, w) = 1$ with overwhelming probability.

We note that a candidate to instantiate $\Pi_\Sigma = (\mathcal{P}_\Sigma, \mathcal{V}_\Sigma)$ is the construction of LS [20] that is delayed-input, and adaptive-input in the variant of [10]. Furthermore if the underling commitment scheme of LS is instantiate from CRHFs, then LS enjoys the statistical WI property. Since we can obtain the description of a CRHF from $\mathsf{GetHash}$, it follows that it is possible to instantiate Π_wi over a blockchain protocol Γ^V without requiring additional computational assumptions.

Corollary 1. *If Assumption 1 holds, then $\Pi_\mathsf{wi} = (\mathcal{P}_\mathsf{wi}, \mathcal{V}_\mathsf{wi})$ is a publicly verifiable off-chain statistical adaptive-input witness indistinguishable AoK over a blockchain protocol $\Gamma^\mathsf{V} = (\mathsf{UpdateState}, \mathsf{GetRecords}, \mathsf{Broadcast}, \mathsf{GetHash})$ for $\mathcal{NP}$*[14].

---

[14] Again, we are implicitly assuming that a CRHF comes for free from a blockchain.

3.1 An On-Chain Publicly Verifiable WI AoK

In order to construct an on-chain publicly verifiable non-interactive witness indistinguishable argument of knowledge $\Pi_{wi} = (\mathcal{P}_{wi}, \mathcal{V}_{wi})$ over blockchain protocol $\Gamma_n^V = (\text{UpdateState}, \text{GetRecords}, \text{Broadcast}, \text{GetHash})$ for the $\mathcal{NP}$-language $\mathcal{L}$ we make use of the following tools:

- A 3-round communication-efficient[15] delayed-input public-coin adaptive-input WI adaptive-input special sound proof system $\Pi_\Sigma = (\mathcal{P}_\Sigma, \mathcal{V}_\Sigma)$ for $\mathcal{L}$ with instance length ℓ;
- An efficient procedure $\texttt{ExtProc}$ that on input a 3-source randomness extractor $\mathsf{E}_{n,\lambda}$ and a sequence of $t = 3 \cdot q^{16}$ blocks $B_1, \ldots, B_t$ computes the following steps:
  1. Construct a set of sub-blocks (through the function s) adding a sub-block for each block in the sequence $\{B_1, \ldots, B_t\}$.
  2. Evaluate $\mathsf{E}_{n,\lambda}$ on all the possible subsets of 3 elements of set of sub-blocks.
  3. Output all the $\binom{t}{3}$ evaluations of $\mathsf{E}_{n,\lambda}$.

$\Pi_{wi} = (\mathcal{P}_{wi}, \mathcal{V}_{wi})$ works as follow.

$\mathcal{P}_{wi}$ on input the parameter ℓ, an instance x and a witness w s.t. $\mathcal{R}(x, w) = 1$ computes the following steps, where x, w are used in the 5th step.

1. Set $st_\mathcal{P} = \epsilon$ and run $st_\mathcal{P} = \text{UpdateState}(1^\lambda, st_\mathcal{P})$.
2. Set $\tau = \binom{t}{3}$. For $i = 1, \ldots, \tau$ compute $\Sigma_i^1 \leftarrow \mathcal{P}_\Sigma(1^\lambda, \ell)$ and post Σ_i^1 on the blockchain by executing $\text{Broadcast}(1^\lambda, \Sigma_i^1)$.
3. Run $st_\mathcal{P} = \text{UpdateState}(1^\lambda, st_\mathcal{P})$ and $\mathbf{B} = \text{GetRecords}(1^\lambda, st_\mathcal{P})$ wait until the messages $\{\Sigma_i^1\}_{i=1}^\tau$ are posted on the blockchain and further the chain is extended by t blocks.
4. Let B^* be the last block of the blockchain $\mathbf{B}$ where the messages $\{\Sigma_i^1\}_{i=1}^\tau$ are posted and let $B_1, \ldots, B_t$ be t blocks of the blockchain $\mathbf{B}$ after B^*. Run $\{\Sigma_i^2\}_{i=1}^\tau = \texttt{ExtProc}(\mathsf{E}_{n,\lambda}, B_1, \ldots, B_t)$.
5. For $i = 1, \ldots, \tau$ compute $\Sigma_i^3 \leftarrow \mathcal{P}_\Sigma(\Sigma_i^2, x, w)$ and post Σ_i^3 on the blockchain executing $\text{Broadcast}(1^\lambda, \Sigma_i^3)$.
6. Run $st_\mathcal{P}' = \text{UpdateState}(1^\lambda, st_\mathcal{P})$, $\mathbf{B}' = \text{GetRecords}(1^\lambda, st_\mathcal{P}')$ and wait for messages $\{\Sigma_i^3\}_{i=1}^\tau$ to be posted on the blockchain.
7. Set $\pi = (\{\Sigma_i^1, \Sigma_i^2, \Sigma_i^3\}_{i=1}^\tau, \mathbf{B}')$.

$\mathcal{V}_{wi}$ on input the statement x, $\pi = (\{\Sigma_i^1, \Sigma_i^2, \Sigma_i^3\}_{i=1}^\tau, \mathbf{B}')$, and a blockchain $\tilde{\mathbf{B}}$. If the messages $\{\Sigma_i^1\}_{i=1}^\tau$ are not posted on the blockchain $\mathbf{B}'$ $\mathcal{V}_{wi}$ outputs 0 otherwise she continues with the following steps.

Let B^* be the last block of the blockchain $\mathbf{B}'$ where the messages $\{\Sigma_i^1\}_{i=1}^\tau$ are posted. Let $B_1, \ldots, B_t$ be t blocks of the blockchain $\mathbf{B}'$ after B^*. $\mathcal{V}_{wi}$ computes $\{\Sigma_i^2\}_{i=1}^\tau = \texttt{ExtProc}(\mathsf{E}_{n,\lambda}, B_1, \ldots, B_t)$ and outputs 1 if the following conditions are satisfied:

---

[15] For this construction we require that the messages of Π_Σ are small enough to be posted in a block of the blockchain.

[16] q is s.t. $q \geq n_0(\lambda)$ where $(\mu(\cdot), n_0(\cdot))$ are the chain quality parameters of Γ^V.

1. $\mathbf{B}' \leq \tilde{\mathbf{B}}$;
2. The blockchain $\mathbf{B}'$ contains the messages $\{\Sigma_i^1, \Sigma_i^3\}_{i=1}^\tau$, and the messages $\{\Sigma_i^3\}_{i=1}^\tau$ are posted at least t blocks after B^*;
3. $\mathcal{V}_\Sigma(x, \Sigma_i^1, \Sigma_i^2, \Sigma_i^3) = 1$ for $i = 1, \dots, \tau$.

Theorem 2. *If Assumption 1 holds, then* $\Pi_{\mathsf{wi}} = (\mathcal{P}_{\mathsf{wi}}, \mathcal{V}_{\mathsf{wi}})$ *is a publicly verifiable on-chain adaptive-input witness indistinguishable argument of knowledge over a blockchain protocol* $\Gamma^\mathsf{V} = (\mathsf{UpdateState}, \mathsf{GetRecords}, \mathsf{Broadcast}, \mathsf{GetHash})$ *for $\mathcal{NP}$-language $\mathcal{L}$.*

The proof is almost identical to the one showed for Theorem 1 and therefore we omit it.

A Note on the Delayed-Input Property of Π_{wi}. Fixing any x, w, s.t. $\mathcal{R}(x, w) = 1$, as for the off-chain construction also in this construction $\mathcal{P}_{\mathsf{wi}}$ is using x, w just to compute the 5th step of Π_{wi}. Therefore, Π_{wi} can compute the first 4 steps of Π_{wi} as a preprocessing phase, without knowing x or w (just the size is required). Then when (in any point in the future) x, w will be available $\mathcal{P}_{\mathsf{wi}}$ computes the last 2 steps of Π_{wi}.

We also want to point out that Theorem 2 holds for any WI Σ-protocol, even without the delayed-input property. However in this case x, w are needed by $\mathcal{P}_{\mathsf{wi}}$ already when she computes the 1st step of Π_{wi}.

On the Instantiation of the Adaptive-Input Special-Sound Π_Σ. We note that the work of [12] shows a compiler that works for a class of delayed-input perfect Σ-protocol described in [14,15,42]. This compiler on input a perfect Σ-protocol Π outputs a variant of Π that is adaptive-input special sound. The compiler does not require any additional assumption.

4   On Publicly Verifiable Zero Knowledge via [29]

Our publicly verifiable WI argument of knowledge in the blockchain model focuses on using a blockchain (as much as possible) as a black-box, therefore using the generic properties that a blockchain offers (in a black-box sense), such as chain consistency and chain quality, and some other natural assumptions that seemingly make sense with respect to known real-world blockchains. A natural challenging open question consists of obtaining a publicly verifiable zero-knowledge argument using a generic blockchain. The reason why we see this very challenging is that there are several subtleties that seem to be very non-trivial to address without making strong assumptions on the underlying blockchain protocol, and therefore losing generality.

Consider the NIZK constructed in [29]. Their construction works for proof-of-stake based blockchains only and the underlying assumption is that no adversary can control the majority of stake, at any point in time, and thus she cannot compute a fork. This assumption is leveraged in the zero-knowledge proof where one assumes that the simulator, controlling the honest parties, controls a majority of the stake (technically the secret keys associated to the public addresses owning a majority of the stake), and this information can be used to compute a fork at any point in time. Given such special power for the simulator, the zero-knowledge argument of [29] consists of a set of n encryptions $e_1, \ldots, e_n$ and a NIWI proof for the theorem: "$(e_1, \ldots, e_n)$ are valid encryptions under public keys of n stakeholders" AND "either they are encryptions of shares of a witness for $x \in L$ or of shares of a valid fork of the blockchain". One of the most appealing properties of this scheme is that the size of the NIZK is independent of the number of total stakeholders, but depends only on parameters concerning the blockchain chain-quality property.

First of all notice that construction of [29] focuses on proof-of-stake based blockchains in order to have a proof that can be sound for ever. Indeed the same approach would fail if a proof-of-work is used instead of a proof-of-stake since clearly in the future an adversary would be able to compute a fork in the past, and therefore an accepting proof of a false theorem.

We note, however, that the approach of [29] has a subtle issue that prevents this construction to be usable in generic proof-of-stake blockchains. The issue stems from the fact that the non-interactive proof consists of encryptions of shares of the witness under the public keys of n stakeholders. The idea behind this approach was that as long as the majority of such keys belongs to a honest "stake" (and assume that the latter will never collude), one can assume that the adversary will never collect enough keys to decrypt the witness. However, this assumption seems to be unsubstantiated in general, if we don't make any assumption on the proof-of-stake blockchain protocol. To see why, assume that honest stakeholders decide to refresh their keys often, in particular, assume that upon each transaction they decide to move their stake from a public key pk_i to a freshly computed public key pk_i' and, in order to publicly disable the old pk_i, they will simply publish sk_i. This behavior could even be required in the blockchain protocol, and therefore always executed by honest parties. Note that, in this case, the assumption on the majority of stake is still preserved. Indeed, the majority of stake is still controlled by the honest parties. However, the keys have *evolved* and thus the keys used at time t in a zero-knowledge proof might be completely exposed at time $t + \delta$ (for some $\delta > 0$) thus invalidating the ZK property. We note that this issue exists even in presence of static adversaries (which is the assumption in [29]) since the honest parties remain honest parties throughout, they simply change their keys and this is not prohibited by the blockchain protocol (and in general it could be even enforced).

More in general, the scenario described above suggests that the above approach to design a non-interactive zero-knowledge proof system cannot retain any security in presence of an adversary who can somehow obtain the keys *after* having observed the zero-knowledge proof. Even assuming that keys do not evolve over time (and a party would never expose her old secret on the blockchain), there are few realistic scenarios that would allow an adversary to obtain such keys, in a blockchain setting. In such setting is indeed more natural to assume that the adversary is adaptive, and the corrupted parties can be chosen over time, for example, depending on the content of the blockchain, or the stake gained or lost by a certain key. Since parties are rational, it might be convenient to them to "sell" their secret keys with lower stake in exchange for a public key with slightly higher stake. Thus, assuming that a zero-knowledge proof was computed using keys $(k_{i_1}, \ldots, k_{i_n})$, an adversary could target such keys, and at later stage, when the total stake of the system has increased, the adversary can corrupt the stakeholders associated to those keys, in such a way that the adversary still does not possess the majority of the stake – and thus the proof of stake assumption is not invalidated– but she has enough information to break the zero-knowledge property (for instance in the case of [29] the adversary has enough informations to decrypt the witness).

Finally we also remark that current blockchains exist because of the rewards that participants hope to obtain sharing their resources for the execution of the blockchain protocol. It is therefore natural to think that an honest party would be fine with giving up the secret key corresponding to a currently empty wallet receiving back a revenue. It is completely unknown to an honest party of a blockchain protocol the fact that there could be a cryptographic protocol designed on top of the blockchain that relies on honest parties keeping private some secret keys for ever, even in case they do not have any value.

A   Standard Tools

Definition 9 (One-way function (OWF)). *A function $f : \{0,1\}^* \to \{0,1\}^*$ is called one way if the following two conditions hold:*

- *there exists a deterministic polynomial-time algorithm that on input y in the domain of f outputs $f(y)$;*
- *for every PPT algorithm $\mathcal{A}$ there exists a negligible function ν, such that for every auxiliary input $z \in \{0,1\}^{\mathsf{poly}(\lambda)}$:*

$$\Pr\left[\, y{\leftarrow}\{0,1\}^* : \mathcal{A}(f(y), z) \in f^{-1}(f(y)) \,\right] < \nu(\lambda).$$

We say, also, that a OWF f is a one-way permutation (OWP) *if f is a permutation.*

Definition 10 (Hash Function [32]). *An hash function is a pair of PPT algorithms $\Pi = (\mathsf{Gen}, H)$ fulfilling the following:*

- *Gen is a probabilistic algorithm which takes as input a security parameter λ and outputs a key s.*
- *There exists $l = \mathsf{poly}(\lambda)$ such that H is (deterministic) polynomial time algorithm that takes as input a key s and any string $x \in \{0,1\}^*$ and outputs a string $H(s,x) \in \{0,1\}^l$.*

Definition 11 (Collision-Resistant Hash Functions (CRHFs) [32]). *A hash function $\Pi = (\mathsf{Gen}, H)$ is collision resistant if for all PPT adversaries $\mathcal{A}$ there exists a negligible function ν such that:*

$$\Pr\left[\, H(s,x) = H(s,x') \wedge x \neq x' : s \leftarrow \mathsf{Gen}(1^\lambda), (x,x') \leftarrow \mathcal{A}(s) \,\right] \leq \nu(\lambda)$$

In this paper we denote by $h(\cdot)$ a CRHFs where the description of the hash function (i.e., the key s) is publicly available either in the blockchain protocol or in the genesis block of the blockchain.

Definition 12 (Witness Indistinguishable (WI)). *An argument/proof system $\Pi = (\mathcal{P}, \mathcal{V})$, is* Witness Indistinguishable (WI) *for a relation $\mathcal{R}$ if, for every malicious* PPT *verifier $\mathcal{V}^*$, there exists a negligible function ν such that for all x, w, w' such that $(x, w) \in \mathcal{R}$ and $(x, w') \in \mathcal{R}$ it holds that:*

$$\left| \Pr \langle \mathcal{P}(w), \mathcal{V}^* \rangle (x) = 1 - \Pr \langle \mathcal{P}(w'), \mathcal{V}^* \rangle (x) = 1 \right| < \nu(|x|).$$

Obviously one can generalize the above definitions of WI to their natural adaptive-input variants, where the adversarial verifier can select the statement and the witnesses adaptively, before the prover plays the last round. We note that [23] prove that WI is preserved under self-concurrent composition, i.e. when multiple instance of Π are played concurrently.

Definition 13 (Proof/argument system). *A pair of* PPT *interactive algorithms $\Pi = (\mathcal{P}, \mathcal{V})$ constitute a* proof system *(resp., an* argument system*) for an $\mathcal{NP}$-language L, if the following conditions hold:*

Completeness: *For every $x \in L$ and w such that $(x, w) \in \mathcal{R}_L$, it holds that:*

$$\Pr [\, \langle \mathcal{P}(w), \mathcal{V} \rangle (x) = 1 \,] = 1.$$

Soundness*: For every interactive (resp.,* PPT *interactive) algorithm $\mathcal{P}^\star$, there exists a negligible function ν such that for every $x \notin L$ and every z:*

$$\Pr [\, \langle \mathcal{P}^\star(z), \mathcal{V} \rangle (x) = 1 \,] < \nu(|x|).$$

A proof/argument system $\Pi = (\mathcal{P}, \mathcal{V})$ for an $\mathcal{NP}$-language L, enjoys *delayed-input* completeness if $\mathcal{P}$ needs x and w only to compute the last round and $\mathcal{V}$ needs x only to compute the output. Before that, $\mathcal{P}$ and $\mathcal{V}$ run having as input only the size of x. The notion of delayed-input completeness was defined in [12].

An interactive protocol $\Pi = (\mathcal{P}, \mathcal{V})$ is *public coin* if, at every round, $\mathcal{V}$ simply tosses a predetermined number of coins (i.e. a random challenge) and sends the outcome to the prover. Moreover we say that the transcript τ of an execution $b = \langle \mathcal{P}(z), \mathcal{V} \rangle (x)$ is *accepting* if $b = 1$.

A *3-round protocol* $\Pi = (\mathcal{P}, \mathcal{V})$ for a relation $\mathcal{R}$ is an interactive protocol played between a prover $\mathcal{P}$ and a verifier $\mathcal{V}$ on common input x and private input w of $\mathcal{P}$ s.t. $(x, w) \in \mathcal{R}$. In a 3-round protocol the first message a and the third message z are sent by $\mathcal{P}$ and the second messages c is played by $\mathcal{V}$. At the end of the protocol $\mathcal{V}$ decides to accept or reject based on the data that he has seen, i.e. $x, \mathsf{a}, \mathsf{c}, \mathsf{z}$.

We usually denote the message c sent by $\mathcal{V}$ as a *challenge*, and as *challenge length* the number of bit of c.

Definition 14 (Σ-Protocol). *A 3-round public-coin protocol $\Pi = (\mathcal{P}, \mathcal{V})$ for a relation $\mathcal{R}$ is a Σ-Protocol if the following properties hold:*

- *Completeness: if $(\mathcal{P}, \mathcal{V})$ follow the protocol on input x and private input w to $\mathcal{P}$ s.t. $(x, w) \in \mathcal{R}$, $\mathcal{V}$ always accepts.*
- *Special soundness: if there exists a polynomial time algorithm such that, for any pair of accepting transcripts on input x, $(\mathsf{a}, \mathsf{c}_1, \mathsf{z}_1)$ $(\mathsf{a}, \mathsf{c}_2, \mathsf{z}_2)$ where $\mathsf{c}_1 \neq \mathsf{c}_2$, outputs witnesses w such that $(x, w) \in \mathcal{R}$.*
- *Special Honest Verifier Zero-knowledge (SHVZK): there exists a PPT simulator algorithm S that for any $x \in L$, security parameter λ and any challenge c works as follow: $(\mathsf{a}, \mathsf{z}) \leftarrow \mathsf{S}(1^\lambda, x, \mathsf{c})$. Furthermore, the distribution of the output of S is computationally indistinguishable from the distribution of a transcript obtained when $\mathcal{V}$ sends S as challenges and $\mathcal{P}$ runs on common input x and any w such that $(x, w) \in \mathcal{R}$.*

Definition 15. *A perfect Σ-Protocol is Σ-Protocol that satisfies a strong SHVZK requirement, that is:*

Perfect Special Honest Verifier Zero-knowledge: there exists a PPT simulator algorithm S that for any $x \in L$, security parameter λ and any challenge c works as follow: $(\mathsf{a}, \mathsf{z}) \leftarrow \mathsf{S}(1^\lambda, x, \mathsf{c})$. Furthermore, the distribution of the output of S is perfect indistinguishable from the distribution of a transcript obtained when $\mathcal{V}$ sends S as challenges and $\mathcal{P}$ runs on common input x and any w such that $(x, w) \in \mathcal{R}$.

Theorem 3 [16]. *Every perfect Σ-protocol is perfect WI.*

Theorem 4 [25]. *The OR-composition of Σ-Protocols is WI.*

Definition 16. *A delayed-input 3-round system $\Pi = (\mathcal{P}, \mathcal{V})$ for relation $\mathcal{R}$ enjoys adaptive-input special soundness if there exists a polynomial time algorithm Ext such that, for any pair of accepting transcripts $\mathsf{a}, \mathsf{c}_1, \mathsf{z}_1$ for input x_1 and $\mathsf{a}, \mathsf{c}_2, \mathsf{z}_2$ for input x_2 with $\mathsf{c}_1 \neq \mathsf{c}_2$, outputs witnesses w_1 and w_2 such that $(x_1, w_1) \in \mathcal{R}$ and $(x_2, w_2) \in \mathcal{R}$.*

Definition 17 (Proof of Knowledge [37]). *A protocol that is complete $\Pi = (\mathcal{P}, \mathcal{V})$ is a proof of knowledge (PoK) for the relation $\mathcal{R}_\mathsf{L}$ if there exist a probabilistic expected polynomial-time machine Ext, called the extractor, such that for every algorithm $\mathcal{P}^\star$, there exists a negligible function ν, every statement $x \in \{0,1\}^\lambda$, every randomness $r \in \{0,1\}^\star$ and every auxiliary input $z \in \{0,1\}^\star$,*

$$\Pr\left[\, \langle \mathcal{P}_r^\star(z), \mathcal{V} \rangle(x) = 1 \,\right] \leq \Pr\left[\, w \leftarrow \mathsf{Ext}^{\mathcal{P}_r^\star(z)}(x) : (x, w) \in \mathcal{R} \,\right] + \nu(\lambda).$$

We also say that an argument system Π is a argument of knowledge (AoK) if the above condition holds w.r.t. any PPT $\mathcal{P}^\star$.

In this paper we also consider the *adaptive-input* PoK/AoK property for all the protocols that enjoy delayed-input completeness. Adaptive-input PoK/AoK ensures that the PoK/AoK property still holds when a malicious prover can choose the statement adaptively at the last round.

Definition 18. *Let X, Y be two random variables that takes values in V (i.e., V is the union of supports of X and Y). The statistical distance between X and Y is defined as follows:*

$$\frac{1}{2} \sum_{v \in V} |\Pr[\,X = v\,] - \Pr[\,Y = v\,]|.$$

Definition 19 [36] *[s - Source Extractor]. A function $\mathsf{E}_{n,\lambda} : \{\{0,1\}^n\}^s \to \{0,1\}^m$ is an extractor for independent (n, λ) sources that uses s sources and outputs m bits with error ϵ, if for any s independent (n, λ) sources $X_1, X_2, \ldots, X_s$, we have that*

$$|\mathsf{E}_{n,\lambda}(X_1, X_2, \ldots, X_s) - \mathcal{U}_m| \leq \epsilon$$

where $|\cdot|$ denotes the statistical distance.

The author of [36] gave a construction of a 3-source extractor, with parameters $\lambda \geq \log^{12} n$, $m = 0.9\lambda$ and $\epsilon = 2^{-\lambda^{\omega(1)}}$.

References

1. Badertscher, C., Garay, J., Maurer, U., Tschudi, D., Zikas, V.: But why does it work? A rational protocol design treatment of bitcoin. In: Nielsen, J.B., Rijmen, V. (eds.) EUROCRYPT 2018. LNCS, vol. 10821, pp. 34–65. Springer, Cham (2018). https://doi.org/10.1007/978-3-319-78375-8_2
2. Badertscher, C., Maurer, U., Tschudi, D., Zikas, V.: Bitcoin as a transaction ledger: a composable treatment. In: Katz, J., Shacham, H. (eds.) CRYPTO 2017. LNCS, vol. 10401, pp. 324–356. Springer, Cham (2017). https://doi.org/10.1007/978-3-319-63688-7_11
3. Ben-Sasson, E., et al.: Zerocash: decentralized anonymous payments from bitcoin. In: 2014 IEEE Symposium on Security and Privacy, SP 2014, Berkeley, CA, USA, 18–21 May 2014, pp. 459–474. IEEE Computer Society (2014)
4. Bentov, I., Gabizon, A., Zuckerman, D.: Bitcoin beacon. CoRR abs/1605.04559 (2016). http://arxiv.org/abs/1605.04559
5. Bitansky, N., Paneth, O.: ZAPs and non-interactive witness indistinguishability from indistinguishability obfuscation. In: Dodis, Y., Nielsen, J.B. (eds.) TCC 2015. LNCS, vol. 9015, pp. 401–427. Springer, Heidelberg (2015). https://doi.org/10.1007/978-3-662-46497-7_16
6. Blum, M., Feldman, P., Micali, S.: Non-interactive zero-knowledge and its applications (extended abstract). In: Simon, J. (ed.) Proceedings of the 20th Annual ACM Symposium on Theory of Computing, pp. 103–112. ACM, New York (1988)
7. Bonneau, J., Clark, J., Goldfeder, S.: On bitcoin as a public randomness source. IACR Cryptology ePrint Archive 2015, 1015 (2015). http://eprint.iacr.org/2015/1015
8. Canetti, R.: Universally composable security: a new paradigm for cryptographic protocols. In: 42nd Annual Symposium on Foundations of Computer Science, FOCS 2001, Las Vegas, Nevada, USA, 14–17 October 2001, pp. 136–145. IEEE Computer Society (2001)
9. Cardano: https://www.cardano.org/en/home/

10. Ciampi, M., Ostrovsky, R., Siniscalchi, L., Visconti, I.: Delayed-input non-malleable zero knowledge and multi-party coin tossing in four rounds. In: Kalai, Y., Reyzin, L. (eds.) TCC 2017. LNCS, vol. 10677, pp. 711–742. Springer, Cham (2017). https://doi.org/10.1007/978-3-319-70500-2_24
11. Ciampi, M., Persiano, G., Scafuro, A., Siniscalchi, L., Visconti, I.: Improved OR-composition of sigma-protocols. In: Kushilevitz, E., Malkin, T. (eds.) TCC 2016. LNCS, vol. 9563, pp. 112–141. Springer, Heidelberg (2016). https://doi.org/10.1007/978-3-662-49099-0_5
12. Ciampi, M., Persiano, G., Scafuro, A., Siniscalchi, L., Visconti, I.: Online/offline OR composition of sigma protocols. In: Fischlin, M., Coron, J.-S. (eds.) EURO-CRYPT 2016. LNCS, vol. 9666, pp. 63–92. Springer, Heidelberg (2016). https://doi.org/10.1007/978-3-662-49896-5_3
13. Ciampi, M., Persiano, G., Siniscalchi, L., Visconti, I.: A transform for NIZK almost as efficient and general as the Fiat-Shamir transform without programmable random oracles. In: Kushilevitz, E., Malkin, T. (eds.) TCC 2016. LNCS, vol. 9563, pp. 83–111. Springer, Heidelberg (2016). https://doi.org/10.1007/978-3-662-49099-0_4
14. Cramer, R.: Modular design of secure yet practical cryptographic protocols. Ph.D. thesis, University of Amsterdam (1996)
15. Cramer, R., Damgård, I.: Zero-knowledge proofs for finite field arithmetic, or: can zero-knowledge be for free? In: Krawczyk, H. (ed.) CRYPTO 1998. LNCS, vol. 1462, pp. 424–441. Springer, Heidelberg (1998). https://doi.org/10.1007/BFb0055745
16. Cramer, R., Damgård, I., Schoenmakers, B.: Proofs of partial knowledge and simplified design of witness hiding protocols. In: Desmedt, Y.G. (ed.) CRYPTO 1994. LNCS, vol. 839, pp. 174–187. Springer, Heidelberg (1994). https://doi.org/10.1007/3-540-48658-5_19
17. Damgård, I.: On Σ-protocol (2010). http://www.cs.au.dk/~ivan/Sigma.pdf
18. Dwork, C., Naor, M.: Zaps and their applications. In: 41st Annual Symposium on Foundations of Computer Science, FOCS 2000, Redondo Beach, California, USA, 12–14 November 2000, pp. 283–293 (2000)
19. Ethereum: https://www.ethereum.org/
20. Feige, U.: Alternative models for zero knowledge interactive proofs. Master's thesis (1990). Ph.D. thesis
21. Feige, U., Lapidot, D., Shamir, A.: Multiple non-interactive zero knowledge proofs based on a single random string (extended abstract). In: 31st Annual Symposium on Foundations of Computer Science, St. Louis, Missouri, USA, 22–24 October 1990, vol. I, pp. 308–317. IEEE Computer Society (1990)
22. Feige, U., Shamir, A.: Zero knowledge proofs of knowledge in two rounds. In: Brassard, G. (ed.) CRYPTO 1989. LNCS, vol. 435, pp. 526–544. Springer, New York (1990). https://doi.org/10.1007/0-387-34805-0_46
23. Feige, U., Shamir, A.: Witness indistinguishable and witness hiding protocols. In: Ortiz, H. (ed.) Proceedings of the 22nd Annual ACM Symposium on Theory of Computing, pp. 416–426. ACM, New York (1990)
24. Garay, J., Kiayias, A., Leonardos, N.: The bitcoin backbone protocol: analysis and applications. In: Oswald, E., Fischlin, M. (eds.) EUROCRYPT 2015. LNCS, vol. 9057, pp. 281–310. Springer, Heidelberg (2015). https://doi.org/10.1007/978-3-662-46803-6_10
25. Garay, J.A., MacKenzie, P., Yang, K.: Strengthening zero-knowledge protocols using signatures. J. Cryptology 19(2), 169–209 (2006)

26. Garg, S., Gentry, C., Halevi, S., Raykova, M., Sahai, A., Waters, B.: Candidate indistinguishability obfuscation and functional encryption for all circuits. In: 54th Annual IEEE Symposium on Foundations of Computer Science, FOCS 2013, Berkeley, CA, USA, 26–29 October 2013, pp. 40–49 (2013)

27. Garg, S., Gentry, C., Sahai, A., Waters, B.: Witness encryption and its applications. In: Symposium on Theory of Computing Conference, STOC 2013, Palo Alto, CA, USA, 1–4 June 2013, pp. 467–476 (2013)

28. Goldwasser, S., Micali, S., Rackoff, C.: The knowledge complexity of interactive proof systems. SIAM J. Comput. 18(1), 186–208 (1989)

29. Goyal, R., Goyal, V.: Overcoming cryptographic impossibility results using blockchains. In: Kalai, Y., Reyzin, L. (eds.) TCC 2017. LNCS, vol. 10677, pp. 529–561. Springer, Cham (2017). https://doi.org/10.1007/978-3-319-70500-2_18

30. Groth, J., Ostrovsky, R.: Cryptography in the multi-string model. In: Menezes, A. (ed.) CRYPTO 2007. LNCS, vol. 4622, pp. 323–341. Springer, Heidelberg (2007). https://doi.org/10.1007/978-3-540-74143-5_18

31. Groth, J., Ostrovsky, R., Sahai, A.: Non-interactive zaps and new techniques for NIZK. In: Dwork, C. (ed.) CRYPTO 2006. LNCS, vol. 4117, pp. 97–111. Springer, Heidelberg (2006). https://doi.org/10.1007/11818175_6

32. Katz, J., Lindell, Y.: Introduction to Modern Cryptography. Chapman and Hall/CRC Press, Boca Raton (2007)

33. Kiayias, A., Panagiotakos, G.: Speed-security tradeoffs in blockchain protocols. IACR Cryptology ePrint Archive 2015, 1019 (2015)

34. Kiayias, A., Russell, A., David, B., Oliynykov, R.: Ouroboros: a provably secure proof-of-stake blockchain protocol. In: Katz, J., Shacham, H. (eds.) CRYPTO 2017. LNCS, vol. 10401, pp. 357–388. Springer, Cham (2017). https://doi.org/10.1007/978-3-319-63688-7_12

35. Lapidot, D., Shamir, A.: Publicly verifiable non-interactive zero-knowledge proofs. In: Menezes, A.J., Vanstone, S.A. (eds.) CRYPTO 1990. LNCS, vol. 537, pp. 353–365. Springer, Heidelberg (1991). https://doi.org/10.1007/3-540-38424-3_26

36. Li, X.: Three-source extractors for polylogarithmic min-entropy. In: IEEE 56th Annual Symposium on Foundations of Computer Science, FOCS 2015, Berkeley, CA, USA, 17–20 October 2015, pp. 863–882 (2015)

37. Lin, H., Pass, R.: Constant-round non-malleable commitments from any one-way function. In: Fortnow, L., Vadhan, S.P. (eds.) Proceedings of the 43rd ACM Symposium on Theory of Computing, STOC 2011, pp. 705–714. ACM, New York (2011)

38. Lindell, Y.: An efficient transform from sigma protocols to NIZK with a CRS and non-programmable random oracle. In: Dodis, Y., Nielsen, J.B. (eds.) TCC 2015. LNCS, vol. 9014, pp. 93–109. Springer, Heidelberg (2015). https://doi.org/10.1007/978-3-662-46494-6_5

39. Lipmaa, H.: Progression-free sets and sublinear pairing-based non-interactive zero-knowledge arguments. In: Cramer, R. (ed.) TCC 2012. LNCS, vol. 7194, pp. 169–189. Springer, Heidelberg (2012). https://doi.org/10.1007/978-3-642-28914-9_10

40. Lipmaa, H.: Efficient NIZK arguments via parallel verification of benes networks. In: Abdalla, M., De Prisco, R. (eds.) SCN 2014. LNCS, vol. 8642, pp. 416–434. Springer, Cham (2014). https://doi.org/10.1007/978-3-319-10879-7_24

41. Lipmaa, H., Zhang, B.: A more efficient computationally sound non-interactive zero-knowledge shuffle argument. J. Comput. Secur. 21(5), 685–719 (2013)

42. Maurer, U.: Zero-knowledge proofs of knowledge for group homomorphisms. Des. Codes Crypt. 1–14 (2015). http://dx.doi.org/10.1007/s10623-015-0103-5

43. Merkle, R.C.: A digital signature based on a conventional encryption function. In: Pomerance, C. (ed.) CRYPTO 1987. LNCS, vol. 293, pp. 369–378. Springer, Heidelberg (1988). https://doi.org/10.1007/3-540-48184-2_32
44. Micali, S.: Computationally sound proofs. SIAM J. Comput. **30**(4), 1253–1298 (2000). https://doi.org/10.1137/S0097539795284959
45. Nakamoto, S.: Bitcoin: a peer-to-peer electronic cash system (2008, unpublished)
46. Pass, R., Seeman, L., Shelat, A.: Analysis of the blockchain protocol in asynchronous networks. In: Coron, J.-S., Nielsen, J.B. (eds.) EUROCRYPT 2017. LNCS, vol. 10211, pp. 643–673. Springer, Cham (2017). https://doi.org/10.1007/978-3-319-56614-6_22
47. Pass, R., Shi, E.: FruitChains: a fair blockchain. In: Proceedings of the ACM Symposium on Principles of Distributed Computing, PODC 2017, Washington, DC, USA, 25–27 July 2017, pp. 315–324 (2017)
48. Pass, R., Shi, E.: The sleepy model of consensus. In: Takagi, T., Peyrin, T. (eds.) ASIACRYPT 2017. LNCS, vol. 10625, pp. 380–409. Springer, Cham (2017). https://doi.org/10.1007/978-3-319-70697-9_14
49. Ripple: https://ripple.com/
50. Schnorr, C.P.: Efficient identification and signatures for smart cards. In: Brassard, G. (ed.) CRYPTO 1989. LNCS, vol. 435, pp. 239–252. Springer, New York (1990). https://doi.org/10.1007/0-387-34805-0_22

Identity-Based Encryption

Identity-Based Broadcast Encryption with Efficient Revocation

Aijun Ge[1,2,3]($\boxtimes$) and Puwen Wei[1]

[1] Key Laboratory of Cryptologic Technology and Information Security,
Ministry of Education, Shandong University, Jinan, China
geaijun@163.com, pwei@sdu.edu.cn
[2] State Key Laboratory of Mathematical Engineering and Advanced Computing,
Zhengzhou, China
[3] Henan Key Laboratory of Network Cryptography Technology, Zhengzhou, China

Abstract. Identity-based broadcast encryption (IBBE) is an effective method to protect the data security and privacy in multi-receiver scenarios, which can make broadcast encryption more practical. This paper further expands the study of scalable revocation methodology in the setting of IBBE, where a key authority releases a key update material periodically in such a way that only non-revoked users can update their decryption keys. Following the binary tree data structure approach, a concrete instantiation of revocable IBBE scheme is proposed using asymmetric pairings of prime order bilinear groups. Moreover, this scheme can withstand decryption key exposure, which is proven to be semi-adaptively secure under chosen plaintext attacks in the standard model by reduction to static complexity assumptions. In particular, the proposed scheme is very efficient both in terms of computation costs and communication bandwidth, as the ciphertext size is constant, regardless of the number of recipients. To demonstrate the practicality, it is further implemented in `Charm`, a framework for rapid prototyping of cryptographic primitives.

Keywords: Broadcast encryption · Revocation ·
Asymmetric pairings · Provable security · Constant size ciphertext

1 Introduction

Broadcast encryption (BE), first introduced by Fiat and Naor [13], is a cryptographic paradigm that enables delivering encrypted content over a broadcast channel in a way that only qualified users are able to decrypt. For a BE in the public key setting, there is a dealer which is employed to generate and distribute decryption keys for users. A sender can encrypt to a set of receivers by choosing their public keys adaptively, and the encrypted data can be decrypted only by the user with the private key in the set of receivers. A BE scheme is collusion resistant if no extra information about the encrypted data is leaked, even if all users that are not qualified collude together. BE has a wide range of applications such as pay-TV, encrypted file systems and digital right management.

© International Association for Cryptologic Research 2019
D. Lin and K. Sako (Eds.): PKC 2019, LNCS 11442, pp. 405–435, 2019.
https://doi.org/10.1007/978-3-030-17253-4_14

Identity-based encryption (IBE) is an advanced form of public key encryption in which the public key of a user is some unique information about the identity of the user (e.g., a user's IP or email address). Moreover, as public keys are derived from identifiers, IBE scheme eliminates the need for a public key infrastructure (PKI). In the IBE system, a trusted third party called the private key generator (PKG) can generate the corresponding secret keys associated with each user's public identities. A sender who has access to the public parameters of the system can encrypt a message using the receiver's identity as the public key, and only the intended receiver who obtains its decryption key from PKG can decrypt.

Identity-based broadcast encryption (IBBE) can be seen as a natural generalization of IBE, i.e., BE in the identity-based setting, which recognizes the users in a BE scheme with their identities, instead of indexes assigned by the system. The number of valid identities in the IBBE scheme can be exponential with the security parameter, while the number of public keys in the public key broadcast setting is only polynomial with the security parameter. IBBE is an effective method to protect the data security and privacy in multi-receiver scenarios. In an IBBE scheme, a sender can broadcast an encrypted message to any set of intended users, which is called privileged set. If the size of the privileged set is 1, the resulting IBBE scheme would be an IBE scheme obviously. For the trivial solution to construct an IBBE scheme which encrypts the message once for each identity using an IBE scheme, the resulting ciphertext would be linear in the privileged set, which is inefficient especially for a large set of receivers.

In 2007, Delerablée [11] presented the first IBBE scheme with constant size ciphertext, though it is only weak selective-ID secure in the random oracle model. This construction makes use of the hybrid encryption paradigm: key encapsulation mechanism (KEM) and data encapsulation mechanism (DEM) framework where the broadcast ciphertext only encrypts a short symmetric key used to encrypt the long messages, which is also adopted by most BE schemes [15]. Very recently, Ramanna [31] proposed a novel IBBE scheme with constant size ciphertext that can achieve adaptive security in the standard model.

One desirable functionality of multi-user cryptosystems is the support for membership revocation. For example, malicious users should be driven out immediately from the system, and even for the honest users should be revoked if their private keys get stolen or lost. Key revocation is well studied in BE such as [19,28]. However, realizing efficient user revocation mechanism in the IBE setting turned out to be very challenging. Compared with traditional public key encryption in the PKI setting, IBE simplifies the key management problem by avoiding public key certificates. Therefore, users cannot be easily revoked by digital certificates and certificate revocation lists. As a result, the key revocation problem in IBE is not as simple as in tradition PKI setting.

The first practical IBE scheme, proposed by Boneh and Franklin [5] from the Weil pairing, also suggested a straightforward revocation method for IBE schemes: dividing the lifetime of the system into discrete time periods and refreshing the private key for non-revoked users periodically. Unfortunately, this approach is not scalable and very inefficient because all non-revoked users should update their private keys via a secure channel, and the workload on the PKG grows linearly in the number of non-revoked users. To address this problem, Boldyreva et al. [6] proposed a scalable revocable IBE (RIBE) scheme which employed the tree based revocation techniques from [28] to reduce the PKG's workload to only logarithmic (instead of linear) in the number of users. Moreover, each non-revoked user can derive a decryption key from the public update key, while revoked users cannot compute their decryption keys. There is no secure channel that is required for non-revoked users to update their private keys.

After the work of Boldyreva et al. [6], Seo and Emura [33] introduced a new security notion called decryption key exposure resistance (DKER), which can better capture the realistic threat of IBE system. Generally speaking, this security definition can guarantee that the confidentiality of ciphertexts is not compromised even if a user's decryption key at some periods has been exposed. Though DKER seems to be a natural security notion, Seo and Emura have proved that Boldyreva et al.'s RIBE scheme is vulnerable against decryption key exposure. Using Boldyreva et al.'s revocation methodology, Seo and Emura [33] also proposed the first RIBE scheme that is adaptive secure with DKER, which has become the default security requirements for RIBE scheme. Since then, a lot of followup works of RIBE schemes with DKER have been proposed. Among them, the most recently scheme by Watanabe et al. [38] based on the modified Jutla-Roy IBE scheme [16] is the first adaptively secure RIBE scheme with DKER that can achieve short public parameters in prime order groups.

As the set of qualified users can change in each broadcast emission, efficient revocation of individual users or user groups is the primary objective of broadcast encryption. For the IBBE scheme, which is a natural generalization of BE in the identity-based setting, however, there is still no provably secure scalable revocation methodology has been proposed so far, even in Boldyreva et al.'s security model. Motivated by this, we further expand the study of revocable IBBE (RIBBE). We mainly focus on the construction of RIBBE scheme with DKER. In particular, we would like to have a construction that has constant size ciphertexts, which is more efficient and less bandwidth consuming compared with schemes of ciphertexts that are linear in the set of receivers.

Our Contribution. In this paper, we propose a novel construction of revocable IBBE scheme with constant size ciphertexts. To prove its security with DKER, we first define the syntax of revocable IBBE scheme using KEM-DEM paradigm and its security model, which takes into account the realistic threat of decryption key exposure for the scenario of IBBE. To the best of our knowledge, this is the first construction of revocable IBBE with provable security. Specifically, our revocable IBBE scheme has the following merits.

1. Our scheme is a KEM which can produce a symmetric key along with a header, thus long messages can be encrypted under the short symmetric key. For simplicity, we only discuss the header size in the KEM, which is constant in our construction, regardless of the number of underlying receivers, which is very efficient both in the communication overheads and computational costs. Furthermore, only 4 group elements together with a tag are needed in the

ciphertexts header of our revocable IBBE scheme, which can be comparable to the revocable IBE scheme in [38]. Moreover, we implement it in Charm framework [2], more details of which can be deferred to Sect. 6.

2. The public parameters in our scheme is linear in the maximum size of the privileged identities set: m, which is predetermined and fixed in the setup phase. The private key for each user is linear in the value of $m * \log_2 N$, where the maximal value of system users N is also a predetermined value in the setup phase of the revocable IBBE system.

3. Our scheme also follows Boldyreval et al.'s revocation methodology [6] with the binary-tree data structure approach, which reduces the amount of work in key update from linear to logarithmic complexity in the maximal number of system users N. For each time period, the PKG will broadcast update key information through a public channel, which is useless for already revoked users. Only the non-revoked user can combine the update key and his private key to derive a decryption key that can be used to decrypt proper ciphertexts. More precisely, according to [33], the size of update key is $O(r\log_2(N/r))$ if $r \leqslant N/2$, or $O(N - r)$ if $r > N/2$, where r is the number of revoked users.

4. Our construction is built upon prime order bilinear groups of Type-3 pairings under mild variants of the Symmetric eXternal Diffie-Hellman (SXDH) assumption: the Augmented Decisional Diffie-Hellman on $\mathbb{G}_1$ (ADDH1) and Decisional Diffie-Hellman on $\mathbb{G}_2$ (DDH2). Note that ADDH1 assumption is first defined by Watanabe et al. in [38], which is proved in the generic bilinear group model.

5. With regard to the security, our revocable IBBE scheme is semi-adaptively secure with DKER under chosen plaintext attacks. Semi-adaptive security, first proposed by Chen and Wee [10], is a notion of security that lies between selective and adaptive security for functional encryption systems. More particularly, if we set the maximum size of receivers m to be $m = 1$, the resulting revocable IBBE scheme is a revocable IBE system, which can achieve adaptive security with DKER.

At a high level, our design approach is very similar to the Seo and Emura's technique of transforming IBE to RIBE in [33,38]. Firstly, there should be a basic IBE scheme that satisfies the requirement of (1) the secret key re-randomization property and (2) applicability of Boneh-Boyen technique [4]. Then, an adaptively secure RIBE scheme with DKER is constructed by applying the Seo-Emura technique. Similarly, we also employ a basic IBBE scheme and the Boneh-Boyen IBE scheme [4] as the building blocks. To achieve short ciphertexts and fast decryption, the basic IBBE is derived from the most recently proposed IBBE scheme of Ramanna [31], with necessary modifications mainly for the public parameters part to achieve the secret key re-randomization property. The security of the revocable IBBE scheme with DKER can be reduced to the adaptive security of the basic IBBE scheme. We note that it is not a trivial work to construct a revocable IBBE with adaptive security even given a revocable IBE scheme. The primary challenge in the security proof is how to simulate decryption keys for identities of the privileged recipients. While there is only one target identity in the setting of RIBE, there will be multiple private keys and decryption keys that can be used to decrypt the challenge ciphertext. Note that the privileged recipients are chosen adaptively by the adversary, even the number of privileged recipients is unknown until the challenge phase, which makes it more complicated to simulate in the security proof. We partially overcome these issues by using the semi-adaptive security model, where the adversary should submit the privileged recipients just after receiving the public parameters. More technique will be needed to achieve adaptive security for revocable IBBE. As a side product, we also propose a new construction of revocable IBE scheme with adaptive security, which can be as a complementary of Watanabe et al.'s revocable IBE scheme [38]. In addition, because of using a different strategy, the adaptive security proof of the resulting RIBE scheme in this paper seems more succinct, compared with the security proof in the full version of [38].

Related Work. Hierarchical identity-based encryption (HIBE) is another extension of IBE which further supports a key delegation functionality. Revocable HIBE can support the revocation of user's private keys to manage the dynamic credentials of users in an HIBE system. Several improvement and variants with different properties have been proposed since the first revocable HIBE scheme with DKER introduced by Seo and Emura in [34]. Among them, the most popular revocable HIBE must be those given in [12,24,35], the security of which are proven in the selective model where an adversary should submits the challenge identity or the revocation list before he receives the public parameters. Revocable HIBE with DKER that is secure in the adaptive adversary model has been proposed in [20,36]. Unfortunately, these constructions are built upon composite order (product of three primes) bilinear groups, which is inefficient to implement compared with prime order groups implementation. We note that, contrary to HIBE, no organization of the users is needed in our revocable IBBE scheme to have constant size of ciphertexts, i.e., no hierarchy between identities in our revocable IBBE system.

Besides bilinear maps on elliptic curve, lattice is also a powerful tool to build cryptographic primitives. Lattice-based constructions, which are conjectured to be resistant to attacks by both classical and quantum computers, are currently important candidates for post-quantum cryptography. Chen et al. [8] proposed the first revocable IBE scheme (without DKER) in the lattice setting. Recently, Katsumata et al. [17] solved the open problem of achieving revocable (H)IBE with DKER in the lattice setting by proposing a new tool called the level conversion keys without relying on the key re-randomization property. In addition, revocable IBE scheme from codes with rank metric is proposed in [7], which is only proven selective security in the random oracle model.

We stress that the notion of revocation in this paper is referred to indirect revocation sometimes, since the key authority indirectly enables revocation by forcing revoked users to be unable to update their keys. A direct revocation mechanism has been studied for attribute-based encryption [3] and predicate encryption [27]. This approach requires the sender to carry out the revocation by specifying a set of revoked users in the ciphertext, and hence it does not need any private key update procedures on the recipients's side. Recently, another notion of recipient-revocable identity-based broadcast encryption has been proposed in [22,32], which mainly focuses on how to remove some of the recipients from the set of receivers stated in the original ciphertext after the ciphertext has been generated, but without revealing the message content. Therefore, these systems [22,32] cannot follow the notion of revocable IBBE in this paper.

Server-aided revocable IBE, recently proposed by Qin et al. [30], is a novel system where most of the workloads on users are outsourced to an untrusted server. The server manages users' public key and key updates sent by the PKG periodically, and users can compute decryption keys without communicating with either the PKG or the server. Server-aided revocable IBE [29] and server-aide directly revocable predicate encryption [23] in the lattice setting have been proposed recently, which can satisfy selective security without DKER. It is possible to employ this construction methodology in our revocable IBBE scheme, which can obtain a server-aided revocable IBBE scheme with DKER.

Organization. The rest of the paper is organized as follows. In the next section, we review some preliminaries used throughout this paper, including the rigorous definitions and security model of revocable IBBE scheme. In Sect. 3, we present an adaptive secure IBBE scheme with short ciphertexts modified from Ramanna's original inner production encryption scheme [31], which is used as the core building block of our revocable IBBE scheme. In Sect. 4, we propose a concrete construction of revocable IBBE with DKER that can achieve constant size of ciphertext, together with proof of security in Sect. 5. To show its practicability we implement the proposed scheme in Sect. 6. Finally, Sect. 7 concludes this paper.

2   Preliminaries

2.1   Asymmetric Pairings and Hardness Assumptions

Let $\mathbb{G}_1, \mathbb{G}_2, \mathbb{G}_T$ be cyclic multiplicative groups of the same prime order p. Let g be a generator of $\mathbb{G}_1$ and h be a generator of $\mathbb{G}_2$. A bilinear map $e : \mathbb{G}_1 \times \mathbb{G}_2 \to \mathbb{G}_T$ has the following properties:

- **Bilinearity**: For all $g \in \mathbb{G}_1$, $h \in \mathbb{G}_2$ and all $a, b \in \mathbb{Z}_p^*$, $e(g^a, h^b) = e(g, h)^{ab}$.
- **Non-degeneracy**: $e(g, h) \neq 1$.
- **Computability**: It is efficient to compute $e(u, v)$ for any $u \in \mathbb{G}_1$ and $v \in \mathbb{G}_2$.

It is called *symmetric* (or Type-1) pairing if $\mathbb{G}_1 = \mathbb{G}_2$; otherwise, the pairing is *asymmetric*. Two types of asymmetric pairing can be further classified: Type-2 and Type-3. If there is an efficiently computable isomorphism either from $\mathbb{G}_2$ to $\mathbb{G}_1$ or from $\mathbb{G}_1$ to $\mathbb{G}_2$, then the bilinear map e is called a Type-2 pairing. If no efficiently computable isomorphism is known, then we call it Type-3 pairing. Our constructions in this work are based on Type-3 pairing, which is the most efficient setting from an implementation point according to [9,14].

The security of our construction is based on the Augmented Decisional Diffie-Hellman on $\mathbb{G}_1$ (ADDH1), which is proved security in the generic bilinear group model by Watanabe et al. [38], and Decisional Diffie-Hellman on $\mathbb{G}_2$ (DDH2) assumptions. Below, we describe these assumptions.

Let $\mathcal{G} = (p, e, \mathbb{G}_1, \mathbb{G}_2, \mathbb{G}_T)$ be a Type-3 pairing with generators $g_1 \in \mathbb{G}_1$ and $g_2 \in \mathbb{G}_2$. Denote $D = (g_1, g_1^\mu, g_1^{\alpha_2}, g_1^{\beta\alpha}, g_2, g_2^\alpha, g_2^{\beta\alpha}, g_2^{\beta\alpha_2}, g_2^{1/\beta})$ with the following distribution: $\alpha, \alpha_2, \mu \xleftarrow{R} \mathbb{Z}_p, \beta, \eta \xleftarrow{R} \mathbb{Z}_p^*$. A PPT algorithm $\mathcal{A}$ given D and Z, whose task is to distinguish $Z = Z_0 = g_1^{\mu\alpha_2}$ (the case $\mathcal{A}$ will output 0) or $Z = Z_1 = g_1^{\mu\alpha_2+\eta}$ (the case $\mathcal{A}$ will output 1), has advantage $Adv_{\mathcal{G},\mathcal{A}}^{ADDH1}(\lambda)$ in solving the ADDH1 problem as:

$$Adv_{\mathcal{G},\mathcal{A}}^{ADDH1}(\lambda) = \left| \Pr\left[\mathcal{A}(\mathcal{G}, D, Z_0) = 1\right] - \Pr\left[\mathcal{A}(\mathcal{G}, D, Z_1) = 1\right] \right|.$$

Definition 1. *We say that the ADDH1 assumption holds if the advantage for all PPT adversaries $Adv_{\mathcal{G},\mathcal{A}}^{ADDH1}(\lambda)$ is negligible in the security parameter λ in solving the ADDH1 problem relative to a Type-3 pairing $\mathcal{G}$ of the group $\mathbb{G}_1$.*

Now we introduce the DDH2 assumption, which is defined as follows.

Definition 2. *We say that the DDH2 assumption holds for the group $\mathbb{G}_2$ of Type-3 pairing $\mathcal{G} = (p, e, \mathbb{G}_1, \mathbb{G}_2, \mathbb{G}_T)$ if the advantage $Adv_{\mathcal{G},\mathcal{A}}^{DDH2}(\lambda)$ which equals $\left| \Pr\left[\mathcal{A}(\mathcal{G}, D, g_2^{\mu\alpha}) = 1\right] - \Pr\left[\mathcal{A}(\mathcal{G}, D, g_2^{\mu\alpha+\eta}) = 1\right] \right|$ is negligible in λ for all PPT algorithms $\mathcal{A}$ with $D = (g_1, g_2, g_2^\mu, g_2^\alpha)$ and the distribution: $\alpha, \mu \xleftarrow{R} \mathbb{Z}_p, \eta \xleftarrow{R} \mathbb{Z}_p^*$.*

Note that the dual of the above Definition 2 with the roles of $\mathbb{G}_1$ and $\mathbb{G}_2$ reversed is Decisional Diffie-Hellman in $\mathbb{G}_1$ (DDH1) assumption. The Symmetric eXternal Diffie-Hellman (SXDH) assumption holds if both DDH1 and DDH2 problems are intractable. It can be easily verified that ADDH1 problem is not harder than DDH1, as an instance of DDH1 is embedded in the instance of ADDH1, and an algorithm to solve DDH1 can also be used to solve the ADDH1.

2.2 KUnodes Algorithm

To achieve scalable user revocation, we follow the node selection algorithm KUNode algorithm by using a binary tree data structure as in the previous RIBE schemes [6,21,33,38]. We employ similar notations as follows. For a binary tree BT with N leaves, we denote by root the root node of BT. For a non-leaf node θ, we write θ_L and θ_R as the left and right child of θ, respectively. For a leaf node η, we write Path(η) as the set of nodes on the path from η to root (both η and root are inclusive). Each user is assigned to a leaf node η of BT. If a user who is associated with η is revoked on a time period t, then (η, t) is in the revocation list RL, i.e., $(\eta, t) \in$ RL.

The KUNode algorithm which takes as input a binary tree BT, a revocation list RL as well as a time period t, is executed as follows. It first sets $X := Y := \emptyset$. For each $(\eta_i, t_i) \in RL$, if $t_i \leqslant t$ then it adds Path(η_i) to X as: $X := X \cup \text{Path}(\eta_i)$. Then, for each $x \in X$, it will add x_L to Y for the case $x_L \notin X$, and it will add

x_R to Y for the case $x_R \notin X$. Finally, it will output Y if $Y \neq \emptyset$. Otherwise, for the case $Y = \emptyset$, it will output $Y = \{root\}$.

Note that the output of KUNode algorithm Y is a minimal set of nodes in BT such that for any leaf node η listed in RL, it must hold that $\texttt{Path}(\eta) \cap Y = \emptyset$. But for the non-revoked leaf node η', there is exactly one node $\theta \in Y$ such that θ is an ancestor of η'. Two instances of the KUNode algorithm for the graphical description are illustrated below in Fig. 1.

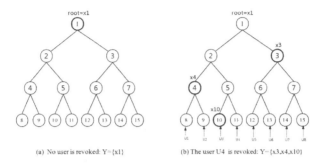

Fig. 1. Two instances of the KUNode algorithm

2.3   Syntax of Revocable IBBE Scheme

A revocable IBBE scheme $\mathcal{RIBBE}$ is described as follows: For simplicity, we omit the description of the security parameter λ and the public parameter PP in the input of all algorithms except for the **Setup** algorithm.

- **Setup**(λ, m, N): The setup algorithm takes as input the security parameter λ, the maximum size m of the set of privileged identities for one encryption together with the maximum number of users N, and it returns the public parameters PP, the master secret key MSK, the initial revocation list $RL = \emptyset$ and a state ST. The algorithm also defines the identity space $\mathcal{ID}$, the time space $\mathcal{T}$ and the key space $\mathcal{K}$ for the DEM.
- **SKGen**(MSK, ID, ST): The secret key generation algorithm takes as input the master secret key MSK, an identity $ID \in \mathcal{ID}$, and the state information ST. It outputs a private key SK_{ID} associated with ID and updated ST.
- **KeyUp**(MSK, T, RL, ST): The key update generation algorithm takes as input the master secret key MSK, a key update time $T \in \mathcal{T}$, the revocation list RL and the state ST, and then outputs the update key KU_T.
- **DKGen**(SK_{ID}, KU_T): The decryption key generation algorithm takes a secret key SK_{ID} and key update KU_T as input, and outputs a decryption key $DK_{ID,T}$ or a symbol $\perp$ indicating that ID has been revoked by time T.
- **Encap**(T, S): The encapsulation algorithm takes as input the current time $T \in \mathcal{T}$ and a set of identities $S = \{ID_1, ..., ID_n\}$ with $n \leq m$, and it returns a pair (Hdr, K), where Hdr is called the header and $K \in \mathcal{K}$ is the session key for the symmetric encryption scheme.

When a message $M \in \{0,1\}^*$ is broadcasted to receivers in S, the sender can compute the encryption C_M of M under the symmetric key $K \in \mathcal{K}$ of DEM and broadcasts (T, S, Hdr, C_M). We will refer to (T, S, Hdr) as the full header and C_M as the broadcast body.

- **Decap**$(T, S, Hdr, DK_{ID,T})$: This algorithm takes as input the full header (T, S, Hdr) with a set of identities $S = \{ID_1, ..., ID_n\}$ (satisfying that $n \leq m$), a decryption key $DK_{ID,T} \neq \bot$ corresponding an identity ID and time T. If $ID \in S$ the algorithm outputs the session key K which is then used to decrypt the broadcast body C_M to obtain the original message M.

- **Revoke**(ID, T, RL, ST): The stateful revocation algorithm takes an identity to be revoked $ID \in \mathcal{ID}$, a revocation time $T \in \mathcal{T}$, the current revocation list RL and the state ST as input, and outputs an updated revocation list RL.

Correctness. The correctness property requires that for all security parameter $\lambda \in \mathbb{N}$, all $(PP, MSK) \leftarrow Setup(\lambda, m, N)$, all possible state ST, a revocation list RL and for all sets $S \subseteq \mathcal{ID}$ with $|S| \leq m$, if $ID \in S$ is not revoked on the time $T \in \mathcal{T}$, then for $(SK_{ID}, ST) \leftarrow SKGen(MSK, ID, ST)$, $(KU_T, ST) \leftarrow KeyUp(MSK, T, RL, ST)$, $DK_{ID,T} \leftarrow DKGen(SK_{ID}, KU_T)$, $(Hdr, K) \leftarrow Encap(T, S)$, it should be satisfied that: $Decap(T, S, Hdr, DK_{ID,T}) = K$.

REMARK. Note that for $m = 1$, the above definition of revocable IBBE scheme is equal to a revocable IBE system, as is used in [33,38].

2.4   Security Models

The security model of RIBE was first introduced by Boldyreva et al. [6] and it was refined by Seo and Emura [33] by considering the realistic threat of decryption key exposure. We define IND-CPA security of a revocable IBBE system with decryption key exposure resistant, which is indistinguishable against chosen plaintext attacks for adaptive adversary. We basically refine the definition of [33], by adding extra restrictions for the scenario of broadcast encryption [15]. We describe the security model using the following **IND-CPA** game between a PPT adversary $\mathcal{A}$ and a challenger $\mathcal{C}$.

Setup: The challenger $\mathcal{C}$ runs Setup(λ, m, N) algorithm of the revocable IBBE scheme $\mathcal{RIBBE}$ to get the public parameters PP, the master secret key MSK, a revocation list RL and a state ST. $\mathcal{C}$ keeps MSK, RL, ST to itself and gives PP to the adversary $\mathcal{A}$.

Key Extraction Phase 1: The adversary $\mathcal{A}$ can make a polynomial number of key extraction queries adaptively, which are processed as follows:

- If this is a private key query for an identity ID, then it gives the corresponding private key SK_{ID} to $\mathcal{A}$ by running SKGen(MSK, ID, ST) algorithm;
- If this is an update key query for the time T, then it gives the corresponding update key KU_T to $\mathcal{A}$ by running KeyUp(MSK, T, RL, ST) algorithm;
- If this is a decryption key query for ID and T, then it gives the corresponding decryption key $DK_{ID,T}$ to $\mathcal{A}$ by running DKGen(SK_{ID}, KU_T) algorithm;

– If this is a revocation key query for an identity to be revoked ID and
a revocation time T, then it updates the revocation list RL by running
Revoke(ID, T, RL, ST) algorithm with the following restriction: The revocation query cannot be queried at a time period T if the update key query
for T was issued.

We note that the update key query and the revocation query can be queried at
a time period which is later or equal to that of all previous queries, which means
they are requested in non-decreasing order of time. In addition, the decryption
key query cannot be queried at T before issuing T to the update key query.

Challenge: When $\mathcal{A}$ decides that phase 1 is over, a challenge time T^* and a
challenge privileged set $S^* = \{ID_1, ID_2, ..., ID_n\}$ with $n \leq m$ are provided with
the following constraints:

– If a private key query for an identity $ID \in S^*$ has been requested, then this
identity ID must be revoked at some time $T \leq T^*$;
– There is no decryption key query for any (ID, T^*) with ID in S^*.

$\mathcal{C}$ runs $Encap$ algorithm to obtain $(Hdr, K_0) = \text{Encap}(S^*, T^*)$ and choose a
random K_1 from the key space $\mathcal{K}$. $\mathcal{C}$ then picks a random coin $\beta \in \{0, 1\}$ and
returns (Hdr, K_β) to $\mathcal{A}$.

Key Extraction Phase 2: The adversary $\mathcal{A}$ can continue to issue a polynomial
number of additional key extraction queries as phase 1 with the same constraints,
$\mathcal{C}$ will respond as before.

Guess: Eventually, the adversary $\mathcal{A}$ outputs a guess $\beta' \in \{0, 1\}$, and wins the
game if $\beta' = \beta$.

Definition 3 *(Adaptive Security). Let $Adv_{\mathcal{A}, RIBBE}^{IND\text{-}CPA} = |\Pr(\beta' = \beta) - 1/2|$ be the
advantage for $\mathcal{A}$ in winning the* IND-CPA *game defined above. We say that a
revocable IBBE scheme is adaptively secure under chosen plaintext attacks if for
all polynomial-time adversary $\mathcal{A}$, the advantage in winning the above experiment
$Adv_{\mathcal{A}, RIBBE}^{IND\text{-}CPA}$ is negligible with respect to the security parameter λ.*

This security model above can capture realistic threat of decryption key
exposure, as the adversary can make decryption key queries. This model reflects
the scenario where all users get together and collude as in ordinary IBBE, since
the adversary can get any user's private key except for S^*. Furthermore, even
users in S^* can be corrupted, as long as they are revoked before the challenge
time T^*. This is called adaptive security as the privileged set S^* is not chosen
at the beginning. We can also define the selective security that is weaker than
adaptive security similarly, except that the challenge S^* and T^* must be declared
by the adversary before it sees the public parameters. In addition, we can define
the semi-adaptive security that lies between selective and adaptive security.

Definition 4 *(Selective Security). The selective security of revocable IBBE under chosen plaintext attacks is similar to the adaptive security except that the adversary $\mathcal{A}$ should submit a challenge set S^* and challenge time T^* before it receives the public parameters. The advantage is defined as $Adv_{\mathcal{A},RIBBE}^{sIND\text{-}CPA} = |\Pr(\beta' = \beta) - 1/2|$. We say that a revocable IBBE scheme is secure under chosen plaintext attacks in the selective model if for all polynomial-time adversary $\mathcal{A}$, the advantage in winning the above experiment $Adv_{\mathcal{A},RIBBE}^{sIND\text{-}CPA}$ is negligible with respect to the security parameter λ.*

Definition 5 *(Semi-adaptive Security). The semi-adaptive security of revocable IBBE under chosen plaintext attacks is similar to the adaptive security except that the adversary $\mathcal{A}$ should submit a challenge set S^* after it receives the public parameters but before it makes any key extraction query. The advantage is defined as $Adv_{\mathcal{A},RIBBE}^{saIND\text{-}CPA} = |\Pr(\beta' = \beta) - 1/2|$. We say that a revocable IBBE scheme is semi-adaptively secure under chosen plaintext attacks if for all polynomial-time adversary $\mathcal{A}$, the advantage in winning the above experiment $Adv_{\mathcal{A},RIBBE}^{saIND\text{-}CPA}$ is negligible with respect to the security parameter λ.*

3   The Basic IBBE Scheme

We now present our construction of identity-based broadcast encryption scheme with short ciphertexts. The core of our construction relies on realizing the inclusion relationship between one identity and a subset of identities from inner product. Note that the technique of deriving an IBBE scheme from the inner production encryption can be traced to the work of Katz et al. [18]. For each identity $ID \in \mathbb{Z}_p$, we can express it by setting a vector $\boldsymbol{x} = (x_0, x_1, \cdots, x_m)$, where $x_i = ID^i \bmod p$ for $i = 0, 1, ..., m$. For a subset $S = \{ID_1, ID_2, ..., ID_n\}$ with $n \leqslant m$, we can define a vector $\boldsymbol{y} = (y_0, y_1, \cdots, y_m)$, where $P_S[Z] = \prod_{ID_j \in S}(Z - ID_j) = \sum_{i=0}^{n} y_i Z^i$. If $n < m$, the coordinates $y_{n+1}, \cdots, y_m$ are all set to 0. It is easy to verify that $P_S[ID] = \sum_{i=0}^{m} y_i(ID)^i = \langle \boldsymbol{x}, \boldsymbol{y} \rangle = 0$ if and only if $ID \in S$.

3.1   Construction

As stated before, our basic IBBE scheme shares the same high level structure as the construction in [31]. In order to achieve the secret key re-randomization property, each component of the master secret key needs to be available in the public parameters in some form of elements in source groups. We note that the extra public group elements, especially for the part of $(g_1^{\beta\alpha}, g_2^{\beta\alpha_1}, g_2^{\beta\alpha_2}, g_2^{1/\beta})$, will play an important role in the security proof of the subsequent revocable IBBE scheme. It is also worth mentioning that the security proof cannot be immediately applied, since some materials of the master secret key from [31] have been exposed in the public parameters. More precisely, our basic IBBE scheme $\prod_{\text{IBBE}}$ is constructed as follows.

- **Setup**(λ, m): Generate a Type-3 pairing $\mathcal{G} = (p, e, \mathbb{G}_1, \mathbb{G}_2, \mathbb{G}_T)$ of prime order $p > 2^\lambda$ with two random generators $g_1 \in \mathbb{G}_1$ and $g_2 \in \mathbb{G}_2$. Let m be the maximum size of the legitimate set for one encryption, two random $(m+1)$-dimensional vectors are chosen from $\mathbb{Z}_p$ with $\boldsymbol{u}_1 = (u_{1,0}, u_{1,1}, \cdots, u_{1,m})$, $\boldsymbol{u}_2 = (u_{2,0}, u_{2,1}, \cdots, u_{2,m})$. Choose $\alpha_1, \alpha_2, w_1, w_2 \xleftarrow{R} \mathbb{Z}_p$, $b, \beta \xleftarrow{R} \mathbb{Z}_p^*$, set $\boldsymbol{u} = \boldsymbol{u}_1 + b\boldsymbol{u}_2 = (u_0, u_1, \cdots, u_m)$, $w = w_1 + bw_2$, $\alpha = \alpha_1 + b\alpha_2$, and compute $U_1 = g_1^{\boldsymbol{u}}$, $W_1 = g_1^w$, $g_T = e(g_1, g_2)^\alpha$. The master key is $MSK = (g_2^{\alpha_1}, g_2^{\alpha_2})$, and the public parameter PP is defined to be:
  $PP = (g_1, g_1^b, \boldsymbol{U}_1, W_1, g_T, g_2, g_2^{\boldsymbol{u}_1}, g_2^{\boldsymbol{u}_2}, g_2^{w_1}, g_2^{w_2}, g_1^{\beta\alpha}, g_2^{\beta\alpha_1}, g_2^{\beta\alpha_2}, g_2^{1/\beta})$.
- **KeyGen**(PP, MSK, ID): For a user with an identity $ID \in \mathbb{Z}_p$, this algorithm chooses $r \xleftarrow{R} \mathbb{Z}_p$ and random tags $ktag_1, \cdots, ktag_m \xleftarrow{R} \mathbb{Z}_p$. The private key $SK_{ID} = \{K_1, K_2, K_3, (K_{4,i}, K_{5,i}, ktag_i)_{i=1}^m\}$ is defined to be: $K_1 = g_2^{\alpha_1} \cdot (g_2^{w_1})^r$, $K_2 = g_2^{\alpha_2} \cdot (g_2^{w_2})^r$, $K_3 = g_2^r$. For $i = 1, 2, ..., m$: $K_{4,i} = ((g_2^{w_1})^{ktag_i} \cdot g_2^{u_{1,i}}/(g_2^{u_{1,0}})^{(ID)^i})^r$, $K_{5,i} = ((g_2^{w_2})^{ktag_i} \cdot g_2^{u_{2,i}}/(g_2^{u_{2,0}})^{(ID)^i})^r$.
- **Encap**(PP, S): Assuming that the privileged set is $S = \{ID_1, ID_2, ..., ID_n\}$ with $n \leqslant m$ for notational simplicity. The algorithm defines a vector $\boldsymbol{y} = (y_0, y_1, \cdots, y_m)$ as the coefficient from $P_S[Z] = \prod_{ID_j \in S}(Z - ID_j) = \sum_{i=0}^n y_i Z^i$. It then picks randomly $s, ctag \in \mathbb{Z}_p$, and computes the session key $K = g_T^s$ which is used to encrypt the message, together with the header $Hdr = (C_1, C_2, C_3, ctag)$, where $C_1 = g_1^s$, $C_2 = g_1^{sb}$, $C_3 = (W_1^{ctag} \cdot \prod_{i=0}^n (g_1^{u_i})^{y_i})^s$.
- **Decap**(PP, S, Hdr, SK_{ID}): The algorithm defines the vector $\boldsymbol{y} = (y_0, y_1, \cdots, y_m)$ according to the set S from the polynomial $P_S[Z]$ as above. It then computes $ktag = \sum_{i=1}^m y_i \cdot ktag_i$. If $ktag = ctag$, the output is $\perp$. Otherwise it computes:
  $A = (e(C_1, \prod_{i=1}^m K_{4,i}^{y_i}) \cdot e(C_2, \prod_{i=1}^m K_{5,i}^{y_i})/e(C_3, K_3))^{\frac{1}{ktag-ctag}}$, and returns the session key: $K = e(C_1, K_1) \cdot e(C_2, K_2) \cdot A^{-1}$.

CORRECTNESS. We observe that if $ID \in S$, we have $\langle \boldsymbol{x}, \boldsymbol{y} \rangle = \sum_{i=0}^m y_i (ID)^i = 0$, and $y_0 = -\sum_{i=1}^m y_i (ID)^i$. Then we have:

$$\prod_{i=1}^m K_{4,i}^{y_i} = ((g_2^{w_1})^{\sum_{i=1}^m y_i ktag_i} \cdot \prod_{i=1}^m (g_2^{u_{1,i}})^{y_i} / \prod_{i=1}^m (g_2^{u_{1,0}})^{\sum_{i=1}^m y_i (ID)^i})^r$$

$$= (g_2^{w_1 \sum_{i=1}^m y_i ktag_i} \cdot g_2^{\sum_{i=0}^m y_i u_{1,i}})^r = (g_2^{w_1 \cdot ktag} \cdot g_2^{\sum_{i=0}^m y_i u_{1,i}})^r;$$

$$\prod_{i=1}^m K_{5,i}^{y_i} = (g_2^{w_2 \cdot ktag} \cdot g_2^{\sum_{i=0}^m y_i u_{2,i}})^r;$$

$$e(C_1, \prod_{i=1}^m K_{4,i}^{y_i}) e(C_2, \prod_{i=1}^m K_{5,i}^{y_i}) = e(g_1^s, g_2^{r(w \cdot ktag + \sum_{i=0}^m y_i u_i)});$$

$$A = (e(C_1, \prod_{i=1}^m K_{4,i}^{y_i}) e(C_2, \prod_{i=1}^m K_{5,i}^{y_i}) \cdot e(C_3, K_3)^{-1})^{\frac{1}{ktag-ctag}} = e(g_1^s, g_2^{rw});$$

$$K = e(C_1, K_1) e(C_2, K_2) A^{-1} = e(g_1^s, g_2^{\alpha_1+rw_1}) e((g_1^b)^s, g_2^{\alpha_2+rw_2}) / e(g_1^s, g_2^{rw})$$

$$= e(g_1^s, g_2^{\alpha_1}) e((g_1^b)^s, g_2^{\alpha_2}) = e(g_1^s, g_2^{\alpha_1+b\alpha_2}) = g_T^s.$$

3.2 Security Proof

We prove the security of the above basic IBBE scheme inspired from Ramanna's original inner production encryption scheme [31] following the theorem:

Theorem 1. *Suppose the DDH1, DDH2 and ADDH1 assumptions hold in the Type-3 pairing $\mathcal{G} = (p, e, \mathbb{G}_1, \mathbb{G}_2, \mathbb{G}_T)$, the basic IBBE scheme $\prod_{IBBE}$ in Sect. 3.1 is adaptively secure.*

Our security proof is obtained by applying the Waters' dual system methodology [37] via a hybrid argument over a sequence of games. Before we describe these games, we introduce the semi-functional headers and secret keys in terms of a transformation on a normal header or key. Note that these algorithms are provided for definitional purposes and only used in the security proof, but not in a real system. In particular, they do not need to be efficiently computable from the public parameters and the master secret key MSK.

SFEncap$(PP, MSK, S, g_1^{w_1}, g_1^{u_1})$: The algorithm first runs the **Encap** algorithm on a set $S = \{ID_1, ..., ID_n\}$ to generate a normal header-session key pair (Hdr', K') with $Hdr' = (C_1', C_2', C_3', ctag')$. Then it randomly chooses $\mu \in \mathbb{Z}_p$, and sets the semi-functional session key $K = K' \cdot e(g_1^\mu, g_2^{\alpha_1})$, together with $C_2 = C_2', ctag = ctag'$. It then sets $C_1 = C_1' \cdot g_1^\mu, C_3 = C_3' \cdot g_1^{\mu(\langle y, u_1 \rangle + ctag \cdot w_1)}$, where $y = (y_0, y_1, \cdots, y_m)$ is the coefficient from $P_S[Z] = \prod_{ID_j \in S} (Z - ID_j) = \sum_{i=0}^n y_i Z^i$. The resulting header $Hdr = (C_1, C_2, C_3, ctag)$ is returned as the semi-functional header. Additionally, $g_1^{w_1}$ and $g_1^{u_1}$ are needed to generate the semi-functional header in this algorithm.

SFKeyGen$(PP, MSK, ID, g_2^{1/b})$: The algorithm first runs the **KeyGen** algorithm to generate a normal private key $SK'_{ID} = \{K_1', K_2', K_3', (K_{4,i}', K_{5,i}', ktag_i')_{i=1}^m\}$. Then it chooses a random $\gamma \in \mathbb{Z}_p$, and sets $K_1 = K_1' \cdot g_2^\gamma, K_2 = K_2' / g_2^{\gamma/b}$, leaving the other elements $\{K_3, (K_{4,i}, K_{5,i})_{i=1}^m\}$ and the tags $\{(ktag_i)_{i=1}^m\}$ unchanged. The resulting key $SK_{ID} = \{K_1, K_2, K_3, (K_{4,i}, K_{5,i}, ktag_i)_{i=1}^m\}$ is returned as the semi-functional secret key. Note that $g_2^{1/b}$ is also needed in this algorithm.

We observe that if one applies the decapsulation procedure with a semi-functional key and a normal header, decapsulation will succeed as $e(C_1, g_2^\gamma) = e(C_2, g_2^{\gamma/b})$. That is, a normal header when decapsulated with a semi-functional user key returns the corresponding normal session key. Similarly, decapsulation of a semi-functional header by a normal key will also succeed because of:

$$A' = e(g_1^\mu, \prod_{i=1}^m K_{4,i}^{y_i})/e(g_1^{\mu(\langle y, u_1 \rangle + ctag \cdot w_1)}, K_3)^{\frac{1}{ktag - ctag}} = e(g_1^{\mu \cdot w_1}, g_2^r),$$

$$e(g_1^\mu, K_1)/A' = e(g_1^\mu, g_2^{\beta \alpha_1} \cdot (g_2^{w_1})^r)/e(g_1^{\mu \cdot w_1}, g_2^r) = e(g_1^\mu, g_2^{\beta \alpha_1}),$$

which equals the extra component of the semi-functional session key. However, when a semi-functional key is used to decapsulate a semi-functional header, the resulting session key will have an additional term of $e(g_1^\mu, g_2^\gamma) \cdot e(g_1^s, g_2^\gamma)$, which means decapsulation will fail when both the header and user's key are semi-functional.

We now present a sequence of games between an adversary $\mathcal{A}$ and a challenger $\mathcal{C}$ defined as follows:

- Game$_{\text{Real}}$: The real IBBE security game, which is basically follows the adaptive security model of [15].
- Game$_0$: The same as Game$_{\text{Real}}$, except that the challenge header and session key are semi-functional.
- Game$_k$: The same as Game$_0$, except that the first k private keys are semi-functional for $1 \leqslant k \leqslant q$, where q is the number of key extraction queries made by the adversary $\mathcal{A}$.
- Game$_{\text{Final}}$: The same as Game$_q$, except that the challenge session key is a random element of $\mathbb{G}_T$.

Our proof will process as follows, which can show that each game defined above is indistinguishable from the next under a complexity assumption. First, we transit from Game$_{\text{Real}}$ to Game$_0$, where the adversary $\mathcal{A}$'s advantage is bounded by the DDH1 assumption. Then we transit from Game$_{k-1}$ to Game$_k$ for each $1 \leqslant k \leqslant q$, and the adversary $\mathcal{A}$'s advantage is bounded by the DDH2 assumption. We note that in Game$_q$ both the challenge header and all the private keys are semi-functional. At this point all private keys the challenger $\mathcal{C}$ gives out are useless in decapsulating the header. Finally, we transit Game$_q$ to Game$_{\text{Final}}$ under the ADDH1 assumption. It is easy to check that the header-session key pair given to the adversary $\mathcal{A}$ is independent with β in Game$_{\text{Final}}$, where the adversary has no advantage unconditionally.

We denote $Adv_{\mathcal{A},IBBE}^{\text{Game}_{\text{Real}}}$, $Adv_{\mathcal{A},IBBE}^{\text{Game}_0}$, $Adv_{\mathcal{A},IBBE}^{\text{Game}_k}$ $(1 \leqslant k \leqslant q)$ and $Adv_{\mathcal{A},IBBE}^{\text{Game}_{\text{Final}}}$ as the advantage in Game$_{\text{Real}}$, Game$_0$, Game$_k$ and Game$_{\text{Final}}$, respectively. Our hybrid argument is accomplished in the following lemmas:

Lemma 1. *If there is an adversary $\mathcal{A}$ with $\left| Adv_{\mathcal{A},IBBE}^{\text{Game}_{\text{Real}}} - Adv_{\mathcal{A},IBBE}^{\text{Game}_0} \right| = \varepsilon$, we can build an algorithm $\mathcal{C}_0$ with advantage $Adv_{\mathcal{C}_0,\mathcal{G}}^{DDH1} = \varepsilon$ in breaking the DDH1 assumption for the Type-3 pairing $\mathcal{G}$.*

Lemma 2. *Suppose that there exists an adversary $\mathcal{A}$ that makes at most q queries with advantage $\left| Adv_{\mathcal{A},IBBE}^{\text{Game}_{k-1}} - Adv_{\mathcal{A},IBBE}^{\text{Game}_k} \right| = \varepsilon$ for some k where $1 \leqslant k \leqslant q$. Then we can build an algorithm $\mathcal{C}_k$ with advantage $Adv_{\mathcal{C}_k,\mathcal{G}}^{DDH2} = \varepsilon$ in breaking the DDH2 assumption for the Type-3 pairing $\mathcal{G}$.*

Lemma 3. *If there is an adversary $\mathcal{A}$ with $\left| Adv_{\mathcal{A},IBBE}^{\text{Game}_q} - Adv_{\mathcal{A},IBBE}^{\text{Game}_{\text{Final}}} \right| = \varepsilon$, we can build an algorithm $\mathcal{C}$ with advantage $Adv_{\mathcal{C},\mathcal{G}}^{ADDH1} = \varepsilon$ in breaking the ADDH1 assumption for the Type-3 pairing $\mathcal{G}$.*

The indistinguishability of Game$_{\text{Real}}$ and Game$_0$ as well as that of Game$_{k-1}$ and Game$_k$ for $1 \leqslant k \leqslant q$ can be proved similarly as the way in [31]. Due to space constraints, the proof for Lemmas 1 and 2 is omitted here, but can be found in the full version. Here we only present the proof for Lemma 3 in Appendix A, which is the most non-trivial part in the theorem.

In addition, we note that the value of β is information theoretically hidden from the adversary $\mathcal{A}$ in $\text{Game}_{\text{Final}}$, the probability in which $\mathcal{A}$ wins is exactly $\frac{1}{2}$. Hence, $\mathcal{A}$ has no advantage in $\text{Game}_{\text{Final}}$: $\left| Adv_{\mathcal{A},\text{IBBE}}^{\text{Game}_{\text{Final}}} - \frac{1}{2} \right| = 0$. Thus, we have the advantage of $\mathcal{A}$ in breaking the security of our basic IBBE scheme $\prod_{\text{IBBE}}$:

$$Adv_{\mathcal{A},\text{IBBE}}^{\text{IND - CPA}} = \left| Adv_{\mathcal{A},\text{IBBE}}^{\text{Game}_{\text{Real}}} - \frac{1}{2} \right| \leqslant \left| Adv_{\mathcal{A},\text{IBBE}}^{\text{Game}_{\text{Real}}} - Adv_{\mathcal{A},\text{IBBE}}^{\text{Game}_{\text{Final}}} \right| + \left| Adv_{\mathcal{A},\text{IBBE}}^{\text{Game}_{\text{Final}}} - \frac{1}{2} \right|$$

$$\leqslant \left| Adv_{\mathcal{A},\text{IBBE}}^{\text{Game}_{\text{Real}}} - Adv_{\mathcal{A},\text{IBBE}}^{\text{Game}_0} \right| + \sum_{k=1}^{q} \left| Adv_{\mathcal{A},\text{IBBE}}^{\text{Game}_{k-1}} - Adv_{\mathcal{A},\text{IBBE}}^{\text{Game}_k} \right| + \left| Adv_{\mathcal{A},\text{IBBE}}^{\text{Game}_q} - Adv_{\mathcal{A},\text{IBBE}}^{\text{Game}_{\text{Final}}} \right|$$

$$= Adv_{\mathcal{C},\mathcal{G}}^{\text{DDH1}} + q \cdot Adv_{\mathcal{C},\mathcal{G}}^{\text{DDH2}} + Adv_{\mathcal{C},\mathcal{G}}^{\text{ADDH1}}.$$

Since the number of key extraction queries q is bounded by polynomial size, the advantage $Adv_{\mathcal{A},\text{IBBE}}^{\text{IND-CPA}}$ defined above is negligible under the DDH1, DDH2 and ADDH1 assumptions. This completes the proof of Theorem 1.   □

4   Construction of Revocable IBBE Scheme

In this section, we present an efficient revocable IBBE scheme with constant size of headers, which is proven semi-adaptively secure in the standard model based on the IBBE scheme described in Sect. 3.1. Here we basically follow the simple two-level HIBE (without delegating property) strategy in our construction. That is, the first level using the adaptively secure IBBE scheme in Sect. 3.1, is assigned for the identity, and the second level using the selectively secure Boneh-Boyen IBE [4], is assigned for the polynomial bounded time period. Our revocable IBBE scheme $\prod_{\text{RIBBE}}$ is described as follows:

- **Setup**(λ, m, N): Given the security parameter λ, $\mathcal{PKG}$ generates a Type-3 pairing $\mathcal{G} = (p, e, \mathbb{G}_1, \mathbb{G}_2, \mathbb{G}_T)$ of prime order p. Also, two random generators $g_1 \in \mathbb{G}_1$ and $g_2 \in \mathbb{G}_2$ are chosen as well as $e(g_1, g_2) \in \mathbb{G}_T$ is computed. As the maximum number of privileged identities is m, $\mathcal{PKG}$ then chooses from $\mathbb{Z}_p$ two random $(m+1)$-dimensional vectors $\boldsymbol{u}_1 = (u_{1,0}, u_{1,1}, \cdots, u_{1,m})$, $\boldsymbol{u}_2 = (u_{2,0}, u_{2,1}, \cdots, u_{2,m})$. Assuming that there are at most N users in the revocable IBBE systems, where N is a power of two for simplicity, a binary tree BT with N leaves is chosen. To generate the system public parameters PP, the authority $\mathcal{PKG}$ does the following:
  1. Choose randomly $b \xleftarrow{R} \mathbb{Z}_p^*$, $\alpha_1, \alpha_2, w_1, w_2, z_1, z_2, \hat{z}_1, \hat{z}_2 \xleftarrow{R} \mathbb{Z}_p$;
  2. Set $\boldsymbol{u} = \boldsymbol{u}_1 + b\boldsymbol{u}_2$, $w = w_1 + bw_2$, $\alpha = \alpha_1 + b\alpha_2$;
  3. Compute $\boldsymbol{U}_1 = g_1^{\boldsymbol{u}}$, $W_1 = g_1^w$, $g_T = e(g_1, g_2)^\alpha$, $Z_1 = g_1^{z_1 + b \cdot z_2}$, $\hat{Z}_1 = g_1^{\hat{z}_1 + b \cdot \hat{z}_2}$;
  4. Finally, output public parameters to be:
     $PP = (g_1, g_1^b, \boldsymbol{U}_1, W_1, Z_1, \hat{Z}_1, g_T, g_2, g_2^{\boldsymbol{u}_1}, g_2^{\boldsymbol{u}_2}, g_2^{w_1}, g_2^{w_2}, g_2^{z_1}, g_2^{z_2}, g_2^{\hat{z}_1}, g_2^{\hat{z}_2})$.
  The master key is defined $MSK = (g_2^{\alpha_1}, g_2^{\alpha_2})$, and the revocation list is $RL = \emptyset$.
- **SKGen**(PP, MSK, ID, ST): Assuming that the domain of identities $\mathcal{ID}$ to be $\mathbb{Z}_p$. For a user associated with an identity $ID \in \mathbb{Z}_p$, $\mathcal{PKG}$ picks an

unassigned leaf node η randomly from BT and stores ID in this node η. For each node $\theta \in Path(BT, \eta)$, the authority does the following:

1. Recall $H_\theta = (H_{1,\theta}, H_{2,\theta})$ from BT if it was defined. Otherwise, choose $H_{1,\theta}, H_{2,\theta} \xleftarrow{R} \mathbb{G}_2$ and store H_θ in the node θ;

2. Choose $r_\theta, ktag_{1,\theta}, \cdots, ktag_{m,\theta} \xleftarrow{R} \mathbb{Z}_p$;

3. Compute $K_{1,\theta} = H_{1,\theta} \cdot (g_2^{w_1})^{r_\theta}, K_{2,\theta} = H_{2,\theta} \cdot (g_2^{w_2})^{r_\theta}, K_{3,\theta} = g_2^{r_\theta}$;
   For each $i = 1, 2, ..., m$:
   $$K_{4,i,\theta} = g_2^{r_\theta(u_{1,i}-(ID)^i \cdot u_{1,0}+ktag_{i,\theta} \cdot w_1)}, K_{5,i,\theta} = g_2^{r_\theta(u_{2,i}-(ID)^i \cdot u_{2,0}+ktag_{i,\theta} \cdot w_2)}.$$
   Return the private secret key SK_{ID} and an updated state ST with
   $$SK_{ID} = \{K_{1,\theta}, K_{2,\theta}, K_{3,\theta}, (K_{4,i,\theta}, K_{5,i,\theta}, ktag_{i,\theta})_{i=1}^m\}_{\theta \in Path(BT,\eta)}.$$

- **KeyUp**(PP, MSK, T, RL, ST): $\mathcal{PKG}$ parses MSK as $(g_2^{\alpha_1}, g_2^{\alpha_2})$, and publishes key updates at time period T for each node $\theta \in KUNode(BT, RL, T)$ in the following steps:
  1. Retrieve $H_\theta = (H_{1,\theta}, H_{2,\theta})$ from the state ST (As noted in [33], H_θ is always pre-defined in the **SKGen** algorithm).
  2. Choose $s_\theta \xleftarrow{R} \mathbb{Z}_p$, and compute:
     $$KU_{1,\theta} = g_2^{\alpha_1} g_2^{s_\theta(z_1+T \cdot \hat{z}_1)} H_{1,\theta}^{-1}, KU_{2,\theta} = g_2^{\alpha_2} g_2^{s_\theta(z_2+T \cdot \hat{z}_2)} H_{2,\theta}^{-1}, KU_{3,\theta} = g_2^{s_\theta}.$$
     Return the key update $KU_T = \{KU_{1,\theta}, KU_{2,\theta}, KU_{3,\theta}\}_{\theta \in KUNode(BT,RL,T)}$.

- **DKGen**(PP, SK_{ID}, KU_T): Parse $KU_T = \{KU_{1,\theta}, KU_{2,\theta}, KU_{3,\theta}\}_{\theta \in J}$ and $SK_{ID} = \{K_{1,\theta}, K_{2,\theta}, K_{3,\theta}, (K_{4,i,\theta}, K_{5,i,\theta}, ktag_{i,\theta})_{i=1}^m\}_{\theta \in I}$ for some set of nodes I and J. The user will return $\perp$ if $I \cap J = \emptyset$. Otherwise, choose $\theta \in I \cap J$, $r'_\theta, s'_\theta \in \mathbb{Z}_p$, compute $DK_{ID,T} = \{DK_1, DK_2, DK_3, DK'_3, (DK_{4,i}, DK_{5,i}, ktag_i)_{i=1}^m\}$:
  $$DK_1 = K_{1,\theta} \cdot KU_{1,\theta} \cdot g_2^{r'_\theta \cdot w_1} g_2^{s'_\theta \cdot (z_1+T \cdot \hat{z}_1)}, \quad DK_2 = K_{2,\theta} \cdot KU_{2,\theta} \cdot g_2^{r'_\theta \cdot w_2} g_2^{s'_\theta \cdot (z_2+T \cdot \hat{z}_2)},$$
  $$DK_3 = K_{3,\theta} \cdot g_2^{r'_\theta}, DK'_3 = KU_{3,\theta} \cdot g_2^{s'_\theta}. \text{ For } i = 1, 2, ..., m: ktag_i = ktag_{i,\theta},$$
  $$DK_{4,i} = K_{4,i,\theta} \cdot g_2^{r'_\theta \cdot (u_{1,i}-(ID)^i \cdot u_{1,0}+ktag_i \cdot w_1)}, DK_{5,i} = K_{5,i,\theta} \cdot g_2^{r'_\theta \cdot (u_{2,i}-(ID)^i \cdot u_{2,0}+ktag_i \cdot w_2)}.$$

- **Encap**(PP, T, S): To encrypt the privileged identity set $S = \{ID_1, ID_2, ..., ID_n\}$ with $n \leqslant m$, the algorithm defines a vector $\boldsymbol{y} = (y_0, y_1, \cdots, y_m)$ as the associated coefficient from: $P_S[Z] = \prod_{ID_j \in S}(Z - ID_j) = \sum_{i=0}^n y_i Z^i$. Note that the coordinates $y_{n+1}, \cdots, y_m$ are all set to 0 if $n < m$. Given the public parameters PP with $\boldsymbol{U_1} = g_1^{\boldsymbol{u}} = (g_1^{u_0}, g_1^{u_1}, \cdots, g_1^{u_m})$, it picks $s, ctag \xleftarrow{R} \mathbb{Z}_p$, and computes the session key $K = g_T^s$ and the header $Hdr = (C_1, C_2, C_3, C_4, ctag)$ with $C_1 = g_1^s, C_2 = (g_1^b)^s, C_3 = (Z_1 \cdot \hat{Z}_1^T)^s, C_4 = (W_1^{ctag} \cdot \prod_{i=0}^n (g_1^{u_i})^{y_i})^s$.

- **Decap**$(PP, T, S, Hdr, DK_{ID,T})$: For $ID \in S$, it parses $DK_{ID,T}$ and Hdr as $\{DK_1, DK_2, DK_3, DK'_3, (DK_{4,i}, DK_{5,i}, ktag_i)_{i=1}^m\}$ and $(C_1, C_2, C_3, C_4, ctag)$, respectively. This algorithm then computes $ktag = \sum_{i=1}^m y_i \cdot ktag_i$, where y_i is the coefficient of the polynomial $P_S[Z]$. If $ktag = ctag$, the output is $\perp$. Otherwise it computes:
  $$A = e(C_1, DK_1) \cdot e(C_2, DK_2)/e(C_3, DK'_3),$$
  $$B = (e(C_1, \prod_{i=1}^n (DK_{4,i})^{y_i}) \cdot e(C_2, \prod_{i=1}^n (DK_{5,i})^{y_i})/e(C_4, DK_3))^{\frac{1}{ktag-ctag}},$$
  and returns $K = A/B$ as the session key.

- **Revoke**(ID, T, RL, ST): This revocation algorithm updates the revocation list RL by adding (η, ID, T), where η is the leaf node associated with ID.

CORRECTNESS. The correctness of our revocable RIBBE scheme follows from the correctness analysis of IBBE in Sect. 3.1, and it is omitted here.

5   Security Analysis

Theorem 2. *If the ADDH1 assumption and DDH2 assumption hold, the proposed revocable IBBE scheme $\prod_{RIBBE}$ is semi-adaptively secure under chosen plaintext attacks. More particularly, if we set the maximum size of the set of receivers for one encryption m to be $m = 1$, the above revocable IBBE scheme $\prod_{RIBBE}$ is a revocable IBE system $\prod_{RIBE}$, which is adaptively secure against chosen plaintext attacks under the same assumptions.*

The proof of Theorem 2 proceeds in the following two lemmas: Lemma 4 and Lemma 5. We first provide a reduction in the semi-adaptive model to the (non-revocable) basic IBBE scheme $\prod_{IBBE}$ described in Sect. 3.1, which has been proven to be adaptively secure in Sect. 3.2 under the ADDH1 and DDH2 assumptions. Therefore, the revocable IBBE scheme $\prod_{RIBBE}$ is semi-adaptivey secure under the ADDH1 and DDH2 assumptions.

Lemma 4. *If the underlying IBBE scheme $\prod_{IBBE}$ described in Sect. 3.1 is adaptively secure against chosen plaintext attacks, then the proposed revocable IBBE scheme $\prod_{RIBBE}$ in Sect. 4 is semi-adaptively secure. Furthermore, if there exists an adversary $\mathcal{A}$ attacking the semi-adaptive security of $\prod_{RIBBE}$ with a non-negligible advantage $Adv_{\mathcal{A},RIBBE}^{saIND-CPA} = \varepsilon$, then there exists an adversary $\mathcal{C}$ against the adaptive security of $\prod_{IBBE}$ with advantage $Adv_{\mathcal{C},IBBE}^{IND-CPA} = \frac{\varepsilon}{2|\mathcal{T}|}$, which is also non-negligible. Here $\mathcal{T}$ is the set of time periods, the size of which is polynomial bounded in the security parameter λ.*

Proof. Suppose there exists an adversary $\mathcal{A}$ that attacks the above revocable IBBE scheme $\prod_{RIBBE}$ with a non-negligible advantage ε, we will construct a PPT algorithm $\mathcal{C}$ to break the adaptive security of the basic IBBE scheme $\prod_{IBBE}$ described in Sect. 3.1.

At the beginning, $\mathcal{C}$ receives public parameters of the IBBE scheme $\prod_{IBBE}$: $(g_1, g_1^b, U_1 = g_1^{u_1 + bu_2}, W_1 = g_1^{w_1 + bw_2}, g_T, g_2, g_2^{u_1}, g_2^{u_2}, g_2^{w_1}, g_2^{w_2}, g_1^{\beta\alpha}, g_2^{\beta\alpha_1}, g_2^{\beta\alpha_2}, g_2^{1/\beta})$. During the process, $\mathcal{C}$ can access to the secret key generation oracle $\text{KeyGen}_{IBBE}(\cdot)$, that is, if $\mathcal{C}$ sends this oracle $\text{KeyGen}_{IBBE}(\cdot)$ an identity ID, then it will receive a private key of $SK_{ID} = \{K_1, K_2, K_3, (K_{4,i}, K_{5,i}, ktag_i)_{i=1}^m\}$ with:
$K_1 = g_2^{\alpha_1} \cdot (g_2^{w_1})^r, K_2 = g_2^{\alpha_2} \cdot (g_2^{w_2})^r, K_3 = g_2^r,$
$K_{4,i} = ((g_2^{w_1})^{ktag_i} \cdot g_2^{u_{1,i}}/(g_2^{u_{1,0}})^{(ID)^i})^r, K_{5,i} = ((g_2^{w_2})^{ktag_i} \cdot g_2^{u_{2,i}}/(g_2^{u_{2,0}})^{(ID)^i})^r.$
   Then $\mathcal{C}$ interacts with $\mathcal{A}$ as follows:

Setup: $\mathcal{C}$ should guess the right time period T^* that $\mathcal{A}$ will submit the target identity in the challenge ciphertext phase. For the rest of the proof, assuming that $\mathcal{C}$'s guess is correct, which holds with probability $1/|\mathcal{T}|$. Note that $\mathcal{C}$ will terminate the simulation once $\mathcal{C}$ finds that the guess is wrong, and a random bit β' will be outputted. $\mathcal{C}$ then proceeds as follows:

1. It first creates a binary tree BT with N leaves. It initializes RL and ST as an empty set respectively.
2. $\mathcal{C}$ chooses $z_1', z_2', \hat{z}_1', \hat{z}_2' \xleftarrow{R} \mathbb{Z}_p$ and computes:
$$Z_1 = g_1^{z_1 + b \cdot z_2} = g_1^{z_1'}(g_1^b)^{z_2'}/(g_1^{\beta\alpha})^{T^*}, \hat{Z}_1 = g_1^{\hat{z}_1 + b \cdot \hat{z}_2} = g_1^{\hat{z}_1'}(g_1^b)^{\hat{z}_2'}(g_1^{\beta\alpha}),$$
$$g_2^{z_1} = g_2^{z_1'}/(g_2^{\beta\alpha_1})^{T^*}, g_2^{z_2} = g_2^{z_2'}/(g_2^{\beta\alpha_2})^{T^*}, g_2^{\hat{z}_1} = g_2^{\hat{z}_1'}g_2^{\beta\alpha_1}, g_2^{\hat{z}_2} = g_2^{\hat{z}_2'}g_2^{\beta\alpha_2},$$
which implicitly sets:
$$z_1 = z_1' - T^* \cdot \beta\alpha_1, z_2 = z_2' - T^* \cdot \beta\alpha_2, \hat{z}_1 = \hat{z}_1' + \beta\alpha_1, \hat{z}_2 = \hat{z}_2' + \beta\alpha_2.$$
3. $\mathcal{C}$ then sends to $\mathcal{A}$ the public parameters of $\prod_{\text{RIBBE}}$ as:
$$PP = (g_1, g_1^b, \boldsymbol{U}_1, W_1, Z_1, \hat{Z}_1, g_T, g_2, g_2^{\boldsymbol{u}_1}, g_2^{\boldsymbol{u}_2}, g_2^{w_1}, g_2^{w_2}, g_2^{z_1}, g_2^{z_2}, g_2^{\hat{z}_1}, g_2^{\hat{z}_2}).$$

Challenge Set: $\mathcal{A}$ submits a challenge set $S^* = \{ID_1^*, ID_2^*, ..., ID_n^*\}$ to the challenger $\mathcal{C}$, which will be used in the challenge ciphertexts. For each identity $ID_i^* \in S^*$, $\mathcal{C}$ assigns ID_i^* to a random leaf η_i^* from BT and saves (ID_i^*, η_i^*) to ST.

Key Extraction Phase 1: $\mathcal{A}$ may adaptively make a polynomial number of queries, which are processed as follows:

- If this is a private key query for an identity ID, $\mathcal{C}$ performs the following:
  1. It first checks whether $ID \in S^*$ or not. If $ID \in S^*$, then the leaf η^* from BT has already been assigned for ID, and $\mathcal{C}$ can retrieve (ID, η^*) from ST. Otherwise, $ID \notin S^*$, $\mathcal{C}$ assigns ID to a random leaf η from BT and saves (ID, η) to ST. We denote N^* as all the nodes from the root node to the leaf nodes which are assigned to identities in the challenge set S^*: $N^* = \bigcup_{i=1}^n Path(BT, \eta_i^*)$, where η_i^* is the leaf node assigned to $ID_i^* \in S^*$.
  2. For each node $\theta \in Path(BT, \eta)$, $\mathcal{C}$ can retrieve H_θ if it was defined. Otherwise, it chooses $H_\theta = (H_{1,\theta}, H_{2,\theta}) \xleftarrow{R} \mathbb{G}_2$ and stores H_θ in the node θ. Note that θ can be further divided into the following two types according to N^*:
     - **Case** $\theta \in N^*$: $\mathcal{C}$ chooses $r_\theta, ktag_{1,\theta}, \cdots, ktag_{m,\theta} \xleftarrow{R} \mathbb{Z}_p$, and computes:
     $$K_{1,\theta} = H_{1,\theta} \cdot (g_2^{w_1})^{r_\theta}, K_{2,\theta} = H_{2,\theta} \cdot (g_2^{w_2})^{r_\theta}, K_{3,\theta} = g_2^{r_\theta};$$
     $$K_{4,i,\theta} = g_2^{r_\theta(u_{1,i}-(ID)^i \cdot u_{1,0}+ktag_{i,\theta} \cdot w_1)}, K_{5,i,\theta} = g_2^{r_\theta(u_{2,i}-(ID)^i \cdot u_{2,0}+ktag_{i,\theta} \cdot w_2)}.$$
     - **Case** $\theta \notin N^*$: In this case, $ID \notin S^*$. $\mathcal{C}$ transfers ID to the oracle: $\text{KeyGen}_{\text{IBBE}}(\cdot)$, and gets the private key $\{K_1, K_2, K_3, (K_{4,i}, K_{5,i}, ktag_i)_{i=1}^m\}$. $\mathcal{C}$ further chooses $r_\theta, ktag_{1,\theta}, \cdots, ktag_{m,\theta} \xleftarrow{R} \mathbb{Z}_p$, sets $ktag_{i,\theta} = ktag_{i,\theta} + ktag_i$, and computes: $K_{1,\theta} = K_1 \cdot (g_2^{w_1})^{r_\theta} \cdot H_{1,\theta}, K_{2,\theta} = K_2 \cdot (g_2^{w_2})^{r_\theta} \cdot H_{2,\theta}, K_{3,\theta} = K_3 \cdot g_2^{r_\theta}, K_{4,i,\theta} = K_{4,i} \cdot g_2^{r_\theta(u_{1,i}-(ID)^i \cdot u_{1,0}+ktag_{i,\theta} \cdot w_1)},$
     $$K_{5,i,\theta} = K_{5,i} \cdot g_2^{r_\theta(u_{2,i}-(ID)^i \cdot u_{2,0}+ktag_{i,\theta} \cdot w_2)}.$$

3. Finally, it stores and outputs the private key SK_{ID} to $\mathcal{A}$ with:
$SK_{ID} = \{K_{1,\theta}, K_{2,\theta}, K_{3,\theta}, (K_{4,i,\theta}, K_{5,i,\theta}, ktag_{i,\theta})_{i=1}^m\}_{\theta \in Path(BT,\eta)}.$

- If this is an update key query for the time T, $\mathcal{C}$ first runs KUNode(BT, RL, T) algorithm with the current revocation list RL and time T. For each node $\theta \in$ KUNode(BT, RL, T), $\mathcal{C}$ can retrieve H_θ if it was defined. Otherwise, it chooses $H_\theta = (H_{1,\theta}, H_{2,\theta}) \xleftarrow{R} \mathbb{G}_2$ and stores H_θ in the node θ. Then it chooses $s_\theta \xleftarrow{R} \mathbb{Z}_p$, checks whether $\theta \in N^*$, and computes:

- **Case $\theta \in N^*$:** $KU_{1,\theta} = (g_2^{z_1}(g_2^{\hat{z}_1})^T)^{s_\theta} H_{1,\theta}^{-1}(g_2^{\frac{1}{\beta}})^{-\frac{z_1' + T\hat{z}_1'}{T-T^*}}$,

$KU_{2,\theta} = (g_2^{z_2}(g_2^{\hat{z}_2})^T)^{s_\theta} H_{2,\theta}^{-1}(g_2^{\frac{1}{\beta}})^{-\frac{z_2' + T\hat{z}_2'}{T-T^*}}$, $KU_{3,\theta} = g_2^{s_\theta}(g_2^{\frac{1}{\beta}})^{-\frac{1}{T-T^*}}$.

  REMARK. Note that for $T = T^*$, there will be no node θ such that $\theta \in$ KUNode(BT, RL, T) $\cap N^*$, as the corresponding SK_{ID} must be revoked before T^* according to the restriction.

- **Case $\theta \notin N^*$:** $KU_{1,\theta} = (g_2^{z_1}(g_2^{\hat{z}_1})^T)^{s_\theta} H_{1,\theta}^{-1}$, $KU_{2,\theta} = (g_2^{z_2}(g_2^{\hat{z}_2})^T)^{s_\theta} H_{2,\theta}^{-1}$, $KU_{3,\theta} = g_2^{s_\theta}$.

Finally, $\mathcal{C}$ stores and outputs the update key KU_T to $\mathcal{A}$ with:
$KU_T = \{KU_{1,\theta}, KU_{2,\theta}, KU_{3,\theta}\}_{\theta \in KUNode(BT,RL,T)}.$

- If this is a decryption key query for an identity ID and time T, on the one hand, $\mathcal{C}$ can generate the corresponding decryption key $DK_{ID,T}$ by running DKGen(SK_{ID}, KU_T) algorithm: $\mathcal{C}$ will create and store the private key SK_{ID} if ID has never been queried to the private key or the decryption key before (otherwise, $\mathcal{C}$ can use the stored SK_{ID}). In addition, $\mathcal{A}$ had to issue the update key query for the time T before issuing the decryption query, and hence KU_T was already generated at that time, which can be retrieved by $\mathcal{C}$. On the other hand, $\mathcal{C}$ can directly generate the decryption key $DK_{ID,T}$ if ID is not revoked before T (otherwise, $\mathcal{C}$ can output $\bot$) without resorting to the DKGen(SK_{ID}, KU_T) algorithm:

- **Case $ID \in S^*$:** $\mathcal{C}$ selects random exponents $s, r, ktag_1, \cdots, ktag_m \xleftarrow{R} \mathbb{Z}_p$ and creates the decryption $DK_{ID,T}$ as:
$DK_1 = (g_2^{z_1}(g_2^{\hat{z}_1})^T)^s (g_2^{w_1})^r (g_2^{\frac{1}{\beta}})^{-\frac{z_1' + T\hat{z}_1'}{T-T^*}}$,

$DK_2 = (g_2^{z_2}(g_2^{\hat{z}_2})^T)^s (g_2^{w_2})^r (g_2^{\frac{1}{\beta}})^{-\frac{z_2' + T\hat{z}_2'}{T-T^*}}$, $DK_3 = g_2^r, DK_3' = g_2^s$,

$DK_{4,i} = g_2^{r(u_{1,i}-(ID)^i \cdot u_{1,0}+ktag_i \cdot w_1)}, DK_{5,i} = g_2^{r(u_{2,i}-(ID)^i \cdot u_{2,0}+ktag_i \cdot w_2)}$.

- **Case $ID \notin S^*$:** In this case, $\mathcal{C}$ transfers ID to the oracle: KeyGen$_{IBBE}(\cdot)$, and gets the private key $\{K_1, K_2, K_3, (K_{4,i}, K_{5,i}, ktag_i)_{i=1}^m\}$. $\mathcal{C}$ further chooses $s \xleftarrow{R} \mathbb{Z}_p$, and computes:
$DK_1 = K_1 \cdot (g_2^{z_1}(g_2^{\hat{z}_1})^T)^s, DK_2 = K_2 \cdot (g_2^{z_2}(g_2^{\hat{z}_2})^T)^s, DK_3 = K_3$, $DK_3' = g_2^s$;
$DK_{4,i} = K_{4,i}, DK_{5,i} = K_{5,i}, ktag_i = ktag_i$.

REMARK. Note that T will never equal to T^* in the case of $ID \in S^*$ according to the restriction in the security model of Sect. 2.4.

Finally, $\mathcal{C}$ stores and outputs the decryption key $DK_{ID,T}$ to $\mathcal{A}$ with:
$DK_{ID,T} = \{DK_1, DK_2, DK_3, DK_3', (DK_{4,i}, DK_{5,i}, ktag_i)_{i=1}^m\}.$

- If this is a revocation key query for an identity to be revoked ID and a revocation time T, then $\mathcal{C}$ updates the revocation list RL by running Revoke(ID, T, RL, ST) algorithm.

Challenge Cihphertexts: Once $\mathcal{A}$ decides that the **Key Extraction Phase 1** is over, $\mathcal{C}$ sends the challenge privileged set $S^* = \{ID_1^*, ID_2^*, ..., ID_n^*\}$ to the challenger in the IND-CPA game of the IBBE scheme $\prod_{\text{IBBE}}$ and gets (Hdr^*, K^*) with $Hdr^* = (C_1^*, C_2^*, C_3^*, ctag^*)$. Note that (Hdr^*, K_0^*) is obtained from the challenger of $\prod_{\text{IBBE}}$ by running $Encap$ algorithm with $(Hdr^*, K_0^*) = \text{Encap}(S^*)$, and K_1^* is a random element from the key space $\mathcal{K}$ of $\prod_{\text{IBBE}}$. It is $\mathcal{C}$'s task to decide $K^* = K_0^*$ or $K^* = K_1^*$. $\mathcal{C}$ sets $C_1 = C_1^*, C_2 = C_2^*, C_3 = (C_1^*)^{z_1' + T^* \hat{z}_1'} \cdot (C_2^*)^{z_2' + T^* \hat{z}_2'}, C_4 = C_3^*, ctag = ctag^*$ and sends $(Hdr = (C_1, C_2, C_3, C_4, ctag), K^*)$ to $\mathcal{A}$ as the challenge header and session key pair.

Key Extraction Phase 2: Same as **Key Extraction Phase 1**.

Guess: Finally, $\mathcal{A}$ outputs a guess $\beta' \in \{0, 1\}$, and $\mathcal{C}$ will transfer it to the challenger in the IND-CPA game of the IBBE scheme $\prod_{\text{IBBE}}$.

Now we show that the simulation is correct. That is, the distribution of all the above transcriptions between $\mathcal{A}$ and $\mathcal{C}$ is identical to the real experiment from the viewpoint of $\mathcal{A}$. Firstly, the public parameters PP is correct as the exponents $z_1', z_2', \hat{z}_1', \hat{z}_2' \in \mathbb{Z}_p$ are randomly chosen. Secondly, we show that the private keys are correct. For each node $\theta \in Path(BT, \eta)$, it can be easily verified that the private keys are of the same distribution in the case of $\theta \in N^*$. In the case of $\theta \notin N^*$, the private key for $(K_{1,\theta}, K_{2,\theta})$ is also correctly distributed from the setting $H_{1,\theta}' = K_{1,\theta} \cdot H_{1,\theta}, H_{2,\theta}' = K_{2,\theta} \cdot H_{2,\theta}, r_\theta' = r + r_\theta$ as

$$K_{1,\theta} = K_1 \cdot (g_2^{w_1})^{r_\theta} \cdot H_{1,\theta} = (g_2^{\alpha_1} \cdot H_{1,\theta}) \cdot (g_2^{w_1})^{r+r_\theta} = H_{1,\theta}' \cdot (g_2^{w_1})^{r_\theta'},$$
$$K_{2,\theta} = K_2 \cdot (g_2^{w_2})^{r_\theta} \cdot H_{2,\theta} = (g_2^{\alpha_1} \cdot H_{1,\theta}) \cdot (g_2^{w_2})^{r+r_\theta} = H_{2,\theta}' \cdot (g_2^{w_2})^{r_\theta'}.$$

Thirdly, we show that the update key is correct. In case of $\theta \in N^*$, we have that a time related update key is correctly distributed from the setting $s_\theta' = s_\theta - \frac{1}{\beta(T - T^*)}$ as it holds that:

$$KU_{1,\theta} = (g_2^{z_1}(g_2^{\hat{z}_1})^T)^{s_\theta} H_{1,\theta}^{-1} (g_2^{\frac{1}{\beta}})^{-\frac{z_1' + T \hat{z}_1'}{T - T^*}} = (g_2^{z_1' - T^* \beta \alpha_1}(g_2^{\hat{z}_1'} g_2^{\beta \alpha_1})^T)^{s_\theta} g_2^{-\frac{z_1' + T \hat{z}_1'}{\beta(T - T^*)}}$$
$$H_{1,\theta}^{-1}$$
$$= g_2^{\alpha_1}(g_2^{z_1' + T \hat{z}_1'} g_2^{(T - T^*)\beta \alpha_1})^{s_\theta} g_2^{-\frac{z_1' + T \hat{z}_1'}{\beta(T - T^*)}} \cdot g_2^{-\alpha_1} \cdot H_{1,\theta}^{-1}$$
$$= g_2^{\alpha_1}(g_2^{z_1' + T \hat{z}_1'} g_2^{(T - T^*)\beta \alpha_1})^{s_\theta} \cdot (g_2^{\alpha_1 \beta(T - T^*) + z_1' + T \hat{z}_1'})^{-\frac{1}{\beta(T - T^*)}} \cdot H_{1,\theta}^{-1}$$
$$= g_2^{\alpha_1}(g_2^{z_1' + T \hat{z}_1'} g_2^{(T - T^*)\beta \alpha_1})^{s_\theta - \frac{1}{\beta(T - T^*)}} \cdot H_{1,\theta}^{-1}$$
$$= g_2^{\alpha_1}(g_2^{z_1' + T \hat{z}_1'} g_2^{(T - T^*)\beta \alpha_1})^{s_\theta'} \cdot H_{1,\theta}^{-1}$$
$$= g_2^{\alpha_1}(g_2^{z_1}(g_2^{\hat{z}_1})^T)^{s_\theta'} \cdot H_{1,\theta}^{-1},$$

$$KU_{2,\theta} = (g_2^{z_2}(g_2^{\hat{z}_2})^T)^{s_\theta} H_{2,\theta}^{-1} (g_2^{\frac{1}{\beta}})^{-\frac{z_2' + T \hat{z}_2'}{T - T^*}} = (g_2^{z_2' - T^* \beta \alpha_2}(g_2^{\hat{z}_2'} g_2^{\beta \alpha_2})^T)^{s_\theta} g_2^{-\frac{z_2' + T \hat{z}_2'}{\beta(T - T^*)}}$$
$$H_{2,\theta}^{-1}$$
$$= g_2^{\alpha_2}(g_2^{z_2' + T \hat{z}_2'} g_2^{(T - T^*)\beta \alpha_2})^{s_\theta} g_2^{-\frac{z_2' + T \hat{z}_2'}{\beta(T - T^*)}} \cdot g_2^{-\alpha_2} \cdot H_{2,\theta}^{-1}$$

$$= g_2^{\alpha_2}(g_2^{z_2'+T\hat{z}_2'}g_2^{(T-T^*)\beta\alpha_2})^{s_\theta'} \cdot H_{2,\theta}^{-1} = g_2^{\alpha_2}(g_2^{z_2}(g_2^{\hat{z}_2})^T)^{s_\theta'} \cdot H_{2,\theta}^{-1},$$

$$KU_{3,\theta} = g_2^{s_\theta}(g_2^{\frac{1}{\beta}})^{-\frac{1}{T-T^*}} = g_2^{s_\theta - \frac{1}{\beta(T-T^*)}} = g_2^{s_\theta'}.$$

In case of $\theta \notin N^*$, the update key is correctly distributed from the setting $H_{1,\theta}' = g_2^{\alpha_1}H_{1,\theta}, H_{2,\theta}' = g_2^{\alpha_1}H_{2,\theta}, s_\theta' = s_\theta$ as:

$$KU_{1,\theta} = (g_2^{z_1}(g_2^{\hat{z}_1})^T)^{s_\theta}H_{1,\theta}^{-1} = g_2^{\alpha_1}(g_2^{z_1}(g_2^{\hat{z}_1})^T)^{s_\theta}g_2^{-\alpha_1}H_{1,\theta}^{-1} = g_2^{\alpha_1}(g_2^{z_1}(g_2^{\hat{z}_1})^T)^{s_\theta}$$
$$(H_{1,\theta}')^{-1},$$

$$KU_{2,\theta} = (g_2^{z_2}(g_2^{\hat{z}_2})^T)^{s_\theta}H_{2,\theta}^{-1} = g_2^{\alpha_2}(g_2^{z_2}(g_2^{\hat{z}_2})^T)^{s_\theta}(H_{2,\theta}')^{-1}, KU_{3,\theta} = g_2^{s_\theta} = g_2^{s_\theta'}.$$

Fourthly, we show that the decryption key is correct. As we have proved before, both the private key SK_{ID} and the update key KU_T are correctly distributed, the resulting decryption key must be correctly distributed by running the $\mathrm{DKGen}(SK_{ID}, KU_T)$ algorithm. Furthermore, if ID is not revoked before T, we can prove that the decryption key for $(DK_{1,\theta}, DK_{2,\theta})$ is also correctly distributed directly with $SK_{ID} = \{K_{1,\theta}, K_{2,\theta}, K_{3,\theta}, (K_{4,i,\theta}, K_{5,i,\theta}, ktag_{i,\theta})_{i=1}^m\}_{\theta \in Path(BT,\eta)}$ and $KU_T = \{KU_{1,\theta}, KU_{2,\theta}, KU_{3,\theta}\}_{\theta \in KUNode(BT,RL,T)}$.

In the case of $ID \in S^*$, there must exist a node $\theta \in \mathrm{KUNode}(BT, RL, T) \cap N^*$ with $KU_{1,\theta} = (g_2^{z_1}(g_2^{\hat{z}_1})^T)^{s_\theta}H_{1,\theta}^{-1}(g_2^{\frac{1}{\beta}})^{-\frac{z_1'+T\hat{z}_1'}{T-T^*}} = g_2^{\alpha_1}(g_2^{z_1}(g_2^{\hat{z}_1})^T)^{s_\theta'} \cdot H_{1,\theta}^{-1}$ and $K_{1,\theta} = H_{1,\theta} \cdot (g_2^{w_1})^{r_\theta}$. According to the $\mathrm{DKGen}(SK_{ID}, KU_T)$ algorithm:

$$K_{1,\theta} \cdot KU_{1,\theta} = H_{1,\theta} \cdot (g_2^{w_1})^{r_\theta} \cdot g_2^{\alpha_1}(g_2^{z_1}(g_2^{\hat{z}_1})^T)^{s_\theta'} \cdot H_{1,\theta}^{-1} = g_2^{\alpha_1} \cdot (g_2^{w_1})^{r_\theta} \cdot (g_2^{z_1}(g_2^{\hat{z}_1})^T)^{s_\theta'},$$
$$K_{2,\theta} \cdot KU_{2,\theta} = H_{2,\theta} \cdot (g_2^{w_2})^{r_\theta} \cdot g_2^{\alpha_2}(g_2^{z_2}(g_2^{\hat{z}_2})^T)^{s_\theta'} \cdot H_{2,\theta}^{-1} = g_2^{\alpha_2} \cdot (g_2^{w_2})^{r_\theta} \cdot (g_2^{z_2}(g_2^{\hat{z}_2})^T)^{s_\theta'}.$$

Thus, $DK_1 = K_{1,\theta} \cdot KU_{1,\theta} \cdot g_2^{r_\theta' \cdot w_1} g_2^{s_\theta' \cdot (z_1 + T \cdot \hat{z}_1)}$ and $DK_2 = K_{2,\theta} \cdot KU_{2,\theta} \cdot g_2^{r_\theta' \cdot w_2} g_2^{s_\theta' \cdot (z_2 + T \cdot \hat{z}_2)}$ have the correct distribution.

In the case of $ID \notin S^*$, as $K_{1,\theta} = K_1 \cdot (g_2^{w_1})^{r_\theta} \cdot H_{1,\theta}, K_{2,\theta} = K_2 \cdot (g_2^{w_2})^{r_\theta} \cdot H_{2,\theta}$ and $KU_{1,\theta} = (g_2^{z_1}(g_2^{\hat{z}_1})^T)^{s_\theta}H_{1,\theta}^{-1}, KU_{2,\theta} = (g_2^{z_2}(g_2^{\hat{z}_2})^T)^{s_\theta}H_{2,\theta}^{-1}$, it is easy to check:

$$K_{1,\theta} \cdot KU_{1,\theta} = K_1 \cdot (g_2^{w_1})^{r_\theta} \cdot H_{1,\theta} \cdot (g_2^{z_1}(g_2^{\hat{z}_1})^T)^{s_\theta}H_{1,\theta}^{-1} = K_1 \cdot (g_2^{w_1})^{r_\theta} \cdot (g_2^{z_1}(g_2^{\hat{z}_1})^T)^{s_\theta},$$
$$K_{2,\theta} \cdot KU_{2,\theta} = K_2 \cdot (g_2^{w_2})^{r_\theta} \cdot H_{1,\theta}(g_2^{z_2}(g_2^{\hat{z}_2})^T)^{s_\theta}H_{1,\theta}^{-1} = K_2 \cdot (g_2^{w_2})^{r_\theta} \cdot (g_2^{z_2}(g_2^{\hat{z}_2})^T)^{s_\theta}.$$

Thus, DK_1 and DK_2 also have the correct distribution.

Finally, we show that the challenge ciphertext is correct. For the challenge session key $K_0^* = g_T^s$, the challenge header $Hdr^* = (C_1^*, C_2^*, C_3^*, ctag^*)$ that $\mathcal{C}$ receives with a privileged set $S^* = \{ID_1^*, ID_2^*, ..., ID_n^*\}$ is of the following distribution: $C_1^* = g_1^s, C_2^* = (g_1^b)^s, C_3^* = (W_1^{ctag} \cdot \prod_{i=0}^n (g_1^{u_i})^{y_i})^s$. Thus, for the same privileged set S^*, the challenge header $Hdr = (C_1, C_2, C_3, C_4, ctag)$ that $\mathcal{A}$ is given from $\mathcal{C}$ is also well formed since:

$$C_3 = (Z_1 \cdot \hat{Z}_1^{T^*})^s = (g_1^{z_1}(g_1^b)^{z_2'}(g_1^{\beta\alpha})^{-T^*} \cdot (g_1^{\hat{z}_1'}(g_1^b)^{\hat{z}_2'}(g_1^{\beta\alpha}))^{T^*})^s$$
$$= (g_1^{z_1'+\hat{z}_1' \cdot T^*}(g_1^b)^{z_2'+\hat{z}_2' \cdot T^*})^s = (C_1^*)^{z_1'+\hat{z}_1' \cdot T^*} \cdot (C_2^*)^{z_2'+\hat{z}_2' \cdot T^*}.$$

From the above simulation, we have $\Pr[\beta = \beta'|\beta = 0] = \frac{1}{2} + Adv_{\mathcal{A},RIBBE}^{saIND\text{-}CPA}/|\mathcal{T}|$ as the simulation is correctly distributed. In addition, $\Pr[\beta = \beta'|\beta = 1] = \frac{1}{2}$ since K_1^* is a random element from the key space $\mathcal{K}$ and is completely independent with Hdr^* in the view of $\mathcal{A}$. Therefore, we have the following equation:

$$Adv_{\mathcal{C},IBBE}^{IND\text{-}CPA} = \left|\Pr[\beta' = \beta] - \frac{1}{2}\right| = \left|\frac{1}{2}\Pr[\beta = \beta'|\beta = 0] + \frac{1}{2}\Pr[\beta = \beta'|\beta = 1] - \frac{1}{2}\right|$$
$$= \left|\frac{1}{2|\mathcal{T}|}Adv_{\mathcal{A},RIBBE}^{saIND\text{-}CPA} + \frac{1}{4} + \frac{1}{4} - \frac{1}{2}\right| = \frac{1}{2|\mathcal{T}|}Adv_{\mathcal{A},RIBBE}^{saIND\text{-}CPA} = \frac{\varepsilon}{2|\mathcal{T}|}.$$

This completes the proof of Lemma 4.   □

Lemma 5. *The resulting revocable IBE scheme $\prod_{RIBE}$ is adaptively secure under chosen plaintext attacks for $m = 1$, if the basic IBBE scheme $\prod_{IBBE}$ described in Sect. 3.1 is adaptively secure. Furthermore, suppose there is an adversary $\mathcal{A}$ attacking the adaptive security of $\prod_{RIBE}$ with a non-negligible advantage $Adv_{\mathcal{A},RIBE}^{IND\text{-}CPA} = \varepsilon$, then there exists an adversary $\mathcal{C}$ against the adaptive security of $\prod_{IBE}$ ($m = 1$ of $\prod_{IBBE}$) with advantage $Adv_{\mathcal{A},RIBE}^{IND\text{-}CPA} = \frac{\varepsilon}{|\mathcal{T}|(q_1+1)}$, which is also non-negligible. Note that q_1 is the maximum number of queries for different identities of private keys and decryption keys before the challenge phase, and $\mathcal{T}$ is the set of time periods, which are both polynomial size.*

Proof. If there exists an adversary $\mathcal{A}$ that attacks the above revocable IBE scheme $\prod_{\text{RIBE}}$ with a non-negligible advantage, we will construct a PPT algorithm $\mathcal{C}$ to break the adaptive security of the IBE scheme $\prod_{\text{IBE}}$ for $m = 1$ described in Sect. 3.1. In the following proof, we will omit some detailed discussion due to page limitation. Especially, we focus on the part that are different from the proof of Lemma 4.

At the beginning, $\mathcal{C}$ receives public parameters of the IBE scheme $\prod_{\text{IBE}}$: $(g_1, g_1^b, U_1 = g_1^{u_1+bu_2}, W_1 = g_1^{w_1+bw_2}, g_T, g_2, g_2^{u_1}, g_2^{u_2}, g_2^{w_1}, g_2^{w_2}, g_1^{\beta\alpha}, g_2^{\beta\alpha_1}, g_2^{\beta\alpha_2}, g_2^{1/\beta})$ with $u_1 = (u_{1,0}, u_{1,1}), u_2 = (u_{2,0}, u_{2,1})$ for $m = 1$. During the process, $\mathcal{C}$ can access to the secret key generation oracle $\text{KeyGen}_{\text{IBE}}(\cdot)$, which can receive a private key of $SK_{ID} = \{K_1, K_2, K_3, K_4, K_5, ktag\}$ with: $K_1 = g_2^{\alpha_1} \cdot (g_2^{w_1})^r, K_2 = g_2^{\alpha_2} \cdot (g_2^{w_2})^r, K_3 = g_2^r, K_4 = ((g_2^{w_1})^{ktag} g_2^{u_{1,1}} (g_2^{-u_{1,0}})^{ID})^r, K_5 = ((g_2^{w_2})^{ktag} g_2^{u_{2,1}} (g_2^{-u_{2,0}})^{ID})^r$.

As the adversary $\mathcal{A}$ won't declare the target identity ID^* and time period T^* at the initial phase for the adaptive security model, $\mathcal{C}$ should first guess the right T^* that $\mathcal{A}$ submits the target identity in the challenge phase, which holds with probability $1/|\mathcal{T}|$ for polynomial-size $\mathcal{T}$.

Furthermore, for the challenge ID^*, $\mathcal{C}$ should guess the exact index of queries i^* that $\mathcal{A}$ issues ID^* to the $SKGen$ or $DKGen$ oracles for the first time. More precisely, $i^* \in \{1, 2, \cdots, q_1\}$ denotes that $\mathcal{A}$ first issues ID^* to $\mathcal{C}$ at the i^*-th identity for the private key query or the decryption key query in the **Key Extraction Phase 1**, where q_1 is the maximum number of private key queries and the decryption key queries before the challenge phase. $i^* = q_1 + 1$ denotes that $\mathcal{A}$ does not query any private key or decryption for ID^*, but it can issue a private key query or decryption key query for ID^* in the **Key Extraction Phase 2**. $\mathcal{C}$ makes a random guess $i^* \in \{1, 2, \cdots, q_1, q_1+1\}$ for the adversary $\mathcal{A}$. Similar as in [33], the adversary $\mathcal{A}$ can be divided into the following two types: $\mathcal{A}$ is a Type-1 adversary if $i^* \in \{1, 2, \cdots, q_1\}$; and $\mathcal{A}$ is a Type-2 adversary if $i^* = q_1 + 1$. Note that $\mathcal{A}$ is a still a Type-2 adversary even $\mathcal{A}$ has never queried ID^* for any private key or decryption key, in which case the target identity ID^* is already known by $\mathcal{C}$ in the challenge phase. In the rest of the proof, we assume that $\mathcal{C}$'s guess for i^* is right, which hold with probability $1/(q_1 + 1)$ (a loss of polynomial in security parameter λ). Once $\mathcal{C}$ finds the guess is wrong, it terminates the simulation and outputs a random bit $\beta' \in \{0, 1\}$.

Setup: $\mathcal{C}$ first creates a binary tree BT with N leaves. It chooses a random leaf node η^* for a target identity ID^* in advance, that is, η^* is pre-assigned to ID^* that will be used in the challenge phase. $\mathcal{C}$ then chooses $z_1', z_2', \hat{z}_1', \hat{z}_2' \xleftarrow{R} \mathbb{Z}_p$ and computes: $Z_1 = g_1^{z_1+b\cdot z_2} = g_1^{z_1'}(g_1^b)^{z_2'}/(g_1^{\beta\alpha})^{T^*}$, $\hat{Z}_1 = g_1^{\hat{z}_1+b\cdot\hat{z}_2} = g_1^{\hat{z}_1'}(g_1^b)^{\hat{z}_2'}(g_1^{\beta\alpha})$, $g_2^{z_1} = g_2^{z_1'}/(g_2^{\beta\alpha_1})^{T^*}, g_2^{z_2} = g_2^{z_2'}/(g_2^{\beta\alpha_2})^{T^*}, g_2^{\hat{z}_1} = g_2^{\hat{z}_1'}g_2^{\beta\alpha_1}, g_2^{\hat{z}_2} = g_2^{\hat{z}_2'}g_2^{\beta\alpha_2}$. Finally, the public parameters PP of $\prod_{RIBE}$ is then sent to $\mathcal{A}$ with:
$$PP = (g_1, g_1^b, U_1, W_1, Z_1, \hat{Z}_1, g_T, g_2, g_2^{u_1}, g_2^{u_2}, g_2^{w_1}, g_2^{w_2}, g_2^{z_1}, g_2^{z_2}, g_2^{\hat{z}_1}, g_2^{\hat{z}_2}).$$

Key Extraction Phase 1 for Type-1 Adversary: $\mathcal{A}$ is a Type-1 adversary in the case of $i^* \leqslant q_1$. $\mathcal{C}$ will keep an integer i to count the number of queries from $\mathcal{A}$ for private key or decryption key up to the current time. $\mathcal{C}$ interacts with $\mathcal{A}$ in the following steps:

- If this is a private key query for an identity ID, $\mathcal{C}$ performs as follows:
  - **Case $i < i^*$**: It assigns ID to a random leaf η from BT and stores ID in the leaf node η if ID is first issued to $\mathcal{C}$ for the private key or decryption key, otherwise, $\mathcal{C}$ uses the stored leaf node η for ID. For each node $\theta \in Path(BT, \eta)$, $\mathcal{C}$ can retrieve H_θ if it was defined. Otherwise, it chooses $H_\theta = (H_{1,\theta}, H_{2,\theta}) \xleftarrow{R} \mathbb{G}_2$ and stores H_θ in the node θ. θ can be further divided into the following two types:
    1. If $\theta \in Path(BT, \eta^*)$: In this situation, $\mathcal{C}$ chooses $r_\theta, ktag_\theta \xleftarrow{R} \mathbb{Z}_p$, and computes: $K_{1,\theta} = H_{1,\theta} \cdot (g_2^{w_1})^{r_\theta}, K_{2,\theta} = H_{2,\theta} \cdot (g_2^{w_2})^{r_\theta}, K_{3,\theta} = g_2^{r_\theta}$, $K_{4,\theta} = g_2^{r_\theta(u_{1,1}-(ID)\cdot u_{1,0}+ktag_\theta \cdot w_1)}, K_{5,\theta} = g_2^{r_\theta(u_{2,1}-(ID)\cdot u_{2,0}+ktag_\theta \cdot w_2)}$.
    2. If $\theta \notin Path(BT, \eta^*)$: In this situation, $\mathcal{C}$ transfers ID to the oracle: $KeyGen_{IBE}(\cdot)$, and gets the private key $\{K_1, K_2, K_3, K_4, K_5, ktag\}$. $\mathcal{C}$ further chooses $r_\theta, ktag_\theta' \xleftarrow{R} \mathbb{Z}_p$, and computes: $ktag_\theta = ktag_\theta' + ktag$, $K_{1,\theta} = K_1 \cdot (g_2^{w_1})^{r_\theta} \cdot H_{1,\theta}, K_{2,\theta} = K_2 \cdot (g_2^{w_2})^{r_\theta} \cdot H_{2,\theta}, K_{3,\theta} = K_3 \cdot g_2^{r_\theta}$, $K_{4,\theta} = K_4 \cdot g_2^{r_\theta(u_{1,1}-ID\cdot u_{1,0}+ktag_\theta \cdot w_1)}, K_{5,\theta} = K_5 \cdot g_2^{r_\theta(u_{2,1}-ID\cdot u_{2,0}+ktag_\theta \cdot w_2)}$.
  - **Case $i = i^*$**: $\mathcal{C}$ identifies this identity ID as the target identity ID^* and stores ID^* in the leaf node η^*, which is pre-assigned in the **Setup** phase. For each node $\theta \in Path(BT, \eta^*)$, $\mathcal{C}$ can retrieve H_θ if it was defined. Otherwise, it chooses $H_\theta = (H_{1,\theta}, H_{2,\theta}) \xleftarrow{R} \mathbb{G}_2$ and stores H_θ in the node θ. $\mathcal{C}$ further chooses $r_\theta, ktag_\theta \xleftarrow{R} \mathbb{Z}_p$, and computes: $K_{1,\theta} = H_{1,\theta} \cdot (g_2^{w_1})^{r_\theta}, K_{2,\theta} = H_{2,\theta} \cdot (g_2^{w_2})^{r_\theta}, K_{3,\theta} = g_2^{r_\theta}$, $K_{4,\theta} = g_2^{r_\theta(u_{1,1}-ID\cdot u_{1,0}+ktag_\theta \cdot w_1)}, K_{5,\theta} = g_2^{r_\theta(u_{2,1}-ID\cdot u_{2,0}+ktag_\theta \cdot w_2)}$.
  - **Case $i > i^*$**: $\mathcal{C}$ does the same process as in the case of $i < i^*$.
  Finally, $\mathcal{C}$ stores and outputs the private key SK_{ID} to $\mathcal{A}$ with:
  $$SK_{ID} = \{K_{1,\theta}, K_{2,\theta}, K_{3,\theta}, K_{4,\theta}, K_{5,\theta}, ktag_\theta\}_{\theta \in Path(BT, \eta)}.$$
- If this is an update key query for the time T, $\mathcal{C}$ first runs $KUNode(BT, RL, T)$ algorithm with the current revocation list RL and time T. For each node $\theta \in KUNode(BT, RL, T)$, $\mathcal{C}$ can retrieve H_θ if it was defined. Otherwise, it chooses $H_\theta = (H_{1,\theta}, H_{2,\theta}) \xleftarrow{R} \mathbb{G}_2$ and stores H_θ in the node θ. Then it chooses $s_\theta \xleftarrow{R} \mathbb{Z}_p$, and computes:
  - If $\theta \in Path(BT, \eta^*)$: $KU_{1,\theta} = (g_2^{z_1}(g_2^{\hat{z}_1})^T)^{s_\theta} \cdot H_{1,\theta}^{-1} \cdot (g_2^{\frac{1}{\beta}})^{-\frac{z_1'+T\hat{z}_1'}{T-T^*}}$,
  $KU_{2,\theta} = (g_2^{z_2}(g_2^{\hat{z}_2})^T)^{s_\theta} \cdot H_{2,\theta}^{-1} \cdot (g_2^{\frac{1}{\beta}})^{-\frac{z_2'+T\hat{z}_2'}{T-T^*}}, KU_{3,\theta} = g_2^{s_\theta} \cdot (g_2^{\frac{1}{\beta}})^{-\frac{1}{T-T^*}}$.

- **If** $\theta \notin Path(BT, \eta^*)$: $KU_{1,\theta} = (g_2^{z_1}(g_2^{\hat{z}_1})^T)^{s_\theta} H_{1,\theta}^{-1}, KU_{2,\theta} = (g_2^{z_2}(g_2^{\hat{z}_2})^T)^{s_\theta} H_{2,\theta}^{-1}$, $KU_{3,\theta} = g_2^{s_\theta}$.

Finally, $\mathcal{C}$ stores and outputs the update key KU_T to $\mathcal{A}$ with:
$KU_T = \{KU_{1,\theta}, KU_{2,\theta}, KU_{3,\theta}\}_{\theta \in \text{KUNode}(BT,RL,T)}$.

- If this is a decryption key query for an identity ID and time T, $\mathcal{C}$ can generate the corresponding decryption key $DK_{ID,T}$ by running DKGen(SK_{ID}, KU_T) algorithm: $\mathcal{C}$ will create and store the private key SK_{ID} following the same process as responding the private key query for ID, if ID has never been queried to the private key or the decryption key before (otherwise, $\mathcal{C}$ can use the stored SK_{ID}). In addition, $\mathcal{A}$ had to issue the update key query for the time T before issuing the decryption query, and hence KU_T was already generated at that time, which can be retrieved by $\mathcal{C}$.
- If this is a revocation key query for an identity to be revoked ID and a revocation time T, then $\mathcal{C}$ updates the revocation list RL by running Revoke(ID, T, RL, ST) algorithm.

Key Extraction Phase 1 for Type-2 Adversary: In this case, $i^* = q_1 + 1$. For a Type-2 adversary $\mathcal{A}$, there is no need for $\mathcal{C}$ to keep an integer i to count the number of queries from $\mathcal{A}$, as the target identity ID^* that $\mathcal{A}$ issues is only after the challenge phase, which is already known by $\mathcal{C}$. $\mathcal{C}$ interacts with $\mathcal{A}$ in the following steps:

- If this is a private key query for an identity ID, $\mathcal{C}$ performs the same procedure as in the case of $i < i^*$ for the Type-1 adversary.
- For the rest of queries, including the update key query, decryption key query and revocation key query, $\mathcal{C}$ acts same as above in the key extraction phase 1 for Type-1 adversary.

Challenge: Now $\mathcal{A}$ sends the challenge identity ID^* and time T^* to $\mathcal{C}$. We assume that $\mathcal{C}$'s guess is right, which holds with probability $1/|\mathcal{T}|(q_1 + 1)$. Once $\mathcal{C}$ finds the guess is wrong, it terminates the simulation and outputs a random bit $\beta' \in \{0,1\}$. $\mathcal{C}$ then sends the challenge identity ID^* to the challenger in the IND-CPA game of the IBE scheme $\prod_{\text{IBE}}$ and gets (Hdr^*, K^*) with $Hdr^* = (C_1^*, C_2^*, C_3^*, ctag^*)$. Note that (Hdr^*, K_0^*) is obtained from the challenger of $\prod_{\text{IBE}}$ by running $Encap$ algorithm with $(Hdr^*, K_0^*) = \text{Encap}(S^*)$, and K_1^* is a random element from the key space $\mathcal{K}$ of $\prod_{\text{IBE}}$. $\mathcal{C}$ sets $C_1 = C_1^*, C_2 = C_2^*, C_3 = (C_1^*)^{z_1' + T^* \hat{z}_1'} \cdot (C_2^*)^{z_2' + T^* \hat{z}_2'}, C_4 = C_3^*, ctag = ctag^*$ and sends $(Hdr = (C_1, C_2, C_3, C_4, ctag), K^*)$ to $\mathcal{A}$ as the challenge header and session key pair.

Key Extraction Phase 2: Same as **Key Extraction Phase 1**.

Guess: Finally, $\mathcal{A}$ outputs a guess $\beta' \in \{0,1\}$, and $\mathcal{C}$ will transfer it to the challenger in the IND-CPA game of the IBE scheme $\prod_{\text{IBE}}$.

We note that during the simulation, $\mathcal{C}$ can access to the secret key generation oracle KeyGen$_{\text{IBE}}(\cdot)$ only for identities that $ID \neq ID^*$. $\mathcal{A}$ can query the private key for ID^* or the decryption key related to ID^* related to time $T \neq T^*$. In this case, $\mathcal{C}$ can also simulate the correct private key SK_{ID^*} or decryption key

$DK_{ID^*,T}$, the distribution of which is identical to those in the real experiment. Furthermore, we can prove that the distribution of all transcriptions between $\mathcal{A}$ and $\mathcal{C}$ is same as those generated by real algorithm. The analysis is very similar to the proof of Lemma 4, and is omitted here.

The reduction loss in our security proof is $\frac{1}{|T|(q_1+1)}$, where q_1 is the maximum number of queries for different identities of private keys and decryption keys. That is, for an adversary $\mathcal{A}$ with advantage $Adv_{\mathcal{A},RIBE}^{IND\text{-}CPA} = \varepsilon$ in breaking IND-CPA security of $\prod_{RIBE}$, there is an algorithm $\mathcal{V}$ with advantage $Adv_{\mathcal{A},RIBE}^{IND\text{-}CPA} = \frac{\varepsilon}{|T|(q_1+1)}$ in breaking adaptive security of $\prod_{IBE}$.

This completes the proof of Lemma 5.   □

6 Experimental and Evaluation

To demonstrate its practicality, we implement the proposed revocable IBBE scheme in Python 3.3.1 using the Charm 0.43 framework [2], a programming framework for cryptographic primitives. For the Type-3 pairings, we choose the default Miyaji-Nakabayashi-Takano elliptic curve group [26] with base field size 224 bits (MNT224) to establish our scheme, which can provide 96-bit security level [39]. All programs are running on a laptop with Intel® Core™ i3-4010U CPU@1.70 GH and 4.0 GB RAM using operating system 32-bit Ubuntu 13.04.

Figures 2 and 3 demonstrate the average time costs of all kinds of algorithms in our scheme. The data is measured by the benchmark tool provided by Charm. The average time cost is recorded after running each program using the MNT224 curve and other related parameters for 100 times. We perform the experiment in the following way: first setup the system with the maximum size of privileged set m and the total number of system users N, then generate a secret key, update key periodically via a public channel for the revocation list RL, generate the decryption key, encrypt a message given a privileged set S and decrypt the ciphertext.

Figure 2 (left) plots the influence of the maximum size of privileged set m on the efficiency of our scheme, where $m \in \{1,2,3,4,5,6,7,8,9,10\}$, the total number of system users is set to be $N = 64$, and there is no users is revoked (i.e., $RL = \emptyset$). For the **Encap** algorithm, the privileged identity is set as

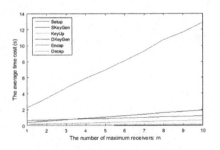 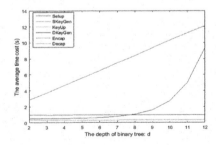

Fig. 2. Average time cost of all algorithms for different choices of m and d

$S = \{$user1@email.com, ..., user$m$@email.com$\}$ for $m = 1, 2, ..., 10$. The user with identity user1@email.com that is not revoked can always correctly decrypt during this experiment. Note that for $m = 1$, this is an adaptively secure revocable IBE scheme, which is proven in Lemma 5. As we see in Fig. 2(a), **SKGen** algorithm consumes the most computation costs. This is because $(3m + 3) * (log_2 N)$ elements are needed for each private key, which will take $O(m * (log_2 N))$ exponentiation operations of $\mathbb{G}_2$. The operations on group $\mathbb{G}_2$ are more expensive than that of $\mathbb{G}_1$, about 11 times for exponentiations according to [1]. Note that the private key is generated only one time from PKG via a secure channel for each user in the system. For the more frequent activity of **KeyUp** algorithm in the PKG side, the average time cost is bounded by just 0.14 s.

Figure 2 (right) plots the time taken by the total number of system users $N \in \{2^2, 2^3, 2^4, 2^5, 2^6, 2^7, 2^8, 2^9, 2^{10}, 2^{11}, 2^{12}\}$, in which case the maximum size of privileged set for one encryption is set to be $m = 10$, and the revocation list $RL = \emptyset$. One can see that the time cost of the **Setup** algorithm grows exponentially in the depth d of the binary tree, which means the computation overhead is still linear in the number of system users N, where $N = 2^d$. The reason is that PKG should assign each identity into a random leaf node in the binary tree, and maintain the state information ST. It is worth mentioning that PKG can use a pseudorandom generator instead of storing the random values for each node in the binary tree, which is suggested in the Libert-Vergnaud scheme [25]. In terms of secret key generation algorithm **SKGen**, the computation overhead is linear in the depth of the binary tree, as the secret key is associated with the path from root to the leaf node. The compution overhead of the **DKGen**, **Decap** and **KeyUp** algorithms are all under 1 s, which are independent of the number of system users. specifically, the average time cost of the **Encap** algorithm is just 31.2 ms, which makes our revocable IBBE scheme very efficient.

Figure 3 (left) demonstrates the time cost of **KeyUp** algorithm for different numbers of users to be revoked r from 1 to 50, where the total number of system users is set to be $N = 64$. Note that the random leaf node assignment technique [33] is used in our scheme. When a new user joins the system, it is assigned a random leaf node in the tree. In our implementation, each identity is pre-assigned a random leaf node via the built-in function

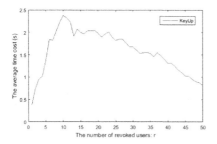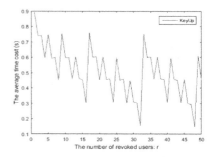

Fig. 3. Average time cost of KeyUp algorithm for different numbers of r

random.shuffle () in the system setup phase. The revocation list is $RL = \{user1@email.com, ..., userj@email.com\}$ for $j = 1, 2, ..., 50$. We can see that the time overhead of this **KeyUp** algorithm in all cases is upper bounded by 2.5 s. More specifically, if each identity is assigned a leaf node in sequence without the random leaf node assignment technique [33], the average time costs of the **KeyUp** algorithm would be present in Fig. 3 (right). We can say that $r = 32$ will have the least computation overhead, as there will be only one node in the KUNode algorithm of the **KeyUp** algorithm.

7 Conclusion

Providing an efficient revocation mechanism is necessary in the IBE setting and BE setting where a large number of users are involved, especially when considering practical deployments of these cryptosystems. It is more desirable that the sender does not need to know the revocation list, and only the receiver needs to check the revocation list of his credential to decrypt ciphertext. We further expand the study of scalable revocation methodology in the setting of IBBE, and then present a concrete instantiation of revocable IBBE scheme with DKER, which is motivated by a new revocable IBE scheme recently proposed in [38]. To build our revocable IBBE scheme, we first propose an adaptive IBBE scheme derived from [31]. Then we can construct a revocable IBBE scheme with a security reduction to the aforementioned IBBE scheme. The proposed scheme is very efficient both in terms of computation costs and communication overheads, as the ciphertext size is constant, independent of the number of recipients. Our scheme can withstand decryption key exposure, which is proved its semi-adaptive security under mild variants of the SXDH assumption. As a side contribution, we also present an adaptive secure revocable IBE scheme with DKER, which can be seen as a complementary of Watanabe et al.'s revocable IBE scheme [38].

Acknowledgment. Part of this work was done while Aijun Ge was visiting Institute for Advanced Study, Tsinghua University. The authors would like to thank Jianghong Wei and Jie Zhang for their helpful discussions on the Charm framework. We also thank anonymous reviewers of PKC 2019 for their insightful comments. The work is partially supported by the National Natural Science Foundation of China (No. 61502529 and No. 61502276), the National Key Research and Development Program of China (No. 2017YFA0303903) and Zhejiang Province Key R&D Project (No. 2017C01062).

A Proof of Lemma 3 in Sect. 3.2

Proof. Given a PPT adversary $\mathcal{A}$ achieving a non-negligible difference ε in advantage between $Game_q$ and $Game_{Final}$, we will create a PPT algorithm $\mathcal{C}$ to break the ADDH1 assumption. Let $(g_1, g_1^{\mu}, g_1^{\alpha_2}, g_1^{\beta\alpha}, g_2, g_2^{\alpha}, g_2^{\beta\alpha}, g_2^{\beta\alpha_2}, g_2^{1/\beta}, Z = g_1^{\mu\alpha_2+\eta})$ be the instance of ADDH1 problem in $\mathcal{G}$ that $\mathcal{C}$ has to solve, i.e., to decide whether $\eta = 0$ or a random value in $\mathbb{Z}_p^*$. Note that in $Game_q$, all the user keys returned to $\mathcal{A}$ are semi-functional and so is the challenge header and session key. $\mathcal{C}$ will simulate either Game_q or $\text{Game}_{\text{Final}}$ with $\mathcal{A}$, depending on the value of η.

Setup: At the beginning, $\mathcal{C}$ chooses random exponents $\boldsymbol{u}_1 = (u_{1,0}, \cdots, u_{1,m})$, $\boldsymbol{u}_2 = (u_{2,0}, \cdots, u_{2,m}), w_1, w_2 \xleftarrow{R} \mathbb{Z}_p$ and $b \xleftarrow{R} \mathbb{Z}_p^*$, and sets the public parameters PP:

$$g_1 := g_1, g_1^b, U_1 := g_1^{\boldsymbol{u}_1 + b\boldsymbol{u}_2}, W_1 := g_1^{w_1 + bw_2}, g_T := e(g_1, g_2^\alpha),$$
$$g_2 := g_2, g_2^{\boldsymbol{u}_1}, g_2^{\boldsymbol{u}_2}, g_2^{w_1}, g_2^{w_2}, g_1^{\beta\alpha}, g_2^{\beta\alpha_1} := g_2^{\beta\alpha}/(g_2^{\beta\alpha_2})^b, g_2^{\beta\alpha_2}, g_2^{1/\beta}.$$

Note that this implicitly sets $\alpha_1 := \alpha - b\alpha_2$, and the secret exponents (α_1, α_2) in MSK are not available to $\mathcal{C}$.

Key Extraction: When the adversary $\mathcal{A}$ requests a secret key extract query for an identity $ID \in \mathbb{Z}_p$, $\mathcal{C}$ creates a semi-functional key. It does this by choosing random exponents $r, \gamma', ktag_1, \cdots, ktag_m \xleftarrow{R} \mathbb{Z}_p$, which implicitly sets $\gamma := \gamma' + b\alpha_2$. The semi-functional key elements are computed as:
$K_1 = g_2^{\alpha_1}(g_2^{w_1})^r g_2^\gamma = g_2^\alpha(g_2^{w_1})^r g_2^{\gamma'}, K_2 = g_2^{\alpha_2}(g_2^{w_2})^r/g_2^{\gamma b^{-1}} = (g_2^{w_2})^r/g_2^{\gamma' b^{-1}},$
$K_3 = g_2^r$.
For $i = 1, 2, ..., m$:
$K_{4,i} = ((g_2^{w_1})^{ktag_i} \cdot g_2^{u_{1,i}}/(g_2^{u_{1,0}})^{(ID)^i})^r, K_{5,i} = ((g_2^{w_2})^{ktag_i} \cdot g_2^{u_{2,i}}/(g_2^{u_{2,0}})^{(ID)^i})^r.$
This is a properly distributed semi-functional key, which can be easily verified.

Challenge: Once the public parameters PP and the keys for all key extraction queries are given, $\mathcal{A}$ provides a challenge privileged set $S^* = \{ID_1, ID_2, ..., ID_n\}$. $\mathcal{C}$ first computes the vector $\boldsymbol{y} = (y_0, y_1, \cdots, y_m)$ according to S^* as the coefficient from $P_{S^*}[Z] = \prod_{ID_j \in S^*} (Z - ID_j)$. It then picks randomly $s, ctag \in \mathbb{Z}_p$, and computes the challenge header $Hdr = (C_1, C_2, C_3, ctag)$ as follows:
$C_1 = g_1^s \cdot g_1^\mu, C_2 = g_1^{sb}, C_3 = (W_1^{ctag} \cdot \prod_{i=0}^n (g_1^{u_i})^{y_i})^s \cdot g_1^{\mu(\langle \boldsymbol{y}, \boldsymbol{u}_1 \rangle + ctag \cdot w_1)})$. In addition, the challenge session key K is set to be: $K = g_T^s \cdot e(g_1^\mu, g_2^\alpha)/e(Z, g_2^b)$.

One can verify that the challenge header $Hdr = (C_1, C_2, C_3, ctag)$ has proper semi-functional forms. Furthermore, if $Z = g_1^{\mu\alpha_2}$ (i.e., $\eta = 0$), then K is a properly distributed semi-functional session key. In this case, $\mathcal{C}$ has properly simulated Game_q. If η is a random value in $\mathbb{Z}_p^*$, which means $Z = g_1^{\mu\alpha_2 + \eta}$ is a random element in G_1, then K is uniformly distributed and is independent of all other components. In this case, $\mathcal{C}$ has properly simulated $\text{Game}_{\text{Final}}$.

Guess: Eventually, the adversary $\mathcal{A}$ will output a guess β' of β. The challenger $\mathcal{C}$ then outputs 0 to guess that $Z = g_1^{\mu\alpha_2}$ if $\beta' = \beta$; otherwise, it outputs 1 to indicate that $Z = g_1^{\mu\alpha_2 + \eta}$ is a random element of G_1. Also, $\mathcal{C}$ simulates Game_q if $\eta = 0$ and $\text{Game}_{\text{Final}}$ if $\eta \in {}_R\mathbb{Z}_p^*$. Therefore, $\mathcal{C}$ can use $\mathcal{A}$'s output to distinguish $Z = g_1^{\mu\alpha_2}$ from random with the same advantage that $\mathcal{A}$ has in distinguishing Game_q from $\text{Game}_{\text{Final}}$.

This completes the proof of Lemma 3.   □

References

1. Agrawal S., Chase M.: FAME: fast attribute-based message encryption. In: Proceedings of the 24th ACM Conference on Computer and Communications Security (CCS 2017), pp. 665–682. ACM, New York (2017)
2. Akinyele, A., Garman, C., Miers, I., et al.: Charm: a framework for rapidly prototyping cryptosystems. J. Cryptogr. Eng. **3**, 111–128 (2013)
3. Attrapadung, N., Imai, H.: Attribute-based encryption supporting direct/indirect revocation modes. In: Parker, M.G. (ed.) IMACC 2009. LNCS, vol. 5921, pp. 278–300. Springer, Heidelberg (2009). https://doi.org/10.1007/978-3-642-10868-6_17
4. Boneh, D., Boyen, X.: Efficient selective-ID secure identity-based encryption without random oracles. In: Cachin, C., Camenisch, J.L. (eds.) EUROCRYPT 2004. LNCS, vol. 3027, pp. 223–238. Springer, Heidelberg (2004). https://doi.org/10.1007/978-3-540-24676-3_14
5. Boneh, D., Franklin, M.: Identity-based encryption from the Weil pairing. In: Kilian, J. (ed.) CRYPTO 2001. LNCS, vol. 2139, pp. 213–229. Springer, Heidelberg (2001). https://doi.org/10.1007/3-540-44647-8_13
6. Boldyreva, A., Goyal, V., Kumar, G.: Identity-based encryption with efficient revocation. In: Proceedings of the 15th ACM Conference on Computer and Communications Security (CCS 2008), pp. 417–426. ACM, New York (2008)
7. Chang, D., Chauhan, A.K., Kumar, S., Sanadhya, S.K.: Revocable identity-based encryption from codes with rank metric. In: Smart, N.P. (ed.) CT-RSA 2018. LNCS, vol. 10808, pp. 435–451. Springer, Cham (2018). https://doi.org/10.1007/978-3-319-76953-0_23
8. Chen, J., Lim, H.W., Ling, S., Wang, H., Nguyen, K.: Revocable identity-based encryption from lattices. In: Susilo, W., Mu, Y., Seberry, J. (eds.) ACISP 2012. LNCS, vol. 7372, pp. 390–403. Springer, Heidelberg (2012). https://doi.org/10.1007/978-3-642-31448-3_29
9. Chatterjee, S., Menezes, A.: On cryptographic protocols employing asymmetric pairings-the role of φ revisited. Discret. Appl. Math. **159**(13), 1311–1322 (2011)
10. Chen, J., Wee, H.: Semi-adaptive attribute-based encryption and improved delegation for boolean formula. In: Abdalla, M., De Prisco, R. (eds.) SCN 2014. LNCS, vol. 8642, pp. 277–297. Springer, Cham (2014). https://doi.org/10.1007/978-3-319-10879-7_16
11. Delerablée, C.: Identity-based broadcast encryption with constant size ciphertexts and private keys. In: Kurosawa, K. (ed.) ASIACRYPT 2007. LNCS, vol. 4833, pp. 200–215. Springer, Heidelberg (2007). https://doi.org/10.1007/978-3-540-76900-2_12
12. Emura, K., Seo, J.H., Youn, T.: Semi-generic transformation of revocable hierarchical identity-based encryption and its DBDH instantiation. IEICE Trans. Fundam. Electron. Commun. Comput. Sci. **99**((A(1))), 83–91 (2016)
13. Fiat, A., Naor, M.: Broadcast encryption. In: Stinson, D.R. (ed.) CRYPTO 1993. LNCS, vol. 773, pp. 480–491. Springer, Heidelberg (1994). https://doi.org/10.1007/3-540-48329-2_40
14. Galbraith, S., Paterson, K., Smart, N.: Pairings for cryptographers. Discret. Appl. Math. **156**(16), 3113–3121 (2008)
15. Gentry, C., Waters, B.: Adaptive security in broadcast encryption systems (with short ciphertexts). In: Joux, A. (ed.) EUROCRYPT 2009. LNCS, vol. 5479, pp. 171–188. Springer, Heidelberg (2009). https://doi.org/10.1007/978-3-642-01001-9_10

16. Jutla, C.S., Roy, A.: Shorter quasi-adaptive NIZK proofs for linear subspaces. In: Sako, K., Sarkar, P. (eds.) ASIACRYPT 2013. LNCS, vol. 8269, pp. 1–20. Springer, Heidelberg (2013). https://doi.org/10.1007/978-3-642-42033-7_1

17. Katsumata, S., Matsuda, T., Takayasu, A.: Lattice-based revocable (hierarchical) identity-based encryption with decryption key exposure resistance. Cryptology ePrint Archive, Report 2018/420 (2018)

18. Katz, J., Sahai, A., Waters, B.: Predicate encryption supporting disjunctions, polynomial equations, and inner products. In: Smart, N. (ed.) EUROCRYPT 2008. LNCS, vol. 4965, pp. 146–162. Springer, Heidelberg (2008). https://doi.org/10.1007/978-3-540-78967-3_9

19. Kogan, N., Shavitt, Y., Wool, A.: A practical revocation scheme for broadcast encryption using smart cards. ACM Trans. Inf. Syst. Secur. **9**(3), 325–351 (2006)

20. Lee, K.: Revocable hierarchical identity-based encryption with adaptive security. Cryptology ePrint Archive, Report 2016/749 (2016)

21. Lee, K., Lee, D., Park, J.: Efficient revocable identity-based encryption via subset difference methods. Des. Codes Cryptogr. **85**, 39–76 (2017)

22. Lai, J., Mu, Y., Guo, F., et al.: Full privacy-preserving and revocable ID-based broadcast encryption for data access control in smart city. Pers. Ubiquitous Comput. **21**, 855–868 (2017)

23. Ling, S., Nguyen, K., Wang, H., Zhang, J.: Server-aided revocable predicate encryption: formalization and lattice-based instantiation. CoRR, abs/1801.07844 (2018)

24. Lee, K., Park, S.: Revocable hierarchical identity-based encryption with shorter private keys and update keys. Des. Codes Cryptogrphy (2018). https://doi.org/10.1007/s10623-017-0453-2

25. Libert, B., Vergnaud, D.: Adaptive-ID secure revocable identity-based encryption. In: Fischlin, M. (ed.) CT-RSA 2009. LNCS, vol. 5473, pp. 1–15. Springer, Heidelberg (2009). https://doi.org/10.1007/978-3-642-00862-7_1

26. Miyaji, A., Nakabayashi, M., Takano, S.: Characterization of elliptic curve traces under FR-reduction. In: Won, D. (ed.) ICISC 2000. LNCS, vol. 2015, pp. 90–108. Springer, Heidelberg (2001). https://doi.org/10.1007/3-540-45247-8_8

27. González-Nieto, J.M., Manulis, M., Sun, D.: Fully private revocable predicate encryption. In: Susilo, W., Mu, Y., Seberry, J. (eds.) ACISP 2012. LNCS, vol. 7372, pp. 350–363. Springer, Heidelberg (2012). https://doi.org/10.1007/978-3-642-31448-3_26

28. Naor, D., Naor, M., Lotspiech, J.: Revocation and tracing schemes for stateless receivers. In: Kilian, J. (ed.) CRYPTO 2001. LNCS, vol. 2139, pp. 41–62. Springer, Heidelberg (2001). https://doi.org/10.1007/3-540-44647-8_3

29. Nguyen, K., Wang, H., Zhang, J.: Server-aided revocable identity-based encryption from lattices. In: Foresti, S., Persiano, G. (eds.) CANS 2016. LNCS, vol. 10052, pp. 107–123. Springer, Cham (2016). https://doi.org/10.1007/978-3-319-48965-0_7

30. Qin, B., Deng, R.H., Li, Y., Liu, S.: Server-aided revocable identity-based encryption. In: Pernul, G., Ryan, P.Y.A., Weippl, E. (eds.) ESORICS 2015. LNCS, vol. 9326, pp. 286–304. Springer, Cham (2015). https://doi.org/10.1007/978-3-319-24174-6_15

31. Ramanna, S.C.: More efficient constructions for inner-product encryption. In: Manulis, M., Sadeghi, A.-R., Schneider, S. (eds.) ACNS 2016. LNCS, vol. 9696, pp. 231–248. Springer, Cham (2016). https://doi.org/10.1007/978-3-319-39555-5_13

32. Susilo, W., Chen, R., Guo, F., et al.: Recipient rovocable identity-based broadcast encryption, or how to revoke some recipient in IBBE without knowledge of the plaintext. In: Proceedings of the 11th ACM on Asia Conference on Computer and Communications Security (AsiaCCS 2016), Xi'an, China, pp. 201–210. ACM (2016)

33. Seo, J.H., Emura, K.: Revocable identity-based encryption revisited: security model and construction. In: Kurosawa, K., Hanaoka, G. (eds.) PKC 2013. LNCS, vol. 7778, pp. 216–234. Springer, Heidelberg (2013). https://doi.org/10.1007/978-3-642-36362-7_14

34. Seo, J.H., Emura, K.: Efficient delegation of key generation and revocation functionalities in identity-based encryption. In: Dawson, E. (ed.) CT-RSA 2013. LNCS, vol. 7779, pp. 343–358. Springer, Heidelberg (2013). https://doi.org/10.1007/978-3-642-36095-4_22

35. Seo, J.H., Emura, K.: Revocable hierarchical identity-based encryption: history-free update, security against insiders, and short ciphertexts. In: Nyberg, K. (ed.) CT-RSA 2015. LNCS, vol. 9048, pp. 106–123. Springer, Cham (2015). https://doi.org/10.1007/978-3-319-16715-2_6

36. Seo, J.H., Emura, K.: Adaptive-ID secure revocable hierarchical identity-based encryption. In: Tanaka, K., Suga, Y. (eds.) IWSEC 2015. LNCS, vol. 9241, pp. 21–38. Springer, Cham (2015). https://doi.org/10.1007/978-3-319-22425-1_2

37. Waters, B.: Dual system encryption: realizing fully secure IBE and HIBE under simple assumptions. In: Halevi, S. (ed.) CRYPTO 2009. LNCS, vol. 5677, pp. 619–636. Springer, Heidelberg (2009). https://doi.org/10.1007/978-3-642-03356-8_36

38. Watanabe, Y., Emura, K., Seo, J.H.: New revocable IBE in prime-order groups: adaptively secure, decryption key exposure resistant, and with short public parameters. In: Handschuh, H. (ed.) CT-RSA 2017. LNCS, vol. 10159, pp. 432–449. Springer, Cham (2017). https://doi.org/10.1007/978-3-319-52153-4_25

39. Yang, B., Yang, K., Qin, Y., Zhang, Z., Feng, D.: DAA-TZ: an efficient DAA scheme for mobile devices using ARM TrustZone. In: Conti, M., Schunter, M., Askoxylakis, I. (eds.) Trust 2015. LNCS, vol. 9229, pp. 209–227. Springer, Cham (2015). https://doi.org/10.1007/978-3-319-22846-4_13

Tightly Secure Hierarchical Identity-Based Encryption

Roman Langrehr[(✉)] and Jiaxin Pan

Karlsruhe Institute of Technology, Karlsruhe, Germany
roman.langrehr@student.kit.edu, jiaxin.pan@kit.edu

Abstract. We construct the *first* tightly secure hierarchical identity-based encryption (HIBE) scheme based on standard assumptions, which solves an open problem from Blazy, Kiltz, and Pan (CRYPTO 2014). At the core of our constructions is a novel randomization technique that enables us to randomize user secret keys for identities with flexible length.

The security reductions of previous HIBEs lose at least a factor of Q, which is the number of user secret key queries. Different to that, the security loss of our schemes is only dependent on the security parameter. Our schemes are adaptively secure based on the Matrix Diffie-Hellman assumption, which is a generalization of standard Diffie-Hellman assumptions such as k-Linear. We have two tightly secure constructions, one with constant ciphertext size, and the other with tighter security at the cost of linear ciphertext size. Among other things, our schemes imply the *first* tightly secure identity-based signature scheme by a variant of the Naor transformation.

Keywords: Hierarchical identity-based encryption · Tight security · Affine message authentication codes

1 Introduction

1.1 Motivation

TIGHT SECURITY. Reductions are useful tools for proving the security of public-key cryptographic schemes. Asymptotically, a reduction shows that if there is an efficient adversary $\mathcal{A}$ that breaks the security of a scheme then we can have another adversary $\mathcal{R}$ that solves the underlying computationally hard problem. Concretely, a reduction provides a security bound for the scheme, $\varepsilon_{\mathcal{A}} \leq \ell \cdot \varepsilon_{\mathcal{R}}$,[1] where $\varepsilon_{\mathcal{A}}$ is the success probability of $\mathcal{A}$ and $\varepsilon_{\mathcal{R}}$ is that of $\mathcal{R}$. Ideally, it is more desirable to have ℓ as small as a constant. We say a reduction is *tight* if ℓ is a small constant and the running time of $\mathcal{A}$ is approximately the same as that of $\mathcal{R}$.

---

[1] Here we ignore the additive negligible terms for simplicity.

J. Pan—Supported by DFG grant HO 4534/4-1.

D. Lin and K. Sako (Eds.): PKC 2019, LNCS 11442, pp. 436–465, 2019.
https://doi.org/10.1007/978-3-030-17253-4_15

Most of the current works have considered the tightness notion called "almost tight security", where ℓ may linearly (or, even better, logarithmically) depend on the security parameter, but not on the size of $\mathcal{A}$.[2] Recently, tightly secure cryptographic schemes drew a large amount of attention (e.g. [1,3,8,11,12,16–18]), since tightly secure schemes do not need to compensate for any security loss.

(HIERARCHICAL) IDENTITY-BASED ENCRYPTION. The concept of identity-based encryption (IBE) was proposed by Shamir [31] to simplify the management of public keys and certificates. With an IBE scheme, one can encrypt a message under a recipient's identity id (for instance, email address or ID card number), and this encrypted message can be decrypted with user id's secret key from a trusted authority. The first constructions of IBE were given in 2001 [4,9,30] in the random oracle model.

A hierarchical IBE (HIBE) scheme [14,22] generalizes the concept of IBE and provides more functionality by forming levels of a hierarchy. In an L-level HIBE, a hierarchical identity is a vector of maximal L identities, and a user at level i can delegate a secret key for its descendants at level i' (where $i < i' \leq L$). Moreover, a user at level i is not supposed to decrypt any encryption from a recipient which is not amongst its descendants. HIBE schemes not only are more general than IBE schemes (for instance, an IBE is simply a 1-level HIBE), but also provide numerous applications. Most famous ones are CCA-secure IBEs [5] and identity-based signatures [24] from HIBE. Both implications are tight.

Adaptive security is a widely accepted security notion for (H)IBEs, where an adversary is allow to adaptively choose a challenge identity id* after it sees the (master) public key and Q-many user secret keys for adversarial chosen identities. To achieve adaptive security in the standard model, the early IBE constructions require either non-tight reductions to the hardness of the underlying assumptions [7,23,27,33], or Q-type, non-static assumptions [13].

In 2013, Chen and Wee constructed the first tightly secure IBE based on static assumptions in the standard model [8]. After that, several works have been done to improve its efficiency and achieve stronger security [3,16,19,21]. However, constructing an L-level HIBE for $L > 1$ with a tight (i.e., independent of Q) security reduction to a standard assumption remains open.

HIBEs MEET TIGHTNESS: DIFFICULTIES AND THE HOPE. Before analyzing the difficulties of achieving tightly secure HIBE, we consider the security loss of the current state-of-the-art HIBEs. The L-level HIBE from [33] has a relatively large security loss, Q^L, which depends on both Q and L. Although the security loss of more recent HIBEs [3,8,15,27,32] does not depends on the number of maximal levels L, they are still not tight and lose a factor of Q.

In general, it is harder to construct HIBEs than IBEs, since HIBEs allow public delegation of user secret keys, given the corresponding ancestor's secret key. Hence, given a tightly secure IBE, there is no (tight) black-box transformation to HIBE. The works of Lewko and Waters [28] show the potential difficulty

---

[2] In this paper, we do not distinguish almost tight security from tight security, but we will detail the security loss in the security proof and comparison of our schemes.

of constructing HIBE with tight reductions. More precisely, [28] proves that it is hard to have an HIBE scheme with security loss less than exponential in L, if the HIBE has rerandomizable user secret keys (over all "functional" user secret keys).

The first attempt of constructing tightly secure HIBEs is due to Blazy, Kiltz, and Pan (cf. the proceeding version and the first full version of [3]), where they tightly transform algebraic message authentication code (MAC) schemes to (H)IBE schemes. As long as the algebraic MAC has tight security, the resulting (H)IBE is tightly secure. The first version of their paper contains a tightly secure delegatable MAC, which results in a tightly secure HIBE. The resulting HIBE has bypassed the impossibility result of [28] and their user secret keys are only rerandomizable over all keys generated by the user secret key generation algorithm, which is only a subspace of all "functional" keys. However, shortly after its publication, a flaw was found in a proof step of the delegatable MAC, and they remove this tightly secure delegatable MAC from their paper. The flaw is basically due to the fact that the BKP randomization technique failed to randomize MAC tags (which is an important part of user secret keys) for hierarchical identities.

The hope of achieving tight security for HIBEs lies in developing a novel method that enables randomization of user secret keys for identities with flexible level.

1.2   Our Contributions

We answer the aforementioned open question affirmatively with two *tightly secure* hierarchical identity-based encryption schemes with identity space $\mathcal{ID} := (\{0,1\}^\alpha)^{\leq L}$: One with constant ciphertext size (in terms of the number of group elements) and $O(\alpha L^2)$ security loss, and the other with ciphertext size linear in L but $O(\alpha L)$ security loss. Both schemes are the *first* tightly secure HIBEs. We compare our schemes with the existing HIBE schemes in prime-order pairing groups in Table 1.

Furthermore, via the known tight transformations from [24] and [5], our HIBEs imply the *first* tightly secure identity-based signature and tightly CCA-secure HIBEs almost for free. We note that an $(L+1)$-level HIBE tightly implies an L-level CCA-secure HIBE via the CHK transformation [5] in the single-challenge setting.

CORE IDEA. In a nutshell, the technical novelty of our constructions is a new randomization technique that enables us to randomize user secret keys with flexible identity length. This technique is motivated by the recent tightly CCA-secure public-key encryption of Gay et al. [11].

At the core of our constructions lie two new pseudorandom message authentication code (MAC) schemes for messages with flexible length. Their pseudorandomness can be proven with tight reductions to the Matrix Decisional Diffie-Hellman (MDDH) assumption [10]. The MDDH assumption is a generalization of the known standard Diffie-Hellman assumptions, such as the k-linear (k-LIN) assumption. Our MAC schemes have algebraic structures compatible with the

Table 1. Comparison of L-level HIBEs with identity-space $\mathcal{ID} = (\{0,1\}^\lambda)^{\leq L}$ in prime-order pairing groups. '$|\mathsf{mpk}|$', '$|\mathsf{usk}|$' and '$|\mathsf{C}|$' stand for the size of master public key, user secret key and ciphertext. We count the number of group elements in $\mathbb{G}_1, \mathbb{G}_2$, and $\mathbb{G}_T$. For a scheme that works in symmetric pairing groups, we write $\mathbb{G} := \mathbb{G}_1 = \mathbb{G}_2$. Q is the number of user secret key queries by the adversary.

Scheme	$\|\mathsf{mpk}\|$	$\|\mathsf{usk}\|$	$\|\mathsf{C}\|$	Loss	Assumption
Wat05 [33]	$O(\alpha L)\|\mathbb{G}_1\|$	$O(\alpha L)\|\mathbb{G}_2\|$	$(1+L)\|\mathbb{G}_1\|$	$O(\alpha Q)^L$	DBDH
Wat09 [32]	$O(L)\|\mathbb{G}_1\|$	$O(L)(\|\mathbb{G}_2\| + \|\mathbb{Z}_q\|)$	$O(L)(\|\mathbb{G}_1\| + \|\mathbb{Z}_q\|)$	$O(Q)$	2-LIN
Lew12 [27]	$60\|\mathbb{G}\| + 2\|\mathbb{G}_T\|$	$(60 + 10L)\|\mathbb{G}\|$	$10L$	$O(Q)$	2-LIN
CW13 [8]	$O(Lk^2)(\|\mathbb{G}_1\| + \|\mathbb{G}_2\|)$	$O(Lk)\|\mathbb{G}_2\|$	$(2k+2)\|\mathbb{G}_1\|$	$O(Q)$	k-LIN
BKP14 [3]	$O(Lk^2)(\|\mathbb{G}_1\| + \|\mathbb{G}_2\|)$	$O(Lk)\|\mathbb{G}_2\|$	$(2k+2)\|\mathbb{G}_1\|$	$O(Q)$	k-LIN
GCTC16 [15]	$18\|\mathbb{G}_1\| + 3\|\mathbb{G}_T\|$	$(18\lceil L/3\rceil + 18 - 3L)\|\mathbb{G}_2\|$	$9\lceil L/3\rceil\|\mathbb{G}_1\|$	$O(Q)$	SXDH
Ours (Fig. 11)	$O(\alpha L^2)(\|\mathbb{G}_1\| + \|\mathbb{G}_2\|)$	$O(\alpha L^2)\|\mathbb{G}_2\|$	$5\|\mathbb{G}_1\|$	$O(\alpha L^2)$	SXDH
Ours (Fig. 12)	$O(\alpha L^2)(\|\mathbb{G}_1\| + \|\mathbb{G}_2\|)$	$O(L)\|\mathbb{G}_2\|$	$(3L+2)\|\mathbb{G}_1\|$	$O(\alpha L)$	SXDH

BKP transformation. In the end, together with a variant of the BKP framework [3], we can tightly randomize user secret keys with hierarchical identities and we have tightly secure HIBEs.

A CLOSER LOOK AT THE BKP FRAMEWORK. The BKP framework proposes the notion of affine MACs and transforms it to an (H)IBE scheme with pairings. Their transformation is tightness-preserving. Under the MDDH assumption, if the affine MAC is tightly secure, then the (H)IBE is also tightly secure. It is worth mentioning that the BKP transformation and its variants are widely used in constructing identity-based encryption [19] with multi-challenge CCA security, predicate encryption [6,34], quasi-adaptive NIZK [26], and structure-preserving signature [12,25] based on standard, static assumptions.

We recall their tightly secure MAC, $\mathsf{MAC_{NR}}$, based on the Naor-Reingold pseudorandom function [29], which is implicitly in the Chen-Wee (CW) IBE [8] as well. $\mathsf{MAC_{NR}}$ is defined over an additive prime-order group $\mathbb{G}_2 := \langle P_2 \rangle$ and its message space is corresponding to the identity space of the resulting IBE. We use the implicit notation $[x]_2 := xP_2$ from [10]. $\mathsf{MAC_{NR}}$ chooses $\mathbf{B} \in \mathbb{Z}_q^{(k+1)\times k}$ according to the underlying assumption. For message space $\mathcal{M} := \{0,1\}^\alpha$, its secret key is defined as

$$\mathsf{sk_{MAC}} := \left((\mathbf{x}_{i,b})_{1 \leq i \leq \alpha, b=0,1}, x_0' \right) \in \left(\mathbb{Z}_q^{k\cdot 2} \right)^\alpha \times \mathbb{Z}_q$$

and its MAC tag contains a message-independent vector $[\mathbf{t}]_2$ and a message-dependent value $[u]_2$ in the form of

$$
\begin{aligned}
\mathbf{t} &= \overline{\mathbf{B}}\mathbf{s} \in \mathbb{Z}_q^k \quad \text{for} \quad \mathbf{s} \xleftarrow{\$} \mathbb{Z}_q^k \\
u &= \sum_i \mathbf{x}_{i,\mathsf{m}_i}^\top \mathbf{t} + x_0' \in \mathbb{Z}_q
\end{aligned}
\tag{1}
$$

where $\overline{\mathbf{B}}$ denotes the first k rows of $\mathbf{B}$. The BKP transformation requires the MAC scheme has psedorandomness against chosen-message attacks (PR-CMA security), which is a decisional variant of the standard existential unforgeability against chosen-message attacks (EUF-CMA security). In order to provide a simpler and more intuitive discussion, we consider the standard EUF-CMA security of $\mathsf{MAC_{NR}}$, where an adversary $\mathcal{A}$ is allowed to see many MAC tags $\tau_\mathsf{m} := ([\mathsf{t_m}]_2, [u_\mathsf{m}]_2)$ on messages m of its choice and tries to forge a fresh and valid forgery (m^*, τ^*) which satisfies Eq. (1).

Following the CW argument [8], by a hybrid argument on the bit length of m, one can show that the value $[u]_2$ is pseudorandom such that it is hard for an adversary to forge. By embedding the problem challenge in $\mathbf{t}$ and $\mathbf{x}_{i+1,1-b}$, the CW argument can manage to develop the following random function RF_{i+1} for $(i+1)$-bit messages from a random function RF_i for i-bit messages on-the-fly:

$$\mathsf{RF}_{i+1}(\mathsf{m}_{|i+1}) = \begin{cases} \mathsf{RF}_i(\mathsf{m}_{|i}) & (\text{if } \mathsf{m}_{i+1} = b) \\ \mathsf{RF}_i(\mathsf{m}_{|i}) + \mathsf{RF}'_i(\mathsf{m}_{|i}) & (\text{if } \mathsf{m}_{i+1} = 1 - b) \end{cases}, \qquad (2)$$

where b is the guess for the $(i+1)$-th bit of m^* and $\mathsf{m}_{|i}$ is the first i bits of m. Such an argument works well if messages have fixed length. For messages m with fixed length, an adversary can see the output of either RF_i (in Hybrid i) or RF_{i+1} (in Hybrid $i+1$), but not both. However, that is not the case for messages m' with flexible length.

Concretely, identities for HIBEs are messages with flexible level. If we follow the CW and BKP arguments, we first need to develop a random function at the 2-level based on that at the 1-level. The critical case happens when we switch from Hybrid α (the end of randomization at the 1-level) to Hybrid $\alpha + 1$ (the beginning of randomization at the 2-level). If we define $\mathsf{RF}_{\alpha+1}$ (with message space $\{0,1\}^\alpha \cup \{0,1\}^{\alpha+1}$) via Eq. (2) based on random functions $\mathsf{RF}_\alpha, \mathsf{RF}'_\alpha$ (with message space $\{0,1\}^\alpha$), then we have $\mathsf{RF}_{\alpha+1}(\mathsf{m}) = \mathsf{RF}_{\alpha+1}(\mathsf{m}||b)$ for a $\mathsf{m} \in \{0,1\}^\alpha$ and that means the resulting $\mathsf{RF}_{\alpha+1}$ is not a random function for messages with flexible level.

1.3   Our Approach: Independent Randomization

To circumvent the aforementioned problem, we propose a suitable pseudorandom MAC, which isolates the tag randomization for messages with different levels. Our strategy is to randomize tags for messages with only one level first, and then for those with two levels, and so on. By a novel use of the recent subspace randomization refined from [11], tags for messages with different levels are randomized independently.

AFFINE MACS WITH LEVELS. We consider a new notion of affine MACs, called *affine MACs with levels*, and we give two constructions of it. This new notion considers messages with flexible levels and enable us to develop independent random functions RF_α for messages with only one level (i.e., in $\{0,1\}^\alpha$), and $\mathsf{RF}'_{2\cdot\alpha}$ for messages with only two levels (i.e., in $\{0,1\}^{2\alpha}$), and so on. For simplicity, we present an overview of our technique in terms of 2-level HIBEs ($L = 2$), namely, the hierarchical identity space $\mathcal{ID} := (\{0,1\}^\alpha)^{\leq 2}$. We denote 1-level messages as $\mathsf{m} \in \{0,1\}^\alpha$ and 2-level messages as $\mathsf{m}' \in \{0,1\}^{\alpha \cdot 2}$.

Our first MAC construction MAC_1's secret keys have the form of

$$\mathsf{sk}_{\mathsf{MAC}_1} := \left((\mathbf{x}_{i,b})_{i,b}, \boxed{(\hat{\mathbf{x}}_{j,b})_{1 \le j \le 2\alpha, b}}, x_0' \right) \in (\mathbb{Z}_q^{k \cdot 2})^\alpha \times \boxed{(\mathbb{Z}_q^{k \cdot 2})^{\alpha \cdot 2}} \times \mathbb{Z}_q.$$

Value u in the MAC tags for $\mathsf{m} \in \{0,1\}^\alpha$ and $\mathsf{m}' \in \{0,1\}^{2\alpha}$ has the form of

$$u_{\mathsf{m}} := \sum_{i=1}^{\alpha} \mathbf{x}_{i,\mathsf{m}_i}^\top \mathbf{t} + x_0' \in \mathbb{Z}_q$$

$$u_{\mathsf{m}'} := \sum_{i=1}^{\alpha} \mathbf{x}_{i,\mathsf{m}_i'}^\top \mathbf{t} + \boxed{\sum_{j=1}^{2\alpha} \hat{\mathbf{x}}_{j,\mathsf{m}_j'}^\top \mathbf{t}} + x_0' \in \mathbb{Z}_q$$

$$(3)$$

By a similar argument as in the BKP we can randomize all the u_{m} for 1-level messages m and, after the first level messages randomization, u_{m} has the form

$$u_{\mathsf{m}} := \sum_{i=1}^{\alpha} \mathbf{x}_{i,\mathsf{m}_i}^\top \mathbf{t} + \mathsf{RF}_\alpha(\mathsf{m}),$$

namely, we replace x_0' with $\mathsf{RF}_\alpha(\mathsf{m})$, but this affects the $u_{\mathsf{m}'}$ for 2-level messages m' as well. More precisely, $u_{\mathsf{m}'}$ carries the random function RF_α and has the form

$$u_{\mathsf{m}'} := \left(\sum_{i=1}^{\alpha} \mathbf{x}_{i,\mathsf{m}_i'}^\top + \sum_{j=1}^{2\alpha} \hat{\mathbf{x}}_{j,\mathsf{m}_j'}^\top \right) \mathbf{t} + \mathsf{RF}_\alpha(\mathsf{m}_{|\alpha}').$$

If we continue to randomize $u_{\mathsf{m}'}$, we will run into the exact same problem as in the CW or BKP randomization.

Motivated by [11], we hide RF_α in some orthogonal space. By switching $\mathbf{t}$ into the "right" span, RF_α appears in u_{m}, but gets canceled in $u_{\mathsf{m}'}$. Concretely, we choose $\mathbf{B} \overset{\$}{\leftarrow} \mathbb{Z}_q^{3k \times k}$ and $\mathbf{B}^\perp \in \mathbb{Z}_q^{3k \times 2k}$ is a kernel matrix of $\mathbf{B}$ such that $(\mathbf{B}^\perp)^\top \mathbf{B} = \mathbf{0}$. We replace $\mathbf{t} \overset{\$}{\leftarrow} \mathbb{Z}_q^k$ with larger $\mathbf{t} \overset{\$}{\leftarrow} \mathbb{Z}_q^{3k}$. We embed the random function RF_α into the kernel of $\mathbf{B}$ and u_{y} ($\mathsf{y} \in \{\mathsf{m}, \mathsf{m}'\}$) has the form

$$u_{\mathsf{y}} := \left(\quad \sim \quad + \quad \mathsf{RF}_\alpha(\mathsf{y}_{|\alpha})(\mathbf{B}^\perp)^\top \right) \mathbf{t} + x_0'$$

where "$\sim$" denotes corresponding summation terms. During the randomization for 1-level messages, if we choose $\mathbf{t} \in \mathsf{Span}(\mathbf{B}) := \{ \mathbf{v} \mid \exists \mathbf{s} \in \mathbb{Z}_q^k : \mathbf{v} = \mathbf{B}\mathbf{s} \}$ for 2-level messages m', then RF_α will get canceled out; and if we choose $\mathbf{t} \notin \mathsf{Span}(\mathbf{B})$ for 1-level messages m, then RF_α will appear and u_{m} gets randomized. After the randomization for 1-level messages, $u_{\mathsf{m}'}$ for 2-level messages m' is distributed the same as in Eq. (3) so that we can start 2-level randomization from a constant random function $\mathsf{RF}_0'(\epsilon)$ multiplying with $(\mathbf{B}^\perp)^\top$, where ϵ denotes the empty string.

The way of developing RF_α (or $\mathsf{RF}_{2 \cdot \alpha}'$, respectively) from RF_0 (or RF_0', respectively) is similar to [11]. Roughly, we choose two random matrices $\mathbf{B}_0, \mathbf{B}_1 \overset{\$}{\leftarrow} \mathbb{Z}_q^{3k \times k}$ and decompose $\mathbb{Z}_q^{3k}$ into the span of $\mathbf{B}, \mathbf{B}_0, \mathbf{B}_1$. The span of

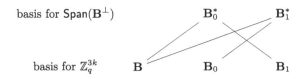

Fig. 1. Solid lines mean orthogonal: $\mathbf{B}^\top \mathbf{B}_0^* = \mathbf{B}_1^\top \mathbf{B}_0^* = \mathbf{0} = \mathbf{B}^\top \mathbf{B}_1^* = \mathbf{B}_0^\top \mathbf{B}_1^* \in \mathbb{Z}_q^{k \times k}$.

$\mathbf{B}^\perp$ is decomposed into that of $\mathbf{B}_0^* \in \mathbb{Z}_q^{3k \times k}$ and $\mathbf{B}_1^* \in \mathbb{Z}_q^{3k \times k}$. An overview of the orthogonal relations between all these matrices is given in Fig. 1. After the decomposition of linear spaces, $\mathsf{RF}_i(\mathsf{m}_{|i})(\mathbf{B}^\perp)^\top = \mathsf{RF}_i^{(0)}(\mathsf{m}_{|i})(\mathbf{B}_0^*)^\top + \mathsf{RF}_i^{(1)}(\mathsf{m}_{|i})(\mathbf{B}_1^*)^\top$. By using the MDDH assumption, we can switch $[\mathbf{t}]_2$ to the right span and develop $\mathsf{RF}_{i+1}(\mathsf{m}_{|i+1})(\mathbf{B}^\perp)^\top$ from $\mathsf{RF}_i(\mathsf{m}_{|i})(\mathbf{B}^\perp)^\top$ in a tight fashion.

In order to have public delegation, the user secret keys at level 1 contain delegation terms $[\hat{\mathbf{x}}_{j,b}^\top \mathbf{t}]_2$. Since our randomization at different levels are isolated, the published terms will not affect our randomization strategy. Details are given in Sect. 3.1. In the end, our security reduction loses a factor of $O(\alpha L^2)$ due to L-many randomization loops and the fact that in each loop a additional factor of $O(\alpha L)$ is required. Applying a variant of the BKP transformation (cf. Sect. 4), we obtain the *first* HIBE scheme with tight security.

ACHIEVING TIGHTER SECURITY. Our second MAC construction (MAC_2 in Sect. 3.2) parallelizes the above randomization strategy and it has a scheme with security loss $O(\alpha L)$. The cost of doing this is to have different $\mathbf{t}_i$ at different level for a message with L levels, which results in an HIBE with $O(L)$-size ciphertext via the BKP transformation.

1.4   More Related Work and Open Problems

Bader et al. [2] use some idea from the BKP HIBE to construct digital signature schemes with corruptions, but it does not involve any randomization for messages with flexible length, and thus it does not have the same issue as the BKP.

Very recently, Hofheinz, Jia, and Pan [19] extend the BKP construction with the information-theoretical Cramer-Shoup-like argument of [11] to answer multiple challenge ciphertext queries for IBE. However, we do not know whether their technique and a similar one from [16] can work directly here to construct tightly multi-challenge secure HIBE. We leave achieving tight multi-challenge security for HIBEs as an open problem. Another interesting direction is to improve the efficiency of our schemes.

2   Preliminaries

NOTATIONS. We use $x \xleftarrow{\$} \mathcal{S}$ to denote the process of sampling an element x from $\mathcal{S}$ uniformly at random if $\mathcal{S}$ is a set. For positive integers $k > 1, \eta \in \mathbb{Z}^+$ and a matrix $\mathbf{A} \in \mathbb{Z}_q^{(k+\eta) \times k}$, we denote the upper square matrix of $\mathbf{A}$ by $\overline{\mathbf{A}} \in \mathbb{Z}_q^{k \times k}$ and the lower η rows of $\mathbf{A}$ by $\underline{\mathbf{A}} \in \mathbb{Z}_q^{\eta \times k}$. Similarly, for a column vector $\mathbf{v} \in \mathbb{Z}_q^{k+\eta}$, we denote the upper k elements by $\overline{\mathbf{v}} \in \mathbb{Z}_q^k$ and the lower η elements of $\mathbf{v}$ by $\underline{\mathbf{v}} \in \mathbb{Z}_q^\eta$. For a string $\mathsf{m} \in \varSigma^n$, m_i denotes the i-th component of m ($1 \le i \le n$) and $\mathsf{m}_{|i}$ denotes the prefix of length i of m.

Furthermore for a p-tuple of bit strings $\mathsf{m} \in (\{0,1\}^n)^p$, we use $[\![\mathsf{m}]\!]$ to denote the string $\mathsf{m}_1\|\ldots\|\mathsf{m}_p$. Thus for $1 \le i \le np$ $[\![\mathsf{m}]\!]_i$ denotes the i-th bit of $\mathsf{m}_1\|\ldots\|\mathsf{m}_p$ and $[\![\mathsf{m}]\!]_{|i}$ denotes the i-bit-long prefix of $\mathsf{m}_1\|\ldots\|\mathsf{m}_p$.

All our algorithms are probabilistic polynomial time unless we stated otherwise. If $\mathcal{A}$ is an algorithm, then we write $a \xleftarrow{\$} \mathcal{A}(b)$ to denote the random variable that outputted by $\mathcal{A}$ on input b.

GAMES. Following [3], we use code-based games to define and prove security. A game G contains procedures INIT and FINALIZE, and some additional procedures $P_1, \ldots, P_n$, which are defined in pseudo-code. Initially all variables in a game are undefined (denoted by $\perp$), all sets are empty (denote by $\emptyset$), and all partial maps (denoted by $f : A \dashrightarrow B$) are totally undefined. An adversary $\mathcal{A}$ is executed in game G (denote by $\mathsf{G}^{\mathcal{A}}$) if it first calls INIT, obtaining its output. Next, it may make arbitrary queries to P_i (according to their specification), again obtaining their output. Finally, it makes one single call to FINALIZE($\cdot$) and stops. We use $\mathsf{G}^{\mathcal{A}} \Rightarrow d$ to denote that G outputs d after interacting with $\mathcal{A}$, and d is the output of FINALIZE.

2.1 Pairing Groups and Matrix Diffie-Hellman Assumptions

Let GGen be a probabilistic polynomial time (PPT) algorithm that on input 1^λ returns a description $\mathcal{G} := (\mathbb{G}_1, \mathbb{G}_2, \mathbb{G}_T, q, P_1, P_2, e)$ of asymmetric pairing groups where $\mathbb{G}_1, \mathbb{G}_2, \mathbb{G}_T$ are cyclic groups of order q for a λ-bit prime q, P_1 and P_2 are generators of $\mathbb{G}_1$ and $\mathbb{G}_2$, respectively, and $e : \mathbb{G}_1 \times \mathbb{G}_2$ is an efficient computable (non-degenerated) bilinear map. Define $P_T := e(P_1, P_2)$, which is a generator in $\mathbb{G}_T$. In this paper, we only consider Type III pairings, where $\mathbb{G}_1 \ne \mathbb{G}_2$ and there is no efficient homomorphism between them. All our constructions can be easily instantiated with Type I pairings by setting $\mathbb{G}_1 = \mathbb{G}_2$ and defining the dimension k to be greater than 1.

We use implicit representation of group elements as in [10]. For $s \in \{1, 2, T\}$ and $a \in \mathbb{Z}_q$ define $[a]_s = aP_s \in \mathbb{G}_s$ as the implicit representation of a in $\mathbb{G}_s$. Similarly, for a matrix $\mathbf{A} = (a_{ij}) \in \mathbb{Z}_q^{n \times m}$ we define $[\mathbf{A}]_s$ as the implicit representation of $\mathbf{A}$ in $\mathbb{G}_s$. $\mathsf{Span}(\mathbf{A}) := \{\mathbf{Ar} | \mathbf{r} \in \mathbb{Z}_q^m\} \subset \mathbb{Z}_q^n$ denotes the linear span of $\mathbf{A}$, and similarly $\mathsf{Span}([\mathbf{A}]_s) := \{[\mathbf{Ar}]_s | \mathbf{r} \in \mathbb{Z}_q^m\} \subset \mathbb{G}_s^n$. Note that it is efficient to compute $[\mathbf{AB}]_s$ given $([\mathbf{A}]_s, \mathbf{B})$ or $(\mathbf{A}, [\mathbf{B}]_s)$ with matching dimensions. We define $[\mathbf{A}]_1 \circ [\mathbf{B}]_2 := e([\mathbf{A}]_1, [\mathbf{B}]_2) = [\mathbf{AB}]_T$, which can be efficiently computed given $[\mathbf{A}]_1$ and $[\mathbf{B}]_2$.

Next we recall the definition of the matrix Diffie-Hellman (MDDH) and related assumptions [10].

Definition 1 (Matrix distribution). *Let $k, \ell \in \mathbb{N}$ with $\ell > k$. We call $\mathcal{D}_{\ell,k}$ a matrix distribution if it outputs matrices in $\mathbb{Z}_q^{\ell \times k}$ of full rank k in polynomial time.*

Without loss of generality, we assume the first k rows of $\mathbf{A} \xleftarrow{\$} \mathcal{D}_{\ell,k}$ form an invertible matrix. The $\mathcal{D}_{\ell,k}$-matrix Diffie-Hellman problem is to distinguish the two distributions $([\mathbf{A}], [\mathbf{A}\mathbf{w}])$ and $([\mathbf{A}], [\mathbf{u}])$ where $\mathbf{A} \xleftarrow{\$} \mathcal{D}_{\ell,k}$, $\mathbf{w} \xleftarrow{\$} \mathbb{Z}_q^k$ and $\mathbf{u} \xleftarrow{\$} \mathbb{Z}_q^\ell$.

Definition 2 ($\mathcal{D}_{\ell,k}$-matrix Diffie-Hellman assumption). *Let $\mathcal{D}_{\ell,k}$ be a matrix distribution and $s \in \{1, 2, T\}$. We say that the $\mathcal{D}_{\ell,k}$-matrix Diffie-Hellman ($\mathcal{D}_{\ell,k}$-MDDH) assumption holds relative to GGen in group $\mathbb{G}_s$ if for all PPT adversaries $\mathcal{A}$, it holds that*

$$\mathsf{Adv}^{\mathsf{mddh}}_{\mathcal{D}_{\ell,k},\mathsf{GGen},s}(\mathcal{A}) := |\Pr[\mathcal{A}(\mathcal{G}, [\mathbf{A}]_s, [\mathbf{A}\mathbf{w}]_s) = 1] - \Pr[\mathcal{A}(\mathcal{G}, [\mathbf{A}]_s, [\mathbf{u}]_s) = 1]|$$

is negligible where the probability is taken over $\mathcal{G} \xleftarrow{\$} \mathsf{GGen}(1^\lambda)$, $\mathbf{A} \xleftarrow{\$} \mathcal{D}_{\ell,k}$, $\mathbf{w} \xleftarrow{\$} \mathbb{Z}_q^k$ and $\mathbf{u} \xleftarrow{\$} \mathbb{Z}_q^\ell$.

The uniform distribution is a particular matrix distribution that deserves special attention, as an adversary breaking the $\mathcal{U}_{\ell,k}$ assumption can also distinguish between real MDDH tuples and random tuples for all other possible matrix distributions. For uniform distributions, they stated in [11] that $\mathcal{U}_k$-MDDH and $\mathcal{U}_{\ell,k}$-MDDH assumptions are equivalent.

Definition 3 (Uniform distribution). *Let $k, \ell \in \mathbb{N}$ with $\ell > k$. We call $\mathcal{U}_{\ell,k}$ a uniform distribution if it outputs uniformly random matrices in $\mathbb{Z}_q^{\ell \times k}$ of rank k in polynomial time. Let $\mathcal{U}_k := \mathcal{U}_{k+1,k}$.*

Lemma 1 ($\mathcal{U}_{\ell,k}$-MDDH $\Leftrightarrow$ $\mathcal{U}_k$-MDDH [11]). *Let $\ell, k \in \mathbb{N}_+$ with $\ell > k$. An $\mathcal{U}_{\ell,k}$-MDDH instance is as hard as an $\mathcal{U}_k$-MDDH instance. Precisely, for each adversary $\mathcal{A}$ there exists an adversary $\mathcal{B}$ and vice versa with*

$$\mathsf{Adv}^{\mathsf{mddh}}_{\mathcal{U}_{\ell,k},\mathsf{GGen},s}(\mathcal{A}) = \mathsf{Adv}^{\mathsf{mddh}}_{\mathcal{U}_k,\mathsf{GGen},s}(\mathcal{B})$$

and $T(\mathcal{A}) \approx T(\mathcal{B})$.

Lemma 2 ($\mathcal{D}_{\ell,k}$-MDDH $\Rightarrow$ $\mathcal{U}_k$-MDDH [10]). *Let $\ell, k \in \mathbb{N}_+$ with $\ell > k$ and let $\mathcal{D}_{\ell,k}$ be a matrix distribution. A $\mathcal{U}_k$-MDDH instance is at least as hard as an $\mathcal{D}_{\ell,k}$ instance. Precisely, for each adversary $\mathcal{A}$ there exists an adversary $\mathcal{B}$ with*

$$\mathsf{Adv}^{\mathsf{mddh}}_{\mathcal{U}_k,\mathsf{GGen},s}(\mathcal{A}) \le \mathsf{Adv}^{\mathsf{mddh}}_{\mathcal{D}_{\ell,k},\mathsf{GGen},s}(\mathcal{B})$$

and $T(\mathcal{A}) \approx T(\mathcal{B})$.

For $Q \in \mathbb{N}$, $\mathbf{W} \xleftarrow{\$} \mathbb{Z}_q^{k \times Q}$, $\mathbf{U} \xleftarrow{\$} \mathbb{Z}_q^{\ell \times Q}$, consider the Q-fold $\mathcal{D}_{\ell,k}$-MDDH problem which is distinguishing the distributions $([\mathbf{A}], [\mathbf{A}\mathbf{W}])$ and $([\mathbf{A}], [\mathbf{U}])$. That is, the Q-fold $\mathcal{D}_{\ell,k}$-MDDH problem contains Q independent instances of the $\mathcal{D}_{\ell,k}$-MDDH problem (with the same $\mathbf{A}$ but different $\mathbf{w}_i$). By a hybrid argument one can show that the two problems are equivalent, where the reduction loses a factor Q. The following lemma gives a tight reduction. For the uniform distribution $\mathcal{U}_{\ell,k}$, the security loss $\ell - k$ can be avoided by applying Lemma 3 to the $\mathcal{U}_k$ distribution and then use Lemma 1 on each of the $\mathcal{U}_k$ instances to get a $\mathcal{U}_{\ell,k}$ instance.

Lemma 3 (Random self-reducibility [10]). *For $\ell > k$ and any matrix distribution $\mathcal{D}_{\ell,k}$, $\mathcal{D}_{\ell,k}$-MDDH is random self-reducible. In particular, for any $Q \geq 1$ and any adversary $\mathcal{A}$ there exists a adversary $\mathcal{B}$ with*

$$(\ell - k)\, \mathrm{Adv}^{\mathrm{mddh}}_{\mathcal{D}_{\ell,k},\mathsf{GGen},s}(\mathcal{A}) + \frac{1}{q-1} \geq \mathrm{Adv}^{\mathrm{mddh},Q}_{\mathcal{D}_{\ell,k},s}(\mathcal{B}) := |\Pr\left[\mathcal{B}\left(\mathcal{G},[\mathbf{A}],[\mathbf{AW}] \Rightarrow 1\right)\right]$$
$$- \Pr\left[\mathcal{B}\left(\mathcal{G},[\mathbf{A}],[\mathbf{U}] \Rightarrow 1\right)\right]|,$$

where $\mathcal{G} \xleftarrow{\$} \mathsf{GGen}\left(1^\lambda\right)$, $\mathbf{A} \xleftarrow{\$} \mathcal{D}_{\ell,k}$, $\mathbf{W} \xleftarrow{\$} \mathbb{Z}_q^{k \times Q}$, $\mathbf{U} \xleftarrow{\$} \mathbb{Z}_q^{(k+1) \times Q}$, and $T(\mathcal{A}) \approx T(\mathcal{B}) + Q \cdot \mathrm{poly}(\lambda)$.

2.2 Hierarchical Identity-Based Key Encapsulation

We recall syntax and security of a hierarchical identity-based key encapsulation mechanism (HIBKEM). We only consider HIBKEM in this paper. By adapting the transformation for public-key encryption in [20] to the HIBE setting, one can easily prove that every HIBKEM can be transformed (tightly) into an HIBE scheme with a (one-time secure) symmetric cipher.

Definition 4 (Hierarchical identity-based key encapsulation mechanism). *A hierarchical identity-based key encapsulation mechanism (HIBE) HIBKEM consists of three PPT algorithms HIBKEM = (Gen, Del, Ext, Enc, Dec) with the following properties.*

- *The probabilistic key generation algorithm Gen(par) returns the (master) public/secret key and delegation key (pk, sk, dk). Note that for some of our constructions dk is empty. We assume that pk implicitly defines a hierarchical identity space $\mathcal{ID} = \mathcal{S}^{\leq L}$, for some base identity set $\mathcal{S}$, and a key space $\mathcal{K}$, and ciphertext space $\mathcal{C}$.*
- *The probabilistic user secret key generation algorithm Ext(sk, id) returns a secret key usk[id] and a delegation value udk[id] for hierarchical identity id $\in \mathcal{ID}$.*
- *The probabilistic key delegation algorithm Del(dk, usk[id], udk[id], id $\in \mathcal{S}^p$, $\mathrm{id}_{p+1} \in \mathcal{S}$) returns a user secret key usk[id|id_{p+1}] for the hierarchical identity id' = id | $\mathrm{id}_{p+1} \in \mathcal{S}^{p+1}$ and the user delegation key udk[id']. We require $1 \leq |\mathrm{id}| \leq m - 1$.*
- *The probabilistic encapsulation algorithm Enc(pk, id) returns a symmetric key $\mathsf{K} \in \mathcal{K}$ together with a ciphertext C with respect to the hierarchical identity id $\in \mathcal{ID}$.*
- *The deterministic decapsulation algorithm Dec(usk[id], id, C) returns a decapsulated key $\mathsf{K} \in \mathcal{K}$ or the reject symbol $\perp$.*

For correctness we require that for all $\lambda \in \mathbb{N}$, all pairs $(\mathsf{pk}, \mathsf{sk})$ generated by $\mathsf{Gen}(\lambda)$, all $\mathsf{id} \in \mathcal{ID}$, all $\mathsf{usk}[\mathsf{id}]$ generated by $\mathsf{Ext}(\mathsf{sk}, \mathsf{id})$ and all (K, c) generated by $\mathsf{Enc}(\mathsf{pk}, \mathsf{id})$:

$$\Pr[\mathsf{Dec}(\mathsf{usk}[\mathsf{id}], \mathsf{id}, \mathsf{C}) = \mathsf{K}] = 1.$$

Moreover, we also require the distribution of $\mathsf{usk}[\mathsf{id}|\mathsf{id}_{p+1}]$ from $\mathsf{Del}(\mathsf{usk}[\mathsf{id}], \mathsf{udk}[\mathsf{id}], \mathsf{id}, \mathsf{id}_{p+1})$ is identical to the one from $\mathsf{Ext}(\mathsf{sk}, \mathsf{id}|\mathsf{id}_{p+1})$.

In our HIBKEM definition we make the delegation key dk explicit to make our constructions more readable. We define indistinguishability (IND-HID-CPA) against adaptively chosen identity and plaintext attacks for a HIBKEM via games IND-HID-CPA$_{\mathsf{real}}$ and IND-HID-CPA$_{\mathsf{rand}}$ from Fig. 2.

<u>INIT:</u>	<u>ENC(id*):</u> //one query
$(\mathsf{pk}, \mathsf{sk}, \mathsf{dk}) \xleftarrow{\$} \mathsf{Gen}(\lambda)$	$(\mathsf{K}^*, \mathsf{C}^*) \xleftarrow{\$} \mathsf{Enc}(\mathsf{pk}, \mathsf{id}^*)$
Return $(\mathsf{pk}, \mathsf{dk})$	$\boxed{\mathsf{K}^* \xleftarrow{\$} \mathcal{K}}$
	Return $(\mathsf{K}^*, \mathsf{C}^*)$
<u>EXT(id):</u>	
$\mathcal{Q}_{\mathcal{ID}} \leftarrow \mathcal{Q}_{\mathcal{ID}} \cup \{\mathsf{id}\}$	<u>FINALIZE($\beta \in \{0,1\}$):</u>
Return $(\mathsf{usk}[\mathsf{id}], \mathsf{udk}[\mathsf{id}]) \xleftarrow{\$} \mathsf{Ext}(\mathsf{sk}, \mathsf{id})$	Return $(\mathsf{Prefix}(\mathsf{id}^*) \cap \mathcal{Q}_{\mathcal{ID}} = \emptyset) \wedge \beta$

Fig. 2. Games IND-HID-CPA$_{\mathsf{real}}$ and $\boxed{\text{IND-HID-CPA}_{\mathsf{rand}}}$ for defining IND-HID-CPA-security. For any identity $\mathsf{id} \in \mathcal{S}^p$, $\mathsf{Prefix}(\mathsf{id})$ denotes the set of all prefixes of id.

Definition 5 (IND-HID-CPA Security). *A hierarchical identity-based key encapsulation scheme HIBKEM is IND-HID-CPA-secure if for all PPT $\mathcal{A}$,*

$$\mathsf{Adv}^{\mathsf{ind\text{-}hid\text{-}cpa}}_{\mathsf{HIBKEM}}(\mathcal{A}) := |\Pr[\mathsf{IND\text{-}HID\text{-}CPA}^{\mathcal{A}}_{\mathsf{real}} \Rightarrow 1] - \Pr[\mathsf{IND\text{-}HID\text{-}CPA}^{\mathcal{A}}_{\mathsf{rand}}]|$$

is negligible.

3   Affine MAC with Levels

The core of our HIBE constructions is a Message Authentication Code with suitable algebraic structures and we call it affine MAC with levels. This is a generalization of the delegatable, affine MAC used in [3], namely, a delegatable, affine MAC is affine MAC with levels with $\ell(p) = 1$ for all $p \in \{1, \dots L\}$.

Definition 6 (Affine MAC with levels). *An affine MAC with levels MAC consists of three PPT algorithms $(\mathsf{Gen}_{\mathsf{MAC}}, \mathsf{Tag}, \mathsf{Ver}_{\mathsf{MAC}})$ with the following properties:*

- $\mathsf{Gen_{MAC}}\,(\mathbb{G}_2, q, P_2)$ *gets a description of a prime-order group* $(\mathbb{G}_2, q, P_2)$ *and returns a secret key* $\mathsf{sk_{MAC}} := \left(\mathbf{B}, (\mathbf{x}_{l,i,j})_{1 \le l \le \ell(L), 1 \le i \le L, 1 \le j \le \ell'(l,i)}, x_0' \right)$ *where* $\mathbf{B} \in \mathbb{Z}_q^{n \times n'}$, $\mathbf{x}_{l,i,j} \in \mathbb{Z}_q^n$ *for* $l \in \{1, \dots, \ell(L)\}$, $i \in \{1, \dots, L\}$, *and* $j \in \{0, \dots, \ell'(l,i)\}$ *and* $x_0' \in \mathbb{Z}_q$.
- $\mathsf{Tag}\,(\mathsf{sk_{MAC}}, \mathsf{m} \in \mathcal{S}^{p \le L})$ *returns a tag* $\tau := \left(([\mathbf{t}_l]_2)_{1 \le l \le \ell(p)}, [u]_2 \right)$ *where*

$$\mathbf{t}_l := \mathbf{B}\mathbf{s}_l \quad \text{for } \mathbf{s}_l \xleftarrow{\$} \mathbb{Z}_q^{n'} \quad (1 \le l \le \ell(p))$$

$$u := \sum_{l=1}^{\ell(p)} \left(\sum_{i=1}^p \sum_{j=1}^{\ell'(l,i)} f_{l,i,j}\,(\mathsf{m}_{|i})\,\mathbf{x}_{l,i,j}^\top \right) \mathbf{t}_l + x_0' \tag{4}$$

- $\mathsf{Ver_{MAC}}\,(\mathsf{sk_{MAC}}, \mathsf{m}, \tau = ([\mathbf{t}]_2, [u]_2))$ *checks, whether Eq. (4) holds.*

The messages of MAC *have the form* $\mathsf{m} = (\mathsf{m}_1, \dots, \mathsf{m}_p)$ *where* $p \le L$ *and* $\mathsf{m}_i \in \mathcal{S}$. *After the transformation to an HIBE,* $\mathcal{S}$ *will be the base set of the identity space and* L *will be the maximum number of levels. The functions* $f_{l,i,j} : \mathcal{S}^i \to \mathbb{Z}_q$ *must be public, efficiently computable functions. The parameters* $\ell : \{1, \dots, p\} \to \mathbb{N}_+$, $n, n' \in \mathbb{N}_+$ *and* $\ell' : \{1, \dots, p\} \times \{1, \dots, L\} \to \mathbb{N}_+$ $(1 \le i \le L)$ *are arbitrary, scheme-depending parameters. The function* ℓ *must be monotonous increasing.*

SECURITY MODEL. As security model for affine MACs with levels we use $\mathsf{HPR_0\text{-}CMA}$-security as defined by the games in Fig. 3. This is a generalization of the $\mathsf{HPR_0\text{-}CMA}$-security for delegatable, affine MACs defined in [3].

INIT:

$\mathsf{sk_{MAC}} \xleftarrow{\$} \mathsf{Gen_{MAC}}(\mathbb{G}_2, q, P_2)$

Parse $\mathsf{sk_{MAC}} =: (\mathbf{B}, \tilde{\mathbf{x}}, x_0')$

Parse $\tilde{\mathbf{x}} =: (\mathbf{x}_{l,i,j})_{1 \le l \le \ell(L), 1 \le i \le L, 1 \le j \le \ell'(l,i)}$

$\mathsf{dk} := \left([\mathbf{x}_{l,i,j}^\top \mathbf{B}]_2 \right)_{1 \le l \le \ell(L), 1 \le i \le L, 1 \le j \le \ell'(l,i)}$

return $([\mathbf{B}]_2, \mathsf{dk})$

EVAL($\mathsf{m} \in \mathcal{S}^p$):

$\mathcal{Q}_\mathcal{M} = \mathcal{Q}_\mathcal{M} \cup \{\mathsf{m}\}$

$([\mathbf{t}]_2, [u]_2) \xleftarrow{\$} \mathsf{Tag}(\mathsf{sk}, \mathsf{m})$

for $l \in \{1, \dots, \ell(p)\}, i \in \{p+1, \dots, L\}, j \in \{1, \dots, \ell'(l,i)\}$ **do** $d_{l,i,j} = \mathbf{x}_{l,i,j}^\top \mathbf{t}_l$

$\mathsf{tdk} := ([d_{l,i,j}]_2)_{1 \le l \le \ell(p), p+1 \le i \le L, 1 \le j \le \ell'(l,i)}$

return $\left(([\mathbf{t}_l]_2)_{1 \le l \le \ell(p)}, [u]_2, \mathsf{tdk} \right)$

CHAL($\mathsf{m}^* \in \mathcal{S}^p$):   // one query

$h \xleftarrow{\$} \mathbb{Z}_q$

for $l \in \{1, \dots, \ell(p)\}$ **do**

$\qquad \mathbf{h}_{0,l} := \left(\sum_{i=1}^L \sum_{j=1}^{\ell'(l,i)} f_{l,i,j}\,(\mathsf{m}_{|i}^*) \mathbf{x}_{l,i,j} \right) h$

$h_1 = x_0' \cdot h \in \mathbb{Z}_q$

$\boxed{h_1 \xleftarrow{\$} \mathbb{Z}_q}$

return $\left([h], ([\mathbf{h}_{0,l}]_1)_{1 \le l \le \ell(p)}, [h_1]_T \right)$

FINALIZE($\beta \in \{0, 1\}$):

return $\beta \wedge (\mathsf{Prefix}(\mathsf{m}^*) \cap \mathcal{Q}_\mathcal{M} = \emptyset)$

Fig. 3. Games $\mathsf{HPR_0\text{-}CMA_{real}}$, and $\boxed{\mathsf{HPR_0\text{-}CMA_{rand}}}$ for defining $\mathsf{HPR_0\text{-}CMA}$ security for affine MACs with levels.

Definition 7 (HPR$_0$-CMA Security). *An affine MAC with levels is* HPR$_0$-CMA *secure in* $\mathbb{G}_2$ *if for all PPT adversaries* $\mathcal{A}$ *the function*

$$\mathsf{Adv}_{\mathsf{MAC},\mathbb{G}_2}^{\mathsf{hpr}_0\text{-}\mathsf{cma}}(\mathcal{A}) := \left| \Pr\left[\mathsf{HPR}_0\text{-}\mathsf{CMA}_{\mathsf{real}}^{\mathcal{A}} \Rightarrow 1 \right] - \Pr\left[\mathsf{HPR}_0\text{-}\mathsf{CMA}_{\mathsf{rand}}^{\mathcal{A}} \Rightarrow 1 \right] \right|$$

is negligible.

3.1 Our First Construction

Let $(\mathbb{G}_2, q, P_2)$ be a group of prime order q. Our first affine MAC with levels $\mathsf{MAC}_1[\mathcal{U}_{3k,k}] := (\mathsf{Gen}_{\mathsf{MAC}}, \mathsf{Tag}, \mathsf{Ver}_{\mathsf{MAC}})$ with message space $\mathcal{ID} := \mathcal{S}^{\leq L} := (\{0,1\}^{\alpha})^{\leq L}$ is defined in Fig. 4. The identity vectors bit-length α and the maximum length L of the identity vectors can be chosen freely.[3] The resulting HIBE from this MAC has constant ciphertext length.

$\mathsf{MAC}_1[\mathcal{U}_{3k,k}]$ has $n := 3k$ and $n' := k$ where $k \in \mathbb{N}_+$ can be chosen arbitrary. To match the formal definition, $\mathbf{x}_{i,j,b}$ should be renamed to $\mathbf{x}_{i,2j-b}$ and $f_{i,2j-b}(\mathsf{m}_{|i}) := \left([\![\mathsf{m}_{|i}]\!]_j \overset{?}{=} b \right)$. Then we get $\ell(p) = 1$ and $\ell'(1, i) = 2i\alpha$.

$\mathsf{Gen}_{\mathsf{MAC}}(\mathbb{G}_2, q, P_2)$:
$\mathbf{B} \xleftarrow{\$} \mathcal{U}_{3k,k}$
for $i \in \{1, \ldots, L\}, j \in \{1, \ldots, i\alpha\}, b \in \{0,1\}$ do $\mathbf{x}_{i,j,b} \xleftarrow{\$} \mathbb{Z}_q^{3k}$
$x_0' \xleftarrow{\$} \mathbb{Z}_q$
return $\mathsf{sk}_{\mathsf{MAC}} := \left(\mathbf{B}, (\mathbf{x}_{i,j,b})_{1 \leq i \leq L, b \in \{0,1\}, 1 \leq j \leq i\alpha}, x_0' \right)$

$\mathsf{Tag}(\mathsf{sk}_{\mathsf{MAC}}, \mathsf{m} \in \mathcal{S}^p)$:
Parse $\mathsf{sk}_{\mathsf{MAC}} =: \left(\mathbf{B}, (\mathbf{x}_{i,j,b})_{1 \leq i \leq L, b \in \{0,1\}, 1 \leq j \leq i\alpha}, x_0' \right)$
$\mathsf{s} \xleftarrow{\$} \mathbb{Z}_q^k; \mathsf{t} := \mathbf{B}\mathsf{s}$
$u := \left(\sum_{i=1}^{p} \sum_{j=1}^{i\alpha} \mathbf{x}_{i,j,[\![\mathsf{m}]\!]_j}^{\top} \right) \mathsf{t} + x_0'$
return $\tau := \left([\mathsf{t}]_2, [u]_2 \right)$

$\mathsf{Ver}_{\mathsf{MAC}}(\mathsf{sk}_{\mathsf{MAC}}, \mathsf{m} \in \mathcal{S}^p, \tau)$:
Parse $\mathsf{sk}_{\mathsf{MAC}} =: \left(\mathbf{B}, (\mathbf{x}_{i,j,b})_{1 \leq i \leq L, b \in \{0,1\}, 1 \leq j \leq i\alpha}, x_0' \right)$
Parse $\mathsf{m} =: (\mathsf{m}_1, \ldots, \mathsf{m}_p)$
Parse $\tau =: \left([\mathsf{t}]_2, [u]_2 \right)$
return $u \overset{?}{=} \left(\sum_{i=1}^{p} \sum_{j=1}^{i\alpha} \mathbf{x}_{i,j,[\![\mathsf{m}]\!]_j}^{\top} \right) \mathsf{t} + x_0'$

Fig. 4. Our first affine MAC

---

[3] A different bitlength on each level is possible as well, but we assume it is α on each level to ease notation.

Theorem 1 (Security of $\mathsf{MAC}_1[\mathcal{U}_{3k,k}]$). $\mathsf{MAC}_1[\mathcal{U}_{3k,k}]$ *is tightly* $\mathsf{HPR}_0\text{-}\mathsf{CMA}$ *secure in* $\mathbb{G}_2$ *under the* $\mathcal{U}_k$-MDDH *assumption for* $\mathbb{G}_2$. *Precisely, for all adversaries* $\mathcal{A}$ *there exists an adversary* $\mathcal{B}$ *with*

$$\mathsf{Adv}^{\mathsf{hpr}_0\text{-}\mathsf{cma}}_{\mathsf{MAC}_1[\mathcal{U}_{3k,k}],\mathbb{G}_2}(\mathcal{A}) \leq \left(4\,(\alpha+1)\,L + 4\alpha L^2\right)\left(\mathsf{Adv}^{\mathsf{mddh}}_{\mathcal{U}_k,\mathsf{GGen},\mathbb{G}_2}(\mathcal{B}) + \frac{1}{q-1}\right)$$

$$+ \frac{LQ}{q^{2k}}$$

and $T(\mathcal{B}) \approx T(\mathcal{A}) + Q \cdot \mathsf{poly}(\lambda)$.

Proof. The proof uses a hybrid argument with the hybrids G_0 (the $\mathsf{HPR}_0\text{-}\mathsf{CMA}_{\text{real}}$ game), G_1, $\mathsf{G}_{2,\hat{\imath},0}$, $\mathsf{G}_{2,\hat{\imath},1}$, $\mathsf{G}_{2,\hat{\imath},2,\hat{\jmath},0}$–$\mathsf{G}_{2,\hat{\imath},2,\hat{\jmath},3}$, $\mathsf{G}_{2,\hat{\imath},3}$, $\mathsf{G}_{2,\hat{\imath},4}$, and $\mathsf{G}_{2,\hat{\imath},5}$ for $\hat{\imath} \in \{1,\dots,L\}$ and $\hat{\jmath} \in \{1,\dots,\hat{\imath}\alpha\}$, and finally G_3. The hybrids are given in Figs. 5 and 6. A summary can be found in Table 2. They make use of random functions $\mathsf{RF}_{\hat{\imath},\hat{\jmath}} : \{0,1\}^{\hat{\jmath}} \to \mathbb{Z}_q^{1\times 2k}$, $\mathsf{RF}^{(0)}_{\hat{\imath},\hat{\jmath}} : \{0,1\}^{\hat{\jmath}} \to \mathbb{Z}_q^{1\times k}$, and $\mathsf{RF}^{(1)}_{\hat{\imath},\hat{\jmath}} : \{0,1\}^{\hat{\jmath}} \to \mathbb{Z}_q^{1\times k}$, defined on-the-fly. $\qquad\square$

Table 2. Summary of the hybrids of Figs. 5 and 6. EVAL queries with $p = \hat{\imath}$ draw $\mathbf{t}$ from the set described by the second column and add the randomness $r_u(\mathsf{m})\,\mathbf{t}$ to u or choose u uniform random. The CHAL query adds the term $r_{\mathbf{h}_0}(\mathsf{m}^\star)^\top$ to $\mathbf{h}_0$ if $\mathsf{m}^\star$ has length $\hat{\imath}$. The column "Transition" displays how we can switch to this hybrid from the previous one. The background colors indicate repeated transitions.

Hybrid	$\mathbf{t}$ uniform in	$r_u(\mathsf{m})$	$r_{\mathbf{h}_0}(\mathsf{m})$	Transition
G_0	$\mathsf{Span}(\mathbf{B})$		0	Original game
G_1	$\mathsf{Span}(\mathbf{B})$		0	Identical
$\mathsf{G}_{2,\hat{\imath},0}$	$\mathsf{Span}(\mathbf{B})$		0	Identical
$\mathsf{G}_{2,\hat{\imath},1}$	$\mathbb{Z}_q^{3k}$		0	$\mathcal{U}_k\text{-}\mathsf{MDDH}$
$\mathsf{G}_{2,\hat{\imath},2,\hat{\jmath},0}$	$\mathbb{Z}_q^{3k}$		$\mathsf{RF}_{\hat{\imath},\hat{\jmath}}\big(\llbracket\mathsf{m}\rrbracket_{|\hat{\jmath}}\big)\big(\mathbf{B}^\perp\big)^\top$	Identical
$\mathsf{G}_{2,\hat{\imath},2,\hat{\jmath},1}$			$\mathsf{RF}_{\hat{\imath},\hat{\jmath}}\big(\llbracket\mathsf{m}\rrbracket_{|\hat{\jmath}}\big)\big(\mathbf{B}^\perp\big)^\top$	$2 \times \mathcal{U}_k\text{-}\mathsf{MDDH}$
$\mathsf{G}_{2,\hat{\imath},2,\hat{\jmath},2}$	if $\llbracket\mathsf{m}\rrbracket_{\hat{\jmath}+1} = 0$ then $\lfloor\mathsf{Span}(\mathbf{B}\|\mathbf{B}_0)$ else $\lfloor\mathsf{Span}(\mathbf{B}\|\mathbf{B}_1)$		$\Big(\mathsf{RF}^{(0)}_{\hat{\imath},\hat{\jmath}+1}\big(\llbracket\mathsf{m}\rrbracket_{|\hat{\jmath}+1}\big)(\mathbf{B}_0^\star)^\top + \mathsf{RF}^{(1)}_{\hat{\imath},\hat{\jmath}}\big(\llbracket\mathsf{m}\rrbracket_{|\hat{\jmath}}\big)(\mathbf{B}_1^\star)^\top\Big)$	Identical
$\mathsf{G}_{2,\hat{\imath},2,\hat{\jmath},3}$			$\Big(\mathsf{RF}^{(0)}_{\hat{\imath},\hat{\jmath}+1}\big(\llbracket\mathsf{m}\rrbracket_{|\hat{\jmath}+1}\big)(\mathbf{B}_0^\star)^\top + \mathsf{RF}^{(1)}_{\hat{\imath},\hat{\jmath}+1}\big(\llbracket\mathsf{m}\rrbracket_{|\hat{\jmath}+1}\big)(\mathbf{B}_1^\star)^\top\Big)$	Identical
$\mathsf{G}_{2,\hat{\imath},2,\hat{\jmath}+1,3}$	$\mathbb{Z}_q^{3k}$		$\mathsf{RF}_{\hat{\imath},\hat{\jmath}+1}\big(\llbracket\mathsf{m}\rrbracket_{|\hat{\jmath}+1}\big)\big(\mathbf{B}^\perp\big)^\top$	$2 \times \mathcal{U}_k\text{-}\mathsf{MDDH}$
$\mathsf{G}_{2,\hat{\imath},3}$	$\mathbb{Z}_q^{3k}$	uniform random	$\mathsf{RF}_{\hat{\imath}}\big(\mathsf{m}_{|\hat{\imath}}\big)\big(\mathbf{B}^\perp\big)^\top$	Identical
$\mathsf{G}_{2,\hat{\imath},4}$	$\mathbb{Z}_q^{3k}$	uniform random	0	Identical
$\mathsf{G}_{2,\hat{\imath},5}$	$\mathsf{Span}(\mathbf{B})$	uniform random	0	$\mathcal{U}_k\text{-}\mathsf{MDDH}$
G_3	$\mathsf{Span}(\mathbf{B})$	uniform random	0	Statistically close

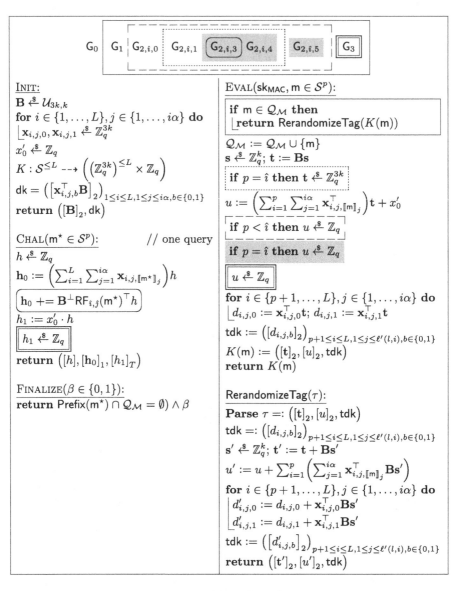

Fig. 5. Hybrids for the security proof of $\mathsf{MAC}_1[\mathcal{U}_{3k,k}]$. The notion $a \mathrel{+}= b$ is shorthand for $a := a + b$. The algorithm RerandomizeTag is only helper function and not an oracle for the adversary.

Lemma 4 ($G_0 \rightsquigarrow G_1$).

$$\Pr[G_0^{\mathcal{A}} \Rightarrow 1] = \Pr[G_1^{\mathcal{A}} \Rightarrow 1]$$

Proof. In game G_1 each time the adversary queries a tag for a message m where he queried a tag for m before, the adversary will get a rerandomized version of the first tag he queried. The rerandomized tag is identically distributed to a fresh tag: $\mathbf{t}' := \mathbf{t} + \mathbf{B}\mathbf{s}'$ is uniformly random in $\mathsf{Span}\,(\mathbf{B})$, when $\mathbf{s}'$ is uniform random in $\mathbb{Z}_q^k$. Together with $u' := u + \sum_{i=1}^{p}\left(\sum_{j=1}^{i\alpha}\mathbf{x}_{i,j,[\![m]\!]_j}^{\top}\mathbf{B}\mathbf{s}'\right)$ we get a valid message tag for m, when $([\mathbf{t}]_2, [u]_2)$ is a valid tag for m.

Note that the rerandomization uses only the "public key" returned by the INIT-Oracle, so it could actually be carried out by the adversary herself. To put it in a nutshell, repeated EVAL-queries for a message m will leak no information, that is not already leaked by the first EVAL-query for m or by the"public key".[4]

$\square$

Lemma 5 ($\mathsf{G}_1 \rightsquigarrow \mathsf{G}_{2,1,0}$).

$$\Pr[\mathsf{G}_1^{\mathcal{A}} \Rightarrow 1] = \Pr[\mathsf{G}_{2,1,0}^{\mathcal{A}} \Rightarrow 1]$$

Proof. These two games are equivalent. $\square$

Lemma 6 ($\mathsf{G}_{2,\hat{\imath},0} \rightsquigarrow \mathsf{G}_{2,\hat{\imath},1}$). *For all adversaries $\mathcal{A}$ there exists an adversary $\mathcal{B}$ with*

$$\left|\Pr\left[\mathsf{G}_{2,\hat{\imath},0}^{\mathcal{A}} \Rightarrow 1\right] - \Pr[\mathsf{G}_{2,\hat{\imath},1}^{\mathcal{A}} \Rightarrow 1]\right| \leq \mathsf{Adv}_{\mathcal{U}_k,\mathsf{GGen},\mathsf{G}_2}^{\mathsf{mddh}}(\mathcal{B}) + \frac{1}{q-1}$$

and $T(\mathcal{B}) \approx T(\mathcal{A}) + Q \cdot \mathsf{poly}(\lambda)$.

Proof. These two games are equivalent except that in EVAL-queries with $p = \hat{\imath}$ the value $\mathbf{t}$ is chosen uniformly random from $\mathsf{Span}\,(\mathbf{B})$ in $\mathsf{G}_{2,\hat{\imath},0}$ and uniformly random from $\mathbb{Z}_q^{3k}$ in game $\mathsf{G}_{2,\hat{\imath},1}$. Since for all computed values it is enough to have $[\mathbf{B}]_2$ instead of $\mathbf{B}$, this leads to a straight forward reduction to the QL-fold $\mathcal{U}_{3k,k}$-MDDH assumption. Remember that by Lemma 1, the $\mathcal{U}_{3k,k}$-MDDH assumption is equivalent to the $\mathcal{U}_k$-MDDH assumption.

The running time of $\mathcal{B}$ is dominated by the running time of $\mathcal{A}$ plus some (polynomial) overhead that is independent of $T(\mathcal{A})$ for the group operations in each oracle query. $\square$

Lemma 7 ($\mathsf{G}_{2,\hat{\imath},1} \rightsquigarrow \mathsf{G}_{2,\hat{\imath},3}$). *For all $\hat{\imath} \in \{1,\ldots,L\}$, $\hat{\jmath} \in \{1,\ldots,\hat{\imath}\alpha - 1\}$ and all adversaries $\mathcal{A}$ there exists an adversary $\mathcal{B}$ with*

$$\left|\Pr\left[\mathsf{G}_{2,\hat{\imath},1}^{\mathcal{A}} \Rightarrow 1\right] - \Pr\left[\mathsf{G}_{2,\hat{\imath},3}^{\mathcal{A}} \Rightarrow 1\right]\right| \leq 4\hat{\imath}\alpha\left(\mathsf{Adv}_{\mathcal{U}_k,\mathsf{GGen},\mathsf{G}_2}^{\mathsf{mddh}}(\mathcal{B}) + \frac{1}{q-1}\right)$$

and $T(\mathcal{B}) \approx T(\mathcal{A}) + Q \cdot \mathsf{poly}(\lambda)$.

Proof. To prove this transition, we introduce new hybrids $\mathsf{G}_{2,\hat{\imath},2,\hat{\jmath},1}$, $\mathsf{G}_{2,\hat{\imath},2,\hat{\jmath},2}$ and $\mathsf{G}_{2,\hat{\imath},2,\hat{\jmath},3}$ for $\hat{\imath} \in \{1,\ldots,L\}$ and $\hat{\jmath} \in \{1,\ldots,\hat{\imath}\alpha - 1\}$. The hybrids are given in Fig. 6.

Lemma 7 follows directly from Lemmas 8, 9, 10, 11, 12 and 13. $\square$

---

[4] The same technique can be used to prove the IBE of [3] secure with duplicated EXT-queries. Thus they work without a pseudorandom function.

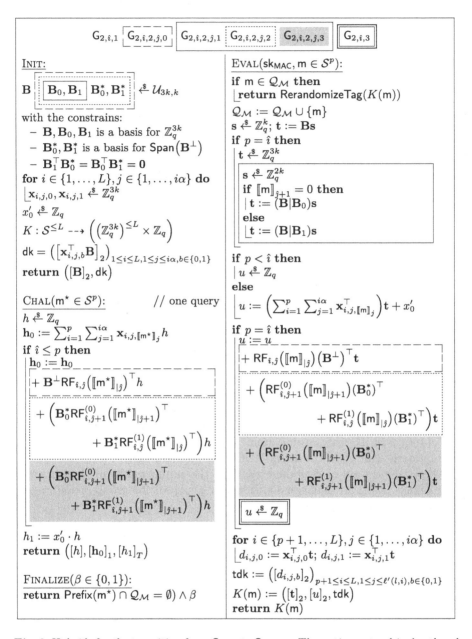

Fig. 6. Hybrids for the transition from $\mathsf{G}_{2,i,\hat{\jmath}}$ to $\mathsf{G}_{2,i,\hat{\jmath}+1}$. The notion $a \mathrel{+}= b$ is shorthand for $a := a + b$. The algorithm RerandomizeTag is defined in Fig. 5.

Lemma 8 $(G_{2,\hat{i},1} \rightsquigarrow G_{2,\hat{i},2,0,0})$.

$$\Pr\left[G_{2,\hat{i},1}^{\mathcal{A}} \Rightarrow 1\right] = \Pr\left[G_{2,\hat{i},2,0,0}^{\mathcal{A}} \Rightarrow 1\right]$$

Proof. These two games are equivalent. When changing in $G_{2,\hat{i},1}$ the secret values $\mathbf{x}_{\hat{i},1,b}$ to $\mathbf{x}_{\hat{i},1,b} + \mathbf{B}^{\perp}\left(\mathsf{RF}_{\hat{i},0}(\varepsilon)\right)^{\top}$ (for $b \in \{0,1\}$), we get game $G_{2,\hat{i},2,0,0}$. The distribution of $\mathbf{x}_{\hat{i},1,b}$ and $\mathbf{x}_{\hat{i},1,b} + \mathbf{B}^{\perp}\left(\mathsf{RF}_{1,0}(\varepsilon)\right)^{\top}$ is identical. Note that the term $\mathbf{B}^{\perp}\left(\mathsf{RF}_{1,0}(\varepsilon)\right)^{\top}$ cancels out in the master public key and in the user delegation keys of EVAL-queries with $p < \hat{i}$. $\qquad\square$

Lemma 9 $(G_{2,\hat{i},2,\hat{j},0} \rightsquigarrow G_{2,\hat{i},2,\hat{j},1})$. *For all adversaries $\mathcal{A}$ there exists an adversary $\mathcal{B}$ with*

$$\left|\Pr\left[G_{2,\hat{i},2,\hat{j},0}^{\mathcal{A}} \Rightarrow 1\right] - \Pr\left[G_{2,\hat{i},2,\hat{j},1}^{\mathcal{A}} \Rightarrow 1\right]\right| \leq 2\left(\mathsf{Adv}_{\mathcal{U}_k,\mathsf{GGen},\mathbb{G}_2}^{\mathsf{mddh}}(\mathcal{B}) + \frac{1}{q-1}\right)$$

and $T(\mathcal{B}) \approx T(\mathcal{A}) + Q \cdot \mathsf{poly}(\lambda)$.

Proof. These two games are equivalent except that the value $\mathbf{t}$ is generated uniformly random from $\mathbb{Z}_q^{3k}$ in game $G_{2,\hat{i},2,\hat{j},0}$ and from either $\mathsf{Span}(\mathbf{B}|\mathbf{B}_0)$ or $\mathsf{Span}(\mathbf{B}|\mathbf{B}_1)$ depending on the bit $\llbracket m \rrbracket_{\hat{j}+1}$ in game $G_{2,\hat{i},2,\hat{j},1}$. We can switch from $G_{2,\hat{i},2,\hat{j},0}$ to $G_{2,\hat{i},2,\hat{j},1}$ with two Q-fold $\mathcal{U}_{3k,k}$-MDDH challenges. Remember that the $\mathcal{U}_{3k,k}$-MDDH assumption is equivalent to the $\mathcal{U}_k$-MDDH assumption by Lemma 1.

To achieve that, we first switch $\mathbf{t}$ for $\llbracket m \rrbracket_{\hat{j}+1} = 0$ from a random vector in $\mathbb{Z}_q^{3k}$ to $\mathbf{t} := \mathbf{B}\mathbf{s}_1 + \mathbf{s}_2$ where $\mathbf{s}_1 \xleftarrow{\$} \mathbb{Z}_q^k$ and $\mathbf{s}_2 \xleftarrow{\$} \mathbb{Z}_q^{3k}$. This change is only conceptual. Then we change $\mathbf{s}_2$ from a random vector in $\mathbb{Z}_q^{3k}$ to a random vector in the span of $\mathbf{B}_0$ via the MDDH assumption. More precisely, let $([\mathbf{B}_0]_2, [\mathbf{Z}]_2) \in \mathbb{G}_2^{3k \times (k+Q)}$ be a Q-fold $\mathcal{U}_{3k,k}$-MDDH challenge. For the i-th EVAL query with $\llbracket m \rrbracket_{\hat{j}+1} = 0$, the reduction $\mathcal{B}$ computes $[\mathbf{t}]_2 := [\mathbf{B}\mathbf{s}_1 + \mathbf{Z}[i]]_2$, where $\mathbf{s}_1 \xleftarrow{\$} \mathbb{Z}_q^k$ and $\mathbf{Z}[i]$ is the i-th column vector of $\mathbf{Z}$. Furthermore, in order to make sure that the column vectors of $(\mathbf{B}|\mathbf{B}_0|\mathbf{B}_1)$ form a random basis of $\mathbb{Z}_q^{3k}$, the reduction $\mathcal{B}$ chooses $\mathbf{B}, \mathbf{B}_1 \xleftarrow{\$} \mathcal{U}_{3k,k}$ such that $(\mathbf{B}|\mathbf{B}_1)$ has rank $2k$ and $(\mathbf{B}|\mathbf{B}_1)^{\perp}\mathbf{b} = \mathbf{0}$ for all column vectors $\mathbf{b}$ of $\mathbf{B}_0$. We note that the latter one can be done over group $\mathbb{G}_2$ by knowing $\mathbf{B}$ and $\mathbf{B}_1$ over $\mathbb{Z}_q$.

Until now, if $\mathbf{Z}$ is uniform then $\mathcal{B}$ simulates the game $G_{2,\hat{i},2,\hat{j},0}$, else if $\mathbf{Z}$ is from $\mathsf{Span}(\mathbf{B}_0)$ then $\mathcal{B}$ simulates the game $G_{2,\hat{i},2,\hat{j},1}$ for messages with $\llbracket m \rrbracket_{\hat{j}+1} = 0$.

By using the same argument, we can switch $\mathbf{t}$ for $\llbracket m \rrbracket_{\hat{j}+1} = 1$ from a random vector in $\mathbb{Z}_q^{3k}$ to a random vector in $\mathsf{Span}(\mathbf{B}|\mathbf{B}_1)$.

The running time of $\mathcal{B}$ is dominated by the running time of $\mathcal{A}$ plus some (polynomial) overhead that is independent of $T(\mathcal{A})$ for the group operations in each oracle query. $\qquad\square$

Lemma 10 $(G_{2,\hat{i},2,\hat{j},1} \rightsquigarrow G_{2,\hat{i},2,\hat{j},2})$.

$$\Pr\left[G_{2,\hat{i},2,\hat{j},1}^{\mathcal{A}} \Rightarrow 1\right] = \Pr\left[G_{2,\hat{i},2,\hat{j},2}^{\mathcal{A}} \Rightarrow 1\right]$$

Proof. First of all, we replace in game $\mathsf{G}_{2,\hat{i},2,\hat{j},1}$ the term $\mathsf{RF}_{\hat{i},\hat{j}}\left([\![m]\!]_{|\hat{j}}\right)(\mathbf{B}^{\perp})^{\top}$ with $\mathsf{RF}_{\hat{i},\hat{j}}^{(0)}\left([\![m]\!]_{|\hat{j}+1}\right)(\mathbf{B}_0^*)^{\top} + \mathsf{RF}_{\hat{i},\hat{j}}^{(1)}\left([\![m]\!]_{|\hat{j}}\right)(\mathbf{B}_1^*)^{\top}$. This does not change the distribution, since $\mathbf{B}_0^*, \mathbf{B}_1^*$ is a basis for $\mathsf{Span}\left(\mathbf{B}^{\perp}\right)$.

We define

$$\mathsf{RF}_{\hat{i},\hat{j}+1}^{(0)}\left([\![m]\!]_{|\hat{j}+1}\right) := \begin{cases} \mathsf{RF}_{\hat{i},\hat{j}}^{(0)}\left([\![m]\!]_{|\hat{j}}\right) & \text{if } [\![m]\!]_{\hat{j}+1} = 0 \\ \mathsf{RF}_{\hat{i},\hat{j}}^{(0)}\left([\![m]\!]_{|\hat{j}}\right) + \mathsf{RF}_{\hat{i},\hat{j}}^{\prime(0)}\left([\![m]\!]_{|\hat{j}}\right) & \text{if } [\![m]\!]_{\hat{j}+1} = 1 \end{cases}$$

where $\mathsf{RF}_{\hat{i},\hat{j}}^{\prime(0)} : \{0,1\}^{\hat{j}+1} \to \mathbb{Z}_q^{1 \times k}$ is another independent random function. Since $\mathsf{RF}_{\hat{i},\hat{j}}^{(0)}$ does not appear in game $\mathsf{G}_{2,\hat{i},2,\hat{j},2}$ anymore, $\mathsf{RF}_{\hat{i},\hat{j}+1}^{(0)}$ is a random function.

The EVAL-queries with $p \neq \hat{i}$ use the same code in both games and EVAL-queries with $p = \hat{i}$ and $[\![m]\!]_{\hat{j}+1} = 0$ are distributed identically in both games, by definition of $\mathsf{RF}_{\hat{i},\hat{j}+1}^{(0)}$.

The EVAL-queries with $p = \hat{i}$ and $[\![m]\!]_{\hat{j}+1} = 1$ are distributed identically in both games, since for those queries $\mathbf{t} \in \mathsf{Span}\left(\mathbf{B}|\mathbf{B}_1\right)$ and both $\mathbf{B}$ and $\mathbf{B}_1$ are orthogonal to $\mathbf{B}_0^*$ and thus $\mathsf{RF}_{\hat{i},\hat{j}+1}^{(0)}\left([\![m]\!]_{|\hat{j}+1}\right)(\mathbf{B}_0^*)^{\top}\mathbf{t} = 0$.

The CHAL query uses the same code if $p \neq \hat{i}$ and otherwise it is distributed identically if $[\![m^*]\!]_{\hat{j}+1} = 0$. For the case $[\![m^*]\!]_{\hat{j}+1} = 1$ note that $\mathbf{x}_{\hat{i},\hat{j}+1,1}$ is identically distributed as $\mathbf{x}_{\hat{i},\hat{j}+1,1} + \mathbf{B}_0^*\mathbf{w}$ for $\mathbf{w} \xleftarrow{\$} \mathbb{Z}_q^k$ and $\mathbf{w}$ is hidden from the adversary except for the CHAL query: In all EVAL-queries with $p \neq \hat{i}$ only $\mathbf{x}_{\hat{i},\hat{j}+1,1}\mathbf{B}$ is used and thus the $\mathbf{B}_0^*$-part cancels out. In the EVAL-queries with $p = \hat{i}$ there is either $[\![m]\!]_{\hat{j}+1} = 0$ which means that $\mathbf{x}_{\hat{i},\hat{j}+1,1}$ is not used to compute the tag or there is $[\![m]\!]_{\hat{j}+1} = 1$ which means that $\mathbf{t} \in \mathsf{Span}\left(\mathbf{B}|\mathbf{B}_1\right)$ and thus the $\mathbf{B}_0^*$-part of $\mathbf{x}_{\hat{i},\hat{j}+1,1}$ cancels out. All in all this means that the value $\mathbf{h}_0$ is the only one in the game that depends on $\mathbf{w}$ and thus the $\mathbf{B}_0^*$-part of $\mathbf{h}_0$ is uniformly random to the adversary. Especially $\mathbf{h}_0$ is distributed identically in both games. $\qquad\square$

Lemma 11 $\left(\mathsf{G}_{2,\hat{i},2,\hat{j},2} \rightsquigarrow \mathsf{G}_{2,\hat{i},2,\hat{j},3}\right)$.

$$\Pr\left[\mathsf{G}_{2,\hat{i},2,\hat{j},2}^{\mathcal{A}} \Rightarrow 1\right] = \Pr\left[\mathsf{G}_{2,\hat{i},2,\hat{j},3}^{\mathcal{A}} \Rightarrow 1\right]$$

Proof. We define

$$\mathsf{RF}_{\hat{i},\hat{j}+1}^{(1)}\left([\![m]\!]_{|\hat{j}+1}\right) := \begin{cases} \mathsf{RF}_{\hat{i},\hat{j}}^{(1)}\left([\![m]\!]_{|\hat{j}}\right) + \mathsf{RF}_{\hat{i},\hat{j}}^{\prime(1)}\left([\![m]\!]_{|\hat{j}}\right) & \text{if } [\![m]\!]_{\hat{j}+1} = 0 \\ \mathsf{RF}_{\hat{i},\hat{j}}^{(1)}\left([\![m]\!]_{|\hat{j}}\right) & \text{if } [\![m]\!]_{\hat{j}+1} = 1 \end{cases}$$

where $\mathsf{RF}_{\hat{i},\hat{j}}^{\prime(1)} : \{0,1\}^{\hat{j}+1} \to \mathbb{Z}_q^{1 \times k}$ is another independent random function. Since $\mathsf{RF}_{\hat{i},\hat{j}}^{(1)}$ in not used in game $\mathsf{G}_{2,\hat{i},2,\hat{j},3}$, $\mathsf{RF}_{\hat{i},\hat{j}+1}^{(1)}$ is a random function.

The argument, that the games $\mathsf{G}_{2,\hat{i},2,\hat{j},2}$ and $\mathsf{G}_{2,\hat{i},2,\hat{j},3}$ are identically distributed, is the same as in Lemma 10, just with the roles of 0 and 1 swapped. $\qquad\square$

Lemma 12 ($G_{2,\hat{\imath},2,\hat{\jmath},3} \rightsquigarrow G_{2,\hat{\imath},2,\hat{\jmath}+1,0}$). *For $\hat{\jmath} < \hat{\imath}\alpha$ and all adversaries $\mathcal{A}$ there exists an adversary $\mathcal{B}$ with*

$$\left| \Pr\left[G^{\mathcal{A}}_{2,\hat{\imath},2,\hat{\jmath},3} \Rightarrow 1 \right] - \Pr\left[G^{\mathcal{A}}_{2,\hat{\imath},\hat{\jmath}+1} \Rightarrow 1 \right] \right| \leq 2 \left(\mathsf{Adv}^{\mathsf{mddh}}_{\mathcal{U}_k,\mathsf{GGen},\mathbb{G}_2}(\mathcal{B}) + \frac{1}{q-1} \right)$$

and $T(\mathcal{B}) \approx T(\mathcal{A}) + Q \cdot \mathsf{poly}(\lambda)$.

Proof. The transition is the reverse of Lemma 9. $\qquad\square$

Lemma 13 ($G_{2,\hat{\imath},2,\hat{\imath}\alpha,3} \rightsquigarrow G_{2,\hat{\imath},3}$).

$$\left| \Pr\left[G^{\mathcal{A}}_{2,\hat{\imath},2,\hat{\imath}\alpha,3} \Rightarrow 1 \right] - \Pr\left[G^{\mathcal{A}}_{2,\hat{\imath},3} \Rightarrow 1 \right] \right| \leq \frac{Q}{q^{2k}}$$

Proof. In game $G_{2,\hat{\imath},2,\hat{\imath}\alpha,3}$ the CHAL-query evaluates $\mathsf{RF}_{\hat{\imath},\hat{\imath}\alpha}$ only for the input value $\mathsf{m}^\star_1 \| \dots \| \mathsf{m}^\star_{\hat{\imath}}$ (if $p \geq \hat{\imath}$, otherwise it does not use $\mathsf{RF}_{\hat{\imath},\hat{\imath}\alpha}$ at all). Assume $\mathsf{Prefix}(\mathsf{m}^\star) \cap \mathcal{Q}_\mathcal{M} = \emptyset$, otherwise the adversary has lost the game anyway. In each user secret key query with $p = \hat{\imath}$ the value $\mathsf{RF}_{\hat{\imath},\hat{\imath}\alpha}(\mathsf{m}) \left(\mathbf{B}^\perp \right)^\top \mathbf{t}$ is part of u. This is the only place where $\mathsf{RF}_{\hat{\imath},\hat{\imath}\alpha}(\mathsf{m})$ is used, since only the first EVAL-query for each message evaluates the random function. Thus each query outputs a uniformly random value for u when $\mathbf{t}_p \notin \mathsf{Span}(\mathbf{B})$, which happens with probability $\geq 1 - 1/\left(q^{2k} \right)$. In this case the games are distributed identically. $\qquad\square$

Lemma 14 ($G_{2,\hat{\imath},3} \rightsquigarrow G_{2,\hat{\imath},4}$).

$$\Pr\left[G^{\mathcal{A}}_{2,\hat{\imath},3} \Rightarrow 1 \right] = \Pr\left[G^{\mathcal{A}}_{2,\hat{\imath},4} \Rightarrow 1 \right]$$

Proof. The games execute the same code if $p < \hat{\imath}$ and otherwise we can argue that $\mathbf{x}_{\hat{\imath},1,[\![\mathsf{m}^\star]\!]_1}$ and $\mathbf{x}_{\hat{\imath},1,[\![\mathsf{m}^\star]\!]_1} - \mathbf{B}^\perp \left(\mathsf{RF}_{\hat{\imath},\hat{\imath}\alpha}(\mathsf{m}^\star) \right)^\top$ are identical distributed. All EVAL-queries and the "public key" returned by INIT make only use of $\mathbf{x}_{\hat{\imath},1,[\![\mathsf{m}^\star]\!]_1}$, $\mathbf{B}$, so the $\mathbf{B}^\perp \left(\mathsf{RF}_{\hat{\imath},\hat{\imath}\alpha}(\cdot) \right)^\top$ part cancels out. $\qquad\square$

Lemma 15 ($G_{2,\hat{\imath},4} \rightsquigarrow G_{2,\hat{\imath},5}$). *For all adversaries $\mathcal{A}$ there exists an adversary $\mathcal{B}$ with*

$$\left| \Pr\left[G^{\mathcal{A}}_{2,\hat{\imath},4} \Rightarrow 1 \right] - \Pr\left[G^{\mathcal{A}}_{2,\hat{\imath},5} \Rightarrow 1 \right] \right| \leq \mathsf{Adv}^{\mathsf{mddh}}_{\mathcal{U}_k,\mathsf{GGen},\mathbb{G}_2}(\mathcal{B}) + \frac{1}{q-1}$$

and $T(\mathcal{B}) \approx T(\mathcal{A}) + Q \cdot \mathsf{poly}(\lambda)$.

Proof. The transition is the reverse of Lemma 6. $\qquad\square$

Lemma 16 ($G_{2,\hat{\imath},5} \rightsquigarrow G_{2,\hat{\imath}+1,0}$). *For $\hat{\imath} < L$*

$$\Pr\left[G^{\mathcal{A}}_{2,\hat{\imath},5} \Rightarrow 1 \right] = \Pr\left[G^{\mathcal{A}}_{2,\hat{\imath}+1,0} \Rightarrow 1 \right].$$

Proof. These two games are equivalent. $\qquad\square$

Lemma 17 ($G_{2,L,5} \rightsquigarrow G_3$).

$$\Pr\left[G_{2,L,5}^{\mathcal{A}} \Rightarrow 1\right] = \Pr\left[G_3^{\mathcal{A}} \Rightarrow 1\right].$$

Proof. In game $G_{2,L,5}$ the value x_0' is only used to compute h_1, thus h_1 is a uniform random value to $\mathcal{A}$ and the games are distributed identical. □

SUMMARY. To prove Theorem 1 combine Lemmas 4, 5, 6, 7, 8, 9, 10, 11, 12, 13, 14, 15, 16 and 17 to change h_1 from real to random and then apply all Lemmas in reverse order to get to the $\mathsf{HPR}_0\text{-}\mathsf{CMA}_{\mathrm{rand}}$ game. □

3.2 Our Second Construction

Let $(\mathbb{G}_2, q, P_2)$ be a group of prime order q. Our second affine MAC with levels $\mathsf{MAC}_1[\mathcal{U}_{3k,k}] := (\mathsf{Gen}_{\mathsf{MAC}}, \mathsf{Tag}, \mathsf{Ver}_{\mathsf{MAC}})$ with message space $\mathcal{ID} := \mathcal{S}^{\leq L} := (\{0,1\}^\alpha)^{\leq L}$ is defined in Fig. 7. The identity vectors bit-length α and the maximum length L of the identity vectors can be chosen freely. The difference to the first construction is that this MAC uses a different $\mathbf{t}_l$ on each level ($\ell(p) = p$) and thus needs no delegation keys. This leads to shorter user secret keys and allows a more efficient reduction. However, this comes at the price of larger ciphertexts. Formally, this MAC uses $\ell'(l,i) = 0$ for $i < p$ and $\ell'(l,i) = 2i\alpha$ for $i = p$.

$\mathsf{Gen}_{\mathsf{MAC}}(\mathbb{G}_2, q, P_2)$:

$\mathbf{B} \xleftarrow{\$} \mathcal{U}_{3k,k}$
for $i \in \{1,\dots,L\}, j \in \{1,\dots,i\alpha\}, b \in \{0,1\}$ **do** $\mathbf{x}_{i,j,b} \xleftarrow{\$} \mathbb{Z}_q^{3k}$
$x_0' \xleftarrow{\$} \mathbb{Z}_q$
return $\mathsf{sk}_{\mathsf{MAC}} := \left(\mathbf{B}, (\mathbf{x}_{i,j,b})_{1 \leq i \leq L, 1 \leq j \leq i\alpha, b \in \{0,1\}}, x_0'\right)$

$\mathsf{Tag}(\mathsf{sk}_{\mathsf{MAC}}, \mathsf{m} \in \mathcal{S}^p)$:

Parse $\mathsf{sk}_{\mathsf{MAC}} =: \left(\mathbf{B}, (\mathbf{x}_{i,j,b})_{1 \leq i \leq L, 1 \leq j \leq i\alpha, b \in \{0,1\}}, x_0'\right)$
for $i \in \{1,\dots,p\}$ **do** $\mathbf{s}_i \xleftarrow{\$} \mathbb{Z}_q^k$; $\mathbf{t}_i := \mathbf{B}\mathbf{s}_i$
$u := \sum_{i=1}^p \left(\sum_{j=1}^{i\alpha} \mathbf{x}_{i,j,[\mathsf{m}]_j}^\top\right) \mathbf{t}_i + x_0'$
return $\left(([\mathbf{t}_i]_2)_{1 \leq i \leq p}, [u]_2\right)$

$\mathsf{Ver}_{\mathsf{MAC}}(\mathsf{sk}_{\mathsf{MAC}}, \mathsf{m} \in \mathcal{S}^p, \tau)$:

Parse $\mathsf{sk}_{\mathsf{MAC}} =: \left(\mathbf{B}, (\mathbf{x}_{i,j,b})_{1 \leq i \leq L, 1 \leq j \leq i\alpha, b \in \{0,1\}}, x_0'\right)$
Parse $\mathsf{m} =: (\mathsf{m}_1, \dots, \mathsf{m}_p)$
Parse $\tau =: \left(([\mathbf{t}_i]_2)_{1 \leq i \leq p}, [u]_2\right)$
return $u \stackrel{?}{=} \sum_{i=1}^p \left(\sum_{j=1}^{i\alpha} \mathbf{x}_{i,j,[\mathsf{m}]_j}^\top\right) \mathbf{t}_i + x_0'$

Fig. 7. Our second affine MAC with levels based on [11]

Theorem 2 (Security of $\mathsf{MAC}_2[\mathcal{U}_{3k,k}]$). $\mathsf{MAC}_2[\mathcal{U}_{3k,k}]$ *is tightly* $\mathsf{HPR}_0\text{-}\mathsf{CMA}$ *secure in* $\mathbb{G}_2$ *under the* $\mathcal{U}_k\text{-}\mathsf{MDDH}$ *assumption for* $\mathbb{G}_2$. *Precisely, for all adversaries* $\mathcal{A}$ *there exists an adversary* $\mathcal{B}$ *with*

$$\mathsf{Adv}^{\mathsf{hpr}_0\text{-}\mathsf{cma}}_{\mathsf{MAC}_2[\mathcal{U}_{3k,k}],\mathbb{G}_2}(\mathcal{A}) \leq (2 + 8\alpha L)\left(\mathsf{Adv}^{\mathsf{mddh}}_{\mathcal{U}_k,\mathsf{GGen},\mathbb{G}_2}(\mathcal{B}) + \frac{1}{q-1}\right) + \frac{Q}{q^{2k}}$$

and $T(\mathcal{B}) \approx T(\mathcal{A}) + Q \cdot \mathsf{poly}(\lambda)$.

The proof uses a hybrid argument with the hybrids G_0 (the $\mathsf{HPR}_0\text{-}\mathsf{CMA}_{\mathsf{real}}$ game), G_1, G_2, $\mathsf{G}_{3,\hat{\jmath}}$ for $\hat{\jmath} \in \{1,\dots,L\alpha\}$, $\mathsf{G}_{3,\hat{\jmath},1}$–$\mathsf{G}_{3,\hat{\jmath},3}$ for $\hat{\jmath} \in \{1,\dots,L\alpha-1\}$, and finally G_4. The hybrids are given in Figs. 8 and 9. A summary can be found in Table 3.

The arguments to switch between the hybrids are similar to the first construction. A detailed proof can be found in the full version.

Table 3. Summary of the hybrids of Figs. 8 and 9. EVAL queries draw $\mathbf{t}$ from the set described by the second column and add the randomness $\sum_{i=1}^{p} r_u(\mathbf{m}, i)\,\mathbf{t}_i$ to u or choose u uniform random. The CHAL query adds the term $r_{\mathbf{h}_0}(\mathbf{m}^\star, i)\,h$ to each $\mathbf{h}_{0,i}$. Throughout this table $g(\hat{\jmath}, i) := \max\{\hat{\jmath}, i\alpha\}$. The background color indicates repeated transitions.

Hybrid	$\mathbf{t}_i$ uniform in	$r_u(\mathbf{m}, i)$	$r_{\mathbf{h}_0}(\mathbf{m}, i)$	Transition
G_0	$\mathsf{Span}(\mathbf{B})$		0	Original game
G_1	$\mathsf{Span}(\mathbf{B})$		0	Identical
G_2	$\mathbb{Z}_q^{3k}$		0	$\mathcal{U}_k\text{-}\mathsf{MDDH}$
$\mathsf{G}_{3,\hat{\jmath}}$	$\mathbb{Z}_q^{3k}$		$\mathsf{RF}_{i,\hat{\jmath}}\big(\llbracket m \rrbracket_{\mid g(\hat{\jmath},i)}\big)\big(\mathbf{B}^\perp\big)^\top$	Identical
$\mathsf{G}_{3,\hat{\jmath},1}$			$\mathsf{RF}_{i,\hat{\jmath}}\big(\llbracket m \rrbracket_{\mid g(\hat{\jmath},i)}\big)\big(\mathbf{B}^\perp\big)^\top$	$2 \times \mathcal{U}_k\text{-}\mathsf{MDDH}$
$\mathsf{G}_{3,\hat{\jmath},2}$	if $\llbracket m \rrbracket_{\hat{\jmath}+1} = 0$ then $\lfloor\mathsf{Span}(\mathbf{B}\mid\mathbf{B}_0)$ else $\lfloor\mathsf{Span}(\mathbf{B}\mid\mathbf{B}_1)$		$\mathsf{RF}^{(0)}_{i,\hat{\jmath}+1}\big(\llbracket m \rrbracket_{\mid g(\hat{\jmath}+1,i)}\big)(\mathbf{B}_0^*)^\top$ $+ \mathsf{RF}^{(1)}_{i,\hat{\jmath}}\big(\llbracket m \rrbracket_{\mid g(\hat{\jmath},i)}\big)(\mathbf{B}_1^*)^\top$	Identical
$\mathsf{G}_{3,\hat{\jmath},3}$			$\mathsf{RF}^{(0)}_{i,\hat{\jmath}+1}\big(\llbracket m \rrbracket_{\mid g(\hat{\jmath}+1,i)}\big)(\mathbf{B}_0^*)^\top$ $+ \mathsf{RF}^{(1)}_{i,\hat{\jmath}+1}\big(\llbracket m \rrbracket_{\mid g(\hat{\jmath}+1,i)}\big)(\mathbf{B}_1^*)^\top$	Identical
G_4	$\mathbb{Z}_q^{3k}$	unif. random	$\mathsf{RF}_{i,i\alpha}\big(m_{\mid i}\big)\big(\mathbf{B}^\perp\big)^\top$	Statistically close

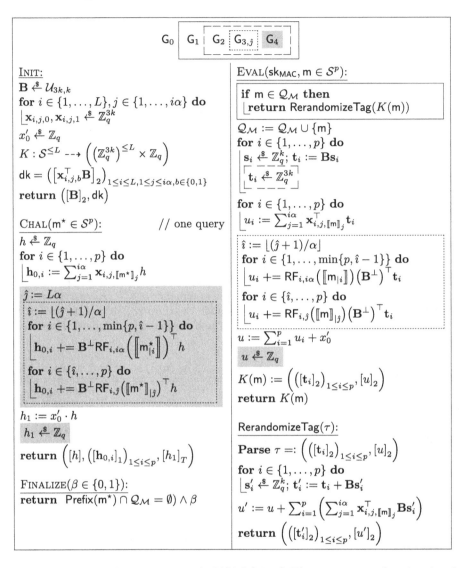

Fig. 8. Hybrids for the security proof of $\mathsf{MAC}_2[\mathcal{U}_{3k,k}]$. The notion $a \mathrel{+}= b$ is shorthand for $a := a + b$.

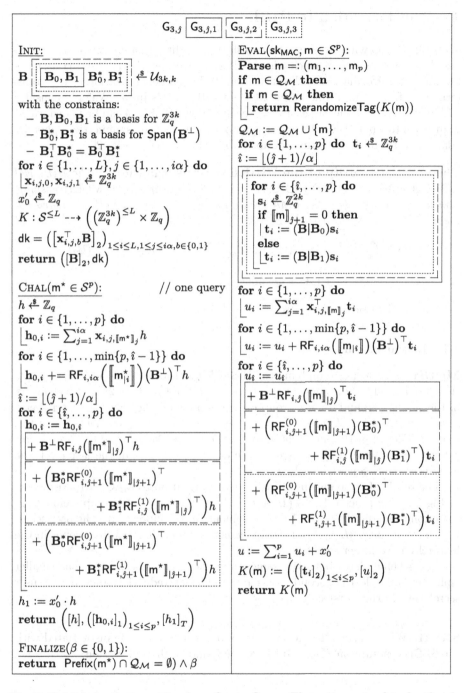

Fig. 9. Hybrids for the transition from $\mathsf{G}_{3,\hat{\jmath}}$ to $\mathsf{G}_{3,\hat{\jmath}+1}$. The notion $a\mathrel{+}=b$ is shorthand for $a:=a+b$.

4   Transformation to HIBE

Any affine MAC with levels can be transformed tightly to a hierarchical identity-based key encapsulation mechanism (HIBKEM) under the $\mathcal{D}_k$-MDDH assumption. The transformation is shown in Fig. 10. It is a generalization of the transformation from delegatable, affine MACs to HIBKEMs in [3]. We only consider HIBKEM here and one can easily prove that every HIBKEM can be transformed (tightly) into an HIBE scheme with a (one-time secure) symmetric cipher by adapting a similar transformation for public-key encryption in [20].

Theorem 3 (Security of the HIBKEM transformation). *The HIBKEM* HIBKEM [MAC, $\mathcal{D}_k$] *is* IND-HID-CPA *secure in* $\mathcal{G}$ *under the* $\mathcal{D}_k$-MDDH *assumption for* $\mathbb{G}_1$ *if* MAC *is* HPR$_0$-CMA *secure in* $\mathbb{G}_2$. *Precisely, for all adversaries* $\mathcal{A}$ *there exists adversaries* $\mathcal{B}_1$ *and* $\mathcal{B}_2$ *with*

$$\mathsf{Adv}^{\text{ind-hid-cpa}}_{\text{HIBKEM}[\text{MAC},\mathcal{D}_k],\mathcal{G}}(\mathcal{A}) \leq \mathsf{Adv}^{\text{hpr}_0\text{-cma}}_{\text{MAC},\mathbb{G}_2}(\mathcal{B}_1) + \mathsf{Adv}^{\text{mddh}}_{\mathcal{D}_k,\text{GGen},\mathbb{G}_1}(\mathcal{B}_2)$$

and $T(\mathcal{B}_1) + T(\mathcal{B}_2) \approx T(\mathcal{A}) + Q \cdot \mathsf{poly}(\lambda)$.

The detailed proof of Theorem 3 can be found in full version.

4.1   Instantiations

MDDH. The result of applying the HIBKEM transformation to $\mathsf{MAC}_1[\mathcal{U}_{3k,k}]$ is shown in Fig. 11. The scheme has $\alpha\left(L^2 + L\right)\left(4k^2 + k\right) + 3k^2 + 2k$ group elements in the public key and $4k + 1$ group elements in the ciphertext. The user secret keys have at most $\alpha\left(L^2/2 + L/2 - 1\right)(k+1) + 4k + 1$ group elements. Identities that are deeper in the hierarchy have smaller secret keys, since the user secret key size is dominated by the size of the delegation keys. On the last level, the user secret keys consist of only $4k + 1$ keys.

The result of applying the HIBKEM transformation to $\mathsf{MAC}_2[\mathcal{U}_{3k,k}]$ is shown in Fig. 12. The scheme has $\alpha\left(L^2 + L\right)\left(4k^2 + k\right) + 3k^2 + 2k$ group elements in the public key and $3Lk + k + 1$ group elements in the ciphertext. The user secret keys have at most $3Lk + k + 1$ group elements. Identities that are deeper in the hierarchy have larger secret keys.

The schemes have both the same public key. The first scheme has smaller ciphertexts, while the second has a more efficient reduction and smaller user secret keys in the worst case.

SXDH. With a type III pairing, both of our schemes can be instantiated with the SXDH assumption. The results can be found in the full version.

$\underline{\text{Gen}(\mathbb{G}_1, \mathbb{G}_2, \mathbb{G}_T, q, P_1, P_2, e):}$

$\text{sk}_{\text{MAC}} \xleftarrow{\$} \text{Gen}_{\text{MAC}}(\mathbb{G}_2, q, P_2)$

Parse $\text{sk}_{\text{MAC}} =: (\mathbf{B}, \widetilde{\mathbf{x}}, x_0')$

Parse $\widetilde{\mathbf{x}} =: (\mathbf{x}_{l,i,j})_{1 \le l \le \ell(L), 1 \le i \le L, 1 \le j \le \ell'(l,i)}$

$\mathbf{A} \xleftarrow{\$} \mathcal{D}_k$

for $l \in \{1, \ldots, \ell(L)\}, i \in \{1, \ldots, L\}, j \in \{1, \ldots, \ell'(l,i)\}$ do

$\quad \mathbf{Y}_{l,i,j} \xleftarrow{\$} \mathbb{Z}_q^{k \times n}; \mathbf{Z}_{l,i,j} := (\mathbf{Y}_{l,i,j}^\top \mid \mathbf{x}_{l,i,j}) \cdot \mathbf{A}$

$\quad \mathbf{d}_{l,i,j} := \mathbf{x}_{l,i,j}^\top \cdot \mathbf{B}; \mathbf{E}_{l,i,j} := \mathbf{Y}_{l,i,j} \cdot \mathbf{B}$

$\mathbf{y}_0' \xleftarrow{\$} \mathbb{Z}_q^k; \mathbf{z}_0' := (\mathbf{y}_0'^\top \mid x_0') \cdot \mathbf{A}$

$\widetilde{\mathbf{Z}} := ([\mathbf{Z}_{l,i,j}]_1)_{1 \le l \le \ell(L), 1 \le i \le L, 1 \le j \le \ell'(l,i)}$

$\text{pk} := (\mathcal{G}, [\mathbf{A}]_1, \widetilde{\mathbf{Z}}, [\mathbf{z}_0']_1)$

$\widetilde{\text{dk}} := ([\mathbf{d}_{l,i,j}]_2, [\mathbf{E}_{l,i,j}]_2)_{1 \le l \le \ell(L), 1 \le i \le L, 1 \le j \le \ell'(l,i)}$

$\text{dk} := ([\mathbf{B}]_2, \widetilde{\text{dk}})$

$\text{sk} := (\text{sk}_{\text{MAC}}, (\mathbf{Y}_{l,i,j})_{1 \le l \le \ell(p), 1 \le i \le L, 1 \le j \le \ell'(l,i)}, \mathbf{y}_0')$

return (pk, dk, sk)

$\underline{\text{Del}(\text{dk}, \text{usk}, \text{udk}, \text{id} \in \mathcal{S}^p, \text{id}_{p+1} \in \mathcal{S}):}$

Parse usk $=: (([\mathbf{t}_l]_2)_{1 \le l \le \ell(p)}, [u]_2, [\mathbf{v}]_2)$

for $l \in \{\ell(p)+1, \ldots, \ell(p+1)\}$ do $\mathbf{t}_l := \mathbf{0}$

for $l \in \{1, \ldots, \ell(p+1)\}$ do

$\quad \mathbf{s}_l' \xleftarrow{\$} \mathbb{Z}_q^{n'}; \mathbf{t}_l' := \mathbf{t}_l + \mathbf{B}\mathbf{s}_l'$

$u' := u + \sum_{l=1}^{\ell(p+1)} \left(\sum_{i=1}^{p+1} \sum_{j=1}^{\ell'(l,i)} f_{l,i,j}(\text{id}_i)\mathbf{d}_{l,i,j} \right) \mathbf{s}_l'$

$\mathbf{v}' := \mathbf{v} + \sum_{l=1}^{\ell(p+1)} \left(\sum_{i=1}^{p+1} \sum_{j=1}^{\ell'(l,i)} f_{l,i,j}(\text{id}_i)\mathbf{E}_{l,i,j} \right) \mathbf{s}_l'$

for $l \in \{1, \ldots, \ell(p)\}, i \in \{p+2, \ldots, L\}, j \in \{1, \ldots, \ell'(l,i)\}$ do

$\quad d_{l,i,j}' := d_{l,i,j} + \mathbf{d}_{l,i,j}\mathbf{s}_l$

$\quad e_{l,i,j}' := e_{l,i,j} + \mathbf{E}_{l,i,j}\mathbf{s}_l$

for $l \in \{\ell(p), \ldots, \ell(p+1)\}, i \in \{p+2, \ldots, L\}, j \in \{1, \ldots, \ell'(l,i)\}$ do

$\quad d_{l,i,j}' := \mathbf{d}_{l,i,j}\mathbf{s}_l; e_{l,i,j}' := \mathbf{E}_{l,i,j}\mathbf{s}_l$

$\text{usk}' := (([\mathbf{t}_l']_2)_{1 \le l \le \ell(p+1)}, [u']_2, [\mathbf{v}']_2)$

$\text{udk}' := ([d_{l,i,j}']_2, [e_{l,i,j}']_2)_{1 \le l \le \ell(p+1), 1 \le i \le L, 1 \le j \le \ell'(l,i)}$

return (usk', udk')

$\underline{\text{Ext}(\text{sk}, \text{id} \in \mathcal{S}^p):}$

$(([\mathbf{t}_l]_2)_{1 \le l \le \ell(p)}, [u]_2) \xleftarrow{\$} \text{Tag}(\text{sk}_{\text{MAC}}, \text{id})$

$\mathbf{v} := \sum_{l=1}^{\ell(p)} \left(\sum_{i=1}^{p} \sum_{j=1}^{\ell'(l,i)} f_{l,i,j}(\mathsf{m}_{|i})\mathbf{Y}_{l,i,j} \right) \mathbf{t}_l + \mathbf{y}_0'$

for $l \in \{1, \ldots, \ell(p)\}, i \in \{p+1, \ldots, L\}, j \in \{1, \ldots, \ell'(l,i)\}$ do

$\quad d_{l,i,j} := \mathbf{x}_{l,i,j}^\top \mathbf{t}_l$

$\quad e_{l,i,j} := \mathbf{Y}_{l,i,j}\mathbf{t}_l$

$\text{usk} := (([\mathbf{t}_l]_2)_{1 \le l \le \ell(p)}, [u]_2, [\mathbf{v}]_2)$

$\text{udk} := ([d_{l,i,j}]_2, [e_{l,i,j}]_2)_{1 \le l \le \ell(p), 1 \le i \le L, 1 \le j \le \ell'(l,i)}$

return (usk, udk)

$\underline{\text{Enc}(\text{pk}, \text{id} \in \mathcal{S}^p):}$

$\mathbf{r} \xleftarrow{\$} \mathbb{Z}_q^k; \mathbf{c}_0 := \mathbf{A}\mathbf{r}$

for $l \in \{1, \ldots, \ell(p)\}$ do

$\quad \mathbf{c}_{1,l} := \sum_{i=1}^{p} \sum_{j=1}^{\ell'(l,i)} f_{l,i,j}(\mathsf{m}_{|i})\mathbf{Z}_{l,i,j}\mathbf{r}$

$\mathsf{C} := ([\mathbf{c}_0]_1, ([\mathbf{c}_{1,l}]_1)_{1 \le l \le \ell(p)})$

$\mathsf{K} := \mathbf{z}_0' \cdot \mathbf{r}$

return $([\mathsf{K}]_T, \mathsf{C})$

$\underline{\text{Dec}(\text{usk}[\text{id}], \text{id} \in \mathcal{S}^p, \mathsf{C}):}$

usk[id] $=: (([\mathbf{t}_l]_2)_{1 \le l \le \ell(p)}, [u]_2, [\mathbf{v}]_2)$

Parse $\mathsf{C} =: ([\mathbf{c}_0]_1, ([\mathbf{c}_{1,l}]_1)_{1 \le l \le \ell(p)})$

$[\mathsf{K}]_T := e\left([\mathbf{c}_0^\top]_1, \begin{bmatrix} \mathbf{v} \\ u \end{bmatrix}_2 \right)$

$\qquad - \sum_{l=1}^{\ell(p)} e([\mathbf{c}_{1,l}^\top]_1, [\mathbf{t}_l]_2)$

return $[\mathsf{K}]_T$

Fig. 10. The transformation of an affine MAC with levels to a HIBKEM.

$\mathsf{Gen}(1^\lambda)$:

$\mathbf{B} \overset{\$}{\leftarrow} \mathcal{U}_{3k,k}$; $\mathbf{A} \overset{\$}{\leftarrow} \mathcal{D}_k$

for $i \in \{1,\dots,L\}, j \in \{1,\dots,i\alpha\}, b \in \{0,1\}$ **do**

$\quad \mathbf{x}_{i,j,b} \overset{\$}{\leftarrow} \mathbb{Z}_q^{3k}$ $\mathbf{Y}_{i,j,b} \overset{\$}{\leftarrow} \mathbb{Z}_q^{k\times n}$

$\quad \mathbf{Z}_{i,j,b} := \left(\mathbf{Y}_{i,j,b}^\top \mid \mathbf{x}_{i,j,b}\right) \cdot \mathbf{A}$

$\quad \mathbf{d}_{i,j,b} := \mathbf{x}_{i,j,b}^\top \mathbf{B}; \mathbf{E}_{i,j,b} := \mathbf{Y}_{i,j,b}\mathbf{B}$

$x_0' \overset{\$}{\leftarrow} \mathbb{Z}_q$; $\mathbf{y}_0' \overset{\$}{\leftarrow} \mathbb{Z}_q^k$; $\mathbf{z}_0' := \left(\mathbf{y}_0'^\top \mid x_0'\right) \cdot \mathbf{A}$

$\widetilde{\mathbf{Z}} := \left([\mathbf{Z}_{i,j,b}]_1\right)_{1\le i\le L, b\in\{0,1\}, 1\le j\le i\alpha}$

$\mathsf{pk} := \left(\mathcal{G}, [\mathbf{A}]_1, \widetilde{\mathbf{Z}}, [\mathbf{z}_0']_1\right)$

$\widetilde{\mathsf{dk}} := \left([\mathbf{d}_{i,j,b}]_2, [\mathbf{E}_{i,j,b}]_2\right)_{\substack{1\le i\le L, b\in\{0,1\}, \\ 1\le j\le i\alpha}}$

$\mathsf{dk} := \left([\mathbf{B}]_2, \widetilde{\mathsf{dk}}\right)$

$\widetilde{\mathbf{Y}} := (\mathbf{Y}_{i,j,b})_{1\le i\le L, b\in\{0,1\}, 1\le j\le i\alpha}$

$\mathsf{sk} := \left(\mathsf{sk}_{\mathsf{MAC}}, \widetilde{\mathbf{Y}}, \mathbf{y}_0'\right)$

return $(\mathsf{pk}, \mathsf{dk}, \mathsf{sk})$

$\mathsf{Ext}(\mathsf{sk}, \mathsf{id} \in \mathcal{S}^p)$:

$\mathbf{s} \overset{\$}{\leftarrow} \mathbb{Z}_q^k$; $\mathbf{t} := \mathbf{B}\mathbf{s}$

$u := \left(\sum_{i=1}^{p}\sum_{j=1}^{i\alpha} \mathbf{x}_{i,j,\llbracket\mathsf{id}\rrbracket_j}^\top\right)\mathbf{t} + x_0'$

$\mathbf{v} := \left(\sum_{i=1}^{p}\sum_{j=1}^{i\alpha} \mathbf{Y}_{i,j,\llbracket\mathsf{id}\rrbracket_j}\right)\mathbf{t} + \mathbf{y}_0'$

for $i \in \{p+1,\dots,L\}, j \in \{1,\dots,i\alpha\}, b\in\{0,1\}$ **do**

$\quad d_{i,j,b} := \mathbf{x}_{i,j,b}^\top\mathbf{t}; e_{i,j,b} := \mathbf{Y}_{i,j,b}^\top\mathbf{t}$

$\mathsf{usk} := \left([\mathbf{t}]_2, [u]_2, [\mathbf{v}]_2\right)$

$\mathsf{udk} := \left([d_{i,j,b}]_2, [e_{i,j,b}]_2\right)_{\substack{p+1\le i\le L, b\in\{0,1\}, \\ 1\le j\le i\alpha}}$

return $(\mathsf{usk}, \mathsf{udk})$

$\mathsf{Del}(\mathsf{dk}, \mathsf{usk}, \mathsf{udk}, \mathsf{id} \in \mathcal{S}^p, \mathsf{id}_{p+1} \in \mathcal{S})$:

Parse $\mathsf{usk} =: \left([\mathbf{t}]_2, [u]_2, [\mathbf{v}]_2\right)$

$\mathbf{s}' \overset{\$}{\leftarrow} \mathbb{Z}_q^{n'}$; $\mathbf{t}' := \mathbf{t} + \mathbf{B}\mathbf{s}'$

$u' := u + \left(\sum_{i=1}^{p+1}\sum_{j=1}^{i\alpha} \mathbf{d}_{i,j,\llbracket\mathsf{id}\rrbracket_j}\right)\mathbf{s}'$

$\mathbf{v}' := \mathbf{v} + \left(\sum_{i=1}^{p+1}\sum_{j=1}^{\ell'(l,i)} \mathbf{E}_{i,j,\llbracket\mathsf{id}\rrbracket_j}\right)\mathbf{s}'$

for $i \in \{p+1,\dots,L\}, j \in \{1,\dots,i\alpha\}, b\in\{0,1\}$ **do**

$\quad d_{i,j,b}' := d_{i,j,b} + \mathbf{d}_{i,j,b}\mathbf{s}'$

$\quad e_{i,j,b}' := e_{i,j,b} + \mathbf{E}_{i,j,b}\mathbf{s}'$

$\mathsf{usk}' := \left([\mathbf{t}']_2, [u']_2, [\mathbf{v}']_2\right)$

$\mathsf{udk}' := \left([d_{i,j,b}']_2, [e_{i,j,b}']_2\right)_{\substack{p+2\le i\le L, \\ 1\le j\le i\alpha, b\in\{0,1\}}}$

return $(\mathsf{usk}', \mathsf{udk}')$

$\mathsf{Enc}(\mathsf{pk}, \mathsf{id} \in \mathcal{S}^p)$:

$\mathbf{r} \overset{\$}{\leftarrow} \mathbb{Z}_q^k$; $\mathbf{c}_0 := \mathbf{A}\mathbf{r}$

$\mathbf{c}_1 := \sum_{i=1}^{p}\sum_{j=1}^{\ell'(l,i)} \mathbf{Z}_{i,j,\llbracket\mathsf{id}\rrbracket_j}^\top \mathbf{r}$

$C := \left([\mathbf{c}_0]_1, [\mathbf{c}_1]_1\right)$

$K := \mathbf{z}_0' \cdot \mathbf{r}$

return $\left([K]_T, C\right)$

$\mathsf{Dec}(\mathsf{usk}, \mathsf{id} \in \mathcal{S}^p, C)$:

Parse $\mathsf{usk} =: \left([\mathbf{t}]_2, [u]_2, [\mathbf{v}]_2\right)$

Parse $C =: \left([\mathbf{c}_0]_1, [\mathbf{c}_1]_1\right)$

$[K]_T := [\mathbf{c}_0^\top]_1 \circ \begin{bmatrix}\mathbf{v}\\u\end{bmatrix}_2 - [\mathbf{c}_1^\top]_1 \circ [\mathbf{t}]_2$

return $[K]_T$

Fig. 11. The resulting scheme HIBKEM $[\mathsf{MAC}_1[\mathcal{U}_{3k,k}], \mathcal{D}_k]$.

Gen(1^λ):

$\mathbf{B} \overset{\$}{\leftarrow} \mathcal{U}_{3k,k}$; $\mathbf{A} \overset{\$}{\leftarrow} \mathcal{D}_k$

for $i \in \{1,\dots,L\}, j \in \{1,\dots,i\alpha\}, b \in \{0,1\}$ do

$\quad \mathbf{x}_{i,j,b} \overset{\$}{\leftarrow} \mathbb{Z}_q^{3k}$ $\mathbf{Y}_{i,j,b} \overset{\$}{\leftarrow} \mathbb{Z}_q^{k\times n}$

$\quad \mathbf{Z}_{i,j,b} := \left(\mathbf{Y}_{i,j,b}^\top \mid \mathbf{x}_{i,j,b}\right) \cdot \mathbf{A}$

$\quad \mathbf{d}_{i,j,b} := \mathbf{x}_{i,j,b}^\top \mathbf{B}$; $\mathbf{E}_{i,j,b} := \mathbf{Y}_{i,j,b}\mathbf{B}$

$x_0' \overset{\$}{\leftarrow} \mathbb{Z}_q$; $\mathbf{y}_0' \overset{\$}{\leftarrow} \mathbb{Z}_q^k$; $\mathbf{z}_0' := \left(\mathbf{y}_0'^\top \mid x_0'\right) \cdot \mathbf{A}$

$\widetilde{\mathbf{Z}} := \left([\mathbf{Z}_{i,j,b}]_1\right)_{1\le i \le L, b \in \{0,1\}, 1 \le j \le i\alpha}$

$\mathsf{pk} := \left(\mathcal{G}, [\mathbf{A}]_1, \widetilde{\mathbf{Z}}, [\mathbf{z}_0']_1\right)$

$\widetilde{\mathsf{dk}} := \left([\mathbf{d}_{i,j,b}]_2, [\mathbf{E}_{i,j,b}]_2\right)_{\substack{1\le i \le L, b \in \{0,1\}, \\ 1 \le j \le i\alpha}}$

$\mathsf{dk} := \left([\mathbf{B}]_2, \widetilde{\mathsf{dk}}\right)$

$\widetilde{\mathbf{Y}} := \left(\mathbf{Y}_{i,j,b}\right)_{1\le i \le L, b \in \{0,1\}, 1 \le j \le i\alpha}$

$\mathsf{sk} := \left(\mathsf{sk}_{\mathsf{MAC}}, \widetilde{\mathbf{Y}}, \mathbf{y}_0'\right)$

return $(\mathsf{pk}, \mathsf{dk}, \mathsf{sk})$

Ext$(\mathsf{sk}, \mathsf{id} \in \mathcal{S}^p)$:

for $i \in \{1,\dots,p\}$ do $\mathbf{s}_i \overset{\$}{\leftarrow} \mathbb{Z}_q^k$; $\mathbf{t}_i := \mathbf{B}\mathbf{s}_i$

$u := \sum_{i=1}^p \left(\sum_{j=1}^{i\alpha} \mathbf{x}_{i,j,[\mathsf{id}]_j}^\top\right)\mathbf{t}_i + x_0'$

$\mathbf{v} := \sum_{i=1}^p \left(\sum_{j=1}^{i\alpha} \mathbf{Y}_{i,j,[\mathsf{id}]_j}\right)\mathbf{t}_i + \mathbf{y}_0'$

return $\left(([\mathbf{t}_i]_2)_{1\le i \le p}, [u]_2, [\mathbf{v}]_2\right)$

Del$(\mathsf{dk}, \mathsf{usk}, \mathsf{udk}, \mathsf{id} \in \mathcal{S}^p, \mathsf{id}_{p+1} \in \mathcal{S})$:

Parse $\mathsf{usk} =: \left(([\mathbf{t}_i]_2)_{1\le i \le p}, [u]_2, [\mathbf{v}]_2\right)$

for $i \in \{1,\dots,p\}$ do

$\quad \mathbf{s}_i' \overset{\$}{\leftarrow} \mathbb{Z}_q^k$; $\mathbf{t}_i' := \mathbf{t}_i + \mathbf{B}\mathbf{s}_i'$

$u' := u + \sum_{i=1}^{p+1}\left(\sum_{j=1}^{i\alpha} \mathbf{d}_{i,j,[\mathsf{id}]_j}\right)\mathbf{s}_i'$

$\mathbf{v}' := \mathbf{v} + \sum_{i=1}^{p+1}\left(\sum_{j=1}^{\ell'(l,i)} \mathbf{E}_{i,j,[\mathsf{id}]_j}\right)\mathbf{s}_i'$

return $\left(([\mathbf{t}']_2)_{1\le i \le p}, [u']_2, [\mathbf{v}']_2\right)$

Enc$(\mathsf{pk}, \mathsf{id} \in \mathcal{S}^p)$:

$\mathbf{r} \overset{\$}{\leftarrow} \mathbb{Z}_q^k$; $\mathbf{c}_0 := \mathbf{A}\mathbf{r}$

for $i \in \{1,\dots,p\}$ do

$\quad \mathbf{c}_{1,i} := \sum_{j=1}^{\ell'(l,i)} \mathbf{Z}_{i,j,[\mathsf{id}]_j}^\top \mathbf{r}$

$C := \left([\mathbf{c}_0]_1, ([\mathbf{c}_1]_1)_{1\le i \le p}\right)$

$K := \mathbf{z}_0' \cdot \mathbf{r}$

return $\left([K]_T, C\right)$

Dec$(\mathsf{usk}, \mathsf{id} \in \mathcal{S}^p, C)$:

Parse $\mathsf{usk} =: \left(([\mathbf{t}_i]_2)_{1\le i \le p}, [u]_2, [\mathbf{v}]_2\right)$

Parse $C =: \left([\mathbf{c}_0]_1, ([\mathbf{c}_1]_1)_{1\le i \le p}\right)$

$[K]_T := [\mathbf{c}_0^\top]_1 \circ \begin{bmatrix}\mathbf{v}\\u\end{bmatrix}_2 - \sum_{i=1}^p \left([\mathbf{c}_{1,i}^\top]_1 \circ [\mathbf{t}]_2\right)$

return $[K]_T$

Fig. 12. The resulting scheme HIBKEM $[\mathsf{MAC}_2[\mathcal{U}_{3k,k}], \mathcal{D}_k]$.

References

1. Abe, M., Hofheinz, D., Nishimaki, R., Ohkubo, M., Pan, J.: Compact structure-preserving signatures with almost tight security. In: Katz, J., Shacham, H. (eds.) CRYPTO 2017. LNCS, vol. 10402, pp. 548–580. Springer, Cham (2017). https://doi.org/10.1007/978-3-319-63715-0_19

2. Bader, C., Hofheinz, D., Jager, T., Kiltz, E., Li, Y.: Tightly-secure authenticated key exchange. In: Dodis, Y., Nielsen, J.B. (eds.) TCC 2015. LNCS, vol. 9014, pp. 629–658. Springer, Heidelberg (2015). https://doi.org/10.1007/978-3-662-46494-6_26

3. Blazy, O., Kiltz, E., Pan, J.: (Hierarchical) identity-based encryption from affine message authentication. In: Garay, J.A., Gennaro, R. (eds.) CRYPTO 2014. LNCS, vol. 8616, pp. 408–425. Springer, Heidelberg (2014). https://doi.org/10.1007/978-3-662-44371-2_23

4. Boneh, D., Franklin, M.: Identity-based encryption from the weil pairing. In: Kilian, J. (ed.) CRYPTO 2001. LNCS, vol. 2139, pp. 213–229. Springer, Heidelberg (2001). https://doi.org/10.1007/3-540-44647-8_13

5. Canetti, R., Halevi, S., Katz, J.: Chosen-ciphertext security from identity-based encryption. In: Cachin, C., Camenisch, J.L. (eds.) EUROCRYPT 2004. LNCS, vol. 3027, pp. 207–222. Springer, Heidelberg (2004). https://doi.org/10.1007/978-3-540-24676-3_13

6. Chen, J., Gay, R., Wee, H.: Improved dual system ABE in prime-order groups via predicate encodings. In: Oswald, E., Fischlin, M. (eds.) EUROCRYPT 2015. LNCS, vol. 9057, pp. 595–624. Springer, Heidelberg (2015). https://doi.org/10.1007/978-3-662-46803-6_20

7. Chen, J., Lim, H.W., Ling, S., Wang, H., Wee, H.: Shorter IBE and signatures via asymmetric pairings. In: Abdalla, M., Lange, T. (eds.) Pairing 2012. LNCS, vol. 7708, pp. 122–140. Springer, Heidelberg (2013). https://doi.org/10.1007/978-3-642-36334-4_8

8. Chen, J., Wee, H.: Fully, (Almost) tightly secure IBE and dual system groups. In: Canetti, R., Garay, J.A. (eds.) CRYPTO 2013. LNCS, vol. 8043, pp. 435–460. Springer, Heidelberg (2013). https://doi.org/10.1007/978-3-642-40084-1_25

9. Cocks, C.: An identity based encryption scheme based on quadratic residues. In: Honary, B. (ed.) Cryptography and Coding 2001. LNCS, vol. 2260, pp. 360–363. Springer, Heidelberg (2001). https://doi.org/10.1007/3-540-45325-3_32

10. Escala, A., Herold, G., Kiltz, E., Ràfols, C., Villar, J.: An algebraic framework for Diffie-Hellman assumptions. In: Canetti, R., Garay, J.A. (eds.) CRYPTO 2013. LNCS, vol. 8043, pp. 129–147. Springer, Heidelberg (2013). https://doi.org/10.1007/978-3-642-40084-1_8

11. Gay, R., Hofheinz, D., Kiltz, E., Wee, H.: Tightly CCA-secure encryption without pairings. In: Fischlin, M., Coron, J.-S. (eds.) EUROCRYPT 2016. LNCS, vol. 9665, pp. 1–27. Springer, Heidelberg (2016). https://doi.org/10.1007/978-3-662-49890-3_1

12. Gay, R., Hofheinz, D., Kohl, L., Pan, J.: More efficient (almost) tightly secure structure-preserving signatures. In: Nielsen, J.B., Rijmen, V. (eds.) EUROCRYPT 2018. LNCS, vol. 10821, pp. 230–258. Springer, Cham (2018). https://doi.org/10.1007/978-3-319-78375-8_8

13. Gentry, C.: Practical identity-based encryption without random oracles. In: Vaudenay, S. (ed.) EUROCRYPT 2006. LNCS, vol. 4004, pp. 445–464. Springer, Heidelberg (2006). https://doi.org/10.1007/11761679_27

14. Gentry, C., Silverberg, A.: Hierarchical ID-based cryptography. In: Zheng, Y. (ed.) ASIACRYPT 2002. LNCS, vol. 2501, pp. 548–566. Springer, Heidelberg (2002). https://doi.org/10.1007/3-540-36178-2_34

15. Gong, J., Cao, Z., Tang, S., Chen, J.: Extended dual system group and shorter unbounded hierarchical identity based encryption. Des. Codes Crypt. **80**(3), 525–559 (2016). https://doi.org/10.1007/s10623-015-0117-z

16. Gong, J., Dong, X., Chen, J., Cao, Z.: Efficient IBE with tight reduction to standard assumption in the multi-challenge setting. In: Cheon, J.H., Takagi, T. (eds.) ASIACRYPT 2016. LNCS, vol. 10032, pp. 624–654. Springer, Heidelberg (2016). https://doi.org/10.1007/978-3-662-53890-6_21

17. Hesse, J., Hofheinz, D., Kohl, L.: On tightly secure non-interactive key exchange. In: Shacham, H., Boldyreva, A. (eds.) CRYPTO 2018, Part II. LNCS, vol. 10992, pp. 65–94. Springer, Heidelberg (Aug (2018)

18. Hofheinz, D., Jager, T.: Tightly secure signatures and public-key encryption. In: Safavi-Naini, R., Canetti, R. (eds.) CRYPTO 2012. LNCS, vol. 7417, pp. 590–607. Springer, Heidelberg (2012). https://doi.org/10.1007/978-3-642-32009-5_35

19. Hofheinz, D., Jia, D., Pan, J.: Identity-based encryption tightly secure under chosen-ciphertext attacks. In: Peyrin, T., Galbraith, S. (eds.) ASIACRYPT 2018. LNCS, vol. 11273, pp. 190–220. Springer, Cham (2018). https://doi.org/10.1007/978-3-030-03329-3_7

20. Hofheinz, D., Kiltz, E.: Secure hybrid encryption from weakened key encapsulation. In: Menezes, A. (ed.) CRYPTO 2007. LNCS, vol. 4622, pp. 553–571. Springer, Heidelberg (2007). https://doi.org/10.1007/978-3-540-74143-5_31

21. Hofheinz, D., Koch, J., Striecks, C.: Identity-based encryption with (almost) tight security in the multi-instance, multi-ciphertext setting. In: Katz, J. (ed.) PKC 2015. LNCS, vol. 9020, pp. 799–822. Springer, Heidelberg (2015). https://doi.org/10.1007/978-3-662-46447-2_36

22. Horwitz, J., Lynn, B.: Toward hierarchical identity-based encryption. In: Knudsen, L.R. (ed.) EUROCRYPT 2002. LNCS, vol. 2332, pp. 466–481. Springer, Heidelberg (2002). https://doi.org/10.1007/3-540-46035-7_31

23. Jutla, C.S., Roy, A.: Shorter quasi-adaptive NIZK proofs for linear subspaces. In: Sako, K., Sarkar, P. (eds.) ASIACRYPT 2013. LNCS, vol. 8269, pp. 1–20. Springer, Heidelberg (2013). https://doi.org/10.1007/978-3-642-42033-7_1

24. Kiltz, E., Neven, G.: Identity-based signatures. In: Joye, M., Neven, G. (eds.) Identity-Based Cryptography. IOS Press, Amsterdam (2009)

25. Kiltz, E., Pan, J., Wee, H.: Structure-preserving signatures from standard assumptions, revisited. In: Gennaro, R., Robshaw, M. (eds.) CRYPTO 2015. LNCS, vol. 9216, pp. 275–295. Springer, Heidelberg (2015). https://doi.org/10.1007/978-3-662-48000-7_14

26. Kiltz, E., Wee, H.: Quasi-adaptive NIZK for linear subspaces revisited. In: Oswald, E., Fischlin, M. (eds.) EUROCRYPT 2015. LNCS, vol. 9057, pp. 101–128. Springer, Heidelberg (2015). https://doi.org/10.1007/978-3-662-46803-6_4

27. Lewko, A.: Tools for simulating features of composite order bilinear groups in the prime order setting. In: Pointcheval, D., Johansson, T. (eds.) EUROCRYPT 2012. LNCS, vol. 7237, pp. 318–335. Springer, Heidelberg (2012). https://doi.org/10.1007/978-3-642-29011-4_20

28. Lewko, A., Waters, B.: Why proving HIBE systems secure is difficult. In: Nguyen, P.Q., Oswald, E. (eds.) EUROCRYPT 2014. LNCS, vol. 8441, pp. 58–76. Springer, Heidelberg (2014). https://doi.org/10.1007/978-3-642-55220-5_4

29. Naor, M., Reingold, O.: On the construction of pseudo-random permutations: Luby-Rackoff revisited (extended abstract). In: 29th ACM STOC, pp. 189–199. ACM Press, May 1997

30. Sakai, R., Ohgishi, K., Kasahara, M.: Cryptosystems based on pairing. In: SCIS 2000, Okinawa, Japan, January 2000

31. Shamir, A.: Identity-based cryptosystems and signature schemes. In: Blakley, G.R., Chaum, D. (eds.) CRYPTO 1984. LNCS, vol. 196, pp. 47–53. Springer, Heidelberg (1985). https://doi.org/10.1007/3-540-39568-7_5

32. Waters, B.: Dual system encryption: realizing fully secure IBE and HIBE under simple assumptions. In: Halevi, S. (ed.) CRYPTO 2009. LNCS, vol. 5677, pp. 619–636. Springer, Heidelberg (2009). https://doi.org/10.1007/978-3-642-03356-8_36

33. Waters, B.: Efficient identity-based encryption without random oracles. In: Cramer, R. (ed.) EUROCRYPT 2005. LNCS, vol. 3494, pp. 114–127. Springer, Heidelberg (2005). https://doi.org/10.1007/11426639_7

34. Wee, H.: Dual system encryption via predicate encodings. In: Lindell, Y. (ed.) TCC 2014. LNCS, vol. 8349, pp. 616–637. Springer, Heidelberg (2014). https://doi.org/10.1007/978-3-642-54242-8_26

Leakage-Resilient Identity-Based Encryption in Bounded Retrieval Model with Nearly Optimal Leakage-Ratio

Ryo Nishimaki and Takashi Yamakawa$^{(\boxtimes)}$

NTT Secure Platform Laboratories, Tokyo, Japan
{ryo.nishimaki.zk,takashi.yamakawa.ga}@hco.ntt.co.jp

Abstract. We propose new constructions of leakage-resilient public-key encryption (PKE) and identity-based encryption (IBE) schemes in the bounded retrieval model (BRM). In the BRM, adversaries are allowed to obtain at most ℓ-bit leakage from a secret key and we can increase ℓ only by increasing the size of secret keys without losing efficiency in any other performance measure. We call $\ell/|\mathsf{sk}|$ leakage-ratio where $|\mathsf{sk}|$ denotes a bit-length of a secret key. Several PKE/IBE schemes in the BRM are known. However, none of these constructions achieve a constant leakage-ratio under a standard assumption in the standard model. Our PKE/IBE schemes are the first schemes in the BRM that achieve leakage-ratio $1 - \epsilon$ for any constant $\epsilon > 0$ under standard assumptions in the standard model.

As previous works, we use identity-based hash proof systems (IB-HPS) to construct IBE schemes in the BRM. It is known that a parameter for IB-HPS called the universality-ratio is translated into the leakage-ratio of the resulting IBE scheme in the BRM. We construct an IB-HPS with universality-ratio $1 - \epsilon$ for any constant $\epsilon > 0$ based on any inner-product predicate encryption (IPE) scheme with compact secret keys. Such IPE schemes exist under the d-linear, subgroup decision, learning with errors, or computational bilinear Diffie-Hellman assumptions. As a result, we obtain IBE schemes in the BRM with leakage-ratio $1 - \epsilon$ under any of these assumptions. Our PKE schemes are immediately obtained from our IBE schemes.

1 Introduction

1.1 Background

Modern cryptography have been placing much importance on provable security. In a traditional theory of provable security, we often assume that secret values (e.g., secret key, randomness etc.) are perfectly hidden from an adversary, and give a security proof in such models. On the other hand, developments of side channel attacks have discovered that an adversary may obtain partial information of these secret values, and some cryptographic schemes can be broken due to the leakage even though they are provably secure in the model where secret

© International Association for Cryptologic Research 2019
D. Lin and K. Sako (Eds.): PKC 2019, LNCS 11442, pp. 466–495, 2019.
https://doi.org/10.1007/978-3-030-17253-4_16

values are perfectly hidden. To withstand these attacks, Akavia et al. [AGV09] initiated the study of leakage resilient cryptography, where leakages from secret values are captured in a security model, and their security is proven even if a certain amount of secret values is leaked to an adversary. There have been vast amount of studies on leakage resilient cryptography including public key encryption, identity-based encryption, attribute-based encryption, digital signatures, identification, zero-knowledge proofs etc. [NS12, ADN+09, HLWW16, LRW11, KP17, KV09, BSW13, ADW09, GJS11].

Relative-Leakage and Absolute-Leakage. If a whole secret key is leaked, then no security remains. Thus we have to bound an amount of leakages an adversary can obtain to prove security in the presence of leakages. There are two possible choices for the way to bound an amount of leakage. In the first choice called the *relative-leakage model*, we bound a *leakage-ratio* $0 < \alpha < 1$, and we allow an adversary to obtain $\alpha \cdot |\mathsf{sk}|$-bit leakage from a secret key sk, where $|\mathsf{sk}|$ denotes a bit-length of sk. In the second choice called the *absolute-leakage model*, we bound an absolute amount ℓ of leakage (which we call a *absolute-leakage-bound*), and we allow an adversary to obtain ℓ-bit leakage from a secret key. This model is especially useful when considering security against malware attacks, where an adversary persistently obtains some parts of secret key remotely. If ℓ is set to be very large (say, many gigabytes), it is difficult for such an adversary to obtain more than ℓ bits of a secret key. We note that any scheme in the relative-leakage model can be also seen as one in the absolute-leakage model. Suppose that one has a scheme resilient to leakage of leakage-ratio α in the relative-leakage model. We can obtain a scheme resilient to absolute-leakage-bound ℓ by simply increasing the security parameter so that $|\mathsf{sk}| > \alpha\ell$.

Bounded Retrieval Model. As seen above, a scheme in the relative-leakage model can also be seen as one in the absolute-leakage model by increasing the security parameter. However, this does not serve as a satisfactory solution considering efficiency. To increase an absolute-leakage-bound ℓ, we have to increase the security parameter, which means that the efficiency of the whole system becomes less efficient when ℓ is set larger. Considering a situation where we set ℓ to be extremely large, it is desirable that we can increase ℓ by just increasing the secret key size without affecting efficiencies of other parts (e.g., public key size, encryption-time, decryption-time in the case of PKE). This goal is usually referred to as the *bounded retrieval model* (BRM) [DLW06, Dzi06].

PKE and IBE in BRM. All known constructions of PKE and IBE schemes in the BRM follow the same template proposed by Alwen et al. [ADN+09]. Specifically, they introduced a primitive called *identity-based hash proof system* (IB-HPS), which is a generalization of a hash proof system [CS02], and gave a generic construction of PKE and IBE schemes in the BRM based on that. Moreover, they gave three concrete constructions of IB-HPS based on (1) truncated augmented bilinear Diffie-Hellman exponent (TABDHE) assumption, (2) learning with errors (LWE) assumption, and (3) quadratic residuosity (QR) assumption, where the second and the third constructions are in the random oracle model.[1] As a result, they obtained PKE and IBE schemes in the BRM based on any of these assumptions. Leakage-ratios of these schemes are $1/2 - \epsilon$, $O(\frac{1}{\mathrm{poly}(\lambda)})$, and $1 - \epsilon$, respectively, where ϵ is an arbitrary constant. Subsequently, Chen et al. [CZLC16] constructed IB-HPSs based on the decisional bilinear Diffie-Hellman (DBDH) and the decisional square bilinear Diffie-Hellman (DSBDH) assumptions in the random oracle model. Based on them, one can construct PKE and IBE schemes in the BRM with leakage-ratio $1/2 - \epsilon$ for an arbitrary constant ϵ.

Hazay et al. [HLWW16] showed that, in fact, an IB-HPS is generically constructed from any IBE scheme.[2] As a result, one can construct PKE and IBE schemes in the BRM from any IBE scheme. However, one drawback of their construction is a poor leakage-ratio. Namely, the leakage-ratio of their scheme is $O(\frac{\log(\lambda)}{\mathrm{poly}(\lambda)})$. In that case, if one wants to set an absolute-leakage-bound to be ℓ, then a secret key size is $O(\frac{\mathrm{poly}(\lambda)}{\log(\lambda)} \cdot \ell)$, which is significantly larger than ℓ. Hopefully, we want to make the leakage-ratio close to 1 so that we can set a secret key size to be almost equal to ℓ for an absolute-leakage-bound ℓ. However, the only known construction of PKE and IBE schemes in the BRM that achieve such high leakage-ratio is the one based on the LWE assumption in the random oracle model. If one only relies on a standard assumption in the standard model, then the only known way to construct PKE and IBE schemes in the BRM is just instantiating the generic construction by Hazay et al. [HLWW16], which results in poor leakage-ratio $O(\frac{\log(\lambda)}{\mathrm{poly}(\lambda)})$. Thus the following problem remains open:

Is it possible to construct PKE and IBE schemes in the BRM whose leakage-ratio is almost equal to 1 based on a standard assumption in the standard model?

1.2   Our Contribution

We give a generic construction of IB-HPS based on any inner product encryption (IPE) scheme. As a result, we obtain PKE and IBE schemes in the BRM based on any IPE scheme. The leakage-ratio of our constructions is $\frac{n}{n+|\mathsf{sk}_{\mathsf{IPE}}(n)|}$ where n is an arbitrary integer and $|\mathsf{sk}_{\mathsf{IPE}}(n)|$ denotes a length of secret key of an underlying IPE scheme associated with an n-dimensional vector. In particular, if an underlying IPE scheme is fully key-compact (i.e., $|\mathsf{sk}_{\mathsf{IPE}}(n)|$ does not depend on n), then leakage-ratio can be made arbitrarily close to 1 by increasing n. For example, there are some known constructions of fully key-compact IPE schemes based on the d-linear (d-Lin) assumption [CGW15] and the subgroup-decision assumption on composite order pairing [Wee14] with adaptive security, and the learning-with-errors (LWE) assumption [AFV11] with selective security. Moreover, we give a construction of a fully key-compact selectively secure IPE

---

[1] They can be proven secure in the standard model if one assumes non-standard interactive versions of these assumptions.

[2] In [HLWW16], IB-HPS is called *identity-based weak hash proof system* (IB-wHPS) for compatibility to their notion of weak hash proof system. We stress that IB-HPS in [ADN+09] and IB-wHPS in [HLWW16] mean completely the identical primitive.

Table 1. The "$|\mathsf{ct}|$" column shows ciphertext-length of IBE schemes in the BRM, Sel and Ad denote selective and adaptive securities, ϵ and δ are arbitrary constants larger than 0, λ denotes the security parameter, N denotes a composite number in underlying hard problems, $|\mathsf{sk}_{\mathsf{IBE}}|$ and $|\mathsf{ct}_{\mathsf{IBE}}|$ denote the length of a secret key and a ciphertext of an underlying IBE scheme, n denotes an arbitrary parameter supposed to be a dimension of vectors in IPE, $|\mathsf{sk}_{\mathsf{IPE}}|(n)$ and $|\mathsf{ct}_{\mathsf{IPE}}|(n)$ denotes the length of a secret key and a ciphertext of an underlying IPE scheme with dimension n, and ROM means the random oracle model.

Reference	Leakage-ratio	$|\mathsf{ct}|$	Sel/Ad	Assumption
[ADN+09]	$\frac{1}{2} - \epsilon$	$O(\lambda^2)$	Ad	TABDHE
[ADN+09]	$\frac{1}{O(N)}$	$O(N)$	Ad	QR (ROM)
[ADN+09]	$1 - \epsilon$	$O(\lambda^4)$	Ad	LWE (ROM)
[CZLC16]	$\frac{1}{2} - \epsilon$	$O(\lambda^2)$	Ad	DBDH (ROM)
[CZLC16]	$\frac{1}{2} - \epsilon$	$O(\lambda^2)$	Ad	DSBDH (ROM)
[HLWW16]	$(1 - \epsilon)\frac{\log(\lambda)}{|\mathsf{sk}_{\mathsf{IBE}}|}$	$O(\lambda^2|\mathsf{ct}_{\mathsf{IBE}}|)$	Sel/Ad	Sel/Ad IBE
Ours	$(1 - \epsilon)\frac{n}{n+|\mathsf{sk}_{\mathsf{IPE}}|(n)}$	$O(n\lambda|\mathsf{ct}_{\mathsf{IPE}}(n)|)$	Sel/Ad	Sel/Ad IPE
Ours + [CGW15]	$1 - \epsilon$	$O(d^3\lambda^4)$	Ad	d-Lin
Ours + [Wee14]	$1 - \epsilon$	$O(N^3\lambda)$	Ad	SD
Ours + [AFV11]	$1 - \epsilon$	$\tilde{O}(\lambda^{4+\delta})$	Sel	LWE
Ours + Appendix A	$1 - \epsilon$	$O(\lambda^4)$	Sel	CBDH

scheme based on the computational bilinear Diffie-Hellman (CBDH) assumption. Each of these schemes gives new PKE and IBE schemes in the BRM model. In particular,

- We obtain the first PKE and selective/adaptive IBE schemes in the BRM whose leakage-ratio is arbitrarily close to 1 based on standard assumptions including d-Lin, LWE and CBDH assumptions in the standard model.
- Our CBDH-based construction is the first selectively secure IBE scheme whose leakage-ratio is arbitrarily close to 1 based on a search assumption on pairing groups even in the relative-leakage model where we allow the efficiency of a scheme to depend on the amount of leakage.

A comparison of IBE schemes in the BRM among known and our constructions is given in Table 1. We omit the comparison among PKE schemes in the BRM since all known constructions of PKE in the BRM are just degenerations of IBE in the BRM. We note that the selective security suffices for this degeneration.

1.3   Technical Overview

IB-HPS. We first roughly explain the definition of IB-HPS. An IB-HPS can be seen as an identity-based key encapsulation mechanism (IB-KEM) with a special "invalid encapsulation algorithm". It consists of a setup algorithm $\mathsf{Setup}(1^\lambda) \xrightarrow{\mathsf{R}} (\mathsf{pp}, \mathsf{msk})$, a key generation algorithm $\mathsf{KeyGen}(\mathsf{msk}, \mathsf{id}) \xrightarrow{\mathsf{R}} \mathsf{sk}_{\mathsf{id}}$, a valid encapsulation algorithm $\mathsf{Encap}(\mathsf{id}) \xrightarrow{\mathsf{R}} (\mathsf{ct}, \mathsf{k})$, an invalid encapsulation algorithm $\mathsf{Encap}^*(\mathsf{id}) \xrightarrow{\mathsf{R}} \mathsf{ct}$, and a decapsulation algorithm $\mathsf{Decap}(\mathsf{sk}_{\mathsf{id}}, \mathsf{id}, \mathsf{ct}) \xrightarrow{\mathsf{R}} \mathsf{k}$. The correctness requires that a ciphertext generated by Encap is correctly decapsulated to the corresponding encapsulated key. A special feature of IB-HPS is that if we decapsulate an invalid ciphertext ct^* generated by Encap^* by a secret key $\mathsf{sk}_{\mathsf{id}}$, then the resulting key $\mathsf{k} \xleftarrow{\mathsf{R}} \mathsf{Decap}(\mathsf{sk}_{\mathsf{id}}, \mathsf{id}, \mathsf{ct}^*)$ has a certain entropy given any fixed pp, id and ct^*. That is, there are many possible values of secret keys $\mathsf{sk}_{\mathsf{id}}$ for each id, and the value of $\mathsf{k} \xleftarrow{\mathsf{R}} \mathsf{Decap}(\mathsf{sk}_{\mathsf{id}}, \mathsf{id}, \mathsf{ct}^*)$ depends on which $\mathsf{sk}_{\mathsf{id}}$ was used for the decapsulation. As security, we require that valid and invalid ciphertexts are computationally indistinguishable even if an adversary can obtain one secret key per identity for all identities including the challenge identity used for generating the ciphertext to distinguish.

IBE in BRM from IB-HPS. Alwen et al. [ADN+09] proved that we can construct a leakage resilient IBE scheme in the BRM based on any IB-HPS. The leakage-ratio of the resulting IBE scheme depends on the parameter called the *universality-ratio* of the underlying IB-HPS. Roughly speaking, the universality-ratio is defined to be $\frac{n}{|\mathsf{sk}_{\mathsf{id}}|}$ where 2^n is the number of possible $\mathsf{sk}_{\mathsf{id}}$ for each id and $|\mathsf{sk}_{\mathsf{id}}|$ denotes the bit-length of $\mathsf{sk}_{\mathsf{id}}$. They proved that the leakage-ratio of the resulting IBE scheme could be made arbitrarily close to the universality-ratio of the underlying IB-HPS. Thus, the problem of constructing IBE schemes in the BRM with high leakage-ratio is translated into the problem of constructing IB-HPS with high universality-ratio.

IB-HPS from Any IBE. Here, we explain the idea of the work by Hazay et al. [HLWW16] that constructed an IB-HPS based on any IBE scheme. The setup algorithm of the IB-HPS (denoted by HPS) is the same as that of the IBE scheme and uses the same pp and msk. Let $\mathsf{Enc}_{\mathsf{IBE}}$ and $\mathsf{KeyGen}_{\mathsf{IBE}}$ denote the encryption and key generation algorithms of the underlying IBE scheme. Then, the key generation algorithm $\mathsf{KeyGen}_{\mathsf{HPS}}$, valid encapsulation algorithm $\mathsf{Enc}_{\mathsf{HPS}}$, and invalid encapsulation algorithm $\mathsf{Enc}^*_{\mathsf{HPS}}$ of HPS work as follows. In the description of $\mathsf{Enc}^*_{\mathsf{HPS}}$, differences from $\mathsf{Enc}_{\mathsf{HPS}}$ are highlighted in red letters.

$\mathsf{KeyGen}_{\mathsf{HPS}}(\mathsf{msk}, \mathsf{id})$: It picks $r \xleftarrow{\mathsf{R}} \{0,1\}$, computes $\mathsf{sk}'_{\mathsf{id}} \xleftarrow{\mathsf{R}} \mathsf{KeyGen}_{\mathsf{IBE}}(\mathsf{id}\|r)$, and sets $\mathsf{sk}_{\mathsf{id}} := (\mathsf{sk}'_{\mathsf{id}}, r)$. That is, $\mathsf{sk}_{\mathsf{id}}$ consists of secret keys for identities that are either $\mathsf{id}\|0$ or $\mathsf{id}\|1$, plus the random bit r that represents which identities were chosen.

$\mathsf{Enc}_{\mathsf{HPS}}(\mathsf{id})$: It picks $\mathsf{k} \in \{0,1\}$, computes $\mathsf{ct}_b \xleftarrow{\mathsf{R}} \mathsf{Enc}_{\mathsf{IBE}}(\mathsf{id}\|b, \mathsf{k})$ for $b \in \{0,1\}$, and outputs a ciphertext $\mathsf{ct} := (\mathsf{ct}_0, \mathsf{ct}_1)$ and an encapsulated key k. That is, ct_0 and ct_1 encrypt the same value k under identities $\mathsf{id}\|0$ and $\mathsf{id}\|1$, respectively. The encapsulated key is defined to be k.

$\mathsf{Enc}^*_{\mathsf{HPS}}(\mathsf{id})$: It picks $k_0, k_1 \in \{0,1\}$ for $b \in \{0,1\}$, computes $\mathsf{ct}_b \xleftarrow{\mathsf{R}}$ $\mathsf{Enc}_{\mathsf{IBE}}(\mathsf{id}\|b, k_b)$ for $b \in \{0,1\}$, and outputs a ciphertext $\mathsf{ct} := (\mathsf{ct}_0, \mathsf{ct}_1)$. That is, ct_0 and ct_1 encrypt independently random values k_0 and k_1 under identities $\mathsf{id}\|0$ and $\mathsf{id}\|1$, respectively. We note that this algorithm does not output an encapsulated key.

It is easy to see that the indistinguishability of valid and invalid ciphertexts can be reduced to the security of the underlying IBE scheme because an adversary never obtains secret keys for identities $\mathsf{id}\|0$ and $\mathsf{id}\|1$ simultaneously.[3] A valid ciphertext generated by $\mathsf{Enc}_{\mathsf{HPS}}$ can be correctly decapsulated because either ct_0 or ct_1, both of which encapsulate the same key k, can be decrypted with $\mathsf{sk}_{\mathsf{id}}$. On the other hand, for an invalid ciphertext, ct_0 and ct_1 encapsulate independent keys k_0 and k_1. Therefore the decapsulation result depends on r that was used as randomness to generate a secret key. This means that the above IB-HPS has 2 different $\mathsf{sk}_{\mathsf{id}}$ for each id, and each of them decapsulate an invalid ciphertext to a different value.[4] However, since the size of $\mathsf{sk}_{\mathsf{id}}$ is $\mathrm{poly}(\lambda)$, the universality-ratio of the above IB-HPS is $\frac{1}{\mathrm{poly}(\lambda)}$, which is far from 1. They also showed that the universality-ratio can be improved to $O(\frac{\log(\lambda)}{\mathrm{poly}(\lambda)})$ by modifying the above scheme to choose r from $[\mathrm{poly}(\lambda)]$ instead of $\{0,1\}$ and modifying other algorithms accordingly. However, this is still far from optimal.

First Step: Parallel Repetition. As a first step to achieve higher universality-ratio, we consider a variant of the above IB-HPS via parallel repetition. Let $n \in \mathbb{N}$ be an arbitrarily chosen parameter and $\mathsf{bin}(i)$ denote a binary representation of i. The setup algorithm of the "n-parallel variant" (denoted by n-HPS) is the same as that of the IBE scheme, and use the same pp and msk. Then, the key generation algorithm $\mathsf{KeyGen}_{n\text{-HPS}}$, valid encapsulation algorithm $\mathsf{Enc}_{n\text{-HPS}}$, and invalid encapsulation algorithm $\mathsf{Enc}^*_{n\text{-HPS}}$ of n-HPS as follows. In the description of $\mathsf{Enc}^*_{n\text{-HPS}}$, differences from $\mathsf{Enc}_{n\text{-HPS}}$ are highlighted in red letters.

$\mathsf{KeyGen}_{n\text{-HPS}}(\mathsf{msk}, \mathsf{id})$: It picks $r_1, ..., r_n \xleftarrow{\mathsf{R}} \{0,1\}$, computes $\mathsf{sk}'_{\mathsf{id},i} \xleftarrow{\mathsf{R}}$ $\mathsf{KeyGen}_{\mathsf{IBE}}(\mathsf{id}\|\mathsf{bin}(i)\|r_i)$ for $i \in [n]$, and outputs a secret key $\mathsf{sk}_{\mathsf{id}} := (\{\mathsf{sk}'_{\mathsf{id},i}\}_{i\in[n]}, \{r_i\}_{i\in[n]})$. That is, $\mathsf{sk}_{\mathsf{id}}$ consists of secret keys for identities that are either $\mathsf{id}\|\mathsf{bin}(i)\|0$ or $\mathsf{id}\|\mathsf{bin}(i)\|1$, plus random bits $\{r_i\}_{i\in[n]}$ that represent which identities were chosen.

$\mathsf{Enc}_{n\text{-HPS}}(\mathsf{id})$: It picks $k_1, ..., k_n \in \{0,1\}$, computes $\mathsf{ct}_{i,b} \xleftarrow{\mathsf{R}} \mathsf{Enc}_{\mathsf{IBE}}(\mathsf{id}\|\mathsf{bin}(i)\|b, k_i)$ for $i \in [n]$ and $b \in \{0,1\}$, and outputs a ciphertext $\mathsf{ct} := \{\mathsf{ct}_{i,b}\}_{i\in[n],b\in\{0,1\}}$ and an encapsulated key $k := \bigoplus_{i\in[n]} k_i$. That is, $\mathsf{ct}_{i,0}$ and $\mathsf{ct}_{i,1}$ encrypt the same value k_i under identities $\mathsf{id}\|\mathsf{bin}(i)\|0$ and $\mathsf{id}\|\mathsf{bin}(i)\|1$, respectively, for each $i \in [n]$. The encapsulated key is defined to be $k := \bigoplus_{i\in[n]} k_i$.

---

[3] Here, it is crucial that an adversary obtains at most one secret key for each identity in the security model of IB-HPS.

[4] Here we assumed that $\mathsf{KeyGen}_{\mathsf{IBE}}$ is deterministic so that $\mathsf{sk}'_{\mathsf{id}}$ is determined by id. This can be assumed without loss of generality since we can derandomize $\mathsf{KeyGen}_{\mathsf{IBE}}$ by using a pseudorandom function.

$\mathsf{Enc}^*_{n\text{-HPS}}(\mathsf{id})$: It picks $\mathsf{k}_{1,b}, ..., \mathsf{k}_{n,b} \in \{0,1\}$ for $b \in \{0,1\}$, computes $\mathsf{ct}_{i,b} \xleftarrow{\mathsf{R}}$ $\mathsf{Enc}_{\mathsf{IBE}}(\mathsf{id}\|\mathsf{bin}(i)\|b, \mathsf{k}_{i,b})$ for $i \in [n]$ and $b \in \{0,1\}$, and outputs a ciphertext $\mathsf{ct} := \{\mathsf{ct}_{i,b}\}_{i\in[n],b\in\{0,1\}}$. That is, $\mathsf{ct}_{i,0}$ and $\mathsf{ct}_{i,1}$ encrypt independently random values $\mathsf{k}_{i,0}$ and $\mathsf{k}_{i,1}$ under identities $\mathsf{id}\|\mathsf{bin}(i)\|0$ and $\mathsf{id}\|\mathsf{bin}(i)\|1$, respectively, for each $i \in [n]$. We note that this algorithm does not output an encapsulated key.

The indistinguishability of valid and invalid ciphertexts can be reduced to the security of the underlying IBE scheme similarly to the case for HPS. Next, we calculate the universality-ratio of n-HPS. For each id, the number of possible $\mathsf{sk}_{\mathsf{id}}$ is 2^n since different $\{r_i\}_{i\in[n]}$ give different $\mathsf{sk}_{\mathsf{id}}$. On the other hand, $\mathsf{sk}_{\mathsf{id}}$ contains n secret keys of the underlying IBE scheme, each of them has a size of $\mathrm{poly}(\lambda)$. As a result, the universality-ratio of n-HPS is still $\frac{1}{\mathrm{poly}(\lambda)}$, which is even not better than that of HPS. Hence, to achieve better universality-ratio, we need an additional idea.

Our Idea: Compressing Secret Keys. As seen above, the reason for the poor universality-ratio of n-HPS is that a secret key of the scheme contains many secret keys of the underlying IBE scheme. Our idea is to compress them. Towards this goal, we introduce a notion called multi-identity-based encryption (MIBE). MIBE works similarly to IBE except that a secret key is associated with multiple identities, and the key can be used to decrypt a ciphertext that is encrypted under any of these identities. If we do not care about the size of a secret key, then it is trivial to construct an MIBE scheme from any IBE scheme: we can just let a secret key of the MIBE consist of a tuple of those of the IBE. The crucial property for our purpose is *key-compactness*, which means that the size of a secret key does not depend on the number of identities the key is associated with. With such a key-compact MIBE, the universality-ratio of n-HPS is dramatically improved because a secret key of the IB-HPS consists of a single secret key of MIBE whose size is $\mathrm{poly}(\lambda)$ that does not depend on n. Then, the universality-ratio is $\frac{n}{n+\mathrm{poly}(\lambda)}$. By increasing n, we can make it arbitrarily close to 1.

MIBE from IPE. The final challenge is to construct a key-compact MIBE. We show that a key-compact MIBE scheme can be constructed from any key-compact IPE scheme where key-compactness of an IPE scheme means that its secret key size does not depend on the dimension of the vector space. In an IPE scheme, a ciphertext and a secret key are associated with vectors $\boldsymbol{x}$ and $\boldsymbol{y}$ respectively, and the ciphertext is decryptable by the secret key if and only if $\boldsymbol{x}^T\boldsymbol{y} = 0$. Suppose that we have a key-compact IPE scheme with vector space $\mathbb{Z}_q^{n+1}$. We construct a key-compact MIBE scheme whose identity space is $\mathbb{Z}_q$ and secret key can be associated with n different identities as follows. To generate a secret key $\mathsf{sk}_{\mathsf{id}_1,...,\mathsf{id}_n}$ associated with a set $(\mathsf{id}_1, ..., \mathsf{id}_n)$ of identities, we first compute a vector $\boldsymbol{y} = (y_0, ..., y_n) \in \mathbb{Z}_q^{n+1}$ such that $\prod_{i=1}^n (X - \mathsf{id}_n) = \sum_{i=0}^n y_i X^i$ as a polynomial in the indeterminate X. The secret key $\mathsf{sk}_{\mathsf{id}_1,...,\mathsf{id}_n}$ is set to be a secret key associated with $\boldsymbol{y}$ of the underlying IPE scheme. To encrypt a message under an identity id^*, we encrypt the message under the vector

$\boldsymbol{x} = (1, \mathsf{id}^*, (\mathsf{id}^*)^2, ..., (\mathsf{id}^*)^n)$ by the encryption algorithm of the underlying IPE. Since we have $\boldsymbol{x}^T \boldsymbol{y} = \sum_{i=0}^{n} y_i(\mathsf{id}^*)^i = \prod_{i=1}^{n}(\mathsf{id}^* - \mathsf{id}_n)$, we have $\boldsymbol{x}^T \boldsymbol{y} = 0$ if and only if $\mathsf{id}^* \in \{\mathsf{id}_1, ..., \mathsf{id}_n\}$. Therefore, this gives a construction of an MIBE scheme. We note that this construction is implicit in the work by Katz, Sahai and Waters [KSW08]. In the above construction, a secret key of the MIBE scheme consists of one secret key of the underlying IPE scheme. Therefore, if the underlying IPE scheme is key-compact, then the resulting MIBE is also key-compact. Finally, we note that IPE schemes with desirable key-compactness are known to exist based on various standard assumptions. Putting everything together, we can construct a leakage resilient IBE scheme in the BRM with leakage-ratio arbitrarily close to 1 based on these standard assumptions.

1.4   Discussion

Notes on Efficiency of Our IBE. One may think that our scheme does not satisfy the definition of IBE in the BRM since the efficiency of our IBE scheme (including encryption time, decryption time, ciphertext size etc.) depends on the parameter n, which is a dimension of a vector space in the underlying IPE. However, our scheme actually satisfies the definition. This is because we *do not directly use* our IB-HPS itself as an IBE scheme, and we use the compiler by Alwen et al. [ADN+09] to *convert* our IB-HPS to IBE scheme (in the BRM). Since their compiler is general and applicable to any IB-HPS, we obtain an IBE scheme in the BRM. To explain this in more detail, we briefly recall their compiler. In their construction of an IBE scheme in the BRM, a "key-size parameter" m and a "locality-parameter" t are set appropriately,[5] and the public parameter is exactly the same as that of the underlying IB-HPS, a secret key for an identity id consists of secret keys for identities $\mathsf{id}\|\mathsf{bin}(1)...\mathsf{id}\|\mathsf{bin}(m)$ generated by the key generation algorithm of the underlying IB-HPS, and an encryption algorithm given a message m, randomly picks $\{r_1, ..., r_t\} \xleftarrow{\mathsf{R}} [m]$, runs the encapsulation algorithm of the underlying IB-HPS under identities $\mathsf{id}\|\mathsf{bin}(r_1)...\mathsf{id}\|\mathsf{bin}(r_t)$ to obtain $(\mathsf{ct}_1, \mathsf{k}_1), ..., (\mathsf{ct}_t, \mathsf{k}_t)$, and outputs a ciphertext $(r_1, ..., r_t, \mathsf{ct}_1, ..., \mathsf{ct}_t, \mathsf{m} \oplus g(\mathsf{k}_1, ..., \mathsf{k}_t))$ where g is a universal hash function. We remark that the efficiency of the scheme (except the secret key size) just depends on t and *does not depend on* m. Their main theorem [ADN+09, Theorem 5.1] shows that we can increase an absolute-leakage-bound ℓ of the scheme just by increasing m and without increasing t, and the leakage-ratio of the IBE scheme is almost the same as the universality-ratio of the underlying IB-HPS. Thus, when we plug our IB-HPS from IPE (with a fixed dimension n) into their construction, we can arbitrarily increase an absolute-leakage-ratio ℓ just by increasing m *neither increasing* n nor t. Since what affect the efficiency of the IBE scheme is only n and t, and *not* m, we can increase an absolute-leakage-ratio ℓ without sacrificing the efficiency.

---

[5] In their paper, they use "n" instead of "m" for representing a "key-size" parameter. We use m for avoiding confusion with the dimension for IPE.

On Further Improving the Leakage-Ratio. In this paper, we propose IBE and PKE schemes in the BRM with leakage-ratio $1 - \epsilon$ for arbitrary constant $\epsilon > 0$. A natural question is if we can further achieve leakage-ratio $1 - \frac{1}{\text{poly}(\lambda)}$ for any polynomial poly, which is optimal. The reason why we cannot achieve such a leakage-ratio is that we rely on Alwen et al.'s theorem [ADN+09] (Theorem 1), which gives an IBE scheme in the BRM with leakage-ratio $\beta(1 - \epsilon)$ where β is the universality-ratio of the underlying IB-HPS and $\epsilon > 0$ is an arbitrary constant. As long as we rely on this theorem, the resulting leakage-ratio cannot be better than $1 - \epsilon$ for constant $\epsilon > 0$. Though it seems that it is possible to achieve leakage-ratio $1 - \frac{1}{\text{poly}(\lambda)}$, by extending the theorem to treat the case of sub-constant ϵ, the analysis is rather complicated, and thus we simply rely on their theorem as a black-box to make the presentation of our results simpler. We note that if we consider schemes in the relative-leakage model where the efficiency of a scheme can depend on a leakage bound ℓ, then our constructions easily yield schemes with leakage-ratio $1 - \frac{1}{\text{poly}(\lambda)}$.

1.5   Related Work

Here, we review existing works on leakage-resilient PKE and IBE schemes in other models. We remark that in all these models, the efficiency of schemes degrades with the leakage bound unlike ones in the BRM.

Leakage Resilient PKE/IBE in the Relative-leakage Model. We review existing works on leakage resilient PKE and IBE schemes in the relative-leakage model. Naor and Segev [NS12] proposed the first PKE scheme whose leakage resilience can be reduced to standard assumptions. Namely, they gave a generic construction of leakage-resilient PKE scheme based on a hash proof system. Subsequently, various constructions of leakage-resilient PKE schemes have been proposed [DHLW10b, BG10, HLWW16, BLSV18, QL13, QL14].

Chow et al. [CDRW10] proposed a leakage resilient IBE scheme based on the DBDH assumption with leakage-ratio $1/3 - o(1)$. Kurosawa and Phong [KP17] proposed leakage resilient IBE and IPE schemes based on the DLIN (2-Lin) and SXDH (1-Lin) assumptions with optimal leakage-ratio $1 - o(1)$ (they also constructed IBE and IPE schemes in an extended leakage model explained below, but its leakage-ratio is not optimal).

Continual Leakage Model. Brakerski et al. [BKKV10] and Dodis et al. [DHLW10a] concurrently introduced the notion of continual leakage model (CLM), where there is a notion of time periods and secret information is updated at the end of each time period. Adversaries are allowed to obtain a limited amount of secret information in each time period, but there is no limitation on the total amount of information that they obtained in all time periods. Brakerski et al. constructed PKE, IBE, and signature schemes from the DLIN or SXDH assumptions in the CLM. Dodis et al. constructed signature and identification schemes and authenticated key agreement protocols from the d-Lin assumption in the CLM.

Subsequently, Lewko et al. [LRW11] constructed adaptively secure IBE and attribute-based encryption (ABE) schemes based on the subgroup decision assumption in the CLM. In their scheme, adversaries are allowed to obtain leakage even from *master-secret keys*. Yu et al. [YAX+16] constructed adaptively secure ABE schemes for wider classes of functionality based on composite-order pairing groups in the CLM. Zhang et al. [ZCG+18] constructed adaptively secure ABE schemes for wider classes of functionality based on prime-order pairing groups (the d-Lin assumption) in the CLM.

Hard-to-Invert Leakage. Dodis et al. [DKL09] introduced the notion of cryptography with hard-to-invert auxiliary inputs, where adversaries are given auxiliary input $h(s)$ such that it is computationally hard to find s from $h(s)$ (s is secret information). Dodis et al. [DKL09] constructed symmetric encryption schemes from a non-standard variant of the learning parity with noise assumption in that model. Dodis et al. [DGK+10] constructed PKE schemes from the DDH or LWE assumption in that model. Yuen et al. [YCZY12] considered IBE schemes in an extended leakage model that is a combination of the CLM and hard-to-invert auxiliary input model.

2 Preliminaries

2.1 Notations

For any natural number n, $[n]$ denotes the set $\{1, \ldots, n\}$. $x \xleftarrow{R} S$ denotes x is randomly chosen from a finite set S, and $y \xleftarrow{R} \mathcal{A}(x; r)$ denotes that y is an output of a randomized algorithm $\mathcal{A}$ with input x and randomness r. We say that a function $f(\cdot) : \mathbb{N} \to [0, 1]$ is negligible if for all positive polynomials $p(\cdot)$ and all sufficiently large $\lambda \in \mathbb{N}$, we have $f(\lambda) < 1/p(\lambda)$. We say that an algorithm $\mathcal{A}$ is probabilistic polynomial time (PPT) if there exists a polynomial p such that a running time of $\mathcal{A}$ with input length λ is less than $p(\lambda)$. For a bit string x, $|x|$ denotes the bit-length of x. The min-entropy of a random variable X is $\mathsf{H}_\infty(X) := -\log(\max_x \Pr[X = x])$. We often denote poly to mean an unspecified polynomial and negl to mean an unspecified negligible function.

2.2 Pseudorandom Function

Definition 1. *An deterministic function* $\mathsf{PRF} : \mathcal{K} \times \mathcal{D} \to \mathcal{R}$ *computable in polynomial time is said to be a pseudorandom function (PRF) if for any PPT adversary* $\mathcal{A}$,

$$\mathsf{Adv}_{\mathsf{PRF},\mathcal{A}}(\lambda) := |\Pr[1 \leftarrow \mathcal{A}^{\mathsf{PRF}(K\cdot)}(1^\lambda)] - \Pr[1 \leftarrow \mathcal{A}^{\mathsf{Rand}(\cdot)}(1^\lambda)]|$$

is negligible where $K \xleftarrow{R} \mathcal{K}$ *and* $\mathsf{Rand} \xleftarrow{R} \mathcal{F}(\mathcal{D}, \mathcal{R})$ *where* $\mathcal{F}(\mathcal{D}, \mathcal{R})$ *denotes the set of all functions from* $\mathcal{D}$ *to* $\mathcal{R}$.

2.3   Identity-Based Encryption

We define IBE, and its leakage-resilient security (in the bounded retrieval model). An IBE scheme consists of the following algorithms.

$\mathsf{Setup}(1^\lambda, 1^\ell) \xrightarrow{\mathsf{R}} (\mathsf{pp}, \mathsf{msk})$: This is the setup algorithm that takes the security parameter 1^λ and the leakage parameter 1^ℓ as input[6] and outputs a public parameter pp and a master secret key msk. All other algorithms implicitly include pp as an input.

$\mathsf{KeyGen}(\mathsf{msk}, \mathsf{id}) \xrightarrow{\mathsf{R}} \mathsf{sk}_\mathsf{id}$: This is the key generation algorithm that takes a master secret key msk and an identity id as input, and outputs a secret key sk_id associated with the identity id.

$\mathsf{Enc}(\mathsf{id}, \mathsf{m}) \xrightarrow{\mathsf{R}} \mathsf{ct}$: This is the encryption algorithm that takes an identity id and a message m, and outputs a ciphertext ct.

$\mathsf{Dec}(\mathsf{sk}_\mathsf{id}, \mathsf{id}, \mathsf{ct}) \to \mathsf{m}$: This is the decryption algorithm that takes a secret key sk_id, an identity id and a ciphertext ct as input, and outputs a message m.

$\mathsf{Expt}^{\mathsf{LR\text{-}CPA}}_{\mathsf{IBE},\mathcal{A}}(\lambda, \ell)$:	$\mathsf{KG}(\mathsf{msk}, \mathsf{id})$
$\quad \mathsf{List} \leftarrow \emptyset$	$\quad$ If there exists $(\mathsf{id}, \mathsf{sk}_\mathsf{id}) \in \mathsf{List}$
$\quad \mathsf{coin} \xleftarrow{\mathsf{R}} \{0,1\}$	$\quad\quad$ Return sk_id
$\quad (\mathsf{pp}, \mathsf{msk}) \xleftarrow{\mathsf{R}} \mathsf{Setup}(1^\lambda)$	$\quad$ Else
$\quad (\mathsf{id}^*, m_0, m_1, \mathsf{st}) \xleftarrow{\mathsf{R}} \mathcal{A}_1^{\mathsf{KG}(\mathsf{msk},\cdot),\mathsf{Leak}(\cdot)}(\mathsf{pp})$	$\quad\quad \mathsf{sk}_\mathsf{id} \xleftarrow{\mathsf{R}} \mathsf{KeyGen}(\mathsf{msk}, \mathsf{id})$
$\quad \mathsf{ct}^* \xleftarrow{\mathsf{R}} \mathsf{Enc}(\mathsf{pp}, \mathsf{id}^*, m_\mathsf{coin})$	$\quad\quad \mathsf{List} \leftarrow \mathsf{List} \cup \{(\mathsf{id}, \mathsf{sk}_\mathsf{id})\}$
$\quad \widehat{\mathsf{coin}} \xleftarrow{\mathsf{R}} \mathcal{A}_2^{\mathsf{KG}(\mathsf{msk},\cdot)}(\mathsf{ct}^*, \mathsf{st})$	$\quad\quad$ Return sk_id
$\quad$ Return $(\widehat{\mathsf{coin}} \stackrel{?}{=} \mathsf{coin})$	$\mathsf{Leak}(\mathsf{id} \in \mathcal{ID}, f)$
	$\quad$ If there exists $(\mathsf{id}, \mathsf{sk}_\mathsf{id}) \in \mathsf{List}$
	$\quad\quad L_\mathsf{id} \leftarrow L_\mathsf{id} + |f(\mathsf{sk}_\mathsf{id})|$
	$\quad\quad$ Return $f(\mathsf{sk}_\mathsf{id})$
	$\quad$ Else
	$\quad\quad \mathsf{sk}_\mathsf{id} \xleftarrow{\mathsf{R}} \mathsf{KeyGen}(\mathsf{msk}, \mathsf{id})$
	$\quad\quad \mathsf{List} \leftarrow \mathsf{List} \cup \{(\mathsf{id}, \mathsf{sk}_\mathsf{id})\}$
	$\quad\quad L_\mathsf{id} \leftarrow |f(\mathsf{sk}_\mathsf{id})|$
	$\quad\quad$ Return $f(\mathsf{sk}_\mathsf{id})$

Fig. 1. The experiment for defining the leakage-resilience for IBE

Remark 1. In our definition, we explicitly give id to Dec as an input, which differs from a commonly-used definition. We define in this way because id need not be hidden, and thus it is natural to separate it from a secret key. We note that this modification does not lose any generality because we can simply include id in sk_id. This modification slightly affects the leakage-ratio defined below, but the difference is negligible when $\ell = \omega(|\mathsf{id}|)$.

---

[6] Since we consider a leakage resilient IBE, we give the leakage parameter 1^ℓ as input, which means a maximum amount of leakage bits the scheme tolerates.

Correctness. For any $(\mathsf{pp}, \mathsf{msk})$ produced by $\mathsf{Setup}(1^\lambda, 1^\ell)$, any $\mathsf{id} \in \mathcal{ID}$, any $\mathsf{m} \in \mathcal{M}$, we have

$$\Pr\left[\mathsf{m} \neq \mathsf{m}' \,\middle|\, \begin{array}{l} \mathsf{sk}_{\mathsf{id}} \xleftarrow{R} \mathsf{KeyGen}(\mathsf{msk}, \mathsf{id}), \\ \mathsf{ct} \xleftarrow{R} \mathsf{Enc}(\mathsf{id}, \mathsf{m}), \mathsf{m}' := \mathsf{Dec}(\mathsf{sk}_{\mathsf{id}}, \mathsf{id}, \mathsf{ct}) \end{array}\right] = \mathrm{negl}(\lambda)$$

Leakage-resilience. Leakage resilience of an IBE scheme IBE is defined by the experiment $\mathsf{Expt}^{\mathsf{LR\text{-}CPA}}_{\mathsf{IBE}, \mathcal{A}}(\lambda, \ell)$ for an adversary $\mathcal{A} = (\mathcal{A}_1, \mathcal{A}_2)$ described in Fig. 1. We say that a PPT adversary $\mathcal{A}$ is admissible if it does not query id^* to $\mathsf{KG}(\mathsf{msk}, \cdot)$, and at the end of the experiment, we have $L_{\mathsf{id}^*} \leq \ell$ or L_{id^*} is undefined (i.e., $\mathcal{A}$ never queries id^* to Leak). We say that an PPT adversary $\mathcal{A}$ is selectively admissible if in addition to the above, $\mathcal{A}_1$ can be divided into two stages $\mathcal{A}_{1\text{-}1}$ and $\mathcal{A}_{1\text{-}2}$: $\mathcal{A}_{1\text{-}1}$ is given 1^λ and not allowed to access to any oracle, and returns $(\mathsf{id}^*, \mathsf{st}_{\mathsf{pre}})$, and $\mathcal{A}_{1\text{-}2}$ is given $(\mathsf{pp}, \mathsf{st}_{\mathsf{pre}})$ and allowed to access to oracles $\mathsf{KG}(\mathsf{msk}, \cdot)$ and $\mathsf{Leak}(\cdot, \cdot)$, and returns $(\mathsf{m}_0, \mathsf{m}_1, \mathsf{st})$.

Definition 2. *We say that an IBE scheme IBE is adaptively leakage resilient if for any polynomial $\ell(\lambda)$, any admissible adversary $\mathcal{A}$, if the advantage*

$$\mathsf{Adv}^{\mathsf{LR\text{-}CPA}}_{\mathsf{IBE}, \mathcal{A}}(\lambda, \ell) := 2 \cdot |\Pr[\mathsf{Expt}^{\mathsf{LR\text{-}CPA}}_{\mathsf{IBE}, \mathcal{A}}(\lambda, \ell) = 1] - 1/2|$$

is negligible in λ. We define selective leakage resilience of IBE analogously by replacing "any admissible adversary $\mathcal{A}$" in the above definition with "any selectively admissible adversary $\mathcal{A}$". We define leakage-ratio α of the scheme to be minimal value of $\frac{\ell}{|\mathsf{sk}_{\mathsf{id}}|}$ where $(\mathsf{pp}, \mathsf{msk}) \xleftarrow{R} \mathsf{Setup}(1^\lambda, 1^\ell)$ and $\mathsf{sk}_{\mathsf{id}} \xleftarrow{R} \mathsf{KeyGen}(\mathsf{msk}, \mathsf{id})$.

Remark 2. In our security model, we assume that an adversary obtains a leakage from one decryption key per one identity, and cannot obtain a leakage from a master secret key. This is the same model as the ones in [CDRW10, ADN+09, KP17]. Some works (e.g., [LRW11]) consider stronger security models where an adversary obtains leakages from many secret keys of the same identity and leakages from a master secret key.

Bounded Retrieval Model.

Next, we define leakage resilient IBE in the BRM [ADN+09][7].

Definition 3 ([ADN+09, Def. 6.2]). *We say that an IBE scheme is adaptively (resp. selectively) leakage-resilient in the bounded retrieval model (BRM), if the scheme is adaptively (resp. selectively) leakage-resilient, and the public parameter size, master secret key size, ciphertext size, encryption time, and decryption time (and the number of secret key bits read by decryption) are independent of the leakage bound ℓ. More formally, there exist polynomials ppsize, $\mathsf{msksize}$, ctsize, encT, decT, such that, for any polynomial ℓ and any $(\mathsf{pp}, \mathsf{msk}) \xleftarrow{R} \mathsf{KeyGen}(1^\lambda, 1^\ell)$, $\mathsf{id} \in \mathcal{ID}$, $\mathsf{m} \in \mathcal{M}$, $\mathsf{ct} \xleftarrow{R} \mathsf{Enc}(\mathsf{id}, m)$, the scheme satisfies:*

---

[7] In [ADN+09], they only consider the adaptive security. We also define the selective security similarly.

1. *Public parameter size is* $|\mathsf{pp}| \leq O(\mathsf{ppsize}(\lambda))$, *master secret key size is* $|\mathsf{msk}| \leq O(\mathsf{msksize}(\lambda))$, *ciphertext size is* $|\mathsf{ct}| \leq O(\mathsf{ctsize}(\lambda, |\mathsf{m}|))$.
2. *Run-time of* $\mathsf{Enc}(\mathsf{id}, \mathsf{m})$ *is* $\leq O(\mathsf{encT}(\lambda, |\mathsf{m}|))$.
3. *Run-time of* $\mathsf{Dec}(\mathsf{ct}, \mathsf{sk})$, *and the number of bits of* sk *accessed, is* $\leq O(\mathsf{decT}(\lambda, |\mathsf{m}|))$.

2.4   Inner Product Encryption

We define inner product encryption (IPE) and its security. We remark that we do not define the leakage resilience for IPE because we do not construct a leakage resilient IPE scheme, and we just use a (non-leakage resilient) IPE scheme as a building block to construct a leakage resilient IBE scheme in the BRM. An IPE scheme consists of the following algorithms.

$\mathsf{Setup}(1^\lambda, 1^n) \xrightarrow{\mathsf{R}} (\mathsf{pp}, \mathsf{msk})$: This is the setup algorithm that takes the security parameter 1^λ and the vector-dimension 1^n as input and outputs a public parameter pp and a master secret key msk. The public parameter pp specifies a vector space $\mathbb{Z}_q^n$. All other algorithms implicitly include pp as an input.

$\mathsf{KeyGen}(\mathsf{msk}, \boldsymbol{y} \in \mathbb{Z}_q^n) \xrightarrow{\mathsf{R}} \mathsf{sk}_{\boldsymbol{y}}$: This is the key generation algorithm that takes a master secret key msk and a vector $\boldsymbol{y} \in \mathbb{Z}_q^n$ as input, and outputs a secret key $\mathsf{sk}_{\boldsymbol{y}}$ associated with the vector $\boldsymbol{y}$.

$\mathsf{Enc}(\boldsymbol{x}, \mathsf{m}) \xrightarrow{\mathsf{R}} \mathsf{ct}$: This is the encryption algorithm that takes a vector $\boldsymbol{x} \in \mathbb{Z}_q^n$ and a message m, and outputs a ciphertext ct.

$\mathsf{Dec}(\mathsf{sk}_{\boldsymbol{y}}, \boldsymbol{y}, \mathsf{ct}) \to \mathsf{m}$: This is the decryption algorithm that takes a secret key $\mathsf{sk}_{\boldsymbol{y}}$, a vector $\boldsymbol{y}$ and a ciphertext ct as input, and outputs a message m.

Correctness. For any $(\mathsf{pp}, \mathsf{msk})$ produced by $\mathsf{Setup}(1^\lambda, 1^n)$, any $\boldsymbol{x}, \boldsymbol{y} \in \mathbb{Z}_q^n$ such that $\boldsymbol{x}^T \cdot \boldsymbol{y} = 0$, any $\mathsf{m} \in \mathcal{M}$, we have

$$\Pr\left[\mathsf{m} \neq \mathsf{m}' \,\middle|\, \begin{array}{l} \mathsf{sk}_{\boldsymbol{y}} \xleftarrow{\mathsf{R}} \mathsf{KeyGen}(\mathsf{msk}, \boldsymbol{y}), \\ \mathsf{ct} \xleftarrow{\mathsf{R}} \mathsf{Enc}(\boldsymbol{x}, \mathsf{m}), \mathsf{m}' := \mathsf{Dec}(\mathsf{sk}_{\boldsymbol{y}}, \boldsymbol{y}, \mathsf{ct}) \end{array}\right] = \mathsf{negl}(\lambda)$$

Security. Security of an IPE scheme IPE is defined by the experiment $\mathsf{Expt}_{\mathsf{IPE}, \mathcal{A}}^{\mathsf{CPA}}(\lambda, n)$ for an adversary $\mathcal{A} = (\mathcal{A}_1, \mathcal{A}_2)$ described in Fig. 2. We say that

$$\begin{array}{l}
\underline{\mathsf{Expt}_{\mathsf{IPE}, \mathcal{A}}^{\mathsf{CPA}}(\lambda, n):} \\
\quad \mathsf{coin} \xleftarrow{\mathsf{R}} \{0, 1\} \\
\quad (\mathsf{pp}, \mathsf{msk}) \xleftarrow{\mathsf{R}} \mathsf{Setup}(1^\lambda, 1^n) \\
\quad (\boldsymbol{x}^*, \mathsf{m}_0, \mathsf{m}_1, \mathsf{st}) \xleftarrow{\mathsf{R}} \mathcal{A}_1^{\mathsf{KeyGen}(\mathsf{msk}, \cdot)}(\mathsf{pp}) \\
\quad \mathsf{ct}^* \xleftarrow{\mathsf{R}} \mathsf{Enc}(\boldsymbol{x}^*, \mathsf{m}_{\mathsf{coin}}) \\
\quad \widehat{\mathsf{coin}} \xleftarrow{\mathsf{R}} \mathcal{A}_2^{\mathsf{KeyGen}(\mathsf{msk}, \cdot)}(\mathsf{ct}_{\mathsf{coin}}, \mathsf{st}) \\
\quad \text{Return } (\widehat{\mathsf{coin}} \stackrel{?}{=} \mathsf{coin}).
\end{array}$$

Fig. 2. The experiment for defining the security for IPE

a PPT adversary $\mathcal{A}$ is admissible if it does not query $\boldsymbol{y}$ satisfying $(\boldsymbol{x}^*)^T \cdot \boldsymbol{y} = 0$ to KeyGen(msk, $\cdot$). We say that a PPT adversary $\mathcal{A}$ is selectively admissible if in addition to the above, $\mathcal{A}_1$ can be divided into two stages $\mathcal{A}_{1\text{-}1}$ and $\mathcal{A}_{1\text{-}2}$: $\mathcal{A}_{1\text{-}1}$ is given $(1^\lambda, 1^n)$ and not allowed to access to any oracle, and returns $(\boldsymbol{x}^*, \mathsf{st}_{\mathsf{pre}})$, and $\mathcal{A}_{1\text{-}2}$ is given $(\mathsf{pp}, \mathsf{st}_{\mathsf{pre}})$ and allowed to access to oracles KeyGen(msk, $\cdot$), and returns $(\mathsf{m}_0, \mathsf{m}_1, \mathsf{st})$.

Definition 4. *We say that an IPE scheme IPE is adaptively secure if for any polynomial $n(\lambda)$, any admissible adversary $\mathcal{A}$, if the advantage*

$$\mathsf{Adv}^{\mathsf{CPA}}_{\mathsf{IPE},\mathcal{A}}(\lambda, n) := 2 \cdot |\Pr[\mathsf{Expt}^{\mathsf{CPA}}_{\mathsf{IBE},\mathcal{A}}(\lambda, n) = 1] - 1/2|$$

is negligible in λ. We define selective security of IPE analogously by replacing "any admissible adversary $\mathcal{A}$" in the above definition with "any selectively admissible adversary $\mathcal{A}$".

Key-Compactness. We say that an IPE scheme is fully key-compact if for any polynomial $n = n(\lambda)$, any $(\mathsf{pp}, \mathsf{msk})$ produced by Setup$(1^\lambda, 1^n)$, any $\boldsymbol{y} \in \mathbb{Z}_q^n$, and any $\mathsf{sk}_{\boldsymbol{y}}$ produced by KeyGen(msk, $\boldsymbol{y}$), we have

$$|\mathsf{sk}_{\boldsymbol{y}}| = \mathrm{poly}(\lambda)$$

where poly is a fixed polynomial that does not depend on n.

2.5 Identity-Based Hash Proof System (IB-HPS)

An identity-based hash proof system (IB-HPS) [ADN+09] consists of five PPT algorithms $\Pi = (\mathsf{Setup}, \mathsf{KeyGen}, \mathsf{Encap}, \mathsf{Encap}^*, \mathsf{Decap})$.

Setup(1^λ): This is the setup algorithm that takes the security parameter 1^λ as an input, and outputs a public parameter pp and a master secret key msk. All other algorithms implicitly include pp as an input.

KeyGen(msk, id): This is the key generation algorithm that takes a master secret key msk and an identity id as inputs, and outputs a identity secret key $\mathsf{sk}_{\mathsf{id}}$.

Encap(id): This is the valid encapsulation algorithm that takes an identity id as an input and outputs a valid ciphertext ct and a encapsulated key k.

Encap*(id): This is the invalid encapsulation algorithm that takes an identity id as an input and outputs an invalid ciphertext ct$'$.

Decap$(\mathsf{sk}_{\mathsf{id}}, \mathsf{id}, \mathsf{ct})$: This is the decapsulation algorithm that takes an identity secret key $\mathsf{sk}_{\mathsf{id}}$, an identity id and a ciphertext ct as inputs, and outputs an encapsulated key k.

We require that an IB-HPS satisfies the following properties.

Correctness. For any $(\mathsf{pp}, \mathsf{msk})$ produced by Setup(1^λ), any $\mathsf{id} \in \mathcal{ID}$, we have

$$\Pr\left[k \neq k' \,\middle|\, \begin{array}{l} \mathsf{sk}_{\mathsf{id}} \xleftarrow{\text{R}} \mathsf{KeyGen}(\mathsf{msk}, \mathsf{id}) \\ (\mathsf{ct}, k) \xleftarrow{\text{R}} \mathsf{Encap}(\mathsf{id}), k' := \mathsf{Decap}(\mathsf{sk}_{\mathsf{id}}, \mathsf{id}, \mathsf{ct}) \end{array}\right] = \mathrm{negl}(\lambda)$$

Valid/Invalid Ciphertext Indistinguishability. The valid ciphertexts generated by Encap and the invalid ciphertexts generated by Encap* should be indistinguishable even given a secret key of a challenge identity. In particular, we define an experiment $\mathsf{Expt}_{\Pi,\mathcal{A}}^{\mathsf{ind}}$ for an IB-HPS Π and an adversary $\mathcal{A} = (\mathcal{A}_1, \mathcal{A}_2)$ as described in Fig. 3.

$$
\begin{array}{|l|}
\hline
\mathsf{Expt}_{\Pi,\mathcal{A}}^{\mathsf{ind}}(\lambda): \\
\quad \mathsf{coin} \xleftarrow{\mathsf{R}} \{0,1\} \\
\quad (\mathsf{pp}, \mathsf{msk}) \xleftarrow{\mathsf{R}} \mathsf{Setup}(1^\lambda) \\
\quad (\mathsf{id}^*, \mathsf{st}) \xleftarrow{\mathsf{R}} \mathcal{A}_1^{\mathsf{KeyGen}(\mathsf{msk},\cdot)}(\mathsf{pp}) \\
\quad \mathsf{ct}_0 \xleftarrow{\mathsf{R}} \mathsf{Encap}(\mathsf{id}^*) \\
\quad \mathsf{ct}_1 \xleftarrow{\mathsf{R}} \mathsf{Encap}^*(\mathsf{id}^*) \\
\quad \widehat{\mathsf{coin}} \xleftarrow{\mathsf{R}} \mathcal{A}_2^{\mathsf{KeyGen}(\mathsf{msk},\cdot)}(\mathsf{ct}_{\mathsf{coin}}, \mathsf{st}) \\
\quad \text{Return } (\widehat{\mathsf{coin}} \stackrel{?}{=} \mathsf{coin}). \\
\hline
\end{array}
$$

Fig. 3. The experiment for defining valid/invalid ciphertext indistinguishability for IB-HPS

We say that a PPT adversary $\mathcal{A}$ is admissible if it does not makes the same query to $\mathsf{KeyGen}(\mathsf{msk}, \cdot)$ twice. We say that a PPT adversary $\mathcal{A}$ is selectively admissible if in addition to that, $\mathcal{A}_1$ is given 1^λ instead of pp and not allowed to access to $\mathsf{KeyGen}(\mathsf{msk}, \cdot)$.

$\mathcal{A}_1$ is only given 1^λ instead of pp and does not make any query. We note that we do not prohibit an adversary from querying id^*. That is, valid and invalid ciphertexts under an identity id^* are indistinguishable even if an adversary is given one secret key that corresponds to id^*.

Definition 5. *We say that an IB-HPS Π is adaptively secure if for any admissible adversary $\mathcal{A}$, the advantage $\mathsf{Adv}_{\Pi,\mathcal{A}}^{\mathsf{ind}}(\lambda) := 2 \cdot |\Pr[\mathsf{Expt}_{\Pi,\mathcal{A}}^{\mathsf{ind}}(\lambda) = 1] - 1/2|$ is negligible. We define selective security of IB-HPS analogously by replacing "any PPT adversary $\mathcal{A}$" in the above definition with "any selectively admissible adversary $\mathcal{A}$".*

Universality. Another property of IB-HPS is *universality*. An IB-HPS is said to be (n, ρ)-universal if the number of possible values of $\mathsf{sk}_{\mathsf{id}} \xleftarrow{\mathsf{R}} \mathsf{KeyGen}(\mathsf{msk}, \mathsf{id})$ is larger than 2^n, and any distinct pair of them decrypts a randomly generated invalid ciphertext to the same message with probability at most ρ. In other words, $\{\mathsf{Decap}(\mathsf{ct}, \mathsf{id}, \cdot) : \mathsf{ct} \xleftarrow{\mathsf{R}} \mathsf{Enc}^*(\mathsf{pp})\}$ is a family of ρ-universal functions.

Definition 6 [ADN+09, Def. 3.1]**.** *We say that an IB-HPS Π is (n, ρ)-universal if for any fixed values of $(\mathsf{pp}, \mathsf{msk})$ produced by $\mathsf{Setup}(1^\lambda)$, $\mathsf{id} \in \mathcal{ID}$, the following hold:*

1. $\mathsf{H}_\infty(\mathsf{sk}_{\mathsf{id}}) \geq n$ where $\mathsf{sk}_{\mathsf{id}} \xleftarrow{\mathsf{R}} \mathsf{KeyGen}(\mathsf{msk}, \mathsf{id})$.

2. *For any fixed distinct* $\mathsf{sk_{id}} \neq \overline{\mathsf{sk}}_{\mathsf{id}}$ *produced by* $\mathsf{KeyGen}(\mathsf{msk}, \mathsf{id})$,

$$\Pr_{\mathsf{ct} \xleftarrow{R} \mathsf{Encap^*}(\mathsf{id})} [\mathsf{Decap}(\mathsf{sk_{id}}, \mathsf{id}, \mathsf{ct}) = \mathsf{Decap}(\overline{\mathsf{sk}}_{\mathsf{id}}, \mathsf{id}, \mathsf{ct})] \leq \rho.$$

We say that Π *has a universality-ratio* β *if there exists* n *and a constant* $\rho < 1$ *such that* Π *is* (n, ρ)*-universal and we have* $\beta < \frac{n}{|\mathsf{sk_{id}}|}$ *for any* $(\mathsf{pp}, \mathsf{msk})$ *produced by* $\mathsf{Setup}(1^\lambda)$, *any* id *and any* $\mathsf{sk_{id}}$ *produced by* $\mathsf{KeyGen}(\mathsf{msk}, \mathsf{id})$.

Alwen et al. [ADN+09] gave a construction of an IBE scheme in the BRM based on an (n, ρ)-universal IB-HPS, and prove that the leakage-ratio α of their IBE scheme can be arbitrarily close to the universality-ratio β of an underlying IB-HPS. More formally, they proved the following theorem[8].

Theorem 1 ([ADN+09, Theorem 6.1]). *If there exists an adaptively (resp. selectively) secure IB-HPS with universality-ratio* $\beta > c$ *for some constant* c, *then for any constant* $\epsilon > 0$ *and any polynomial* v, *there exists an adaptively (resp. selectively) leakage-resilient IBE scheme in the BRM with message space* $\mathcal{M} = \{0, 1\}^v$ *and:*

1. *Master public/secret key size is the same as that of the underlying IB-HPS.*
2. *Ciphertext-size/encryption-time/decryption-time are* $t = O(v + \lambda)$ *times larger than that of the underlying IB-HPS.*
3. *Leakage-ratio is* $\alpha \geq \beta(1-\epsilon)$ *for sufficiently large values of the leakage parameter* ℓ.

3   Generic Construction of IB-HPS from IPE

In this section, we give a generic construction of IB-HPS based on any IPE scheme. Interestingly, universality-ratio of a resulting IB-HPS is related to key-compactness of an underlying IPE scheme. Especially, if an underlying IPE is fully key-compact, then the universality-ratio of the resulting IB-HPS can be arbitrarily close to 1. We give our construction through an intermediate primitive called *multi-identity-based encryption* (MIBE).

3.1   Multi-identity-Based Encryption

Here, we introduce a notion of MIBE, which is a variant of IBE such that a secret key is associated with multiple identities. Then we show a key-compactness-preserving conversion from IPE to MIBE. An MIBE scheme consists of four PPT algorithms ($\mathsf{Setup}, \mathsf{KeyGen}, \mathsf{Enc}, \mathsf{Dec}$).

$\mathsf{Setup}(1^\lambda, 1^n) \xrightarrow{R} (\mathsf{pp}, \mathsf{msk})$: This is the setup algorithm that takes the security parameter 1^λ and the identity-multiplicity 1^n as inputs and outputs a public parameter pp and a master secret key msk. All other algorithms implicitly include pp as an input.

---

[8] Though Alwen et al. [ADN+09] only gave a proof for the case of the adaptive security, the proof can be straightforwardly extended to the selective case.

$\mathsf{KeyGen}(\mathsf{msk}, (\mathsf{id}_1, ..., \mathsf{id}_n)) \xrightarrow{\mathsf{R}} \mathsf{sk}_{(\mathsf{id}_1,...,\mathsf{id}_n)}$: This is the key generation algorithm that takes a master secret key msk and identities $\mathsf{id}_1, ..., \mathsf{id}_n$ as inputs, and outputs secret key $\mathsf{sk}_{(\mathsf{id}_1,...,\mathsf{id}_n)}$ associated with the set $\{\mathsf{id}_1, ..., \mathsf{id}_n\}$.

$\mathsf{Enc}(\mathsf{id}, \mathsf{m}) \xrightarrow{\mathsf{R}} \mathsf{ct}$: This is the encryption algorithm that takes an identity id and a message m as inputs, and outputs a ciphertext ct.

$\mathsf{Dec}(\mathsf{sk}_{\mathsf{id}_1,...,\mathsf{id}_n}, (\mathsf{id}_1, ..., \mathsf{id}_n), \mathsf{ct}) \to \mathsf{m}$: This is the decryption algorithm that takes a secret key $\mathsf{sk}_{(\mathsf{id}_1,...,\mathsf{id}_n)}$, a set of identities $(\mathsf{id}_1, ..., \mathsf{id}_n)$ and a ciphertext ct as inputs, and outputs a message m.

Correctness. For any $(\mathsf{pp}, \mathsf{msk})$ produced by $\mathsf{Setup}(1^\lambda)$, any $n \in \mathbb{N}$, any $\mathsf{id}_1, ..., \mathsf{id}_n \in \mathcal{ID}^n$, any $i \in [n]$, and any message m, we have

$$\Pr\left[\mathsf{m} \neq \mathsf{m}' \middle| \begin{array}{l} \mathsf{sk}_{(\mathsf{id}_1,...,\mathsf{id}_n)} \xleftarrow{\mathsf{R}} \mathsf{KeyGen}(\mathsf{msk}, (\mathsf{id}_1, ..., \mathsf{id}_n)) \\ (\mathsf{ct}, \mathsf{k}) \xleftarrow{\mathsf{R}} \mathsf{Enc}(\mathsf{id}_i, \mathsf{m}), \mathsf{m}' := \mathsf{Dec}(\mathsf{sk}_{(\mathsf{id}_1,...,\mathsf{id}_n)}, (\mathsf{id}_1, ..., \mathsf{id}_n), \mathsf{ct}) \end{array} \right] = \mathsf{negl}(\lambda)$$

$$\boxed{\begin{array}{l} \mathsf{Expt}^{\mathsf{CPA}}_{\mathsf{MIBE},\mathcal{A}}(\lambda): \\ \quad \mathsf{coin} \xleftarrow{\mathsf{R}} \{0, 1\} \\ \quad (\mathsf{pp}, \mathsf{msk}) \xleftarrow{\mathsf{R}} \mathsf{Setup}(1^\lambda) \\ \quad (\mathsf{id}^*, \mathsf{m}_0, \mathsf{m}_1, \mathsf{st}) \xleftarrow{\mathsf{R}} \mathcal{A}_1^{\mathsf{KeyGen}(\mathsf{msk}, \cdot)}(\mathsf{pp}) \\ \quad \mathsf{ct}^* \xleftarrow{\mathsf{R}} \mathsf{Enc}(\mathsf{pp}, \mathsf{id}^*, \mathsf{m}_{\mathsf{coin}}) \\ \quad \widehat{\mathsf{coin}} \xleftarrow{\mathsf{R}} \mathcal{A}_2^{\mathsf{KeyGen}(\mathsf{msk}, \cdot)}(\mathsf{ct}^*, \mathsf{st}) \\ \quad \mathrm{Return}\ (\widehat{\mathsf{coin}} \stackrel{?}{=} \mathsf{coin}). \end{array}}$$

Fig. 4. The experiment for defining the security for MIBE

Security. The security of an MIBE scheme MIBE is defined by the experiment $\mathsf{Expt}^{\mathsf{CPA}}_{\mathsf{MIBE},\mathcal{A}}(\lambda)$ for an adversary $\mathcal{A} = (\mathcal{A}_1, \mathcal{A}_2)$ described in Fig. 4. We say that a PPT adversary $\mathcal{A}$ is admissible if for any query $(\mathsf{id}_1, ..., \mathsf{id}_n)$ made by $\mathcal{A}$, we have $\mathsf{id}^* \notin \{\mathsf{id}_1, ..., \mathsf{id}_n\}$. We say that $\mathcal{A}$ is selectively admissible if in addition to the above, $\mathcal{A}_1$ can be divided into two stages $\mathcal{A}_{1\text{-}1}$ and $\mathcal{A}_{1\text{-}2}$: $\mathcal{A}_{1\text{-}1}$ is given 1^λ and not allowed to access to any oracle, and returns $(\mathsf{id}^*, \mathsf{st}_{\mathsf{pre}})$, and $\mathcal{A}_{1\text{-}2}$ is given $(\mathsf{pp}, \mathsf{st}_{\mathsf{pre}})$ and allowed to access to oracles $\mathsf{KeyGen}(\mathsf{msk}, \cdot)$, and returns $(\mathsf{m}_0, \mathsf{m}_1, \mathsf{st})$.

Definition 7. *We say that a MIBE scheme MIBE is adaptively secure if for any admissible adversary $\mathcal{A}$, if the advantage*

$$\mathsf{Adv}^{\mathsf{CPA}}_{\mathsf{MIBE},\mathcal{A}}(\lambda) := 2 \cdot |\Pr[\mathsf{Expt}^{\mathsf{CPA}}_{\mathsf{MIBE},\mathcal{A}}(\lambda) = 1] - 1/2|$$

is negligible. We define selective security of MIBE analogously by replacing "any admissible adversary $\mathcal{A}$" in the above definition with "any selectively admissible adversary $\mathcal{A}$".

Key-Compactness. We say that an MIBE scheme is fully key-compact if for any polynomial $n = n(\lambda)$, any $(\mathsf{pp}, \mathsf{msk})$ produced by $\mathsf{Setup}(1^\lambda, 1^n)$, any $\mathsf{id}_1, ..., \mathsf{id}_n$, and $\mathsf{sk}_{\mathsf{id}_1,...,\mathsf{id}_n}$ produced by $\mathsf{KeyGen}(\mathsf{msk}, (\mathsf{id}_1, ..., \mathsf{id}_n))$, we have

$$|\mathsf{sk}_{\mathsf{id}_1,...,\mathsf{id}_n}| = \mathrm{poly}(\lambda)$$

where poly is a fixed polynomial that does not depend on n.

Remark 3. If we do not require the key-compactness, it is trivial to construct an MIBE scheme from any IBE scheme.

3.2 MIBE from IPE

Here, we give a key-compactness-preserving construction of an MIBE scheme based on an IPE scheme. Actually, this construction is implicit in the work by Katz, Sahai and Waters [KSW08]. We give the full description for completeness. Let $\mathsf{IPE} = (\mathsf{Setup}_{\mathsf{IPE}}, \mathsf{KeyGen}_{\mathsf{IPE}}, \mathsf{Enc}_{\mathsf{IPE}}, \mathsf{Dec}_{\mathsf{IPE}})$ be an IPE scheme. We construct an MIBE scheme $\mathsf{MIBE} = (\mathsf{Setup}_{\mathsf{MIBE}}, \mathsf{KeyGen}_{\mathsf{MIBE}}, \mathsf{Enc}_{\mathsf{MIBE}}, \mathsf{Dec}_{\mathsf{MIBE}})$ as follows.

$\mathsf{Setup}_{\mathsf{MIBE}}(1^\lambda, 1^n)$: This algorithm runs $(\mathsf{pp}, \mathsf{msk}) \xleftarrow{\mathsf{R}} \mathsf{Setup}_{\mathsf{IPE}}(1^\lambda, 1^{n+1})$ and outputs $(\mathsf{pp}, \mathsf{msk})$. If pp specifies vector space $\mathbb{Z}_q^n$ as an IPE scheme, an identity-space of MIBE is specified to be $\mathbb{Z}_q$.

$\mathsf{KeyGen}_{\mathsf{MIBE}}(\mathsf{msk}, (\mathsf{id}_1, ..., \mathsf{id}_n) \in \mathbb{Z}_q^n)$: This algorithm computes $\{y_i \in \mathbb{Z}_q\}_{i \in \{0,...,n\}}$ such that $\prod_{i=1}^n (X - \mathsf{id}_n) = \sum_{i=0}^n y_i X^i$ as a polynomial in the indeterminate X, sets $\boldsymbol{y} := (y_0, ..., y_n)$, runs $\mathsf{sk}_{\boldsymbol{y}} \xleftarrow{\mathsf{R}} \mathsf{KeyGen}_{\mathsf{IPE}}(\mathsf{msk}, \boldsymbol{y})$ and outputs $\mathsf{sk}_{(\mathsf{id}_1,...,\mathsf{id}_n)} := \mathsf{sk}_{\boldsymbol{y}}$.

$\mathsf{Enc}_{\mathsf{MIBE}}(\mathsf{id}, \mathsf{m})$: This algorithm sets $\boldsymbol{x} := (1, \mathsf{id}, \mathsf{id}^2, ..., \mathsf{id}^n)$, where id^i denotes the i-th power of id on $\mathbb{Z}_q$, runs $\mathsf{ct} \xleftarrow{\mathsf{R}} \mathsf{Enc}_{\mathsf{IPE}}(\boldsymbol{x}, \mathsf{m})$ and outputs ct.

$\mathsf{Dec}_{\mathsf{MIBE}}(\mathsf{sk}_{(\mathsf{id}_1,...,\mathsf{id}_n)}, (\mathsf{id}_1, ..., \mathsf{id}_n), \mathsf{ct})$: This algorithm computes $\boldsymbol{y}$ similarly to in $\mathsf{KeyGen}_{\mathsf{MIBE}}$, runs $\mathsf{m} \xleftarrow{\mathsf{R}} \mathsf{Dec}_{\mathsf{IPE}}(\mathsf{sk}_{(\mathsf{id}_1,...,\mathsf{id}_n)}, \boldsymbol{y}, \mathsf{ct})$ and outputs m.

Correctness. Suppose that we have $\mathsf{id} \in \{\mathsf{id}_1, ..., \mathsf{id}_n\}$. Let $\boldsymbol{x} := (1, \mathsf{id}, \mathsf{id}^2, ..., \mathsf{id}^n)$ and $\boldsymbol{y}$ be the vector associated with $\{\mathsf{id}_1, ..., \mathsf{id}_n\}$ specified as in the description of $\mathsf{KeyGen}_{\mathsf{MIBE}}$. Then we have $\boldsymbol{x}^T \boldsymbol{y} = \sum_{i=0}^n y_i \mathsf{id}^i = \prod_{i=1}^n (\mathsf{id} - \mathsf{id}_n) = 0$. Therefore the correctness of MIBE follows from the correctness of IPE.

Security

Theorem 2. *If* IPE *is adaptively (resp. selectively) secure, then* MIBE *is adaptively (resp. selectively) secure. Moreover, if* IPE *is fully key-compact, then* MIBE *is fully key-compact.*

Proof. First, it is easy to see that MIBE is fully key-compact if IPE is fully key-compact since a decryption key $\mathsf{sk}_{(\mathsf{id}_1,...,\mathsf{id}_n)}$ of MIBE consists of a single secret key $\mathsf{sk}_{\boldsymbol{y}}$ of IPE whose size is polynomial in λ due to the full key-compactness of IPE. Then, we reduce the security of MIBE to IPE. Here, we only give the proof for the adaptive case because the selective case can be proven similarly. Let $\mathcal{A} = (\mathcal{A}_1, \mathcal{A}_2)$ be an admissible adversary against the adaptive security of MIBE. Then we construct an adversary $\mathcal{B} = (\mathcal{B}_1, \mathcal{B}_2)$ against the adaptive security of IPE as follows.

$\mathcal{B}_1^{\mathsf{KeyGen}_{\mathsf{IPE}}(\mathsf{msk}, \cdot)}(\mathsf{pp})$: This algorithm runs $\mathcal{A}_1^{\mathsf{KeyGen}_{\mathsf{MIBE}}(\mathsf{msk}, \cdot)}(\mathsf{pp})$. When $\mathcal{A}_1$ queries $(\mathsf{id}_1, ..., \mathsf{id}_n)$ to $\mathsf{KeyGen}_{\mathsf{MIBE}}(\mathsf{msk}, \cdot)$, $\mathcal{B}_1$ computes $\{y_i \in \mathbb{Z}_q\}_{i \in \{0,...,n\}}$ such that $\prod_{i=1}^{n}(X - \mathsf{id}_n) = \sum_{i=0}^{n} y_i X^i$, sets $\boldsymbol{y} := (y_0, ..., y_n)$, queries $\boldsymbol{y}$ to its own oracle $\mathsf{KeyGen}_{\mathsf{IPE}}(\mathsf{msk}, \cdot)$ to obtain $\mathsf{sk}_{\boldsymbol{y}}$, sets $\mathsf{sk}_{(\mathsf{id}_1,...,\mathsf{id}_n)} := \mathsf{sk}_{\boldsymbol{y}}$, and returns $\mathsf{sk}_{(\mathsf{id}_1,...,\mathsf{id}_n)}$ as a response by the oracle $\mathsf{KeyGen}_{\mathsf{MIBE}}(\mathsf{msk}, \cdot)$. When $\mathcal{A}_1$ outputs $(\mathsf{id}^*, \mathsf{m}_0, \mathsf{m}_1, \mathsf{st})$, $\mathcal{B}_1$ sets $\boldsymbol{x}^* := (1, \mathsf{id}^*, (\mathsf{id}^*)^2, ..., (\mathsf{id}^*)^n)$ and outputs $(\boldsymbol{x}^*, \mathsf{m}_0, \mathsf{m}_1, \mathsf{st})$.

$\mathcal{B}_2^{\mathsf{KeyGen}_{\mathsf{IPE}}(\mathsf{msk}, \cdot)}(\mathsf{ct}^*, \mathsf{st})$: This algorithms runs $\mathcal{A}_2^{\mathsf{KeyGen}_{\mathsf{MIBE}}(\mathsf{msk}, \cdot)}(\mathsf{ct}^*, \mathsf{st})$. When $\mathcal{A}_2$ queries $(\mathsf{id}_1, ..., \mathsf{id}_n)$ to $\mathsf{KeyGen}_{\mathsf{MIBE}}(\mathsf{msk}, \cdot)$, $\mathcal{B}_2$ computes $\{y_i \in \mathbb{Z}_q\}_{i \in \{0,...,n\}}$ such that $\prod_{i=1}^{n}(X - \mathsf{id}_n) = \sum_{i=0}^{n} y_i X^i$, sets $\boldsymbol{y} := (y_0, ..., y_n)$, queries $\boldsymbol{y}$ to its own oracle $\mathsf{KeyGen}_{\mathsf{IPE}}(\mathsf{msk}, \cdot)$ to obtain $\mathsf{sk}_{\boldsymbol{y}}$, sets $\mathsf{sk}_{(\mathsf{id}_1,...,\mathsf{id}_n)} := \mathsf{sk}_{\boldsymbol{y}}$, and returns $\mathsf{sk}_{(\mathsf{id}_1,...,\mathsf{id}_n)}$ as a response by the oracle $\mathsf{KeyGen}_{\mathsf{MIBE}}(\mathsf{msk}, \cdot)$. When $\mathcal{A}_2$ outputs $\widehat{\mathsf{coin}}$, $\mathcal{B}_2$ outputs $\widehat{\mathsf{coin}}$.

It is easy to see that $\mathcal{B}$ perfectly simulates $\mathsf{KeyGen}_{\mathsf{MIBE}}(\mathsf{msk}, \cdot)$ for $\mathcal{A}$, and the challenge ciphertext simulated by $\mathcal{B}$ is a correct encryption of $\mathsf{m}_{\mathsf{coin}}$ where coin is the random coin chosen by the challenger in the experiment $\mathcal{B}$ is involved. Therefore, we have $\mathsf{Adv}_{\mathsf{MIBE}, \mathcal{A}}^{\mathsf{CPA}}(\lambda) = \mathsf{Adv}_{\mathsf{IPE}, \mathcal{B}}^{\mathsf{CPA}}(\lambda)$. What is left is to prove that $\mathcal{B}$ is admissible if $\mathcal{A}$ is admissible. Let $\boldsymbol{y} = (y_0, ..., y_n)$ be the corresponding vector to a queried set of identities $(\mathsf{id}_1, ..., \mathsf{id}_n)$ by $\mathcal{A}$, i.e., $\boldsymbol{y}$ satisfies $\prod_{i=1}^{n}(X - \mathsf{id}_n) = \sum_{i=0}^{n} y_i X^i$, and $\boldsymbol{x}^* := (1, \mathsf{id}^*, (\mathsf{id}^*)^2, ..., (\mathsf{id}^*)^n)$. Then we have $(\boldsymbol{x}^*)^T \boldsymbol{y} = \sum_{i=0}^{n} y_i (\mathsf{id}^*)^i = \prod_{i=1}^{n}(\mathsf{id}^* - \mathsf{id}_n) \neq 0$ where the last inequality holds because we have $\mathsf{id}^* \notin \{\mathsf{id}_1, ..., \mathsf{id}_n\}$ due to the admissibility of $\mathcal{A}$. This completes the proof. ∎

3.3   IB-HPS from MIBE

Here, we give a construction of an IB-HPS based on any MIBE scheme. Moreover, we show that if the underlying MIBE scheme is fully key-compact, then the universality-ratio of the resulting IB-HPS can be made arbitrarily close to 1.

Let $\mathsf{MIBE} = (\mathsf{Setup}_{\mathsf{MIBE}}, \mathsf{KeyGen}_{\mathsf{MIBE}}, \mathsf{Enc}_{\mathsf{MIBE}}, \mathsf{Dec}_{\mathsf{MIBE}})$ be an MIBE scheme with a message space $\mathcal{M}$ and an identity space $\{0,1\}^{\ell_{\mathsf{id}}}$. We assume that there exists a positive integer ℓ_{k} such that $\{0,1\}^{\ell_{\mathsf{k}}}$ can be embedded into $\mathcal{M}$, i.e., there exists an efficiently computable injective function $\sigma : \{0,1\}^{\ell_{\mathsf{k}}} \to \mathcal{M}$. In the following, we often identify $\mathsf{k} \in \{0,1\}^{\ell_{\mathsf{k}}}$ with $\sigma(\mathsf{k})$ and treat k as an element of $\mathcal{M}$. Let $\mathsf{PRF} : \mathcal{K} \times \{0,1\}^{\ell_{\mathsf{id}}} \to \mathcal{R}$ where $\mathcal{R}$ denotes the randomness space for $\mathsf{KeyGen}_{\mathsf{MIBE}}$. Then for any positive integer n, we construct an IB-HPS $\Pi_n = (\mathsf{Setup}_{\mathsf{HPS}}, \mathsf{KeyGen}_{\mathsf{HPS}}, \mathsf{Encap}_{\mathsf{HPS}}, \mathsf{Encap}_{\mathsf{HPS}}^*, \mathsf{Decap}_{\mathsf{HPS}})$ with identity space $\{0,1\}^{\ell_{\mathsf{id}} - \lceil \log n \rceil - 1}$ and key space $\{0,1\}^{\ell_{\mathsf{k}}}$ as follows, where $\mathsf{bin}(m)$ denotes a binary representation of an integer m.

$\mathsf{Setup}_{\mathsf{HPS}}(1^\lambda)$: This algorithm generates $(\mathsf{pp}, \mathsf{msk}) \xleftarrow{\text{R}} \mathsf{Setup}_{\mathsf{MIBE}}(1^\lambda, 1^n)$, chooses a PRF key $K \xleftarrow{\text{R}} \mathcal{K}$, and outputs pp and (msk, K) as its public parameter and master secret key.

$\mathsf{KeyGen}_{\mathsf{HPS}}((\mathsf{msk}, K), \mathsf{id})$: This algorithm picks $r_i \xleftarrow{\text{R}} \{0,1\}$ for $i \in [n]$, generates $\mathsf{sk}'_{\mathsf{id}} \xleftarrow{\text{R}} \mathsf{KeyGen}_{\mathsf{MIBE}}(\mathsf{msk}, (\mathsf{id}\|\mathsf{bin}(1)\|r_1, ..., \mathsf{id}\|\mathsf{bin}(n)\|r_n); \mathsf{PRF}(K, \mathsf{id}))$, and outputs $\mathsf{sk}_{\mathsf{id}} := (\mathsf{sk}'_{\mathsf{id}}, \{r_i\}_{i \in [n]})$.

$\mathsf{Encap}_{\mathsf{HPS}}(\mathsf{id})$: This algorithm picks $\mathsf{k}_i \in \{0,1\}^{\ell_\mathsf{k}}$ for $i \in [n]$, generates $\mathsf{ct}_{i,b} \xleftarrow{\text{R}} \mathsf{Enc}_{\mathsf{MIBE}}(\mathsf{id}\|\mathsf{bin}(i)\|b, \mathsf{k}_i)$ for $i \in [n]$ and $b \in \{0,1\}$, sets $\mathsf{ct} := \{\mathsf{ct}_{i,b}\}_{i \in [n], b \in \{0,1\}}$ and $\mathsf{k} := \bigoplus_{i \in [n]} \mathsf{k}_i$, and outputs $(\mathsf{ct}, \mathsf{k})$.

$\mathsf{Encap}^*_{\mathsf{HPS}}(\mathsf{id})$: This algorithm picks $\mathsf{k}_{i,b} \in \{0,1\}^{\ell_\mathsf{k}}$ for $i \in [n]$ and $b \in \{0,1\}$, generates $\mathsf{ct}_{i,b} \xleftarrow{\text{R}} \mathsf{Enc}_{\mathsf{MIBE}}(\mathsf{id}\|\mathsf{bin}(i)\|b, \mathsf{k}_{i,b})$ for all $i \in [n]$, $b \in \{0,1\}$, sets $\mathsf{ct} := \{\mathsf{ct}_{i,b}\}_{i \in [n], b \in \{0,1\}}$, and outputs ct.

$\mathsf{Decap}_{\mathsf{HPS}}(\mathsf{sk}_{\mathsf{id}}, \mathsf{id}, \mathsf{ct})$:

This algorithm parses $(\mathsf{sk}'_{\mathsf{id}}, \{r_i\}_{i \in [n]}) \leftarrow \mathsf{sk}_{\mathsf{id}}$ and $\{\mathsf{ct}_{i,b}\}_{i \in [n], b \in \{0,1\}} \leftarrow \mathsf{ct}$, runs $\mathsf{k}'_i \leftarrow \mathsf{Dec}_{\mathsf{MIBE}}(\mathsf{sk}'_{\mathsf{id}}, (\mathsf{id}\|\mathsf{bin}(1)\|r_1, ..., \mathsf{id}\|\mathsf{bin}(n)\|r_n), \mathsf{ct}_{i,r_i})$, and outputs $\mathsf{k} := \bigoplus_{i \in [n]} \mathsf{k}'_i$

Correctness. Correctness of Π_n is easy to see given the correctness of MIBE.

Security

Theorem 3. *If* MIBE *is adaptively (resp. selectively) secure MIBE scheme, then Π_n is an adaptively (resp. selectively) secure and $(n, 2^{-\ell_\mathsf{k}})$-universal IB-HPS with the universality-ratio $\frac{n}{n + \ell_{\mathsf{sk}}(n)}$ where $\ell_{\mathsf{sk}}(n)$ denotes the maximum length of* sk *generated by* $\mathsf{KeyGen}_{\mathsf{MIBE}}(\mathsf{msk}, \cdot)$ *where* $(\mathsf{pp}, \mathsf{msk}) \xleftarrow{\text{R}} \mathsf{Setup}_{\mathsf{MIBE}}(1^\lambda, 1^n)$. *Especially, if* MIBE *is fully key-compact, then we can make the universality-ratio arbitrarily close to 1 by increasing n.*

Proof

Valid/Invalid Ciphertext Indistinguishability. First, we prove that Π_n is adaptively (resp. selectively) secure if MIBE is adaptively (resp. selectively) secure. Here, we only give the proof for the adaptive case because the selective case can be proven similarly. We assume that there exists a PPT adversary $\mathcal{A} = (\mathcal{A}_1, \mathcal{A}_2)$ that breaks the adaptive security of Π_n. We consider the following sequence of hybrid games.

Game_0: This game simulates the environment of $\mathsf{Expt}^{\mathsf{ind}}_{\Pi_n, \mathcal{A}}(\lambda)$ for the case of $\mathsf{coin} = 0$ (where $\mathcal{A}$ is always given a valid ciphertext) to $\mathcal{A}$. $\widehat{\mathsf{coin}}$ output by $\mathcal{A}$ is treated as the output of this game.

Game'_0: This game is the same as Game_0 except that the challenger uses a fresh randomness instead of $\mathsf{PRF}(K, \mathsf{id})$ when responding to $\mathcal{A}$'s key generation queries. We denote this modified key generation oracle by $\mathsf{KeyGen}'_{\mathsf{HPS}}(\mathsf{msk}, \cdot)$. We note that K is not needed for simulating $\mathsf{KeyGen}'_{\mathsf{HPS}}(\mathsf{msk}, \cdot)$.

Game'_x: For $x = 0, ..., n$, we consider the following games. We remark that the definitions of Game'_0 given above and below is consistent.

Game$'_x$:

$(\mathsf{pp}, \mathsf{msk}) \xleftarrow{\mathsf{R}} \mathsf{Setup}_{\mathsf{MIBE}}(1^\lambda)$

$(\mathsf{id}^*, \mathsf{st}_{\mathcal{A}}) \xleftarrow{\mathsf{R}} \mathcal{A}_1^{\mathsf{KeyGen}'_{\mathsf{HPS}}(\mathsf{msk}, \cdot)}(\mathsf{pp})$

For $i = 1$ to x

  $\mathsf{k}_{i,0}, \mathsf{k}_{i,1} \xleftarrow{\mathsf{R}} \{0,1\}^{\ell_k}$

For $i = x+1$ to n

  $\mathsf{k}_{i,0} \xleftarrow{\mathsf{R}} \{0,1\}^{\ell_k}$

  $\mathsf{k}_{i,1} := \mathsf{k}_{i,0}$

For $i \in [n]$, $b \in \{0,1\}$

  $\mathsf{ct}^*_{i,b} \xleftarrow{\mathsf{R}} \mathsf{Enc}_{\mathsf{MIBE}}(\mathsf{id}^* \| \mathsf{bin}(i) \| b, \mathsf{k}_{i,b})$

$\mathsf{ct}^* := \{\mathsf{ct}^*_{i,b}\}_{i \in [n], b \in \{0,1\}}$

$\widetilde{\mathsf{coin}} \xleftarrow{\mathsf{R}} \mathcal{A}_2^{\mathsf{KeyGen}'_{\mathsf{HPS}}(\mathsf{msk}, \cdot)}(\mathsf{ct}^*, \mathsf{st}_{\mathcal{A}})$

Return $\widetilde{\mathsf{coin}}$.

It is easy to see that Game$'_n$ simulates the environment of $\mathsf{Expt}^{\mathsf{ind}}_{\Pi_n, \mathcal{A}}(\lambda)$ given $\mathsf{coin} = 1$ (where $\mathcal{A}$ is always given an invalid ciphertext) to $\mathcal{A}$. Therefore, we have $|\Pr[1 \xleftarrow{\mathsf{R}} \mathsf{Game}_0] - \Pr[1 \xleftarrow{\mathsf{R}} \mathsf{Game}'_n]| = \mathsf{Adv}^{\mathsf{ind}}_{\Pi_n, \mathcal{A}}(\lambda)$. We prove that this is negligible by showing the following lemmas.

Lemma 1. *There exists a PPT adversary $\mathcal{B}$ against PRF such that* $|\Pr[\mathsf{Game}_0 = 1] - \Pr[\mathsf{Game}'_0 = 1]| = \mathsf{Adv}_{\mathsf{PRF}, \mathcal{B}}(\lambda)$.

Proof. The PRF key K is used only when simulating the key generation oracle, and evaluations of the PRF on the same input id is not repeated more than once since $\mathcal{A}$ is not allowed to query the same identity more than once. Therefore, it is straightforward to reduce the distinguishing advantage between these two games to the security of PRF. ∎

Lemma 2. *For $x \in [n]$, there exists an admissible adversary $\mathcal{B}$ against MIBE such that* $|\Pr[\mathsf{Game}'_{x-1} = 1] - \Pr[\mathsf{Game}'_x = 1]| = \mathsf{Adv}^{\mathsf{CPA}}_{\mathsf{MIBE}, \mathcal{B}}(\lambda)$.

Proof. We assume that $\mathcal{A}$ distinguishes Game$'_x$ and Game$'_{x+1}$, and construct a PPT adversary $\mathcal{B} = (\mathcal{B}_1, \mathcal{B}_2)$ that breaks the adaptive security of MIBE. We describe $\mathcal{B}$ below.

$\mathcal{B}_1^{\mathsf{KeyGen}_{\mathsf{MIBE}}(\mathsf{msk}, \cdot)}(\mathsf{pp})$: It runs $(\mathsf{id}^*, \mathsf{st}_{\mathcal{A}}) \xleftarrow{\mathsf{R}} \mathcal{A}_1^{\mathsf{KeyGen}'_{\mathsf{HPS}}(\mathsf{msk}, \cdot)}(\mathsf{pp})$ where $\mathcal{B}$ simulates $\mathsf{KeyGen}'_{\mathsf{HPS}}$ to $\mathcal{A}_1$ as follows. When $\mathcal{A}_1$ makes its j-th query $\mathsf{id}^{(j)}$ to $\mathsf{KeyGen}'_{\mathsf{HPS}}$, it randomly picks $r_i^{(j)} \xleftarrow{\mathsf{R}} \{0,1\}$ for $i \in [n]$, queries $(\mathsf{id}^{(j)} \| \mathsf{bin}(1) \| r_1^{(j)}, ..., \mathsf{id}^{(j)} \| \mathsf{bin}(n) \| r_n^{(j)})$ to its own oracle $\mathsf{KeyGen}_{\mathsf{MIBE}}$ to obtain $\mathsf{sk}_{\mathsf{id}}^{(j)'}$, and gives $(\mathsf{sk}_{\mathsf{id}}^{(j)'}, \{r_i^{(j)}\}_{i \in [n]})$ to $\mathcal{A}_1$ as a response from the oracle $\mathsf{KeyGen}'_{\mathsf{HPS}}$. If there exists $j \in [Q]$ such that $\mathsf{id}^* = \mathsf{id}^{(j)}$, then it sets $r_x^* := r_x^{(j)}$. Otherwise it picks $r_x^* \xleftarrow{\mathsf{R}} \{0,1\}$. It picks $\mathsf{k}_{x,0}, \mathsf{k}_{x,1} \xleftarrow{\mathsf{R}} \{0,1\}^{\ell_k}$ and sets $\mathsf{st}_{\mathcal{B}} := (\mathsf{st}_{\mathcal{A}}, r_x^*, \mathsf{k}_{x,0}, \mathsf{k}_{x,1})$. Then, $\mathcal{B}_1$ outputs $(\mathsf{id} \| \mathsf{bin}(x) \| (1 - r_x^*), \mathsf{k}_{x, r_x^*}, \mathsf{k}_{x, 1 - r_x^*}, \mathsf{st}_{\mathcal{B}})$.

$\mathcal{B}_2^{\mathsf{KeyGen}_{\mathsf{MIBE}}(\mathsf{msk}, \cdot)}(\mathsf{ct}^*_{\mathsf{MIBE}}, \mathsf{st}_{\mathcal{B}})$: It parses $\{\mathsf{ct}_{i,b}\}_{i \in [n], b \in \{0,1\}} \leftarrow \mathsf{ct}^*$ and $(\mathsf{st}_{\mathcal{A}}, r_x^*) \leftarrow \mathsf{st}_{\mathcal{B}}$. It picks $\mathsf{k}_{i,0}, \mathsf{k}_{i,1} \xleftarrow{\mathsf{R}} \{0,1\}^{\ell_k}$ for $i = 1, ..., x - 1$. It picks $\mathsf{k}_{i,0} \xleftarrow{\mathsf{R}} \{0,1\}^{\ell_k}$ and sets $\mathsf{k}_{i,1} := \mathsf{k}_{i,0}$ for $i = x + 1, ..., n$. It computes $\mathsf{ct}^*_{i,b} \xleftarrow{\mathsf{R}} \mathsf{Enc}_{\mathsf{MIBE}}(\mathsf{id} \| \mathsf{bin}(i) \| b, \mathsf{k}_{i,b})$ for all $(i, b) \in ([n] \times \{0,1\}) \setminus \{(x, 1 - r_x^*)\}$, and sets $\mathsf{ct}^*_{x, 1 - r_x^*} := \mathsf{ct}^*_{\mathsf{MIBE}}$. Then, it sets $\mathsf{ct}^*_{\mathsf{HPS}} := \{\mathsf{ct}^*_{i,b}\}_{i \in [n], b \in \{0,1\}}$ and runs

$\widehat{\mathsf{coin}} \xleftarrow{\mathsf{R}} \mathcal{A}_2^{\mathsf{KeyGen}'_{\mathsf{HPS}}(\mathsf{msk},\cdot)}(\mathsf{ct}^*_{\mathsf{HPS}}, \mathsf{st}_\mathcal{A})$ where $\mathcal{B}_2$ simulates $\mathsf{KeyGen}'_{\mathsf{HPS}}(\mathsf{msk},\cdot)$ as follows. When $\mathcal{A}_2$ makes a j-th query $\mathsf{id}^{(j)}$ to $\mathsf{KeyGen}'_{\mathsf{HPS}}(\mathsf{msk},\cdot)$ (where the number of query is counted through $\mathcal{A}_1$ and $\mathcal{A}_2$), if $\mathsf{id}^{(j)} \neq \mathsf{id}^*$, then $\mathcal{B}_2$ randomly picks $r_i^{(j)} \xleftarrow{\mathsf{R}} \{0,1\}$ for $i \in [n]$, and otherwise it randomly picks $r_i^{(j)} \xleftarrow{\mathsf{R}} \{0,1\}$ for $i \in [n] \setminus \{x\}$ and sets $r_x^{(j)} := r_x^*$. Then, $\mathcal{B}_2$ queries $(\mathsf{id}^{(j)}\|\mathsf{bin}(1)\|r_1^{(j)}, ..., \mathsf{id}^{(j)}\|\mathsf{bin}(n)\|r_n^{(j)})$ to its own oracle $\mathsf{KeyGen}_{\mathsf{MIBE}}(\mathsf{msk},\cdot)$ to obtain $\mathsf{sk}_{\mathsf{id}}^{(j)'}$, and gives $(\mathsf{sk}_{\mathsf{id}}^{(j)'}, \{r_i^{(j)}\}_{i\in[n]})$ to $\mathcal{A}_2$ as a response from the oracle $\mathsf{KeyGen}'_{\mathsf{HPS}}(\mathsf{msk},\cdot)$. Finally, $\mathcal{B}_2$ outputs coin'.

This completes the description of $\mathcal{B}$. First, we can see that $\mathcal{B}$ is admissible because $\mathcal{B}$'s query to its oracle never contains $\mathsf{id}^*\|\mathsf{bin}(x)\|(1-r_x^*)$. If the random coin chosen by the challenger of $\mathsf{Expt}^{\mathsf{CPA}}_{\mathsf{MIBE},\mathcal{B}}$, which is the experiment $\mathcal{B}$ is involved in, is 0, then $\mathcal{B}$ perfectly simulates Game'_{x-1} to $\mathcal{A}$, and if the coin is 1, then $\mathcal{B}$ perfectly simulates Game'_x to $\mathcal{A}$. Therefore we have $|\Pr[\mathsf{Game}'_{x-1} = 1] - \Pr[\mathsf{Game}'_x = 1]| = \mathsf{Adv}^{\mathsf{CPA}}_{\mathsf{MIBE},\mathcal{B}}(\lambda)$ as desired.   ∎

Due to the above lemmas and the triangle inequality, if PRF is a secure PRF and MIBE is adaptively secure, then $|\Pr[1 \xleftarrow{\mathsf{R}} \mathsf{Game}_0] - \Pr[1 \xleftarrow{\mathsf{R}} \mathsf{Game}'_n]| = \mathsf{Adv}^{\mathsf{ind}}_{\Pi,\mathcal{A}}(\lambda)$ is negligible, and thus Π_n is adaptively secure.

Universality. We prove that Π_n is $(n, 2^{-\ell_k})$-universal. First, for any fixed $(\mathsf{msk}, \mathsf{pp})$ and $\mathsf{id} \in \{0,1\}^{\ell_{\mathsf{id}}}$, we have $\mathsf{H}_\infty(\mathsf{sk}_{\mathsf{id}}) = n$ where $\mathsf{sk}_{\mathsf{id}} \xleftarrow{\mathsf{R}} \mathsf{KeyGen}_{\mathsf{HPS}}(\mathsf{msk}, \mathsf{id})$ because a different choice of $\{r_i\}_{i\in[n]} \in \{0,1\}^n$ gives a different value of $\mathsf{sk}_{\mathsf{id}}$. For any fixed $(\mathsf{msk}, \mathsf{pp})$ and $\mathsf{id} \in \{0,1\}^{\ell_{\mathsf{id}}}$, let $\mathsf{sk}_{\mathsf{id}} = (\mathsf{sk}'_{\mathsf{id}}, \{r_i\}_{i\in[n]})$ and $\overline{\mathsf{sk}}_{\mathsf{id}} = (\overline{\mathsf{sk}}'_{\mathsf{id}}, \{\overline{r}_i\}_{i\in[n]})$ be distinct secret keys produced by $\mathsf{KeyGen}_{\mathsf{HPS}}(\mathsf{msk}, \mathsf{id})$. Since the first component $\mathsf{sk}'_{\mathsf{id}}$ in a secret key $\mathsf{sk}_{\mathsf{id}}$ is deterministically derived from msk, id, and $\{r_i\}_{i\in[n]}$, we must have $\{r_i\}_{i\in[n]} \neq \{\overline{r}_i\}_{i\in[n]}$. Let ct be an invalid ciphertext generated by $\mathsf{Encap}^*(\mathsf{id})$, i.e., we pick $\mathsf{k}_{i,b} \in \{0,1\}^{\ell_k}$ for $i \in [n]$ and $b \in \{0,1\}$, generate $\mathsf{ct}_{i,b} \xleftarrow{\mathsf{R}} \mathsf{Enc}_{\mathsf{MIBE}}(\mathsf{id}\|\mathsf{bin}(i)\|b, \mathsf{k}_{i,b})$ for all $i \in [n]$, $b \in \{0,1\}$ and set $\mathsf{ct} := \{\mathsf{ct}_{i,b}\}_{i\in[n],b\in\{0,1\}}$. Then, we have $\mathsf{Decap}(\mathsf{sk}_{\mathsf{id}}, \mathsf{id}, \mathsf{ct}) = \bigoplus_{i=1}^n \mathsf{k}_{i,r_i}$ and $\mathsf{Decap}(\overline{\mathsf{sk}}_{\mathsf{id}}, \mathsf{id}, \mathsf{ct}) = \bigoplus_{i=1}^n \mathsf{k}_{i,\overline{r}_i}$ by the correctness of MIBE. Since there exists $i^* \in [n]$ such that $r_{i^*} \neq \overline{r}_{i^*}$ and $\mathsf{k}_{i^*,0}$ and $\mathsf{k}_{i^*,1}$ are independently random, $\mathsf{Decap}(\mathsf{sk}_{\mathsf{id}}, \mathsf{id}, \mathsf{ct})$ and $\mathsf{Decap}(\overline{\mathsf{sk}}_{\mathsf{id}}, \mathsf{id}, \mathsf{ct})$ are independently random. Therefore, we have

$$\Pr_{\mathsf{ct} \xleftarrow{\mathsf{R}} \mathsf{Encap}^*(\mathsf{id})}[\mathsf{Decap}(\mathsf{sk}_{\mathsf{id}}, \mathsf{id}, \mathsf{ct}) = \mathsf{Decap}(\overline{\mathsf{sk}}_{\mathsf{id}}, \mathsf{id}, \mathsf{ct})] \leq 2^{-\ell_k}.$$

Therefore Π_n is $(n, 2^{-\ell_k})$-universal. Since a secret key $\mathsf{sk}_{\mathsf{id}}$ of Π_n consists of a secret key $\mathsf{sk}'_{\mathsf{id}}$ of MIBE and an n-bit string $\{r_i\}_{i\in[n]}$, the secret key size of Π_n is $n + \ell_{\mathsf{sk}}(n)$. Therefore, the universality-ratio of Π_n is $\frac{n}{n+\ell_{\mathsf{sk}}(n)}$. Especially, if MIBE is fully key-compact, then $\ell_{\mathsf{sk}}(n)$ is a fixed polynomial in λ that does not depend on n, and thus we can make the universality-ratio arbitrarily close to 1 by increasing n.   ∎

4 Leakage Resilient IBE in BRM

Here, we first observe that combining Theorems 1, 2, and 3, we can construct a leakage resilient IBE scheme in the BRM based on any IPE scheme, and the leakage-ratio of the resulting IBE scheme can be made arbitrary close to 1 if the underlying IPE is fully key-compact. Then we give some instantiations for it.

4.1 Construction from IPE

Combining Theorems 1, 2, and 3, we obtain the following corollary.

Corollary 1. *Suppose we have an adaptively (resp. selectively) secure fully key-compact IPE scheme with vector space $\mathbb{Z}_q^n$ whose secret key size is $|\mathsf{sk}_{\mathsf{IPE}}(n)|$ where $q = \lambda^{\omega(1)}$ and the dimension $n \in \mathbb{N}$ can be flexibly chosen by the setup algorithm. Then for any $n = \mathrm{poly}(\lambda)$ and constant $\epsilon > 0$, we can construct an adaptively (resp. selectively) secure leakage resilient IBE scheme in the BRM with identity-space $\{0,1\}^{\lfloor \frac{\log q}{2} \rfloor}$ and message space $\{0,1\}^v$ such that*

1. *Public parameter/master secret key size is almost the same as that of the underlying IPE scheme.*
2. *Ciphertext-size/encryption-time/decryption-time are $O(n(v+\lambda))$ times larger than that of the underlying IPE with dimension n.*
3. *leakage-ratio is $(1 - \epsilon)(\frac{n}{n+|\mathsf{sk}_{\mathsf{IPE}}(n)|})$ for sufficiently large values of the leakage parameter ℓ.*

Especially, by choosing sufficiently large $n = O(|\mathsf{sk}_{\mathsf{IPE}}(n)|)$, we can make the leakage-ratio $1 - \epsilon$ for any constant $\epsilon > 0$.

Proof. Suppose we have an adaptively (resp. selectively) secure fully key-compact IPE scheme with vector space $\mathbb{Z}_q^n$. By Theorem 2, we can construct an adaptively (resp. selectively) secure fully key-compact MIBE scheme whose identity-space is $\{0,1\}^{\lfloor \log q \rfloor}$ and public parameter/master secret key size, ciphertext-size/encryption-time/decryption-time, are almost the same as those of the underlying IPE. Then by Theorem 3, for any $n \in \mathbb{N}$, we can construct an adaptively (resp. selectively) secure IB-HPS whose identity-space is $\{0,1\}^{\lfloor \log q \rfloor - \lfloor \log(n) \rfloor - 1}$, master public/secret key size is the same as that of the underlying IPE scheme, ciphertext-size/encryption-time/decryption-time differ by a factor of $O(n)$ from those of the underlying IPE with dimension n, and universality-ratio $\frac{n}{n+|\mathsf{sk}_{\mathsf{IPE}}(n)|}$. Here, for sufficiently large λ, we have $\lfloor \log q \rfloor - \lfloor \log n \rfloor - 1 > \lfloor \frac{\log q}{2} \rfloor$ since we have $q = \lambda^{\omega(1)}$ and $n = \mathrm{poly}(\lambda)$. Therefore the identity-space of IB-HPS can be restricted to $\{0,1\}^{\lfloor \frac{\log q}{2} \rfloor}$. Finally, by applying Theorem 1 to this IB-HPS, we obtain Corollary 1. Especially, for any constant $\epsilon' > 0$, if we set $n > \frac{|\mathsf{sk}_{\mathsf{IPE}}(n)|}{\epsilon'}$ then we have $\frac{n}{n+|\mathsf{sk}_{\mathsf{IPE}}(n)|} > \frac{1}{1+\epsilon'}$. Thus we can make the leakage-ratio arbitrarily close to 1.   ∎

4.2   Instantiations

By Corollary 1, we can construct a leakage resilient IBE scheme in the BRM whose leakage-ratio is arbitrarily close to 1 based on any fully key-compact IPE scheme. We give a list of possible instantiations below. Note that all constructions are secure in the standard model. In the following, $|\mathsf{sk_{IPE}}|$ and $|\mathsf{ct_{IPE}}(n)|$ denotes the size of a secret key and a ciphertext when the dimension is set to be n. (Remark that since these schemes are fully-key-compact, $|\mathsf{sk_{IPE}}|$ does not depend on n.)

1. Wee constructed an adaptively secure IPE scheme from the subgroup decision assumption on composite-order pairing groups [Wee14]. The construction is fully key-compact since a secret key for vector $\boldsymbol{y} \in \mathbb{Z}_N^n$ consists of 2 group elements where N is the order of a group and consists of three distinct primes. A ciphertext of the scheme consists of n elements of the group. Namely, we have $|\mathsf{sk_{IPE}}| = O(N)$ and $|\mathsf{ct_{IPE}}(n)| = O(nN)$. For any constant $\epsilon > 0$, we can set $n = O(N)$ to achieve the leakage-ratio $1 - \epsilon$. In this case, the ciphertext size of the resulting IBE scheme is $O(N^3\lambda)$.

2. Chen et al. constructed an adaptively secure IPE scheme from the d-Lin assumption on prime-order pairing groups [CGW15]. The construction is fully key-compact since a secret key for vector $\boldsymbol{y} \in \mathbb{Z}_q^n$ consists of $2(d+1)$ group elements where q is the order of a group. If we use the 1-Lin (i.e., SXDH) assumption, only 4 group elements. A ciphertext of the scheme consists of $(n+1)(d+1)$ group elements and a message masking part. Namely, we have $|\mathsf{sk_{IPE}}| = O(d\lambda)$ and $|\mathsf{ct_{IPE}}(n)| = O(nd\lambda)$. For any constant $\epsilon > 0$, we can set $n = O(d\lambda)$ to achieve the leakage-ratio $1 - \epsilon$. In this case, the ciphertext size of the resulting IBE scheme is $O(d^3\lambda^4)$.

3. Agrawal et al. constructed a selectively secure IPE scheme from the LWE assumption [AFV11]. The construction is fully key-compact since a secret key for a vector $\boldsymbol{y} \in \mathbb{Z}_q^n$ is a vector of small length in $\mathbb{Z}^m$ where m does not depend on n. More precisely, a secret key consists of a vector of length of $O(\sigma\sqrt{m})$ (with overwhelming probability) in $\mathbb{Z}^{2m}$, and a ciphertext consists of $O(n \log q)$ vectors in $\mathbb{Z}_q^m$ where we can set $q = \mathrm{poly}(\lambda, n)$, $m = O(\lambda^{1+\delta})$ and $\sigma = \mathrm{poly}(\lambda, n)$ where $\delta > 0$ is an arbitrary constant. Namely, we have $|\mathsf{sk_{IPE}}| = \tilde{O}(\lambda^{1+\delta})$ and $|\mathsf{ct_{IPE}}(n)| = O(n\lambda^{1+\delta})$. For any constant $\epsilon > 0$, we can set $n = \tilde{O}(\lambda^{1+\delta})$ to achieve the leakage-ratio $1 - \epsilon$. In this case, the ciphertext size of the resulting IBE scheme is $\tilde{O}(\lambda^{4+3\delta})$.

4. We constructed a selectively secure IPE scheme from the CBDH assumption. This construction is an extension of Boneh-Boyen selectively secure IBE [BB04] and can be seen as a selectively secure variant of the scheme proposed by Chen et al. [CGW15] (which is an adaptively secure IPE scheme under the d-Lin assumption). The construction is fully key compact since a secret key for vector $\boldsymbol{y} \in \mathbb{Z}_q^n$ consists of 2 group elements where q is the order of a group. A ciphertext consists of $n+1$ group elements and a message masking part. Namely, we have $|\mathsf{sk_{IPE}}| = O(\lambda)$ and $|\mathsf{ct_{IPE}}(n)| = O(n\lambda)$. For any constant $\epsilon > 0$, we can set $n = O(\lambda)$ to achieve the leakage-ratio $1 - \epsilon$. In this case, the ciphertext size of the resulting IBE scheme is $O(\lambda^4)$.

Acknowledgments. We thank Daniel Wichs for helpful comments on the presentation.

A   Key-Compact IPE from CBDH or DBDH

Here, we give constructions of a fully key-compact selectively secure IPE scheme based on the CBDH or DBDH assumptions. The constructions are simple extensions of the Boneh-Boyen IBE [BB04] and can be seen as selectively secure variants of the adaptively secure short secret key IPE scheme by Chen, Gay, and Wee [CGW15].

A.1   Definitions

First, we define pairing groups and CBDH and DBDH assumptions for it. Let $\mathbb{G}_1$, $\mathbb{G}_2$ and $\mathbb{G}_T$ be groups of prime order q associated with a pairing $e : \mathbb{G}_1 \times \mathbb{G}_2 \to \mathbb{G}_T$. We require e to satisfy the following two properties.

Bilinearity For all $g_1 \in \mathbb{G}_1$, $g_2 \in \mathbb{G}_2$ and $a, b \in \mathbb{Z}_q$, it holds that $e(g_1^a, g_2^b) = e(g_1, g_2)^{ab}$.

Non-degeneracy If g_1 and g_2 generate $\mathbb{G}_1$ and $\mathbb{G}_2$ respectively, then $e(g_1, g_2) \neq 1$.

Definition 8 *(Computational Bilinear Diffie-Hellman Assumption). We say that the computational bilinear Diffie-Hellman (CBDH) assumption holds if for any PPT adversary $\mathcal{A}$, we have*

$$\mathsf{Adv}_{\mathcal{A}}^{\mathsf{cbdh}}(\lambda) := \Pr[e(g_1, g_2)^{xyz} \xleftarrow{\mathsf{R}} \mathcal{A}(g_1, g_1^\alpha, g_1^\beta, g_1^\gamma, g_2, g_2^\alpha, g_2^\beta, g_2^\gamma)] = \mathsf{negl}(\lambda)$$

where $g_1 \xleftarrow{\mathsf{R}} \mathbb{G}_1$, $g_2 \xleftarrow{\mathsf{R}} \mathbb{G}_2$ and $\alpha, \beta, \gamma \xleftarrow{\mathsf{R}} \mathbb{Z}_q$.

Definition 9 *(Decisional Bilinear Diffie-Hellman Assumption). We say that the decisional bilinear Diffie-Hellman (DBDH) assumption holds if for any PPT adversary $\mathcal{A}$, we have*

$$| \Pr[\mathcal{A}(g_1, g_1^\alpha, g_1^\beta, g_1^\gamma, g_2, g_2^\alpha, g_2^\beta, g_2^\gamma, T_0) = 1]$$
$$- \Pr[\mathcal{A}(g_1, g_1^\alpha, g_1^\beta, g_1^\gamma, g_2, g_2^\alpha, g_2^\beta, g_2^\gamma, T_1) = 1]| = \mathsf{negl}(\lambda)$$

where $g_1 \xleftarrow{\mathsf{R}} \mathbb{G}_1$, $g_2 \xleftarrow{\mathsf{R}} \mathbb{G}_2$, $\alpha, \beta, \gamma \xleftarrow{\mathsf{R}} \mathbb{Z}_q$, $T_0 := e(g_1, g_2)^{\alpha\beta\gamma}$, and $T_1 \xleftarrow{\mathsf{R}} \mathbb{G}_T$.

By the Goldreich-Levin theorem [GL89], the following lemma holds.

Lemma 3 *(Hardcore security of CBDH). If the CBDH assumption holds, then there exists a family $\mathcal{GL}$ of functions $\mathsf{hc} : \mathbb{G}_T \to \{0,1\}$ such that*

$$| \Pr[\mathcal{A}(g_1, g_1^\alpha, g_1^\beta, g_1^\gamma, g_2, g_2^\alpha, g_2^\beta, g_2^\gamma, \mathsf{hc}, T_0) = 1]$$
$$- \Pr[\mathcal{A}(g_1, g_1^\alpha, g_1^\beta, g_1^\gamma, g_2, g_2^\alpha, g_2^\beta, g_2^\gamma, \mathsf{hc}, T_1) = 1]| = \mathsf{negl}(\lambda)$$

where $g_1 \xleftarrow{\mathsf{R}} \mathbb{G}_1$, $g_2 \xleftarrow{\mathsf{R}} \mathbb{G}_2$, $\alpha, \beta, \gamma \xleftarrow{\mathsf{R}} \mathbb{Z}_q$, $\mathsf{hc} \xleftarrow{\mathsf{R}} \mathcal{GL}$, $T_0 := \mathsf{hc}(e(g_1, g_2)^{\alpha\beta\gamma})$, and $T_1 \xleftarrow{\mathsf{R}} \{0,1\}$.

A.2 Construction

We first describe our IPE scheme based on the CBDH assumption.

Setup($1^\lambda, 1^n$): It generates parameters of a pairing group $\mathsf{pp}_{\mathsf{bm}} := (q, \mathbb{G}_1, \mathbb{G}_2,$ $\mathbb{G}_T, e, g_1, g_2)$, chooses $\mathsf{hc} \xleftarrow{R} \mathcal{GL}$, $\alpha, \beta \xleftarrow{R} \mathbb{Z}_q$ and $r_i \xleftarrow{R} \mathbb{Z}_q$ for $i \in [n]$, sets $v := g_1^\alpha$, $w := e(g_1, g_2)^{\alpha\beta}$ and $u_i := g_1^{r_i}$ for $i \in [n]$, and outputs $\mathsf{pp} := (\mathsf{pp}_{\mathsf{bm}}, v, w, u_1, ..., u_n)$ and $\mathsf{msk} := (g_2^{\alpha\beta}, r_1, ..., r_n)$. All other algorithms implicitly include pp as an input. The message space is $\{0, 1\}$ and the vector space $\mathbb{Z}_q^n$.

KeyGen($\mathsf{msk}, \boldsymbol{y} = (y_1, ..., y_n)$): It chooses $s \xleftarrow{R} \mathbb{Z}_q$, sets $k_0 := g_2^s$, $k_1 := g_2^{\alpha\beta} \cdot (g_2^{\sum_{i=1}^n y_i r_i})^s$, and outputs $\mathsf{sk}_{\boldsymbol{y}} := (k_0, k_1)$.

Enc($\boldsymbol{x} = (x_1, ..., x_n), \mathsf{m} \in \mathbb{G}_T$): It chooses $\gamma \xleftarrow{R} \mathbb{Z}_q$, computes $C_0 := g_1^\gamma$, $C_i := (v^{x_i} u_i)^\gamma$ for $i \in [n]$, and $C_{\mathsf{m}} := \mathsf{m} \oplus \mathsf{hc}(w^\gamma)$, and outputs $\mathsf{ct}_{\boldsymbol{x}} := (C_0, C_1, ..., C_n, C_{\mathsf{m}})$.

Dec($\mathsf{sk}_{\boldsymbol{y}}, \boldsymbol{y} = (k_0, k_1), \mathsf{ct}_{\boldsymbol{x}} = (C_0, C_1, ..., C_n, C_{\mathsf{m}})$): It outputs $\mathsf{m} := C_{\mathsf{m}} \oplus \mathsf{hc}(e(C_0, k_1)e(\prod_{i=1}^n (C_i^{y_i}), k_0)^{-1})$.

Correctness. Let $\boldsymbol{x} \in \mathbb{Z}_q^n$ and $\boldsymbol{y} \in \mathbb{Z}_q^n$ be vectors such that $\boldsymbol{x}^T \cdot \boldsymbol{y} = 0$ and $\mathsf{m} \in \{0, 1\}$ be any message. Suppose that $\mathsf{ct}_{\boldsymbol{x}} = (C_0, C_1, ..., C_n, C_{\mathsf{m}})$ and $\mathsf{sk}_{\boldsymbol{y}} = (k_1, k_2)$ are generated as $(\mathsf{msk}, \mathsf{pp}) \xleftarrow{R} \mathsf{Setup}(1^\lambda, 1^n)$, $\mathsf{ct}_{\boldsymbol{x}} \xleftarrow{R} \mathsf{Enc}(\boldsymbol{x}, \mathsf{m})$, and $\mathsf{sk}_{\boldsymbol{y}} \xleftarrow{R} \mathsf{KeyGen}(\mathsf{msk}, \boldsymbol{y} = (y_1, ..., y_n))$. Then we have

$$e(C_0, k_1) \cdot e(\prod_{i=1}^n (C_i^{y_i}), k_0)^{-1}$$
$$= e(g_1^\gamma, g_2^{\alpha\beta + s\sum_{i=1}^n y_i r_i}) \cdot e(g_1^{\sum_{i=1}^n y_i \gamma(\alpha x_i + r_i)}, g_2^s)^{-1}$$
$$= e(g_1, g_2)^{\alpha\beta\gamma + \gamma s\sum_{i=1}^n y_i r_i} \cdot e(g_1, g_2)^{-\gamma s(\alpha\sum_{i=1}^n x_i y_i + \sum_{i=1}^n y_i r_i)}$$
$$= e(g_1, g_2)^{\alpha\beta\gamma}.$$

Thus, the decryption correctly works since $w^\gamma = e(g_1, g_2)^{\alpha\beta\gamma}$.

Key-Compactness. A secret key $\mathsf{sk}_{\boldsymbol{y}}$ for a vector $\boldsymbol{y}$ consists of two group elements of $\mathbb{G}_2$, and its size is independent from the demension n. Therefore the scheme is fully key-compact.

Security

Theorem 4. *If the CBDH assumption holds, then the above scheme is selectively secure.*

Proof. Suppose that there exists a PPT adversary $\mathcal{A} = ((\mathcal{A}_{1\text{-}1}, \mathcal{A}_{1\text{-}2}), \mathcal{A}_2)$ that breaks the selective security of the above IPE scheme. We construct a PPT algorithm $\mathcal{B}$ that breaks the hardcore security of CBDH as follows.

$\mathcal{B}(g_1, g_1^\alpha, g_1^\beta, g_1^\gamma, g_2, g_2^\alpha, g_2^\beta, g_2^\gamma, \mathsf{hc}, T)$: The goal of $\mathcal{B}$ is to distinguish if $T = \mathsf{hc}(e(g_1, g_2)^{\alpha\beta\gamma})$ or $T \xleftarrow{\mathrm{R}} \{0,1\}$. It first runs $(\boldsymbol{x}^*, \mathsf{st}_{\mathcal{A},\mathsf{pre}}) \xleftarrow{\mathrm{R}} \mathcal{A}_{\text{1-1}}(1^\lambda, 1^n)$. Then it picks $r_i' \xleftarrow{\mathrm{R}} \mathbb{Z}_q$ for $i \in [n]$, sets $v \xleftarrow{\mathrm{R}} g_1^\alpha$, $w := e(g_1^\alpha, g_2^\beta)$, $u_i := g_1^{r_i'} \cdot (g_1^\alpha)^{-x_i^*}$ (this implicitly sets $r_i := r_i' - \alpha x_i^* \bmod q$), and $\mathsf{pp} := (v, w, u_1, ..., u_n)$, and runs $(\mathsf{m}_0, \mathsf{m}_1, \mathsf{st}) \xleftarrow{\mathrm{R}} \mathcal{A}_{\text{1-2}}^{\mathsf{KeyGen}(\mathsf{msk}, \cdot)}(\mathsf{pp}, \mathsf{st}_{\mathcal{A},\mathsf{pre}})$ where the way to simulate the oracle $\mathsf{KeyGen}(\mathsf{msk}, \cdot)$ is described below. Then $\mathcal{B}$ picks coin $\xleftarrow{\mathrm{R}} \{0,1\}$, sets $C_0^* := g^\gamma$, $C_i^* := (g^\gamma)^{r_i'}$ for $i \in [n]$, $C_{\mathsf{m}}^* := \mathsf{m}_{\mathsf{coin}} \oplus T$, and $\mathsf{ct}^* := (C_0^*, C_1^*, ..., C_n^*, C_{\mathsf{m}}^*)$, and runs $\widehat{\mathsf{coin}} \xleftarrow{\mathrm{R}} \mathcal{A}_2^{\mathsf{KeyGen}(\mathsf{msk}, \cdot)}(\mathsf{ct}^*, \mathsf{st})$ where the way to simulate the oracle $\mathsf{KeyGen}(\mathsf{msk}, \cdot)$ is described below. Finally, $\mathcal{B}$ outputs $(\widehat{\mathsf{coin}} \stackrel{?}{=} \mathsf{coin})$.

$\mathsf{KeyGen}(\mathsf{msk}, \cdot)$: Here, we describe the way to simulate $\mathsf{KeyGen}(\mathsf{msk}, \cdot)$ by $\mathcal{B}$. Given a key query $\boldsymbol{y} = (y_1, ..., y_n)$, it first computes $\eta := (\boldsymbol{x}^*)^T \cdot \boldsymbol{y}$. If $\eta = 0$, then it aborts. Otherwise it picks $s' \xleftarrow{\mathrm{R}} \mathbb{Z}_q$, sets $k_0 := g_2^{s'} \cdot (g_2^\beta)^{1/\eta}$ and $k_1 := (g^{\sum_{i=1}^n y_i r_i'} \cdot (g^\alpha)^{-\eta})^{s'} \cdot (g^\beta)^{\sum_{i=1}^n y_i r_i'/\eta}$, and returns $\mathsf{sk}_{\boldsymbol{y}} := (k_0, k_1)$. We omit sub/super-script of $\sum_{i=1}^n$ below for ease of notation. Now, we set $s := s' + \beta/\eta$, then we can rewrite

$$k_1 = g^{s' \sum y_i(r_i + \alpha x_i^*) - s'\alpha\eta + \beta/\eta \sum y_i(r_i + \alpha x_i^*)}$$
$$= g^{(s' + \beta/\eta) \sum y_i r_i + s'\alpha(\sum y_i x_i^* - \eta) + \alpha\beta/\eta \sum y_i x_i^*}$$
$$= g^{s \sum y_i r_i + \alpha\beta} \quad (\because (\boldsymbol{x}^*)^T \cdot \boldsymbol{y} = \sum y_i x_i^* = \eta)$$

This perfectly simulate secret keys.
For the target ciphertext, $C_0^* = g^\gamma$, and for $i = 1, ..., n$, we have

$$C_i^* = (g^{r_i'})^\gamma$$
$$= (g_1^{\alpha x_i^*} \cdot g_1^{r_i' - \alpha x_i^*})^\gamma$$
$$= (v^{x_i^*} u_i)^\gamma$$

If $T = \mathsf{hc}(e(g_1, g_2)^{\alpha\beta\gamma})$, then C_{m}^* is also simulated correctly. On the other hand, if $T \xleftarrow{\mathrm{R}} \{0,1\}$, no information of coin is given to $\mathcal{A}$, and thus the probability that $\mathcal{B}$ outputs 1 is $1/2$. Therefore we have

$$\Pr[1 \xleftarrow{\mathrm{R}} \mathcal{B} | T = \mathsf{hc}(e(g_1, g_2)^{\alpha\beta\gamma})] - \Pr[1 \xleftarrow{\mathrm{R}} \mathcal{B} | T \xleftarrow{\mathrm{R}} \{0,1\}] = \frac{\mathsf{Adv}_{\mathsf{IPE}, \mathcal{A}}^{\mathsf{CPA}}(\lambda)}{2}.$$

i Thus, $\mathcal{B}$ can break the hardcore security of CBDH if $\mathcal{A}$ breaks the selective security of the IPE scheme. This immediately implies that if the CBDH assumption holds, then the scheme is selectively secure by Lemma 3. ∎

If we use the DBDH assumption, we can set the message space of the scheme to $\mathbb{G}_T$.

References

[ADN+09] Alwen, J., Dodis, Y., Naor, M., Segev, G., Walfish, S., Wichs, D.: Public-key encryption in the bounded-retrieval model. In: Gilbert, H. (ed.) EUROCRYPT 2010. LNCS, vol. 6110, pp. 113–134. Springer, Heidelberg (2010). https://doi.org/10.1007/978-3-642-13190-5_6. IACR Cryptology ePrint Archive, 2009:512, 2009. Version 20091028:202321

[ADW09] Alwen, J., Dodis, Y., Wichs, D.: Leakage-resilient public-key cryptography in the bounded-retrieval model. In: Halevi, S. (ed.) CRYPTO 2009. LNCS, vol. 5677, pp. 36–54. Springer, Heidelberg (2009). https://doi.org/10.1007/978-3-642-03356-8_3

[AFV11] Agrawal, S., Freeman, D.M., Vaikuntanathan, V.: Functional encryption for inner product predicates from learning with errors. In: Lee, D.H., Wang, X. (eds.) ASIACRYPT 2011. LNCS, vol. 7073, pp. 21–40. Springer, Heidelberg (2011). https://doi.org/10.1007/978-3-642-25385-0_2

[AGV09] Akavia, A., Goldwasser, S., Vaikuntanathan, V.: Simultaneous hardcore bits and cryptography against memory attacks. In: Reingold, O. (ed.) TCC 2009. LNCS, vol. 5444, pp. 474–495. Springer, Heidelberg (2009). https://doi.org/10.1007/978-3-642-00457-5_28

[BB04] Boneh, D., Boyen, X.: Efficient selective-ID secure identity based encryption without random oracles. In: Cachin, C., Camenisch, J. (eds.) EURO-CRYPT 2004. LNCS, vol. 3027, pp. 223–238. Springer, Heidelberg (2004). https://doi.org/10.1007/978-3-540-24676-3_14

[BG10] Brakerski, Z., Goldwasser, S.: Circular and leakage resilient public-key encryption under subgroup indistinguishability - (or: Quadratic residuosity strikes back). In: Rabin, T. (ed.) CRYPTO 2010. LNCS, vol. 6223, pp. 1–20. Springer, Heidelberg (2010). https://doi.org/10.1007/978-3-642-14623-7_1

[BKKV10] Brakerski, Z., Kalai, Y.T., Katz, J., Vaikuntanathan, V.: Overcoming the hole in the bucket: public-key cryptography resilient to continual memory leakage. In: 51st FOCS, pp. 501–510. IEEE Computer Society Press, October 2010

[BLSV18] Brakerski, Z., Lombardi, A., Segev, G., Vaikuntanathan, V.: Anonymous IBE, leakage resilience and circular security from new assumptions. In: Nielsen, J.B., Rijmen, V. (eds.) EUROCRYPT 2018, Part I. LNCS, vol. 10820, pp. 535–564. Springer, Cham (2018). https://doi.org/10.1007/978-3-319-78381-9_20

[BSW13] Boyle, E., Segev, G., Wichs, D.: Fully leakage-resilient signatures. J. Cryptol. **26**(3), 513–558 (2013)

[CDRW10] Chow, S.S.M., Dodis, Y., Rouselakis, Y., Waters, B.: Practical leakage-resilient identity-based encryption from simple assumptions. In: Al-Shaer, E., Keromytis, A.D., Shmatikov, V. (eds.) ACM CCS 2010, pp. 152–161. ACM Press, October 2010

[CGW15] Chen, J., Gay, R., Wee, H.: Improved dual system ABE in prime-order groups via predicate encodings. In: Oswald, E., Fischlin, M. (eds.) EUROCRYPT 2015, Part II. LNCS, vol. 9057, pp. 595–624. Springer, Heidelberg (2015). https://doi.org/10.1007/978-3-662-46803-6_20

[CS02] Cramer, R., Shoup, V.: Universal hash proofs and a paradigm for adaptive chosen ciphertext secure public-key encryption. In: Knudsen, L.R. (ed.) EUROCRYPT 2002. LNCS, vol. 2332, pp. 45–64. Springer, Heidelberg (2002). https://doi.org/10.1007/3-540-46035-7_4

[CZLC16] Chen, Y., Zhang, Z., Lin, D., Cao, Z.: Generalized (identity-based) hash proof system and its applications. Secur. Commun. Netw. **9**(12), 1698–1716 (2016)

[DGK+10] Dodis, Y., Goldwasser, S., Tauman Kalai, Y., Peikert, C., Vaikuntanathan, V.: Public-key encryption schemes with auxiliary inputs. In: Micciancio, D. (ed.) TCC 2010. LNCS, vol. 5978, pp. 361–381. Springer, Heidelberg (2010). https://doi.org/10.1007/978-3-642-11799-2_22

[DHLW10a] Dodis, Y., Haralambiev, K., López-Alt, A., Wichs, D.: Cryptography against continuous memory attacks. In: 51st FOCS, pp. 511–520. IEEE Computer Society Press, October 2010

[DHLW10b] Dodis, Y., Haralambiev, K., López-Alt, A., Wichs, D.: Efficient public-key cryptography in the presence of key leakage. In: Abe, M. (ed.) ASIACRYPT 2010. LNCS, vol. 6477, pp. 613–631. Springer, Heidelberg (2010). https://doi.org/10.1007/978-3-642-17373-8_35

[DKL09] Dodis, Y., Kalai, Y.T., Lovett, S.: On cryptography with auxiliary input. In: Mitzenmacher, M. (ed.) 41st ACM STOC, pp. 621–630. ACM Press, May/June 2009

[DLW06] Di Crescenzo, G., Lipton, R., Walfish, S.: Perfectly secure password protocols in the bounded retrieval model. In: Halevi, S., Rabin, T. (eds.) TCC 2006. LNCS, vol. 3876, pp. 225–244. Springer, Heidelberg (2006). https://doi.org/10.1007/11681878_12

[Dzi06] Dziembowski, S.: Intrusion-resilience via the bounded-storage model. In: Halevi, S., Rabin, T. (eds.) TCC 2006. LNCS, vol. 3876, pp. 207–224. Springer, Heidelberg (2006). https://doi.org/10.1007/11681878_11

[GJS11] Garg, S., Jain, A., Sahai, A.: Leakage-resilient zero knowledge. In: Rogaway, P. (ed.) CRYPTO 2011. LNCS, vol. 6841, pp. 297–315. Springer, Heidelberg (2011). https://doi.org/10.1007/978-3-642-22792-9_17

[GL89] Goldreich, O., Levin, L.A.: A hard-core predicate for all one-way functions. In: 21st ACM STOC, pp. 25–32. ACM Press, May 1989

[HLWW16] Hazay, C., López-Alt, A., Wee, H., Wichs, D.: Leakage-resilient cryptography from minimal assumptions. J. Cryptol. **29**(3), 514–551 (2016)

[KP17] Kurosawa, K., Phong, L.T.: Anonymous and leakage resilient IBE and IPE. Des. Codes Crypt. **85**(2), 273–298 (2017)

[KSW08] Katz, J., Sahai, A., Waters, B.: Predicate encryption supporting disjunctions, polynomial equations, and inner products. In: Smart, N. (ed.) EUROCRYPT 2008. LNCS, vol. 4965, pp. 146–162. Springer, Heidelberg (2008). https://doi.org/10.1007/978-3-540-78967-3_9

[KV09] Katz, J., Vaikuntanathan, V.: Signature schemes with bounded leakage resilience. In: Matsui, M. (ed.) ASIACRYPT 2009. LNCS, vol. 5912, pp. 703–720. Springer, Heidelberg (2009). https://doi.org/10.1007/978-3-642-10366-7_41

[LRW11] Lewko, A., Rouselakis, Y., Waters, B.: Achieving leakage resilience through dual system encryption. In: Ishai, Y. (ed.) TCC 2011. LNCS, vol. 6597, pp. 70–88. Springer, Heidelberg (2011). https://doi.org/10.1007/978-3-642-19571-6_6

[NS12] Naor, M., Segev, G.: Public-key cryptosystems resilient to key leakage. SIAM J. Comput. **41**(4), 772–814 (2012)

[QL13]   Qin, B., Liu, S.: Leakage-resilient chosen-ciphertext secure public-key encryption from hash proof system and one-time lossy filter. In: Sako, K., Sarkar, P. (eds.) ASIACRYPT 2013, Part II. LNCS, vol. 8270, pp. 381–400. Springer, Heidelberg (2013). https://doi.org/10.1007/978-3-642-42045-0_20

[QL14]   Qin, B., Liu, S.: Leakage-flexible CCA-secure public-key encryption: simple construction and free of pairing. In: Krawczyk, H. (ed.) PKC 2014. LNCS, vol. 8383, pp. 19–36. Springer, Heidelberg (2014). https://doi.org/10.1007/978-3-642-54631-0_2

[Wee14] Wee, H.: Dual system encryption via predicate encodings. In: Lindell, Y. (ed.) TCC 2014. LNCS, vol. 8349, pp. 616–637. Springer, Heidelberg (2014). https://doi.org/10.1007/978-3-642-54242-8_26

[YAX+16] Yu, Z., Au, M.H., Xu, Q., Yang, R., Han, J.: Leakage-resilient functional encryption via pair encodings. In: Liu, J.K.K., Steinfeld, R. (eds.) ACISP 2016, Part I. LNCS, vol. 9722, pp. 443–460. Springer, Cham (2016). https://doi.org/10.1007/978-3-319-40253-6_27

[YCZY12] Yuen, T.H., Chow, S.S.M., Zhang, Y., Yiu, S.M.: Identity-based encryption resilient to continual auxiliary leakage. In: Pointcheval, D., Johansson, T. (eds.) EUROCRYPT 2012. LNCS, vol. 7237, pp. 117–134. Springer, Heidelberg (2012). https://doi.org/10.1007/978-3-642-29011-4_9

[ZCG+18] Zhang, J., Chen, J., Gong, J., Ge, A., Ma, C.: Leakage-resilient attribute based encryption in prime-order groups via predicate encodings. Des. Codes Crypt. 86(6), 1339–1366 (2018)

Additively Homomorphic IBE from Higher Residuosity

Michael Clear[1]([⊠]) and Ciaran McGoldrick[2]

[1] Georgetown University, Washington, D.C., USA
clearm@tcd.ie
[2] Trinity College Dublin, Dublin, Ireland

Abstract. We present an identity-Based encryption (IBE) scheme that is group homomorphic for addition modulo a "large" (i.e. superpolynomial) integer, the first such group homomorphic IBE. Our first result is the construction of an IBE scheme supporting homomorphic addition modulo a poly-sized prime e. Our construction builds upon the IBE scheme of Boneh, LaVigne and Sabin (BLS). BLS relies on a hash function that maps identities to e^{th} residues. However there is no known way to securely instantiate such a function. Our construction extends BLS so that it can use a hash function that can be securely instantiated. We prove our scheme IND-ID-CPA secure under the (slightly modified) e^{th} residuosity assumption in the random oracle model and show that it supports a (modular) additive homomorphism. By using multiple instances of the scheme with distinct primes and leveraging the Chinese Remainder Theorem, we can support homomorphic addition modulo a "large" (i.e. superpolynomial) integer. We also show that our scheme for $e > 2$ is anonymous by additionally assuming the hardness of deciding solvability of a special system of multivariate polynomial equations. We provide a justification for this assumption by considering known attacks.

1 Introduction

Identity-Based Encryption (IBE), first proposed by Shamir [1], and first constructed by Boneh and Franklin [2] (based on bilinear pairings) and Cocks [3] (based on quadratic residuosity), is centered around the notion that a user's public key can be efficiently derived from an identity string and system-wide public parameters. The public parameters are chosen by a Trusted Authority (TA) along with a master secret key, which is used to extract secret keys for user identities. In this work, we present an IBE that is group homomorphic for addition modulo a smooth square-free integer. An encryption scheme is said to be *group homomorphic* if its decryption algorithm is a group homomorphism (known as Group Homomorphic Encryption (GHE) [4]). Although GHE only permits evaluation of a single algebraic operation, it is a very powerful primitive for the following reasons:

© International Association for Cryptologic Research 2019
D. Lin and K. Sako (Eds.): PKC 2019, LNCS 11442, pp. 496–515, 2019.
https://doi.org/10.1007/978-3-030-17253-4_17

1. It is used as a building block in protocols for Private Information Retrieval [5], Electronic Voting [6–10], Oblivious Polynomial Evaluation [11], Private Outsourced Computation [12] and the Millionaire's Problem [13].
2. Fully Homomorphic Encryption (FHE) is currently impractical for many applications, and even if it were to become more practical, it may add unnecessary overhead, especially in applications that only require a single algebraic operation.

GHE is the "classical" flavor of homomorphic encryption. It allows unbounded applications of the group operation. Goldwasser and Micali [14] constructed the first GHE scheme. The Goldwasser-Micali (GM) cryptosystem supports addition modulo 2 i.e. the XOR operation. Other additively-homomorphic GHE schemes from the literature include Benaloh [6], Naccache-Stern [15], Okamoto-Uchiyama [16], Paillier [17] and Damgård-Jurik [10]. Other instances of GHE include [18–20].

Existing identity-based GHE (IBGHE) schemes such as those based on pairings are typically multiplicatively homomorphic. It is a well-known that a scheme with a multiplicative homomorphism can be transformed into one with an additive homomorphism, where the addition takes place in the exponent, and a discrete logarithm problem must be solved to recover the result. In this case, we usually get a bounded (aka "quasi") additively homomorphic scheme, but it is not group homomorphic in the sense of the definition considered in this paper since one cannot perform an unbounded number of homomorphic operations. However, to the best of our knowledge, the only existing "pure" (i.e. supporting modular addition) additively-homomorphic instance of IBGHE in the literature is the variant of the Cocks scheme due to Clear, Hughes and Tewari [21] that is XOR-homomorphic i.e. it supports addition modulo 2. Applications of IBGHE are explored in [21] but can be extended to private information retrieval (PIR) [22] (instantiating the protocol from [5] with an IBGHE scheme instead of a public-key GHE scheme), data aggregation in wireless sensor networks (IBE has been applied to wireless sensor networks already in [23–26]) and participatory sensing (Günther et al. [27] use additively homomorphic IBE for data aggregation in a participatory sensing system).

1.1 Our Results

Our main contribution is the construction of an IBGHE for addition modulo a poly-sized prime e. Our construction builds on the IBE scheme of Boneh, LaVigne and Sabin (BLS) [28], which uses a hash function that maps identities to e^{th} residues; there is no known way to securely instantiate such a function. We extend BLS so that it uses a hash function that can be securely instantiated. We prove our scheme IND-ID-CPA secure under a (slightly modified) e^{th} residuosity assumption in the random oracle model. Indeed this is the same assumption that BLS is proved secure under. We then show that our scheme supports homomorphic addition modulo a poly-sized prime e and prove that it satisfies the properties of an IBGHE.

Our second contribution is to use multiple instances of the scheme with distinct primes and to leverage the Chinese Remainder Theorem to support homomorphic addition modulo a "large" (i.e. superpolynomial) integer, the first such IBE scheme supporting an unbounded number of operations[1], solving an open problem mentioned in [21]. Below we consider the advantages of a scheme that supports homomorphic addition with such a "large" range.

Our third contribution is to show that our scheme for $e > 2$ is anonymous by additionally assuming the hardness of deciding solvability of a special system of multivariate polynomial equations. We investigate this problem from a cryptanalytic perspective and provide justification in light of known attacks for assuming its hardness.

1.2 Practicality and Applications

While the space complexity of ciphertexts in our scheme is high, requiring e^2 group elements, there are contexts where it may be of import, which we now discuss.

Pairings-based IBE schemes that support an additive homomorphism in the exponent rely on Pollard's lambda algorithm to extract the result. Let B be a bound on the result. Pollard's lambda algorithm has time complexity of $O(\sqrt{B})$. Suppose we require B to be exponentially large. The runtime for extracting the result with Pollard's lambda algorithm is exponential for such B. In contrast, our CRT scheme gives polynomial running time for this case. We also compare with LWE-based IBE schemes. The GPV scheme [29] is perhaps the simplest LWE-based IBE scheme and its security is also proved in the random oracle model. We consider a comparison for 80 bits of security and $B = 2^{80}$. We used the estimator of Albrecht, Player and Scott [30] to derive suitable parameters for LWE for an instantiation of GPV. For 80 bits of security and $B = 2^{80}$, the size of a ciphertext in GPV (modified to support an additive homomorphism with bound B) is approximately the same as ours (of the order of 3 MB). Our scheme however has significantly smaller public parameters - by a factor of several thousand but has considerably worse running time for encryption, decryption and evaluation.

An example real-world application is that of data aggregation, a common practice in Machine Learning and related fields. Günther et al. [27] use additively homomorphic IBE for data aggregation in participatory sensing. A bound of 2^{80} might be required if the data were real numbers with high precision requirements, which can be represented as integers in fixed point form.

2 Preliminaries

2.1 Notation

A quantity is said to be negligible with respect to some parameter λ, written $\mathsf{negl}(\lambda)$, if it is asymptotically bounded from above by the reciprocal of all polynomials in λ.

---

[1] LWE-based additively homomorphic IBE can be constructed with an a superpolynomial range but supporting only a theoretically bounded number of operations, albeit the bound is more than sufficient for practical purposes.

For a probability distribution D, we denote by $x \xleftarrow{\$} D$ that x is sampled according to D. If S is a set, $y \xleftarrow{\$} S$ denotes that y is sampled from x according to the uniform distribution on S.

The support of a predicate $f : A \to \{0,1\}$ for some domain A is denoted by $\mathsf{supp}(f)$, and is defined by the set $\{a \in A : f(a) = 1\}$.

The set of contiguous integers $\{1, \ldots, k\}$ for some $k > 1$ is denoted by $[k]$.

2.2 Identity Based Encryption

Definition 1. *An Identity Based Encryption (IBE) scheme is a tuple of PPT algorithms* (G, K, E, D) *defined with respect to a message space* $\mathcal{M}$, *an identity space* $\mathcal{I}$ *and a ciphertext space* $\hat{\mathcal{C}}$ *as follows:*

- $\mathsf{G}(1^\lambda)$:
  On input (in unary) a security parameter λ, *generate public parameters* PP *and a master secret key* MSK. *Output* (PP, MSK).
- $\mathsf{K}(\mathsf{MSK}, \mathsf{id})$:
  On input master secret key MSK *and an identity* $\mathsf{id} \in \mathcal{I}$: *derive and output a secret key* $\mathsf{sk}_{\mathsf{id}}$ *for identity* id.
- $\mathsf{E}(\mathsf{PP}, \mathsf{id}, m)$:
  On input public parameters PP, *an identity* $\mathsf{id} \in \mathcal{I}$, *and a message* $m \in \mathcal{M}$, *output a ciphertext* $c \in \mathcal{C} \subseteq \hat{\mathcal{C}}$ *that encrypts* m *under identity* id.
- $\mathsf{D}(\mathsf{sk}_{\mathsf{id}}, c)$:
  On input a secret key $\mathsf{sk}_{\mathsf{id}}$ *for identity* $\mathsf{id} \in \mathcal{I}$ *and a ciphertext* $c \in \hat{\mathcal{C}}$, *output* m' *if* c *is a valid encryption under identity* id; *output a failure symbol* $\bot$ *otherwise.*

2.3 Public-Key GHE

An important subclass of partial homomorphic encryption is the class of public-key encryption schemes that admit a group homomorphism between their ciphertext space and plaintext space. This class corresponds to what is considered "classical" HE [4], where a single group operation is supported, most usually addition. Gjøsteen [18] examined the abstract structure of these cryptosystems in terms of groups, and characterized their security as relying on the hardness of a subgroup membership problem. Armknecht, Katzenbeisser and Peter [4] rigorously formalized the notion, and called it *group homomorphic encryption* (GHE). We recap with the formal definition of GHE by Armknecht, Katzenbeisser and Peter [4].

Definition 2 (GHE, Definition 1 in [4]). *A public-key encryption scheme* $\mathcal{E} = (G, E, D)$ *is called* group homomorphic, *if for every* $(\mathsf{pk}, \mathsf{sk}) \leftarrow G(1^\lambda)$, *the plaintext space* $\mathcal{M}$ *and the ciphertext space* $\hat{\mathcal{C}}$ *(written in multiplicative notation) are non-trivial groups such that*

- *the set of all encryptions* $\mathcal{C} := \{c \in \hat{\mathcal{C}} \mid c \leftarrow E_{\mathsf{pk}}(m), m \in \mathcal{M}\}$ *is a non-trivial subgroup of* $\hat{\mathcal{C}}$

- *the restricted decryption* $D_{sk}^* := D_{sk|\mathcal{C}}$ *is a group epimorphism (surjective homomorphism) i.e.*

$$D_{sk}^* \text{ is surjective and } \forall c, c' \in \mathcal{C} : D_{sk}(c \cdot c') = D_{sk}(c) \cdot D_{sk}(c')$$

- sk *contains an efficient* decision function $\delta : \hat{\mathcal{C}} \to \{0, 1\}$ *such that*

$$\delta(c) = 1 \iff c \in \mathcal{C}$$

- *the decryption on* $\hat{\mathcal{C}} \setminus \mathcal{C}$ *returns the symbol* $\perp$.

2.4   Identity-Based Group Homomorphic Encryption (IBGHE)

Definition 3 (Identity Based Group Homomorphic Encryption (IBGHE), Based on [21]). *Let* $\mathcal{E} = (G, K, E, D)$ *be an IBE scheme with message space* $\mathcal{M}$, *identity space* $\mathcal{I}$ *and ciphertext space* $\hat{\mathcal{C}}$. *The scheme* $\mathcal{E}$ *is group homomorphic if for every* $(\mathsf{PP}, \mathsf{MSK}) \leftarrow G(1^\lambda)$, *every* $\mathsf{id} \in \mathcal{I}$, *and every* $\mathsf{sk}_{\mathsf{id}} \leftarrow K(\mathsf{MSK}, \mathsf{id})$, *the message space* $(\mathcal{M}, \cdot)$ *is a non-trivial group, and there is a binary operation* $* : \hat{\mathcal{C}}^2 \to \hat{\mathcal{C}}$ *such that the following properties are satisfied for the restricted ciphertext space* $\widehat{\mathcal{C}_{\mathsf{id}}} = \{c \in \hat{\mathcal{C}} : D_{\mathsf{sk}_{\mathsf{id}}}(c) \neq \perp\}$:

GH.1: *The set of all encryptions* $\mathcal{C}_{\mathsf{id}} = \{c \mid c \leftarrow E(\mathsf{PP}, \mathsf{id}, m), m \in \mathcal{M}\} \subseteq \widehat{\mathcal{C}_{\mathsf{id}}}$ *is a non-trivial group with respect to the operation* $*$.
GH.2: *The restricted decryption* $D_{\mathsf{sk}_{\mathsf{id}}}^* := D_{\mathsf{sk}_{\mathsf{id}}|\mathcal{C}_{\mathsf{id}}}$ *is surjective and* $\forall c, c' \in \mathcal{C}_{\mathsf{id}}$ $D_{\mathsf{sk}_{\mathsf{id}}}(c * c') = D_{\mathsf{sk}_{\mathsf{id}}}(c) \cdot D_{\mathsf{sk}_{\mathsf{id}}}(c')$.

We are interested in schemes whose plaintext space forms a group and which allow that operation to be homomorphically applied an unbounded number of times. There exist schemes however that do not satisfy all the requirements of GHE, namely their ciphertext space does not form a group but instead forms a quasigroup (a group without associativity). We can define what we call Quasigroup Homomorphic Encryption (QHE) analogously to Definition 2 by replacing the term 'group' with 'quasigroup' in the definition. An example of such a scheme is the Cocks' IBE [3], which was shown to be inherently XOR-homomorphic by Joye [31].

2.5 e^{th} Residuosity

An integer x is said to be a quadratic residue modulo an integer m if x is congruent to a square modulo m. We denote the set of quadratic residues modulo p as $\mathbb{QR}(m)$. The Legendre symbol of an integer x modulo a prime p is defined as

$$\left(\frac{x}{p}\right) = \begin{cases} 0 & \text{if } p|x \\ 1 & \text{if } x \in \mathbb{QR}(p) \\ -1 & \text{otherwise} \end{cases}$$

The Jacobi symbol generalizes the Legendre symbol to composite moduli. For a composite modulus $m = p_1^{a_1} \cdots p_n^{a_n}$, it is defined as

$$\left(\frac{x}{m}\right) = \left(\frac{x}{p_1}\right)^{a_1} \cdots \left(\frac{x}{p_n}\right)^{a_n}$$

We now generalize quadratic residues to e^{th} power residues. We define the eth power residue symbol as follows:

Definition 4 (Based on Definition 4.1 in [32]). *Let $e \geq 2$ be an integer, and let $\zeta_e \in \bar{\mathbb{Q}}$ be a primitive e^{th} root of unity (note that $\bar{\mathbb{Q}}$ is the algebraic closure of $\mathbb{Q}$). Let K be the number field $\mathbb{Q}(\zeta_e)$, and let $\mathcal{O}_K = \mathbb{Z}[\zeta_e]$ be the ring of integers in K. Let $\mathfrak{p}$ be a prime ideal of $\mathcal{O}_K$ that does not contain e. For $x \in \mathcal{O}_K$, the eth power residue symbol of $x \bmod \mathfrak{p}$, denoted $\left(\dfrac{x}{\mathfrak{p}}\right)_e$ is defined as*

$$\left(\frac{x}{\mathfrak{p}}\right)_e = \begin{cases} 0 & \text{if } x \in \mathfrak{p} \\ \zeta_e^i & \text{if } x \notin \mathfrak{p} \end{cases}$$

where i is the unique integer modulo e such that $\zeta_e^i \equiv x^{(\mathcal{N}(\mathfrak{p})-1)/e} \pmod{\mathfrak{p}}$ and $\mathcal{N}(\mathfrak{p})$ is the norm of $\mathfrak{p}$.

If $\mathfrak{a}$ is an ideal that factors as $\mathfrak{a} = \mathfrak{p_1}^{k_1} \cdots \mathfrak{p_n}^{k_n}$ where $\mathfrak{p_1}, \ldots, \mathfrak{p_n}$ are prime ideals, then $\left(\dfrac{x}{\mathfrak{a}}\right)_e$ is defined as

$$\left(\frac{x}{\mathfrak{a}}\right)_e := \left(\frac{x}{\mathfrak{p_1}}\right)_e^{k_1} \cdots \left(\frac{x}{\mathfrak{p_n}}\right)_e^{k_n}$$

Let $e \geq 2$ be an integer. Let N be a positive integer. An integer $x \in \mathbb{Z}_N^*$ is said to be an eth residue modulo N if there is an integer $y \in \mathbb{Z}_N^*$ such that $y^e \equiv x \bmod N$. We denote the set of eth residues in $\mathbb{Z}_N^*$ by $\mathbb{ER}(N)$. A superset of $\mathbb{ER}(N)$ is the set of integers in $\mathbb{Z}_N^*$ with a power residue symbol of 1, which we denote as $\mathbb{PR}(N)$.

Definition 5 (e^{th} Residuosity (ER) Assumption). *For a PPT algorithm $\mathsf{RSAgen}(\lambda)$ that generates two equally sized primes p and q, the eth residuosity assumption is that the following two distributions are computationally indistinguishable[2]*

$$\{(N, v) : (p, q) \leftarrow \mathsf{RSAgen}(\lambda), N \leftarrow pq, v \xleftarrow{\$} \mathbb{ER}(N)\}$$

$$\underset{C}{\approx}$$

$$\{(N, v) : (p, q) \leftarrow \mathsf{RSAgen}(\lambda), N \leftarrow pq, v \xleftarrow{\$} \mathbb{PR}(N) \setminus \mathbb{ER}(N)\}.$$

---

[2] Any PPT distinguisher has only a negligible advantage (in λ) of distinguishing the distributions.

Let $N = pq$ be a product of two primes p and q with $p \equiv q \equiv 1 \bmod e$. An eth root of unity in $\mathbb{Z}_N$ is an integer μ such that $\mu^e \equiv 1 \bmod N$. The trivial root of unity is 1. A root of unity μ is said to be *degenerate* if either $\mu \equiv 1 \bmod p$ or $\mu \equiv 1 \bmod q$ since given such a μ one can trivially learn the factorization of N. For one of the schemes in this work, it is necessary to publish a nontrivial, non-degenerate root of unity as part of the public parameters. This is in order to compute the eth power residue symbol which is needed for the scheme. It is believed that revealing such a root of unity does not make factorization of N easier, but nevertheless it serves as additional information for the adversary, and therefore must be made explicit in the assumption we use for security. Hence, we follow [28] and modify the ER assumption to incorporate this information.

Definition 6 (Modified e^{th} Residuosity (MER) Assumption, [28]). *Let $\mathcal{Z}$ be the set of nontrivial, non-degenerate roots of unity in $\mathbb{Z}_N$. For a PPT algorithm $\mathsf{RSAgen}(\lambda)$ that generates two equally sized primes p and q, the modified e^{th} residuosity assumption is that the following two distributions are computationally indistinguishable*

$$\{(N, v, \mu) : (p, q) \leftarrow \mathsf{RSAgen}(\lambda), N \leftarrow pq, v \xleftarrow{\$} \mathbb{ER}(N), \mu \xleftarrow{\$} \mathcal{Z}\}$$

$$\underset{C}{\approx}$$

$$\{(N, v, \mu) : (p, q) \leftarrow \mathsf{RSAgen}(\lambda), N \leftarrow pq, v \xleftarrow{\$} \mathbb{PR}(N) \setminus \mathbb{ER}(N), \mu \xleftarrow{\$} \mathcal{Z}\}.$$

3   Our Additively Homomorphic IBE

Boneh, LaVigne and Sabin [28] presented an IBE scheme whose security relies on the MER assumption. However, their scheme uses a hash function that maps identity strings to e^{th} residues in $\mathbb{Z}_N$. It is not known how such a function can be instantiated without compromising security. We extend their construction so that it uses a hash function that can be instantiated. We then prove our construction secure under the MER assumption in the random oracle model. We show that the construction is group homomorphic for the additive group $(\mathbb{Z}_e, +)$ for prime e i.e. we show it meets the criteria for IBGHE. This is the only additively group-homomorphic IBE we are aware of with a message space larger than 2 elements. First, we need to introduce some functions that are used by the scheme along with an overview on how e^{th} power residue symbols are computed for integers in $\mathbb{Z}_N$.

3.1 e^{th} Power Residue Symbols in $\mathbb{Z}_N$

Let $e \geq 2$ be an integer. Let $N = pq$ be a product of two primes p and q with $p \equiv q \equiv 1 \bmod e$. The symbol $\left(\dfrac{x}{N}\right)_e$ for integers x is always 1 for odd e and ± 1 for even e, so for $e > 2$, we need to find a way to extract more information about x so we can map it to one of e symbols. We follow the approach taken in [32].

Let ζ_e and K be as defined in Definition 4. Note that we can take K to be $\mathbb{Q}[x]/\Phi_e(x)$ where $\Phi_e(x)$ is the eth cyclotomic polynomial; accordingly, we have $\zeta_e = x$. Given p and q, we can compute an element $\mu \in \mathbb{Z}_N^*$ that is a primitive root of unity modulo p and modulo q. In schemes described later, we require that μ be published as part of the public parameters. For a fixed μ, we define the ideal $\mathfrak{N} = N\mathcal{O}_K + (\zeta_e - \mu)\mathcal{O}_K$. Let $\mu_p = \mu \bmod p$ and $\mu_q = \mu \bmod q$. We also define the ideals $\mathfrak{p} = p\mathcal{O}_K + (\zeta_e - \mu_p)\mathcal{O}_K$ and $\mathfrak{q} = q\mathcal{O}_K + (\zeta_e - \mu_q)\mathcal{O}_K$. It holds that $\mathfrak{N} = \mathfrak{p}\mathfrak{q}$. Squirrel [33] gives a polynomial time algorithm for computing the eth residue symbol $\left(\dfrac{x}{\mathfrak{a}}\right)_e$ for any $x \in \mathcal{O}_K$ and any ideal in $\mathcal{O}_K$ (such as $\mathfrak{N}$ for example). It is an interesting problem for future work to find a more efficient algorithm tailored to the ideal $\mathfrak{N}$.

Furthermore, we define a function $J_N : \mathbb{Z}_N \to \{0, \dots, e-1\}$ as follows

$$J(x) = \begin{cases} 0 \text{ if } \gcd(x, N) \neq 1 \\ i \text{ if } \gcd(x, N) = 1 \text{ and } \left(\dfrac{x}{\mathfrak{N}}\right)_e = \zeta_e^i \end{cases}$$

Additionally, we define J_p analogous to J_N except with ideal $\mathfrak{p}$ and modulus p, and similarly, we define J_q using ideal $\mathfrak{q}$ and modulus q. When an integer x is an eth power residue modulo N, we have $J_N(x) = 0$. We establish some important properties:

●

$$J_N(x) \equiv J_p(x) + J_q(x) \mod e \quad \forall x \in \mathbb{Z}_N \tag{3.1}$$

● **Homomorphic property**

$$J_N(xy) \equiv J_N(x) + J_N(y) \mod e \quad \forall x, y \in \mathbb{Z}_N^* \tag{3.2}$$

The homomorphic property is also satisfied by J_p and J_q.

3.2   Boneh, LaVigne and Sabin (BLS) Scheme

We now describe the BLS scheme. While the scheme is described as an IBE in [28], as aforementioned, there is no efficient means to securely realize the hash function it depends on[3]. We present it here as a public-key scheme, and in fact the security proof in [28] treats it as such.

The scheme is parameterized by a prime e. Note the scheme employs the function J_N which implicitly uses the root of unity μ published in the public key.

---

[3] This is with absolute correctness. There is an alternative approach to the one we present here that achieves probabilistic correctness, but the parameters can be set so that it is correct with all but negligible probability. It is however less space efficient. The idea is that the hash function gives multiple (say $k = \mathsf{poly}(\lambda)$) elements whose e^{th} residue symbol is 1 and at least one of them will be an eth residue with all but negligible probability. The ciphertext contains k encryptions, as opposed to $e < k$ in our approach, thus making this approach less space-efficient than ours.

- Gen(1^λ): Generate two RSA primes p and q with $e|p-1$ and $e|q-1$ and let $N = pq$. Uniformly choose a nontrivial, nondegenerate root of unity $\mu \in \mathbb{Z}_N$. Uniformly sample an integer $r \xleftarrow{\$} \mathbb{Z}_N^*$ and set $v \leftarrow r^e \bmod N$. Output (pk $:= (N, \mu, v)$, sk $:= r$).
- Encrypt(pk, m): Given public key pk $:= (N, \mu, v)$ and message $m \in \{0, \dots, e-1\}$, perform the following steps. Generate a uniformly random polynomial $f(x) \xleftarrow{\$} \mathbb{Z}_N^*[x]$ of degree $e-1$ and compute $g(x) \leftarrow f(x)^e \bmod x^e - v$. Choose a uniformly random $t \xleftarrow{\$} \mathbb{Z}_N^*$ and compute the polynomial $c(x) \leftarrow \frac{g(x)}{t}$. Output CT $:= (c(x), d := m + J_N(t) \bmod e)$.
- Decrypt(sk, CT): Given secret key sk $:= r$ and ciphertext CT $:= (c(x), d)$, output $d + J_N(c(r)) \bmod e$.

BLS is proven semantically secure under the MER assumption in the standard model.

3.3 Our Construction

Our approach to circumventing the uninstantiability of the hash function employed in the IBE-version of BLS is akin to the original Cocks scheme. As part of the public parameters, we publish $e-1$ e^{th} non-residues (with $J_N(x) = 0$ for all non-residues x). Then for any integer a satisfying $J(a) = 0$, either a is an eth residue or its product with one of the $e-1$ non-residues is an eth residue. We also make some simplifications to BLS such as removing an element of $\mathbb{Z}_e$ from the ciphertext. We assume a hash function $H : \{0, 1\}^* \to \{x \in \mathbb{Z}_N : J_N(x) = 0\}$ that maps identity strings to elements of $x \in \mathbb{Z}_N$ with $J_N(x) = 0$ (i.e. the power residue symbol of the element is 1).

The scheme is parameterized with a prime e. We make use of the functions J_N and J_p defined earlier which implicitly use a root of unity μ published in the public parameters.

Remark 1. We sometimes omit "mod N" for ease of presentation. This is particularly the case for products involving the elements α_i (as described below) to avoid clutter.

- Setup(1^λ): Generate two RSA primes p and q with $e|p-1$ and $e|q-1$ and let $N = pq$. Sample uniformly an element $\gamma \xleftarrow{\$} \mathbb{Z}_N^*$ with $J_N(\gamma) = 0$ and $J_p(\gamma) \neq 0$. For every $i \in [e]$, set $\alpha_i \leftarrow \gamma^{i-1} \bmod N$. Uniformly choose a nontrivial, nondegenerate root of unity $\mu \in \mathbb{Z}_N$. Output PP $:= (N, \mu, \alpha_1, \dots, \alpha_e)$ and MSK $:= (p, q, \alpha_1, \dots \alpha_e)$.
- KeyGen(MSK, id): Given master secret key MSK $:= (p, q, \alpha_1, \dots, \alpha_e)$ and an identity string id $\in \{0, 1\}^*$, compute $a \leftarrow H(\text{id})$. Check which of $\alpha_1 \cdot a, \dots, \alpha_e \cdot a$ is an eth residue and let the index in the list be i. Then compute the eth root of $\alpha_i \cdot a$ using p and q; denote this root by r. Output sk$_{\text{id}} := (i, r)$.
- Encrypt(PP, id, m): Given public parameters PP $:= (N, \mu, \alpha_1, \dots, \alpha_e)$, an identity string id $\in \{0, 1\}^*$ and a message $m \in \{0, \dots, e-1\}$, first compute

$a \leftarrow H(\mathsf{id})$. We define the subalgorithm $\mathcal{E}$ that takes an integer v and message m' as input and outputs a polynomial in $\mathbb{Z}_N[x]$.

$\mathcal{E}(v, m')$:

- Generate a uniformly random polynomial $f(x) \stackrel{\$}{\leftarrow} \mathbb{Z}_N^*[x]$ of degree $e - 1$.
- Compute $g(x) \leftarrow f(x)^e \bmod x^e - v$.
- Choose a uniformly random $t \stackrel{\$}{\leftarrow} \mathbb{Z}_N^*$ such that $J(t) = m'$.
- Output the polynomial $c(x) = t \cdot g(x)$.

The encryption algorithm outputs $\mathsf{CT} = (a, \mathcal{E}(\alpha_1 \cdot a, m), \ldots, \mathcal{E}(\alpha_e \cdot a, m))$.

- Decrypt($\mathsf{sk}_{\mathsf{id}}, \mathsf{CT}$) : On input a secret key $\mathsf{sk}_{\mathsf{id}} := (i, r)$ and a ciphertext $\mathsf{CT} := (a, c_1(x), \ldots, c_e(x))$, output $m \leftarrow J_N(c_i(r))$.

Correctness The correctness of decryption follows in the same way as BLS; since, $f(x)^3 = g(x)^3 + (x^3 - \alpha_i \cdot a)$, we have $f(r)^3 = g(r)^3$ when $r^3 \equiv \alpha_i \cdot a$ and $J_N(tg(r)^3) = J_N(t)$. It is necessary that the product of one of the α_i's with a gives an eth residue. An element of $v \in \mathbb{Z}_N^*$ is an eth residue iff $J_N(v) = J_p(v) = 0$. Let $k = J_p(a)$. Then multiplying a with an element α satisfying $J_N(\alpha) = 0$ and $J_p(\alpha) = e - k$ guarantees that the resulting element is an eth residue (recall that $J_p(xy) = Jp(x) + Jp(y) \bmod e$). So we need to show that for each $z \in \mathbb{Z}_e$, there is an α_i with $J_p(\alpha_i) = z$. In the setup, we sample a γ with $J_N(\gamma) = 0$ and $J_p(\gamma) \neq 0$. Let $g = J_p(\gamma)$. Then $J_p(\gamma^j) = jg \bmod e$ for $j \in \{0, \ldots, e - 1\}$ and since e is prime, this generates all elements in the additive group $\mathbb{Z}_e$.

Security Now we will reduce the security of our construction to that of BLS. When we refer to BLS hereafter, we will assume that its encryption algorithm is the same as $\mathcal{E}$ above i.e. it outputs a polynomial $\mathsf{CT} := c(x) = t \cdot g(x)$. This does not affect its security. However, there is an obstacle that we must contend with in the security reduction. Given a BLS public key, we cannot generate a $\gamma \in \mathbb{PR}(N) \setminus \mathbb{ER}(N)$ (note that this is precisely the set $\{x : J_N(x) = 0 \wedge J_p(x) \neq 0\}$) with probability 1 which is needed to correctly simulate the public parameters of our scheme. To address this, we consider a modified BLS scheme, denoted BLS', that generates such a γ and outputs it as part of the public key. We first show that BLS' is semantically secure under the MER assumption. Then we will base our security reduction on BLS'.

Lemma 1. *BLS' is IND-CPA secure under the MER assumption.*

Proof. We will prove the lemma via a hybrid argument.

Game 0: This is the real IND-CPA game.

Game 1: We make one change from Game 0, namely we set $\gamma \leftarrow u^e \bmod N$ for a uniformly chosen $u \stackrel{\$}{\leftarrow} \mathbb{Z}_N^*$.

Game 0 and Game 1 are computationally indistinguishable due to MER. In Game 0, γ is sampled uniformly from $\mathbb{PR}(N) \setminus \mathbb{ER}(N)$ and in Game 1, γ is sampled uniformly from $\mathbb{ER}(N)$.

Game 2: The change we make in this game is to encrypt a fixed element $w \in \mathbb{Z}_e$ instead of m_b, where $m_0 \in \mathbb{Z}_e$ and $m_1 \in \mathbb{Z}_e$ are the challenge messages and b is a random bit. The adversary has a zero advantage in this game.

Game 1 and Game 2 are computationally indistinguishable by the semantic security of BLS. Given a BLS public key (N, μ, v), we use these values in the public key and generate γ as in Game 2. When the adversary provides the challenge plaintexts (m_0, m_1), we choose a random b and forward the challenge plaintexts (m_b, w) to the BLS challenger, and return the challenge ciphertext CT^* provided by the BLS challenger. If CT^* encrypts m_b then Game 1 is perfectly simulated whereas if it encrypts w, Game 2 is perfectly simulated. Therefore, a non-negligible advantage distinguishing the hybrids implies a non-negligible advantage breaking the semantic security of BLS. □

Theorem 1. *Our scheme is IND-ID-CPA secure under the MER assumption in the random oracle model.*

Proof. Let $\mathcal{A}$ be the adversary in the IND-ID-CPA game against our scheme. We show that a non-negligible advantage by $\mathcal{A}$ implies a non-negligible advantage against the IND-CPA security of BLS$'$. We construct a simulator $\mathcal{S}$ that interacts in the IND-CPA game and simulates the view of $\mathcal{A}$. The hash function H in our IBE scheme is modeled as a random oracle. We now describe how $\mathcal{S}$ works.

Given a public key (N, μ, v, γ) of BLS$'$ by the IND-CPA challenger, $\mathcal{S}$ uses this information to construct public parameters $(N, \mu, \alpha_1, \ldots, \alpha_e)$, which it gives to $\mathcal{A}$. Let Q be the number of non-adaptive calls to the random oracle H. We assume that $\mathcal{A}$ makes a call to H for identity id prior to making a secret key query for id. The simulator picks a random $k \in [Q]$. The simulator answers calls to H as follows. On the j-th call to H with identity string id_j, perform the following steps:

- If $j = k$:
    - Choose a random $i \xleftarrow{\$} [e]$.
    - Add tuple $(\mathsf{id}_k, \perp, i)$ to table T.
    - Output $v \cdot \alpha_i^{-1} \bmod N$.
- Else:
    - Choose a random $i \xleftarrow{\$} [e]$.
    - Choose a random $r \xleftarrow{\$} \mathbb{Z}_N^*$.
    - Add tuple (id_j, r, i) to T.
    - Output $r^e \cdot \alpha_i^{-1}$.

The simulator handles secret key queries as follows. On querying the secret key for identity id, perform the following steps.

- If $\mathsf{id} = \mathsf{id}_k$, output a random bit and abort the simulation.
- Fetch tuple (id_j, r, i) from T with $\mathsf{id}_j = \mathsf{id}$.
- Output r.

When $\mathcal{A}$ sends its target identity id^* and pair of challenge plaintexts (m_0, m_1), the simulator checks if $\mathsf{id}^* = \mathsf{id}_k$. If this is not the case, $\mathcal{S}$ outputs a random bit and aborts. Otherwise, it forwards (m_0, m_1) to the IND-CPA challenger. Subsequently, the IND-CPA challenger gives $\mathcal{S}$ its challenge ciphertext $\mathsf{CT}^* := c^*(x)$. The simulator performs the following steps:

- Fetch $(\mathsf{id}_k, \bot, i)$ from T.
- Set $c_i(x) \leftarrow c^*(x)$.
- Set $a \leftarrow v \cdot \alpha_i^{-1} \bmod N$
- Compute $c_j(x) \leftarrow \mathcal{E}(\alpha_j \cdot a, u_j)$ with $u_j \overset{\$}{\leftarrow} \mathbb{Z}_e$ for all $j \in [e] \setminus \{i\}$.
- Set $\mathsf{CT} \leftarrow (a, c_1(x), \ldots, c_e(x))$.

The simulator then gives CT to $\mathcal{A}$ as its challenge ciphertext. We claim that CT is identically distributed to a ciphertext in the real game. Firstly, since $a \cdot \alpha_i \equiv v \bmod N$, we have that $c_i(x)$ is perfectly simulated. For all other $j \in [e]$ with $j \neq i$, the element $a \cdot \alpha_j$ is an eth non-residue. It is shown in [28] that ciphertext polynomials computed with an eth non-residue give no information about the plaintext. Therefore, in the view of $\mathcal{A}$, the challenge ciphertext CT is perfectly simulated. Finally, $\mathcal{S}$ outputs $\mathcal{A}$'s guess bit. The probability that the simulation does not abort is $1/Q$. It follows that if $\mathcal{A}$ has advantage ϵ attacking the IND-ID-CPA security of our scheme then $\mathcal{S}$ has advantage ϵ/Q attacking the IND-CPA security of BLS'. Since a non-negligible ϵ would contradict Lemma 1 assuming MER holds, the result follows. $\qquad\square$

3.4 Homomorphism

We now show that our construction is additively homomorphic for the group $(\mathbb{Z}_e, +)$. Given two ciphertexts $\mathsf{CT}_1 := (a, c_1(x), \ldots, c_e(x))$ and $\mathsf{CT}_2 := (a, d_1(x), \ldots, d_e(x))$ encrypted with the same identity id with $a = H(\mathsf{id})$, we compute the i-th component of the resulting ciphertext as $e_i(x) = c_i(x) \cdot d_i(x) \pmod{x^e - \alpha_i \cdot a}$ for $i \in [e]$. Consider the i-th component of the ciphertexts such that $\alpha_i \cdot a \in \mathbb{Z}_N$ is an eth residue. Suppose we have that $c_i(x) = t_1 \cdot f_1(x)^e \pmod{x^e - \alpha_i \cdot a}$ and $d_i(x) = t_2 \cdot f_2(x)^e \pmod{x^e - \alpha_i \cdot a}$. Let r be the eth root of $\alpha_i \cdot a$. To see that multiplication modulo $(x^e - \alpha_i \cdot a)$ is homomorphic, observe that

$$J_N(c_i(x)d_i(x) \ (\bmod \ x^e - \alpha_i \cdot a)(r)) = J_N((t_1 \cdot f_1(x)^e) \cdot (t_2 \cdot f_2(x)^e) \pmod{x^e - \alpha_i \cdot a}(r)) \tag{3.3}$$

$$= J_N((t_1 \cdot t_2)(f_1(x) \cdot f_2(x))^e \pmod{x^e - \alpha_i \cdot a}(r)) \tag{3.4}$$

$$= J_N((t_1 \cdot t_2) \cdot (f_1(r) \cdot f_2(r))^e) \tag{3.5}$$

$$= J_N(t_1 \cdot t_2) \tag{3.6}$$

$$= J_N(t_1) + J_N(t_2) \pmod{e} \tag{3.7}$$

Recall the homomorphic property of J_N i.e. $J_N(xy) = J_N(x) + J_N(y) \bmod e$.

Keeping with the notation we have established so far, let us first fix some identity id $\in \{0,1\}^*$. Let (i, r) be a secret key for id. The ciphertext space $\hat{\mathcal{C}}_{id}$ is defined as follows:

$$\hat{\mathcal{C}}_{id} \triangleq \{(a, (c_1(x), \ldots, c_e(x)) \in \mathbb{Z}_N^e : \deg(c_1) = \cdots = \deg(c_e) = e - 1,$$
$$\left(\frac{c_i(r)}{\mathfrak{N}}\right)_e \neq 0,$$
$$c_j(x) \text{ is invertible in } \mathbb{Z}_N[x]/(x^e - \alpha_j \cdot a) \; \forall j \in [e]\}.$$

The binary operation $*$ can be defined on $\hat{\mathcal{C}}$ as follows: given two ciphertexts $\mathsf{CT}_1 := (a_1, c_1(x), \ldots, c_e(x))$ and $\mathsf{CT}_2 := (a_2, d_1(x), \ldots, d_e(x))$, their product under $*$ is defined as $\mathsf{CT}' := (a_1, c_1(x) \cdot d_1(x) \pmod{x^e - \alpha_1 \cdot a_1}), \ldots, c_e(x) \cdot d_e(x) \pmod{x^e - \alpha_e \cdot a_1}$ if $a_1 = a_2$, and $\mathsf{CT}' := Z$ otherwise, where $Z \in \hat{\mathcal{C}}$ is the null ciphertext.

Lemma 2. *$(\hat{\mathcal{C}}_{id}, *)$ is a group.*

Proof. It is sufficient to consider a single component of the ciphertext because the same analysis applies for each component. Let $v = \alpha_i \cdot a$ for some j. We can view the j-th component as an element in the ring $R_a = \mathbb{Z}_N[x]/(x^e - v)$. Let $c(x)$ be the j-th polynomial component of a ciphertext in $\hat{\mathcal{C}}_{id}$. By definition, $c(x)$ is invertible. Consider the case where $j = i$. By definition, we have $\left(\frac{c(r)}{\mathfrak{N}}\right)_e \neq 0$. Applying $*$ to $c(x)$ and any other element of $\hat{\mathcal{C}}_{id}$ preserves this condition. Therefore $\hat{\mathcal{C}}_{id}$ is closed under $*$. It follows $(\hat{\mathcal{C}}_f, *)$ is a group. $\qquad\square$

We denote the set of legal encryptions under identity id by $\mathcal{C}_{id}$. We have the following straightforward lemma:

Lemma 3. *$(\mathcal{C}_{id}, *)$ is a subgroup of $\hat{\mathcal{C}}_{id}$.*

Proof. We focus on a single component, say the j-th, of a ciphertext. Let $c(x)$ be such a component. Then $c(x)$ is of the form $t \cdot f(x)^e$ for some $f(x)$ that is a unit[4] in $\mathbb{Z}_N[x]/(x^e - \alpha_j \cdot a)$ and $t \in \mathbb{Z}_N^*$. Naturally we have that $c(x) \in \hat{\mathcal{C}}_{id}$. Multiplying $c(x)$ by another element $d(x)$ with the same form yields an element of the same form. $\qquad\square$

Theorem 2. *Our scheme is an IBGHE scheme i.e. it satisfies Definition 3.*

Proof. By Lemma 3 the scheme satisfies GH.1. By the derivation given in Eqs. 3.3–3.7 the scheme satisfies GH.2. Therefore the scheme is an IBGHE. $\qquad\square$

---

[4] We omitted an explicit check for this in the encryption algorithm since a non-unit occurs with negligible probability.

3.5   Homomorphic Addition Modulo a "Large" Modulus

Our scheme supports homomorphic addition modulo a "small" (i.e. poly-sized) prime. However if we use multiple instances of the scheme with distinct primes, we can leverage the Chinese Remainder Theorem to support addition modulo a square-free integer M provided M factors into a polynomial number of poly-sized primes. Hence we can support modular addition with an exponentially-large modulus. This is the first IBE scheme admitting a modular additive homomorphism with a superpolynomial modulus, solving an open problem mentioned in [21].

Concretely, suppose our desired square-free modulus is $M = p_1 \cdots p_n$. We employ n instances of our scheme $\{\mathcal{E}_i\}_{i\in[n]}$ with the e parameter for $\mathcal{E}_i$ set to p_i for all $i \in [n]$.

- Setup(1^λ): Output (PP $:= (PP_1, \ldots, PP_n)$, MSK $:= (MSK_1, \ldots, MSK_n)$ where $(PP_i, MSK_i) \leftarrow \mathcal{E}_i.Setup(1^\lambda)$ for $i \in [n]$.
- KeyGen(MSK $:= (MSK_1, \ldots, MSK_n)$, id): Output sk $:= (sk_1, \ldots, sk_n)$ where $sk_i \leftarrow \mathcal{E}_i.KeyGen(MSK_i, id)$ for $i \in [n]$.
- Encrypt(PP $:= (PP_1, \ldots, PP_n)$, id, m): Output $c := (c_1, \ldots, c_n)$ where $c_i \leftarrow \mathcal{E}_i.Encrypt(PP_i, m \bmod p_i)$ for $i \in [n]$.
- Decrypt(sk $:= (sk_1, \ldots, sk_n), c := (c_1, \ldots, c_n)$) : Output CRT$((m_1, \ldots, m_n),$ $(p_1, \ldots, p_n))$ where $m_i \leftarrow \mathcal{E}_i.Decrypt(sk_i, c_i)$ for $i \in [n]$.
- **Additive Homomorphism:** Let $*^i$ denote the binary operation on the ciphertext space of $\mathcal{E}_i$. We define $*$, the binary operation on the ciphertext space of this construction, as follows:
  - $c * c' = (c_1, \ldots, c_n) * (c'_1, \ldots, c'_n) \triangleq (c_1 *^1 c'_1, \ldots, c_n *^n c'_n)$

The ciphertext space complexity of this scheme is $\sum p_i^2$.

3.6   Anonymity

The XOR-homomorphic scheme CHT mentioned earlier is not anonymous as a result of a test due to Galbraith[5]. Consider an identity id and let $a = H(id)$. Ciphertexts in CHT are a pair of polynomials $(c(x), d(x)) \in (\mathbb{Z}_N[x])^2$. We will consider only a single ciphertext component here, say the first ($c(x)$), which is encrypted with respect to a. The observations also hold with respect to the second component by replacing a with $-a$. We define Galbraith's Test for ciphertext polynomials as the function GT $: \mathbb{Z}_N \times \mathbb{Z}_N[x] \to \{-1, 0, +1\}$ given by

$$GT(a, c(x)) = \left(\frac{c_0^2 - c_1^2 a}{N}\right).$$

For encryptions $c(x)$ (recall we are just considering one component) encrypted under identity id, we have GT$(a, c(x)) = 1$. For encryptions $c'(x)$ under a different identity, it is the case that GT$(a, c'(x)) = 1$ with probability negligibly close to $1/2$.

---

[5] Reported as emerging from personal communication in [34].

For convenience, let us denote our scheme that extends BLS, as described above, for the case of $e = 2$ (i.e. admitting an XOR homomorphism) by $\mathcal{E}_2$. Although $\mathcal{E}_2$ is algorithmically different to CHT, it shares many of the same properties. In particular it is easy to see that Galbraith's test is applicable in the same way. An anonymous variant of CHT was proposed in [35] and the techniques are also applicable to $\mathcal{E}_2$. However the approach to achieve anonymity in [35] loses the homomorphic property i.e. one cannot homomorphically operate on anonymized ciphertexts.

We now turn our attention to investigating whether our scheme for the case of $e > 2$ is anonymous. We will denote our scheme for this case by $\mathcal{E}_e$. As usual, for identity id, we let $a = H(\text{id})$. We define the ciphertext space $\hat{C}$ for a single component as $\hat{C} := \{c(x) \in \mathbb{Z}_N^*[x] : \deg(c(x)) = e - 1\}$ (the analysis holds analogously for the other components). Now consider the subset $C_a \subset \hat{C}$, which are the set of polynomials (for a single component) in the image of the encryption algorithm with respect to a; that is, we have $C_a := \{t \cdot f(x)^e \bmod x^e - a : t \in \mathbb{Z}_N^*, f(x) \in \mathbb{Z}_N^*[x], \deg(f(x)) = e - 1\}$. Also we need to define a subset $C_a^{(0)} \subset C_a$ of C_a that corresponds to encryptions of the identity element 0 with respect to a.

Definition 7 (Algebraic Equation Set). *The algebraic equation set for a ciphertext $c(x) \in \hat{C}$ with respect to a is derived as follows. The unknowns are the coefficients $z_0, ..., z^{e-1}$ of the polynomial $f(x)$ generated during encryption. Raising $f(x)$ to the power of e and reducing according to the equivalence relation $x^e \equiv a$ induced by the quotient of the ring $\mathbb{Z}_N^*[x]/(x^e - a)$ yields a set of e multivariate polynomials in $z_0, ..., z^{e-1}$ of degree e, one for each coefficient of the result. The algebraic equation set is formed by letting the polynomial for the i-th coefficient of the result equal to c_i for $i \in 0, ..., e - 1$. For example, the algebraic equation set for $e = 3$ is*

$$z_0^3 + a z_1^3 + a^2 z_2^3 + 6a z_0 z_1 z_2 = c_0$$
$$3z_0^2 z_1 + 3a z_0 z_2^2 + 3a z_1^2 z_2 = c_1$$
$$3z_0^2 z_2 + 3z_0 z_1^2 + 3a z_1 z_2^2 = c_2$$

We now define a subset $C_a^{(0)\prime} \subset C_a^{(0)}$ of the honest encryptions of 0 as $C_a^{(0)\prime} := \{t \cdot f(x)^e \bmod x^e - a : t \in \mathbb{ER}(N), f(x) \in \mathbb{Z}_N^*[x], \deg(f(x)) = e - 1\}$ i.e. the $t \in \mathbb{Z}_N^*$ used during encryption is an eth residue. We have the following lemma.

Lemma 4. *The algebraic equation set for $c(x) \in \hat{C}$ with respect to a has a solution if and only if $c(x) \in C_a^{(0)\prime}$.*

Proof. Let $R = \mathbb{Z}_N^*[x]/(x^e - a)$. A solution to the algebraic equation set for $c(x)$ is a polynomial $f(x)$ such that $f(x)^e = c(x)$ (in R). Therefore $t = 1$, an eth residue and thus we have $c(x) \in C_a^{(0)\prime}$. Conversely, let $c(x)$ be an element of $C_a^{(0)\prime}$. We can write $c(x) = t \cdot f(x)^e \in R$. Since $t = r^e$ is an eth residue for some $r \in \mathbb{Z}_N^*$, we have that $r \cdot f(x) \in R$ is a solution to the algebraic equation set, which secures the lemma. $\qquad\square$

We have an additional lemma.

Lemma 5. *The sets $C_a^{(0)}$ and $C_a^{(0)\prime}$ are computationally indistinguishable assuming the hardness of MER.*

Proof. An algorithm that distinguishes between $C_a^{(0)}\backslash C_a^{(0)\prime}$ and $C_a^{(0)\prime}$ can be used to construct an algorithm that solves MER. Given a MER challenge $t \in \{x \in \mathbb{Z}_N : J_N(t) = 0\}$, an element $c(x)$ is generated by computing $t \cdot f(x)^e \bmod x^e - a$ for $f(x) \xleftarrow{\$} \mathbb{Z}_N^*[x]$, $\deg(f(x)) = e - 1$. If t is a non-residue then $c(x)$ is uniformly distributed in the first distribution. Otherwise, it is uniformly distributed in the second distribution. An algorithm that distinguishes the distributions can thus solve MER. By extension, the statement of the lemma follows. □

Let $A = \{x \in \mathbb{Z}_N^* : J_N(x) = 0\}$. We are now ready to define the assumption under which we prove anonymity of $\mathcal{E}_e$.

Definition 8. (Special Polynomial Equations Solvability (SPES(e) Assumption). *Given $(a, c(x)) \in A \times \hat{C}$ where $a \xleftarrow{\$} A$, consider an algorithm $\mathcal{A}$ that decides the solvability of the algebraic equation set for $c(x)$ with respect to a. Let S be the set of instances in $A \times \hat{C}_a$ that are solvable and let $\bar{S}$ be the unsolvable instances. The advantage of $\mathcal{A}$ deciding correctly $\mathsf{Adv}_\mathcal{A}$ is defined as*

$$\mathsf{Adv}_\mathcal{A} \triangleq \Pr[s \xleftarrow{\$} S : \mathcal{A}(s) \to 1] - \Pr[\bar{s} \xleftarrow{\$} \bar{S} : \mathcal{A}(\bar{s}) \to 1].$$

The SPES(e) assumption for prime $e > 2$ is that for every PPT algorithm $\mathcal{A}$ it holds that $\mathsf{Adv}_\mathcal{A} < \mathsf{negl}(\lambda)$.

Remark 2. Deciding solvability of a system of multivariate polynomial equations in general is NP-complete. However for the special system of equations of interest here, with certain structure, we must make an explicit assumption about the hardness of deciding its solvability.

Lemma 6. *The sets C_a and $\hat{C} \backslash C_a$ are computationally indistinguishable for $a \xleftarrow{\$} A$ assuming the hardness of SPES and MER.*

Proof. By semantic security of $\mathcal{E}_e$, via the MER assumption, shown in Theorem 1, it holds that C_a is computationally instinguishable from $C_a^{(0)}$. Then by invoking Lemma 5, we have that $C_a^{(0)}$ is computationally indistinguishable from $C_a^{(0)\prime}$. Now Lemma 4 tells us that the solvable instances for SPES are the set $C_a^{(0)\prime}$. The unsolvable instances are $\hat{C}\backslash C_a^{(0)\prime}$. By the hardness of SPES, these sets are therefore computationally indistinguishable. The result follows. □

Theorem 3. *$\mathcal{E}_e$ for $e > 2$ is anonymous under the SPES and MER assumptions.*

Proof. In the anonymity security game, the adversary chooses two target identities id and id$'$.

Game 0: This is the real game.

Game 1: In this game, we change how the challenge ciphertext is generated if the challenger's bit $\beta = 0$ (i.e. using identity id). If $\beta = 0$, we sample the challenge ciphertext uniformly from $\hat{C}$ instead of C_a where a is what is returned by $H(\text{id})$.

To invoke Lemma 6 to argue indistinguishability of $\hat{C}$ and C_a, we need to program the output of the random oracle H on identity id to be a, which is distributed correctly. In a similar manner to the proof of Theorem 1, we must guess one of the identities the adversary chooses from its queries to H and abort with a random bit if we guessed incorrectly. This step loses a factor of roughly $1/Q$ where Q is the number of queries to H prior choosing the target identities.

Game 2: In this game, we change how the challenge ciphertext is generated if the challengers bit $\beta = 1$ (i.e. using identity id'). If $\beta = 1$, we sample the challenge ciphertext uniformly from $\hat{C}$ instead of C_b where b is what is returned by $H(\text{id}')$.

Indistinguishability follows in the same manner as the transition between Game 0 to Game 1.

The adversary has zero advantage in this game as it learns no information about β. The result follows.   □

3.7   Cryptanalytic Investigation of SPES

The main practical approach for solving a system of multivariate polynomial equations is via computing a reduced Gröbner basis. For a sufficient number of equations, solvability can be decided by checking if the reduced Gröbner basis is $\{1\}$ [36], which means the system is inconsistent (no solution exists). Buchberger [36,37] introduced an algorithm for computing a Gröbner basis. The time complexity of this algorithm is difficult to analyze but is estimated to be doubly exponential in the number of variables. Therefore for $e = \Omega(\log \lambda)$ with security parameter λ this approach is intractable. For such values of e, a standard technique is to use resultants to eliminate variables. However to eliminate variables such that only a constant number remain, leads to polynomials with superpolynomial degree in λ. In view of this state of affairs, since Gröbner basis computation is the best known practical approach for solving multivariate equations, we conjecture that $\text{SPES}(e)$ is hard for $e = \Omega(\log \lambda)$. We now focus on small (constant) values of e. For example we are interested in knowing whether $\text{SPES}(3)$ is hard.

We used a variant of Buchberger's algorithm in Sage to compute Gröbner bases and conduct experimental analysis. Our experimental results show that with overwhelming probability the reduced Gröbner basis in the lexicographic monomial ordering for the $\text{SPES}(e)$ system consists of e polynomials where the last polynomial (when ordered lexicographically) in the basis is a univariate polynomial in z_{e-1} of the form $\sum_{i=0}^{e-1} a_i z_{e-1}^{i \cdot e}$ for coefficients $a_i \in Z_N$. This is the case whether the system is solvable or not. Buchberger's criterion for unsolvability, i.e. checking if the reduced Gröbner basis is $\{1\}$, does not pertain because we have an insufficient number of equations. We now have a univariate polynomial over Z_N. However to the best of our knowledge, there are no known feasible attacks on deciding solvability of such polynomials when N is an RSA modulus. Inspecting the form of the univariate polynomial above, it is not difficult to see that deciding solvability of polynomials of this form for general coefficients a_i is at least as hard as the eth residuosity problem. This gives evidence that the problem we are faced with (for a certain distribution of coefficients) has the *potential* to be hard but we cannot provide a reduction or firmer conclusion on its exact hardness for the distribution of coefficients encountered. Nevertheless, in light of the evidence, we conjecture that $SPES(e)$ is hard for constant prime $e > 2$. We invite the community to conduct further cryptanalysis.

References

1. Shamir, A.: Identity-based cryptosystems and signature schemes. In: Blakley, G.R., Chaum, D. (eds.) CRYPTO 1984. LNCS, vol. 196, pp. 47–53. Springer, Heidelberg (1985). https://doi.org/10.1007/3-540-39568-7_5
2. Boneh, D., Franklin, M.: Identity-based encryption from the Weil pairing. In: Kilian, J. (ed.) CRYPTO 2001. LNCS, vol. 2139, pp. 213–229. Springer, Heidelberg (2001). https://doi.org/10.1007/3-540-44647-8_13
3. Cocks, C.: An identity based encryption scheme based on quadratic residues. In: Honary, B. (ed.) Cryptography and Coding 2001. LNCS, vol. 2260, pp. 360–363. Springer, Heidelberg (2001). https://doi.org/10.1007/3-540-45325-3_32
4. Armknecht, F., Katzenbeisser, S., Peter, A.: Group homomorphic encryption: characterizations, impossibility results, and applications. Des. Codes Cryptogr. **67**, 1–24 (2012)
5. Kushilevitz, E., Ostrovsky, R.: Replication is not needed: single database, computationally-private information retrieval. In: Proceedings of the 38th Annual Symposium on Foundations of Computer Science, FOCS 1997, pp. 364–373. IEEE Computer Society, Washington, DC (1997)
6. Benaloh, J.D.C.: Verifiable secret-ballot elections. Ph.D. thesis, Yale University, New Haven, CT, USA (1987). AAI8809191
7. Cohen, J.D., Fischer, M.J.: A robust and verifiable cryptographically secure election scheme. In: Proceedings of the 26th Annual Symposium on Foundations of Computer Science, pp. 372–382. IEEE Computer Society, Washington, DC (1985)
8. Cramer, R., Franklin, M., Schoenmakers, B., Yung, M.: Multi-authority secret-ballot elections with linear work. In: Maurer, U. (ed.) EUROCRYPT 1996. LNCS, vol. 1070, pp. 72–83. Springer, Heidelberg (1996). https://doi.org/10.1007/3-540-68339-9_7
9. Cramer, R., Gennaro, R., Schoenmakers, B.: A secure and optimally efficient multi-authority election scheme. In: Fumy, W. (ed.) EUROCRYPT 1997. LNCS, vol. 1233, pp. 103–118. Springer, Heidelberg (1997). https://doi.org/10.1007/3-540-69053-0_9
10. Damgård, I., Jurik, M.: A generalisation, a simplification and some applications of Paillier's probabilistic public-key system. In: Kim, K. (ed.) PKC 2001. LNCS, vol. 1992, pp. 119–136. Springer, Heidelberg (2001). https://doi.org/10.1007/3-540-44586-2_9

11. Naor, M., Pinkas, B.: Oblivious polynomial evaluation. SIAM J. Comput. **35**, 1254–1281 (2006)
12. Sander, T., Young, A.L., Yung, M.: Non-interactive cryptocomputing for nc^1. In: FOCS, pp. 554–567. IEEE Computer Society (1999)
13. Fischlin, M.: A cost-effective pay-per-multiplication comparison method for millionaires. In: Naccache, D. (ed.) CT-RSA 2001. LNCS, vol. 2020, pp. 457–471. Springer, Heidelberg (2001). https://doi.org/10.1007/3-540-45353-9_33
14. Goldwasser, S., Micali, S.: Probabilistic encryption. J. Comput. Syst. Sci. **28**, 270–299 (1984). See also preliminary version in 14th STOC, 1982
15. Naccache, D., Stern, J.: A new public key cryptosystem based on higher residues. In: Gong, L., Reiter, M.K., (eds.) ACM Conference on Computer and Communications Security, pp. 59–66. ACM (1998)
16. Okamoto, T., Uchiyama, S.: A new public-key cryptosystem as secure as factoring. In: Nyberg, K. (ed.) EUROCRYPT 1998. LNCS, vol. 1403, pp. 308–318. Springer, Heidelberg (1998). https://doi.org/10.1007/BFb0054135
17. Paillier, P.: Public-key cryptosystems based on composite degree residuosity classes. In: Stern, J. (ed.) EUROCRYPT 1999. LNCS, vol. 1592, pp. 223–238. Springer, Heidelberg (1999). https://doi.org/10.1007/3-540-48910-X_16
18. Gjøsteen, K.: Homomorphic cryptosystems based on subgroup membership problems. In: Dawson, E., Vaudenay, S. (eds.) Mycrypt 2005. LNCS, vol. 3715, pp. 314–327. Springer, Heidelberg (2005). https://doi.org/10.1007/11554868_22
19. Gjøsteen, K.: Symmetric subgroup membership problems. In: Vaudenay, S. (ed.) PKC 2005. LNCS, vol. 3386, pp. 104–119. Springer, Heidelberg (2005). https://doi.org/10.1007/978-3-540-30580-4_8
20. Damgård, I.: Towards practical public key systems secure against chosen ciphertext attacks. In: Feigenbaum, J. (ed.) CRYPTO 1991. LNCS, vol. 576, pp. 445–456. Springer, Heidelberg (1992). https://doi.org/10.1007/3-540-46766-1_36
21. Clear, M., Hughes, A., Tewari, H.: Homomorphic encryption with access policies: characterization and new constructions. In: Youssef, A., Nitaj, A., Hassanien, A.E. (eds.) AFRICACRYPT 2013. LNCS, vol. 7918, pp. 61–87. Springer, Heidelberg (2013). https://doi.org/10.1007/978-3-642-38553-7_4
22. Chor, B., Kushilevitz, E., Goldreich, O., Sudan, M.: Private information retrieval. J. Assoc. Comput. Mach. **45**, 965–981 (1998)
23. Oliveira, L., Scott, M., Lopez, J., Dahab, R.: TinyPBC: pairings for authenticated identity-based non-interactive key distribution in sensor networks. In: 5th International Conference on Networked Sensing Systems, INSS 2008, pp. 173–180 (2008)
24. Liu, A., Ning, P.: TinyECC: a configurable library for elliptic curve cryptography in wireless sensor networks. In: IPSN 2008: Proceedings of the 7th International Conference on Information Processing in Sensor Networks, pp. 245–256. IEEE Computer Society, Washington, DC (2008)
25. Oliveira, L.B., Aranha, D.F., Morais, E., Daguano, F., López, J., Dahab, R.: TinyTate: computing the tate pairing in resource-constrained sensor nodes. In: IEEE International Symposium on Network Computing and Applications, pp. 318–323 (2007)
26. Szczechowiak, P., Kargl, A., Scott, M., Collier, M.: On the application of pairing based cryptography to wireless sensor networks. In: WiSec 2009: Proceedings of the Second ACM Conference on Wireless Network Security, pp. 1–12. ACM, New York (2009)

27. Günther, F., Manulis, M., Peter, A.: Privacy-enhanced participatory sensing with collusion resistance and data aggregation. In: Gritzalis, D., Kiayias, A., Askoxylakis, I. (eds.) CANS 2014. LNCS, vol. 8813, pp. 321–336. Springer, Cham (2014). https://doi.org/10.1007/978-3-319-12280-9_21

28. Boneh, D., LaVigne, R., Sabin, M.: Identity-based encryption with eth residuosity and its incompressibility. (TRUST Conference, poster presentation). http://www.truststc.org/education/reu/13/Papers/SabinM_Paper.pdf

29. Gentry, C., Peikert, C., Vaikuntanathan, V.: Trapdoors for hard lattices and new cryptographic constructions. In: STOC 2008: Proceedings of the 40th Annual ACM Symposium on Theory of Computing, pp. 197–206. ACM, New York (2008)

30. Albrecht, M.R., Player, R., Scott, S.: On the concrete hardness of learning with errors. J. Math. Cryptol. **9**, 169–203 (2015)

31. Joye, M.: On Identity-Based Cryptosystems from Quadratic Residuosity. http://joye.site88.net/papers/gcocks.pdf

32. Freeman, D.M., Goldreich, O., Kiltz, E., Rosen, A., Segev, G.: More constructions of lossy and correlation-secure trapdoor functions. J. Cryptol. **26**, 39–74 (2013)

33. Squirrel, D.: Computing reciprocity symbols in number fields. Thesis (B.A.) Reed College (1997)

34. Boneh, D., Gentry, C., Hamburg, M.: Space-efficient identity based encryption without pairings. In: FOCS, pp. 647–657. IEEE Computer Society (2007)

35. Clear, M., Tewari, H., McGoldrick, C.: Anonymous IBE from quadratic residuosity with improved performance. In: Pointcheval, D., Vergnaud, D. (eds.) AFRICACRYPT 2014. LNCS, vol. 8469, pp. 377–397. Springer, Cham (2014). https://doi.org/10.1007/978-3-319-06734-6_23

36. Buchberger, B.: An algorithmic criterion for the solvability of a system of algebraic equations. In: Buchberger, B., Winkler, F. (eds.) Gröbner Bases and Applications. London Mathematical Society Lecture Notes Series, vol. 251, pp. 535–545. Cambridge University Press (1998)

37. Buchberger, B.: Introduction to Gröbner bases. In: Buchberger, B., Winkler, F. (eds.) Gröbner Bases and Applications. London Mathematical Society Lecture Notes Series, vol. 251, pp. 3–31. Cambridge University Press (1998)

Fundamental Primitives (I)

Upper and Lower Bounds for Continuous Non-Malleable Codes

Dana Dachman-Soled and Mukul Kulkarni[(✉)]

University of Maryland, College Park, USA
danadach@ece.umd.edu, mukul@terpmail.umd.edu

Abstract. Recently, Faust et al. (TCC'14) introduced the notion of *continuous* non-malleable codes (CNMC), which provides stronger security guarantees than standard non-malleable codes, by allowing an adversary to tamper with the codeword in a continuous way instead of one-time tampering. They also showed that CNMC with information theoretic security cannot be constructed in the 2-split-state tampering model, and presented a construction in the common reference string (CRS) model from collision-resistant hash functions and non-interactive zero-knowledge proofs.

In this work, we ask if it is possible to construct CNMC from weaker assumptions. We answer this question by presenting lower as well as upper bounds. We show that it is impossible to construct 2-split-state CNMC, with no CRS, for one-bit messages from any falsifiable assumption, thus establishing the lower bound. We additionally provide an upper bound by constructing 2-split-state CNMC for one-bit messages, assuming only the existence of a family of injective one way functions. We note that in a recent work, Ostrovsky et al. (CRYPTO'18) considered the construction of a relaxed notion of 2-split-state CNMC from minimal assumptions.

We also present a construction of 4-split-state CNMC for multi-bit messages in CRS model from the same assumptions. Additionally, we present definitions of the following new primitives: (1) *One-to-one commitments*, and (2) *Continuous Non-Malleable Randomness Encoders*, which may be of independent interest.

Keywords: Continuous non-malleable codes ·
Black-box impossibility · Split-state

1 Introduction

Non-Malleable Codes (NMC). Non-malleable codes were introduced by Dziembowski, Pietrzak and Wichs [37] as a relaxation of error-correcting codes,

D. Dachman-Soled—This work is supported in part by NSF grants #CNS-1840893, #CNS-1453045 (CAREER), by a research partnership award from Cisco and by financial assistance award 70NANB15H328 from the U.S. Department of Commerce, National Institute of Standards and Technology.

D. Lin and K. Sako (Eds.): PKC 2019, LNCS 11442, pp. 519–548, 2019.
https://doi.org/10.1007/978-3-030-17253-4_18

and are useful in settings where privacy—but not necessarily correctness—is desired. The main application of non-malleable codes proposed in the literature is for protecting a secret key stored on a device against tampering attacks, although non-malleable codes have also found applications in other of areas of cryptography [24,25,49] and theoretical computer science [20].

Continuous Non-Malleable Codes (CNMC). Importantly, standard non-malleable codes achieve security only against one-time tampering. So in applications, the non-malleable encoding of a secret key must be continually decoded and re-encoded, incurring overhead in computation and in generation of randomness for re-encoding. This motivated a stronger notion of non-malleable codes, *continuous non-malleable codes (CNMC)*, introduced by Faust et al. [40]. This definition allows many-time tampering–i.e. the adversary can continuously tamper with the codeword and observe the effects of the tampering. Due to known impossibility results, there must also be a "self-destruct" mechanism: If, upon decode, the device detects an error, then a "self-destruct" mechanism, which erases the secret key, is triggered, rendering the device useless.

The notion of CNMC with respect to a tampering class $\mathcal{F}$ is as follows: Given a coding scheme $\Pi = (\mathsf{E}, \mathsf{D})$, where E is the encoding function and D is the decoding function, the adversary interacts with an oracle $\mathcal{O}_\Pi(C)$, parameterized by Π and an encoding of a message m, $C \leftarrow \mathsf{E}(m)$. We refer to the encoding C as the "challenge" encoding. In each round, the adversary submits a tampering function $f \in \mathcal{F}$. The oracle evaluates $C' = f(C)$. If $\mathsf{D}(C') = \bot$, the oracle outputs $\bot$ and a "self-destruct" occurs, aborting the experiment. If $C' = C$, the oracle outputs a special message "same." Otherwise, the oracle outputs C'. We emphasize that the entire tampered codeword is returned to the adversary in this case. A CNMC is secure if for every pair of messages m_0, m_1, the adversary's view in the above game is computationally indistinguishable when the message is m_0 or m_1.

Recently, Ostrovsky et al. [63] proposed a relaxed definition of CNMC (sufficient for many applications) along with a construction, in which the oracle $\mathcal{O}_\Pi(C)$ returns, if valid, the decoding of the tampered codeword $\mathsf{D}(C')$ (or "same") instead of the tampered codeword C' as in the standard (original) definition of [40]. In terms of applications, the difference between the original notion (which we consider in this paper) and the notion of [63], is that the notion we consider captures stronger types of side-channel attacks: Our notion provides security against an adversary who tampers and additionally learns information about the modified codeword C' through other side-channels. As a concrete example, an interesting research direction is to compose a split-state CNMC (under the original definition) with a leakage-resilient circuit compiler, such as the compiler of Ishai, Sahai and Wagner [51], in order to yield a compiler that simultaneously provides security against tampering with memory and leakage on computation. For more discussion and comparison of this paper with [63] see Sect. 1.2.

Split-State Tampering. One of the most well-studied tampering classes for non-malleable codes is *split-state tampering*. Here, the codeword is split into sections and the adversarial tampering function may tamper each section independently. The case of 2-split-state tampering, where the codeword is split into two sections, is of particular interest. See Sect. 1.4 for a discussion of prior work on NMC and CNMC against split-state tampering.

Information-Theoretic Impossibility. The original CNMC paper of [40] showed an information-theoretic impossibility result for 2-split-state CNMC. To aid the subsequent discussion, we present an outline of this result. The impossibility result considers a property of 2-split-state CNMC known as (perfect) "uniqueness." Informally, perfect uniqueness means that there do not exist triples (x, y, z) such that either (1) $y \neq z \wedge \mathsf{D}(x,y) \neq \bot \wedge \mathsf{D}(x,z) \neq \bot$ OR (2) $x \neq y \wedge \mathsf{D}(x,z) \neq \bot \wedge \mathsf{D}(y,z) \neq \bot$. First, a perfectly unique CNMC cannot be information-theoretically secure since, given L, the split-state tampering function can find the unique R such that $\mathsf{D}(L, R) \neq \bot$ and then tamper based on $m = \mathsf{D}(L, R)$. On the other hand, if the CNMC is not perfectly unique, then the following is an efficient attack (with non-uniform advice): Given a tuple L_1', L_2', R' such that $\mathsf{D}(L_1', R') \neq \bot$ and $\mathsf{D}(L_2', R') \neq \bot$, the adversary can learn L bit-by-bit by using the following tampering function in the i-th round: f_L does the following: If the i-th bit of L is equal to 0, replace L with L_1'. Otherwise, replace L' with L_2'. f_R always replaces R with R'. Now, in the i-th round, if the oracle returns (L_1', R'), then the adversary learns that the i-th bit of L is equal to 0. If the oracle returns (L_2', R'), then the adversary learns that the i-th bit of L is equal to 1. Once L is fully recovered, the adversary can tamper based on $m = \mathsf{D}(L, R)$.

The Computational Setting. The above shows that the CNMC setting is distinguished from other NMC settings, since information-theoretic (unconditional) security is impossible. Prior work has shown how to construct 2-split-state CNMC in the *CRS model* under the assumptions of collision-resistant hash functions and NIZK. On the other hand, CNMC's imply commitment schemes, which in turn imply OWF. It remains to determine where CNMC lies in terms of complexity assumptions and what are the minimal computational assumptions needed to achieve CNMC. As mentioned previously, a very recent work of Ostrovsky et al. [63] addressed minimizing computational assumptions under a relaxed definition of CNMC. See Sect. 1.2 for more details.

Black-Box Reductions. In general, it is not feasible to unconditionally rule out the construction of a primitive G from a cryptographic assumption H, since unconditionally ruling it out is as hard as proving $P \neq NP$. Despite this, we can still show that the proof techniques we have at hand cannot be used to construct G from assumption H. In the literature, this is typically done by showing that there is no black-box reduction from primitive G to assumption H. In this work, what we mean by a black-box reduction is a reduction that accesses the *adversary* in an input/output fashion only. However, we allow non-black-box usage of the assumption H in both the construction and the proof (see Definition 6 for a formal definition tailored to CNMC). While there are some exceptions [12,14], the vast majority of cryptographic reductions are black-box in the adversary.

1.1   Our Results

We present upper and lower bounds for CNMC in the 2-split-state model. First, we show that with no CRS, single-bit CNMC in the 2-split-state model (with a black-box security proof) is impossible to construct from any falsifiable assumption.

Theorem 1 (Informal). *There is no black-box reduction from a single-bit, 2-split-state, CNMC scheme $\Pi = (\mathsf{E}, \mathsf{D})$ to any falsifiable assumption.*

On the other hand, in the CRS model, we show how to achieve single-bit CNMC in the 2-split-state model from injective one-way functions.

Theorem 2. *Assuming the existence of an injective one-way function family, there is a construction of a 2-split-state CNMC for encoding single bit, in the CRS model. Moreover, the corresponding reduction is black-box.*

Actually, we show a somewhat more general result: First, we define a (to the best of our knowledge) new type of commitment scheme called *one-to-one commitment schemes in the CRS model*. Informally, these commitment schemes have the additional property that with all but negligible probability over Σ produced by CRS generation, for every string *com*, there is at most a *single* string d that will be accepted as a valid decommitment for *com* (See Definition 9 for a formal definition). We also define the notion of a 2-split-state CNM Randomness Encoder, which is the continuous analogue of the non-malleable randomness encoder recently introduced by [54] (See Definition 5). We then show the following:

Theorem 3. *Assuming the existence of one-to-one commitment schemes in the CRS model, there is a construction of a 2-split-state CNM Randomness Encoder in the CRS model. Moreover, the corresponding reduction is black-box.*

One-to-one commitment schemes in the CRS model can be constructed from any injective one-way function family. Furthermore, we show (see the full version of this paper [27]) that 2-split-state CNM Randomness Encoders in the CRS model imply 2-split-state CNMC for encoding single bit, in the CRS model. We therefore obtain Theorem 2 as a corollary. Moreover, CNMC with *perfect* uniqueness in the CRS model implies one-to-one commitment schemes in the CRS model in a straightforward way (refer to the full version of this paper [27]).

We leave open the question of constructing CNMC in the CRS model from (non-injective) one-way functions and/or showing a black-box separation between the two primitives. Finally, we extend the techniques from our single-bit construction above to achieve the following:

Theorem 4. *Assuming the existence of one-to-one commitment schemes in the CRS model, there is a construction of a multi-bit, 4-split-state CNMC in the CRS model. Moreover, the corresponding reduction is black-box.*

Are Prior CNMC Reductions "black-box"? Prior CNMC reductions often proceed in a sequence of hybrids, where in the final hybrid, the description of the adversary is incorporated in the definition of a leakage function. It is then shown that the leakage-resilience properties of an underlying encoding imply that the view of the adversary is statistically close when the encoded message is set to m_0 or m_1. While this may seem like non-black-box usage of the adversary, we note that typically the leakage-resilience of the underlying encoding is information-theoretic. When converting a hybrid-style proof to a reduction, the reduction will choose one of the hybrid steps at random and use the fact that a distinguisher between some pair of consecutive hybrids implies an adversary breaking an underlying assumption. Therefore, reductions of the type discussed above are still black-box in the adversary, pairs of consecutive hybrids whose indistinguishability is implied by a *computational* assumption yield a reduction in which the adversary is used in a black-box manner.

1.2   Comparison with Ostrovsky et al. [63]

The CNMC notion considered in this work is the original continuous non-malleable codes notion, first introduced in [40] and then further studied in several follow-up works (including [35,41,52]). Recently, Ostrovsky et al. [63] introduced a relaxed notion of CNMC,[1] which is sufficient for many applications. In the work of Ostrovsky et al. [63], they refer to the original notion as "continuous super-non-malleability" (since it is analogous to "super-non-malleability", a notion that was introduced in the non-continuous setting [42]). They then presented a construction achieving the relaxed definition (which they simply call "continuous non-malleability"), against 2-split-state tampering functions, assuming the existence of injective one-way functions in the plain model (without CRS).

The difference between the two CNMC notions is that in the original CNMC notion, the tampering oracle returns the entire modified codeword C' if $C' = f(C) \neq C$ and $\mathsf{D}(C) \neq \perp$, whereas the relaxation only requires the oracle to return $\mathsf{D}(C')$ but not C' itself. The original notion captures stronger types of tampering attacks; specifically, it provides security against an adversary who learns arbitrary additional information about the modified codeword C' through other side-channels.

Our result and the result of [63] are complementary and together give a full picture of the landscape of assumptions required for CNMC. Our work shows that it is *necessary* to rely on setup assumptions (CRS) in order to achieve the original, stronger security definition of CNMC. Moreover, if one is willing to assume the existence of a CRS, we show that this type of CNMC can be achieved from nearly minimal computational assumptions. In contrast, if one is not willing to assume the existence of a CRS, the work of [63] achieves weaker security guarantees in the plain model (with no setup assumptions) from

---

[1] A similar relaxed definition was previously given for a variant of CNMC, known as R- CNMC [38], but in this setting it was shown that it is actually impossible to achieve the stronger notion.

the same computational assumptions. We also note that the work of Ostrovsky et al. [63] explicitly lists the question we address in this work as an interesting open problem. They state:

> Interesting open questions related to our work are, for instance, whether continuous non-malleability can be achieved, under minimal assumptions, together with additional properties, such as strong non-malleability, **super-non-malleability**, augmented non-malleability, and locality ...

1.3   Technical Overview

Lower Bound. Recall that prior work has shown that if a CNMC is not perfectly unique, then there is an efficient attack (with non-uniform advice). Thus, it remains to show that there is no black-box reduction from a single-bit, *perfectly unique* CNMC scheme to any falsifiable assumption. We use the meta-reduction approach, which is to prove impossibility by showing that given only black-box access to the split-state adversary, $A = (A_L, A_R)$, the reduction cannot distinguish between the actual adversary and a *simulated* (efficient) adversary (which is possibly stateful). Since the view of the reduction is indistinguishable in the two cases, the reduction must also break the falsifiable assumption when interacting with the simulated adversary. But this in turn means that there is an efficient adversary (obtained by composing the reduction and the simulated adversary), which contradicts the underlying falsifiable assumption. Consider the following stateless, inefficient, split-state adversary $A = (A_L, A_R)$, which leverages the uniqueness property of the CNMC scheme: The real adversary, given L (resp. R), recovers the corresponding unique valid codeword (L, R) (if it exists) and decodes to get the bit b. If $b = 0$, the real adversary encodes a random bit b' using internal randomness that is tied to (L, R), and outputs the left/right side as appropriate. If $b = 1$ or there is no corresponding valid codeword, the real adversary outputs the left/right side of a random encoding of a random bit, b'' (generated using internal randomness that is tied to L or R respectively). The simulated adversary is stateful and keeps a table containing all the L and R values that it has seen. Whenever a L (resp. R) query is made, the simulated adversary first checks the table to see if a matching query to R (resp. L) such that $\mathsf{D}(L, R) \neq \bot$ was previously made. If not, the simulated adversary chooses a random encoding, (L', R'), of a random bit b', stores it in the table along with the L/R query that was made and returns either L' or R' as appropriate. If yes, the simulated adversary finds the corresponding R (resp. L) along with the pair (L', R') stored in the table. The simulated adversary then decodes (L, R) to find out b. If $b = 0$, the simulated adversary returns either L' or R' as appropriate. Otherwise, the simulated adversary returns the left/right side of an encoding of a random bit b''. The uniqueness property allows us to prove that the input/output behavior of the real adversary is identical to that of the simulated adversary. See Sect. 3 for additional details. For a discussion on why our impossibility result does not hold for the relaxed CNMC notion considered by [63], see the full version of this paper [27].

Upper Bound. For the upper bound, we construct a new object called a continuous non-malleable randomness encoder (see Definition 5), which is the continuous analogue of the non-malleable randomness encoder recently introduced by [54]. Informally, a continuous non-malleable randomness encoder is just a non-malleable code for randomly chosen messages. It is then straightforward to show that a continuous non-malleable randomness encoder implies a single-bit continuous non-malleable code (see the full version of this paper [27] for details).

At a high level, the difficulty in proving continuous non-malleability arises from the need of the security reduction to simulate the interactive tampering oracle, without knowing the message underlying the "challenge" encoding. The approach of prior work such as [40] was to include a NIZK Proof of Knowledge in each part of the codeword to allow the simulator to extract the second part of the encoding, given the first. This then allowed the simulator (with some additional leakage) to respond correctly to a tampering query, while knowing only one of the two split-states of the original encoding. In our setting, we cannot use NIZK, since our goal is to reduce the necessary complexity assumptions; therefore, we need a different extraction technique.[2] Our main idea is as follows: To respond to the i-th tampering query, we run the adversarial tampering function on random (simulated) codewords (L', R') that are consistent with the output seen thus far (denoted Out_A^{i-1}) and keep track of frequent outcomes (occurring with non-negligible probability) of the tampering function, $\widehat{L}, \widehat{R}$. I.e. S_L (resp. S_R) is the set of values of $\widehat{L}$ (resp. $\widehat{R}$) such that with non-negligible probability over choice of L' (resp. R'), it is the case that $\widehat{L} = f_L(L')$ (resp. $\widehat{R} = f_R(R')$). We then show that if the outcome of the tampering function applied to the actual "challenge" split-state L or R is not equal to one of these frequent outcomes (i.e. $f_L(L) \notin S_L$ or $f_R(R) \notin S_R$), then w.h.p. the decode function D outputs $\bot$. This will allow us to simulate the experiment with only a small amount of leakage (to determine which of the values in S_L/S_R should be outputted). Note that, while the sets S_L/S_R are small, and so only a few bits are needed to specify the outcome, conditioned on the outcome being in S_L/S_R, the CNMC experiment runs for an *unbounded* number of times, and so even outputting a small amount of information in each round can ultimately lead to unbounded leakage. To solve this problem, we also consider the *most frequent* outcome in the sets S_L/S_R. This is the value of $\widehat{L}$ (resp. $\widehat{R}$) that occurs with the highest probability when $f_L(L')$ (resp. $f_R(R')$) is applied to consistent L' (resp. R'). Note that if a value $\widehat{L}'$ (resp. $\widehat{R}'$) is *not* the most frequent value, then it occurs with probability at most $1/2$. We argue that, for each round i of the CNMC experiment, the probability that a value $\widehat{L}'$ (resp. $\widehat{R}'$) that is not the most frequent value is outputted by f_L (resp. f_R) *and* self-destruct does not occur is at most $1/2$. This allows us to bound, w.h.p., the number of times in the entire tampering experiment that

---

[2] Note that our extraction technique is inefficient. This is ok, since the goal of the extraction technique is simply to show that the view of the adversary can be simulated given a small amount of leakage on each of the two split-states. Then, information-theoretic properties of the encoding are used to show that the view of the adversary must be independent of the random encoded value.

the value outputted by f_L (resp. f_R) is not the most frequent value. Thus, when the value outputted by f_L (resp. f_R) *is* the most frequent value, the leakage function outputs *nothing*, since the most frequent value can be reconstructed from the given information. In contrast, if the value outputted by f_L (resp. f_R) is *not* the most frequent value, but is in the sets S_L/S_R, then it has a small description and, moreover, this event occurs a bounded number of times. Therefore, we can afford to leak this information up to some upperbounded number of rounds, while the total amount of leakage remains small relative to the length of the encoding. Looking ahead, our construction will use a two-source extractor, whose properties will guarantee that even given the leakage (which contains all the information needed to simulate the CNMC experiment), the decoded value remains uniform random.

To show that if the outcome of the tampering function is not in S_L or S_R, then decode outputs $\perp$ w.h.p., we first use the "uniqueness" property, which says that for every $\widehat{L} = f_L(L)$ (resp. $\widehat{R} = f_R(R)$), there is at most a single "match", $\widehat{R}'$ (resp. $\widehat{L}'$), such that $\mathsf{D}_\Sigma(\widehat{L}, \widehat{R}') \neq \perp$ (resp. $\mathsf{D}_\Sigma(\widehat{L}', \widehat{R}) \neq \perp$). Given the "uniqueness" property, it is sufficient to show that for every setting of L, Out_A^{i-1}

$$\Pr[f_R(R) = \widehat{R}' \wedge \widehat{R}' \notin S_R \mid L \wedge \mathsf{Out}_A^{i-1}] \leq \mathsf{negl}(n) \tag{1}$$

and that for every setting of $R \wedge \mathsf{Out}_A^{i-1}$

$$\Pr[f_L(L) = \widehat{L}' \wedge \widehat{L}' \notin S_L \mid R \wedge \mathsf{Out}_A^{i-1}] \leq \mathsf{negl}(n). \tag{2}$$

To prove the above, we first argue that for the "challenge" codeword, (L, R), the split-states L and R are conditionally independent, given Out_A^{i-1} (assuming no $\perp$ has been outputted thus far) and an additional simulated part of the codeword. This means that the set of frequent outcomes S_L (resp. S_R) conditioned on Out_A^{i-1} is the same as the set of frequent outcomes S_L (resp. S_R) conditioned on *both* Out_A^{i-1} and R (resp. L). So for any $\widehat{R} \notin S_R$,

$$\Pr[f_R(R) = \widehat{R} \mid L \wedge \mathsf{Out}_A^{i-1}] \leq \mathsf{negl}(n)$$

and for any $\widehat{L} \notin S_L$,

$$\Pr[f_L(L) = \widehat{L} \mid R \wedge \mathsf{Out}_A^{i-1}] \leq \mathsf{negl}(n).$$

Since $\widehat{R}'$ (resp. $\widehat{L}'$) is simply a particular setting of $\widehat{R} \notin S_R$ (resp. $\widehat{L} \notin S_L$), we have that (1) and (2) follow.

For the above analysis, we need the encoding scheme to possess the following property: The L, R sides of the "challenge" codeword are conditionally independent given Out_A^{i-1} (and an additional simulated part of the codeword), but any tampered split-state $f_L(L)$ or $f_R(R)$ created by the adversary has at most a single "match," $\widehat{R}'$ or $\widehat{L}'$.

To explain how we achieve this property, we briefly describe our construction. Our construction is based on a non-interactive, equivocal commitment scheme in the CRS model and a two-source (inner product) extractor. Informally, an equivocal commitment scheme is a commitment scheme with the normal binding and hiding properties, but for which there exists a simulator that can output simulated commitments which can be opened to both 0 and 1. In the CRS model, the simulator also gets to sample a simulated CRS. Moreover, the CRS and commitments produced by the simulator are indistinguishable from real ones.

To encode a random value m, random vectors c_L, c_R such that $\langle c_L, c_R \rangle = m$ are chosen. We generate a commitment com to $c_L \| c_R$. The commitment scheme has the additional property that adversarially produced commitments are statistically binding (even if an equivocal commitment has been released) and have at most a *single* valid decommitment string. The left (resp. right) split-state L (resp. R) consists of com and an opening of com to the bits of c_L (resp. c_R). The special properties of the commitment scheme guarantee the "perfect uniqueness" property of the code. In the security proof, we replace the statistically binding commitment com in the "challenge" codeword with an equivocal commitment. Thus, each split-state of the challenge encoding, L (resp. R), contains no information about c_R (resp. c_L). Moreover, assuming "$\perp$" is not yet outputted, the output received by the adversary in the experiment at the point that the i-th tampering function is submitted, denoted Out_A^{i-1} is of the form $(f_L^1(L) = v_1, f_R^1(R) = w_1), \ldots, (f_L^{i-1}(L)) = v_{i-1}, f_R^{i-1}(R) = w_{i-1})$, where for $j \in [i-1]$, v_j is equal to the left value outputted in response to the j-th query and w_j is equal to the right value outputted in response to the j-th query. (note that v_j/w_j can be set to "same" if the tampering function leaves L/R unchanged). This allows us to argue that the distribution of $L \mid \mathsf{Out}_A^{i-1}, R$ (resp. $R \mid \mathsf{Out}_A^{i-1}, L$) is identical to the distribution of $L \mid \mathsf{Out}_A^{i-1}$ (resp. $R \mid \mathsf{Out}_A^{i-1}$) which implies that the left and right hand sides are conditionally independent given Out_A^{i-1} and the equivocal commitment, as desired. See Sect. 4 for additional details.

Extension to 4-State CNMC in CRS Model from OWF. To encode a message m we now generate random $(c_{L,1}, c_{R,1}, c_{L,2}, c_{R,2})$ conditioned on $\langle c_{L,1}, c_{R,1} \rangle + \langle c_{L,2}, c_{R,2} \rangle = m$ (where addition is over a finite field). Now, we generate a commitment com to $c_{L,1} \| c_{R,1} \| c_{L,2} \| c_{R,2}$. Each of the four split states now consists of com and an opening of com to the bits of $c_{L,b}$ (resp. $c_{R,b}$). The analysis is similar to the previous case and requires the property that at each point in the experiment the distribution of $\langle c_{L,1}, c_{R,1} \rangle$ (resp. $\langle c_{L,2}, c_{R,2} \rangle$) is uniform random, conditioned on the output thus far. Our techniques are somewhat similar to those used in [35] in their construction of $2t$-split-state continuously non-malleable codes from t-split-state one-way continuously non-malleable codes. See the full version of this paper [27] for additional details.

1.4 Additional Related Work

Non-Malleable Codes. The notion of non-malleable codes (NMC) was formalized in the seminal work of Dziembowski, Pietrzak and Wichs [37]. Split-state classes of tampering functions subsequently received a lot of attention with a long line of works, including [2–4,8,19,36,53,57,60]. Other works focused on various other classes of tampering functions, including [7,9–11,18,39]. NMC have also been considered in several other models for various applications such as in [15,17,30]. Other works on non-malleable codes include [6,16,17,22,28,29,35,40,41,52,55].

Continuous Non-Malleable Codes. Continuous Non-Malleable codes (*CNMC*) were introduced by Faust et al. [40]. They gave a construction based on collision resistant hash functions and non-interactive zero knowledge proof systems in the CRS model. They also showed the impossibility of constructing 2-split state CNMC information theoretically. Subsequently, Jafargholi and Wichs [52] presented a general study of CNMCs and its variants with some existential results. Aggarwal et al. [5] gave the first information theoretic construction in the 8-split-state model. Recently, Damgård et al. [31] gave the first construction of information theoretic CNMC against permutations. Faonio et al. [38] considered a variant of CNMC against split-state tampering where the codeword is refreshed (to avoid self-destruct) in the CRS model. For a discussion related to the recent work of Ostrovsky et al. [63], see Sect. 1.2 and refer to the full version of this paper [27] for further details.

Non-Malleable Randomness Encoders (NMRE). NMRE were introduced recently by Kanukurthi et al. [54] as a building block for constructing efficient (constant-rate) split-state NMC. In this work, we present the stronger variant *Continuous NMRE* which allows continual tampering in split-state model.

Bounds on Non-Malleable Codes. Cheragachi and Guruswami [21] studied the "capacity" of non-malleable codes and their work has been instrumental in asserting the claims of efficient constructions for non-malleable codes since then (cf. [2,7,8]). A similar study was presented in [28] for locally decodable and updatable NMC. This work studies bounds for *continuous non-malleable codes* in terms of *complexity assumptions*.

Black-Box Separations. Impagliazzo and Rudich ruled out black-box reductions from key agreement to one-way function in their seminal work [50]. Their oracle separation technique was subsequently used to rule out black-box reductions between various other primitives (cf. [48,69] and many more). The meta-reduction technique (cf. [1,13,26,43,45–47,64,65,68]) has been useful for ruling out larger classes of reductions—where the construction is arbitrary (non-black-box), but the reduction uses the adversary in a black-box manner. The meta-reduction technique is often used to provide evidence that construction of some cryptographic primitive is impossible under "standard assumptions" (e.g. falsifiable assumptions or non-interactive assumptions).

2   Definitions and Preliminaries

We present some standard notations and definitions, along with important lemmas related to randomness extractors, and the definition of strong one-time signature schemes in the full version of this paper [27] due to lack of space.

We present some more definitions in the following sections.

2.1   CNMC

Definition 1 (Coding Scheme [37]). *A coding scheme,* $\mathsf{Code} = (\mathsf{E}, \mathsf{D})$*, consists of two functions: a randomized encoding function* $\mathsf{E} : \{0,1\}^\lambda \to \{0,1\}^n$*, and a deterministic decoding function* $\mathsf{D} : \{0,1\}^n \to \{0,1\}^\lambda \cup \{\bot\}$ *such that, for each* $m \in \{0,1\}^\lambda$*,* $\Pr[\mathsf{D}(\mathsf{E}(m)) = m] = 1$ *(over the randomness of encoding function).*

Definition 2 (Split-State Encoding Scheme in the CRS model [40]). *A split-state encoding scheme in* common reference string *(CRS) model is a tuple of algorithms,* $\mathsf{Code} = (\mathsf{CRSGen}, \mathsf{E}, \mathsf{D})$ *specified as follows:*

- CRSGen *takes the security parameter as input and outputs the CRS,* $\Sigma \leftarrow \mathsf{CRSGen}(1^\lambda)$*.*
- E *takes a message* $x \in \{0,1\}^\lambda$ *as input along with the CRS* Σ*, and outputs a codeword consisting of two parts* (X_0, X_1) *such that* $X_0, X_1 \in \{0,1\}^n$*.*
- D *takes a codeword* $(X_0, X_1) \in \{0,1\}^{2n}$ *as input along with the CRS* Σ *and outputs either a message* $x' \in \{0,1\}^\lambda$ *or a special symbol* $\bot$*.*

Consider the following oracle, $\mathcal{O}_{\mathsf{CNM}}((X_0, X_1), (\mathsf{T}_0, \mathsf{T}_1))$ which is parametrized by the CRS Σ and "challenge" codeword (X_0, X_1) and takes functions $\mathsf{T}_0, \mathsf{T}_1 : \{0,1\}^n \to \{0,1\}^n$ as inputs.

$\mathcal{O}_{\mathsf{CNM}}(\Sigma, (X_0, X_1), (\mathsf{T}_0, \mathsf{T}_1)) :$

$(X'_0, X'_1) = (\mathsf{T}_0(X_0), \mathsf{T}_1(X_1))$
If $(X'_0, X'_1) = (X_0, X_1)$ return same*
If $\mathsf{D}_\Sigma(X'_0, X'_1) = \bot$, return $\bot$ and "self destruct"
Else return (X'_0, X'_1).

"Self destruct" here means that once $\mathsf{D}_\Sigma(X'_0, X'_1)$ outputs $\bot$, the oracle answers all the future queries with $\bot$.

Definition 3 (Continuous Non Malleability [40]). *Let* $\mathsf{Code} = (\mathsf{CRSGen}, \mathsf{E}, \mathsf{D})$ *be a split-state encoding scheme in the CRS model. We say that* Code *is* q*-continuously non-malleable code, if for all messages* $x, y \in \{0,1\}^\lambda$ *and all PPT adversary* $\mathcal{A}$ *it holds that*

$$\left\{ \mathsf{CTamper}_{\mathcal{A},x}(\lambda) \right\}_{\lambda \in \mathbb{N}} \approx_c \left\{ \mathsf{CTamper}_{\mathcal{A},y}(\lambda) \right\}_{\lambda \in \mathbb{N}} \qquad \text{where,}$$

$$\mathsf{CTamper}_{\mathcal{A},x}(\lambda) \stackrel{def}{=} \left\{ \begin{array}{c} \Sigma \leftarrow \mathsf{CRSGen}(1^\lambda); \ (X_0, X_1) \leftarrow \mathsf{E}_\Sigma(x); \\ \mathsf{out}_\mathcal{A} \leftarrow \mathcal{A}^{\mathcal{O}_{\mathsf{CNM}}(\Sigma,(X_0,X_1),(\cdot,\cdot))}; \ \text{OUTPUT} : \mathsf{out}_\mathcal{A} \end{array} \right\}$$

and $\mathcal{A}$ *asks total of* q *queries to* $\mathcal{O}_{\mathsf{CNM}}$*.*

The following is an equivalent formulation

Definition 4 (Continuous Non Malleability [40], equivalent formulation). *Let* $\mathsf{Code} = (\mathsf{CRSGen}, \mathsf{E}, \mathsf{D})$ *be a split-state encoding scheme in the CRS model. We say that* Code *is* q*-continuously non-malleable code, if for all messages* $m_0, m_1 \in \{0,1\}^\lambda$*, all PPT adversary* $\mathcal{A}$ *and all PPT distinguishers* D *it holds that*

$$\Pr[D(\mathsf{out}_\mathcal{A}^b) = b] \leq 1/2 + \mathsf{negl}(\lambda)$$

where $b \leftarrow \{0,1\}$ *and*

$$\mathsf{out}^b_{\mathcal{A}} \leftarrow \mathcal{A}^{\mathcal{O}_{\mathsf{CNM}}(\Sigma,(X^b_0,X^b_1),(\cdot,\cdot))} : \Sigma \leftarrow \mathsf{CRSGen}(1^\lambda); (X^b_0,X^b_1) \leftarrow \mathsf{E}_\Sigma(m_b)$$

and $\mathcal{A}$ *asks total of* q *queries to* $\mathcal{O}_{\mathsf{CNM}}$.

2.2 Continuous Non-Malleable Randomness Encoder

The following definition is an adaptation of the notion of Non-Malleable Randomness Encoders [54] to the continuous setting.

Definition 5. *Let* $\mathsf{Code} = (\mathsf{CRSGen}, \mathsf{CNMREnc}, \mathsf{CNMRDec})$ *be such that* CRSGen *takes security parameter* λ *as input and outputs a string of length* $\Sigma_1 = \mathrm{poly}(\lambda)$ *as CRS.* $\mathsf{CNMREnc} : \{0,1\}^{\Sigma_1} \times \{0,1\}^r \rightarrow \{0,1\}^\lambda \times (\{0,1\}^{n_1}, \{0,1\}^{n_2})$ *is defined as* $\mathsf{CNMREnc}(r) = (\mathsf{CNMREnc}_{1,\Sigma}(r), \mathsf{CNMREnc}_{2,\Sigma}(r)) = (m, (x_0, x_1))$ *and* $\mathsf{CNMRDec} : \{0,1\}^{\Sigma_1} \times \{0,1\}^{n_1} \times \{0,1\}^{n_2} \rightarrow \{0,1\}^\lambda$.

We say that $(\mathsf{CRSGen}, \mathsf{CNMREnc}, \mathsf{CNMRDec})$ *is a* continuous non-malleable randomness encoder *with message space* $\{0,1\}^\lambda$ *and codeword space* $\{0,1\}^{n_1} \times \{0,1\}^{n_2}$, *for the distribution* $\mathcal{R}$ *on* $\{0,1\}^r$ *with respect to the 2-split-state family* $\mathcal{F}$ *if the following holds true:*

- *Correctness:*

$$\Pr_{r \leftarrow \mathcal{R}}[\mathsf{CNMRDec}_\Sigma(\mathsf{CNMREnc}_{2,\Sigma}(r)) = \mathsf{CNMREnc}_{1,\Sigma}(r)] = 1$$

- *Continuous Non-Malleability:*

$$(\Sigma, \mathsf{CNMREnc}_{1,\Sigma}(R), \mathsf{out}_{\Sigma,\mathcal{A}}(R)) \approx_c (\Sigma, U_\lambda, \mathsf{out}_{\Sigma,\mathcal{A}}(R))$$

where $\Sigma \leftarrow \mathsf{CRSGen}(1^\lambda)$, R *is a uniform random variable over* $\{0,1\}^r$, U_λ *is a uniform random variable over* $\{0,1\}^\lambda$ *and* $\mathsf{out}_{\Sigma,\mathcal{A}}(R)$ *is defined as follows:*

$$\mathsf{out}_{\Sigma,\mathcal{A}}(R) \leftarrow \mathcal{A}^{\mathcal{O}_{\mathsf{CNM}}(\Sigma,(X_0,X_1),(\cdot,\cdot))} : (X_0,X_1) \leftarrow \mathsf{CNMREnc}_{2,\Sigma}(R)$$

where $\mathcal{O}_{\mathsf{CNM}}$ *runs with* $\mathsf{CNMRDec}$ *as decoding algorithm.*

2.3 Falsifiable Assumptions and Black-Box Reductions

Definition 6. *A falsifiable assumption consists of* PPT *interactive challenger* $\mathcal{C}(1^\lambda)$ *that runs in time* $\mathrm{poly}(\lambda)$ *and a constant* $0 \leq \delta < 1$. *The challenger* $\mathcal{C}$ *interacts with a machine* $\mathcal{A}$ *and may output special symbol* win. *If this occurs,* $\mathcal{A}$ *is said to win* $\mathcal{C}$. *For any adversary* $\mathcal{A}$, *the advantage of* $\mathcal{A}$ *over* $\mathcal{C}$ *is defined as:*

$$\mathrm{Adv}^{(\mathcal{C},\delta)}_{\mathcal{A}} = |\Pr[\mathcal{A}(1^\lambda) \text{ wins } \mathcal{C}(1^\lambda)] - \delta|,$$

where the probability is taken over the random coins of $\mathcal{A}$ *and* $\mathcal{C}$. *The assumption associated with the tuple* $(\mathcal{C}, \delta)$ *states that for every (non-uniform) adversary* $\mathcal{A}(1^\lambda)$ *running in time* $\mathrm{poly}(\lambda)$,

$$\mathrm{Adv}^{(\mathcal{C},\delta)}_{\mathcal{A}} = \mathsf{negl}(\lambda).$$

If the advantage of $\mathcal{A}$ *is non-negligible in* λ *then* $\mathcal{A}$ *is said to* break *the assumption.*

Definition 7. *Let $\Pi = (\mathsf{E}, \mathsf{D})$ be a split-state CNMC. We say that the non-malleability of Π can be proven via a* black-box reduction *to a falsifiable assumption, if there is an oracle access machine $\mathcal{M}^{(\cdot)}$ such that for every (possibly inefficient) Π-adversary $\mathcal{P}^*$, the machine $\mathcal{M}^{\mathcal{P}^*}$ runs in time $\mathrm{poly}(\lambda)$ and breaks the assumption.*

2.4 Equivocal Commitment Scheme

Definition 8 (Commitment Scheme). *A (non-interactive) commitment scheme in the CRS model for the message space $\mathcal{M}$, is a triple (CRSGen, Commit, Open) such that:*

- *$\Sigma \leftarrow \mathsf{CRSGen}(1^k)$ generates the CRS.*
- *For all $m \in \mathcal{M}$, $(c, d) \leftarrow \mathsf{Commit}_\Sigma(m)$ is the commitment/opening pair for the message m. Specifically; c is the* commitment value *for m, and d is the* opening.
- *$\mathsf{Open}_\Sigma(c, d) \rightarrow \tilde{m} \in \mathcal{M} \cup \{\bot\}$, where $\bot$ is returned when c is not a valid commitment to any message.*

The commitment scheme must satisfy the standard correctness requirement,

$$\forall k \in \mathbb{N}, \forall m \in \mathcal{M} \text{ and } \Sigma \in \mathcal{CRS}, \ \Pr\left[\mathsf{Open}_\Sigma(\mathsf{Commit}_\Sigma(m)) = m\right] = 1$$

where, $\mathcal{CRS}$ is the set of all possible valid CRS's generated by $\mathsf{CRSGen}(1^k)$ and where the probability is taken over the randomness of Commit.

The commitment scheme provides the following 2 security properties:

- *Hiding: It is computationally hard for any adversary $\mathcal{A}$ to generate two messages $m_0, m_1 \in \mathcal{M}$ such that $\mathcal{A}$ can distinguish between their corresponding commitments. Formally, for any PPT adversary $\mathcal{A} = (\mathcal{A}_1, \mathcal{A}_2)$ it should hold that:*

$$\Pr\left[b = b' \ \middle| \ \begin{array}{l} \Sigma \leftarrow \mathsf{CRSGen}(1^k), (m_0, m_1, \alpha) \leftarrow \mathcal{A}_1(\Sigma), \\ b \leftarrow_r \{0, 1\}, (c, d) \leftarrow \mathsf{Commit}_\Sigma(m_b), b' \leftarrow \mathcal{A}_2(c, \alpha) \end{array} \right] \leq \frac{1}{2} + \mathsf{negl}(k)$$

- *Binding: It is computationally hard for any adversary $\mathcal{A}$ to find a triple (c, d, d') such that* both *(c, d) and (c, d') are valid commitment/opening pairs for some $m, m' \in \mathcal{M}$ respectively, and $m \neq m'$. Formally, for any PPT adversary $\mathcal{A}$ it should hold that:*

$$\Pr\left[\begin{array}{l} m \neq m' \wedge \\ m, m' \neq \bot \end{array} \ \middle| \ \begin{array}{l} \Sigma \leftarrow \mathsf{CRSGen}(1^k), (c, d, d') \leftarrow \mathcal{A}(\Sigma), \\ m \leftarrow \mathsf{Open}_\Sigma(c, d), m' \leftarrow \mathsf{Open}_\Sigma(c, d') \end{array} \right] \leq \mathsf{negl}(k)$$

Definition 9 (One-to-One Commitment Scheme in the CRS Model). *Let (CRSGen, Commit, Open) be a bit-commitment scheme in CRS model. We say that (CRSGen, Commit, Open) is a one-to-one commitment scheme if with all but negligible probability over $b \leftarrow \{0, 1\}$, $\Sigma \leftarrow \mathsf{CRSGen}(1^\lambda)$, $(com, d) \leftarrow \mathsf{Commit}_\Sigma(b)$, $d' = d$ is the unique string such that $\mathsf{Open}(com, d') \neq \bot$.*

Definition 10. *Let* (CRSGen, Commit, Open) *be a bit-commitment scheme in CRS model. We say that* (CRSGen, Commit, Open) *is a* non-interactive equiv-ocable bit-commitment scheme *in the CRS model if there exists an efficient probabilistic algorithm* S_{Eq} *which on input* 1^λ *outputs a 4-tuple* $(\Sigma', c', d'_0, d'_1)$ *satisfying the following:*

- $\Pr[\mathsf{Open}_{\Sigma'}(c', d'_b) = b] = 1$ *for* $b \in \{0,1\}$.
- *For* $b \in \{0,1\}$, *it holds that* $\mathsf{out}_{\mathsf{Commit}}(b) \approx_\varepsilon \mathsf{out}_{S_{Eq}}(b)$ *where the random variables* $\mathsf{out}_{\mathsf{Commit}}(b)$ *and* $\mathsf{out}_{S_{Eq}}(b)$ *are defined as follows:*

$$\left\{ \begin{array}{c} \Sigma \leftarrow \mathsf{CRSGen}(1^\lambda); (c,d) \leftarrow \mathsf{Commit}_\Sigma(b); \\ \mathsf{out}_{\mathsf{Commit}}(b) : (\Sigma, c, d) \end{array} \right\} \approx \left\{ \begin{array}{c} (\Sigma', c', d'_0, d'_1) \leftarrow S_{Eq}(1^\lambda); \\ \mathsf{out}_{S_{Eq}}(b) : (\Sigma', c', d'_b) \end{array} \right\}$$

We now present variant of the commitment scheme presented by Naor in [61], specifically we present the same construction in CRS model. This is also presented in [32].

Let $n > 0$ be an integer, let $G : \{0,1\}^n \to \{0,1\}^{3n}$ be a PRG.

- CRSGen(1^n): Output a uniform random string Σ of length $3n$.
- Commit$_\Sigma(b)$: Choose uniform random seed $s \in \{0,1\}^n$ and compute $t = G(s)$. If $b = 0$, set $c := t$. If $b = 1$, set $c := t \oplus \Sigma$. Output c. Output decommitment $d = s$.
- Open$_\Sigma(c,d)$: If $c = G(d)$, then output 0. Else if, $c = G(d) \oplus \Sigma$, then output 1. Output $\bot$ otherwise.

Claim 2.1. The scheme presented above is an *equivocal* commitment scheme.

The proof of Claim 2.1 can be found in the full version of this paper [27].

2.5   One-to-One Equivocal Commitment

The scheme presented in Sect. 2.4 is not necessarily a one-to-one commitment scheme, since for PRG G, there may exist two different seeds s and s' such that $G(s) = G(s')$. In this case both s, s' are valid decommitments of the same bit.

We therefore, present a modification of the above scheme that allows us to achieve an equivocal commitment scheme with the one-to-one property: for every statistically binding commitment, there is at most a single opening string that will be accepted by the receiver during the decommitment phase. As an underlying ingredient, we use any commitment scheme $\Pi = (\mathsf{CRSGen}_\Pi, \mathsf{Commit}_\Pi, \mathsf{Open}_\Pi)$ (not necessarily equivocal) with the above property. Such a commitment scheme can be constructed straightforwardly e.g. from *injective* one-way functions. Let $n > 0$ be an integer, let $G : \{0,1\}^n \to \{0,1\}^{3n}$ be PRG.

- CRSGen(1^n): Run CRSGen$_\Pi(1^n)$ to generate Σ_Π. Output $\Sigma = \Sigma_\Pi, \Sigma_1, \Sigma_2$ where Σ_1, Σ_2 are uniform random strings of length $3n$.
- Commit(Σ, b): Choose uniform random seeds $s_1, s_2 \in \{0,1\}^n$ and compute $t_1 = G(s_1), t_2 = G(s_2)$. Choose $\beta \in \{0,1\}$. Set $c^1 = t_1 \oplus (b \cdot \Sigma_1)$. Set $c^2 = t_2 \oplus (\beta \cdot \Sigma_2)$. Generate $(com_\beta, s_\Pi) \leftarrow \mathsf{Commit}(\Sigma_\Pi, s_1 || s_2)$ and

$(com_{1-\beta}, \cdot) \leftarrow \mathsf{Commit}(\Sigma_\Pi, 0^{2n})$. Output commitment (c^1, c^2, com_0, com_1) along with decommitment information $(\beta||s_1||s_2||s_\Pi)$. In the following, we sometimes write $\mathsf{Commit}(\Sigma, b; \beta)$, explicitly including the randomness β in the input.

- $\mathsf{Open}(\Sigma, c, s)$: Parse $c = (c^1, c^2, com_0, com_1)$ and $s = \beta||s_1||s_2||s_\Pi$. If $c^2 = G(s_2)$, check that $\beta = 0$. If $c^2 = G(s_2) \oplus \Sigma_2$, check that $\beta = 1$. Run $\mathsf{Open}(\Sigma_\Pi, com_\beta, s_\Pi)$ and check that it outputs $s_1||s_2$. Otherwise, output $\bot$. If $c^1 = G(s_1)$, output 0. If $c^1 = G(s_1) \oplus \Sigma_1$, output 1. Output $\bot$ otherwise.

Clearly, by the binding of the original commitment scheme and the one-to-one property of Π, the modified scheme has the one-to-one property.

To create equivocal commitments/openings one can do the following: Run $\mathsf{CRSGen}_\Pi(1^n)$ to generate Σ_Π. Choose uniform random seeds $s_1^0, s_1^1, s_2^0, s_2^1 \in \{0,1\}^n$ and compute $t_1^0 = G(s_1^0)$, $t_2^0 = G(s_2^0)$, $t_1^1 = G(s_1^1)$, $t_2^1 = G(s_2^1)$. Choose $\beta \leftarrow \{0,1\}$ Generate $com_\beta = \mathsf{Commit}(\Sigma_\Pi, s_1^0||s_2^\beta)$ and $com_{1-\beta} = \mathsf{Commit}(\Sigma_\Pi, s_1^1||s_2^{1-\beta})$. Set $c^1 = t_1^0$. Set $c^2 = t_2^0$. Set $\Sigma_1 = c^1 \oplus t_1^1$. Set $\Sigma_2 = c^2 \oplus t_2^1$. Output (c^1, c^2, com_0, com_1).

To open the commitment to a 0, output $(\beta||s_1^0||s_2^\beta||open_\beta)$, where $open_\beta$ is the decommitment information for com_β.

To open the commitment to a 1, output $(1 - \beta||s_1^1||s_2^{1-\beta}||open_{1-\beta})$, where $open_{1-\beta}$ is the decommitment information for $com_{1-\beta}$.

We note the following important property: For any commitment string c, and any CRS Σ, any two valid openings for c $s = \beta||s_1||s_2||s_\Pi$, $s' = \beta'||s_1'||s_2'||s_\Pi'$, it must be the case that $\beta \neq \beta'$.

2.6   Equivocal Commitment (with Extra Properties) in the CRS Model

Let $\Pi' = (\mathsf{Gen}'_{Com}, \mathsf{Com}', \mathsf{Open}', \mathsf{S}'_{Eq})$, be an equivocal, one-to-one bit commitment scheme in the CRS model (given in Sect. 2.5). Let $(\mathsf{Gen}_{\mathsf{Sign}}, \mathsf{Sign}, \mathsf{Verify})$ be a strong, one-time signature scheme (for definition, see the full version [27]). We construct $\Pi = (\mathsf{Gen}_{Com}, \mathsf{Com}, \mathsf{Open}, \mathsf{S}_{Eq})$, which is an equivocal commitment scheme, with several additional properties that we describe at the end of the section and which will be useful for our constructions in Sect. 4.

Key Generation Gen_{Com} is as Follows: On input security parameter 1^λ, run Gen'_{Com} $2t \cdot \ell$ times to generate t pairs of vectors of CRS's $[(\Sigma_{Eq}^{0,i,j}, \Sigma_{Eq}^{1,i,j})]_{i \in [\ell], j \in [t]}$, where t is the length of the verification key vk output by $\mathsf{Gen}_{\mathsf{Sign}}$.

Commitment Com is as Follows: To commit to a message $m := m_1, \ldots, m_\ell$ of length ℓ, generate a key pair $(\mathsf{vk}, \mathsf{sk}) \leftarrow \mathsf{Gen}_{\mathsf{Sign}}$. For $i \in [\ell]$, choose $\beta_i \leftarrow \{0,1\}$ at random. For $i \in [\ell], j \in [t]$, generate $(com_{i,j}, d_{i,j}) \leftarrow \mathsf{Com}'(\Sigma^{\mathsf{vk}_j, i, j}, m_i; \beta_i)$, where for each $i \in [\ell]$, $[com_{i,j}]_{j \in [t]}$ is the (bit-by-bit) commitment and $[d_{i,j}]_{j \in [t]}$ is the (bit-by-bit) decommitment information. Generate $\sigma \leftarrow \mathsf{Sign}_{\mathsf{sk}}([com_{i,j}]_{i \in [\ell], j \in [t]})$. Output commitment $com = (\mathsf{vk}, [com_{i,j}]_{i \in [\ell], j \in [t]}, \sigma)$. A sender can decommit separately to any set of bits of the message m. Decommitment information for a set S of message bits consists of $d[S] = [d_{i,j}]_{i \in S, j \in [t]}$, where $d_{i,j}$ is the decommitment information corresponding to the j-th bit of the i-th instance. We also denote the decommitment for the m_i as $d_i := d_{i,1}, d_{i,2}, \ldots d_{i,t}$.

Decommitment Open w.r.t. a Set S: Given a set S, a commitment com, and an opening $[d_{i,j}]_{i \in S, j \in [t]}$, Open does the following: Parse commitment as $(\mathsf{vk}, [com_{i,j}]_{i \in [\ell], j \in [t]}, \sigma)$. (1) Check that $\mathsf{Verify}_{\mathsf{vk}}([com_{i,j}]_{i \in [\ell], j \in [t]}, \sigma) = 1$ (2) For $i \in S$, $j \in [t]$, check that $d_{i,j}$ is a valid decommitment for $com_{i,j}$ w.r.t. CRS $\Sigma^{\mathsf{vk}_j, i, j}$.

Equivocal CRS Generation and Commitment S_{Eq} is as Follows: On input security parameter 1^λ, generate a key pair $(\mathsf{vk}, \mathsf{sk}) \leftarrow \mathsf{Gen}_{\mathsf{Sign}}$. Run S'_{Eq} $t \cdot \ell$ times to generate $[\Sigma^{\mathsf{vk}_j, i, j}]_{i \in [\ell], j \in [t]}$, equivocal commitments $[com_{i,j}]_{i \in [\ell], j \in [t]}$ and decommitments $[(d^0_{i,j}, d^1_{i,j})]_{i \in [\ell], j \in [t]}$. Note that for each $i \in [\ell]$, all equivocal commitments use the same value of $\beta := \beta_i$. Run Gen'_{Com} $t \cdot \ell$ times to generate $[\Sigma^{1 - \mathsf{vk}_j, i, j}]_{i \in [\ell], j \in [t]}$. Set $\Sigma_{Eq} := [(\Sigma^{0, i, j}_{Eq}, \Sigma^{1, i, j}_{Eq})]_{i \in [\ell], j \in [t]}$. Compute $\sigma \leftarrow \mathsf{Sign}_{\mathsf{sk}}([com_{i,j}]_{i \in [\ell], j \in [t]})$. Output $(\Sigma = \Sigma_{Eq}, \overline{com} = (\mathsf{vk}, [com_{i,j}]_{i \in [\ell], j \in [t]}, \sigma), d^0 = [d^0_{i,j}]_{i \in [\ell], j \in [t]}, d^1 = [d^1_{i,j}]_{i \in [\ell], j \in [t]})$.

Additional Check Functionality: Given a Σ and commitments $com = (\mathsf{vk}, [com_{i,j}]_{i \in [\ell], j \in [t]}, \sigma)$, $com' = (\mathsf{vk}', [com'_{i,j}]_{i \in [\ell], j \in [t]}, \sigma')$, $\mathsf{Check}_\Sigma(com, com')$ outputs 1 if (1) $\mathsf{vk} = \mathsf{vk}'$; (2) $\mathsf{Verify}_{\mathsf{vk}}([com'_{i,j}]_{i \in [\ell], j \in [t]}, \sigma') = 1$.

Additional Properties:

1. With overwhelming probability over generation of Σ, for every set $S \subseteq [\ell]$ and every string com, there is at most a *single* string $d[S]$ such that $\mathsf{Open}_\Sigma(S, com, d[S]) = 1$. This property is achieved by using the equivocal, one-to-one, commitment scheme given in Sect. 2.5 as the underlying commitment scheme.
2. Given a pair (Σ, com), a PPT adversary outputs com' such that $com \neq com'$ but $\mathsf{Check}_\Sigma(com, com') = 1$ with negligible probability. This property follows from the security of the one-time signature scheme.
3. Given equivocal commitment $(\Sigma_{Eq}, \overline{com})$, for every string com', if $\mathsf{Check}_{\Sigma_{Eq}}(\overline{com}, com') = 0$ then (with overwhelming probability over generation of Σ_{Eq}) com' has at most one valid opening. Specifically, for every set $S \subseteq [\ell]$, there is at most a *single* string $d[S]$ such that $\mathsf{Open}_{\Sigma_{Eq}}(S, com', d[S]) = 1$. Again, this property is achieved by using the equivocal, one-to-one, commitment scheme given in Sect. 2.5 as the underlying commitment scheme.

We elaborate on the third property, since it is less straightforward than the first two. First, note that the third property is a type of "simulation soundness" property, which essentially says that given an equivocal commitment, the only way to construct a *different* commitment with more than one valid opening is by forging a signature. This type of construction, where the CRS is indexed by bits of a signature verification key, has been used in various settings in the literature, such as in the construction of one-time simulation-sound NIZK, as well as CCA-secure encryption and non-malleable encryption [23,34,58,66,67]. In more detail, assume the adversary is given an equivocal commitment $(\Sigma_{Eq}, \overline{com})$, where $\Sigma_{Eq} = [(\Sigma_{Eq}^{0,i,j}, \Sigma_{Eq}^{1,i,j})]_{i \in [\ell], j \in [t]}$, and $\overline{com} = (\mathsf{vk}, [com_{i,j}]_{i \in [\ell], j \in [t]}, \sigma)$. It is sufficient to show that any commitment output by the adversary $com' = (\mathsf{vk}', [com'_{i,j}]_{i \in [\ell], j \in [t]}, \sigma')$, where $\mathsf{vk}' \neq \mathsf{vk}$ can have at most a single valid opening relative to any set $S \subseteq [\ell]$. Assume $\mathsf{vk}' \neq \mathsf{vk}$ and that com' has two valid openings relative to a set S. These openings must be of the form $[s^{i,j,0}]_{i \in S, j \in [t]} = [\beta_i || s_1^{i,j,0} || s_2^{i,j,0} || s_{\Pi}^{i,j,0}]_{i \in S, j \in [t]}$ $[s^{i,j,0}]_{i \in S, j \in [t]} = [1 - \beta_i || s_1^{i,j,1} || s_2^{i,j,1} || s_{\Pi}^{i,j,1}]_{i \in S, j \in [t]}$. Since $\mathsf{vk}' \neq \mathsf{vk}$ there must be at least one $j \in [t]$ such that $\mathsf{vk}'_j = 1 - \mathsf{vk}_j$. But $[\Sigma^{1-\mathsf{vk}_j,i,j}]_{i \in [\ell], j \in [t]}$ were generated via Gen'_{Com}, so it is guaranteed with overwhelming probability that any string $com'_{i,j}$ relative to $\Sigma^{1-\mathsf{vk}_j,i,j}$ has at most a single valid decommitment. Therefore $\beta_i || s_1^{i,j,0} || s_2^{i,j,0} || s_{\Pi}^{i,j,0}$ and $1 - \beta_i || s_1^{i,j,1} || s_2^{i,j,1} || s_{\Pi}^{i,j,1}$ cannot both be valid decommitments, leading to contradiction.

3 Impossibility of CNMC with No CRS

In this section we present Theorem 5, stating the impossibility of constructing CNMC without CRS.

Theorem 5. *There is no black-box reduction from a single-bit CNMC scheme $\Pi = (\mathsf{E}, \mathsf{D})$ to any falsifiable assumption, unless the assumption is false.*

We know from prior work that continuous NMC are impossible in the info-theoretic setting. Assume we have a construction of single-bit, continuous NMC from some falsifiable assumption with no CRS. We only allow black-box usage of the adversary in the reduction. However, the underlying assumption can be used in a non-black-box way in the construction/proof.

Preliminaries. Given adversary $A = (A_L, A_R)$, we say that A has advantage α in the *simplified no-Σ CNMC game* against construction $\Pi = (\mathsf{E}, \mathsf{D})$ if:

$$\Big| \Pr[\mathsf{D}(A_L(L), A_R(R)) \neq \perp \mid (L, R) \leftarrow \mathsf{E}(1^n, 0)]$$

$$- \Pr[\mathsf{D}(A_L(L), A_R(R)) \neq \perp \mid (L, R) \leftarrow \mathsf{E}(1^n, 1)] \Big| = \alpha,$$

Clearly, if $A = (A_L, A_R)$ has non-negligible advantage in the *simplified no-Σ CNMC game*, it can be used to break the CNMC security of $\Pi = (\mathsf{E}, \mathsf{D})$.

Definition 11. *A tuple (x, y, z) is bad relative to CNMC scheme $\Pi = (\mathsf{E}, \mathsf{D})$ if either:*

- $y \neq z \wedge \mathsf{D}(x, y) \neq \perp \wedge \mathsf{D}(x, z) \neq \perp$ OR
- $x \neq y \wedge \mathsf{D}(x, z) \neq \perp \wedge \mathsf{D}(y, z) \neq \perp$.

Definition 12. *A single-bit CNMC $\Pi = (\mathsf{E}, \mathsf{D})$ in the standard (no CRS model) is perfectly unique if there exist no bad tuples relative to $\Pi = (\mathsf{E}, \mathsf{D})$.*

We next present the following two lemmas, which, taken together, imply Theorem 5.

Lemma 1. *If a single-bit CNMC scheme $\Pi = (\mathsf{E}, \mathsf{D})$ is* not *perfectly unique then it is insecure.*

This is immediate, since if a bad tuple exists, it can be given to the adversary as non-uniform advice. Then the same attack from the literature (reviewed in the introduction) can be run.

Lemma 2. *There is no BB reduction from a single-bit CNMC scheme $\Pi = (\mathsf{E}, \mathsf{D})$ which is perfectly unique to any falsifiable assumption.*

The basic idea is that, given only black-box access to the split-state adversary, $A = (A_L, A_R)$, the reduction cannot tell the difference between the actual adversary and a *simulated* adversary. The simulated adversary simply waits to get matching L and R queries from the reduction, decodes, and re-encodes a fresh value that is related to the decoded value. The challenges are that the L and R queries are not received simultaneously. In fact, there could be many queries interleaved between a L and R match. So the simulated adversary must return a value upon seeing the L or R half *before* seeing the other half and *before* knowing whether the encoded value is a 0 or a 1. Therefore, the simulated adversary does the following: It keeps a table containing all the L and R values that it has seen. Whenever a L or R query is made, the simulated adversary first checks the table to see if a matching query was previously made. If not, the simulated adversary chooses a random encoding, (L', R'), of a random bit b', stores it in the table along with the L/R query that was made and returns either L' or R' as appropriate. If yes, the simulated adversary finds the corresponding L/R along with the pair (L', R') stored in the table. The simulated adversary then decodes (L, R) to find out b. If $b = 0$, the simulated adversary returns either L' or R' as appropriate. Otherwise, the simulated adversary returns the left/right side of an encoding of a random bit b''. We prove that the view generated by the reduction interacting with this adversary is identical to the view of the reduction interacting with the following real adversary: The real adversary, given L or R, recovers the corresponding unique valid codeword (L, R) (if it exists) and decodes to get the bit b. If $b = 0$, the real adversary encodes a random bit $b' = \mathsf{RO}_1(L\|R)$ using randomness $r = \mathsf{RO}_2(L\|R)$ (where $\mathsf{RO}_1, \mathsf{RO}_2$ are random oracles internal to the real adversary that are used to generate consistent randomness across invocations) and outputs the left/right side as appropriate. Otherwise (i.e. if the corresponding unique codeword does not exist or if $\mathsf{D}(L, R) = 1$), the real adversary outputs the left/right side of encoding of a random bit, $b'' = \mathsf{RO}_3(L)$ (or $b'' = \mathsf{RO}_3(R)$) using randomness $r'' = \mathsf{RO}_4(L)$ (or $r'' = \mathsf{RO}_4(R)$) (where $\mathsf{RO}_3, \mathsf{RO}_4$ are random oracles internal to the real adversary that are used to generate consistent randomness across invocations). Note that since the CNMC is perfectly unique, the real adversary obtains non-negligible advantage of $1 - \mathsf{negl}(n)$ in the simplified no-Σ CNMC game.

Proof. We will construct a *meta-reduction* as follows:

Consider the following inefficient, split state adversary $A = (A_L, A_R)$ with internal random oracles $\mathsf{RO}_1, \mathsf{RO}_2, \mathsf{RO}_3$, and RO_4:

A_L: On input L, find the unique R such that $\mathsf{D}(L, R) \neq \perp$ (if it exists). Let $b :=$ $\mathsf{D}(L, R)$. If $b = 0$, encode $b' = \mathsf{RO}_1(L\|R)$ using randomness $r = \mathsf{RO}_2(L\|R)$ to obtain $(L', R') := \mathsf{E}(b'; r)$ and output L'. If such R does not exist or if $b = 1$, compute a random encoding of a random bit $b'' = \mathsf{RO}_3(L)$ using randomness $r'' = \mathsf{RO}_4(L)$ to obtain $(L'', R'') := \mathsf{E}(b'', r'')$ and output L''.

A_R: On input R, find the unique L such that $\mathsf{D}(L, R) \neq \perp$ (if it exists). Let $b :=$ $\mathsf{D}(L, R)$. If $b = 0$, encode $b' = \mathsf{RO}_1(L\|R)$ using randomness $r = \mathsf{RO}_2(L\|R)$ to obtain $(L', R') := \mathsf{E}(b'; r)$ and output R'. If such L does not exist or if $b = 1$, compute a random encoding of a random bit $b'' = \mathsf{RO}_3(R)$ using randomness $r'' = \mathsf{RO}_4(R)$ to obtain $(L'', R'') := \mathsf{E}(b'', r'')$ and output R''.

Clearly, A succeeds with advantage $1 - \mathsf{negl}(n)$ in the simplified no-Σ CNMC game.

The following adversary A' simulates the above efficiently: Let T be a table that records internal randomness. T is initialized to empty. A' is a stateful adversary that proceeds as follows:

1. On input L, check if the corresponding R such that $\mathsf{D}(L, R) \neq \perp$ has been queried. If yes, decode to get bit $b := \mathsf{D}(L, R)$. If $b = 0$, check the table T to recover (R, L', R'). Output L'. Otherwise, if $L \in T$ then output L'' corresponding to entry (L, L'', R''). If $L \notin T$, choose a random encoding of a random bit b'': $(L'', R'') \leftarrow \mathsf{E}(b'')$. Store (L, L'', R'') in T. and output L''.
2. On input R, check if the corresponding L such that $\mathsf{D}(L, R) \neq \perp$ has been queried. If yes, decode to get bit $b := \mathsf{D}(L, R)$. If $b = 0$, check the table T to recover (L, L', R'). Output R'. Otherwise, if $R \in T$ then output R'' corresponding to entry (R, L'', R''). If $R \notin T$, choose a random encoding of a random bit b'': $(L'', R'') \leftarrow \mathsf{E}(b'')$. Store (R, L'', R'') in T and output R''.

By properties of the random oracle, the view of the reduction **Red** when interacting with A versus A' are equivalent.

Since the reduction succeeds when interacting with Real adversary A with non-negligible probability p and since the view of the reduction is identical when interacting with A or A', **Red** interacting with A' must also succeed with non-negligible probability p. But **Red** composed with A' yields an efficient adversary, leading to an efficient adversary breaking the underlying falsifiable assumption, which is a contradiction.

4   2-State CNMC for One-Bit Messages

In this section we prove the following theorem:

Theorem 6. *Assuming the existence of one-to-one commitment schemes in the CRS model, there is a construction of a 2-split-state CNM Randomness Encoder in the CRS model.*

The corollary is immediate, given the transformation in the full version [27].

Corollary 1. *Assuming the existence of one-to-one commitment schemes in the CRS model, there is a construction of a single-bit, 2-split-state CNMC in the CRS model.*

Notation and Parameters. λ is security parameter and length of encoded randomness. $\ell = \ell(\lambda) \in \Theta(\lambda^2)$ and we assume for simplicity that $\lambda | \ell$. Sets $S_L, S_R \subseteq [2\ell]$ are defined as follows: $S_L = [\ell], S_R = [2\ell] \setminus [\ell]$. $y_o = y_o(\ell) \in \Theta(\ell^{1/2})$, $y_t = y_t(\ell) \in \Theta(\ell^{1/2})$.

The construction of the 2-state CNM Randomness Encoder is given in Fig. 1.

Let $(\mathsf{CRSGen}_{\mathsf{Com}}, \mathsf{Com}, \mathsf{Open}, \mathsf{S}_{Eq})$ be the non-interactive, equivocal, one-to-one commitment in the CRS model given in Section 2.6.

$\mathsf{CRSGen}(1^\lambda)$: $\Sigma \leftarrow \mathsf{CRSGen}_{\mathsf{Com}}(1^\lambda)$. Output Σ.

$\mathsf{E}_\Sigma(c_L \| c_R \| r_{com})$:

1. Parse c_L, c_R as strings in $\mathbb{F}_{2\lambda}^{\frac{\ell}{\lambda}}$.
2. $(com, d = d_1, \ldots, d_{2\ell}) \leftarrow \mathsf{Com}_\Sigma(c_L \| c_R; r_{com})$
3. Let $d[S_L]$ (resp. $d[S_R]$) correspond to the decommitment of com to the bits corresponding to S_L (resp. S_R).
4. $\mathsf{E}_{2,\Sigma}$ outputs $L = (com, d[S_L])$; $R = (com, d[S_R])$. $\mathsf{E}_{1,\Sigma}$ outputs $\langle c_L, c_R \rangle$.

$\mathsf{D}_\Sigma(\widetilde{L}, \widetilde{R})$:

1. Parse $\widetilde{L} = (\widetilde{com}, \widetilde{d}[S_L])$, $\widetilde{R} = (\widetilde{com}', \widetilde{d}[S_R])$.
2. Check that $\widetilde{com} = \widetilde{com}'$.
3. Let $\widetilde{c}_L = \mathsf{Open}_\Sigma(S_L, \widetilde{com}, \widetilde{d}[S_L])$ and $\widetilde{c}_R = \mathsf{Open}_\Sigma(S_R, \widetilde{com}, \widetilde{d}[S_R])$. Check that $\widetilde{c}_L \neq \bot$ and $\widetilde{c}_R \neq \bot$.
4. If all the above checks pass, output $\langle \widetilde{c}_L, \widetilde{c}_R \rangle$. Otherwise, output $\bot$.

Fig. 1. Construction of 2-State, Continuous, Non-Malleable Randomness Encoder.

To prove Theorem 6, we show that the construction above is a secure CNM Randomness Encoder, via the following sequence of hybrids.

Hybrid 0: This is the "Real" security experiment.

Hybrid 1: The experiment is identical to Hybrid 0 except we modify the decode algorithm from D_Σ to D_Σ^1 to abort if the tampered codeword submitted is different from the challenge codeword and the Check function outputs 1. Specifically, let $(L := (com, d[S_L]), R = (com, d[S_R]))$ be the "challenge" codeword (i.e. the codeword generated by the security experiment) (Fig. 2).

$\mathsf{D}^1_\Sigma(\widetilde{L}, \widetilde{R})$:

1. Parse $\widetilde{L} = (\widetilde{com}, \widetilde{d}[S_L])$, $\widetilde{R} = (\widetilde{com}', \widetilde{d}[S_R])$.
2. If $\widetilde{L} \neq L$ and $\mathsf{Check}_\Sigma(com, \widetilde{com}) = 1$ or $\widetilde{R} \neq R$ and $\mathsf{Check}_\Sigma(com, \widetilde{com}') = 1$
   then output $\perp$.
3. Check that $\widetilde{com} = \widetilde{com}'$.
4. Let $\widetilde{c}_L = \mathsf{Open}_\Sigma(S_L, \widetilde{com}, \widetilde{d}[S_L])$ and $\widetilde{c}_R = \mathsf{Open}_\Sigma(S_R, \widetilde{com}, \widetilde{d}[S_R])$. Check that
   $\widetilde{c}_L \neq \perp$ and $\widetilde{c}_R \neq \perp$.
5. If all the above checks pass, output $\langle \widetilde{c}_L, \widetilde{c}_R \rangle$. Otherwise, output $\perp$.

Fig. 2. Decode in Hybrid 1.

Hybrid 2: The experiment is identical to Hybrid 1, except we switch to equivocal commitments in the codeword (L, R) that is given to the adversary. Specifically, CRSGen is replaced with CRSGen^2 and the challenge codeword is generated as shown in Fig. 3.

$\mathsf{CRSGen}^2(1^\lambda)$: $(\Sigma_{Eq}, \overline{com}, d^0 = d^0_1 \ldots d^0_{2\ell}, d^1 = d^1_1 \ldots d^1_{2\ell}) \leftarrow \mathsf{S}_{Eq}(1^\lambda)$. Output Σ_{Eq}.
Challenge codeword:

1. Sample c_L, c_R uniform randomly from $\mathbb{F}^{\frac{\ell}{\lambda}}_{2^\lambda}$.
2. Set $d[S_L] := [d^{c_L[i]}_i]_{i \in S_L}$; Set $d[S_R] := [d^{c_R[i]}_i]_{i \in S_R}$;
3. Output $L = (\overline{com}, d[S_L])$; $R = (\overline{com}, d[S_R])$.

Fig. 3. Gen and Challenge Codeword generation in Hybrid 2.

Hybrid 3: The experiment is identical to Hybrid 2, except we modify D^1 to D^3, which aborts if the outcome of $f^i_L(L)$ or $f^i_R(R)$ is not a "likely value."

Specifically, given $(\Sigma_{Eq}, \overline{com}, d^0 = d^0_1 \ldots d^0_{2\ell}, d^1 = d^1_1 \ldots d^1_{2\ell})$ and the adversary's current output $\mathsf{Out}^{i-1}_A = \widehat{Out}^{i-1}_A$, we define the sets $\mathcal{S}_L, \mathcal{S}_R, \mathcal{S}'_L, \mathcal{S}'_R$ as:

- $\mathcal{S}_L$ contains all values of $\widehat{L}'$ that occur with probability at least $\epsilon = 1/2^{y_o/3}$, where values of $\widehat{L}'$ are sampled as follows: Sample $\widehat{c}_L$ conditioned on the output of the experiment in Hybrid 2 thus far being equal to $\mathsf{Out}^{i-1}_A = \widehat{Out}^{i-1}_A$. Compute equivocal decommitment of $\overline{com}$: $\widehat{d}[S_L] := [d^{\widehat{c}_L[i]}_i]_{i \in S_L}$. Apply f^i_L to $\widehat{L} = (\overline{com}, \widehat{d}[S_L])$ to obtain $\widehat{L}'$ (or "same" if the output is $\widehat{L}$ itself).
- $\mathcal{S}_R$ contains all values of $\widehat{R}'$ that occur with probability at least $\epsilon = 1/2^{y_o/3}$, where values of $\widehat{R}'$ are sampled as follows: Sample $\widehat{c}_R$ conditioned on the output of the experiment in Hybrid 2 thus far being equal to $\mathsf{Out}^{i-1}_A = \widehat{Out}^{i-1}_A$. Compute equivocal decommitment of $\overline{com}$: $\widehat{d}[S_R] := [d^{\widehat{c}_R[i]}_i]_{i \in S_R}$. Apply f^i_R to $\widehat{R} = (\overline{com}, \widehat{d}[S_R])$ to obtain $\widehat{R}'$ (or "same" if the output is $\widehat{R}$ itself).

- Let $\mathcal{S}'_L \subseteq \mathcal{S}_L$ be the set of $\widehat{L}'$ such that there is a "matching" $\widehat{R}' \in \mathcal{S}_R$ such that $\mathsf{D}^1_{\Sigma_{Eq}}(\widehat{L}', \widehat{R}') \neq \perp$.
- Let $\mathcal{S}'_R \subseteq \mathcal{S}_R$ be the set of $\widehat{R}'$ such that there is a "matching" $\widehat{L}' \in \mathcal{S}_L$ such that $\mathsf{D}^1_{\Sigma_{Eq}}(\widehat{L}', \widehat{R}') \neq \perp$.

Note that the decode oracle is now stateful and depends on the current round of interaction, as well as the outputs returned in previous rounds. Specifically, note that the sets $\mathcal{S}'_L, \mathcal{S}'_R$ change in each round i, since the likely outputs depend on the tampering function (f_L^i, f_R^i) submitted by the adversary in round i, and are conditioned on the output $\mathsf{Out}_A^{i-1} = \widehat{Out}_A^{i-1}$ seen by the adversary thus far in rounds $1, \ldots, i-1$ (Fig. 4).

$\mathsf{D}^3_{\Sigma_{Eq}}((f_L^i, f_R^i), \widetilde{L}, \widetilde{R})$:

1. Check that $\widetilde{L} \in \mathcal{S}'_L$ and that $\widetilde{R} \in \mathcal{S}'_R$. If not, output $\perp$.
2. Parse $\widetilde{L} = (\widetilde{com}, \widetilde{d}[S_L])$, $\widetilde{R} = (\widetilde{com}', \widetilde{d}[S_R])$.
3. Check that $\widetilde{com} = \widetilde{com}'$.
4. Let $\widetilde{c}_L = \mathsf{Open}_\Sigma(S_L, \widetilde{com}, \widetilde{d}[S_L])$ and $\widetilde{c}_R = \mathsf{Open}_\Sigma(S_R, \widetilde{com}, \widetilde{d}[S_R])$. Check that $\widetilde{c}_L \neq \perp$ and $\widetilde{c}_R \neq \perp$.
5. If all the above checks pass, output $\langle \widetilde{c}_L, \widetilde{c}_R \rangle$. Otherwise, output $\perp$.

Fig. 4. Decode in Hybrid 3.

Hybrid 4: The experiment is identical to Hybrid 3, except we modify D^3 to D^4 which aborts if there are more than y_t number of queries f_L^i (resp. f_R^i) such that the outcome of $f_L^i(L)$ (resp. $f_R^i(R)$) is not the most "likely value". Specifically, at the beginning of the experiment, we initialize counters $\mathsf{count}_L, \mathsf{count}_R$ to 0. We also define L^* (resp. R^*) to be the element of $\mathcal{S}'_L$ (resp. $\mathcal{S}'_R$) that occurs most frequently. More precisely, we consider the sets

$$\mathcal{L}^* := \mathsf{argmax}_{L' \in \mathcal{S}'_L} \Pr[f_L^i(\widehat{L}) = L' \mid \mathsf{Out}_A^{i-1} = \widehat{Out}_A^{i-1}].$$

$$\mathcal{R}^* := \mathsf{argmax}_{R' \in \mathcal{S}'_R} \Pr[f_R^i(\widehat{R}) = R' \mid \mathsf{Out}_A^{i-1} = \widehat{Out}_A^{i-1}].$$

Then L^* (resp. R^*) is defined to be the lexicographically first element in $\mathcal{L}^*$ (resp. $\mathcal{R}^*$) (Fig. 5).

Claim 4.1. Hybrids 0 and 1 are computationally indistinguishable.

This follows from the additional properties of the equivocal commitment scheme given in Sect. 2.6.

Claim 4.2. Hybrids 1 and 2 are computationally indistinguishable.

This follows from the security of the equivocal commitment scheme.

$\mathsf{D}^4_{\Sigma_{Eq}}((f^i_L, f^i_R), \widetilde{L}, \widetilde{R})$:

1. Check that $\widetilde{L} \in \mathcal{S}'_L$ and that $\widetilde{R} \in \mathcal{S}'_R$. If not, output $\perp$.
2. If $\widetilde{L} \neq L^*$, then set $\mathsf{count}_L := \mathsf{count}_L + 1$.
3. If $\widetilde{R} \neq R^*$, then set $\mathsf{count}_R := \mathsf{count}_R + 1$.
4. If $\mathsf{count}_L > y_t$ or $\mathsf{count}_R > y_t$, output $\perp$.
5. Parse $\widetilde{L} = (\widetilde{com}, \widetilde{d}[S_L])$, $\widetilde{R} = (\widetilde{com}', \widetilde{d}[S_R])$.
6. Check that $\widetilde{com} = \widetilde{com}'$.
7. Let $\widetilde{c}_L = \mathsf{Open}_\Sigma(S_L, \widetilde{com}, \widetilde{d}[S_L])$ and $\widetilde{c}_R = \mathsf{Open}_\Sigma(S_R, \widetilde{com}, \widetilde{d}[S_R])$. Check that $\widetilde{c}_L \neq \perp$ and $\widetilde{c}_R \neq \perp$.
8. If all the above checks pass, output $\langle \widetilde{c}_L, \widetilde{c}_R \rangle$. Otherwise, output $\perp$.

Fig. 5. Decode in Hybrid 4.

Claim 4.3. Hybrids 2 and 3 are $\epsilon \cdot 2q$-close, where $\epsilon = 1/2^{y_o/3}$ and $y_o \in O(\ell^{1/2})$.

Proof. To prove indistinguishability of Hybrids 2 and 3, it is sufficient to show that for each $i \in [q]$, $\Pr[f^i_L(L) \notin \mathcal{S}'_L \wedge \mathsf{D}^1_{\Sigma_{Eq}}(f^i_L(L), f^i_R(R)) \neq \perp] \leq \epsilon$ and $\Pr[f^i_L(R) \notin \mathcal{S}'_R \wedge \mathsf{D}^1_{\Sigma_{Eq}}(f^i_L(L), f^i_R(R)) \neq \perp] \leq \epsilon$. The result then follows by a union bound over the q LHS and q RHS queries.

To bound the above, we in fact show something stronger: (1) for each $i \in [q]$, each value of $\mathsf{Out}^{i-1}_A = \widehat{Out}^{i-1}_A$ (which does not contain a $\perp$ output) and each value of $R = \widehat{R}$,

$$\Pr[f^i_L(L) \notin \mathcal{S}'_L \wedge \mathsf{D}^1_{\Sigma_{Eq}}(f^i_L(L), f^i_R(R)) \neq \perp \mid R = \widehat{R} \wedge \mathsf{Out}^{i-1}_A = \widehat{Out}^{i-1}_A)] \leq \epsilon;$$

and (2) for each $i \in [q]$, each value of $\mathsf{Out}^{i-1}_A = \widehat{Out}^{i-1}_A$ (which does not contain a $\perp$ output) and each value of $L = \widehat{L}$,

$$\Pr[f^i_R(R) \notin \mathcal{S}'_R \wedge \mathsf{D}^1_{\Sigma_{Eq}}(f^i_L(L), f^i_R(R)) \neq \perp \mid L = \widehat{L} \wedge \mathsf{Out}^{i-1}_A = \widehat{Out}^{i-1}_A)] \leq \epsilon.$$

We first fix $(\Sigma_{Eq}, \overline{com}, d^0 = d^0_1 \ldots d^0_{2\ell}, d^1 = d^1_1 \ldots d^1_{2\ell})$. Note that for fixed $\Sigma_{Eq}, \overline{com}, d^0 = d^0_1 \ldots d^0_{2\ell}, d^1 = d^1_1 \ldots d^1_{2\ell}$, there is a bijection ϕ_L (resp. ϕ_R) between c_L (resp. c_R) and $(\overline{com}, d[S_L])$ (where $d[S_L] := [d^{c_L[i]}_i]_{i \in S_L}$). Therefore the probability of a particular value of c_L (resp. c_R) occurring is equivalent to the probability of $L = \phi_L(c_L)$ (resp. $R = \phi_R(c_R)$) occurring. Additionally, Let ρ_L (resp. ρ_R) be the function that given $f^i_R(R)$ (resp. $f^i_L(L)$) returns the unique L' (resp. R') if it exists such that, $\mathsf{D}^1_{\Sigma_{Eq}}(L', f^i_R(R)) \neq \perp$ (resp. $\mathsf{D}^1_{\Sigma_{Eq}}(f^i_L(L), R') \neq \perp$). Note that L' (resp. R') is equal to "same" if and only if $f^i_R(R) =$ "same" (resp. $f^i_L(L) =$ "same"). To see why this is so, recall that in D^1, $\perp$ is outputted if $\widetilde{L} \neq L$ and $\mathsf{Check}_\Sigma(com, \widetilde{com}) = 1$ or $\widetilde{R} \neq R$ and $\mathsf{Check}_\Sigma(com, \widetilde{com}') = 1$. Now, if L' is equal to same, then it must be that $\mathsf{Check}_\Sigma(com, \widetilde{com}) = 1$. Therefore, by the above, the only value of $f^i_R(R)$, for which $\perp$ will not be output is $f_R^i(R) =$ "same". The same is true for the case that $f_R^i(R) =$ "same".

We first show that for $i \in [q]$, c_L, c_R are conditionally independent given $\mathsf{Out}_A^i = \widehat{\mathsf{Out}}_A^i$. This follows from the fact that the information contained in $\widehat{\mathsf{Out}}_A^i$ is of the form $(f_L^1(\phi_L(c_L)) = v_1, f_R^1(\phi_R(c_R)) = w_1), \ldots, (f_L^i(\phi_L(c_L)) = v_i, f_R^i(\phi_R(c_R)) = w_i)$, where for $j \in [i]$, v_j is equal to the L' value outputted in response to the j-th query and w_j is equal to the R' value outputted in response to the j-th query. (note that v_j/w_j can be set to "same" if the tampering function leaves L/R unchanged). Thus, the distribution of c_L, c_R conditioned on $(f_L^1(\phi_L(c_L)) = v_1, f_R^1(\phi_R(c_R)) = w_1), \ldots, (f_L^i(\phi_L(c_L)) = v_i, f_R^i(\phi_R(c_R)) = w_i)$ is equal to $(U_\ell \mid (f_L^1(\phi_L(U_\ell)) = v_1, \ldots, f_L^i(\phi_L(U_\ell)) = v_i)) \times (U_\ell \mid (f_R^1(\phi_R(U_\ell)) = w_1, \ldots, f_R^i(\phi_R(U_\ell)) = w_i))$. Moreover, due to the discussion above, L, R are also conditionally independent given $\mathsf{Out}_A^{i-1} = \widehat{\mathsf{Out}}_A^{i-1}$. Therefore, to show (1), we note that for every $(\widehat{L}, \widehat{R}, \widehat{\mathsf{Out}}_A^{i-1})$, $\Pr[L = \widehat{L} \mid R = \widehat{R} \wedge \mathsf{Out}_A^{i-1} = \widehat{\mathsf{Out}}_A^{i-1})] = \Pr[L = \widehat{L} \mid \mathsf{Out}_A^{i-1} = \widehat{\mathsf{Out}}_A^{i-1})]$. So we have that for every fixed $R = \widehat{R}$ (for which $\Pr[R = \widehat{R} \wedge \mathsf{Out}_A^{i-1} = \widehat{\mathsf{Out}}_A^{i-1})] > 0$), and every $L' \notin S_L'$, $\Pr[f^i(L) = L' \mid R = \widehat{R} \wedge \mathsf{Out}_A^{i-1} = \widehat{\mathsf{Out}}_A^{i-1})] \leq \epsilon$. Therefore,

$$\Pr[f_L^i(L) \notin S_L' \wedge \mathsf{D}_{\Sigma_{Eq}}^1(f_L^i(L), f_R^i(R)) \neq \perp \mid R = \widehat{R} \wedge \mathsf{Out}_A^{i-1} = \widehat{\mathsf{Out}}_A^{i-1})]$$
$$= \Pr[f_L^i(L) \notin S_L' \wedge (f_L^i(L) = \rho_L(f_R^i(R))) \mid R = \widehat{R} \wedge \mathsf{Out}_A^{i-1} = \widehat{\mathsf{Out}}_A^{i-1})]$$
$$\leq \epsilon.$$

The proof for (2) is analogous.

Claim 4.4. Hybrids 3 and 4 are statistically indistinguishable.

Proof. To prove indistinguishability of Hybrids 3 and 4, we must show that the probability that the event (1) $f_L^i(L)$ is not most frequent and $\mathsf{D}_{\Sigma_{Eq}}^3(f_L^i(L), f_R^i(R)) \neq \perp$ or event (2) $f_R^i(R)$ is not most frequent and $\mathsf{D}_{\Sigma_{Eq}}^3(f_L^i(L), f_R^i(R)) \neq \perp$ occurs more than y_t times in a single execution is at most $(1/2)^{y_t}$.

We first analyze the event (1). Recall that set S_L' contains values, L', that occur with probability p in some experiment. By "most frequent value" in S_L', we mean the value L' in S_L' with the maximum associated probability p. Note that if L' is not the most frequent value, the associated probability p is at most $1/2$, since otherwise, the probabilities will sum to more than 1. More precisely, if $f_L^i(L) = L'$ is not the most frequent query in S_L' then, by definition of the set S_L' and the above argument, $\Pr[f_L^i(\widehat{L}) = L' \mid \mathsf{Out}_A^{i-1} = \widehat{\mathsf{Out}}_A^{i-1}] \leq 1/2$. Recall that in the proof of the previous claim, we have shown that for $i \in \{0, \ldots, q\}$, L, R are conditionally independent given Out_A^i. Therefore, $\Pr[f_L^i(L) = L' \mid \mathsf{Out}_A^{i-1} = \widehat{\mathsf{Out}}_A^{i-1} \wedge R = \widehat{R}] \leq 1/2$. This implies that for every fixed $R = \widehat{R}$ (for which $\Pr[R = \widehat{R} \wedge \mathsf{Out}_A^{i-1} = \widehat{\mathsf{Out}}_A^{i-1}] > 0$),

$$\Pr[f_L^i(L) \neq L^* \wedge \mathsf{D}^3_{\Sigma_{Eq}}(f_L^i(L), f_R^i(R)) \neq \bot \mid R = \widehat{R} \wedge \mathsf{Out}_A^{i-1} = \widehat{Out}_A^{i-1})]$$

$$\leq \Pr[f_L^i(L) \neq L^* \wedge f_L^i(L) = \rho_L(f_R^i(R)) \mid R = \widehat{R} \wedge \mathsf{Out}_A^{i-1} = \widehat{Out}_A^{i-1})]$$

$$\leq 1/2.$$

We consider the number of adversarial queries such that both $f_L^i(L) = L'$ is not the most frequent value $(L^*) \in \mathcal{S}_L'$ and $\mathsf{D}^3_{\Sigma_{Eq}}(f_L^i(L), f_R^i(R)) \neq \bot$. (note that the total number of adversarial queries can be much higher). By the above argument, the probability that there are y_t number of rounds i such that both $f_L^i(L) = L'$ is not the most frequent value $(L^*) \in \mathcal{S}_L'$ and $\mathsf{D}^3_{\Sigma_{Eq}}(f_L^i(L), f_R^i(R)) \neq \bot$ is at most $(1/2)^{y_t} \in \mathsf{negl}(\lambda)$. Thus, we have concluded the proof for event (1). The proof for event (2) is analogous.

We finally show the main technical claim of this section, which completes the proof of Theorem 6.

Claim 4.5. In Hybrid 4, the encoded randomness $\langle c_L, c_R \rangle$ is statistically close to uniform, given the view of the adversary.

Proof. Towards proving the claim, we consider the following leakage functions:

Leakage Function on c_L: Fix $\Sigma_{Eq}, \overline{com}, d^0, d^1$, universal hash $h : \{0,1\}^\alpha \to \{0,1\}^{y_o} \in \mathcal{H}$ (where α is the length of a single split-state of the encoding) and adversary A. On input c_L, set output Out_A to "" and Out_L to "". Set $L = (\overline{com}, [d_i^{c_L[i]}]_{i \in [\ell]})$. Repeat the following in rounds $i = 1, 2, \ldots$:

1. Obtain the next tampering function (f_L, f_R) from adversary A. If A terminates then terminate with output Out_L.
2. Set $L' := f_L(L)$. If $L' \in \mathcal{S}_L'$, then:
   (a) Find the unique $\widehat{R}' \in \mathcal{S}_R'$ such that $\mathsf{D}^1_{\Sigma_{Eq}}(L', \widehat{R}') \neq \bot$. Return $(L', \widehat{R}')$ to the adversary. Set $\mathsf{Out}_A = \mathsf{Out}_A || (L', \widehat{R}')$.
   (b) If L' is not the most frequent output in $\mathcal{S}_L'$, set $\mathsf{Out}_L := \mathsf{Out}_L || (i || h(L'))$ If $|\mathsf{Out}_L| > (\log(q) + y_o) \cdot y_t$ then terminate with output $\mathsf{Out}_L := \mathsf{Out}_L || (i || \bot)$.
3. If $L' \notin \mathcal{S}_L'$, output $\bot$ to the adversary and terminate with output $\mathsf{Out}_L := \mathsf{Out}_L || (i || \bot)$.

The leakage function for the RHS is analogous.

We now show that given Out_L and Out_R we can reconstruct the full output sequence for the adversary's view with probability $1 - \frac{2q}{\epsilon^2 \cdot 2^{y_o}} = 1 - \frac{2q}{2^{y_o/3}}$ in the following way:

Fix $\Sigma_{Eq}, \overline{com}, d^0 = d_1^0 \ldots d_{2\ell}^0, d^1 = d_1^1 \ldots d_{2\ell}^1$, universal hash $h \leftarrow \mathcal{H}$ and adversary A. Set output Out_A to "" and Out_L to "". Repeat the following in rounds $i = 1, 2, \ldots, q$:

1. Obtain the next tampering function (f_L, f_R) from adversary A given its current view, Out_A.
2. If $(i, \bot) \in \mathsf{Out}_L$ or $(i, \bot) \in \mathsf{Out}_R$, set $\mathsf{Out}_A = \mathsf{Out}_A || \bot$ and abort.

3. If $(i, y) \in \mathsf{Out}_L$, for some $y \neq \perp$, set $L' = \widehat{L}'$ such that $\widehat{L}' \in \mathcal{S}'_L$ and $h(\widehat{L}') = y$.
4. If $(i, \cdot) \notin \mathsf{Out}_L$, set $L' = \widehat{L}'$ such that $\widehat{L}' \in \mathcal{S}'_L$ is the most frequent value.
5. If $(i, y) \in \mathsf{Out}_R$, for some $y \neq \perp$, set $R' = \widehat{R}'$ such that $\widehat{R}' \in \mathcal{S}'_R$ and $h(\widehat{R}') = y$.
6. If $(i, \cdot) \notin \mathsf{Out}_R$, set $R' = \widehat{R}'$ such that $\widehat{R}' \in \mathcal{S}'_R$ is the most frequent value.
7. If $L' = $ "same" and $R' = $ "same" output "same" and set $\mathsf{Out}_A = \mathsf{Out}_A ||$ "same".
8. Else if one of L', R' is "same" and not the other, set $\mathsf{Out}_A = \mathsf{Out}_A || \perp$ and abort.
9. Else Parse $L' := (com, d[S_L])$ and $R' := (com', d[S_R])$. If $com \neq com'$, set $\mathsf{Out}_A = \mathsf{Out}_A || \perp$ and abort.
10. Otherwise, set $\mathsf{Out}_A = \mathsf{Out}_A || (L', R')$.

It can be determined by inspection that the incorrect value is output only if in one of the at most $2q$ instances, there are two distinct values $\widehat{L}', \widehat{L}'' \in \mathcal{S}'_L$ or $\widehat{R}', \widehat{R}'' \in \mathcal{S}'_R$ such that $h(\widehat{L}') = h(\widehat{L}'')$ or $h(\widehat{R}') = h(\widehat{R}'')$. Due to universality of h and the fact that $|\mathcal{S}'_L| = |\mathcal{S}'_R| = 1/\epsilon$, this can occur with probability at most $\frac{2q}{\epsilon^2 \cdot 2^{y_o}}$, as claimed.[3]

Since $|\mathsf{Out}_L| \leq (\log(q) + y_o) \cdot y_t \leq 2y_o \cdot y_t \leq c \cdot \ell$ for constant $c < 1$ and $|\mathsf{Out}_R| \leq (\log(q) + y_o) \cdot y_t \leq 2y_o \cdot y_t \leq c \cdot \ell$ for constant $c < 1$, we can use the properties of the inner product extractor (check the full version of this paper [27] for more details.) to argue that $\langle c_L, c_R \rangle$ is statistically close to uniform random, given $\mathsf{Out}_L, \mathsf{Out}_R$. Moreover, since we have shown that the view of the adversary in the Hybrid 4 can be fully reconstructed given $\mathsf{Out}_L, \mathsf{Out}_R$, we have that, in the Hybrid 4, the encoded randomness $\langle c_L, c_R \rangle$ is statistically close to uniform, given the adversary's view in the CNMC experiment.

Acknowledgments. We thank the anonymous PKC 2019 reviewers for pointing out an error and fix to our lower bound proof. We also thank them for extensive comments that helped to significantly improve our presentation.

References

1. Abe, M., Groth, J., Ohkubo, M.: Separating short structure-preserving signatures from non-interactive assumptions. In: Lee, D.H., Wang, X. (eds.) ASIACRYPT 2011. LNCS, vol. 7073, pp. 628–646. Springer, Heidelberg (2011). https://doi.org/10.1007/978-3-642-25385-0_34
2. Aggarwal, D., Agrawal, S., Gupta, D., Maji, H.K., Pandey, O., Prabhakaran, M.: Optimal computational split-state non-malleable codes. [56], pp. 393–417
3. Aggarwal, D., Dodis, Y., Kazana, T., Obremski, M.: Non-malleable reductions and applications. In: Servedio, R.A., Rubinfeld, R. (eds.) 47th ACM STOC, pp. 459–468. ACM Press, June 2015

---

[3] Recall that $\mathcal{S}'_L \subseteq \mathcal{S}_L$, and $\mathcal{S}_L$ contains all the values of $\widehat{L}'$ which occur with probability at least ϵ. Therefore $|\mathcal{S}_L| \leq 1/\epsilon$ (and thus $|\mathcal{S}'_L| \leq 1/\epsilon$), since otherwise the sum of the probabilities would exceed 1. A similar argument is true for $\mathcal{S}'_R$.

4. Aggarwal, D., Dodis, Y., Lovett, S.: Non-malleable codes from additive combinatorics. In: Shmoys, D.B. (ed.) 46th ACM STOC, pp. 774–783. ACM Press, May/June 2014
5. Aggarwal, D., Dottling, N., Nielsen, J.B., Obremski, M., Purwanto, E.: Continuous non-malleable codes in the 8-split-state model. Cryptology ePrint Archive, Report 2017/357 (2017). https://eprint.iacr.org/2017/357
6. Aggarwal, D., Dziembowski, S., Kazana, T., Obremski, M.: Leakage-resilient non-malleable codes. [33], pp. 398–426
7. Agrawal, S., Gupta, D., Maji, H.K., Pandey, O., Prabhakaran, M.: Explicit non-malleable codes against bit-wise tampering and permutations. In: Gennaro, R., Robshaw, M. (eds.) CRYPTO 2015, Part I. LNCS, vol. 9215, pp. 538–557. Springer, Heidelberg (2015). https://doi.org/10.1007/978-3-662-47989-6_26
8. Agrawal, S., Gupta, D., Maji, H.K., Pandey, O., Prabhakaran, M.: A rate-optimizing compiler for non-malleable codes against bit-wise tampering and permutations. [33], pp. 375–397
9. Ball, M., Dachman-Soled, D., Guo, S., Malkin, T., Tan, L.Y.: Non-malleable codes for small-depth circuits. In: Thorup, M. (ed.) 59th FOCS, pp. 826–837. IEEE Computer Society Press, October 2018
10. Ball, M., Dachman-Soled, D., Kulkarni, M., Malkin, T.: Non-malleable codes for bounded depth, bounded fan-in circuits. In: Fischlin, M., Coron, J.-S. (eds.) EUROCRYPT 2016, Part II. LNCS, vol. 9666, pp. 881–908. Springer, Heidelberg (2016). https://doi.org/10.1007/978-3-662-49896-5_31
11. Ball, M., Dachman-Soled, D., Kulkarni, M., Malkin, T.: Non-malleable codes from average-case hardness: AC^0, decision trees, and streaming space-bounded tampering. [62], pp. 618–650
12. Barak, B.: How to go beyond the black-box simulation barrier. In: 42nd FOCS, pp. 106–115. IEEE Computer Society Press, October 2001
13. Barak, B., Mahmoody-Ghidary, M.: Merkle puzzles are optimal — an $O(n^2)$-query attack on any key exchange from a random oracle. In: Halevi, S. (ed.) CRYPTO 2009. LNCS, vol. 5677, pp. 374–390. Springer, Heidelberg (2009). https://doi.org/10.1007/978-3-642-03356-8_22
14. Bitansky, N., Paneth, O.: From the impossibility of obfuscation to a new non-black-box simulation technique. In: 53rd FOCS, pp. 223–232. IEEE Computer Society Press, October 2012
15. Chandran, N., Goyal, V., Mukherjee, P., Pandey, O., Upadhyay, J.: Block-wise non-malleable codes. In Chatzigiannakis, I., Mitzenmacher, M., Rabani, Y., Sangiorgi, D. (eds.) ICALP 2016. LIPIcs, vol. 55, pp. 31:1–31:14, Schloss Dagstuhl, July 2016
16. Chandran, N., Kanukurthi, B., Ostrovsky, R.: Locally updatable and locally decodable codes. [59], pp. 489–514
17. Chandran, N., Kanukurthi, B., Raghuraman, S.: Information-theoretic local non-malleable codes and their applications. [59], pp. 367–392
18. Chattopadhyay, E., Li, X.: Non-malleable codes and extractors for small-depth circuits, and affine functions. In: Hatami, H., McKenzie, P., King, V. (eds.) 49th ACM STOC, pp. 1171–1184. ACM Press, June 2017
19. Chattopadhyay, E., Zuckerman, D.: Non-malleable codes against constant split-state tampering. In: 55th FOCS, pp. 306–315. IEEE Computer Society Press, October 2014
20. Chattopadhyay, E., Zuckerman, D.: Explicit two-source extractors and resilient functions. [70], pp. 670–683
21. Cheraghchi, M., Guruswami, V.: Capacity of non-malleable codes. In: Naor, M. (ed.) ITCS 2014, pp. 155–168. ACM, January 2014

22. Cheraghchi, M., Guruswami, V.: Non-malleable coding against bit-wise and split-state tampering. [59], pp. 440–464

23. Choi, S.G., Dachman-Soled, D., Malkin, T., Wee, H.: Black-box construction of a non-malleable encryption scheme from any semantically secure one. In: Canetti, R. (ed.) TCC 2008. LNCS, vol. 4948, pp. 427–444. Springer, Heidelberg (2008). https://doi.org/10.1007/978-3-540-78524-8_24

24. Coretti, S., Dodis, Y., Tackmann, B., Venturi, D.: Non-malleable encryption: simpler, shorter, stronger. In: Kushilevitz, E., Malkin, T. (eds.) TCC 2016-A, Part I. LNCS, vol. 9562, pp. 306–335. Springer, Heidelberg (2016). https://doi.org/10.1007/978-3-662-49096-9_13

25. Coretti, S., Maurer, U., Tackmann, B., Venturi, D.: From single-bit to multi-bit public-key encryption via non-malleable codes. [33], pp. 532–560

26. Coron, J.-S.: Security proof for partial-domain hash signature schemes. In: Yung, M. (ed.) CRYPTO 2002. LNCS, vol. 2442, pp. 613–626. Springer, Heidelberg (2002). https://doi.org/10.1007/3-540-45708-9_39

27. Dachman-Soled, D., Kulkarni, M.: Upper and lower bounds for continuous non-malleable codes. Cryptology ePrint Archive, Report 2018/517 (2018). https://eprint.iacr.org/2018/517

28. Dachman-Soled, D., Kulkarni, M., Shahverdi, A.: Tight upper and lower bounds for leakage-resilient, locally decodable and updatable non-malleable codes. In: Fehr, S. (ed.) PKC 2017, Part I. LNCS, vol. 10174, pp. 310–332. Springer, Heidelberg (2017). https://doi.org/10.1007/978-3-662-54365-8_13

29. Dachman-Soled, D., Kulkarni, M., Shahverdi, A.: Local non-malleable codes in the bounded retrieval model. In: Abdalla, M., Dahab, R. (eds.) PKC 2018, Part II. LNCS, vol. 10770, pp. 281–311. Springer, Cham (2018). https://doi.org/10.1007/978-3-319-76581-5_10

30. Dachman-Soled, D., Liu, F.H., Shi, E., Zhou, H.S.: Locally decodable and updatable non-malleable codes and their applications. [33], pp. 427–450

31. Damgård, I., Kazana, T., Obremski, M., Raj, V., Siniscalchi, L.: Continuous NMC secure against permutations and overwrites, with applications to CCA secure commitments. In: Beimel, A., Dziembowski, S. (eds.) TCC 2018, Part II. LNCS, vol. 11240, pp. 225–254. Springer, Cham (2018). https://doi.org/10.1007/978-3-030-03810-6_9

32. Di Crescenzo, G., Ishai, Y., Ostrovsky, R.: Non-interactive and non-malleable commitment. In: 30th ACM STOC, pp. 141–150. ACM Press, May 1998

33. Dodis, Y., Nielsen, J.B. (eds.): TCC 2015, Part I. LNCS, vol. 9014. Springer, Heidelberg (2015). https://doi.org/10.1007/978-3-662-46494-6

34. Dolev, D., Dwork, C., Naor, M.: Non-malleable cryptography (extended abstract). In: 23rd ACM STOC, pp. 542–552. ACM Press, May 1991

35. Döttling, N., Nielsen, J.B., Obremski, M.: Information theoretic continuously non-malleable codes in the constant split-state model. Cryptology ePrint Archive, Report 2017/357 (2017). https://eprint.iacr.org/2017/357

36. Dziembowski, S., Kazana, T., Obremski, M.: Non-malleable codes from two-source extractors. In: Canetti, R., Garay, J.A. (eds.) CRYPTO 2013, Part II. LNCS, vol. 8043, pp. 239–257. Springer, Heidelberg (2013). https://doi.org/10.1007/978-3-642-40084-1_14

37. Dziembowski, S., Pietrzak, K., Wichs, D.: Non-malleable codes. In: Yao, A.C.C. (ed.) ICS 2010, pp. 434–452. Tsinghua University Press, Beijing (2010)

38. Faonio, A., Nielsen, J.B., Simkin, M., Venturi, D.: Continuously non-malleable codes with split-state refresh. In: Preneel, B., Vercauteren, F. (eds.) ACNS 2018. LNCS, vol. 10892, pp. 121–139. Springer, Cham (2018). https://doi.org/10.1007/978-3-319-93387-0_7

39. Faust, S., Hostáková, K., Mukherjee, P., Venturi, D.: Non-malleable codes for space-bounded tampering. In: Katz, J., Shacham, H. (eds.) CRYPTO 2017, Part II. LNCS, vol. 10402, pp. 95–126. Springer, Cham (2017). https://doi.org/10.1007/978-3-319-63715-0_4

40. Faust, S., Mukherjee, P., Nielsen, J.B., Venturi, D.: Continuous non-malleable codes. [59], pp. 465–488

41. Faust, S., Mukherjee, P., Nielsen, J.B., Venturi, D.: A tamper and leakage resilient von Neumann architecture. In: Katz, J. (ed.) PKC 2015. LNCS, vol. 9020, pp. 579–603. Springer, Heidelberg (2015). https://doi.org/10.1007/978-3-662-46447-2_26

42. Faust, S., Mukherjee, P., Venturi, D., Wichs, D.: Efficient non-malleable codes and key-derivation for poly-size tampering circuits. In: Nguyen, P.Q., Oswald, E. (eds.) EUROCRYPT 2014. LNCS, vol. 8441, pp. 111–128. Springer, Heidelberg (2014). https://doi.org/10.1007/978-3-642-55220-5_7

43. Fischlin, M., Schröder, D.: On the impossibility of three-move blind signature schemes. In: Gilbert, H. (ed.) EUROCRYPT 2010. LNCS, vol. 6110, pp. 197–215. Springer, Heidelberg (2010). https://doi.org/10.1007/978-3-642-13190-5_10

44. Fortnow, L., Vadhan, S.P. (eds.): 43rd ACM STOC. ACM Press, June 2011

45. Fuchsbauer, G., Konstantinov, M., Pietrzak, K., Rao, V.: Adaptive security of constrained PRFs. In: Sarkar, P., Iwata, T. (eds.) ASIACRYPT 2014, Part II. LNCS, vol. 8874, pp. 82–101. Springer, Heidelberg (2014). https://doi.org/10.1007/978-3-662-45608-8_5

46. Garg, S., Bhaskar, R., Lokam, S.V.: Improved bounds on security reductions for discrete log based signatures. In: Wagner, D. (ed.) CRYPTO 2008. LNCS, vol. 5157, pp. 93–107. Springer, Heidelberg (2008). https://doi.org/10.1007/978-3-540-85174-5_6

47. Gentry, C., Wichs, D.: Separating succinct non-interactive arguments from all falsifiable assumptions. [44], pp. 99–108

48. Gertner, Y., Kannan, S., Malkin, T., Reingold, O., Viswanathan, M.: The relationship between public key encryption and oblivious transfer. In: 41st FOCS, pp. 325–335. IEEE Computer Society Press, November 2000

49. Goyal, V., Pandey, O., Richelson, S.: Textbook non-malleable commitments. [70], pp. 1128–1141

50. Impagliazzo, R., Rudich, S.: Limits on the provable consequences of one-way permutations. In: 21st ACM STOC, pp. 44–61. ACM Press, May 1989

51. Ishai, Y., Sahai, A., Wagner, D.: Private circuits: securing hardware against probing attacks. In: Boneh, D. (ed.) CRYPTO 2003. LNCS, vol. 2729, pp. 463–481. Springer, Heidelberg (2003). https://doi.org/10.1007/978-3-540-45146-4_27

52. Jafargholi, Z., Wichs, D.: Tamper detection and continuous non-malleable codes. [33], pp. 451–480

53. Kanukurthi, B., Obbattu, S.L.B., Sekar, S.: Four-state non-malleable codes with explicit constant rate. In: Kalai, Y., Reyzin, L. (eds.) TCC 2017, Part II. LNCS, vol. 10678, pp. 344–375. Springer, Cham (2017). https://doi.org/10.1007/978-3-319-70503-3_11

54. Kanukurthi, B., Obbattu, S.L.B., Sekar, S.: Non-malleable randomness encoders and their applications. [62], pp. 589–617

55. Kiayias, A., Liu, F.H., Tselekounis, Y.: Practical non-malleable codes from l-more extractable hash functions. In: Weippl, E.R., Katzenbeisser, S., Kruegel, C., Myers, A.C., Halevi, S. (eds.) ACM CCS 2016, pp. 1317–1328. ACM Press, October 2016

56. Kushilevitz, E., Malkin, T. (eds.): TCC 2016-A, Part II. LNCS, vol. 9563. Springer, Heidelberg (2016). https://doi.org/10.1007/978-3-662-49099-0

57. Li, X.: Non-malleable extractors and non-malleable codes: partially optimal constructions. Cryptology ePrint Archive, Report 2018/353 (2018). https://eprint.iacr.org/2018/353

58. Lindell, Y.: A simpler construction of CCA2-secure public-key encryption under general assumptions. J. Cryptol. **19**(3), 359–377 (2006)

59. Lindell, Y. (ed.): TCC 2014. LNCS, vol. 8349. Springer, Heidelberg (2014). https://doi.org/10.1007/978-3-642-54242-8

60. Liu, F.-H., Lysyanskaya, A.: Tamper and leakage resilience in the split-state model. In: Safavi-Naini, R., Canetti, R. (eds.) CRYPTO 2012. LNCS, vol. 7417, pp. 517–532. Springer, Heidelberg (2012). https://doi.org/10.1007/978-3-642-32009-5_30

61. Naor, M.: Bit commitment using pseudo-randomness. In: Brassard, G. (ed.) CRYPTO 1989. LNCS, vol. 435, pp. 128–136. Springer, New York (1990). https://doi.org/10.1007/0-387-34805-0_13

62. Nielsen, J.B., Rijmen, V. (eds.): EUROCRYPT 2018, Part III. LNCS, vol. 10822. Springer, Cham (2018). https://doi.org/10.1007/978-3-319-78372-7

63. Ostrovsky, R., Persiano, G., Venturi, D., Visconti, I.: Continuously non-malleable codes in the split-state model from minimal assumptions. In: Shacham, H., Boldyreva, A. (eds.) CRYPTO 2018, Part III. LNCS, vol. 10993, pp. 608–639. Springer, Cham (2018). https://doi.org/10.1007/978-3-319-96878-0_21

64. Paillier, P., Vergnaud, D.: Discrete-log-based signatures may not be equivalent to discrete log. In: Roy, B. (ed.) ASIACRYPT 2005. LNCS, vol. 3788, pp. 1–20. Springer, Heidelberg (2005). https://doi.org/10.1007/11593447_1

65. Pass, R.: Limits of provable security from standard assumptions. [44], pp. 109–118

66. Pass, R., Shelat, A., Vaikuntanathan, V.: Construction of a non-malleable encryption scheme from any semantically secure one. In: Dwork, C. (ed.) CRYPTO 2006. LNCS, vol. 4117, pp. 271–289. Springer, Heidelberg (2006). https://doi.org/10.1007/11818175_16

67. Sahai, A.: Non-malleable non-interactive zero knowledge and adaptive chosen-ciphertext security. In: 40th FOCS, pp. 543–553. IEEE Computer Society Press, October 1999

68. Seurin, Y.: On the Exact security of Schnorr-type signatures in the random oracle model. In: Pointcheval, D., Johansson, T. (eds.) EUROCRYPT 2012. LNCS, vol. 7237, pp. 554–571. Springer, Heidelberg (2012). https://doi.org/10.1007/978-3-642-29011-4_33

69. Simon, D.R.: Finding collisions on a one-way street: can secure hash functions be based on general assumptions? In: Nyberg, K. (ed.) EUROCRYPT 1998. LNCS, vol. 1403, pp. 334–345. Springer, Heidelberg (1998). https://doi.org/10.1007/BFb0054137

70. Wichs, D., Mansour, Y. (eds.): 48th ACM STOC. ACM Press, June 2016

Improved Security Evaluation Techniques for Imperfect Randomness from Arbitrary Distributions

Takahiro Matsuda[1](✉), Kenta Takahashi[2], Takao Murakami[1],
and Goichiro Hanaoka[1]

[1] National Institute of Advanced Industrial Science and Technology (AIST),
Tokyo, Japan
{t-matsuda,takao-murakami,hanaoka-goichiro}@aist.go.jp
[2] Hitachi, Ltd., Yokohama, Japan
kenta.takahashi.bw@hitachi.com

Abstract. Dodis and Yu (TCC 2013) studied how the security of cryptographic primitives that are secure in the "ideal" model in which the distribution of a randomness is the uniform distribution, is degraded when the ideal distribution of a randomness is switched to a "real-world" (possibly biased) distribution that has some lowerbound on its min-entropy or collision-entropy. However, in many constructions, their security is guaranteed only when a randomness is sampled from some non-uniform distribution (such as Gaussian in lattice-based cryptography), in which case we cannot directly apply the results by Dodis and Yu.

In this paper, we generalize the results by Dodis and Yu using the *Rényi divergence*, and show how the security of a cryptographic primitive whose security is guaranteed when the ideal distribution of a randomness is a general (possibly non-uniform) distribution Q, is degraded when the distribution is switched to another (real-world) distribution R. More specifically, we derive two general inequalities regarding the Rényi divergence of R from Q and an adversary's advantage against the security of a cryptographic primitive. As applications of our results, we show (1) an improved reduction for switching the distributions of distinguishing problems with public samplability, which is simpler and much tighter than the reduction by Bai et al. (ASIACRYPT 2015), and (2) how the differential privacy of a mechanism is degraded when its randomness comes from not an ideal distribution Q but a real-world distribution R. Finally, we show methods for approximate-sampling from an arbitrary distribution Q with some guaranteed upperbound on the Rényi divergence (of the distribution R of our sampling methods from Q).

Keywords: Rényi divergence · Security evaluation · Security reduction

© International Association for Cryptologic Research 2019
D. Lin and K. Sako (Eds.): PKC 2019, LNCS 11442, pp. 549–580, 2019.
https://doi.org/10.1007/978-3-030-17253-4_19

1 Introduction

1.1 Background and Motivation

Most cryptographic primitives such as encryption and signature schemes, are defined using a probabilistic algorithm that internally generates and uses randomness, and their security is typically defined and analyzed assuming that the randomness used by the algorithm is sampled from some pre-determined "ideal" distribution. Let us call it an ideal model. For example, in the case of encryption and signature schemes, their key generation algorithm is typically defined as a probabilistic algorithm that takes a randomness chosen from the uniform distribution as input, and we evaluate their security by estimating the probability of any possible adversary (with some resource constraint, e.g. running time, memory size, the number of oracle queries) violating the security of the considered schemes is sufficiently small. However, randomness available in the real world may not necessarily come from the ideal distribution with which the security of cryptographic primitives is analyzed. It is often the case that randomness used for generating some secret parameter (such as a secret key) could be biased and/or estimating its exact distribution could be difficult, for example, a situation of using randomness generated based on some physical phenomena (radiation, thermal noise, etc.) [5], a situation in which its partial information is possibly leaked, or a situation of using randomness generated from biometric information [8], to name a few. Even if a cryptographic primitive is guaranteed to be secure in the ideal model via a formal security proof, the security of the primitive is no longer guaranteed in the real world when such a "real-world" randomness is used.

Regarding such "ideal" vs. "real-world" randomness problem, Dodis and Yu [11] studied how the security of a cryptographic primitive in the ideal model where the distribution of its randomness is the uniform distribution $\mathcal{U}$, is degraded when the distribution is switched to another ("real-world") possibly biased distribution $\mathcal{R}$. In particular, they showed that for all cryptographic primitives categorized as *unpredictability applications* (e.g. one-way functions, message authentication codes, and signature schemes) and for some (but not all) cryptographic primitives categorized as *indistinguishability applications* satisfying the so-called "square-friendly" property [4,9,11] (e.g. pseudorandom functions and IND-CPA secure encryption schemes), their security is not totally lost even if the distribution of a randomness is switched to a real-world distribution $\mathcal{R}$ that satisfies some entropy criteria. More specifically, Dodis and Yu showed two inequalities that show how an adversary's advantage against the security of a cryptographic primitive could increase when the min-entropy or collision-entropy of the real-world distribution $\mathcal{R}$ is decreased, compared to the ideal model in which its distribution is the uniform distribution $\mathcal{U}$ and has the maximum entropy.

However, an ideal distribution, which we denote by $\mathcal{Q}$ throughout this paper, of a randomness used by cryptographic primitives is in general not necessarily the uniform distribution. For example, there are constructions in lattice-based cryptography in which a secret key is sampled from the (discrete) Gaussian distribution (e.g. [2,16]), and randomness (a noise vector) used in the encryption procedure is chosen according to a biased distribution so that 0 appears more often than other values (e.g. [15]). When implementing these constructions in practice, again the real-world distribution $\mathcal{R}$ of a randomness may not necessarily follow the ideal distribution $\mathcal{Q}$. However, for these constructions, we cannot directly apply the results by Dodis and Yu [11], since their results are restricted to the case in which the ideal distribution $\mathcal{Q}$ of a randomness is the uniform distribution.

The main motivation of our work is to generalize and extend the results by Dodis and Yu [11], so that we can apply the analogues of their results to a wider class of distributions as the ideal distribution $\mathcal{Q}$.

1.2 Our Results

As mentioned above, we generalize and extend the results by Dodis and Yu [11] so that the analogues of their results can be applied to a wider class of distributions as the ideal distribution $\mathcal{Q}$ of a randomness. The main tool we use in this paper is the *Rényi divergence* [21,23], which is a measure of divergence between distributions, and has recently been found useful in security evaluations of cryptographic primitives [1,3,6,19,22].

Our results are summarized as follows:

- In Sect. 3, we show two general lemmas that serve as the main tools throughout the paper, which are inequalities on two expectations each taken over arbitrary distribution $\mathcal{Q}$ and over $\mathcal{R}$, respectively (where intuitively, $\mathcal{Q}$ is an "ideal" distribution and $\mathcal{R}$ is a "real-world" distribution), and involve the Rényi divergence of $\mathcal{R}$ from $\mathcal{Q}$. These lemmas are generalizations of the lemmas shown by Dodis and Yu [11], who showed similar inequalities involving the min-entropy and collision-entropy of the "real-world" distribution $\mathcal{R}$, and theirs can only handle the case where the "ideal" distribution $\mathcal{Q}$ is the uniform distribution.
- Based on our general lemmas, in Sect. 4, we show general techniques for evaluating security of a cryptographic primitive (or, we use the term "application" following the style of [11] from here on) in case the distribution of a parameter (such as a secret key and/or a randomness) is switched from an ideal distribution $\mathcal{Q}$ to an arbitrary "real-world" distribution $\mathcal{R}$, using the Rényi divergence. As in [11], we show two types of results, one regarding unpredictability applications and the other regarding "square-friendly" indistinguishability applications. These results are generalizations of the corresponding results by Dodis and Yu [11], where their results only capture the case in which the ideal distribution $\mathcal{Q}$ is the uniform distribution.
- In Sect. 5, we show two applications of the above general results: one application from our general security evaluation technique for square-friendly indistinguishability applications from Sect. 4, and the other application from one of our lemmas in Sect. 3.

- Our first application is for switching the distribution of a problem instance in distinguishing problems that satisfy the property called *public samplability*, formalized by Bai et al. [3]. Using the Rényi divergence, they showed a reduction from the hardness of a problem in this class to the hardness of the same problem but in which the distribution of a parameter behind a problem instance is switched from an original distribution $\mathcal{Q}$ to another distribution $\mathcal{R}$. We show that distinguishing problems with public samplability are square-friendly in the sense of [4,9,11], thereby we can apply our above result on the general security evaluation technique of square-friendly applications under switching distributions to obtain a quantitatively improved reduction. Although our results are not applicable to the case in which the order α of the Rényi divergence is less than 2, our result gives a simpler and much tighter reduction than that of [3] for all $\alpha \geq 2$. Concretely, if we compare the ratio of the running time and the advantage of the reduction algorithm (which is sometimes called the "work factor", and a smaller value means a tighter reduction) for the same order of the Rényi divergence, the work factor of our reduction (solving the problem under distribution $\mathcal{Q}$) is always at least $\mathcal{O}(\epsilon^{-2})$ times smaller than that of the reduction shown in [3], where ϵ denotes the advantage of an underlying adversary (solving the problem under distribution $\mathcal{R}$). For the details, see Sect. 5.1.
- As the second application, we show that how differential privacy [12–14] of a mechanism is degraded when the randomness used by the mechanism comes from not an ideal distribution $\mathcal{Q}$ but a real-world distribution $\mathcal{R}$, using the Rényi divergence of order ∞. It is typical that non-uniform distributions that are uncommon in the constructions of cryptographic primitives (e.g. the Laplace distribution, the matrix Bingham distribution [7]), are used in the literature of differential privacy. Thus, although simple, we believe that this result is useful. For the details, see Sect. 5.2.
- Finally, motivated by the difficulty of sampling randomness from non-uniform distributions in computer implementations in practice, and in the light of the usefulness and versatility of the Rényi divergence in cryptography, in Sect. 6, we show two methods for approximate sampling from an arbitrary distribution $\mathcal{Q}$ by using a uniformly chosen random string via the inversion sampling (a.k.a. inverse transform sampling), with the guarantee that the Rényi divergence of the distribution of our sampling method (which we denote by $\mathcal{R}$) from the target ideal distribution $\mathcal{Q}$, is upperbounded. We show two results: one for the Rényi divergence of order 2 and the other for the Rényi divergence of order ∞.

We remark that previously, Yao and Li [24] showed some generalization of Dodis and Yu's lemmas [11] using *Rényi entropy* (which incorporates min-entropy and collision-entropy as special cases), and corresponding techniques for evaluating security of unpredictability and square-friendly indistinguishability applications, in a similar way we do in this paper. Interestingly, [24] uses the Hölder inequality as a main tool, which we also use for showing one of our technical lemmas in Sect. 3. Like [11], however, the results of [24] are only applicable to the case in which the ideal distribution is the uniform distribution (and the real-world distribution has some high Rényi entropy), and our results in this paper are more general than their main theorems [24, Theorems 3.2 and 3.3] in the sense that the latter can be derived from ours. On the other hand, Yao and Li also studied the application of their results to a setting where the real-world distribution only has some high *computational* version of Rényi entropy, which is a setting we do not explore in this work. It would be interesting to investigate whether results with computational variants of Rényi divergence analogous to [24] can be established.

1.3   Paper Organization

The rest of the paper is organized as follows. In Sect. 2, we review basic notation and the definitions used in the paper. In Sect. 3, we show two general lemmas that are used throughout the subsequent sections. In Sect. 4, we show two general techniques for evaluating the security of cryptographic primitives, one for unpredictability applications and the other for "square-friendly" indistinguishability applications. In Sect. 5, we show two applications of the results from the previous sections, one for an improved reduction for a class of distinguishing problems called distinguishing problems with public samplability, and the other for differential privacy. In Sect. 6, we propose two inversion sampling methods for arbitrary discrete distributions, with some guaranteed upperbounds on the Rényi divergence.

2   Preliminaries

In this section, we review the basic notation and the definitions for the Rényi divergence and entropy, and some useful lemmas.

2.1   Basic Notation

$\mathbb{N}$, $\mathbb{Z}_{\geq 0}$, $\mathbb{R}$, and $\mathbb{R}_{\geq 0}$ denote the set of all natural numbers, all non-negative integers, all real numbers, and all non-negative real numbers, respectively. For $n \in \mathbb{N}$, we define $[n] := \{1, \ldots, n\}$. If S is a finite set, then "$|S|$" denotes its size, and "$x \leftarrow_R S$" denotes that x is chosen uniformly at random from S. If $\mathcal{X}$ is a distribution (over some set), then "$x \leftarrow_R \mathcal{X}$" denotes that x is chosen according to the distribution $\mathcal{X}$, and "$[\mathcal{X}]$" denotes the support of $\mathcal{X}$, i.e. $[\mathcal{X}] := \{x \mid \Pr[\mathcal{X} = x] > 0\}$. In this paper, we only treat discrete distributions.

   If A is a probabilistic algorithm, then "A(x)" denotes the distribution of A's output when it takes x as input and uses an internal randomness chosen according to some prescribed distribution, and if we need to specify a particular randomness r used by A, we denote it by "A$(x; r)$" (in which case the computation of A is deterministic that takes x and r as input).

2.2   Hölder Inequality

Here, we recall the Hölder inequality.

Lemma 1 (Hölder Inequality). *Let $n \in \mathbb{N}$, and let $(a_1, \ldots, a_n)$ and $(b_1, \ldots, b_n)$ be sequences of real numbers. Let $\alpha, \beta \in (1, \infty)$ be real numbers such that $\frac{1}{\alpha} + \frac{1}{\beta} = 1$. Then, it holds that*

$$\sum_{i \in [n]} |a_i \cdot b_i| \leq \left(\sum_{i \in [n]} |a_i|^\alpha \right)^{\frac{1}{\alpha}} \cdot \left(\sum_{i \in [n]} |b_i|^\beta \right)^{\frac{1}{\beta}}.$$

Note that the case of $\alpha = \beta = 2$ implies the Cauchy-Schwarz inequality.

2.3   Rényi Divergence

Here, we recall the definition of Rényi divergence in the form typically used in cryptography.[1]

Definition 1. *Let $\mathcal{Q}$ and $\mathcal{R}$ be distributions such that $[\mathcal{R}] \subseteq [\mathcal{Q}]$, and let $\alpha > 1$ be a real number. The* Rényi divergence of order α *(or α-Rényi divergence, for short) of the distribution $\mathcal{R}$ from the distribution $\mathcal{Q}$, denoted by $\mathrm{RD}_\alpha(\mathcal{R}\|\mathcal{Q})$, is defined by*

$$\mathrm{RD}_\alpha(\mathcal{R}\|\mathcal{Q}) := \left(\sum_{z \in [\mathcal{Q}]} \frac{\Pr[\mathcal{R} = z]^\alpha}{\Pr[\mathcal{Q} = z]^{\alpha-1}} \right)^{\frac{1}{\alpha-1}},$$

and the ∞-Rényi divergence of $\mathcal{R}$ from $\mathcal{Q}$ is given by

$$\mathrm{RD}_\infty(\mathcal{R}\|\mathcal{Q}) := \max_{z \in [\mathcal{Q}]} \frac{\Pr[\mathcal{R} = z]}{\Pr[\mathcal{Q} = z]}.$$

It is known that the Rényi divergence is non-decreasing in its order, and not less than 1 when $\alpha > 1$ (see [23]). Thus, for any distributions $\mathcal{Q}$ and $\mathcal{R}$ and $1 < \alpha < \alpha'$, we have $1 \leq \mathrm{RD}_\alpha(\mathcal{R}\|\mathcal{Q}) \leq \mathrm{RD}_{\alpha'}(\mathcal{R}\|\mathcal{Q})$.

It is also known that the Rényi divergence enjoys several (multiplicative) analogues of the properties satisfied by the statistical distance (see [3, Lemma 2.9]). Here, we recall the so-called probability preservation property of the Rényi divergence.

Lemma 2 (Probability Preservation). *Let $\mathcal{Q}$ and $\mathcal{R}$ be distributions over the same set X such that $[\mathcal{R}] \subseteq [\mathcal{Q}] \subseteq X$. Then, for all $E \subseteq X$ and $\alpha \in (1, \infty)$, it holds that*

$$\Pr[\mathcal{R} \in E] \leq \min\left\{ \left(\mathrm{RD}_\alpha(\mathcal{R}\|\mathcal{Q}) \cdot \Pr[\mathcal{Q} \in E] \right)^{\frac{\alpha-1}{\alpha}}, \ \mathrm{RD}_\infty(\mathcal{R}\|\mathcal{Q}) \cdot \Pr[\mathcal{Q} \in E] \right\}.$$

---

[1] In a non-cryptographic context, it is typical to define the α-Rényi divergence as the logarithm of the quantity RD_α defined here [23].

2.4 Entropy

Here, we recall the definitions of entropy.

Definition 2. *Let $\mathcal{X}$ (resp. $\mathcal{Y}$) be a distribution defined over a set X (resp. Y).*

- *The* min-entropy *of $\mathcal{X}$, denoted by $\mathbf{H}_\infty(\mathcal{X})$, is defined by*

$$\mathbf{H}_\infty(\mathcal{X}) := -\log_2\left(\max_{x \in X} \Pr[\mathcal{X} = x]\right).$$

- *The* average collision-entropy *of $\mathcal{X}$ given $\mathcal{Y}$, denoted by $\mathbf{H}_2(\mathcal{X}|\mathcal{Y})$, is defined by*

$$\mathbf{H}_2(\mathcal{X}|\mathcal{Y}) := -\log_2\left(\mathop{\mathbf{E}}_{y \leftarrow_{\mathbb{R}} \mathcal{Y}}\left[\sum_{x \in X} \Pr[\mathcal{X} = x | \mathcal{Y} = y]^2\right]\right).$$

3 General Lemmas for Switching Distributions

In this section, we show two lemmas that are used as the main tools for showing our results in the subsequent sections. Our lemmas are generalizations of the lemmas shown by Dodis and Yu [11]. Thus, for reference we first recall their lemmas in Sect. 3.1. We then show our lemmas in Sect. 3.2.

3.1 Lemmas by Dodis and Yu

Dodis and Yu [11] showed the following lemmas. Actually, they only state the lemmas for functions taking bitstrings as input, but the lemmas straightforwardly generalize for functions with any domain. Thus, we state such versions.

Lemma 3 (Lemma 1 in [11]). *Let X be a finite set, $\mathcal{R}$ be a distribution over X, and $\mathcal{U}$ be the uniform distribution over X. Then, for any (deterministic) non-negative function $f : X \to \mathbb{R}_{\geq 0}$, we have*

$$\mathbf{E}[f(\mathcal{R})] \leq |X| \cdot 2^{-\mathbf{H}_\infty(\mathcal{R})} \cdot \mathbf{E}[f(\mathcal{U})].$$

Lemma 4 (Adapted from Lemmas 5 and 7 in [11][2]). *Let X and Y be finite sets, and $(\mathcal{R}, \mathcal{S})$ be a joint distribution over $X \times Y$. Let $\mathcal{U}$ be the uniform distribution over X. Then, for any (deterministic) real-valued function $f : X \times Y \to \mathbb{R}$, we have*

$$\left|\mathbf{E}[f(\mathcal{R}, \mathcal{S})]\right| \leq \sqrt{|X| \cdot 2^{-\mathbf{H}_2(\mathcal{R}|\mathcal{S})} \cdot \mathbf{E}[f(\mathcal{U}, \mathcal{S})^2]} \qquad and$$

$$\left|\mathbf{E}[f(\mathcal{R}, \mathcal{S})] - \mathbf{E}[f(\mathcal{U}, \mathcal{S})]\right| \leq \sqrt{(|X| \cdot 2^{-\mathbf{H}_2(\mathcal{R}|\mathcal{S})} - 1) \cdot \mathbf{E}[f(\mathcal{U}, \mathcal{S})^2]}.$$

---

[2] Lemma 7 in [11] is attributed to Barak et al. [4].

3.2   Our Lemmas

Our first lemma is as follows.

Lemma 5. *Let $\mathcal{Q}$ and $\mathcal{R}$ be distributions over the same set X such that $[\mathcal{R}] \subseteq [\mathcal{Q}] \subseteq X$. Then, for any (deterministic) real-valued function $f : X \to \mathbb{R}$ and any $\alpha \in (1, \infty)$, we have*

$$\left| \mathbf{E}[f(\mathcal{R})] \right| \leq \min \left\{ \left(\mathrm{RD}_\alpha(\mathcal{R} \| \mathcal{Q}) \cdot \mathbf{E}\left[|f(\mathcal{Q})|^{\frac{\alpha}{\alpha-1}} \right] \right)^{\frac{\alpha-1}{\alpha}}, \ \mathrm{RD}_\infty(\mathcal{R} \| \mathcal{Q}) \cdot \mathbf{E}\left[|f(\mathcal{Q})| \right] \right\}. \tag{1}$$

Relation to Dodis and Yu's Lemma. Before providing the proof, let us remark that the above lemma is a generalization of Lemma 3 and the first inequality in Lemma 4. To see this, note that for any distribution $\mathcal{R}$ over some set X and the uniform distribution $\mathcal{U}$ over X, we have $\mathrm{RD}_\infty(\mathcal{R} \| \mathcal{U}) = \max_{x \in X} \frac{\Pr[\mathcal{R}=x]}{\Pr[\mathcal{U}=x]} = |X| \cdot 2^{-\mathbf{H}_\infty(\mathcal{R})}$, and thus Lemma 3 can be obtained by setting $\mathcal{Q} = \mathcal{U}$ in our lemma for non-negative functions. Also, let $\mathcal{S}$ be an arbitrary distribution over some set Y that forms a joint distribution $(\mathcal{R}, \mathcal{S})$ over $X \times Y$. Then, we have

$$
\begin{aligned}
\mathrm{RD}_2\big((\mathcal{R}, \mathcal{S}) \| (\mathcal{U}, \mathcal{S})\big) &= \sum_{(x,y) \in X \times Y} \frac{\Pr[\mathcal{R}=x \wedge \mathcal{S}=y]^2}{\Pr[\mathcal{U}=x \wedge \mathcal{S}=y]} \\
&= \sum_{(x,y) \in X \times Y} \frac{(\Pr[\mathcal{R}=x|\mathcal{S}=y] \cdot \Pr[\mathcal{S}=y])^2}{\frac{1}{|X|} \cdot \Pr[\mathcal{S}=y]} \\
&= |X| \cdot \sum_{y \in Y} \Pr[\mathcal{S}=y] \cdot \left(\sum_{x \in X} \Pr[\mathcal{R}=x|\mathcal{S}=y]^2 \right) \\
&= |X| \cdot 2^{-\mathbf{H}_2(\mathcal{R}|\mathcal{S})},
\end{aligned}
$$

and thus, the first inequality in Lemma 4 can be obtained by setting $\mathcal{R}$ in our lemma to be $(\mathcal{R}, \mathcal{S})$ explained here, setting $\mathcal{Q} = (\mathcal{U}, \mathcal{S})$, and then invoking our lemma for general real-valued functions and $\alpha = 2$.

Proof of Lemma 5. For each $z \in [\mathcal{Q}]$, let $r_z := \Pr[\mathcal{R} = z]$ and $q_z := \Pr[\mathcal{Q} = z]$. The bound regarding the ∞-Rényi divergence can be shown as follows:

$$\left| \mathbf{E}[f(\mathcal{R})] \right| \leq \sum_{z \in [\mathcal{Q}]} r_z \cdot |f(z)| \overset{(*)}{\leq} \sum_{z \in [\mathcal{Q}]} \mathrm{RD}_\infty(\mathcal{R} \| \mathcal{Q}) \cdot q_z \cdot |f(z)|$$

$$= \mathrm{RD}_\infty(\mathcal{R} \| \mathcal{Q}) \cdot \mathbf{E}\left[|f(\mathcal{Q})| \right],$$

where the inequality (*) uses the probability preservation property (Lemma 2), which implies $r_z \leq \mathrm{RD}_\infty(\mathcal{R} \| \mathcal{Q}) \cdot q_z$.

The bound for a general $\alpha \in (1, \infty)$ does not simply follow from the probability preservation property, but can be shown using the Hölder inequality (Lemma 1). Specifically, we have

$$\left| \mathbf{E}[f(\mathcal{R})] \right| \leq \sum_{z \in [\mathcal{Q}]} \left(r_z \cdot q_z^{-\frac{\alpha-1}{\alpha}} \right) \cdot q_z^{\frac{\alpha-1}{\alpha}} \cdot |f(z)|$$

$$\overset{(*)}{\leq} \left(\sum_{z \in [\mathcal{Q}]} \left(r_z \cdot q_z^{-\frac{\alpha-1}{\alpha}} \right)^\alpha \right)^{\frac{1}{\alpha}} \cdot \left(\sum_{z \in [\mathcal{Q}]} \left(q_z^{\frac{\alpha-1}{\alpha}} \cdot |f(z)| \right)^{\frac{\alpha}{\alpha-1}} \right)^{\frac{\alpha-1}{\alpha}}$$

$$= \left(\sum_{z \in [\mathcal{Q}]} r_z^\alpha \cdot q_z^{-(\alpha-1)} \right)^{\frac{1}{\alpha}} \cdot \left(\sum_{z \in [\mathcal{Q}]} q_z \cdot |f(z)|^{\frac{\alpha}{\alpha-1}} \right)^{\frac{\alpha-1}{\alpha}}$$

$$= \left(\mathrm{RD}_\alpha(\mathcal{R}\|\mathcal{Q})^{\alpha-1} \right)^{\frac{1}{\alpha}} \cdot \left(\mathbf{E}\left[|f(\mathcal{Q})|^{\frac{\alpha}{\alpha-1}} \right] \right)^{\frac{\alpha-1}{\alpha}},$$

where the inequality (*) is due to the Hölder inequality. Note that the rightmost is equivalent to the first bound in Eq. (1). □ **(Lemma 5)**

Note that if the range of a function f is $[0,1]$, then $f(z)^a \leq f(z)$ holds for every $a \geq 1$, and thus the inequalities in Lemma 5 can be slightly simplified. For our purpose, it is useful to formally state it as a corollary, which can be seen as a generalization of the probability preservation property (Lemma 2).

Corollary 1 (Special Case of Lemma 5**).** *Let $\mathcal{Q}$ and $\mathcal{R}$ be the same as in Lemma 5. Then, for any (deterministic) function $f : X \to [0,1]$ and any $\alpha \in (1,\infty)$, we have*

$$\mathbf{E}[f(\mathcal{R})] \leq \min\left\{ \left(\mathrm{RD}_\alpha(\mathcal{R}\|\mathcal{Q}) \cdot \mathbf{E}[f(\mathcal{Q})] \right)^{\frac{\alpha-1}{\alpha}}, \ \mathrm{RD}_\infty(\mathcal{R}\|\mathcal{Q}) \cdot \mathbf{E}[f(\mathcal{Q})] \right\}.$$

Our second lemma is as follows. Similarly to our first lemma, the lemma here is a generalization of the second inequality in Lemma 4.

Lemma 6. *Let $\mathcal{Q}$ and $\mathcal{R}$ be distributions over the same set X such that $[\mathcal{R}] \subseteq [\mathcal{Q}] \subseteq X$. Then, for any (deterministic) real-valued function $f : X \to \mathbb{R}$, we have*

$$\left| \mathbf{E}[f(\mathcal{R})] - \mathbf{E}[f(\mathcal{Q})] \right| \leq \sqrt{(\mathrm{RD}_2(\mathcal{R}\|\mathcal{Q}) - 1) \cdot \mathbf{E}[f(\mathcal{Q})^2]}. \tag{2}$$

Proof of Lemma 6. Let $c \in \mathbb{R}_{\geq 0}$. Using the same notation as in the proof of Lemma 5, we have

$$\left| \mathbf{E}[f(\mathcal{R})] - c \cdot \mathbf{E}[f(\mathcal{Q})] \right| = \left| \sum_{z \in [\mathcal{Q}]} \left(\frac{r_z}{\sqrt{q_z}} - c \cdot \sqrt{q_z} \right) \cdot \sqrt{q_z} \cdot f(z) \right|$$

$$\leq \sqrt{\sum_{z \in [\mathcal{Q}]} \left(\frac{r_z}{\sqrt{q_z}} - c \cdot \sqrt{q_z} \right)^2} \cdot \sqrt{\sum_{z \in [\mathcal{Q}]} q_z \cdot f(z)^2}$$

$$= \sqrt{\sum_{z \in [\mathcal{Q}]} \frac{r_z^2}{q_z} - 2c \cdot \sum_{z \in [\mathcal{Q}]} r_z + c^2 \cdot \sum_{z \in [\mathcal{Q}]} q_z} \cdot \sqrt{\mathbf{E}[f(\mathcal{Q})^2]}$$

$$= \sqrt{(\mathrm{RD}_2(\mathcal{R}\|\mathcal{Q}) - 2c + c^2) \cdot \mathbf{E}[f(\mathcal{Q})^2]},$$

where the inequality is due to the Cauchy-Schwarz inequality (Lemma 1 with $\alpha = \beta = 2$), and the last equality uses $\sum_{z \in [\mathcal{Q}]} r_z = \sum_{z \in [\mathcal{Q}]} q_z = 1$. Then, Eq. (2) is obtained by taking $c = 1$.[3]   □ (**Lemma 6**)

4 General Security Evaluation Techniques via Rényi Divergence

In this section, we show general techniques for evaluating security in case the distribution of a parameter (e.g. a secret key, randomness etc.) in a security game is switched from an "ideal" distribution $\mathcal{Q}$ to an arbitrary "real-world" distribution $\mathcal{R}$, using the Rényi divergence.

Specifically, in Sect. 4.1, we first recall the definition of an abstract security game in the style of [11] that abstractly captures most security games used in cryptography, in particular unpredictability applications and indistinguishability applications. There, we also recall the notion of "square-security" [4,11]. It plays an important role when showing results for "square-friendly" applications, which is a class of applications including all unpredictability applications and many indistinguishability applications.

Then, in Sects. 4.2 and 4.3, we show general results on how the security of applications in the "ideal" model in which a parameter is drawn from an ideal distribution $\mathcal{Q}$, is "degraded" in the "real-world" model in which a parameter is drawn from an arbitrary distribution $\mathcal{R}$. Our result for unpredictability applications is given in Sect. 4.2, and our result for square-friendly indistinguishability applications is given in Sect. 4.3.

4.1 Definitions

Abstract Security Game. We define a general type of cryptographic applications in the same manner as [11]. The security of a cryptographic application Π is defined via an interactive *security game* between a probabilistic adversary A and a probabilistic challenger $C(r)$, where C is fixed by the definition of Π, and $r \in X$ is a "parameter"[4] in the security game that is drawn from some distribution, which we wish to switch to another distribution using the Rényi divergence. The game can have an arbitrary structure, and after the interaction with the adversary A, the challenger $C(r)$ outputs a bit. If $C(r)$ outputs 1 (resp. 0), A is said to win (resp. lose) the game. As usual, we consider two types of cryptographic applications: *unpredictability* applications and *indistinguishability* applications. The former type captures applications in which it is hard for an adversary to compute some value (e.g. a preimage of a one-way function, forging a signature on a fresh message), and the latter type captures applications in which

---

[3] We can also obtain the proof of the case $\alpha = 2$ of our first lemma by setting $c = 0$ in this proof. Setting other values for c does not seem to give us any merit.

[4] In [11], r was called a "secret key". Since r can be any value sampled in the security game, we call it just a "parameter".

it is hard for an adversary to guess the challenge bit chosen by the challenger (e.g. security of a pseudorandom function, IND-CPA security of an encryption scheme).

Given a particular parameter $r \in X$, let $\mathtt{Win_A}(r)$ be the probability that A wins in the security game played with the challenger $C(r)$, where the probability is over the choice of the randomness consumed by A and $C(r)$. Then, we define the *advantage* $\mathtt{Adv_A}(r)$ *of* A *on* r (against particular C fixed by an application Π) as follows:

$$\mathtt{Adv_A}(r) := \begin{cases} \mathtt{Win_A}(r) & \text{(for unpredictability applications)} \\ 2 \cdot \mathtt{Win_A}(r) - 1 & \text{(for indistinguishability applications)} \end{cases}.$$

The actual advantage of an adversary in a security game is defined by taking (the absolute value of) the expectation over the choice of the parameter r in the game. In this paper, as in [11], we will treat ordinary security and "square-security", the latter of which takes the expectation of the squared value of the advantage and plays an important role for the results on indistinguishability applications that are "square-friendly". The (square-)security of Π in case the parameter r is chosen according to a distribution $\mathcal{X}$, is called (square-)security in the $\mathcal{X}$-model.

Definition 3 (Security and Square-Security (Adapted from [11])). *Let $\mathcal{X}$ be a distribution over the parameter space X. We say that an application Π is*

- *(T, ϵ)-secure in the $\mathcal{X}$-model, if for all adversaries A with resource[5] T, it holds that $|\mathbf{E}[\mathtt{Adv_A}(\mathcal{X})]| \le \epsilon$.*
  $|\mathbf{E}[\mathtt{Adv_A}(\mathcal{X})]|$ is called the advantage of A in the $\mathcal{X}$-model.
- *(T, σ)-square-secure in the $\mathcal{X}$-model, if for all adversaries A with resource T, it holds that $\mathbf{E}[\mathtt{Adv_A}(\mathcal{X})^2] \le \sigma$.*
  $\mathbf{E}[\mathtt{Adv_A}(\mathcal{X})^2]$ is called the square-advantage of A in the $\mathcal{X}$-model.

4.2 General Result for Unpredictability Applications

Our result for unpredictability applications is stated as follows.

Theorem 1. *Let Π be an unpredictability application. Let $\mathcal{Q}$ and $\mathcal{R}$ be distributions over the parameter space X satisfying $[\mathcal{R}] \subseteq [\mathcal{Q}] \subseteq X$. Then, for any adversary A against the security of Π, it holds that[6]*

$$\mathbf{E}[\mathtt{Adv_A}(\mathcal{R})] \le F_{\mathcal{Q} \to \mathcal{R}}\Big(\mathbf{E}[\mathtt{Adv_A}(\mathcal{Q})]\Big),$$

---

[5] Resource of an adversary abstractly models all of an adversary's efficiency measures, e.g. the running time, the circuit size, the number of oracle queries, etc.

[6] Note that for unpredictability applications, the absolute value of an adversary A's advantage can be removed.

where the function $F_{\mathcal{Q} \to \mathcal{R}}(\cdot)$ is defined by

$$F_{\mathcal{Q} \to \mathcal{R}}(\epsilon) := \min \left\{ \begin{array}{c} \min_{\alpha \in (1,\infty)} \left(\mathrm{RD}_\alpha(\mathcal{R} \| \mathcal{Q}) \cdot \epsilon \right)^{\frac{\alpha-1}{\alpha}}, \\ \mathrm{RD}_\infty(\mathcal{R} \| \mathcal{Q}) \cdot \epsilon, \\ \epsilon + \sqrt{(\mathrm{RD}_2(\mathcal{R} \| \mathcal{Q}) - 1) \cdot \epsilon} \end{array} \right\}.$$

In particular, if Π is (T, ϵ)-secure in the $\mathcal{Q}$-model, then Π is also $(T, F_{\mathcal{Q} \to \mathcal{R}}(\epsilon))$-secure in the $\mathcal{R}$-model.

This theorem shows how the security of an unpredictability application under a real-world distribution $\mathcal{R}$ is guaranteed in terms of its security under an ideal distribution $\mathcal{Q}$, via the Rényi divergence. In particular, this theorem gives us an implication to the standard asymptotic-style security: If an unpredictability application is secure in the $\mathcal{Q}$-model in the asymptotic sense (i.e. any efficient adversary's advantage in the $\mathcal{Q}$-model is bounded by a negligible function of a security parameter), it remains secure in the $\mathcal{R}$-model as long as the Rényi divergence of some order $\alpha \in (1, \infty]$ is bounded by a polynomial of the security parameter.

Proof of Theorem 1. Let A be any adversary against the security of Π. Since Π is an unpredictability application, the range of $\mathsf{Adv}_{\mathsf{A}}(\cdot)$ is $[0,1]$. Thus, A's advantage in the $\mathcal{R}$-model (resp. $\mathcal{Q}$-model) is $\mathbf{E}[\mathsf{Adv}_{\mathsf{A}}(\mathcal{R})]$ (resp. $\mathbf{E}[\mathsf{Adv}_{\mathsf{A}}(\mathcal{Q})]$). Then, $\mathbf{E}[\mathsf{Adv}_{\mathsf{A}}(\mathcal{R})] \leq \min_{\alpha \in (1,\infty)}(\mathrm{RD}_\alpha(\mathcal{R} \| \mathcal{Q}) \cdot \mathbf{E}[\mathsf{Adv}_{\mathsf{A}}(\mathcal{Q})])^{\frac{\alpha-1}{\alpha}}$ and $\mathbf{E}[\mathsf{Adv}_{\mathsf{A}}(\mathcal{R})] \leq \mathrm{RD}_\infty(\mathcal{R} \| \mathcal{Q}) \cdot \mathbf{E}[\mathsf{Adv}_{\mathsf{A}}(\mathcal{Q})]$, are obtained by applying Corollary 1 to the advantage function $\mathsf{Adv}_{\mathsf{A}}(\cdot)$.

To complete the proof, it remains to show $\mathbf{E}[\mathsf{Adv}_{\mathsf{A}}(\mathcal{R})] \leq \mathbf{E}[\mathsf{Adv}_{\mathsf{A}}(\mathcal{Q})] + \sqrt{(\mathrm{RD}_2(\mathcal{R} \| \mathcal{Q}) - 1) \cdot \mathbf{E}[\mathsf{Adv}_{\mathsf{A}}(\mathcal{Q})]}$. By the triangle inequality, we have

$$\mathbf{E}[\mathsf{Adv}_{\mathsf{A}}(\mathcal{R})] \leq \mathbf{E}[\mathsf{Adv}_{\mathsf{A}}(\mathcal{Q})] + \left| \mathbf{E}[\mathsf{Adv}_{\mathsf{A}}(\mathcal{R})] - \mathbf{E}[\mathsf{Adv}_{\mathsf{A}}(\mathcal{Q})] \right|.$$

Regarding the second term in the right hand side, due to Lemma 6, we have

$$\left| \mathbf{E}[\mathsf{Adv}_{\mathsf{A}}(\mathcal{R})] - \mathbf{E}[\mathsf{Adv}_{\mathsf{A}}(\mathcal{Q})] \right| \leq \sqrt{(\mathrm{RD}_2(\mathcal{R} \| \mathcal{Q}) - 1) \cdot \mathbf{E}[\mathsf{Adv}_{\mathsf{A}}(\mathcal{Q})^2]}$$

$$\leq \sqrt{(\mathrm{RD}_2(\mathcal{R} \| \mathcal{Q}) - 1) \cdot \mathbf{E}[\mathsf{Adv}_{\mathsf{A}}(\mathcal{Q})]},$$

where we use $\mathsf{Adv}_{\mathsf{A}}(\cdot)^2 \leq \mathsf{Adv}_{\mathsf{A}}(\cdot)$, which is in turn because its range is $[0,1]$. Combining the two inequalities yields the desired inequality. $\square$ **(Theorem 1)**

4.3 General Result for Square-Friendly Indistinguishability Applications

Here, we show our general result for "square-friendly" indistinguishability applications, which is done via the notion of square-security.

We first show how the security of any application (including both unpredictability and indistinguishability applications) under a real-world distribution $\mathcal{R}$ is guaranteed from its square-security (and ordinary security) under an ideal distribution $\mathcal{Q}$, via the 2-Rényi divergence $\mathrm{RD}_2(\mathcal{R} \| \mathcal{Q})$.

Lemma 7. *Let Π be an (unpredictability/indistinguishability) application. Let $\mathcal{Q}$ and $\mathcal{R}$ be distributions over the parameter space X satisfying $[\mathcal{R}] \subseteq [\mathcal{Q}] \subseteq X$. Then, for any adversary A against the security of Π, it holds that*

$$\left| \mathbf{E}[\mathsf{Adv}_\mathsf{A}(\mathcal{R})] \right| \leq G_{\mathcal{Q} \to \mathcal{R}}\left(\left| \mathbf{E}[\mathsf{Adv}_\mathsf{A}(\mathcal{Q})] \right|, \; \mathbf{E}[\mathsf{Adv}_\mathsf{A}(\mathcal{Q})^2] \right),$$

where the function $G_{\mathcal{Q} \to \mathcal{R}}(\cdot, \cdot)$ is defined by

$$G_{\mathcal{Q} \to \mathcal{R}}(\epsilon, \sigma) := \min\left\{ \sqrt{\mathrm{RD}_2(\mathcal{R}\|\mathcal{Q}) \cdot \sigma}, \; \epsilon + \sqrt{(\mathrm{RD}_2(\mathcal{R}\|\mathcal{Q}) - 1) \cdot \sigma} \right\}. \quad (3)$$

In particular, if Π is (simultaneously) (T, ϵ)-secure and (T, σ)-square-secure in the $\mathcal{Q}$-model, then Π is also $(T, G_{\mathcal{Q} \to \mathcal{R}}(\epsilon, \sigma))$-secure in the $\mathcal{R}$-model.[7]

Proof of Lemma 7. Let A be any adversary against the security of Π. Then, applying the first bound in Eq. (1) in Lemma 5 with $\alpha = 2$ to the advantage function $\mathsf{Adv}_\mathsf{A}(\cdot)$, we immediately obtain $|\mathbf{E}[\mathsf{Adv}_\mathsf{A}(\mathcal{R})]| \leq \sqrt{\mathrm{RD}_2(\mathcal{R}\|\mathcal{Q}) \cdot \mathbf{E}[\mathsf{Adv}_\mathsf{A}(\mathcal{Q})^2]}$.

To complete the proof, it remains to show $|\mathbf{E}[\mathsf{Adv}_\mathsf{A}(\mathcal{R})]| \leq |\mathbf{E}[\mathsf{Adv}_\mathsf{A}(\mathcal{Q})]| + \sqrt{(\mathrm{RD}_2(\mathcal{R}\|\mathcal{Q}) - 1) \cdot \mathbf{E}[\mathsf{Adv}_\mathsf{A}(\mathcal{Q})^2]}$. By the triangle inequality, we have

$$\left| \mathbf{E}[\mathsf{Adv}_\mathsf{A}(\mathcal{R})] \right| \leq \left| \mathbf{E}[\mathsf{Adv}_\mathsf{A}(\mathcal{Q})] \right| + \left| \mathbf{E}[\mathsf{Adv}_\mathsf{A}(\mathcal{R})] - \mathbf{E}[\mathsf{Adv}_\mathsf{A}(\mathcal{Q})] \right|.$$

Regarding the second term in the right hand side, due to Lemma 6, we have

$$\left| \mathbf{E}[\mathsf{Adv}_\mathsf{A}(\mathcal{R})] - \mathbf{E}[\mathsf{Adv}_\mathsf{A}(\mathcal{Q})] \right| \leq \sqrt{(\mathrm{RD}_2(\mathcal{R}\|\mathcal{Q}) - 1) \cdot \mathbf{E}[\mathsf{Adv}_\mathsf{A}(\mathcal{Q})^2]}.$$

Combining the two inequalities yields the desired inequality. $\square$ **(Lemma 7)**

Next, we would like to establish the implication of the security of an indistinguishability application to its square-security, but unfortunately it is known that for some indistinguishability applications, their square-security is not necessarily implied by the ordinary security. Fortunately, however, the works of Barak et al. [4] and Dodis and Yu [11] showed that for some indistinguishability applications in which the so-called "double-run trick" is applicable, ordinary (non-square) security *does* imply its corresponding square-security. Dodis and Yu formalized a sufficient condition for such indistinguishability applications as what they call *simulatability*. It is this property that makes indistinguishability applications square-friendly. We recall the definition here.

Definition 4 (Simulatability [11]). *Consider an indistinguishability application Π in the security game of which possibly there is a "failure predicate"*[8] *F*

---

[7] Note that the first bound does not involve the (non-square) advantage $|\mathbf{E}[\mathsf{Adv}_\mathsf{A}(\mathcal{Q})]|$, and hence is true regardless of the (non-square) security of Π in the $\mathcal{Q}$-model.

[8] A failure predicate models the restrictions in a security game that typically prevent an adversary from winning the game trivially, e.g., submitting the challenge ciphertext as a decryption query in the IND-CCA security game of an encryption scheme.

(that is efficiently checkable by both an adversary A *and the challenger* C(r)*)* *such that* C(r) *regards* A *as winning the game if* A *succeeds in guessing the challenge bit* and *does not violate* F, *while if* A *violates* F, *the challenger flips a random coin on behalf of* A *and uses it to decide if* A *wins the game or not*[9]. *We say that* Π *is* (T', T, γ)-*simulatable, if for any parameter r and any adversary* A *whose resource is* T *and that never violates the failure predicate* F, *there exists an adversary* B *(against the security of* Π*) with resource* T' *(for some* T' ≥ T*) such that:*

1. *The execution between* B *and "real"* C(r) *defines two independent executions between a copy* A_i *of* A *and a "simulated" challenger* $C_i(r)$, *for* $i = 1, 2$. *In particular, except reusing the same r,* A_1, $C_1(r)$, A_2, *and* $C_2(r)$ *use fresh and independent randomness, including independent challenge bits* b_1 *and* b_2.
2. *The challenge bit b used by the "real"* C(r) *is equal to the challenge bit* b_2 *used by the "simulated"* C_2.
3. *Before making its guess b' of the challenge bit b,* B *learns the values* b_1, b'_1, *and* b'_2, *where each* b'_i *denotes* A_i*'s guess for* b_i.
4. *The probability of* B *violating the failure predicate* F *is at most* γ.

Though it might look somewhat complicated, as noted in [11], simulatability is satisfied by many natural indistinguishability applications, such as IND-CPA and IND-CCA security of encryption schemes, (weak) pseudorandom functions. Looking ahead, in Sect. 5.1, we will see another example of indistinguishability applications with simulatability, which is called "distinguishing problems with public samplability" formalized by Bai et al. [3].

We now show that for indistinguishability applications that satisfy simulatability as defined above, their square-security is indeed implied by the ordinary security. This is a generalized version of [11, Lemma 4].

Lemma 8. *Let* $\mathcal{X}$ *be a distribution over the parameter space X. If an indistinguishability application* Π *is* (T', T, γ)-*simulatable (with* T' ≥ T*), then for any adversary* A *with resource* T *against the security of* Π, *there exists another adversary* B *with resource* T' *against the security of* Π, *such that*

$$\mathbf{E}[\mathsf{Adv}_\mathsf{A}(\mathcal{X})^2] \leq \left| \mathbf{E}[\mathsf{Adv}_\mathsf{B}(\mathcal{X})] \right| + \gamma.$$

In particular, if Π *is* (T', ε)-*secure in the* $\mathcal{X}$-*model and* (T', T, γ)-*simulatable, then* Π *is also* (T, ε + γ)-*square-secure in the* $\mathcal{X}$-*model.*

Proof of Lemma 8. This theorem can be shown via the "double-run trick" [4,11]. Let Π be an indistinguishability application that is (T, T', γ)-simulatable. Let A be any adversary with resource T against the security of Π, and let B be

---

[9] This is to offset an adversary's advantage in case it violates the failure predicate F. How an adversary's advantage is affected in case it violates the failure predicate F is not explicit in the definition of [11], and thus we adopt (seemingly) the most natural choice which is also convenient for our purpose.

the adversary (corresponding to A and the challenger $C(r)$, where r is chosen according to $\mathcal{X}$) with resource T' against the security of Π, which is guaranteed to exist by the (T', T, γ)-simulatability of Π. We augment B as an adversary against the security of Π so that when B successfully finishes the two executions of A (without violating the failure predicate), if $b'_1 = b_1$ then B sets $b' := b'_2$, otherwise sets $b' := 1 - b'_2$, and outputs b' as its guess for the challenge bit, which we denote by b_2. Let F be the event that B violates the failure predicate. Then, due to the (T', T, γ)-simulatability, both of B's simulations of the challenger $C(r)$ for A are perfect as long as F does not happen, and whether F happens is independent of the choice of r and whether $b'_1 = b_1$ or $b'_2 = b_2$ occurs. Hence, B's advantage on a fixed parameter r can be calculated as follows:

$$\mathsf{Adv_B}(r) = 2 \cdot \mathsf{Win_B}(r) - 1 = 2 \cdot \Pr[b' = b_2] - 1$$

$$= 2 \cdot \left(\Pr[b'_1 = b_1 \wedge b'_2 = b_2 \wedge \overline{\mathsf{F}}] + \Pr[b'_1 \neq b_1 \wedge b'_2 \neq b_2 \wedge \overline{\mathsf{F}}] + \frac{1}{2} \Pr[\mathsf{F}] \right) - 1$$

$$= (1 - \Pr[\mathsf{F}]) \cdot \left(2 \cdot \Pr[b'_1 = b_1 \wedge b'_2 = b_2] + 2 \cdot \Pr[b'_1 \neq b_1 \wedge b'_2 \neq b_2] - 1 \right).$$

Here, $\Pr[b'_1 = b_1 \wedge b'_2 = b_2]$ (resp. $\Pr[b'_1 \neq b_1 \wedge b'_2 \neq b_2]$) corresponds to the probability (which does not include the choice of r) that A wins (resp. loses) the game played with $C(r)$ twice, and thus is equal to $\mathsf{Win_A}(r)^2$ (resp. $(1 - \mathsf{Win_A}(r))^2$). Hence, we have

$$\mathsf{Adv_B}(r) = (1 - \Pr[\mathsf{F}]) \cdot \left(2 \cdot \mathsf{Win_A}(r)^2 + 2 \cdot (1 - \mathsf{Win_A}(r))^2 - 1 \right)$$

$$= (1 - \Pr[\mathsf{F}]) \cdot \left(2 \cdot \mathsf{Win_A}(r) - 1 \right)^2$$

$$= (1 - \Pr[\mathsf{F}]) \cdot \mathsf{Adv_A}(r)^2.$$

From this equality, $\Pr[\mathsf{F}] \leq \gamma$, and the fact that the square-advantage is at most 1, we obtain

$$\left| \mathbf{E}[\mathsf{Adv_B}(\mathcal{X})] \right| = (1 - \Pr[\mathsf{F}]) \cdot \mathbf{E}[\mathsf{Adv_A}(\mathcal{X})^2] \geq \mathbf{E}[\mathsf{Adv_A}(\mathcal{X})^2] - \gamma,$$

which is equivalent to the inequality stated in the theorem.   □ **(Lemma 8)**

Combining Lemma 8 with Lemma 7, we obtain our general result for square-friendly indistinguishability applications. Specifically, the following theorem shows how the security of an indistinguishability application satisfying simulatability under a real-world distribution $\mathcal{R}$ is guaranteed in terms of its security under an ideal distribution $\mathcal{Q}$, via the 2-Rényi divergence $\mathsf{RD}_2(\mathcal{R} \| \mathcal{Q})$.

Theorem 2. *Let $\mathcal{Q}$ and $\mathcal{R}$ be distributions over the parameter space X satisfying $[\mathcal{R}] \subseteq [\mathcal{Q}] \subseteq X$. If an indistinguishability application Π is (T', T, γ)-simulatable (with $T' \geq T$), then for any adversary A with resource T against the security of Π, there exists an adversary B with resource T' against the security of Π, such that*

$$\left| \mathbf{E}[\mathsf{Adv_A}(\mathcal{R})] \right| \leq G_{\mathcal{Q} \to \mathcal{R}} \left(\left| \mathbf{E}[\mathsf{Adv_A}(\mathcal{Q})] \right|, \left| \mathbf{E}[\mathsf{Adv_B}(\mathcal{Q})] \right| + \gamma \right),$$

where the function $G_{\mathcal{Q}\to\mathcal{R}}(\cdot,\cdot)$ is defined as in Eq. (3) of Lemma 7. In particular, if Π is (T',ϵ)-secure in the $\mathcal{Q}$-model and (T',T,γ)-simulatable, then Π is also $(T,G_{\mathcal{Q}\to\mathcal{R}}(\epsilon,\epsilon+\gamma))$-secure in the $\mathcal{R}$-model.

It would be an interesting question whether our general result for indistinguishability applications can be extended to those without simulatability.

5   Applications

In this section, we show some applications of our results from Sects. 3 and 4.

Specifically, in Sect. 5.1, we show an improved reduction for a class of distinguishing problems, called *distinguishing problems with public samplability* formalized by Bai et al. [3], using our results for indistinguishability applications with simulatability given in Sect. 4. Next, in Sect. 5.2, we show how one of the general lemmas shown in Sect. 3 is useful for assessing the differential privacy [12–14] of a privacy mechanism in which randomness (a.k.a. "noise") comes from a "real-world" distribution in terms of its differential privacy with an ideal randomness distribution.

5.1   Tighter Reduction for Distinguishing Problems with Public Samplability

In [3], Bai et al. formalized a class of distinguishing problems called *distinguishing problems with public samplability*. Informally, a distinguishing problem is said to have public samplability if given a problem instance x which is generated according to one of distributions $\mathcal{D}_0(r)$ or $\mathcal{D}_1(r)$ where r denotes a parameter chosen from some distribution common to both $\mathcal{D}_0$ and $\mathcal{D}_1$, we can efficiently sample a "fresh" sample from both $\mathcal{D}_0(r)$ and $\mathcal{D}_1(r)$, regardless of whether the original x comes from $\mathcal{D}_0(r)$ or $\mathcal{D}_1(r)$. One example of such a problem is the learning with errors (LWE) problem, which is a problem to decide, given a matrix/vector pair $(A,\mathbf{b})$, whether the vector $\mathbf{b}$ is of the form $\mathbf{b}=A\cdot\mathbf{s}+\mathbf{e}$ where $\mathbf{s}$ is a secret vector and $\mathbf{e}$ is a small "noise" vector, or $\mathbf{b}$ is chosen uniformly at random. It has public samplability because given a problem instance $x=(A,\mathbf{b})$, one can sample fresh LWE problem instances having the same A. (In this example, r is the matrix A.)

Bai et al. showed a reduction that reduces the hardness of a distinguishing problem with public samplability to the hardness of the same problem in which the distribution of a parameter r is changed to another distribution, using the Rényi divergence.

Our result in this subsection is a tighter reduction than the one by Bai et al. To formally show our result and give a comparison, we first recall the formal definition of distinguishing problems with public samplability, and then recall the result by Bai et al.

Definition 5 (Distinguishing Problem with Public Samplability [3]). *A distinguishing problem is a type of indistinguishability application and consists* of a tuple $D = (X, \mathcal{D}_0, \mathcal{D}_1)$ where X is the parameter space, and $\mathcal{D}_0$ and $\mathcal{D}_1$ are (possibly probabilistic) functions with domain X. In the security game of D, the challenger $\mathsf{C}(r)$ (which receives a parameter $r \in X$ as input) first picks the challenge bit $b \in \{0, 1\}$ uniformly at random, samples $x \leftarrow_\mathsf{R} \mathcal{D}_b(r)$, and gives x to an adversary A. When A returns its guess b' for b, $\mathsf{C}(r)$ decides that A wins (resp. loses) the game if $b' = b$ (resp. $b' \neq b$) and outputs 1 (resp. 0).

We say that a distinguishing problem $D = (X, \mathcal{D}_0, \mathcal{D}_1)$ is publicly samplable, if there exists a probabilistic algorithm S (called the sampling algorithm) satisfying the following properties:

- S takes a bit b and a sample x (output by $\mathcal{D}_0$ or $\mathcal{D}_1$) as input, and outputs some value x'.[10]
- For any $(r, b) \in X \times \{0, 1\}$ and any values x output by $\mathcal{D}_b(r)$,
  - The output of $\mathsf{S}(0, x)$ is distributed identically to a fresh sample chosen according to the distribution $\mathcal{D}_0(r)$.
  - The output of $\mathsf{S}(1, x)$ is distributed identically to a fresh sample chosen according to the distribution $\mathcal{D}_1(r)$.

Theorem 3 (Theorem 4.2 of [3]). *Let $D = (X, \mathcal{D}_0, \mathcal{D}_1)$ be a distinguishing problem with public samplability, and let S be the corresponding sampling algorithm whose running time is T_S. Let $\mathcal{Q}$ and $\mathcal{R}$ be distributions over the parameter space X such that $[\mathcal{R}] \subseteq [\mathcal{Q}] \subseteq X$. Then, for any adversary A against the security of D with running time T_A and advantage $|\mathbf{E}[\mathsf{Adv}_\mathsf{A}(\mathcal{R})]| = \epsilon_\mathsf{A}$ in the $\mathcal{R}$-model, and for any $\alpha \in (1, \infty]$, there exists another adversary B against the security of D with running time T_B and advantage $|\mathbf{E}[\mathsf{Adv}_\mathsf{B}(\mathcal{Q})]| = \epsilon_\mathsf{B}$ in the $\mathcal{Q}$-model, such that:*

$$T_\mathsf{B} \leq \frac{64}{\epsilon_\mathsf{A}^2} \log_2 \left(\frac{8 \cdot \mathsf{RD}_\alpha(\mathcal{R}\|\mathcal{Q})}{\epsilon_\mathsf{A}^{2+\frac{1}{\alpha-1}}} \right) \cdot (T_\mathsf{A} + T_\mathsf{S}), \quad and$$

$$\epsilon_\mathsf{B} \geq \frac{1}{2^{3+\frac{1}{\alpha-1}} \cdot \mathsf{RD}_\alpha(\mathcal{R}\|\mathcal{Q})} \cdot \epsilon_\mathsf{A}^{2+\frac{1}{\alpha-1}}.$$

Now, we show our result.

Theorem 4. *Let $D = (X, \mathcal{D}_0, \mathcal{D}_1)$, $\mathcal{R}$, and $\mathcal{Q}$ be the same as in Theorem 3. Then, for any adversary A against the security of D with running time T_A and advantage $|\mathbf{E}[\mathsf{Adv}_\mathsf{A}(\mathcal{R})]| = \epsilon_\mathsf{A}$ in the $\mathcal{R}$-model, there exists another adversary B against the security of D with running time T_B and advantage $|\mathbf{E}[\mathsf{Adv}_\mathsf{B}(\mathcal{Q})]| = \epsilon_\mathsf{B}$ in the $\mathcal{Q}$-model, such that:*

$$T_\mathsf{B} = 2T_\mathsf{A} + T_\mathsf{S} + \tau,$$

$$\epsilon_\mathsf{B} \geq \frac{1}{\mathsf{RD}_2(\mathcal{R}\|\mathcal{Q})} \cdot \epsilon_\mathsf{A}^2 \quad \left(\geq \frac{1}{\mathsf{RD}_\alpha(\mathcal{R}\|\mathcal{Q})} \cdot \epsilon_\mathsf{A}^2 \ for \ any \, \alpha \in [2, \infty] \right), \qquad (4)$$

where τ represents some (small) constant independent of T_A and ϵ_A.

---

[10] We stress that S is not given as input the parameter r used to generate a sample x, but may instead infer whatever it needs to know from x for generating x'.

Note that the Rényi divergence is non-decreasing regarding the order α (see [23]), and thus $\mathrm{RD}_\alpha(\mathcal{R}\|\mathcal{Q}) \leq \mathrm{RD}_{\alpha'}(\mathcal{R}\|\mathcal{Q})$ holds for all $\alpha < \alpha'$. Thus, Eq. (4) implies $\epsilon_B \geq \frac{1}{\mathrm{RD}_\alpha(\mathcal{R}\|\mathcal{Q})} \cdot \epsilon_A^2$ for every $\alpha \in [2, \infty]$ as well. Hence, although our reduction is not applicable for $\alpha \in (1, 2)$, otherwise ours strictly improves and is much simpler and tighter than the reduction of Bai et al. [3] for every $\alpha \in [2, \infty]$, both in terms of the running time and the distinguishing advantage of the reduction algorithm B. More concretely, the ratio $T_B \cdot \epsilon_B^{-1}$ (sometimes called the *work factor*, and a smaller value means a tighter reduction) of our reduction is $\approx 2 \cdot \mathrm{RD}_2(\mathcal{R}\|\mathcal{Q}) \cdot T_A \cdot \epsilon_A^{-2}$, while that of Bai et al. is as large as $\widetilde{O}(\mathrm{RD}_\alpha(\mathcal{R}\|\mathcal{Q}) \cdot T_A \cdot \epsilon_A^{-(4+\frac{1}{\alpha-1})})$.[11] It is $\widetilde{O}(\mathrm{RD}_2(\mathcal{R}\|\mathcal{Q}) \cdot T_A \cdot \epsilon_A^{-5})$ for $\alpha = 2$ and $\widetilde{O}(\mathrm{RD}_\infty(\mathcal{R}\|\mathcal{Q}) \cdot T_A \cdot \epsilon_A^{-4})$ for $\alpha = \infty$.

Proof of Theorem 4. We will show that a distinguishing problem with public samplability satisfies $(2T + T_S + \tau, T, 0)$-simulatability in the sense of Definition 4, and then invoke Theorem 2 to conclude the proof.

To see that any distinguishing problem with public samplability $D = (X, \mathcal{D}_0, \mathcal{D}_1)$ satisfies $(2T + T_S + \tau, T, 0)$-simulatability, consider an adversary A against the security of D with running time T, and consider the corresponding adversary B′ against the security of D for showing $(2T + T_S + \tau, T, 0)$-simulatability, which interacts with the challenger $\mathsf{C}(r)$ as follows:

B′ is initially given a sample x chosen according to $\mathcal{D}_b(r)$, where b is the challenge bit chosen by $\mathsf{C}(r)$ in the security game of B′ (and r is sampled according to $\mathcal{Q}$, possibly unknown to B′). Then, B′ picks the challenge bit $b_1 \in \{0, 1\}$ in the "first run" for A uniformly at random, and generates $x_1 \leftarrow_R \mathsf{S}(b_1, x)$. B′ then executes A twice, first with input x_1 and second with input x, where for each execution B′ uses a fresh randomness for A. Let b_1' (resp. b_2') be the output of A in the first (resp. second) run of A.

By design, the running time of this B′ is $2T + T_S + \tau$ for some small τ independent of A. Furthermore, due to the property of S, B′ simulates the challenger $\mathsf{C}(r)$ perfectly for A in both of the executions, so that the challenge bit for A in the first (resp. second) execution is b_1 (resp. b). Also, there is no notion of failure predicate in a distinguishing problem. Consequently, B′ satisfies all the properties of $(2T + T_S + \tau, T, 0)$-simulatability.

Then, by Theorem 2, for any adversary A against the security of D with running time T_A and advantage $|\mathbf{E}[\mathsf{Adv}_A(\mathcal{R})]| = \epsilon_A$ in the $\mathcal{R}$-model, there exists another adversary B against the security of D with running time $T_B = 2T_A + T_S + \tau$ and advantage $|\mathbf{E}[\mathsf{Adv}_B(\mathcal{Q})]| = \epsilon_B$ in the $\mathcal{Q}$-model satisfying $\epsilon_A \leq \sqrt{\mathrm{RD}_2(\mathcal{R}\|\mathcal{Q}) \cdot \epsilon_B}$. This inequality is equivalent to Eq. (4). □ (**Theorem 4**)

---

[11] If we adopt the approach of Micciancio and Walter [18] that regards ("running time") · ("advantage")$^{-2}$ (which corresponds to the steps needed to solve a distinguishing problem with a constant advantage) of the best adversary as the "bit security" of a problem, the difference between our reduction and that of Bai et al. will be even larger.

5.2 Switching Distributions in Differential Privacy

Intuitively, a differentially private mechanism (for some statistical task) takes a data set D as input, and uses its internal randomness r (typically called "noise" in the context of differential privacy) to produce a "sanitized" version of a true answer computed from D so that it is hard to tell whether any individual's data was included in D. It is often the case that the distribution of a randomness r used in a differentially private mechanism is not the uniform distribution, e.g. the Laplace distribution [12].

Here, we would like to consider the problem of how differential privacy in the setting where a randomness is drawn from an ideal distribution $\mathcal{Q}$ is degraded if we use a randomness drawn from another distribution $\mathcal{R}$. Using one of our lemmas in Sect. 3, we show a simple technique to assess differential privacy under such switching of distributions of a randomness via the ∞-Rényi divergence.

We note that the connection between differential privacy and the ∞-Rényi divergence is almost immediate from their definitions, and has already been mentioned in existing works (say, [17]). However, we are not aware of any work that formally states a statement in the form that we show below. We also note that our result only covers the case where randomness distributions are discrete, while many works on differential privacy use continuous distributions.

Below, we recall the definition of a differentially private mechanism and then give our result. (We adopt the so-called *approximate differential privacy* [13].)

Let $n \geq 1$ and let $\mathcal{D}$ be the data space. We say that two data sets $D, D' \in \mathcal{D}^n$ are *neighboring* if D and D' have exactly one distinct entry. As in [10], we parameterize differential privacy with not only the privacy budget (ϵ and δ) but also the distribution of randomness used by a mechanism.

Definition 6. *Let $n \geq 1$ and $\mathcal{D}$ be as above. Let $\mathsf{M} : \mathcal{D}^n \to R$ be a probabilistic algorithm whose randomness space is some finite set X. Let $\epsilon, \delta \geq 0$ be real numbers, and let $\mathcal{X}$ be a distribution over X. We say that M satisfies $(\mathcal{X}, \epsilon, \delta)$-differential privacy if for every neighboring data sets $D, D' \in \mathcal{D}^n$ and for every $T \subseteq R$, we have*

$$\Pr_{r \leftarrow_{\mathrm{R}} \mathcal{X}}[\mathsf{M}(D; r) \in T] \leq e^\epsilon \cdot \Pr_{r \leftarrow_{\mathrm{R}} \mathcal{X}}[\mathsf{M}(D'; r) \in T] + \delta.$$

Theorem 5. *Let $n \geq 1$ and $\mathcal{D}$ be as above, and let M be a probabilistic algorithm whose randomness space is some set X. Let $\mathcal{R}$ and $\mathcal{Q}$ be distributions such that $[\mathcal{R}] = [\mathcal{Q}] \subseteq X$. Let $\epsilon, \delta \geq 0$. Then, if M satisfies $(\mathcal{Q}, \epsilon, \delta)$-differential privacy, then M also satisfies $(\mathcal{R}, \epsilon', \delta')$-differential privacy, where*

$$\epsilon' = \epsilon + \ln \mathrm{RD}_\infty(\mathcal{R}\|\mathcal{Q}) + \ln \mathrm{RD}_\infty(\mathcal{Q}\|\mathcal{R}) \qquad and \qquad \delta' = \mathrm{RD}_\infty(\mathcal{R}\|\mathcal{Q}) \cdot \delta.$$

Proof of Theorem 5. Fix arbitrarily neighboring data sets $D, D' \in \mathcal{D}^n$ and $T \subseteq R$. For each $r \in X$, define $f_D(r) := \Pr[\mathsf{M}(D; r) \in T]$ and $f_{D'}(r) := \Pr[\mathsf{M}(D'; r) \in T]$. Note that the range of these functions is $[0, 1]$, and we have $\mathbf{E}[f_D(\mathcal{R})] = \Pr_{r \leftarrow_{\mathrm{R}} \mathcal{R}}[\mathsf{M}(D; r) \in T]$, $\mathbf{E}[f_D(\mathcal{Q})] = \Pr_{r \leftarrow_{\mathrm{R}} \mathcal{Q}}[\mathsf{M}(D; r) \in T]$, and we have similar equations for $f_{D'}$. Now, for D, D', T, we have

$$\Pr_{r \leftarrow_{\mathsf{R}} \mathcal{R}} \Pr[\mathsf{M}(D; r) \in T] = \mathbf{E}[f_D(\mathcal{R})]$$

$$\overset{(*)}{\leq} \mathrm{RD}_\infty(\mathcal{R}\|\mathcal{Q}) \cdot \mathbf{E}[f_D(\mathcal{Q})]$$

$$\overset{(\dagger)}{\leq} \mathrm{RD}_\infty(\mathcal{R}\|\mathcal{Q}) \cdot \left(e^\epsilon \cdot \mathbf{E}[f_{D'}(\mathcal{Q})] + \delta \right)$$

$$\overset{(\ddagger)}{\leq} \mathrm{RD}_\infty(\mathcal{R}\|\mathcal{Q}) \cdot e^\epsilon \cdot \mathrm{RD}_\infty(\mathcal{Q}\|\mathcal{R}) \cdot \mathbf{E}[f_{D'}(\mathcal{R})] + \mathrm{RD}_\infty(\mathcal{R}\|\mathcal{Q}) \cdot \delta$$

$$= \mathrm{RD}_\infty(\mathcal{R}\|\mathcal{Q}) \cdot e^\epsilon \cdot \mathrm{RD}_\infty(\mathcal{Q}\|\mathcal{R}) \cdot \Pr_{r \leftarrow_{\mathsf{R}} \mathcal{R}}[\mathsf{M}(D'; r) \in T] + \mathrm{RD}_\infty(\mathcal{R}\|\mathcal{Q}) \cdot \delta,$$

where the inequalities (*) and (‡) use Corollary 1 and the inequality (†) uses the $(\mathcal{Q}, \epsilon, \delta)$-differential privacy of M that implies $\mathbf{E}[f_D(\mathcal{Q})] = \Pr_{r \leftarrow_{\mathsf{R}} \mathcal{Q}}[\mathsf{M}(D; r) \in T] \leq e^\epsilon \cdot \Pr_{r \leftarrow_{\mathsf{R}} \mathcal{Q}}[\mathsf{M}(D'; r) \in T] + \delta = e^\epsilon \cdot \mathbf{E}[f_{D'}(\mathcal{Q})] + \delta$. Since the choice of D, D', and T is arbitrary, we can conclude that M satisfies $(\mathcal{R}, \epsilon', \delta')$-differential privacy with the claimed ϵ' and δ'.   □ (**Theorem 5**)

6   Approximate Sampling with Guaranteed Rényi Divergence Bound Using Uniform Randomness

There are a number of (not necessarily cryptographic) applications in which we wish to sample random elements from distributions that are not the uniform distribution, e.g. the discrete Gaussian distribution in lattice-based cryptography (e.g. [20]), the Laplace distribution [12,14] (and other complicated distributions such as the matrix Bingham distribution [7]) in the literature of differential privacy, to name a few. However, it is not always easy (and sometimes impossible) for computers to sample a randomness that exactly follows a target distribution. Thus, a lot of efforts have been made for approximately sampling a randomness from the target distribution using a randomness drawn from the uniform distribution (over bitstrings), so that the sampling method is implementable by computers. One of the basic approaches used for such approximate sampling of a randomness is the *inversion sampling* method (a.k.a. inverse transform sampling), which is the focus in this section.

We propose two computer-friendly inversion sampling methods for an arbitrary discrete distribution $\mathcal{Q}$ using a randomness drawn from the uniform distribution over bitstrings.

– The first method, given in Sect. 6.1, has the guarantee that the actual distribution $\mathcal{R}$ of a randomness sampled by our method has a guarantee that the 2-Rényi divergence $\mathcal{R}$ from $\mathcal{Q}$ is upperbounded by some number that depends on the size of the support of the distribution and the bit-length of the randomness. More concretely, when using an n-bit string for each sampling from a distribution $\mathcal{Q}$ the size of whose support is m, then the distribution $\mathcal{R}$ of our first sampling method guarantees $\mathrm{RD}_2(\mathcal{R}\|\mathcal{Q}) \leq 1 + m/2^n$.
– The second method, given in Sect. 6.2, has a similar property to the first method, but it has a guaranteed ∞-Rényi divergence bound. Concretely, under the same setting as above, our second sampling method guarantees $\mathrm{RD}_\infty(\mathcal{R}\|\mathcal{Q}) \leq (1 + \sqrt{m/2^n})^2$.

Throughout this section, for simplicity, we work with distributions over $[m]$ for some $m \in \mathbb{N}$ (but our proposals straightforwardly generalize to distributions with an arbitrary finite support). Note that in this case, a distribution $\mathcal{D}$ can be identified with an m-dimensional vector $(p_1, \ldots, p_m) \in [0,1]^m$ such that $\sum_{i \in [m]} p_i = 1$, where $p_i := \Pr[\mathcal{D} = i]$ for each $i \in [m]$.

Our Approach. Recall that the inversion sampling method is based on the inverse of the cumulative distribution function (CDF) of a distribution $\mathcal{D} = (p_1, \ldots, p_m)$. More specifically, let $c_0 = 0$ and $c_i := \Pr[1 \leq \mathcal{D} \leq i] = \sum_{j \in [i]} p_i$ for all $i \in [m]$, then given a uniformly random value x in the interval $[0, 1)$, the sampling method outputs k such that $c_{k-1} \leq x < c_k$. Hence, the problem is reduced to showing how to construct a table of the CDF of a distribution.

Given a target distribution $\mathcal{Q} = (q_1, \ldots, q_m)$, our approach is to consider an approximated version $\mathcal{R} = (r_1, \ldots, r_m)$ of $\mathcal{Q}$ such that (1) each r_i can be described by an n-bit string, and (2) the α-Rényi divergence ($\alpha \in \{2, \infty\}$) of $\mathcal{R}$ from $\mathcal{Q}$ has an upperbound dependent on m and n. Note that (1) means that each r_i is of the form $R_i/2^n$ for some $R_i \in \mathbb{Z}_{\geq 0}$ with $R_i \leq 2^n$ and it holds that $\sum_{i \in [m]} R_i = 2^n$, which in turn implies that any value of the CDF of $\mathcal{R}$ can be expressed by an n-bit string, and thus $\mathcal{R}$ can be exactly sampled by using a uniformly random n-bit string. Hence, to achieve the goal, it is sufficient to show how to construct such $\mathcal{R}$ given $\mathcal{Q}$.

The high-level structure for both of our proposed methods is common, and quite simple and intuitive. For convenience, instead of working with a distribution, we work with its scaled-up version, i.e. a vector $(Q_1, \ldots, Q_m) = (2^n \cdot q_1, \ldots, 2^n \cdot q_m) \in ([0, 2^n])^m$.

1. From the original vector $(Q_1, \ldots, Q_m)$, we construct its "tail-cut" version $(\widetilde{Q}_1, \ldots, \widetilde{Q}_m)$. That is, if some value Q_i is too small, $\widetilde{Q}_i$ is set as 0, while the suppressed values are distributed (added) to the non-zero positions in $(\widetilde{Q}_1, \ldots, \widetilde{Q}_m)$ so that $\sum_{i \in [m]} \widetilde{Q}_i = 2^n$ holds.

2. We construct an *integer* vector $(R_1, \ldots, R_m) \in (\mathbb{Z}_{\geq 0})^m$ from $(\widetilde{Q}_1, \ldots, \widetilde{Q}_m)$, so that each R_i is "close" to $\widetilde{Q}_i$ and $\sum_{i \in [m]} R_i = 2^n$ holds. The resulting integer vector $(R_1, \ldots, R_m)$ is a scaled-up version of our desired distribution $\mathcal{R} = (r_1, \ldots, r_m)$. Note that the distribution $\mathcal{R}$ obtained in this way satisfies the property that each r_i can be represented by an n-bit string.

Although simple in a high-level structure, the details are quite different between our first and second proposed methods due to the difference between the 2-Rényi divergence and the ∞-Rényi divergence. For each method, we have to carefully choose the definition of $(\widetilde{Q}_i)_{i \in [m]}$ (in particular, the threshold for the tail cutting), and how to approximate $(\widetilde{Q}_i)_{i \in [m]}$ by the integer vector $(R_i)_{i \in [m]}$, so that we have the desired upperbound of the α-Rényi divergence ($\alpha \in \{2, \infty\}$). For the details, see the actual proofs.

Supporting Lemma. In the proofs of both of our sampling methods, we will use the following supporting lemma, whose proof is given in Appendix A.

Lemma 9. *Let $k \in \mathbb{N}$, and let $A = (a_1, \ldots, a_k) \in (\mathbb{R}_{\geq 0})^k$ be a vector satisfying $\sum_{i \in [k]} a_i \in \mathbb{N}$. Then, there exists a constructive procedure for constructing a vector $B = (b_1, \ldots, b_k) \in (\mathbb{Z}_{\geq 0})^k$ satisfying the following two properties:*

1. *$\sum_{i \in [k]} b_i = \sum_{i \in [k]} a_i$.*
2. *For each $i \in [k]$, let $d_i := b_i - a_i$. Then, $|d_i| \leq 1$ holds for all $i \in [k]$, and $|d_i - d_j| \leq 1$ holds for all $i, j \in [k]$.*

6.1 Approximate Sampling with a 2-Rényi-Divergence Bound

The following theorem captures our first sampling method.

Theorem 6. *Let $n, m \in \mathbb{N}$. Let $\mathcal{Q} = (q_1, \ldots, q_m)$ be a distribution whose support is $[m]$. Then, there is a constructive procedure for constructing a distribution $\mathcal{R} = (r_1, \ldots, r_m)$ over $[m]$ satisfying the following two properties:*

- **(Samplable Using Uniform Random Bits):** *Each r_i can be described by using at most n-bits. Namely, for all $i \in [m]$, r_i is of the form $r_i = \frac{R_i}{2^n}$, where $R_i \in \mathbb{Z}_{\geq 0}$ and $R_i \leq 2^n$.*
- **(Upperbound of 2-Rényi Divergence):** *The 2-Rényi divergence of $\mathcal{R}$ from $\mathcal{Q}$ is upperbounded as follows:*

$$\mathrm{RD}_2(\mathcal{R} \| \mathcal{Q}) \leq 1 + \frac{m}{2^n}. \tag{5}$$

Proof of Theorem 6. If $m = 1$, then $q_1 = 1$, and thus by defining $r_1 := 1$, the theorem trivially holds. Hence, from here on we assume $m \geq 2$, i.e. the support of $\mathcal{Q}$ contains at least two elements. Then, first of all, note that for proving the theorem, it is sufficient to consider the case that $\mathcal{Q} = (q_1, \ldots, q_m)$ is "ordered" in the following way:

$$0 < q_1 \leq \cdots \leq q_m < 1. \tag{6}$$

Specifically, for a general "non-ordered" distribution $\mathcal{Q}' = (q_1', \ldots, q_m')$ with support $[m]$, let $\pi : [m] \to [m]$ be a permutation such that $\mathcal{Q} = (q_1, \ldots, q_m) = (q_{\pi^{-1}(1)}', \ldots, q_{\pi^{-1}(m)}')$ satisfying Eq. (6). Then, we construct a distribution $\mathcal{R} = (r_1, \ldots, r_m)$ satisfying the two properties guaranteed by the theorem with respect to the ordered distribution $\mathcal{Q}$, and finally obtain the desired distribution $\mathcal{R}' = (r_1', \ldots, r_m')$ by defining $r_i' = r_{\pi(i)}$ for every $i \in [m]$. Then, $\mathcal{R}'$ obtained in this way satisfies the two properties with respect to the original distribution $\mathcal{Q}'$: π preserves the first property of $\mathcal{R}$, and we have $\mathrm{RD}_2(\mathcal{R}' \| \mathcal{Q}') = \sum_{i \in [m]} \frac{r_i'^2}{q_i'} = \sum_{i \in [m]} \frac{r_{\pi(i)}^2}{q_{\pi(i)}} = \sum_{i \in [m]} \frac{r_i^2}{q_i} = \mathrm{RD}_2(\mathcal{R} \| \mathcal{Q})$. Hence, we can focus on the case that $\mathcal{Q}$ is ordered in the sense of Eq. (6).

Let $N := 2^n$, and let $Q_i := N \cdot q_i$ for all $i \in [m]$. Then, $\sum_{i \in [m]} Q_i = N$ holds due to the fact that $\mathcal{Q}$ is a probability distribution, and Eq. (6) implies

$$0 < Q_1 \leq \cdots \leq Q_m < N. \tag{7}$$

Next, we note that showing how to construct a distribution $\mathcal{R} = (r_1, \ldots, r_m)$ satisfying the desired properties with respect to $\mathcal{Q}$, is reduced to showing how to construct an integer vector $(R_1, \ldots, R_m) \in (\mathbb{Z}_{\geq 0})^m$ satisfying $\sum_{i \in [m]} R_i = N$ and

$$Z := \sum_{i \in [m]} \frac{(R_i - Q_i)^2}{Q_i} \leq m. \tag{8}$$

To see this, define the probability distribution $\mathcal{R} = (r_1, \ldots, r_m)$ by $r_i = R_i/N$ for every $i \in [m]$ (which guarantees $\sum_{i \in [m]} r_i = 1$). Then, we have

$$RD_2(\mathcal{R}\|\mathcal{Q}) = \sum_{i \in [m]} \frac{r_i^2}{q_i} = \sum_{i \in [m]} \frac{(R_i/N)^2}{Q_i/N} = \frac{1}{N} \sum_{i \in [m]} \frac{((R_i - Q_i) + Q_i)^2}{Q_i}$$

$$= \frac{1}{N} \left(\sum_{i \in [m]} \frac{(R_i - Q_i)^2}{Q_i} + 2 \cdot \sum_{i \in [m]} R_i - \sum_{i \in [m]} Q_i \right)$$

$$\overset{(*)}{=} \frac{1}{N}(Z + 2N - N) = 1 + \frac{Z}{N},$$

where the equality $(*)$ is due to $\sum_{i \in [m]} R_i = \sum_{i \in [m]} Q_i = N$. Since $N = 2^n$, the right hand side of the above equality is exactly that of Eq. (5) if $Z \leq m$.

Hence, our task is to show how to construct a vector $(R_1, \ldots, R_m) \in (\mathbb{Z}_{\geq 0})^m$ satisfying $\sum_{i \in [m]} R_i = N$ and Eq. (8). To this end, we introduce the following values m^* and S:

$$m^* := \max \left\{ \ell \in \{0\} \cup [m] \mid Q_\ell \leq \frac{1}{2} \wedge \sum_{i \in [\ell]} Q_i \leq \frac{m - \ell - 1}{2} \right\},$$

$$S := \sum_{i \in [m^*]} Q_i,$$

where for convenience we define $Q_0 := 0$. Note that the definition of m^* implies $m^* \leq m - 1$. Indeed, $m = m^*$ cannot hold because this and the condition $\sum_{i \in [m^*]} Q_i \leq \frac{m - m^* - 1}{2}$ imply $\sum_{i \in [m]} Q_i < 0$, which contradicts $\sum_{i \in [m]} Q_i = N$. Furthermore, due to the definitions of m^* and S, the following inequalities hold, which will be used later in the proof:

Lemma 10.

$$Q_{m^*+1} > \min \left\{ \frac{1}{2}, \frac{m - m^*}{2(m^* + 1)} \right\} \quad and \quad S \leq \min \left\{ \frac{m^*}{2}, \frac{m - m^* - 1}{2} \right\}.$$

Proof of Lemma 10. The definitions of m^* and S directly imply (a) $S = \sum_{i \in [m^*]} Q_i \leq \frac{m - m^* - 1}{2}$, (b) $Q_{m^*} \leq \frac{1}{2}$, and (c) either $Q_{m^*+1} > \frac{1}{2}$ or $\sum_{i \in [m^*+1]} Q_i > \frac{m - m^*}{2}$. Here, the condition (b) and Eq. (7) imply $S \leq m^* \cdot Q_{m^*} \leq \frac{m^*}{2}$. Combining this with the condition (a), we immediately obtain $S \leq \min\{\frac{m^*}{2}, \frac{m - m^* - 1}{2}\}$.

It remains to show $Q_{m^*+1} > \min\{\frac{1}{2}, \frac{m - m^*}{2(m^* + 1)}\}$. Assume towards a contradiction that $Q_{m^*+1} \leq \frac{1}{2}$ and $Q_{m^*+1} \leq \frac{m - m^*}{2(m^* + 1)}$ simultaneously hold. Then, on the one hand, $Q_{m^*+1} \leq \frac{1}{2}$ and the condition (c) imply $\sum_{i \in [m^*+1]} Q_i > \frac{m-m^*}{2}$. On the other hand, $Q_{m^*+1} \leq \frac{m-m^*}{2(m^*+1)}$ and Eq. (7) imply $\sum_{i \in [m^*+1]} Q_i \leq (m^*+1) \cdot Q_{m^*+1} \leq \frac{m-m^*}{2}$, and thus we have reached a contradiction. Hence, we can conclude that $Q_{m^*+1} > \min\{\frac{1}{2}, \frac{m-m^*}{2(m^*+1)}\}$ holds as well. ☐ (**Lemma** 10)

Now, as an intermediate step for constructing the desired vector $(R_1, \ldots, R_m)$, we consider the following modified vector $(\widetilde{Q}_1, \ldots, \widetilde{Q}_m)$, which is the "tail-cut" version of $(Q_1, \ldots, Q_m)$, such that for every $i \in [m]$:

$$
\widetilde{Q}_i := \begin{cases} 0 & \text{if } 1 \leq i \leq m^* \\ Q_i + \frac{S}{m-m^*} & \text{if } m^*+1 \leq i \leq m \end{cases}.
$$

(We note that the above definition covers the case of $m^* = 0$, which implies $S = 0$ and thus $\widetilde{Q}_i = Q_i$ for all $i \in [m]$.) Note that $0 \leq \widetilde{Q}_i \leq N$ for all $i \in [m]$, and they preserve the sum N of the original vector $(Q_1, \ldots, Q_m)$:

$$
\sum_{i \in [m]} \widetilde{Q}_i = \sum_{i=m^*+1}^{m} \widetilde{Q}_i = \sum_{i=m^*+1}^{m} \left(Q_i + \frac{S}{m-m^*} \right) = \sum_{i=m^*+1}^{m} Q_i + S
$$

$$
= \sum_{i=m^*+1}^{m} Q_i + \sum_{i=1}^{m^*} Q_i = N.
$$

Our target vector $(R_1, \ldots, R_m)$ is constructed by approximating the above defined modified vector $(\widetilde{Q}_1, \ldots, \widetilde{Q}_m)$ by integers. Specifically, we define $R_1 = \cdots = R_{m^*} = 0$. The remaining values R_i for $i \geq m^*+1$, are constructed by using the supporting lemma (Lemma 9). Specifically, by setting $k := m - m^*$ and $a_i := \widetilde{Q}_{m^*+i}$ for every $i \in [m - m^*]$, we have a vector $A = (a_1, \ldots, a_k)$ satisfying $\sum_{i \in [k]} a_i = \sum_{i=m^*+1}^{m} \widetilde{Q}_i = N$. Then, we apply Lemma 9 to this vector A and obtain a vector $B = (b_1, \ldots, b_k) \in (\mathbb{Z}_{\geq 0})^k$, from which we define $R_{m^*+i} := b_i$ for every $i \in [k] = [m - m^*]$. Note that the first property guaranteed by Lemma 9 implies $\sum_{i \in [k]} b_i = \sum_{i=m^*+1}^{m} R_i = N$, and the second property of the lemma guarantees that we have $|d_i - d_j| \leq 1$ for all $i, j \in [m - m^*]$, where $d_i := b_i - a_i = R_{m^*+i} - \widetilde{Q}_{m^*+i}$ for each $i \in [m - m^*]$.

So far, we have defined the vector $(R_1, \ldots, R_m) \in (\mathbb{Z}_{\geq 0})^m$ that satisfies $\sum_{i \in [m]} R_i = \sum_{i=m^*+1}^{m} R_i = N$. Hence, it remains to show that Eq. (8), i.e., $Z \leq m$, is satisfied. Calculating Z gives us the following inequality:

$$
Z = \sum_{i=1}^{m} \frac{(R_i - Q_i)^2}{Q_i} = \sum_{i=1}^{m^*} \frac{(0 - Q_i)^2}{Q_i} + \sum_{i=m^*+1}^{m} \frac{(R_i - Q_i)^2}{Q_i}
$$

$$
\leq S + \frac{1}{Q_{m^*+1}} \cdot \sum_{i=m^*+1}^{m} (R_i - Q_i)^2 \tag{9}
$$

where the inequality uses $S = \sum_{i=1}^{m^*} Q_i$ and $Q_{m^*+1} \leq Q_i$ for every $i \geq m^*+1$.

In order to show that Eq. (9) is further upperbounded by m, we wish to upperbound the sum $\sum_{i=m^*+1}^{m}(R_i - Q_i)^2$. For doing this, we do some preparation. Notice that for every $i \in [m - m^*]$, we have

$$R_{m^*+i} - Q_{m^*+i} = R_{m^*+i} - \widetilde{Q}_{m^*+i} + \widetilde{Q}_{m^*+i} - Q_{m^*+i} = d_i + \frac{S}{m - m^*}.$$

Due to the second property satisfied by a vector obtained via Lemma 9, for all $i, j \in [m - m^*]$, we have

$$\left| (R_{m^*+i} - Q_{m^*+i}) - (R_{m^*+j} - Q_{m^*+j}) \right| = |d_i - d_j| \leq 1. \tag{10}$$

Moreover, we have

$$\sum_{i=m^*+1}^{m}(R_i - Q_i) = \sum_{i=1}^{m}(R_i - Q_i) - \sum_{i=1}^{m^*}(R_i - Q_i) \overset{(*)}{=} N - N + \sum_{i=1}^{m^*} Q_i \overset{(\dagger)}{=} S, \tag{11}$$

where the equality $(*)$ uses $\sum_{i=1}^{m} R_i = \sum_{i=1}^{m} Q_i = N$ and the property that $R_i = 0$ for all $i \in [m^*]$, and the equality $(\dagger)$ is due to the definition of S.

We now use the following supporting lemma to upperbound $\sum_{i=m^*+1}^{m}(R_i - Q_i)^2$, whose proof is given in Appendix B.

Lemma 11. Let $k \in \mathbb{N}$. Let $A = (a_1, \ldots a_k) \in \mathbb{R}^k$ be any vector satisfying $|a_i - a_j| \leq 1$ for all $i, j \in [k]$. Let $\alpha := \sum_{i \in [k]} a_i$. Then,

$$\sum_{i \in [k]} a_i^2 \leq \frac{\alpha^2}{k} + \frac{k}{4}.$$

Let $k := m - m^*$ and $a_i' := (R_{m^*+i} - Q_{m^*+i})$ for every $i \in [k]$. By Eq. (11), we have $\alpha := \sum_{i \in [k]} a_i' = \sum_{i=m^*+1}^{m}(R_i - Q_i) = S \leq \frac{m-m^*-1}{2} \leq \frac{m-m^*}{2}$. Also, Eq. (10) guarantees that $|a_i' - a_j'| \leq 1$ holds for all $i, j \in [k]$. Then, by applying Lemma 11 to the vector $(a_1', \ldots, a_k')$, we obtain

$$\sum_{i=m^*+1}^{m}(R_i - Q_i)^2 = \sum_{i \in [k]} a_i'^2 \leq \frac{\alpha^2}{k} + \frac{k}{4} = \frac{S^2}{m - m^*} + \frac{m - m^*}{4} \leq \frac{m - m^*}{2}.$$

Using this inequality and Lemma 10 in Eq. (9), we have

$$Z \leq S + \frac{1}{Q_{m^*+1}} \cdot \sum_{i=m^*+1}^{m}(R_i - Q_i)^2$$

$$\leq \min\left\{ \frac{m^*}{2}, \frac{m - m^* - 1}{2} \right\} + \max\left\{ 2, \frac{2(m^* + 1)}{m - m^*} \right\} \cdot \frac{m - m^*}{2}$$

$$= \min\left\{ \frac{m^*}{2}, \frac{m - m^* - 1}{2} \right\} + \max\left\{ m - m^*, m^* + 1 \right\}$$

$$= \begin{cases} m - \frac{m^*}{2} & \text{if } m^* \leq \frac{m-1}{2} \\ \frac{m+m^*+1}{2} & \text{if } m^* > \frac{m-1}{2} \end{cases}.$$

Recall that we have $0 \leq m^* \leq m - 1$. Hence, regardless of the value m^*, we have $Z \leq m$, as required. This completes the proof of the theorem. $\square$ (**Theorem** 6)

6.2   Approximate Sampling with a ∞-Rényi-Divergence Bound

The following theorem captures our second sampling method.

Theorem 7. *Let $n, m \in \mathbb{N}$. Let $\mathcal{Q} = (q_1, \ldots, q_m)$ be a distribution whose support is $[m]$. Then, there is a constructive procedure for constructing a distribution $\mathcal{R} = (r_1, \ldots, r_m)$ over $[m]$ satisfying the following two properties:*

- **(Samplable Using Uniform Random Bits):** *Each r_i can be described by using at most n-bits. Namely, for all $i \in [m]$, r_i is of the form $r_i = \frac{R_i}{2^n}$, where $R_i \in \mathbb{Z}_{\geq 0}$ and $R_i \leq 2^n$.*
- **(Upperbound of ∞-Rényi Divergence):** *The ∞-Rényi divergence of $\mathcal{R}$ from $\mathcal{Q}$ is upperbounded as follows:*

$$\mathrm{RD}_\infty(\mathcal{R} \| \mathcal{Q}) \leq \left(1 + \sqrt{\frac{m}{2^n}} \right)^2. \tag{12}$$

Proof of Theorem 7. If $m = 1$, then $q_1 = 1$, and thus by defining $r_1 := 1$, the theorem trivially holds. Hence, from here on we assume $m \geq 2$. Then, with exactly the same reason as in the proof of Theorem 6, it is sufficient to consider the case that $\mathcal{Q} = (q_1, \ldots, q_m)$ satisfies the "ordered" condition $0 < q_1 \leq \cdots \leq q_m < 1$.

Let $N = 2^n$, and let $Q_i = N \cdot q_i$ for all $i \in [m]$. Then, $\sum_{i \in [m]} Q_i = N$ holds due to the fact that $\mathcal{Q}$ is a probability distribution, and the "ordered" condition implies

$$0 < Q_1 \leq \cdots \leq Q_m < N. \tag{13}$$

Next, we note that due to the definition of the ∞-Rényi divergence, showing how to construct a distribution $\mathcal{R} = (r_1, \ldots, r_m)$ satisfying Eq. (12), is equivalent to showing how to construct an integer vector $(R_1, \ldots, R_m) \in (\mathbb{Z}_{\geq 0})^m$ satisfying $\sum_{i \in [m]} R_i = N$ and

$$\max_{i \in [m]} \frac{R_i}{Q_i} \leq \left(1 + \sqrt{\frac{m}{N}} \right)^2, \tag{14}$$

since it holds that $\mathrm{RD}_\infty(\mathcal{R} \| \mathcal{Q}) = \max_{i \in [m]} \frac{r_i}{q_i} = \max_{i \in [m]} \frac{R_i/N}{Q_i/N} = \max_{i \in [m]} \frac{R_i}{Q_i}$.

To this end, we introduce the following values S^*, m^*, and S:

$$S^* := \frac{\sqrt{m}}{\sqrt{N} + \sqrt{m}} \cdot N,$$

$$m^* := \max\left\{ \ell \in \{0\} \cup [m] \ \Big| \ \sum_{i \in [\ell]} Q_i \leq S^* < \sum_{i \in [\ell+1]} Q_i \right\},$$

$$S := \sum_{i \in [m^*]} Q_i,$$

where for convenience we define $Q_0 := 0$. Here, the definition of S^* may look somewhat sudden and bizarre. This is the value of x that minimizes the function

$f(x) := \frac{N}{N-x} + \frac{m}{x}$ in the interval $x \in (0, N)$, so that $f(S^*) = (1 + \sqrt{\frac{m}{N}})^2$ holds (which can be checked by considering the zero of the first-order derivative of f). Note that this is the desired upperbound of $\max_{i \in [m]} \frac{R_i}{Q_i}$ to be shown.

Our proof from here on is heading to showing how to bound $\mathrm{RD}_\infty(\mathcal{R} \| \mathcal{Q})$ by using the above minimum. We note that the definition of m^* implies that m^* is strictly smaller than m, because $\sum_{i \in [m^*]} Q_i \leq S^* < N = \sum_{i \in [m]} Q_i$. Furthermore, the definitions of m^* and S imply the following inequality, which will be used later in the proof.

Lemma 12.

$$Q_{m^*+1} \geq \frac{S^*}{m}. \tag{15}$$

Proof of Lemma 12. If $m^* = 0$, then we have $Q_1 > S^*$, and thus $Q_{m^*+1} \geq \frac{S^*}{m}$ is trivially satisfied. Hence, from here on we consider the case $m^* \geq 1$.

By the definitions of m^* and S, we have $S = \sum_{i \in [m^*]} Q_i \leq S^* < \sum_{i \in [m^*+1]} Q_i = S + Q_{m^*+1}$. This implies $Q_{m^*+1} > S^* - S$. Furthermore, we also have $Q_{m^*+1} \geq \frac{S}{m^*}$ because otherwise (i.e., $Q_{m^*+1} < \frac{S}{m^*}$) we have $0 < Q_1 \leq \cdots \leq Q_{m^*} < \frac{S}{m^*}$, which implies $\sum_{i \in [m^*]} Q_i = Q_1 + \cdots + Q_{m^*} < m^* \cdot \frac{S}{m^*} = S$, contradicting the definitions of m^* and S.

So far, we have seen $Q_{m^*+1} > S^* - S$ and $Q_{m^*+1} \geq \frac{S}{m^*}$, equivalently,

$$Q_{m^*+1} \geq \max\left\{ S^* - S, \frac{S}{m^*} \right\}. \tag{16}$$

We now show that Eq. (15) holds regardless of the values m^* and S. This is shown by considering the following two cases covering all possibilities:

Case $S \leq \frac{m-1}{m} \cdot S^*$: Note that

$$S \leq \frac{m-1}{m} \cdot S^* \quad \Longleftrightarrow \quad S \leq \left(1 - \frac{1}{m}\right) \cdot S^* \quad \Longleftrightarrow \quad S^* - S \geq \frac{S^*}{m}.$$

Hence, by Eq. (16), we have $Q_{m^*+1} \geq S^* - S \geq \frac{S^*}{m}$.

Case $S > \frac{m-1}{m} \cdot S^*$: By dividing both sides of the condition of this case by $m^* \geq 1$, we obtain

$$\frac{S}{m^*} > \frac{m-1}{m^*} \cdot \frac{S^*}{m} \overset{(*)}{\geq} \frac{S^*}{m},$$

where the inequality (*) uses $\frac{m-1}{m^*} \geq 1$, which holds because of the condition $m^* < m$. Hence, by Eq. (16), we have $Q_{m^*+1} \geq \frac{S}{m^*} > \frac{S^*}{m}$.

As seen above, $Q_{m^*+1} \geq \frac{S^*}{m}$ holds in any case. $\quad\square$ **(Lemma 12)**

Now, as an intermediate step for constructing the desired vector $(R_1, \ldots, R_m)$, we consider the following modified vector $(\widetilde{Q}_1, \ldots, \widetilde{Q}_m)$, which is the "tail-cut" version of $(Q_1, \ldots, Q_m)$, such that for every $i \in [m]$:

$$\widetilde{Q}_i := \begin{cases} 0 & \text{if } 1 \leq i \leq m^* \\ Q_i \cdot \frac{N}{N-S} & \text{if } m^* + 1 \leq i \leq m \end{cases}.$$

(We note that the above definition covers the case of $m^* = 0$, which implies $S = 0$ and thus $\widetilde{Q}_i = Q_i$ for all $i \in [m]$.) Note that $0 \leq \widetilde{Q}_i \leq N$ for all $i \in [m]$, and they preserve the sum N of the original vector $(Q_1, \ldots, Q_m)$:

$$\sum_{i \in [m]} \widetilde{Q}_i = \sum_{i=m^*+1}^{m} \widetilde{Q}_i = \frac{N}{N-S} \cdot \sum_{i=m^*+1}^{m} Q_i = \frac{N}{N-S} \cdot \left(\sum_{i \in [m]} Q_i - \sum_{i \in [m^*]} Q_i \right)$$

$$= \frac{N}{N-S} \cdot (N-S) = N.$$

Our target vector $(R_1, \ldots, R_m)$ is constructed by approximating the above defined modified vector $(\widetilde{Q}_1, \ldots, \widetilde{Q}_m)$ by integers, in the same manner as what we do in the proof of Theorem 6. Specifically, we define $R_1 = \cdots = R_{m^*} = 0$. The remaining values R_i for $i \geq m^* + 1$, are constructed by using the supporting lemma (Lemma 9). Specifically, by setting $k := m - m^*$ and $a_i := \widetilde{Q}_{m^*+i}$ for every $i \in [m - m^*]$, we have a vector $A = (a_1, \ldots, a_k)$ satisfying $\sum_{i \in [k]} a_i = \sum_{i=m^*+1}^{m} \widetilde{Q}_i = N$. Then, we apply Lemma 9 to this vector A and obtain a vector $B = (b_1, \ldots, b_k) \in (\mathbb{Z}_{\geq 0})^k$, from which we define $R_{m^*+i} := b_i$ for every $i \in [k] = [m - m^*]$. Note that the first property guaranted by Lemma 9 implies $\sum_{i \in [k]} b_i = \sum_{i=m^*+1}^{m} R_i = N$, and the second property of the lemma guarantees that we have $|d_i| \leq 1$ for all $i \in [m - m^*]$, where $d_i := b_i - a_i = R_{m^*+i} - \widetilde{Q}_{m^*+i}$ for each $i \in [m - m^*]$.

So far, we have defined the vector $(R_1, \ldots, R_m) \in (\mathbb{Z}_{\geq 0})^m$ that satisfies $\sum_{i \in [m]} R_i = \sum_{i=m^*+1}^{m} R_i = N$. Hence, it remains to show $\max_{i \in [m]} \frac{R_i}{Q_i} \leq (1 + \sqrt{\frac{m}{N}})^2$. To this end, we use the following lemma as an intermediate step.

Lemma 13. *For every* $i \in [m]$, *we have*

$$\frac{R_i}{Q_i} \leq \frac{N}{N-S} + \frac{1}{Q_{m^*+1}}. \tag{17}$$

Proof of Lemma 13. For $i \in [m^*]$, we have $\frac{R_i}{Q_i} = 0$ due to $R_i = 0$, and thus Eq. (17) is trivially satisfied.

For showing the remaining case, fix any $i \in \{m^* + 1, \ldots, m\}$. Recall that $|R_i - \widetilde{Q}_i| \leq 1$ holds due to the second property of the vector obtained from Lemma 9, and thus we have $R_i \leq \widetilde{Q}_i + 1$. Dividing both sides of this inequality by $Q_i > 0$, we have

$$\frac{R_i}{Q_i} \leq \frac{\widetilde{Q}_i}{Q_i} + \frac{1}{Q_i} \overset{(*)}{=} \frac{N}{N-S} + \frac{1}{Q_i} \overset{(\dagger)}{\leq} \frac{N}{N-S} + \frac{1}{Q_{m^*+1}},$$

where the equality $(*)$ uses the definition of $\widetilde{Q}_i$ for $i \in \{m^* + 1, \ldots, m\}$, and the inequality $(\dagger)$ uses $Q_{m^*+1} \leq Q_i$ for all $i \in \{m^* + 1, \ldots, m\}$, which is due to the "ordered" condition (Eq. (13)). The above shows that Eq. (17) is satisfied for $i \in \{m^* + 1, \ldots, m\}$ as well. $\square$ (**Lemma** 13)

Now, combining Lemmas 12 and 13, we obtain

$$\max_{i \in [m]} \frac{R_i}{Q_i} \le \frac{N}{N-S} + \frac{m}{S^*} \overset{(*)}{\le} \frac{N}{N-S^*} + \frac{m}{S^*} \overset{(\dagger)}{=} \left(1 + \sqrt{\frac{m}{N}}\right)^2,$$

where the inequality (*) is due to $S \le S^*$, and the equality (†) is just a direct calculation. (As mentioned earlier, S^* is the value minimizing the function $f(x) = \frac{N}{N-x} + \frac{m}{x}$ in the domain $0 < x < N$ such that we have $f(S^*) = (1 + \sqrt{\frac{m}{N}})^2$.) This completes the proof of the theorem.   □ (**Theorem 7**)

Acknowledgement. The authors would like to thank the anonymous reviewers of PKC 2019 for their helpful comments.

A   Proof of Lemma 9

Let $k \in \mathbb{N}$ and $A = (a_1, \ldots, a_k) \in (\mathbb{R}_{\ge 0})^k$ such that $\sum_{i \in [k]} a_i \in \mathbb{N}$. For each $i \in [k]$, let $\delta_i := \lceil a_i \rceil - a_i$. Also, define

$$\Delta := \sum_{i \in [k]} \delta_i = \sum_{i \in [k]} \lceil a_i \rceil - \sum_{i \in [k]} a_i.$$

Note that since $\sum_{i \in [k]} a_i \in \mathbb{N}$ and $\delta_i \in [0, 1)$ for every $i \in [k]$, the definition of Δ implies $\Delta \in \mathbb{Z}_{\ge 0}$ and $\Delta < k$. Furthermore, let $\mathcal{S}_{\mathrm{up}}$ and $\mathcal{S}_{\mathrm{low}}$ be subsets of $[k]$ satisfying the following four conditions:

- (1) $\mathcal{S}_{\mathrm{up}} \cup \mathcal{S}_{\mathrm{low}} = [k]$
- (2) $\mathcal{S}_{\mathrm{up}} \cap \mathcal{S}_{\mathrm{low}} = \emptyset$
- (3) $|\mathcal{S}_{\mathrm{up}}| = \Delta$
- (4) $\max\{\delta_i | i \in \mathcal{S}_{\mathrm{low}}\} \le \min\{\delta_i | i \in \mathcal{S}_{\mathrm{up}}\}$.

Using them, define the vector $B = (b_1, \ldots, b_k)$ such that for every $i \in [k]$,

$$b_i := \begin{cases} \lceil a_i \rceil & \text{if } i \in \mathcal{S}_{\mathrm{low}} \\ \lceil a_i \rceil - 1 & \text{if } i \in \mathcal{S}_{\mathrm{up}} \end{cases}.$$

By definition, every b_i is an integer. Since $a_i \in \mathbb{R}_{\ge 0}$ for every $i \in [k]$, we have $b_i \in \mathbb{Z}_{\ge 0}$ for every $i \in \mathcal{S}_{\mathrm{low}}$. Note also that by the definitions of Δ and $\mathcal{S}_{\mathrm{up}}$, we have $|\{i \in [k] | \delta_i > 0\}| \ge \Delta = |\mathcal{S}_{\mathrm{up}}|$, and thus $a_i > 0$ holds for every $i \in \mathcal{S}_{\mathrm{up}}$, which implies $b_i = \lceil a_i \rceil - 1 \ge 0$ for every $i \in \mathcal{S}_{\mathrm{up}}$. Hence, we have $B = (b_1, \ldots, b_k) \in (\mathbb{Z}_{\ge 0})^k$.

In the following we confirm that the vector B defined above satisfies both of the properties. Regarding the first property, we have

$$\sum_{i \in [k]} b_i = \sum_{i \in \mathcal{S}_{\mathrm{low}}} \lceil a_i \rceil + \sum_{i \in \mathcal{S}_{\mathrm{up}}} (\lceil a_i \rceil - 1)$$

$$\overset{(*)}{=} \sum_{i \in [k]} \lceil a_i \rceil - \Delta = \sum_{i \in [k]} (a_i + \delta_i) - \sum_{i \in [k]} \delta_i = \sum_{i \in [k]} a_i,$$

where the equality (*) uses $|\mathcal{S}_{\mathrm{up}}| = \Delta$. Hence, B satisfies the first property.

It remains to show that B satisfies the second property. For each $i \in [k]$, let

$$d_i := b_i - a_i = \begin{cases} \delta_i & \text{if } i \in \mathcal{S}_{\mathrm{low}} \\ \delta_i - 1 & \text{if } i \in \mathcal{S}_{\mathrm{up}} \end{cases}.$$

Recall that $\delta_i \in [0,1)$ holds for every $i \in [k]$. Thus, we have $|d_i| \leq 1$ for all $i \in [k]$. Furthermore, for every $(i,j) \in [k]^2$, we have

$$|d_i - d_j| = \begin{cases} |\delta_i - \delta_j| & \text{if } (i,j) \in (\mathcal{S}_{\mathrm{low}})^2 \text{ or } (i,j) \in (\mathcal{S}_{\mathrm{up}})^2 \\ |1 - (\delta_j - \delta_i)| & \text{if } (i,j) \in \mathcal{S}_{\mathrm{low}} \times \mathcal{S}_{\mathrm{up}} \\ |\delta_i - \delta_j - 1| & \text{if } (i,j) \in \mathcal{S}_{\mathrm{up}} \times \mathcal{S}_{\mathrm{low}} \end{cases}.$$

From the above, it is immediate that $|d_i - d_j| \leq 1$ holds for the cases $(i,j) \in (\mathcal{S}_{\mathrm{low}})^2$ and $(i,j) \in (\mathcal{S}_{\mathrm{up}})^2$. Also, for the case $(i,j) \in \mathcal{S}_{\mathrm{low}} \times \mathcal{S}_{\mathrm{up}}$, we have $\delta_i \leq \delta_j$ due to the condition (4) of $\mathcal{S}_{\mathrm{low}}$ and $\mathcal{S}_{\mathrm{up}}$, and thus we have $|1 - (\delta_j - \delta_i)| \leq 1$. Similarly, for the case $(i,j) \in \mathcal{S}_{\mathrm{up}} \times \mathcal{S}_{\mathrm{low}}$, we have $\delta_i \geq \delta_j$, and thus we have $|\delta_i - \delta_j - 1| \leq 1$. Hence, we have $|d_i - d_j| \leq 1$ for any pair $(i,j) \in [k]^2$. This shows that the vector B satisfies the second property as well.   □ (**Lemma 9**)

B   Proof of Lemma 11

Fix arbitrarily a number $k \in \mathbb{N}$ and a vector $(a_1, \ldots, a_n) \in \mathbb{R}^k$ satisfying $|a_i - a_j| \leq 1$ for all $i, j \in [k]$, and let $\alpha := \sum_{i \in [k]} a_i$. We will show that $\sum_{i \in [k]} a_i^2 \leq \frac{\alpha^2}{k} + \frac{k}{4}$ holds, which proves the lemma.

Let $a_{\min} := \min\{a_i\}_{i \in [k]}$, and $\delta_i := a_i - a_{\min}$ for each $i \in [k]$. Note that due to the given condition of the vector $(a_1, \ldots, a_k)$, $\delta_i \in [0,1]$ holds for all $i \in [k]$. We also have

$$\alpha = \sum_{i \in [k]} a_i = \sum_{i \in [k]} \left(a_{\min} + \delta_i \right) = k a_{\min} + \sum_{i \in [k]} \delta_i$$

$$\Longleftrightarrow \quad \sum_{i \in [k]} \delta_i = \alpha - k a_{\min}. \tag{18}$$

Furthermore, for each $i \in [k]$, we have

$$a_i^2 = (a_{\min} + \delta_i)^2 = a_{\min}^2 + 2 a_{\min} \delta_i + \delta_i^2$$
$$\leq a_{\min}^2 + (2 a_{\min} + 1) \cdot \delta_i, \tag{19}$$

where the inequality uses $\delta_i^2 \leq \delta_i$, which is due to $\delta_i \in [0,1]$.

Now, consider the sum of squares $\sum_{i \in [k]} a_i^2$. We have

$$\sum_{i \in [k]} a_i^2 \overset{(*)}{\leq} \sum_{i \in [k]} \left(a_{\min}^2 + (2a_{\min} + 1) \cdot \delta_i \right)$$

$$= ka_{\min}^2 + (2a_{\min} + 1) \cdot \sum_{i \in [k]} \delta_i$$

$$\overset{(\dagger)}{=} ka_{\min}^2 + (2a_{\min} + 1) \cdot (\alpha - ka_{\min})$$

$$= -k \left(a_{\min} - \left(\frac{\alpha}{k} - \frac{1}{2} \right) \right)^2 + \frac{\alpha^2}{k} + \frac{k}{4}$$

$$\leq \frac{\alpha^2}{k} + \frac{k}{4},$$

where the inequality (*) uses Eq. (19), and the equality (†) uses Eq. (18).

$$\square \ (\textbf{Lemma } 11)$$

References

1. Alkim, E., Ducas, L., Pöppelmann, T., Schwabe, P.: Post-quantum key exchange - a new hope. In: Proceedings of USENIX Security 2016, pp. 327–343. USENIX Association (2016)
2. Applebaum, B., Cash, D., Peikert, C., Sahai, A.: Fast cryptographic primitives and circular-secure encryption based on hard learning problems. In: Halevi, S. (ed.) CRYPTO 2009. LNCS, vol. 5677, pp. 595–618. Springer, Heidelberg (2009). https://doi.org/10.1007/978-3-642-03356-8_35
3. Bai, S., Langlois, A., Lepoint, T., Stehlé, D., Steinfeld, R.: Improved security proofs in lattice-based cryptography: using the Rényi divergence rather than the statistical distance. In: Iwata, T., Cheon, J.H. (eds.) ASIACRYPT 2015, Part I. LNCS, vol. 9452, pp. 3–24. Springer, Heidelberg (2015). https://doi.org/10.1007/978-3-662-48797-6_1
4. Barak, B., et al.: Leftover hash lemma, revisited. In: Rogaway, P. (ed.) CRYPTO 2011. LNCS, vol. 6841, pp. 1–20. Springer, Heidelberg (2011). https://doi.org/10.1007/978-3-642-22792-9_1
5. Barak, B., Shaltiel, R., Tromer, E.: True random number generators secure in a changing environment. In: Walter, C.D., Koç, Ç.K., Paar, C. (eds.) CHES 2003. LNCS, vol. 2779, pp. 166–180. Springer, Heidelberg (2003). https://doi.org/10.1007/978-3-540-45238-6_14
6. Bogdanov, A., Guo, S., Masny, D., Richelson, S., Rosen, A.: On the hardness of learning with rounding over small modulus. In: Kushilevitz, E., Malkin, T. (eds.) TCC 2016, Part I. LNCS, vol. 9562, pp. 209–224. Springer, Heidelberg (2016). https://doi.org/10.1007/978-3-662-49096-9_9
7. Chaudhuri, K., Sarwate, A.D., Sinha, K.: Near-optimal differentially private principal components. In: Proceedings of NIPS 2012, pp. 998–1006 (2012)
8. Dodis, Y., Ostrovsky, R., Reyzin, L., Smith, A.: Fuzzy extractors: how to generate strong keys from biometrics and other noisy data. SIAM J. Comput. 38(1), 97–139 (2008)
9. Dodis, Y., Ristenpart, T., Vadhan, S.: Randomness condensers for efficiently samplable, seed-dependent sources. In: Cramer, R. (ed.) TCC 2012. LNCS, vol. 7194, pp. 618–635. Springer, Heidelberg (2012). https://doi.org/10.1007/978-3-642-28914-9_35

10. Dodis, Y., Yao, Y.: Privacy with imperfect randomness. In: Gennaro, R., Robshaw, M. (eds.) CRYPTO 2015, Part II. LNCS, vol. 9216, pp. 463–482. Springer, Heidelberg (2015). https://doi.org/10.1007/978-3-662-48000-7_23

11. Dodis, Y., Yu, Y.: Overcoming weak expectations. In: Sahai, A. (ed.) TCC 2013. LNCS, vol. 7785, pp. 1–22. Springer, Heidelberg (2013). https://doi.org/10.1007/978-3-642-36594-2_1

12. Dwork, C.: Differential privacy. In: Bugliesi, M., Preneel, B., Sassone, V., Wegener, I. (eds.) ICALP 2006, Part II. LNCS, vol. 4052, pp. 1–12. Springer, Heidelberg (2006). https://doi.org/10.1007/11787006_1

13. Dwork, C., Kenthapadi, K., McSherry, F., Mironov, I., Naor, M.: Our data, ourselves: privacy via distributed noise generation. In: Vaudenay, S. (ed.) EUROCRYPT 2006. LNCS, vol. 4004, pp. 486–503. Springer, Heidelberg (2006). https://doi.org/10.1007/11761679_29

14. Dwork, C., McSherry, F., Nissim, K., Smith, A.: Calibrating noise to sensitivity in private data analysis. In: Halevi, S., Rabin, T. (eds.) TCC 2006. LNCS, vol. 3876, pp. 265–284. Springer, Heidelberg (2006). https://doi.org/10.1007/11681878_14

15. Gentry, C., Halevi, S.: Implementing Gentry's fully-homomorphic encryption scheme. In: Paterson, K.G. (ed.) EUROCRYPT 2011. LNCS, vol. 6632, pp. 129–148. Springer, Heidelberg (2011). https://doi.org/10.1007/978-3-642-20465-4_9

16. Gentry, C., Peikert, C., Vaikuntanathan, V.: Trapdoors for hard lattices and new cryptographic constructions. In: Proceedings of STOC 2008, pp. 197–206. ACM (2008)

17. Micciancio, D., Walter, M.: Gaussian sampling over the integers: efficient, generic, constant-time. In: Katz, J., Shacham, H. (eds.) CRYPTO 2017, Part II. LNCS, vol. 10402, pp. 455–485. Springer, Cham (2017). https://doi.org/10.1007/978-3-319-63715-0_16

18. Micciancio, D., Walter, M.: On the bit security of cryptographic primitives. In: Nielsen, J.B., Rijmen, V. (eds.) EUROCRYPT 2018, Part I. LNCS, vol. 10820, pp. 3–28. Springer, Cham (2018). https://doi.org/10.1007/978-3-319-78381-9_1

19. Prest, T.: Sharper bounds in lattice-based cryptography using the Rényi divergence. In: Takagi, T., Peyrin, T. (eds.) ASIACRYPT 2017, Part I. LNCS, vol. 10624, pp. 347–374. Springer, Cham (2017). https://doi.org/10.1007/978-3-319-70694-8_13

20. Regev, O.: On lattices, learning with errors, random linear codes, and cryptography. In: Proceedings of STOC 2005, pp. 84–93. ACM (2005)

21. Rényi, A.: On measures of entropy and information. In: Proceedings of Fourth Berkeley Symposium on Mathematical Statistics and Probability, vol. 1, pp. 547–561. University of California Press (1961)

22. Takashima, K., Takayasu, A.: Tighter security for efficient lattice cryptography via the Rényi divergence of optimized orders. In: Au, M.-H., Miyaji, A. (eds.) ProvSec 2015. LNCS, vol. 9451, pp. 412–431. Springer, Cham (2015). https://doi.org/10.1007/978-3-319-26059-4_23

23. van Erven, E., Harremoës, P.: Rényi divergence and Kullback-Leibler divergence. IEEE Trans. Inf. Theory **60**(7), 3797–3820 (2014)

24. Yao, Y., Li, Z.: Overcoming weak expectations via the Rényi entropy and the expanded computational entropy. In: Padró, C. (ed.) ICITS 2013. LNCS, vol. 8317, pp. 162–178. Springer, Cham (2014). https://doi.org/10.1007/978-3-319-04268-8_10

On Tightly Secure Primitives
in the Multi-instance Setting

Dennis Hofheinz[1]([⊠]) and Ngoc Khanh Nguyen[2]

[1] Karlsruhe Institute of Technology, Karlsruhe, Germany
dennis.hofheinz@kit.edu
[2] IBM Research Zurich, Rüschlikon, Switzerland

Abstract. We initiate the study of *general* tight reductions in cryptography. There already exist a variety of works that offer tight reductions for a number of cryptographic tasks, ranging from encryption and signature schemes to proof systems. However, our work is the first to provide a universal definition of a tight reduction (for arbitrary primitives), along with several observations and results concerning primitives for which tight reductions have not been known.

Technically, we start from the general notion of reductions due to Reingold, Trevisan, and Vadhan (TCC 2004), and equip it with a quantification of the respective reduction loss, and a canonical multi-instance extension to primitives. We then revisit several standard reductions whose tight security has not yet been considered. For instance, we revisit a generic construction of signature schemes from one-way functions, and show how to tighten the corresponding reduction by assuming collision-resistance from the used one-way function. We also obtain tightly secure pseudorandom generators (by using suitable rerandomisable hard-core predicates), and tightly secure lossy trapdoor functions.

1 Introduction

Motivation. To argue for the security of a cryptographic scheme, we usually employ a security reduction (or simply reduction). A reduction formalises that the only way to break the scheme is to solve an underlying computational problem (such as factoring a large integer). More specifically, a reduction turns any adversary A on the scheme into a problem solver B. Hence, if the problem is hard to solve, then the scheme must be secure.

Most existing reductions are however *loose*, in the sense that B's success is much lower (or its runtime much higher) than that of A. For instance, for most existing encryption schemes, the best known reduction in a multi-user, multiciphertext scenario yields Bs whose success degrades linearly in the number of users and/or ciphertexts. Hence, in a large-scale setting, this reduction loss can easily be in the order of, say, 2^{30}.

N. K. Nguyen—This work was carried out when the author was doing an internship at the KIT.

D. Lin and K. Sako (Eds.): PKC 2019, LNCS 11442, pp. 581–611, 2019.
https://doi.org/10.1007/978-3-030-17253-4_20

In contrast, a *tight* reduction yields problem solvers B which have the same success (and running time) as A.[1] A loose reduction gives quantitatively lower guarantees than a tight one. For instance, suppose one would like to give a key length recommendation for a scheme based on the currently best attacks on the underlying computational problem. In this case, loose reductions lead to larger key length recommendations, and thus to a (perhaps substantially) less efficient scheme.

In this work, we are interested in tight reductions, in particular in a setting in which the scheme or primitive is used multiple times.

State of the Art. The tightness of reductions (in particular for schemes in a multi-instance scenario) has first been considered by Bellare, Boldyreva, and Micali [6]. Since their work, a variety of tightly secure constructions for concrete cryptographic building blocks (such as encryption [1,17,18,26,27,34,35], identity-based encryption [3,7,11,22,28], digital signatures [2,25,34,35], or zero-knowledge proofs [17,27]) have been proposed.

On the other hand, the notion of a reduction has been formalised early on in cryptography (e.g., in the context of black-box separations such as [31,43, 45]).[2] We note that these works were mostly interested in the (non-)existence of reductions for certain types of schemes, and do not take into account reduction loss. Hence, currently there is no *general* (i.e., formal but primitive-independent) definition of a tight reduction.

Our Contribution. We provide the first general definition of a tight reduction, and revisit several classical reductions (with an emphasis on their tightness). We obtain the following results:

- We obtain a new (and tighter) security reduction for the classical construction of signatures from one-way functions [23,32,44].
- We also obtain tightly secure pseudorandom generators by instantiating the classical construction of Blum and Micali [8] with a suitable (i.e., rerandomisable) hard-core predicate.
- Finally, we show that the DDH-based lossy trapdoor functions of Peikert and Waters [42] are tightly secure in a multi-instance scenario.

In the following, we will outline our definition and results.

Our New Definition. Our definition of tight security adapts the general definition of reductions due to Reingold, Trevisan, and Vadhan [43]. First, we will consider the tightness of a reduction as an additional property of that reduction. Additionally, we will formalise the "multi-instance version" of a given primitive (taking into account a suitably modified multi-instance security game and potential global parameters).

---

[1] Of course, there are other interesting properties (such as memory usage [4]) of a given adversary A one would want a reduction to preserve.

[2] We also remark that other formalisations of cryptographic *assumptions* exist, e.g., [14,38].

Perhaps most interestingly, this modification allows to define the notion of a "tightly extensible primitive". Intuitively, a primitive X is tightly extensible relative to another primitive Y if the multi-instance version of X can be tightly reduced to Y. For instance, it is easy to see that one-way functions are tightly extensible relative to collision-resistant hash functions (CRHFs). In fact, a simple extension of an argument of Damgård [12] shows that any compressing CRHF h already is a one-way function in the multi-instance setting: suppose an algorithm A successfully finds a preimage x_i' for one of potentially many given images $h(x_i)$. Since h is compressing, we have $x_i' \neq x_i$ with probability at least $1/2$, so that (x_i, x_i') forms a collision. This holds even if we require "adaptive" one-wayness[3], in the sense that A may get selected preimages x_i upon request (and then loses the inversion game in those instances of course).

Our Results. We now outline the results mentioned above.

First, we revisit the classical construction of signatures from one-way functions from [23,32,44]. This construction uses the one-time signature scheme of Lamport [33], which in turn uses many (i.e., $L = O(\lambda)$, where λ is the security parameter) instances of a given one-way function f. Each forged (one-time) signature implies an inversion of one instance of f. The problem here is that it is not clear a priori *which* instance is inverted. Hence, the corresponding security reduction for the one-time signature scheme (as formalized, e.g., in [20]) loses a factor of L, which of course is inherited by the security reduction of the overall signature scheme.

This loss of L can essentially be avoided if we assume that f is collision-resistant. Concretely, recall our observation above that f (when viewed as an adaptive one-way function) is tightly extensible relative to itself (when viewed as a CRHF). In particular, an adversary that inverts one out of many f-instances can be turned into a collision finder for f with a reduction loss of only 2. Hence, any forged one-time signature can be converted into an f-collision with probability of at least $1/2$, and we can save a factor of $L/2$ in the overall reduction.

Next, we consider pseudorandom generators (PRGs) G that are tightly extensible (relative to themselves). In other words, we are looking for a G such that the pseudorandomness of many $G(x_i)$ instances (for independently chosen seeds x_i) can be tightly reduced to the pseudorandomness of a single $G(x)$. This property leads to tighter reductions whenever G is used multiple times (e.g., in one or many instances of a larger scheme).

Note that an almost trivial solution to this problem can be found under the DDH assumption (assuming groups with dense representations, such that random group elements are random bitstrings). Namely, recall that the DDH assumption states that for a generator g and random exponents a, b, c, the tuple (g^a, g^b, g^{ab}) is computationally indistinguishable from (g^a, g^b, g^c). Now the DDH assumption is known to be rerandomisable (e.g., [6, Lemma 1]), in the sense a distinguisher between many $(g^{a_i}, g^{b_i}, g^{a_i b_i})$ and many $(g^{a_i}, g^{b_i}, g^{c_i})$ can be

---

[3] This notion is not related to the notion of adaptive one-way functions from [40] in which an adversary gets access to a full inversion oracle for the function.

converted into a DDH distinguisher, with (almost) no reduction loss. Hence, defining $G(a, b) = g^a || g^b || g^{ab}$ yields a tightly extensible PRG.

Here, however, we are interested in constructions from (potentially) weaker assumptions. To this end, we revisit the PRG of Blum and Micali [8]. This PRG assumes a one-way permutation f with a hard-core predicate b, and defines $G(x) = f(x) || b(x)$.[4] We set $f(x) = g^x$ (which also means we require a group with dense representations), and $b(x)$ to be the Legendre symbol $\left(\frac{x}{p}\right)$ of x modulo the group order p.[5] Under a suitable computational assumption (that appears to lie in between the CDH and DDH assumptions), b is indeed a hard-core predicate of f. Most importantly, and unlike with other hard-core predicates, f and b are rerandomisable: given $f(x)$ and $b(x)$, it is easy to compute $f(ax)$ and $b(ax)$ (for a known random a). Hence, by rerandomising PRG images, we can show the tight extensibility of this G.[6]

Finally, we consider the tight extensibility of lossy trapdoor functions (LTDFs) relative to themselves. Our motivation to consider LTDFs is that they form an abstract tool which is already known to imply tightly (IND-CPA-)secure encryption in the single-user (but multi-ciphertext) setting [42]. A tightly extensible LTDF can be additionally useful in settings with many instances (e.g., users). Here, our main result is that the DDH-based LTDF construction of Peikert and Waters [42] is already tightly extensible. The corresponding argument is somewhat technical, but relies on the rerandomisability of the DDH assumption (as outlined already above).

We note that this last result does not yield interesting new tightly secure encryption schemes. In fact, already the ElGamal scheme is tightly IND-CPA-secure under the DDH assumption [6]. Rather, we view our last result as conceptual: it shows that an abstract building block (that was already known to enable "partially tight" reductions) is tightly secure even in a multi-instance setting.

There are areas of cryptography where we have not looked at applying tight extensibility. For example, a natural question would be if we can build tightly extensible symmetric encryption schemes or even more complicated protocols (e.g. zero-knowledge). More importantly, it is an open question whether this notion can be used in constructing more efficient and more secure primitives which could not be shown using current state-of-the-art methods.

2   Preliminaries

In this section we review standard notation and cryptographic definitions we use in later sections. We also provide relevant background related to formal notion of black-box reductions.

---

[4] For simplicity, we only consider a PRG that stretches its seed x by one bit.

[5] Slightly simplifying, we ignore the unlikely case $x = 0$ and treat $\left(\frac{x}{p}\right)$ as a bit.

[6] We note that the Legendre symbol has already been considered as a hard-core predicate by Damgård [13], although, to the best of our knowledge, its rerandomisability has not been investigated before.

2.1   Notation

Let $\mathbb{N}$ be the set of natural numbers and $\mathbb{Z}_n$ be the set of integers modulo n. We denote the security parameter by $\lambda \in \mathbb{N}$ and assume that it is implicitly given to all algorithms in the unary representation 1^λ, unless stated otherwise. An algorithm here is defined as a stateless Turing machine. Algorithms are randomised and PPT means "probabilistic polynomial time" in the (unary) security parameter λ. For a randomised algorithm $\mathcal{A}$, we denote $\mathbf{T}(\mathcal{A})$ for the worst-case runtime of $\mathcal{A}$, parametrized over λ. Also, we describe $(y_1, \dots) \leftarrow_\$ \mathcal{A}(1^\lambda, x_1, \dots; r)$ as an event when $\mathcal{A}$ gets $(1^\lambda, x_1, \dots)$ as input, uses fresh random coins r and outputs $(y_1, \dots)$. If $\mathcal{A}$ is determininstic then we simply write $(y_1, \dots) \leftarrow \mathcal{A}(1^\lambda, x_1, \dots)$. Let us write $\mathcal{A}^B$ to denote that $\mathcal{A}$ has black-box access to algorithm B, meaning it sees only its input-output behaviour. We define $\mathsf{queries}(\mathcal{A}^B, B)$ to be the worst-case number of messages/queries sent by B to $\mathcal{A}$ (parametrized by λ). On the other hand, $\mathcal{A}^{(\cdot)}$ means that $\mathcal{A}$ expects a black-box access to some other algorithm.

For a finite set S, we denote its cardinality by $|S|$ and write $s \leftarrow_\$ S$ meaning that we choose an element s from S uniformly at random. For a function $f : A \to B$ and $C \subset A$, we define $f|_C : C \to B$ as $f|_C(x) = f(x)$. We write $\mathsf{poly}(\lambda)$ to denote the set of polynomials in λ. A function $v : \mathbb{N} \to \mathbb{R}^{\geq 0}$ is negligible if for any $c \in \mathbb{N}$, $\lim_{\lambda \to \infty} v(\lambda)\lambda^c = 0$. We let $\mathsf{negl}(\lambda)$ denote an unspecified negligible function in λ. Throughout the paper, $\perp$ denotes an error symbol.

Denote $\mathcal{X} = \{X_\lambda\}_{\lambda \in \mathbb{N}}, \mathcal{Y} = \{Y_\lambda\}_{\lambda \in \mathbb{N}}$ as ensembles of random variables over some countable set S indexed by λ. Then, $\mathcal{X}$ and $\mathcal{Y}$ are statistically indistinguishable $(\mathcal{X} \overset{s}{\approx} \mathcal{Y})$ if $\Delta(X_\lambda, Y_\lambda) = \frac{1}{2}\sum_{s \in S} |\Pr[X = s] - \Pr[Y = s]| = \mathsf{negl}(\lambda)$. Moreover, $\mathcal{X}$ and $\mathcal{Y}$ are computationally indistinguishable $(\mathcal{X} \overset{c}{\approx} \mathcal{Y})$ if for every PPT algorithm $\mathcal{A}$:

$$| \Pr[1 \leftarrow_\$ \mathcal{A}(1^\lambda, X_\lambda)] - \Pr[1 \leftarrow_\$ \mathcal{A}(1^\lambda, Y_\lambda)]| = \mathsf{negl}(\lambda).$$

2.2   Cryptographic Primitives

ONE-WAY FUNCTIONS. Intuitively, we say that a function is one-way (OWF) if it is easy to compute but hard to invert. Using our notation, we formalise it as follows:

Definition 1. *A function $f : \{0,1\}^* \to \{0,1\}^*$ is one-way if:*

- *There exists a deterministic polynomial-time algorithm f so that*

$$\forall \lambda \in \mathbb{N}, \Pr[f(x) \leftarrow \mathsf{f}(1^\lambda, x) : x \leftarrow_\$ \{0,1\}^\lambda] = 1.$$

- *For every PPT algorithm $\mathcal{A}$,*

$$\Pr[f(y) = f(x) : x \leftarrow_\$ \{0,1\}^\lambda, y \leftarrow_\$ \mathcal{A}(1^\lambda, f(x))] = negl(\lambda).$$

Most of the time, we do not deal with a single one-way function but rather with a collection of one-way functions. That is, we consider a set $\mathcal{F} = \{f\}$ of functions f that each have a finite domain, but may be parameterized over the security parameter (and other public parameters such as a fixed group). In that case, we choose f at random for the currently given security parameter (and potentially other parameters), and sample x uniformly at random from f's domain.

In the case of a family $\mathcal{F}$ of parameterized one-way functions f (with finite domain $\mathcal{D}_f$), we say that $\mathcal{F}$ is a family of one-way permutations if f is bijective and $f(\mathcal{D}_f) = \mathcal{D}_f$.

We also recall the notion of a hard-core predicate introduced by Goldreich et al. [21].

Definition 2. *Let* $b : \{0,1\}^* \to \{0,1\}$ *be a function and* $u \leftarrow_\$ \{0,1\}$. *Then,* b *is a hardcore-bit predicate for function* $f : \{0,1\}^* \to \{0,1\}^*$ *if*

$$(f(x), b(x)) \stackrel{c}{\approx} (f(x), u)$$

Goldreich et al. provide in [21] a construction of a one-way function with hard-core predicate from any given one-way function.

LOSSY TRAPDOOR FUNCTIONS. We say that a function f is a trapdoor function if it is easy to compute $f(x)$ and also easy to invert if we know some "special information" (called trapdoor) but hard to invert without trapdoor. The notion of a lossy trapdoor function was introduced by Peikert et al. [41]. A tuple of PPT algorithms $(S_{inj}, S_{loss}, F, F^{-1})$ is called a collection of $(n, k)-$lossy trapdoor functions (LTDF) if:

- S_{inj} outputs (s, t) where s is a function index and t its trapdoor, $F(s, \cdot)$ computes a deterministic injective function f over the domain $\{0,1\}^n$, and $F^{-1}(t, \cdot)$ computes f^{-1},
- S_{loss} outputs $(s, \perp)$ and $F(s, \cdot)$ computes a deterministic function f over the domain $\{0,1\}^n$ whose image has size at most 2^{n-k},
- For $(s_1, t_1) \leftarrow_\$ S_{inj}$ and $(s_2, \perp) \leftarrow_\$ S_{loss}$,

$$s_1 \stackrel{c}{\approx} s_2.$$

Peikert et al. also define all-but-one trapdoor functions in order to construct an IND-CCA encryption scheme. In this paper we concentrate more on LTDFs but our results can be easily generalised to the second notion.

PSEUDORANDOM GENERATORS. A function $G : \{0,1\}^k \to \{0,1\}^l$, where $k < l$, is a pseudorandom generator (PRG) if given random x from $\{0,1\}^k$, no PPT adversary can distinguish $G(x)$ and a random element from $\{0,1\}^l$.

Definition 3. *Let* $G : \{0,1\}^k \to \{0,1\}^l$ *be a function where* $k < l$, *and let* $x \leftarrow_\$ \{0,1\}^k$ *and* $u \leftarrow_\$ \{0,1\}^l$ *be uniformly chosen. Then,* G *is a pseudorandom generator if*

$$G(x) \stackrel{c}{\approx} u.$$

Håstad et al. [24] show that one can construct a pseudorandom generator from any one-way function. Unfortunately, their security reduction has a large loss, i.e., is far from tight. Since then, more efficient constructions of PRGs from OWFs with much tighter reductions have been discovered [29] but they still suffer from a large reduction loss. On the other hand, Blum and Micali [8] provide a construction of a PRG from a one-way permutation which loses a factor of l.

HASHING. A family of functions $\mathcal{H} = \{h_i : A \to B\}$ is universal if for every distinct $x, x' \in A, \Pr_{h \leftarrow_{\$} \mathcal{H}}[h(x) = h(x')] = 1/|B|$. Moreover, we say that $\mathcal{H}$ is pairwise independent if, for every distinct $x, x' \in A$ and every $y, y' \in B$, $\Pr_{h \leftarrow_{\$} \mathcal{H}}[h(x) = y \land h(x') = y'] = 1/|B|^2$.

A hash function $H : \{0,1\}^k \to \{0,1\}^l$, where $k > l$, is collision resistant if for any PPT adversary $\mathcal{A}$, $\Pr[(x,y) \leftarrow_{\$} \mathcal{A}(1^\lambda, h) : h(x) = h(y)] = \mathsf{negl}(\lambda)$. Similarly we can define a collection of collision-resistant hash functions.

2.3 Cryptographic Assumptions

We briefly state the most common computational and decisional problems in public-key cryptography. Let G be a cyclic group (that may depend on the security parameter λ) of order p where p is a λ-bit prime. Also, let $g \in G$ be a generator of G. We denote $\langle G \rangle$ to be the description of G.

- Discrete Logarithm Problem (DLOG) - we say that the discrete logarithm problem is hard in G if for every PPT algorithm $\mathcal{A}$:

$$\Pr[x \leftarrow_{\$} \mathcal{A}(\langle G \rangle, p, g, g^x) : x \leftarrow_{\$} \mathbb{Z}_p] = \mathsf{negl}(\lambda).$$

- Computational Diffie-Hellman Problem (CDH) - we say that the computational Diffie-Hellman problem is hard in G if for every PPT algorithm $\mathcal{A}$:

$$\Pr[g^{xy} \leftarrow_{\$} \mathcal{A}(\langle G \rangle, p, g, g^x, g^y) : x, y \leftarrow_{\$} \mathbb{Z}_p] = \mathsf{negl}(\lambda).$$

- Decisional Diffie-Hellman Problem (DDH) - we say that the decisional Diffie-Hellman problem is hard in G if for $z \leftarrow_{\$} \mathbb{Z}_p$:

$$(\langle G \rangle, p, g, g^x, g^y, g^{xy}) \stackrel{c}{\approx} (\langle G \rangle, p, g, g^x, g^y, g^z).$$

2.4 Public Key Schemes

PUBLIC-KEY ENCRYPTION. A public-key encryption scheme for a given security parameter λ is a triple of PPT algorithms (Gen; Enc; Dec) such that:

- $(pk, sk) \leftarrow_{\$} \mathsf{Gen}(1^\lambda)$ is the key generation algorithm which takes a security parameter λ and outputs a pair (pk, sk) where pk and sk are called public and secret keys respectively,
- $c \leftarrow_{\$} \mathsf{Enc}(pk, m)$ is the encryption algorithm which takes a public key pk, a message m and returns a ciphertext c,

- $m \leftarrow \mathsf{Dec}(sk, c)$ is the decryption algorithm which takes a secret key sk, ciphertext c and returns a message m or $\perp$ if given ciphertext is invalid.

A public-key encryption must satisfy the correctness condition, meaning that for every message m and every security parameter λ, if $(pk, sk) \leftarrow_\$ \mathsf{Gen}(1^\lambda)$ then $\mathsf{Dec}(sk, \mathsf{Enc}(pk, m)) = m$.

We recall basic notions of security for public-key encryption schemes. We say that an encryption scheme $\mathcal{E} = (\mathsf{Gen}; \mathsf{Enc}; \mathsf{Dec})$ is IND-CPA secure (has indistinguishable ciphertexts under chosen plaintext attack) if there exists no PPT adversary $\mathcal{A}$ which wins the following game with non-negligible probability:

1. Challenger C generates $(pk, sk) \leftarrow_\$ \mathsf{Gen}(1^\lambda)$ and sends pk to $\mathcal{A}$.
2. Adversary $\mathcal{A}$ sends messages (m_0, m_1) to C. Challenger then selects a bit b uniformly at random and returns $c \leftarrow_\$ \mathsf{Enc}(pk, m_b)$.
3. At the end, $\mathcal{A}$ sends a bit b' to the challenger. Then, $\mathcal{A}$ wins if $b = b'$ and loses otherwise.

Similarly, we define IND-CCA security (indistinguishability under chosen ciphertext attack). We say that $\mathcal{E}$ is IND-CCA secure if there exists no PPT adversary $\mathcal{A}$ which wins a similar game to the one described above (with non-negligible probability), but this time $\mathcal{A}$ also has access to decryption oracle $\mathcal{O}_{\mathsf{Dec}}$ which on input c' returns $\perp$ if $c = c'$ and $\mathsf{Dec}(sk, c')$ otherwise.

ONE-TIME SIGNATURES. A signature scheme consists of a tuple of PPT algorithms $(\mathsf{Gen}; \mathsf{Sign}; \mathsf{Ver})$ satisfying the following conditions:

- $(vk, sk) \leftarrow_\$ \mathsf{Gen}(1^\lambda)$ is the key generation algorithm, which takes a security parameter λ and outputs a pair (vk, sk) where vk and sk are called verification and signing keys respectively,
- $c \leftarrow_\$ \mathsf{Sign}(sk, m)$ is the signing algorithm which takes the signing key sk, a message m and returns a signature σ,
- $b \leftarrow \mathsf{Ver}(vk, m, \sigma)$ is the verification algorithm which takes the verification key vk, message m and signature σ and returns a bit b.

Any signature scheme must satisfy the correctness condition meaning that for every message m and every security parameter λ, if $(vk, sk) \leftarrow_\$ \mathsf{Gen}(1^\lambda)$ then $\mathsf{Ver}(vk, m, \mathsf{Sign}(sk, m)) = 1$.

We now define a security notion for signature schemes called existential unforgeability under a one-time chosen message attack (EUF-OTCMA). We say that the signature scheme $\mathcal{E} = (\mathsf{Gen}; \mathsf{Sign}; \mathsf{Ver})$ is EUF-OTCMA secure if there is no PPT adversary $\mathcal{A}$ which wins the following game with non-negligible probability:

1. Challenger C generates $(vk, sk) \leftarrow \mathsf{Gen}(1^\lambda)$ and sends vk to $\mathcal{A}$.
2. Adversary $\mathcal{A}$ sends message a m to C. Challenger then returns $\sigma = \mathsf{Sign}(sk, m)$.
3. Finally, $\mathcal{A}$ outputs a pair (m', σ') b'. Then, $\mathcal{A}$ wins if $\mathsf{Ver}(vk, m', \sigma') = 1$ and $m' \neq m$ and loses otherwise.

Strong unforgeable one-time signatures can be constructed from a one-way function as well as collision-resistant hash functions.

2.5 Fully Black-Box Reductions

We review the framework of Reingold et al. [43] on security reductions. For simplicity, we only consider fully black-box reductions against uniform adversaries. There are many formal definitions of reductions (such as [5,16,30,43]) but in this paper we focus on work by Reingold et al. [43], mainly due to its simplicity and the ease to modify their framework to suit our needs. Using their notation, primitive P is a pair $\langle F_P, R_P \rangle$ where F_P is a set of functions $f : \{0,1\}^* \to \{0,1\}^*$ and R_P is a relation over pairs (f, M) for $f \in F_P$ and machine M. One can think of F_P as implementations of primitive P and R_P as security conditions on F_P. For example, if we think of P as a one-way function, the set of implementations could be a set of one-way functions. On the other hand, R_P would be the standard one-wayness game. Depending on the application, it might be useful to define F_P such that it only corresponds to *efficient* (e.g., realizable through PPT machines) implementations.

There is a fully-BB reduction from a primitive $P = \langle F_P, R_P \rangle$ to $Q = \langle F_Q, R_Q \rangle$ if there exist PPT machines G, S such that:

- for every function $f \in F_Q$, $G^f \in F_P$,
- for every function $f \in F_Q$ and every adversary $\mathcal{A}$, $(G^f, \mathcal{A}) \in R_P \implies (f, S^{\mathcal{A}}) \in R_Q$.

As mentioned in [43], this definition of reduction does not apply to non-uniform or information-theoretic notions of security. They also define different types of reductions such as semi-black-box or relativizing reductions.

3 Notion of Tight Reduction

In this section we formalise the notion of tight reduction by adapting the framework of Reingold et al. (RTV) [43]. Roughly speaking, we represent security conditions as a security game instead of a set of relations. Thus, we could formally define what we mean by "breaking one primitive with about the same success as the other primitive" in terms of probabilities. Then, we define what a multi-instance version of a primitive is. At the end, we give a few examples of cryptographic primitives which satisfy our framework.

3.1 Primitives and Reductions

We start by stating what a primitive is and what it means for it to be secure.

Definition 4. *A primitive P is a tuple $\langle \mathbb{P}, S_P, F_P, R_P, \sigma \rangle$ where:*

- $\mathbb{P}$ *is a triple of sets (A, B, C) where $C \subset A$,*
- F_P *is a subset of $\{f : A \to B\}$,*
- S_P *is a PPT setup algorithm which sends parameters $(r_1, \ldots)$ to R_P,*
- $R_P^{(\cdot, \cdot)}$ *is a PPT security algorithm which gets parameters $(r_1, \ldots)$ from S_P.*
- $\sigma : \mathbb{N} \to \mathbb{R}$ *is a security threshold.*

We say that f is an implementation of P if $f \in F_P$.

There are three main differences between this definition and the one proposed by Reingold et al. Firstly, $\mathbb{P} = (A, B, C)$ is a triple of sets which describe the domain, co-domain and the challenge space respectively. Indeed, an implementation f is a function from A to B and the security game R_P can call f only on inputs in C (e.g. $A = \{0,1\}^*$ and $C = \{0,1\}^\lambda$). This modification enables us to characterize implementations which are defined on more abstract mathematical models (e.g. groups, rings) rather than on $\{0,1\}^*$. Secondly, R_P is now an algorithm which expects black-box access to both an implementation f and an adversary $\mathcal{A}$. One can think of R_P as a security game, e.g. one-wayness game or IND-CCA game. Here, we want to associate for each pair $(f, \mathcal{A})$ a value in $[0, 1]$ which corresponds to the probability of $\mathcal{A}$ winning the R_P game against f (see Definition 5). This adjustment helps us introduce the notion of a security loss. Eventually, we introduce a setup algorithm S_P which sends some values to R_P. This machine could as well send nothing or just provide fresh random coins which R_P would use in its game. However, this addition will be very useful in defining the multi-instance setting of a primitive. Informally, we can define a new security game R' which represents the security of P in the multi-user setting as follows: given parameters $(r_1, \ldots)$ from S_P, run n independent copies of R_P and send $(r_1, \ldots)$ as setup parameters to each of them. Then, R' returns a bit depending on what the n copies returned earlier. This idea is formally defined in Subsect. 3.2.

Definition 5. *Let* $P = \langle \mathbb{P}, S_P, F_P, R_P, \sigma \rangle$ *be a primitive and* $\mathbb{P} = (A, B, C)$. *Take* $f \in F_P$ *and any algorithm* $\mathcal{A}$. *We define the advantage of* $\mathcal{A}$ *in breaking* f *as*

$$\mathsf{Adv}^{\mathrm{P}}_{f,\mathcal{A}}(\lambda) := |\Pr[R_P^{f|_C, \mathcal{A}} = 1] - \sigma(\lambda)|$$

where the probability is defined over random coins in the system. We say that $\mathcal{A}$ $P-breaks$ f *if* $\mathsf{Adv}^{\mathrm{P}}_{f,\mathcal{A}}(\lambda)$ *is non-negligible. Primitive* P *is called secure if there exists an implementation* f *of* P *such that there are no PPT algorithms* $\mathcal{A}$ *that* $P-break$ f.

From the definition above one observes that we do not assign each pair $(f, \mathcal{A})$ a binary value (that would indicate, e.g., whether it satisfies a relation or not), but a probability. Therefore, the notion of a primitive from [43] is a generalisation of our definition. Indeed, any primitive in our sense can be easily transformed into a primitive from RTV definition: let $P = \langle \mathbb{P}, S_P, F_P, R_P, \sigma \rangle$ be a primitive in our sense and define a primitive $P' = \langle F'_P, R'_P \rangle$ such that $F'_P = F_P$ and $R'_P = \{(f, \mathcal{A}) | \mathcal{A}$ P-breaks $f\}$. Then, primitives P and P' are equivalent. On the other hand, it is not clear if implication in the opposite direction holds. It is unknown if given relation set $\mathcal{R}$ we can construct a PPT algorithm R which could be equivalent to $\mathcal{R}$, meaning that $(f, \mathcal{A}) \in \mathcal{R} \iff |\Pr[R^{f, \mathcal{A}} = 1] - \sigma(\lambda)|$ is not negligible. An obvious brute force solution would be to check all elements of R but this could take exponential time. Despite the fact that our definition of a primitive is less general, it allows us to spot relations between two distinct advantages and consequently, to formally define a security loss.

Using our previous definitions we formalise the notion of a (tight) fully black-box reduction.

Definition 6 (*C*-**tightness**). *Let* $P = \langle \mathbb{P}_1, S_P, F_P, R_P, \sigma \rangle$ *and* $Q = \langle \mathbb{P}_2, S_Q, F_Q, R_Q, \tau \rangle$ *be primitives. Then, there is a fully black-box reduction from* P *to* Q *if there exist algorithms* $G^{(\cdot)}, S^{(\cdot)}$ *such that:*

- *for every implementation* f *of* Q, G^f *is an implementation of* P,
- *for every implementation* f *of* Q *and every (unbounded) algorithm* $\mathcal{A}$, *if* $\mathcal{A}$ *P-breaks* G^f *then* $S^{\mathcal{A}}$ *Q-breaks* f.

We require that G^f *is PPT for every* $f \in F_Q$, *and that* $S^{\mathcal{A}}$ *is PPT for every PPT* $\mathcal{A}$. *Let* $C \colon \mathbb{N} \to \mathbb{R}$ *be a function. We say that the reduction is* C-*tight (and write* $P \overset{C}{\hookrightarrow} Q$ *) if:*

- *for every algorithm* $\mathcal{A}$, $\mathbf{T}(S^{\mathcal{A}}) = \mathbf{T}(\mathcal{A}) + \mathsf{queries}(S^{\mathcal{A}}, \mathcal{A}) \cdot n_1(\lambda) + n_2(\lambda)$ *for some* $n_1, n_2 \in \mathsf{poly}(\lambda)$ *that do not depend on* $\mathcal{A}$[78],
- *for every implementation* f *of* Q *and every algorithm* $\mathcal{A}$:

$$\mathsf{Adv}^{\mathrm{p}}_{G^f, \mathcal{A}}(\lambda) \leq C(\lambda) \cdot \mathsf{Adv}^{\mathrm{q}}_{f, S^{\mathcal{A}}}(\lambda) + \mathsf{negl}(\lambda). \tag{1}$$

In particular, we say that the reduction is **fully-tight** *if* $C = 1$, **tight** *if* $C = a$ *for* $a \in \mathbb{N}$ *and* **almost-tight** *if* $C \in \mathsf{poly}(\lambda)$.

We say that G is a generic construction of P from Q and S is an actual reduction. The first condition for a tight reduction states that the runtime of $S^{\mathcal{A}}$ should be about the same as the runtime of the adversary $\mathcal{A}$. This prevents the reduction S from running many copies of $\mathcal{A}$. An alternative way to formalise this condition would be to use the definition of a *time-success ratio* from [24] and combine it with the security loss C. However, in this paper we do not calculate exactly the runtime of $S^{\mathcal{A}}$[9] and thus, we omit such formalities. Note that we allow a tight reduction to do some *small enough* amount of work proportional to the number of queries it gets from $\mathcal{A}$. Hence, some reductions, which are commonly considered as tight (e.g. ElGamal encryption scheme to DDH), would be also classified as tight by our definition. Further, the second condition from the definition of tight reduction assures that the success of an adversary $\mathcal{A}$ breaking the primitive is always about as large as the success of the reduction $S^{\mathcal{A}}$ breaking the other one.

We note that reductions with security loss L, which depends on the number of queries made by $\mathcal{A}$, are still almost-tight as long as $L = \mathsf{poly}(\lambda)$. This observation includes recent identity-based encryption (IBE) schemes [10,19] with security loss $O(\log Q)$, where Q is the number of IBE secret key queries. In these reductions, we have that $Q \leq 2^\lambda$ and consequently, they are still almost-tight in our definition.

We can get some simple but useful properties of tight reductions from the definition above. For example, they satisfy the transitivity property.

---

[7] Recall that $\mathsf{queries}(S^{\mathcal{A}}, \mathcal{A})$ denotes the worst-case number of queries/messages from $\mathcal{A}$ to S.

[8] Runtime of $\mathcal{A}$ is included in $\mathbf{T}(S^{\mathcal{A}})$.

[9] As long as it is similar to the runtime of $\mathcal{A}$.

Lemma 1. *Let P, Q, R be primitives such that $P \overset{C}{\hookrightarrow} Q$ and $Q \overset{D}{\hookrightarrow} R$, where $C, D \in \mathsf{poly}(\lambda)$. Then, $P \overset{E}{\hookrightarrow} R$, where $E(\lambda) = C(\lambda) \cdot D(\lambda)$.*

Proof. Let (G, S) be a tight reduction from P to Q and (G', S') be a tight reduction from Q to R. Define:

$$\bar{G}^{(\cdot)} = G^{G'^{(\cdot)}}, \bar{S}^{(\cdot)} = S'^{S^{(\cdot)}}.$$

We claim that $(\bar{G}, \bar{S})$ gives a reduction from P to R.

Take $f \in F_R$. Then, G'^f is an implementation of Q. Therefore, $\bar{G}^f = G^{G'^f}$ is an implementation of P. Now, take any $f \in F_R$ and algorithm $\mathcal{A}$. Note that there are some negligible functions $\mathsf{negl}_1(\lambda), \mathsf{negl}_2(\lambda)$ and $\mathsf{negl}(\lambda)$ such that:

$$\begin{aligned}
\mathsf{Adv}^{\mathsf{p}}_{\bar{G}^f, \mathcal{A}}(\lambda) &\le C(\lambda) \cdot \mathsf{Adv}^{\mathsf{q}}_{G'^f, S^{\mathcal{A}}}(\lambda)| + \mathsf{negl}_1(\lambda) \\
&\le C(\lambda) \cdot (D(\lambda) \cdot \mathsf{Adv}^{\mathsf{r}}_{f, \bar{S}^{\mathcal{A}}}(\lambda) + \mathsf{negl}_1(\lambda)) + \mathsf{negl}_2(\lambda) \\
&= C(\lambda) D(\lambda) \cdot \mathsf{Adv}^{\mathsf{r}}_{f, \bar{S}^{\mathcal{A}}}(\lambda) + \mathsf{negl}(\lambda) \\
&= E(\lambda) \cdot \mathsf{Adv}^{\mathsf{r}}_{f, \bar{S}^{\mathcal{A}}}(\lambda) + \mathsf{negl}(\lambda)
\end{aligned} \tag{2}$$

by the definition of the almost-tight reduction. Therefore, we have shown that $(\bar{G}, \bar{S})$ is a $E-$tight reduction from P to R. □

The notion of computational indistinguishability ($\approx$, see Sect. 2) can also be recast in our definitional framework. Let Ω_1, Ω_2, S be finite sets and $X_\lambda : \Omega_1 \to S, Y_\lambda : \Omega_2 \to S$ be random variables (parametrized over λ). We define $f_{X,Y} : \Omega_1 \times \Omega_2 \to S \times S$ as $f_{X,Y}(u) = (X_\lambda(u), Y_\lambda(u))$. Then, the $[X_\lambda; Y_\lambda]$ primitive is a tuple $\langle \mathbb{P}, S_{X,Y}, F_{X,Y}, R_{X,Y}, \frac{1}{2} \rangle$, where $\mathbb{P} = (\Omega_1 \times \Omega_2, S \times S, \Omega_1 \times \Omega_2)$, $F_{X,Y} = \{f_{X,Y}\}$, $S_{X,Y}$ sends $b \leftarrow_\$ \{0, 1\}$ to $R_{X,Y}$, and $R_{X,Y}$ is the following game: generate $(u_0, u_1) \leftarrow_\$ \Omega_1 \times \Omega_2$ and send (u_0, u_1) to an implementation $f \in F_{X,Y}$. Then, get back (v_1, v_2) from f and take b from $S_{X,Y}$. Output v_b to an adversary $\mathcal{A}$ and eventually get back b' from $\mathcal{A}$. Then, the adversary $\mathcal{A}$ wins if $b = b'$.

3.2 Multi-instance Setting

Using notions from Subsect. 3.1 we define the multi-instance setting of a primitive. Informally, this means that an adversary now interacts with (polynomially) many independent copies of the security game, so it gets more information. However, the winning condition would be almost the same as in the single-instance case, e.g. returning a preimage or guessing a bit (see Fig. 1). We define it formally for a primitive $P = \langle \mathbb{P}, S_P, F_P, R_P, \sigma \rangle$ in terms of the security algorithm R_P. We, however, provide two definitions of the multi-instance setting due to the differences between computational and decisional problems.

Definition 7. ($\exists/\forall$-**Multi-instance Setting**). *Let $n(\lambda)$ be a polynomial in λ and $P = \langle \mathbb{P}, S_P, F_P, R_P, \sigma \rangle$ be a primitive. Then, the $\exists\mathsf{MI}_n(P)$ primitive (resp. $\forall\mathsf{MI}_n(P)$) is a primitive $\langle \mathbb{P}, \mathcal{S}, \mathcal{F}, \mathcal{R}_\exists, \sigma \rangle$ (resp. $\langle \mathbb{P}, \mathcal{S}, \mathcal{F}, \mathcal{R}_\forall, \sigma \rangle$) such that $\mathcal{F} = F_P, \mathcal{S} = S_P$ and $\mathcal{R}_\exists$ (resp. $\mathcal{R}_\forall$) is defined in Fig. 2 (left) (resp. right).*

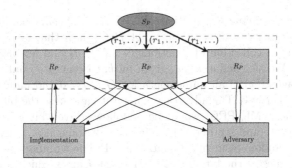

Fig. 1. New security game for the three-instance version of primitive $P = \langle \mathbb{P}, S_P, F_P, R_P, \sigma \rangle$ is described as the green dashed box. (Color figure online)

$\mathcal{R}_{\exists}^{f|_C, \mathcal{A}}(1^\lambda, r_1, \ldots)$	$\mathcal{R}_{\forall}^{f|_C, \mathcal{A}}(1^\lambda, r_1, \ldots)$
1 : Initialise $n(\lambda)$ ind. copies of $R_P^{f|_C, \mathcal{A}}$	1 : Initialise $n(\lambda)$ ind. copies of $R_P^{f|_C, \mathcal{A}}$
2 : send $(r_1, \ldots)$ to each of them	2 : send $(r_1, \ldots)$ to each of them
3 : as the setup parameters	3 : as the setup parameters
4 : **if** one of the copies returns 1	4 : **if** all of the copies return 1
5 : **return** 1	5 : **return** 1
6 : **else return** 0	6 : **else return** 0

Fig. 2. Security algorithms for $\exists\mathsf{MI}_n(P)$ (on the left) and $\forall\mathsf{MI}_n(P)$ (on the right). They get as input the security parameter λ (in unary) and parameters $(r_1, \ldots)$ from the setup algorithm S_Q. Here, we assume that $\mathcal{R}$ has black-box access to implementation f (restricted to the domain C, where $\mathbb{P} = (A, B, C)$) and adversary $\mathcal{A}$.

Now we provide examples of cryptographic primitives in the multi-instance setting using definitions above.

Example 1. Let $\mathsf{OWF} = \langle \mathbb{P}_{\mathsf{OWF}}, S_{\mathsf{OWF}}, F_{\mathsf{OWF}}, R_{\mathsf{OWF}}, 0 \rangle$ be the primitive of a one-way function. That is, $\mathbb{P}_{\mathsf{OWF}} = (A, B, C)$, F_{OWF} is a collection of functions $f : A \to B$, and R_{OWF} is a standard one-wayness game (i.e. R_{OWF} generates x uniformly at random from C, gets $f(x)$ by calling an implementation f and returns 1 only if adversary can guess the preimage of $f(x)$). For simplicity, when we write $\mathsf{OWF}_{p(\lambda)}$, where $p = \mathsf{poly}(\lambda)$, we mean OWF with $\mathbb{P}_{\mathsf{OWF}} = (\{0,1\}^*, \{0,1\}^*, \{0,1\}^{p(\lambda)})$ which is closer to the standard definition of a one-way function. The security game for $\exists\mathsf{MI}_n(\mathsf{OWF})$ would be as follows: it generates $x_1, \ldots, x_n$ independently and uniformly at random from C, then it gets $f(x_1), \ldots, f(x_n)$ by calling f and sends to adversary. The winning condition is that adversary returns a preimage of *one* of the values it was given i.e. x satisfying $f(x) = f(x_i)$ for some i. On the other hand, in $\forall\mathsf{MI}_n(\mathsf{OWF}_{p(\lambda)})$, the adversary wins if it returns preimages for *all* values $f(x_1), \ldots, f(x_n)$. In practice, the $\exists\mathsf{MI}_n(\mathsf{OWF}_{p(\lambda)})$ setting is more common and therefore we focus on the former case.

Example 2. Let us define a primitive $\mathsf{PRG} = \langle \mathbb{P}_{\mathsf{PRG}}, S_{\mathsf{PRG}}, F_{\mathsf{PRG}}, R_{\mathsf{PRG}}, \frac{1}{2} \rangle$ of a pseudorandom generator where $\mathbb{P}_{\mathsf{PRG}} = (A, B, C)$ such that $C = A$ and $|B| > |A|$. Let F_{PRG} be a collection of functions $G : A \to B$ and let S_{PRG} generate a bit $b \leftarrow_\$ \{0, 1\}$. We also define R_{PRG}, given bit b, to generate random $x \in C$ and output the image $G(x)$ of an implementation G if $b = 0$ and uniformly random value from B otherwise. The adversary wins if it can guess the bit b. Then, the security game for $\forall \mathsf{MI}_n(\mathsf{PRG})$ would be as follows: given bit b from the setup algorithm, generate and send $G(x_1), \dots, G(x_n)$ for some $x_1, \dots, x_n \in A$ if $b = 0$ or n uniformly random elements from B if $b = 1$. The winning condition here is that adversary guesses the bits for *all* of the n subgames which is equivalent to guessing the bit b.

Now, consider $\exists \mathsf{MI}_n(\mathsf{PRG})$. We claim that it is not secure. Note that in this case adversary wins if it guesses the bit b for *one* of the n subgames. In other words, it has n chances to guess b. Thus, an adversary which just sends 1 to a random subgame and 0 to another one will always win one of these two games (because $b \in \{0, 1\}$) and consequently, break $\exists \mathsf{MI}_n(\mathsf{PRG})$. Therefore, we only analyse the security of $\forall \mathsf{MI}_n(\mathsf{PRG})$.

Example 3. We define a primitive corresponding to an IND-CPA secure public-key encryption scheme as $\mathsf{PKE} = \langle \mathbb{P}_{\mathsf{PKE}}, S_{\mathsf{PKE}}, F_{\mathsf{PKE}}, R_{\mathsf{PKE}}, \frac{1}{2} \rangle$ where, as before, S_{PKE} does the sampling $b \leftarrow_\$ \{0, 1\}$, R_{PKE} is the IND-CPA game and F_{PKE} contains encryption schemes. Note that $\exists \mathsf{MI}_n(\mathsf{PKE})$ is not secure due to the same reasons as the $\exists$-multi instance pseudorandom generator. On the other hand, $\forall \mathsf{MI}_n(\mathsf{PKE})$ yields the definition of an encryption scheme in the multi-user setting by Bellare et al. [6]. In a similar fashion we can define IND-CCA secure PKE schemes.

One observes that one can slightly change the definition of a primitive in order to get a definition of "multi-ciphertext setting". If we give S_{PKE} black-box access to an implementation and let it also generate keys (pk, sk) instead of R_{PKE} then the security game for $\forall \mathsf{MI}_n(\mathsf{PKE})$ is indeed an IND-CPA game with many ciphertexts. However, we do not consider the multi-ciphertext security in this paper so we omit defining it formally here.

We also introduce the notion of a primitive being *tightly extensible*, meaning that a reduction from its multi-instance setting admits the same security loss as in the single-instance case.

Definition 8. *Let P be a primitive and $C : \mathbb{N} \to \mathbb{R}$ be a function. Then, P is $(C, \forall)$-tightly extensible (resp. $(C, \exists)$-tightly extensible) with respect to primitive Q if:*

- $P \overset{C}{\hookrightarrow} Q$,
- $\forall n \in \mathsf{poly}(\lambda)$, $\forall MI_n(P) \overset{C}{\hookrightarrow} Q$ (resp.$\exists MI_n(P) \overset{C}{\hookrightarrow} Q$).

Based on what we have already defined, we can formally state the main problem of this paper:

> **Problem.** Suppose that $P \overset{C}{\hookrightarrow} Q$. Show that P is $(C, \exists (\text{ or } \forall))$-tightly extensible w.r.t. Q.

There are two standard approaches to show that P is tightly extensible w.r.t. Q. Namely, (i) somehow tightly reduce the multi-instance primitive to the single case, (ii) modify the former reduction and apply re-randomisation/self-reducibility techniques to eventually obtain the same security loss, or (iii) hide the factor of n in the statistical difference. In Sect. 4 we discuss these methods used in practical examples. When we apply (i), we use the following simple lemma.

Lemma 2. *Let n be a polynomial in λ and let P and Q be primitives such that $P = \langle \mathbb{P}_1, S_P, F_P, R_P, \sigma \rangle \overset{C}{\hookrightarrow} Q = \langle \mathbb{P}_2, S_Q, F_Q, R_Q, \tau \rangle$ and let (G, S) be such a reduction. Define P/Q to be the primitive $\langle \mathbb{P}_1, S_P, \mathcal{F}, R_P, \sigma \rangle$ such that $\mathcal{F} = \{G^f : f \in F_Q\}$. Then, if $\exists MI_n(P) \overset{D}{\hookrightarrow} P/Q$ (resp. $\forall MI_n(P) \overset{D}{\hookrightarrow} P/Q$) then $\exists MI_n(P) \overset{C \cdot D}{\longrightarrow} Q$ (resp. $\forall MI_n(P) \overset{C \cdot D}{\longrightarrow} Q$). In particular, if $D = 1$ then P is $(C, \exists)$ (resp. $(C, \forall)$)-tightly extensible w.r.t. Q.*

Proof. Using the notation above, it is easy to see that $P \overset{C}{\hookrightarrow} Q$ implies $P/Q \overset{C}{\hookrightarrow} Q$. The result holds by this simple observation and by Lemma 1. □

4   Tightly Extensible Primitives

We provide a few constructions of tightly extensible primitives from more general primitives. In principle, we first take a tight reduction from the single-instance primitive and see if we can extend it (in a tight way) to the multi-instance setting or otherwise, use the Lemma 2. In the first subsection, we demonstrate the use of definitions from Sect. 3, and derive formal proofs. In the later subsections, however, we focus more on showing novel techniques to extend reductions to the multi-instance setting.

4.1   One-Wayness of Collision-Resistant Hash Functions

It is well-known that signatures schemes can be constructed from one-way functions [23,32,44]. Concretely, we can use the Lamport construction [33] of a one-time signature scheme from one-way functions, and then extend these one-time signatures to full signatures using Merkle trees [37]. The corresponding reduction is far from tight, and not known to scale well to the multi-user setting. Here, we consider the same construction under a slightly stronger assumption (namely, collision-resistance) of the used one-way function. We will show that this stronger assumption enables a much tighter security reduction.

We start by defining collision-resistant hash functions w.r.t. the definition of a primitive from Sect. 3. Define $\mathsf{CRHF} = \langle \mathbb{P}_{\mathsf{CRHF}}, S_{\mathsf{CRHF}}, F_{\mathsf{CRHF}}, R_{\mathsf{CRHF}}, 0 \rangle$ as follows: $\mathbb{P}_{\mathsf{CRHF}} = (\{0,1\}^*, \{0,1\}^\lambda, \{0,1\}^*), S_{\mathsf{CRHF}}$ returns no parameters, $F_{\mathsf{CRHF}} = \{h : \{0,1\}^* \rightarrow \{0,1\}^\lambda\}$ and R_{CRHF} is the collision resistance game, i.e. it waits until it gets (x, x') from adversary, checks if $x \neq x'$ and then calls the implementation h to check if $h(x) = h(x')$.

Let us define an *adaptive one-way function*. Specifically, we denote $\mathsf{AOWF} = \langle \mathbb{P}_{\mathsf{OWF}}, S_{\mathsf{OWF}}, F_{\mathsf{OWF}}, R_{\mathsf{AOWF}}, 0 \rangle$, where $\mathbb{P}_{\mathsf{OWF}}, S_{\mathsf{OWF}}, F_{\mathsf{OWF}}$ are defined in Example 1. Also, R_{AOWF} is defined identically as R_{OWF}, but here adversary can also send a message $\mathtt{lose}$, in which case R_{AOWF} outputs back the challenge preimage x and automatically returns 0. Similarly as in Example 1, we use the notation $\mathsf{AOWF}_{p(\lambda)}$ when $\mathbb{P}_{\mathsf{OWF}} = (\{0,1\}^*, \{0,1\}^*, \{0,1\}^{p(\lambda)})$. Clearly, security of OWF implies (tightly) the AOWF security. Interestingly, we cannot conclude the same for $\exists \mathsf{MI}_n(\mathsf{OWF})$ and $\exists \mathsf{MI}_n(\mathsf{AOWF})$.

Damgård [12] showed that h, when considered as a function with domain $\{0,1\}^{\lambda+1}$, is also a (adaptive) one-way function. Indeed, if there exists an adversary $\mathcal{A}$ which can find preimage of $h(x)$ for uniformly random x, then we can construct adversary $S^{\mathcal{A}}$ which breaks the collision-resistance of h as follows: given h, choose random x and send $h(x)$ to $\mathcal{A}$. Let x' be the output of $\mathcal{A}$. Then, return the pair (x, x'). Note that with non-negligible probability (over x and x'), we have $x \neq x'$. Hence, adversary $S^{\mathcal{A}}$ wins the collision-resistance game and additionally, the reduction itself is clearly tight.

Damgård's argument in fact nicely extends to the multi-instance setting:

Theorem 1. *Let CRHF be the primitive of a collision-resistant hash function and $\mathsf{AOWF}_{2\lambda}$ be the primitive of a one-way function defined in Example 1. Then, $\mathsf{AOWF}_{2\lambda}$ is $(2, \exists)$-tightly extensible w.r.t. CRHF.*

Proof. We first reprove that $\mathsf{AOWF}_{2\lambda} \overset{2}{\hookrightarrow} \mathsf{CRHF}$. Let us define PPT algorithms G and S as in Fig. 3. Clearly, both G and S run in polynomial time. One can observe that G is a generic construction. Indeed, G only forwards all the queries from/to an implementation and hence, $\forall h \in F_{\mathsf{CRHF}}$, $G^h = h$. In particular, $G^h : \{0,1\}^* \rightarrow \{0,1\}^\lambda$ is a function, so $G^h \in F_{\mathsf{OWF}}$. Now, suppose that there

$G^h(1^\lambda)$	$S^{\mathcal{A}}(1^\lambda)$
1: **if** G is queried on x:	1: $x \leftarrow_\$ \{0,1\}^{2\lambda}$
2: send x to h	2: send $h(x)$ to $\mathcal{A}$
3: get y from h	3: if $\mathcal{A}$ outputs $\mathtt{lose}$, send x to $\mathcal{A}$ and abort
4: **return** y	4: Othewise, get x' from $\mathcal{A}$ and **return** (x, x')

Fig. 3. PPT algorithms G and S.

exists an algorithm $\mathcal{A}$ which $\mathsf{OWF}_{2\lambda}$-breaks G^h. We want to prove that $S^{\mathcal{A}}$ CRHF-breaks h. Using the variables x and x' from Fig. 3, one observes that:

$$
\begin{aligned}
\mathsf{Adv}^{\mathsf{crhf}}_{h,S^{\mathcal{A}}}(\lambda) &= \Pr[R^{h,S^{\mathcal{A}}}_{\mathsf{CRHF}} = 1] \\
&= \Pr[x \neq x' \wedge h(x) = h(x')] \\
&\geq \Pr[x \neq x' \wedge h(x) = h(x') \mid |h^{-1}(h(x))| \geq 2] \cdot \Pr[|h^{-1}(h(x))| \geq 2],
\end{aligned}
\tag{3}
$$

where $h^{-1}(u) = \{v \in \{0,1\}^{2\lambda} : h(v) = u\}$. Clearly, $|h^{-1}(h(x))| \geq 1$. Note that $\Pr[x \neq x' \mid h(x) = h(x') \wedge |h^{-1}(h(x))| \geq 2] \geq \frac{1}{2}$ since adversary $\mathcal{A}$ does not know, given $h(x)$, if S chose exactly x or some other element in $h^{-1}(h(x))$ (it exists $h^{-1}(h(x)) \geq 2$). Hence, if we denote $X = |h^{-1}(h(x))|$, then we eventually have $\frac{X-1}{X} \geq 1/2$. Using this observation and the fact that $h(x)$ is generated by S with the same distribution as the challenge by R_{OWF}, we deduce that:

$$
\begin{aligned}
\mathsf{Adv}^{\mathsf{crhf}}_{h,S^{\mathcal{A}}}(\lambda) &\geq \frac{1}{2}\Pr[h(x) = h(x') \mid |h^{-1}(h(x))| \geq 2] \cdot \Pr[|h^{-1}(h(x))| \geq 2] \\
&\geq \frac{1}{2}\Pr[h(x) = h(x')] - \frac{1}{2}\Pr[|h^{-1}(h(x))| = 1] \\
&\geq \frac{1}{2}\mathsf{Adv}^{\mathsf{owf}}_{G^h,\mathcal{A}}(\lambda) - \frac{1}{2}\Pr[|h^{-1}(h(x))| = 1].
\end{aligned}
\tag{4}
$$

The only thing to compute here is $\Pr[|h^{-1}(h(x))| = 1]$. Let $a_1,\ldots,a_m \in \{0,1\}^{2\lambda}$ be the bit-strings such that $|h^{-1}(h(a_i))| = 1$ for $i = 1,\ldots,m$. Clearly, we have that $h(a_1),\ldots,h(a_m)$ are pairwise distinct. Also $\{h(a_1),\ldots,h(a_m)\} \subset \{0,1\}^{\lambda}$, and therefore $m \leq 2^{\lambda}$. Thus, $\Pr[|h^{-1}(h(x))| = 1] = \frac{m}{2^{2\lambda}} \leq \frac{2^{\lambda}}{2^{2\lambda}} = \frac{1}{2^{\lambda}}$. By substituting this result into Eq. 4 and reordering both sides we get:

$$
2\mathsf{Adv}^{\mathsf{crhf}}_{h,S^{\mathcal{A}}}(\lambda) + \frac{1}{2^{\lambda}} \geq \mathsf{Adv}^{\mathsf{aowf}}_{G^h,\mathcal{A}}(\lambda),
$$

which concludes that $\mathsf{AOWF}_{2\lambda} \overset{2}{\hookrightarrow} \mathsf{CRHF}$.

Now, we have to prove that $\exists \mathsf{MI}_n(\mathsf{AOWF}_{2\lambda}) \overset{2}{\hookrightarrow} \mathsf{CRHF}$ for any $n \in \mathsf{poly}(\lambda)$. Denote $n = n(\lambda)$. We define the reduction $(\bar{G}, \bar{S})$ as in the Fig. 4. One observes that $\bar{G}$ and $\bar{S}$ are both PPT algorithms, and also $\bar{G} = G$ is a generic construction of $\exists \mathsf{MI}_n(\mathsf{AOWF}_{2\lambda})$ from CRHF. Suppose that there exists an algorithm $\mathcal{A}$ which $\mathsf{OWF}_{2\lambda}$-breaks G^h for some $h \in F_{\mathsf{CRHF}}$. We extend the previous argument for many instances as follows (the probabilities are calculated over $x_1,\ldots,x_n,x'$ which are defined in Fig. 4):

$$
\begin{aligned}
\mathsf{Adv}^{\mathsf{crhf}}_{h,\bar{S}^{\mathcal{A}}}(\lambda) &= \Pr[R^{h,\bar{S}^{\mathcal{A}}}_{\mathsf{CRHF}} = 1] \\
&= \Pr[x_i \neq x' \wedge h(x_i) = h(x')] \\
&\geq \Pr[x_i \neq x' \wedge h(x_i) = h(x') \mid E] \cdot \Pr[E],
\end{aligned}
\tag{5}
$$

$\bar{G}^h(1^\lambda)$
1: **if** G is queried on x:
2:     send x to h
3:     get y from h
4: **return** y

$\bar{S}^{\mathcal{A}}(1^\lambda)$
1: $x_1,\ldots,x_n \leftarrow_{\$} \{0,1\}^{2\lambda}, U = \emptyset$
2: send $h(x_1),\ldots,h(x_n)$ to $\mathcal{A}$
3: if $\mathcal{A}$ returns **lose** in the i-th subgame:
4:     send back x_i and set $U \leftarrow U \cup \{i\}$
5: if $\mathcal{A}$ returns some x' in the i-th subgame:
6:     **if** $h(x') = h(x_i), \mathbf{return}\ (x', x_i)$

Fig. 4. PPT algorithms G and S.

where $E = \bigwedge\limits_{i=1}^{n} |h^{-1}(h(x_i))| \geq 2$. In the similar fashion as before, we have that $\Pr[x_i \neq x' \mid h(x_i) = h(x') \wedge E] \geq \frac{1}{2}$. Hence,

$$
\begin{aligned}
\mathsf{Adv}_{h,\bar{S}^{\mathcal{A}}}^{\mathsf{crhf}}(\lambda) &\geq \frac{1}{2}\Pr[h(x_i) = h(x') \mid E] \cdot \Pr[E] \\
&\geq \frac{1}{2}\mathsf{Adv}_{\bar{G}^h,\mathcal{A}}^{\min(\mathsf{aowf})}(\lambda) - \frac{1}{2}\Pr[\neg E].
\end{aligned}
\tag{6}
$$

By the union bound, we compute:

$$
\Pr[\neg E] = \Pr[\bigvee_{i=1}^{n} |h^{-1}(h(x_i))| = 1] \leq \sum_{i=1}^{n} \Pr[|h^{-1}(h(x_i))| = 1] = \frac{n}{2^\lambda}.
\tag{7}
$$

Eventually, by reordering both sides of Eq. 6 we get that $\exists \mathsf{MI}_n(\mathsf{AOWF}_{2\lambda}) \overset{2}{\hookrightarrow} \mathsf{CRHF}$:

$$
2\mathsf{Adv}_{h,\bar{S}^{\mathcal{A}}}^{\mathsf{crhf}}(\lambda) + \frac{n}{2^\lambda} \geq \mathsf{Adv}_{\bar{G}^h,\mathcal{A}}^{\min(\mathsf{aowf})}(\lambda).
$$

$\square$

Even though this proof is not complicated, the theorem itself can be useful in constructing secure one-time signature schemes (OTS) with small security loss. Let us first define OTS using the definition of a primitive from Sect. 3. That is, $\mathsf{OTS} = \langle \mathbb{P}_{\mathsf{OTS}}, S_{\mathsf{OTS}}, F_{\mathsf{OTS}}, R_{\mathsf{OTS}}, 0 \rangle$, where $\mathbb{P} = (\{0,1\}^*, \{0,1\}^*, \{0,1\}^*)$, S_{OTS} does not send any global parameters, F_{OTS} is the set of all signature schemes and R_{OTS} represents the EUF-OTCMA game.

Let f be a one-way function and let n be a polynomial in λ. Consider the Lamport's one-time signature scheme [33] ($\mathsf{Gen}_L; \mathsf{Sign}_L; \mathsf{Ver}_L$) for messages of length $n = n(\lambda)$, meaning:

- $\mathsf{Gen}_L(\lambda)$: generate $2n$ random values $x_{i,j}$ and compute $y_{i,j} = f(x_{i,j})$ for $j \in \{0,1\}, i \in \{1,\ldots,n\}$. Then, set $sk = \{x_{1,0},\ldots,x_{n,0}, x_{1,1},\ldots,x_{n,1}\}$ and $vk = \{y_{1,0},\ldots,y_{n,0}, y_{1,1},\ldots,y_{n,1}\}$.

- $\mathsf{Sign}_L(m, sk)$: for message $m = m_1 m_2 \ldots m_n$, output $\sigma = \sigma_1 \sigma_2 \ldots \sigma_n$ where $\sigma_i = x_{i,m_i}$.
- $\mathsf{Ver}_L(vk, m, \sigma)$: for signature $\sigma = \sigma_1 \sigma_2 \ldots \sigma_n$ and message $m = m_1 m_2 \ldots m_n$, check if $f(\sigma_i) = y_{i,m_i}$ for all $i = 1, \ldots, n$. If so, return 1 and 0 otherwise.

Lamport proved that this scheme is EUF-OTCMA secure by giving a reduction to the one-wayness of f which admits the security loss of $2n$. We show how to tightly reduce it to the adaptive one-wayness of f in the multi-instance setting.

Theorem 2. *Let $n \in \mathsf{poly}(\lambda)$ and OTS and $\mathsf{AOWF}_{2\lambda}$ be the primitives of a one-time signature scheme and one-way function respectively. Then, there exists a fully-tight fully black-box reduction from OTS to $\exists \mathsf{MI}_{2n}(\mathsf{AOWF}_{2\lambda})$.*

Proof. As usual, let us define PPT algorithms G and S as in Fig. 5. We can see that G represents the Lamport construction of a one-time signature scheme. In particular, G is a signature scheme and also, G is a generic construction of OTS from $\exists \mathsf{MI}_{2n}(\mathsf{AOWF}_{2\lambda})$. Now, let us consider S and suppose that S is given $f(x_{1,0}), \ldots, f(x_{n,1})$ from $R_{\exists \mathsf{MI}_{2n}(\mathsf{AOWF}_{2\lambda})}$. If $\mathcal{A}$ requests a signature on $m' = m'_1 \ldots m'_n$ then we abort $1 + m'_1 \cdot n$-th, ..., $n + m'_n \cdot n$-th subgames of $R_{\exists \mathsf{MI}_{2n}(\mathsf{AOWF}_{2\lambda})}$ and consequently, get back preimages $x_{i,m'_i}, \ldots, x_{n,m'_n}$. Eventually, when $\mathcal{A}$ outputs a valid forgery (m, σ), then we must have $m \neq m'$. So, there exists some index i such that $m_i \neq m'_i{}^{10}$. This means that $f(\sigma_i) = y_{i,m_i}$ and therefore, S wins the $i + m_i \cdot n$-th subgame of $R_{\exists \mathsf{MI}_{2n}(\mathsf{AOWF}_{2\lambda})}$. Hence, we end up with a tight reduction which admits security loss 1. □

Combining the previous two results we get that it is possible to construct a one-time signature scheme, which can be reduced to a collision-resistant hash

$G^f(1^\lambda)$	$S^{\mathcal{A}}(1^\lambda)$
1 : **if** G is queried on $\mathsf{Gen}(1^\lambda)$:	1 : receive $(y_{1,0}, \ldots, y_{n,0}, y_{1,1}, \ldots, y_{n,1})$
2 : run $\mathsf{Gen}_L(\lambda)$ by calling f	2 : $vk = (y_{1,0}, \ldots, y_{n,1})$
3 : **if** G is queried on $\mathsf{Sign}(m, sk)$:	3 : send vk to $\mathcal{A}$
4 : run $\mathsf{Sign}_L(m, sk)$	4 : **if** $\mathcal{A}$ requests a signature on m':
5 : **if** G is queried on $\mathsf{Ver}(vk, m, \sigma)$:	5 : **for** $i = 1, \ldots, n$
6 : run $\mathsf{Ver}_L(vk, m, \sigma)$	6 : send $\mathtt{lose}$ to $i + m'_i \cdot n$-th subgame
	7 : get back x_{i,m'_i}
	8 : send $\sigma = x_{1,m'_1} \ldots x_{n,m'_n}$ to $\mathcal{A}$
	9 : **if** $\mathcal{A}$ outputs $(m, \sigma = \sigma_1, \ldots, \sigma_n)$:
	10 : find i so that $m_i \neq m'_i$
	11 : send σ_i to $i + m_i \cdot n$-th subgame

Fig. 5. PPT algorithms G and S. Here, $(\mathsf{Gen}_L; \mathsf{Sign}_L; \mathsf{Ver}_L)$ is the Lamport signature scheme.

---

[10] If $\mathcal{A}$ has not requested a signature before, then we just set $i = 1$.

function with the loss of 2. Thus, we managed to eliminate the factor n and if one wants to apply Merkle trees, the overall reduction to CRHF from a secure signature scheme would have the security loss of $O(l)$, where l is the number of signing queries.

4.2   A Rerandomisable Hard-Core Predicate

Blum and Micali [8] provided a construction of a pseudorandom generator from a one-way permutation. Let f be a one-way permutation and b be its hard-core predicate. Then, the function $G(x) = f(x)||b(x)$ is a pseudo-random generator. Now, our aim is to construct, given f and b, a tightly extensible pseudo-random generator w.r.t. some certain mathematical assumption. We find suitable f and b such that we can apply Lemma 2. Note that in order to do this, we need a rerandomisation property from these functions. For instance, given $b(x)$ and a value a, we should somehow be able to compute $b(ax)$. We will choose a one-way permutation on a group where the discrete logarithm problem is hard and use properties of Legendre symbol to construct a rerandomisable hard-core predicate.

BACKGROUND. Let $a \in \mathbb{Z}$ be an integer and p be a prime number such that $p \nmid a$. We say that a is a quadratic residue mod p if there exists $x \in \mathbb{Z} \setminus \{0\}$ so that $x^2 \equiv a \pmod{p}$. If there is no such x, then a is a quadratic non-residue mod p. It is a well-known fact that in $\{1, \ldots, p-1\}$ there are exactly $(p-1)/2$ quadratic residues (and also $(p-1)/2$ quadratic non-residues) mod p. Clearly, the quadratic residues form a subgroup of $\mathbb{Z}_p^*$.

The Legendre symbol is defined as follows:

$$\left(\frac{a}{p}\right) = \begin{cases} 0 & \text{if } p|a \\ 1 & \text{if } a \text{ is a quadratic residue mod } p \\ -1 & \text{if } a \text{ is a quadratic non-residue mod } p \end{cases}$$

One of useful properties of the Legendre symbol is that it is homomorphic, meaning $\left(\frac{a}{p}\right)\left(\frac{b}{p}\right) = \left(\frac{ab}{p}\right)$ for any a, b. Moreover, by the Euler's criterion, the Legendre symbol can be computed efficiently.

THE LGR PROBLEM. We propose a new computational problem, called Legendre Problem (LGR).

Definition 9. *Let p be a λ-bit prime number and let G be a group of order p with generator g. We say that the Legendre Problem (LGR) is hard in G if for all PPT algorithms $\mathcal{A}$,*

$$Adv_{G,\mathcal{A}}^{lgr}[(\lambda)] := \Pr[b \leftarrow_\$ \mathcal{A}(\langle G \rangle, p, g, g^x) : x \leftarrow_\$ \mathbb{Z}_p, b = \frac{1 + \left(\frac{x}{p}\right)}{2}] = \frac{1}{2} + negl(\lambda).$$

Equivalently, define a primitive $LGR_G = \langle \mathbb{P}_{LGR}, S_{LGR}, F_{LGR}, R_{LGR}, \frac{1}{2} \rangle$ such that $\mathbb{P}_{LGR} = (\mathbb{Z}_p, G, \mathbb{Z}_p)$, S_{LGR} sends parameters (G, p, g) to R_P and $F_{LGR} = \{f_g\}$, where f_g is defined by $a \mapsto g^a$. The security game R_{LGR} first chooses random

$x \leftarrow_{\$} \mathbb{Z}_p$, *sends* x *to an implementation* $f \in F_{LGR}$ *of* LGR_G *and gets back* y. *Then, it outputs* y *to adversary* $\mathcal{A}$. *When it receives* $b \in \{0,1\}$ *from* $\mathcal{A}$, *it returns a value of the statement* $b = (1 + (\frac{x}{p}))/2$.

One observes that the Legendre Problem is not harder than the discrete logarithm problem. Indeed, given g^x, solving the discrete logarithm problem yields x, from which one can directly compute $(\frac{x}{p})$. A more interesting question is whether LGR is as hard as DLOG. We first show that LGR is at least as hard as DDH.

Lemma 3. *Let* G *be a group of prime order* p *and suppose that DDH is hard in* G. *Then, the Legendre Problem is also hard in* G.

Proof. Suppose there exists a PPT algorithm $\mathcal{A}$ which solves LGR with a non-negligible advantage. We construct a PPT algorithm $S^{\mathcal{A}}$ which wins the DDH game as follows. S first generates random $a, b, c \leftarrow_{\$} \mathbb{Z}_p$. Next, given g^x, g^x, g^z, where $z = xy$ or z is random, S sends g^{ax}, g^{by}, g^{cz} to $\mathcal{A}$ and gets $(\frac{ax}{p}), (\frac{by}{p}), (\frac{cz}{p})$ respectively. Then, S simply extracts $(\frac{x}{p}), (\frac{y}{p}), (\frac{z}{p})$ (e.g. by $(\frac{x}{p})(\frac{a}{p}) = (\frac{ax}{p})$) and returns the value of statement $(\frac{x}{p})(\frac{y}{p}) = (\frac{z}{p})$. Note that if $z = xy$ then this will always be true. On the other hand, if z is random, then the probability that $(\frac{z}{p}) = b$ for $b \in \{-1, 1\}$ is $1/2$. All in all, S wins the DDH game with non-negligible probability. The reduction itself, however, is far from tight[11]. $\square$

Legendre's symbol has already been used in building pseudorandom generators [13,36,46]. For example, Damgård [13] applied specific subsequences of the sequence of Legendre symbols modulo a prime to obtain a pseudorandom generator. Security of such constructions, however, rely on empirical results or additional unproven conjectures.

OUR CONSTRUCTION. We build a tightly extensible pseudorandom generator with respect to the Legendre assumption. Let G be a *densely presentable* group with generator g of prime order p, i.e. a group which satisfies the property that for $x \in \mathbb{Z}_p$, the map $x \mapsto g^x$ is a permutation (e.g. [9]). We define PRG_G to be the primitive from Example 2 with $\mathbb{P} = (\mathbb{Z}_p, G \times \{0,1\}, \mathbb{Z}_p)$. Then, the construction is presented as follows.

Theorem 3. *Let* G *be a densely presentable group of prime order* p *where the Legendre problem is hard. Denote* $g \in G$ *to be a generator of* G. *Then,* PRG_G *is* $(2, \forall)$*-tightly extensible w.r.t.* LGR_G.

Proof. Define $f : \mathbb{Z}_p \to G$ as $x \mapsto g^x$, $b : \mathbb{Z}_p \to \{0,1\}$ as $x \mapsto (1 + (\frac{x}{p}))/2$ and eventually, $F(x) := f(x) \| b(x)$. Clearly, if the Legendre Problem is hard in G then f is a one-way permutation and b is a hard-core predicate for f.

---

[11] On the other hand, one can actually derive a simple tight reduction from $\forall \mathsf{MI}_3(\mathsf{LGR})$ to DDH.

Blum and Micali [8] showed that F is a pseudorandom generator. In this case, the generic reduction is fully-tight. Thus, by Lemma 2 it is enough to reduce the multi-instance setting of F to the single-instance with security loss 2. Suppose that there exists an adversary $\mathcal{A}$ which can win the n-multi-instance game for the pseudorandom generator F. We construct an adversary $S^{\mathcal{A}}$ that wins a single-instance game as follows. Given $(u\|v)$ $(u \in G, v \in \{0,1\})$, toss a fair coin n times. For the i-th trial, where $i = 1, \ldots, n$, if we get heads - generate random $x_i \leftarrow_{\$} \mathbb{Z}_p$ and set $y_i = F(x_i)$. On the other hand, if the coin comes out tails, we choose random $a_i \leftarrow_{\$} \mathbb{Z}_p$ and set $y_i = u^{a_i}\|v_i$ where $v_i = (1 + (\frac{a_i}{p})(2v - 1))/2$. Then, send $y_1, \ldots, y_n$ to adversary $\mathcal{A}$ and eventually output what $\mathcal{A}$ returns.

Let us assume that $x \neq 0^{12}$. In order to analyse correctness of this reduction, we have to consider two cases. First, suppose that $u = g^x$ for some x. Then, $v = (1 + (\frac{x}{p}))/2$ or $v = (1 - (\frac{x}{p}))/2$.

Case 1: $v = (1 + (\frac{x}{p}))/2$. Let us fix i and consider the i-th trial of flipping the coin. If it comes out heads, then $y_i = F(x_i)$ for randomly chosen x_i. Otherwise, we get that $v_i = (1 + (\frac{a_i}{p})(\frac{x}{p}))/2 = (1 + (\frac{a_i x}{p}))/2$ and thus $y_i = F(x_i)$ where $x_i = a_i x$ for uniformly random a_i. Therefore, for each i we have $y_i = F(x_i)$ and also $x_1, \ldots, x_n$ are independently, uniformly random in $\mathbb{Z}_p$.

Case 2: $v = (1 - (\frac{x}{p}))/2$. Let us denote $y_i = g^{s_i}\|t_i$ where $s_i \in \mathbb{Z}_p, t \in \{0,1\}$. We need to show that for every $\alpha_1, \ldots, \alpha_n \in \mathbb{Z}_p$ and $\beta_1, \ldots, \beta_n \in \{0,1\}$ we have

$$\Pr[s_1 = \alpha_1, \ldots, s_n = \alpha_n, t_1 = \beta_1, \ldots, t_n = \beta_n] = \frac{1}{2^n p^n}.$$

This is the same as showing $\Pr[t_1 = \beta_1, \ldots, t_n = \beta_n | s_1 = \alpha_1, \ldots, s_n = \alpha_n] \cdot \Pr[s_1 = \alpha_1, \ldots, s_n = \alpha_n] = \frac{1}{2^n p^n}$. Note that $\Pr[s_1 = \alpha_1, \ldots, s_n = \alpha_n] = 1/p^n$ because $x \neq 0$ and $s_i = a_i x$ or $s_i = x_i$ for random a_i, x_i. Now, consider $\Pr[t_1 = \beta_1, \ldots, t_n = \beta_n | s_1 = \alpha_1, \ldots, s_n = \alpha_n]$. Clearly, this is the same as $\Pr[t_1 = \beta_1 | s_1 = \alpha_1, \ldots, s_n = \alpha_n]^n$. Firstly, assume that $\beta_1 = (1 + (\frac{\alpha_1}{p}))/2$ and let X denote the output of tossing a coin for the first time (and say H - heads, T - tails). Then, $\Pr[t_1 = \beta_1 | X = H, s_1 = \alpha_1, \ldots, s_n = \alpha_n] = 1$ because if $S^{\mathcal{A}}$ gets heads then it generates fresh $F(x_1)$ and in this case $x_1 = s_1 = \alpha_1$ so $t_1 = (1 + (\alpha_1/p))/2 = \beta_1$. On the other hand, if the coin comes out tails then we have $\alpha_i = s_i = a_i x$. Also, $t_1 = v_1 = (1 - (\frac{a_i}{p})(\frac{x}{p})/2 = (1 - (\frac{\alpha_1}{p}))/2 \neq \beta_1$ and hence $\Pr[t_1 = \beta_1 | X = T, s_1 = \alpha_1, \ldots, s_n = \alpha_n] = 0$. Consequently, we get $\Pr[t_1 = (1 + (\frac{\alpha_1}{p}))/2 | s_1 = \alpha_1, \ldots, s_n = \alpha_n] = (1 + 0)/2 = 1/2$. Using a similar argument it can be shown that $\Pr[t_1 = (1 - (\frac{\alpha_1}{p}))/2 | s_1 = \alpha_1, \ldots, s_n = \alpha_n] = 1/2$. Thus, $\Pr[t_1 = \beta_1, \ldots, t_n = \beta_n | s_1 = \alpha_1, \ldots, s_n = \alpha_n] = 1/2^n$ and the result holds. In particular, if $v = (1 - (\frac{x}{p}))/2$ then all the values y_i sent to $\mathcal{A}$ look independently and uniformly random.

---

[12] This occurs with an overwhelming probability.

In conclusion, we obtain the following results:

$$\Pr[1 \leftarrow_\$ S^{\mathcal{A}}(u||v) \mid (u||v) \leftarrow_\$ F] = \Pr[1 \leftarrow_\$ \mathcal{A}(y_1, ..., y_n) \mid (y_1, ..., y_n) \leftarrow_\$ F],$$

and also $\Pr[1 \leftarrow_\$ S^{\mathcal{A}}(u||v) \mid (u||v) \leftarrow_\$ G \times \{0,1\}] = \alpha$, where

$$\alpha \geq \frac{1}{2} \Pr[1 \leftarrow_\$ S^{\mathcal{A}}(u||v) \mid (u||v) \leftarrow_\$ G \times \{0,1\} \wedge v = (1 - (\frac{x}{p}))/2]$$

$$= \frac{1}{2} \Pr[1 \leftarrow_\$ \mathcal{A}(y_1, ..., y_n) \mid (y_1, ..., y_n) \leftarrow_\$ G \times \{0,1\}]. \tag{8}$$

Thus, we get a tight fully black-box reduction from $\forall \mathsf{MI}_n(\mathsf{PRG}_G)$ to $\mathsf{PRG}_G/\mathsf{LGR}_G$ which admits the security loss of 2. Hence, by Lemma 2 the result holds. $\square$

A rerandomisable hard-core predicate can be potentially also very useful in constructing a tightly extensible encryption scheme out of a computational problem (rather than a decisional one). However, it is not known how it can concretely be used, for example, because we do not have any information about functions related to DLOG being trapdoor one-way functions.

4.3 Tightly Extensible Lossy Trapdoor Functions

Our aim is to construct IND-CPA secure encryption schemes in the multi-user setting from lossy trapdoor functions in a tight way. In order to do so, we introduce tightly secure LTDFs in the multi-instance setting. Let $\mathsf{LTDF} = \langle \mathbb{P}_{\mathsf{LTDF}}, S_{\mathsf{LTDF}}, F_{\mathsf{LTDF}}, R_{\mathsf{LTDF}}, \frac{1}{2} \rangle$ be a primitive of lossy trapdoor functions, i.e. $\mathbb{P}_{\mathsf{LTDF}}$ defines the domain, codomain and challenge space, F_{LTDF} is a collection of LTDFs, S_{LTDF} provides a random bit to R_{LTDF} and R_{LTDF} runs a game where the goal is to distinguish a lossy function from an injective one. As before, let PKE be a public-key encryption scheme with its security game being IND-CPA. For exact same reasons as in PRGs or PKE cases, it is sensible only to consider $\forall \mathsf{MI}_n(\mathsf{LTDF})$ for the multi-instance setting. Also, denote DDH as a primitive representing the DDH assumption (formal definition is not required here). Peikert et al. [41] showed that:

$$\mathsf{PKE} \overset{2}{\hookrightarrow} \mathsf{LTDF} \overset{\lambda}{\hookrightarrow} \mathsf{DDH}.$$

Using these results, we show the following:

$$\forall \mathsf{MI}_n(\mathsf{PKE}) \overset{2}{\hookrightarrow} \forall \mathsf{MI}_n(\mathsf{LTDF}) \overset{1}{\hookrightarrow} \mathsf{LTDF}/\mathsf{DDH} \overset{\lambda}{\hookrightarrow} \mathsf{DDH}. \tag{9}$$

Primitive LTDF/DDH is a construction of a lossy trapdoor function from a DDH group by Peikert et al.

Clearly, $\mathsf{LTDF} \overset{2}{\hookrightarrow} \mathsf{DDH}$ implies $\mathsf{LTDF}/\mathsf{DDH} \overset{2}{\hookrightarrow} \mathsf{DDH}$ and so we concentrate on proving the first two reductions.

Theorem 4. *Let $n \in \mathrm{poly}(\lambda)$. Then, $\forall MI_n(PKE) \overset{2}{\hookrightarrow} \forall MI_n(LTDF)$.*

Proof. We use the construction of Peikert et al. Let $(S_{inj}, S_{loss}, F, F^{-1})$ be a collection of (m, k)-lossy trapdoor functions. Let $\mathcal{H}$ be a family of pairwise independent hash functions from $\{0,1\}^m$ to $\{0,1\}^l$ for $l \leq k - 2\log(1/\epsilon)$ where $\epsilon = \texttt{negl}(\lambda)$. The message space is $\{0,1\}^l$. Define the encryption scheme $\mathcal{E} = (\mathsf{Gen}; \mathsf{Enc}; \mathsf{Dec})$ where:

- $\mathsf{Gen}(1^\lambda)$ takes an injective trapdoor function $(s, t) \leftarrow_\$ S_{inj}$ and a hash function $h \leftarrow_\$ \mathcal{H}$. Then, it sets $pk = (s, h)$ and $sk = (t, h)$.
- $\mathsf{Enc}(pk, m)$ first generates random $x \leftarrow_\$ \{0,1\}^m$. Then, it sets $c_1 = F(s, x)$ and $c_2 = m \oplus h(x)$. It outputs $c = (c_1, c_2)$.
- $\mathsf{Dec}(sk, c)$ computes $x = F^{-1}(t, c_1)$ and returns $c_2 \oplus h(x)$.

Peikert et al. proved that $\mathcal{E}$ is an IND-CPA secure scheme. We show that if $(S_{inj}, S_{loss}, F, F^{-1})$ is a LTDF in the multi-instance setting then $\mathcal{E}$ is a IND-CPA tightly secure scheme in the multi-user setting. We do it using the same technique as Peikert et al. Consider the following variables:

- Variable X_0: choose $(s_1, t_1), \ldots, (s_n, t_n) \leftarrow_\$ S_{inj}, x_1, \ldots, x_n \leftarrow_\$ \{0,1\}^m$ and also $h_1, \ldots, h_n \in \mathcal{H}$. Then the value of X_0 is

$$(s_1, \ldots, s_n, h_1, \ldots, h_n, F(s_1, x_1), \ldots, F(s_n, x_n), h(x_1), \ldots, h(x_n)).$$

- Variable X_1: choose $(s_1, t_1), \ldots, (s_n, t_n) \leftarrow_\$ S_{loss}, x_1, \ldots, x_n \leftarrow_\$ \{0,1\}^m$ and also $h_1, \ldots, h_n \in \mathcal{H}$. Then the value of X_1 is

$$(s_1, \ldots, s_n, h_1, \ldots, h_n, F(s_1, x_1), \ldots, F(s_n, x_n), h(x_1), \ldots, h(x_n)).$$

- Variable X_2: choose $(s_1, t_1), \ldots, (s_n, t_n) \leftarrow_\$ S_{loss}, x_1, \ldots, x_n \leftarrow_\$ \{0,1\}^m$ and also $r_1, \ldots, r_n \in \{0,1\}^l$. Then the value of X_2 is

$$(s_1, \ldots, s_n, h_1, \ldots, h_n, F(s_1, x_1), \ldots, F(s_n, x_n), r_1, \ldots, r_n).$$

- Variable X_3: choose $(s_1, t_1), \ldots, (s_n, t_n) \leftarrow_\$ S_{inj}, x_1, \ldots, x_n \leftarrow_\$ \{0,1\}^m$ and also $r_1, \ldots, r_n \in \{0,1\}^l$. Then the value of X_3 is

$$(s_1, \ldots, s_n, h_1, \ldots, h_n, F(s_1, x_1), \ldots, F(s_n, x_n), r_1, \ldots, r_n).$$

Lemma 4 ([41], generalized). *Let X_0, X_1, X_2, X_3 be random variables defined as above. Then,* $\{X_0\} \overset{c}{\approx} \{X_1\} \overset{s}{\approx} \{X_2\} \overset{c}{\approx} \{X_3\}$.

Proof. Note that X_0 and X_1 are computationally indistinguishable because of the multi-setting indistinguishability property of LTDFs. Identical argument works for X_2 and X_3. In order to show that X_1 and X_2 are statistically indistinguishable we use the result by Peikert et al. ([41], Lemma 3.4) for the single-instance case. Then, by the standard hybrid argument we get $\Delta(X_1, X_2) \leq n \cdot \epsilon(\lambda)$ which is still negligible. $\square$

One observes that, by Lemma 4, the encryption scheme $\mathcal{E}$ is indeed IND-CPA in the multi-user setting. Moreover, the reduction is still tight because only the statistical difference between X_1 and X_2 is dependent on the number of instances n. This completes the proof.   □

In a similar way we can define the multi-instance All-But-One LTDFs and use them to construct IND-CCA secure scheme in the multi-user setting. One could take the construction provided by Peikert et al. and extend the proof of security to many instances. This approach would give us a reduction with security loss $O(q_{\mathsf{dec}})$, the same as in the single-instance case. However, we omit the formal proof here.

Let us consider the construction of a pseudorandom generator provided by Peikert et al., i.e. define $G(x) = (h_1(F(s,x)), h_2(x))$, for $h_1, h_2 \leftarrow_{\$} \mathcal{H}$. By Lemma 3.4 in [41] and the Leftover Hash Lemma (e.g. [15]), if $(S_{inj}, S_{loss}, F, F^{-1})$ is a collection of lossy trapdoor functions then G is a pseudorandom generator. One observes that this result can be easily extended to the multi-instance setting thanks to Lemma 4. This example and Theorem 4 show that multi-instance LTDFs can be useful in constructing more general primitives in the multi-instance setting. We now present how to build such primitives from a standard assumption, namely DDH.

CONSTRUCTING TIGHTLY EXTENSIBLE LTDFs. We focus on proving the second reduction in (2) which involves encrypting matrices in a way similar to ElGamal encryption scheme. Suppose we work with a group G of prime order p and generator g. For simplicity, we write $[x] = g^x$ for $x \in \mathbb{Z}_p$. We write small bold letters (e.g. $\mathbf{x}, \mathbf{y}$) for column vectors and capital bold letters (e.g. $\mathbf{A}, \mathbf{U}$) for matrices. We denote $\mathbf{A}^t$ to be the transpose of $\mathbf{A}$. For simplicity, we write $[x] = g^x$ for $x \in \mathbb{Z}_p$ and similarly $[\mathbf{x}] = ([x_1], \ldots, [x_m])$ for $\mathbf{x} = (x_1, \ldots, x_m)$. We use identical notation $[\mathbf{A}]$ also for matrix $\mathbf{A}$.

For a matrix $\mathbf{A}$ with at least 2 rows, we write $\mathtt{WLR}(\mathbf{A})$ for a matrix $\mathbf{A}$ without last row. Similarly, we define $\mathtt{WLC}(\mathbf{A})$ for $\mathbf{A}$ without last column. We will use the following simple observation.

Observation 1. *Let $m, n, k \geq 2$ and $\mathbf{A}, \mathbf{B}$ be $m \times n$ and $n \times k$ matrices in G respectively. Then, $\mathtt{WLR}(\mathbf{A}\mathbf{B}) = \mathtt{WLR}(\mathbf{A})\mathbf{B}$ and $\mathtt{WLC}(\mathbf{A}\mathbf{B}) = \mathbf{A}\,\mathtt{WLC}(\mathbf{B})$*

We briefly recall the method for encrypting matrix $\mathbf{M} \in \mathbb{Z}_p^{m \times m}$ by Peikert et al. Firstly, we generate secret keys $\mathbf{z} = (z_1, \ldots, z_m) \in \mathbb{Z}_p^m$ and set $sk = \mathbf{z}, pk = [\mathbf{z}]$. Also, denote $h_i = [z_i]$. Then, choose uniformly random $r_1, \ldots, r_m \in \mathbb{Z}_p$. The encryption of $\mathbf{M}$ is a matrix $\mathbf{C} = (C_{i,j})$ where $C_{i,j} = ([r_i], [m_{i,j}][z_i]^{r_i})$. The construction of a LTDF $(S_{inj}, S_{loss}, F, F^{-1})$ from a DDH group looks as follows.

- S_{inj} first selects group parameters (G, p, g). Then, it returns $(\mathbf{C}, t)$ where $\mathbf{C}$ is a matrix encryption of the identity $\mathbf{I}$ and t consists of secret keys $\mathbf{z}$.
- S_{loss} selects group parameters (G, p, g) and returns $(\mathbf{C}, \perp)$ where $\mathbf{C}$ is a matrix encryption of zero matrix $\mathbf{0}$.
- F takes as input $(\mathbf{C}, \mathbf{x})$, where $\mathbf{C}$ is a function index and $\mathbf{x} \in \{0, 1\}^m$, and returns $\mathbf{y} = \mathbf{x}\mathbf{C}$.

- F^{-1} takes as input $\mathbf{y} = ((y_{1,0}, y_{1,1}), \dots, (y_{m,0}, y_{m,1}))$ and the trapdoor $\mathbf{z} = (z_1, \dots, z_m)$. Then, it returns $\mathbf{x} = (x_1, \dots, x_m)$ where $x_i = \log_g(y_{i,1}/y_{i,0}^{z_i})$ (it can be efficiently computed since x_i is a bit).

Security of this lossy trapdoor function relies heavily on the fact that the matrix encryption scheme described above gives indistinguishable ciphertexts if the DDH assumption holds [39, 41]. The key observation is that if DDH is hard in G, then for randomly chosen $\mathbf{x}, \mathbf{y} \in \mathbb{Z}_p^m$, $[\mathbf{x}\mathbf{y}^t]$ is indistinguishable from a uniformly random chosen matrix $\mathbf{U} \leftarrow_\$ G^{m \times m}$. We claim that this is also true for many instances, i.e. for randomly chosen $\mathbf{x}_i, \mathbf{y}_i \in \mathbb{Z}_p^m$ where $i = 1, \dots, n$, $([\mathbf{x}_1\mathbf{y}_1^t], \dots, [\mathbf{x}_n\mathbf{y}_n^t])$ is indistinguishable from a uniformly random chosen matrix $([\mathbf{U}_1], \dots, [\mathbf{U}_n])$ where $U_i \leftarrow_\$ \mathbb{Z}_p^{m \times m}$. We write it formally as follows.

Theorem 5. *Let n be a polynomial in λ and $m \geq 2$. Define primitive $P_m = \langle \mathbb{P}, S_P, F_P R_P, \frac{1}{2} \rangle$ where:*

- $\mathbb{P} = (\mathbb{Z}_p^m \times \mathbb{Z}_p^m, \mathbb{Z}_p^{m \times m}, \mathbb{Z}_p^m \times \mathbb{Z}_p^m)$,
- *S_P sends group information (G, p, g) to R_P,*
- *F_P contains only a function f defined by $f(\mathbf{x}, \mathbf{y}) = \mathbf{x}\mathbf{y}^t$,*
- *R_P first generates $\mathbf{x}, \mathbf{y} \leftarrow_\$ \mathbb{Z}_p^m$, calls f to get $\mathbf{x}\mathbf{y}^t$, samples $b \leftarrow_\$ \{0,1\}$ and sets $U = \mathbf{x}\mathbf{y}^t$ if $b = 0$ and $U \leftarrow_\$ \mathbb{Z}_p^{m \times m}$ if $b = 1$. Finally, it sends $([\mathbf{x}], [\mathbf{y}], [\mathbf{U}])$ along with (G, p, g) to adversary $\mathcal{A}$. Security game R_P returns 1 if $\mathcal{A}$ guesses the bit b.*

Then, $\forall MI_n(P_m) \xrightarrow{1} P_m$.

Proof. Assume first that there exists a PPT algorithm $\mathcal{C}_1$, which given a triple $([\mathbf{x}], [\mathbf{y}], [\mathbf{U}])$ sent by R_P, returns another triple $([\mathbf{x}'], [\mathbf{y}'], [\mathbf{U}'])$ such that: (i) $\mathbf{y}' = \mathbf{y}$, (ii) $\mathbf{x}'$ is uniformly random, (iii) if $b = 0$ then $\mathbf{U}' = \mathbf{x}'\mathbf{y}'^t$ and if $b = 1$ then $\mathbf{U}'$ is uniformly random with probability $1 - \texttt{negl}(\lambda)$. In a similar fashion we can define a PPT algorithm $\mathcal{C}_2$ which does the same thing as $\mathcal{C}_1$ but it fixes $\mathbf{x}$ instead of $\mathbf{y}$. Note that if $\mathcal{C}_1$ exists then clearly $\mathcal{C}_2$ also exists.

Now, suppose there exists an adversary $\mathcal{A}$ which $\forall MI_n(P_m)$−breaks f. We construct an adversary $S^{\mathcal{A}}$ which P_m-breaks f as follows. Given a triple $\mathbf{v} = ([\mathbf{x}], [\mathbf{y}], [\mathbf{U}])$ from R_P, it runs n independent copies of $\mathcal{C}_1$ on input $\mathbf{v}$ and gets back outputs $\mathbf{v}_1, \dots, \mathbf{v}_n$. Next, it runs n independent copies of $\mathcal{C}_2$ where the i-th copy of $\mathcal{C}_2$ gets as input $\mathbf{v}_i$. Then, collect the outputs $\mathbf{w}_1, \dots, \mathbf{w}_n$ and pass them to $\mathcal{A}$. Eventually, when $\mathcal{A}$ returns a bit b', output b'. Note that this reduction is tight by the property (iii) of $\mathcal{C}_1$ and by standard hybrid argument. Therefore, what we have left is to construct an algorithm $\mathcal{C}_1$ (Fig. 6).

Consider the following algorithm for $\mathcal{C}_1$ in Fig. 6. Note that we are able to compute $[\mathbf{x}']$ and $[\mathbf{U}']$ in lines 3 and 4 even though we do not know values for $\mathbf{x}', \mathbf{U}'$. Clearly, property (i) is satisfied. Also, $\mathbf{x}'$ is uniformly random because of the randomness of $\tilde{\mathbf{r}}$. The most challenging part is to show (iii).

First, suppose that $b = 0$. So we have $\mathbf{U} = \mathbf{x}\mathbf{y}^t$. Hence, $\mathbf{U}' = \mathbf{R}\mathbf{U} + \tilde{\mathbf{r}}\mathbf{y}^t = \mathbf{R}\mathbf{x}\mathbf{y}^t + \tilde{\mathbf{r}}\mathbf{y}^t = (\mathbf{R}\mathbf{x} + \tilde{\mathbf{r}})\mathbf{y}^t = \mathbf{x}'\mathbf{y}^t$. Now, consider the case $b = 1$. Then, $\mathbf{U}$ is a uniformly random matrix. We want to show that $\mathbf{U}'$ is also a uniformly random

$$
\begin{array}{l}
\hline
\mathcal{C}_1(1^\lambda, G, p, g, [\mathbf{x}], [\mathbf{y}], [\mathbf{U}]) \\
\hline
1: \quad \mathbf{R} \leftarrow_\$ \mathbb{Z}_p^{m \times m} \\
2: \quad \tilde{\mathbf{r}} \leftarrow_\$ \mathbb{Z}_p^m \\
3: \quad [\mathbf{x}'] = [\mathbf{Rx} + \tilde{\mathbf{r}}] \\
4: \quad [\mathbf{U}'] = [\mathbf{RU} + \tilde{\mathbf{r}}\mathbf{y}^t] \\
5: \quad \textbf{return } ([\mathbf{x}'], [\mathbf{y}], [\mathbf{U}']) \\
\hline
\end{array}
$$

Fig. 6. PPT algorithm for $\mathcal{C}_1$.

matrix with overwhelming probability. Denote $\mathbf{x} = (x_1, \ldots, x_m)$ and assume that $x_m \neq 0$ (this occurs with an overwhelming probability). We slightly change the algorithm for $\mathcal{C}_1$: we first choose random $\mathbf{x}' = (x_1', \ldots, x_m')$, $\tilde{\mathbf{r}} = (\tilde{r}_1, \ldots, \tilde{r}_m)$ from $\mathbb{Z}_p^m$ and $\tilde{\mathbf{R}} = (\tilde{R}_{i,j}) \in \mathbb{Z}_p^{m \times (m-1)}$. Next, we set $\mathbf{r} = (r_1, \ldots, r_m)$, where $r_i = x_m^{-1}(x_i' - \tilde{r}_i - \sum_{j=1}^{m-1} x_j \tilde{R}_{i,j})$, and $\mathbf{R} = (\tilde{\mathbf{R}} \,|\, \mathbf{r})$. Note that this change does not affect the input/output behaviour of $\mathcal{C}_1$. Moreover, we can rewrite $\mathbf{R}$ as:

$$
\mathbf{R} =
\begin{pmatrix}
\tilde{r}_1 & \tilde{R}_{1,1} & \tilde{R}_{1,2} & \cdots & \tilde{R}_{1,m-1} & x_1' \\
\tilde{r}_2 & \tilde{R}_{2,1} & \tilde{R}_{2,2} & \cdots & \tilde{R}_{2,m-1} & x_2' \\
\vdots & \vdots & \vdots & \vdots & & \vdots \\
\tilde{r}_m & \tilde{R}_{m,1} & \tilde{R}_{m,2} & \cdots & \tilde{R}_{m,m-1} & x_m'
\end{pmatrix}
\begin{pmatrix}
0 & 0 & \cdots & 0 & -x_m^{-1} \\
1 & 0 & \cdots & 0 & -x_1 x_m^{-1} \\
0 & 1 & \cdots & 0 & -x_2 x_m^{-1} \\
\vdots & \vdots & \ddots & \vdots & \vdots \\
0 & 0 & \cdots & 1 & -x_{m-1} x_m^{-1} \\
0 & 0 & \cdots & 0 & x_m^{-1}
\end{pmatrix}
\tag{10}
$$

Denote $\bar{\mathbf{R}}$ and $\mathbf{M}$ as the left-hand side and the right-hand side matrices respectively. Also, define $\mathbf{A} = \mathbf{MU}$ and $\hat{\mathbf{R}}$ such that $\bar{\mathbf{R}} = (\hat{\mathbf{R}} \,|\, \mathbf{x}')$. Note that the first column of $\mathbf{M}$ is the (additive) inverse of the last column of $\mathbf{M}$. Consequently, we get the same property in $\mathbf{A}$. Moreover, $\mathrm{WLR}(\mathbf{M})$ is clearly invertible and thus $\mathbf{U}$ being uniformly random matrix implies that $\mathrm{WLR}(\mathbf{A}) = \mathrm{WLR}(\mathbf{M})\mathbf{U}$ is also uniformly random. For simplicity, let us denote $\mathbf{a}$ to be the last row of $\mathbf{A}$, $\mathbf{A}_1 = \mathrm{WLR}(\mathbf{A})$ and $\mathbf{A}_2$ be the matrix $\mathbf{A}_1$ without the first row (which is the inverse of the last row of $\mathbf{A}$). Then, by the observations above we can expand $\mathbf{U}'$ as follows:

$$
\begin{aligned}
\mathbf{U}' &= \mathbf{RU} + \tilde{\mathbf{r}}\mathbf{y}^t \\
&= \left((\hat{\mathbf{R}} \,|\, \mathbf{0}) + (\mathbf{0} \,|\, \mathbf{x}') \right) \mathbf{A} + \tilde{\mathbf{r}}\mathbf{y}^t \\
&= \hat{\mathbf{R}}\mathbf{A}_1 + \mathbf{x}'\mathbf{a}^t + \tilde{\mathbf{r}}\mathbf{y}^t \\
&= \left((\tilde{\mathbf{r}} \,|\, \mathbf{0}) + (\mathbf{0} \,|\, \tilde{\mathbf{R}}) \right) \mathbf{A}_1 + \mathbf{x}'\mathbf{a}^t + \tilde{\mathbf{r}}\mathbf{y}^t \\
&= \tilde{\mathbf{r}}(\mathbf{y}^t - \mathbf{a}^t) + \tilde{\mathbf{R}}\mathbf{A}_2 + \mathbf{x}'\mathbf{a}^t.
\end{aligned}
\tag{11}
$$

This is equivalent to $\mathbf{U}'^t = (\mathbf{y} - \mathbf{a} \,|\, \mathbf{A}_2^t) (\tilde{\mathbf{r}} \,|\, \tilde{\mathbf{R}})^t + \mathbf{a}\mathbf{x}'^t$. Note that $(\mathbf{y} - \mathbf{a} \,|\, \mathbf{A}_2^t)$ is with high probability an invertible matrix because $\mathbf{A}_1$ is uniformly random.

Moreover, we chose $\left(\tilde{\mathbf{r}} \mid \tilde{\mathbf{R}}\right)$ uniformly at random and therefore $\mathbf{U}'$ is also uniformly random (with probability $1 - \mathsf{negl}(\lambda)$). □

Similarly as in [41], we obtain $\forall \mathsf{MI}_n(\mathsf{LTDF}) \overset{1}{\hookrightarrow} \forall \mathsf{MI}_n(P_m)$. Hence, $\forall \mathsf{MI}_n(\mathsf{LTDF}) \overset{1}{\hookrightarrow} \mathsf{LTDF/DDH}$ follows from the Theorem 5 applied to the construction by Peikert et al. along with the random self-reducibility of DDH. Thus, combining (9) with Lemma 2 we obtain the following.

Theorem 6. *LTDF is* $(\lambda, \forall)$-*tightly extensible w.r.t. DDH and PKE is* $(2\lambda, \forall)$-*tightly extensible w.r.t. DDH.*

All in all, we have provided a new way of constructing multi-user IND-CPA encryption schemes out of a DDH group using tightly extensible lossy trapdoor functions. We leave it as an open question whether it is possible to obtain tightly extensible LTDFs from different standard assumptions, such as lattices.

References

1. Abe, M., David, B., Kohlweiss, M., Nishimaki, R., Ohkubo, M.: Tagged one-time signatures: tight security and optimal tag size. In: Kurosawa, K., Hanaoka, G. (eds.) PKC 2013. LNCS, vol. 7778, pp. 312–331. Springer, Heidelberg (2013). https://doi.org/10.1007/978-3-642-36362-7_20

2. Abe, M., Hofheinz, D., Nishimaki, R., Ohkubo, M., Pan, J.: Compact structure-preserving signatures with almost tight security. In: Katz, J., Shacham, H. (eds.) CRYPTO 2017, Part II. LNCS, vol. 10402, pp. 548–580. Springer, Cham (2017). https://doi.org/10.1007/978-3-319-63715-0_19

3. Attrapadung, N., Hanaoka, G., Yamada, S.: A framework for identity-based encryption with almost tight security. In: Iwata, T., Cheon, J.H. (eds.) ASIACRYPT 2015, Part I. LNCS, vol. 9452, pp. 521–549. Springer, Heidelberg (2015). https://doi.org/10.1007/978-3-662-48797-6_22

4. Auerbach, B., Cash, D., Fersch, M., Kiltz, E.: Memory-tight reductions. In: Katz, J., Shacham, H. (eds.) CRYPTO 2017, Part I. LNCS, vol. 10401, pp. 101–132. Springer, Cham (2017). https://doi.org/10.1007/978-3-319-63688-7_4

5. Baecher, P., Brzuska, C., Fischlin, M.: Notions of black-box reductions, revisited. In: Sako, K., Sarkar, P. (eds.) ASIACRYPT 2013, Part I. LNCS, vol. 8269, pp. 296–315. Springer, Heidelberg (2013). https://doi.org/10.1007/978-3-642-42033-7_16

6. Bellare, M., Boldyreva, A., Micali, S.: Public-key encryption in a multi-user setting: security proofs and improvements. In: Preneel, B. (ed.) EUROCRYPT 2000. LNCS, vol. 1807, pp. 259–274. Springer, Heidelberg (2000). https://doi.org/10.1007/3-540-45539-6_18

7. Blazy, O., Kiltz, E., Pan, J.: (Hierarchical) identity-based encryption from affine message authentication. In: Garay, J.A., Gennaro, R. (eds.) CRYPTO 2014, Part I. LNCS, vol. 8616, pp. 408–425. Springer, Heidelberg (2014). https://doi.org/10.1007/978-3-662-44371-2_23

8. Blum, M., Micali, S.: How to generate cryptographically strong sequences of pseudo random bits. In: 23rd FOCS, pp. 112–117. IEEE Computer Society Press, November 1982

9. Boyen, X., Mei, Q., Waters, B.: Direct chosen ciphertext security from identity-based techniques. In: Atluri, V., Meadows, C., Juels, A. (eds.) ACM CCS 2005, pp. 320–329. ACM Press, November 2005

10. Chen, J., Gong, J., Weng, J.: Tightly secure IBE under constant-size master public key. In: Fehr, S. (ed.) PKC 2017, Part I. LNCS, vol. 10174, pp. 207–231. Springer, Heidelberg (2017). https://doi.org/10.1007/978-3-662-54365-8_9

11. Chen, J., Wee, H.: Fully, (almost) tightly secure IBE and dual system groups. In: Canetti, R., Garay, J.A. (eds.) CRYPTO 2013, Part II. LNCS, vol. 8043, pp. 435–460. Springer, Heidelberg (2013). https://doi.org/10.1007/978-3-642-40084-1_25

12. Damgård, I.B.: Collision free hash functions and public key signature schemes. In: Chaum, D., Price, W.L. (eds.) EUROCRYPT 1987. LNCS, vol. 304, pp. 203–216. Springer, Heidelberg (1988). https://doi.org/10.1007/3-540-39118-5_19

13. Damgård, I.B.: On the randomness of Legendre and Jacobi sequences. In: Goldwasser, S. (ed.) CRYPTO 1988. LNCS, vol. 403, pp. 163–172. Springer, New York (1990). https://doi.org/10.1007/0-387-34799-2_13

14. Dodis, Y., Oliveira, R., Pietrzak, K.: On the generic insecurity of the full domain hash. In: Shoup, V. (ed.) CRYPTO 2005. LNCS, vol. 3621, pp. 449–466. Springer, Heidelberg (2005). https://doi.org/10.1007/11535218_27

15. Dodis, Y., Reyzin, L., Smith, A.: Fuzzy extractors: how to generate strong keys from biometrics and other noisy data. In: Cachin, C., Camenisch, J.L. (eds.) EUROCRYPT 2004. LNCS, vol. 3027, pp. 523–540. Springer, Heidelberg (2004). https://doi.org/10.1007/978-3-540-24676-3_31

16. Fischlin, M., Lehmann, A., Ristenpart, T., Shrimpton, T., Stam, M., Tessaro, S.: Random oracles with(out) programmability. In: Abe, M. (ed.) ASIACRYPT 2010. LNCS, vol. 6477, pp. 303–320. Springer, Heidelberg (2010). https://doi.org/10.1007/978-3-642-17373-8_18

17. Gay, R., Hofheinz, D., Kiltz, E., Wee, H.: Tightly CCA-secure encryption without pairings. In: Fischlin, M., Coron, J.-S. (eds.) EUROCRYPT 2016, Part I. LNCS, vol. 9665, pp. 1–27. Springer, Heidelberg (2016). https://doi.org/10.1007/978-3-662-49890-3_1

18. Gay, R., Hofheinz, D., Kohl, L.: Kurosawa-Desmedt meets tight security. In: Katz, J., Shacham, H. (eds.) CRYPTO 2017, Part III. LNCS, vol. 10403, pp. 133–160. Springer, Cham (2017). https://doi.org/10.1007/978-3-319-63697-9_5

19. Gay, R., Hofheinz, D., Kohl, L., Pan, J.: More efficient (almost) tightly secure structure-preserving signatures. In: Nielsen, J.B., Rijmen, V. (eds.) EUROCRYPT 2018. LNCS, vol. 10821, pp. 230–258. Springer, Cham (2018). https://doi.org/10.1007/978-3-319-78375-8_8

20. Goldreich, O.: Foundations of Cryptography: Basic Applications, vol. 2. Cambridge University Press, Cambridge (2004)

21. Goldreich, O., Levin, L.A.: A hard-core predicate for all one-way functions. In: 21st ACM STOC, pp. 25–32. ACM Press, May 1989

22. Gong, J., Chen, J., Dong, X., Cao, Z., Tang, S.: Extended nested dual system groups, revisited. In: Cheng, C.-M., Chung, K.-M., Persiano, G., Yang, B.-Y. (eds.) PKC 2016, Part I. LNCS, vol. 9614, pp. 133–163. Springer, Heidelberg (2016). https://doi.org/10.1007/978-3-662-49384-7_6

23. Haitner, I., Holenstein, T., Reingold, O., Vadhan, S., Wee, H.: Universal one-way hash functions via inaccessible entropy. In: Gilbert, H. (ed.) EUROCRYPT 2010. LNCS, vol. 6110, pp. 616–637. Springer, Heidelberg (2010). https://doi.org/10.1007/978-3-642-13190-5_31

24. Håstad, J., Impagliazzo, R., Levin, L.A., Luby, M.: A pseudorandom generator from any one-way function. SIAM J. Comput. 28(4), 1364–1396 (1999)

25. Hofheinz, D.: Algebraic partitioning: fully compact and (almost) tightly secure cryptography. In: Kushilevitz, E., Malkin, T. (eds.) TCC 2016, Part I. LNCS, vol. 9562, pp. 251–281. Springer, Heidelberg (2016). https://doi.org/10.1007/978-3-662-49096-9_11
26. Hofheinz, D.: Adaptive partitioning. In: Coron, J.-S., Nielsen, J.B. (eds.) EURO-CRYPT 2017, Part III. LNCS, vol. 10212, pp. 489–518. Springer, Cham (2017). https://doi.org/10.1007/978-3-319-56617-7_17
27. Hofheinz, D., Jager, T.: Tightly secure signatures and public-key encryption. In: Safavi-Naini, R., Canetti, R. (eds.) CRYPTO 2012. LNCS, vol. 7417, pp. 590–607. Springer, Heidelberg (2012). https://doi.org/10.1007/978-3-642-32009-5_35
28. Hofheinz, D., Koch, J., Striecks, C.: Identity-based encryption with (almost) tight security in the multi-instance, multi-ciphertext setting. In: Katz, J. (ed.) PKC 2015. LNCS, vol. 9020, pp. 799–822. Springer, Heidelberg (2015). https://doi.org/10.1007/978-3-662-46447-2_36
29. Holenstein, T.: Pseudorandom generators from one-way functions: a simple construction for any hardness. In: Halevi, S., Rabin, T. (eds.) TCC 2006. LNCS, vol. 3876, pp. 443–461. Springer, Heidelberg (2006). https://doi.org/10.1007/11681878_23
30. Impagliazzo, R., Rudich, S.: Limits on the provable consequences of one-way permutations. In: 21st ACM STOC, pp. 44–61. ACM Press, May 1989
31. Impagliazzo, R., Rudich, S.: Limits on the provable consequences of one-way permutations. In: Goldwasser, S. (ed.) CRYPTO 1988. LNCS, vol. 403, pp. 8–26. Springer, New York (1990). https://doi.org/10.1007/0-387-34799-2_2
32. Katz, J., Koo, C.-Y.: On constructing universal one-way hash functions from arbitrary one-way functions. Cryptology ePrint Archive, Report 2005/328 (2005). http://eprint.iacr.org/2005/328
33. Lamport, L.: Constructing digital signatures from a one-way function. Technical report SRI-CSL-98, SRI International Computer Science Laboratory, October 1979
34. Libert, B., Joye, M., Yung, M., Peters, T.: Concise multi-challenge CCA-secure encryption and signatures with almost tight security. In: Sarkar, P., Iwata, T. (eds.) ASIACRYPT 2014, Part II. LNCS, vol. 8874, pp. 1–21. Springer, Heidelberg (2014). https://doi.org/10.1007/978-3-662-45608-8_1
35. Libert, B., Peters, T., Joye, M., Yung, M.: Compactly hiding linear spans. In: Iwata, T., Cheon, J.H. (eds.) ASIACRYPT 2015, Part I. LNCS, vol. 9452, pp. 681–707. Springer, Heidelberg (2015). https://doi.org/10.1007/978-3-662-48797-6_28
36. Mauduit, C., Sárközy, A.: On finite pseudorandom binary sequences i: measure of pseudorandomness, the Legendre symbol. Acta Arith. $\mathbf{82}$(4), 365–377 (1997)
37. Merkle, R.C.: A digital signature based on a conventional encryption function. In: Pomerance, C. (ed.) CRYPTO 1987. LNCS, vol. 293, pp. 369–378. Springer, Heidelberg (1988). https://doi.org/10.1007/3-540-48184-2_32
38. Naor, M.: On cryptographic assumptions and challenges. In: Boneh, D. (ed.) CRYPTO 2003. LNCS, vol. 2729, pp. 96–109. Springer, Heidelberg (2003). https://doi.org/10.1007/978-3-540-45146-4_6
39. Naor, M., Reingold, O.: Synthesizers and their application to the parallel construction of psuedo-random functions. In: 36th Annual Symposium on Foundations of Computer Science, Milwaukee, Wisconsin, 23–25 October 1995, pp. 170–181 (1995)
40. Pandey, O., Pass, R., Vaikuntanathan, V.: Adaptive one-way functions and applications. In: Wagner, D. (ed.) CRYPTO 2008. LNCS, vol. 5157, pp. 57–74. Springer, Heidelberg (2008). https://doi.org/10.1007/978-3-540-85174-5_4
41. Peikert, C., Waters, B.: Lossy trapdoor functions and their applications. Cryptology ePrint Archive, Report 2007/279 (2007). http://eprint.iacr.org/2007/279

42. Peikert, C., Waters, B.: Lossy trapdoor functions and their applications. In: Ladner, R.E., Dwork, C. (eds.) 40th ACM STOC, pp. 187–196. ACM Press, May 2008
43. Reingold, O., Trevisan, L., Vadhan, S.: Notions of reducibility between cryptographic primitives. In: Naor, M. (ed.) TCC 2004. LNCS, vol. 2951, pp. 1–20. Springer, Heidelberg (2004). https://doi.org/10.1007/978-3-540-24638-1_1
44. Rompel, J.: One-way functions are necessary and sufficient for secure signatures. In: 22nd ACM STOC, pp. 387–394. ACM Press, May 1990
45. Simon, D.R.: Finding collisions on a one-way street: can secure hash functions be based on general assumptions? In: Nyberg, K. (ed.) EUROCRYPT 1998. LNCS, vol. 1403, pp. 334–345. Springer, Heidelberg (1998). https://doi.org/10.1007/BFb0054137
46. van Dam, W., Hallgren, S., Ip, L.: Quantum algorithms for some hidden shift problems. In: 14th SODA, pp. 489–498. ACM-SIAM, January 2003

Author Index

Printed in the United States
By Bookmasters